The Complete Directory to Prime Time Network TV Shows

1946–present

The Complete Directory to Prime Time Network TV Shows
1946–present

Tim Brooks and Earle Marsh

BALLANTINE BOOKS • NEW YORK

Cover photographs, from left to right:

Tonight Show, Perry Mason, All in the Family, Little House on the Prairie, I Love Lucy, The Honeymooners, Mary Tyler Moore Show, Milton Berle Show, Gunsmoke

Courtesy of Viacom International, Inc. and NBC.

 Published in the United States by Ballantine Books, a division of Random House, Inc., New York, and simultaneously in Canada by Random House of Canada Limited, Toronto, Canada.

Library of Congress Cataloging in Publication Data

Brooks, Tim.
The complete directory to prime time network TV shows, 1946–present.

Includes index.
1. Television broadcasting—United States—Dictionaries. I. Marsh, Earle, joint author. II. Title.

PN1992.18.B68 791.45'7'03 78-25664

ISBN 0-345-28248-5

ISBN 0-345-29004-6 pbk

This edition published simultaneously in hardcover and trade paperback.

Manufactured in the United States of America

First Edition: May 1979

4 5 6 7 8 9 10

CONTENTS

ACKNOWLEDGMENTS

Like a TV show, this book should have its own roll of credits, in acknowledgment of the help and encouragement we have received from many of our friends in the broadcasting industry. Foremost have been the patient and helpful staffs at the program information departments of all three networks, who made their files and memories available to us at all hours of the day and night: Dan Rustin and Mitch Praver of ABC-TV; Betsy Broesamle, John Behrens, and the late Dorothy Boyle of CBS-TV; and Betty Jane Reed and staff of NBC-TV. Also most helpful were Vera Mayer and Judy Friedman of the NBC-TV Library, who opened to us their unparalleled collection of trade literature from all periods of television history.

Others who contributed in large ways and small included Melvin Goldberg, Cathy Korda, and Roann Levinsohn of ABC-TV; Arnold Becker of CBS-TV; Curt Block, Owen Comora, Winifred Craig, Donald Eddy, Steve Flynn, Edward Frank, Betty Furness, Stuart Gray, Doris Katz, and Alfred Ordover of NBC-TV; Hugh Beville of the Broadcast Rating Council; Dr. Thomas Coffin; Gedeon de Margitay; Jack Fishman of Universal Television; William Fishman of Sundance Computer Systems, Inc.; Margaret Heron of Teleklew Productions; bandleader Elliot Lawrence; James W. Seiler of Mediastat; William Behanna of the A. C. Nielsen Company; and Theodore Bergmann, former head of the DuMont Television Network, and now a highly successful producer in Hollywood (responsible for, among other things, *Three's Company*). Mr. Bergmann not only gave us his recollections of DuMont operations, but led us to an excellent Ph.D. dissertation on the history of the DuMont network, written by Gary Newton Hess at Northwestern University in 1960.

INTRODUCTION

"What's on TV tonight?"

Within these pages are 10,000 nights, a panorama of television programs and stars from the earliest pioneers of the mid-1940s to the very latest contemporary hits. What's on? A pretty, pixie-ish ingenue named Helen Parrish, introducing television's first "big time" series ever for a hardy little band of set owners in 1946 (see *Hour Glass*); a loud, brash comic who never quite made it in radio, becoming TV's first superstar, and causing millions of Americans to buy their first TV set (see *Milton Berle*); a laconic non-actor named Jack Webb droning "Just the facts, ma'am," and ushering in a whole era of grippingly real dramas (see *Dragnet*); a veteran actor who is to lose his career—and his life—when he is driven from his hit series by McCarthy-era blacklisting (see *The Goldbergs*); a towering, unknown actor in a role intended for John Wayne, opening an entire decade of "adult" westerns (see *Gunsmoke*); Richard M. Nixon saying "Sock it to me" on nationwide TV (see *Laugh-In*); a blue collar bigot railing about "spics and spades"—and changing the nature of TV comedy forever after (see *All in the Family*); the "Fonz" giving his thumbs-up signal and bringing a wave of nostalgia about the simpler days of the 1950s into our living rooms (see *Happy Days*).

They are all here, and a great many more.

We have set out to give you the most complete and accurate history of night time television series ever assembled. But this is not simply a book of nostalgia, for current shows are here as well, and many of TV's great series of the past are still very much with us, in reruns. We suggest that you keep this book by your set, and when a favorite repeat or star turns up in your evening's viewing, take a moment to see what the background of that show was, its stars and story development during its run. You may even want to catch the movie or read the book on which it was based.

We hope that this book can help you enjoy today's TV a little more.

This volume has been carefully researched for the scholar who wants to know what happened and when. But it is also—like TV itself—for your enjoyment.

What Is in This Book

This is an encyclopedia of every nighttime program series aired on the four commercial networks since the beginning of regular television networking in the United States in 1946. Although the book focuses on "prime time" (7:00–11:00 P.M.), many other programs are here as well. Included are all network programs that aired after 6 P.M. and ran for at least four consecutive weeks in the same time slot (or were intended to). Thus, the entries range from the early evening *Small Fry Club* to the late night *Tonight* Show and *Tomorrow Show*.

A few generic program types are found under general headings. Newscasts are summarized under *News;* sports events such as football, boxing, wrestling, etc., under the name of the sport; and feature film series under *Movies*. All other series are arranged by title in alphabetical order. There is a full index in the back to every cast member, plus appendixes listing the highest rated programs each season, network schedules for each season at a glance, major TV awards, and other information.

Only network series are listed, those that were fed out by ABC, CBS, or NBC (and, in the early days, DuMont), and which were seen simultaneously in most parts of the country. Other programs that may have been seen in your city were local programs, or syndicated shows—programs bought by local stations from independent producers, seen only in certain cities and shown at different times in each locality.

This is the first book to trace programming back to the very founding of the networks, and, consequently, it includes some very early series that were seen in only two or three cities on the east coast. The networks spread quickly, however, first by sending out kinescopes (films) of their shows to non-connected stations, and soon after with live connections to stations in the midwest (in 1949) and on the west coast (in 1951).

Under each series main heading you will find the following:

First/Last Telecast: The dates on which the series was first and last seen on a *network.* This includes repeats on a network, but not later reruns on local stations, which will be at a different time in each city, and may go on long after the program has ceased production. Generally the first/last telecast dates indicate the original production run of the series.

Broadcast History: The days, times, and networks on which the series was carried (eastern time). Special episodes which ran for only one or two weeks in other than the normal time slot are not reflected. DUM indicates the DuMont TV network, and (OS) indicates that the program was off during the summer months.

Cast: Regular cast members, those who were seen on a recurring basis, are listed along with the years in which they were seen during the original run. We have gone to considerable effort to separate regulars from guests making one-time only appearances, as the latter were not part of the continuing casts. Notable guests may be listed in the series description, however.

Principal sources of scheduling information were the files of the three surviving networks (ABC, CBS, NBC), cross-checked against detailed four-network logs maintained over the years by NBC and by the A.C. Nielsen Company. For the very earliest programs, listings in *TV Guide* and various newspapers were consulted, with listings in different cities being compared to establish network status. Cast and content data were drawn from network files, press releases, listings in *TV Guide*, reviews in *Variety*, *Billboard*, and *Television* magazine, and elsewhere. To all of these organizations, we express our sincere gratitude.

A Short History of Network Television

Television goes back a good deal further than most people realize. There was no single inventor of television, although Dr. Vladimir Zworykin's invention of the iconoscope in 1923 provided a basic element, the "eye" of the TV camera. Demonstrations of various kinds of experimental TV were made in the late 1920s, including even primitive color television in 1929. General Electric began semi-regular telecasts from its laboratories in Schenectady in May 1928, mostly for the benefit of a few nearby engineers who had receiving sets. NBC opened experimental TV station W2XBS in New York in 1930, followed by a similar CBS station in 1931. But for the next several years TV seemed to go nowhere. Pictures were fuzzy, screens tiny, and costs astronomical. In addition, there were several incompatible types of transmission, and engineers spent much time arguing over a single set of technical standards—something we take for granted today.

For the public at large the 1930s was the decade of radio, when virtually every home had a set, and superstars and hit shows became a familiar phenomenon. Comedies, dramas, quiz shows, and variety hours were all developed for a mass market, establishing formats that would later be transferred virtually intact to television. While radio and TV are only vaguely related technically, there is no doubt that the great radio networks of the 1930s were the direct entertainment predecessors of today's TV.

By the end of the 1930s interest in TV was picking up. In 1938 NBC transmitted several notable telecasts from its New York station, including scenes from the Broadway play *Susan and God* starring Gertrude Lawrence and Paul McGrath from the original cast. Also in that year the NBC station carried the first live, unscheduled coverage of a news event in progress. An NBC mobile unit happened to be working in a park in Queens, New York, when a fire broke out on Ward's Island, across the river. The TV crew swung their cameras around and telecast live pictures of the raging fire to surprised viewers.

Looking for a memorable event with which to inaugurate regular TV service, NBC decided upon the official opening of the World's Fair in New York on April 30, 1939. President Franklin D. Roosevelt was seen arriving and delivering the opening address, thus becoming the first incumbent president to appear on television. NBC announcer Bill Farren described the proceedings and also conducted interviews at the fairground. Thereafter, from 1939–1941, both NBC and CBS presented a surprisingly extensive schedule of programs over their New York stations for the several thousand sets then in use. There were few regular "series" however—every night was an event. If you had a set, you simply turned it on at night (there was seldom anything telecast during the day) and saw what was being sent out from the studios that night. Anything that moved was worth watching.

A sample night's entertainment, shortly after the World's Fair inaugural, was called simply *The Wednesday Night Program* and ran from 8:00–9:07 P.M. It opened with a fashion show described by commentators Renee Macredy and Nancy Turner, followed by songs by The Three Smoothies, a sketch called "The Smart Thing" (cast included Martha Sleeper, Ned Wever, and Burford Hampden), dancer Hal Sherman from the show *Helzapoppin'*, and finally a magic act by Robert Reinhart, who also served as emcee of the program. If you've never heard of most of these names, neither had most viewers in 1939. Appearances by stars, especially the big names of radio, were few and far between, and television had to rely primarily on cabaret talent and young, lesser-known Broadway actors and actresses for many years to come.

Viewers didn't mind. There was a common bond of pioneering between viewers and broadcasters in those days, and in fact a good deal of communication both ways. NBC kept a card file listing every known set owner and sent out postcards each week listing the programs to be telecast, asking the viewer's opinion of each one. These were the first TV "ratings."

Most television programs were seen in New York only, which was, throughout the 1940s, America's TV "capital." It was the first city with more than one station operating, and it had by far the largest number of sets in people's homes. However, the possibility of networking, along the lines of the great radio chains, was pursued from the very beginning. As early as 1940 NBC began to relay some telecasts to the General Electric station in Schenectady, thus forming history's first network of sorts. (The feasibility of transmitting pictures between two widely separated cities had been demonstrated in 1927, when Secretary of Commerce Herbert Hoover, speaking in Washington, D.C., was seen in a New York laboratory, by special hookup.) The New York-Schenectady link was accomplished by the simple method of having General Electric pick up the signal off the air from New York, 130 miles away, and rebroadcast it. The picture quality thus obtained was not very good. In 1941 some NBC New York telecasts began to be fed to the Philco station in Philadelphia as well, giving NBC a three station "network." But all of this was intermittent, and there were still no regular series as we know them today.

Commercial television first saw the light of day in 1941, when both NBC and CBS were granted commercial licenses for their New York stations, both on July 1st (so neither could claim a "first"). NBC's call letters became WNBT on channel one (now WNBC-TV on channel four), and CBS got WCBW on channel two (now WCBS-TV).

Just as commercial television was beginning to take root, World War II put a stop to everything. Little was telecast during the war years, except for some training programs. The DuMont Laboratories, which had been experimenting with TV for years, received a commercial license in 1944 for WABD, New York (now WNEW-TV on channel five), serving as the cornerstone of that company's ill-fated network venture.

With the war over, work started anew. The year 1946 marked the true beginnings of regular network service. NBC's WNBT began feeding its programs on a more or less regular basis to Philadelphia and Schenectady, forming NBC's "East Coast Network." DuMont opened a second station, WTTG, in Washington, D.C., to which it fed programs—even though there were in mid-1946 only a bare dozen sets in the nation's capital. Network television's first major series effort, and the program which set many precedents for programs to come, was a regular Thursday night big budget variety hour called *Hour Glass,* which ran for ten months beginning in May 1946. It was a pioneer in many ways and helped spread the word that television could provide not only a novelty gadget for the gadget-minded, but regular high-quality family entertainment as well.

Several other network series began in 1946, including the long running *You Are an Artist,* Mrs. Carveth Wells' *Geographically Speaking, Television Screen Magazine* (an early version of *60 Minutes*), *Play the Game* (charades), *Cash and Carry* (quiz), *Face to Face* (drawings), *I Love to Eat* (cooking), and *Faraway Hill* (the first network soap opera). All of these programs can be found under their individual headings in this book.

Most early programming was quite experimental, just to see what would work in the new medium. Costs were kept to a minimum, and advertising agencies were given free time by the stations, just to get them into the studio to try out TV. (Programs were often produced by the advertisers themselves.) Such visual formats as charades, cartooning, and fashion shows were favorites, along with sports events and adaptations of radio shows, telecast on a one-time tryout basis.

A landmark was the premiere of *Kraft Television Theater* in May 1947. This was not only the first regularly scheduled drama series to go out over a network, but was also blessed with sufficient money from a sponsor to insure uniformly high-quality productions.

Gradually stations were added to NBC's and DuMont's chains, two more stations in Washington, D.C., additional facilities in Philadelphia, then Baltimore, then Boston. Stations not connected with the east coast opened in the midwest and far west, often receiving network programs on kinescope.

But where were CBS and ABC?

Both were fully committed to the idea of networking, but each hung back for a different reason. ABC did not yet have a New York flagship station on the air from which to originate programming. ABC had in fact been buying time on other stations and producing programs on their schedules just to give its own technicians experience in studio production techniques, against the day when ABC would have its own station. An early example was *Play the Game* (1946), which was produced by ABC using DuMont's facilities. In early 1948 ABC lined up a network of four stations, a curious amalgam of DuMont and independent stations, for a series called *On the Corner* with radio star Henry Morgan—which it now considers its first "network" program (although *Play the Game* was also seen over a network). Finally, in August 1948 ABC got its own New York station and production center on the air and began network service on a regular basis.

CBS delayed its entry into network television for quite a different reason. It had had an active New York station for years. But CBS was committed to the idea of color TV, and tried hard to get its own color system accepted by the Federal Communications Commission as the industry standard. This would have meant color TV from the start for everyone, and would also have made obsolete all of the equipment in use by CBS' rivals because the different systems were incompatible. The choice had to be color or black and white, but not both. Unfortunately, the CBS system was clumsy and unreliable compared with the fairly well-developed black and white TV of the day, and its adoption would probably have set TV back several years. (Eventually the CBS electro-mechanical system, with its spinning disc within every set, was discarded altogether. It is RCA's all-electronic, black and white compatible color system that we use today.) While the verdict was out, CBS delayed investment in a network.

Two events changed CBS' mind. First, a critical government decision went against the CBS color system. Then the NBC network's coverage of the 1947 World Series—the first World Series on TV—suddenly made it very apparent that an explosion in TV set ownership was about to take place. CBS, if it did not move quickly, was in danger of being left at the starting gate. A crash program of series development was instituted, and early in 1948 CBS began feeding programs out over its own small network.

The 1947 World Series brought in television's first mass audience. It was carried in New York, Philadelphia, Schenectady, and Washington, D.C., and was seen by an estimated 3.9 million people—3.5 million of them in bars! The TV set over the corner bar was a first introduction to the new medium for many people, and it helped sell thousands of sets for the home. After that, TV ownership was contagious. The first set on the block always brought in dozens of curious neighbors, who eventually went out and bought sets of their own.

By 1948 television networking was on its way. Several of the longest running programs included in this book premiered in that year, including Ted Mack's *Original Amateur Hour* in January, Milton Berle's *Texaco Star Theater* in June, Ed Sullivan's *Toast of the Town* in June, and *Arthur Godfrey's Talent Scouts* in December. NBC opened its midwest network of stations in September 1948, and in a special ceremonial telecast on January 11, 1949, east and midwest were linked. For a time Chicago was an important production center for network programs, but without the talent pool available in New York it could not compete for long. *Kukla, Fran & Ollie* and *Garroway at Large* were probably the most important series to come out of Chicago in its TV heyday.

In September 1951 the link was completed to the west coast, and America at last had nationwide television. Los Angeles was not to become the principal network production center until Hollywood-produced filmed dramatic shows became the TV norm during the second half of the 1950s, however.

In the early years of network operation NBC had the largest audiences, with *Milton Berle, Kraft Television Theater, Your Show of Shows, Dragnet,* and other top hits. But by the mid 1950s, through a combination of astute program development *(I Love Lucy, Ed Sullivan)* and carry-overs from its top radio shows *(Arthur Godfrey, Jack Benny)* CBS took the lead, which it proudly retained for two decades thereafter. Nevertheless, NBC and CBS, the two giants of TV, were never far apart. ABC and DuMont were far behind, fighting for survival—for it was rapidly becoming apparent that there was room for only one other network in the U.S. There were several reasons for this. For one thing the talent pool available for successful TV shows was severely limited and very high priced. NBC and CBS had so many of the trump cards that there just wasn't very much left over for another network, much less for two others. Whenever a new talent emerged on DuMont or ABC, such as Ted Mack *(Original Amateur Hour)* or Jackie Gleason, he would soon be stolen away by the "majors" with the promise of much more money.

Even more important, there were a limited number of stations to go around. Outside of New York and a few other large cities, very few places in the U.S. were serviced by more than two, or perhaps three, stations (many areas still aren't). NBC and CBS always got the best stations in each city, leaving ABC and DuMont to fight for the scraps, or perhaps be seen only part-time on a "shared" station.

In many ways DuMont seemed to be in a good position to become America's third network. The company was led by a brilliant and progressive engineer, Dr. Allen B. DuMont, who seemed to have made all the right decisions at the right times. He was involved in experimental television broadcasting from his laboratory in New Jersey in the early 1930s, long before ABC was even founded (in 1943, as a spinoff from NBC). DuMont had a base in manufacturing, and in fact marketed the first large screen (14 inch) home TV set in 1938. Knowing that large amounts of capital would be needed for television development, he obtained financing from giant Paramount Pictures in 1938 and began active TV programming in the early 1940s. DuMont was close on the heels of NBC in setting up a network in 1946/1947, and its production facilities were the most elaborate in the industry. What went wrong?

One important factor working against DuMont was the fact that the company did not operate a radio network, as did NBC, CBS, and ABC. An established radio network not only provided its competitors with a ready talent pool to draw on, but also gave them a foot in the door in signing up choice affiliates (which were usually associated with network radio stations) in many cities. Another devastating blow was a ruling by the government that DuMont, unlike the other three networks, could not own the legal maximum of five television stations.

Most of the affiliates over which the TV networks send their programs are locally-owned. Each network can by law own outright only five VHF stations. These five are critically important because they provide the base of revenues to support the network (for years the networks themselves all lost money). They also guarantee that all of the network's programs will be seen in at least those five markets. NBC, CBS, and ABC each obtained their quota of five stations early in the game. But because of a series of complicated legal rulings involving its relationship with Paramount Pictures (which also owned stations), DuMont could not, and thus was denied both the revenues and guaranteed program clearances that a full roster of five big market stations could provide. In addition, Paramount refused to give DuMont any further financial support after 1939.

ABC had financial problems too, but in 1953 it got the boost it needed by merging with United Paramount Theaters. With a heavy infusion of capital provided by the merger, ABC began developing programs in earnest, including the landmark deal in 1954 that brought *Walt Disney* to television and in 1955 the arrangement with Warner Brothers that produced many hit series (see under *Warner Brothers Presents*). With the ABC-Paramount Theaters merger, DuMont's fate was sealed, and the latter network finally went out of business in 1956.

Structurally, little has changed in TV networking since that time. In the mid 1950s compatible color TV was introduced, pushed hard by NBC (whose parent company, RCA, manufactured the sets). Video tape effected a behind-the-scenes revolution in the 1960s by freeing producers from the cumbersome aspects of film and the hectic uncertainty of live production. There has been periodic talk of a fourth national network, such as the ill-fated Overmyer Network ("ON") in the 1960s, but this has so far come to naught. Even network ownership has remained unchanged. The giant conglomerate ITT, and later billionaire Howard Hughes, each tried to buy ABC, but neither succeeded. It took ABC nearly thirty years to reach parity with CBS and NBC in audience size. It did not have a number one rated series until *Marcus Welby, M.D.*, in the 1970s, and it did not rank number one as a network for a full season until 1976–1977, when longtime leader CBS was finally deposed.

Over the years America's love affair with television has matured from initial infatuation to an accepted, and pervasive, part of everyday life. It happened very fast. The percentage of U.S. homes with one or more TV sets leaped from 1 percent to 50 percent in five short years (1948–1953), and passed 90 percent in the early 1960s. Today 98 percent of U.S. homes have TV—it is everywhere. And the average home has its set on six and a quarter hours a day, every day.

As for the programs we've watched, they're all in these pages. Leaf through the book, guided perhaps by the year-by-year network schedules and top program rankings in the back. A panorama of the series and the stars who captivated America for thirty-plus years is on display.

The Complete Directory to Prime Time Network TV Shows

1946–present

ABC ALBUM

see *Plymouth Playhouse*

ABC BARN DANCE

Music

FIRST TELECAST: *February 21, 1949*

LAST TELECAST: *November 14, 1949*

BROADCAST HISTORY:

Feb 1949–Jun 1949, ABC Mon 8:30–9:00
Jul 1949–Oct 1949, ABC Mon 9:00–9:30
Oct 1949–Nov 1949, ABC Mon 9:30–10:00

The *National Barn Dance,* begun in 1924 on radio station WLS, Chicago, and long a radio favorite, was carried on ABC television in 1949 as the *ABC Barn Dance.* Among the *Barn Dance* favorites appearing on this half-hour Monday night version were the Sage Riders instrumental quartet, Lulu Belle and Scotty, Cousin Tifford, the De Zurick Sisters (a yodeling duet), and John Dolce. The series was telecast from Chicago.

ABC COMEDY HOUR

Comedy Variety

FIRST TELECAST: *January 12, 1972*

LAST TELECAST: *August 9, 1972*

BROADCAST HISTORY:

Jan 1972–Apr 1972, ABC Wed 8:30–9:30
Jun 1972–Aug 1972, ABC Wed 9:30–10:30

REGULARS:

Rich Little
Frank Gorshin
George Kirby
Marilyn Michaels
Charlie Callas
Joe Baker
Fred Travalena

Most of the telecasts that were aired under the title *ABC Comedy Hour* featured a guest host plus a regular repertory company of impressionists called The Kopycats, listed above. (Fred Travalena replaced Charlie Callas in the company in mid-series.) The series also included a number of other comedy specials, among them two Friars' Roasts, an Alan King special, and an updated version of *Hellzapoppin'.* Reruns of the Kopycats episodes were aired during the summer of 1972 under the title *ABC Comedy Hour Presents the Kopycats.*

ABC DRAMATIC SHORTS—1952–1953

Dramatic Films

ABC had problems in the early 1950s. It had fewer stations than NBC or CBS, few advertisers, and therefore little revenue with which to pay for new programming. In order just to stay on the air, the "other network" was forced to schedule dozens of low-budget quiz shows, interview programs, and documentary films (most obtained free from government and industry). Needless to say, this did not attract much of an audience to the network. In 1952 ABC tried an experiment. It assembled a package of several dozen low-budget 30-minute dramatic films, most of them made by MCA Films in Hollywood. Many of them had been seen on TV before, on ABC (*Gruen Guild Theater*), DuMont (*Gruen Playhouse*), and some even on NBC (*Campbell Soundstage*). These shopworn films were sprinkled liberally throughout the ABC schedule during the 1952–1953 season, on multiple "theater" series. Each film ran up to half a dozen times on different nights and on different series. Not every film would turn up on every series, but if you watched ABC long enough you would frequently get the impression that you had "seen that film before."

Most of the films were grade "B" productions, starring some Hollywood old-timers as well as lesser-known young actors and actresses (some of whom were to gain fame in later years). Among them were Buddy Ebsen, Raymond Burr, Cesar Romero, Ann Rutherford, Helen Parrish, Vincent Price, Anita Louise, Hans Conried, Cliff Arquette, Onslow Stevens, and many others. The scripts included mysteries (such as "The Cavorting Statue" with Cesar Romero), romantic tales ("A Little Pig Cried" with Frances Rafferty), and comedies.

Following is a list of the theater series among which the films rotated during 1952–1953. It is not guaranteed to be complete!

APPOINTMENT WITH LOVE

Dec 1952–Sep 1953, ABC Fri 9:00–9:30

CARNIVAL

Feb 1953–Sep 1953, ABC Thu 8:00–8:30

DARK ADVENTURE

Jan 1953–Jul 1953, ABC Mon 8:30–9:00

DOUBLE EXPOSURE

Jan 1953–Sep 1953, ABC Wed 9:00–9:30

FABLE FOR A SUMMER NIGHT

Jul 1953–Oct 1953, ABC Thu 10:30–11:00

FEAR AND FANCY

May 1953–Aug 1953, ABC Wed 8:00–8:30

FILM FESTIVAL
Jul 1953–Sep 1953, ABC Sun 6:30–7:00
GRUEN GUILD THEATER
Sep 1951–Dec 1951, ABC Thu 9:30–10:00
HALF HOUR THEATRE
Jun 1953–Sep 1953, ABC Fri 9:30–10:00
HOUR GLASS
Jan 1953–Sep 1953, ABC Wed 8:30–9:00
LITTLE THEATRE
Dec 1952–Jan 1953, ABC Wed 7:30–8:00
Aug 1953–Sep 1953, ABC Tue 9:00–10:30 (3 films)
PLAYHOUSE NUMBER 7
Oct 1952–Nov 1952, ABC Sun 9:00–9:30
Nov 1952–Jan 1953, ABC Wed/Sun 9:00–9:30
Jan 1953–Mar 1953, ABC Sun 7:30–8:00
RETURN ENGAGEMENT
Jul 1953–Sep 1953, ABC Mon 9:30–10:00
STRAW HAT THEATER
Jul 1953–Sep 1953, ABC Sun 7:30–8:00
SUMMER FAIR
Jun 1953–Sep 1953, ABC Thu 9:30–10:00
TURNING POINT, THE
Jan 1953–Mar 1953, ABC Thu 9:00–9:30
May 1953–Jun 1953, ABC Sat 7:30–8:00
TWENTIETH CENTURY TALES
Jan 1953–Jul 1953, ABC Wed 8:00–8:30
Jul 1953–Sep 1953, ABC Mon 8:30–9:00
WHITE CAMELLIA, THE
Jan 1953–Mar 1953, ABC Tue 8:30–9:30 (2 films)

ABC FEATURE FILM
see *Movies—Prior to 1961*

ABC LATE NIGHT SPECIALS
see *ABC Wide World of Entertainment*

ABC MONDAY NIGHT COMEDY SPECIAL, THE
Various

FIRST TELECAST: *May 16, 1977*
LAST TELECAST: *September 5, 1977*
BROADCAST HISTORY:
May 1977–Sep 1977, ABC Mon 8:00–8:30

This was an umbrella title, covering an assortment of films for proposed series that did not make the schedule and leftovers from series that had been canceled. Included was a John Byner situation comedy, an unusual rock music show (30 minutes of music—no dialogue), and leftover episodes from the canceled *Blansky's Beauties*, *Nancy Walker Show*, and *Holmes and Yoyo*.

ABC NEWS REPORTS
Documentary/Public Affairs

FIRST TELECAST: *July 7, 1963*
LAST TELECAST: *August 13, 1964*
BROADCAST HISTORY:
Jul 1963–Dec 1963, ABC Sun 10:30–11:00
Jan 1964–Aug 1964, ABC Thu 10:30–11:00
ANCHORMAN:
Bob Young (1963)

Some of the documentaries in this ABC News series were newly produced; others had been aired previously under the title *ABC Closeup*. A major production during August and September 1963 was a five-part series of special reports entitled "Crucial Summer: The 1963 Civil Rights Crisis," produced by Bill Kobin and anchored by newsman Ron Cochran. From September through December 1963, correspondent Bob Young, who was reportedly being groomed as a major on-camera news "personality" by ABC, served as the regular host. Later the anchor responsibilities rotated among various ABC correspondents.

ABC PENTHOUSE PLAYERS
see *ABC Television Players*

ABC PRESENTS
Documentary

FIRST TELECAST: *July 22, 1957*
LAST TELECAST: *October 3, 1957*
BROADCAST HISTORY:
Jul 1957–Sep 1957, ABC Mon 9:00–9:30
Sep 1957–Oct 1957, ABC Thu 8:00–8:30

A documentary film series seen during the summer of 1957, this program was also known as *Quest for Adventure*.

ABC SATURDAY COMEDY SPECIAL, THE
Comedy Anthology

FIRST TELECAST: *June 24, 1978*
LAST TELECAST: *August 5, 1978*
BROADCAST HISTORY:
Jun 1978–Jul 1978, ABC Sat 8:30–9:00
Jul 1978–Aug 1978, ABC Sat 8:00–9:00

This was a collection of pilots for shows which did not make ABC's Fall 1978 schedule, along with miscellaneous reruns. Included were three Harvey Korman comedy episodes and a comedy-variety hour featuring characters from the Archie comic strip, with Dennis Bowen as Archie,

Mark Winkworth as Reggie and Hilary Thompson as Veronica.

ABC SCOPE

Documentary/Public Affairs

FIRST TELECAST: *November 11, 1964*

LAST TELECAST: *March 2, 1968*

BROADCAST HISTORY:

Nov 1964–Sep 1965, ABC Wed 10:30–11:00
Sep 1965–Mar 1968, ABC Sat 10:30–11:00

Filmed reports, interviews, and roundtable discussions of current issues were all part of the format of this weekly public affairs series. ABC has also run many one-time documentary specials under this umbrella title over the years.

ABC SHOWCASE

Drama/Variety

FIRST TELECAST: *June 22, 1950*

LAST TELECAST: *July 26, 1950*

BROADCAST HISTORY:

Jun 1950–Jul 1950, ABC Thu 9:00–9:30

This was a blanket title for a series of dramatic and variety specials run during the summer of 1950 and starring, among others, Betty Furness, Peter Donald, and George O'Hanlon.

ABC STAGE 67

Various

FIRST TELECAST: *September 14, 1966*

LAST TELECAST: *May 11, 1967*

BROADCAST HISTORY:

Sep 1966–Jan 1967, ABC Wed 10:00–11:00
Jan 1967–May 1967, ABC Thu 10:00–11:00

This was an umbrella title for a potpourri of assorted specials. Among them were serious dramas with distinguished international casts, musical comedies and musical variety shows, an occasional documentary, and such unique formats as Jack Paar with examples of the Kennedy wit and David Frost on a tour of London with Peter Sellers, Albert Finney, and Laurence Olivier. The program had no regular host.

ABC TELE-PLAYERS

see *ABC Television Players*

ABC TELEVISION PLAYERS

Dramatic Anthology

FIRST TELECAST: *January 16, 1949*

LAST TELECAST: *October 30, 1949*

BROADCAST HISTORY:

Jan 1949–Mar 1949, ABC Sun 9:00–9:30
Mar 1949–Oct 1949, ABC Sun 7:30–8:00

This was a series of low-budget live dramatic presentations from Chicago, fed to the East Coast network in the months immediately following the opening of the East-Midwest coaxial cable. Little-known Midwestern actors and actresses were used.

In April the title of the series was changed to *ABC Tele-Players*, and in August to *ABC Penthouse Players*.

ABC WIDE WORLD OF ENTERTAINMENT

Various

FIRST TELECAST: *January 1, 1973*

LAST TELECAST:

BROADCAST HISTORY:

Jan 1973– ABC Mon–Fri 11:30–1:00 (approx.)

With the failure of Les Crane, Joey Bishop, or Dick Cavett to attract a substantial following for ABC in the late-night area, the network decided in 1972 to try a new tack. Johnny Carson could have the talk-show audience; ABC countered with a diversified potpourri that, it was hoped, would offer something of interest to everyone. There were nights, in fact whole weeks, with Cavett or Jack Paar hosting talk shows, but there were also comedy specials, mysteries, documentaries, rock-music shows, and just about anything else that could be done on a low budget. The first telecast was in two parts: "Let's Celebrate," a comedy-variety show starring Tony Roberts, followed by a short "Bedtime Story" in which a young married couple talked about their day as they prepared for bed. Other specials included "In Concert" (rock music), "Comedy News," Truman Capote interviewing convicts, and "The Roger Miller Show."

It soon became apparent that the improvisational comedy and offbeat specials were not attracting weary viewers, but the occasional mystery thrillers and TV-movie repeats were. Eventually these became the bulk of the presentations. In recent years quite a few reruns of prime-time dramatic series have also been seen, including *Dan August, Toma, The Rookies, Mannix, Streets of San Francisco, S.W.A.T.*, and others.

The *Wide World of Entertainment* received a three week try-out run from November 21–December 8, 1962, under the title *ABC Late Night Specials*, then returned on January 1, 1973, as a regular feature. The name *Wide World of Entertainment* has lately fallen into disuse in favor of individual titles for each night's presentation.

ABC'S NIGHTLIFE

Talk

FIRST TELECAST: *November 9, 1964*
LAST TELECAST: *November 12, 1965*
BROADCAST HISTORY:
Nov 1964–Nov 1965, ABC Mon–Fri 11:15–1:00
HOST:
Les Crane (Nov 1964–Feb 1965, Jun–Nov 1965)
REGULARS:
William B. Williams (1965)
Nipsey Russell (1965)
Jimmy Cannon (1965)
ORCHESTRA:
Cy Coleman (1965)
Donn Trenner (Mar–Jun 1965)
Elliot Lawrence (Jun–Nov 1965)

ABC's Nightlife was an early and abortive attempt by that network to compete in the late-night area long dominated by NBC's *Tonight Show*. The star was Les Crane, a handsome young talk-show host from San Francisco who had attracted considerable attention there. Les' style was informal, highly spontaneous, and often controversial. The setting was a sort of studio-in-the-round, with the audience seated in circular tiers surrounding the stage, arena-style. Les, perched on his stool, often conversed with audience members by using a long-nosed "shotgun microphone," which he could focus on someone a long distance off. He strove for diversity and intelligence in his guests; the first show featured conservative commentator William Buckley and liberal Representative John V. Lindsay, actress Betsy Palmer, columnist Max Lerner, and comedian Groucho Marx, who acted as "instant critic" of the show.

Other critics were not very friendly, and Les left the show after only four months, to be replaced by a succession of guest hosts, including Shelley Berman, Dave Garroway, and Pat Boone, among others. Radio personality William B. Williams acted as aide-de-camp for all of them. At the end of June, however, Les was back, with Nipsey Russell as his sidekick. Soon after, the program moved from New York to Hollywood, but that couldn't save it. It ended its run just a year and three days after its premiere. Johnny Carson remained king of late-night television.

During its first four months the program was known as *The Les Crane Show*.

A.E.S. HUDSON STREET

Situation Comedy

FIRST TELECAST: *March 23, 1978*
LAST TELECAST: *April 20, 1978*
BROADCAST HISTORY:
Mar 1978–Apr 1978, ABC Thu 9:30–10:00
CAST:
Dr. Antonio "Tony" Menzies .... Gregory Sierra
Nurse Rosa Santiago ....Rosana Soto
J. Powell Karbo ....Stefan Gierasch
Ambulance Driver Foshko ....Susan Peretz
Ambulance Aide Stanke .....Ralph Manza
Nurse Newton ....Ray Stewart
Dr. Mackler ....Bill Cort
Dr. Glick ....Allan Miller

This medical comedy starred Gregory Sierra as Dr. Menzies, the harried chief resident of an inner city emergency ward; "A.E.S." stood for Adult Emergency Services. The location was Hudson Street, New York City, an area as run down as the hospital itself. Perpetually short of funds and surrounded by a staff of lunatics, Dr. Menzies nevertheless dealt with the various accident victims coming through the door as best he could, with good humor and only an occasional yearning to be somewhere else in the medical profession—anywhere else. Dr. Glick was the resident psychiatrist and J. Powell Karbo the bureaucratic hospital administrator.

ABE BURROWS' ALMANAC

Comedy Variety

FIRST TELECAST: *January 4, 1950*
LAST TELECAST: *March 29, 1950*
BROADCAST HISTORY:
Jan 1950–Mar 1950, CBS Wed 9:00–9:30
REGULARS:
Abe Burrows
Milton Delugg and His Orchestra

This live variety series starred comedian

Abe Burrows, "the bald-headed baritone from Brooklyn," who chatted with orchestra leader Milton Delugg and welcomed different guest stars each week. Burrows had hosted two short-lived radio series in the late 1940's, but his greatest fame came as a writer-director for radio (*Duffy's Tavern*), Broadway (*Guys and Dolls, How to Succeed in Business Without Really Trying*), and Hollywood (*The Solid Gold Cadillac*).

ACADEMY THEATRE

Dramatic Anthology

FIRST TELECAST: *July 25, 1949*

LAST TELECAST: *September 12, 1949*

BROADCAST HISTORY:

Jul 1949–Sep 1949, NBC Mon 8:00–8:30

This series of eight live half-hour dramas replaced *Chevrolet on Broadway* for the summer of 1949. It had a different cast each week, consisting of lesser-known actors and actresses in playlets by such authors as Thorton Wilder, Edna St. Vincent Millay, and Robert Finch. *Academy Theatre* was produced by Curtis Canfield, Professor of Dramatics at Amherst College.

ACAPULCO

Adventure

FIRST TELECAST: *February 27, 1961*

LAST TELECAST: *April 24, 1961*

BROADCAST HISTORY:

Feb 1961–Apr 1961, NBC Mon 9:00–9:30

CAST:

Patrick Malone ....Ralph Taeger
Gregg Miles ....James Coburn
Mr. Carver ....Telly Savalas
Chloe ....Allison Hayes
Bobby ....Bobby Troup
Max ....Jason Robards, Jr.

Ralph Taeger and James Coburn starred as two Korean War buddies turned action-prone "beachcombers" in sunny Acapulco. Mr. Carver, a retired criminal lawyer, had supplied them with a beach cottage adjoining his sumptuous estate in return for their help in protecting him from enemies made during his career as a gang-busting lawyer. The two ex-GI's were constantly forced to give up their girl-chasing to protect Mr. Carver, but they still managed to spend much time at a small club run by musician Bobby Troup and at a more opulent club run by Chloe, a beautiful woman who knew everything about everybody in Acapulco.

ACCENT ON AN AMERICAN SUMMER

Travelogue

FIRST TELECAST: *June 7, 1962*

LAST TELECAST: *September 6, 1962*

BROADCAST HISTORY:

Jun 1962–Sep 1962, CBS Thu 7:30–8:00

HOST:

John Ciardi

Accent on an American Summer was a summer series that took viewers on tours of various places of historic or general interest. Hosted by John Ciardi, the series went to Monticello, Thomas Jefferson's home; the American Shakespeare Festival, to see excerpts from two plays; the wilds of Yellowstone National Park; the gambling environment of Reno, Nevada; and other varied locales.

ACCIDENTAL FAMILY

Situation Comedy

FIRST TELECAST: *September 15, 1967*

LAST TELECAST: *January 5, 1968*

BROADCAST HISTORY:

Sep 1967–Jan 1968, NBC Fri 9:30–10:00

CAST:

Jerry Webster ....Jerry Van Dyke
Sue Kramer ....Lois Nettleton
Sandy Webster ....Teddy Quinn
Tracy Kramer ....Susan Benjamin
Ben McGrath ....Ben Blue
Marty Warren ....Larry D. Mann

Jerry Van Dyke played nightclub comedian Jerry Webster, one of TV's many widowers confronted with the problems of raising a young son, Sandy, played by Teddy Quinn. In this series Father decided literally to "farm out" his son by purchasing a farm in California's San Fernando Valley as a full-time home for the boy and part-time home for himself, between performing commitments. Farm manager Sue Kramer, a pretty divorcée whose daughter, Tracy, just happened to be Sandy's age, served as de facto governess for the boy and foil for Jerry. Ben McGrath, the farm handyman, and Marty Warren, Jerry's friend and lawyer, rounded out the cast of regulars.

ACCUSED

Courtroom Drama

FIRST TELECAST: *December 10, 1958*

LAST TELECAST: *September 30, 1959*
BROADCAST HISTORY:
Dec 1958–Sep 1959, ABC Wed 9:30–10:00
CAST:
Presiding Judge ......Edgar Allan Jones Jr.
Presiding Judge (occasional)
.... William Gwinn
Bailiff ....Tim Farrell
Clerk ....Jim Hodson
Reporter ....Violet Gilmore

Accused was a prime-time spin-off from *Day in Court*, a popular ABC daytime program that presented filmed reenactments of actual cases. Realism was the keynote of the series; the judge for most of the trials was Edgar Allan Jones, Jr., a UCLA law professor, and the prosecution and defense attorneys were also real-life lawyers. Only the defendants and witnesses were actors, usually obscure ones but occasionally such well-known performers as Pamela Mason and Robert Culp (who appeared with his wife, actress Nancy Ash). The cases were almost invariably criminal proceedings.

Accused was produced by Selig J. Seligman, a former State Department attorney and ABC-TV Vice President, who kept a whole staff of lawyers and law students busy digging through court records and law books to provide authenticity for the show.

During its first few weeks on the air the nighttime series was known as *Day in Court*. The daytime version continued under that name from 1958 until 1965.

ACT IT OUT

see *Say It with Acting*

ACTION AUTOGRAPHS

Documentary
FIRST TELECAST: *April 24, 1949*
LAST TELECAST: *January 8, 1950*
BROADCAST HISTORY:
Apr 1949–Jun 1949, ABC Sun 10:00–10:15
Sep 1949–Jan 1950, ABC Sun 6:30–6:45
HOST:
Ed Prentiss

This short filmed program was sponsored by Bell & Howell Cameras, evidently to show how the medium of film could allow viewers to drop in on many interesting people and watch their activities. Interviews, demonstrations, and performances were included. Among the subjects were the national barbershop quartet champions, a water show, singer Burl Ives, and Dr. Beryl Orris psychoanalyzing the thoughts and actions of a character played by actor Richard Basehart in a scene from the play *She Walks at Night*.

ACTION TONIGHT

Dramatic Anthology
FIRST TELECAST: *July 15, 1957*
LAST TELECAST: *September 2, 1957*
BROADCAST HISTORY:
Jul 1957–Sep 1957, NBC Mon 8:30–9:00

This series presented filmed reruns of dramas originally seen on *Schlitz Playhouse* and *Pepsi-Cola Playhouse*.

ACTORS STUDIO

Dramatic Anthology
FIRST TELECAST: *September 26, 1948*
LAST TELECAST: *June 23, 1950*
BROADCAST HISTORY:
Sep 1948–Mar 1949, ABC Sun 8:30–9:00
Mar 1949–Apr 1949, ABC Thu 8:30–9:00
May 1949, ABC Thu 9:30–10:00
Sep 1949–Oct 1949, ABC Wed 8:00–8:30
Nov 1949–Jan 1950, CBS Tue 9:00–9:30
Feb 1950–Jun 1950, CBS Fri 9:00–10:00
PRODUCER:
Donald Davis

This was one of the first "prestige" dramatic showcases on the fledgling ABC network. It was produced live each week by the Actors Studio, Inc., a nonprofit organization for professional actors and actresses. Most productions were serious dramas, encompassing both adaptations of classic stories and occasional original scripts. Among the authors represented were William Saroyan, James Thurber, Ring Lardner, Edgar Allan Poe, Irwin Shaw, and Budd Schulberg. Performers included such first-rate talent as Julie Harris, Cloris Leachman, Martin Balsam, Marc Connelly, and Kim Hunter. The first telecast was "Portrait of a Madonna" and starred Jessica Tandy.

Actors Studio made a strong impression during its first months on the air, and received a Peabody Award for its "uninhibited and brilliant pioneering in the field of televised drama" during the year 1948.

During its final four months the program expanded to a full hour and was seen every other week, alternating with *Ford Theatre*.

The series name was changed to *The Play's the Thing* in March 1950.

ACTUALITY SPECIALS

Documentary

FIRST TELECAST: *July 16, 1962*
LAST TELECAST: *September 13, 1968*
BROADCAST HISTORY:
Jul 1962–Sep 1962, NBC Mon 10:00–11:00
Oct 1965–Jun 1967, NBC Sun 6:30–7:30 (OS)
Sep 1967–Sep 1968, NBC Fri 10:00–11:00

Actuality Specials was a collection of NBC News documentary specials. Some were reruns of programs shown earlier; others were new programs made specifically for this series. Narrators were usually NBC newsmen such as Robert MacNeil, Edwin Newman, Frank McGee, and Chet Huntley; however, celebrities such as Lorne Greene or Raymond Burr sometimes provided narration. *Actuality Specials* frequently alternated with other documentary series such as *NBC White Paper, NBC News Special, Campaign and the Candidates*, and *American Profile*.

AD LIBBERS

Improvisation

FIRST TELECAST: *August 3, 1951*
LAST TELECAST: *August 31, 1951*
BROADCAST HISTORY:
Aug 1951, CBS Fri 8:00–8:30
HOST:
Peter Donald
REGULARS:
Charles Mendick
Patricia Hosley
Joe Silver
Jack Lemmon
Cynthia Stone
Earl Hammond

This live series of improvisations was the 1951 summer replacement for *Mama*. Peter Donald, the host, would read a brief outline of a situation to the performers, who would then ad-lib dialogue to fit the situation. There were three or four sketches performed during each episode of this five-week show.

ADAM 12

Police Drama

FIRST TELECAST: *September 21, 1968*
LAST TELECAST: *August 26, 1975*
BROADCAST HISTORY:
Sep 1968–Sep 1969, NBC Sat 7:30–8:00
Sep 1969–Jan 1971, NBC Sat 8:30–9:00
Jan 1971–Sep 1971, NBC Thu 9:30–10:00
Sep 1971–Jan 1974, NBC Wed 8:00–8:30
Jan 1974–Aug 1975, NBC Tue 8:00–8:30
CAST:
Officer Pete Malloy ....Martin Milner
Officer Jim Reed ....Kent McCord
Sgt. MacDonald ....William Boyett
Officer Ed Wells ....Gary Crosby
Officer Woods (1974–1975)
..........................Fred Stromsoe

Produced by Jack Webb, whose realistic portrayal of police work had scored a major hit in *Dragnet*, *Adam 12* dealt with the day-to-day working world of two uniformed policemen assigned to patrol-car duty. Officer Pete Malloy was a senior officer who at the start of the series was teamed with a probationary rookie cop, Jim Reed. As members of the Los Angeles Police Department, they encountered a wide range of cases in each episode, some serious, some trivial, some amusing, and some tragic. Running as it did for seven seasons, *Adam 12* saw changes in the status of the officers as the years passed. During the 1970–1971 season Jim Reed was promoted from rookie to officer, and in the following year Officer Malloy was upped to Policeman 3, one notch below the rank of sergeant.

ADAM'S RIB

Situation Comedy

FIRST TELECAST: *September 14, 1973*
LAST TELECAST: *December 28, 1973*
BROADCAST HISTORY:
Sep 1973–Dec 1973, ABC Fri 9:30–10:00
CAST:
Adam Bonner ....Ken Howard
Amanda Bonner ....Blythe Danner
Gracie ....Dena Dietrich
Asst. D.A. Roy Mendelsohn .....Ron Rifkin
Kip Kipple ....Edward Winter
District Attorney Donahue
........................Norman Bartold
CREATOR/PRODUCER/DIRECTOR:
Peter H. Hunt
THEME:
"Two People," by Perry Botkin, Jr., and Gil Garfield

This romantic comedy was based on the Spencer Tracy–Katharine Hepburn movie classic of the same title. The show concerned a young Assistant D.A. and his wife, a junior partner in a law firm, whose jobs often put them on opposite sides in the courtroom as well as at home. *Adam's Rib* made overtures to the Women's Lib movement by building many stories around Amanda's crusades for women's rights (50 percent of the show's writers were women), but the program never found an audience.

Dena Dietrich ("Mother Nature" of commercials fame) played Amanda's secretary, and Edward Winter her law partner, while Norman Bartold and Ron Rifkin were on Adam's side.

ADDAMS FAMILY, THE

Situation Comedy

FIRST TELECAST: *September 18, 1964*
LAST TELECAST: *September 2, 1966*
BROADCAST HISTORY:

Sep 1964–Sep 1966, ABC Fri 8:30–9:00

CAST:

Morticia ....Carolyn Jones
Gomez ....John Astin
Uncle Fester ....Jackie Coogan
Lurch ....Ted Cassidy
Grandmama ....Blossom Rock
Pugsley ....Ken Weatherwax
Wednesday ....Lisa Loring

The strange, macabre, but somehow amusing cartoon characters created by Charles Addams for *The New Yorker* magazine made their live-action debut in the fall of 1964, one of two almost identical "ghoul comedies" to premiere that year (see also CBS's *Munsters*). Morticia was the beautiful but somber lady of the house. Her husband Gomez had strange eyes and rather destructive instincts, as did Uncle Fester. Lurch, the butler, was a seven-foot-tall warmed-over Frankenstein monster whose dialogue usually consisted solely of the two words, "You rang?" The children also had a rather ghoulish quality about them. Grandmama, although a witch, was the most normal-looking one of the bunch. They all lived in a musty, castlelike home full of strange objects—such as a disembodied hand, called "Thing," which kept popping out of a black box—and they scared almost everyone—except viewers —half to death.

ADMIRAL BROADWAY REVUE

Variety

FIRST TELECAST: *January 28, 1949*
LAST TELECAST: *June 3, 1949*
BROADCAST HISTORY:

Jan 1949–Jun 1949, NBC & DUM Fri 8:00–9:00

REGULARS:

Sid Caesar
Imogene Coca
Mary McCarty
Marge and Gower Champion

Sid Caesar won his first regular starring role in this program, which united him in a comedy team with Imogene Coca for the first time.

Neither of them was new to television in 1949, Caesar having guest-starred on Milton Berle's show during the previous fall and Coca having appeared on television as early as 1939.

Though short-lived, *Admiral Broadway Revue* was one of early television's most spectacular productions, completely dominating Friday night viewing the way that Milton Berle dominated Tuesday and Ed Sullivan, Sunday. The series was produced and directed by Max Liebman and was built along the lines of a Broadway music and comedy revue, with top-name guest stars and big production numbers. For example, the opening program included half a dozen comedy skits and closed with an elaborate burlesque on opera in the style of Billy Rose, called "No No Rigoletto." The program was telecast live from the newly completed International Theatre in New York and was one of the few major programs ever to be carried on two networks simultaneously (NBC and DuMont). It was seen in every city in the United States that had television facilities, either live from the networks or on kinescope in markets not yet having network connections.

ADMIRAL PRESENTS THE FIVE STAR REVUE—WELCOME ABOARD

see *Welcome Aboard*

ADMISSION FREE

see *Movies—Prior to 1961*

ADORN PLAYHOUSE

Dramatic Anthology

FIRST TELECAST: *May 13, 1958*
LAST TELECAST: *July 1, 1958*

BROADCAST HISTORY:
May 1958–Jul 1958, CBS Tue 8:30–9:00

This 1958 summer series consisted of reruns of episodes from other CBS anthologies, primarily *Schlitz Playhouse*.

ADVENTURE
Wildlife/Adventure
FIRST TELECAST: *June 28, 1953*
LAST TELECAST: *September 27, 1953*
BROADCAST HISTORY:
Jun 1953–Sep 1953, CBS Sun 6:00–7:00
NARRATOR:
Charles Collingwood

Produced in cooperation with the American Museum of Natural History, *Adventure* was composed of interviews with naturalists, anthropologists, and other authorities, coupled with filmed reports of expeditions to remote areas and primitive peoples. Charles Collingwood was the host of the series, which actually had its premiere as a late-Sunday-afternoon program on May 10, 1953. Following its run as an evening program, it returned to Sunday afternoons where it remained on the air until June of 1955.

ADVENTURE PLAYHOUSE
see *Movies—Prior to 1961*

ADVENTURE SHOWCASE
Adventure Anthology
FIRST TELECAST: *August 11, 1959*
LAST TELECAST: *September 1, 1959*
BROADCAST HISTORY:
Aug 1959–Sep 1959, CBS Tue 9:00–9:30

This four-week summer series consisted of unsold pilots for proposed adventure series.

ADVENTURE THEATER
Adventure Anthology
FIRST TELECAST: *June 16, 1956*
LAST TELECAST: *August 31, 1957*
BROADCAST HISTORY:
Jun 1956–Sep 1956, NBC Sat 10:30–11:00
Jun 1957–Aug 1957, NBC Sat 10:30–11:00
HOST:
Paul Douglas

Aired as a summer replacement for *Your Hit Parade*, this program presented filmed, two-act plays that were produced in England. Host Paul Douglas introduced the plays, appearing as a storyteller who had been to England and returned with various objects such as a fur coat or a scarf, each of which led into the story with which it was associated. The 1957 series consisted of repeats of the 1956 episodes.

ADVENTURE THEATER
Dramatic Anthology
FIRST TELECAST: *August 4, 1960*
LAST TELECAST: *September 22, 1961*
BROADCAST HISTORY:
Aug 1960–Sep 1960, CBS Thu 10:00–10:30
Jul 1961–Sep 1961, CBS Fri 9:30–10:00

The dramas seen in this summer series were all reruns of episodes originally telecast on *Schlitz Playhouse*. There was no host.

ADVENTURES AT SCOTT ISLAND
see *Harbourmaster*

ADVENTURES IN JAZZ
Music
FIRST TELECAST: *January 28, 1949*
LAST TELECAST: *June 24, 1949*
BROADCAST HISTORY:
Jan 1949–Jun 1949, CBS Fri 8:00–8:30
HOST:
Fred Robbins
Bill Williams

Disc jockey Fred Robbins—noted for his unique chatter, concocted vocabulary, and floppy bow tie—was host of this live show, which brought jazz musicians and singers to television. After appearing on the show's premiere telecast, Robbins departed for other commitments and did not return to the series until May. Bill Williams hosted in Robbins' absence.

ADVENTURES IN PARADISE
Adventure
FIRST TELECAST: *October 5, 1959*
LAST TELECAST: *April 1, 1962*
BROADCAST HISTORY:
Oct 1959–Sep 1961, ABC Mon 9:30–10:30
Oct 1961–Apr 1962, ABC Sun 10:00–11:00
CAST:
Capt. Adam Troy ....Gardner McKay
Oliver Lee (1959–1961) ....Weaver Levy
Renee (1960–1961) ....Linda Lawson
Lovey (1960–1961) ....Henry Slate
Clay Baker (1960–1962) .....James Holden

Trader Penrose (1960–1961)
.... George Tobias
Sondi (1960–1961) .... Sondi Sodsai
Kelly (1960–1962) .... Lani Kai
Chris Parker (1961–1962) ... Guy Stockwell
Inspector Bouchard (1961–1962)
.... Marcel Hillaire

This series featured handsome Gardner McKay as Adam Troy, the captain of a free-lance schooner plying the South Pacific in search of passengers, cargo, and adventure. Troy was a Korean War veteran who had found the Pacific to his liking. His schooner, the *Tiki*, ranged across the area from Hong Kong to Pitcairn Island with all sorts of adventurers, schemers, and island beauties aboard. Troy's original partner was a Chinese-American named Oliver Lee. In 1960 he hired a first mate named Clay Baker. The following season Baker went ashore to become manager of the Bali Miki hotel (replacing Trader Penrose), and Troy took on Chris Parker as his first mate. The females in the cast were young Tahitians and other lovely young women who seemed to abound in this series.

James A. Michener created *Adventures in Paradise* and sold the original idea to television, but then he apparently dropped out of the project. Critics complained that the series contained none of the scripting one would expect from such an eminent author. Even the sets looked like the 20th Century Fox back lot—which it was—though, after a couple of years, some location filming was actually done in the South Pacific.

ADVENTURES OF CHAMPION, THE

Adventure

FIRST TELECAST: *September 30, 1955*
LAST TELECAST: *February 3, 1956*
BROADCAST HISTORY:
Sep 1955–Feb 1956, CBS Fri 7:30–8:00
CAST:
Ricky North .... Barry Curtis
Sandy North .... Jim Bannon
Will Calhoun .... Francis McDonald
Sheriff Powers .... Ewing Mitchell

This series was produced by Gene Autry and starred Champion the Wonder Horse, his mount. In *The Adventures of Champion*, the talented horse was owned by 12-year-old Ricky North, the only person Champion would allow to ride him. Ricky also owned a German shepherd named Rebel, and both the horse and the dog were his constant companions. Ricky, who lived on a ranch owned by his Uncle Sandy, had a penchant for getting involved in dangerous situations. But whether he was faced with natural disasters or with evil men who would steal, murder, or in some other way cause trouble, Champion and Rebel would come to his rescue by performing some feat not normally associated with horses or dogs.

ADVENTURES OF ELLERY QUEEN, THE

Detective Drama

FIRST TELECAST: *October 14, 1950*
LAST TELECAST: *September 5, 1976*
BROADCAST HISTORY:
Oct 1950–Dec 1951, DUM Thu 9:00–9:30 (OS)
Dec 1951–Mar 1952, ABC Sun 7:30–8:00
Apr 1952–Dec 1952, ABC Wed 9:00–9:30
Sep 1958–Aug 1959, NBC Fri 8:00–9:00
Sep 1975–Dec 1975, NBC Thu 9:00–10:00
Jan 1976–Sep 1976, NBC Sun 8:00–9:00
CAST:
Ellery Queen (1950–1951) .... John Hart
Ellery Queen (1951–1952) .... Lee Bowman
Inspector Richard Queen
(1950–1952) .... Florenz Ames
Ellery Queen (1958–1959) ... George Nader
Inspector Richard Queen
(1958–1959) .... Les Tremayne
Ellery Queen (1959) .... Lee Philips
Ellery Queen (1975–1976) ...... Jim Hutton
Inspector Richard Queen
(1975–1976) .... David Wayne
Sgt. Velie (1975–1976) .... Tom Reese

Fictional mystery writer-supersleuth Ellery Queen had been the main character in a number of popular mystery novels, written by Frederic Dannay and Manfred Bennington Lee, before he became a regular feature on the CBS Radio Network in 1939. A decade later he made the first of four appearances on television. Ellery was a slightly absentminded mystery writer who would sort through a mass of evidence and a large collection of suspects to determine the guilty party in a crime, usually murder. His aid was regularly sought by his father, an inspector with the New York Police Department. Inspector Queen never ceased to marvel at the way his son could reach the proper conclusion by unearthing the most obscure clues—often left by the dying victim—and piecing them together.

John Hart was television's first Ellery Queen, portraying the role in *The Adventures of Ellery Queen*, a live series that premiered on DuMont in the fall of 1950. The following January, Hart died of a sudden and unexpected heart attack—he was in his 30s—and was replaced by Lee Bowman. Bowman stayed with the series when it moved to ABC in December of 1951 and played Ellery until its cancellation in December 1952. In 1954 a syndicated film version appeared, also titled *The Adventures of Ellery Queen*, and starring Hugh Marlowe, one of four actors who had played the role on radio. The title of the syndicated version was changed in 1956 to *Mystery Is My Business*.

Ellery returned to live network television on NBC in the fall of 1958 with George Nader in the title role. To distinguish it from its predecessors, this edition was titled *The Further Adventures of Ellery Queen* but, effective with the October 24, 1958, telecast, the title was shortened to *Ellery Queen*. When production of this edition shifted from Hollywood to New York, and went from live to videotape, both of the principal actors—George Nader and Les Tremayne—left the series. The role of Ellery was assumed by Lee Philips and that of Inspector Queen was dropped.

After a gap of 16 years, NBC once more brought the series back to television, with Jim Hutton in the title role. This version, also titled *Ellery Queen*, was done as a period piece set in New York City in the late 1940s. Sergeant Velie, the plainclothes assistant to Inspector Queen, was now a regular in the cast; he had appeared in the novels and the radio series, but had not been seen regularly in any of the previous TV versions. At the climax of each episode, just before resolving the case, Ellery would turn to the television audience and ask, "Have you figured it out? Do you know who the murderer is?"

ADVENTURES OF HIRAM HOLIDAY, THE

Situation Comedy

FIRST TELECAST: *October 3, 1956*

LAST TELECAST: *February 27, 1957*

BROADCAST HISTORY:

Oct 1956–Feb 1957, NBC Wed 8:00–8:30

CAST:

Hiram Holiday ....Wally Cox
Joel Smith ....Ainslie Pryor

Hiram was a meek, mild-mannered proofreader for a New York newspaper who was discovered to possess physical and technical skills in a remarkable assortment of activities, such as fencing, scuba diving, airplane piloting, and art forgery. This so impressed his publisher that the newspaper sent him on a trip around the world, along with reporter Joel Smith as companion and recorder of his adventures.

ADVENTURES OF JIM BOWIE, THE

Western

FIRST TELECAST: *September 7, 1956*

LAST TELECAST: *August 29, 1958*

BROADCAST HISTORY:

Sep 1956–Aug 1958, ABC Fri 8:00–8:30

CAST:

Jim Bowie ....Scott Forbes
John James Audubon ...Robert Cornthwaite
Rezin Bowie ....Peter Hanson

This Western was unusual in at least two respects: it was based—somewhat loosely, to be sure—on a real historical character, and its hero wielded a knife instead of a gun. According to the scriptwriters, Jim Bowie invented his famous knife after an encounter with a grizzly bear in which his standard blade broke at a critical moment. His new Bowie knife became his favorite weapon, although ABC, sensitive to parental reaction, played down its explicit use as a weapon in this series.

The Adventures of Jim Bowie was set in the Louisiana Territory of the 1830s, which provided backdrops of French-American New Orleans, and backwoods settings. Bowie was a wealthy young planter and adventurer, and his path crossed those of many interesting people, including his good friend John James Audubon (the naturalist painter), pirate Jean Lafitte, Sam Houston, Andrew Jackson, and even Johnny Appleseed. In one episode Jim ran for Congress against Davy Crockett. A young Michael Landon appeared in a 1956 episode.

The show was adapted from the book *Tempered Blade*, by Monte Barrett.

ADVENTURES OF MCGRAW, THE

see *Meet McGraw*

ADVENTURES OF OKY DOKY

Children's

FIRST TELECAST: *November 4, 1948*

LAST TELECAST: *May 26, 1949*
BROADCAST HISTORY:
Nov 1948–Mar 1949, DUM Thu 7:00–7:30
Mar 1949–May 1949, DUM Tue/Thu 6:45–7:00
HOSTESS:
Wendy Barrie
VOICE OF OKY DOKY:
Dayton Allen

Oky Doky was a large (30-inch) mustachioed puppet created by Raye Copeland, which was first seen on a local New York kids' fashion show called *Tots, Tweens and Teens*. He later got his own show on the DuMont network, called first *Adventures of Oky Doky* and later *Oky Doky Ranch*. The setting was a dude ranch to which the kids flocked, to watch Oky's latest Western adventure and to take part in games and junior talent performances. There was a certain amount of roughhouse in Oky's sketches, including knock-down drag-out fights with the bad guys and lots of smashed furniture, but Oky triumphed in the end, thanks to his magic strength pills (they contained good wholesome MILK, kids!).

ADVENTURES OF OZZIE & HARRIET, THE

Situation Comedy
FIRST TELECAST: *October 3, 1952*
LAST TELECAST: *September 3, 1966*
BROADCAST HISTORY:
Oct 1952–Jun 1956, ABC Fri 8:00–8:30 (OS)
Oct 1956–Sep 1958, ABC Wed 9:00–9:30
Sep 1958–Sep 1961, ABC 8:00–8:30
Sep 1961–Sep 1963, ABC Thu 7:30–8:00
Sep 1963–Jan 1966, ABC Wed 7:30–8:00
Jan 1966–Sep 1966, ABC Sat 7:30–8:00
CAST:
Ozzie Nelson .... Himself
Harriet Nelson .... Herself
David Nelson .... Himself
Eric "Ricky" Nelson .... Himself
"Thorny" Thornberry (1952–1958) .... Don DeFore
Darby (1955–1961) .... Parley Baer
Joe Randolph (1956–1966) ..... Lyle Talbot
Clara Randolph (1956–1966) .... Mary Jane Croft
Doc Williams (1956–1965) ..... Frank Cady
Wally (1957–1966) .... Skip Young
Butch (1959–1960) .... Gordon Jones
June (Mrs. David Nelson) (1961–1966) .... June Blair
Kris (Mrs. Rick Nelson) (1964–1966) .... Kristin Harmon
PRODUCER/DIRECTOR/HEAD WRITER:
Ozzie Nelson

One of TV's longest-running family comedies, this program was as much a picture of reality in its own way as the "relevance" comedies of the 1970s. *The Adventures of Ozzie & Harriet* was the real-life Nelson family on the air, with all the little adventures that an active and interesting middle-class American family might have, and two young boys growing up before their parents'—and the television audience's—eyes. Even the house they lived in was modeled on the Nelson's real-life home in Hollywood. About the only liberties taken with reality, for dramatic purposes, was in Ozzie's role. On TV he had no defined source of income, and always seemed to be hanging around the house. In real life Ozzie Nelson was a hard worker indeed, having been the nation's youngest Eagle Scout at age 13, an honor student and star quarterback at Rutgers, and a nationally known bandleader in the 1930s. His wife, Harriet, had once been his band's vocalist.

Their two sons were the real stars of the program. When *The Adventures of Ozzie & Harriet* began on radio in 1944, the boys' roles were played by professional actors, but in 1949 Ozzie finally allowed his actual offspring to go on the air. From then until the TV version ended, America watched the two boys grow up. From 1952 to 1966 Ricky went from a crew-cut 11-year-old, to a real-life teenage singing idol, to a 25-year-old husband.

In the early episodes the stories revolved mostly around the four Nelsons, with only a few friends and neighbors featured—notably Thorny Thornberry, a holdover from radio days, who regularly offered Ozzie bits of ill-timed advice. Later, as the boys began to date, a succession of girl friends and school buddies began to appear. In 1956 David went off to college, followed four years later by Ricky. In the meantime Ricky had begun a show business career of his own, which gave *The Adventures of Ozzie & Harriet* quite a boost among younger viewers. A fall 1956 episode had him organizing a rock 'n' roll band in high school. Then in an April 1957 telecast he picked up a guitar and sang a currently popular Fats Domino hit, "I'm Walkin' "—which, backed with "A Teenager's Romance," promptly became a real-life million-selling record for him. It was no flash-in-the-pan. Ricky went on to become one of the biggest stars of the rock era, and all of his songs were featured in *Ozzie & Harriet* episodes, or in an unconnected short segment tacked on to the end of the show.

In time both David and Ricky were married, and both real-life wives (June and Kris) appeared on the show. David emerged from "college" as a lawyer, and opened a law office, in which Ricky later worked as a part-time clerk. Toward the end *The Adventures of Ozzie & Harriet* became almost a living exercise in nostalgia, with a number of episodes from the early 1950s being rerun during the last two seasons. The final original telecast in 1966 was wistful; it had Ozzie deciding to buy a pool table and convert David and Ricky's now vacant bedroom into a game room—until he met with stiff opposition from Harriet.

For a short time in 1960 the series ran under the title *The Adventures of the Nelson Family*.

ADVENTURES OF RIN TIN TIN, THE

Western

FIRST TELECAST: *October 15, 1954*
LAST TELECAST: *August 28, 1959*
BROADCAST HISTORY:
Oct 1954–Aug 1959, ABC Fri 7:30–8:00
CAST:
Rusty .... Lee Aaker
Lt. Rip Masters .... James Brown
Sgt. Biff O'Hara .... Joe Sawyer
Cpl. Boone .... Rand Brooks
TRAINER:
Lee Duncan

The Adventures of Rin Tin Tin was TV's "other" dog show. Despite some similarities to *Lassie*—it featured a heroic dog, with a small boy as his companion—there were considerable differences between the two shows. *Rin Tin Tin* was set in the Old West and was full of violent action, including gunfights, rampaging Indians, and the like. The boy, Rusty, had in fact been orphaned in an Indian raid, after which he and his dog Rin Tin Tin ("Yo ho, Rinty!") were adopted by the cavalry soldiers at Fort Apache, Arizona. The two were made honorary troopers and for the next five seasons proceeded to help the cavalry and the townspeople of nearby Mesa Grande establish law and order on the frontier.

Rin Tin Tin was a movie favorite of long standing, the first Rin Tin Tin feature having been made in 1922. Three different German shepherds filled the role in the TV series, two of them descendants of the original Rinty (who died in 1932) and the other the offspring of another movie canine, Flame, Jr.

ADVENTURES OF ROBIN HOOD, THE

Adventure

FIRST TELECAST: *September 26, 1955*
LAST TELECAST: *September 22, 1958*
BROADCAST HISTORY:
Sep 1955–Sep 1958, CBS Mon 7:30–8:00
CAST:
Robin Hood .... Richard Greene
Maid Marian (1955–1957)
.... Bernadette O'Farrell
Maid Marian (1957–1958)
.... Patricia Driscoll
Sir Richard .... Ian Hunter
Friar Tuck .... Alexander Gauge
Little John .... Archie Duncan
Sheriff of Nottingham ...... Alan Wheatley
Prince John .... Donald Pleasence

Filmed completely on location in England, *The Adventures of Robin Hood* brought the famous swashbuckler to American television. Robin and his Merry Men made their home in Sherwood Forest. Their efforts to rob from the rich to give to the poor were frowned upon by Prince John and the Sheriff of Nottingham. Robin's true love, Maid Marian, was a member of Prince John's court who provided Robin with useful information, which helped him frustrate the efforts of the sheriff to capture him.

ADVENTURES OF SIR FRANCIS DRAKE, THE

Adventure

FIRST TELECAST: *June 24, 1962*
LAST TELECAST: *September 9, 1962*
BROADCAST HISTORY:
Jun 1962–Sep 1962, NBC Sun 8:30–9:00
CAST:
Sir Francis Drake .... Terence Morgan
Queen Elizabeth I .... Jean Kent
Richard Trevelyan .... Patrick McLoughlin

Walsingham ....Richard Warner
Morton, Earl of Lenox ....Ewan Roberts
Mendoza, the Spanish Ambassador
..........................Roger Delgado

Filmed in England, and used as a summer replacement for *Car 54, Where Are You?*, this series consisted of fictional stories about Sir Francis Drake, the 16th-century adventurer. His varied skills as a seaman, soldier, pirate, explorer, and spy made him an invaluable asset to the court of Queen Elizabeth I. Included in his exploits were the rescue of Sir Walter Raleigh's lost colony in Virginia; an attack on the Spanish fort at St. Augustine in what is now Florida; and the release of a captive Seminole Indian princess. The producers made every effort to replicate exactly Drake's ship, *The Golden Hind*, and emphasis was placed on accuracy in historical detail.

ADVENTURES OF SIR LANCELOT, THE

Adventure

FIRST TELECAST: *September 24, 1956*
LAST TELECAST: *June 24, 1957*
BROADCAST HISTORY:
Sep 1956–Jun 1957, NBC Mon 8:00–8:30
CAST:
Sir Lancelot ....William Russell
Queen Guinevere ....Jane Hylton
King Arthur ....Ronald Leigh-Hunt
Merlin ....Cyril Smith
Leonides ....Peter Bennett
Brian ....Bobby Scroggins

This series, consisting of stories of the most famous knight of the Round Table, was filmed in England after extensive research had been done by Oxford University to guarantee the authenticity of the sixth- and seventh-century settings. Themes for the episodes came from assorted legends surrounding the chivalrous acts of Sir Lancelot and the other members of King Arthur's court.

ADVENTURES OF THE NELSON FAMILY, THE

see *Adventures of Ozzie & Harriet, The*

AIR POWER

Documentary

FIRST TELECAST: *November 11, 1956*
LAST TELECAST: *October 19, 1958*
BROADCAST HISTORY:
Nov 1956–May 1957, CBS Sun 6:30–7:00
May 1958–Oct 1958, CBS Sun 6:30–7:00
NARRATOR:
Walter Cronkite

Air Power was a documentary series produced with the cooperation of the U.S. Air Force. Using filmed footage from all over the world, it traced the history of the airplane and gave an appraisal of its impact on the history and life-styles of the 20th century. From its infancy at the turn of the century to the jet planes that were flying when the series was produced in the 1950s, the airplane was portrayed as both a weapon and a servant. The 1958 summer series consisted of reruns of the 1956–1957 films.

AIR TIME '57

Musical Variety

FIRST TELECAST: *December 27, 1956*
LAST TELECAST: *April 4, 1957*
BROADCAST HISTORY:
Dec 1956–Apr 1957, ABC Thu 10:00–10:30
REGULARS:
Vaughn Monroe
Bobby Hackett
Elliot Lawrence Orchestra

Singer Vaughn Monroe was the host and star of this live musical variety series. Jazz trumpet player Bobby Hackett and his group were featured regulars, and there were one or more guest stars each week.

AL MORGAN

Music

FIRST TELECAST: *September 5, 1949*
LAST TELECAST: *August 30, 1951*
BROADCAST HISTORY:
Sep 1949–Feb 1951, DUM Mon 8:30–9:00
May 1951–Aug 1951, DUM Thu 8:00–8:30
HOST:
Al Morgan

This musical variety program from Chicago featured popular singer-pianist Al Morgan (whose big hit, in 1949, was a song called "Jealous Heart"). Most of the program consisted of Al's own easygoing playing and singing, although guests also appeared.

ALAN DALE SHOW, THE

Music

FIRST TELECAST: *August 10, 1948*
LAST TELECAST: *January 16, 1951*
BROADCAST HISTORY:

Aug 1948–Sep 1948, DUM Tue 7:00–7:15
Jun 1950–Nov 1950, CBS Fri 11:00–11:30
Dec 1950–Jan 1951, CBS Mon/Wed/Fri 6:30–6:45
Dec 1950–Jan 1951, CBS Tue/Thu 6:30–7:00

HOST:

Alan Dale

REGULARS:

Janie Ford (1948)
Milt Green Trio (1950–1951)

Young Alan Dale (whose real name was Aldo Sigismundi) was considered one of the more promising crooners of the late 1940s and early 1950s. He was only 21 when he began his first local television show over DuMont's New York station in May 1948. The setting was a record shop supposedly run by Alan and his singing partner Janie Ford, which gave him plenty of opportunities to demonstrate his smooth baritone (actually he lip-synched to his own recordings). This series, which continued until March 1949, was fed out over the DuMont network for a time during the fall of 1948. Later Alan Dale was seen on CBS, in late-night and early-evening shows. Guest singers and comedians also appeared on his shows.

ALAN YOUNG SHOW, THE

Comedy Variety

FIRST TELECAST: *April 6, 1950*
LAST TELECAST: *June 21, 1953*
BROADCAST HISTORY:

Apr 1950–Mar 1952, CBS Thu 9:00–9:30 (OS)
Feb 1953–Jun 1953, CBS Sun 9:30–10:00

REGULARS:

Alan Young .... Himself
Kay Prindall (1953) .... Dawn Addams

WRITERS:

Leo Solomon, David R. Schwartz, Alan Young

Young Canadian comedian Alan Young seemed to have a very bright future when he first moved to the new medium of television in 1950 (he had previously been on radio for a number of years). Critics applauded his gentle, intelligent humor, his versatility, and the excellent writing for his shows. "The Charlie Chaplin of television," *TV Guide* called him. "Without benefit of purloined gags, squirting seltzer, bad grammar, insults, references to his family, worn-out guest stars or women's hats, [he has] quietly become the rave of a growing legion of loving fans."

Young generally played a well-meaning young man who constantly wound up in a predicament. His half-hour shows consisted of a brief monologue, a song or two by a vocalist, and two complete skits—ranging from the first-time airline passenger who turns a peaceful flight into chaos, to a small boy in a world of very large furniture.

Despite his talents, Young's shows never caught on really. After two and a half seasons of the skits format, he returned in the spring of 1953 in a situation comedy, cast as a bank teller, with a girl friend played by Dawn Addams. This version of the *Alan Young Show* was aired on alternate weeks with the *Ken Murray Show* under the umbrella title, *Time to Smile*. After two unsuccessful months Young returned to his familiar two-skit format, but this failed to save the series from final cancellation in June 1953.

ALASKANS, THE

Adventure

FIRST TELECAST: *October 4, 1959*
LAST TELECAST: *September 25, 1960*
BROADCAST HISTORY:

Oct 1959–Sep 1960, ABC Sun 9:30–10:30

CAST:

Silky Harris .... Roger Moore
Reno McKee .... Jeff York
Nifty Cronin .... Ray Danton
Rocky Shaw .... Dorothy Provine

The Alaskan gold rush of the 1890s brought adventurers Silky Harris and Reno McKee to less-than-beautiful Skagway, Alaska, in search of their fortunes. With them went a singer friend, Rocky Shaw. Hunting for gold did not really appeal to the trio—it was too much like work—so they cast about for other means of obtaining money. Rocky went to work for saloon owner Nifty Cronin, who was only slightly more devious than Rocky's two friends but noticeably less honest. Silky and Reno would fleece their victims gently and rarely did anything completely harmful. Nifty would resort to robbery, murder and any other means to attain his ends.

ALCOA HOUR, THE

Dramatic Anthology

FIRST TELECAST: *October 16, 1955*
LAST TELECAST: *September 22, 1957*
BROADCAST HISTORY:

Oct 1955–Sep 1957, NBC Sun 9:00–10:00

One of the major drama series of TV's "Golden Age," *The Alcoa Hour* was telecast live from New York on alternate Sundays. The premiere presented Ann Todd in her American TV debut in "The Black Wings," co-starring Wendell Corey. Among the others who performed on *Alcoa* during its two-year run were Laurence Harvey (in his United States TV debut), Martin Balsam, Walter Matthau, Joanne Woodward, Sal Mineo, Helen Hayes, Eddie Albert, and Maureen Stapleton.

Although the majority of plays presented on *Alcoa Hour* were dramas, there were some musicals as well. These included "Amahl and the Night Visitors"; an adaptation of Dickens's *Christmas Carol* entitled "The Stingiest Man in Town," starring Vic Damone, Johnny Desmond, and Basil Rathbone (singing!); and an original TV musical entitled "He's for Me," with Roddy McDowall, Jane Kean, and Larry Blyden.

ALCOA PREMIERE

Dramatic Anthology

FIRST TELECAST: *October 10, 1961*
LAST TELECAST: *September 12, 1963*
BROADCAST HISTORY:

Oct 1961–Sep 1962, ABC Tue 10:00–11:00
Oct 1962–Sep 1963, ABC Thu 10:00–11:00

HOST:

Fred Astaire

This filmed dramatic series featured Fred Astaire as host and occasional star. The premiere telecast was "People Need People," a powerful drama about the rehabilitation of psychologically disturbed war veterans, starring Lee Marvin and Arthur Kennedy and directed by Alex Segal. Subsequent telecasts maintained this high standard, with appearances by Charlton Heston, Brian Keith, Shelley Winters, Cliff Robertson, Janis Paige, Telly Savalas, and many others. Among the notable productions were "End of a World," a big-budget documentary drama about the assassination of Archduke Ferdinand, the event that triggered World War I; "Hornblower," based on the C. S. Forester books and pilot for a series that never materialized; "The Jail," by science-fiction writer Ray Bradbury; and "Flashing Spikes," a baseball drama starring James Stewart and real-life pitcher Don Drysdale, directed by movie giant John Ford.

Astaire generally appeared in dramatic roles too, but perhaps his most notable performance was in a comedy called "Mr. Lucifer," co-starring Elizabeth Montgomery—in which he played the Devil, in six different disguises.

ALCOA PRESENTS

Occult Anthology

FIRST TELECAST: *January 20, 1959*
LAST TELECAST: *October 3, 1961*
BROADCAST HISTORY:

Jan 1959–Oct 1961, ABC Tue 10:00–10:30

HOST:

John Newland

Actual case histories of supernatural phenomena and the occult were dramatized for this filmed series. Confrontations with ghosts and various forms of ESP were frequent themes, and the stories were always told with a suitably eerie and mysterious air. The subtitle of the show (later used as the title when the series went into syndication) was more descriptive of its contents: *One Step Beyond.*

ALCOA THEATRE

Dramatic Anthology

FIRST TELECAST: *October 7, 1957*
LAST TELECAST: *September 19, 1960*
BROADCAST HISTORY:

Oct 1957–Sep 1960, NBC Mon 9:30–10:00

ROTATING STARS:

David Niven (1957–1958)
Robert Ryan (1957–1958)
Jane Powell (1957–1958)
Jack Lemmon (1957–1958)
Charles Boyer (1957–1958)

When Alcoa transferred its dramatic efforts from Sunday (see *Alcoa Hour*) to Monday nights in 1957, several major changes were made. A rotating company of five stars was introduced, and the format was reduced from a full hour live to half an hour on film. Though the quality remained high, the program had a less spectacular air. Many of the presentations were dramas, with titles such as "On Edge," "Circumstantial," "In the Dark," and "Ten Miles to Doomsday."

However, there were occasional light comedies as well.

In 1958 the rotating stars were dropped and the program became a true anthology once again, featuring such varied talents as Cornel Wilde, Janet Blair, John Cassavetes, Jack Carson, Cliff Robertson, Agnes Moorehead, Walter Slezak, and Gary Merrill, among others. Throughout its run *Alcoa Theatre* was seen on alternate weeks. During its first four months it alternated with *Goodyear Theatre* under the umbrella title *A Turn of Fate.*

ALDRICH FAMILY, THE

Situation Comedy

FIRST TELECAST: *October 2, 1949*

LAST TELECAST: *May 29, 1953*

BROADCAST HISTORY:

Oct 1949–Jun 1951, NBC Sun 7:30–8:00
Sep 1951–May 1953, NBC Fri 9:30–10:00

CAST:

Henry Aldrich (1949–1950) .... Robert Casey
Henry Aldrich (1950–1951) ... Richard Tyler
Henry Aldrich (1951–1952) .... Henry Girard
Henry Aldrich (1952) ..... Kenneth Nelson
Henry Aldrich (1952–1953) ..... Bobby Ellis
Mr. Sam Aldrich .... House Jameson*
Mrs. Alice Aldrich (1949–1950) .... Lois Wilson
Mrs. Alice Aldrich (1950–1951) .... Nancy Carrol
Mrs. Alice Aldrich (1951) ..... Lois Wilson
Mrs. Alice Aldrich (1951–1953) .... Barbara Robbins
Mary Aldrich (1949–1950) .... Charita Bauer
Mary Aldrich (1950–1952) .... Mary Malone
Mary Aldrich (1952–1953) ..... June Dayton
Homer Brown (1949–1951) ..... Jackie Kelk*
Homer Brown (1951–1952) .... Robert Barry
Homer Brown (1952–1953) ... Jackie Grimes
Mrs. Brown .... Leona Powers*
Mr. Brown .... Howard Smith
Kathleen .... Marcia Henderson
Aunt Harriet .... Ethel Wilson
Anna Mitchell .... Ann Sorg
George Bigelow .... Lionel Wilson
Mr. Bradley (1949) .... Richard Midgley
Mr. Bradley (1950–1953) ..... Joseph Foley

*Same role in radio series.

This television version of the long-running radio situation comedy concerned the adventures of teenager Henry Aldrich, his "typical American family," his high school buddies (including best friend Homer Brown), and his puppy loves. The locale was the Aldrich household on Elm Street, Centerville. There was considerable turnover in casting of the principal roles, with only House Jameson remaining throughout the television run as Henry's long-suffering father. Viewers must have wondered at Mr. Aldrich's marital life, what with five different sons, three daughters, and three wives all within the space of four years!

Still another actress was supposed to play the role of Henry's mother, but was dropped at the last minute in one of the television industry's most celebrated cases of political blacklisting. Jean Muir, a movie and radio actress for nearly 20 years, was hired during the summer of 1950 to portray Mrs. Aldrich in the coming season. Immediately, protests began to come in from right-wing groups, accusing Miss Muir of left-wing sympathies—it seems her name was listed in *Red Channels,* a vicious pamphlet that cited the alleged left-wing activities of dozens of performers. The sponsor, General Foods, and its advertising agency, Young and Rubicam, canceled the opening episode of the season as a result, and Miss Muir was summarily fired—with no opportunity to defend herself. Later, before a Congressional committee, she stated that she was not and had never been a Communist. But the truth didn't really matter. As in the cases of Philip Loeb of *The Goldbergs* and Ireene Wicker, *The Singing Lady,* the accusations alone had been enough to virtually destroy her career.

The Aldrich Family was created by Clifford Goldsmith, based on his play *What a Life.* The opening lines each week became something of a national catch phrase, with Mrs. Aldrich's call, "Henry! Henry Aldrich!," and Henry's pained reply, "Coming, Mother!"

ALFRED HITCHCOCK HOUR, THE

see *Alfred Hitchcock Presents*

ALFRED HITCHCOCK PRESENTS

Suspense Anthology

FIRST TELECAST: *October 2, 1955*

LAST TELECAST: *September 6, 1965*

BROADCAST HISTORY:

Oct 1955–Sep 1960, CBS Sun 9:30–10:00
Sep 1960–Sep 1962, NBC Tue 8:30–9:00
Sep 1962–Dec 1962, CBS Thu 10:00–11:00

Jan 1963–Sep 1963, CBS Fri 9:30–10:30
Sep 1963–Sep 1964, CBS Fri 10:00–11:00
Oct 1964–Sep 1965, NBC Mon 10:00–11:00

HOST:
Alfred Hitchcock

MUSICAL THEME:
Based on Gounod's "Funeral March of a Marionette"

The benign countenance of pudgy film director Alfred Hitchcock welcomed viewers to stories of terror, horror, suspense, and twisted endings for an entire decade. His clipped British accent and catlike theme music became television standbys as the series appeared on two different networks and was later seen for years in syndication. The stories would often appear to end with evil triumphant, in strict violation of the television code of ethics. This situation was always resolved following the last commercial, when Hitchcock would return to explain, in his deadpan sardonic way, what silly mistake or chance occurrence had finally done the villain in. When the show was expanded to an hour in the fall of 1962, the title was changed to *The Alfred Hitchcock Hour*.

ALIAS SMITH AND JONES

Western

FIRST TELECAST: *January 21, 1971*
LAST TELECAST: *January 13, 1973*
BROADCAST HISTORY:
Jan 1971–Sep 1971, ABC Thu 7:30–8:30
Sep 1971–Aug 1972, ABC Thu 8:00–9:00
Sep 1972–Jan 1973, ABC Sat 8:00–9:00

CAST:
Hannibal Heyes (Joshua Smith) (1971–1972) .... Peter Duel
Hannibal Heyes (Joshua Smith) (1972–1973) .... Roger Davis
Jed "Kid" Curry (Thaddeus Jones) .... Ben Murphy
Clementine Hale .... Sally Field

NARRATOR:
Roger Davis (1971–1972)
Ralph Story (1972–1973)

CREATOR/PRODUCER:
Glen A. Larson

The main characters in this Western adventure were two gallant and amiable ex-outlaws trying to go straight. The governor had promised them a pardon for their past crimes if they could stay out of trouble for one year, but what with a price still on their heads, a lot of grudges against them, and a bit of larceny still in their hearts, that was no easy proposition. Chased across two TV seasons by posses, bounty hunters, and old outlaw friends who wanted them to join in on some escapade, they never did get their pardon. The occasional role of Clementine Hale, another lovable rogue, was added in October 1971 to give the program some continuing female interest.

On December 31, 1971, star Peter Duel, age 31, was found shot to death in his Hollywood Hills apartment. With only a few advance episodes in the can, the role of Joshua Smith quickly had to be recast. Roger Davis, who had been doing the program's opening and closing narrations, was chosen, and a partially completed episode was finished with Davis redoing scenes already filmed by Duel.

ALICE

Situation Comedy

FIRST TELECAST: *August 31, 1976*
LAST TELECAST:
BROADCAST HISTORY:
Aug 1976, CBS Mon 9:30–10:00
Sep 1976–Oct 1976, CBS Wed 9:30–10:00
Nov 1976–Sep 1977, CBS Sat 9:30–10:00
Oct 1977–Oct 1978, CBS Sun 9:30–10:00
Oct 1978– , CBS Sun 8:30–9:00

CAST:
Alice Hyatt .... Linda Lavin
Tommy Hyatt .... Philip McKeon
Mel .... Vic Tayback
Flo .... Polly Holliday
Vera .... Beth Howland
Henry (1977–) .... Marvin Kaplan

Alice Hyatt was a recently widowed aspiring singer with a very precocious 12-year-old son. She had moved from her home in New Mexico to look for work in Phoenix. While attempting to find a singing job, she kept her household together by working at Mel's Cafe. The two other waitresses at Mel's provided quite a contrast; Flo, the old hand, was loud-mouthed but softhearted, while Vera was young, impressionable, and rather quiet. Also seen rather frequently was Henry, a regular customer at the diner.

The series was based on the movie *Alice Doesn't Live Here Anymore*, the title role of which was played by Ellen Burstyn, who received an Academy Award for her performance. The only member of the movie cast to appear in the TV series was Vic Tayback, recreating his role as the owner of Mel's Cafe.

ALICE PEARCE

Musical Variety

FIRST TELECAST: *January 28, 1949*

LAST TELECAST: *March 4, 1949*

BROADCAST HISTORY:

Jan 1949–Mar 1949, ABC Fri 9:45–10:00

REGULARS:

Alice Pearce
Mark Lawrence, piano

This short—and short-lived—program presented fifteen minutes of music and comedy, hosted by comedienne Alice Pearce.

ALKALI IKE

Comedy

FIRST TELECAST: *April 17, 1950*

LAST TELECAST: *May 11, 1950*

BROADCAST HISTORY:

Apr 1950–May 1950, CBS Mon/Thu/Fri 7:45–8:00

REGULARS:

Al Robinson
The Slim Jackson Quartet

Ventriloquist Al Robinson was a discovery of Arthur Godfrey's. For a short time in the spring of 1950 he had his own live show featuring his Western dummy, Alkali Ike. Ike was trying to learn to live a varied and interesting life with the help of Al and an attractive female tutor. The action took place at Ike's ranch "somewhere in the West" and included vocal numbers by The Slim Jackson Quartet.

ALL AROUND THE TOWN

Interview

FIRST TELECAST: *November 10, 1951*

LAST TELECAST: *June 7, 1952*

BROADCAST HISTORY:

Nov 1951–Jan 1952, CBS Sat 6:00–6:45
May 1952–Jun 1952, CBS Sat 9:00–9:30

REGULARS:

Mike Wallace
Buff Cobb

Mike Wallace and his wife Buff Cobb hosted this live interview show on CBS during the 1951–1952 season. They traveled around New York City to places such as Coney Island, City Center, and numerous restaurants from which they telecast their informal interviews with patrons and promoters.

ALL IN ONE

Comedy Variety

FIRST TELECAST: *December 27, 1952*

LAST TELECAST: *April 2, 1953*

BROADCAST HISTORY:

Dec 1952–Jan 1953, CBS Sat 9:00–9:30
Apr 1953, CBS Thu 8:00–8:30

HOST:

George de Witt

In addition to functioning as host, George de Witt participated in sketches with the guest comics who were the stars of this short-lived variety show. Everything was done on a bare stage, and the audience was required to use its imagination to visualize sets and props. *All in One* had a four-week run and then returned in April for a single encore. It originated live from New York.

ALL IN THE FAMILY

Situation Comedy

FIRST TELECAST: *January 12, 1971*

LAST TELECAST:

BROADCAST HISTORY:

Jan 1971–Jul 1971, CBS Tue 9:30–10:00
Sep 1971–Sep 1975, CBS Sat 8:00–8:30
Sep 1975–Sep 1976, CBS Mon 9:00–9:30
Sep 1976–Oct 1976, CBS Wed 9:00–9:30
Nov 1976–Sep 1977, CBS Sat 9:00–9:30
Oct 1977–Oct 1978, CBS Sun 9:00–9:30
Oct 1978– , CBS Sun 9:00–9:30

CAST:

Archie Bunker .... Carroll O'Connor
Edith Bunker (Dingbat) ...... Jean Stapleton
Gloria Bunker Stivic (1971–1978) .... Sally Struthers
Mike Stivic (Meathead) (1971–1978) .... Rob Reiner
Lionel Jefferson (1971–1975) ... Mike Evans
Louise Jefferson (1971–1975) .... Isabel Sanford
Henry Jefferson (1971–1973) ... Mel Stewart
George Jefferson (1973–1975) .... Sherman Hemsley
Irene Lorenzo (1973–1975) .... Betty Garrett
Frank Lorenzo (1973–1974) .... Vincent Gardenia
Bert Munson (1972–1977) ...... Billy Halop
Tommy Kelsey (1972–1973) .... Brendon Dillon
Tommy Kelsey (1973–1977) .... Bob Hastings

Justin Quigley (1973–1976) .... Bert Mustin
Barney Hefner (1973–)
.... Allan Melvin
Jo Nelson (1973–1975) ....Ruth McDevitt
Stretch Cunningham (1974)
.... James Cromwell
Teresa Betancourt (1976–1977)
.... Liz Torres
Stephanie Mills (1978–)
.... Danielle Brisebois
Harry (1977–) .... Jason Wingreen
Hank Pivnik (1977–) ... Danny Dayton

THEME:

"Those Were the Days," by Strouse and Adams, sung at the opening of each show by Archie and Edith

PRODUCER:

Norman Lear

All in the Family changed the course of television comedy. It brought a sense of harsh reality to a TV world which previously had been populated largely by homogenized, inoffensive characters and stories that seemed to have been laundered before they ever got on the air. Its chief character, Archie Bunker, was anything but bland. A typical working-class Joe, he was uneducated, prejudiced and blatantly outspoken. He was constantly lambasting virtually every minority group in existence. His views on blacks (or, as he often called them, "jungle bunnies" or "spades"), Puerto Ricans ("spics"), Chinese ("chinks") and any other racial or religious group not his own, were clear and consistent. Archie believed in every negative racial and ethnic stereotype he had ever heard.

Unfortunately, he could never get away from the people he despised. Archie was a dock foreman for the Prendergast Tool and Die Company, and he had to work with a racially mixed group of people. Next door to his small house at 704 Houser Street, in the Corona section of Queens, New York, lived a black family, the Jeffersons. His daughter Gloria had married a Pole. On top of it all, Archie, the bigoted arch-conservative, even had to share his house with his "egghead" liberal son-in-law, Mike Stivic. (Mike was studying for his degree in sociology, and so was unemployed.) Completing the Bunker household was Archie's slow-witted but honest and unprejudiced wife, Edith.

The Jefferson family next door consisted of Louise, one of Edith's closest friends, her husband George, who ran a small dry-cleaning store, and their son Lionel, a close friend of Mike's. Lionel loved to come to the Bunker house to tease Archie about his prejudices, while George Jefferson's brother Henry, who was as opinionated from the black point of view as Archie was from the white, also provided conflict.

Over the years changes took place. Edith's cousin Maude Findlay, played by Bea Arthur, appeared in several episodes, provoking Archie with her loud, liberal opinions. She got her own show, *Maude*, in 1972. The Jeffersons moved away to Manhattan and into their own show, *The Jeffersons*, early in 1975, whereupon Mike, who had finally graduated from college, moved into their old house. This allowed Mike to continue to torment Archie, but as a next door neighbor. Then Gloria became pregnant; the baby, Joey, was born in December 1975. The Lorenzos, an Italian couple, moved in as neighbors for awhile. Frank Lorenzo loved to clean and cook (woman's work, according to Archie) while his wife Irene was an accomplished fixer of anything mechanical. Irene also possessed a sarcastic wit, with which she put down Archie regularly. When Archie was temporarily laid off from his job in October 1976, the Bunkers were forced to take in a Puerto Rican boarder, Teresa Betancourt, which provided still another source of irritation.

The 1977–1978 season brought a major change to *All in the Family*. In the opening three-part story, Archie gave up his job to pursue the American dream of owning his own business. Along with Harry the bartender, he purchased Kelsey's Bar from an ailing Tommy Kelsey, and reopened it as Archie's Place. This season included episodes with some very adult themes, including one in which an intruder attempted to rape Edith. Then at the end of the season Rob Reiner and Sally Struthers announced that they were leaving *All in the Family* for ventures of their own. The final episode of the season saw Mike, Gloria and little Joey (played by twins Jason and Justin Draeger) moving to California, where Mike was to take a teaching position. The episode was a tearful and sentimental farewell, leaving Archie and Edith with an "empty nest." The nest did not remain completely empty, however, as in the fall of 1978, Archie and Edith were joined by little Stephanie Mills, a niece who had been abandoned by her father.

Throughout all of these changes *All in the Family* remained one of the top hits on television. It did not begin that way, however. It took 1971 audiences several months to adjust to the blunt, outrageous humor of the show. There was considerable publicity about Archie's railings against "spics and spades," and it seemed possible that the show might be canceled. But by the summer of 1971 *All in the Family* had become a controversial hit, and the number one program on television—a position it retained for five years. Part of its appeal was based on the fact that it could be interpreted in several different ways. Liberals and intellectuals could cite it as an example of the absurdity of prejudice, while another large segment of the viewing audience could agree with Archie's attitudes and enjoy him as their kind of guy. Like *The Honeymooners'* Ralph Kramden in the 1950s, the loud-mouthed yet vulnerable Archie Bunker was a man for all audiences.

All in the Family was based on the British series, *Till Death Do Us Part.*

ALL STAR REVUE

Comedy Variety

FIRST TELECAST: *October 4, 1950*

LAST TELECAST: *April 18, 1953*

BROADCAST HISTORY:

Oct 1950–Jul 1951, NBC Wed 8:00–9:00
Sep 1951–Apr 1953, NBC Sat 8:00–9:00

STARS:

Ed Wynn (1950–1952)
Danny Thomas (1950–1952)
Jack Carson (1950–1952)
Jimmy Durante
Martha Raye (1951–1953)
George Jessel (1952–1953)
Tallulah Bankhead (1952–1953)

This variety series originally featured a rotating roster of four famous comedians—Ed Wynn, Danny Thomas, Jack Carson, and Jimmy Durante—who alternated as hosts. First known as *Four Star Revue*, the series was retitled *All Star Revue* in the fall of 1951 when a number of additional entertainers began to headline episodes. Among them were Martha Raye (who starred in four episodes), Olson & Johnson, Spike Jones, Victor Borge, Bob Hope, the Ritz Brothers, and Paul Winchell.

During the summer of 1952 there was no regular star and the program adopted a vaudeville flavor, with both new and established performers appearing. This summer version was titled *All Star Summer Revue*. When the fall season began there was a new lineup of regular hosts, with only Jimmy Durante remaining from prior seasons. The other performers starring in single episodes of the series in 1952–1953 were Dennis Day, the Ritz Brothers, Walter O'Keefe, Perry Como, Sonja Henie, and Ben Blue.

ALL'S FAIR

Situation Comedy

FIRST TELECAST: *September 20, 1976*

LAST TELECAST: *August 15, 1977*

BROADCAST HISTORY:

Sep 1976–Aug 1977, CBS Mon 9:30–10:00

CAST:

Richard C. Barrington .....Richard Crenna
Charlotte (Charley) Drake .... Bernadette Peters
Lucy ....Lee Chamberlain
Allen Brooks ....J. A. Preston
Ginger ....Judy Kahan
Sen. Wayne Joplin ....Jack Dodson
Lanny Wolf (1977) ....Michael Keaton

As if the difference in their ages wasn't enough of a problem, 49-year-old political columnist Richard Barrington and his vivacious 23-year-old girl friend Charley, a freelance photographer, were also at the opposite ends of the political spectrum: he was an archconservative and she was a "liberated" liberal. Love somehow managed to keep them together, despite the stormy outbursts that occurred when the subject of government and governmental policies happened to come up, which was quite often, since this series was set in Washington, D.C. Al Brooks was Richard's black assistant; Al's girl friend Lucy was a reporter for CBS News in Washington. Charley's roommate Ginger was involved with a married Congressman; Wayne Joplin was a liberal senator and a friend of Richard's who usually sided with Charley in any disagreement between the couple. When Richard became a special assistant to President Carter, Ginger became his secretary and "superhip" Carter aide Lanny

Wolf became a permanent member of the cast.

ALMOST ANYTHING GOES

Competition

FIRST TELECAST: *July 31, 1975*

LAST TELECAST: *April 10, 1976*

BROADCAST HISTORY:

Jul 1975–Aug 1975, ABC Thu 8:00–9:00

Jan 1976–Apr 1976, ABC Sat 8:00–9:00

PLAY BY PLAY:

Charlie Jones

COLOR COMMENTATOR:

Lynn Shackleford

FIELD INTERVIEWER:

Dick Whittington (1975)

Regis Philbin (1976)

Originally conceived as a one-month summer fill-in show, this uninhibited free-for-all was sufficiently popular to win a regular season tryout in early 1976 and also give birth to a Saturday morning kid's edition (called *Junior Almost Anything Goes.*) The format was an expansion of the old *Beat the Clock*, pitting teams from different towns and states against each other in all sorts of bizarre stunts. The setting was outdoors and the coverage was handled as in a sports event, complete with play-by-play, color, and field interviews. Winning teams got to participate in regional championships.

The first telecast, for example, had contestants carry a loaf of bread while sliding across a greased pole suspended over a pool; balance an egg on the head while riding down an obstacle course in a golf cart; and dive into a pool and climb onto a raft to dress up in formal garb. Greased runways, swimming pools filled with peanuts, and chocolate pies in the face were also stock-in-trade for this series.

ALVIN SHOW, THE

Cartoon

FIRST TELECAST: *October 4, 1961*

LAST TELECAST: *September 5, 1962*

BROADCAST HISTORY:

Oct 1961–Sep 1962, CBS Wed 7:30–8:00

VOICES:

Ross Bagdasarian

Shepard Menken

Ross Bagdasarian, whose professional name is David Seville, had a huge success with a novelty record "The Chipmunk Song." In the seven weeks following its original release in 1958, it sold over four million copies. Subsequent success with chipmunk albums and singles eventually resulted in this animated series. Bagdasarian was the voice of three chipmunks: Alvin, an aggressive, ambitious, impulsive, and often foolish little fellow, and his more conservative brothers Simon and Theodore. Bagdasarian was also the voice of the animated David Seville in whose home Alvin and his brothers lived. In addition to stories about their relationship and one or two musical numbers, each episode included an adventure of Clyde Crashcup, a nutty inventor who took credit for inventing anything and everything. His voice was done by Shepard Menken.

AMATEUR HOUR, THE

see *Original Amateur Hour, The*

AMAZING DUNNINGER, THE

Mind Reading/Audience Participation

FIRST TELECAST: *June 25, 1955*

LAST TELECAST: *October 10, 1956*

BROADCAST HISTORY:

Jun 1955–Sep 1955, NBC Sat 8:30–9:00

May 1956–Oct 1956, ABC Wed 8:30–9:00

REGULAR:

Joseph Dunninger

Titled *The Dunninger Show* on NBC and *The Amazing Dunninger* on ABC, this summer series featured the unique skills of the famed mentalist. His ability to read minds was tested each week by celebrity guests and by members of the studio audience.

AMAZING MR. MALONE, THE

Crime Drama

FIRST TELECAST: *September 24, 1951*

LAST TELECAST: *March 10, 1952*

BROADCAST HISTORY:

Sep 1951–Mar 1952, ABC Mon 8:00–8:30

CAST:

John J. Malone .... Lee Tracy

Lee Tracy, who perhaps was better known as *Martin Kane—Private Eye*, enacted the role of the "brilliant criminal lawyer" John J. Malone in this live mystery series. Malone, who had been a cynical, humorless character on radio, became a lighthearted sleuth with a ready quip and an affinity for pretty girls in this TV version.

It was based on the Malone novels by Craig Rice, and on the radio series which began in 1947. The TV version alternated with *Mr. District Attorney*.

AMAZING POLGAR, THE

Hypnosis

FIRST TELECAST: *September 16, 1949*

LAST TELECAST: *October 21, 1949*

BROADCAST HISTORY:

Sep 1949–Oct 1949, CBS Fri 7:45–7:55

STAR:

Dr. Franz Polgar

This extremely short, live series—it was only ten minutes long and was on the air for five weeks—examined the effects of hypnosis, the power of suggestion, immunity to pain, the ability to recall incidents that the conscious mind does not remember, and other mental feats. It starred professional hypnotist Dr. Franz Polgar, who possessed doctorates in psychology and economics.

AMAZING SPIDER-MAN, THE

Adventure

FIRST TELECAST: *April 5, 1978*

LAST TELECAST: *May 3, 1978*

BROADCAST HISTORY:

Apr 1978–May 1978, CBS Wed 8:00–9:00

CAST:

Peter Parker/Spider-Man .... Nicholas Hammand
Capt. Barbera ....Michael Pataki
J. Jonah Jameson ....Robert F. Simon
Rita ....Chip Fields

Spider-Man, the Marvel comic creation of Stan Lee, was brought to life for this limited run CBS series. Peter Parker was a young college science major and a part-time news photographer for the *Daily Bugle*. When he was accidentally bitten by a radioactive spider, he suddenly found himself endowed with superhuman abilities. He could sense the presence of danger and possessed strength far superior to that of ordinary men; he could scale sheer walls without ropes and had a magic web concealed in a wrist band that helped him to "fly" and to subdue attackers. But the transformation to Spider-Man was a mixed blessing for young Peter. He was, by nature, a rather simple, nonviolent man who found himself forced to lead a double life, possessing powers he didn't quite understand and didn't really want.

Peter's boss at the *Daily Bugle* was publisher J. Jonah Jameson. Jameson's secretary, Rita, was Peter's good friend and protector.

AMERICA

Documentary

FIRST TELECAST: *November 14, 1972*

LAST TELECAST: *April 10, 1973*

BROADCAST HISTORY:

Nov 1972–Apr 1973, NBC Tue 10:00–11:00

HOST:

Alistair Cooke

Through pictures and the commentary of Englishman Alistair Cooke, these documentaries traced the history of the United States from the last of the Mohicans to the hippies of the 1970s; they were filmed on location over a period of two years. Cooke, who had spent the previous 35 years living in the United States as a foreign correspondent and reporter, narrated the series, which he regarded as a "personal history of America."

America was one of the few series ever to be shown first on commercial television and later rerun on public television (the Public Broadcasting Service network).

AMERICA IN VIEW

Travelogue

FIRST TELECAST: *May 31, 1951*

LAST TELECAST: *October 28, 1953*

BROADCAST HISTORY:

May 1951–Jul 1951, ABC Thu 10:30–11:00
Aug 1951–Oct 1951, ABC Fri 10:30–11:00
Jan 1952–Mar 1952, ABC Sat 10:45–11:00
Jun 1952–Jun 1953, ABC Sun 9:00–9:30 (most weeks)
Oct 1953, ABC Wed 8:00–8:30

Film travelogues of the United States.

AMERICA SONG

Music

FIRST TELECAST: *April 21, 1948*

LAST TELECAST: *April 25, 1949*

BROADCAST HISTORY:

Apr 1948–Jul 1948, NBC Wed 8:00–8:15
Jul 1948–Sep 1948, NBC Tue 7:30–7:50
Oct 1948–Feb 1949, NBC Mon 7:30–7:50
Mar 1949–Apr 1949, NBC various 15-minute spots

REGULARS:
Paul Arnold
Nellie Fisher, dancer

A program of traditional American folk songs and dances, hosted by singer-guitarist Paul Arnold. A number of singers and dancers rotated in and out of the cast during the program's run, including 12-year-old Jimsey Somers and 8-year-old Dickie Orlan in early 1949. The program was renamed *American Songs* during its last four months.

AMERICA SPEAKS

Opinion Poll

FIRST TELECAST: *September 5, 1948*
LAST TELECAST: *October 31, 1948*
BROADCAST HISTORY:
Sep 1948–Oct 1948, CBS Sun 10:00–10:15
HOST:
Dr. George Gallup

George Gallup is probably the most famous poll taker in America. In the fall of 1948, a presidential election year, he was the star of a nine-week live series in which he presented the results of a series of public opinion polls he had taken to the television audience. In addition to displaying the results, the series showed reenactments of the actual polling techniques.

AMERICAN BANDSTAND

Music

FIRST TELECAST: *October 7, 1957*
LAST TELECAST: *December 30, 1957*
BROADCAST HISTORY:
Oct 1957–Dec 1957, ABC Mon 7:30–8:00
HOST:
Dick Clark

American Bandstand had started as a local dance show in Philadelphia in the early 1950s. It moved to the full ABC network as a Monday–Friday late-afternoon show in August of 1957, and its immediate success prompted ABC to give it a brief run in prime time that fall. The nighttime version was identical to its daytime counterpart, which is still aired on Saturdays. Clark hosted one or two guest performers whose records were on the pop music charts. They lip-synched their current hits, chatted with him about their careers, and signed autographs. The remainder of the time was devoted to playing other current hit records and watching the studio audience dance to the music. Clark had not yet moved the show to California; both the nighttime and afternoon versions of *American Bandstand* were telecast live from Philadelphia.

AMERICAN FORUM OF THE AIR

Discussion

FIRST TELECAST: *February 4, 1950*
LAST TELECAST: *September 21, 1952*
BROADCAST HISTORY:
Feb 1950–Sep 1950, NBC Sat 7:00–7:30
Sep 1950–Oct 1950, NBC Sat 6:00–6:30
Jul 1951–Sep 1951, NBC Sun 10:00–10:30
May 1952–Sep 1952, NBC Sun 10:30–11:00
MODERATOR:
Theodore Granik

This long-running discussion program was founded and moderated by Theodore Granik. It originated in Washington, D.C., usually before a live audience, with Granik interviewing two distinguished guests, one on each side of a major national or international issue. *Forum* began on radio in 1928 and appeared on television from 1949 to 1957, generally on Sunday afternoons. However, during the period indicated above it was a prime-time series. Granik, who was also founder and moderator of *Youth Wants to Know*, relinquished the role of moderator in 1953 due to ill health, but continued to produce the program with newsman Stephen McCormick as moderator.

AMERICAN GIRLS, THE

Adventure-Drama

FIRST TELECAST: *September 23, 1978*
LAST TELECAST: *November 10, 1978*
BROADCAST HISTORY:
Sep 1978–Nov 1978, CBS Sat 9:00–10:00
CAST:
Rebecca Tomkins ....Priscilla Barnes
Amy Waddell ....Debra Clinger
Francis X. Casey ....David Spielberg

Rebecca and Amy were two very attractive young reporters working for *The American Report*, a fictitious TV news magazine similar to the real life *60 Minutes*. Rebecca was the older and more experienced of the two, a witty and sophisticated big city girl. Amy was fresh out of college, a small-town girl who was eager to succeed. The two of them travelled around the country on assignments in an elaborately equipped van that provided them with a remote production studio to work on their stories. Casey was the show's producer in New York, who gave the girls their assignments and helped them out of dangerous or embarrassing situations.

AMERICAN INVENTORY

Documentary/Drama

FIRST TELECAST: *July 1, 1951*

LAST TELECAST: *August 23, 1952*

BROADCAST HISTORY:

Jul 1951–Aug 1951, NBC Sun 8:00–8:30

Jun 1952–Aug 1952, NBC Sat 7:30–8:00

HOST:

Ray Morgan (1951)

Produced by NBC in cooperation with the Alfred P. Sloan Foundation, *American Inventory* was an experimental series that tried out new techniques in adult education. Episodes included panel discussions on various issues, documentary films, ballet, drama, and other features making it, according to its producers, "the living newspaper." It premiered as a Sunday evening show in July of 1951 and moved to an earlier time period on Sunday afternoons in September. The host of the original series was Ray Morgan, who left in May 1952 when the program ended. When the series returned to nighttime television on June 28, 1952, it was as a series of documentary-style dramatizations under the broad subtitle "American Gallery." The dramatizations dealt with the people who contributed, in their modest ways, to the betterment of American society—doctors, lawyers, teachers, and so on. In September 1952 it again moved into an earlier time slot on Sunday afternoons, where it remained on the air until December 1955.

AMERICAN MINSTRELS OF 1949

Variety

FIRST TELECAST: *January 13, 1949*

LAST TELECAST: *March 17, 1949*

BROADCAST HISTORY:

Jan 1949–Mar 1949, ABC Thu 8:00–9:00

EMCEE:

Jack Carter

REGULARS:

Pick and Pat
Mary Small
Jimmy Burrell
Estelle Sloan

This was more vaudeville than a true minstrel show, but it featured some real old-time acts, such as Smith and Dale in their "Doctor Kronkheit" routine. Regulars included blackface comics Pick and Pat, singers Mary Small and Jimmy Burrell, and dancer Estelle Sloan. Also seen were such big-time TV acts as Nelson's Cats.

AMERICAN ODYSSEY

Documentary

FIRST TELECAST: *March 24, 1958*

LAST TELECAST: *June 9, 1958*

BROADCAST HISTORY:

Mar 1958–Jun 1958, ABC Mon 7:30–8:00

American Odyssey focused on the various roles played by American institutions and individuals and presented a half-hour filmed documentary on a given topic each week. Subjects ranged from the grueling experiences of a plebe at West Point to dramatized cases from the files of the American Medical Association to a tour of the famous sights in Washington, D.C.

AMERICAN PROFILE

Documentary

FIRST TELECAST: *September 29, 1967*

LAST TELECAST: *July 5, 1968*

BROADCAST HISTORY:

Sep 1967–Jul 1968, NBC Fri 10:00–11:00

Various aspects of American life and the natural beauty of the country were covered in this series of seven documentaries, which were aired on a rotating basis with *The Bell Telephone Hour, Actuality Specials*, and *NBC News Reports*. The subjects included an examination of endangered species of American wildlife, discussions of politics, and a tour through the National Gallery of Art in Washington, D.C. NBC newsmen narrated most of the telecasts; however, Eddy Arnold was host for "Music from the Land" and Robert Culp led the tour through the National Gallery of Art.

AMERICAN SCENE, THE

Documentary

FIRST TELECAST: *July 6, 1952*

LAST TELECAST: *September 28, 1952*

BROADCAST HISTORY:

Jul 1952–Sep 1952, ABC Sun 6:30–7:00

American Scene presented documentary films on assorted subjects. The title was also used by ABC for various one-time telecasts of films in 1952–1953.

AMERICAN WEEK, THE

News/Commentary

FIRST TELECAST: *April 4, 1954*

LAST TELECAST: *October 10, 1954*

BROADCAST HISTORY:

Apr 1954–Oct 1954, CBS Sun 6:00–6:30

CORRESPONDENT:

Eric Sevareid

A summary of the major happenings in the world during the previous week was presented each Sunday evening by CBS News' chief Washington correspondent, Eric Sevareid. In addition to summarizing the news, Mr. Sevareid included observations and analysis of his own. The show featured original filmed interviews with people prominent in the week's news. Although it left the nighttime slot in the middle of October 1954, this series remained on the air in an earlier time period on Sunday afternoons until the following May.

AMERICAN YOUTH FORUM

see *Youth Wants to Know*

AMERICANA

Quiz

FIRST TELECAST: *December 8, 1947*

LAST TELECAST: *July 4, 1949*

BROADCAST HISTORY:

Dec 1947, NBC Mon 8:10–8:40
Jan 1948–Apr 1948, NBC Wed 8:00–8:30
Apr 1948–Nov 1948, NBC Mon 8:30–9:00
Dec 1948–Jul 1949, NBC Mon 9:30–10:00

MODERATOR:

John Mason Brown (Dec 1947–Jan 1948)
Ben Grauer (1948–1949)

This quiz program dealt with American history and folklore, using questions submitted by viewers. The person submitting "the most interesting question of the week" received a set of the *Encyclopedia Americana*. At first the questions were put to a panel of adult experts, but in February 1948 this was changed to teams of high school students.

AMERICANS, THE

Civil War Drama

FIRST TELECAST: *January 23, 1961*

LAST TELECAST: *September 11, 1961*

BROADCAST HISTORY:

Jan 1961–Sep 1961, NBC Mon 7:30–8:30

CAST:

Ben Canfield ....Darryl Hickman
Jeff Canfield ....Dick Davalos

Two young brothers who grew up in Harpers Ferry, then in the state of Virginia, were faced with a major decision when Virginia seceded from the Union in 1861. Jeff, the younger brother, somewhat impetuous and rebellious, decided to fight for the Confederacy. Ben, the elder brother, was torn between loyalty to his home state and loyalty to the Union. After their father died in a fire during the first episode, Ben swam across the river to Maryland and enlisted in the Union Army. During the remainder of the series each brother was showcased on alternate weeks, Ben fighting for the Union and Jeff with the Confederates in the Virginia Militia.

AMERICA'S GREATEST BANDS

Music

FIRST TELECAST: *June 25, 1955*

LAST TELECAST: *September 24, 1955*

BROADCAST HISTORY:

Jun 1955–Sep 1955, CBS Sat 8:00–9:00

HOST:

Paul Whiteman

Serving as the 1955 summer replacement for *The Jackie Gleason Show*, *America's Greatest Bands* presented four different big-name bands each week. Appearing on a giant rotating stage, each of the bands took turns performing. The permanent host of the series was bandleader Paul Whiteman, whose own band was featured on the first telecast. Among the other bands that appeared were those of Duke Ellington, Sammy Kaye, Xavier Cugat, Perez Prado, Bob Crosby, Les Brown, and Count Basie.

AMERICA'S HEALTH

Documentary

FIRST TELECAST: *August 20, 1951*

LAST TELECAST: *March 6, 1952*

BROADCAST HISTORY:

Aug 1951–Sep 1951, ABC Mon 10:00–10:30
Sep 1951–Oct 1951, ABC Sat 9:30–10:00
Feb 1952–Mar 1952, ABC Thu 10:00–10:15

This series consisted of documentary films on health subjects, provided by such organizations as the Veterans Administration and the American Cancer Society. A sample title was "Doctor Speaks His Mind."

AMERICA'S TOWN MEETING

Debate

FIRST TELECAST: *October 5, 1948*

LAST TELECAST: *July 6, 1952*

BROADCAST HISTORY:

Oct 1948–Jun 1949, ABC Tue 8:30–9:30

Jan 1952–Jul 1952, ABC Sun 6:30–7:00

MODERATOR:

George V. Denny, Jr. (1948–1952)

John Daly (Apr–Jul 1952)

This venerable radio series, which began in 1935 and ran for 21 years thereafter, had two runs on network television, in 1948–1949 and in 1952. The format was the same as that of the radio show, consisting of debates by politicians, writers, and other prominent persons on such topics as "Are We Too Hysterical About Communism?", "Has the Korean War Been a Failure?", and "Should We Have Uniform Federal Divorce Laws?" The program originated from New York's Town Hall Auditorium before a vociferous and involved audience. George V. Denny, Jr., who created the series, served as moderator for all telecasts except for a brief period in 1952 when ABC newsman John Daly took over.

AMOS BURKE—SECRET AGENT

see *Burke's Law*

AMOS 'N' ANDY

Situation Comedy

FIRST TELECAST: *June 28, 1951*

LAST TELECAST: *June 11, 1953*

BROADCAST HISTORY:

Jun 1951–Jun 1953, CBS Thu 8:30–9:00

CAST:

Amos Jones .... Alvin Childress

Andy Brown .... Spencer Williams

George "The Kingfish" Stevens .... Tim Moore

Lawyer Algonquin Calhoun .... Johnny Lee

Sapphire Stevens .... Ernestine Wade

Lightnin' .... Horace Stewart

Sapphire's Mama ...... Amanda Randolph

Madame Queen .... Lillian Randolph

Amos 'n' Andy, one of the most popular and long-running radio programs of all time, was brought to television in the summer of 1951. The series was produced by Freeman Gosden and Charles Correll, the two actors who had created and starred in the radio version. Since they were white, and the entire cast of the show on television had to be black, a much ballyhooed search was held, over a period of four years, to find the right actors to play the parts.

Set in Harlem, *Amos 'n' Andy* centered around the activities of George Stevens, a conniving character who was always looking for a way to make a fast buck. As head of the Mystic Knights of the Sea Lodge, where he held the position of "Kingfish," he got most of the lodge brothers involved in his schemes. This put him at odds not only with them, but with his wife Sapphire and her mother. Mama, in particular, didn't trust him at all. Andy Brown was the most gullible of the lodge members, a husky, well-meaning, but rather simple soul. His girl friend was Madame Queen. Amos was the philosophical cabdriver who narrated most of the episodes, and Lightnin' was the janitor at the lodge.

AMY PRENTISS

Police Drama

FIRST TELECAST: *December 1, 1974*

LAST TELECAST: *July 6, 1975*

BROADCAST HISTORY:

Dec 1974–Jul 1975, NBC Sun 8:30–10:30

CAST:

Amy Prentiss .... Jessica Walter

Det. Tony Russell .... Steve Sandor

Det. Rod Pena .... Arthur Metrano

Det. Contreras .... Johnny Seven

Jill Prentiss .... Helen Hunt

When the chief of detectives of the San Francisco Police Department died unexpectedly, the person at the top of the service list was Amy Prentiss, an attractive 35-year-old widow with a young daughter. There had never been a woman chief of detectives before, and many of the male officers who suddenly found themselves reporting to Amy resented it. A measure of grudging respect gradually emerged, however, when her skill as an investigator became apparent in a series of cases that otherwise constituted standard crime-show fare. Unfortunately, viewers took less readily to the idea of woman as boss, and the program was canceled after a short run.

Amy Prentiss was one of the four rotating elements that made up the 1974–1975 edition of *NBC Sunday Mystery Movie.* The others were *Columbo*, *McCloud*, and *McMillan and Wife*.

AND EVERYTHING NICE

Fashions

FIRST TELECAST: *March 15, 1949*

LAST TELECAST: *January 2, 1950*

BROADCAST HISTORY:

Mar 1949–Jun 1949, DUM Tue 7:00–7:30
Jul 1949–Aug 1949, DUM Mon 8:30–9:00
Sep 1949–Jan 1950, DUM Mon 9:00–9:30

HOSTESS:

Maxine Barrat

An early television program that presented fashions, style tips, and guests.

AND HERE'S THE SHOW

Comedy Variety

FIRST TELECAST: *July 9, 1955*

LAST TELECAST: *September 24, 1955*

BROADCAST HISTORY:

Jul 1955–Sep 1955, NBC Sat 10:00–10:30

REGULARS:

Ransom Sherman
Jonathan Winters
The Double Daters
John Scott Trotter, musical director
Bob LeMond, announcer

This live variety program served as a summer replacement for the *George Gobel Show*. Ransom Sherman and Jonathan Winters were the co-stars, with Sherman also acting as host. Both of the stars functioned as monologists and appeared together in skits. The Double Daters introduced the guest stars and the comedy skits and performed a featured musical number each week. The program's title was derived from one of George Gobel's familiar lines.

ANDROS TARGETS, THE

Newspaper Drama

FIRST TELECAST: *January 31, 1977*

LAST TELECAST: *July 9, 1977*

BROADCAST HISTORY:

Jan 1977–May 1977, CBS Mon 10:00–11:00
Jul 1977, CBS Sat 10:00–11:00

CAST:

Mike Andros .... James Sutorius
Sandi Farrell .... Pamela Reed
Chet Reynolds .... Roy Poole
Norman Kale .... Alan Mixon
Wayne Hillman .... Ted Beniades

Mike Andros was an investigative reporter for *The New York Forum*. Much in the style of the real-life reporters who had become celebrities in the aftermath of the Watergate scandal, Andros focused his efforts on the corruption in the biggest city in the nation. Unethical use of amphetamines by doctors, underworld activities in areas of pornography, prostitution, and narcotics, and unusual criminal cases that had been hushed up by the police all came under his scrutiny. Sandi Farrell was Mike's young assistant and Chet and Norman were the managing and city editors, respectively, of *The New York Forum*. Wayne Hillman was a fellow reporter and a friend.

ANDY AND DELLA RUSSELL

Music

FIRST TELECAST: *December 18, 1950*

LAST TELECAST: *June 15, 1951*

BROADCAST HISTORY:

Dec 1950–Jun 1951, ABC Mon–Fri 7:00–7:05

REGULARS:

Andy Russell
Della Russell

Andy Russell, a radio and recording star of the 1940s, and his wife Della hosted this brief but pleasant musical interlude, which originated live from New York every weeknight. A month after its premiere the series' name was changed to *Cook's Champagne Party*, in honor of the sponsor.

ANDY GRIFFITH SHOW, THE

Situation Comedy

FIRST TELECAST: *October 3, 1960*

LAST TELECAST: *September 16, 1968*

BROADCAST HISTORY:

Oct 1960–Jul 1963, CBS Mon 9:30–10:00 (OS)
Sep 1963–Sep 1964, CBS Mon 9:30–10:00
Sep 1964–Jun 1965, CBS Mon 8:30–9:00
Sep 1965–Sep 1968, CBS Mon 9:00–9:30

CAST:

Andy Taylor .... Andy Griffith
Opie Taylor .... Ronny Howard
Barney Fife(1960–1965) .... Don Knotts
Ellie Walker (1960–1961) .. Elinor Donahue
Aunt Bee Taylor .... Frances Bavier
Gomer Pyle (1963–1964) .... Jim Nabors
Helen Crump (1964–1968) ... Anita Corsaut
Goober Pyle (1965–1968) .. George Lindsey
Floyd Lawson (1965–1968)
.... Howard McNear
Otis Campbell (1965–1967) ..... Hal Smith

Howard Sprague (1967–1968)
.... Jack Dodson

The small town of Mayberry, North Carolina, was the setting of this highly successful homespun situation comedy. Sheriff Andy Taylor was a widower with a young son, Opie. They lived with Andy's Aunt Bee, a combination housekeeper and foster mother for Opie. Andy's deputy was his cousin Barney Fife, the most inept, hypertense deputy sheriff ever seen on television. The tone of the show was very gentle, giving Andy the opportunity to state and practice his understanding, philosophical outlook on life. Since there was practically no crime in Mayberry, the stories revolved mostly around the personal relationships of its citizens.

Two of the show's regulars graduated to series of their own. The first was Jim Nabors. He had become a member of the cast in the spring of 1963 in the role of Gomer Pyle, the naive, lovable gas station attendant at Wally's filling station. After a year and a half he left to join the marines and become *Gomer Pyle, U.S.M.C.* Co-star Don Knotts left the show in 1965 for his own variety series, *The Don Knotts Show*. Among the other regulars, Andy's original girl friend, druggist Ellie Walker, was seen only during the first season, and for the following three years Andy had no regular romantic interest. Schoolteacher Helen Crump filled the void in 1964, and, when Andy Griffith decided to quit the show in 1968, she also provided his means of escape. On the first episode of *Mayberry R.F.D.*, the successor to *The Andy Griffith Show*, Andy and Helen married and moved away, leaving the supporting cast to carry on with a new star, Ken Berry, in the role of Sam Jones—another widower with a young son.

Daytime reruns of this series, as well as some syndicated versions, were titled *Andy of Mayberry*.

ANDY OF MAYBERRY

see *Andy Griffith Show, The*

ANDY WILLIAMS AND JUNE VALLI SHOW, THE

Music

FIRST TELECAST: *July 2, 1957*

LAST TELECAST: *September 5, 1957*

BROADCAST HISTORY:

Jul 1957–Sep 1957, NBC Tue/Thu 7:30–7:45

REGULARS:

Andy Williams
June Valli
Alvy West, orchestra conductor

On this live summer series, Andy Williams and June Valli sang both individually and together. The theme song for the program was "On a Summer Evening."

ANDY WILLIAMS PRESENTS RAY STEVENS

Comedy Variety

FIRST TELECAST: *June 20, 1970*

LAST TELECAST: *August 8, 1970*

BROADCAST HISTORY:

Jun 1970–Aug 1970, NBC Sat 7:30–8:30

REGULARS:

Ray Stevens
Lulu
Dick Curtis
Steve Martin
Carol Robinson
Solari and Carr
Billy Van
"Mama" Cass Elliot

Singer-composer-comedian-impressionist Ray Stevens starred in this summer replacement for *The Andy Williams Show*. Ray, who was a frequent guest on Andy's show, was featured in production numbers and comedy skits in the summer program, which was taped in Toronto. The skits tended to be very broad and often verged on the physical violence associated with Mack Sennett slapstick.

ANDY WILLIAMS SHOW, THE

Musical Variety

FIRST TELECAST: *July 3, 1958*

LAST TELECAST: *July 17, 1971*

BROADCAST HISTORY:

Jul 1958–Sep 1958, ABC Thu 9:00–9:30
Jul 1959–Sep 1959, CBS Tue 10:00–11:00
Sep 1962–Jun 1963, NBC Thu 10:00–11:00
Sep 1963–May 1964, NBC Tue 10:00–11:00
Oct 1964–May 1966, NBC Mon 9:00–10:00
Sep 1966–May 1967, NBC Sun 10:00–11:00
Sep 1969–Jul 1971, NBC Sat 7:30–8:30 (OS)

STAR:

Andy Williams

REGULARS:

Dick Van Dyke (1958)
The Bob Hamilton Trio (1958)

The Mort Lindsey Orchestra (1958)
The Dick Williams Singers (1959)
The Peter Gennaro Dancers (1959)
The Jack Kane Orchestra (1959)
Randy Sparks and the New Christy Minstrels (1962–1963)
Jimmy Gaines (1962–1963)
Marian Mercer (1962–1963)
R. C. Brown (1962–1963)
The Osmond Brothers (1962–1971)
The Colin Romoff Orchestra (1962–1963)
The Dave Grusin Orchestra (1963–1966)
The Allyn Ferguson Orchestra (1966–1967)
The Mike Post Orchestra (1969–1971)
The Good Time Singers (1963–1966)
Jonathan Winters (1965–1967, 1970–1971)
Irwin Corey (1969–1970)
Janos Prohaska (1969–1971)
Ray Stevens (1969–1971)
The Lennon Sisters (1970–1971)
Charlie Callas (1970–1971)
The Nick Castle Dancers (1963–1966)
The James Starbuck Dancers (1966–1967)
The Jaime Rogers Dancers (1969–1970)
The Andre Tayri Dancers (1970–1971)

THEME (after 1962):
"Moon River," by Henry Mancini and Johnny Mercer

Smooth-voiced popular singer Andy Williams starred in a number of variety shows in the late 1950s and 1960s. The first two were summer shows, in 1958 and 1959, followed by his own regular season series on NBC beginning in 1962. Big-name guest stars appeared, usually of the adult variety (rarely a rock act), and a large number of regulars were seen. Originally the New Christy Minstrels were the chief backup act, but they were soon superseded by a quartet of talented youngsters discovered by Williams performing at Disneyland (they had also appeared once on a *Disneyland* TV special). The Osmond Brothers, billed as a "youthful barbershop harmony group from Ogden, Utah," were first seen on December 20, 1962, singing "I'm a Ding Dong Daddy from Dumas" and "Side by Side." They stayed with Williams for the rest of his run. The original four were periodically augmented by brothers and sisters, with six-year-old Donny Osmond making his debut on December 10, 1963.

In 1967 Andy cut back to a schedule of only three specials per year, but in 1969 he returned with a regular weekly series once again. This time the look was decidedly contemporary, including rock acts, psychedelic lighting, and a futuristic set that had the audience seated on movable platforms which followed Andy around through the show. Among the regular features were "The Informal Spot" and "The Williams Weirdos"—Little General, Walking Suitcase, Big Bird, and The Bear.

Williams's 1958 summer show, which had filled in for vacationing Pat Boone, was titled *The Chevy Showroom Starring Andy Williams.* All of his subsequent series were simply titled *The Andy Williams Show.*

ANGEL

Situation Comedy

FIRST TELECAST: *October 6, 1960*
LAST TELECAST: *September 20, 1961*
BROADCAST HISTORY:
Oct 1960–Dec 1960, CBS Thu 9:00–9:30
Dec 1960–Apr 1961, CBS Thu 8:00–8:30
Apr 1961–Sep 1961, CBS Wed 9:00–9:30

CAST:
Angel .... Annie Farge
John Smith .... Marshall Thompson
Susie .... Doris Singleton
George .... Don Keefer

Angel was a petite French girl who had just moved to America and become the bride of a young architect, John Smith. Her efforts to adjust to the American way of life provided the humor in this series. Her problems with English, misunderstanding of situations, and attempts to be a responsible housewife all contributed to the amusement of her husband and their next-door neighbors, Susie and George, who were also their closest friends.

ANIMAL KINGDOM

see *Animal World*

ANIMAL SECRETS

Wildlife Documentary

FIRST TELECAST: *July 2, 1967*
LAST TELECAST: *August 27, 1967*
BROADCAST HISTORY:
Jul 1967–Aug 1967, NBC Sun 7:00–7:30

HOST:
Dr. Loren Eiseley

The mysteries of animal behavior were explored in this nature series hosted by Dr. Loren Eiseley, Professor of Anthropology at the University of Pennsylvania. Each episode dealt with a specific mystery—

why do birds migrate, what makes bees buzz, how do fish talk. The episodes seen in prime time were repeats from the Saturday afternoon series of the same name in the prior season.

ANIMAL WORLD

Wildlife Documentary

FIRST TELECAST: *June 16, 1968*

LAST TELECAST: *September 12, 1971*

BROADCAST HISTORY:

Jun 1968–Sep 1968, NBC Sun 6:30–7:00
May 1969–Sep 1969, CBS Thu 7:30–8:00
Apr 1970–Sep 1970, ABC Thu 7:30–8:00
Jul 1971–Sep 1971, CBS Sun 7:30–8:00

HOST:

Bill Burrud

Bill Burrud, who had previously made several true-life adventure films for theatrical release, produced and hosted this nature series, which showed wild animals in their natural habitats from locations all over the world. The title of the series was originally *Animal Kingdom,* but was changed to *Animal World* with the telecast that was aired on August 11, 1968. After a season on NBC, it moved to CBS as a late Sunday afternoon series in the fall of 1968. It returned to prime time on three occasions; on CBS in the summers of 1969 and 1971, and on ABC in the summer of 1970.

ANN SOTHERN SHOW, THE

Situation Comedy

FIRST TELECAST: *October 6, 1958*

LAST TELECAST: *September 25, 1961*

BROADCAST HISTORY:

Oct 1958–Jul 1960, CBS Mon 9:30–10:00 (OS)
Oct 1960–Dec 1960, CBS Thu 9:30–10:00
Dec 1960–Mar 1961, CBS Thu 7:30–8:00
Jul 1961–Sep 1961, CBS Mon 9:30–10:00

CAST:

Katy O'Connor ....Ann Sothern
Jason Macauley (1958–1959) ..Ernest Truex
Olive Smith ....Ann Tyrrell
Johnny ....Jack Mullaney
Paul Martine (1958–1959) ....Jacques Scott
Flora Macauley (1958–1959) ....Reta Shaw
James Devery (1959–1961) ......Don Porter
Dr. Delbert Gray (1960–1961) ...Louis Nye

Katy O'Connor was the assistant manager of the plush Bartley House hotel in New York. Her first boss, Jason Macauley, was transferred to Calcutta in the March 9, 1959, episode, but Katy's hopes of succeeding him as manager were torpedoed when James Devery arrived to fill the job. Katy's secretary, roommate, and best friend was Olive Smith, who developed a romantic interest during the 1960–1961 season in the person of dentist Delbert Gray. Don Porter and Ann Tyrrell had been Ann Sothern's co-stars in her previous series, *Private Secretary,* and they joined her here in amusing tales of the problems encountered in running a big-city hotel.

ANNA AND THE KING

Situation Comedy

FIRST TELECAST: *September 17, 1972*

LAST TELECAST: *December 31, 1972*

BROADCAST HISTORY:

Sep 1972–Dec 1972, CBS Sun 7:30–8:00

CAST:

King of Siam ....Yul Brynner
Anna Owens ....Samantha Eggar
Kralahome ....Keye Luke
Louis Owens ....Eric Shea
Crown Prince Chulalongkorn ..Brian Tochi
Lady Thiang ....Lisa Lu

It was in 1951, while preparing for his starring role in Rodgers and Hammerstein's new musical *The King And I,* that Yul Brynner first shaved his head, to add realism to his portrayal. The role and the bald pate both became Brynner trademarks; he brought them to the film version of the musical in 1956 and to this short-lived television comedy version in 1972. Based on Margaret Landon's novel *Anna and the King of Siam,* the story was set in the 1860s and involved a young schoolteacher, a widow with a 12-year-old son, who had been hired by the King of Siam to educate his royal offspring. (The King's many wives, of whom Lady Thiang was most important, had borne him a whole schoolful of children.) There was much conflict between the autocratic king and the stubborn, strong-willed teacher, but there was also a developing respect and affection.

ANOTHER DAY

Situation Comedy

FIRST TELECAST: *April 8, 1978*

LAST TELECAST: *April 29, 1978*

BROADCAST HISTORY:

Apr 1978, CBS Sat 9:00–9:30

CAST:

Don Gardner ....David Groh

Ginny Gardner ....Joan Hackett
Olive Gardner ....Hope Summers
Kelly Gardner ....Lisa Lindgren
Mark Gardner ....Al Eisenmann

Don Gardner was a somewhat old-fashioned young businessman trying to live up to his expectations of the American dream despite limited finances. Even with the extra income provided by his wife Ginny, who had recently returned to work, there never seemed to be enough money. With an inhibited 12-year-old son, Mark, and a totally uninhibited teenage daughter, Kelly, things were never normal in the Gardner family. Adding to the confusion was Don's complaining mother, Olive, who completed the household.

ANSWER YES OR NO

Quiz

FIRST TELECAST: *April 30, 1950*
LAST TELECAST: *July 23, 1950*
BROADCAST HISTORY:
Apr 1950–Jul 1950, NBC Sun 10:30–11:00
EMCEE:
Moss Hart

This quiz show featured a celebrity panel. Arlene Francis was the only panelist to remain for the entire three-month run of the program. The typical question asked of the panel was "What would you do in this situation?", to which they responded with comic answers.

ANSWERS FOR AMERICANS

Discussion

FIRST TELECAST: *November 11, 1953*
LAST TELECAST: *February 24, 1954*
BROADCAST HISTORY:
Nov 1953–Feb 1954, ABC Wed 8:30–9:00
MODERATOR:
Hardy Burt
PERMANENT PANEL:
Brig. General Frank Howley, Vice Chancellor, New York University
Devin Garrity, publisher
John K. Norton, Columbia University
Dr. Charles Hodges, New York University

This public affairs program was presented in cooperation with *Facts Forum*. The prestigious panel discussed with equally prestigious guests such lofty issues as "Where Does the Eisenhower Administration Stand Today?", "Should Red China Be Admitted to the UN?", and "What Can Be Done About Korea?" After a brief prime-time run the program continued on Sunday afternoon until June 1954.

ANYBODY CAN PLAY

Quiz/Audience Participation

FIRST TELECAST: *July 6, 1958*
LAST TELECAST: *December 8, 1958*
BROADCAST HISTORY:
Jul 1958–Sep 1958, ABC Sun 8:30–9:00
Oct 1958–Dec 1958, ABC Mon 9:30–10:00
EMCEE:
George Fenneman
ASSISTANT:
Judy Bamber (Nov–Dec)

In this quiz show, four studio contestants competed for cash and prizes by answering questions on a point system. The questions ranged over many subjects; for instance, contestants were asked to name a celebrity, identify a song or movie from short clips, or identify an object solely by touch. Contestants remained on the show for four weeks (later reduced to two), and viewers at home had the opportunity to participate in a $10,000 jackpot competition by sending in estimates of the contestants' age, weight, ability, and related data. Judy Bamber joined George Fenneman as co-host during the program's final month.

ANYONE CAN WIN

Quiz/Audience Participation

FIRST TELECAST: *July 14, 1953*
LAST TELECAST: *September 1, 1953*
BROADCAST HISTORY:
Jul 1953–Sep 1953, CBS Tue 9:00–9:30
MODERATOR:
Al Capp

Each week a different panel of four celebrities competed in a general quiz, with cartoonist Al Capp serving as moderator. Before the show started, all members of the studio audience were asked to pick which celebrity they thought would answer the most questions correctly. At the end of each show, those who had correctly guessed the winner shared $2,000 in cash.

ANYWHERE, U.S.A.

Documentary Drama

FIRST TELECAST: *November 9, 1952*
LAST TELECAST: *December 14, 1952*

BROADCAST HISTORY:

Nov 1952–Dec 1952, ABC Sun 10:30–11:00

CAST:

Doctor ....Eddie Dowling

Dramatized documentary films on health subjects, produced by the Health Information Foundation and covering such topics as physical therapy, the need for checkups, and new drugs. Robert Preston also appeared as a doctor on some telecasts of this series.

APPLE PIE

Situation Comedy

FIRST TELECAST: *September 23, 1978*

LAST TELECAST: *September 30, 1978*

BROADCAST HISTORY:

Sept 1978, ABC Sat 8:30–9:00

CAST:

Ginger-Nell Hollyhock ... Rue McClanahan
"Fast Eddie" Murtaugh ... Dabney Coleman
Grandpa Hollyhock .... Jack Gilford
Anna Marie Hollyhock ... Caitlin O'Heaney
Junior Hollyhock .... Derrel Maury

"You can't pick your own relatives," goes the old saying, but that's exactly what a lonely hairdresser named Ginger-Nell Hollyhock did in this 1978 comedy. Placing classified ads in the local papers, she recruited a con man husband ("Fast Eddie"), a tap dancing daughter (Anna Marie), a son who wanted to fly like a bird (Junior), and a tottering old grandfather (Grandpa), all of whom came to live together—for the laughs. The setting was Kansas City, Missouri, in 1933, which added period color.

The program was based on the play "Nourish the Beast," by Steve Tesich.

APPLE'S WAY

General Drama

FIRST TELECAST: *February 10, 1974*

LAST TELECAST: *January 12, 1975*

BROADCAST HISTORY:

Feb 1974–Jan 1975, CBS Sun 7:30–8:30

CAST:

George Apple ....Ronny Cox
Barbara Apple ....Lee McCain
Paul Apple ....Vincent Van Patten
Cathy Apple ....Patti Cohoon
Patricia Apple (1974) ....Franny Michel
Steven Apple ....Eric Olson
Grandfather Aldon .....Malcolm Atterbury
Patricia Apple (1974–1975)
.......................Kristy McNichol

This drama concerned successful architect George Apple, who decided to leave the rat race of big-city life and return with his wife Barbara and their four children to his home town of Appleton, Iowa. This small rural community, which had been founded by George's ancestors, was a far cry from Los Angeles. It provided even more adjustment problems for George's city-bred children than for his wife and himself, but in time the entire family came to appreciate their new surroundings. George was an idealist, with compassion for his fellow man and strong religious convictions. He found himself getting involved in numerous causes, and sometimes was looked upon by the townspeople as a bit of a kook.

APPOINTMENT WITH ADVENTURE

Dramatic Anthology

FIRST TELECAST: *April 3, 1955*

LAST TELECAST: *April 1, 1956*

BROADCAST HISTORY:

Apr 1955–Apr 1956, CBS Sun 10:00–10:30

This live half-hour series, using studio sets, took viewers to various parts of the world, as well as different locations in the United States. Its contemporary and period stories were set in such locales as World War II Europe and Civil War America. Among the better-known performers who appeared in these plays were Polly Bergen, Betsy Palmer, Gena Rowlands, Phyllis Kirk, Dane Clark, Tony Randall, Gene Barry, and Paul Newman.

APPOINTMENT WITH LOVE

see *ABC Dramatic Shorts—1952–1953*

AQUANAUTS, THE

Adventure

FIRST TELECAST: *September 14, 1960*

LAST TELECAST: *September 27, 1961*

BROADCAST HISTORY:

Sep 1960–Sep 1961, CBS Wed 7:30–8:30

CAST:

Drake Andrews ....Keith Larsen
Larry Lahr ....Jeremy Slate
Mike Madison (1961) ....Roy Ely
The Captain (1961) .....Charles Thompson

Taking the same format as the highly successful syndicated series *Sea Hunt, The Aquanauts* told stories of the adventures of two professional salvage divers based in Southern California. The human and marine perils they faced on assignments created the suspense and action. Drake Andrews and Larry Lahr were the two young divers at the start of the season. Andrews was last seen in the episode that was aired on January 18. The following week Larry Lahr recruited Mike Madison as a replacement. On February 15, the title of the series was changed to *Malibu Run*. Although the principals still participated in salvage operations, they had moved into the Malibu Beach area and set up an aquatic sports shop. A new member of the cast was the Captain, an old salt who lived nearby and who became their good friend.

ARCHER

Detective Drama

FIRST TELECAST: *January 30, 1975*

LAST TELECAST: *March 13, 1975*

BROADCAST HISTORY:

Jan 1975–Mar 1975, NBC Thu 9:00–10:00

CAST:

Lew Archer .... Brian Keith
Lt. Barney Brighton .... John P. Ryan

Lew Archer was the antithesis of the slick, sexy, superefficient detective so often seen on television. He was a real person, a man of simple tastes, who used his analytic ability rather than brute strength or gimmicks to solve crimes. Although he was a former cop, and generally worked with the police, Archer was not above bending the law if it would help him nail the culprit. Perhaps the lack of gimmicks is why the program failed to catch on.

The series was based on the central character in Ross MacDonald's highly successful mystery novels.

ARE YOU POSITIVE

Sports Quiz/Audience Participation

FIRST TELECAST: *July 6, 1952*

LAST TELECAST: *August 24, 1952*

BROADCAST HISTORY:

Jul 1952–Aug 1952, NBC Sun 6:00–6:30

EMCEE:

Bill Stern
Frank Coniff

REGULAR PANELISTS:

Jimmy Cannon (New York *Post* columnist)
Frank Frisch (radio and TV sports commentator)

This weekly live sports quiz program, which premiered as *Bill Stern's Sports Quiz*, featured Stern and a panel of three people familiar with all aspects of sports. The panelists were asked to identify a sports personality from photographs taken when he/she was a child, or occasionally from a negative of a photograph. Suggestions for personalities to be used were sent in by the viewing audience. Frank Coniff replaced Bill Stern as emcee of the program on July 27.

ARMCHAIR DETECTIVE

Detective Drama

FIRST TELECAST: *July 6, 1949*

LAST TELECAST: *September 28, 1949*

BROADCAST HISTORY:

Jul 1949–Sep 1949, CBS Wed 9:00–9:30

CAST:

Mr. Crime Interrogator .... John Milton Kennedy
Mr. Crime Authority .... H. Allen Smith

Each week two one-act whodunit plays were presented in this series of films. The plays contained clues that pointed to the solution, which was explained in detail at the end of each story by H. Allen Smith, a member of the California State Legislature.

ARMED FORCES HOUR, THE

Musical Variety

FIRST TELECAST: *February 4, 1951*

LAST TELECAST: *May 6, 1951*

BROADCAST HISTORY:

Feb 1951–May 1951, DUM Sun 8:30–9:00

This was a frankly promotional half-hour for the U.S. Armed Forces, produced by the Department of Defense and using a musical variety format to lure viewers to watching short films about the services. Entertainment was by servicemen-performers such as The Singing Sergeants and the U.S. Navy Dance Band appearing on a USO Club set, joined by professional entertainers such as Frances Langford and Marion Morgan. Acts were interspersed with films about the army, the navy, and the air force.

ARMSTRONG BY REQUEST

Dramatic Anthology

FIRST TELECAST: *July 8, 1959*

LAST TELECAST: *September 16, 1959*

BROADCAST HISTORY:

Jul 1959–Sep 1959, CBS Wed 10:00–11:00

The summer 1959 replacement for *Armstrong Circle Theatre* was a series of repeats of six documentary dramas that had been presented on that program during the 1958–1959 season. The program alternated with *The U.S. Steel Hour.*

ARMSTRONG CIRCLE THEATRE

Dramatic Anthology

FIRST TELECAST: *June 6, 1950*

LAST TELECAST: *August 28, 1963*

BROADCAST HISTORY:

Jun 1950–Jun 1955, NBC Tue 9:30–10:00
Sep 1955–Jun 1957, NBC Tue 9:30–10:30
Oct 1957–Aug 1963, CBS Wed 10:00–11:00 (OS)

HOST/NARRATOR:

Douglas Edwards (1957–1961)
Ron Cochran (1961–1962)
Henry Hamilton (1962–1963)

Armstrong Circle Theatre was one of the major dramatic anthology series of television's "Golden Age." At the outset it featured original dramas set in the contemporary world, many by noted writers. Serious treatments of such sensitive subjects as mental illness and racial intolerance alternated with occasional spoofs and comedies. Violence and morbidity were specifically avoided, as Armstrong intended its program to be suitable for family viewing. Among the early telecasts was "The Parrot" (March 24, 1953), the first operetta commissioned for commercial television.

In 1955, when *Armstrong Circle Theatre* expanded to an hour, the format was changed to emphasize dramas based on real-life events, both headline-making ("S.O.S. from the *Andrea Doria*") and personal ("I Was Accused," the story of an immigrant threatened with deportation). One of the most notable telecasts of this period was "Nightmare in Red," a documentary on the history of Communism in Russia (December 27, 1955).

With the move to CBS in 1957, as the program alternating with *The U.S. Steel Hour, Armstrong Circle Theatre* retained the documentary drama format but acquired a regular host/narrator in the person of CBS newsman Doug Edwards. The most popular topics during this period were related to the cold war: "The Vanished," about an Iron Curtain victim; "Thunder Over Berlin"; "Security Risk," about army counterintelligence; "The Spy Next Door"; "Crime Without a Country," about Interpol; "Window on the West," about Radio Free Europe; "Tunnel to Freedom," about refugees escaping to West Berlin; and "The Assassin," about a Soviet espionage agent. The other most prevalent format was the exposé: "The Meanest Crime in the World," about fraudulent medical practices; "Sound of Violence: The Juke Box Rackets"; "Full Disclosure," about security swindles; "The Antique Swindle"; "Smash-Up," about auto insurance company fraud; and "The Thief of Charity," among others.

ARNIE

Situation Comedy

FIRST TELECAST: *September 19, 1970*

LAST TELECAST: *September 9, 1972*

BROADCAST HISTORY:

Sep 1970–Sep 1971, CBS Sat 9:00–9:30
Sep 1971–Dec 1971, CBS Mon 10:30–11:00
Dec 1971–Sep 1972, CBS Sat 9:30–10:00

CAST:

Arnie Nuvo ....Herschel Bernardi
Lillian Nuvo ....Sue Ane Langdon
Hamilton Majors, Jr. ....Roger Bowen
Felicia ....Elaine Shore
Neil Ogilvie ....Herb Voland
Richard Nuvo ....Del Russell
Andrea Nuvo ....Stephanie Steele
Julius ....Tom Pedi

Arnie Nuvo, a perfectly content loading dock foreman for the Continental Flange Company, unexpectedly found himself promoted to head of the Product Improvement Division. The sudden shift from blue-collar worker to white-collar executive made many drastic changes in Arnie's life. Suddenly he had all sorts of new challenges, new responsibilities, new sources of aggravation, and a substantial increase in pay. His social status was changed, and, with the exception of his good friend Julius, he was removed from contact with his former co-workers. The adjustments he and his wife Lillian had to make, and the problems they had making them, provided the material for the comedy in this series.

AROUND THE TOWN

see *Girl about Town* for 1949 program by this name

AROUND THE TOWN

Documentary

FIRST TELECAST: *January 7, 1950*

LAST TELECAST: *February 18, 1950*

BROADCAST HISTORY:

Jan 1950–Feb 1950, NBC Sat 9:30–10:00

HOST:

Bob Stanton

In this program, a mobile unit visited interesting places around New York City.

ARREST AND TRIAL

Crime Drama

FIRST TELECAST: *September 15, 1963*

LAST TELECAST: *September 6, 1964*

BROADCAST HISTORY:

Sep 1963–Sep 1964, ABC Sun 8:30–10:00

CAST:

Det. Sgt. Nick Anderson ......Ben Gazzara
Attorney John Egan ....Chuck Connors
Deputy D.A. Jerry Miller ....John Larch
Assistant Deputy D.A. Barry Pine
.... John Kerr
Det. Sgt. Dan Kirby ....Roger Perry
Det. Lt. Bone ....Noah Keen
Mitchell Harris ....Don Galloway
Jake Shakespeare ....Joe Higgins
Janet Okada ....Jo Anne Miya

Arrest and Trial was actually two separate but interwoven 45-minute programs, the first showing the commission of a crime, the police investigation, and the arrest; and the second depicting the trial. Ben Gazzara starred as Los Angeles police detective Nick Anderson in the first part, while Chuck Connors portrayed defense attorney John Egan (who tried to get Anderson's arrestees off the hook) in the second.

ARROW SHOW, THE

Comedy Variety

FIRST TELECAST: *November 24, 1948*

LAST TELECAST: *May 19, 1949*

BROADCAST HISTORY:

Nov 1948–May 1949, NBC Thu 8:00–8:30

HOST:

Phil Silvers (Nov 1948–Mar 1949)
Hank Ladd (Apr–May 1949)

REGULAR:

Jack Gilford

This was a comedy variety show with guest stars and a rotating stable of "regulars," of whom only Jack Gilford remained for the full season. Also known as *The Phil Silvers Arrow Show* and *Arrow Comedy Theatre.*

ART BAKER SHOW, THE

see *You Asked for It*

ART FORD ON BROADWAY

Interview

FIRST TELECAST: *April 5, 1950*

LAST TELECAST: *June 30, 1950*

BROADCAST HISTORY:

Apr 1950–Jun 1950, ABC Wed/Thu/Fri 7:15–7:30

HOST:

Art Ford

On this short-lived Broadway chatter program, host Art Ford interviewed such guests as the manager of the Astor Hotel, a Broadway detective, and the author of a new book. During its final month on the air the program's title was altered to *Art Ford on the Broadways of the World.*

ART FORD SHOW, THE

Quiz/Audience Participation

FIRST TELECAST: *July 28, 1951*

LAST TELECAST: *September 15, 1951*

BROADCAST HISTORY:

Jul 1951–Sep 1951, NBC Sat 7:30–8:00

EMCEE:

Art Ford

Each week three disc jockeys from stations around the country served as panelists trying to guess composers, vocalists, and orchestras of various records played on the air. The disc jockey with the most correct answers at the end of the program received a special "Disc Jockey Oscar." Mr. Ford, himself a disc jockey on radio station WNEW in New York, also introduced each week a recording artist with a "million seller" who performed on the show.

An unusual feature of this program was that it also sought to publicize the good works done by many disc jockeys, such as their support of charities and their involvement in other public service activities.

ART LINKLETTER SHOW, THE

Quiz/Audience Participation

FIRST TELECAST: *February 18, 1963*

LAST TELECAST: *September 16, 1963*

BROADCAST HISTORY:

Feb 1963–Sep 1963, NBC Mon 9:30–10:00

HOST:
Art Linkletter
REGULARS:
Carl Reiner (Apr–Sep)
Jayne Meadows (Apr–Sep)

This short-lived variation on *Candid Camera* presented amusing incidents in everyday life, some filmed with a hidden camera and some acted out by a group of players. Celebrity guests and the studio audience then tried to guess the outcome; by April the guessing was being done by a celebrity panel alone. In a typical episode, the panel had to guess whether a woman would buy an atrocious hat, if told it was by a famous French designer; whether a man with both his arms in slings could persuade a stranger to feed him ice cream; and if a customer in a pet shop would be willing to conduct his business with a chimpanzee, in the absence of the proprietor.

ART LINKLETTER'S HOLLYWOOD TALENT SCOUTS

see *Hollywood Talent Scouts*

ARTHUR GODFREY AND HIS FRIENDS

Musical Variety
FIRST TELECAST: *January 12, 1949*
LAST TELECAST: *April 28, 1959*
BROADCAST HISTORY:
Jan 1949–Jun 1957, CBS Wed 8:00–9:00 (OS)
Sep 1958–Apr 1959, CBS Tue 9:00–9:30
HOST:
Arthur Godfrey
REGULARS:
Tony Marvin
The Chordettes (Virginia Osborn, Dorothy Schwartz, Carol Hagedorn, Janet Ertel) (1949–1953)
Janette Davis (1949–1957)
Bill Lawrence (1949–1950)
The Mariners (Jim Lewis, Tom Lockard, Nat Dickerson, Martin Karl) (1949–1955)
Haleloke (1950–1955)
Frank Parker (1950–1956)
Marion Marlowe (1950–1955)
Julius LaRosa (1952–1953)
Lu Ann Sims (1952–1955)
The McGuire Sisters (Christine, Dorothy, Phyllis) (1952–1957)
Carmel Quinn (1954–1957)
Pat Boone (1955–1957)
The Toppers (1955–1957)
Miyoshi Umeki (1955)
Frank Westbrook Dancers (1958–1959)
ORCHESTRA:
Archie Bleyer (1949–1954)
Jerry Bresler (1954–1955)
Will Roland and Bert Farber (1955–1957)
Bernie Green (1958–1959)

The arrival of Arthur Godfrey on television was the most widely publicized event of the 1948–1949 season. Godfrey had been one of the biggest stars on radio in the late 1940s, and his folksy, person-to-person style looked like a natural for TV. It was.

Both *Arthur Godfrey and His Friends* and its companion show, *Arthur Godfrey's Talent Scouts,* shot to the top of the TV ratings and stayed there for several years. Part of the appeal was in Godfrey's repertory company of singers, all of them good clean kids who had been lifted out of obscurity by Godfrey (he never hired an established performer as a regular). But mostly it was "the old redhead" himself that the viewers adored. Ben Gross of the New York *Daily News* summed up his appeal: "It is his friendliness, his good cheer, his small-boy mischievousness and his kindly philosophy . . . or maybe it's his magnetism, his personal attractiveness." As on radio, Godfrey frequently kidded his sponsors and refused to advertise any product for which he could not personally vouch. Frequently he would throw away the script and improvise his way through a testimonial. When Godfrey talked about how much he liked that cup of Lipton Tea, he sounded as if he meant it.

The show itself was a variety hour built around Godfrey and his "friends." Frank Parker and Marion Marlowe were the mature, romantic duet, Julius LaRosa was the bright young boy singer, Haleloke the shy, exotic Hawaiian, and the Chordettes the well-scrubbed young barbershop harmonizers from Sheboygan, Wisconsin. Tony Marvin was the deep-voiced announcer who added a certain urbanity to the show. In and out of the proceedings flitted Godfrey, sometimes plunking his ukulele, sometimes singing (the term is used generously), sometimes just adding encouragement or folksy chatter.

For several years there seemed to be no stopping him. Arthur Godfrey was practically deified by the press. When he underwent surgery in May 1953 for an old hip injury (the painful result of an auto smashup 20 years before), the whole country, it seemed, sent get-well cards.

Then, in one of the most dramatic turnarounds in any star's career, Godfrey became the subject of tremendous controversy, vilified by the same columnists who had heaped praise on him only a few years before. Probably no personality got more press coverage in the mid-1950s, often with sensational headlines. Godfrey brought it on himself. Most publicized was his firing of the "little Godfreys," one by one, for what often seemed petty reasons. By far the most dramatic incident was the on-the-air dismissal in October 1953 of Julius LaRosa, who, Godfrey said, had gotten to be too big a star. His remark to the press that LaRosa had lost his "humility" was to haunt Godfrey for the rest of his days. (LaRosa, who had only humble praise for his former boss, immediately went on to some well-publicized appearances on the *Ed Sullivan Show*, several hit records, and a series of his own, but his career faded after a few years.) Others who got the ax included orchestra leader Archie Bleyer, who was running a record company on the side and who made the mistake of recording Godfrey's archrival, Don McNeil (Bleyer's dating of Chordette Janet Ertel, whom he later married, was also given as a reason); producer Larry Puck (who was dating Marion Marlowe); and the Chordettes (they never could figure out why). Then, in April 1955, in one fell swoop he fired Marion Marlowe, Haleloke, and the Mariners, plus three writers.

All this might not have been so bad if Godfrey had not been so thin-skinned about press criticism. A regular feud erupted, with the vituperous star variously labeling his detractors as "Dope!" (Ed Sullivan), "Liar!" (or words to that effect, for Dorothy Kilgallen), "Fatuous ass!" (John Crosby), "These jerk newspapermen!" and "Muckrakers!" for all and sundry. When his private pilot's license was suspended because he allegedly buzzed an airport tower in his private DC-3, the papers had a field day with that, too.

Godfrey's bad press adversely affected his image, and his ratings began to drop. The fired "friends" were all replaced, almost on a one-for-one basis. Pretty Marion Marlowe with her long, flowing black hair was replaced by pretty Carmel Quinn with long flowing red hair; earnest young Julius LaRosa by earnest young Pat Boone; the harmonizing Chordettes by the harmonizing McGuire Sisters. Godfrey even signed up a Japanese girl, Miyoshi Umeki, to take the place of the Hawaiian Haleloke. It was not quite the same, though, and while Godfrey kept both his shows until he voluntarily decided to give them up, their popularity in the later days never matched that of the spectacular early 1950s.

After a final season in a half-hour format in 1958–1959, with only Tony Marvin as a regular, Godfrey left nighttime TV. He turned up briefly on *Candid Camera* in 1960–1961, then continued on radio for many years, until a tearful farewell broadcast on CBS in 1972. In recent years, having survived a bout with cancer, he has devoted himself to conservationist causes.

ARTHUR GODFREY AND HIS UKULELE

Instruction

FIRST TELECAST: *April 4, 1950*

LAST TELECAST: *June 30, 1950*

BROADCAST HISTORY:

Apr 1950, CBS Tue/Thu 7:45–8:00

Apr 1950–Jun 1950, CBS Tue/Fri 7:45–8:00

STAR:

Arthur Godfrey

For a three-month period in 1950, in addition to his other CBS radio and television programs, Arthur Godfrey appeared twice a week to give lessons on how to play the ukulele. For the first three weeks these live lessons ran on Tuesday and Thursday nights at 7:45, after which the Thursday lesson moved to Friday.

ARTHUR GODFREY SHOW, THE

see *Arthur Godfrey and His Friends*

ARTHUR GODFREY'S TALENT SCOUTS

Talent

FIRST TELECAST: *December 6, 1948*

LAST TELECAST: *July 21, 1958*

BROADCAST HISTORY:

Dec 1948–Jul 1958, CBS Mon 8:30–9:00 (OS)

HOST:

Arthur Godfrey

ANNOUNCER:

Tony Marvin

ORCHESTRA:

Archie Bleyer (1948–1954)

Jerry Bresler (1954–1955)

Will Roland and Bert Farber (1955–1958)

Arthur Godfrey was the only personality in TV history to have two top-rated programs running simultaneously in prime time for an extended period (eight and a half seasons). On Mondays viewers could see him on the *Talent Scouts,* on Wednesdays on *Arthur Godfrey and His Friends. Talent Scouts* was slightly higher-rated, reaching No. 1 for the 1951–1952 season. But it was hard to tell the two programs apart. In 1952–1953 *Talent Scouts* and *Friends* ranked No. 2 and 3 among all programs on TV, just behind *I Love Lucy.*

Talent Scouts had "scouts" bring on their discoveries to perform before a live national audience. Most of these "discoveries" were aspiring professionals with some prior experience, and the quality of the acts was therefore quite high. Godfrey's folksy banter and interviews added the icing to the cake. Winners for each show were chosen by audience applause meter. Several of the winners were invited to join Godfrey as regulars on his other show, and of these some went on to become major stars in their own right. Among the Godfrey regulars who were discovered on *Talent Scouts* were the Chordettes, Carmel Quinn, Pat Boone, and the McGuire Sisters.

ARTHUR MURRAY PARTY, THE

Musical Variety

FIRST TELECAST: *July 20, 1950*

LAST TELECAST: *September 6, 1960*

BROADCAST HISTORY:

Jul 1950–Sep 1950, ABC Thu 9:00–9:30
Oct 1950–Jan 1951, DUM Sun 9:00–10:00
Jan 1951–Mar 1951, DUM Sun 9:00–9:30
Apr 1951–Jun 1951, ABC Mon 9:00–9:30
Sep 1951–Dec 1951, ABC Wed 9:00–9:30
Jan 1952–May 1952, ABC Sun 9:00–9:30
Jul 1952–Aug 1952, CBS Fri 8:00–8:30
Oct 1952–Apr 1953, DUM Sun 10:00–10:30
Jun 1953–Oct 1953, CBS Sun 9:30–10:00
Oct 1953–Apr 1954, NBC Mon 7:30–7:45
Jun 1954–Sep 1954, NBC Tue 8:30–9:00
Jun 1955–Sep 1955, NBC Tue 8:30–9:00
Apr 1956–Sep 1956, CBS Thu 10:00–10:30
Apr 1957–Jun 1957, NBC Tue 8:00–8:30
Jul 1957–Sep 1957, NBC Mon 9:30–10:00
Sep 1958–Sep 1959, NBC Mon 10:00–10:30
Sep 1959–Jan 1960, NBC Tue 9:00–9:30
Jan 1960–Sep 1960, NBC Tue 9:30–10:00

REGULARS:

Kathryn Murray
Arthur Murray
The Arthur Murray Dancers
The Stanley Melba Orchestra (1950)
The Emil Coleman Orchestra (1951–1952)
The Ray Carter Orchestra (1953–1960)

This was, without a doubt, the longest-running commercial in the history of television. For a full decade, Arthur and Kathryn Murray built an entire program around dancing as an incentive for viewers to take courses with the Arthur Murray Dance Studio. In the early years, through the spring of 1953, the show was actually sponsored by the dance studios. A regular feature was a mystery dance segment, in which viewers could win two free lessons at their nearest Arthur Murray Studio by mailing in a postcard correctly identifying the week's mystery dance.

Throughout its long run, the format of *The Arthur Murray Party* remained virtually unchanged. The setting was a large party at which Kathryn was the cheerful, vivacious hostess. There were always one or two guest stars on hand, from the world of show business or sports, and a substantial group of Arthur Murray dance instructors from the various studios in the New York area. Kathryn chatted with the guests; they in turn sang, danced, and occasionally participated in comedy sketches. Arthur acted as the instructor who taught the home audience, and often the guest stars as well, a particular dance step. The instructors who appeared in the party group would often be singled out to demonstrate their proficiency at unusual or complex dances. As the show drew to a close, Arthur and Kathryn would glide majestically into a Strauss waltz with the rest of the party group joining in. There were subtle additions and subtractions to the format over the years but the basic structure remained intact. Kathryn's closing line each week was, "Till then, to put a little fun in your life, try dancing."

The Arthur Murray Party was the perennial summer replacement series. It was easy to produce and always attracted a respectable audience. It was one of only four series to appear, at one time or another, on all four television networks. When it premiered on ABC in 1950 it was called *Authur Murray Party Time.* That fall, the first DuMont version was titled *The Arthur Murray Show,* but by the autumn of 1951 it had become *The Arthur Murray Party,* the name it retained throughout the rest of its ten years on the air.

ASIA PERSPECTIVE

Documentary/Public Affairs

FIRST TELECAST: *September 4, 1966*

LAST TELECAST: *September 25, 1966*

BROADCAST HISTORY:

Sep 1966, CBS Sun 6:00–6:30

The four documentaries that were shown under the collective title *Asia Perspective* covered the then-current ideological purges in Communist China, the elections taking place in South Vietnam, and a two-part history of the political, economic, and social changes that had taken place on the Chinese mainland since the fall of Manchuria in 1931. Various CBS correspondents contributed to the reports.

ASK ME ANOTHER

Quiz/Audience Participation

FIRST TELECAST: *July 3, 1952*

LAST TELECAST: *September 25, 1952*

BROADCAST HISTORY:

Jul 1952–Sep 1952, NBC Thu 10:30–11:00

EMCEE:

Joe Boland

REGULAR PANELISTS:

Johnny Lujack (football player)
Warren Brown (sports editor, *Chicago Tribune*)
Kay Westfall (TV actress)
Tom Duggan (sports commentator)

The four panelists on this quiz show tried to guess the identities of famous sports personalities, who appeared as guests. Each guest would stand behind a shadow curtain while the panelists asked questions to try to figure out his or her identity. A special feature of the show was the appearance of one "performing guest" each week, who would perform his or her specialty behind the shadow curtain while the panelists tried to guess who it was.

ASPHALT JUNGLE, THE

Police Drama

FIRST TELECAST: *April 2, 1961*

LAST TELECAST: *September 24, 1961*

BROADCAST HISTORY:

Apr 1961–Sep 1961, ABC Sun 9:30–10:30

CAST:

Matthew Gower ....Jack Warden
Capt. Gus Honochek ....Arch Johnson
Sgt. Danny Keller ....Bill Smith

Fighting crime in a big city is often a job that requires specialists. Deputy Police Commissioner Matthew Gower was one of them. Helping him break up the large organized crime rings that infiltrated his town was a special squad of select men headed by Gus Honochek and Danny Keller. Often they had undercover assignments, and Commissioner Gower, not one to leave the dirty work to his men, would pitch in and go undercover with them. The most memorable aspect of this police series was the background music, composed by the great jazz musician Duke Ellington.

ASSIGNMENT FOREIGN LEGION

Adventure Anthology

FIRST TELECAST: *October 1, 1957*

LAST TELECAST: *December 24, 1957*

BROADCAST HISTORY:

Oct 1957–Dec 1957, CBS Tue 10:30–11:00

HOSTESS:

Merle Oberon

Actress Merle Oberon was the narrator of and occasional performer in this British dramatic series about the French Foreign Legion. Each episode opened with Miss Oberon, as a foreign correspondent stationed in North Africa, introducing a story about the officers and men of the Legion. Occasionally, as the foreign correspondent, she appeared in the story as well. The series was filmed on location in Morocco, Algiers, and Spain and was first seen on British television.

ASSIGNMENT MANHUNT

see *Manhunt*

ASSIGNMENT VIENNA

Spy Drama

FIRST TELECAST: *September 28, 1972*

LAST TELECAST: *June 9, 1973*

BROADCAST HISTORY:

Sep 1972–Dec 1972, ABC Thu 9:00–10:00
Jan 1973–Jun 1973, ABC Sat 10:00–11:00

CAST:

Jake Webster ....Robert Conrad
Maj. Caldwell ....Charles Cioffi
Inspector Hoffman ....Anton Diffring

This international spy drama was one of three rotating elements of the series *The*

Men. It starred Robert Conrad as Jake Webster, a rugged, independent American expatriate with a shady past who operated Jake's Bar & Grill in Vienna. Jake's bistro was only a cover for his undercover work for the United States government, however, as he tracked down assorted spies and international criminals in convoluted plots. He maintained an uneasy liaison with Major Caldwell of U.S. Intelligence, who in return for Jake's services kept the American out of jail. The series was filmed on location in Vienna.

AT HOME SHOW

see *Earl Wrightson Show*

AT ISSUE

Interview

FIRST TELECAST: *July 12, 1953*
LAST TELECAST: *February 24, 1954*
BROADCAST HISTORY:
Jul 1953–Aug 1953, ABC Sun 9:00–9:15
Oct 1953–Feb 1954, ABC Wed 8:00–8:15
HOST:
Martin Agronsky

News commentator Agronsky interviewed public figures on important issues of the day in this 15-minute public-affairs program. After its prime-time run the program continued on Sunday afternoons until June 1954.

AT LIBERTY CLUB

Music

FIRST TELECAST: *June 25, 1948*
LAST TELECAST: *September 16, 1948*
BROADCAST HISTORY:
Jun 1948–Jul 1948, NBC Fri 8:00–8:30
Jul 1948–Sep 1948, NBC Thu 8:00–8:15
HOSTESS:
Jacqueline (Turner)

This short musical interlude was set in a mythical nightclub for "at liberty" youngsters, presided over by Parisian singer Jacqueline, with guests. The program was formerly local on WPTZ, Philadelphia.

AUCTION-AIRE

Auction

FIRST TELECAST: *September 30, 1949*
LAST TELECAST: *June 23, 1950*
BROADCAST HISTORY:
Sep 1949–Jun 1950, ABC Fri 9:00–9:30
EMCEE:
Jack Gregson
REGULAR:
"Rebel" (Charlotte) Randall

In this fast-paced auction program from Chicago, the audience had a chance to bid on valuable merchandise—using, instead of cash, the labels from products of The Libby Company, the program's sponsor. Among the bargains was a $250 home freezer that went for 88 labels, a $355 refrigerator for 225 labels, and a $450 sterling silver set for 225 labels. Auction-Aire Gregson's assistant, buxom model "Rebel" Randall, was mainly decorative.

AUTHOR MEETS THE CRITICS

Book Discussion

FIRST TELECAST: *April 4, 1948*
LAST TELECAST: *October 10, 1954*
BROADCAST HISTORY:
Apr 1948–Mar 1949, NBC Sun 8:00–8:30
Mar 1949–Jul 1949, NBC Sun 8:30–9:00
Oct 1949–Nov 1949, ABC Mon 7:30–8:00
Nov 1949–Dec 1949, ABC Wed 9:00–9:30
Dec 1949–Mar 1950, ABC Thu 9:30–10:00
Mar 1950–Sep 1950, ABC Wed 8:30–9:00
Sep 1951–Dec 1951, NBC Mon 10:00–10:30
Mar 1952–Oct 1952, DUM Thu 10:30–11:00
Oct 1952–May 1953, DUM Thu 10:00–10:30
May 1953–Oct 1953, DUM Wed 9:30–10:00
Mar 1954–Jul 1954, DUM Sun 7:00–7:30
Jul 1954–Oct 1954, DUM Sun 10:00–10:30
MODERATOR:
John K. M. McCaffery (1948–1951)
Faye Emerson (1952)
Virgilia Peterson (1952–1954)

An author defending his current work against a panel of critics was the premise of this durable program, which began on local television in New York on July 10, 1947, and later saw service on an assortment of nights and networks. The critics, one pro and one con each week, were generally literary figures, although some were TV celebrities as well, such as Bennett Cerf and Dr. Mason Gross. Authors ranged from Ezra Stone and Cornelia Otis Skinner to Henry Morgan (whose latest movie was dissected) and cartoonist Al Capp. Their debates sometimes generated real verbal fireworks.

In addition to current books, such as *U.S.A. Confidential* and *The Execution of Private Slovik*, occasional movies and magazine articles were considered. John K. M. McCaffery, who had been one of the hosts of *Author Meets the Critics* on radio, where it originated in 1946, was the first host of the TV series; he was later succeeded by actress Faye Emerson and then by Virgilia Peterson.

AVENGERS, THE

Spy Drama

FIRST TELECAST: *March 28, 1966*

LAST TELECAST:

BROADCAST HISTORY:

Mar 1966–Jul 1966, ABC Mon 10:00–11:00
Jul 1966–Sep 1966, ABC Thu 10:00–11:00
Jan 1967–Sep 1967, ABC Fri 10:00–11:00
Jan 1968–Sep 1968, ABC Wed 7:30–8:30
Sep 1968–Sep 1969, ABC Mon 7:30–8:30
Sep 1978– , CBS Fri 11:30–12:30

CAST:

Jonathan Steed ....Patrick Macnee
Emma Peel (1966–1968) ....Diana Rigg
Tara King (1968–1969) .....Linda Thorson
Purdey (1978–) ....Joanna Lumley
Mike Gambit (1978–) .....Gareth Hunt

The Avengers first appeared on British television more than five years before it was imported to the United States in 1966. Pure escapist entertainment, it centered on Jonathan Steed, a suave, imperturbable, and very proper British secret agent, and his partner Mrs. Peel. Their missions, whether planned or accidental, involved all sorts of diabolical geniuses who planned to take over the world through various fantastic schemes. Improbable technical devices, wittily absurd villains, and the clever and efficient Steed combined to make this fantasized espionage series unique. Like the American-made *Man from U.N.C.L.E.*, it attempted to out-James-Bond James Bond.

Macnee's original partner in the British version of the series was Honor Blackman, who played Pussy Galore in the James Bond film *Goldfinger*. By the time *The Avengers* reached American audiences she had been replaced by the lithe, jumpsuited Diana Rigg. Steed and Mrs. Peel were separated in the March 20, 1968, episode, when the lady agent was reunited with her long-lost husband. Linda Thorson, a younger and more voluptuous woman, then became the female partner.

The series was resurrected in Britain in 1976 with a new title, *The New Avengers*, and a new supporting cast for Mr. Steed—young agents Purdey and Gambit. It was this version that joined the CBS late night lineup in the fall of 1978, the only original programming (at least to American audiences) amid CBS' late night movie reruns and episodes of former prime time network series.

AWARD THEATER

syndicated title for *Alcoa Theatre* and *Goodyear Theater*

AWAY WE GO

Musical Variety

FIRST TELECAST: *June 3, 1967*

LAST TELECAST: *September 2, 1967*

BROADCAST HISTORY:

Jun 1967–Sep 1967, CBS Sat 7:30–8:30

REGULARS:

George Carlin
Buddy Greco
Buddy Rich

Comedian George Carlin, singer Buddy Greco, and drummer Buddy Rich and his orchestra were the stars of this variety show, which was the 1967 summer replacement for *The Jackie Gleason Show*. The series title was based on one of Gleason's pet expressions, "And away we go!"

BAA BAA BLACK SHEEP

War Drama

FIRST TELECAST: *September 21, 1976*

LAST TELECAST: *September 1, 1978*

BROADCAST HISTORY:

Sep 1976–Aug 1977, NBC Tue 8:00–9:00
Dec 1977–Mar 1978, NBC Wed 9:00–10:00
Mar 1978–Apr 1978, NBC Thu 9:00–10:00
Jul 1978, NBC Wed 9:00–10:00
Aug 1978–Sep 1978, NBC Fri 8:00–9:00

CAST:

Maj. Gregory "Pappy" Boyington
........................Robert Conrad
Col. Lard, USMC ....Dana Elcar
Capt. Gutterman (1976–1977)
..................James Whitmore, Jr.
Lt. Jerry Bragg ....Dirk Blocker
Lt. T. J. Wiley ....Robert Ginty
Lt. Bob Anderson ....John Larroquette
Lt. L. Casey ....W. K. Stratton
Gen. Moore ....Simon Oakland
Hutch (1976–1977) ....Joey Aresco
Lt. Don French ....Jeff MacKay

Lt. Bob Doyle ....Larry Manetti
Sgt. Andy Micklin (1977–1978)
............................Red West
Capt. Dottie Dixon (1977–1978)
.....................Katherine Cannon
Lt. Jeb Pruitt (1978) ....Jeb Adams
Nurse Samantha (1978) ....Denise DuBarry
Nurse Ellie (1978) ....Kathy McCullem
Nurse Susan (1978) ....Brianne Leary
Nurse Nancy (1978) ....Nancy Conrad

TECHNICAL ADVISOR:
Gregory Boyington

Based loosely on the book *Baa Baa Black Sheep*, by World War II Marine Corps flying ace Gregory Boyington, this series was the story of a squadron of misfit flyers in the South Pacific. Squadron 214 was composed of men who had been on the verge of court martial before Boyington provided them with reprieves. They had been charged with everything from fighting with officers, to stealing booze, to being general nuisances and nonconformists. Pappy (he was so named because at age 35 he was an "old man" by the standards of his men) maintained almost no discipline, ignored military regulations, and did not care what his men did when they weren't on missions. As long as they could fly and do the job when necessary, nothing else mattered. Given this personal code, Pappy was completely at home with his men, whether they were chasing women, getting into brawls, conning the military hierarchy or civilian populations, or—in a more serious vein—intercepting the Japanese.

Baa Baa Black Sheep was dropped from the NBC lineup at the end of the 1976–1977 season, only to be revived in December 1977 when most of NBC's new 1977–1978 series failed and the network ran short of programming. It was retitled *Black Sheep Squadron*, and Capt. Dottie Dixon was added to the cast. She was in charge of the nursing force on Vella La Cava, the island where Pappy and his men were based, and her young charges were seemingly always available for fun and games with the men of the 214th Squadron. Four of the girls became regular cast members in early 1978. They were christened "Pappy's Lambs," perhaps as a parody of ABC's popular *Charlie's Angels*, who were scheduled opposite *Black Sheep Squadron*. One of the lambs, Nurse Nancy, was played by the daughter of Robert Conrad.

BABY, I'M BACK

Situation Comedy

FIRST TELECAST: *January 30, 1978*
LAST TELECAST: *August 12, 1978*
BROADCAST HISTORY:
Jan 1978–Aug 1978, CBS Mon 8:30–9:00

CAST:
Raymond Ellis ....Demond Wilson
Olivia Ellis ....Denise Nicholas
Luzelle Carter ....Helen Martin
Angie Ellis ....Kim Fields
Jordan Ellis ....Tony Holmes
Col. Wallace Dickey ....Ed Hall

Seven years after he had deserted his wife because he couldn't take the pressures of being married, Raymond Ellis discovered that she had just had him declared legally dead. His interest in reconciliation suddenly revived, Raymond moved into the apartment building where his ex-wife, Olivia, lived with their two young children, Angie and Jordan, and her mother Luzelle. Not only did Ray try to rekindle a romance with his estranged wife, but he also had to contend with a mother-in-law who had never thought very much of him in the first place, and with Olivia's fiancé, Col. Dickey. Col. Dickey was a Pentagon official for whom Olivia worked and to whom she was planning to get married—until Ray showed up. A backdrop to this romantic conflict was Ray's attempts to have himself legally declared alive.

BACHELOR FATHER

Situation Comedy

FIRST TELECAST: *September 15, 1957*
LAST TELECAST: *September 25, 1962*
BROADCAST HISTORY:
Sep 1957–Jun 1959, CBS Sun 7:30–8:00 (OS)
Jun 1959–Sep 1961, NBC Thu 9:00–9:30
Oct 1961–Sep 1962, ABC Tue 8:00–8:30

CAST:
Bentley Gregg ....John Forsythe
Kelly Gregg ....Noreen Corcoran
Peter Tong ....Sammee Tong
Ginger Farrell/Loomis/Mitchell
...................Bernadette Withers
Howard Meechim (1958–1961)
..........................Jimmy Boyd
Elaine Meechim (1959) ....Joan Vohs
Cal Mitchell (1960–1962) ....Del Moore
Adelaide Mitchell (1960–1962)
..........................Evelyn Scott

Cousin Charlie Fong (1961–1962)
........................Victor Sen Yung
Warren Dawson (1962) ......Aron Kincaid
Vickie (1957–1958) ....Alice Backus
Kitty Deveraux (1958–1959)
........................Shirley Mitchell
Kitty Marsh (1959–1961)
......................Sue Ane Langdon
Suzanne Collins (1961) ....Jeanne Bal
Connie (1961–1962) ....Sally Mansfield

Bentley Gregg was a wealthy, successful Hollywood attorney, whose clients included many glamorous and available women. He lived with his niece Kelly, his houseboy Peter, and a large shaggy dog named Jasper in posh Beverly Hills. Uncle Bentley had become Kelly's legal guardian after her parents had been killed in an automobile accident when she was 13 years old. Between his large and active law practice, his social life with beautiful women, and the responsibilities of raising a teenage girl, Bentley's time was more than adequately filled. Peter, the helpful but often inscrutable Oriental houseboy, was a jack-of-all-trades who ran the Gregg home and was indispensible to his boss.

Kelly was a typical teenager—exuberant and enthusiastic—who at times tried to find a wife for her uncle. During her high school years she had a regular boyfriend, lanky Howard Meechim. Her best friend was Ginger, whose parents and last name were changed twice during the five-year run of the show; only the last set of parents, Cal and Adelaide Mitchell, appeared often enough to be listed as regulars. At the end of the 1960–1961 season, in the last episode aired on NBC, Kelly graduated from high school. Two weeks later, when new episodes began on ABC, she had started college. The following spring brought her true love, in the person of Warren Dawson, a young lawyer who became Bentley's junior partner and Kelly's fiancé. *Bachelor Father* concluded its network run at the end of that season, however, so that Kelly and Warren never did get married.

As for Bentley, he may have been an irresistible ladies' man, but he certainly had trouble holding on to a secretary. Five different actresses filled that role in succession: Alice Backus, Shirley Mitchell, Sue Ane Langdon, Jeanne Bal, and Sally Mansfield.

BACK THAT FACT

Audience Participation

FIRST TELECAST: *October 22, 1953*
LAST TELECAST: *November 26, 1953*
BROADCAST HISTORY:
Oct 1953–Nov 1953, ABC Thu 9:00–9:30
EMCEE:
Joey Adams

As host of this short-lived audience-participation show, Joey Adams interviewed members of the studio audience about such matters as their backgrounds, hobbies, and accomplishments. From time to time an offstage voice would challenge a statement they made, calling on them to "back that fact." If they could (in the estimation of a panel chosen from the audience), they won a prize. The program was presented live from New York.

BACKGROUND

News/Documentary

FIRST TELECAST: *August 16, 1954*
LAST TELECAST: *September 6, 1954*
BROADCAST HISTORY:
Aug 1954–Sep 1954, NBC Mon 8:30–9:00
COMMENTATOR:
Joseph C. Harsch

On this program, Joseph C. Harsch each week presented an analysis of a different issue of current world importance. Special film reports produced by NBC News were used; the thrust of the program was to take the audience beyond the headlines to the people who were actually living the news. After a brief run in prime time the series moved to Sunday afternoons, where it continued until June 1955.

BACKSTAGE WITH BARRY WOOD

Variety

FIRST TELECAST: *March 1, 1949*
LAST TELECAST: *May 24, 1949*
BROADCAST HISTORY:
Mar 1949–May 1949, CBS Tue 10:00–10:15
HOST:
Barry Wood

Singer Barry Wood was the producer and host of this series, which gave young entertainers an opportunity to perform on live television before a full network audience. The slogan of the show was that it featured "tomorrow's stars today."

BADGE 714

syndicated title for *Dragnet* (before 1967)

BAILEYS OF BALBOA, THE

Situation Comedy

FIRST TELECAST: *September 24, 1964*
LAST TELECAST: *April 1, 1965*
BROADCAST HISTORY:
Sep 1964–Apr 1965, CBS Thu 9:30–10:00
CAST:
Sam Bailey ....Paul Ford
Buck Singleton ....Sterling Holloway
Jim Bailey ....Les Brown, Jr.
Stanley ....Clint Howard
Commodore Cecil Wyntoon ...John Dehner
Barbara Wyntoon ....Judy Carne

Paul Ford portrayed crusty old Sam Bailey, a widower who ran a small charter fishing boat called *The Island Princess*. The boat was based on a little island Sam owned in the middle of Balboa, an exclusive yachting community. Sam's unpretentious nature and dislike for fancy society trappings antagonized the surrounding community, particularly the aristocratic Commodore Wyntoon. Sam's son Jim was infatuated with the commodore's daughter Barbara, however, and their romance forced a degree of civility on the two fathers. Buck was the forgetful first mate and entire crew of *The Island Princess*, and Stanley was an obnoxious little boy who was one of Sam's neighbors.

BALANCE YOUR BUDGET

Quiz/Audience Participation

FIRST TELECAST: *October 18, 1952*
LAST TELECAST: *May 2, 1953*
BROADCAST HISTORY:
Oct 1952–May 1953, CBS Sat 10:00–10:30
EMCEE:
Bert Parks

Contestants on *Balance Your Budget* were asked to describe what had caused their personal or family budgets to slip "into the red"; they were then given an opportunity to win some money by answering a series of questions asked by emcee Bert Parks. Winners were also given the opportunity to pick from among a large number of keys, one of which would open the show's "Treasure Chest," containing an additional jackpot of $1,500 or more. Because the contestants had the chance to explain why they needed the money, CBS billed this as a "human interest" quiz show.

BALL FOUR

Situation Comedy

FIRST TELECAST: *September 22, 1976*
LAST TELECAST: *October 27, 1976*
BROADCAST HISTORY:
Sep 1976–Oct 1976, CBS Wed 8:30–9:00
CAST:
Jim Barton ....Jim Bouton
"Cap" Capogrosso ....Jack Somack
Bill Westlake ....David-James Carroll
"Rhino" Rhinelander ....Ben Davidson
Coach Pinky Pinkney ....Bill McCutcheon
Lenny "Birdman" Siegel ....Lenny Schultz
Rayford Plunkett ....Marco St. John
Orlando Lopez ....Jaime Tirelli
C. B. Travis ....Sam Wright

Ball Four was truly "locker-room" comedy, since most of its action took place in the locker room of a major league baseball team, the Washington Americans. In the first episode pitcher Jim Barton informed his teammates and coaches that he was going to write a series of articles on baseball life "off the field." Manager Capogrosso and most of the others were not very keen on the idea, and neither was the viewing audience. The show folded after less than two months on the air. *Ball Four* was based on a book of the same title by former major league pitcher Jim Bouton. Not only did he star in a semi-autobiographical role in the series, he was also one of the writers.

BANACEK

Detective Drama

FIRST TELECAST: *September 13, 1972*
LAST TELECAST: *September 3, 1974*
BROADCAST HISTORY:
Sep 1972–Dec 1973, NBC Wed 8:30–10:00
Jan 1974–Sep 1974, NBC Tue 8:30–10:00
CAST:
Thomas Banacek ....George Peppard
Jay Drury ....Ralph Manza
Felix Mulholland ....Murray Matheson
Carlie Kirkland (1973–1974)
......................Christine Belford

The gimmick in this private-eye series was ethnic: Banacek was a cool, smooth, shrewd Polish-American. His game was collecting rewards from insurance companies by solving crimes involving stolen property, and he was successful enough to live in the exclusive Beacon Hill section of Boston. Banacek's buddies were his chauffeur Jay and his good friend Felix, who ran a bookstore. During the show's second season Carlie, an insurance agent, was added for romantic interest. Polish proverbs were liberally sprinkled throughout the series, and the positive image of its hero made the show very popular with such groups as the Polish-American Congress, which gave the program an award for portraying Polish-Americans in a positive manner. Banacek originally aired as one of the rotating segments of NBC's *Wednesday Mystery Movie*.

BAND OF AMERICA

see *Cities Service*

BAND OF THE WEEK

see *Music at the Meadowbrook*

BANK ON THE STARS

Quiz/Audience Participation

FIRST TELECAST: *June 20, 1953*

LAST TELECAST: *August 21, 1954*

BROADCAST HISTORY:

Jun 1953, CBS Sat 9:00–9:30
Jun 1953–Aug 1953, CBS Sat 9:30–10:00
May 1954–Aug 1954, NBC Sat 8:00–8:30

EMCEE:

Jack Paar (1953)
Bill Cullen (May–Jul 1954)
Jimmy Nelson (Jul–Aug 1954)

Contestants on this game show were drawn from the studio audience and divided into teams. Each two-person team would be shown a film clip from a famous motion picture and asked questions about the scene, for cash prizes. A bonus round involved answering more difficult questions about a different movie scene, which the contestants could only hear and not see. Jack Paar was the emcee during the summer of 1953, when the series was on CBS. It moved to NBC the following summer, with Bill Cullen as emcee until July 10. He was replaced the following week by ventriloquist Jimmy Nelson.

BANYON

Detective Drama

FIRST TELECAST: *September 15, 1972*

LAST TELECAST: *January 12, 1973*

BROADCAST HISTORY:

Sep 1972–Jan 1973, NBC Fri 10:00–11:00

CAST:

Miles C. Banyon .... Robert Forster
Peggy Revere .... Joan Blondell
Lt. Pete McNeil .... Richard Jaeckel
Abby Graham .... Julie Gregg

This period private-eye series was set in Los Angeles during the late 1930s. Banyon, a tough but honest detective, would take on any case, from murder to missing persons, for $20 a day. Peggy Revere, whose secretarial school was located in the same building as Banyon's office, provided him each week with a new free secretary, ranging from sexpot to country farm girl. But Banyon's eyes were fixed on his girl friend Abby Graham, a nightclub singer—though he successfully evaded her constant efforts to get him to marry and settle down.

BARBARA STANWYCK SHOW, THE

Dramatic Anthology

FIRST TELECAST: *September 19, 1960*

LAST TELECAST: *September 11, 1961*

BROADCAST HISTORY:

Sep 1960–Sep 1961, NBC Mon 10:00–10:30

HOSTESS/STAR:

Barbara Stanwyck

Hollywood leading lady Barbara Stanwyck hosted this anthology of original 30-minute filmed teleplays and starred in all but four of them. The four were pilots for possible series and starred Lloyd Nolan ("The Seventh Miracle"), Milton Berle ("Dear Charlie"), Peggy Cass ("Call Me Annie"), and Andy Devine ("Big Jake"). None of them made it on to the next fall's schedule.

The dramas in which Miss Stanwyck appeared tended to be on the serious side. Three of them were pilots for a proposed new series of her own, in which she was to star as an American adventuress running an import-export business in exotic Hong Kong. The original pilot was aired on November 14, 1960, as "The Miraculous Journey of 'Tadpole Chan' " and established the character of Josephine Little. Viewers were requested to write to the network if they liked the idea, and the response was strong enough to result in two other episodes, in January and March. However, the Josephine Little series never went into full production.

BARBARY COAST, THE

Western

FIRST TELECAST: *September 8, 1975*
LAST TELECAST: *January 9, 1976*
BROADCAST HISTORY:
Sep 1975–Oct 1975, ABC Mon 8:00–9:00
Oct 1975–Jan 1976, ABC Fri 8:00–9:00
CAST:
Cash Conover .... Doug McClure
Jeff Cable .... William Shatner
Moose Moran .... Richard Kiel
Thumbs, the piano player .... Dave Turner

This Western was set in the 1870s in a square-mile section of San Francisco called the Barbary Coast, a wide-open, rip-roaring district whose inhabitants ranged from flashy ladies to sourdoughs. Cable was a special agent working for the Governor of California, gathering information on criminals in the district. He traveled incognito and was a master of disguise. Conover was the flamboyant owner of the Golden Gate Casino (which he had won in a poker game) and was Cable's unlikely ally.

BAREFOOT IN THE PARK

Situation Comedy

FIRST TELECAST: *September 24, 1970*
LAST TELECAST: *January 14, 1971*
BROADCAST HISTORY:
Sep 1970–Jan 1971, ABC Thu 9:00–9:30
CAST:
Paul Bratter .... Scoey Mitchlll
Corie Bratter .... Tracy Reed
Mabel Bates .... Thelma Carpenter
Honey Robinson .... Nipsey Russell
Mr. Kendricks .... Harry Holcombe
Mr. Velasquez .... Vito Scotti

This all-black version of Neil Simon's hit play and movie concerned two young newlyweds trying to establish their life on a shoestring budget in New York. Their home was a one room walk-up apartment on the top floor of an old brownstone . At least they had each other—plus Corie's busybody mother Mabel, Mabel's persistent suitor Honey, Paul's boss Mr. Kendricks, and the bumbling building superintendent Mr. Velasquez.

BARETTA

Police Drama

FIRST TELECAST: *January 17, 1975*
LAST TELECAST: *June 1, 1978*
BROADCAST HISTORY:
Jan 1975–Mar 1975, ABC Fri 10:00–11:00
Apr 1975–Jul 1975, ABC Wed 10:00–11:00
Sep 1975–Aug 1977, ABC Wed 9:00–10:00
Aug 1977–Jan 1978, ABC Wed 10:00–11:00
Feb 1978–Jun 1978, ABC Thu 10:00–11:00
CAST:
Det. Tony Baretta .... Robert Blake
Inspector Shiller (1975) .... Dana Elcar
Lt. Hal Brubaker .... Edward Grover
Billy Truman .... Tom Ewell
Rooster .... Michael D. Roberts
THEME:
"Keep Your Eye on the Sparrow," sung by Sammy Davis, Jr.

Baretta was half-a-spinoff from another detective show. Robert Blake had originally been scheduled to take over the lead role in *Toma* after Tony Musante left that series. But *Toma* had not been a big hit, and rather than risk being tied to an unsuccessful series the title was changed and alterations were made in the locale and other details. In essence, *Toma* became *Baretta*, moved to California.

Tony Baretta was, like Toma, an unconventional cop. He was streetwise, single, with a decidedly funky life-style: he holed up in a run-down old hotel when he wasn't on the job, which was seldom. He was usually seen in T-shirt and jeans, with his trademark cap pulled down over his forehead. The orphaned son of poor Italian immigrants, Tony knew the city inside out. He was a master of disguise, and because of his rough appearance was able to infiltrate such groups as motorcycle gangs and even "the Mob." Needless to say, he refused to have a partner and always worked alone. Inspector Shiller was his original boss, later succeeded by Lt. Brubaker. Billy Truman was a retired cop who was a combination manager and house detective at the hotel where Baretta lived.

There was plenty of hard action in this series, despite Blake's public protestations that he opposed wanton violence on TV. The show had a "with-it" light sense of humor; comic relief was provided by Tony's fancy-dude informant-friend Rooster and by Fred, Tony's pet cockatoo. Blake's real-life wife Sondra Blake was an occasional guest star.

BARNABY JONES

Detective Drama

FIRST TELECAST: *January 28, 1973*
LAST TELECAST:
BROADCAST HISTORY:

Jan 1973–Jun 1974, CBS Sun 9:30–10:30
Jul 1974–Sep 1974, CBS Sat 10:00–11:00
Sep 1974–Aug 1975, CBS Tue 10:00–11:00
Sep 1975–Nov 1975, CBS Fri 10:00–11:00
Dec 1975– , CBS Thu 10:00–11:00

CAST:

Barnaby Jones ....Buddy Ebsen
Betty Jones ....Lee Meriwether
Jedediah Romano (J.R.) Jones (1976–) ....Mark Shera
Lt. Biddle (1974–) ....John Carter

EXECUTIVE PRODUCER:

Quinn Martin

After a long and successful career as a private investigator, Barnaby Jones had retired, leaving the business to his son Hal. When Hal was murdered while on a case, Barnaby came out of retirement to help track down his son's killer. Hal's widow, Betty, worked with her father-in-law to solve the case and remained with him, as his assistant, when he decided to keep his Los Angeles-based firm in operation. His keen analytic skills were often masked by a homespun exterior, drawing guilty parties into a false sense of security that led to their downfall. Until *Cannon*—another Los Angeles detective series—went off the air in the fall of 1975, there was occasional interplay between it and *Barnaby Jones*.

In the fall of 1976 Barnaby's young cousin J.R. joined the firm, initially to track down the murderer of *his* father, but eventually as a permanent partner. One of the things that most fascinated him was Barnaby's home crime laboratory, something rarely seen in other detective series. It was in the lab that various clues were analyzed and possible bits of evidence evaluated. J.R., in addition to his work with Barnaby, was also studying to pass the bar exam and become a lawyer.

BARNEY BLAKE, POLICE REPORTER

Crime Drama

FIRST TELECAST: *April 22, 1948*
LAST TELECAST: *July 8, 1948*
BROADCAST HISTORY:

Apr 1948–Jul 1948, NBC Thu 9:30–10:00

CAST:

Barney Blake ....Gene O'Donnell
Jennifer Allen ....Judy Parrish

Reporter Barney Blake, assisted by his secretary Jennifer, solved assorted homicides in this live series, which NBC claims was television's first regularly scheduled mystery series. It set at least one precedent when it was canceled by the sponsor, American Tobacco Company, after only thirteen weeks.

BARNEY MILLER

Situation Comedy

FIRST TELECAST: *January 23, 1975*
LAST TELECAST:
BROADCAST HISTORY:

Jan 1975–Jan 1976, ABC Thu 8:00–8:30 (OS)
Jan 1976–Dec 1976, ABC Thu 8:30–9:00 (OS)
Dec 1976– , ABC Thu 9:00–9:30

CAST:

Capt. Barney Miller ....Hal Linden
Det. Phil Fish (1975–1977) ....Abe Vigoda
Det. Sgt. Chano Amenguale (1975–1976) ....Gregory Sierra
Det. Wojohowicz ("Wojo") ...Maxwell Gail
Det. Nick Yemana ....Jack Soo
Det. Ron Harris ....Ron Glass
Elizabeth Miller (1975–1976; portrayed in pilot by Abby Dalton) ....Barbara Barrie
Rachael Miller (1975) .....Anne Wyndham
David Miller (1975) ....Michael Tessier
Bernice Fish (1975–1977) .... Florence Stanley
Det. Janice Wentworth (1975–1976) ....Linda Lavin
Inspector Luger ....James Gregory
Officer Carl Levitt (1976–) .... Ron Carey
Det. Baptista (1976–1977) ......June Gable
Det. Arthur Dietrich (1976–) .... Steve Landesberg

Barney Miller grew out of a rejected comedy pilot called "The Life and Times of Captain Barney Miller," which aired as part of an ABC summer anthology called *Just for Laughs* in 1974. In that pilot the action revolved equally around Barney's problems at the police precinct house and his home life, with his wife Elizabeth and kids prominently featured. But when *Barney Miller* made it to the regular ABC schedule the following January, the family played a much smaller role (eventually they were written out) and the locale became the Greenwich Village station house where Barney and his motley crew spent their day.

Three actors besides Hal Linden came over from the pilot to the series: Barney's two kids, David and Rachael, who soon disappeared, and a broken-down old cop named Fish. Fish was the hit of the show. Not only did he look incredible, he sounded and acted like every breath might be his last. Fish was always on the verge of retirement, and his worst day was when the station house toilet broke down. He was constantly complaining about everything, especially his seldom-seen wife Bernice.

There were ironies in Abe Vigoda's portrayal of Fish. Vigoda, 54, was in real life an active athlete (he jogs and plays handball), and the role for which he was previously best known was quite different indeed—that of the ruthless Mafia leader Tessio, in *The Godfather*. Vigoda became so popular that he eventually got his own series, *Fish*, though he also continued on *Barney Miller* for a time. He left the series ("retiring" from the police force) in September 1977.

Others around the 12th Precinct station house were Det. Amenguale, the Puerto Rican; Wojo, the naive, trusting one; Yemana, the philosophical one who made coffee for them all; and Harris, the wisecracking, ambitious black. Seen occasionally were Inspector Luger, the hard nosed superior; Levitt, the 5′3″ uniformed officer who wanted to be a detective, but was "too short"; and female officers Wentworth and Baptista. A continuous parade of crazies, crooks, conmen, hookers, juvenile muggers, and other street denizens passed through.

BARON, THE

Spy Drama

FIRST TELECAST: *January 20, 1966*
LAST TELECAST: *July 14, 1966*
BROADCAST HISTORY:

Jan 1966–Jul 1966, ABC Thu 10:00–11:00

CAST:

John Mannering, "The Baron" .... Steve Forrest
Cordelia Winfield .... Sue Lloyd
John Alexander Templeton-Green .... Colin Gordon
David Marlowe .... Paul Ferris

John Mannering, otherwise known as The Baron, was the handsome, cultured, American-born owner of fine antiques shops in London, Paris, and Washington, D.C. When not appraising expensive *objets d'art* for his exclusive clientele, he was pursuing dangerous missions around the world on behalf of British Intelligence. He was called in whenever priceless art objects were involved, as often seemed to happen in cases of espionage, blackmail, and murder. His contact at British Intelligence was John Templeton-Green, to whom the beautiful secret agent Cordelia Winfield also reported. David Marlowe served occasionally as Mannering's assistant. The name "The Baron" derived from the Mannering family's sprawling ranch in Texas, where John grew up.

The series was filmed in England and was based on the novels of John Creasy.

BASEBALL

Sports

FIRST TELECAST: *May 26, 1951*
LAST TELECAST:
BROADCAST HISTORY:

May 1951–Sep 1951, ABC Sat 9:00–11:00
May 1952–Jun 1952, ABC Sat 8:30–10:30
Jun 1972–Sep 1975, NBC Mon 8:15–Conclusion (summers only)
Apr 1976– , ABC Mon 8:30–Conclusion (summers only)

SPORTSCASTERS:

Pat Flanagan (1951)
Don Dunphy (1952)
Bob Finnegan (1952)
Curt Gowdy (1972–1975)
Tony Kubek (1972–1975)
Jim Simpson (1972–1975)
Sandy Koufax (1972)
Maury Wills (1973–1975)
Joe Garagiola (1975)
Bob Prince (1976)
Warner Wolf (1976–1977)
Bob Uecker (1976–)
Al Michaels (1976–)
Norm Cash (1976)
Bob Gibson (1976–1977)
Bill White (1977–)
Howard Cosell (1977–)
Keith Jackson (1978–)
Don Drysdale (1978–)
Jim Lampley (1978–)

Baseball has always had a home on television, at both the local and the network level. The first baseball game ever telecast was a college, rather than a professional, game. On May 17, 1939, NBC telecast a game between Princeton and Columbia to the few sets in operation in the New York City area. In 1947 the World Series had its first network telecast, over a four-city network; it has been a popular fall attraction ever since. Although locally originated baseball networks were set up in the late 1940s and early 1950s, they were primarily weekend afternoon games and were beamed to the limited area in which the originating team had most of its fans. Later, on both local stations and networks, Saturday and Sunday afternoons were reserved for "the national pastime."

The first nighttime network baseball series, aired on ABC in 1951 and 1952, featured women rather than men. There was a women's professional league at that time, and the ABC series, known popularly as *Girls' Baseball*, was officially titled *National Women's Professional Baseball League Games*. In 1951 it was telecast from Chicago and followed the home games of the Queens of America. The following year it originated from New York, with Don Dunphy doing the play-by-play and Bob Finnegan providing color commentary on home games of the Arthur Murray Girls.

It was not until two decades later that NBC decided to bring men's major league baseball to prime-time television as the regular summer replacement for *NBC Monday Night at the Movies*. Curt Gowdy and Tony Kubek provided coverage of the major game telecast each week, with other sportscasters covering secondary games. After four years on NBC, *Monday Night Baseball* moved to ABC in the spring of 1976. ABC expanded the number of people in the broadcast booth from two to three, as they had done with *Monday Night Football*, and during the summer of 1976 the primary game team was composed of Bob Prince, Warner Wolf, and Bob Uecker. By 1977 Uecker was the only surviving member of the ABC "first team"; Al Michaels was moved up, Warner Wolf demoted, and Howard Cosell added to the group. Cosell was the only returning member of the primary game team in 1978, with Keith Jackson and Don Drysdale joining him.

BASEBALL CORNER

Sports Discussion

FIRST TELECAST: *June 1, 1958*
LAST TELECAST: *August 27, 1958*
BROADCAST HISTORY:
Jun 1958–Jul 1958, ABC Sun 9:00–9:30
Jul 1958–Aug 1958, ABC Wed 9:30–10:00
HOST:
Buddy Blattner

Buddy Blattner broadcast sports news, narrated films, and conducted interviews with a panel of four guests. The program emanated from Chicago.

BASEBALL WORLD OF JOE GARAGIOLA, THE

Sports Commentary

FIRST TELECAST: *June 12, 1972*
LAST TELECAST: *September 1, 1975*
BROADCAST HISTORY:
Jun 1972–Sep 1972, NBC Mon 8:00–8:15
May 1973–Sep 1973, NBC Mon 8:00–8:15
May 1974–Sep 1974, NBC Mon 8:00–8:15
Jun 1975–Sep 1975, NBC Mon 8:00–8:15
HOST:
Joe Garagiola

Former major-league baseball player Joe Garagiola was the host of this show that preceded the Monday night *NBC Major League Baseball* game. The show featured interviews with players and the humorous anecdotes and observations of Mr. Garagiola.

BASKETBALL

Sports

FIRST TELECAST: *November 13, 1948*
LAST TELECAST: *March 15, 1952*
BROADCAST HISTORY:
Nov 1948–Mar 1949, NBC Sat 9:00–Conclusion
Feb 1949–Mar 1949, CBS Thu 9:00–Conclusion
Dec 1951–Mar 1952, ABC Sat 9:00–Conclusion

Basketball has rarely been seen on a regular basis on nighttime network television, and not at all in the last 25 years. Back in the early days of network television it was tried by three different networks, all four networks if its frequent appearance on DuMont's *Saturday Night at the Garden* is considered.

The earliest appearance of network basketball was on NBC during the 1948–1949 season, with Bob Stanton announcing the games of the semipro New York Gothams. That same spring CBS gave Mel Allen the mike to cover various college games during the college tournament season. College games did somewhat better than the semipros in terms of audience appeal, and ABC gave them another try during the 1951–1952 college season, with Curt Gowdy and Vince Garrity doing the play-by-play.

BAT MASTERSON

Western

FIRST TELECAST: *October 8, 1959*
LAST TELECAST: *September 21, 1961*
BROADCAST HISTORY:

Oct 1958–Sep 1959, NBC Wed 9:30–10:00
Oct 1959–Sep 1960, NBC Thu 8:00–8:30
Sep 1960–Sep 1961, NBC Thu 8:30–9:00

CAST:

Bat Masterson .... Gene Barry

Bat Masterson was a lawman, Indian fighter, scout, and professional gambler. He was also, by Western standards, quite a dandy. With a derby hat, a gold-topped cane, and clothes that were more at home in New York than in Tombstone, Arizona, he did not look like he belonged in the Old West. Preferring to disarm opponents with his wits and his cane rather than his gun, Masterson provided quite a contrast to the general run of violent Western heroes. He was a debonair charmer of women and roamed the Southwest romancing the ladies and helping to protect the innocent, especially in situations where they had been wrongly accused of crimes. The real William Bartley "Bat" Masterson may not have been quite as glamorous a personality as Gene Barry's portrayal indicated, but he was quite a character in his own right. The derby, cane, and a specially designed gun were presented to him by the grateful citizens of Dodge City during his tenure as sheriff; he was a close friend of Wyatt Earp, another legendary Western hero; and his own exploits created the legend upon which this series was based.

BATMAN

Fantasy Adventure

FIRST TELECAST: *January 12, 1966*
LAST TELECAST: *March 14, 1968*
BROADCAST HISTORY:

Jan 1966–Aug 1967, ABC Wed/Thu 7:30–8:00
Sep 1967–Mar 1968, ABC Thu 7:30–8:00

CAST:

Bruce Wayne (Batman) .... Adam West
Dick Grayson (Robin) .... Burt Ward
Alfred .... Alan Napier
Aunt Harriet Cooper .... Madge Blake
Police Commissioner Gordon .... Neil Hamilton
Chief O'Hara .... Stafford Repp
Barbara Gordon (Batgirl) (1967–1968) .... Yvonne Craig

MUSICAL THEME:

"Batman," by Neal Hefti

Cartoonist Bob Kane's *Batman* first appeared in comic-book form in *Detective Comics* in 1939 and was featured on radio's *Superman* series and in two movie serials in the 1940s. In January of 1966 it took television by storm. But in slightly over two years it blew itself out. *Batman* was the ultimate "camp" show of the 1960s and was definitely not to be taken seriously, even by those who acted in it. The fight scenes were punctuated by animated "Pows," "Bops," "Bangs," and "Thuds" that flashed on the screen when a blow was struck, obliterating the actors. The situations were incredibly contrived and the acting was intentionally overdone by everyone except Adam West, who was so wooden that he was hilarious.

The general structure of the series was true to Bob Kane's original comics. Bruce Wayne had been orphaned in his teens when his parents were killed by a criminal. Inheriting their fortune, Bruce built a complex crime lab under the Wayne mansion and, as the mysterious Batman, waged war on the evil-doers who plagued Gotham City. His young ward, the orphaned Dick Grayson, joined him; they were known individually as the Caped Crusader and The Boy Wonder, and together as The Dynamic Duo. The only person who knew their real identity was the Wayne family butler, Alfred, who had raised Bruce after his parents' murder. In addition to the underground Batlab (where every device was carefully labeled with its function), they used a marvelously equipped car, the Batmobile, to chase and apprehend criminals. Whenever their services were needed, Police Commissioner Gordon could summon them with the searchlight-like Batsignal or call them on the special Batphone.

Batman was an overnight sensation when it premiered in 1966, airing two-part stories that ran on Wednesday and Thursday. The climax of the first part always left the pair in a dire predicament from which they managed to extricate themselves on the following night. The public's fancy was caught by the silliness, the absurdity, and Robin's horrible puns (attempting to scale a building with Batman in the first episode, he was heard to say "Holy fire escape, Batman!"). Both the Wednesday and Thursday episodes ranked among the ten most popular programs of the 1965–1966 season. Appearing as a guest villain on the show became something of a status symbol. Among the more celebrated foes were The Penguin (Burgess Meredith), The Joker (Cesar Romero), The Riddler (Frank Gorshin and, later, John Astin), Egghead (Vincent Price), King Tut (Victor Buono), and the Catwoman (played variously by Julie Newmar, Lee Ann Meriwether, and Eartha Kitt).

By the fall of 1967, however, the novelty had passed and the ratings began to fall. A new role was added, the part of Commissioner Gordon's daughter Barbara, a young librarian who fought crime on her own as Batgirl and who regularly teamed up with Batman and Robin (she had also been in Kane's comics). But it didn't help. Cut back to once a week in the fall of 1967, the surprise hit of 1966 was gone by the following spring.

BATTLE OF THE AGES

Talent

FIRST TELECAST: *January 1, 1952*

LAST TELECAST: *November 29, 1952*

BROADCAST HISTORY:

Jan 1952–Jun 1952, DUM Tue 9:00–9:30

Sep 1952–Nov 1952, CBS Sat 10:30–11:00

EMCEE:

John Reed King (Jan–Jun)

Morey Amsterdam (Sep–Nov)

Each week *Battle of the Ages* presented two teams of professional performers competing for audience applause. The teams' distinguishing characteristic was the age of the participants. All members of one team had to be over 35 (veterans), and all members of the other team under 35 (youngsters). When the older team won the sponsor made a donation to the Actors Fund of America, and when the younger team won a similar donation was made to the Scholarship Fund of the Professional Children's School.

BATTLE REPORT

Documentary/Public Affairs

FIRST TELECAST: *August 13, 1950*

LAST TELECAST: *August 31, 1951*

BROADCAST HISTORY:

Aug 1950–Sep 1950, NBC Sun 8:00–8:30

Jun 1951–Aug 1951, NBC Fri 9:30–10:00

HOST:

Robert McCormick

This weekly documentary program on the United States' involvement in the Korean War used filmed interviews and reports from both the home front and battle front. Although produced by NBC News, it was virtually an official government presentation, with regular weekly commentary by Dr. John Steelman, assistant to President Truman, and reports from many high-ranking officials. The series was telecast on Sunday afternoon during most of its 1950–1952 run, but moved to prime time during the periods shown above.

BATTLESTAR GALACTICA

Science Fiction

FIRST TELECAST: *September 17, 1978*

LAST TELECAST:

BROADCAST HISTORY:

Sep 1978– , ABC Sun 8:00–9:00

CAST:

Commander Adama ....Lorne Greene
Capt. Apollo ....Richard Hatch
Lt. Starbuck ....Dirk Benedict
Lt. Boomer ....Herb Jefferson, Jr.
Athena ....Maren Jensen
Flight Sgt. Jolly ....Tony Swartz
Boxey ....Noah Hathaway
Col. Tigh ....Terry Carter
Cassiopea ....Laurette Spang
Count Baltar ....John Colicos

SPECIAL EFFECTS:

John Dykstra

MUSIC:

The Los Angeles Philharmonic Orchestra

Battlestar Galactica was the most highly publicized new series of the fall 1978 schedule. Reported to have cost one million dollars per hour to produce—the highest budget ever for a regular series—it used spectacular special effects to depict a mighty life and death struggle between the forces of good and evil in outer space, thousands of years in the future. Lasers flashed, majestic space ships lumbered through deep space, and dashing, caped heroes fought half-human, half-robot villains for no less than the survival of mankind.

If this sounds like a copy of the movie *Star Wars*, it was. *Battlestar Galactica* was such a literal imitation of *Star Wars* that the producers of the movie sued ABC for "stealing" their film. Part of the similarity lay in the special effects, such as laser battles and closeups of the spacecraft, which were created by John Dykstra, the same man who worked on *Star Wars*.

The setting was the seventh millennium, A.D. Galactica was the only surviving battlestar after a surprise attack by the evil Cylons, aided by the treacherous Count Baltar, had shattered the interplanetary peace and wiped out most of humankind. Now the Cylons were pursuing Galactica and her attendant fleet of 220 smaller spacecraft as they sped through space toward a last refuge, a distant, unknown planet called Earth.

Commanding the mile-wide Galactica was the stoic, silver haired Adama. His son Apollo led Galactica's fighter squadron (another son was killed off by the Cylons in the premiere). Starbuck was his ace pilot, as well as a smooth talking con artist and ladies' man. Many other characters came and went from the large cast, including the singing Anroid Sisters, who entertained with two sets of mouths apiece, in a surrealistic outer space bar peopled by oddly shaped creatures from other civilizations (Remember *that* scene in *Star Wars*?).

BE OUR GUEST

Musical Variety

FIRST TELECAST: *January 27, 1960*
LAST TELECAST: *June 1, 1960*
BROADCAST HISTORY:
Jan 1960–Jun 1960, CBS Wed 7:30–8:30
HOST:
George de Witt (Jan–Mar)
Keefe Brasselle (Mar–Jun)
REGULARS:
Mary Ann Mobley
Ray McKinley and the Glenn Miller Orchestra

A number of performers, some well known and some not, some professional and some amateur, some very young and others very old, were invited each week to *Be Our Guest* and participate in this informal musical variety program. George de Witt was the original host, replaced by Keefe Brasselle on March 16; Mary Ann Mobley (a former Miss America) was the featured singer.

BEACON HILL

General Drama

FIRST TELECAST: *August 2, 1975*
LAST TELECAST: *November 4, 1975*
BROADCAST HISTORY:
Aug 1975, CBS Mon 9:00–11:00
Sep 1975–Nov 1975, CBS Tue 10:00–11:00
CAST:
Trevor Bullock .... Roy Cooper
Robert Lassiter .... David Dukes
Benjamin Lassiter .... Stephen Elliott
Richard Palmer .... Edward Herrmann
Mary Lassiter .... Nancy Marchand
Maude Palmer .... Maeve McGuire
Emily Bullock .... Deann Mears
Giorgio Bellonci .... Michael Nouri
Betsy Bullock .... Linda Purl
Mr. Hacker .... George Rose
Terence O'Hara .... David Rounds
Brian Mallory .... Paul Rudd
Harry Emmet .... Barry Snider
Mrs. Hacker .... Beatrice Straight
Eleanor .... Sydney Swire
Marilyn Gardiner .... Holland Taylor
Fawn Lassiter .... Kathryn Walker
William Piper .... Richard Ward
Rosamond Lassiter .... Kitty Winn

Hoping to capitalize on the success that public television had had with the British import *Upstairs, Downstairs*, CBS launched this lavish, period soap opera in prime time in the fall of 1975. *Beacon Hill* was set in Boston in the early 1920s. The various continuing storylines revolved around the lives of the wealthy Lassiter family and the members of their household staff, led by Mr. Hacker, the Lassiters' head butler. The cast was huge, the sets and production values the best, and a special two-hour advance premiere on August 2 received top ratings. But after that the audience shrank steadily with each succeeding episode. CBS, which had hoped to parlay a successful British program into a new trend in American television (as it had done with *All in the Family*), was forced to cancel the program after only 13 episodes.

BEANY & CECIL

see *Matty's Funday Funnies*

BEARCATS

Adventure

FIRST TELECAST: *September 16, 1971*

LAST TELECAST: *December 30, 1971*

BROADCAST HISTORY:

Sep 1971–Dec 1971, CBS Thu 8:00–9:00

CAST:

Hank Brackett ....Rod Taylor

Johnny Reach ....Dennis Cole

Set in the American Southwest around 1914, *Bearcats* was the story of two adventurers who traveled around looking for lucrative, difficult, and dangerous assignments. Their mode of transportation was a fancy Stutz Bearcat. Rather than charge a fee for taking on an assignment, they requested a blank check from each of their clients. After completing the job they filled in the amount according to what they felt their services were worth. In one episode they were hired to find out who was setting fire to oil wells in a small border town; in another, their task was to stop mercenaries from sabotaging medical supplies that were being shipped overseas to the Allies during World War I.

BEAT THE CLOCK

Quiz/Audience Participation

FIRST TELECAST: *March 23, 1950*

LAST TELECAST: *February 16, 1958*

BROADCAST HISTORY:

Mar 1950, CBS Thu 9:45–10:30

Apr 1950–Sep 1950, CBS Sat 8:00–9:00

Sep 1950–Mar 1951, CBS Fri 10:30–11:00

Mar 1951–Sep 1956, CBS Sat 7:30–8:00

Sep 1956–Feb 1957, CBS Sat 7:00–7:30

Feb 1957–Sep 1957, CBS Fri 7:30–8:00

Oct 1957–Feb 1958, CBS Sun 6:00–6:30

EMCEE:

Bud Collyer

ASSISTANT:

Roxanne Arlen (1950–1955)

Beverly Bentley (1956–1958)

PRODUCERS:

Mark Goodson and Bill Todman

This durable game show started on CBS radio in 1949 with Bud Collyer as emcee and moved to television in March 1950. The format was certainly simple. Contestants were chosen from the studio audience and attempted to perform various stunts within a given time limit (in most cases 60 seconds or less), which depended on the difficulty of the stunt. Prizes were awarded for succeeding within the time limit, and occasionally there was a bonus if the contestant completed it faster than that. A large clock ticked off the seconds so that the audience and contestants could see how much time was left.

What made *Beat the Clock* a hit were the stunts themselves, which were full of whipped cream, custard pies, and exploding balloons, always frantic yet always ingenious. Most of them were dreamed up by production staffers Frank Wayne and Bob Howard, who maintained a "stunt factory" where each feat was tried out before the show to make sure that it wasn't either too hard or too easy. Unemployed actors were used for the testing (including a young unknown named James Dean, who was described as so well-coordinated he could do *anything* the producers dreamed up). The stunts were so popular that the sponsor even issued a book of them.

A typical stunt had a contestant put on an oversize set of long underwear, then try to stuff 12 inflated balloons into it without breaking any, all in 45 seconds. Another presented the contestant with a fishing pole and line, with a frankfurter tied at the end. He would then have to lower the frankfurter onto a series of mousetraps and try to spring a total of six of them in 40 seconds. His teammate would release the frankfurter from each trap after it sprang. Yet a third stunt, one that was pretty messy, involved three marshmallows and a bowl of Jell-O. The marshmallows were buried deep in the bowl and the contestant had to dig out two of them with a spoon held in his mouth, and deposit them carefully on the table next to the bowl. If a marshmallow fell off the spoon it was reburied in the gelatin (time limit: 35 seconds). Some stunts were even messier. One interesting statistic quoted in 1955 was that, up to that time, approximately 1,100 gallons of whipped cream had been squirted into the faces of hapless contestants on the program, an average of three and a half gallons per week.

Before the advent of the big-money quiz shows in 1955, the prizes on *Beat the Clock* had always been secondary to the game. Even the "bonus stunt," which was harder than most, had rarely been worth more than $100. By 1956 however, with competition from NBC's *The Big Surprise,* the ante for successfully completing the "bonus stunt" had gone up considerably, starting at $5,000 and rising by $1,000 for every attempt until somebody finally managed to complete it successfully. In September 1956 one winning couple took home $64,000, by far the biggest prize ever given on the show.

Bud Collyer's original assistant and the show's official photographer, who snapped photos of contestants amid the debris after their stunts, was a shapely blonde named Roxanne. She became a celebrity in her own right, often appearing in magazine articles about beauty or fashion and making personal appearance tours with her boss. At one time there were rumors that her celebrity status did not endear her to Collyer, who was, after all, supposed to be the star of the show. In August 1955 she left the show on maternity leave and was replaced by Beverly Bentley.

A daytime version of *Beat the Clock* remained on the air until 1961, and the show has been periodically revived in syndicated versions since its departure from network television.

BEAUTIFUL PHYLLIS DILLER SHOW, THE

Comedy Variety

FIRST TELECAST: *September 15, 1968*
LAST TELECAST: *December 22, 1968*
BROADCAST HISTORY:
Sep 1968–Dec 1968, NBC Sun 10:00–11:00
REGULARS:
Phyllis Diller
Norm Crosby
Rip Taylor
The Curtain Calls

This comedy variety hour had as its star the comedienne Phyllis Diller, known for her fright-wig hair and rasping cackle; the supporting performers were comics Norm Crosby and Rip Taylor, guest stars, and the Curtain Calls, a song-and-dance group. Each week's show featured a big production-number "salute" to a famous person, ranging from Ponce de León to Luther Burbank to P. T. Barnum—all classified, at least as far as Phyllis was concerned, as forgotten Americans.

BEHIND CLOSED DOORS

Spy Drama

FIRST TELECAST: *October 2, 1958*
LAST TELECAST: *April 9, 1959*
BROADCAST HISTORY:
Oct 1958–Apr 1959, NBC Thu 9:00–9:30
CAST:
Commander Matson ....Bruce Gordon

Incidents of American counterespionage were dramatized in this series based on the files of Rear Admiral Ellis M. Zacharias, USN (Ret.), who had spent 25 years in naval intelligence. The stories were connected with the cold war, which required updating and relocating the real-life incidents supplied by Adm. Zacharias, who served as technical consultant for the series. Commander Matson was the program host and was occasionally featured in the stories themselves.

BEHIND THE NEWS WITH HOWARD K. SMITH

News Analysis

FIRST TELECAST: *April 12, 1959*
LAST TELECAST: *September 20, 1959*
BROADCAST HISTORY:
Apr 1959–Jun 1959, CBS Sun 6:00–6:30
Sep 1959, CBS Sun 6:00–6:30
HOST:
Howard K. Smith

The purpose of this series was to take the most significant news story of the previous week and do an in-depth analysis of its background, significance, and consequences. CBS News Washington correspondent Howard K. Smith served as analyst, host, moderator, or discussion leader, depending on the way in which the story was presented. Film coverage, interviews, and round-table discussions were all used at one time or another. The program was originally seen on Sunday afternoons, beginning in January 1959.

BELIEVE IT OR NOT

Variety/Drama

FIRST TELECAST: *March 1, 1949*
LAST TELECAST: *September 28, 1950*
BROADCAST HISTORY:
Mar 1949–Jun 1949, NBC Tue 9:30–10:00
Jul 1949–Sep 1949, NBC Wed 10:00–10:30
Oct 1949–Nov 1949, NBC various
Jan 1950–May 1950, NBC Wed 8:00–8:30
May 1950–Sep 1950, NBC Thu 8:00–8:30
HOST:
Robert L. Ripley (Mar–May 1949)
Robert St. John (Jul–Nov 1949)

This highly successful radio series moved to television in March 1949. Seen seated in a living room decorated with oriental antiques and mementoes of his worldwide travels, Ripley recounted for viewers a number of strange stories each week, sometimes with the aid of exhibits or dramatizations. At times the program had a freak-show atmosphere. Among the early guests were Kuda Bux, the Indian fakir with "X-ray vision"; a man who could thread a needle with one hand while balancing his body parallel to the floor with the other; and a four-eyed Mongolian. However, there were also stories of ordinary people who had triumphed over great adversity to lead normal, and even exceptional, lives.

On May 27, 1949, less than three months after the series began, Bob Ripley died suddenly. He had already prepared the next week's program and it was presented, along with a tribute to his long career. The series continued, hosted by "guest custodians" of Ripley's sketchbook until Robert St. John became permanent host in July 1949. The program left the air briefly at the end of the year and returned in January 1950 as a dramatic series loosely based on Ripley's stories. Each week a guest cast enacted one of his remarkable true tales, usually one involving murder, romance, or both.

BELL AND HOWELL CLOSEUP

Documentary

FIRST TELECAST: *November 14, 1961*

LAST TELECAST: *June 4, 1963*

BROADCAST HISTORY:

Nov 1961–Dec 1961, ABC Tue 10:30–11:00
Oct 1962–Dec 1962, ABC Tue 10:30–11:00
Apr 1963–Jun 1963, ABC Tue 10:30–11:00

This series of documentaries, produced by ABC News, covered subjects ranging from international politics to a day in the life of a concert pianist. It began on an occasional basis in September 1960 and was seen in sporadic regular runs from 1961–1963.

BELL SUMMER THEATRE

see *Bell Telephone Hour, The*

BELL TELEPHONE HOUR, THE

Music

FIRST TELECAST: *October 9, 1959*

LAST TELECAST: *April 26, 1968*

BROADCAST HISTORY:

Oct 1959–Apr 1960, NBC Fri 8:30–9:30
Sep 1960–Apr 1961, NBC Fri 9:00–10:00
Sep 1961–Apr 1962, NBC Fri 9:30–10:30
Oct 1963–May 1965, NBC Tue 10:00–11:00
Sep 1965–Apr 1967, NBC Sun 6:30–7:30 (OS)
Sep 1967–Apr 1968, NBC Fri 10:00–11:00

FEATURING:

The Bell Telephone Orchestra conducted by Donald Voorhees

EXECUTIVE PRODUCER:

Barry Wood (1959–1967)
Henry Jaffe (1967–1968)

THEME:

"The Bell Waltz," by Donald Voorhees

For nearly a decade *The Bell Telephone Hour* provided a prestigious television showcase for fine music, always presented with elegance and style. The music ranged across the spectrum from popular to jazz to classical, performed by the top names among established Broadway, Hollywood, and recording stars (no rock 'n' roll here). A different host presided over each telecast. The featured performers appearing over the years included Benny Goodman, Mahalia Jackson, Carol Lawrence, Paul Whiteman (conducting "Rhapsody in Blue"), Marge and Gower Champion, the Kingston Trio, Ray Bolger, Richard Tucker, and Bing Crosby.

Among the classical highlights were the American TV debuts of ballet dancer Rudolf Nureyev in January 1961 (he was a last-minute substitute for the injured Erik Bruhn), Joan Sutherland in March 1961, and pianists Albert Casadesus in February 1964 and Clifford Curzon in April 1965.

Just as the performers tended to be standard adult favorites, so did the music. *The Bell Telephone Hour,* though certainly classy, was not overly adventuresome. During the first few seasons, popular and show music predominated, though there was usually a classical spot in each telecast. Programs were built around tributes to popular composers such as Gershwin, Berlin, and Porter, or around holiday themes or topics such as small-town shindigs. In 1966 a new format was introduced—that of filmed musical documentaries, generally of great performers—and the emphasis was shifted to more classical music. Among the subjects were Van Cliburn, Pablo Casals, Zubin Mehta, Arturo Toscanini, Duke Ellington, and even George Plimpton (in his brief career as a percussionist with the New York Symphony Orchestra).

The Bell Telephone Hour had been a radio standby for 19 years when it moved to television in 1959, first as a series of specials in the spring and then as a regular alternate weekly series in the fall. Bell had previously sponsored a series of science specials and for a time these alternated with the music hour. Later, news and other programs ran on the alternate weeks; *Bell* continued as a biweekly or monthly series throughout its television history. During the summer of 1964 the program featured some newer talent and was subtitled *The Bell Summer Theatre*.

Conductor Donald Voorhees, who was associated with the program throughout its radio and TV history, was also composer of its lilting theme, "The Bell Waltz."

BEN CASEY

Medical Drama

FIRST TELECAST: *October 2, 1961*

LAST TELECAST: *March 21, 1966*

BROADCAST HISTORY:

Oct 1961–Sep 1963, ABC Mon 10:00–11:00
Sep 1963–Sep 1964, ABC Wed 9:00–10:00
Sep 1964–Mar 1966, ABC Mon 10:00–11:00

CAST:

Dr. Ben Casey ....Vince Edwards
Dr. David Zorba (1961–1965) ....Sam Jaffe
Dr. Maggie Graham ......Bettye Ackerman
Dr. Ted Hoffman ....Harry Landers
Nick Kanavaras ....Nick Dennis
Nurse Wills ....Jeanne Bates
Jane Hancock (1965) ....Stella Stevens
Dr. Mike Rogers (1965) ....Ben Piazza
Dr. Daniel Niles Freeland (1965–1966) .... Franchot Tone
Dr. Terry McDaniel (1965–1966) .... Jim McMullan
Sally Welden (1965–1966) ..Marlyn Mason

One of the great medical dramas in television history, *Ben Casey* premiered in October 1961 and quickly became the most popular program on the ABC network. Much of its success was due to its lead, the handsome, virile Vince Edwards, who was discovered by Bing Crosby (the show was produced by Crosby's production company). Casey's original mentor, in the Kildare-Gillespie tradition, was Dr. David Zorba, who guided the gifted young resident surgeon in his battles with disease and the medical establishment. *Ben Casey* frequently tackled controversial subjects and exuded a feeling of realism and tension, which was emphasized by extreme close-up shots in moments of crisis. A *Time* review noted that it "accurately captures the feeling of sleepless intensity in a metropolitan hospital."

Some important changes took place at County General Hospital at the beginning of the 1965–1966 season. Dr. Zorba departed and was replaced as Chief of Surgery by Dr. Daniel Freeland. A greater thread of continuity from week to week was introduced, including some "cliffhangers," and Casey was even allowed a brief love affair with Jane Hancock, a beautiful young woman who had just awakened from a 13-year coma. This was established in a five-part story early in the season, which involved a romantic triangle between Casey, Hancock, and the young intern Mike Rogers. (There had always been a hint of love between Casey and Dr. Maggie Graham, but it was not openly stated.) There was also a stormy romance between the new doctor Terry McDaniel and a disturbed patient, Sally Welden. The role of the orderly Nick Kanavaras was downplayed, although quiet, likable Dr. Ted Hoffman and Nurse Wills remained.

Ben Casey was produced by James Moser, who also created *Medic*.

BEN GRAUER SHOW, THE

Talk

FIRST TELECAST: *January 3, 1950*

LAST TELECAST: *June 27, 1950*

BROADCAST HISTORY:

Jan 1950–Jun 1950, NBC Tue 11:00–11:15

HOST:

John Gnagy (Jan)
Warren Hull (Jan–Feb)
Ben Grauer (Feb–Jun)

This show was nothing more than an extended commercial for its sponsor, the book publishers Doubleday and Company. It started as a local program in New York, with John Gnagy as the host and the title *You Are an Artist*, the same title as Gnagy's previous art-instruction program on NBC. In this case, since Doubleday had published Gnagy's new book, the emphasis was on convincing the viewing audience to run out and buy it to help them learn to draw. The show started in October 1949 and went network at the start of the new year.

At the end of January, Warren Hull took over, with the title changed to *The Warren Hull Show*. Hull had no book to plug but, instead, chatted each week about a new book (offered by Doubleday) and then interviewed the author. Hull left the show after a month and was replaced by Ben Grauer. Again the title was changed, to identify the host, but the format remained the same. Grauer would interview authors about their new books, and there were plugs for both the books themselves and the various Doubleday book clubs—such as the Doubleday Dollar Book Club and the Mystery Guild—through which books could be obtained at a discount.

BEN VEREEN . . . COMIN' AT YA

Musical Variety

FIRST TELECAST: *August 7, 1975*

LAST TELECAST: *August 28, 1975*

BROADCAST HISTORY:

Aug 1975, NBC Thu 8:00–9:00

HOST:

Ben Vereen

REGULARS:

Lola Falana

Liz Torres

Avery Schreiber

This was a summer musical variety hour hosted by the versatile black actor/singer Ben Vereen.

BENNY RUBIN SHOW, THE

Comedy Variety

FIRST TELECAST: *April 29, 1949*

LAST TELECAST: *June 24, 1949*

BROADCAST HISTORY:

Apr 1949–Jun 1949, NBC Fri 9:00–9:30

HOST:

Benny Rubin

In this comedy variety program, a succession of singers, dancers, and comedians visited Benny Rubin's Theatrical Agency to show him their latest routines.

BERT D'ANGELO/SUPERSTAR

Police Drama

FIRST TELECAST: *February 21, 1976*

LAST TELECAST: *July 10, 1976*

BROADCAST HISTORY:

Feb 1976–Jul 1976, ABC Sat 10:00–11:00

CAST:

Sgt. Bert D'Angelo .... Paul Sorvino

Inspector Larry Johnson .... Robert Pine

Capt. Jack Breen .... Dennis Patrick

EXECUTIVE PRODUCER:

Quinn Martin

The superstar in this case was a TV cop, this one a 10-year veteran of the New York City force who had transferred to new turf—San Francisco. Tough, direct, and often in trouble with his superiors, D'Angelo handled cases that cut across departmental lines, including homicides, narcotics, and robberies. He found lots of action but not much audience, and was canceled after half a season.

BEST IN MYSTERY, THE

Dramatic Anthology

FIRST TELECAST: *July 16, 1954*

LAST TELECAST: *August 31, 1956*

BROADCAST HISTORY:

Jul 1954–Sep 1954, NBC Fri 9:00–9:30

Jul 1955–Sep 1955, NBC Fri 9:00–9:30

Jul 1956–Aug 1956, NBC Fri 9:00–9:30

This program was aired for three years as a summer replacement for *The Big Story*. During 1954 and 1955 it was a true anthology composed of reruns from other dramatic series. The suspense dramas during this period included "Lullaby," starring Agnes Moorehead and Tom Drake; "Death Makes a Pass," starring Jay Novello and Lloyd Corrigan; "Accounts Closed," starring George Nader and Carolyn Jones; and "Passage Home," starring John Doucette, James McCallion, and Brian Keith. The 1956 version, however, consisted solely of episodes of *Four Star Playhouse*, seen previously on CBS, starring Dick Powell as the gambling-house owner Willie Dante. See also under series: *Dante*.

BEST OF GROUCHO, THE

see *You Bet Your Life*

BETTER HOME SHOW, THE

Instruction

FIRST TELECAST: *May 5, 1951*

LAST TELECAST: *April 26, 1952*

BROADCAST HISTORY:

May 1951–Apr 1952, ABC Sat 6:30–7:00

REGULARS:

Norman Brokenshire

Dick Wilson
Doreen Wilson

An interesting "how-to" program with kindly old radio announcer Norman Brokenshire, assisted by his neighbors the Wilsons, who often dropped in. "Broke's" topics ranged from how to build cabinets out of orange crates to how to use luminous paint on garden tools and how to get bats out of your belfry. The program was previously aired locally.

BETTER LIVING TV THEATRE

Documentary/Discussion

FIRST TELECAST: *April 21, 1954*
LAST TELECAST: *August 29, 1954*
BROADCAST HISTORY:
Apr 1954–Jun 1954, DUM Wed 10:30–11:00
Jun 1954–Aug 1954, DUM Sun 10:30–11:00
HOST:
Fischer Black

The program promoted private industry through interviews, discussions, and film clips illustrating the contribution made by industry toward better living in the United States. Fischer Black, editor of *Electrical World*, served as moderator.

BETTY HUTTON SHOW, THE

Situation Comedy

FIRST TELECAST: *October 1, 1959*
LAST TELECAST: *June 30, 1960*
BROADCAST HISTORY:
Oct 1959–Jun 1960, CBS Thu 8:00–8:30
CAST:
Goldie ....Betty Hutton
Pat Strickland ....Gigi Perreau
Nicky Strickland ....Richard Miles
Roy Strickland ....Dennis Joel
Lorna ....Joan Shawlee
Rosemary ....Jean Carson
Howard Seaton ....Tom Conway
Hollister ....Gavin Muir

The leading lady in this comedy was Goldie, an outspoken showgirl turned manicurist. When Mr. Strickland, one of her regular customers, died suddenly, Goldie found herself the inheritor of his considerable estate, as well as legal guardian of his three teenage children. The adjustments made by all concerned—Goldie to the luxury and social status of her new wealth, the children to their unsophisticated and unconventional guardian, and family lawyer Howard Seaton to his new employer—created many comic story situations. Goldie's ex-roommates, Lorna and Rosemary, also spent time at the Strickland mansion and remained her closest friends.

BETTY WHITE SHOW, THE

Comedy Variety

FIRST TELECAST: *February 5, 1958*
LAST TELECAST: *April 30, 1958*
BROADCAST HISTORY:
Feb 1958–Apr 1958, ABC Wed 9:30–10:00
HOSTESS:
Betty White
REGULARS:
Johnny Jacobs
Del Moore
Reta Shaw
Frank Nelson
ORCHESTRA:
Frank DeVol

After the cancellation of her situation comedy *Date with the Angels*, comedienne Betty White filled the same time slot by starring for a few months in this comedy variety show. Each show generally consisted of three skits, in which Miss White portrayed a variety of roles, assisted by her regulars and guest stars, such as Charles Coburn and Billy DeWolfe. Jimmy Boyd, who had played the role of Wheeler in *Angels*, was a regular guest, and orchestra leader Frank DeVol also took part in the skits.

BETTY WHITE SHOW, THE

Situation Comedy

FIRST TELECAST: *September 12, 1977*
LAST TELECAST: *January 9, 1978*
BROADCAST HISTORY:
Sep 1977–Nov 1977, CBS Mon 9:00–9:30
Dec 1977–Jan 1978, CBS Mon 9:30–10:00
CAST:
Joyce Whitman ....Betty White
John Elliot ....John Hillerman
Mitzi Maloney ....Georgia Engel
Tracy Garrett ....Caren Kaye
Doug Porterfield ....Alex Henteloff
Fletcher Huff ....Barney Phillips
Hugo Muncy ....Charles Cyphers

Betty White and Georgia Engel, two alumnae from *The Mary Tyler Moore Show*, starred in this comedy spoof of television and the people who work in it. Joyce Whitman was a 40-ish movie actress whose career had been on the decline until she was offered the starring role in a new television series, *Undercover Woman* (a loose parody on the real TV series, *Police Woman*). Joyce jumped at the chance, only to discover that the director was her suave, sarcastic ex-husband, John Elliot. None of the mutual antagonism that had ended their marriage had ebbed, and the two of them spent much of their time on the set putting each other down. Others working on *Undercover Woman* were Joyce's TV "partner," Tracy Garrett, a sexy young actress who was mindlessly clawing her way to the top, using anybody and anything to get there; Fletcher Huff, a fidgety actor who played the police chief for whom Undercover Woman worked; and Hugo Muncy, her stuntman double. Also wandering around the set was Doug Porterfield, the network liaison man assigned to the series by CBS (yes, they did refer to the network producing the mythical series as CBS). Doug was forever trying to assert himself as a network "executive," but his weak, bumbling personality kept getting in his way, making it difficult for anyone to take him seriously.

Away from the studio, Joyce's best friend was flaky Mitzi Maloney, a lovable dumb blonde (virtually the same role Georgia Engel had played on *The Mary Tyler Moore Show*). Mitzi had worked at the unemployment office when Joyce was collecting unemployment checks, prior to getting the part in *Undercover Woman*, and she subsequently became Joyce's roommate.

BEULAH

Situation Comedy

FIRST TELECAST: *October 3, 1950*

LAST TELECAST: *September 22, 1953*

BROADCAST HISTORY:

Oct 1950–Sep 1953, ABC Tue 7:30–8:00

CAST:

Beulah (1950–1952) .... Ethel Waters
Beulah (1952–1953) .... Louise Beavers
Harry Henderson (1950–1952)
.... William Post, Jr.
Harry Henderson (1952–1953)
.... David Bruce
Alice Henderson (1950–1952)
.... Ginger Jones
Alice Henderson (1952–1953)
.... June Frazee
Donnie Henderson (1950–1952)
.... Clifford Sales
Donnie Henderson (1952–1953)
.... Stuffy Singer
Oriole ....Butterfly McQueen
Bill Jackson (1950–1951)
.... Percy (Bud) Harris
Bill Jackson (1951–1953) ... Dooley Wilson

"Somebody bawl fo' Beulah?" she exclaimed, as TV's favorite black maid came once again to the rescue of her ever-bumbling employers. *Beulah*, one of the most popular comedy characters of the 1940s and 1950s, originated as a supporting role on radio's *Fibber McGee and Molly* program in 1944. Its creator was a white male actor, Marlin Hurt, who eventually began a separate *Beulah* series on radio. When ABC brought the popular show to television in 1950 the role was filled by veteran singer-actress Ethel Waters, with Percy Harris as her shiftless boyfriend Bill and Butterfly McQueen as her girlfriend Oriole. Her employers, the Hendersons, were a virtual caricature of a white middle-class family, giving Beulah plenty to do as one crisis after another overtook the household (such as Mr. Henderson's burning the steaks at a picnic, falling into the water while fishing, or trying to stop his young son Donnie from running away from home—with a home like that, why shouldn't he?).

In April 1952, there was a major cast change. Hattie McDaniel, another Hollywood veteran *(Gone with the Wind)*, was scheduled to take over the role of Beulah, but she suddenly became ill and the part went to Louise Beavers, who had a long list of movie credits of her own. At the same time the entire Henderson family changed faces. *Beulah* was still receiving high ratings in September 1953, when it went off the air because Miss Beavers decided to leave the role.

BEVERLY HILLBILLIES, THE

Situation Comedy

FIRST TELECAST: *September 26, 1962*

LAST TELECAST: *September 7, 1971*

BROADCAST HISTORY:

Sep 1962–Sep 1964, CBS Wed 9:00–9:30
Sep 1964–Sep 1968, CBS Wed 8:30–9:00
Sep 1968–Sep 1969, CBS Wed 9:00–9:30
Sep 1969–Sep 1970, CBS Wed 8:30–9:00
Sep 1970–Sep 1971, CBS Tue 7:30–8:00

CAST:

Jed Clampett ....Buddy Ebsen

Granny Clampett ....Irene Ryan
Elly May Clampett ....Donna Douglas
Jethro Bodine ....Max Baer, Jr.
Milton Drysdale ....Raymond Bailey
Jane Hathaway ....Nancy Kulp
Cousin Pearl Bodine (1962–1963)
.... Bea Benadaret
Mrs. Drysdale ....Harriet MacGibbon

One of CBS's longest-running situation comedies, this was the slapstick treatment of a hillbilly family from the Ozarks who struck it rich (an oil well sprouted in their front yard) and moved to a Beverly Hills mansion. Ebsen portrayed Jed Clampett, a widower and patriarch of the Clampett clan, surrounded by the slightly scatterbrained members of his family and his comparatively "straight" neighbor and banker, Milton Drysdale. The Clampetts' encounters with corrupt politics, unfamiliar fashions, indoor plumbing, and the other trappings of modern life provided grist for years of comedy.

Beverly Hillbillies was an instantaneous hit, and during its first two seasons ranked as the number one program on television, attracting as many as 60 million viewers per week. It entertained viewers for nine years in prime time; it was finally canceled because its ratings declined gradually and its audience was too heavily concentrated in rural areas to suit Madison Avenue advertisers. The only member of the original cast who did not stay with the show through its entire run was Bea Benadaret, who played cousin Jethro's mother Pearl. She left the series at the end of its first season to star in *Petticoat Junction*, another CBS rural comedy.

The theme song, "The Ballad of Jed Clampett," was especially composed for the program by bluegrass musicians Lester Flatt and Earl Scruggs and was on the national hit parade in early 1963.

BEWITCHED

Situation Comedy

FIRST TELECAST: *September 17, 1964*
LAST TELECAST: *July 1, 1972*
BROADCAST HISTORY:

Sep 1964–Jan 1967, ABC Thu 9:00–9:30
Jan 1967–Sep 1971, ABC Thu 8:30–9:00
Sep 1971–Jan 1972, ABC Wed 8:00–8:30
Jan 1972–Jul 1972, ABC Sat 8:00–8:30

CAST:

Samantha Stephens/Serena
.... Elizabeth Montgomery
Darrin Stephens (1964–1969)
.... Dick York
Darrin Stephens (1969–1972)
.... Dick Sargent
Endora ....Agnes Moorehead
Maurice ....Maurice Evans*
Larry Tate ....David White
Louise Tate (1964–1966) .....Irene Vernon
Louise Tate (1966–1972) .....Kasey Rogers
Tabitha Stephens (1966–1972)
.... Erin and Diane Murphy
Adam Stephens (1971–1972)
.... David Lawrence
Abner Kravitz ....George Tobias
Gladys Kravitz (1964–1966)
.... Alice Pearce (d. 3/66)
Gladys Kravitz (1966–1972) ..Sandra Gould
Aunt Clara (1964–1968) .....Marion Lorne
Uncle Arthur (1965–1972) ....Paul Lynde*
Esmerelda (1969–1972) ....Alice Ghostley*

PRODUCER/DIRECTOR:

William Asher

*Occasional role

Bewitched was a comedy about an exceptionally pretty young witch named Samantha and her earnest attempts to abandon her witchcraft to please her mortal husband, Darrin. The couple was married on the first telecast, but that was the last "normal" event in their union. Samantha was continually tempted to use her witchly powers, invoked by a twitch of her nose, to get her way around the house. There was also a bevy of her relatives, none of whom wanted her to go straight: her mother Endora, her father Maurice, practical-joking Uncle Arthur, and forgetful Aunt Clara, witches and warlocks all. Esmerelda the housekeeper, who came along in 1969, was also a witch, but her powers were declining; a timid soul, she would fade away when spoken to harshly. Samantha's mischievous lookalike, cousin Serena, was also played by Miss Montgomery.

Also in the cast were Larry Tate, Darrin's long-suffering boss at the New York advertising agency of Tate & Mann, Larry's wife Louise, and the Stephens's easygoing but somewhat nosy neighbors, the Kravitzes.

Samantha's first child, Tabitha, "born" on the telecast of January 13, 1966, was played by twins Erin and Diane Murphy (later by Erin alone), who were only one and a half years old when they first appeared on the show. A son, Adam, came along on the night of October 16, 1969, although he was not seen regularly until the 1971–1972 season.

Visitors to the Stephens household included Julius Caesar (summoned up by mistake when Samantha asked Esmerelda to make a Caesar salad), George Washington, and Henry VIII.

Bewitched was an imaginative and well-written show that earned several Emmys. Extremely popular, it was in fact the biggest hit series produced by the ABC network up to that time (it ranked number two among all programs on the air during its first season). Reruns have entertained viewers during the daytime and on local stations for many years—all with a witch's twitch.

Elizabeth Montgomery, the star of the series, was in real life married to its producer/director, William Asher.

BID 'N' BUY

Quiz/Audience Participation

FIRST TELECAST: *July 1, 1958*

LAST TELECAST: *September 23, 1958*

BROADCAST HISTORY:

Jul 1958–Sep 1958, CBS Tue 10:00–10:30

EMCEE:

Bert Parks

At the start of each telecast of this auction game show, each of four contestants was given $10,000 in real money, which they then used to bid for clues that would help them identify a silhouette of some common object. The winner received an expensive prize, such as a sportscar, a fancy wardrobe, or a cabin cruiser, plus the right to return the following week.

BIFF BAKER U.S.A.

Adventure

FIRST TELECAST: *November 13, 1952*

LAST TELECAST: *March 26, 1953*

BROADCAST HISTORY:

Nov 1952–Mar 1953, CBS Thu 9:00–9:30

CAST:

Biff Baker .... Alan Hale, Jr.
Louise Baker .... Randy Stewart

Traveling all over the world in search of goods for his profitable importing business, Biff Baker often found himself involved in some form of international intrigue. Never looking for trouble, he nevertheless encountered it with remarkable frequency, and was always ready to deal with it. Biff and his wife Louise, with whom he traveled, most often found themselves caught up in some form of espionage, which was bad for the importing business but good for the plot.

BIG BEAT, THE

Music

FIRST TELECAST: *July 12, 1957*

LAST TELECAST: *August 2, 1957*

BROADCAST HISTORY:

Jul 1957–Aug 1957, ABC Fri 10:00–10:30

HOST:

Alan Freed

Alan Freed was the New York City disc jockey who is credited with coining the term "rock 'n' roll" and who did much to popularize "the big beat" in the mid-1950s. A flamboyant showman and promoter, Freed packaged this series of four rock spectaculars for ABC in the summer of 1957. The list of guests reads like a Who's Who of rock in the 1950s; the first show alone starred Connie Francis, The Everly Brothers ("Bye Bye Love"), Ferlin Husky ("Gone"), Don Rondo ("White Silver Sands"), the Billy Williams Quartet ("I'm Gonna Sit Right Down and Write Myself a Letter"), Nancy Wiskey ("Freight Train"), and Johnnie and Joe ("Over the Mountain"). Later guests included Andy Williams, Chuck Berry, Frankie Lymon and the Teenagers, Bobby Darin, the Fontane Sisters, Fats Domino, Clyde McPhatter, Dale Hawkins, Gogi Grant, Mickey and Sylvia, Jerry Lee Lewis, and more—all in four half-hour telecasts! *The Big Beat* was probably a better representation of the current hit parade, all with original artists doing their own hits, than was ever heard on *Your Hit Parade*. In addition to serving as host, Freed led his own orchestra on the show, which included star saxophonists "Big Al" Sears and Sam "the Man" Taylor.

BIG EDDIE

Situation Comedy

FIRST TELECAST: *August 23, 1975*

LAST TELECAST: *November 7, 1975*

BROADCAST HISTORY:

Aug 1975–Sep 1975, CBS Sat 8:30–9:00
Sep 1975–Nov 1975, CBS Fri 8:00–8:30

CAST:

Eddie Smith ....Sheldon Leonard
Honey Smith ....Sheree North
Ginger Smith ....Quinn Cummings
Monte "Bang Bang" Valentine .... Billy Sands
Jessie Smith ....Alan Oppenheimer
Raymond McKay ....Ralph Wilcox

Eddie Smith was a reformed gambler who was trying to make it as the owner-promoter of New York's Big E Sports Arena. Despite the gruff exterior, accentuated by the thickest New York accent ever heard on television, Eddie was a softie at heart and really wanted to broaden his intellectual horizons and improve his manners. His family consisted of his wife Honey, an ex-stripper; his granddaughter Ginger; and his brother Jessie, the accountant for Eddie's business. Bang Bang was Eddie's cook, and Raymond a stereotyped, jive-talking young black man working for Eddie. *Big Eddie* was given a preseason preview run on Saturday nights before moving into a Friday time period, but it faded quickly when pitted against *Sanford and Son*, its regular competition, in September.

BIG EVENT, THE

Various

FIRST TELECAST: *September 26, 1976*

LAST TELECAST:

BROADCAST HISTORY:

Sep 1976– , NBC Sun various times
Jan 1978– , NBC Tue various times

The Big Event was NBC's regular weekly showcase for special programming. Many of the specials lumped under this generic title were two hours in length, and some were even longer. "The First Fifty Years," a retrospective of NBC's half-century in broadcasting, occupied the entire evening of November 21, 1976, from 7:00 to 11:30 P.M. Major theatrical motion pictures were aired as *Big Events; Earthquake, 2001: A Space Odyssey*, and *Gone with the Wind* made their network television debuts here. In addition several major original television films were produced for the show (*Sybil, The Moneychangers, Holocaust*, and *Jesus of Nazareth*—the latter having previously aired in Europe) as well as more standard specials ("An Evening with Diana Ross," "The Father Knows Best Reunion," "The Story of Princess Grace").

The *Big Event* concept soon spread to other nights of the week as NBC, which was suffering from a shortage of hit series at the time, sought to boost its ratings with short-run but spectacular programming. A number of two- and three-part series such as "Harvest Home" and "The Godfather Saga" (an amalgam of the two *Godfather* theatrical films plus unused footage left over from the making of the films), ran partly or entirely under the *Big Event* title, usually extending from Saturday through Monday or Tuesday nights. In 1978 a second regular weekly *Big Event* time was added on Tuesday night.

BIG GAME, THE

Quiz/Audience Participation

FIRST TELECAST: *June 13, 1958*

LAST TELECAST: *September 12, 1958*

BROADCAST HISTORY:

Jun 1958–Sep 1958, NBC Fri 7:30–8:00

EMCEE:

Tom Kennedy

An unusual variation on quiz shows, this program tried to create the atmosphere of a big-game hunt. Each contestant was first given three plastic animals to place wherever he chose in his "jungle" (game board). He then answered multi-part questions, giving him opportunities to "shoot" at his opponent's animals. Although unable to see his opponent's board, a contestant could "shoot" at specific locations on the board (marked by a grid), hoping that the animals had been placed there. The first hunter to bag all of his opponent's animals won $2,000 and the right to face a new challenger.

BIG HAWAII

Adventure

FIRST TELECAST: *September 21, 1977*

LAST TELECAST: *November 16, 1977*

BROADCAST HISTORY:

Sep 1977–Nov 1977, NBC Wed 10:00–11:00

CAST:

Mitch Fears ....Cliff Potts
Barrett Fears ....John Dehner
Karen "Keke" Fears ....Lucia Stralser
Oscar Kalahani ....Bill Lucking
Lulu Kalahani ....Elizabeth Smith

Garfield Kalahani ....Moe Keale
Kimo Kalahani ....Remi Abellira

The sprawling Paradise Ranch on the island of Hawaii was the private domain of autocratic Barrett Fears. He had built it into an empire that had made him one of the richest and most powerful men in all the Hawaiian islands. Recently returned to help him run the ranch was his only son, 29-year-old Mitch, a free spirit whose anti-establishment, radical attitudes were a source of constant conflict with his traditional father. Mitch's best friend, and the mediator between the two strong-willed Fears men, was Oscar Kalahani, the foreman of Paradise Ranch. Keke was Mitch's spoiled, tomboyish 18-year-old cousin who also lived on the ranch; Big Lulu, Oscar's mother and the family housekeeper, whose son Garfield did odd jobs around the ranch; and Kimo, Lulu's son and a good friend of Keke. Stories revolved around the problems of running the ranch, the conflicts between its owners, and the adjustments forced on the traditional Hawaiian life-style by the inroads of change.

BIG IDEA, THE

Inventions

FIRST TELECAST: *December 15, 1952*
LAST TELECAST: *October 15, 1953*
BROADCAST HISTORY:
Dec 1952–May 1953, DUM Mon 9:00–9:30
May 1953–Oct 1953, DUM Thu 10:00–10:30
HOST:
Donn Bennett
REGULAR PANELIST:
Ray Wood

This unusual program displayed new inventions, with commentary by a panel and interviews with guest inventors. The presentations were entirely straight, and most of the inventions shown were useful, if prosaic, aids to everyday life, though there were some screwball exceptions. A sample of what the viewer might see on *The Big Idea:* a women's inflatable bathing suit, an inflatable coat hanger, a dart board that lit up, a golf bag that stood up by itself, a complete miniature orchestra, a lunch box with self-contained hot plate, a refrigerated lunch box, a self-snuffing ashtray, a collapsible smoking pipe, spring-loaded shoe heels, rotating shoe heels, a clothesline with permanently attached clothespins, a device for preventing storm windows from falling off, a device to allow cars to park sideways, the "Dickey-Dout" (a device to hold blouses and shirts in place), and individual plastic nose filters for allergy sufferers.

The Big Idea was first scheduled against CBS's *I Love Lucy*, where it was probably seen by nobody except friends and families of the inventors. It later moved to Thursday night but expired after a year's run.

BIG ISSUE, THE

Public Affairs

FIRST TELECAST: *April 7, 1953*
LAST TELECAST: *January 18, 1954*
BROADCAST HISTORY:
Apr 1953–Jun 1953, DUM Tue 8:30–9:00
Sep 1953–Jan 1954, DUM Mon 8:30–9:00
MODERATOR:
Martha Rountree
REGULAR PANELIST:
Lawrence E. Spivak

This discussion program covered important issues of the day and was moderated for most of its run by Martha Rountree, who is better known for her *Meet the Press*. Two guests, on opposing sides of the "big issue," appeared on each telecast. DuMont considered this to be "throwaway" programming, scheduling it first against *Milton Berle* on Tuesday and then opposite *Arthur Godfrey's Talent Scouts* on Monday.

BIG MOMENT, THE

Sports Drama

FIRST TELECAST: *July 5, 1957*
LAST TELECAST: *September 13, 1957*
BROADCAST HISTORY:
Jul 1957–Sep 1957, NBC Fri 9:30–10:00
HOST:
Bud Palmer

Films of sports highlights from the early 1920s to the present were featured on this summer replacement for *The Big Story*. Among the stories covered were famous finishes, arguments and riots, upsets, comebacks, sports characters, and women athletes.

BIG PARTY, THE

Variety

FIRST TELECAST: *October 8, 1959*
LAST TELECAST: *December 31, 1959*

BROADCAST HISTORY:

Oct 1959–Dec 1959, CBS Thu 9:30–11:00

The full title of this biweekly series was *The Big Party by Revlon*, paying homage to its sponsor. Each telecast presented a different host or hostess and a large roster of guest stars in a lavish 90-minute variety show. The program filling the alternate weeks was the prestigious *Playhouse 90*. Originally there were to have been a total of 20 of these live variety shows, but the series was canceled with the New Year's Eve telecast. Despite the appearance of such well-known performers as Rock Hudson, Tallulah Bankhead, Sammy Davis, Jr., Mort Sahl, and Esther Williams, all of whom were on the first telecast, *The Big Party* never found a big audience.

BIG PAYOFF, THE

Quiz/Audience Participation

FIRST TELECAST: *June 29, 1952*

LAST TELECAST: *September 27, 1953*

BROADCAST HISTORY:

Jun 1952–Sep 1952, NBC Sun 8:00–9:00
Jun 1953–Sep 1953, NBC Sun 8:00–9:00

EMCEE:

Randy Merriman

HOSTESS:

Bess Myerson

Contestants for this summer series were selected from letters in which men told why the women in their lives deserved the wonderful prizes offered by the program. The Big Payoff itself included jewelry, clothes, a mink coat for the woman, a new car for the man, and a trip to anywhere in the world via Pan American World Airways. To win, the man had to answer a series of progressively more difficult questions. Added features were the Big Little Payoff for children and the Turn About Payoff, in which women had a chance to win prizes for their men. Bert Parks had been the emcee of the daytime version of this show, which premiered earlier in 1952. Bess Myerson appeared on both the daytime and the nighttime versions, chatting with contestants and displaying prizes.

BIG PICTURE, THE

Documentary

FIRST TELECAST: *October 5, 1953*

LAST TELECAST: *September 30, 1959*

BROADCAST HISTORY:

Oct 1953–Dec 1954, ABC Mon 9:30–10:00
Jan 1954–Aug 1954, ABC Wed 9:00–9:30
Aug 1954–Feb 1955, ABC Sun 8:30–9:00
Mar 1955–Jun 1955, ABC Sat 7:30–8:00
Aug 1955, ABC Tue 8:30–9:00
Sep 1955–Jan 1956, ABC Mon 10:00–10:30
Mar 1956–Apr 1956, ABC Sun 10:00–10:30
Jun 1956–Oct 1956, ABC Tue 10:00–10:30
Jul 1957, ABC Thu 8:00—8:30
Aug 1957–Oct 1957, ABC Fri 10:00–10:30
Sep 1958–Oct 1958, ABC Fri 9:00–9:30
Jun 1959–Aug 1959, ABC Sat 10:00–10:30
Aug 1959–Sep 1959, ABC Wed 7:30–8:00

Many films produced by government and industry to promote their own interests were shown on television during the 1950s, especially by the impoverished ABC and DuMont networks. Probably no such series had as long a run or was as well received by viewers as the U.S. Army's *Big Picture*. This program aired straight documentary films produced by the Army Pictorial Center and depicting various facets of the U.S. Army in action, including great battles, biographies of generals, new weaponry, and the roles played by various divisions and branches. Professional actors were rarely used; instead most of the footage came from the army's own vast historical and training film libraries.

The Big Picture was the brainchild of Lt. Carl Bruton, a commercial broadcaster called to active duty at the Pentagon during the Korean War. Seeing the vast amount of film available, and realizing the impact made by such privately made documentaries as *Crusade in Europe*, he sensed an excellent public relations opportunity for the army. (The films were also used for training purposes and were shown to foreign audiences.) The series began on WTOP in Washington, D.C., in 1951 and was soon being offered free to stations all over the country, to be shown in any manner they pleased. ABC picked it up in 1953 and ran it off and on for six years, seemingly whenever there was a hole to plug in the network schedule.

BIG QUESTION, THE

News/Discussion

FIRST TELECAST: *September 9, 1951*

LAST TELECAST: *October 21, 1951*

BROADCAST HISTORY:

Sep 1951–Oct 1951, CBS Sun 6:00–6:30

MODERATOR:
Charles Collingwood

This live discussion program, which originated from Washington, D.C., attempted to cover a major issue of domestic or world importance each week. CBS White House correspondent Charles Collingwood served as moderator. When the subject warranted, the program might be filmed in advance on location, as in the case of a discussion with the delegates to the San Francisco conference on the Japanese Peace Treaty. At the end of October 1951 the program moved to an afternoon time slot, where it remained until early 1952.

BIG RECORD, THE

Music

FIRST TELECAST: *September 18, 1957*
LAST TELECAST: *June 11, 1958*
BROADCAST HISTORY:
Sep 1957–Mar 1958, CBS Wed 8:00–8:30
Mar 1958–Jun 1958, CBS Wed 8:30–9:00
HOSTESS:
Patti Page

Singer Patti Page, who had sold millions of her own records, was the hostess of this live musical showcase. The program's guest stars were well-established recording artists singing their biggest-selling or trademark songs; those currently on the popular record charts; and up-and-coming young singers who were, in the words of the producers, "due to hit the jukebox jackpot within the near future." The range of selections included show music and standards in addition to rock 'n' roll, then a fairly new trend in music. Emphasis was placed on standards, however, to attract a wider audience than the teenage-oriented top-40 songs.

BIG STORY, THE

Dramatic Anthology

FIRST TELECAST: *September 16, 1949*
LAST TELECAST: *June 28, 1957*
BROADCAST HISTORY:
Sep 1949–Mar 1951, NBC Fri 9:30–10:00
Mar 1951–Jul 1956, NBC Fri 9:00–9:30
Sep 1956–Jun 1957, NBC Fri 9:30–10:00
NARRATOR:
Bob Sloane (1949–1954)
Norman Rose (1954–1955)
Ben Grauer (1955–1957)

This long-running documentary-drama series was based on the actual case histories of reporters who solved crimes, uncovered corruption, or otherwise performed significant public service through their diligent reporting. Some episodes were local human-interest stories, and some were national scandals, such as the story of labor columnist Victor Riesel, who was blinded by racketeers for his exposés. Each week, the sponsor, American Tobacco Company, gave a $500 cash award (initially called the Pall Mall Award) to the reporter whose story was used. Starting in 1955 Ben Grauer appeared in a newsroom at the beginning and end of each episode, in the role of the program's editor. He introduced the evening's "big story," and then, after the drama, would present the real-life reporter with his "Big Story Award." The series was presented on alternate weeks during part of its run.

BIG SURPRISE, THE

Quiz/Audience Participation

FIRST TELECAST: *October 8, 1955*
LAST TELECAST: *April 2, 1957*
BROADCAST HISTORY:
Oct 1955–Jun 1956, NBC Sat 7:30–8:00
Sep 1956–Apr 1957, NBC Sat 8:00–8:30
EMCEE:
Jack Barry (1955–1956)
Mike Wallace (1956–1957)

In the wake of the sudden and dramatic success of CBS's *The $64,000 Question*, which had premiered during the summer of 1955, NBC brought out its own big-money quiz show that fall. During its first six months on the air *The Big Surprise* underwent numerous modifications in format. There was a period during which the contestant could be "rescued" if he or she missed a question, by having someone else correctly answer a substitute question; the "rescuer" then got 10 percent of the regular contestant's total winnings. There was a period when the contestant could be asked easy or hard questions. Missing an easy question cost the contestant all his or her winnings, while missing a hard one cost only half the winnings. There were other variations as well. In April 1956 the program finally settled down with a less complicated format. The subject area was chosen by the contestant. There were ten questions ranging in value from $100 to

$100,000, and the contestant could also answer two insurance questions. Correct answers to the insurance questions guaranteed the contestants all the money they had won up to that point, regardless of future misses.

Unlike *The $64,000 Question*, *The Big Surprise* had no isolation booths. Contestants stood on a pedestal while pondering the answers to questions. Jack Barry left the show on March 3, 1956, and was replaced the following week by Mike Wallace.

BIG TOP

Circus

FIRST TELECAST: *July 1, 1950*
LAST TELECAST: *January 6, 1951*
BROADCAST HISTORY:
Jul 1950–Sep 1950, CBS Sat 7:00–8:00
Sep 1950–Jan 1951, CBS Sat 6:30–7:30
REGULARS:
Jack Sterling
Dan Lurie
Ed McMahon
Chris Keegan

Each week a full hour of live circus acts was presented on this series, which originated from the Camden, New Jersey, Convention Hall. Jack Sterling was the ringmaster, Ed McMahon (later of *The Tonight Show*) and Chris Keegan were the resident clowns, and Dan Lurie was the strongman. In addition to the regulars, at least six different acts, ranging from trapeze to trained animals, were presented on each show. After its six-month run at night, *Big Top* moved to Saturday afternoons (noon–1:00 P.M.), where it remained a fixture on the CBS lineup for the next seven years.

BIG TOWN

Newspaper Drama

FIRST TELECAST: *October 5, 1950*
LAST TELECAST: *October 2, 1956*
BROADCAST HISTORY:
Oct 1950–Sep 1954, CBS Thu 9:30–10:00
Feb 1953–Jul 1953, DUM Fri 8:00–8:30
Oct 1954–Sep 1955, NBC Wed 10:30–11:00
Sep 1955–Oct 1956, NBC Tue 10:30–11:00
CAST:
Steve Wilson (1950–1954) .... Patrick McVey
Steve Wilson (1954–1956) .... Mark Stevens
Lorelei Kilbourne (1950–1951) .... Mary K. Wells
Lorelei Kilbourne (1951–1952) .... Julie Stevens
Lorelei Kilbourne (1952–1953) .... Jane Nigh
Lorelei Kilbourne (1953–1954) .... Beverly Tyler
Lorelei Kilbourne (1954–1955) .... Trudy Wroe
Charlie Anderson (1954–1956) .... Barry Kelly
Diane Walker (1955–1956) ....Doe Avedon

This long-running melodrama centered on *The Illustrated Press*, the largest and most influential newspaper in Big Town, whose driving force was crusading editor Steve Wilson. Steve's concerns were thwarting the spread of organized crime, exposing political corruption, establishing various types of reforms, and any other cause that seemed worthy. His star reporter was Lorelei Kilbourne, who had a certain romantic interest in her boss. *Big Town* had run from 1937 to 1948 on radio (where Steve Wilson had once been played by Edward G. Robinson), and when it moved to television as a live weekly series in 1950 it was an immediate hit. In April 1952 series production moved from New York to Hollywood, and *Big Town* was thereafter a filmed rather than live show. Patrick McVey portrayed editor Wilson throughout the CBS run, but Lorelei Kilbourne's face kept changing. After the end of its first season on NBC, her part was dropped completely from the show and Steve's love interest became Diane Walker, a commercial artist. City editor Charlie Anderson was also added as a regular cast member by NBC.

Repeats of *Big Town* were seen on DuMont under the title *City Assignment* while the program was still running on CBS.

BIG VALLEY, THE

Western

FIRST TELECAST: *September 15, 1965*
LAST TELECAST: *May 19, 1969*
BROADCAST HISTORY:
Sep 1965–Jul 1966, ABC Wed 9:00–10:00
Jul 1966–May 1969, ABC Mon 10:00–11:00
CAST:
Victoria Barkley ....Barbara Stanwyck
Jarrod Barkley ....Richard Long
Nick Barkley ....Peter Breck
Heath Barkley ....Lee Majors

Audra Barkley .... Linda Evans
Silas .... Napoleon Whiting

This action-filled Western adventure was set on the sprawling Barkley ranch in California's San Joaquin Valley in the 1870s. The matriarch of the clan was Victoria Barkley, who ran the family empire with a strong hand and the help of her four adult offspring; lawyer Jarrod, bold, brawling young Nick, ruggedly handsome Heath, and beautiful daughter Audra. (Another son, 19-year-old Eugene, played by Charles Briles, was seen occasionally in early episodes.) Like other settlers, the Barkleys were continually fighting the lawless elements of the Old West, and *Big Valley* stories were peopled with schemers, murderers, bank robbers, Mexican revolutionaries, and con men; one of the latter was delightfully portrayed by Milton Berle, in a guest appearance.

The Big Valley was Lee Majors's first TV series, and was in fact the first acting role he read for after completing a mere six months of drama instruction. He played the illegitimate son of Victoria's late husband, Tom.

BIGELOW SHOW, THE

Variety

FIRST TELECAST: *October 14, 1948*
LAST TELECAST: *December 28, 1949*
BROADCAST HISTORY:

Oct 1948–Jul 1949, NBC Thu 9:30–10:00
Oct 1949–Dec 1949, CBS Wed 9:00–9:30

REGULARS:

Paul Winchell and Jerry Mahoney
Dunninger

This two-part program featured the ventriloquist Paul Winchell and his dummy Jerry Mahoney in one segment, and mental telepathist Dunninger in another. Winchell and Mahoney did a regular weekly comedy routine, sometimes with the aid of a guest star. Dunninger's act consisted of reading the minds of members of the studio audience or special guests, and sometimes other tricks, always with a noted personality present to judge the honesty of the performance; he had a standing offer of $10,000 to anyone who could prove that he used an accomplice. In one telecast a United States Congressman was shown on the steps of the Capitol in Washington, while from New York Dunninger read his mind—via split screen.

BIGELOW THEATRE, THE

Dramatic Anthology

FIRST TELECAST: *December 10, 1950*
LAST TELECAST: *December 27, 1951*
BROADCAST HISTORY:

Dec 1950–Jun 1951, CBS Sun 6:00–6:30
Sep 1951–Dec 1951, DUM Thu 10:00–10:30

This series of filmed dramas appeared first on CBS and then moved to DuMont. Some of the telecasts in the DuMont run had originally been seen on CBS—among them, "The Big Hello" with Cesar Romero, "Charming Billy" with Spring Byington, and "A Man's First Debt" with Lloyd Bridges; others were originals appearing for the first time. Ward Bond, Gig Young, Lynn Bari, Chico Marx, and Gale Storm were among those appearing in episodes.

BILL COSBY SHOW, THE

Situation Comedy

FIRST TELECAST: *September 14, 1969*
LAST TELECAST: *August 31, 1971*
BROADCAST HISTORY:

Sep 1969–May 1971, NBC Sun 8:30–9:00
Jun 1971–Aug 1971, NBC Tue 7:30–8:00

CAST:

Chet Kincaid .... Bill Cosby
Chet's mother (1969–1970)
.... Lillian Randolph
Chet's mother (1970–1971)
.... Beah Richards
Brian Kincaid .... Lee Weaver
Verna Kincaid .... Olga James
Mr. Langford .... Sid McCoy
Mrs. Peterson .... Joyce Bulifant

Comic Bill Cosby, who scored his first TV success in the adventure series *I Spy,* played a high school physical education teacher and coach, Chet Kincaid, in this warmhearted comedy. The setting was a school in a lower-middle-class neighborhood of Los Angeles. Chet's relationships with family, students, and fellow teachers were emphasized, giving free reign to Cosby's gentle sense of humor and philosophy. His family life with his mother, his brother Brian, and his sister-in-law Verna were as much a part of the program as his professional life with the principal, Mr. Langford; the guidance counselor, Mrs. Peterson; and lots of kids.

BILL DANA SHOW, THE

Situation Comedy

FIRST TELECAST: *September 22, 1963*

LAST TELECAST: *January 17, 1965*

BROADCAST HISTORY:

Sep 1963–Sep 1964, NBC Sun 7:00–7:30
Sep 1964–Jan 1965, NBC Sun 8:30–9:00

CAST:

Jose Jimenez .... Bill Dana
Mr. Phillips .... Jonathan Harris
Eddie (1963–1964) .... Gary Crosby
Byron Glick .... Don Adams
Susie .... Maggie Peterson

Writer-comedian Bill Dana, whose character Jose Jimenez had a very successful career on records and in nightclubs following its creation on *The Steve Allen Show*, brought Jose to life for this series. Jose was a Mexican immigrant who worked as a bellhop at the Park Central Hotel. Not only did he work there, it was practically his entire world: he lived in special bachelor quarters provided for hotel employees, ate in the hotel kitchen, and had social contact only with employees and guests of the hotel. In his goodhearted naiveté he saw only the good in the people around him. His biggest problems were his fellow bellhop Eddie, who was constantly trying to get him to wise up; the less-than-understanding hotel manager Mr. Phillips; and the not-too-brilliant hotel detective Byron Glick. Walter Mitty-like dream sequences were occasionally used to extricate Jose from the hotel environment.

BILL GWINN SHOW, THE

Audience Participation

FIRST TELECAST: *February 5, 1951*

LAST TELECAST: *April 21, 1952*

BROADCAST HISTORY:

Feb. 1951–Mar 1951, ABC Mon 10:30–11:00
Mar 1951–Jun 1951, ABC Mon 8:30–9:30
Jun 1951–Sep 1951, ABC Wed 9:00–9:30
Oct 1951–Mar 1952, ABC Mon 10:00–10:30
Mar 1952–Apr 1952, ABC Mon 9:30–10:00

EMCEE:

Bill Gwinn

In this audience-participation show, three couples competed for prizes by enacting scenes showing how favorite songs had influenced their lives. The program underwent several title changes, beginning as *It Could Be You*, changing to *This Could Be You* two weeks later, *The Bill Gwinn Show* in April 1951, and *This Is My Song* shortly before its demise in April 1952.

BILL STERN'S SPORTS QUIZ

see *Are You Positive?*

BILLY BOONE AND COUSIN KIB

Children's

FIRST TELECAST: *July 9, 1950*

LAST TELECAST: *August 27, 1950*

BROADCAST HISTORY:

Jul 1950–Aug 1950, CBS Sun 6:30–7:00

REGULARS:

Carroll "Kib" Colby
Patti Milligan

As the 1950 summer replacement for *Mr. I Magination*, another children's show, this series featured cartoonist "Kib" Colby and Patti Milligan as Suzy, his ten-year-old helper and friend. Each episode consisted of Billy Boone comic strips sketched by Mr. Colby, drawing games with members of the studio audience, and children's folk songs sung by the audience.

BILLY DANIELS SHOW, THE

Music

FIRST TELECAST: *October 5, 1952*

LAST TELECAST: *December 28, 1952*

BROADCAST HISTORY:

Oct 1952–Dec 1952, ABC Sun 6:30–6:45

FEATURING:

Billy Daniels

HOST:

Jimmy Blaine

This brief program consisted of songs performed by "That Old Black Magic" singer, Billy Daniels, with rhythm accompaniment.

BILLY GRAHAM CRUSADE, THE

Religion

FIRST TELECAST: *June 1, 1957*

LAST TELECAST: *April 11, 1959*

BROADCAST HISTORY:

Jun 1957–Aug 1957, ABC Sat 8:00–9:00
May 1958–Jun 1958, ABC Sat 10:00–11:00
Sep 1958–Oct 1958, ABC Sat 8:00–9:00
Feb 1959–Apr 1959, ABC Sat 10:00–11:00

HOST:

Rev. Billy Graham

On four occasions in the late 1950s, the world-famous evangelist Dr. Billy Graham had a regular series of televised religious services from his various crusades.

BILLY ROSE SHOW, THE

Dramatic Anthology

FIRST TELECAST: *October 3, 1950*

LAST TELECAST: *March 27, 1951*

BROADCAST HISTORY:

Oct 1950–Mar 1951, ABC Tue 9:00–9:30

DIRECTOR:

Jed Harris

Billy Rose, the legendary Broadway producer and songwriter, had a brief fling with television in this early dramatic series, most of whose stories were adaptations from his syndicated newspaper column, "Pitching Horseshoes." Sample titles were "The Night They Made a Bum out of Helen Hayes" and "The Night Billy Rose Shoulda Stood in Bed." Billy had a reputation for doing things in a big way. The talent he used here was respectable—Burgess Meredith, Alfred Drake, Leo G. Carroll—but the project never quite measured up to the Rose reputation. What did Billy, the producer of so many theatrical spectaculars, finally think of the new medium? "It shapes up like a shortcut to an ulcer," he told *TV Guide*, ". . . but a darn interesting one."

BING CROSBY SHOW, THE

Situation Comedy

FIRST TELECAST: *September 14, 1964*

LAST TELECAST: *June 14, 1965*

BROADCAST HISTORY:

Sep 1964–Jun 1965, ABC Mon 9:30–10:00

CAST:

Bing Collins . . . . Bing Crosby
Ellie Collins . . . . Beverly Garland
Janice Collins . . . . Carol Faylen
Joyce Collins . . . . Diane Sherry
Willie Walters . . . . Frank McHugh

Bing Collins was a former singer who had left the hectic world of show business to settle down with his family and work as an electrical engineer. But life around the Collins household was hardly peaceful. Bing's wife Ellie had visions of making it in show business herself. Their two daughters provided quite a contrast: Janice was a normal, boy-crazy 15-year-old, but 10-year-old Joyce was so intellectual she seemed to belong in college. Willie Walters was the family's live-in handyman. Bing managed to sneak a song into almost every episode of this series, in between mediating disputes and dispensing sage advice to all.

BIONIC WOMAN, THE

Adventure

FIRST TELECAST: *January 14, 1976*

LAST TELECAST: *September 2, 1978*

BROADCAST HISTORY:

Jan 1976–May 1977, ABC Wed 8:00–9:00
Sep 1977–Mar 1978, NBC Sat 8:00–9:00
May 1978–Sep 1978, NBC Sat 8:00–9:00

CAST:

Jaime Sommers, the Bionic Woman
. . . . Lindsay Wagner
Oscar Goldman . . . . Richard Anderson
Dr. Rudy Wells . . . . Martin E. Brooks
Jim Elgin (1976) . . . . Ford Rainey
Helen Elgin (1976) . . . . Martha Scott

The Bionic Woman was one of a wave of comic-book-style superheroes brought to TV in the wake of the enormous success of *The Six Million Dollar Man. The Bionic Woman* was in fact a spinoff from, and closely linked to, that program. Jaime Sommers was originally introduced on *The Six Million Dollar Man* as Steve Austin's one-time fiancée. The couple had drifted apart when Steve became an astronaut, while Jaime went to college and then became a successful tennis pro. Then Jaime was nearly killed in a sky-diving accident, and the doctors who had reconstructed Steve bionically after his accident decided to try again with Jaime. Steve and Jaime renewed their romance, but too late it seemed, for when the four-part story ended in early 1975 Jaime was in a coma and apparently near death.

Unbeknownst to Steve, Jaime recovered and began a new life as a schoolteacher on an army base near her home town of Ojai, California. Her bionic operation had given her superhuman abilities—two legs for great speed, a right arm of great strength, and an ear for acute, long-distance hearing. Grateful for having been saved, she, like Steve, undertook dangerous underground missions for the government's Office of Scientific Information (OSI), fighting international spies, smugglers, kidnappers, and an occasional extraterrestrial being. Among her disguises were those of a nun, a roller-derby queen, and a lady wrestler.

When Steve Austin learned of all this he

rushed to her, but Jaime's problems had left her with a partial memory loss, and she had forgotten her love for Steve. So for the time being there was no bionic marriage. They sometimes were seen jointly on missions, however, and Jaime for a time lived in an apartment over the coach house at the farm of Steve's mother and stepfather, the Elgins, in Ojai.

Other regulars in the cast were Oscar Goldman, Jaime's supervisor at OSI, and Dr. Rudy Wells, who had devised the bionic operations, both of whom also appeared on *The Six Million Dollar Man*. Peggy Callahan (played by Jennifer Darling) was seen occasionally as Oscar's secretary on both series.

When *The Bionic Woman* moved to NBC another regular character was added to the cast in the person of Max, the bionic dog, a German Shepherd that became Jaime's loyal pet. Toward the end of that NBC season, with the popularity of science fiction movies on theater screens, more and more episodes of *The Bionic Woman* found Jaime encountering visitors from other planets.

The series was based on the novel *Cyborg*, by Martin Caidin.

BIRTHDAY PARTY

Children's

FIRST TELECAST: *May 15, 1947*
LAST TELECAST: *June 23, 1949*
BROADCAST HISTORY:

May 1947–Jan 1948, DUM Thu 7:30–8:00
Jan 1948–Aug 1948, DUM Thu 7:00–7:30
Sep 1948–Mar 1949, DUM Wed 7:00–7:30
Mar 1949–May 1949, DUM Sun 6:00–6:30
May 1949–Jun 1949, DUM Thu 7:00–7:30

HOST:

Bill Slater (1947)
Aunt Grace (1948)

This early children's show was built around a birthday party for a visiting child, complete with ice cream and cake, with performances by talented youngsters. Although it began on DuMont's New York station in May 1947, the exact date when it was first fed over the network is not known; it was a network entry by early in 1948. It was also known as *King Cole's Birthday Party*.

BLACK ROBE, THE

Courtroom Re-enactments

FIRST TELECAST: *May 18, 1949*
LAST TELECAST: *March 30, 1950*
BRODADCAST HISTORY:

May 1949–Aug 1949, NBC Wed 8:30–9:00
Aug 1949–Oct 1949, NBC Mon, various times
Nov 1949–Dec 1949, NBC Sat 10:00–10:30
Jan 1950–Mar 1950, NBC Thu 8:00–8:30

REGULARS:

Judge ....Frank Thomas
Police Officer ....John Green

Dramatic re-enactments of cases tried in New York City's Police Night Court. Although the judge and court officers were portrayed by actors, the persons appearing in court were often actual defendants and witnesses recreating their own cases; their names and appearance were "altered for reasons in the public interest." Various public figures appeared as guests of the court, and on at least one occasion a remorseful criminal was induced to surrender to authorities as the result of an appeal made on the show. The a›pearance of three orphans on another telecast drew 500 offers of adoption in the New York City area *The Black Robe* received a number of commendations for its public service and humanitarian work, but could not find a sponsor and so was canceled after ten months on the air.

BLACK SADDLE

Western

FIRST TELECAST: *January 10, 1959*
LAST TELECAST: *September 30, 1960*
BROADCAST HISTORY:

Jan 1959–Sep 1959, NBC Sat 9:00–9:30
Oct 1959–Sep 1960, ABC Fri 10:30–11:00

CAST:

Clay Culhane ....Peter Breck
Marshal Gib Scott ....Russell Johnson
Nora Travers ....Anna Lisa

Clay Culhane came from a family of gunfighters, but after losing his brothers in a shootout he decided that the practice of law might be a less violent way to settle personal disputes. Carrying his law books in his saddle bags, he traveled throughout the New Mexico Territory during the post-Civil War years, helping those in need of legal assistance. U.S. Marshal Gib Scott, who could not quite believe that Clay had really given up the gun for good, was never far behind.

BLACK SHEEP SQUADRON

see *Baa Baa Black Sheep*

BLANSKY'S BEAUTIES

Situation Comedy

FIRST TELECAST: *February 12, 1977*

LAST TELECAST: *May 21, 1977*

BROADCAST HISTORY:

Feb 1977–May 1977, ABC Sat 8:00–8:30

CAST:

Nancy Blansky ....Nancy Walker
Bambi Benton ....Caren Kaye
Ethel "Sunshine" Akalino
.... Lynda Goodfriend
Emilio ....Johnny Desmond
Joey DeLuca ....Eddie Mekka
Anthony DeLuca ....Scott Baio
Horace "Stubbs" Wilmington
.... George Pentecost
Hillary S. Prentiss ....Taaffe O'Connell
Arkansas ....Rhonda Bates
Lovely Carson ....Bond Gideon
Jackie Outlaw ....Gerri Reddick
Gladys "Cochise" Littlefeather
.... Shirley Kirkes
Sylvia Silver ....Antoinette Yuskis
Misty Karamazov ....Jill Owens
Bridget Muldoon ....Elaine Bolton
Arnold ....Pat Morita

Nancy Blansky was den mother to a bevy of beautiful Las Vegas showgirls in this short-lived comedy. In addition to keeping order in the chaotic apartment complex where they all lived, Nancy staged the girls' big numbers at the Oasis Hotel, where her boss—the second-in-command at the hotel—was Horace Wilmington. Emilio, the *maître d'*, was Nancy's boy friend. To help Nancy defray the costs of her apartment, Sunshine and Bambi shared it with her, along with her nephews Joey DeLuca (a choreographer) and leering, 12-year-old ("going on 28") Anthony. Anthony was forever trying to make time with Bambi, who much to his chagrin treated him like a kid brother, as did almost all of Nancy's girls. Also sharing Nancy's apartment was a huge Great Dane named Black Jack.

Pat Morita, after the failure of his series *Mr. T. and Tina*, was added to the cast as Arnold, the same name (and virtually the same character) he had had in a similar supporting role on *Happy Days*. There he had run a drive-in restaurant, while here he ran the coffee shop at the Oasis. His presence on *Blansky's Beauties* gave both him and star Nancy Walker the dubious distinction of being in two program failures in the same season; she had starred in *The Nancy Walker Show* five months before the premiere of *Blansky's Beauties*.

BLIND DATE

Audience Participation

FIRST TELECAST: *May 5, 1949*

LAST TELECAST: *September 15, 1953*

BROADCAST HISTORY:

May 1949–Jul 1949, ABC Thu 7:30–8:00
Jul 1949–Sep 1949, ABC Thu 9:30–10:00
Sep 1949–Feb 1950, ABC Fri 8:30–9:00
Mar 1950–Jun 1950, ABC Thu 9:00–9:30
Aug 1950–Sep 1951, ABC Thu 9:30–10:00
Jun 1952–Jul 1952, NBC Sat 9:00–9:30
May 1953–Sep 1953, DUM Tue 8:00–8:30

EMCEE:

Arlene Francis (1949–1952)
Melvyn Douglas (May–Jun 1953)
Jan Murray (Jun–Sep 1953)

REGULAR:

Ray Bloch Orchestra (1953)

College boys attempted to win a date with an unseen—but beautiful—model in this audience-participation program, which was adapted from the radio series of the same name. The boys and their quarry were separated by a wall, but they could talk to each other via a special telephone hookup. The boys with the best "line" won the date and a night on the town. During the Korean War the program did its patriotic bit by substituting eager young servicemen for the college crowd, as its radio predecessor had done during World War II.

After a two-year run on ABC, *Blind Date* returned in 1952 as an NBC summer replacement and in 1953 as a DuMont summer show. The DuMont version began under the title *Your Big Moment*, with a slightly different format; the host helped arrange blind dates for people writing in requesting a certain type of individual—a sort of TV dating service. After a few weeks the title was changed back to *Blind Date* and the duties of host passed from Melvyn Douglas to Jan Murray.

BLONDIE

Situation Comedy

FIRST TELECAST: *January 4, 1957*

LAST TELECAST: *January 9, 1969*

BROADCAST HISTORY:

Jan 1957–Sep 1957, NBC Fri 8:00–8:30
Sep 1968–Jan 1969, CBS Thu 7:30–8:00

CAST:

1957

Dagwood Bumstead .... Arthur Lake
Blondie .... Pamela Britton
J. C. Dithers .... Florenz Ames
Alexander .... Stuffy Singer
Cookie .... Ann Barnes
Cora Dithers .... Elvia Allman
Herb Woodley .... Hal Peary
Mr. Beasley .... Lucien Littlefield

1968

Dagwood Bumstead .... Will Hutchins
Blondie .... Patricia Harty
J. C. Dithers .... Jim Backus
Alexander .... Peter Robbins
Cookie .... Pamelyn Ferdin
Cora Dithers .... Henny Backus
Tootsie Woodley .... Bobbi Jordan
Mr. Beasley .... Bryan O'Bourne

There were two attempts to bring to television the adventures of the Bumstead household, long a favorite of comic-strip readers and movie fans. In 1957 NBC brought Dagwood, Blondie, their children Alexander and Cookie, and Daisy and the other dogs to TV. Arthur Lake, the Dagwood of this version, had played the role in the movie series of the 1940s. The stories were all familiar to regular readers of the strip, with Dagwood getting into misunderstandings both at home and at work with Mr. Dithers, his boss. CBS gave *Blondie* a second chance a decade later, with a completely different cast, but that version also failed to catch on.

BLUE ANGEL, THE

Variety

FIRST TELECAST: *July 6, 1954*
LAST TELECAST: *October 12, 1954*
BROADCAST HISTORY:

Jul 1954–Aug 1954, CBS Tue 10:30–11:00
Sep 1954–Oct 1954, CBS Tue 8:30–9:00

HOST:

Orson Bean

This variety series was the 1954 summer replacement for *See It Now*. In a nightclub setting patterned after the famous Blue Angel in the 1930 movie of the same title, host Orson Bean introduced and chatted with the various guest stars and occasionally added his own humor to the show. After *See It Now* returned to the air, *The Blue Angel* was given an additional four-week run at an earlier time.

BLUE KNIGHT, THE

Police Drama

FIRST TELECAST: *December 17, 1975*
LAST TELECAST: *October 27, 1976*
BROADCAST HISTORY:

Dec 1975–Oct 1976, CBS Wed 10:00–11:00

CAST:

Bumper Morgan .... George Kennedy
Sgt. Newman .... Phillip Pine
Sgt. Cabe (1976) .... Charles Siebert
Lt. Hauser (1976) .... Lin McCarthy

Joseph Wambaugh, the author of the novel *The Blue Knight*, had once been a member of the Los Angeles Police Department, and his portrayal of police officers at work bore a note of strong realism missing from many TV police series. Wambaugh's first brush with TV was as consultant for NBC's police anthology *Police Story*, where he continued to write about the day-to-day world of big-city cops. Bumper Morgan, *The Blue Knight's* leading chararacter, first came to television in an NBC mini-series of the same name in the spring of 1973, with William Holden in the lead role. In both the mini-series and the series itself, Bumper Morgan was a cop who walked his beat, had no squad car for transportation, and knew virtually everyone in his territory. He was not beyond overlooking the existence of "good" prostitutes and other harmless types living on the fringes of the law, for his main concern was maintaining order in his inner-city neighborhood. He was stubborn, loyal, and determined, often resorting to physical force when it served his needs. An old-fashioned cop, he had a certain amount of trouble adjusting to the red tape and concern for suspects' rights that had grown up over the years.

BLUE LIGHT

Spy Drama

FIRST TELECAST: *January 12, 1966*
LAST TELECAST: *August 31, 1966*
BROADCAST HISTORY:

Jan 1966–Aug 1966, ABC Wed 8:30–9:00

CAST:

David March .... Robert Goulet
Suzanne Duchard .... Christine Carere

Filmed in Germany and set in Europe during World War II, *Blue Light* was the story of American espionage agent David March. March posed as a foreign correspondent who had officially renounced his American citizenship, but he actually belonged to a highly secret organization called "Code: Blue Light," whose purpose was to infiltrate the German high command and pass information on to the Allies. In addition to eluding German counterintelligence, who managed to uncover and execute 17 members of the Blue Light unit, March also had to watch out for Allied intelligence agencies, who never seemed to realize that he was on their side. Suzanne Duchard was his Girl Friday.

BLUE MEN, THE

see *Brenner*

BLUE RIBBON BOUTS

see *Boxing*

BLUES BY BARGY

Music

FIRST TELECAST: *April 23, 1949*
LAST TELECAST: *April 22, 1950*
BROADCAST HISTORY:

Apr 1949–Aug 1949, CBS Sat 7:45–8:00
Aug 1949–Feb 1950, CBS Sat 7:45–7:55
Mar 1950–Apr 1950, CBS Sat 7:15–7:30

HOSTESS:

Jean Bargy

Jean Bargy, daughter of veteran pianist-conductor Roy Bargy, sang ballads and played the piano in this short musical interlude that ran for a full year on CBS. She was also seen locally in New York on other nights of the week in an end-of-the-evening "filler" program on WCBS-TV.

BOB & CAROL & TED & ALICE

Situation Comedy

FIRST TELECAST: *September 26, 1973*
LAST TELECAST: *November 7, 1973*
BROADCAST HISTORY:

Sep 1973–Nov 1973, ABC Wed 8:00–8:30

CAST:

Bob Sanders .... Robert Urich
Carol Sanders .... Anne Archer
Ted Henderson .... David Spielberg
Alice Henderson .... Anita Gillette
Sean Sanders, son .... Brad Savage
Elizabeth Henderson, daughter
.... Jodie Foster

This comedy concerned two Los Angeles couples who were close friends, but rather distant in values and attitudes. Filmmaker Bob Sanders and his wife Carol were in their twenties, young, aware, and "with it." Lawyer Ted Henderson and his wife Alice, in their thirties, were much more conventional. Overly cute stories about nude swimming, premarital sex, and unmarried friends living together helped hasten this generation-gap comedy to an early end. The program was based on the movie of the same name.

BOB AND RAY

Comedy Variety

FIRST TELECAST: *November 26, 1951*
LAST TELECAST: *September 28, 1953*
BROADCAST HISTORY:

Nov 1951–Feb 1952, NBC Mon–Fri 7:15–7:30
Feb 1952–May 1952, NBC Tue/Thu 7:15–7:30
Jul 1952–Aug 1952, NBC Sat 7:30–8:00
Apr 1953–Sep 1953, NBC Mon 7:30–7:45

REGULARS:

Bob Elliott
Ray Goulding
Audrey Meadows
Cloris Leachman (1952)

Satirists Bob Elliott and Ray Goulding were already well known to radio audiences when they first appeared on television in the early 1950s. Although their gentle, intelligent humor had always relied more on puns and vocal delivery than on sight gags, they nevertheless adapted well enough to the new medium to survive nearly two years on NBC, first on a Monday-through-Friday show, then on Tuesdays and Thursdays, and later once a week. Among their stock characters were Mary Margaret McGoon, cooking "expert," commentator, and all-purpose giver of advice; Tex, the drawling cowboy; and an assortment of travesties on current radio and TV personalities. Singer and actress Audrey Meadows played the part of Linda Lovely in Bob and Ray's continuing satire of soap operas. During the summer of 1952, when the show served as summer replacement for the soap opera *One Man's Family* (their version was *One Feller's Family*), Miss Meadows' place was taken by Cloris Leachman. Her primary role was in their spoof *Mary Backstage, Noble Wife* (a takeoff on the indomitable heroine of the radio serial *Mary Noble, Backstage Wife*).

Audrey Meadows returned to the cast in the spring of 1953.

BOB CRANE SHOW, THE

Situation Comedy

FIRST TELECAST: *March 6, 1975*

LAST TELECAST: *June 19, 1975*

BROADCAST HISTORY:

Mar 1975–Jun 1975, NBC Thu 8:30–9:00

CAST:

Bob Wilcox ....Bob Crane
Ellie Wilcox ....Trisha Hart
Marvin Susman ....Todd Susman
Dean Lyle Ingersoll ....Jack Fletcher
Mr. Busso ....Ronny Graham
Pam Wilcox ....Erica Petal
Jerry Mallory ....James Sutorius

In this short-lived series, Bob Crane played a fortyish insurance executive who abruptly decided to quit his job and enter medical school. The family pitched in, but the problems inherent in being twice the age of the other students and dependent on his working wife Ellie created constant comic situations, as did such resident characters as the overzealous Dean Ingersoll and nutty landlord Mr. Busso.

BOB CROSBY SHOW, THE

Musical Variety

FIRST TELECAST *June 14, 1958*

LAST TELECAST: *September 6, 1958*

BROADCAST HISTORY:

Jun 1958–Sep 1958, NBC Sat 8:00–9:00

REGULARS:

Bob Crosby
The Bobcats
Gretchen Wyler

Singer-bandleader Bob Crosby hosted and starred in this 1958 summer replacement for *The Perry Como Show*. With Bob were his band, The Bobcats, and musical-comedy star Gretchen Wyler.

BOB CUMMINGS SHOW, THE

Situation Comedy

FIRST TELECAST: *January 2, 1955*

LAST TELECAST: *September 15, 1959*

BROADCAST HISTORY:

Jan 1955–Sep 1955, NBC Sun 10:30–11:00
Jul 1955–Sep 1957, CBS Thu 8:00–8:30
Sep 1957–Sep 1959, NBC Tue 9:30–10:00

CAST:

Bob Collins ....Bob Cummings
Margaret MacDonald ...Rosemary DeCamp
Charmaine "Shultzy" Schultz
..........................Ann B. Davis
Chuck MacDonald ......Dwayne Hickman
Pamela Livingston ....Nancy Kulp
Paul Fonda ....Lyle Talbot
Collette DuBois ....Lisa Gaye
Francine Williams (1955–1956)
.........................Diane Jergens
Harvey Helm (1955–1958) ...King Donovan
Ruth Helm (1956–1958) ....Mary Lawrence
Mary Beth Hall (1956–1957)
.......................Gloria Marshall
Shirley Swanson (1956–1959)
.............................Joi Lansing
Olive Sturgess (1956–1957)
........................Carol Henning
Ingrid Goude, Miss Sweden 1956 (1957–1958) ....Herself
Tammy Johnson (1959)
................Tammy Lea Marihugh

Clean-cut Bob Cummings played swinging bachelor Bob Collins in this comedy about a professional photographer who spent all his working time with beautiful models. In his spare time Bob squired the lovely ladies around town, but he never seemed able to settle on any one woman, causing endless problems at home and in the "harem." Bob lived with his widowed sister Margaret and her son Chuck; Margaret never quite understood her brother's social life, and Chuck was always trying to get in on Uncle Bob's action, despite the fact that he had attractive, wholesome girl friends of his own (Francine and later Olive). Bob's devoted assistant was Shultzy, who had a crush on her boss but couldn't compete with glamorous models like Collette, Mary Beth, Shirley, and Ingrid.

Bob had his own private plane and occasionally flew to his home town of Joplin, Missouri, to visit his grandfather, Josh Collins (also played by Bob Cummings). Despite his age, the elder Collins had not lost his eye for the ladies, which he proved when it was his turn to visit his grandson—and all the sexy young models at the photography studio. When this series moved to daytime after concluding its evening run, the title was changed to *Love That Bob*, the same title later used in syndication.

BOB HOPE PRESENTS THE CHRYSLER THEATRE

Dramatic Anthology

FIRST TELECAST: *September 27, 1963*
LAST TELECAST: *September 6, 1967*
BROADCAST HISTORY:
Sep 1963–Sep 1965, NBC Fri 8:30–9:30
Sep 1965–Sep 1967, NBC Wed 9:00–10:00
HOST:
Bob Hope

A mixed bag of drama, variety, and "event" specials, all involving Bob Hope in one role or another. In addition to serving as host on the dramatic telecasts, he starred in several of them. Among the more memorable telecasts of the series were "One Day in the Life of Ivan Denisovich," starring Jason Robards, Jr., Albert Paulson, and Harold J. Stone (from the novel by Alexander Solzhenitsyn, later made into a movie); "The Seven Little Foys," with Mickey Rooney, Eddie Foy, Jr., and the Osmond Brothers; and "Think Pretty," a musical with Fred Astaire and Barrie Chase. Performers who starred in at least two of the episodes in this series were Peter Falk, Hugh O'Brien, Shelley Winters, Cliff Robertson, John Cassavetes, Jack Lord, William Shatner, Angie Dickinson, Suzanne Pleshette, Robert Stack, Dina Merrill, Darren McGavin, Broderick Crawford, and Stuart Whitman.

The variety shows were pure Hope, full of his topical one-liners, beautiful girls, sports heroes, and elaborate skits. The title of the variety hours was altered slightly to *Chrysler Presents a Bob Hope Special*. The highlight of the year, however, must be classed as one of TV's annual "events." This was the Bob Hope Christmas Show, filmed before an audience of G.I.'s in Vietnam and carried as a 90-minute special telecast in January.

BOB NEWHART SHOW, THE

Comedy Variety
FIRST TELECAST: *October 11, 1961*
LAST TELECAST: *June 13, 1962*
BROADCAST HISTORY:
Oct 1961–Jun 1962, NBC Wed 10:00–11:00
HOST:
Bob Newhart
REGULARS:
Mickey Manners (1961)
Joe Flynn
Jackie Joseph
Andy Albin
Dan Sorkin
Kay Westfall (1961)
Jack Grinnage (1961)
Ken Berry (1962)
Paul Weston and His Orchestra

On the heels of the success of his "Button Down Mind" comedy albums, young comic Bob Newhart was given this variety hour in the fall of 1961. Borrowing the format of his nightclub and album routines, each telecast opened with a monologue in which Newhart talked on the telephone with an unseen, and unheard, adversary. The conversation usually concluded with Newhart's regular tag line, "Same to you, fella." The show featured guest musical talent and a large group of comic actors and actresses who appeared in various sketches about contemporary life. None of them were truly regulars appearing on each telecast, but those listed above showed up at least half a dozen times during the season.

BOB NEWHART SHOW, THE

Situation Comedy
FIRST TELECAST: *September 16, 1972*
LAST TELECAST: *August 26, 1978*
BROADCAST HISTORY:
Sep 1972–Oct 1976, CBS Sat 9:30–10:00
Nov 1976–Sep 1977, CBS Sat 8:30–9:00
Sep 1977–Apr 1978, CBS Sat 8:00–8:30
Jun 1978–Aug 1978, CBS Sat 8:00–8:30
CAST:
Robert (Bob) Hartley ....Bob Newhart
Emily Hartley ....Suzanne Pleshette
Howard Borden ....Bill Daily
Jerry Robinson ....Peter Bonerz
Carol Kester Bondurant ....Marcia Wallace
Margaret Hoover (1972–1973) .... Patricia Smith
Dr. Bernie Tupperman (1972–1976) .... Larry Gelman
Ellen Hartley (1974–1976) ....Pat Finley
Larry Bondurant (1975–1977) .... Will Mackenzie
Elliot Carlin ....Jack Riley
Mrs. Bakerman ....Florida Friebus
Miss Larson (1972–1973) ...Penny Marshall
Michelle Nardo (1973–1976) .... Renee Lippin
Mr. Peterson (1973–1978) .....John Fiedler
Mr. Gianelli (1972–1973) ......Noam Pitlik
Mr. Vickers (1974–1975) ......Lucien Scott
Mr. Herd (1976–1977) ....Oliver Clark

Bob Hartley was a successful Chicago psychologist who lived in a high-rise apartment with his wife Emily, an elementary schoolteacher. Bob shared the services of his receptionist Carol with a bachelor dentist, Jerry Robinson. Carol was a brash, nutty individual who could dish it out pretty well to both her bosses. In the fall of 1975, she married Larry Bondurant, a travel agent, after a whirlwind courtship. Originally two of the Hartleys' neighbors were seen on a regular basis: Howard Borden, a divorced commercial airline pilot who had an annoying habit of barging into their apartment without knocking; and Margaret Hoover, a friend of Emily's. For a period Bob's sister Ellen lived with him and Emily, and at one point almost married Howard, but that passed.

Bob was a very low-key fellow, which was handy at the office but did not always prove effective in dealings with his wife and friends. He had a number of regular patients, including all the above cast of characters from Elliot Carlin to the bottom of the list. Bob's patients had problems ranging from ordinary, everyday neuroses to homosexuality to extreme paranoia. They were all trying to find themselves. The character who appeared most regularly—and the one with the biggest problems—was Elliot, without doubt one of the most neurotic individuals ever seen on television. He was completely lacking in self-confidence, had a persecution complex, and was forever putting himself down.

In addition to treating his patients individually, Bob was a firm believer in group therapy, and his patients interacted in various groups in hilarious fashion.

BOBBIE GENTRY SHOW, THE

Musical Variety

FIRST TELECAST: *June 5, 1974*
LAST TELECAST: *June 26, 1974*
BROADCAST HISTORY:
Jun 1974, CBS Wed 8:00–9:00
REGULARS:
Bobbie Gentry
Michael Greer
Earl Pomerantz
Valri Bromfield

The star and host of this short summer variety series was Country and Western singer Bobbie Gentry, whose biggest hit was "Ode to Billy Joe," a ballad she had written herself.

The series was also known as *Bobbie Gentry's Happiness.*

BOBBY DARIN AMUSEMENT COMPANY, THE

see *Dean Martin Presents the Bobby Darin Amusement Company*

BOBBY DARIN SHOW, THE

Musical Variety

FIRST TELECAST: *January 19, 1973*
LAST TELECAST: *April 27, 1973*
BROADCAST HISTORY:
Jan 1973–Apr 1973, NBC Fri 10:00–11:00
REGULARS:
Bobby Darin
Dick Bakalyan
Geoff Edwards
Tommy Amato

Pop singer Bobby Darin appeared as both a singer and a sketch comedian in this short-lived series. In the sketches he became Groucho, Dusty John the hippie poet, Angie the tenement dweller, or the Godmother. He also performed several musical numbers each week, backed by a full orchestra. A consistent theme of the show was a salute to a different city each week, in song and in blackout comedy sketches.

BOBBY SHERMAN SHOW, THE

see *Getting Together*

BOING BOING SHOW, THE

Cartoon

FIRST TELECAST: *May 30, 1958*
LAST TELECAST: *October 3, 1958*
BROADCAST HISTORY:
May 1958–Oct 1958, CBS Fri 7:30–8:00
NARRATOR:
Bill Goodwin

The Gerald McBoing-Boing cartoon series—a combination of animation and live action—made its debut on CBS in December 1956, on Sunday afternoons. Unable to talk, little Gerald would make himself understood by using pantomime and various noises rather than speech. When this didn't work, actor-announcer Bill Goodwin was always on hand to serve as a live interpreter. The series was aired in prime time during the summer of 1958.

BOLD JOURNEY

Travel Documentary

FIRST TELECAST: *July 16, 1956*
LAST TELECAST: *August 31, 1959*

BROADCAST HISTORY:

Jul 1956–Feb 1957, ABC Mon 7:30–8:00
Feb 1957–Jun 1957, ABC Thu 9:30–10:00
Jun 1957–Aug 1959, ABC Mon 8:30–9:00

HOST:

John Stephenson (1955–1957)
Jack Douglas (1957–1959)

Home movies were shown on this series, but not normal everyday home movies. These films were taken by explorers and adventurers on trips to remote or highly unusual places around the world. The host of the show would introduce each week's guest, interview him about his experiences during the expedition, and then help narrate the film that had been taken during the trip. The show's producer, Jack Douglas, took over as host on October 28, 1957.

BOLD ONES, THE

General Drama

FIRST TELECAST: *September 14, 1969*
LAST TELECAST: *June 22, 1973*
BROADCAST HISTORY:

Sep 1969–Sep 1972, NBC Sun 10:00–11:00
Sep 1972–Jan 1973, NBC Tue 9:00–10:00
May 1973–Jun 1973, NBC Fri 10:00–11:00

The Bold Ones was the umbrella title for a number of rotating series that were aired within the same time slot. During the 1969–1970 season there were three elements in the program: *The New Doctors, The Lawyers,* and *The Protectors.* In its second season, *The Senator* replaced *The Protectors.* For 1971–1972 only two elements were aired—*The New Doctors* and *The Lawyers*—and in its last season the program was composed solely of new episodes of *The New Doctors.* For information on specific elements in this series, see their respective titles.

BON VOYAGE

see *Treasure Quest*

BONANZA

Western

FIRST TELECAST: *September 12, 1959*
LAST TELECAST: *January 16, 1973*
BROADCAST HISTORY:

Sep 1959–Sep 1961, NBC Sat 7:30–8:30
Sep 1961–Sep 1972, NBC Sun 9:00–10:00
May 1972–Aug 1972, NBC Tue 7:30–8:30
Sep 1972–Jan 1973, NBC Tue 8:00–9:00

CAST:

Ben Cartwright .... Lorne Greene
Little Joe Cartwright ...... Michael Landon
"Hoss" Cartwright (1959–1972) .... Dan Blocker
Adam Cartwright (1959–1965) .... Pernell Roberts
Hop Sing .... Victor Sen Yung
Candy (1967–1970, 1972–1973) .... David Canary
Dusty Rhoades (1970–1972) ... Lou Frizzell
Jamie Hunter (1970–1973) .... Mitch Vogel
Griff King (1972–1973) ...... Tim Matheson

THEME SONG:

"Bonanza," by Jay Livingston and Ray Evans

Set in the vicinity of Virginia City, Nevada, during the years of the Civil War, soon after the discovery of the fabulous Comstock Silver Lode, *Bonanza* was the story of a prosperous family of ranchers. Widower Ben Cartwright was the patriarch of the all-male clan and owner of the thousand-square-mile Ponderosa Ranch. Each of his three sons had been borne by a different wife, none of whom were still alive. Adam, the oldest of the half-brothers, was the most serious and introspective, the likely successor to his father as the controlling force behind the sprawling Cartwright holdings. Hoss, the middle son, was a mountain of a man who was as gentle as he was huge, at times naive, and not particularly bright. Little Joe was the youngest, most impulsive, and most romantic of the Cartwright offspring. The adventures of these men, individually and collectively, their dealings with the mining interests and the ranching interests, and the people whose paths crossed theirs made up the stories on *Bonanza.*

The program was not a traditional shoot-em-up Western; it relied more on the relationships between the principals and the stories of the characters played by weekly guest stars than it did on violence. Many of the episodes explored serious dramatic themes.

Bonanza premiered on Saturday night in the fall of 1959, and was the first Western to be televised in color. It was at first only moderately successful, but two years later, when it moved to Sunday night as the replacement for *The Dinah Shore Chevy Show,* it soared in popularity. For most of the 1960s *Bonanza* ranked as one of the highest-rated programs on television, placing number one for three seasons between 1964–1967. Its driving theme song, written by two Hollywood songsmiths who had written many top movie hits of the 1940s and 1950s, was on the hit parade. *Bonanza* finished second only to *Gunsmoke* as the longest-running, most successful Western in the history of television.

There were cast changes over the years. Pernell Roberts left the series at the end of the 1964–1965 season and his role was written out of the show. At the start of the 1967–1968 season a wanderer named Candy was hired as a ranch hand for the Cartwrights and practically became one of the family. Three years later, when Candy left the series (he later returned), two other new cast members arrived to join the Ponderosa household. Dusty Rhoades was a friend of Ben's, and Jamie Hunter, his charge, was an orphaned teenaged son of a rainmaker who had been killed. Prior to the start of production for the 1972–1973 season Dan Blocker died unexpectedly. His loss, coupled with a move to a new day and time, after 11 years on Sunday night, may have contributed to the poor rating performance that resulted in *Bonanza*'s cancellation in the middle of its 14th season.

During the summer of 1972, while *Bonanza* was still being aired on Sundays, reruns from the 1967–1970 period were shown on Tuesdays at 7:30 P.M. under the title *Ponderosa*. *Bonanza* itself moved to Tuesdays that September.

BONINO

Situation Comedy

FIRST TELECAST: *September 12, 1953*
LAST TELECAST: *December 26, 1953*
BROADCAST HISTORY:
Sep 1953–Dec 1953, NBC Sat 8:00–8:30
CAST:

Bonino .... Ezio Pinza
Edward .... Conrad Janis
Doris .... Lenka Peterson
Jerry .... Chet Allen
Jerry (beg. 11/18) .... Donald Harris
Carlo .... Oliver Andes
Francesco .... Gaye Huston
Andrew .... Van Dyke Parks
Martha, the maid .... Mary Wickes
Rusty, the former valet .... Mike Kellin
Walter Rogers .... David Opatashu
John Clinton .... Fred Eisley

This live situation comedy starred the operatic basso Ezio Pinza as Bonino, a world-famous concert singer. Bonino's wife had died, leaving him with eight children to support. He abandoned his professional touring—much to the chagrin of his concert manager, Walter Rogers, and his valet—but found that his children had grown very independent during his absence. Mr. Pinza sang once during each episode.

BONNY MAID VERSATILE VARIETIES

see *Versatile Varieties*

BORDEN SHOW, THE

Various

FIRST TELECAST: *July 6, 1947*
LAST TELECAST: *September 28, 1947*
BROADCAST HISTORY:
Jul 1947–Sep 1947, NBC Sun 9:00–9:30
DIRECTOR:
Fred Coe

The Borden Show was the overall title for a 1947 series, sponsored by Borden, that presented a different format each week. Such "sampler" programs were typical in the early days of TV broadcasting when networks and sponsors alike were experimenting with the new medium. Among the formats tried out on *The Borden Show* were variety shows, dramas, films, and marionette shows. The first telecast, subtitled "Borden Club," is illustrative. Set in an intimate supper club, it opened outside the club with a shot of a group of autograph-seekers besieging an unseen celebrity—who turned out to be Elsie the Borden Cow, in marionette form. The camera then moved inside where emcee Wally Boag entertained with his rubber balloons, followed by singer Lisa Kirk, impressionist Patricia Bright, and the Dominicans dance team.

The Elsie marionette also appeared on other *Borden Show* telecasts, providing a thread of continuity for the series.

BORN FREE

Adventure

FIRST TELECAST: *September 9, 1974*
LAST TELECAST: *December 30, 1974*
BROADCAST HISTORY:
Sep 1974–Dec 1974, NBC Mon 8:00–9:00
CAST:

George Adamson .... Gary Collins
Joy Adamson .... Diana Muldaur

Makedde ....Hal Frederick
Nuru ....Peter Lukoye
Awaru ....Nelson Kajuna
Joe Kanini ....Joseph De Craft

Filmed entirely on location in East Africa, where the action took place, *Born Free* chronicled the adventures of George and Joy Adamson with the lioness Elsa. The Adamsons were game wardens whose job was to watch over the wildlife in the area and protect the animals from poachers and natural disasters. The show was based on the popular book and movie of the same name.

BOSS LADY

Situation Comedy

FIRST TELECAST: *July 1, 1952*

LAST TELECAST: *September 23, 1952*

BROADCAST HISTORY:

Jul 1952–Sep 1952, NBC Tue 9:00–9:30

CAST:

Gwen F. Allen ....Lynn Bari
Gwen's Father ....Nicholas Joy
Jeff Standish ....Glenn Langan
Chester Allen ....Charlie Smith
Aggie ....Lee Patrick
Roger ....Richard Gaines

In this summer replacement for *Fireside Theatre,* Lynn Bari played Gwen F. Allen, the beautiful chief executive of a highly successful construction firm, Hillandale Homes. Her two major problems, around which most of the stories were based, were finding a general manager who would not fall in love with her and maintaining her well-intentioned but inept father in his position as chairman of the board.

BOTH SIDES

Debate

FIRST TELECAST: *March 15, 1953*

LAST TELECAST: *June 21, 1953*

BROADCAST HISTORY:

Mar 1953–Jun 1953, ABC Sun 10:30–11:00

MODERATOR:

Quincy Howe

This public-affairs debate was sponsored by the American Federation of Labor. Prominent politicians, organized into opposing teams of two members each (the debater and his "counsel"), engaged in lively verbal jousting on a major issue of the day. On the first telecast Sen. Hubert Humphrey (D–Minn.) and Sen. Homer Ferguson (R–Mich.) practically tore each other apart.

BOURBON STREET BEAT

Detective Drama

FIRST TELECAST: *October 5, 1959*

LAST TELECAST: *September 26, 1960*

BROADCAST HISTORY:

Oct 1959–Sep 1960, ABC Mon 8:30–9:30

CAST:

Cal Calhoun ....Andrew Duggan
Rex Randolph ....Richard Long
Melody Lee Mercer ....Arlene Howell
Kenny Madison ....Van Williams

Bourbon Street Beat was the least successful of the imitation *77 Sunset Strip* detective shows churned out by Warner Brothers for ABC in the late 1950s and early 1960s. It had the requisite team of detectives (Cal and Rex), the aspiring young junior-grade detective (Kenny), the attractive female (Melody), and was set in an interesting locale (New Orleans), but somehow it just never caught on. The only survivor of the series was Kenny. He decided to move to Miami Beach and set up his own agency. He was seen in the same time slot during the next season as one of the stars of *Surfside Six.*

BOWLING HEADLINERS

Sports

FIRST TELECAST: *January 2, 1949*

LAST TELECAST: *October 30, 1949*

BROADCAST HISTORY:

Jan 1949–Apr 1949, ABC Sun 10:00–10:30
May 1949–Jun 1949, ABC Sun 10:15–11:00
Jul 1949–Oct 1949, ABC Sun 10:30–11:00 (OS)
Oct 1949, ABC Sun 11:00–12:00

ANNOUNCERS:

Al Cirillo
Jimmy Powers
Joe Hasel

This show, broadcast live from the Rego Park Lanes in Queens, New York, has the distinction of being television's first regularly scheduled bowling show. Each week two nationally known professional bowlers competed in matches of a round-robin elimination tournament. There was prize money, but it was minimal by today's standards, since bowling in the late 1940s was still a sport with limited appeal that was trying to change its lower-middle-class image. It was during this period, as a matter of fact, that the first major effort to change bowling terminology was launched to give it universal appeal; "lanes" was substituted for "alleys," "channel ball" for "gutter ball," and so on.

Al Cirillo, who produced the show, was the announcer throughout its run, assisted by sportswriter Jimmy Powers until the middle of March, and by Joe Hasel thereafter. For a two-month period, from mid-July until mid-September, when the heat in an unairconditioned bowling establishment became unbearable, the show took a summer break.

BOWLING STARS

see *National Bowling Champions*

BOXING

Sports

FIRST TELECAST: *November 8, 1946*
LAST TELECAST: *September 11, 1965*
BROADCAST HISTORY:

Monday—
Nov 1946–May 1949, NBC 9:00–Conclusion
Mar 1949–May 1949, DUM 10:00–Conclusion
May 1952–Aug 1956, DUM 9:00–Conclusion
May 1954–May 1955, ABC 9:30–11:00

Tuesday—
Jul 1948–Jan 1949, DUM 9:00–11:00
Jan 1949–Sep 1950, ABC 10:00–Conclusion
Apr 1949–May 1949, DUM 9:30–Conclusion
Feb 1953–Aug 1953, ABC 9:00–10:00

Wednesday—
Jul 1948–Jan 1949, DUM 9:00–11:00
Jun 1949–Aug 1949, DUM 9:30–Conclusion
Oct 1948–May 1949, CBS 9:00–Conclusion
Oct 1949–May 1950, CBS 9:30–Conclusion
Sep 1950–May 1955, CBS 10:00–Conclusion
Jun 1955–Sep 1960, ABC 10:00–Conclusion

Thursday—
Aug 1949–Sep 1950, DUM 9:30–Conclusion
Jan 1952–Jun 1952, ABC 9:30–10:00
Mar 1953–Jun 1953, ABC 9:00–10:00

Friday—
Nov 1946–Jan 1949, NBC 9:30–Conclusion
Jan 1949–May 1949, NBC 10:00–Conclusion
Sep 1949–Jun 1960, NBC 10:00–Conclusion (OS)
Sep 1949–Jul 1950, DUM 10:00–Conclusion
Oct 1963–Sep 1964, ABC 10:00–Conclusion

Saturday—
Jan 1953–Jan 1955, ABC 9:00–Conclusion
Oct 1960–Sep 1963, ABC 10:00—Conclusion

Boxing was an institution on early television for several reasons. It was easy to produce, the camera-coverage area was limited to the relatively small space occupied by the ring, and it had tremendous appeal to the first purchasers of television sets in the late 1940s—bars. Even a TV with a ten-inch screen could become a magnet to sports-minded drinkers. All the great names of the era—Sugar Ray Robinson, Rocky Marciano, Willie Pep, Rocky Graziano, and Archie Moore—appeared on the screen, as well as multitudes of lesser-known boxers who would probably not have had careers if it were not for the voracious appetite of television. Unlike today, when the only interest is in the heavyweight class, boxers in all weight divisions had strong fan appeal when television was new.

There were periods in the late 1940s and early 1950s when it was common to have as many as five or six network boxing shows on during the same week, not to mention the local shows that were also available. Those who complain about the saturation of football on television today need only look at the boxing picture in the early 1950s to see what *real* saturation was. A summary of the boxing shows carried by each network follows.

NBC was the first network to carry televised boxing. *Cavalcade of Sports* began on local TV in the mid-1940s and added network coverage in 1946, with Bob Stanton at the TV mike from St. Nicholas Arena in Manhattan on Mondays and from Madison Square Garden on Fridays. The Friday telecasts, which became the *Gillette Cavalcade of Sports* in 1948, ran for 14 years, by far the longest continuous run of any televised boxing show. When Stanton, who worked with Ray Forrest for part of the 1948–1949 season, left the series in 1949, he was replaced by Jimmy Powers. Powers remained the principal NBC announcer until the show went off the air in 1960. In its later years, the *Gillette Cavalcade of Sports* traveled all over the country to cover top bouts, and other announcers occasionally substituted for Powers.

CBS's boxing coverage was aired exclusively on Wednesday nights. Russ Hodges was the first CBS announcer for bouts originating from White Plains, New York, and St. Nicholas Arena. The series was given the title *International Boxing Club Bouts* in the fall of 1949, not long before Hodges left to be replaced by Ted Husing in March 1950. Husing remained for roughly 16 months; Hodges returned in the summer of 1951, when the title was changed to *Blue Ribbon Bouts;* and Jack Drees arrived in 1954. Drees and Hodges shared announcing duties during that last CBS year, and both stayed with the show when ABC took it over in June 1955. As was true on NBC, origination was extended beyond the New York area in the early 1950s, to locations where the most promotable fights were being staged.

DuMont's programming was heavy with both boxing and wrestling in the late 1940s and early 1950s. With its limited finances, inexpensive programming that had a ready audience was something that DuMont could not resist. Dennis James was DuMont's sports announcer for boxing and wrestling. The DuMont boxing shows, however, could not afford traveling to locations where there were no DuMont stations, so that most of them originated from the New York area. Dennis James covered bouts from Jamaica Arena, Queens, on Mondays, from Park Arena on Tuesdays, from White Plains, New York, on Wednesdays, and from Sunnyside Gardens and Dexter Arena on Thursdays. The longest-running DuMont boxing show, however, did not have James at the helm. Ted Husing was the announcer when *Boxing from Eastern Parkway* (Brooklyn) went on the air in May 1952. He left in March 1953 and was replaced by young Chris Schenkel. When ABC picked up the show in May 1954, DuMont and Schenkel moved shop to St. Nicholas Arena where they stayed until DuMont went out of the network business in 1956. *Boxing from St. Nicholas Arena* was the last DuMont network series, its last network telecast coming on August 6, 1956, though it remained on as a local program in New York for another two months.

ABC's first major entry into the boxing wars came with *Tomorrow's Boxing Champions,* a show featuring young, unranked boxers that was aired on Tuesday nights in 1949. It originated from Chicago, with Bob Elson at the mike. January 1952 brought *Meet the Champ,* a collection of bouts involving members of the armed forces, on Thursday nights, with Wally Butterfield announcing. In 1953 ABC's boxing coverage really expanded. In January *The Saturday Night Fights* premiered, with Bill Stern doing the blow-by-blow; Jack Gregson took over from Stern in the fall. In February a series of *Boxing from Ridgewood Grove* bouts began on Tuesdays, with Jason Owen as the announcer in the first month and Bob Finnegan taking over until its cancellation in August. March brought *Motor City Boxing* from Detroit for three months of Thursdays, with Don Wattrick at the mike. In 1954 *Boxing from Eastern Parkway* moved to ABC from DuMont, with the announcing chores taken over by Tommy Logran, occasionally helped by Bob Finnegan and Fred Sayles. ABC also picked up the CBS *Blue Ribbon Bouts* when it was canceled and renamed it *The Wednesday Night Fights.* Russ Hodges and Jack Drees both stayed with the show, but Hodges left in October and Drees was the only regular announcer for the five years it stayed on ABC. When it moved to Saturday, and eventually Friday, the title was again changed, this time to *The Fight of the Week.* Don Dunphy, released from NBC radio with the cancellation of the *Cavalcade of Sports* show on Fridays, took over the television commentary in the fall of 1960 and remained with it until it faded in September 1964, the last regular nighttime network boxing series on the air.

BRACKEN'S WORLD

General Drama

FIRST TELECAST: *September 19, 1969*
LAST TELECAST: *December 25, 1970*
BROADCAST HISTORY:

Sep 1969–Dec 1970, NBC Fri 10:00–11:00

CAST:

Sylvia Caldwell (1969–1970) .... Eleanor Parker
Kevin Grant .... Peter Haskell
Davey Evans (1969–1970) ..... Dennis Cole
Laura Deane .... Elizabeth Allen
John Bracken (voice only) (1969–1970) .... Warren Stevens
John Bracken (1970–1971) ... Leslie Nielsen
Diane Waring .... Laraine Stephens
Rachel Holt .... Karen Jensen
Paulette Douglas .... Linda Harrison
Marjorie Grant (1969–1970) .. Madlyn Rhue
Tom Hudson (1970–1971) ... Stephen Oliver
Grace Douglas (1970–1971) .... Jeanne Cooper
Mark Grant (1970–1971) .... Gary Dubin

The personal and professional lives of fictitious people in the movie business were the focus of this melodrama. Filmed at 20th Century Fox, and featuring many real-life movie stars in cameo roles, *Bracken's World* was set at fictional Century Studios. Studio head John Bracken, though never seen, dominated the lives of the principals in the series through his executive secretary, Sylvia Caldwell. Among his many scheming underlings were writer-producer Kevin Grant; Laura Deane, who ran the studio's new-talent school; stunt man Davey Evans; and a number of aspiring young actors and starlets.

Bracken's World was only moderately successful during its first season, and so major surgery was performed at the start of the second. Bracken, now played by Leslie Nielsen, became visible as he struggled to guide the studio through troubled economic times. Gone were his executive secretary, stunt man Evans, and Kevin Grant's alcoholic wife Marjorie—who was killed off in the season's premiere episode. The series itself outlived her by only three months.

BRADY BUNCH, THE

Situation Comedy

FIRST TELECAST: *September 26, 1969*
LAST TELECAST: *August 30, 1974*
BROADCAST HISTORY:

Sep 1969–Sep 1970, ABC Fri 8:00–8:30
Sep 1970–Sep 1971, ABC Fri 7:30–8:00
Sep 1971–Aug 1974, ABC Fri 8:00–8:30

CAST:

Mike Brady .... Robert Reed
Carol Brady .... Florence Henderson
Alice .... Ann B. Davis
Marcia Brady .... Maureen McCormick
Jan Brady .... Eve Plumb
Cindy Brady .... Susan Olsen
Greg Brady .... Barry Williams
Peter Brady .... Christopher Knight
Bobby Brady .... Mike Lookinland

The Brady Bunch was one of the last of the old-style fun-around-the-house situation comedies, full of well-scrubbed children, trivial adventures, and relentlessly middle-class parents. The premise here was a kind of conglomerate family, formed by a widow with three daughters who married a widower with three sons; a nutty housekeeper, Alice, thrown in to act as referee; plus, of course, the family cat and a shaggy dog, Tiger.

All of these smiling faces lived in a four-bedroom, two-bathroom house in the Los Angeles suburbs, from which Dad pursued his nice, clean profession as a designer and architect. Typical stories revolved around the children going steady, family camping trips, competition for the family telephone (at one point Dad installed a pay phone), and of course war in the bathroom.

The children ranged in age from 7 to 14 at the series' start, and the oldest son, Greg, played by Barry Williams, soon became something of a teenage idol; he was receiving 6,500 fan letters per week during 1971. Barry and several of the others tried to parlay their TV success into recording careers in the early 1970s, but without notable success.

BRADY BUNCH HOUR, THE

Comedy Variety

FIRST TELECAST: *January 23, 1977*
LAST TELECAST: *May 25, 1977*
BROADCAST HISTORY:

Jan 1977–Feb 1977, ABC Sun 7:00–8:00
Mar 1977–Apr 1977, ABC Mon 8:00–9:00
May 1977, ABC Wed 8:00–9:00

CAST:

Carol Brady .... Florence Henderson
Mike Brady .... Robert Reed
Alice .... Ann B. Davis
Marcia Brady .... Maureen McCormick
Jan Brady .... Geri Reischl
Cindy Brady .... Susan Olsen
Greg Brady .... Barry Williams
Peter Brady .... Christopher Knight
Bobby Brady .... Mike Lookinland

This was an attempt to revive the *Brady Bunch* comedy of the early 1970s, in hour-long format. The original cast returned intact except for Eve Plumb, who was replaced by Geri Reischl as Jan. The format now contained more variety than situation comedy, as father Mike had given up his career as an architect so that the family could star in their own TV variety show. The setting also changed, to a new beachfront home in California, and a group called the Water Follies Swimmers made regular appearances.

Originally scheduled to be seen only every fifth week in the *Nancy Drew/Hardy Boys Mysteries* time slot on Sunday, *The Brady Bunch Hour* later turned up in various ABC time periods on different nights.

BRAINS & BRAWN

Quiz/Audience Participation

FIRST TELECAST: *September 13, 1958*

LAST TELECAST: *December 27, 1958*

BROADCAST HISTORY:

Sep 1958–Dec 1958, NBC Sat 10:30–11:00

EMCEE:

Jack Lescoulie ("brawn")
Fred Davis ("brains")

Each team on this unusual show consisted of an athlete (the "brawn") and someone with high intellectual skills (the "brains"). The teams were determined by lot before the show went on the air. Two such teams were then pitted against each other, the "brawn" competing in athletic events and the "brains" answering questions. Two emcees handled the two parts of the competition.

BRANDED

Western

FIRST TELECAST: *January 24, 1965*

LAST TELECAST: *September 4, 1966*

BROADCAST HISTORY:

Jan 1965–Sep 1966, NBC Sun 8:30–9:00 (OS)

CAST:

Jason McCord ....Chuck Conners

Set in America in the 1880s, this series was the story of Jason McCord, who had had a successful military career following his graduation from West Point. He had risen to the rank of captain before he was dismissed from the service after being unjustly accused of cowardice. McCord traveled around the country in his attempt to gain proof that he was not a coward. In his travels he encountered people who believed in him and others who accepted his cowardice as fact. His previous experience as an engineer and mapmaker also led him into assorted adventures.

BRAVE EAGLE

Western

FIRST TELECAST: *September 28, 1955*

LAST TELECAST: *June 6, 1956*

BROADCAST HISTORY:

Sep 1955–Jun 1956, CBS Wed 7:30–8:00

CAST:

Brave Eagle ....Keith Larsen
Keena ....Keena Nomkeena
Morning Star ....Kim Winona
Smokey Joe ....Bert Wheeler

In a turnabout from the normal pattern of TV Westerns, *Brave Eagle* presented the white man's expansion into the American Southwest during the middle of the 19th century from the Indian point of view. Brave Eagle was the young chief of a peaceful tribe of Cheyenne, Keena was his foster son, Morning Star was the attractive young Indian girl in whom he showed some romantic interest, and Smokey Joe was an old half-breed who was the tribal sage. Stories told in the series detailed their struggles with nature, other Indian tribes, and the ever-encroaching white man.

BREAK THE BANK

Quiz

FIRST TELECAST: *October 22, 1948*

LAST TELECAST: *January 15, 1957*

BROADCAST HISTORY:

Oct 1948–Sep 1949, ABC Fri 9:00–9:30
Oct 1949–Jan 1952, NBC Wed 10:00–10:30
Jan 1952–Feb 1953, CBS Sun 9:30–10:00
Jun 1953–Sep 1953, NBC Tue 8:30–9:00
Jan 1954–Oct 1955, ABC Sun 10:00–10:30
Oct 1955–Jun 1956, ABC Wed 9:30–10:00
Oct 1956–Jan 1957, NBC Tue 10:30–11:00

HOST:

Bert Parks

CO-HOST:

Bud Collyer (1948–1953)

PAYING TELLER:

Janice Wolfe (1949–1953)
Janice Gilbert (1953–1957)

ORCHESTRA:

Peter Van Steeden

This popular quiz show began on radio in 1945 and started television simulcasts in 1948. Bert Parks, who had begun as one of several radio hosts in 1945, when he was fresh out of the army, was closely associated with the program throughout its television run.

Break the Bank was always considered a big-money show, with cash prizes sometimes running over $10,000 even in the early days. The questions were tough, too. Contestants, who were drawn from the studio audience, chose a category and were asked a series of questions in that category for increasing amounts of money. If successful, they eventually had a chance to "break the bank," which was usually worth thousands of dollars (depending on how long it was since it had last been "broken").

A number of gimmicks were added to the show from time to time, including guest celebrities during the early years, and a "Wish Bowl Couple." These were viewers chosen by postcard drawing who won an expense-paid trip to New York to compete on the show.

In October 1956 *Break the Bank* jumped on the super-money bandwagon and was renamed *Break the $250,000 Bank*. Instead of studio contestants, "experts" were brought in to answer complex questions worth thousands of dollars. They did this while standing in a specially designed "Hall of Knowledge" and could sometimes be assisted by members of their families seated to the side of the stage. Among the unusual contestants during this period were two Hungarian refugees just arrived in the United States (their category was "Fight for Freedom") and the veteran actress-singer Ethel Waters, who said she needed the money to pay off back taxes (she won $10,000). No one ever reached $250,000 during the program's brief run.

There was a daytime version of *Break the Bank* in the 1950s and, briefly, in the 1970s.

BREAKING POINT

Medical Drama

FIRST TELECAST: *September 16, 1963*

LAST TELECAST: *September 7, 1964*

BROADCAST HISTORY:

Sep 1963–Sep 1964, ABC Mon 10:00–11:00

CAST:

Dr. McKinley Thompson .... Paul Richards
Dr. Edward Raymer .... Eduard Franz

McKinley Thompson, called Dr. Mac by almost everyone on the staff, was the chief resident psychiatrist at fictitious York Hospital in Los Angeles. His superior, the director of the hospital's psychiatric clinic, was Dr. Edward Raymer. Running what amounted to an out-patient service for the emotionally distraught, they tried to help the various people who came to the clinic. Their roles in the series were rather peripheral, as the action dealt more with the situations that had caused people to seek their help than with life at the hospital.

BRENNER

Police Drama

FIRST TELECAST: *June 6, 1959*

LAST TELECAST: *September 13, 1964*

BROADCAST HISTORY:

Jun 1959–Oct 1959, CBS Sat 9:00–9:30
Jun 1961–Sep 1961, CBS Mon 10:30–11:00
Jun 1962–Sep 1962, CBS Thu 9:00–9:30
May 1964–Sep 1964, CBS Sun 9:30–10:00

CAST:

Det. Lt. Roy Brenner .... Edward Binns
Officer Ernie Brenner ..... James Broderick

Filmed entirely on location in New York, *Brenner* was the story of two generations of police officers learning from each other. Roy Brenner was a career cop who had risen to the rank of detective lieutenant. His son Ernie was a rookie patrolman. The approach of the veteran father, who had been hardened by the experiences of more than 20 years on the force, was often radically different from that of the young, inexperienced, and idealistic son. Nevertheless, their love and respect for each other enabled both of them to grow as individuals and learn from each other. The series was produced in 1959 and selected reruns were aired by CBS in the summers of 1961, 1962, and 1964. In order to freshen the series during its 1964 run, ten new episodes were produced and aired in addition to the original 1959 shows.

BRIAN KEITH SHOW, THE

Situation Comedy

FIRST TELECAST: *September 15, 1972*

LAST TELECAST: *August 30, 1974*

BROADCAST HISTORY:

Sep 1972–Aug 1973, NBC Fri 8:30–9:00
Sep 1973–May 1974, NBC Fri 9:30–10:00
May 1974–Aug 1974, NBC Fri 8:30–9:00

CAST:

Dr. Sean Jamison ....Brian Keith
Dr. Anne Jamison ....Shelley Fabares
Nurse Puni ....Victoria Young
Ronnie (1972–1973) ....Michael Gray
Alfred (1972–1973) ....Steven Hague
Stewart ....Sean Tyler Hall
Dr. Austin Chaffee (1973–1974)
.... Roger Bowen
Mrs. Gruber (1973–1974) ......Nancy Kulp

Titled *The Little People* during its first season, this was a "heartwarming" comedy about two pediatricians, a father and a daughter, who ran a free clinic as well as private practices on the Hawaiian island of Oahu. The concern that the Jamisons had for their "little people" formed the crux of most of the stories. The type of humor was similar to that on *Family Affair*, Mr. Keith's previous hit series. In its second season the situation changed somewhat, as did the title, which became *The Brian Keith Show*. The very proper Dr. Chaffee now shared office space with Sean and found that adjusting to Sean's informality could be rather difficult. Wealthy widow Mrs. Gruber, owner of the free clinic, as well as of much of Hawaii, was added to the cast to help provide problem situations for the easygoing doctor and his attractive and equally competent daughter.

BRIDGET LOVES BERNIE

Situation Comedy

FIRST TELECAST: *September 16, 1972*
LAST TELECAST: *September 8, 1973*
BROADCAST HISTORY:

Sep 1972–Sep 1973, CBS Sat 8:30–9:00

CAST:

Bernie Steinberg ....David Birney
Bridget Fitzgerald Steinberg
.... Meredith Baxter
Sam Steinberg ....Harold J. Stone
Sophie Steinberg ....Bibi Osterwald
Amy Fitzgerald ....Audra Lindley
Walt Fitzgerald ....David Doyle
Uncle Moe ....Ned Glass
Father Mike Fitzgerald ....Robert Sampson
Otis Foster ....William Elliott

This show was part of a wave of "ethnic" comedies in the early 1970s that followed on the success of *All in the Family* and *Sanford and Son*. Bernie was Jewish, a struggling young writer who supplemented his income by driving a cab. Bridget, his young bride, was an elementary schoolteacher whose parents were wealthy Irish Catholics. The couple shared a small apartment above a New York City delicatessen owned by Bernie's parents. The widely divergent ethnic, cultural, and social backgrounds of the Steinberg and Fitzgerald families, and their attempts to reconcile for the sake of the young couple, provided most of the plot situations. Any resemblance to the vintage Broadway play *Abie's Irish Rose* was hardly coincidental.

Despite reasonably good ratings, *Bridget Loves Bernie* was canceled at the end of its first season. One contributing factor may have been the furor created by the unhappiness of religious groups, primarily Jewish, over the show's condoning and publicizing mixed marriages. An interesting sidelight is that the two stars of the series, David Birney and Meredith Baxter, later married each other in real life.

BRINGING UP BUDDY

Situation Comedy

FIRST TELECAST: *October 10, 1960*
LAST TELECAST: *September 25, 1961*
BROADCAST HISTORY:

Oct 1960–Sep 1961, CBS Mon 8:30–9:00

CAST:

Aunt Violet Flower ....Enid Markey
Aunt Iris Flower ....Doro Merande
Buddy Flower ....Frank Aletter

Making his home with two lovable but wacky maiden aunts kept investment counselor Buddy Flower pretty busy. As if he didn't have enough to cope with at the office, when he came home he was likely to discover that they had found the perfect girl for him to marry, had made some other major decision about the way he was to live, or had gotten themselves into some kind of trouble from which he would have to extricate them.

BRISTOL-MYERS TELE-VARIETIES

Various

FIRST TELECAST: *January 5, 1947*
LAST TELECAST: *April 13, 1947*
BROADCAST HISTORY:

Jan 1947–Mar 1947, NBC Sun 8:15–8:30
Mar 1947–Apr 1947, NBC Sun 8:00–8:15

This was a series of short program tryouts by sponsor Bristol-Myers in the new medium of television. The variety show was the most common format, using an assortment of little-known talent, but perhaps the most successful experiment was a TV adaptation in March of Tex and Jinx McCrary's radio talk show, *Hi Jinx.* The McCrarys were naturals for TV, and with their combination of friendly chatter, interviews, and features, they later became two of the leading personalities in the new medium.

Tele-Varieties was first seen as a local show in New York in December 1946.

BROADSIDE

Situation Comedy

FIRST TELECAST: *September 20, 1964*

LAST TELECAST: *September 5, 1965*

BROADCAST HISTORY:

Sep 1964–Sep 1965, ABC Sun 8:30–9:00

CAST:

Lt. (j.g.) Anne Morgan ....Kathy Nolan
Cdr. Rogers Adrian ......Edward Andrews
Lt. Maxwell Trotter ....Dick Sargent
Machinist's Mate Molly McGuire
.... Lois Roberts
Machinist's Mate Selma Kowalski
.... Sheila James
Machinist's Mate Roberta Love
.... Joan Staley
Machinist's Mate Marion Botnik
.... Jimmy Boyd
Ship's Cook 1st Class Stanley Stubbs (1965)
.... Arnold Stang
Ensign Beasley ....George Furth

This military comedy featured a group of U.S. Navy WAVES who were assigned to a South Pacific island during World War II and found themselves surrounded by thousands of sailors and an unappreciative CO. As an experiment, Lt. Morgan and her girls had been sent to Ranakai Island as replacements for male motor pool personnel, but Cdr. Adrian, the base CO, did not appreciate the resulting disruption. Ranakai was one of the quietest posts in the Pacific, and until they arrived Adrian had had a soft tour, complete with a Persian rug in his office, Rolls-Royce staff car, and gourmet meals (prepared by his eccentric but world-famous chef, Stanley Stubbs).

Most episodes consisted of Adrian's attempts to get the WAVES to transfer Stateside, by such clever ploys as cutting off their lipstick supply. Some concerned the "plight" of M/M Marion Botnik, who had been assigned to the WAVES by mistake when a personnel clerk mistook his name for that of a female.

Broadside was produced by the creator of *McHale's Navy,* Edward J. Montagne.

BROADWAY JAMBOREE

Musical Variety

FIRST TELECAST: *May 10, 1948*

LAST TELECAST: *June 28, 1948*

BROADCAST HISTORY:

May 1948–Jun 1948, NBC Mon 8:00–8:30

This short-lived early musical revue was originally conceived to feature an all-black cast, under the title *Broadway Minstrels.* It switched titles after two weeks and thereafter featured both black and white performers.

BROADWAY MINSTRELS

see *Broadway Jamboree*

BROADWAY OPEN HOUSE

Talk/Variety

FIRST TELECAST: *May 29, 1950*

LAST TELECAST: *August 24, 1951*

BROADCAST HISTORY:

May 1950–May 1951, NBC Mon–Fri 11:00–12:00
May 1951–Aug 1951, NBC Tue/Thu/Fri 11:00–12:00

REGULARS:

Jerry Lester
Morey Amsterdam (1950)
Dave Street
Jane Harvey (1950)
Andy Roberts
The Mello Larks
Bob Warren (1951)
Richard Hayes (1951)
Helen Wood (1951)
Elaine Dunn (1951)
Jack Leonard (1951)
Eileen Barton (1951)
Buddy Greco (1951)
The Milton Delugg Quartet
Dagmar
Ray Malone
Wayne Howell
The Honeydreamers
Dell and Abbott (1951)
Estelle Sloane (1951)
Earl Barton (1951)
The Kirby Stone Quintet (1951)
Maureen Cannon (1951)
Marion Colby (1951)
Ray Malone (1951)

Frank Gallop (1951)
Barbara Nichols (1951)

Broadway Open House was the granddaddy of all of television's informal talk shows, and preceded *The Tonight Show* as NBC's post-11 P.M. nightly attraction. Actually, however, it was two shows in one. Jerry Lester was on three days a week (Tuesday, Thursday, and Friday), while Morey Amsterdam was the initial emcee on Mondays and Wednesdays. They each had their own group of regulars, the most famous being the statuesque "dumb" blonde Dagmar, on Lester's nights. Stars were invited to drop in and chat, or perform if they felt like it, and the regulars performed in comedy skits, songs, and dances. There was also by-play with orchestra leader/accordionist Milton Delugg. Delugg was a songwriter as well and at least one of his numbers, "Orange Colored Sky," was plugged so much on this show that it became a major record hit.

Morey Amsterdam left in November 1950, and the cast on his two nights underwent a number of changes. Finally, in May 1951, Jerry Lester also left the show; he was replaced by Jack Leonard as star, and the entire show was cut back to three nights a week. Original cast member Dagmar was retained, new singers, dancers, and musicians were added, and the Kirby Stone Quintet moved over from the canceled Monday and Wednesday show.

The circumstances surrounding Jerry Lester's departure from *Broadway Open House* involved an ongoing feud with Dagmar, the show's biggest star next to Jerry. A young actress named Jennie Lewis (although her real name was Virginia Ruth Egnor), Dagmar had been signed by Jerry to do a walk-on early in the run of the show, reading inane poetry with a deadpan delivery. It was for that part that Jerry renamed her Dagmar. She was an instant hit and became a regular feature, her salary rising quickly to the point where only Jerry made more. A veteran performer, Jerry resented the publicity and popularity of what he felt was his "creation" and tried to minimize her role. In the spring of 1951, to divert attention from Dagmar, he even added another statuesque blonde to the cast, Barbara Nichols (whom he renamed Agathon). The friction became intolerable, for Dagmar had become Jerry's Frankenstein monster, too popular for him to deal with, and Jerry abandoned the series to pursue other interests. Neither the show nor Dagmar's newfound career survived without him.

BROADWAY SPOTLIGHT

Variety

FIRST TELECAST: *March 10, 1949*
LAST TELECAST: *September 4, 1949*
BROADCAST HISTORY:
Mar 1949–Apr 1949, NBC Wed 8:00–8:30
May 1949–Jul 1949, NBC Sun 7:00–7:30
Jul 1949–Sep 1949, NBC Sun 7:30–8:00
HOST:
Danton Walker (Mar–Jun)
Richard Kollmar (Jun–Sep)
REGULARS:
Ving Merlin Orchestra
Joey Faye, comedian (Jun–Sep)
June Taylor Dancers (Jul–Sep)

This live variety program was originally hosted by Broadway columnist Danton Walker, later by radio personality Richard Kollmar. Singers, comedians, and stage actors and actresses appeared as guests, with the emphasis on past and present stars of the Broadway stage. One early feature involved a major star performing one of his or her great successes of the past, together with a newcomer whom that star had discovered. The title of the series varied from *Show Business, Inc.* (March–April) to *Danton Walker's Broadway Scrapbook* (April–June) to *Broadway Spotlight* (June–September).

BROADWAY TO HOLLYWOOD—HEADLINE CLUES

News/Interview/Quiz

FIRST TELECAST: *July 20, 1949*
LAST TELECAST: *July 15, 1954*
BROADCAST HISTORY:
Jul 1949–Sep 1949, DUM Wed 8:30–9:00
Oct 1949–May 1950, DUM Fri 8:30–9:00
May 1950–Jan 1951, DUM Wed 10:00–10:30
Jan 1951–Jul 1954, DUM Thu 8:30–9:00
HOST:
George F. Putnam (1949–1951)
Bill Slater (1951–1953)
Conrad Nagel (1953–1954)

This magazine show featuring news, gossip, and quiz elements ran for five years on the DuMont TV network. Early in the program's history the quiz element was stressed; host-commentator George Putnam would call viewers at home and offer prizes for the correct answers to news-related questions or identification of photos shown on the air. There were also guest celebrities and new talent discoveries; Eddie Fisher is said to have made his first TV appearance on this show.

By the time Bill Slater took over as host in March 1951, the quiz segment had been dropped, and emphasis was placed on late-breaking news stories and timely features on world and national issues and show business. The day assassins attempted to kill President Truman, for instance, *Headline Clues* flew an eyewitness to its New York studios to give a firsthand account of the incident. Human-interest stories were also featured, as in the meeting—on the show—of two doctors who had developed the wonder drug cortisone and a little girl who had been cured of a crippling infirmity by their discovery. New movies and nightclub acts were reviewed, and guest celebrities performed.

First known simply as *Headline Clues*, the program changed its name to *Broadway to Hollywood—Headline Clues* in October 1949.

BROKEN ARROW

Western

FIRST TELECAST: *September 25, 1956*
LAST TELECAST: *September 18, 1960*
BROADCAST HISTORY:

Sep 1956–Sep 1958, ABC Tue 9:00–9:30
Apr 1960–Sep 1960, ABC Sun 7:00–7:30

CAST:

Tom Jeffords .... John Lupton
Cochise .... Michael Ansara
Duffield .... Tom Fadden

The cowboys and Indians got together to battle injustice in this Western, which starred John Lupton as Indian agent Tom Jeffords and Michael Ansara as Apache Chief Cochise. Jeffords was originally an army officer given the assignment of getting the U.S. Mail safely through Apache territory in Arizona. Adopting the novel approach of making friends with the Indians instead of shooting at them, Jeffords soon became blood brother to Cochise. Together they fought both renegades from the Chiricahua Reservation and dishonest "white eyes" who preyed upon the Indians. The show was based on the novel *Blood Brother*, by Elliott Arnold, which had been made into a movie in 1950.

Repeats of *Broken Arrow* were seen on the network on Sunday afternoons in 1959–1960 and in an early-evening time slot during the summer of 1960.

BRONCO

Western

FIRST TELECAST: *September 23, 1958*
LAST TELECAST: *August 20, 1962*
BROADCAST HISTORY:

Sep 1958–Sep 1960, ABC Tue 7:30–8:30
Oct 1960–Aug 1962, ABC Mon 7:30–8:30

CAST:

Bronco Layne .... Ty Hardin

Bronco, as portrayed by newcomer Ty Hardin, was born of the fight between Clint Walker and Warner Brothers Studios over the series *Cheyenne* (see *Cheyenne* for details). When Walker quit his successful series in 1958, Hardin was brought in to replace him. Although the series continued under the title *Cheyenne*, Hardin starred in it as Bronco Layne, an ex-Confederate Army captain who had wandered west after the war in search of adventure. There were no other regulars, but the handsome young Bronco did encounter plenty of interesting characters in his exploits, including Billy the Kid, Jesse James (played by James Coburn), Cole Younger, Belle Starr, and Wild Bill Hickok.

In 1959 Clint Walker returned to *Cheyenne*, and *Bronco* became a separate series. In both the 1958–1959 and 1959–1960 seasons Hardin's series alternated with another western, *Sugarfoot*. Then in 1960 *Bronco* was brought back under the *Cheyenne* umbrella title, as part of a rotating anthology consisting of Walker's *Cheyenne*, Will Hutchin's *Sugarfoot*, and Hardin's *Bronco*; the three stars were seen separately, in different episodes. *Sugarfoot* was dropped from the rotation in 1961, leaving only *Bronco* and *Cheyenne*, to alternate in 1961–1962.

BRONK

Detective Drama

FIRST TELECAST: *September 21, 1975*
LAST TELECAST: *July 18, 1976*
BROADCAST HISTORY:

Sep 1975–Jul 1976, CBS Sun 10:00–11:00

CAST:

Lt. Alex Bronkov .... Jack Palance

Mayor Pete Santori ....Joseph Mascolo
Harry Mark ....Henry Beckman
Sgt. John Webber ....Tony King
Ellen Bronkov ....Dina Ousley

Tough guy Jack Palance, who frequently played heavies in movies, turned contemplative cop for this single-season series. Pipe-smoking Lt. Alex Bronkov had been enlisted by his old friend Pete Santori, mayor of Ocean City, in Southern California, to help clean up that corruption-ridden town. Bronk worked on special assignments from the mayor, with the assistance of fellow officer Sgt. John Webber. Also featured in the cast were retired policeman Harry Mark, a close friend of Bronk's who was now in the auto-junkyard business, and Bronk's crippled daughter Ellen, who had been confined to a wheelchair by an accident that had crippled her and killed Bronk's wife.

BROTHERS, THE

Situation Comedy

FIRST TELECAST: *October 2, 1956*
LAST TELECAST: *September 7, 1958*
BROADCAST HISTORY:
Oct 1956–Mar 1957, CBS Tue 8:30–9:00
Jun 1958–Sep 1958, CBS Sun 7:30–8:00
CAST:
Harvey Box ....Gale Gordon
Gilmore Box ....Bob Sweeney
Dr. Margaret Kleeb ....Ann Morriss
Captain Sam Box ....Frank Orth
Marilee Dorf ....Nancy Hadley
Carl Dorf ....Oliver Blake

Harvey and Gilly Box were two brothers who owned a photography studio in San Francisco. Harvey, the older brother, was somewhat blustery and overbearing, but at heart was a good man whose bark was worse than his bite. Gilly was a shy, naive, and inoffensive soul who seemed happy to let his older brother run things. Both of them had girlfriends whose personalities seemed well matched to those of their men; Harvey's the strong-willed Dr. Margaret Kleeb, and Gilly's the quiet Marilee Dorf. Most of the episodes of *The Brothers* revolved around their social and personal lives, their friends and family. During the summer of 1958, reruns of this series alternated with *Bachelor Father.*

BUCCANEERS, THE

Adventure

FIRST TELECAST: *September 22, 1956*
LAST TELECAST: *September 14, 1957*
BROADCAST HISTORY:
Sep 1956–Sep 1957, CBS Sat 7:30–8:00
CAST:
Captain Dan Tempest ....Robert Shaw
Lt. Beamish ....Peter Hammond

Set in the West Indies during the early 1700s, *The Buccaneers* featured adventure on the high seas as well as swashbuckling on land. After clearing the island of New Providence (Nassau) of pirates, the original governor was sent back to England by the Admiralty and replaced by young Lt. Beamish. Fresh out of the Royal Navy's Midshipman's School, the inexperienced Beamish found that, with Blackbeard threatening to take over the island, the situation there was more than he could handle. To cope with it, he made an ally of Dan Tempest, a reformed pirate who had been pardoned by the previous governor. Tempest helped rout the pirates and enjoyed himself so much in the process that he decided to return permanently to the sea on his ship *The Sultana.* His travels to places as far away as New York, and battles with pirates and Spaniards, provided the central plots of episodes in this series. *The Buccaneers* was filmed entirely in England.

BUCK ROGERS

Science Fiction

FIRST TELECAST: *April 15, 1950*
LAST TELECAST: *January 30, 1951*
BROADCAST HISTORY:
Apr 1950–Sep 1950, ABC Sat 7:00–7:30
Sep 1950–Jan 1951, ABC Tue 8:30–9:00
CAST:
Buck Rogers (1950) ....Kem Dibbs
Buck Rogers (1950-1951) ...Robert Pastene
Wilma Deering ....Lou Prentis
Dr. Huer ....Harry Sothern
Black Barney ....Harry Kingston

This was the TV version of the famous hero of comic books, radio, and movie serials, also known as *Buck Rogers in the Twenty-fifth Century.* As in the other versions Buck alone was responsible for the safety of the universe; aided by various pseudo-scientific gadgets, he always managed to outwit such interstellar villains as Killer

Kane. Lou Prentis played Buck's beautiful companion Wilma; Harry Sothern his ally, the brilliant Dr. Huer; and Harry Kingston his Martian crony, Barney. His home base was Niagara, capital of the world. Handsome Kem Dibbs first played the role of Buck on television with suitable derring-do, but was nevertheless replaced after a few months by Robert Pastene.

Production was on the cheap side, though perhaps not as cheap as for DuMont's long-running hit *Captain Video*, which *Buck Rogers* preceded on Saturdays for a time. *Buck Rogers* was also seen in later years as a local series, consisting of edited versions of the movie serials starring Buster Crabbe in the title role.

BUCKSKIN

Western

FIRST TELECAST: *July 3, 1958*
LAST TELECAST: *August 29, 1965*
BROADCAST HISTORY:

Jul 1958–Sep 1958, NBC Thu 9:30–10:00
Oct 1958–Jan 1959, NBC Fri 7:30–8:00
Jan 1959–Sep 1959, NBC Mon 7:30–8:00
Jul 1965–Aug 1965, NBC Sun 8:30–9:00

CAST:

Jody O'Connell ....Tommy Nolan
Mrs. Annie O'Connell ....Sallie Brophy
Marshal Tom Sellers ....Michael Road

Jody O'Connell was a ten-year-old boy living in his mother's boardinghouse in the frontier town of Buckskin, Montana, in 1880. Annie's boardinghouse was the center of social and business activity for the area, and the series showed life through the eyes of young Jody as he became involved both with guests passing through town and with residents of Buckskin. The series ran for about a year in 1958–1959 and was rerun during the summer of 1965.

BUDWEISER SUMMER THEATRE

see *Movies—Prior to 1961*

BUGS BUNNY/ROADRUNNER SHOW, THE

Cartoon

FIRST TELECAST: *April 27, 1976*
LAST TELECAST: *June 1, 1976*
BROADCAST HISTORY:

Apr 1976–Jun 1976, CBS Tue 8:00–8:30

For a five-week period in the spring of 1976, CBS aired a collection of cartoon shorts from the Warner Brothers cartoon library as a prime-time series. Although titled *The Bugs Bunny/Roadrunner Show*, the series included appearances by such famous cartoon characters as Elmer Fudd, Sylvester and Tweety, Yosemite Sam, Daffy Duck, and Pepe le Pew. Voice characterizations were done by veteran Mel Blanc. This series ran concurrently with other Warner Bros. cartoons that were aired on Saturday mornings by CBS under the same title.

BUGS BUNNY SHOW, THE

Cartoon

FIRST TELECAST: October 11, 1960
LAST TELECAST: *September 25, 1962*
BROADCAST HISTORY:

Oct 1960–Sep 1962, ABC Tue 7:30–8:00

VOICES:

Mel Blanc

Bugs Bunny and the entire Warner Brothers inventory of theatrical cartoon characters first appeared on network television in this prime-time series, which premiered in the fall of 1960; the same season that saw the premiere of ABC's most successful venture in prime-time animation, *The Flintstones*. Along with Bugs were Porky Pig, Tweety and Sylvester, Yosemite Sam, the Roadrunner, Henry Hawk, Hippity Hopper, Daffy Duck, and others. All voices were done by veteran Mel Blanc. By the time this series departed from prime time in September 1962 a Saturday morning version had already started (in April 1962). That Saturday morning version, still on the air, has become the longest continuously running Saturday morning children's program in the history of network television.

BUICK ACTION THEATER

Dramatic Anthology

FIRST TELECAST: *August 22, 1958*
LAST TELECAST: *October 3, 1958*
BROADCAST HISTORY:

Aug 1958–Oct 1958, ABC Fri 9:30–10:00

The plays telecast in this short summer series consisted of filmed reruns of episodes from other anthology series.

BUICK BERLE SHOW, THE

See *Milton Berle Show, The*

BUICK CIRCUS HOUR, THE

Musical Drama

FIRST TELECAST: *October, 7, 1952*

LAST TELECAST: *June 16, 1953*

BROADCAST HISTORY:

Oct 1952–Jun 1953, NBC Tue 8:00–9:00

CAST:

The Clown .... Joe E. Brown
Bill Sothern .... John Raitt
Kim O'Neill .... Dolores Gray
The Ringmaster .... Frank Gallop

Set within the framework of a circus, this was the story of an aging clown who tries to help a young singer, Kim O'Neill, who has just joined the troupe. Kim had joined the circus to be near its owner, Bill Sothern, a boisterous, fun-loving giant of a man with whom she had fallen in love. Musical production numbers as well as real circus acts were featured in this series, all interwoven with the stories of the personal and professional conflicts of circus life. Originating live from New York, the series was aired every fourth week in the time slot normally occupied by Milton Berle's *Texaco Star Theatre.*

BULLWINKLE SHOW, THE

Cartoon

FIRST TELECAST: *September 24, 1961*

LAST TELECAST: *September 16, 1962*

BROADCAST HISTORY:

Sep 1961–Sep 1962, NBC Sun 7:00–7:30

VOICES:

Bullwinkle J. Moose, Dudley Doright, Mr. Peabody .... Bill Scott
Rocky Squirrel, Natasha Fatale .... June Foray
Boris Badenov .... Paul Frees
Aesop .... Charles Ruggles
Snidley Whiplash .... Hans Conried
Sherman .... Walter Tetley
Narrator of "Fractured Fairy Tales" .... Edward Everett Horton

This cartoon show included clever satire designed to appeal to adults as well as children. The principal characters in the series were Bullwinkle and his friend Rocket J. (Rocky) Squirrel. Boris and Natasha were the cynical but rather ineffectual spies with whom they were most often involved. Other featured segments, not seen in every episode, included "Fractured Fairy Tales"; "Peabody's Improbable History," in which a wealthy dog, Mr. Peabody, traveled back through time with his adopted boy, Sherman; "Adventures of Dudley Doright," a noble mountie confronted with the evil Snidley Whiplash; and "Aesop and Son," in which fables were recounted in unusual ways. Following its departure from prime time in 1962 *Bullwinkle* was aired on Sunday afternoons and then Saturday mornings until September 5, 1964.

BURKE'S LAW

Police/Detective Drama

FIRST TELECAST: *September 20, 1963*

LAST TELECAST: *January 12, 1966*

BROADCAST HISTORY:

Sep 1963–Sep 1964, ABC Fri 8:30–9:30
Sep 1964–Sep 1965, ABC Wed 9:30–10:30
Sep 1965–Jan 1966, ABC Wed 10:00–11:00

CAST:

Capt. Amos Burke .... Gene Barry
Det. Tim Tilson (1963–1965) .... Gary Conway
Det. Sgt. Les Hart (1963–1965) .... Regis Toomey
Henry (1963–1965) .... Leon Lontoc
Sgt. Ames (1964–1965) ...... Eileen O'Neill
"The Man" (1965–1966) .... Carl Benton Reid

Gene Barry played a Los Angeles chief of detectives who also was a millionaire, a role not unlike his cowboy-dandy in the earlier *Bat Masterson* series. The character of Amos Burke was first seen two seasons earlier in a *Dick Powell Theatre* presentation ("Who Killed Julia Greer"), where it was played by Dick Powell. As portrayed by Barry, Amos Burke was high-living, elegant, and witty, yet cagey and tough when required. He lived in a palatial mansion and habitually arrived at the scene of a crime in a Rolls-Royce driven by his chauffeur, Henry. Burke also had a magnetic attraction for beautiful women, and interrupted his romances only for interesting homicide cases, usually involving the elite.

His sidekicks were Det. Tim Tilson, a smart young college type; Det. Les Hart, a seasoned veteran of the force; and in 1964–1965 a pretty policewoman, Sgt. Ames. *Burke's Law* was highly promoted during its first season and featured dozens of Hollywood stars as guests, ranging from Annette Funicello to Sir Cedric Hardwicke; 63 stars appeared in the first eight episodes, according to one press release.

An important change in format and title was made in September 1965. Glamour and sophistication remained the series' trademarks, but Amos Burke severed his connection with the police and became a debonair, globe-trotting secret agent for a United States intelligence agency. His only contact at the agency, and the only other regular during the last season, was known simply as "The Man." The title of the series was simultaneously changed to *Amos Burke—Secret Agent*.

BURNS AND ALLEN SHOW, THE

see *George Burns and Gracie Allen Show, The*

BURNS AND SCHREIBER COMEDY HOUR, THE

Comedy Variety

FIRST TELECAST: *June 30, 1973*
LAST TELECAST: *September 1, 1973*
BROADCAST HISTORY:
Jun 1973–Sep 1973, ABC Sat 9:00–10:00
REGULARS:
Jack Burns
Avery Schreiber

Comedians Jack Burns (the thin one) and Avery Schreiber (the rotund, mustachioed one) starred in this summer series, which featured their own brand of off-beat humor in sketches and blackouts. Various guest stars, including many popular singers, also appeared.

BUS STOP

Drama

FIRST TELECAST: *October 1, 1961*
LAST TELECAST: *March 25, 1962*
BROADCAST HISTORY:
Oct 1961–Mar 1962, ABC Sun 9:00–10:00
CAST:
Grace Sherwood ....Marilyn Maxwell
Will Mayberry ....Rhodes Reason
Elma Gahringer ....Joan Freeman
Glenn Wagner ....Richard Anderson

The bus stop of this series was a diner in Sunrise, Colorado, a small town in Rocky Mountain country. The continuing characters included Grace Sherwood, the working owner of the diner; Elma Gahringer, its only waitress; Sheriff Will Mayberry, and District Attorney Glenn Wagner. The stories revolved around the people passing through Sunrise, and many an unusual character stepped off that interstate bus. The program earned national notoriety—and probably an early cancellation—due to an episode titled "A Lion Walks Among Us," which was based on a Tom Wicker novel and starred rock singer Fabian Forte as a youthful psychopath bent on murder and mayhem. This segment was widely denounced for its explicit violence and sadism and was cited in Congressional hearings on violence in television. The president of ABC-TV, when challenged by an angry senator as to whether he allowed his own children to watch such a series, stammered and admitted no—he did not.

Bus Stop was based on the successful play of the same name and had the original playwright, William Inge, as a script consultant.

BUSTING LOOSE

Situation Comedy

FIRST TELECAST: *January 17, 1977*
LAST TELECAST: *November 16, 1977*
BROADCAST HISTORY:
Jan 1977–May 1977, CBS Mon 8:30–9:00
Jul 1977–Nov 1977, CBS Wed 8:30–9:00
CAST:
Lenny Markowitz ....Adam Arkin
Melody Feebeck ....Barbara Rhoades
Sam Markowitz ....Jack Kruschen
Pearl Markowitz ....Pat Carroll
Lester Bellman ....Danny Goldman
Allan Simmonds ....Steve Nathan
Vinnie Mordabito ....Greg Antonacci
Woody Warshaw ....Paul Sylvan
Ralph Cabell ....Paul B. Price
Raymond ....Ralph Wilcox
Jackie Gleason ....Louise Williams

After graduating from engineering school, young Lenny Markowitz decided it was time to find his own place, away from his overprotective parents Sam and Pearl. He secretly moved into a run-down apartment building and set up housekeeping. Since he could not even afford to cover up the ducks on the wallpaper left by the previous tenant, it was not exactly a swinger's pad. It did have compensations, however, most notably his next-door neighbor Melody, a beautiful young woman who worked for an escort service. To make money on a temporary basis, until he could find more suitable employment, Lenny went to work as a salesman at Mr. Cabell's shoe store, where he worked with a "hip" black named Raymond. Lenny's buddies, Lester, Allan, Vinnie, and Woody, were frequent visitors to his place and partners in mischief, as when they left the New York setting of the series to hunt girls at a fashionable Catskills resort. In the fall of 1977, Lenny found a regular girl friend in a curvaceous young beauty named "Jackie Gleason" (no relation, or resemblance, to the famous TV comedian).

BUZZY WUZZY

Comedy Variety

FIRST TELECAST: *November 17, 1948*

LAST TELECAST: *December 8, 1948*

BROADCAST HISTORY:

Nov 1948–Dec 1948, ABC Wed 7:30–7:45

HOST:

Jerry Bergen
Imogene Coca

Hollywood comedian Jerry Bergen had just finished work on *The Pirate*, a Judy Garland film, when he was recruited to try television in this short comedy variety show. It lasted only four weeks. Imogene Coca was seen with him.

BY POPULAR DEMAND

Variety

FIRST TELECAST: *July 2, 1950*

LAST TELECAST: *September 22, 1950*

BROADCAST HISTORY:

Jul 1950–Aug 1950, CBS Sun 7:30–8:00
Aug 1950–Sep 1950, CBS Fri 10:00–10:30
Sep 1950, CBS Fri 10:30–11:00

HOST:

Robert Alda
Arlene Francis (Sep)

Robert Alda was the master of ceremonies for this series, which featured four professional entertainment acts competing with each other in an elimination competition to determine which act would return the following week. Winners were determined by the applause-meter vote of the studio audience. Robert Alda left the show at the beginning of September and was replaced by Arlene Francis for the last three telecasts.

BYLINE

Drama

FIRST TELECAST: *November 4, 1951*

LAST TELECAST: *December 9, 1951*

BROADCAST HISTORY:

Nov 1951–Dec 1951, ABC Sun 7:30–8:00

CAST:

Betty Furness

Betty Furness starred in this five-week series of live mysteries, which filled in ABC's Sunday 7:30 P.M. time slot until *Ellery Queen* moved over from DuMont in December 1951. Miss Furness was introduced in the first episode as a reporter on the trail of international criminals.

The official title of the program must surely be one of the longest in TV history: *Your Kaiser Dealer Presents Kaiser-Frazer "Adventures in Mystery" Starring Betty Furness in "Byline."*

BY-LINE—STEVE WILSON

syndicated title for *Big Town*

CBS CARTOON THEATRE

Cartoons

FIRST TELECAST: *June 13, 1956*

LAST TELECAST: *September 5, 1956*

BROADCAST HISTORY:

Jun 1956–Sep 1956, CBS Wed 7:30–8:00

HOST:

Dick Van Dyke

This summer cartoon series featured the characters from Hollywood's "Terrytunes," Heckle and Jeckle, Gandy Goose, Sour Puss, Dinky Duck, and Little Roquefort. Through the use of special film techniques, host Dick Van Dyke was seen chatting with the animated characters between cartoons.

CBS NEWCOMERS

Variety

FIRST TELECAST: *July 12, 1971*

LAST TELECAST: *September 6, 1971*

BROADCAST HISTORY:

Jul 1971–Sep 1971, CBS Mon 10:00–11:00

REGULARS:

Dave Garroway
David Arlen
Cynthia Clawson
Raul Perez
Gay Perkins
Nelson Riddle and His Orchestra
Peggy Sears
The Californians
Joey Garza
Rodney Winfield
The Good Humor Company

This summer variety show marked the return to a regular network series of Dave Garroway after a nine-year absence. He introduced performances by a wide range of young entertainers, all new to network television, who had been discovered in nightclubs and theaters during the previous year. None of them, alas, went on to become a major star.

CBS NEWS ADVENTURE

Documentary

FIRST TELECAST: *March 20, 1970*

LAST TELECAST: *April 17, 1970*

BROADCAST HISTORY:

Mar 1970–Apr 1970, CBS Fri 7:30–8:30

NARRATOR:

Charles Kuralt

This adventure documentary series examined in depth one or two subjects each week. Among the topics were an auto race from London, England, to Sydney, Australia; people who dive to remarkable depths without diving equipment; and a round-the-world sailing trip by five men and a woman, using a 47-foot boat.

CBS NEWS RETROSPECTIVE

Documentary/Public Affairs

FIRST TELECAST: *July 8, 1973*

LAST TELECAST: *September 1, 1974*

BROADCAST HISTORY:

Jul 1973–Sep 1973, CBS Sun 6:00–7:00
Jul 1974–Sep 1974, CBS Sun 6:00–7:00

HOST:

John Hart

The documentaries that were aired in this summer series had originally been telecast during the 1950s and 1960s and were considered classics of TV journalism. Many of them came from Edward R. Murrow's *See It Now;* others were from the *CBS News Reports* and *CBS News Special* series that succeeded it. John Hart was the host, setting the background for the period in which the specials had originally been aired and putting them in historical perspective.

CBS REPORTS/NEWS HOUR/NEWS SPECIAL

Documentary

FIRST TELECAST: *January 5, 1961*

LAST TELECAST: *September 7, 1971*

BROADCAST HISTORY:

Jan 1961–Sep 1962, CBS Thu 10:00–11:00
Sep 1962–Dec 1964, CBS Wed 7:30–8:30
Dec 1964–Aug 1965, CBS Mon 10:00–11:00
Sep 1965–Jun 1970, CBS Tue 10:00–11:00
Apr 1966–May 1966, CBS Fri 10:00–11:00
Sep 1970–Sep 1971, CBS Tue 10:00–11:00

On October 27, 1959, fifteen months after the demise of Edward R. Murrow's *See It Now,* the CBS News Department premiered a new, incisive, in-depth documentary program entitled *CBS Reports.* It was patterned after Murrow's precedent-setting program and employed many of the same production staff, including Murrow's former partner Fred Friendly. It was aired during 1950–1960 on an irregular basis as a series of specials. Murrow himself appeared on the first telecast, "Biography of a Missile," though he was later only an infrequent participant in the new series.

In January 1961 CBS began airing *CBS Reports* as a regular alternate-week series on Thursday nights, opposite ABC's enormously successful *The Untouchables.* The rationale seemed to be that since CBS could not compete for the escapist-entertainment audience, it would at least telecast something worthwhile opposite the violence on ABC. For almost a full decade *CBS Reports* remained a regular series on various nights, at times alternating with *CBS News Hour, CBS News Special,* and other shows and at times as a weekly series. It remained CBS's most prestigious news analysis program and generally ran for a full hour, while the other CBS news programs varied between 30 and 60 minutes depending on subject. *CBS Reports* has continued to appear since 1971 on an irregular basis, in the form of specials.

During its ten-year run as a regular series, a number of the documentaries aired on *CBS Reports* won Emmy awards. Among them were "KKK—The Invisible Empire" (1966), "Eric Hoffer, the Passionate State of Mind" (1968), "CBS Reports: What About Ronald Reagan" (1968), "Gauguin in Tahiti: The Search for Paradise" (1968), "CBS Reports: Hunger in America" (1969), "Justice Black and the Bill of Rights" (1969), "The Great American Novel" (1969), "The Japanese" (1970), and "The Selling of the Pentagon" (1971).

C.P.O. SHARKEY

Situation Comedy

FIRST TELECAST: *December 1, 1976*
LAST TELECAST: *July 28, 1978*
BROADCAST HISTORY:

Dec 1976–Jan 1977, NBC Wed 8:00–8:30
Feb 1977–Apr 1977, NBC Wed 9:00–9:30
Jul 1977–Aug 1977, NBC Wed 9:00–9:30
Oct 1977–Jan 1978, NBC Fri 8:00–8:30
Feb 1978–Apr 1978, NBC Fri 8:30–9:00
Jun 1978–Jul 1978, NBC Fri 8:00–8:30

CAST:

C.P.O. Otto Sharkey .... Don Rickles
Seaman Pruitt .... Peter Isacksen
Daniels .... Jeff Hollis
Kowalski .... Tom Ruben
Skolnick .... David Landsberg
Capt. Quinlan (1976–1977)
.... Elizabeth Allen
Chief Robinson .... Harrison Page
Mignone (1976–1977) .... Barry Pearl
Apodaca (1977–1978) .... Philip Simms
Rodriguez .... Richard Beauchamp
Lt. Whipple .... Jonathan Daly
Chief Gypsy Koch .... Beverly Sanders
Capt. "Buck" Buckner (1977–1978)
.... Richard X. Slattery

Insult comic Don Rickles found the perfect vehicle for his humor in this situation comedy, in which he was cast as Chief Petty Officer Sharkey of the U.S. Navy. Sharkey, a 24-year veteran of navy service, was stationed at the Navy Training Center in San Diego, California. He was in charge of a company of new recruits, and it was his job to make sailors out of a collection of diverse ethnic types, most of whom had never been away from home before. The various ethnic backgrounds and stereotypes were all targets for Sharkey's verbal barbs, but beneath that nasty exterior beat the heart of an old softie, especially when he sensed the suffering of a recruit who either could not take his bluster or was having problems adjusting to life away from home. Sharkey's immediate superior was the long-winded and overbearing Lt. Whipple; the base commander was Capt. Quinlan, who was of all things, an attractive woman.

When *C.P.O. Sharkey* returned in October 1977, to replace the short-lived *Sanford Arms*, Sharkey had a new, and male, commanding officer in Capt. "Buck" Buckner.

CACTUS JIM

Children's

FIRST TELECAST: *October 31, 1949*
LAST TELECAST: *October 26, 1951*
BROADCAST HISTORY:

Oct 1949–Oct 1951, NBC Mon-Fri 6:00–6:30

HOST:

Cactus Jim (1949–1951)
.... Clarence Hartzell
Cactus Jim (1951) .... Bill Bailey

This children's program was built around Western feature movies, which were shown in segments on succeeding days. Cactus Jim, a "range-riding old-timer," introduced each episode and spun a few yarns. The program emanated from WNBQ, Chicago.

CADE'S COUNTY

Police Drama

FIRST TELECAST: *September 19, 1971*
LAST TELECAST: *September 4, 1972*
BROADCAST HISTORY:

Sep 1971–Aug 1972, CBS Sun 9:30–10:30
Aug 1972–Sep 1972, CBS Mon 10:00–11:00

CAST:

Sam Cade .... Glenn Ford
J. J. Jackson .... Edgar Buchanan
Arlo Pritchard .... Taylor Lacher
Rudy Davillo .... Victor Campos
Pete .... Peter Ford
Joannie Little Bird .... Sandra Ego
Betty Ann Sundown .... Betty Ann Carr

Sprawling Madrid County, California, was the setting for this contemporary Western/police drama. Sheriff Sam Cade, based in the town of Madrid, was responsible for law enforcement throughout the county. He was assisted by veteran deputy J. J. Jackson and three younger deputies, Arlo, Rudy, and Pete. Sandra Ego initially had the role of police dispatcher but was replaced early on by Betty Ann Carr. Both of them were American Indians. The role of Pete, one of Cade's young deputies, was played by the son of Glenn Ford, the show's star.

CAESAR PRESENTS

Comedy Variety

FIRST TELECAST: *July 4, 1955*
LAST TELECAST: *September 12, 1955*
BROADCAST HISTORY:

Jul 1955–Sep 1955, NBC Mon 8:00–9:00

HOST:

Bobby Sherwood

CAST:

Charles Williams ....Phil Foster
Barbara Williams ....Barbara Nichols
Sandy Williams ....Sandra Deel
Vocalist ....Bill Hayes
Various parts ....Sid Gould
Various parts ....Cliff Norton
Various parts ....Judy Tyler

This combination variety and situation-comedy show was a summer replacement for *Caesar's Hour*. In addition to production numbers and comedy skits, a weekly feature of the program was the situation-comedy sketch "The Pharmacist," starring Phil Foster as an overworked and underpaid pharmacist with problems at home and at work. Sid Caesar, who produced this show, appeared live to introduce each episode.

CAESAR'S HOUR

Comedy Variety

FIRST TELECAST: *September 27, 1954*
LAST TELECAST: *May 25, 1957*
BROADCAST HISTORY:

Sep 1954–Jun 1956, NBC Mon 8:00–9:00
Sep 1956–May 1957, NBC Sat 9:00–10:00

CAST:

Bob Victor ....Sid Caesar
George Hansen ....Carl Reiner
Fred Brewster ....Howard Morris
Ann Victor (1954–1956) ....Nanette Fabray
Betty Hansen (1954–1955) ...Virginia Curtis
Betty Hansen (1955–1956) .....Sandra Deel
Betty Hansen (1956–1957) ...Shirl Conway
Alice Brewster (1954–1956) ...Ellen Parker
Alice Brewster (1956–1957) .....Pat Carroll
Jane Victor (1956–1957) ....Janet Blair

REGULARS:

William Lewis (1955–1957)
Earl Wild (1955–1957)
Dave Caesar (1955–1957)
Paul Reed (1955–1957)
Milt Kamen (1956–1957)
Bea Arthur (1956–1957)
Hugh Downs (1956–1957); announcer

The highly imaginative and creative comedy of Sid Caesar was the moving force in this successor to his famous *Your Show of Shows*. With him in this venture, also from *Your Show of Shows*, were comedians Carl Reiner and Howard Morris. The format of the series varied from a full hour of situation comedy, to musical revues, to a variety show or any combination of the three. Although the three male leads remained the same throughout the duration of the series, there was considerable turnover among the women.

The most successful sketch used in the series was "The Commuters," in which Caesar, Reiner, and Morris typified suburbanites who take the same train to work in the big city every morning and the same train home every evening. The lives of these people became to *Caesar's Hour* what "The Honeymooners" was to *The Jackie Gleason Show*. A featured part of the program, this sketch was sometimes expanded to fill the entire hour. The cast credits above are for the parts played by the participants in this sketch. Other featured comedy skits were "The Three Haircuts," in which Caesar, Reiner, and Morris satirized rock'n'roll musicians, and Caesar's characterization of "The Professor."

CAIN'S HUNDRED

Police Drama

FIRST TELECAST: *September 19, 1961*
LAST TELECAST: *September 11, 1962*
BROADCAST HISTORY:

Sep 1961–Sep 1962, NBC Tue 10:00–11:00

CAST:

Nicholas "Nick" Cain ......Mark Richman

Nick Cain had spent years as a gangland lawyer. He knew who the important people in organized crime were; and now that he had become an agent of the federal government, he was determined to ferret out and bring to prosecution the 100 men controlling the many-tentacled monster of organized crime in America. Roving about the country with a special squad of assistants, Nick Cain assembled the necessary evidence to help the government bring big-time gangsters to justice. Based on actual case histories, *Cain's Hundred* dramatized, often in quasi-documentary fashion, the personalities, lives, and methods of the members of the underworld fraternity in the United States.

CALIFORNIANS, THE

Western

FIRST TELECAST: *September 24, 1957*
LAST TELECAST: *August 27, 1959*

BROADCAST HISTORY:

Sep 1957–Mar 1959, NBC Tue 10:00–10:30
Apr 1959–Jun 1959, NBC Tue 9:00–9:30
Jul 1959–Aug 1959, NBC Thu 7:30–8:00

CAST:

Dion Patrick (1957–1958)... Adam Kennedy
Jack McGivern (1957–1958) ....Sean McClory
Martha McGivern (1957–1958) .... Nan Leslie
Sam Brennan (1957–1958) .... Herbert Rudley
Matthew Wayne ....Richard Coogan
Schaab (1957–1958) ....Howard Caine
Wilma Fansler (1958–1959) ....Carole Mathews
Jeremy Pitt (1958–1959) ...Arthur Fleming

Set in San Francisco during the 1850s, at the height of the Gold Rush, *The Californians* was the story of honest men trying to clean up a wild city overrun by criminals and con men. Dion Patrick had been drawn to San Francisco by the prospect of Gold Rush riches, but went to work instead as a crusading reporter for newspaperman Sam Brennan—and also joined storekeeper Jack McGivern's vigilantes, the only functioning law-enforcement organization in town. In the middle of the first season Matthew Wayne arrived and was elected sheriff of San Francisco; he became the leading character as vigilantes Patrick and McGivern were eased out of the show. In the second season Wayne, by then city marshal, continued his fight against crime with a newly reorganized 50-man police force. He remained the focal point with the addition of love interest Wilma Fansler, a young widow who ran a gambling house, and attorney Jeremy Pitt, friend and foil to the marshal.

CALL MR. D

Syndicated title for *Richard Diamond, Private Detective*

CALUCCI'S DEPARTMENT

Situation Comedy

FIRST TELECAST: *September 14, 1973*
LAST TELECAST: *December 28, 1973*
BROADCAST HISTORY:

Sep 1973–Dec 1973, CBS Fri 8:00–8:30

CAST:

Joe Calucci ....James Coco
Shirley Balukis ....Candy Azzara
Ramon Gonzales ....Jose Perez
Cosgrove ....Jack Fletcher
Elaine Fusco ....Peggy Pope
Woods ....Bill Lazarus
Frohler ....Bernard Wexler
Mitzi Gordon ....Rosetta Lenoir

Roly-poly comic James Coco portrayed the supervisor of a branch of the New York State Unemployment Office in this ethnic comedy. Calucci had to cope with the problems of unemployed claimants, the frictions among various members of his staff (who were carefully picked to represent every race, religion, and creed imaginable), and the frustrations of governmental red tape. As if that wasn't enough, he was in love with his secretary Shirley—or at least infatuated with her—but the series was canceled before their relationship really developed. Apparently most Americans did not find an unemployment office very amusing.

CALVIN AND THE COLONEL

Cartoon

FIRST TELECAST: *October 3, 1961*
LAST TELECAST: *September 22, 1962*
BROADCAST HISTORY:

Oct 1961–Nov 1961, ABC Tue 8:30–9:00
Jan 1962–Sep 1962, ABC Sat 7:30–8:00

VOICES:

The Colonel ....Freeman Gosden
Calvin ....Charles Correll
Maggie Belle ....Virginia Gregg
Sister Sue ....Beatrice Kay
Oliver Wendell Clutch ....Paul Frees

This animated feature concerned the exploits of a bunch of animals from the Deep South who had taken up residence in a large Northern city. The Colonel was a very foxy fox, and Calvin was his best friend, a lovable but not particularly bright bear. Other regulars on the series were the Colonel's wife Maggie Belle, her sister Sue, and Oliver Wendell Clutch, a lawyer who was a weasel. If the plot line sounds vaguely like that of *Amos 'n' Andy*, don't be surprised. Gosden and Correll, the creators and principal voices of this series, played *Amos 'n' Andy* on the radio for years. The use of animals have avoided creating what could have been a touchy racial situation in the early 1960s.

CAMEO THEATRE

Dramatic Anthology

FIRST TELECAST: *May 16, 1950*
LAST TELECAST: *August 21, 1955*
BROADCAST HISTORY:
May 1950–Sep 1950, NBC Wed 8:30–9:00
Jun 1951–Aug 1951, NBC Mon 8:00–8:30
Jan 1952–Apr 1952, NBC Sun 10:00–10:30
Jul 1955–Aug 1955, NBC Sun 10:00–10:30
CREATOR AND PRODUCER:
Albert McCleery

An interesting early experiment in the unique dramatic possibilities of television, this occasional series of live plays was produced in the round, using a minimum of props. It made considerable use of close-ups and other camera techniques to focus attention on the characterizations of individual actors. High-quality scripts were used, both originals and adaptations for television. The first telecast was "It Takes a Thief," by Arthur Miller; later presentations included a three-part adaptation of Ibsen's *Peer Gynt* and a version of the Broadway musical *Dark of the Moon*.

After an absence of three years the series returned for a final run during the summer of 1955, as a replacement for *The Loretta Young Show*.

CAMP RUNAMUCK

Situation Comedy
FIRST TELECAST: *September 17, 1965*
LAST TELECAST: *September 2, 1966*
BROADCAST HISTORY:
Sep 1965–Sep 1966, NBC Fri 7:30–8:00
CAST:
Senior Counselor Spiffy ....Dave Ketchum
Commander Wivenhoe ......Arch Johnson
Mahala May Gruenecker ......Alice Nunn
Pruett ....David Madden
Doc Joslyn ....Leonard Stone
Caprice Yeudleman ....Nina Wayne

Nuttiness abounded in this comedy of two summer camps for children, Camp Runamuck for boys and, on the other side of the lake bordering it, Camp Divine for girls. The four characters in charge of the boys' camp, Spiffy, Wivenhoe, Pruett, and Doc Joslyn, created constant chaos in their own camp and maintained a strong, and often hilarious, rivalry with the counselors of Camp Divine.

CAMPAIGN AND THE CANDIDATES, THE

News
FIRST TELECAST: *September 17, 1960*
LAST TELECAST: *November 5, 1960*
BROADCAST HISTORY:
Sep 1960–Nov 1960, NBC Sat 9:30–10:30
ANCHORMAN:
Frank McGee

This series of weekly summaries followed the campaigns of presidential candidates John F. Kennedy and Richard M. Nixon as they stated their cases to the American public in the fall of 1960. Coverage was narrated by numerous NBC reporters assigned to the campaigns, with Frank McGee acting as host and coordinator.

CAMPAIGN ROUNDUP

News Analysis
FIRST TELECAST: *May 12, 1958*
LAST TELECAST: *June 9, 1958*
BROADCAST HISTORY:
May 1958–Jun 1958, ABC Mon 8:00–8:30
MODERATOR:
Quincy Howe

Continuing analysis of the various congressional and gubernatorial campaigns taking place throughout the country was provided by the ABC news staff during the 1958 primary season. Different correspondents contributed information regarding the races in different parts of the country.

CAMPAIGN '72

News
FIRST TELECAST: *June 25, 1972*
LAST TELECAST: *September 17, 1972*
BROADCAST HISTORY:
Jun 1972–Sep 1972, CBS Sun 6:00–7:00

During the summer of 1972, a presidential election year, CBS aired a regular series of reports on the activities of both parties as they prepared for their conventions, planned their campaign strategies, and sought to determine the way in which their respective nominees would handle themselves in the post-convention campaign.

CAMPAIGN '76

News
FIRST TELECAST: *September 3, 1976*
LAST TELECAST: *October 31, 1976*
BROADCAST HISTORY:
Sep 1976–Oct 1976, CBS Fri 7:30–8:00

As the 1976 presidential campaign drew to a close, CBS News provided a weekly report on the activities of Gerald Ford and Jimmy Carter in their "Race for the White House." In addition to the latest poll results, CBS correspondents were shown on location with the candidates and in various parts of the country discussing issues with citizens and evaluating how regional climate of opinion was affected by the rhetoric. Various CBS News correspondents served as anchormen on individual telecasts.

CAMPBELL PLAYHOUSE

see *Campbell Soundstage*

CAMPBELL SOUNDSTAGE

Dramatic Anthology

FIRST TELECAST: *June 6, 1952*
LAST TELECAST: *September 3, 1954*
BROADCAST HISTORY:
Jun 1952–Aug 1952, NBC Fri 9:30–10:00
Jul 1953–Sep 1954, NBC Fri 9:30–10:00

This dramatic series premiered in 1952 as the summer replacement for the vacationing *Aldrich Family*. Initially it was a collection of filmed dramas under the title *Campbell Playhouse*. Among the dramas were "The Cavorting Statue," starring Cesar Romero and Ann Rutherford, "Return to Vienna," with Ruth Warrick and Cameron Mitchell, and "This Little Pig Cried," with Frances Rafferty and Robert Rockwell.

The show returned in 1953 under the title *Campbell Soundstage*, this time as the permanent replacement for the canceled *Aldrich Family*. With the new name came a change in format. The plays were produced live in New York, starred big-name talent, and all had surprise endings reminiscent of O. Henry's short stories. Among the performers who starred in these live plays were Jack Lemmon, Walter Matthau, James Dean, E. G. Marshall, Betsy Palmer, Roddy McDowall, Brian Keith, and Lillian Gish.

On June 4, 1954, the title became *Campbell Summer Soundstage* and the presentations reverted to film. Many of these were reruns of episodes previously aired on *Ford Theatre*.

CAMPUS CORNER

Music

FIRST TELECAST: *March 18, 1949*
LAST TELECAST: *April 11, 1949*
BROADCAST HISTORY:
Mar 1949–Apr 1949, CBS Mon/Fri 7:45–8:00
STAR:
Beverly Fite

Singer Beverly Fite was the hostess and star of this short-lived musical series, which was aired twice a week in the spring of 1949. She sang, with an unspecified musical quartet as backup, and chatted with a guest or two. The series was also called *The Quadrangle*.

CAMPUS HOOPLA

Sports/Variety

FIRST TELECAST: *December 27, 1946*
LAST TELECAST: *December 19, 1947*
BROADCAST HISTORY:
Dec 1946–Dec 1947, NBC Fri 8:00–8:30 (OS)
HOST:
Bob Stanton

Campus Hoopla was a combination sports and variety show aimed at teenage viewers. The setting was a campus soda shop, complete with "cheerleaders" and "students" who talked about sports, participated in quiz segments, and sang and danced to the music of a jukebox. The latest sports scores were given by NBC sportscaster Bob Stanton, who also narrated films of recent games.

CAN DO

Quiz/Audience Participation

FIRST TELECAST: *November 26, 1956*
LAST TELECAST: *December 31, 1956*
BROADCAST HISTORY:
Nov 1956–Dec 1956, NBC Mon 9:00–9:30
EMCEE:
Robert Alda

This short-lived game show offered contestants the opportunity to win up to $50,000 for correctly guessing whether famous show-business personalities could successfully perform certain stunts. The first round was worth $1,500, with the prize doubling on each successive round. A contestant could quit at any time, with the threat of losing most of his winnings to be weighed against doubling his money. An incorrect guess meant that the contestant only took home 10 percent of the amount he was trying for, or roughly 20 percent of what he had already won. Among the celebrities featured were Sal Mineo operating a construction crane and Rory Calhoun performing an archery feat.

CAN YOU TOP THIS?

Comedy

FIRST TELECAST: *October 3, 1950*
LAST TELECAST: *March 26, 1951*
BROADCAST HISTORY:
Oct 1950–Dec 1950, ABC Tue 9:30–10:00
Dec 1950–Mar 1951, ABC Mon 8:00–8:30
EMCEE:
Ward Wilson
PANEL:
Joe Laurie, Jr.
Harry Hershfield
Peter Donald
"Senator" Ed Ford

In the simple format of this show, four old-time gagsters sat around a table and told funny stories, including some sent in by viewers. A laugh meter measured the audience reaction to each and determined the winner of each round. The program was based on the radio show of the same name.

Here's a typical story: A very fussy school inspector arrived to inspect a little country schoolhouse. Hearing a commotion in one of the classrooms, he walked in and found the boys and girls raising a ruckus. One of them, a little taller than the rest, was making most of the noise. So the inspector promptly took this lad into another room, bent him over his knee and spanked him. "Now, you stand in that corner and behave yourself or else I'll spank you again," the inspector warned sternly. So the fellow stood in the corner. Awhile later, there was a timid knock on the door. A little girl stuck her head in and said, "Please, sir, can we have our teacher back now?"

CANDID CAMERA

Humor

FIRST TELECAST: *August 10, 1948*
LAST TELECAST: *September 3, 1967*
BROADCAST HISTORY:
Aug 1948–Sep 1948, ABC Sun 8:00–8:30
Oct 1948, ABC Wed 8:30–8:45
Nov 1948–Dec 1948, ABC Fri 8:00–8:30
May 1949–Jul 1949, NBC Sun 7:30–8:00
Jul 1949–Aug 1949, NBC Thu 9:00–9:30
Sep 1949–Sep 1950, CBS Mon 9:00–9:30
Jun 1953, NBC Tue 9:30–10:00
Jul 1953, NBC Wed 10:00–10:30
Oct 1960–Sep 1967, CBS Sun 10:00–10:30
PRODUCER AND HOST:
Allen Funt
CO-HOST:
Arthur Godfrey (1960–1961)
Durward Kirby (1961–1966)
Bess Myerson (1966–1967)

A patron at a bowling alley would roll a ball, and back down the chute it would come—minus finger holes. *Candid Camera* viewers watched as the poor fellow tried to figure out *what the* ———!

A tiny foreign car would pull into a service station and the driver would casually ask for a "fill up." The hidden camera focused on the attendant's growing astonishment as the midget auto practically drained the station dry. (There was a giant tank concealed in the trunk.)

"Smile, you're on *Candid Camera!*"

The premise of Allen Funt's long-running *Candid Camera* was simply to snoop on unsuspecting citizens with hidden cameras and see how they would react to bizarre situations. Cars were a favorite device. In one sequence, innocent-looking Dorothy Collins (frequently seen on the show during the 1960s) would come driving down a hill and pull up in front of a passerby, asking for help—the car "won't seem to start." Up went the hood to reveal . . . no engine. Other ploys included vending machines that talked back, actors who got into unbelievable predicaments and then asked passersby for help, diners served impossibly small portions, and so on—*ad infinitum.* The reactions of the surprised victims were often hilarious.

Allen Funt, who appeared in many of the gags, may have been one of the nerviest actors in TV history. Yet he got few rejections, much less punches in the nose, for his presumptions upon innocent citizens. His greatest coup was a special filmed in Moscow—without the permission, or even knowledge, of the Russian authorities. Funt managed to smuggle himself, cameramen, hidden cameras, and 90,000 feet of film into and out of the Soviet Union undetected (the border guards, taking him for a tourist, never opened his bags). On the streets of the Russian capital he staged many of his favorite stunts, including the newspaper routine (start reading someone's paper over their shoulder, gradually get your hands on it to position it better, and then work it away from them entirely) and the two-suitcase caper. (A pretty girl with two suitcases asks a passing male to help her carry one; hers is empty, his is filled with 200 pounds of concrete. To Funt's astonishment, a burly Russian blithely picked up the trick suitcase and trotted off with it, never blinking an eye.)

Some of the best sequences were not setups, but simply cameos from life; for instance the husky traffic cop at a busy intersection who seemed to perform a classical ballet as he motioned cars hither and yon.

Allen Funt first brought his established *Candid Microphone* radio program to television in 1948, and it continued off and on for 19 years thereafter. The first TV version was in fact called *Candid Microphone*, but the title was changed to *Candid Camera* when it moved to NBC in 1949. In addition to its prime-time runs, listed above, *Candid Camera* was aired as a local program in New York in the mid-1950s; as part of the commercials within *Pontiac Presents Playwrights '56* in 1955–1956; as a segment within the *Garry Moore Show* in 1959–1960; and in countless reruns on CBS daytime TV.

CANDID MICROPHONE

see *Candid Camera*

CANNON

Detective Drama

FIRST TELECAST: *September 14, 1971*

LAST TELECAST: *September 19, 1976*

BROADCAST HISTORY:

Sep 1971–Sep 1972, CBS Tue 9:30–10:30

Sep 1972–Sep 1973, CBS Wed 10:00–11:00

Sep 1973–Jul 1976, CBS Wed 9:00–10:00

Jul 1976–Sep 1976, CBS Sun 10:00–11:00

CAST:

Frank Cannon ....William Conrad

Balding, middle-aged and portly, detective Frank Cannon represented quite a change from the traditional suave, handsome private detectives TV had brought to its viewers. He occasionally let his conscience dictate his choice of cases, but more often his wallet took precedence. To most clients he charged a high fee, in order to provide himself with the money to indulge in personal luxuries such as an expensive convertible and fine cuisine. Cannon rarely fired a shot, was in no condition to beat up his adversaries, and was generally seen driving around Los Angeles in his big shiny Continental. The car took more physical abuse than Cannon did, often getting dented, scraped, and mangled during chase sequences.

William Conrad, the only regular in the series, had previously been more familiar to the ears than to the eyes of Americans. During the 1950s he had been the voice of Matt Dillon in the radio version of *Gunsmoke*, but was manifestly unsuited to portray the tough Western marshal when the series moved to television—so young James Arness got the role, in what became the longest-running dramatic series in TV history.

CAPITOL CAPERS

Music

FIRST TELECAST: *August 1, 1949*

LAST TELECAST: *September 7, 1949*

BROADCAST HISTORY:

Aug 1949–Sep 1949, NBC Mon/Wed 7:30–7:45

REGULARS:

Cliff Quartet, instrumental

Gene Archer, baritone

This live musical program emanated from NBC's Washington, D.C., studios.

CAPITOL CLOAK ROOM

Public Affairs Discussion

FIRST TELECAST: *October 14, 1949*

LAST TELECAST: *September 8, 1950*

BROADCAST HISTORY:

Oct 1949–Sep 1950, CBS Fri 10:30–11:00

PANELISTS:

Griffing Bancroft

Eric Sevareid

Willard Shadel

CBS simulcast this live political discussion program from Washington, D.C., on both its television and radio networks. Each week a key political figure was interviewed by a panel of three CBS correspondents. The panel was chaired by Griffing Bancroft.

CAPTAIN AND TENNILLE, THE

Musical Variety

FIRST TELECAST: *September 20, 1976*

LAST TELECAST: *March 14, 1977*

BROADCAST HISTORY:

Sep 1976–Mar 1977, ABC Mon 8:00–9:00

REGULARS:

Daryl Dragon
Toni Tennille

This youth-oriented variety hour was built around the "soft rock" husband-and-wife team of Daryl Dragon and Toni Tennille, who had several big record hits in 1975–1976 and who, ABC hoped, might become another Sonny and Cher on TV. They didn't.

Toni was a pretty but somewhat antiseptic version of Cher, while Daryl ("The Captain," after his ever-present captain's hat) was decidedly quieter than Sonny. In fact, he scarcely said a word, and much of the comedy was built around his extremely taciturn nature. He also had a chance to show off his musical wizardry—he was a master of all sorts of keyboard instruments. Daryl came from a background of music, if not comedy, being the son of the well-known concert conductor Carmen Dragon.

Among the featured segments on the show were "The Charcoal House," with Daryl and Toni as two struggling young performers, and "Masterjoke Theater." The only other regulars on the show were the Dragons' two English bulldogs, Elizabeth and Broderick.

CAPTAIN BILLY'S MISSISSIPPI MUSIC HALL

Variety

FIRST TELECAST: *October 1, 1948*
LAST TELECAST: *November 26, 1948*
BROADCAST HISTORY:

Oct 1948–Nov 1948, CBS Fri 8:30–9:00

HOST:

Ralph Dumke

Loosely based on incidents related in the book *Old Man River and His Chillun*, written by Captain Billy Bryant, this live variety series was set on a Mississippi paddle-wheel showboat. It was hosted by Ralph Dumke, in the role of Captain Billy, and included musical numbers, comedy, and dramatic interludes performed by guest stars. The series had premiered on August 16 as a local show under the title *Captain Billy's Showboat*, changed its name on September 17, and two weeks later became a network program.

CAPTAIN NICE

Situation Comedy

FIRST TELECAST: *January 9, 1967*
LAST TELECAST: *August 28, 1967*
BROADCAST HISTORY:

Jan 1967–Aug 1967, NBC Mon 8:30–9:00

CAST:

Carter Nash (Captain Nice) .... William Daniels
Mrs. Nash .... Alice Ghostley
Sgt. Candy Kane .... Ann Prentiss
Mayor Finney .... Liam Dunn
Chief Sagal .... William Zuckart

Captain Nice was created and written by Buck Henry, co-creator of *Get Smart*, and it was to superheroes what *Get Smart* was to secret agents—a parody. Carter Nash was a police department chemist who had accidentally discovered a liquid that, when drunk, would transform him into Captain Nice. Unfortunately Captain Nice was no stronger a personality than Carter was normally—shy, quiet, unassuming, and mother-dominated. In fact if it had not been for his mother, who demanded that her son wage war on the evil forces that constantly threatened society, he would not have gotten actively involved in fighting crime at all. The sight of Captain Nice trying to maintain his composure while flying over Bigtown (he had an acute fear of heights) in his baggy, moth-eaten, red-white-and-blue leotards (made for him by his mother) did not exactly terrify evil-doers.

CAPTAIN VIDEO AND HIS VIDEO RANGERS

Children's

FIRST TELECAST: *June 27, 1949*
LAST TELECAST: *April 1, 1955*
BROADCAST HISTORY:

Jun 1949–Aug 1949, DUM Mon/Tu/Th/Fri 7:00–7:30
Aug 1949–Sep 1953, DUM Mon–Fri 7:00–7:30
Sep 1953–Apr 1955, DUM Mon–Fri 7:00–7:15 also
Feb 1950–Sep 1950, DUM Sat 7:30–8:00
Sep 1950–Nov 1950, DUM Sat 7:00–7:30

CAST:

Captain Video (1949–1950) .... Richard Coogan
Captain Video (1951–1955) ...... Al Hodge
The Ranger .... Don Hastings
Dr. Pauli .... Hal Conklin

CREATOR/PRODUCER:

James Caddigan

WRITER:

Maurice C. Brock

THEME:

Overture to *The Flying Dutchman* by Richard Wagner

"Guardian of the Safety of the World"—on a prop budget of $25 per week! *Captain Video* was one of the low-budget wonders of television history, and one of the most popular children's programs of the early 1950s. It was the first of a trio of "space operas" popular at the time—*Space Patrol* and *Tom Corbett—Space Cadet* were mere imitations—and the one most frequently seen (Monday–Friday during most of its run).

Captain Video, as played by handsome, jut-jawed Richard Coogan, and later by handsome, jut-jawed Al Hodge (formerly the voice of radio's *Green Hornet*), was a scientific genius who took it upon himself, as a private citizen, to insure the safety of the universe. Operating from his secret, mountaintop headquarters, sometime in the 21st or 22nd century, he controlled a vast network of "Video Rangers" as well as an impressive arsenal of futuristic weaponry of his own invention. His sidekick The Ranger—idol of half the kids in America—was played by young Don Hastings, who was 15 when the series began.

Captain Video's adversaries were legion, among them Nargola, Mook the Moon Man, Kul of Eos, Heng Foo Seeng, Dr. Clysmok, and Dahoumie. But the most persistent was Dr. Pauli, head of the Astroidal Society and an evil genius whose scientific weaponry was almost equal to Video's own.

Captain Video and The Ranger were constantly coming up with new devices with which to fight off these assorted villains. The Opticon Scillometer (which looked suspiciously like a length of pipe with some spare parts bolted on) allowed one to see through things; the Atomic Rifle could blow up almost anything; the Discatron was a sort of portable TV set; the Radio Scillograph was a long range two-way radio that fit in the palm of the hand; and the Cosmic Ray Vibrator a handy device that literally shook adversaries into submission—seldom was anyone killed outright on *Captain Video*. Not to be outdone, Dr. Pauli countered with his Trisonic Compensator, which could curve bullets around a house; his Barrier of Silence, so he couldn't be heard; and the Cloak of Invisibility—how many kids would have liked to get their hands on *that!*

Perhaps the most terrifying piece of machinery seen on *Captain Video*, however, was Tobor ("robot" spelled backward). Designed as the ultimate, unstoppable, indestructible robot to work for the good of mankind, he had been appropriated by a beautiful villainess named Atar. She programmed him, naturally, to "get Captain Video." But the Captain also managed to get on Tobor's secret frequency and in a magnificent climactic scene, the hulking brute was reduced to a pile of scrap metal by conflicting orders from Atar and Video.

Since DuMont was perpetually impoverished, the sets and props on *Captain Video* were constructed on the smallest possible budget. Most of the controls in the Captain's spaceship, the *Galaxy*, were painted on, and one suspected that a single swift kick at his master control board would destroy the entire headquarters. The unkindest limitations were on the network of Video Rangers, whom the Captain would look in on, using his Remote Carrier Beam, once during each telecast. Most of them looked exactly like cowboys in the Old West—DuMont was running pieces of ancient Westerns to pad out the half hour! (This practice ceased after a time.)

There was tremendous viewer interest in *Captain Video*, heightened by offers of premiums such as plastic replicas of the Captain's weapons, his decoder ring, and his space helmet. A theatrical serial was made based on his exploits. The program won several awards from impressed adults, too, for the Captain's regular short talks to "Rangers at home" on the value of tolerance, fair play, and personal integrity.

Captain Video was, in all, a splendid example of innovative programming that was perfect for the TV medium. Had DuMont been able to devise more such breakthroughs, the network might have survived longer than it did. As it was, *Captain Video and His Video Rangers* lasted until the network itself crumbled away, in 1955. During the last stages of its run it was also known as *The Secret Files of Captain Video*.

The reader interested in a detailed, and loving, description of *Captain Video* and other "space operas" is referred to the book *The Great Television Heroes*, by Donald F. Glut and Jim Harmon.

CAPTAINS AND THE KINGS

Drama

FIRST TELECAST: *September 30, 1976*

LAST TELECAST: *April 25, 1977*

BROADCAST HISTORY:

Sep 1976–Nov 1976, NBC Thu 9:00–10:00
Mar 1977–Apr 1977, NBC Thu 9:00–11:00
Apr 1977, NBC Mon 9:00–11:00

CAST:

Joseph Armagh ....Richard Jordan
Katherine Hennessey ....Joanna Pettet
Big Ed Healey ....Charles Durning
Martinique ....Barbara Parkins
Tom Hennessey ....Vic Morrow
Harry Zieff ....Harvey Jason
Miss Emmy ....Beverly D'Angelo
Charles Desmond ....Robert Vaughn
Elizabeth Healey Hennessey ... Blair Brown
Bernadette Hennessey Armagh
.... Patty Duke Astin
Moira/Mary Armagh
.... Katherine Crawford
Marjorie Chisholm Armagh
.... Jane Seymour
Rory Armagh ....Perry King
Claudia Desmond ....Cynthia Sikes
Kevin Armagh ....Douglas Heyes, Jr.

Adapted from Taylor Caldwell's novel, *Captains and the Kings* was the saga of Joseph Armagh, a poor Irish immigrant who rose to great prominence in America in the latter part of the nineteenth century. Episodes chronicled the period from his arrival in New York as a young man in 1857 till the death of his last son around 1912. His rise to wealth and power through investments in the oil industry, his affairs both public and private, and his consuming desire to have one of his sons become the first Irish Catholic president of the United States were all woven into the story. That latter plan, on the verge of success, was abruptly destroyed when Rory was assassinated during the campaign.

Captains and the Kings was one of the four novels dramatized under the collective title *NBC's Best Sellers*. Although most of the chapters ran only one hour, as indicated in the broadcast history above, the first and last chapters ran from 9–11 P.M. It was also the only one of the four novels to be rerun, in the spring of 1977, with all rerun installments running two hours in length. The concluding chapter of the *Captains and the Kings* reruns aired on Monday night, April 25, 1977.

CAPTURED

syndicated title for *Gangbusters*

CAR 54, WHERE ARE YOU?

Situation Comedy

FIRST TELECAST: *September 17, 1961*

LAST TELECAST: *September 8, 1963*

BROADCAST HISTORY:

Sep 1961–Sep 1963, NBC Sun 8:30–9:00

CAST:

Officer Gunther Toody ....Joe E. Ross
Officer Francis Muldoon .....Fred Gwynne
Lucille Toody ....Bea Pons
Captain Block ....Paul Reed
Officer O'Hara ....Albert Henderson
Officer Anderson (1961–1962)
.... Nipsey Russell
Officer Antonnucci (1961–1962)
.... Jerome Guardino
Officer Leo Schnauser ....Al Lewis
Officer Kissel ....Bruce Kirby
Officer Nicholson ....Hank Garrett
Officer Nelson ....Jim Gormley
Sylvia Schnauser ....Charlotte Rae
Officer Wallace (1962–1963)
.... Frederick O'Neal

CREATOR AND PRODUCER:

Nat Hiken

Officers Toody and Muldoon were among the most unlikely patrol-car partners ever seen on a police force. Toody was short, stocky, friendly, and just a bit nosy, a marked contrast to the tall, quiet Muldoon. Although they were assigned to New York's 53rd precinct—a run-down area in the Bronx not generally considered a hotbed of hilarity—they always seemed to encounter more comedy than crime. Much of the action took place in the precinct house itself, particularly in the locker room as the officers got into uniform, and the comedy was invariably of the broad slapstick variety reminiscent of Mack Sennett.

One unusual aspect of this series was the partners' patrol car, which looked identical to those used by real-life New York City police—but only because the show was filmed in black and white. The car was actually painted red and white, to distinguish it from real police cars during shooting (all of which was done on location). On the home screen the red and white car looked identical to the dark green and white of genuine New York City police cars.

Nat Hiken of the *Phil Silvers Show* was the

creator, producer, and one of the writers of *Car 54, Where Are You?*

CARA WILLIAMS SHOW, THE

Situation Comedy

FIRST TELECAST: *September 23, 1964*

LAST TELECAST: *September 10, 1965*

BROADCAST HISTORY:

Sep 1964–Apr 1965, CBS Wed 9:30–10:00

May 1965–Sep 1965, CBS Fri 8:30–9:00

CAST:

Cara Bridges/Wilton ....Cara Williams
Frank Bridges ....Frank Aletter
Damon Burkhardt ....Paul Reed
Mrs. Burkhardt ....Reta Shaw
Fletcher Kincaid ....Jack Sheldon
Mary Hammilmeyer ....Jeanne Arnold
Agnes ....Audrey Christie

A secret marriage in the face of a company rule against employing married couples provided the basis for much of the comedy in this series. Cara and Frank Bridges, the secret spouses, had to pretend to be singles as they went to work each day at Fenwick Diversified Industries. Frank was the company efficiency expert, and Cara, who used her maiden name of Wilton in the office, was a secretary with an incredibly complex filing system. She was indispensable to her boss, Mr. Burkhardt, because she was the only one who could find anything in her files. The Bridges's problems at home and at work, as they tried to protect their secret, made for amusing and complicated situations.

CARIBE

Police Drama

FIRST TELECAST: *February 17, 1975*

LAST TELECAST: *August 11, 1975*

BROADCAST HISTORY:

Feb 1975–Aug 1975, ABC Mon 10:00–11:00

CAST:

Lt. Ben Logan ....Stacy Keach
Sgt. Mark Walters ....Carl Franklin
Deputy Commissioner Ed Rawlings, Miami P.D. ....Robert Mandan

This action-adventure series was set in Miami and throughout the Caribbean. Ben Logan and his black partner, Sgt. Mark Walters, constituted a two-man law-enforcement unit working for Caribbean Force, an international agency fighting crime wherever Americans were involved.

CARMEL MYERS SHOW, THE

Interviews

FIRST TELECAST: *June 26, 1951*

LAST TELECAST: *February 21, 1952*

BROADCAST HISTORY:

Jun 1951–Oct 1951, ABC Tue 7:15–7:30

Oct 1951–Feb 1952, ABC Thu 10:45–11:00

HOSTESS:

Carmel Myers

Carmel Myers, formerly a queen of the silent movies, hosted this weekly 15-minute program of interviews, chats, and reminiscenses on ABC in 1951–1952. Among her guests were Abe Burrows, Jule Styne, and Richard Rodgers.

CARNIVAL

see *ABC Dramatic Shorts—1952–1953*

CAROL BURNETT SHOW, THE

Comedy Variety

FIRST TELECAST: *September 11, 1967*

LAST TELECAST: *August 9, 1978*

BROADCAST HISTORY:

Sep 1967–May 1971, CBS Mon 10:00–11:00 (OS)

Sep 1971–Nov 1972, CBS Wed 8:00–9:00 (OS)

Dec 1972–Dec 1977, CBS Sat 10:00–11:00 (OS)

Dec 1977–Mar 1978, CBS Sun 10:00–11:00

Jun 1978–Aug 1978, CBS Wed 8:00–9:00

REGULARS:

Carol Burnett
Harvey Korman (1967–1977)
Lyle Waggoner (1967–1974)
Vicki Lawrence
Tim Conway (1975–1978)
The Ernest Flatt Dancers
The Harry Zimmerman Orchestra (1967–1971)
The Peter Matz Orchestra (1971–1978)
Dick Van Dyke (1977)

THEME:

"Carol's Theme," by Joe Hamilton

In an era in which variety shows were rapidly disappearing from television, *The Carol Burnett Show* survived for more than a decade. The life span for other variety series in the 1970s rarely exceeded two seasons, and their total number had dwindled substantially from their heyday in the 1950s. Only Carol managed to remain popular and successful. The small nucleus of her regular cast remained constant for seven years, with none of her original supporting troupe leaving until 1974. Their chemistry helped hold the show together. The binding force, however, was Carol, one of television's most versatile variety performers, who could sing, dance, act, clown, and mime with equal facility.

Over the years certain basic aspects of the show remained the same. There was one point in each telecast, usually at the beginning, when Carol and the evening's guest star would answer questions from the studio audience. There were comedy sketches that spoofed TV series, popular movies, or other forms of mass entertainment. Among Carol's extensive repertoire of comic characterizations, were two recurring sketches that persisted for years. In one of them she and Harvey Korman portrayed two elderly people rocking on the porch and contemplating what might have been had they made other decisions early in life. In the other, she and Harvey were an uptight married couple who fought with each other constantly and who had problems with their independent teenage daughter, played by Vicki Lawrence (who, disconcertingly, looked very much like Carol).

Jim Nabors, one of Carol's close friends, was her good-luck charm and always appeared as the guest star on the opening telecast of each season. Tim Conway, who had been a frequent guest in *The Carol Burnett Show*'s early years, joined the regular cast in the fall of 1975. Harvey Korman decided to leave the series in the spring of 1977, a loss that was felt deeply by Carol, who had worked so well with him for so long. The resulting need for a strong lead actor-comic was met by Dick Van Dyke, who was signed to be Carol's co-star that fall.

The chemistry that had existed between Carol and Harvey Korman was not present with her new co-star, and Dick Van Dyke left the show only three months after he had arrived. For the first time in years, Carol's ratings faltered, forcing the move to Sunday nights in December 1977. Semi-regular guest stars Ken Berry and Steve Lawrence tried to help fill the void caused by the lack of a strong male lead, but by the following spring, after eleven years on the air, Carol decided to give up the weekly grind. In a special two-hour finale, on March 29, 1978, highlights from past shows were intermixed with new material. With the series no longer in production, reruns were aired during the summer of 1978, the only time *The Carol Burnett Show* was ever aired during the summer.

CAROLYN GILBERT SHOW, THE

Music

FIRST TELECAST: *January 15, 1950*
LAST TELECAST: *July 30, 1950*
BROADCAST HISTORY:
Jan 1950–Jul 1950, ABC Sun 7:30–7:45
REGULARS:
Carolyn Gilbert
Don Tennant

This musical variety program was hosted by singer-pianist Carolyn Gilbert. The young puppeteer and vocalist Don Tennant provided skits to introduce Miss Gilbert's numbers.

CARTER COUNTRY

Situation Comedy

FIRST TELECAST: *September 15, 1977*
LAST TELECAST:
BROADCAST HISTORY:
Sep 1977–Mar 1978, ABC Thur 9:30–10:00
May 1978–Aug 1978, ABC Tue 9:30–10:00
Sep 1978, ABC Sat 8:00–8:30
Oct 1978– , ABC Sat 8:30–9:00
CAST:
Chief Roy Mobey ....Victor French
Sgt. Curtis Baker ....Kene Holliday
Mayor Teddy Burnside ......Richard Paul
Deputy Jasper DeWitt, Jr. ....Harvey Vernon
Deputy Harley Puckett ......Guich Koock
Cloris Phebus ....Barbara Cason
Lucille Banks ....Vernee Watson

This racial comedy was set in the small Georgia town of Clinton Corners, "just down the road from Plains" (home of President Jimmy Carter). Chief Roy Mobey was the lovable redneck police chief and Sgt. Baker his ultra-sharp black deputy, who had been trained in big-city police methods in New York. Despite the obvious points of conflict—black *vs.* white, big city *vs.* backwoods—the two had a basic respect for each other. Also on the force was Cloris Phebus, a man-hungry policewoman; young Harley; and "Good ole boy" Jasper. Teddy Burnside was the chubby, weak-willed mayor, a mama's boy who was elected because nobody else wanted the job, and Curtis's girlfriend Lucille was the mayor's secretary.

CARTOON TELETALES

Children's

FIRST TELECAST: *November 14, 1948*
LAST TELECAST: *September 24, 1950*
BROADCAST HISTORY:

Nov 1948–Sep 1949, ABC Sun 6:00–6:30
May 1950–Aug 1950, ABC Sun 6:30–7:00
Aug 1950–Sep 1950, ABC Sun 6:00–6:30

HOSTS:

Chuck Luchsinger
Jack Luchsinger

This children's program was hosted by the cartoonist Chuck Luchsinger and his brother Jack. Jack, a professional actor, narrated stories from the big *Cartoon Tele-Tales* storybook while his brother drew amusing illustrations to match. For a time the program was highly popular with both children and their parents, and a continuing art contest drew as many as 5,600 entries a month during 1949. Among the characters introduced were Usta the Rooster, Bumsniff the Bloodhound, Madcap the Mountain Goat, and Mimi the Mole. *Cartoon TeleTales* began in Philadelphia in May 1948, moved to New York as a late-afternoon entry in June, and became a 6:00 P.M. network entry in November.

CASABLANCA

International Intrigue

FIRST TELECAST: *September 27, 1955*
LAST TELECAST: *April 24, 1956*
BROADCAST HISTORY:

Sep 1955–Apr 1956, ABC Tue 7:30–8:30

CAST:

Rick Jason .... Charles McGraw
Capt. Renaud .... Marcel Dalio
Ferrari .... Dan Seymour
Sasha .... Michael Fox
Sam .... Clarence Muse
Ludwig .... Ludwig Stossel

Casablanca, based on the classic 1942 film of the same name, presented stories of romance and adventure in a North African setting. Charles McGraw recreated the Bogart role of Rick Jason, owner of the Club Américain in Casablanca, a bistro that attracted both intrigue and beautiful women. Capt. Renaud was the unsympathetic police captain, and Sam, the inimitable piano player.

Casablanca was seen approximately every third week as one of three rotating elements of *Warner Brothers Presents.*

CASE HISTORIES OF SCOTLAND YARD

syndicated title for *Scotland Yard*

CASH AND CARRY

Quiz/Audience Participation

FIRST TELECAST: *June 20, 1946*
LAST TELECAST: *July 1, 1947*
BROADCAST HISTORY:

Jun 1946–Jan 1947, DUM Thu 9:00–9:30
Apr 1947–Jul 1947, DUM Tue 7:30–8:00

EMCEE:

Dennis James

Sponsored by Libby's, this early quiz show was set in a grocery store, its shelves lined with cans of the sponsor's products to which were attached questions worth $5, $10, or $15. There were also studio stunts, such as a man assigned to pantomime a woman taking off her clothes for a bath, or a blindfolded wife trying to feed her husband ice cream. At-home viewers could also participate, via phone, in a segment that involved guessing what was under a large barrel.

As with some other early programs, it is not known whether this was fed over a network from the start, though it was being networked by early 1947 at the latest.

CAVALCADE OF AMERICA

Dramatic Anthology

FIRST TELECAST: *October 1, 1952*
LAST TELECAST: *June 4, 1957*
BROADCAST HISTORY:

Oct 1952–Jun 1953, NBC Wed 8:30–9:00
Sep 1953–Jun 1955, ABC Tue 7:30–8:00 (OS)
Sep 1955–Jun 1957, ABC Tue 9:30–10:00 (OS)

Cavalcade of America was one of the most prestigious dramatic shows of network radio, sponsored for 18 years (1935–1953) by DuPont as a means of enhancing the company's image and bringing great events in American history to an audience of millions. In 1952 DuPont brought the *Cavalcade* to TV, and viewers were treated to the same meticulously accurate stories of American heroes both famous and obscure, in historical periods ranging from colonial days to the Revolution to the early 1900s. The first telecast was a humorous piece about Benjamin Franklin's lighter side.

In 1955 the format was modified to include contemporary stories, such as a biography of Dr. Ralphe Bunche and an account of a 1948 Olympic swimming star's battle with polio. In this season and the one following, an increasing number of episodes dealt with ordinary people unconnected with great events, but triumphing over some adversity or showing some act of courage.

Actors and actresses appearing on *Cavalcade* were generally lesser-known talent, as the focus was always on the story.

For the first season the program was seen every two weeks, alternating with *Scott Music Hall*. In 1955 it changed its name to *DuPont Cavalcade Theater* and in 1956 to *DuPont Theater*.

CAVALCADE OF BANDS

Musical Variety

FIRST TELECAST: *January 17, 1950*

LAST TELECAST: *September 25, 1951*

BROADCAST HISTORY:

Jan 1950–Sep 1951, DUM Tues 9:00–10:00

EMCEE:

Fred Robbins (Jan 1950)
Warren Hull (Jan–Apr 1950)
Ted Steele (May 1950–Feb 1951)
Buddy Rogers (Feb–Sep 1951)

This was one of the DuMont network's major efforts in the musical variety field, and was designed to lure some of the NBC audience away following the top-rated Milton Berle hour (which ran Tuesday 8–9 P.M.). The "star" of this series was a different big-name band each week, ranging from the "sweet" music of Guy Lombardo and Lawrence Welk to the big-band swing of Lionel Hampton and Duke Ellington. Virtually every major dance band in the country appeared on this program at one time or another.

In addition to the "Band of the Week," top-line singers and comedians filled out the bill, including such names as Jackie Gleason, Kitty Kallen, and Peggy Lee, as well as a number of lesser lights. Four different hosts presided over the *Cavalcade of Bands* during its year-and-a-half run: New York disc jockey Fred Robbins at the beginning, replaced almost immediately by Warren Hull, who was followed by Ted Steele and finally by former matinee idol Buddy Rogers.

CAVALCADE OF SPORTS

see *Boxing* and *Gillette Summer Sports Reel*

CAVALCADE OF STARS

Comedy Variety

FIRST TELECAST: *June 4, 1949*

LAST TELECAST: *September 26, 1952*

BROADCAST HISTORY:

Jun 1949–Sep 1950, DUM Sat 9:00–10:00
Sep 1950–Sep 1952, DUM Fri 10:00–11:00

EMCEE:

Jack Carter (1949–1950)
Jerry Lester (1950)
Jackie Gleason (1950–1952)
Larry Storch (summer 1951, 1952)

REGULARS:

Art Carney (1950–1952)
Pert Kelton (1950–1952)
June Taylor Dancers (1950–1952)

ORCHESTRA:

Sammy Spear/Charlie Spear

Big-budget variety shows seemed to be taking over television in 1949. DuMont's answer to such hits as NBC's *Texaco Star Theatre* and CBS's *Ed Sullivan Show* was the *Cavalcade of Stars*, which gave early exposure to a number of talented performers who later became major TV celebrities.

The first host was Jack Carter, who maintained a lightning pace throughout the 60 minutes, mugging, tossing off gags, and working with the guests in skits. Just as he began to build a following, NBC stole him away in February 1950, to front the first hour of its *Saturday Night Revue*, on the same night as *Cavalcade*. His replacement was round-faced comic Jerry Lester, who was no less manic but who remained on the show for only four months, until July 1950. (He later became TV's first late-night star, on NBC's original *Broadway Open House*.) Lester's replacement, and one of the major talents on DuMont during the next two years, was Jackie Gleason.

Gleason, who had starred in the first, unsuccessful version of *The Life of Riley* in 1949–1950, immediately began to build a large and loyal following, a process that was helped when *Cavalcade* moved to a more propitious time period on Friday night, away from the competition of Saturday's Sid Caesar–Imogene Coca hour. One of the chief delights of *Cavalcade* was the variety of comic characterizations Gleason introduced on the show, many of which he was to continue throughout his TV career. The first to become enormously popular, in 1950, was "The Bachelor," in which he portrayed a helpless, spouseless male bedeviled by the necessities of housekeeping for one. Typical routines, all in pantomime, were "The Bachelor Gets His Own Breakfast," "Doing the Laundry," and "Dressing for a Date," all to the soft music of "Somebody Loves Me."

Later additions included the dissolute, top-hatted playboy Reggie Van Gleason III; The Poor Soul; the garrulous Joe the Bartender, talking about his patrons Crazy Guggenheim, Moriarty the undertaker, Duddy Duddleston, and Bookshelf Robinson; the continually oppressed Fenwick Babbitt; and Charlie Bratten, "The Loudmouth." The best, however, was probably "The Honeymooners," introduced in the fall of 1951. Bus driver Ralph Kramden was the perfect incarnation of the always boastful, always scheming, always thwarted "poor slob" who would never get away from his dingy apartment and nagging wife.

Part of Gleason's success lay with his excellent supporting cast—which included Pert Kelton as the original Alice Kramden and Art Carney as his foil in many of the sketches—and his stable of topnotch writers (Joe Bigelow and Harry Crane helped him develop "The Honeymooners"). But most of the appeal lay with Gleason himself, and when CBS lured him away in 1952—with a reported offer of $8,000 per week instead of the $1,600 he was getting from DuMont—there was nowhere for *Cavalcade* to go but down. After lingering through the summer with comedian Larry Storch as host, it ended in September 1952.

CAVALIER THEATRE

Dramatic Anthology

FIRST TELECAST: *December 5, 1951*

LAST TELECAST: *December 26, 1951*

BROADCAST HISTORY:

Dec 1951, NBC Wed 10:30–11:00

A short-lived anthology series that filled NBC's Wednesday 10:30 P.M. time slot between the last telecast of *The Freddy Martin Show* and the premiere of *Pantomime Quiz* on January 2, 1952.

CELANESE THEATRE

Dramatic Anthology

FIRST TELECAST: *October 3, 1951*

LAST TELECAST: *June 25, 1952*

BROADCAST HISTORY:

Oct 1951–Dec 1951, ABC Wed 10:00–11:00
Dec 1951–Jun 1952, ABC Wed 10:00–10:30

A live dramatic series telecast from New York, *Celanese Theatre* presented high-quality plays by leading playwrights. The first *Celanese* telecast was Eugene O'Neill's *Ah, Wilderness!*, followed by such classics as O'Neill's *Anna Christie*, Maxwell Anderson's *Winterset*, and Elmer Rice's *Street Scene*. Stars appearing included Alfred Drake, David Niven, Mickey Rooney, and Lillian Gish. *Celanese Theatre* appeared on alternate weeks throughout its run.

CELEBRITY CHALLENGE OF THE SEXES

Sports

FIRST TELECAST: January 31, 1978

LAST TELECAST: February 28, 1978

BROADCAST HISTORY:

Jan 1978–Feb 1978, CBS Tue 8:00–8:30

HOST:

Tom Brookshier

COACHES:

McLean Stevenson (men)
Barbara Rhoades (women)

This series was an offshoot of the CBS Sunday afternoon sports series *Challenge of the Sexes*. As the title implies, *Celebrity Challenge of the Sexes* pitted show business personalities against each other in various sporting events. To make the contests more competitive, the men were given handicaps to compensate for their superior size or strength. Sports announcer Tom Brookshier acted as host and commentator, while McLean Stevenson and Barbara Rhoades coached the competitors, although the "coaches" played their roles primarily for laughs. Among the stars participating were Karen Black and Don Adams in ping pong, Barbi Benton and baseball star Reggie Jackson in a bicycle race, and Elke Sommer and Pat Harrington on an obstacle course.

CELEBRITY GAME, THE

Quiz/Audience Participation

FIRST TELECAST: *April 5, 1964*

LAST TELECAST: *September 9, 1965*

BROADCAST HISTORY:

Apr 1964–Sep 1964, CBS Sun 9:00–9:30
Apr 1965–Sep 1965, CBS Thu 9:30–10:00

EMCEE:

Carl Reiner

At times this series seemed more like a comedy program than a quiz show. There were three contestants each week and a rotating panel of nine celebrities. Reiner would pose a question such as "Can a man love two women at the same time?," "Should nude scenes be banned from Hollywood movies?," or "Can most women keep a secret?" The individual panelists decided yes or no, and each contestant tried to guess which way a given panelist had voted, and why. The "why" gave the panelists the opportunity to make funny responses. Contestants won money for correct guessing but the money was incidental to the humor.

CELEBRITY TALENT SCOUTS

Variety

FIRST TELECAST: *August 1, 1960*

LAST TELECAST: *September 26, 1960*

BROADCAST HISTORY:

Aug 1960–Sep 1960, CBS Mon 9:00–9:30

HOST:

Sam Levenson

This series was the 1960 summer replacement for *The Danny Thomas Show*. Each week Sam Levenson introduced three or four celebrities who had new young "discoveries" they felt deserved national television exposure. The "discoveries" then performed their specialties, generally comedy, singing, or dancing.

CELEBRITY TIME

Quiz/Audience Participation

FIRST TELECAST: *January 23, 1949*

LAST TELECAST: *September 21, 1952*

BROADCAST HISTORY:

Jan 1949–Mar 1949, CBS Sun 8:30–9:00
Mar 1949–Jun 1949, ABC Sun 8:30–9:00
Jul 1949–Mar 1950, ABC Sun 10:00–10:30
Apr 1950–Jun 1950, CBS Sun 10:00–10:30
Oct 1950–Sep 1952, CBS Sun 10:00–10:30

EMCEE:

Conrad Nagel

PANELISTS:

John Daly (1948–1950)
Ilka Chase (1948–1950)
Kyle MacDonnell (1950–1951)
Herman Hickman (1950–1952)
Martha Wright (1950–1951)
Mary McCarty (1951–1952)
Jane Wilson (1951–1952)

This program began as a combination guessing game and battle of the sexes, teaming regular panelists with guest celebrities of their own sex to compete against a similar team of the opposite sex. Guests ranged from Sir Thomas Beecham to Slapsie Maxie Rosenbloom. At first the questions were reasonably intelligent, involving, for example, guessing names in the news, identifying famous places from film clips, or providing information about live demonstrations or skits performed on the show. Later, skits and performances by the guests began to predominate until the proceedings more resembled a variety show than a quiz. Finally, in June, 1952, the panel was dropped altogether; during its final months *Celebrity Time* became a straight musical variety program, with Conrad Nagel as host.

The series underwent quite a few title changes during its career, beginning in November 1948 as a local New York program called *The Eyes Have It* (Douglas Edwards, host), quickly changing to *Stop, Look and Listen* (Paul Gallico, host), then *Riddle Me This* in December 1948 (with Nagel), *Goodrich Celebrity Time* in March 1949, and finally *Celebrity Time* in April 1950.

CENTER STAGE

Dramatic Anthology

FIRST TELECAST: *June 1, 1954*

LAST TELECAST: *September 21, 1954*

BROADCAST HISTORY:

Jun 1954–Sep 1954, ABC Tue 9:30–10:30

Center Stage consisted of filmed dramas presented on alternate weeks during the summer of 1954, as a replacement for *Motorola TV Theatre*. An assortment of notable actors and actresses were seen, including Walter Matthau, Lee Marvin, Vivian Blaine, and Charles Coburn.

CHAMBER MUSIC HOUR

see *Chicago Symphony Chamber Orchestra*

CHAMPAGNE AND ORCHIDS

Music

FIRST TELECAST: *September 6, 1948*
LAST TELECAST: *January 10, 1949*
BROADCAST HISTORY:

Sep 1948–Nov 1948, DUM Mon 8:00–8:15
Nov 1948–Jan 1949, DUM Mon 7:45–8:00

HOSTESS:

Adrienne (Meyerberg)

ANNOUNCER:

Robert Turner

ALSO:

David Lippman on the theremin

This musical interlude featured Adrienne, a svelte brunette who sang sultry torch songs in French, Spanish, and English. The setting was a fancy nightclub, and the atmosphere of elegance was enhanced by Adrienne's glamorous gowns, lent by some of New York's leading stores. Even the announcer, with whom she sometimes danced, wore a tux.

Seen originally as a local New York show beginning in December 1947, *Champagne and Orchids* was sent out over the DuMont network beginning in September 1948.

CHAMPIONS, THE

Adventure

FIRST TELECAST: *June 10, 1968*
LAST TELECAST: *September 9, 1968*
BROADCAST HISTORY:

Jun 1968–Sep 1968, NBC Mon 8:00–9:00

CAST:

Craig Stirling ....Stuart Damon
Sharon Macready ......Alexandra Bastedo
Richard Barrett ....William Gaunt
Tremayne ....Anthony Nicholls

Craig, Sharon, and Richard were three international crime fighters with special "powers," which had been given to them by members of an unknown race from a lost civilization deep in the wastelands of Tibet. The powers included extraordinary mental abilities, the ability to see in the dark, superhuman strength, and assorted other physical talents. All these special skills were put to good use by the trio in their missions for Nemesis, a Geneva-based international agency similar to Interpol. Tremayne, head of Nemesis, was their boss and principal contact.

CHANCE OF A LIFETIME

Quiz/Audience Participation

FIRST TELECAST: *September 6, 1950*
LAST TELECAST: *November 28, 1951*
BROADCAST HISTORY:

Sep 1950–Nov 1951, ABC Wed 7:30–8:00

EMCEE:

John Reed King

REGULARS:

Dick Collier
Russell Arms
Liza Palmer

This quiz show, which was also heard on radio, used singers and comedians to provide clues for contestants. A female contestant might be placed in a mock-Egyptian setting and wooed by rotund comic Dick Collier, to hint that the correct answer was "Cleopatra." Or, a couple of professional wrestlers might come on stage and the contestant would be asked to name the holds they were using. Singers Russell Arms and Liza Palmer gave musical clues.

CHANCE OF A LIFETIME

Talent

FIRST TELECAST: *May 8, 1952*
LAST TELECAST: *June 23, 1956*
BROADCAST HISTORY:

May 1952–Aug 1953, ABC Thu 8:30–9:00
Sep 1953–Jun 1955, DUM Fri 10:00–10:30
Jul 1955–Feb 1956, ABC Sun 9:00–9:30
Mar 1956–Jun 1956, ABC Sat 10:00–10:30

EMCEE:

Dennis James

This talent show gave network exposure to aspiring young performers who had some prior professional experience. Winners, chosen by the studio audience, got $1,000 and a week's engagement at New York's Latin Quarter, while runners-up often landed bookings at lesser night spots. Those competing ranged from banjo players to opera singers, but surprisingly, despite their professional orientation, none seems to have gone on to become a big name in show business. According to a review of the show after its first year, the top "find" up to that time was a comedienne named Helen Halpin, who subsequently had a minor career on Broadway and TV.

CHANNING

Drama

FIRST TELECAST: *September 18, 1963*
LAST TELECAST: *April 8, 1964*
BROADCAST HISTORY:
Sep 1963–Apr 1964, ABC Wed 10:00–11:00
CAST:
Dean Fred Baker ....Henry Jones
Prof. Joseph Howe ....Jason Evers

Mythical Channing University was the setting for this series of dramas revolving around life on a college campus. Fred Baker was the school's dean, and Joseph Howe was a professor of English. Their personal and professional lives provided the bases for many stories, as they related to students, faculty, and the nonacademic world. At times the action focused more strongly on the students or other faculty members.

CHARADE QUIZ

Charades

FIRST TELECAST: *December 4, 1947*
LAST TELECAST: *June 23, 1949*
BROADCAST HISTORY:
Dec 1947–May 1948, DUM Thu 8:30–9:00
May 1948–Jul 1948, DUM Thu 8:00–8:30
Aug 1948–Jan 1949, DUM Thu 8:30–9:00
Jan 1949–Apr 1949, DUM Wed 8:00–8:30
May 1949–Jun 1949, DUM Thu 8:30–9:00
EMCEE:
Bill Slater
PANEL:
Minnabess Lewis
Herb Polesie
Bob Shepard
Jackson Beck
REPERTORY COMPANY:
Allan Frank
Richard Seff
Ellen Fenwick

Charades were a favorite type of program on early television, since they were so obviously visual. This show used subjects suggested by viewers and acted out by a varying repertory company of young actors (those remaining on the show for several months are listed above). If the actors stumped the panel, the viewer who sent in the suggestion got $15.

CHARLEY WEAVER SHOW, THE

see *Hobby Lobby*

CHARLIE FARRELL SHOW, THE

Situation Comedy

FIRST TELECAST: *July 2, 1956*
LAST TELECAST: *September 19, 1960*
BROADCAST HISTORY:
Jul 1956–Sep 1956, CBS Mon 9:00–9:30
Jul 1957–Sep 1957, NBC Mon 8:00–8:30
Aug 1960–Sep 1960, CBS Mon 7:30–8:00
CAST:
Charlie Farrell ....Himself
Dad Farrell ....Charles Winninger
Sherman Hull ....Richard Deacon
Mrs. Papernow ....Kathryn Card
Pierre ....Leon Askin
Rodney ....Jeff Silver

The Charlie Farrell Show was originally telecast as the 1956 summer replacement for *I Love Lucy.* It was the semi-autobiographical story of its star, as the stories were all based on actual incidents that had occurred at the Racquet Club, the exclusive Palm Springs, California, resort owned and managed by Mr. Farrell. Charlie had problems with everybody—the resort's manager, Sherman Hull; the chef, Pierre; his nephew, Rodney; his housekeeper, Mrs. Papernow; and even his lovable father. Reruns of the series were aired by NBC in 1957 and by CBS in 1960.

CHARLIE WILD, PRIVATE DETECTIVE

Detective Drama

FIRST TELECAST: *December 22, 1950*
LAST TELECAST: *June 19, 1952*
BROADCAST HISTORY:
Dec 1950–Mar 1951, CBS Fri 9:00–9:30
Apr 1951–Jun 1951, CBS Wed 9:00–9:30
Sep 1951–Mar 1952, ABC Tue 8:00–8:30
Mar 1952–Jun 1952, DUM Thu 10:00–10:30
CAST:
Charlie Wild (1950–1951)
.... Kevin O'Morrison
Charlie Wild (1951–1952)
.... John McQuade
Effie Perrine ....Cloris Leachman

Charlie Wild was a tough New York City private eye who got into a fight in almost every episode of this live detective series, one of many on the air in the late 1940s and early 1950s. The series had started on CBS radio in the late 1940s and was brought to television with Kevin O'Morrison, who had played the lead in the radio version. He was replaced in January 1951 by John McQuade, who remained in the part through the show's rapid movement from CBS to ABC to DuMont. The show's only other regular cast member was Charlie's secretary, Effie Perrine.

CHARLIE'S ANGELS

Detective Drama

FIRST TELECAST: *September 22, 1976*

LAST TELECAST:

BROADCAST HISTORY:

Sep 1976–Aug 1977, ABC Wed 10:00–11:00
Aug 1977– , ABC Wed 9:00–10:00

CAST:

Sabrina Duncan ....Kate Jackson
Jill Munroe (1976–1977) .... Farrah Fawcett-Majors
Kelly Garrett .. ..Jaclyn Smith
John Bosley ....David Doyle
Charlie Townsend (voice only) .... John Forsythe
Kris Munroe (1977–) ......Cheryl Ladd

Sex, pure and simple, seemed to be the principal ingredient in the considerable success of this detective show. Denunciations of "massage parlor television" and "voyeurism" only brought more viewers to the screen, to see what the controversy was about. Often they were rather disappointed, as a lot more seemed to be promised than delivered, but *Charlie's Angels* nevertheless ended its first season as one of the top hits on television.

The plot involved three sexy police-trained detectives working for an unseen boss named Charlie, who relayed assignments by telephone. Charlie's assistant, Bosley, was on hand to help the girls and fret about costs, but he hardly seemed likely to make a pass at any of them. Most of the cases involved health spas, Las Vegas night spots, or other places where the girls could appear in bikinis or other scanty attire.

Sabrina was the cool, multilingual leader, Jill the athletic type, and Kelly the former showgirl who had "been around." Usually they worked as an undercover team. When they investigated a killing in the army, Jill and Kelly became recruits and Sabrina a base nurse; when it was the death of a roller-derby queen, Sabrina posed as an insurance investigator, Kelly as a magazine writer, and Jill as a derby competitor.

Farrah Fawcett-Majors was the last of the angels to be cast (the show needed a blonde) and was little known compared to the lead, Kate Jackson, when the series began. Farrah quickly became the object of a tremendous fad, based partially on her gorgeous flowing blonde hair, and partially on some cheesecake publicity photos, including one now-famous swimsuit pose which showed the fine points of her anatomy in marvelous detail. Farrah Fawcett-Majors dolls were marketed, as were T-shirts with her picture and dozens of other gimmicks. Heady with all the sudden adulation, she walked out on the series, with the intention of launching a career in feature films. This started a series of lawsuits, which ended when she finally agreed to make a limited number of guest appearances on the show. Meanwhile her place as a regular was taken over by Cheryl Ladd, who was introduced to viewers as Kris Munroe, Jill's younger sister. Kris's qualifications for the role seemed to fit the show's standards: 35-23-34.

CHASE

Police Drama

FIRST TELECAST: *September 11, 1973*

LAST TELECAST: *August 28, 1974*

BROADCAST HISTORY:

Sep 1973–Jan 1974, NBC Tue 8:00–9:00
Jan 1974–Aug 1974, NBC Wed 8:00–9:00

CAST:

Capt. Chase Reddick ....Mitchell Ryan
Officer Norm Hamilton ....Reid Smith
Officer Steve Baker ....Michael Richardson
Officer Fred Sing ....Brian Fong
Sgt. Sam MacCray ....Wayne Maunder
Inspector Frank Dawson ......Albert Reed
Officer Ed Rice ....Gary Crosby
Officer Tom Wilson ....Craig Gardner

One of the variations on the police-show format so popular in the early 1970s was the "special cop," the policeman or unit with special skills solving otherwise unsolvable crimes with unconventional means. Capt. Chase Reddick's plainclothes unit, though nominally part of the Los Angeles Police Department, was accountable only to the Chief of Detectives and had a virtual free hand in solving cases none of the other police divisions could crack. Reddick had only four men, each with a useful skill: Sam MacCray, a specialist in the training and handling of police dogs; Norm Hamilton, a former Vietnam War helicopter pilot; Steve Baker, a hot-rod car driver; and Fred Sing, an expert motorcycle rider. Occasional "straight" cops also appeared in the series, including officer Ed Rice, played by Gary Crosby—who on other duty tours turned up in Jack Webb's *Adam 12*, the model of the "straight cop" genre.

CHECKMATE

Detective Drama

FIRST TELECAST: *September 17, 1960*
LAST TELECAST: *September 19, 1962*
BROADCAST HISTORY:
Sep 1960–Sep 1961, CBS Sat 8:30–9:30
Oct 1961–Sep 1962, CBS Wed 8:30–9:30
CAST:
Don Corey ....Anthony George
Jed Sills ....Doug McClure
Carl Hyatt ....Sebastian Cabot

Checkmate, Inc. was the name of a very fancy, very expensive investigative agency operated in San Francisco by Don Corey and Jed Sills. The goal of the company was to prevent crimes and to forestall death. In most of their cases, Don and Jed tried to protect the lives of people who had been threatened or who suspected they were possible targets of criminals. Helping them with the analytical side of the operation was Carl Hyatt, a bearded and very British former Oxford professor of criminology, who acted as special consultant to the firm.

CHEER TELEVISION THEATRE

Dramatic Anthology

FIRST TELECAST: *May 30, 1954*
LAST TELECAST: *June 27, 1954*
BROADCAST HISTORY:
May 1954–Jun 1954, NBC Sun 7:00–7:30

This five-week series of filmed dramas filled the period between the cancellation of *The Paul Winchell Show* and the start of *Kollege of Musical Knowledge*.

CHER

Musical Variety

FIRST TELECAST: *February 16, 1975*
LAST TELECAST: *January 4, 1976*
BROADCAST HISTORY:
Feb 1975–Jun 1975, CBS Sun 7:30–8:30
Sep 1975–Jan 1976, CBS Sun 8:00–9:00
REGULARS:
Cher Bono
Gailard Sartain
The Tony Charmoli Dancers (1975)
The Anita Mann Dancers (1975–1976)
The Jimmy Dale Orchestra (1975)
The Jack Eskew Orchestra (1975–1976)

Following their divorce in 1974, pop singers Sonny and Cher Bono, who had formerly starred together on *The Sonny and Cher Comedy Hour*, each hosted a series of their own. His was a short-lived variety series on ABC in the fall of 1974 (see *The Sonny Comedy Revue*), and hers was *Cher*, a musical variety hour with guest stars that premiered the following February. Steve Martin, Teri Garr, and Sonny and Cher's daughter Chastity were frequent guest stars during Cher's solo period.

The magic Sonny and Cher had had together did not survive the transition to singles. Cher's solo venture limped along on CBS for almost a year, with a new dance group and orchestra in the fall of 1975, by which time she and Sonny decided to try it again as a team, at least professionally. One month after *Cher* left the air, *The Sonny and Cher Show* reappeared in the time period that *Cher* had vacated.

CHESTERFIELD PRESENTS

Dramatic Anthology

FIRST TELECAST: *January 10, 1952*
LAST TELECAST: *March 6, 1952*
BROADCAST HISTORY:
Jan 1952–Mar 1952, NBC Thu 9:00–9:30

This dramatic anthology series, also known as *Dramatic Mystery*, alternated with *Dragnet* on Thursday nights during the latter's first two months on network television.

CHESTERFIELD SOUND OFF TIME

Comedy Variety

FIRST TELECAST: *October 14, 1951*
LAST TELECAST: *January 6, 1952*
BROADCAST HISTORY:
Oct 1951–Jan 1952, Sun 7:00–7:30
STARS:
Bob Hope
Jerry Lester
Fred Allen

This half-hour comedy variety series was emceed on a rotating basis by three major stars. The programs involved skits, monologues, and production numbers keyed to each star's brand of comedy. The original version of *Dragnet* was previewed as a special edition of *Chesterfield Sound Off Time* on December 16, 1951. Jack Webb starred in the preview, while his superior was played by Raymond Burr, later of *Perry Mason* and *Ironside*.

CHESTERFIELD SUPPER CLUB

see *Perry Como*

CHET HUNTLEY REPORTING

News/Documentary

FIRST TELECAST: *December 22, 1957*
LAST TELECAST: *June 18, 1963*
BROADCAST HISTORY:

Dec 1957–Sep 1959, NBC Sun 6:30–7:00
Jan 1962–Sep 1962, NBC Fri 10:30–11:00
Oct 1962–Jun 1963, NBC Tue 10:30–11:00

HOST/REPORTER:

Chet Huntley

This documentary series premiered on Sunday afternoons in April 1956 under the title *Outlook*. It began as a weekend news program that included news headlines and covered four or five stories at greater length, with filmed reports. Narration and commentary was by Huntley. When the program moved to Sunday evenings in December 1957, the format was changed to provide in-depth exploration of a single subject. From 1959 to 1961 the program was aired on Sunday afternoons at 5:30 P.M. On January 12, 1962, it moved to Friday nights and continued in the evening hours for another year and a half, retaining the same news-documentary format with Huntley interviewing news personalities and exploring topical issues in depth.

The program title changed several times during its seven-year run. Originally *Outlook*, it later became *Chet Huntley . . . Reporting* (November 1958) and *Time: Present . . . Chet Huntley Reporting* (October 1959) before going back to *Chet Huntley Reporting* (September 1960).

CHEVROLET ON BROADWAY

Musical Variety

FIRST TELECAST: *July 17, 1956*
LAST TELECAST: *September 13, 1956*
BROADCAST HISTORY:

Jul 1956, NBC Tue/Thu 7:30–7:45
Aug 1955–Sep 1956, NBC Thu 7:30–7:45

REGULARS:

Snooky Lanson
Mello Larks, vocal quartet

This summer replacement for *The Dinah Shore Show* featured Snooky Lanson, star of the popular *Your Hit Parade*. For its first three weeks it ran as a twice-weekly series on Tuesdays and Thursdays, then switched to once a week for the duration of the summer.

CHEVROLET ON BROADWAY

see *Chevrolet Tele-Theatre*

CHEVROLET SHOWROOM

see *Your Chevrolet Showroom*

CHEVROLET TELE-THEATRE

Dramatic Anthology

FIRST TELECAST: *September 27, 1948*
LAST TELECAST: *June 26, 1950*
BROADCAST HISTORY:

Sep 1948–Jan 1949, NBC Mon 8:00–8:30
Jan 1949–Apr 1949, NBC Mon 8:30–9:00
May 1949–Jun 1950, NBC Mon 8:00–8:30

Chevrolet Tele-Theatre was a big-budget live dramatic series that presented an original play or adaptation each week during the 1948–1949 and 1949–1950 seasons. Top-flight writers and actors were used, the latter including such names as Paul Muni, Eddie Albert, Nanette Fabray, Basil Rathbone, Mercedes McCambridge, Rex Harrison, and E. G. Marshall. Gertrude Berg made her TV debut on the October 18, 1948, telecast in the comedy "Whistle, Daughter, Whistle." This was based on her highly popular radio series *The Goldbergs* and became the prototype for the TV series of the same name which premiered a few months later. *Chevrolet Tele-Theatre* was known as *Chevrolet on Broadway* during parts of the 1948–1949 season.

CHEVY MYSTERY SHOW, THE

Dramatic Anthology

FIRST TELECAST: *May 29, 1960*
LAST TELECAST: *September 17, 1961*
BROADCAST HISTORY:

May 1960–Sep 1960, NBC Sun 9:00–10:00
Jul 1961–Sep 1961, NBC Sun 9:00–10:00

HOSTS:

Walter Slezak
Vincent Price

Aired as a summer replacement for *The Dinah Shore Chevy Show*, these dramas were hosted by Walter Slezak through September 4, 1960, and by Vincent Price for the last three telecasts. The host introduced the program, introduced each act, and then closed the program. Reruns of the plays hosted by Walter Slezak were aired the following summer under the title *Sunday Mystery Hour.* Among the plays, which emphasized suspense and mystery without resorting to violence, were: "The Summer Hero," written by Charlotte Armstrong and starring Zachary Scott and Patty McCormack; "Dead Man's Walk," starring Robert Culp and Abby Dalton; "Trial by Fury," starring Agnes Moorehead and Warren Stevens; and an adaptation of the A. A. Milne story "The Perfect Alibi," starring Janet Blair.

CHEVY SHOW, THE

Variety

FIRST TELECAST: *October 4, 1955*
LAST TELEECAST: *September 4, 1956*
BROADCAST HISTORY:
Oct 1955–Sep 1956, NBC Tue 8:00–9:00

There was no regular star on this variety series, which aired every third Tuesday during the 1955–1956 season on a rotating basis with *The Milton Berle Show* and *The Martha Raye Show.* Bob Hope and Dinah Shore—who later had her own *Chevy Show* series—appeared frequently during the winter season, and Betty Hutton and Ethel Merman each starred in one show apiece. During the summer of 1956 *The Chevy Show* continued to appear every third week, alternating with assorted specials. Gisele Mackenzie, Fred Waring, and Janet Blair appeared as hosts for the summer edition.

CHEVY SHOW, THE

Musical Variety

FIRST TELECAST: *June 22, 1958*
LAST TELECAST: *September 27, 1959*
BROADCAST HISTORY:
Jun 1958–Sep 1958, NBC Sun 9:00–10:00
Jun 1959–Sep 1959, NBC Sun 9:00–10:00
REGULARS:
Janet Blair
John Raitt
Edie Adams (1958)
Dorothy Kirsten
Stan Freberg (1958)
Rowan and Martin (1958)

This *Chevy Show* was the summer replacement for *The Dinah Shore Chevy Show* in 1958 and 1959. The format was a mixed bag of popular and classical music, skits, and monologues. During the summer of 1958 the show had three musical-comedy stars—Janet Blair, John Raitt and Edie Adams—who appeared each week and took turns as host. The opera singer Dorothy Kirsten was a featured regular; Stan Freberg and Rowan and Martin provided humor. During the summer of 1959 Blair and Raitt returned as co-hosts, with Miss Kirsten the only other returning regular.

CHEVY SHOWROOM STARRING ANDY WILLIAMS, THE

see *Andy Williams Show, The*

CHEYENNE

Western

FIRST TELECAST: *September 20, 1955*
LAST TELECAST: *September 13, 1963*
BROADCAST HISTORY:
Sep 1955–Sep 1959, ABC Tue 7:30–8:30
Sep 1959–Dec 1962, ABC Mon 7:30–8:30
Apr 1963–Sep 1963, ABC Fri 7:30–8:30
CAST:
Cheyenne Bodie ....Clint Walker
Smitty (1955–1956) ....L. Q. Jones

The behind-the-scenes story of this series was fully as interesting as what appeared on the screen. Probably no series in TV history has undergone so much production turmoil and absorbed and spun off as many other series as did *Cheyenne.*

The on-screen story was simple enough. Cheyenne Bodie was a tall, strapping Western adventurer in the days following the Civil War—he was 6′7″ (or 6′5″, or 6′8″, depending on the press release) and a mean hombre. He drifted from job to job, encountering plenty of villains, beautiful girls, and gunfights. In one episode he might be seen as the foreman on a ranch, in another as trail scout for a wagon train, in another as a recently deputized lawman. The show was lavishly produced, movie-style, by Warner Brothers, but the attraction was obviously Clint Walker himself. He had a sidekick, Smitty, for the first season, but after that he worked alone.

Cheyenne was first seen as one of three rotating elements of *Warner Brothers Presents,* the studio's first venture into TV, and quickly emerged as the most popular of the three. Hour-long Westerns were difficult to produce on a once-a-week basis, however, so the program continued to alternate with other series, first *Conflict* (1956–1957) and then *Sugarfoot* (1957–1959). In fact, Clint Walker's *Cheyenne* was seldom seen on an every-week basis at any time during its original run.

In 1958 the brooding fighter of the screen walked out on Warner Brothers, after they refused to release him from some of the more stringent requirements of his contract, which had been signed before *Cheyenne* became a hit. Among other things, Walker did not want to have to kick back 50 percent of all personal-appearance fees to the studio, wanted higher payment for reruns, and wanted permission to make records for labels other than Warners' own. Stripped of its star, the studio nevertheless refused to give an inch and continued the series under the name *Cheyenne*, with an unknown actor named Ty Hardin in the leading role, which was now that of Bronco Layne. Walker, meanwhile, was legally prevented from working anywhere else.

In early 1959 Walker and the studio finally came to terms, and Walker returned to the series. Ty Hardin continued in a series of his own called *Bronco*. Clint Walker was obviously not happy with the settlement, for although the pot had been sweetened somewhat he felt he had simply worn out the Cheyenne character and was becoming typecast. But the program was in the top 20, and Warner Brothers was not about to let him go. "I am like a caged animal," he complained to reporters.

For part of the 1959–1960 season *Cheyenne* alternated with *Shirley Temple's Storybook*. Then for 1960–1961 *Cheyenne* became *The Cheyenne Show*, a rotating anthology in which Walker was seen on a majority of weeks, interspersed with episodes of Ty Hardin as *Bronco* and Will Hutchins as *Sugarfoot*. In 1961–1962 *Sugarfoot* was dropped and only *Cheyenne* and *Bronco* were seen. Finally, in the fall of 1962, for the last three months, the series consisted of episodes of Walker's *Cheyenne* alone. Reruns of *Cheyenne* episodes were also seen during the summer of 1963.

Cheyenne was based, rather loosely, on a 1947 movie of the same name that starred Dennis Morgan.

See *Bronco* and *Sugarfoot* for details of those series, including the period when they ran under the *Cheyenne* title.

CHICAGO JAZZ

Music

FIRST TELECAST: *November 26, 1949*

LAST TELECAST: *December 31, 1949*

BROADCAST HISTORY:

Nov 1949–Dec 1949, NBC Sat 8:30–8:45

REGULARS:

Art Van Damme Quintette
The Tailgate Seven

A live musical interlude from Chicago, this short-lived program was also known as *Sessions*. The Art Van Damme Quintette was featured on the first telecast, and The Tailgate Seven on the rest.

CHICAGO SYMPHONY

Music

FIRST TELECAST: *January 6, 1954*

LAST TELECAST: *April 6, 1955*

BROADCAST HISTORY:

Jan 1954–Mar 1954, DUM Wed 8:30–9:00
Sep 1954–Apr 1955, DUM Wed 9:00–10:00

CONDUCTORS:

Fritz Reiner
George Schick

COMMENTATOR:

George Kuyper

George Kuyper, orchestra manager of the Chicago Symphony, introduced the various pieces performed in this weekly classical-music series. During the intermissions, he also provided commentary and information about the composers and their works, from "The Music Room." The principal conductor of the Chicago Symphony at this time was Fritz Reiner, who for most of this series shared the podium with associate conductor George Schick. During the first four weeks of the 1954–1955 season, before the start of the Chicago Symphony season, this time period was occupied by *Concert Tonight*, performances by the New York Concert Choir and Orchestra under the baton of Margaret Hillis.

CHICAGO SYMPHONY CHAMBER ORCHESTRA

Music

FIRST TELECAST: *September 25, 1951*

LAST TELECAST: *March 18, 1952*

BROADCAST HISTORY:

Sep 1951–Mar 1952, ABC Tue 10:30–11:00

With 25 to 30 members of the Chicago Symphony under the baton of Rafael Kubelik, this program featured soloists from the orchestra and guest vocalists. Some of the presentations were not carried over the full ABC network. ABC also carried occasional telecasts of the Chicago Symphony during the fall of 1948 under the titles *Chamber Music Hour* and *Chamber Music*. The 1951–1952 series was also known simply as *The Symphony*.

CHICAGO TEDDY BEARS, THE

Situation Comedy

FIRST TELECAST: *September 17, 1971*

LAST TELECAST: *December 17, 1971*

BROADCAST HISTORY:

Sep 1971–Dec 1971, CBS Fri 8:00–8:30

CAST:

Linc McCray .... Dean Jones
Nick Marr .... Art Metrano
Marvin .... Marvin Kaplan
Duke .... Mickey Shaughnessy
Lefty .... Jamie Farr
Julius .... Mike Mazurki
Dutch .... Huntz Hall
Uncle Latzi .... John Banner

Linc McCray and his Uncle Latzi were partners in a Chicago speakeasy during the late 1920s in this period comedy. The speakeasy did good business and was coveted by a small-time gangster, Big Nick Marr, whose efforts to muscle in on the operation provided much of the action. It was all a family affair, since Linc and Nick were cousins and both were nephews of Uncle Latzi, who couldn't believe that his nephew Nicholas could be anything but a nice young man. Everyone else was terrified of Big Nick, however, including Marvin, Linc's bookkeeper, and the club's four inept bodyguards, Duke, Lefty, Julius, and Dutch.

CHICAGOLAND MYSTERY PLAYERS

Police Drama

FIRST TELECAST: *September 18, 1949*

LAST TELECAST: *July 30, 1950*

BROADCAST HISTORY:

Sep 1949–Jul 1950, DUM Sun 8:00–8:30

CAST:

Jeffrey Hall .... Gordon Urquhart
Sgt. Holland .... Bob Smith

Chicagoland Mystery Players was a good example of Chicago-based dramatic programming in the early days of television. The format was that of a straight crime drama, with criminologist Jeffrey Hall and his partner, Sgt. Holland, tracking down criminals in stories such as "The Fangs of Death," "Tryst with a Dummy," and "Kiss of Death." The program had been seen locally on Chicago television for two years before its network run. During its local days viewers were not shown the solution of the night's crime, but were told to pick up a copy of the next day's *Chicago Tribune* for the outcome—a nice commercial tie-in.

CHICO AND THE MAN

Situation Comedy

FIRST TELECAST: *September 13, 1974*

LAST TELECAST: *July 21, 1978*

BROADCAST HISTORY:

Sep 1974–Jan 1976, NBC Fri 8:30–9:00
Jan 1976–Mar 1976, NBC Wed 9:00–9:30
Apr 1976–Aug 1976, NBC Wed 9:30–10:00
Aug 1976–Feb 1978, NBC Fri 8:30–9:00
Jun 1978–Jul 1978, NBC Fri 8:30–9:00

CAST:

Ed Brown (The Man) .... Jack Albertson
Chico Rodriguez (1974–1977) .... Freddie Prinze
Louie .... Scatman Crothers
Mabel (1974–1975) .... Bonnie Boland
Mando (1974–1977) .... Isaac Ruiz
Rev. Bemis (1975–1976) .... Ronny Graham
Della Rogers (1976–1978) .... Della Reese
Raul Garcia (1977–1978) .... Gabriel Melgar
Aunt Charo (1977–1978) .... Charo

THEME:

"Chico and the Man," written and performed by Jose Feliciano

Set in the barrio of East Los Angeles, *Chico and the Man* was the story of two men from radically different cultural backgrounds who grew to respect each other. Chico, the enterprising young Chicano, was determined to go into partnership with cranky, sarcastic, cynical Ed Brown. Ed operated a small run-down garage and spent most of his time complaining and alienating people. A lonely widower, he at first fought Chico's determined efforts to help him make the business work, but underneath it all he was both flattered and touched to have someone show genuine interest in him. Chico cleaned the place up, moved into a beat-up old truck in the garage, and brought in business. As often as Ed complained about Chico, and as often as he made token efforts to get rid of him, he felt an attachment that he would never publicly admit.

Regularly seen were Louie the garbageman, Mabel the mailwoman, and Chico's friend Mando. Della Rogers was added to the cast in the fall of 1976 as the civic-minded owner of the diner across the street from Ed's Garage, who also happened to be the new owner of the property on which the garage was located. She was more than capable of dishing out as much as she took from Ed.

When Freddy Prinze took his own life early in 1977, prior to the completion of the season's episodes, there was serious consideration given to cancellation of the series. That was not done, however, as a new "Chico" was added to the cast for the following fall.

He was not an adult, though, or even someone whose name was really Chico. In the opening episode of the 1977–1978 season it was established that Chico had left Ed's garage to go into business with his successful father, a character introduced the previous year and played by Cesar Romero. Later, Ed and Louie returned from a fishing trip to Tijuana to discover a 12-year-old stowaway in their car trunk. The boy, Raul, ingratiated himself with Ed and became his personal resident alien. At the end of that first episode, when the two of them were preparing to go to bed, Ed inadvertently said "Good night, Chico" to his new friend and, when corrected, simply said, "You're all Chicos to me." Thus a new "Chico" for "The Man." Ed eventually adopted Raul and found himself contending with Raul's protective, and very sexy, Aunt Charo, an entertainer who had recently arrived from Spain to work in Los Angeles. She spent so much time at Ed's garage with her nephew that she, too, became part of the family.

CHILDREN'S SKETCH BOOK

Children's

FIRST TELECAST: *January 7, 1950*

LAST TELECAST: *February 4, 1950*

BROADCAST HISTORY:

Jan 1950–Feb 1950, NBC Sat 7:00–7:30

STORYTELLER:

Edith Skinner

ILLUSTRATOR:

Lisl Weil

In this live children's program, Edith Skinner told stories in rhyme, accompanied by songs and drawings made by Lisl Weil. The show had formerly been on the network during the afternoon.

CHILD'S WORLD

Children's Discussion

FIRST TELECAST: *November 1, 1948*

LAST TELECAST: *April 27, 1949*

BROADCAST HISTORY:

Nov 1948–Jan 1949, ABC Tue 7:30–7:45
Jan 1949–Apr 1949, ABC Wed 7:15–7:30

HOSTESS:

Helen Parkhurst

Child's World was an experiment in drawing out children's real feelings through spontaneous discussions. Youngsters ranging in age from 8 to 13 met in Miss Parkhurst's apartment and discussed such topics as jealousy, God, prejudice, and school.

CHIPS

Police Drama

FIRST TELECAST: *September 15, 1977*

LAST TELECAST:

BROADCAST HISTORY:

Sep 1977–Mar 1978, NBC Thu 8:00–9:00
Apr 1978, NBC Sat 8:00–9:00
May 1978–Aug 1978, NBC Thu 8:00–9:00
Sep 1978– , NBC Sat 8:00–9:00

CAST:

Officer Jon Baker .... Larry Wilcox
Officer Frank "Ponch" Poncherello .... Erik Estrada
Sgt. Joe Getraer .... Robert Pine
Officer Gene Fritz .... Lew Saunders
Officer Barickza .... Brodie Greer
Officer Sindy Cahill (1978–) .... Brianne Leary
Harlan (1978–) .... Lou Wagner

CHiPs, an acronym for California Highway Patrol, was the motorcycle equivalent to a previous episodic police series, *Adam 12*. Jon Baker and "Ponch" Poncherello were two state motorcycle patrolmen, both young bachelors, whose adventures helping citizens, fighting crime, and leading active social lives were all woven into the series. The two men worked as a team, and spent most of their working time around the vast Los Angeles freeway system. Each episode was a composite of four or five separate incidents, both on the job and off, with violence downplayed in favor of human interest and the humorous elements of their work. Jon was rather straight and serious, while "Ponch" was the romantic free spirit, whose happy-go-lucky attitude did not always sit well with their superior, Sgt. Getraer. Added in 1978 were Harlan, a police mechanic who worked on their "choppers," and Sindy, a female "Chippie" who worked out of a patrol car.

CHOPPER ONE

Police Drama

FIRST TELECAST: *January 17, 1974*

LAST TELECAST: *July 11, 1974*

BROADCAST HISTORY:

Jan 1974–Jul 1974, ABC Thu 8:00–8:30

CAST:

Officer Don Burdick ....Jim McMullan
Officer Gil Foley ....Dirk Benedict
Capt. McKeegan ....Ted Hartley
Mitch ....Lou Frizzel

In this action drama, two young "chopper cops" were assigned to police helicopter duty in a large California city. Among their adversaries were rooftop snipers, muggers in the parks, and other desperados foolish enough to work in the open—including one sniper whose goal in life was to shoot down police helicopters. Lou Frizzel played Mitch, the copter mechanic.

CHRONICLE

Documentary

FIRST TELECAST: *October 2, 1963*

LAST TELECAST: *April 22, 1964*

BROADCAST HISTORY:

Oct 1963–Apr 1964, CBS Wed 7:30–8:30

HOST:

Charles Collingwood

Chronicle was aired during the 1963–1964 season on an alternating basis with *CBS Reports*. Whereas *CBS Reports* was known for its hard-news documentaries, *Chronicle* sought to look at the cultural side of contemporary society and the roots from which that culture developed. Episodes in the series covered such diverse subjects as the British music hall, the writings of Edgar Allan Poe, political and social revolution in the 20th century, and the Constitution of the United States.

CHRONOSCOPE

Discussion

FIRST TELECAST: *June 11, 1951*

LAST TELECAST: *April 29, 1955*

BROADCAST HISTORY:

Jun 1951–Sep 1951, CBS Mon 11:00–11:15
Sep 1951–Jun 1953, CBS Mon/Wed/Fri 11:00–11:15
Aug 1953–Apr 1955, CBS Mon/Wed/Fri 11:00–11:15

MODERATOR:

Frank Knight (1951)
William Bradford Huie (1951–1953)
Edward P. Morgan (1953)
Larry Le Sueur (1953–1955)

Current issues in world affairs were discussed on this late evening series. Each telecast featured a guest who was either personally involved in, or an expert on, a situation of major significance on the world scene—politics, finance, natural disasters, or the Korean War, for example. Two other panelists from a rotating group of journalists chatted with the guest panelist about the implications of the event or trend under discussion.

CHRYSLER THEATRE

see *Bob Hope Presents The Chrysler Theatre*

CHUCK BARRIS RAH RAH SHOW, THE

Comedy Variety

FIRST TELECAST: *February 28, 1978*

LAST TELECAST: *April 11, 1978*

BROADCAST HISTORY:

Feb 1978–Apr 1978, NBC Tue 8:00–9:00

HOST:

Chuck Barris

REGULARS:

Jave P. Morgan
Milton Delugg Orchestra

The Chuck Barris Rah Rah Show was one of the less conventional variety shows of recent years, as well as one of the shortest lived. Barris was a longtime producer of game shows who had first been seen on camera on *The Gong Show*, a parody on talent shows which was seen on the NBC daytime lineup. He was supposed to be simply the program's producer, but had taken over as host at the last minute before the premiere when the original host proved unsuitable. He was perfect in the role.

The *Gong Show* idea—a succession of no-talent amateurs doing dreadful acts (and often getting "gonged" off the stage)—caught on, and soon produced both a syndicated version and this nighttime adaptation. Unlike *Gong*, the *Rah Rah Show* included professional acts doing their bits in quick succession on a simple stage. Barris's choice of guests was a bit odd, combining old timers such as Slim Gaillard ("Flat Foot Floogie") and Cab Calloway with 1950s rock artists such as the Coasters and Chuck Berry, along with contemporary talent such as Jose Feliciano and Anson Williams. Comics Fred Travalena and Henny Youngman made repeat appearances, and singer Jaye P. Morgan was a regular. In addition there were always several amateurs displaying their questionable talents, such as the lady who chirped and barked while singing "The Sound of Music" and Dr. Flame-O, who played "Smoke Gets in Your Eyes" on a row of burning candles.

CIMARRON CITY

Western

FIRST TELECAST: *October 11, 1958*

LAST TELECAST: *September 16, 1960*

BROADCAST HISTORY:

Oct 1958–Sep 1959, NBC Sat 9:30–10:30

Jun 1960–Sep 1960, NBC Fri 7:30–8:30

CAST:

Matthew Rockford ....George Montgomery
Beth Purcell ....Audrey Totter
Lane Temple ....John Smith
Art Sampson ....Stuart Randall
Martin Kingsley ....Addison Richards
Burt Purdy ....Fred Sherman
Alice Purdy ....Claire Carleton
Tiny Budinger ....Dan Blocker
Jesse Williams ....George Dunn
Dody Hamer ....Pete Dunn
Silas Perry ....Tom Fadden
Jed Fame .... Wally Brown

George Montgomery was both star and narrator of this saga of a boom town on the western frontier during the 1890s. Oil and gold had created a booming economy in the Oklahoma Territory, and Cimarron City had mushroomed into a sprawling, rough-hewn metropolis, with hopes of becoming the capital of the future state of Oklahoma. Matthew Rockford, son of the town's founder, was mayor and a leading cattle rancher; Beth Purcell, the owner of a boardinghouse; and Lane Temple, the town sheriff. These three, singly or together, were the focus of most episodes. Dan Blocker, who later starred as Hoss on *Bonanza*, was featured as a local citizen who often helped the sheriff in the cause of law and order. Montgomery narrated the episodes from the perspective of an older man recalling the adventures and happenings of his younger days. Those that were telecast during the summer of 1960 were reruns of earlier shows.

CIMARRON STRIP

Western

FIRST TELECAST: *September 7, 1967*

LAST TELECAST: *September 7, 1971*

BROADCAST HISTORY:

Sep 1967–Sep 1968, CBS Thu 7:30–9:00

Jul 1971–Sep 1971, CBS Tue 8:30–10:00

CAST:

U.S. Marshal Jim Crown ...Stuart Whitman
Mac Gregor ....Percy Herbert
Francis Wilde ....Randy Boone
Dulcey Coopersmith ....Jill Townsend

The Cimarron Strip was the border region between the Kansas Territory and Indian territory during the late 19th century. Patrolling this vast area was the job of U.S. Marshal Jim Crown, who was based in Cimarron City. Marshal Crown had no full-time deputies but he often availed himself of the assistance of Mac Gregor, an itinerant Scot, and Francis Wilde, a young photographer. Also seen as a regular in this series was Dulcey, a young woman from the East who had moved to the frontier to take over an inn that had been run by her late father. *Cimarron Strip* was an attempt by CBS to copy the success of NBC's *The Virginian* (the first 90-minute Western series), and like *The Virginian* it centered largely on characters portrayed by guest stars. Reruns of the original series aired during the summer of 1971.

CINEMA VARIETIES

see *Movies—Prior to 1961*

CINEMA-SCOPE

see *Movies—Prior to 1961*

CIRCLE OF FEAR

see *Ghost Story*

CIRCLE THEATER

see *Armstrong Circle Theater*

CIRCUIT RIDER

Religion

FIRST TELECAST: *March 5, 1951*
LAST TELECAST: *May 7, 1951*
BROADCAST HISTORY:
Mar 1951–May 1951, ABC Mon 11:00–11:30

This program consisted of dramatizations that emphasized the significance of Christianity in everyday life, plus a weekly guest who discussed current religious problems and activities. The sponsor was America for Christ, Inc.

CIRCUS BOY

Adventure

FIRST TELECAST: *September 23, 1956*
LAST TELECAST: *September 11, 1958*
BROADCAST HISTORY:
Sep 1956–Sep 1957, NBC Sun 7:30–8:00
Sep 1957–Sep 1958, ABC Thu 7:30–8:00
CAST:
Corky .... Mickey Braddock
Joey, the Clown .... Noah Beery, Jr.
Big Tim Champion .... Robert Lowery
Hank Miller .... Leo Gordon
Little Tom, the Midget .... Billy Barty
Swifty .... Olin Howlin
Barker .... Eddie Marr
Big Boy .... Guinn Williams

Circus life at the turn of the century as seen through the eyes of a young boy. Corky, a 12-year-old orphan, had been adopted by the members of a traveling circus owned by Big Tim Champion. His life with the colorful performers and behind-the-scenes workers, as the circus traveled from town to town, formed the basis for the series. Corky's personal pet was Bimbo, a baby elephant, for whom he was water boy.

Although the series left prime time after two seasons on two networks, reruns continued on Saturday mornings until September 1960.

CIRCUS TIME

Variety

FIRST TELECAST: *October 4, 1956*
LAST TELECAST: *June 27, 1957*
BROADCAST HISTORY:
Oct 1956–Jun 1957, ABC Thu 8:00–9:00
HOST:
Paul Winchell
REGULARS:
Betty Ann Grove (1957)
Ralph Herman Orchestra

This variety show with the flavor of a traditional circus presented both circus performers and traditional entertainment acts. Paul Winchell was the "ringmaster-host," assisted by his dummies Jerry Mahoney and Knucklehead Smith. Guests included popular music acts such as Mickey and Sylvia and the Dell Vikings.

CITIES SERVICE BAND OF AMERICA

Music

FIRST TELECAST: *October 17, 1949*
LAST TELECAST: *January 9, 1950*
BROADCAST HISTORY:
Oct 1949–Jan 1950, NBC Mon 9:30–10:00
CONDUCTOR:
Paul Lavalle
ANNOUNCER:
Ford Bond

This simulcast of the popular NBC radio program featured Paul Lavalle and the 48-piece Band of America. Various soloists from the band were spotlighted, as well as the Green and White Vocal Quartette and a 12-voice glee club. Baton-twirling majorettes and an occasional film clip were added as a concession to television, but the program faced withering competition from *The Goldbergs*, running opposite it on CBS, and was soon canceled.

CITY ASSIGNMENT

see *Big Town*

CITY HOSPITAL

Medical Drama

FIRST TELECAST: *March 25, 1952*
LAST TELECAST: *October 1, 1953*
BROADCAST HISTORY:
Mar 1952–Jun 1953, CBS Tue 9:00–9:30
Jun 1953–Oct 1953, CBS Thu 10:30–11:00
CAST:
Dr. Barton Crane .... Melville Ruick
Dr. Kate Morrow .... Ann Burr

The daily crises of a large metropolitan hospital, and the personal and professional lives of its staff members, were dramatized in this live series. Dr. Barton Crane was the medical director of City Hospital, and it was from his position, either as an active participant or advisor to those involved, that the stories were developed. The presence of a female doctor, Kate Morrow, was rather uncommon for medical shows of this period. *City Hospital* was aired on a biweekly basis throughout its run, alternating with *Crime Syndicated* on Tuesdays and with *Place the Face* on Thursdays.

CITY OF ANGELS

Detective Drama

FIRST TELECAST: *February 3, 1976*

LAST TELECAST: *August 10, 1976*

BROADCAST HISTORY:

Feb 1976–Aug 1976, NBC Tue 10:00–11:00

CAST:

Jake Axminster .... Wayne Rogers
Marsha .... Elaine Joyce
Lt. Quint .... Clifton James
Michael Brimm .... Philip Sterling

Set in Los Angeles (the "City of Angels") in the 1930s, this period detective series was patterned after the hit motion picture *Chinatown*. It concerned the exploits of Jake Axminster, an often broke but always free-wheeling private investigator who was not above stretching the law and his ethics to get the information he wanted. Possibly as a reflection of his own standards, Jake trusted nobody completely, not even his attorney, Michael Brimm. Jake's office was run by a beautiful but daffy secretary, Marsha, who also ran a switchboard that took messages for call girls. A mid-season replacement, *City of Angels* was notable more for its vintage automobiles and period fashions than for dramatic involvement, and it was soon canceled.

CLAUDIA, THE STORY OF A MARRIAGE

Drama

FIRST TELECAST: *January 6, 1952*

LAST TELECAST: *June 30, 1952*

BROADCAST HISTORY:

Jan 1952–Mar 1952, NBC Sun 6:30–7:00
Mar 1952–Jun 1952, CBS Mon 9:30–10:00

CAST:

Claudia Naughton .... Joan McCracken
David Naughton .... Hugh Reilly
Mrs. Brown .... Margaret Wycherly
Bertha .... Lilia Skala
Julia Naughton .... Faith Brook
Harley Naughton .... Alex Clark
Fritz .... Paul Andor
Roger .... Mercer McCloud

Claudia was a study in contrasts, at once both very childish and remarkably mature for her age. She married aspiring architect David Naughton at the age of 18, and the problems and joys of their young marriage were explored realistically in this series. Claudia's dealings with her new family, including David's sister Julia and brother Harley, and her attempts to break away from her possessive mother, Mrs. Brown, all served as subject matter. The series was broadcast live from New York.

Claudia had had a highly successful career before coming to TV, having been the heroine in three novels by Rose Franken (published between 1939–1941), a Broadway play, a radio series and two movies starring Dorothy McGuire and Robert Young. On television, however, her story was brief.

CLIFF EDWARDS SHOW, THE

Music

FIRST TELECAST: *May 23, 1949*

LAST TELECAST: *September 19, 1949*

BROADCAST HISTORY:

May 1949–Sep 1949, CBS Mon/Wed/Fri 7:45–8:00
Sep 1949, CBS Mon 7:45–8:00

REGULARS:

Cliff Edwards
The Tony Mottola Trio

Show-business veteran Cliff "Ukulele Ike" Edwards was the host of this informal live musical series, which filled out the remainder of the half-hour in which CBS aired its nightly network news program. Cliff would recount homespun stories, play his ukulele, and model some of his huge collection of unusual hats. He also sang songs and occasionally chatted with a guest. Some of the songs were no doubt taken from Cliff's long career on records, radio, and in movies, during which he had introduced such hits as "Fascinating Rhythm" (in a 1924 Broadway show), "Singin' in the Rain" (in a 1929 movie musical), and "When You Wish Upon A Star" (in the 1939 Disney feature *Pinocchio*, for which Edwards provided the voice of Jiminy Cricket).

CLIMAX

Dramatic Anthology

FIRST TELECAST: *October 7, 1954*

LAST TELECAST: *June 26, 1958*

BROADCAST HISTORY:

Oct 1954–Jun 1958, CBS Thu 8:30–9:30

HOSTS:

William Lundigan

Mary Costa (1956–1958)

Climax was one of the longer-running dramatic series aired on network television during the 1950s. Hosted by William Lundigan, who was joined by co-host Mary Costa in the summer of 1956, it presented a weekly one-hour drama originating from CBS's facilities in Hollywood. When it first went on the air, *Climax* was produced live every week, but as time wore on, filmed (and later taped) productions were added to the mix. Even in its last season, however, there were several live programs presented. Among the plays aired were adaptations of *Casino Royale*, with Barry Nelson playing an American James Bond; *A Farewell to Arms*, with Guy Madison and Diana Lynn; and *Dr. Jekyll and Mr. Hyde*, with Michael Rennie playing the dual role.

CLOAK OF MYSTERY

Dramatic Anthology

FIRST TELECAST: *May 11, 1965*

LAST TELECAST: *August 8, 1965*

BROADCAST HISTORY:

May 1965, NBC Tue 9:30–10:00

May 1965–Aug 1965, NBC Tue 9:00–10:00

This summer anthology series consisted of reruns of episodes of *Alcoa Premiere*, *Alfred Hitchcock Presents*, *Pepsi-Cola Playhouse*, and *G. E. Theatre*. In addition, two episodes were pilots for series that were never sold.

CLOCK, THE

Suspense Drama

FIRST TELECAST: *May 16, 1949*

LAST TELECAST: *January 9, 1952*

BROADCAST HISTORY:

May 1949–Aug 1949, NBC Mon 8:30–9:00

Aug 1949–Mar 1950, NBC Wed 8:30–9:00

Apr 1950–Feb 1951, NBC Fri 9:30–10:00

Jul 1951–Aug 1951, NBC Fri 8:30–9:00

Oct 1951–Jan 1952, ABC Wed 9:30–10:00

NARRATOR:

Larry Semon

THEME:

"Sands of Time"

"Sunrise and sunset, promise and fulfillment, birth and death—the whole drama of life is written in the Sands of Time." So began this mystery-suspense series, composed for the most part of live original dramas written for TV and starring a wide range of guest actors and actresses. A clock was prominently featured, and time played a vital role in each story. Typically, murder or insanity was the theme. The program was based on an ABC radio series that was heard from 1946–1948.

CLORETS SUMMER THEATRE

Dramatic Anthology

FIRST TELECAST: *July 12, 1955*

LAST TELECAST: *August 23, 1955*

BROADCAST HISTORY:

Jul 1955–Aug 1955, NBC Tue 9:00–9:30

Clorets Summer Theatre alternated with *Kleenex Summer Theatre* as a summer replacement series for *Fireside Theatre*. The dramas shown were all filmed reruns of episodes from *Four Star Playhouse*.

CLUB EMBASSY

Variety

FIRST TELECAST: *October 7, 1952*

LAST TELECAST: *June 23, 1953*

BROADCAST HISTORY:

Oct 1952–Jun 1953, NBC Tue 10:30–10:45

REGULARS:

Bob Elliott (Oct–Dec)

Ray Goulding (Oct–Dec)

Audrey Meadows (Oct–Dec)

Florian Zabach

Julia Meade (Oct–Dec)

Mindy Carson (Dec–May)

The Embassy Quartet (Dec–Jun)

Danny Hoctor (Dec–June)

Connie Russell (May–June)

This comedy variety show originally starred Bob and Ray doing their own brand of off-beat, satirical humor, in the setting of a nightclub (the first telecast was under the title *Embassy Club*). Audrey Meadows sang and acted in various skits, violinist Florian Zabach (famous for his showpiece number "The Hot Canary") was the featured instrumental soloist, and Julia Meade was the emcee and cigarette girl. On December 30, 1952, the cast and format underwent major changes. Bob and Ray, Audrey Meadows, and Julia Meade were replaced by singer Mindy Carson, and the emphasis was shifted from comedy to music. Backing up Miss Carson were the Embassy Quartet and dancer Danny Hoctor. On May 19, 1953, Miss Carson was in turn replaced by singer Connie Russell, but the "club" closed down a month later.

CLUB OASIS

Variety

FIRST TELECAST: *September 28, 1957*

LAST TELECAST: *September 6, 1958*

BROADCAST HISTORY:

Sep 1957–Aug 1958, NBC Sat 9:00–9:30
Sep 1958, NBC Sat 10:30–11:00

REGULARS:

Spike Jones and His City Slickers (1958)
Helen Grayco (1958)
Joyce Jameson (1958)
Billy Barty (1958)

Club Oasis was a simulated nightclub that headlined a different popular entertainer each week. Depending on the performer, the material might be comedy or singing or full-scale production numbers. Among those featured were Jimmy Durante, Martha Raye, Eddie Fisher, Jo Stafford, Dean Martin, Kay Starr, and Frank Sinatra, along with supporting acts each week to fill out the bill. During the summer of 1958 Spike Jones became the permanent star of the show and the title was changed to *Club Oasis Starring Spike Jones.* Featured along with Spike's lunatic band were his wife, singer Helen Grayco; comedienne Joyce Jameson; and midget comic Billy Barty. *Club Oasis* was a biweekly series throughout its run, first alternating with *The Polly Bergen Show* and during the summer of 1958 with *Opening Night.*

CLUB SEVEN

Musical Variety

FIRST TELECAST: *August 12, 1948*

LAST TELECAST: *August 24, 1951*

BROADCAST HISTORY:

Aug 1948–Sep 1948, ABC Thu 8:00–8:30
Oct 1948, ABC Thu 8:30–9:00
Nov 1948–Jan 1949, ABC Wed 8:00–8:30
Jan 1949–Mar 1949, ABC Thu 10:30–11:00
Sep 1950–Aug 1951, ABC Mon–Fri 7:00–7:30 (approx.)

REGULARS:

Johnny Thompson (1948–1949)
Bobby Byrne Orchestra (1948–1949)
Tony Bavaar (1950–1951)
Eadie and Rack, piano team (1950–1951)

This informal, low-budget musical variety program in the early days of the ABC network featured new talent, ranging from singers and dancers to acrobats and "Hank the Mule." After a hiatus in 1949–1950 the program returned as a nightly feature, hosted by vocalist Tony Bavaar. This later version varied in length from 10 to 30 minutes, since it was often truncated by five- or ten-minute newscasts or other series on either end.

CODE R

Adventure

FIRST TELECAST: *January 21, 1977*

LAST TELECAST: *June 10, 1977*

BROADCAST HISTORY:

Jan 1977–Jun 1977, CBS Fri 8:00–9:00

CAST:

Rick Wilson ....James Houghton
George Baker ....Martin Kove
Walt Robinson ....Tom Simcox
Suzy ....Susanne Reed
Ted Milbank ....Ben Davidson
Bobby Robinson ....Robbie Rundle
Harry ....W. T. Zacha

Scenic Channel Island, off the southern California coast, was the setting for this adventure series, which resembled NBC's *Emergency* but took place in a more limited locale. Rick Wilson was the fire chief, George Baker the chief of beaches, and Walt Robinson the police chief on Channel Island. They all managed to get involved in at least one of the several stories that unfolded in any given episode. Suzy was the dispatcher for the Island's Emergency Services Department and doubled as secretary to all three men, since their offices were all in the same building. Ted was a deputy of police, Bobby was Walt's ten-year-old son, and Harry was the owner and bartender at the Lighthouse Bar, a favorite off-duty hangout of the three chiefs. Typical situations included rescuing two young boys floating out to sea on a homemade raft, tracking down a bootleg whiskey operation, coping with an arsonist, and helping a man trapped in the water in his dune buggy.

COKE TIME WITH EDDIE FISHER

Music

FIRST TELECAST: *April 29, 1953*

LAST TELECAST: *February 22, 1957*

BROADCAST HISTORY:

Apr 1953–Feb 1957, NBC Wed/Fri 7:30–7:45 (OS)

REGULARS:

Eddie Fisher
Don Ameche (Apr–Oct 1953)
Freddy Robbins (1953–1957)
Axel Stordahl and His Orchestra
The Echoes (1956–1957)

Handsome young Eddie Fisher was fresh out of the army and at the height of his career when this popular 15-minute show began in 1953. The idol of bobbysoxers all over the country, he sang many of his million-selling recordings here, including "I'm Walking Behind You" (which reached number one on the hit parade shortly after the series began), "Oh! My Papa," and "Anytime." Each live telecast—occasionally the show was filmed in advance or on location—opened with Eddie singing his theme song, "May I Sing to You." Guest stars appeared frequently and a permanent backup group, the Echoes, was added in the fall of 1956. Actor Don Ameche was the original host of the show, through October 23, 1953. Freddy Robbins, who had been announcing the commercials, subsequently took on the added duty of host.

COLGATE COMEDY HOUR, THE

Variety

FIRST TELECAST: *September 10, 1950*

LAST TELECAST: *December 25, 1955*

BROADCAST HISTORY:

Sep 1950–Dec 1955, NBC Sun 8:00–9:00

PRINCIPAL HOSTS:

Eddie Cantor (1950–1954)
Dean Martin and Jerry Lewis (1950–1955)
Fred Allen (1950)
Donald O'Connor (1951–1954)
Abbott and Costello (1951–1954)
Bob Hope (1952–1953)
Jimmy Durante (1953–1954)
Gordon MacRae (1954–1955)
Robert Paige (1955)

This big-budget series of comedy spectaculars, featuring most of the top names in show business, was NBC's first successful counterprogramming against *The Ed Sullivan Show,* which ran opposite it on Sunday nights. It boasted numerous television firsts, and was the first starring vehicle for such names as Eddie Cantor, Fred Allen, Abbott and Costello, Spike Jones, Tony Martin, and Ray Bolger. It was also the first commercial series to originate in Hollywood (September 30, 1951), and it included the first network color telecast, on November 22, 1953 (as an experimental test of RCA's new compatible color system, under special permission from the FCC).

When *The Colgate Comedy Hour* began in the fall of 1950 the intention was to have three rotating elements, each a complete series of its own, starring Eddie Cantor, Martin and Lewis, and Fred Allen, respectively. Allen was dropped in December 1950, and the series thereafter began to include other big-name hosts on an occasional basis, in addition to the principals, who appeared approximately once a month. Among those hosting one or two shows during 1950–1951, for example, were Abbott and Costello, Jerry Lester, Spike Jones, Tony Martin, and Phil Silvers. In September 1951 the program began telecasts from the El Capitan Theatre in Hollywood, though there continued to be occasional telecasts from the International Theatre in New York.

In September 1952 Eddie Cantor suffered a heart attack immediately following one of his telecasts and was off the air for several months. He returned in January 1953 and completed one more season with the show. Beginning with the 1952–1953 season Colgate also began to vary the revue format, with occasional "book" musicals, such as *Anything Goes,* starring Ethel Merman and Frank Sinatra (February 28, 1954); *Revenge With Music,* with Anna Maria Alberghetti (October 24, 1954); and *Roberta,* with Gordon MacRae (April 10, 1955). In early 1954 the program began to "hit the road," with special broadcasts from all over the United States, including Pebble Beach, California; the Cocoanut Grove and Hollywood Bowl in Hollywood; Miami; Las Vegas; Jones Beach, New York; and the liner *S.S. United States* docked at a pier in New York. Some shows featured special events, such as the Ice Capades or various awards presentations and salutes. Always the emphasis was on big names and "event" television.

In the summer of 1955 Colgate began a tie-in with Paramount Pictures, in which scenes from a new film were shown, and stars from the movie appeared. Charlton Heston even hosted several telecasts. The name of the series was changed at this time to *Colgate Variety Hour*. However, a super-budget series such as this proved harder and harder to sustain, and in December 1955 one of TV's most notable early comedy variety programs finally reached the end of its run—with a December 25th hour devoted to Christmas music by Fred Waring and his Pennsylvanians, from Hollywood.

COLGATE THEATRE

Dramatic Anthology

FIRST TELECAST: *January 3, 1949*
LAST TELECAST: *October 7, 1958*
BROADCAST HISTORY:

Jan 1949–Oct 1949, NBC Mon 9:00–9:30
Oct 1949–Jun 1950, NBC Sun 8:30–9:00
Aug 1958–Oct 1958, NBC Tue 9:00–9:30

The first program to use this name was a live dramatic series presenting adaptations of short stories and plays, as well as scripts especially written for television. Comedies, dramas, and mysteries alternated, and a wide variety of talent appeared (usually not top names, however). A "Broadway Theater" theme opened the show, with the camera following theatergoers into their seats, scanning the program for the title of the night's production, and then focusing on the stage as the curtain began to rise. Among the first season's productions were the first TV adaptations of two popular radio series, *Mr. and Mrs. North* (July 4, 1949) and *Vic and Sade* (July 11–July 25, 1949).

The second *Colgate Theatre* was a summer film series in 1958, consisting primarily of pilots for projected series that did not make it to the network's fall schedule. However, one episode, "Fountain of Youth," written, directed, and narrated by Orson Welles, won a Peabody Award.

COLGATE VARIETY HOUR, THE

see *Colgate Comedy Hour, The*

COLGATE WESTERN THEATRE

Western Anthology

FIRST TELECAST: *July 3, 1959*
LAST TELECAST: *September 4, 1959*
BROADCAST HISTORY:

Jul 1959–Sep 1959, NBC Fri 9:30–10:00

This summer series consisted of reruns of films of Western dramas originally seen, for the most part, on *G.E. Theatre* and *Schlitz Playhouse*.

COLISEUM

Variety

FIRST TELECAST: *January 26, 1967*
LAST TELECAST: *June 1, 1967*
BROADCAST HISTORY:

Jan 1967–Jun 1967, CBS Thu 7:30–8:30

Each week a different star hosted this variety series, which traveled around the world to film such spectacles as the New Vienna Ice Extravaganza and the Moscow State Circus. In addition there were many New York-based programs featuring popular entertainers in a straight variety format.

COLLEGE BOWL, THE

Musical Comedy

FIRST TELECAST: *October 2, 1950*
LAST TELECAST: *March 26, 1951*
BROADCAST HISTORY:

Oct 1950–Mar 1951, ABC Mon 9:00–9:30

STARRING:

Chico Marx

REGULARS:

Jimmy Brock
Stanley Prager
Barbara Ruick
Kenny Buffert
Evelyn Ward
Andy Williams
Paula Huston
Tommy Morton
Joan Holloway
Lee Lindsey

PRODUCER:

Martin Gosch

A weekly musical comedy show featuring Chico Marx, of the Marx Brothers, as the proprietor of a campus soda shop. The supporting cast was a lively group of young actors and actresses from Broadway shows and nightclubs, including 18-year-old Andy Williams. The show was telecast live from New York.

COLLEGE OF MUSICAL KNOWLEDGE, THE

see *Kay Kyser's Kollege of Musical Knowledge*

COLLEGE PRESS CONFERENCE

see *Junior Press Conference*

COLONEL HUMPHREY FLACK

Situation Comedy

FIRST TELECAST: *October 7, 1953*
LAST TELECAST: *July 2, 1954*
BROADCAST HISTORY:

Oct 1953–Dec 1953, DUM Wed 9:00–9:30
Jan 1954–May 1954, DUM Sat 10:00–10:30
May 1954–Jul 1954, DUM Fri 10:30–11:00

CAST:

Col. Humphrey Flack ......Alan Mowbray
Uthas P. Garvey ....Frank Jenks

By 1953, Britisher Alan Mowbray was one of Hollywood's most experienced character actors, having appeared in nearly 300 B-films since 1923. (Contrary to popular belief, in only five of them did he play the butler.) DuMont could not have picked a more suitable performer to play Col. Humphrey Flack, a dapper, witty, somewhat paunchy modern-day Robin Hood. Flack was a con man's con man, outswindling assorted swindlers in order to aid the poor—and retaining a percentage for himself, of course, to "cover expenses." His sidekick was Uthas P. (for Patsy) Garvey, who was no slouch himself, but not up to the colonel's suave standards.

The program was based on a series of *Saturday Evening Post* stories by Everett Rhodes Castle and was telecast live.

COLT .45

Western

FIRST TELECAST: *October 18, 1957*
LAST TELECAST: *September 27, 1960*
BROADCAST HISTORY:

Oct 1957–Dec 1957, ABC Fri 10:00–10:30
Jan 1958–Apr 1958, ABC Fri 8:30–9:00
Oct 1958–Sep 1959, ABC Sun 9:00–9:30
Oct 1959–Mar 1960, ABC Sun 7:00–7:30
Apr 1960–Sep 1960, ABC Tue 9:30–10:00

CAST:

Christopher Colt ....Wayde Preston
Sam Colt, Jr. (1959–1960) .....Donald May

Christopher Colt was a handsome young government undercover agent posing as a gun salesman in this Western adventure. Most of his missions involved tracking down notorious outlaws, and in the process he had plenty of opportunities to use his famous Colt .45 pistol.

Not long after the series began, Warner Brothers Studios began to have trouble with its star. Eventually Wayde Preston joined the growing list of "Warner Brothers walkouts" (for some others see *Cheyenne*, *Maverick*, and *77 Sunset Strip*), and a considerable number of repeats had to be interspersed with original episodes to keep the series on the air through the 1958–1959 season. In 1959 Christopher Colt was gradually replaced as the leading character by his cousin Sam Colt, Jr. Also a government agent, Sam was the focal point of some episodes and appeared jointly with Christopher Colt at least once. Although actor Preston did rejoin the fold, Donald May eventually took over as the lead full time.

COLUMBIA UNIVERSITY SEMINAR

Instruction

FIRST TELECAST: *October 4, 1952*
LAST TELECAST: *January 3, 1953*
BROADCAST HISTORY:

Oct 1952–Jan 1953, ABC Sat 6:30–7:00

This series was a course on great American literature, presented by the faculty of Columbia University. Academic credit was given to viewers actively participating in the course. After its prime-time run the series continued on Sunday afternoons until May 1953.

COLUMBO

Police Drama

FIRST TELECAST: *September 15, 1971*
LAST TELECAST: *September 4, 1977*
BROADCAST HISTORY:

Sep 1971–Sep 1972, NBC Wed 8:30–10:00
Sep 1972–Jul 1974, NBC Sun 8:30–10:00
Aug 1974–Aug 1975, NBC Sun 8:30–10:30
Sep 1975–Sep 1976, NBC Sun 9:00–11:00
Oct 1976–Sep 1977, NBC Sun 8:00–9:30

CAST:

Lt. Columbo ....Peter Falk

At the beginning of each *Columbo* episode the audience witnessed a clever murder and saw the ingenious measures the murderer took to prevent detection by the police. Then into the case came Lt. Columbo (he never did have a first name). He drove a beat-up old car, wore a dirty, rumpled trench coat that looked at least ten years old, and acted for all the world like an incompetent bumbler. He was excessively polite to everyone, went out of his way not to offend any of the suspects, and seemed like a hopeless choice to solve any crime, much less a well-conceived murder. But all that was superficial, designed to lull the murderer into a false sense of security. Despite his appearance, Columbo was one of the shrewdest, most resourceful detectives on the Los Angeles police force. Slowly and methodically he pieced together the most minute clues leading to the identity of the killer, who, when his guilt was revealed, was always incredulous that such an unlikely cop had managed to find him out.

Columbo was one of the three original rotating elements of the *NBC Mystery Movie*, the other two being *McMillan and Wife* and *McCloud*. It was by far the most popular of the elements and would have become a separate series in its own right if actor Peter Falk had permitted it to. But a 60- or 90-minute movie every week was too much for one actor to carry, not to mention the dangers of being typecast in such a distinctive role. Toward the end of the program's run Falk was said to be making more than a quarter of a million dollars per episode, but even at that he refused to do more than a few per year. He continued to film an occasional new episode after the last date shown above.

An interesting sidelight is that Peter Falk was the producers' second choice to portray Columbo. The first actor approached for the role was Bing Crosby. Crosby, 67 years old and a millionaire many times over, declined, reportedly because it would interfere with his golf game. And so Falk got the part, and stardom.

COMBAT

War Drama

FIRST TELECAST: *October 2, 1962*
LAST TELECAST: *August 29, 1967*
BROADCAST HISTORY:

Oct 1962–Aug 1967, ABC Tue 7:30–8:30

CAST:

Lt. Gil Hanley .... Rick Jason
Sgt. Chip Saunders .... Vic Morrow
Caje (Caddy Cadron) .... Pierre Jalbert
Kirby (1963–1967) .... Jack Hogan
Littlejohn (1963–1967) .... Dick Peabody
Doc Walton (1962–1963) .... Steven Rogers
Doc (1963–1965) .... Conlon Carter
Pvt. Braddock (1962–1963) .... Shecky Greene
Nelson (1963–1964) .... Tom Lowell

Combat depicted the exploits of a U.S. Army platoon fighting its way across Europe during World War II, following D-Day. Realism was the keynote of this mud-splattered series, whose cast was sent to army camp for a week of actual "boot camp" training before production began. Original World War II battle footage was included in some episodes. The stories ranged from straight combat adventure to human interest and sometimes humorous themes. Among the regulars were Pvt. Braddock, the platoon comic and resident hustler, played by nightclub comedian Shecky Greene; Caje, the sly, dark-haired Cajun; and Doc Walton, the young, sensitive medical aidman. Out in front were the tough, hard-boiled leaders, Lt. Gil Hanley and Sgt. Chip Saunders.

COMBAT SERGEANT

War Drama

FIRST TELECAST: *June 29, 1956*
LAST TELECAST: *September 27, 1956*
BROADCAST HISTORY:

Jun 1956–Aug 1956, ABC Fri 8:00–8:30
Sep 1956, ABC Thu 9:00–9:30

CAST:

Sgt. Nelson .... Michael Thomas
Gen. Harrison .... Cliff Clark

This wartime adventure was set in North Africa during World War II. Sgt. Nelson, receiving his orders direct from Gen. Harrison, found himself involved in various dangerous assignments, including coordination between the Allied forces, espionage against the Germans, and sometimes even romance. Actual World War II film footage was used in this series.

COME CLOSER

Quiz/Audience Participation

FIRST TELECAST: *September 20, 1954*
LAST TELECAST: *December 13, 1954*
BROADCAST HISTORY:

Sep 1954–Dec 1954, ABC Mon 8:00–8:30

EMCEE:

Jimmy Nelson

DUMMIES:

Danny O'Day
Humphrey Higby
Farfel the Dog

This audience-participation show starred the ventriloquist Jimmy Nelson and his dummies, with questions calling for comic answers by studio contestants. The contestant "coming closest" to the correct answer won cash and prizes. A jackpot prize, based on a clue given in song by "Danny O'Day," was also featured.

COMEBACK STORY, THE

Drama/Interview

FIRST TELECAST: *October 2, 1953*
LAST TELECAST: *February 5, 1954*
BROADCAST HISTORY:
Oct 1953–Feb 1954, ABC Fri 9:30–10:00
EMCEE:
George Jessel (Oct 1953–Jan 1954)
Arlene Francis (Jan–Feb 1954)

This heartwarming series presented, through interviews and dramatizations, the stories of persons stricken with physical disabilities or bad fortune who had fought to rebuild their lives. Some of the guests were ordinary people, but most were notable personalities such as Norman Brokenshire, the pioneer radio announcer who won his battle with alcoholism; athlete Mildred "Babe" Didrikson Zaharias; and blind jazz pianist George Shearing. The program was telecast live from New York.

COMEDY CIRCUS

Films

FIRST TELECAST: *July 13, 1951*
LAST TELECAST: *September 28, 1951*
BROADCAST HISTORY:
Jul 1951, ABC Fri 7:30–8:00
Aug 1951–Sep 1951, ABC Fri 8:00–8:30

Comedy Circus consisted of vintage comedy films starring such actors as Buster Keaton and Harry Langdon.

COMEDY HOUR SPECIAL

Comedy Variety

FIRST TELECAST: *July 29, 1963*
LAST TELECAST: *September 16, 1963*
BROADCAST HISTORY:
Jul 1963–Sep 1963, CBS Mon 9:00–10:00

Reruns of eight specials formed the contents of this summer series. Originally aired during the 1959–1960 season, they starred Jack Benny and Phil Silvers, appearing both separately and together.

COMEDY PARADE

see *Movies—Prior to 1961*

COMEDY PLAYHOUSE

Comedy Anthology

FIRST TELECAST: *August 1, 1971*
LAST TELECAST: *September 5, 1971*
BROADCAST HISTORY:
Aug 1971–Sep 1971, CBS Sun 8:00–8:30

The situation comedies that made up this 1971 summer anthology were all pilots for proposed series that had not made it to the fall schedule. Around the networks this kind of summer runoff of busted pilots—which every network has in quantity—is irreverently known as "garbage can theater."

COMEDY SPOT, THE

Comedy Anthology

FIRST TELECAST: *June 28, 1960*
LAST TELECAST: *September 18, 1962*
BROADCAST HISTORY:
Jun 1960–Sep 1960, CBS Tue 9:30–10:00
Jul 1961–Sep 1961, CBS Tue 9:00–9:30
Jul 1962–Sep 1962, CBS Tue 9:00–9:30
HOST:
Art Gilmore (1960)

This series filled in for *The Red Skelton Show* for three consecutive summers. The 1960 and 1962 versions were called *The Comedy Spot*, while the 1961 edition was titled *Comedy Spotlight*. Although some of the episodes were reruns of previously aired episodes from other anthologies, most were pilots for proposed comedy series that had not made it to the fall schedule. There was one notable exception: the July 19, 1960, comedy titled "Head of the Family," starring Carl Reiner as a television comedy writer, Robert Petrie. This was the pilot for what would become, the following season, *The Dick Van Dyke Show*. Reiner, the creator of the show, was the only member of the pilot's cast to have a role in *The Dick Van Dyke Show* when it went on the air, though it was not the role he had had in the pilot. Instead of the series' star, he played Rob's tyrannical boss, Alan Brady (Alan Sturdy in the pilot), star of the variety show for which Rob was head writer.

COMEDY THEATRE

Comedy Anthology

FIRST TELECAST: *July 26, 1976*
LAST TELECAST: *September 6, 1976*

BROADCAST HISTORY:

Jul 1976–Sep 1976, NBC Mon 8:00–9:00

Each episode of this summer series was composed of two half-hour pilots for proposed situation-comedy series that were not scheduled by NBC.

COMEDY TIME

Comedy Anthology

FIRST TELECAST: *July 6, 1977*

LAST TELECAST: *September 1, 1977*

BROADCAST HISTORY:

Jul 1977, NBC Wed 9:30–10:00

Jul 1977–Sep 1977, NBC Thu 8:00–9:00

NBC used this blanket title for a collection of situation-comedy pilots that were aired during the summer of 1977 on two different nights. All of them were half-hour shows, with two different pilots running back-to-back on Thursdays. None of them made the fall schedule as regular series.

COMEDY TONIGHT

Comedy Variety

FIRST TELECAST: *July 5, 1970*

LAST TELECAST: *August 23, 1970*

BROADCAST HISTORY:

Jul 1970–Aug 1970, CBS Sun 9:00–10:00

REGULARS:

Robert Klein
Peter Boyle
Macintyre Dixon
Judy Graubart
Madeline Kahn
Lynn Lipton
Marty Barris
Barbara Cason
Boni Enten
Laura Greene

Comedian Robert Klein was the host and star of this summer comedy series that spoofed such things as soap operas, politics, and almost anything else that its cast felt topical and worth satirizing. The tone was highly improvisational. Two members of the cast, Peter Boyle and Madeline Kahn, went on to successful careers in motion pictures.

COMMAND POST

Instruction

FIRST TELECAST: *February 14, 1950*

LAST TELECAST: *April 4, 1950*

BROADCAST HISTORY:

Feb 1950–Apr 1950, CBS Tue 8:00–9:00

Produced by and for the U.S. Army, this series was designed as an eight-week course to train the army reserves via television. Subjects covered in the series included planning attacks, self-defense, and combat theory and technique.

COMMENT

Public Affairs

FIRST TELECAST: *June 17, 1954*

LAST TELECAST: *September 10, 1972*

BROADCAST HISTORY:

Jun 1954–Aug 1954, NBC Mon 8:30–9:00

Jan 1958–Aug 1958, NBC Fri 10:45–11:00

Jan 1971–Sep 1971, NBC Sun 6:00–6:30

Jan 1972–Sep 1972, NBC Sun 6:00–6:30

HOST:

Edwin Newman (1971–1972)

In the first two series aired by NBC under the title *Comment*, NBC News correspondents made personal observations about current news issues. That was in 1954 and 1958. More than a decade later, when *Comment* returned to the NBC lineup, the personal opinions voiced were those of spokesmen for various causes or noted public figures discussing significant issues. NBC newsman Edwin Newman was the host for the 1970s version of *Comment* but rarely voiced any opinions of his own on the series.

COMPASS

Travelogue

FIRST TELECAST: *October 23, 1954*

LAST TELECAST: *October 6, 1957*

BROADCAST HISTORY:

Oct 1954–Feb 1955, ABC Sat 7:30–8:00

Mar 1955–Sep 1955, ABC Sat 10:00–10:30

Jul 1956–Sep 1956, ABC Thu 10:00–10:30

Jun 1957–Jul 1957, ABC Thu 9:30–10:00

Jul 1957–Oct 1957, ABC Sun 9:00–9:30

These documentary travel films were fed out over the ABC network for the benefit of stations that did not wish to schedule local series in these time periods. *Compass* was never carried on ABC's flagship station in New York.

CONCENTRATION

Quiz/Audience Participation

FIRST TELECAST: *October 30, 1958*

LAST TELECAST: *September 11, 1961*
BROADCAST HISTORY:
Oct 1958–Nov 1958, NBC Thu 8:30–9:00
Apr 1961–Sep 1961, NBC Mon 9:30–10:00
EMCEE:
Jack Barry (1958)
Hugh Downs (1961)

Concentration, a fixture on the NBC daytime lineup from August 1958 until March 1973, had two runs as a nighttime network series. It first appeared in the fall of 1958 as a temporary replacement for *Twenty-One*, after the latter was suddenly pulled off the air because of the quiz-show scandals that were developing at the time. The host of this version of *Concentration*, which ran for only four weeks, was Jack Barry, who had been host of the suspended *Twenty-One*. *Concentration* made its second appearance on the nighttime schedule as a summer show in 1961, with Hugh Downs, who had hosted the daytime version since its inception.

The format of the show was based on an old children's game of the same name. Two contestants were faced with a game board containing 30 squares. Behind each square was a prize. There were two squares on the board for each prize, and to win the prize the contestant had to match the two correct squares. In order to keep the prizes, however, the contestant also had to be first to guess a rebus, which was gradually revealed as the chosen squares were rotated.

CONCERT TONIGHT
see *Chicago Symphony*

CONFESSION
Interview/Discussion
FIRST TELECAST: *June 19, 1958*
LAST TELECAST: *January 13, 1959*
BROADCAST HISTORY:
Jun 1958–Sep 1958, ABC Thu 10:00–10:30
Sep 1958–Jan 1959, ABC Tue 10:00–10:30
HOST:
Jack Wyatt

This series sought to probe the underlying causes of criminal acts. Filmed in Dallas, Texas, and moderated by Jack Wyatt, each show opened with an interview between Mr. Wyatt and a convicted criminal. Following the interview, Mr. Wyatt led a discussion group that attempted to analyze the reasons for the crime. The discussion group consisted of a lawyer, a clergyman, a penologist or sociologist, and a psychiatrist or psychologist.

CONFLICT
Dramatic Anthology
FIRST TELECAST: *September 18, 1956*
LAST TELECAST: *September 3, 1957*
BROADCAST HISTORY:
Sep 1956–Sep 1957, ABC Tue 7:30–8:30

These hour-long dramas, produced in Hollywood by Warner Brothers, featured varying casts and were seen on alternate weeks with *Cheyenne*. The general theme was people in conflict, in settings ranging across time from Elizabethan England to the present. One of the better productions was "The Magic Brew," starring Jim Backus as a medicine-show pitchman attempting to peddle his wares in a small town. At least two episodes served as prototypes for future series; in one, Will Hutchins appeared as an inept cowboy (his role a year later in *Sugarfoot*), and in the other Efrem Zimbalist, Jr., portrayed private detective Stuart Bailey (as he did in 1958's *77 Sunset Strip*). Among the others seen on *Conflict* were Tab Hunter, Virginia Mayo and Jack Lord.

CONGRESSIONAL REPORT
Discussion
FIRST TELECAST: *June 15, 1969*
LAST TELECAST: *August 31, 1969*
BROADCAST HISTORY:
Jun 1969–Aug 1969, NBC Sun 6:00–6:30
MODERATOR:
Bill Monroe

Each week four members of Congress participated in a round-table discussion of an issue of current interest to the congressmen and their constituencies. Two members of the panel supported the issue and the other two opposed it. NBC newsman Bill Monroe was the moderator of this series, which had premiered as a Sunday afternoon show on April 13, 1969.

CONTINENTAL, THE
Romantic Monologue
FIRST TELECAST: *January 22, 1952*
LAST TELECAST: *January 6, 1953*
BROADCAST HISTORY:
Jan 1952–Apr 1952, CBS Tue/Thu 11:15–11:30

Oct 1952–Jan 1953, ABC Tue/Fri 11:00–11:15

HOST:

Renzo Cesana

For bored housewives looking to add a little excitement to their lives, CBS offered this live program, which followed the 11:00 P.M. local news twice a week. Suave, debonair, sultry-voiced Renzo Cesana, Italian by birth but American by choice, was the only performer. Each night, in a glamorous setting, he would provide a romantic monologue directed to the women in the audience. He was promoted as an Italian count and member of one of the leading families of Rome, and had been doing a similar program on a local station in Los Angeles for several months before CBS brought him to New York to perform on the network.

After a short tenure on that network he showed up on ABC in the fall for another brief run, this time meeting with couples out on their first date.

CONTINENTAL SHOWCASE

Variety

FIRST TELECAST: *June 11, 1966*

LAST TELECAST: *September 10, 1966*

BROADCAST HISTORY:

Jun 1966–Sep 1966, CBS Sat 7:30–8:30

HOST:

Jim Backus

Continental Showcase was the 1966 summer replacement for *The Jackie Gleason Show*. Host Jim Backus traveled throughout Europe with the production company filming many popular local acts, including singers, dancers, acrobats, and other European (and occasionally Oriental) performers.

CONVERSATIONS WITH ERIC SEVAREID

Discussion

FIRST TELECAST: *July 13, 1975*

LAST TELECAST: *August 31, 1975*

BROADCAST HISTORY:

Jul 1975–Aug 1975, CBS Sun 6:00–7:00

HOST:

Eric Sevareid

CBS News correspondent Eric Sevareid had an informal chat each Sunday with a person who had a background in, and understanding of, world affairs. Their talks usually dealt with developing economic and political situations. Among the guests were former West German President Willy Brandt and novelist Leo Rosten.

CONVOY

War Drama

FIRST TELECAST: *September 17, 1965*

LAST TELECAST: *December 10, 1965*

BROADCAST HISTORY:

Sep 1965–Dec 1965, NBC Fri 8:30–9:00

CAST:

Comdr. Dan Talbot ....John Gavin
Merchant Capt. Ben Foster .....John Larch
Chief Officer Steve Kirkland ....Linden Chiles
Lt. Dick O'Connor ....James Callahan

The problems of transporting troops and supplies across the high seas during World War II provided the thrust for this series. Commander Dan Talbot of the U.S. Navy Destroyer Escort *DD 181* was responsible for insuring the safety of a convoy of merchant ships, while civilian Captain Ben Foster ran the merchant freighter *Flagship*, the nerve center for the entire convoy. These two men, one military and one civilian, contended with the problems caused by war—air and U-boat attacks—as well as fogs, high seas, and other perils of the ocean. Foster's chief aide was Chief Officer Steve Kirkland; his counterpart on the destroyer escort was Lt. Dick O'Connor.

COOK'S CHAMPAGNE PARTY

see *Andy and Della Russell*

COOL MILLION

Detective Drama

FIRST TELECAST: *October 25, 1972*

LAST TELECAST: *July 11, 1973*

BROADCAST HISTORY:

Oct 1972–Jul 1973, NBC Wed 8:30–10:00

CAST:

Jefferson Keyes ....James Farentino
Elena ....Adele Mara
Tony ....Ed Bernard

Jefferson Keyes was a former CIA agent who had become an extremely successful private investigator. He was so successful, in fact, that he demanded a $1-million fee for his services. With that kind of money he could afford to have his own executive jet, which he piloted himself to whatever destination, business or pleasure, he had in mind. His popularity as a raconteur as well as a sleuth created strong demands on his time whenever he was not occupied professionally. *Cool Million* was one of the three elements in the 1972–1973 version of *NBC Wednesday Mystery Movie,* along with *Banacek* and *Madigan.*

COP AND THE KID, THE

Situation Comedy

FIRST TELECAST: *December 4, 1975*
LAST TELECAST: *March 4, 1976*
BROADCAST HISTORY:
Dec 1975, NBC Thu 8:30–9:00
Jan 1976–Mar 1976, NBC Thu 8:00–8:30
CAST:
Officer Frank Murphy ....Charles Durning
Lucas Adams ....Tierre Turner
Mrs. Brigid Murphy ....Patsy Kelly
Mary Goodhew ....Sharan Spelman

This was another of the ethnic comedies so popular in the 1970s. Through a strange circumstance, portly, middle-aged Irish cop Frank Murphy found himself assigned custody of Lucas, a young, black, streetwise orphan. Murphy had suffered an asthma attack while chasing Lucas following a shoplifting incident. Knowing that the asthma could be cause for Murphy's dismissal from the force, Lucas blackmailed Murphy into asking for leniency for him at his trial. Murphy did this so well that the court made him Lucas's guardian. The efforts of Murphy and his mother to reform young Lucas provided the comedy.

CORLISS ARCHER

see *Meet Corliss Archer*

CORNER BAR, THE

Situation Comedy

FIRST TELECAST: *June 21, 1972*
LAST TELECAST: *September 7, 1973*
BROADCAST HISTORY:
Jun 1972–Aug 1972, ABC Wed 8:30–9:00
Aug 1973–Sep 1973, ABC Fri 9:30–10:00
CAST:
Harry Grant (1972) ....Gabriel Dell
Fred Costello ....J. J. Barry
Phil Bracken ....Bill Fiore
Joe (1972) ....Joe Keyes
Peter Panama (1972) .....Vincent Schiavelli
Meyer ....Shimen Ruskin
Mary Ann (1972) ....Langhorn Scruggs
Mae (1973) ....Anne Meara
Frank Flynn (1973) ....Eugene Roche
Donald Hooten (1973) ....Ron Carey
EXECUTIVE PRODUCER:
Alan King
PRODUCER:
Howard Morris

This comedy about contemporary life focused on the patrons who frequented Grant's Toomb, a neighborhood tavern in New York City. During the summer of 1972 Gabriel Dell (one of the original Bowery Boys) portrayed bartender-owner Harry Grant, but in 1973 the place was taken over by Mae and Frank (Anne Meara and Eugene Roche). The regular patrons in one or both seasons were Fred, a griping, hard-hat cabdriver; Phil, a scheming Wall Street lawyer; Peter Panama, a gay set designer; and Donald, a flamboyant actor. The hired help included Joe, the "liberated" black cook; Meyer, the long-suffering waiter; and Mary Ann, the sexy and slightly daft waitress.

CORONET BLUE

Mystery

FIRST TELECAST: *May 29, 1967*
LAST TELECAST: *September 4, 1967*
BROADCAST HISTORY:
May 1967–Sep 1967, CBS Mon 10:00–11:00
CAST:
Michael Alden ....Frank Converse
Anthony ....Brian Bedford
Max Spier ....Joe Silver

Michael Alden was not his real name. It was the name he used because he had suffered almost total amnesia after having been dumped off a freighter in New York harbor by someone trying to kill him. The only clue he could remember was that he had been mumbling the words "Coronet Blue" when the police fished him out of the water. In his attempt to ascertain his identity, Alden was befriended by a monk named Anthony and a coffee-shop owner named Max Spier. Danger and intrigue were the keynotes of this summer series as the unknown villains who had dumped Alden into the river pursued him to finish the job. *Coronet Blue* never made it to a full season's run and no conclusion was ever filmed, so Alden—and the viewers—never did find out the meaning of those mysterious words.

CORRUPTORS, THE

see *Target: The Corruptors*

COS

Comedy Variety

FIRST TELECAST: *September 19, 1976*

LAST TELECAST: *November 7, 1976*

BROADCAST HISTORY:

Sep 1976–Nov 1976, ABC Sun 7:00–8:00

HOST:

Bill Cosby

REGULARS:

Jeffrey Altman
Tim Thomerson
Marion Ramsey
Buzzy Linhart
Willie Bobo
Mauricio Jarrin

Cos was one of the few attempts in recent years to design a prime-time television series specifically for two- to twelve-year-olds. It was essentially a variety program, with guest celebrities, sports stars, puppets, and comedy and music that would appeal to the younger set. Bill Cosby opened each show with a monologue, which he never got to finish, because he was invariably interrupted in some fashion. Then he went through a "magic door" to various adventures. A "Cos" Repertory Company of youngsters was on hand to assist in the skits.

COSMOPOLITAN THEATRE

Dramatic Anthology

FIRST TELECAST: *October 2, 1951*

LAST TELECAST: *December 25, 1951*

BROADCAST HISTORY:

Oct 1951–Dec 1951, DUM Tue 9:00–10:00

This major dramatic effort by DuMont presented live TV adaptations of stories from the pages of *Cosmopolitan* magazine, many of them mysteries or romantic dramas. Among the stars that appeared were Lee Tracy, Marsha Hunt, and Lon Chaney, Jr.

COUNTRY MUSIC JUBILEE

see *Ozark Jubilee*

COUNTRY STYLE

Musical Variety

FIRST TELECAST: *July 29, 1950*

LAST TELECAST: *November 25, 1950*

BROADCAST HISTORY:

Jul 1950–Nov 1950, DUM Sat 8:00–9:00

REGULARS:

Peggy Ann Ellis
Gordon Dilworth
Pat Adair
Emily Barnes
Bob Austin
The Folk Dancers
Alvy West and the Volunteer Firemen

This rustic musical variety hour was designed to simulate a Saturday night's entertainment in a small town. The town bandstand, manned by the Volunteer Fireman's band, was the setting around which musical numbers, square dancing, and comedy vignettes took place.

COUPLE OF JOES, A

Variety

FIRST TELECAST: *October 27, 1949*

LAST TELECAST: *July 12, 1950*

BROADCAST HISTORY:

Oct 1949–Dec 1949, ABC Thu 11:15–12 Mid
Dec 1949–Feb 1950, ABC Wed 8:00–9:00
Mar 1950–Jul 1950, ABC Wed 9:00–9:30

REGULARS:

"Big" Joe Rosenfield
Joe Bushkin
Joan Barton (Dec–Feb)
Warren Hull (Dec–Mar)
Beryl Richards (Mar–Jul)
Pat Harrington (Mar–May)
Allyn Edwards (Mar–Jul)
Morgan the Dog

This combination music, variety, and giveaway program starred "Big" Joe Rosenfield and jazz pianist Joe Bushkin, with an assortment of regulars that included singer Joan Barton and, later, comic Pat Harrington. One of the biggest stars of the show seemed to be Morgan the Dog, who attracted much publicity and survived numerous cast changes. *A Couple of Joes* premiered as a local New York show in August 1949, moved to the network in a late-night time slot in October, and in December became a prime-time entry.

COURT-MARTIAL

Drama

FIRST TELECAST: *April 8, 1966*

LAST TELECAST: *September 2, 1966*

BROADCAST HISTORY:

Apr 1966–Sep 1966, ABC Fri 10:00–11:00

CAST:

Capt. David Young ...... Bradford Dillman
Maj. Frank Whittaker .... Peter Graves
M/Sgt. John MacCaskey .... Kenneth J. Warren
Sgt. Wendy .... Diane Clare

At the center of this World War II drama were the officer-lawyers of the U.S. Army Judge Advocate General's Office, headquartered in England, who investigated and prosecuted crimes committed during wartime. The court-martial itself, the climactic part of each show, was preceded by lengthy investigations ranging across war-torn Europe. The series was filmed in England.

COURT OF CURRENT ISSUES

Debate

FIRST TELECAST: *February 9, 1948*
LAST TELECAST: *June 26, 1951*
BROADCAST HISTORY:

Feb 1948–Jul 1948, DUM Tue 8:00–8:30
Jul 1948–Nov 1948, DUM Mon 9:30–10:00
Nov 1948–Jan 1949, DUM Mon 8:00–9:00
Jan 1949–Feb 1949, DUM Mon 10:00–11:00
Mar 1949–Apr 1949, DUM Mon 9:00–10:00
May 1949–Jun 1949, DUM Wed 9:00–10:00
Jun 1949–Jun 1951, DUM Tue 8:00–9:00

CREATOR/PRODUCER:

Irvin Paul Sulds

Court of Current Issues was one of a number of early programs that presented debates on public affairs, this one within the framework of a courtroom trial. A real judge or attorney sat on the bench, prominent persons on each side of the issue represented opposing counsel and witnesses, and a jury of 12 drawn from the audience handed down a verdict. During its last two years *Court* was scheduled on Tuesday night, opposite NBC's Milton Berle, and a reviewer complained that a fine public-affairs show was being wasted—not a single person called in an audience survey was watching it.

The program was known during its early months as *Court of Public Opinion*.

COURT OF LAST RESORT, THE

Crime Drama

FIRST TELECAST: *October 4, 1957*
LAST TELECAST: *February 17, 1960*
BROADCAST HISTORY:

Oct 1957–Apr 1958, NBC Fri 8:00–8:30
Aug 1959–Sep 1959, ABC Wed 8:00–8:30
Oct 1959–Feb 1960, ABC Wed 7:30–8:00

CAST:

Sam Larson .... Lyle Bettger
Erle Stanley Gardner .... Paul Birch
Dr. LeMoyne Snyder ...... Charles Meredith
Raymond Schindler ...... Robert H. Harris
Harry Steeger .... Carleton Young
Marshall Houts .... John Launer
Alex Gregory .... John Maxwell
Park Street, Jr. .... Robert Anderson

The Court of Last Resort, in real life, is a committee of crime experts who investigate cases in which there is a possibility that the convicted prisoner is innocent. This series dramatized some of the actual cases taken on by this renowned group, founded in the early 1950s by the famous mystery writer Erle Stanley Gardner. Each episode depicted the crime for which a given person was imprisoned, and then followed the efforts of the members of the Court of Last Resort to verify his guilt or find evidence of his innocence. The names of the people involved were changed, since the cases were all based on real situations.

In the series Sam Larsen was a special investigator working with the seven members of the Court in their search for truth. At the close of each story, the actual seven-member board was seen briefly and one of them would discuss a specific point of law that was crucial in the drama just finished. On occasion this function was taken over by judges, law-enforcement officers, or district attorneys.

The ABC telecasts consisted of reruns from the original NBC series.

COURT OF PUBLIC OPINION

see *Court of Current Issues*

COURTSHIP OF EDDIE'S FATHER, THE

Situation Comedy

FIRST TELECAST: *September 17, 1969*
LAST TELECAST: *June 14, 1972*
BROADCAST HISTORY:

Sep 1969–Sep 1970, ABC Wed 8:00–8:30
Sep 1970–Sep 1971, ABC Wed 7:30–8:00
Sep 1971–Jan 1972, ABC Wed 8:30–9:00
Jan 1972–Jun 1972, ABC Wed 8:00–8:30

CAST:

Tom Corbett .... Bill Bixby
Eddie Corbett .... Brandon Cruz

Mrs. Livingston .... Miyoshi Umeki
Norman Tinker .... James Komack
Tina .... Kristina Holland

THEME:

"Best Friend," by Harry Nilsson

Magazine publisher Tom Corbett was one of television's many widowers saddled with the responsibility of running a motherless household. In this case his son, freckle-faced young Eddie (played by Brandon Cruz, who was seven years old when the series began), did most of the plotting. Eddie had a special penchant for getting his father romantically involved with prospective brides, which led to many warm and comic moments. Mrs. Livingston was Tom's dependable, philosophical, but sometimes confused housekeeper, Tina his secretary, and Norman Tinker a mod photographer at the magazine. The series was based on a novel by Mark Toby, and had a theme song ("Best Friend") written by pop singer Harry Nilsson.

COWBOY IN AFRICA

Adventure

FIRST TELECAST: *September 11, 1967*
LAST TELECAST: *September 16, 1968*
BROADCAST HISTORY:

Sep 1967–Sep 1968, ABC Mon 7:30–8:30

CAST:

Jim Sinclair .... Chuck Connors
John Henry .... Tom Nardini
Wing Comdr. Howard Hayes
.... Ronald Howard
Samson .... Gerald Edwards

After TV had run through adult Westerns, dude Westerns, "empire" Westerns, contemporary Westerns, and comedy Westerns, ABC decided to try an African Western. *Cowboy in Africa* starred Chuck Connors as the world champion rodeo cowboy Jim Sinclair, who had been hired by an English landowner, Commander Hayes, to bring modern ranching methods to his game ranch in Kenya. Sinclair was assisted by his Navajo blood brother John Henry and was "adopted" by an orphaned, ten-year-old Kikuyu native boy named Samson.

The series was based on Ivan Tors's theatrical film *Africa—Texas Style* and was shot in Africa (for the backgrounds) and the Africa, U.S.A., park in southern California.

COWBOY THEATRE

Western Anthology

FIRST TELECAST: *June 9, 1957*
LAST TELECAST: *September 15, 1957*
BROADCAST HISTORY:

Jun 1957, NBC Sun 6:30–7:00
Jun 1957–Sep 1957, NBC Sun 6:30–7:30

HOST:

Monty Hall

Re-edited Western feature films produced by Columbia Pictures in the 1930s and 1940s provided the material for this anthology, which was hosted and narrated by Monty Hall. The series began on Saturday afternoons in September 1956.

COWBOYS, THE

Western

FIRST TELECAST: *February 6, 1974*
LAST TELECAST: *August 14, 1974*
BROADCAST HISTORY:

Feb 1974–Aug 1974, ABC Wed 8:00–8:30

CAST:

Jebediah Nightlinger .... Moses Gunn
Mrs. Annie Andersen .... Diana Douglas
U.S. Marshal Bill Winter .... Jim Davis
Cimarron .... A Martinez
Slim .... Robert Carradine
Jimmy .... Sean Kelly
Homer .... Kerry MacLane
Steve .... Clint Howard
Hardy .... Mitch Brown
Weedy .... Clay O'Brien

The Cowboys was a kind of teenage Western in which seven young boys, aged 9 to 17 years, faced the trials of growing into manhood while helping a widow run a ranch in the New Mexico Territory of the 1870s. The ranch foreman, Jebediah Nightlinger, and the widow, Mrs. Andersen, were around for adult supervision as the boys fought off teenage Comanches and adult rustlers. The series was based on the novel by William Dale Jennings and the movie starring John Wayne. Four of the boys in the series—Martinez, Carradine, Kelly, and O'Brien—also appeared in the film.

COWBOYS & INJUNS

Children's

FIRST TELECAST: *October 15, 1950*

LAST TELECAST: *December 31, 1950*
BROADCAST HISTORY:
Oct 1950–Dec 1950, ABC Sun 6:00–6:30
HOST:
Rex Bell

This was an unusually informative children's show, consisting of demonstrations of real cowboy and Indian folklore. It was filmed in an outdoor corral and an Indian village as well as in indoor settings. Originally it was a local program in Los Angeles.

COWTOWN RODEO

Rodeo
FIRST TELECAST: *August 1, 1957*
LAST TELECAST: *September 8, 1958*
BROADCAST HISTORY:
Aug 1957–Sep 1957, ABC Thu 8:00–9:00
Jun 1958–Sep 1958, ABC Mon 7:30–8:30
COMMENTATORS:
Marty Glickman
Howard "Stony" Harris

Top rodeo performers competed for cash prizes on this summertime show. Bronco busting, saddle and bareback riding, and calf roping were among the featured events. The program was produced at Cowtown Ranch in New Jersey, whose owner, Stony Harris, was one of the commentators.

CRASH CORRIGAN'S RANCH

Children's
FIRST TELECAST: *July 15, 1950*
LAST TELECAST: *September 29, 1950*
BROADCAST HISTORY:
Jul 1950–Aug 1950, ABC Sat 7:00–7:30
Aug 1950–Sep 1950, ABC Sun 6:30–7:00
Sep 1950, ABC Fri 7:30–8:00
HOST:
Ray (Crash) Corrigan

This variety show for children, starring Ray (Crash) Corrigan, featured musical and other acts in a Western setting.

CRAWFORD MYSTERY THEATRE

Drama/Quiz
FIRST TELECAST: *September 6, 1951*
LAST TELECAST: *September 27, 1951*
BROADCAST HISTORY:
Sep 1951, DUM Thu 9:30–10:00
HOST/MODERATOR:
John Howard
Warren Hull

Detective-fiction writers and other guests guessed solutions to filmed mysteries in this early series, which was sponsored by Crawford Clothes. John Howard was host for the first two telecasts, after which he was replaced by Warren Hull (Howard later appeared as an actor in some of the dramas). The program was also known as *Public Prosecutor.* It was under the latter title that it remained on the air locally in New York until the end of February 1952.

CRIME PHOTOGRAPHER

Newspaper Drama
FIRST TELECAST: *April 19, 1951*
LAST TELECAST: *June 5, 1952*
BROADCAST HISTORY:
Apr 1951–Jun 1952, CBS Thu 10:30–11:00
CAST:
Casey (Apr–Jun 1951) .....Richard Carlyle
Casey (Jun 1951–1952) ....Darren McGavin
Ethelbert (Apr–Jun 1951) ......John Gibson
Ethelbert (Jun 1951–1952) ....Cliff Hall
Ann Williams ....Jan Miner
Captain Logan ....Donald McClelland
Jack Lipman ....Archie Smith

The adventures of Casey, crack photographer for *The Morning Express,* were told in this series, which moved to television after a highly successful run on radio in the 1940s. Casey hung out at the Blue Note Cafe, where the music was provided by the Tony Mottola Trio, and was friendly with Ethelbert the bartender, to whom he recounted his various exploits. Richard Carlyle and John Gibson portrayed the roles when the series premiered in April of 1951, but by June they were replaced by Darren McGavin and Cliff Hall. Ann Williams, a reporter on *The Morning Express,* was Casey's girlfriend. During the summer of 1951, he acquired a partner in cub reporter Jack Lipman, who wrote copy to go with Casey's pictures. This live series was set in, and broadcast from, New York City.

CRIME SYNDICATED

Police Anthology
FIRST TELECAST: *September 18, 1951*
LAST TELECAST: *June 23, 1953*
BROADCAST HISTORY:
Sep 1951–Jun 1953, CBS Tue 9:00–9:30
NARRATOR:
Rudolph Halley
Herbert R. O'Conor

Dramatizations of actual cases from the files of the Senate Crime Investigating Committee, the FBI, and local law-enforcement agencies were presented each week on this live series. Rudolph Halley, former chief counsel for the Senate Crime Investigating Committee, was the original host. When he became president of the New York City Council in late 1951 he decided to alternate narrator responsibilities with Sen. Herbert R. O'Conor of Maryland, former chairman of the Senate Crime Investigating Committee. In March 1952 *Crime Syndicated* was cut back from a weekly series to a biweekly series, alternating with *City Hospital*.

CRIME WITH FATHER

Police Drama

FIRST TELECAST: *August 31, 1951*
LAST TELECAST: *January 18, 1952*
BROADCAST HISTORY:
Aug 1951–Jan 1952, ABC Fri 9:00–9:30
CAST:
Capt. Jim Riland .... Rusty Lane
Chris Riland .... Peggy Lobbin

This father-and-daughter detective show revolved around the cases of Capt. Jim Riland of the homicide squad. Jim's daughter Chris was of greater help in solving cases than any of his plainclothesmen.

CRISIS

syndicated title for *Kraft Mystery Theater*

CRISIS, THE

Drama

FIRST TELECAST: *October 5, 1949*
LAST TELECAST: *December 28, 1949*
BROADCAST HISTORY:
Oct 1949–Dec 1949, NBC Wed 8:00–8:30
INTERVIEWER:
Adrian Spies
"DIRECTOR":
Arthur Peterson (Oct)
Bob Cunningham (Nov–Dec)

This unusual series used a real-life crisis as the subject of a studio dramatization. First a guest would describe for interviewer Spies the events leading up to a critical moment in his or her life. At the major turning point in the story the guest's narrative was stopped, and professional actors—who were unaware of what actually happened next—would carry on, playing the scene as they imagined it might have been resolved. The actors worked unrehearsed and without scripts, improvising dialogue. An on-camera "director" provided some instructions and called for props. After each scene was played, the guest would return to explain what had actually happened. The show was produced live in Chicago and was directed by Norman Felton.

CRITIC AT LARGE

Discussion

FIRST TELECAST: *August 18, 1948*
LAST TELECAST: *April 20, 1949*
BROADCAST HISTORY:
Aug 1948–Nov 1948, ABC Wed 7:30–8:00
Nov 1948–Jan 1949, ABC Thu 8:30–9:00
Jan 1949–Apr 1949, ABC Wed 8:30–9:00
MODERATOR:
John Mason Brown

Author and critic John Mason Brown, who once commented that "some television programs are so much chewing gum for the eyes," offered this intellectual alternative in 1948–1949. It consisted of an informal living-room discussion on the arts with two or three guests, of the caliber of author James Michener, producer Billy Rose, publisher Bennett Cerf, and critic Bosley Crowther. The subjects ranged from modern art to new novels, films, the theater, and fashions.

CROSS QUESTION

see *They Stand Accused*

CROSSROADS

Dramatic Anthology

FIRST TELECAST: *October 7, 1955*
LAST TELECAST: *September 27, 1957*
BROADCAST HISTORY:
Oct 1955–Sep 1957, ABC Fri 8:30–9:00

Crossroads would have been indistinguishable from many other competently done dramatic anthologies of the early and mid-1950s were it not for its unusual subject matter. The series dealt exclusively with dramatizations of the experiences of clergymen. The problems they faced in both their personal and professional lives were depicted by many fine actors, Vincent Price and Luther Adler among them. Clergymen of all faiths were treated at one time or another, and the dramas successfully made the point that these were real people, as well as representatives of their respective faiths.

CRUSADE IN EUROPE
Documentary
FIRST TELECAST: *May 5, 1949*
LAST TELECAST: *October 27, 1949*
BROADCAST HISTORY:
May 1949–Oct 1949, ABC Thu 9:00–9:30
PRODUCER:
Richard de Rochemont
ADAPTED BY:
Fred Feldkamp

This film documentary series on the European theater of action during World War II was assembled from combat footage shot during the war. *Crusade in Europe* was one of the first major documentary series produced especially for television (by the March of Time film unit), and was based on General Dwight D. Eisenhower's best-selling book of the same name. Its success led to a syndicated sequel titled *Crusade in the Pacific.*

CRUSADER
International Intrigue
FIRST TELECAST: *October 7, 1955*
LAST TELECAST: *December 28, 1956*
BROADCAST HISTORY:
Oct 1955–Dec 1956, CBS Fri 9:00–9:30
CAST:
Matt Anders ....Brian Keith

Freelance writer Matt Anders devoted much of his time to one cause: helping the oppressed peoples living under dictatorial or Communist regimes escape to free countries. The reason for his devotion to this cause was simple. After overthrowing the Polish government the Communists had kept his mother in Poland and sent her to a concentration camp, where she died. Holding the Communists responsible for her death, Matt used every means at his disposal to help save others from her fate.

CRYSTAL ROOM
Variety
FIRST TELECAST: *August 15, 1948*
LAST TELECAST: *September 12, 1948*
BROADCAST HISTORY:
Aug 1948–Sep 1948, ABC Sun 8:30–9:00
HOSTESS:
Maggi McNellis

This short-lived variety program was set in an imaginary nightclub and featured Maggi McNellis, one of early TV's most ubiquitous personalities, and guests.

CURTAIN CALL
syndicated title for *Lux Video Theater*

CURTAIN CALL
Dramatic Anthology
FIRST TELECAST: *June 20, 1952*
LAST TELECAST: *September 26, 1952*
BROADCAST HISTORY:
Jun 1952–Sep 1952, NBC Fri 8:00–8:30

Curtain Call, the 1952 summer replacement for *The RCA Victor Show,* was composed of live plays telecast from Hollywood.

CURTAIN UP
see *Movies—Prior to 1961*

CUSTER
Western
FIRST TELECAST: *September 6, 1967*
LAST TELECAST: *December 27, 1967*
BROADCAST HISTORY:
Sep 1967–Dec 1967, ABC Wed 7:30–8:30
CAST:
Lt. Col. George A. Custer
.......................Wayne Maunder
California Joe Milner ....Slim Pickens
Sgt. James Bustard ....Peter Palmer
Crazy Horse ....Michael Dante
Brig. Gen. Alfred Terry ....Robert F. Simon
Capt. Miles Keogh ....Grant Woods

This action Western was based on the career of George A. Custer between 1868 and 1875, the year before his death in the Battle of the Little Big Horn. In 1868, after losing his Civil War rank of brevet major general, Custer was posted to Fort Hays, Kansas, to take command of the 7th Cavalry Regiment. The 7th was a ragtag outfit of low reputation, made up of ex-Confederates, thieves, and renegades. With the help of California Joe Milner, a leathery old army scout and friend; Capt. Keogh, a shrewd and witty Irishman; and towering Sgt. Bustard, Custer managed to whip this sorry regiment into an effective force capable of protecting the settlers on the surrounding plains. Gen. Terry, commanding officer of Fort Hays, disliked Custer's unconventional methods and appearance (including his shoulder-length blond hair), but supported him in his battles with Crazy Horse's Sioux.

D.A., THE

Courtroom Drama

FIRST TELECAST: *September 17, 1971*

LAST TELECAST: *January 7, 1972*

BROADCAST HISTORY:

Sep 1971–Jan 1972, NBC Fri 8:00–8:30

CAST:

Deputy D.A. Paul Ryan ..... Robert Conrad
Chief Deputy D.A. "Staff" Stafford ..... Harry Morgan
D.A. Investigator Bob Ramirez ..... Ned Romero
Public Defender Katherine Benson ..... Julie Cobb

Collecting the evidence necessary to bring criminals to trial and following the course of the trial provided the thrust for this short-lived series. The program had two segments: first Deputy D.A. Ryan and his team would investigate the crime, then Ryan would function as prosecuting attorney. His courtroom adversary in most cases was Public Defender Katherine Benson, representing the accused. The courtroom portion of the series was done in quasi-documentary style with Ryan doing voice-over narration to explain legal terminology and procedures to the audience. The series was replaced after a few months by the highly successful *Sanford and Son*.

D.A.'S MAN, THE

Police Drama

FIRST TELECAST: *January 3, 1959*

LAST TELECAST: *August 29, 1959*

BROADCAST HISTORY:

Jan 1959–Aug 1959, NBC Sat 10:30–11:00

CAST:

Shannon ..... John Compton
Al Bonacorsi ..... Ralph Manza
Frank LaValle ..... Herb Ellis

Working as an undercover investigator for the New York City District Attorney's Office, ex-private eye Shannon spent most of his time infiltrating the New York underworld. Hijacking rings, prostitution, narcotics, and any other source of "mob" income were appropriate targets for his sleuthing. Shannon's contact at the D.A.'s office was First Assistant D.A. Al Bonacorsi.

DAGMAR'S CANTEEN

Variety

FIRST TELECAST: *March 22, 1952*

LAST TELECAST: *June 14, 1952*

BROADCAST HISTORY:

Mar 1952–Jun 1952, NBC Sat 12:15–12:45 A.M.

REGULARS:

Dagmar (Jennie Lewis)
Ray Malone
Tim Herbert
Jeanne Lewis
Milton Delugg and His Orchestra

Dagmar, the statuesque, well-endowed blonde made famous on Jerry Lester's *Broadway Open House*, starred in this late-night live variety show as the hostess of a real canteen for servicemen. She interviewed, sang songs, and danced, but the most amusing part of the show was her weekly reading of one of her original plays (similar to her hilarious "poetry readings" on *Broadway Open House*). Roles in the plays were also read by servicemen chosen from the audience, as well as by the other cast members. One of the regulars was Dagmar's sister Jeanne, who was the assistant hostess.

DAKOTAS, THE

Western

FIRST TELECAST: *January 7, 1963*

LAST TELECAST: *September 9, 1963*

BROADCAST HISTORY:

Jan 1963–Sep 1963, ABC Mon 7:30–8:30

CAST:

Marshal Frank Ragan ..... Larry Ward
Deputy J. D. Smith ..... Jack Elam
Deputy Del Stark ..... Chad Everett
Deputy Vance Porter ..... Mike Greene

This Western adventure depicted the efforts of a U.S. Marshal and his three deputies to maintain law and order across the Black Hills and Badlands of the Dakota Territory. The deputies were a study in contrasts: young, volatile Del Stark; big, gruff Vance Porter; and J. D. Smith, an ex-gunfighter.

DAKTARI

Adventure

FIRST TELECAST: *January 11, 1966*

LAST TELECAST: *January 15, 1969*

BROADCAST HISTORY:

Jan 1966–Sep 1968, CBS Tue 7:30–8:30

Sep 1968–Jan 1969, CBS Wed 7:30–8:30

CAST:

Dr. Marsh Tracy ......Marshall Thompson
Paula Tracy ....Cheryl Miller
Jack Dane (1965–1968) .....Yale Summers
Hedley ....Hedley Mattingly
Mike ....Hari Rhodes
Bert Jason (1968–1969) ....Ross Hagen
Jenny (1968–1969) ....Erin Moran

Filmed at Africa, U.S.A., a wild-animal park south of Los Angeles, *Daktari* told the story of an American doctor and his daughter living in Africa. "Daktari" is a native word for doctor. Marsh Tracy was a veterinarian who ran an animal study center with the assistance of his daughter Paula, an American named Jack Dane, and a native named Mike. The Tracys had two distinctive pets, a lion named Clarence and a chimpanzee named Judy. (Clarence had previously starred in an Ivan Tors movie called *Clarence the Crosseyed Lion*.) Also featured was Hedley, the British game warden, who often called on Marsh for help in dealing with animals, natives, and poachers. Added to the cast in 1968 were Bert Jason, a former ranger and hunter who had become a guide for camera safaris, and Jenny, a seven-year-old orphan who became part of the Tracy household.

DALLAS

Drama

FIRST TELECAST: *April 2, 1978*

LAST TELECAST:

BROADCAST HISTORY:

Apr 1978, CBS Sun 10:00–11:00
Sep 1978–Oct 1978, CBS Sat 10:00–11:00
Oct 1978– , CBS Sun 10:00–11:00

CAST:

Eleanor Southworth Ewing
.... Barbara Bel Geddes
John "Jock" Ewing ....Jim Davis
Bobby Ewing ....Patrick Duffy
Pamela Barnes Ewing ... Victoria Principal
Lucy Ewing ....Charlene Tilton
Sue Ellen Ewing ....Linda Grey
J. R. Ewing ....Larry Hagman
Ray Krebbs ....Steve Kanaly
Cliff Barnes ....Ken Kercheval
Julie (April 1978) .... Tina Louise
Digger Barnes ....David Wayne

The Ewing family owned one of the richest oil and cattle empires in contemporary Texas. They had the power and prestige to do virtually anything, except to keep peace among themselves. Patriarch Jock Ewing and his oldest son, J.R., ruled the family empire, through means that were often unscrupulous. When Jock's younger son, Bobby, arrived home with a new wife and plans to participate more actively in the family's operations, things got complicated. J.R. resented his younger brother's intrusion into a business he had planned to take over himself, and the entire family resented Bobby's bride Pamela. Her father had been ruined years before in business dealings with Jock, and her brother Cliff was legal counsel to a government committee which was attempting to expose the Ewings' corruption of public officials and their other illegal business practices.

DAMON RUNYON THEATRE

Dramatic Anthology

FIRST TELECAST: *April 16, 1955*

LAST TELECAST: *June 30, 1956*

BROADCAST HISTORY:

Apr 1955–Jun 1956, CBS Sat 10:30–11:00

HOST:

Donald Woods

Most of the episodes in this filmed anthology were based on the short stories of Damon Runyon. Best known through the musical *Guys and Dolls*, which was adapted from his writings, Runyon was unique in his use of hip New York language and characters. Vivian Blaine, who created the role of Adelaide in *Guys and Dolls*, appeared in a variation on that role in the premiere episode of the program.

DAN AUGUST

Police Drama

FIRST TELECAST: *September 23, 1970*

LAST TELECAST: *June 25, 1975*

BROADCAST HISTORY:

Sep 1970–Jan 1971, ABC Wed 10:00–11:00
Jan 1971–Aug 1971, ABC Thu 9:30–10:30
May 1973–Oct 1973, CBS Wed 9:00–10:00
Apr 1975–Jun 1975, CBS Wed 10:00–11:00

CAST:

Det. Lt. Dan August ....Burt Reynolds
Sgt. Charles Wilentz ....Norman Fell
Sgt. Joe Rivera ....Ned Romero
Chief George Untermeyer
.... Richard Anderson
Katy Grant ....Ena Hartmann

Burt Reynolds portrayed Dan August, a police detective, in this straight police-action show. Since August had grown up with many of the people he had to deal with officially in Santa Luisa, California, he became more personally involved in his cases than would most big-city detectives. Despite—or perhaps because of—this, he always got his man, in true TV-detective fashion.

Dan August was aired on ABC during the 1970–1971 season to mediocre ratings and was not renewed. However, shortly thereafter Reynolds became a major celebrity through feature-film and other exposure, and CBS telecast reruns during two subsequent summers to larger audiences than had seen the original series.

DAN RAVEN

Police Drama

FIRST TELECAST: *September 23, 1960*

LAST TELECAST: *January 6, 1961*

BROADCAST HISTORY:

Sep 1960–Jan 1961, NBC Fri 7:30–8:30

CAST:

Lt. Dan Raven .... Skip Homeier
Det. Sgt. Burke .... Dan Barton
Perry Levitt .... Quinn Redeker

The Sunset Strip in Hollywood provided the setting for this police-action series. Lt. Dan Raven and his partner Sgt. Burke were assigned by the Los Angeles Sheriff's Office (West Hollywood Division) to the maze of jazz spots, nightclubs, coffee houses, and other entertainment emporiums that lined the famous Strip. While covering his beat, Raven often became involved with show business personalities—such as Bobby Darin, Paul Anka, Buddy Hackett, and Gogi Grant—who worked on the Strip. The plots often revolved around these guest stars, some of whom played themselves and some of whom portrayed fictional characters. Magazine photographer Perry Levitt, who also had the Hollywood beat, was often seen where the action was.

DANCING ON AIR

Instruction

FIRST TELECAST: *February 2, 1947*

LAST TELECAST: *March 2, 1947*

BROADCAST HISTORY:

Feb 1947–Mar 1947, NBC Sun 8:00–8:15

EMCEE:

Ed Sims

Dancing on Air was a five-week dance-instruction program, with instructors from the Fred Astaire Studios.

DANGER

Dramatic Anthology

FIRST TELECAST: *September 19, 1950*

LAST TELECAST: *May 31, 1955*

BROADCAST HISTORY:

Sep 1950–Aug 1954, CBS Tue 10:00–10:30
Aug 1954–Dec 1954, CBS Tue 9:30–10:00
Jan 1955–May 1955, CBS Tue 10:00–10:30

HOST/NARRATOR:

Richard Stark

The title of this series was fully descriptive of its content. Psychological dramas and various types of murder mysteries were the weekly fare in these live plays telecast from New York. "Death and Murder," in fact, might have been an even more appropriate title, since those words kept popping up in titles of individual episodes. There were "Murder Takes the 'A' Train," "Operation Murder," "Murder's Face," "Motive for Murder," and "Inherit Murder" on the one hand, and "Death Gamble," "Death Among the Relics," "Death Beat," "Prelude to Death," "Death for the Lonely," "Flowers of Death," and "Death Signs an Autograph" on the other. The players were not particularly well known and, at the time, neither were the directors. Three of the directors subsequently did become highly successful. Yul Brynner, who worked frequently as a director in the early days of television, was the director of *Danger* when it went on the air in the fall of 1950. He was replaced early on by Sidney Lumet, who later gave way to John Frankenheimer.

DANGER MAN

International Intrigue

FIRST TELECAST: *April 5, 1961*

LAST TELECAST: *September 13, 1961*

BROADCAST HISTORY:

Apr 1961–Sep 1961, CBS Wed 8:30–9:00

CAST:

John Drake .... Patrick McGoohan

Filmed on diverse locations around the world, ranging from major European capitals to remote African jungles, *Danger Man* told of the exploits of John Drake, an internationally famous security investigator whose services were available only to governments or highly placed government officials. Working in affiliation with NATO, the suave, calculating, and highly efficient Mr. Drake was equally at home in the best restaurants or eating raw meat with a native tribe in some remote outpost as he pursued his quarry to the four corners of the earth. This British-produced series was the first of three similar series starring Patrick McGoohan to reach American audiences in the 1960s. The other two were *Secret Agent* and *The Prisoner*.

DANIEL BOONE

Western

FIRST TELECAST: *September 24, 1964*
LAST TELECAST: *August 27, 1970*
BROADCAST HISTORY:
Sep 1964–Aug 1970, NBC Thu 7:30–8:30
CAST:
Daniel Boone ....Fess Parker
Yadkin (1964–1965) ....Albert Salmi
Mingo (1964–1968) ....Ed Ames
Rebecca Boone ....Patricia Blair
Jemima Boone (1964–1966)
.....................Veronica Cartwright
Israel Boone ....Darby Hinton
Cincinnatus ....Dal McKennon
Jericho Jones (1965–1966) ....Robert Logan
Gideon (1968–1969) .....Don Pedro Colley
Gabe Cooper (1969–1970)
.... Roosevelt Grier
Josh Clements (1968–1970) .... Jimmy Dean

Fess Parker, who gained fame portraying Davy Crockett for Walt Disney in the mid-1950s, became even more successful as another frontiersman, Daniel Boone, in the 1960s. Like Crockett, Daniel Boone was one of America's great folk heroes. He lived in the North Carolina-Tennessee-Kentucky area just before and during the Revolutionary War, and his exploits were legendary. The stories in this series revolved around Boone's encounters with Indians, both friendly and hostile, his survey work and pioneering expeditions, and his relationships with family and friends.

The family included his wife Rebecca, his daughter Jemima, and his son Israel. The friends were originally his traveling companion Yadkin, his Indian friend Mingo, and Cincinnatus, tavernkeeper of Boonesborough, Daniel's home base. Only Cincinnatus remained through the entire six-year run of the show. Later added to the cast were young pioneer Jericho Jones; Gideon, a black Indian; Josh Clements, a fur trapper; and Gabe Cooper, a runaway slave living with the Indians.

DANNY KAYE SHOW, THE

Musical Variety

FIRST TELECAST: *September 25, 1963*
LAST TELECAST: *June 7, 1967*
BROADCAST HISTORY:
Sep 1963–Jun 1967, CBS Wed 10:00–11:00 (OS)
REGULARS:
Danny Kaye
Harvey Korman (1964–1967)
Joyce Van Patten (1964–1967)
Paul Weston and His Orchestra

The multitalented Danny Kaye starred for four seasons in his own musical comedy–variety series on CBS. He did monologues, pantomime, and comedy sketches; he sang, danced, and even played an instrument or two. The most remarkable aspect of the series was its use of inventive comedy sketches with Danny's guest stars. Although neither Harvey Korman nor Joyce Van Patten appeared on every episode during the three years in which they frequented the series, they were given featured performer status by CBS in all press releases about the show.

DANNY THOMAS HOUR, THE

Various

FIRST TELECAST: *September 11, 1967*
LAST TELECAST: *June 10, 1968*
BROADCAST HISTORY:
Sep 1967–Jun 1968, NBC Mon 9:00–10:00
HOST/STAR:
Danny Thomas

This weekly series was a potpourri of different entertainment forms. Included were musical-variety specials, dramatic plays, and light comedies. Danny Thomas starred in all the musical-variety episodes and comedies and was host of the serious dramas. A number of comedies were long versions of his own previous hit series, *Make Room for Daddy (The Danny Thomas Show)*.

DANNY THOMAS SHOW, THE

Situation Comedy

FIRST TELECAST: *September 29, 1953*
LAST TELECAST: *September 2, 1971*
BROADCAST HISTORY:
Sep 1953–Jun 1956, ABC Tue 9:00–9:30

Oct 1956–Feb 1957, ABC Mon 8:00–8:30
Feb 1957–Jul 1957, ABC Thu 9:00–9:30
Oct 1957–Sep 1964, CBS Mon 9:00–9:30 (OS)
Apr 1965–Sep 1965, CBS Mon 9:30–10:00
Sep 1970–Jan 1971, ABC Wed 8:00–8:30
Jan 1971–Sep 1971, ABC Thu 9:00–9:30

CAST:

Danny Williams .... Danny Thomas
Mrs. Margaret Williams (1953–1956) .... Jean Hagen
Mrs. Kathy Williams ("Clancey") (1957–1971) .... Marjorie Lord
Rusty Williams .... Rusty Hamer
Terry Williams (1953–1958) .... Sherry Jackson
Terry Williams (1959–1960) .... Penney Parker
Linda Williams (1957–1971) .... Angela Cartwright
Louise (1953–1964) ..... Amanda Randolph
Horace (1953–1954) ..... Horace McMahon
Benny (1953–1957) .... Ben Lessy
Jesse Leeds (1955–1957) .... Jesse White
Uncle Tonoose (1958–1971) .... Hans Conried
Phil Brokaw (1959–1961) .... Sheldon Leonard
Pat Hannigan (1959–1960) .... Pat Harrington, Jr.
Gina (1959) .... Annette Funicello
"Uncle Charley" Halper (1959–1971) .... Sid Melton
Bunny Halper (1961–1964) ..... Pat Carroll
Rosey Robbins (1970–1971) .... Roosevelt Grier
Michael (1970–1971) ...... Michael Hughes
Henry (1970–1971) .... Stanley Myron Handleman

THEME:

"Danny Boy" ("Londonderry Air")

Danny Thomas's first major exposure on television had been as one of the hosts of NBC's *All Star Revue*. His nightclub routine was a flop on TV, as a result of which he blasted the new medium as being suitable "only for idiots" and vowed never to return. But return he did, in 1953, with one of the longest-running family comedies of the 1950s and 1960s. *Make Room for Daddy*, as it was called for its first three seasons, was a reflection of Danny's own life as an entertainer and the problems created by his frequent absences from his children. The title came from a phrase used in the real-life Thomas household: whenever Danny returned home from a tour, his children had to shift bedrooms, to "make room for Daddy." In the series, Danny played nightclub entertainer Danny Williams, a sometimes loud but ultimately softhearted lord of the household, who was constantly being upstaged by his bratty but lovable kids. The kids were, at the outset, 6-year-old Rusty and 11-year-old Terry. Jean Hagen played Danny's loving wife, Margaret.

A number of major changes took place as the show matured. In 1956 Jean Hagen quit. Instead of replacing her, Danny had her written out of the show as having died, which led to a season (1956–1957) of his courting eligible women—with frequent assistance from the kids. He eventually proposed to an Irish lass, Kathy. The wedding did not take place on the show, but when the program returned in the fall of 1957 Danny and Kathy were just returning from their honeymoon, and little Linda, Kathy's daughter by a previous marriage, had also joined the Williams household.

Sherry Jackson left the cast in 1958. At first the character she played, Terry, was supposed to be away at school, but in 1959 a new actress assumed the role. Terry then had a season-long courtship with a young nightclub performer named Pat Hannigan, whom she eventually married. Terry then left the household for good.

A number of other youngsters also passed through the series, including Gina, a foreign exchange student living in the Williams home. Piccola Pupa, a young Italian singer discovered by Danny, was also seen in a few episodes. Other regulars included a succession of Danny's agents, the first played by Horace McMahon, and later ones by Jesse White—who simultaneously was appearing as the agent on *Private Secretary*—and Sheldon Leonard. (Leonard was the real-life producer of *The Danny Thomas Show* and had appeared in 1953 episodes as Danny's masseur.) Benny was Danny's original accompanist, Louise the family housekeeper, and Charley Halper the owner of the Copa Club, where Danny Williams frequently performed.

No doubt the most memorable regular was Hans Conried in the role of Uncle Tonoose, eccentric patriarch of the Williams family. Conried had previously been seen in several guest roles on the show, including those of ne'er-do-well Cousin Carl,

Uncle Oscar, and visiting Derik Campbell, before he turned up as Tonoose in a fall 1958 telecast. The role was perfect, and he continued to appear in it, periodically, for the rest of the series' run. Others who made guest appearances were songwriter Harry Ruby as himself, Bill Dana as Jose Jiminez, the elevator operator, and many top names from the entertainment world, playing themselves.

The Danny Thomas Show ended its original run in 1964, although repeat telecasts were seen on CBS during 1965. Then in 1970 Danny Williams returned in a new series called *Danny Thomas in Make Room for Granddaddy*, complete with Kathy, Rusty (now 23 and married), and Linda (now 17) from the original cast. A newcomer was a roguishly cute little terror named Michael, age 6. Michael made Danny the "Granddaddy," since he was cast as Terry's son, left with the Williams while Terry and her soldier husband were abroad. Charley Halper and Uncle Tonoose were back, joined by a new accompanist (played by ex-football star Roosevelt Grier) and Henry, the neurotic elevator operator in Danny's apartment building. Despite guest appearances by such stars as Bob Hope, Frank Sinatra, Milton Berle, and Lucille Ball, the format was rather old-hat for the 1970s, and *Make Room for Granddaddy* expired after a single season.

DANTE

Mystery Adventure

FIRST TELECAST: *October 3, 1960*
LAST TELECAST: *April 10, 1961*
BROADCAST HISTORY:
Oct 1960–Apr 1961, NBC Mon 9:30–10:00
CAST:
Willie Dante .... Howard Duff
Stewart Styles .... Alan Mowbray
Biff .... Tom D'Andrea

Adventurer Willie Dante had a history of running clip joints and gambling casinos around the country, a reputation he planned to change when he opened his own legitimate nightclub in San Francisco. With him were his two sidekicks from the gambling days, Biff the bartender and Stewart the maître d'. Unfortunately, neither the police nor the underworld believed that Dante had really gone straight, and his confrontations with both provided much of the action of the show. Played in a tongue-in-cheek manner, *Dante* had more humor than violence. The contrast between the three leads—suave, urbane, ladies' man Willie Dante; Biff, who kept bringing up incidents from their sordid past; and Stewart, whose proper British image did not fit with his encyclopedic knowledge of underworld characters and activities—was the source of much of the humor.

The role of Willie Dante had been played by Dick Powell in a number of episodes of *Four Star Playhouse* during the 1950s.

DARK ADVENTURE

see *ABC Dramatic Shorts—1952–1953*

DARK OF NIGHT

Dramatic Anthology

FIRST TELECAST: *October 10, 1952*
LAST TELECAST: *May 1, 1953*
BROADCAST HISTORY:
Oct 1952–May 1953, DUM Fri 8:30–9:00

The stars of this unusual drama series were its locations. *Dark of Night* was telecast live each week from locations all over the New York City area, such as stores, factories, railroad yards, docks, and hospitals. Apparently most of the budget was used in getting the cameras and crew to the locations, since the performers and writers were for the most part unknowns. Among the starring locations were Brentano's Book Store on Fifth Avenue, a hangar at Idlewild (now Kennedy) Airport, an old English-style castle in Paterson, New Jersey, the Parke-Bernet art galleries in Manhattan, a Coca-Cola bottling plant, a coffee company (for a comedy about the trials of a coffee taster), the F. & M. Shaeffer Brewing Company, and the American Red Cross Blood Bank. Appropriately, the final telecast was from the DuMont television set factory in East Paterson, New Jersey.

During a two-month period, from mid-November 1952 to mid-January 1953, *Dark of Night* was seen on alternate weeks.

DATE WITH JUDY, A

Situation Comedy

FIRST TELECAST: *July 10, 1952*
LAST TELECAST: *September 30, 1953*
BROADCAST HISTORY:
Jul 1952–Oct 1952, ABC Thu 8:00–8:30
Jan 1953–Sep 1953, ABC Wed 7:30–8:00

CAST:

Judy Foster ....Mary Linn Beller
Melvyn Foster ....John Gibson
Dora Foster ....Flora Campbell
Randolph Foster ....Peter Avramo
Oogie Pringle ....Jimmy Sommers

WRITER:

Aleen Leslie

The trials of a hyperactive bobbysoxer and her harassed parents were the subject of this live situation comedy, which was the TV version of a popular radio series begun in 1941. In addition to Judy and her sedate, middle-class parents, the characters included her pesky younger brother Randolph and her boyfriend Oogie. First seen as a Saturday daytime series on June 2, 1951 (with Pat Crowley as Judy), *A Date With Judy* changed casts and moved to prime time in July 1952.

DATE WITH THE ANGELS

Situation Comedy

FIRST TELECAST: *May 10, 1957*

LAST TELECAST: *January 29, 1958*

BROADCAST HISTORY:

May 1957–Jun 1957, ABC Fri 10:00–10:30
Jul 1957–Dec 1957, ABC Fri 9:30–10:00
Jan 1958, ABC Wed 9:30–10:00

CAST:

Vicki Angel ....Betty White
Gus Angel ....Bill Williams
Wilma Clemson ....Natalie Masters
George Clemson ....Roy Engle
Mrs. Murphy ....Maudie Prickett
Mr. Murphy (Murph) ......Richard Reeves
Mrs. Drake ....Lillian Bronson
Dr. Gordon ....Gage Clark
Mr. Finley ....Burt Mustin
Roger Finley ....Richard Deacon
Wheeler ....Jimmy Boyd

Betty White starred in this domestic comedy about a new bride and her husband, an insurance salesman. An unusually wide assortment of neighbors and friends passed through the series, usually serving as foils for one of Vicki's or Gus's schemes. Most frequently seen were their friend Murph, the Clemsons, and an erratic neighbor, Mr. Finley. Jimmy Boyd appeared periodically as their teenage nephew Wheeler.

DATING GAME, THE

Quiz/Audience Participation

FIRST TELECAST: *October 6, 1966*

LAST TELECAST: *January 17, 1970*

BROADCAST HISTORY:

Oct 1966–Jan 1967, ABC Thu 8:30–9:00
Jan 1967–Jan 1970, ABC Sat 7:30–8:00

HOST:

Jim Lange

PRODUCER:

Chuck Barris

The premise of *The Dating Game* was to take one young person plus three "candidates" of the opposite sex and arrange a date. There were two rounds in each show, one in which a girl asked questions of three guys, and one in which a guy asked questions of three girls. The questioner could not see the three candidates, which eliminated appearance as a consideration. At the end of each round the questioner picked the date he or she thought would be most interesting, and the newly matched pair were then sent off on a night on the town or an expense-paid trip to some exotic fun spot. (Follow-up reports in later months told how many of these first dates blossomed into romance and marriage.) The questions, which were prepared by the show's staff, were generally of the titillating variety.

Originally a daytime program on ABC, *The Dating Game* came to prime time as a stop-gap replacement for *The Tammy Grimes Show*, the first casualty of the 1966–1967 season. It was popular enough to remain on the nighttime lineup for more than three years, after which it continued in daytime only. For the companion program by the same producers, which ran in the adjacent time slot on Saturday night, see *The Newlywed Game*.

DAVE GARROWAY SHOW, THE

see *Garroway at Large*

DAVE KING SHOW, THE

see *Kraft Music Hall Presents the Dave King Show*

DAVID BRINKLEY'S JOURNAL

Documentary

FIRST TELECAST: *October 11, 1961*

LAST TELECAST: *August 26, 1963*

BROADCAST HISTORY:

Oct 1961–Sep 1962, NBC Wed 10:30–11:00
Oct 1962–Aug 1963, NBC Mon 10:00–11:00

COMMENTATOR:

David Brinkley

David Brinkley, who had been the co-anchor of NBC's nightly *Huntley-Brinkley Report* since 1956, hosted his own prime-time documentary series in the early 1960s. From one to three stories were examined each week, each of them treated from Brinkley's own unique perspective. His caustic wit and incisive observations gave the program a very personal flavor, quite different from the run of TV documentaries. The subject matter ranged from light pieces on professional wrestler Antonino Rocca, the birth of a Broadway musical, and after-dinner speeches by political figures, to probing evaluations of domestic and foreign political issues.

The critical response to *David Brinkley's Journal* was positive, and the program won Emmy Awards in both 1962 and 1963 as the best public-affairs series on television. However, viewership was low and the series survived as a weekly entry for only two seasons. It was later seen on an occasional basis, until 1965.

DAVID NIVEN SHOW, THE

Dramatic Anthology

FIRST TELECAST: *April 7, 1959*

LAST TELECAST: *September 15, 1959*

BROADCAST HISTORY:

Apr 1959–Sep 1959, NBC Tue 10:00–10:30

HOST:

David Niven

David Niven appeared before each episode of this summer anthology series to introduce the drama being presented, and personally starred in one of the episodes.

DAVID STEINBERG SHOW, THE

Comedy Variety

FIRST TELECAST: *July 19, 1972*

LAST TELECAST: *August 16, 1972*

BROADCAST HISTORY:

Jul 1972–Aug 1972, CBS Wed 8:00–9:00

REGULAR:

David Steinberg

Controversial comedian David Steinberg was referred to in *TV Guide* as "off beat, racy, outrageous and establishment-baiting—all of which makes him a particular favorite of the young and disenchanted." In 1972 he starred in his own summer comedy series, introducing two or three guest stars each week and performing with them.

DAY DREAMING WITH LARAINE DAY

Interviews/Variety

FIRST TELECAST: *May 17, 1951*

LAST TELECAST: *July 19, 1951*

BROADCAST HISTORY:

May 1951–Jul 1951, ABC Thu 7:15–7:30

HOSTESS:

Laraine Day

Celebrity interviews, songs, and Broadway and Hollywood gossip with actress Laraine Day were the features of this program. Among other things, Miss Day asked her guests to describe alternative careers they might wish they had chosen. A similar series with Miss Day ran concurrently on Saturday afternoons.

DAY IN COURT

see *Accused*

DEADLINE FOR ACTION

see *Wire Service*

DEAN MARTIN COMEDY WORLD, THE

Comedy Variety

FIRST TELECAST: *June 6, 1974*

LAST TELECAST: *August 15, 1974*

BROADCAST HISTORY:

Jun 1974–Aug 1974, NBC Thu 10:00–11:00

HOSTS:

Jackie Cooper
Nipsey Russell
Barbara Feldon

Jackie Cooper served as "anchorman in the control room from the center of the comedy world," coordinating and introducing many of the comedy acts that appeared on this summer replacement for *The Dean Martin Comedy Hour*. The show included taped performances by new comedy talent from all over the world, excerpts from both old and new comedy films, and performances by well-established comedy stars. Nipsey Russell and Barbara Feldon were on location to do introductions from such diverse spots as London, Hollywood, and San Francisco.

DEAN MARTIN PRESENTS

Musical Variety

FIRST TELECAST: *June 20, 1968*

LAST TELECAST: *September 6, 1973*

BROADCAST HISTORY:

Jun 1968–Sep 1968, NBC Thu 10:00–11:00
Jul 1969–Sep 1969, NBC Thu 10:00–11:00

Jul 1970–Sep 1970, NBC Thu 10:00–11:00
Jul 1972–Sep 1972, NBC Thu 10:00–11:00
Jul 1973–Sep 1973, NBC Thu 10:00–11:00

REGULARS:

Joey Heatherton (1968)
Frank Sinatra, Jr. (1968)
Paul Lynde (1968, 1969)
The Golddiggers (1968, 1969, 1970)
Barbara Heller (1968)
Stu Gilliam (1968)
Stanley Myron Handleman (1968)
Skiles and Henderson (1968)
Times Square Two (1968)
Gail Martin (1969)
Lou Rawls (1969)
Tommy Tune (1969)
Albert Brooks (1969)
Danny Lockin (1969)
Joyce Ames (1969)
Charles Nelson Reilly (1970)
Marty Feldman (1970)
Julian Chagrin (1970)
Bobby Darin (1972)
Rip Taylor (1972)
Steve Landsburg (1972)
Sara Hankboner (1972)
Cathy Cahill (1972)
Dick Bakalyan (1972)
Schnecklegruber (1972)
Loretta Lynn (1973)
Lynn Anderson (1973)
Jerry Reed (1973)
Ray Stevens (1973)

Dean Martin Presents . . . was the umbrella title for a series of summer replacements for *The Dean Martin Show*. They were all musical variety shows featuring mostly young talent; their actual titles were as follows:

1968—*Dean Martin Presents the Golddiggers*
1969—*Dean Martin Presents the Golddiggers*
1970—*Dean Martin Presents the Golddiggers in London*
1972—*Dean Martin Presents the Bobby Darin Amusement Co.*
1973—*Dean Martin Presents Music Country*

The regular casts of these summer shows remained relatively stable through 1972. The Country and Western version aired during the summer of 1973 had, in addition to the four regulars who appeared in almost every episode, a large number of Country music performers who appeared irregularly.

DEAN MARTIN SHOW, THE

Comedy Variety

FIRST TELECAST: *September 16, 1965*
LAST TELECAST: *May 24, 1974*
BROADCAST HISTORY:

Sep 1965–Jul 1973, NBC Thu 10:00–11:00 (OS)
Sep 1973–May 1974, NBC Fri 10:00–11:00

REGULARS:

Dean Martin
The Golddiggers (1967–1971)
The Ding-a-Ling Sisters (1970–1973)
Kay Medford (1970–1973)
Lou Jacobi (1971–1973)
Marian Mercer (1971–1972)
Tom Bosley (1971–1972)
Dom DeLuise (1972–1973)
Nipsey Russell (1972–1973)
Rodney Dangerfield (1972–1973)
Ken Lane
Les Brown and His Band

Singer-comedian Dean Martin was host and star of this long-lived variety hour, which was for most of its run a fixture on the NBC Thursday night lineup. At first Dean had no regular supporting cast other than his accompanist, pianist Ken Lane. Guest stars were featured each week in comedy skits and songs, both alone and with Dean. Some of the young talent appearing during the regular season also starred in Dean's summer replacement series, *The Dean Martin Summer Show* and later *Dean Martin Presents*. A bevy of pretty young dancers called the Golddiggers were added as regulars in 1967, and four of these later became the Ding-a-Ling Sisters (1970–1973).

Beginning in 1970 a supporting cast of comics and singers was gradually assembled around Dean, some of whom appeared regularly (see credits) and others occasionally, such as Foster Brooks with his "drunk" routine. The hallmark of the show remained Dean's own easy informality, as he welcomed guests into his cozy living room through the ever-present door, or sang or clowned beside (or on, or under) Ken Lane's grand piano. In fact, a stipulation in Dean's contract helped foster this air of informality by allowing Dean not to show up until the day of the taping each week, when the show would be done with only minimal rehearsal.

In 1973 the title and format were changed, as well as the time slot. The new title was *The Dean Martin Comedy Hour,* and Dean and Ken Lane were once again the only regulars. Two new features were added. The first was a Country music spot, with top-name Country performers, to hold some of the audience that had been attracted to Dean's summer replacement in 1973, *Dean Martin Presents Music Country*. The second was the "Man of the Week Celebrity Roast," in which several celebrities seated at a banquet dais tossed comic insults at the guest of honor. This feature proved so popular that after Dean's regular series ended in 1974, the "roasts" continued on NBC as a series of occasional specials.

DEAN MARTIN SUMMER SHOW, THE

Variety

FIRST TELECAST: *June 16, 1966*
LAST TELECAST: *August 19, 1971*
BROADCAST HISTORY:

Jun 1966–Sep 1966, NBC Thu 10:00–11:00
Jun 1967–Sep 1967, NBC Thu 10:00–11:00
Jul 1971–Aug 1971, NBC Thu 10:00–11:00

REGULARS:

Dan Rowan (1966)
Dick Martin (1966)
Dom DeLuise (1966)
Lainie Kazan (1966)
Frankie Randall (1966)
Judi Rolin (1966)
Wisa D'Orso (1966)
Vic Damone (1967)
Carol Lawrence (1967)
Gail Martin (1967)
Don Cherry (1967)

Nearly two years before their hit *Laugh-In*, comedians Dan Rowan and Dick Martin starred as the 1966 summer replacements for Dean Martin. Because of the stars, the emphasis was more on comedy than on music. The 1967 replacement, however, which was aired under the title *The Dean Martin Summer Show Starring Your Host Vic Damone,* relied more on music. Selected episodes of the Vic Damone series were rerun as Dean's summer replacement during the summer of 1971.

DEAR PHOEBE

Situation Comedy

FIRST TELECAST: September 10, 1954
LAST TELECAST: September 11, 1956
BROADCAST HISTORY:

Sep 1954–Sep 1955, NBC Fri 9:30–10:00
Jun 1956–Sep 1956, NBC Tue 8:00–8:30

CAST:

Bill Hastings ....Peter Lawford
Mickey Riley ....Marcia Henderson
Mr. Fosdick ....Charles Lane
Humphrey Humpsteader ....Joe Corey

In this comedy, a college instructor gave up teaching to become the writer of the advice-to-the-lovelorn column in The *Los Angeles Daily Blade*. Bill Hastings, who wrote under the name Phoebe Goodheart, had a lovelorn admirer of his own in the person of the paper's female sports writer, Mickey Riley. Mickey tried to hide her affection by being extremely competitive with Bill for choice assignments from Mr. Fosdick, the flinty old managing editor. Bill made no secret of his love for Mickey, however, and many of the episodes developed around their rocky romance. Humphrey Humpsteader was the eager copyboy trying to make it in the newspaper game. The 1956 edition of *Dear Phoebe* was composed entirely of reruns.

DEBBIE REYNOLDS SHOW, THE

Situation Comedy

FIRST TELECAST: *September 16, 1969*
LAST TELECAST: *September 1, 1970*
BROADCAST HISTORY:

Sep 1969–Sep 1970, NBC Tue 8:00–8:30

CAST:

Debbie Thompson ....Debbie Reynolds
Jim Thompson ....Don Chastain
Charlotte Landers ....Patricia Smith
Bob Landers ....Tom Bosley
Bruce Landers ....Bobby Riha

Debbie Reynolds made her series television debut in this comedy about the unpredictable wife of a successful sports columist for the *Los Angeles Sun*. Debbie's efforts to create more excitement for herself than her life in the suburbs offered got her into all sorts of strange situations, much to the consternation of her husband Jim. Debbie's schemes, which were in some ways reminiscent of Lucille Ball's screwball exploits in the old *I Love Lucy* series, were often helped along by her sister Charlotte. The long-suffering members of Charlotte's family were her husband Bob and their son Bruce.

DECEMBER BRIDE

Situation Comedy

FIRST TELECAST: *October 4, 1954*
LAST TELECAST: *April 20, 1961*
BROADCAST HISTORY:

Oct 1954–Jun 1958, CBS Mon 9:30–10:00 (OS)
Oct 1958–Sep 1959, CBS Thu 8:00–8:30
Jul 1960–Sep 1960, CBS Fri 9:30–10:00
Apr 1961, CBS Thu 7:30–8:00

CAST:

Lily Ruskin .... Spring Byington
Ruth Henshaw .... Frances Rafferty
Matt Henshaw .... Dean Miller
Hilda Crocker .... Verna Felton
Pete Porter .... Harry Morgan

Lily Ruskin was that truly rare individual, a mother-in-law who could live with and be loved by her son-in-law. An attractive widow who was very popular with the older set—hence her potential as a "December bride"—Lily's social life revolved around her family as well. Her daughter Ruth and son-in-law Matt were always looking for suitable marriage prospects for Lily as was her friend and peer, Hilda Crocker. Pete Porter, the next-door neighbor who couldn't stand *his* mother-in-law, was often seen around the Henshaw household, and he became so popular that he eventually got his own series, *Pete and Gladys,* after *December Bride* went off the air. Pete complained constantly about his wife, Gladys, but she was never seen on *December Bride*—only heard. Reruns of this series were aired during 1960 and 1961.

DECISION

Dramatic Anthology

FIRST TELECAST: *July 6, 1958*
LAST TELECAST: *September 28, 1958*
BROADCAST HISTORY:

Jul 1958–Sep 1958, NBC Sun 10:00–10:30

This series of filmed dramas was the 1958 summer replacement for *The Loretta Young Show.* Half the shows were reruns of episodes from other dramatic-anthology series; the remainder were pilots for proposed series. One of the latter was a short version of *The Virginian* starring James Drury, who played the same role when the show became a series in the fall of 1962.

DEFENDERS, THE

Courtroom Drama

FIRST TELECAST: *September 16, 1961*
LAST TELECAST: *September 9, 1965*
BROADCAST HISTORY:

Sep 1961–Sep 1963, CBS Sat 8:30–9:30
Sep 1963–Nov 1963, CBS Sat 9:00–10:00
Nov 1963–Sep 1964, CBS Sat 8:30–9:30
Sep 1964–Sep 1965, CBS Thu 10:00–11:00

CAST:

Lawrence Preston .... E. G. Marshall
Kenneth Preston .... Robert Reed
Helen Donaldson (1961–1962)
.... Polly Rowles
Joan Miller (1961–1962) ...... Joan Hackett

The law firm of Preston & Preston was composed of a father and son, two lawyers involved in a weekly courtroom drama. Lawrence, the father, was a knowledgeable, seasoned attorney with more than 20 years of experience at the bar. Kenneth, the son, was a recent law school graduate. The learning process he went through as his father's partner was an integral part of this series. During the first season the firm's secretary, Helen Donaldson, and Kenneth's girlfriend, Joan Miller, had regular featured roles.

The Defenders was based on an original story by Reginald Rose, which was first telecast as a two-part episode of *Studio One* in February-March, 1957. That presentation was titled "The Defender," and starred Ralph Bellamy and William Shatner as the father and son attorneys, with Steve McQueen as a young defendent accused of murder.

DELL O'DELL SHOW

Variety

FIRST TELECAST: *September 14, 1951*
LAST TELECAST: *December 14, 1951*
BROADCAST HISTORY:

Sep 1951–Dec 1951, ABC Fri 10:00–10:30

EMCEE:

Dell O'Dell

Lady magician Dell O'Dell performed on this short-lived variety program, which included audience participation in the stunts as well as special guests. Wonder if she sawed only men in half?

DELORA BUENO

Music

FIRST TELECAST: *March 10, 1949*
LAST TELECAST: *May 5, 1949*
BROADCAST HISTORY:

Mar 1949–May 1949, DUM Thu 7:00–7:15

HOSTESS:
Delora Bueno

Songs and piano stylings were performed by Delora Bueno, a Latin beauty born in Dubuque, Iowa. (She was raised, however, in Brazil.)

DELPHI BUREAU, THE

Spy Drama

FIRST TELECAST: *October 5, 1972*
LAST TELECAST: *September 1, 1973*
BROADCAST HISTORY:
Oct 1972–Jan 1973, ABC Thu 9:00–10:00
Mar 1973–Sep 1973, ABC Sat 10:00–11:00
CAST:
Glenn Garth Gregory ...Laurence Luckinbill
Sybil Van Loween ....Anne Jeffreys

The Delphi Bureau was an obscure government agency ostensibly intended to do research for the President of the United States; in fact it carried out super-secret missions to protect and defend the security of the nation against various foes. Its office was a moving limousine, and its chief operative, Glenn Gregory, a most reluctant hero. Gregory's only contact at the Delphi Bureau was Sybil Van Loween, a delightful but slightly mysterious Washington hostess. Secret ciphers, hidden islands, and bizarre international operators showed up regularly in the plots.

Celeste Holm was originally announced to play the role of Sybil, but she never appeared in the series, being replaced by Anne Jeffreys. *The Delphi Bureau* was one of three rotating elements of *The Men.*

DELVECCHIO

Police Drama

FIRST TELECAST: *September 9, 1976*
LAST TELECAST: *July 17, 1977*
BROADCAST HISTORY:
Sep 1976, CBS Thu 9:00–10:00
Sep 1976–Jul 1977, CBS Sun 10:00–11:00
CAST:
Sgt. Dominick Delvecchio ..... Judd Hirsch
Sgt. Shonski ....Charles Haid
Lt. Macavan ....Michael Conrad
Tomaso Delvecchio ....Mario Gallo
Sgt. Rivera ....Jay Varela

Delvecchio was the story of a tough, independent, big-city police detective fighting crime in Los Angeles. Delvecchio and his partner Shonski were assigned cases that ranged from narcotics investigations to murders to auto thefts. His boss, and the man who assigned most of his cases, was Lt. Macavan. Also seen regularly was Delvecchio's father, Tomaso, an Old World type who ran a small barbershop and was constantly perplexed about why his stubborn, determined son had become a cop. The series was shot on location in Los Angeles.

DENNIS DAY SHOW, THE

see *RCA Victor Show, The*

DENNIS O'KEEFE SHOW, THE

Situation Comedy

FIRST TELECAST: *September 22, 1959*
LAST TELECAST: *June 7, 1960*
BROADCAST HISTORY:
Sep 1959–Jun 1960, CBS Tue 8:00–8:30
CAST:
Hal Towne ....Dennis O'Keefe
Sarge ....Hope Emerson
Randy Towne ....Rickey Kelman
Karen Hadley ....Eloise Hardt
Eliot ....Eddie Ryder

This comedy starred Dennis O'Keefe as syndicated columnist Hal Towne, one of TV's many widowers, with a precocious, friendly ten-year-old son named Randy. Helping Hal keep his home together while he was out getting material for his column was a housekeeper aptly named Sarge. Karen Hadley, an aggressive, career-oriented publicity agent, was Hal's regular girlfriend, but his work on his column, called "All Around Towne," was constantly introducing Hal to some very attractive competition. The story was set in Los Angeles.

DENNIS THE MENACE

Situation Comedy

FIRST TELECAST: *October 4, 1959*
LAST TELECAST: *September 22, 1963*
BROADCAST HISTORY:
Oct 1959–Sep 1963, CBS Sun 7:30–8:00
CAST:
Dennis Mitchell ....Jay North
Henry Mitchell ....Herbert Anderson
Alice Mitchell ....Gloria Henry
George Wilson (1959–1962)
.... Joseph Kearns
Martha Wilson (1961–1962) ....Sylvia Field
Joey McDonald (1959–1960) ..... Gil Smith
Mrs. Elkins (1961–1963) ......Irene Tedrow

Tommy Anderson (1961–1963)
.... Billy Booth
John Wilson (1962–1963) ..... Gale Gordon
Eloise Wilson (1962–1963) ..... Sara Seeger

Cartoonist Hank Ketcham's mischievous imp was brought to television in 1959 in the person of Jay North. *Dennis the Menace* had been a comic-strip fixture for years, with its little boy who was always trying to help out but who usually managed to make everything worse. Dennis's long-suffering parents put up with him as best they could, which was more than could be said for Mr. Wilson, their next-door neighbor in suburban Hillsdale. If Mr. Wilson planted some fancy tulips, Dennis was sure to uproot them and plant some "prettier" potatoes in their place. If Dennis happened upon some of Mr. Wilson's rare coins, he was sure to donate them to the March of Dimes. Adding to the general confusion was Dennis' dog, Freemont.

Joseph Kearns, the first Mr. Wilson, died before filming was completed for the 1961–1962 season. He was replaced in May 1962 by Gale Gordon, who was initially introduced as Mr. Wilson's brother John, a house guest of Mrs. Wilson. The next fall, John returned complete with a wife of his own, Eloise, as if he had always been the sole Mr. Wilson.

DEPUTY, THE

Western

FIRST TELECAST: *September 12, 1959*
LAST TELECAST: *September 16, 1961*
BROADCAST HISTORY:
Sep 1959–Sep 1961, NBC Sat 9:00–9:30
CAST:
Simon Fry .... Henry Fonda
Clay McCord .... Allen Case
Herk Lamson (1959–1960) ..... Wallace Ford
Fran McCord (1959–1960) ... Betty Lou Keim
Sgt. Hapgood Tasker (1960–1961)
.... Read Morgan

Set in the Arizona Territory in the early 1880s, *The Deputy* was built around the conflict in ideals between Chief Marshal Simon Fry, a dedicated lawman, and young storekeeper Clay McCord. Although an expert shot, Clay was opposed to the use of weapons because they contributed to the high level of violence on the frontier. Despite his pacifist feelings, however, Clay was frequently persuaded to serve as "the deputy" in Silver City to help the aging town marshal, Herk Lamson, defend the local populace when Marshal Fry was out of town. The basis for many of the stories was the ongoing conflict between the old-timers in Silver City and the younger townspeople, who wanted to see it settle down, grow, and prosper. Added to the cast at the start of the second season was "Sarge" Tasker, an army sergeant assigned to set up a supply office in Silver City. At the same time, Herk Lamson and Clay's younger sister Fran were dropped from the cast. Henry Fonda appeared as narrator in all episodes but was featured in the cast only when Marshal Fry was in town.

DES O'CONNER SHOW, THE

see *Kraft Music Hall Presents The Des O'Conner Show*

DESILU PLAYHOUSE

see *Westinghouse Desilu Playhouse*

DESTINY

Dramatic Anthology

FIRST TELECAST: *July 5, 1957*
LAST TELECAST: *September 26, 1958*
BROADCAST HISTORY:
Jul 1957–Sep 1957, CBS Fri 8:30–9:00
Jul 1958–Sep 1958, CBS Fri 8:30–9:00
HOST:
Francis C. Sullivan

Reruns of episodes from other anthologies were aired by CBS in this time slot for two summers, as replacement for *Dick Powell's Zane Grey Theater.*

DESTRY

Western

FIRST TELECAST: *February 14, 1964*
LAST TELECAST: *September 11, 1964*
BROADCAST HISTORY:
Feb 1964–Sep 1964, ABC Fri 7:30–8:30
CAST:
Harrison Destry .... John Gavin

At the center of this comedy-Western was Harrison Destry, a tall, easygoing chap who wasn't exactly a coward—just a mite careful. He'd just as soon dive under the table as shoot it out. Young Destry, the son of famed lawman Tom Destry, had once been a sheriff, until he was packed off to prison on a trumped-up embezzlement charge. In this series he wandered about the West trying to stay out of further trouble as he looked for the scalawags who had framed him.

The Destry character has had a lengthy career; he was portrayed in films by Tom Mix, James Stewart (in a 1939 movie classic co-starring Marlene Dietrich), and Audie Murphy, and later in a hit Broadway musical starring Andy Griffith. The character was originally based on the Max Brand novel, *Destry Rides Again*.

DETECTIVE'S DIARY

see *Mark Saber*

DETECTIVES, THE, STARRING ROBERT TAYLOR

Police Drama

FIRST TELECAST: *October 16, 1959*
LAST TELECAST: *September 21, 1962*
BROADCAST HISTORY:
Oct 1959–Sep 1961, ABC Fri 10:00–10:30
Sep 1961–Sep 1962, NBC Fri 8:30–9:30
CAST:
Capt. Matt Holbrook ....Robert Taylor
Lt. John Russo ....Tige Andrews
Lt. James Conway (1959–1960) .....Lee Farr
Lt. Otto Lindstrom (1959–1961) ....Russell Thorson
Sgt. Chris Ballard (1960–1962) ....Mark Goddard
Lisa Bonay (1960–1961) ......Ursula Thiess
Sgt. Steve Nelson (1961–1962) ..Adam West

Screen star Robert Taylor played a humorless, hard-nosed, doggedly effective captain on a big-city police force in this unassuming series. He led a team of three plainclothes detectives, which allowed individual episodes of the program to vary the lead (seldom were all four men assigned to the same case). The original trio consisted of Lt. Jim Conway of Homicide, a young ladies' man; Lt. Johnny Russo of Burglary, cigar smoking and tough talking; and Lt. Otto Lindstrom of the Bunco Squad, an old-timer. Each week one or more of them would tackle a murder, con game, drug operation, or other crime.

Capt. Holbrook was a widower with little time for anything but his job. His only romantic involvement during the three-year run of the series was a brief, antiseptic affair with a police reporter named Lisa Bonay—played by Taylor's real-life wife, German actress Ursula Thiess.

During its season on NBC the program was retitled *Robert Taylor's Detectives*.

DETECTIVE'S WIFE

Detective/Comedy

FIRST TELECAST: *July 7, 1950*
LAST TELECAST: *September 29, 1950*
BROADCAST HISTORY:
Jul 1950–Sep 1950, CBS Fri 8:30–9:00
CAST:
Lynn Conway ....Lynn Bari
Adam Conway ....Donald Curtis

Detective's Wife was the live summer replacement in 1950 for the popular detective series *Man Against Crime*. Adam Conway was a private detective who wanted to run a peaceful little agency but had received so much publicity after solving a murder that homicides were the only kind of cases he could get. The emphasis in this series was mostly on Adam's wife Lynn, who got more involved in his cases than either of them would have preferred.

DIAGNOSIS: UNKNOWN

Detective Drama

FIRST TELECAST: *July 5, 1960*
LAST TELECAST: *September 20, 1960*
BROADCAST HISTORY:
Jul 1960–Sep 1960, CBS Tue 10:00–11:00
CAST:
Dr. Daniel Coffee ....Patrick O'Neal
Doris Hudson ....Phyllis Newman
Dr. Motilal Mookerji ....Cal Bellini
Link ....Martin Huston
Det. Capt. Max Ritter ......Chester Morris

Daniel Coffee, the head pathologist at a large metropolitan hospital, worked closely with the police department to solve bizarre murders. Working with him were his two close friends and assistants, Motilal Mookerji and Doris Hudson. Also seen regularly was Link, the young boy who cleaned up the lab and worked as a handyman for Dr. Coffee. Dr. Coffee's contact on the New York City police department was Capt. Ritter.

DIAHANN CARROLL SHOW, THE

Musical Variety

FIRST TELECAST: *August 14, 1976*
LAST TELECAST: *September 3, 1976*
BROADCAST HISTORY:
Aug 1976–Sep 1976, CBS Sat 10:00–11:00

STAR:

Diahann Carroll

Singer Diahann Carroll was the star of this four-week mini-series, which included comedy and repartee with guest performers as well as musical numbers.

DIANA

Situation Comedy

FIRST TELECAST: *September 10, 1973*

LAST TELECAST: *January 7, 1974*

BROADCAST HISTORY:

Sep 1973–Jan 1974, NBC Mon 8:30–9:00

CAST:

Diana Smythe ....Diana Rigg
Norman Brodnik ....David Sheiner
Howard Tolbrook ....Richard B. Shull
Norma Brodnik ....Barbara Barrie
Marshall Tyler ....Robert Moore
Holly Green ....Carol Androsky

Diana Rigg had been introduced to American audiences as Emma Peel in the British spy-adventure series *The Avengers*. In *Diana* she played an English divorcee in her mid-30s who had moved to New York to begin a new life and a new career. Soon after taking over her absent brother's Manhattan apartment, however, Diana discovered that a number of his men friends had duplicate keys to the place, a situation that resulted in both embarrassing and comic confrontations. Commercial model Holly Green was Diana's friendly neighbor, helping her cope with the unexpected visitors. Diana's co-workers at Butley's Department Store on Fifth Avenue, where she was employed as a fashion coordinator, included Norman Brodnik, the president of the store; Norma, his wife; Howard Tolbrook, a cantankerous copywriter who shared an office with Diana; and Marshall Tyler, a window dresser.

DIANE DOXEE SHOW, THE

Music

FIRST TELECAST: *August 6, 1950*

LAST TELECAST: *September 24, 1950*

BROADCAST HISTORY:

Aug 1950–Sep 1950, ABC Sun 7:30–8:00

REGULARS:

Diane Doxee
Jimmy Blade

This program featured songs by Miss Doxee, accompanied by Jimmy Blade on piano.

DICK AND THE DUCHESS

Comedy Adventure

FIRST TELECAST: *September 28, 1957*

LAST TELECAST: *May 16, 1958*

BROADCAST HISTORY:

Sep 1957–Mar 1958, CBS Sat 8:30–9:00
Mar 1958–May 1958, CBS Fri 7:30–8:00

CAST:

Dick Starrett ....Patrick O'Neal
Jane Starrett ....Hazel Court
Peter Jamison ....Richard Wattis
Inspector Stark ....Michael Shepley
Mathilda ....Beatrice Varley

Dick Starrett was an American living in London and married to Jane, an English duchess. He often found himself in perplexing situations with members of Jane's upper-crust family, who were less than enchanted with her marriage to a commoner—and an American at that. Dick was employed as an insurance investigator/adjustor by a large multinational company, and to complicate matters, Jane frequently managed to get herself involved in his claims investigations, trying to help but only causing problems. Peter Jamison was Dick's friend and associate at the office, and Inspector Stark was a Scotland Yard investigator with whom he often worked.

DICK CAVETT SHOW, THE

Talk/Variety

FIRST TELECAST: *May 26, 1969*

LAST TELECAST: *December 29, 1972*

BROADCAST HISTORY:

May 1969–Sep 1969, ABC Mon/Tue/Fri 10:00–11:00
Dec 1969–Dec 1972, ABC Mon–Fri 11:30 P.M.–1:00 A.M.

HOST:

Dick Cavett

REGULARS:

Bobby Rosengarden
Fred Foy

Dick Cavett was one of the few TV personalities ever to star in major programs in daytime, prime time, and late nighttime, all in quick succession, and to fail to attract a large audience with any of them. His shows were well received by the critics and were generally acknowledged to be witty, intelligent, and interesting as compared to what was scheduled around them. Perhaps it was his intelligence that did Cavett in, for he never hesitated to bring in thought-provoking people as well as show-biz types as guests. Viewers, evidently, didn't much care to have their thoughts provoked.

All three of Cavett's ABC shows were essentially talk programs with some singing or performing guests. The daytime version was a 90-minute affair, five days a week, and lasted from March 1968 until January 1969. The prime-time summer show was on three nights a week from May until September 1969, and the late-night edition (11:30 P.M.–1:00 A.M.) lasted from December 1969, until December 1972. Guests in prime time included the usual run of movie and sports stars (including a full hour with Groucho Marx) mixed in with such heady fare as political pundit I. F. Stone, maverick Federal Communications Commission member Nicholas Johnson, and Cavett's own former philosophy professor, Paul Weiss.

In December 1969 Cavett moved to late night television, with Bobby Rosengarden as orchestra leader and Fred Foy as announcer. The guests continued to be diverse. At one point Cavett presented a series of one-guest shows with Anthony Quinn, Fred Astaire, Charlton Heston, Jack Lemmon and Woody Allen, followed by a program on which a group of children gave their views of contemporary life. On another famous occasion, in December 1971, former Governor Lester Maddox of Georgia walked off the show when challenged on his segregationist views.

While the show continued to receive excellent reviews, ABC continued to run a poor third behind NBC and CBS in late night viewership. Finally in April 1972 the network announced that unless audience levels improved by July 28th, the program would be cancelled. This set off a controversy almost unparalled in TV history. ABC was deluged with more than 15,000 letters in a few weeks, running nine to one in favor of Cavett. Several ABC affiliates ran "Save the Dick Cavett Show" advertisements, and notable public figures urged that the series be continued. Columnists around the country had a field day, castigating ABC and the Nielsen audience measurement system, and lauding Cavett as—in the words of one—"infinitely more valuable than another old movie." Perhaps Cavett could not attract as many viewers as Johnny Carson, editorialized *Time* magazine, but "should the more than 3,200,000 viewers who want his brand of intelligent alternative programming be summarily disenfranchised?"

Viewership did not increase significantly, and after a temporary reprieve, *The Dick Cavett Show* was cut back to occasional status in January 1973, when it became part of the new *ABC Wide World of Entertainment*. It left ABC entirely in 1975. In recent years Cavett has been seen with a similar program on Public television.

DICK CAVETT SHOW, THE

Variety

FIRST TELECAST: *August 16, 1975*

LAST TELECAST: *September 6, 1975*

BROADCAST HISTORY:

Aug 1975–Sep 1975, CBS Sat 10:00–11:00

REGULARS:

Dick Cavett
Leigh French

Host Dick Cavett did a little bit of everything in this four-week summer series. He interviewed guest stars, sang a little, and acted in comedy sketches with comedienne Leigh French, the only other regular on the show.

DICK CLARK PRESENTS THE ROCK AND ROLL YEARS

Music

FIRST TELECAST: *November 28, 1973*

LAST TELECAST: *January 9, 1974*

BROADCAST HISTORY:

Nov 1973–Jan 1974, ABC Wed 8:00–8:30

HOST/EXECUTIVE PRODUCER:

Dick Clark

REGULARS:

Jeff Kutash Dancers

This series presented a nostalgic portrait of the rock and roll era through performances by its top artists, laced with chatter about the styles, dances, and news events of the period. Each program consisted of three acts taped before a live audience at Santa Monica Civic Auditorium in California, five acts from the past shown in film clips, and one spot titled "The Immortal," in which a superstar of the past performed. Many of the top recording stars of the 1950s and 1960s appeared, such as Chuck Berry, Pat Boone, Danny and the Juniors, the Shirelles, Duane Eddy, and Little Richard; there were also some more recent acts, such as Chicago and Three Dog Night. The "Immortals" (most of them deceased) included Jimi Hendrix, James Dean, Clyde McPhatter, and Jim Croce. Unfortunately, Clark never managed to sign Elvis.

DICK CLARK SHOW, THE

Music

FIRST TELECAST: *February 16, 1958*

LAST TELECAST: *September 10, 1960*

BROADCAST HISTORY:

Feb 1958–Sep 1960, ABC Sat 7:30–8:00

HOST:

Dick Clark

Dick Clark, host of the highly successful afternoon series *American Bandstand*, moved into nighttime television with this derivative of his daytime show. Each week a number of recording artists, whose records were currently on the "Top 40" charts, performed their hits on *The Dick Clark Show*. Although some of them actually sang on the show, most of them lip-synched to their own recordings. Some of the numbers were performed simply; others were done as production numbers. The highlight of the show was the unveiling of the "American Bandstand Top Ten" records for the following week at the conclusion of the program. The series was also known as *The Dick Clark Saturday Night Beechnut Show*.

DICK CLARK'S LIVE WEDNESDAY

Variety

FIRST TELECAST: *September 20, 1978*

LAST TELECAST:

BROADCAST HISTORY:

Sept 1978– NBC Wed 8:00–9:00

HOST/PRODUCER:

Dick Clark

Dick Clark, who was a major force in bringing rock 'n' roll to TV in the 1950s, became the chief exponent of nostalgia for the music of that decade, twenty years later. Looking just as young as he had on *American Bandstand* in 1957, Clark hosted a series of highly popular specials which led to his own live prime time musical variety series in 1978. The program featured a mix of current popular music and that of the 1950s and 1960s, performed by the original artists. Sometimes a singer would be introduced with clips of themselves performing years before, as when Ricky Nelson was seen as a child on *The Adventures of Ozzie & Harriet*, before he came on to perform. There was chatter about the fads of the past, and a feature called "Where Are They Now?", but all was not nostalgia. Current stars performed as well. Dozens of famous faces flashed across the screen each week, many in cameo appearances, ranging from such current teenage favorites as Jimmy and Kristy McNichol to old pros like Bob Hope and Danny Kaye, and old rock 'n' rollers like Chuck Berry and Bo Diddley. To emphasize the show's live origination (from Hollywood), a death-defying stunt was performed on each telecast by a professional stuntman.

DICK CLARK'S WORLD OF TALENT

Variety

FIRST TELECAST: *September 27, 1959*

LAST TELECAST: *December 20, 1959*

BROADCAST HISTORY:

Sep 1959–Dec 1959, ABC Sun 10:30–11:00

HOST:

Dick Clark

REGULAR:

Jack E. Leonard

Each week Dick Clark was the host to three young performers, who presented their acts to the viewing audience and a panel composed of Jack E. Leonard and two celebrity guests. The panel would then comment on the performances and offer suggestions to the entertainers. Most of the performers had already begun their professional careers; they ranged from 15-year-old concert pianist Lorin Hollander to folk singers Bud and Travis. Comedians, dancers and soloists were also seen (despite Clark's identification with the current hit parade, there were few rock acts). Some of the performers had been in show business quite awhile, in fact, stretching the "young artist" theme a bit; among these were singers Don Cornell, Della Reese, Alan Dale and the Four Aces.

DICK POWELL SHOW, THE

Dramatic Anthology

FIRST TELECAST: *September 26, 1961*

LAST TELECAST: *September 17, 1963*

BROADCAST HISTORY:

Sep 1961–Sep 1962, NBC Tue 9:00–10:00
Sep 1962–Sep 1963, NBC Tue 9:30–10:30

HOST/STAR:

Dick Powell

Dick Powell, the boyish star of some of the 1930s' most glittering movie musicals, was a seasoned veteran when he appeared in this, his last TV series. Many of the episodes aired were pilots, and two of them actually became regular series in their own right. Powell himself starred in the first telecast, "Who Killed Julie Greer," playing the role of wealthy policeman Amos Burke; the following fall Gene Barry took on the same role in the series *Burke's Law*. "Savage Sunday" starred Nick Adams as a crusading New York newspaper reporter, a role he kept when *Saints and Sinners* premiered the next fall. Among the pilots that didn't succeed was "Safari," based on the movie *The African Queen* and starring Glynis Johns and James Coburn. A noteworthy episode was titled, "The Price of Tomatoes," for which a young Peter Falk won an Emmy.

In addition to serving as host, Powell periodically appeared in individual episodes. During the first season he co-starred with his wife June Allyson in a play called "A Time to Die." It is not known whether Powell knew at the time that he had cancer, but by the beginning of the second season he was in declining health. His last acting role was in "The Court-Martial of Captain Wycliff," which was aired on December 12, 1962, and his last appearance as host (on film) was on New Year's Day 1963. He died the following day. In deference to his family the filmed introductions that he had already prepared for future telecasts were deleted, and a succession of guest stars appeared as hosts for the remainder of the season. The title of the program was also changed to *The Dick Powell Theatre*.

DICK POWELL'S ZANE GREY THEATER

Western Anthology

FIRST TELECAST: *October 5, 1956*

LAST TELECAST: *September 20, 1962*

BROADCAST HISTORY:

Oct 1956–Jul 1958, CBS Fri 8:30–9:00 (OS)
Oct 1958–Sep 1960, CBS Thu 9:00–9:30
Oct 1960–Jul 1961, CBS Thu 8:30–9:00
Apr 1962–Sep 1962, CBS Thu 9:30–10:00

HOST/STAR:

Dick Powell

During its early seasons, *Dick Powell's Zane Grey Theater* was comprised completely of adaptations of the short stories and novels of famous Western author Zane Grey. Eventually, when the Grey material began to run out, Western stories from other authors were included. Host Dick Powell was frequently the star of individual episodes, more often in the early years than later in its run. The episodes telecast in the summer of 1962 were all reruns.

DICK TRACY

Police Drama

FIRST TELECAST: *September 11, 1950*

LAST TELECAST: *February 12, 1951*

BROADCAST HISTORY:

Sep 1950–Oct 1950, ABC Wed 8:30–9:00
Oct 1950–Dec 1950, ABC Mon 8:30–9:00
Jan 1951–Feb 1951, ABC Tue 8:00–8:30

CAST:

Dick Tracy .... Ralph Byrd

Chester Gould's famous comic-strip hero appeared briefly on television in 1950–1951. With him were the famous supporting characters, including his sidekick Sam Catchem, Chief Murphy, and an array of incredible villains ranging from The Mole (a counterfeiter who tunneled underground) to the laughing Joker. Ralph Byrd, who had been starring in Dick Tracy theatrical movies and serials since the 1930s, also appeared in this TV version.

Dick Tracy had also been heard on radio from 1935–1948, the latter part of its run on ABC. Edited versions of the theatrical movies, as well as a cartoon version, have been seen on TV in more recent years.

DICK VAN DYKE SHOW, THE

Situation Comedy

FIRST TELECAST: *October 3, 1961*

LAST TELECAST: *September 7, 1966*

BROADCAST HISTORY:

Oct 1961–Dec 1961, CBS Tue 8:00–8:30
Jan 1962–Sep 1964, CBS Wed 9:30–10:00
Sep 1964–Sep 1965, CBS Wed 9:00–9:30
Sep 1965–Sep 1966, CBS Wed 9:30–10:00

CAST:

Rob Petrie .... Dick Van Dyke
Laura Petrie .... Mary Tyler Moore
Sally Rogers .... Rose Marie

Buddy Sorrell ....Morey Amsterdam
Ritchie Petrie ....Larry Mathews
Melvin Cooley ....Richard Deacon
Jerry Helper ....Jerry Paris
Millie Helper ....Ann Morgan Guilbert
Alan Brady ....Carl Reiner

CREATOR:

Carl Reiner

PRODUCER/DIRECTOR/WRITER (VARIOUS EPISODES):

Carl Reiner
Sheldon Leonard
Jerry Paris

This highly successful series is often considered one of television's classic comedies, primarily because of its first-class scripting and excellent casting. Most of the principals were show-business veterans and several went on to star in series of their own. The setting, appropriately enough, was behind the scenes on a mythical TV comedy show. Rob Petrie was the head comedy writer for *The Alan Brady Show*, a popular New York-based comedy-variety series whose neurotic star was seldom seen here. Working with Rob were two other writers, Sally and Buddy, both of whom were close friends of Rob and his wife Laura. Their nemesis at the office, and the butt of much humor, was balding Melvin Cooley, the pompous producer of *The Alan Brady Show* and the brother-in-law of its star. Episodes generally revolved around the problems of the writers and the home life of the Petries in New Rochelle. Early episodes often included flashbacks to Rob's and Laura's courtship, while Rob was still in the army, the early days of their marriage, and the development of Rob's career. Frequently seen were their next-door neighbors, Jerry and Millie Helper. Writer-director Carl Reiner played the occasional role of Alan Brady, who was heard but never seen until the show had been on for several seasons.

The Dick Van Dyke Show took several seasons to develop into a major hit and was still very popular in 1966, when it finally left the air because Van Dyke and other cast members wanted to try new material. Van Dyke was never able to repeat the spectacular success of this series, but his co-star Mary Tyler Moore went on to greater fame on her own *Mary Tyler Moore Show* in the 1970s. See the index for other series starring Morey Amsterdam and Sheldon Leonard.

DINAH AND HER NEW BEST FRIENDS

Musical Variety

FIRST TELECAST: *June 5, 1976*
LAST TELECAST: *July 31, 1976*
BROADCAST HISTORY:

Jun 1976–Jul 1976, CBS Sat 10:00–11:00

STAR:

Dinah Shore

REGULARS:

Diane Canova
Bruce Kimmel
Gary Mule Deer
Mike Neun
Leland Palmer
Michael Preminger

This 1976 summer variety series, a replacement for the vacationing Carol Burnett, starred the most successful female variety series performer of the 1950s and 1960s, the versatile Dinah Shore. Working with Miss Shore was a company of regular players who had had little, if any, previous television exposure. They participated in comedy sketches, did their own solos, and blended their talents with those of the guest stars for the week.

DINAH SHORE CHEVY SHOW, THE

Musical Variety

FIRST TELECAST: *October 5, 1956*
LAST TELECAST: *May 12, 1963*
BROADCAST HISTORY:

Oct 1956–Jun 1957, NBC Fri 10:00–11:00
Oct 1957–May 1960, NBC Sun 9:00–10:00 (OS)
Oct 1960–Jun 1961, NBC Sun 9:00–10:00
Oct 1961–Jun 1962, NBC Fri 9:30–10:30
Dec 1962–May 1963, NBC Sun 10:00–11:00

REGULAR:

Dinah Shore

Dinah Shore, one of the few women to achieve major success as a variety-series host on TV, starred in her own full-hour musical variety show on NBC for seven seasons, following a successful run with the much simpler and shorter *Dinah Shore Show* which was only 15 minutes long. A full hour enabled Dinah to play host to top-name guest stars, include skits and large production numbers, and expand on her own varied talents. Besides her warm and friendly style, her trademarks on this series were the theme song "See the U.S.A. in your Chevrolet" and the resounding kiss she gave the audience at the end of each show.

When *The Dinah Shore Chevy Show* premiered in 1956 it was as a series of monthly specials. The following fall it moved to Sunday night and became a weekly series. It vacated the Sunday time slot to *Bonanza* in 1961, moved to Friday with the new title *The Dinah Shore Show*, and continued on a rotating basis with assorted specials for two more seasons.

DINAH SHORE SHOW, THE

Music

FIRST TELECAST: *November 27, 1951*
LAST TELECAST: *July 18, 1957*
BROADCAST HISTORY:

Nov 1951–Jul 1957, NBC Tue/Thu 7:30–7:45 (OS)

REGULARS:

Dinah Shore
The Notables, vocal quintet (1951–1955)
The Skylarks, vocal quintet (1955–1957)
Ticker Freeman, pianist

Twice weekly for six years, Dinah Shore starred in this live 15-minute musical show that occupied the remainder of the half hour that included the NBC network news. Dinah sang, often gave her accompanist Ticker Freeman a chance to do featured solos, and occasionally had guest stars with whom she chatted and performed.

DINNER DATE WITH VINCENT LOPEZ

see *Vincent Lopez*

DIONE LUCAS SHOW, THE

see *To The Queen's Taste*

DIRTY SALLY

Western

FIRST TELECAST: *January 11, 1974*
LAST TELECAST: *July 19, 1974*
BROADCAST HISTORY:

Jan 1974–Jul 1974, CBS Fri 8:00–8:30

CAST:

Sally Fergus .... Jeanette Nolan
Cyrus Pike .... Dack Rambo

Dirty Sally was a far cry from the traditional violent Western. Sally Fergus was a hard-drinking, crusty old lady who was traveling west to the California gold fields in a wagon pulled by her faithful mule, Worthless. Her traveling companion was Cyrus Pike, a young ex-gunfighter. His desire to reach their destination met with constant frustration from Sally, who got herself involved in the lives of almost everyone they met along the way.

DISC MAGIC

see *Musical Merry-Go-Round*

DISNEYLAND

see *Walt Disney*

DO IT YOURSELF

Comedy/Information

FIRST TELECAST: *June 26, 1955*
LAST TELECAST: *September 18, 1955*
BROADCAST HISTORY:

Jun 1955–Sep 1955, NBC Sun 7:30–8:00

REGULARS:

Dave Willock
Cliff Arquette (as Charley Weaver)

Do It Yourself was a short-lived attempt to mix situation comedy with useful household information. Hobbyist-builder Dave Willock was seen each week in his workshop with two or three projects on his schedule, ranging from the repair of broken appliances to building various objects from scratch. He was "helped" by his friend Charley Weaver, who spent most of the time clowning around, and by other friends who happened to drop by. Despite the horseplay. Wollock managed to convey all the information to build or repair the projects at hand.

DO YOU TRUST YOUR WIFE?

Quiz/Audience Participation

FIRST TELECAST: *January 3, 1956*
LAST TELECAST: *March 26, 1957*
BROADCAST HISTORY:

Jan 1956–Mar 1957, CBS Tue 10:30–11:00

EMCEE:

Edgar Bergen

ANNOUNCER:

Ed Reimers

Ventriloquist Edgar Bergen was the host of this comedy quiz show, which derived its title from the fact that when Mr. Bergen asked each married team of contestants to answer questions on a given topic, the husband had to decide whether he—or his wife—would try to answer. The jackpot available at the end of each telecast was $100 per week for a full year. Featured on the series along with Mr. Bergen were his assorted dummies: Charlie McCarthy, Mortimer Snerd, and Effie Klinker. The program later moved to daytime where it was seen under the title *Who Do You Trust?* During most of its run as a daytime show, Johnny Carson was the emcee and Ed McMahon the onstage announcer.

DOBIE GILLIS

syndicated title for *Many Loves Of Dobie Gillis, The*

DOC

Situation Comedy

FIRST TELECAST: *August 16, 1975*
LAST TELECAST: *October 30, 1976*
BROADCAST HISTORY:
Aug 1975–Oct 1976, CBS Sat 8:30–9:00
CAST:
"Doc" Joe Bogert ....Barnard Hughes
Annie Bogert ....Elizabeth Wilson
Miss Tully ....Mary Wickes
"Happy" Miller ....Irwin Corey
Laurie Bogert Fenner ....Judy Kahan
Fred Fenner ....John Harkins
Ben Goldman ....Herbie Faye
Janet Scott (1976) ....Audra Lindley
Stanley Moss (1976) ...David Ogden Stiers
Woody Henderson (1976) ....Ray Vitte
Teresa Ortega (1976) ....Lisa Mordente

During its first season, *Doc* was the story of an old-fashioned doctor practicing medicine in New York City. Joe Bogert was a kindly, soft-spoken doctor who was more concerned with his patients' health than with his fees (similar to *The Practice*, which premiered the following January). He was happily married to a woman who was much tougher with his patients than he was; his daughter and son-in-law (a fellow he disliked intensely) rented the apartment above his. Doc often sought refuge in the company of his friends Ben and Happy.

Marginal ratings during the first season prompted a major overhaul in the fall of 1976. Doc now worked at the Westside Clinic, run by Stanley Moss, and had a new nurse in Janet Scott. Gone were his wife and family and friends from the previous season. The new characters in the series consisted of the people who worked at the clinic with him, including Woody and Teresa. The change didn't help the show, which lasted only two months in the new format before being canceled.

DOC CORKLE

Situation Comedy

FIRST TELECAST: *October 5, 1952*
LAST TELECAST: *October 19, 1952*
BROADCAST HISTORY:
Oct 1952, NBC Sun 7:30–8:00
CAST:
Doc Corkle ....Eddie Mayehoff
Melinda ....Billie Burke
Winfield Dill ....Arnold Stang
Nellie Corkle ....Hope Emerson
Laurie Corkle ....Connie Marshall

Doc Corkle was a neighborhood dentist who was continually beset with money problems and a collection of nutty relatives. The wackiest was his stepsister Melinda, whose well-meaning blunders got Doc and his sister Nellie in all sorts of trouble. His teenage daughter Laurie was engaged to marry Winfield Dill, a youthful millionaire who had inherited six businesses.

This filmed series ran only three weeks. The sponsor, Reynolds Metals, was so disappointed with it that it was quickly canceled and replaced with *Mr. Peepers*. The part of Melinda was played by the famous and, by this time, aging film and theater star, Billie Burke.

DOC ELLIOT

Medical Drama

FIRST TELECAST: *January 23, 1974*
LAST TELECAST: *August 14, 1974*
BROADCAST HISTORY:
Jan 1974–Aug 1974, ABC Wed 10:00–11:00
CAST:
Dr. Benjamin Elliot .....James Franciscus
Mags Brimble ....Neva Patterson
Barney Weeks ....Noah Beery
Eldred McCoy ....Bo Hopkins
PRODUCER:
Sandor Stern, M.D.
MAIN THEME:
by Marvin Hamlisch

This contemporary drama concerned a drop-out doctor who gave up his career in New York City to become a blue-jeaned G.P. in Gideon, Colorado. Doc's new patients, most of them as independent as he, were spread over a 600-square-mile area of rugged terrain, and his house calls (better named cabin calls) were made by plane or in a four-wheel-drive camper outfitted with medical equipment. Mags Brimble was the widow of the area's former G.P. and Doc's helper and confidante; Barney Weeks the owner of the general store; and Eldred McCoy a bush pilot. There was lots of attactive mountain scenery in this series.

DOCTOR, THE

Medical Anthology

FIRST TELECAST: *August 24, 1952*

LAST TELECAST: *June 28, 1953*

BROADCAST HISTORY:

Aug 1952–Jun 1953, NBC Sun 10:00–10:30

CAST:

The Doctor ....Warner Anderson

The Doctor was a series of dramas centering more on situations of high emotional stress than on physical ailments. An assortment of actors and actresses appeared, among them Jay Jostyn, Anne Jackson, Ernest Truex, Mildard Natwick and Lee Marvin. Except for the infrequent occasions on which he also starred in the story, Warner Anderson appeared only at the beginning and end of each episode, to set the scene and discuss the outcome.

DR. FIX-UM

Information

FIRST TELECAST: *May 3, 1949*

LAST TELECAST: *August 6, 1950*

BROADCAST HISTORY:

May 1949–Jun 1949, ABC Tues 9:30–10:00

Nov 1949–Jan 1950, ABC Sun 6:45–7:00

Jan 1950–Aug 1950, ABC Sun 7:45–8:00

HOST:

Arthur Youngquist

Dr. Fix-Um was a program of helpful household hints in which Arthur Youngquist showed how to repair broken gadgets and gave solutions to various other household problems. The program was telecast from Chicago.

DOCTOR I.Q.

Quiz/Audience Participation

FIRST TELECAST: *November 4, 1953*

LAST TELECAST: *March 23, 1959*

BROADCAST HISTORY:

Nov 1953, ABC Wed 9:30–10:00

Dec 1953–Jan 1954, ABC Thu 9:00–9:30

Jan 1954–Mar 1954, ABC Mon 8:30–9:00

Apr 1954–Oct 1954, ABC Sun 9:30–10:00

Dec 1958–Mar 1959, ABC Sun 9:30–10:00

EMCEE:

Jay Owen (1953–1954)

James McClain (1954)

Tom Kennedy (1958–1959)

Doctor I.Q. one of radio's more popular quiz shows, came to television for two brief runs in the 1950s. The "Doctor" stood behind a podium on the stage and fired questions at people seated in the studio audience. Roving assistants with hand microphones located the contestants and shot back to the Doctor such familiar phrases as "I have a lady in the balcony, Doctor." The questions were reasonably intelligent, and winners were always paid off in silver dollars ("Give that lady ten silver dollars!").

DR. KILDARE

Medical Drama

FIRST TELECAST: *September 28, 1961*

LAST TELECAST: *August 30, 1966*

BROADCAST HISTORY:

Sep 1961–Sep 1965, NBC Thu 8:30–9:30

Sep 1965–Aug 1966, NBC Mon/Tue 8:30–9:00

CAST:

Dr. James Kildare ....Richard Chamberlain

Dr. Leonard Gillespie ....Raymond Massey

Dr. Simon Agurski (1961–1962) ....Eddie Ryder

Dr. Thomas Gerson (1961–1962) ....Jud Taylor

Receptionist Susan Deigh (1961–1962) ....Joan Patrick

Nurse Zoe Lawton (1965–1966) ....Lee Kurty

PRODUCER:

Norman Felton

Dr. Kildare came to television after having been an extremely successful series of movies in the 1940s. There was something immensely appealing about the story of a young intern in a large metropolitan hospital trying to learn his profession, deal with the problems of the patients, and win the respect of the senior doctor in his specialty, internal medicine. Kildare was the young intern, Dr. Gillespie the father figure, and Blair General the hospital in which they practiced medicine. The series did not flinch from realistic portrayals of hospital life and the life-and-death aspect of the work. Interestingly, both *Dr. Kildare* and *Ben Casey*, two of the most successful medical shows ever aired on television, arrived in the same season.

During the course of its run, *Dr. Kildare* went through an evolutionary process. By the third season Kildare was promoted to resident. His intern buddies from the first season, Drs. Agurski and Gerson, were not seen in subsequent seasons as the program came to center more closely on the patients and their families. In the 1965–1966 season the show was aired twice a week as a half-hour program rather than once a week for an hour, as previously. Although each episode was self-contained, the series began to take on more of a serial nature, with consecutive episodes developing an overall story. Some of these extended stories ran for only two episodes, others for as many as six.

DOCTORS AND THE NURSES, THE

see *Nurses, The*

DOCTORS' HOSPITAL

Medical Drama

FIRST TELECAST: *September 10, 1975*
LAST TELECAST: *January 14, 1976*
BROADCAST HISTORY:
Sep 1975–Jan 1976, NBC Wed 9:00–10:00
CAST:
Dr. Jake Goodwin ....George Peppard
Dr. Norah Purcell ....Zohra Lampert
Dr. Felipe Ortega ....Victor Campos
Janos Varga ....Albert Paulsen
Scotty ....Maxine Stuart

Set at fictitious Lowell Memorial Hospital in Los Angeles, this medical series sought a unique approach to hospital life: it examined all aspects of that life—the good and the bad—through the eyes of the doctors rather than those of the patients. Dr. Jake Goodwin was the chief of neurosurgical services at the hospital, and Norah Purcell was a second-year resident and his most gifted student. Dr. Ortega was the chief resident at Lowell Memorial and Janos Varga its director. To minimize the roles of the patients, a large number of them were treated in each episode, thereby shifting the emphasis to the work and personalities of the doctors and the other members of the hospital staff.

DOG AND CAT

Police Drama

FIRST TELECAST: *March 5, 1977*
LAST TELECAST: *May 14, 1977*
BROADCAST HISTORY:
Mar 1977–May 1977, ABC Sat 10:00–11:00
CAST:
Det. Sgt. Jack Ramsey ....Lou Antonio
Officer J. Z. Kane ....Kim Basinger
Lt. Arthur Kipling ....Matt Clark

This was a police show with a light sense of humor. It had to be, to team an experienced veteran plainclothes cop (Ramsey) with a bright, sexy and, of course, competent female rookie (Kane) and expect nothing but police work to occur. Lt. Kipling was the boss. The program was filmed in Southern California.

DOLLAR A SECOND

Quiz/Audience Participation

FIRST TELECAST: *September 20, 1953*
LAST TELECAST: *September 28, 1957*
BROADCAST HISTORY:
Sep 1953–Apr 1954, DUM Sun 10:00–10:30
Apr 1954–Jun 1954, DUM Mon 8:00–8:30
Jul 1954–Aug 1954, NBC Sun 10:00–10:30
Oct 1954–Jun 1955, ABC Fri 9:00–9:30
Jul 1955–Aug 1955, NBC Tue 9:30–10:00
Sep 1955–Sep 1956, ABC Fri 9:00–9:30
Jun 1957–Sep 1957, NBC Sat 9:30–10:00
Sep 1957, NBC Sat 10:00–10:30
EMCEE:
Jan Murray

In this comedy quiz show the contestant could win money in two ways: he won a dollar for every correct answer and another dollar for every second he stayed on the show. There was a catch, however, and that was called "the outside event." While the contestant was answering questions, and paying funny but embarrassing penalties for wrong answers (as in *Truth or Consequences*), something was going on outside the studio that might cause him or her to forfeit all winnings. The contestant could choose to quit at any time and keep all winnings up to that point, or continue in the hope that the outside event would not take place until after the show was over. The contestant did not know the nature of the outside event, but viewers did. It might be the arrival of a train at a specified point, or the landing of a given plane at LaGuardia Airport, or the birth of a baby at a designated hospital. A remote camera looked in periodically on the event about to take place, to heighten the suspense for the viewing audience.

DOM DELUISE SHOW, THE

Comedy Variety

FIRST TELECAST: *May 1, 1968*

LAST TELECAST: *September 18, 1968*

BROADCAST HISTORY:

May 1968–Sep 1968, CBS Wed 10:00–11:00

REGULARS:

Dom DeLuise
Marian Mercer
Bill McCutcheon
Carol Arthur
The June Taylor Dancers
Sammy Spear and His Orchestra

Pudgy comedian Dom DeLuise hosted and starred in this summer variety series. The emphasis was on comedy, with DeLuise's pantomime routines frequently featured. Guest stars appeared on each telecast, along with a cast of regulars.

DON AMECHE'S MUSICAL PLAYHOUSE

see *Holiday Hotel*

DON KNOTTS SHOW, THE

Comedy Variety

FIRST TELECAST: *September 15, 1970*

LAST TELECAST: *July 6, 1971*

BROADCAST HISTORY:

Sep 1970–Jan 1971, NBC Tue 7:30–8:30
Jan 1971–Jul 1971, NBC Tue 8:00–9:00

REGULARS:

Don Knotts
Elaine Joyce
Bob Williams and his dog Louie
Frank Walker
Ken Mars
Mickey Deems

Don Knotts hosted and starred in this comedy variety show. There were two regular features each week: Don and his guest stars in skits about his frustrations caused by the grind of doing a weekly TV show, and "The Front Porch," in which Don and his guest star would sit in rocking chairs and exchange "philosophies."

DON McNEILL TV CLUB

Variety

FIRST TELECAST: *September 13, 1950*

LAST TELECAST: *December 19, 1951*

BROADCAST HISTORY:

Sep 1950–Jun 1951, ABC Wed 9:00–10:00
Sep 1951–Dec 1951, ABC Wed 9:00–9:30 (alternate weeks)

REGULARS:

Don McNeill
Johnny Desmond
Fran Allison
Sam Cowling
Patsy Lee
Eddie Ballantine Orchestra

Don McNeill seemed like a natural for TV. His easygoing, homey style was much like that of Arthur Godfrey, who in 1950 was scoring an enormous hit with his *Arthur Godfrey and His Friends* and *Talent Scouts* programs. McNeill, like Godfrey, had been a radio fixture for years; his *Breakfast Club*, which began in 1933, had almost single-handedly turned early-morning network radio into a profitable medium. Thus, in the fall of 1950 ABC brought McNeill and his *Breakfast Club* gang to nighttime network television, live from his home town of Chicago.

Music and variety acts were featured, all delivered with the down-home charm and sincerity that had endeared McNeill to millions of radio fans. Among the regulars were Fran Allison doing her rural Aunt Fanny characterization, singer Johnny Desmond, portly comic Sam Cowling, singer-comedienne Patsy Lee, plus show-business guests. The guests never overshadowed the regular cast. Perhaps that was part of the problem; perhaps there was only room for one Godfrey. In any event, McNeill never caught on in television, and after a season and a half in prime time and an attempt at a daytime version of the *Breakfast Club* in 1954, he abandoned the medium to concentrate solely on his radio show (which had continued in the meantime). He continued with it until 1968, a run of over 34 years. His signature was the same on radio and television: "Be good to yourself."

DON RICKLES SHOW, THE

Comedy Variety

FIRST TELECAST: *September 27, 1968*

LAST TELECAST: *January 31, 1969*

BROADCAST HISTORY:

Sep 1968–Jan 1969, ABC Fri 9:00–9:30

REGULARS:

Don Rickles
Pat McCormick
Vic Mizzy Orchestra

This was a kind of one-man roast, in which Don Rickles directed his famous "insult humor" at guests and audience. Everyone was a "dummy" to Don. Pat McCormick was his gargantuan foil-announcer-factotum, as well as being one of the writers of the show. Apparently the viewing audience did not take kindly to this kind of assault, and the show was soon canceled. Those involved bore no grudge, however; at the end of the final telecast the writers and the entire crew and staff carried Rickles off the stage on their shoulders. What they did with him afterward was not revealed.

DON RICKLES SHOW, THE

Situation Comedy

FIRST TELECAST: *January 14, 1972*

LAST TELECAST: *May 26, 1972*

BROADCAST HISTORY:

Jan 1972–May 1972, CBS Fri 10:30–11:00

CAST:

Don Robinson .... Don Rickles
Barbara Robinson .... Louise Sorel
Janie Robinson .... Erin Moran
Tyler Benedict .... Robert Hogan
Audrey .... Judy Cassmore

The life and endless problems of a New York advertising-agency executive were the premise for this comedy starring Don Rickles. Don Robinson's loving wife Barbara and his cute young daughter Janie stood by more or less helplessly while Don, the master of insult humor, did constant battle with the frustrations of corporate society. Battlegrounds included his office at Kingston, Cohen and Vanderpool, Inc., and his pleasant Long Island home. Apparently viewers quickly wearied of the fray, as the series was canceled after only four months.

DONALD O'CONNOR TEXACO SHOW, THE

Situation Comedy

FIRST TELECAST: *October 9, 1954*

LAST TELECAST: *September 10, 1955*

BROADCAST HISTORY:

Oct 1954–Sep 1955, NBC Sat 9:30–10:00

CAST:

Donald O'Connor .... Himself
Sid Miller .... Himself
Doreen .... Joyce Smight

During the 1954–1955 season the *Texaco Star Theatre* consisted of two alternating series, *The Donald O'Connor Show* and *The Jimmy Durante Show*. O'Connor's half of the venture, which was subtitled "Here Comes Donald," was a loosely structured situation comedy whose primary function was to let Donald perform as a singer and dancer with his songwriting partner Sid Miller. The basic story line presented Donald and Sid as two young songwriters trying to find buyers for their songs and winding up in situations where they had the opportunity to sing, dance, and be comedians. Joyce Smight had the continuing role of their secretary, Doreen.

DONNA REED SHOW, THE

Situation Comedy

FIRST TELECAST: *September 24, 1958*

LAST TELECAST: *September 3, 1966*

BROADCAST HISTORY:

Sep 1958–Sep 1959, ABC Wed 9:00–9:30
Oct 1959–Jan 1966, ABC Thu 8:00–8:30
Jan 1966–Sep 1966, ABC Sat 8:00–8:30

CAST:

Donna Stone .... Donna Reed
Dr. Alex Stone .... Carl Betz
Mary Stone (1958–1963) .... Shelley Fabares
Jeff Stone .... Paul Petersen
Trisha Stone (1963–1966) ... Patty Petersen
Dr. Dave Kelsey (1963–1965) .... Bob Crane
Midge Kelsey (1963–1966) .... Ann McCrea
Karen Holmby (1964–1965) .. Janet Langard
Smitty (1965–1966) .... Darryl Richard

PRODUCER/EXEC. PRODUCER:

Tony Owen

THEME SONG:

"Happy Days," by William Loose and John Seely

At the center of this family comedy were Donna Stone, her husband Alex, a pediatrician, and their rambunctious teenage kids. The adventures of the Stone family were similar to those of other TV families—measles, girl friends, school problems, little white lies, and so on—compounded by the fact that Dr. Alex was always running off at odd hours to attend to his patients. The show was set in the small town of Hilldale, and it had a wholesome quality that endeared it to audiences. It won many awards from youth, women's, educational, and medical groups; the president of the American Medical Association even appeared in a cameo role in one telecast.

Over the years changes in the series took

place. Mary, the older child, went off to college in 1962, followed by Jeff two years later. About the time that Mary left the series for good, in 1963, the character of Trisha, an eight-year-old orphan who "adopted" the Stones, was added. Played by Patty Petersen, Paul's real-life sister, she was first seen in a January 1963 telecast and stayed for the rest of the series. Dave Kelsey was Alex's colleague and the Stones' next-door neighbor, and Midge was Dave's wife. Various friends and romances of Mary and Jeff appeared from time to time, the most regular of whom were Paul's girlfriend Karen (1964–1965) and his college buddy Smitty (1965–1966).

Both of Donna Reed's original TV offspring had short but spectacular recording careers in 1962–1963 with songs introduced on the series. On a January 1962 telecast Paul Petersen sang the novelty ditty "She Can't Find Her Keys," as part of a dream sequence in which Jeff dreamed he was a teenage recording star out on a date. His recording of the song became a major hit during early 1962. Later he had several other best sellers, including the top-ten hit "My Dad," about Dr. Alex. Shelley Fabares did even better with a teenage love song called "Johnny Angel," which went to number one on the charts in early 1962 and earned her a gold record, denoting sales of more than a million copies.

DONNY AND MARIE

Musical Variety

FIRST TELECAST: *January 16, 1976*
LAST TELECAST:
BROADCAST HISTORY:

Jan 1976–May 1977, ABC Fri 8:00–9:00
Jun 1977–Aug 1977, ABC Wed 8:00–9:00
Aug 1977– , ABC Fri 8:00–9:00 (OS)

CO-HOSTS:

Donny Osmond
Marie Osmond

REGULARS:

Alan Osmond
Wayne Osmond
Merrill Osmond
Jay Osmond
Johnny Dark (1978–
Jimmy Osmond
The Ice Vanities (1976–1977)
The Ice Angels (1977–1978)
The Disco Dozen (1978–
Jim Connell
Larry Larsen

Sid and Marty Krofft of animated cartoon fame originally produced this teenage variety hour. Eighteen-year-old Donny and his 16-year-old sister Marie were co-hosts of the show, which also featured other members of the popular musical family, ranging in age from Jimmy (12) to Alan (26). Despite his youth, Donny was a show-business veteran by the time the program premiered, having made his TV debut at the age of four singing "You Are My Sunshine" on *The Andy Williams Show*. In order to keep up the clan's youthful appearance, Merrill introduced another Osmond—his six month old son Travis—to the cast on an early telecast.

The format was the usual mixture of comedy and songs, with a liberal sprinkling of the Osmonds' teenybopper hits. The comedy often made fun of Donny's toothy, super-wholesome appearance, as when his brothers ganged up and dumped him into a gigantic nine-foot whipped cream pie in one 1976 broadcast. "I think I finally made a big splash on television," Donny said. Although not credited as a regular, Paul Lynde appeared as a guest star on many of the *Donny and Marie* episodes.

The second season brought changes, as a new production team took over in an attempt to give the show a more "adult" look. Much was made of Marie's stunning new wardrobe, designed by Bob Mackie (Cher's former designer), and her eighteenth birthday party was telecast in October. However *Donny and Marie* remained, at heart, a homey affair. Tired of the tinsel and glitter of Hollywood, the entire Osmond clan packed up and moved back to their hometown of Orem, Utah, in late 1977; all subsequent telecasts originated from the elaborate studio facility built there by the Osmonds at a cost of $2.5 million, to house their various TV and film activities. The first episode taped in Orem was the 1977 Christmas show, which starred Paul Lynde, the Mormon Tabernacle Choir and 28 members of the Osmond family.

DON'T CALL ME CHARLIE

Situation Comedy

FIRST TELECAST: *September 21, 1962*
LAST TELECAST: *January 25, 1963*
BROADCAST HISTORY:

Sep 1962–Jan 1963, NBC Fri 9:30–10:00

CAST:

Judson McKay .... Josh Peine
Pat Perry .... Linda Lawson
Col. U. Charles Barker ...... John Hubbard
First Sgt. Wozniak .... Cully Richards
Gen. Steele .... Alan Napier
Cpl. Lefkowitz .... Artie Johnson
Selma Yossarian .... Louise Glenn
Madame Fatima .... Penny Santon

This "military" comedy centered on Judson McKay, a young veterinarian from Iowa, who was drafted by mistake and assigned to a U.S. Army veterinary station in Paris. The principal conflict was between good-natured country boy McKay and his pompous commander, Col. U. Charles Barker, the "Charlie" of the title. Arte Johnson (who had not at this point in his career changed the spelling of his first name from Artie) played the supporting role of Cpl. Lefkowitz. Pat Perry was the general's secretary, Selma Yossarian another secretary, and Mme. Fatima the concierge.

DOODLES WEAVER

Comedy Variety

FIRST TELECAST: *June 9, 1951*

LAST TELECAST: *September 1, 1951*

BROADCAST HISTORY:

Jun 1951–Jul 1951, NBC Sat 10:00–10:15
Aug 1951–Sep 1951, NBC Sat 10:00–10:30

REGULARS:

Doodles Weaver
Marion Colby
Milton Delugg and His Orchestra
Red Marshall
Dick Dana
Peanuts Mann

In the premiere telecast, Doodles Weaver was informed that he had to put together a low-budget summer show without sets, scenery, or dancing girls. He was left with an empty television studio and discarded sets and props from other shows. Although this was supposed to be a joke, it set the tone for a rather formless improvisational comedy series. Veteran burlesque comics Marshall, Dana, and Mann contributed laughs and singer Marion Colby provided musical support.

DOOR WITH NO NAME

see *Doorway To Danger*

DOORWAY TO DANGER

International Intrigue

FIRST TELECAST: *July 6, 1951*

LAST TELECAST: *October 1, 1953*

BROADCAST HISTORY:

Jul 1951–Aug 1951, NBC Fri 9:00–9:30
Jul 1952–Aug 1952, NBC Fri 9:00–9:30
Jul 1953–Oct 1953, ABC Thu 8:30–9:00

CAST:

John Randolph (1951) .... Mel Ruick
John Randolph (1952) ..... Roland Winters
John Randolph (1953) ... Raymond Bramley
Doug Carter (1951) .... Grant Richards
Doug Carter (1953) .... Stacy Harris

NARRATOR:

Westbrook Van Voorhis (1951)

Doorway to Danger was a summer replacement series during the early 1950s. It told, in quasi-documentary style, stories of international intrigue involving operatives of federal agencies. The title referred to the door to the office of John Randolph, chief of a top-secret government agency, who supervised the agents assigned to track down enemies of the United States. These enemies might be either domestic criminals or agents of a foreign power; smugglers and spies seemed to be the usual opponents in this series.

Doug Carter was Randolph's number one agent during the first and third seasons, and episodes followed Carter around the world on his dangerous assignments. During the second season there was no regular agent, and each week Chief Randolph sent a different trench-coated operative scurrying off to defend the nation.

During its first season this series was known as *Door With No Name.*

DOORWAY TO FAME

Talent

FIRST TELECAST: *May 2, 1947*

LAST TELECAST: *July 11, 1949*

BROADCAST HISTORY:

May 1947–Sep 1947, DUM Fri 7:30–8:00 (approximately)
Oct 1947–Jan 1948, DUM Mon 7:30–8:00
Jan 1948–Mar 1949, DUM Mon 7:00–7:30
Mar 1949–Jul 1949, DUM Mon 8:30–9:00

EMCEE:

Johnny Olsen

This was one of the many talent shows that populated early television. Through the doorway came all manner of hopefuls, plus one guest star each week who offered words of encouragement. Some 20,000 New York-area residents were said to have auditioned for the show during its first year, but none is known to have gone on to stardom.

DORIS DAY SHOW, THE

Situation Comedy

FIRST TELECAST: *September 24, 1968*

LAST TELECAST: *September 10, 1973*

BROADCAST HISTORY:

Sep 1968–1969 CBS Tue 9:30–10:00

Sep 1969–Sep 1973, CBS Mon 9:30–10:00

CAST:

Doris Martin .... Doris Day
Buck Webb (1968–1970) .... Denver Pyle
Aggie Thompson (1968) .... Fran Ryan
Leroy B. Simpson (1968–1969) .... James Hampton
Billy Martin (1968–1971) .... Philip Brown
Toby Martin (1968–1971) ..... Todd Starke
Juanita (1968–1969) .... Naomi Stevens
Myrna Gibbons (1969–1971) .... Rose Marie
Michael Nicholson (1969–1971) .... McLean Stevenson
Ron Harvey (1970–1971) .... Paul Smith
Cy Bennett (1971–1973) ...... John Dehner
Jackie Parker (1971–1973) .... Jackie Joseph

When *The Doris Day Show* premiered in the fall of 1968, Miss Day was cast as a widow with two young sons who had decided to move back to the family ranch after spending most of her life in big cities. The adjustments to rural living provided much of the comedy. The ranch was run by her father Buck, their hired hand Leroy, and the housekeeper Aggie (replaced in December by a new housekeeper, Juanita).

At the start of the second season Doris became a commuter. She got a job as a secretary at *Today's World* magazine in San Francisco and commuted daily from the farm. Mr. Nicholson, the editor of the magazine, was her boss, and Myrna Gibbons was a secretary with whom she became friendly. At the start of the third season Doris, her two boys, and their huge dog Lord Nelson left the farm and moved into an apartment in San Francisco. Doris's activities expanded from merely being Mr. Nicholson's secretary to include some writing for the magazine, on assignment from the assistant editor, Ron Harvey.

Still another major change was made at the start of the fourth season, in the fall of 1971, as the show edged still closer to the urban career-girl format popularized by *Mary Tyler Moore*. Doris continued to work for *Today's World*, but she suddenly became a carefree, single staff writer; the children, the dog, and the entire cast from previous seasons disappeared. Her new boss was editor Cy Bennett, and the only other regular was his secretary Jackie.

At the end of the fifth season the entire show disappeared.

DO'S AND DON'TS

Instruction

FIRST TELECAST: *July 3, 1952*

LAST TELECAST: *August 28, 1952*

BROADCAST HISTORY:

Jul 1952–Aug 1952, ABC Thu 9:30–10:00

This was a brief series of films on safety.

DOTTO

Quiz/Audience Participation

FIRST TELECAST: *July 1, 1958*

LAST TELECAST: *August 12, 1958*

BROADCAST HISTORY:

Jul 1958–Aug 1958, NBC Tue 9:00–9:30

EMCEE:

Jack Narz

In *Dotto* two contestants competed to guess the identity of a famous personality whose caricature was drawn on a screen by connecting fifty dots on each contestant's "Dotto" board. The contestants answered questions that allowed them progressively to connect the dots, and the first to identify the picture of the person won. There was also a home game in which viewers sent in postcards, hoping to be called on the phone to identify a special dotted caricature shown on the air. *Dotto*'s biggest claim to fame was that a disgruntled former contestant on the daytime version of the show (which had begun earlier and ran concurrently with this nighttime version) started the famous quiz show scandals by publicly declaring that the game was rigged. His name was Edward Hilgemeier Jr. and, ironically, he had never actually appeared on the show at all. While waiting in the studio for his opportunity to go on as a contestant, he found a notebook belonging to a woman contestant that contained answers to questions she had been asked on the show. He informed the contestant who had been defeated by the woman and both he and the defeated contestant confronted the producers. They were both paid off but, when Mr. Hilgemeier found out the defeated contestant had been given $4000 while he had only been given $1500, he became angry and precipitated the quiz show scandals by protesting to the New York State Attorney General's office.

DOTTY MACK SHOW, THE

Music

FIRST TELECAST: *February 16, 1953*

LAST TELECAST: *September 3, 1956*

BROADCAST HISTORY:

Feb 1953–Jun 1953, DUM Mon 10:45–11:00
Jul 1953–Aug 1953, DUM Tue 9:00–9:30
Aug 1953–Oct 1953, ABC Thu 9:00–9:30
Oct 1953–Mar 1954, ABC Sat 6:30–7:00
Apr 1954–Oct 1954, ABC Sat 7:30–8:00
Oct 1954–Jun 1955, ABC Sat 8:00–9:00
Jun 1955–Sep 1955, ABC Tue 9:30–10:00
Sep 1955–Mar 1956, ABC Mon 9:00–9:30
Apr 1956–Jul 1956, ABC Thu 10:00–10:30
Jul 1956–Sep 1956, ABC Mon 8:00–8:30

REGULARS:

Dotty Mack
Bob Braun
Colin Male

Dotty Mack had one of the simpler acts on early television: she pantomimed to other performers' hit records. She began her miming on *The Paul Dixon Show* out of Cincinnati, then landed a 15-minute spot by herself on DuMont called, appropriately, *Girl Alone*. Five months later, in July 1953, the program was expanded to 30 minutes, two assistants (Bob Braun and Colin Male) were added, and the title was changed to *The Dotty Mack Show*. Shortly thereafter ABC picked it up. At times the program was a full hour in length, although 30 minutes was normal.

Most of the songs pantomimed were currently popular favorites or novelty songs by such stars as Eddie Fisher, Perry Como, or Patti Page; sometimes puppets or other visual aids accompanied the pantomimes. Things began to get complicated when rock 'n' roll started taking over the hit parade in 1955. Although Dotty gamely included such records as "Rock Around the Clock" in her repertoire, the sight of pleasant young people pantomiming to Bill Haley or Elvis Presley records became slightly ludicrous, and the show quietly passed from the scene in 1956.

DOUBLE EXPOSURE

see *ABC Dramatic Shorts—1952–1953*

DOUBLE LIFE OF HENRY PHYFE, THE

Situation Comedy

FIRST TELECAST: *January 13, 1966*

LAST TELECAST: *September 1, 1966*

BROADCAST HISTORY:

Jan 1966–Sep 1966, ABC Thu 8:30–9:00

CAST:

Henry Wadsworth Phyfe ......Red Buttons
Gerald B. Hannahan ....Fred Clark
Judy Kimball ....Zeme North
Mrs. Florence Kimball ....Marge Redmond

This short-lived comedy focused on the adventures of Henry Phyfe, a mild-mannered accountant who was recruited by the CIS, a United States counterintelligence agency, to impersonate U-31, a recently deceased foreign agent to whom Henry bore a striking resemblance. The trouble was that U-31 in most other respects had been the opposite of Henry: bon vivant, Don Juan, master linguist, and crack shot. Henry's girl friend Judy, his future mother-in-law Florence, and his boss at the accounting firm had no idea of his double life. Only Gerald B. Hannahan, the balding, bombastic regional director of CIS, linked him with the world of spies and adventure. Judy and her mother were phased out of the series in March.

DOUBLE OR NOTHING

Quiz/Audience Participation

FIRST TELECAST: *June 5, 1953*

LAST TELECAST: *July 3, 1953*

BROADCAST HISTORY:

Jun 1953–Jul 1953, NBC Fri 9:30–10:00

EMCEE:

Bert Parks
Bob Williams (asst.)

The summer of 1953 brought this familiar radio quiz show—and its emcee, Bert Parks—to television for a five-week stay. Each contestant was asked a series of four questions, respectively worth $10, $20, $40, and double or nothing, for a possible total of $140 in the first round. All contestants, whether or not they were successful in the first round, then participated in the "Red and White Sweepstakes" at the end (the colors referred to those on the label of the sponsor's product, Campbell soups). In the sweepstakes, a question was asked and each contestant wrote his answer on a card shaped like a horse. The "race" was won by whoever could provide the correct answer first.

DOWN YOU GO

Quiz/Panel

FIRST TELECAST: *May 30, 1951*
LAST TELECAST: *September 8, 1956*
BROADCAST HISTORY:

May 1951–Jul 1951, DUM Wed 9:00–9:30
Jul 1951–Sep 1951, DUM Thu 9:00–9:30
Sep 1951–Jun 1952, DUM Fri 9:00–9:30
Jul 1952–Sep 1952, DUM Fri 8:00–8:30
Oct 1952–Apr 1954, DUM Fri 10:30–11:00
May 1954–Jun 1954, DUM Wed 9:30–10:00
Sep 1954–Jan 1955, DUM Wed 10:00–10:30
Jan 1955–May 1955, DUM Fri 10:30–11:00
Jun 1955–Sep 1955, CBS Sat 9:30–10:00
Sep 1955–Jun 1956, ABC Thu 9:30–10:00
Jun 1956–Sep 1956, NBC Sat 7:30–8:00

EMCEE:

Dr. Bergen Evans (1951–1956)
Bill Cullen (1956)

REGULAR PANELISTS:

Francis Coughlin
Prof. Robert Breen (1951–1954)
Toni Gilman (1951–1954)
Carmelita Pope (1951–1954)
Fran Allison (1954)
Phil Rizzuto (1954–1955)
Boris Karloff (1954–1955)
Jean Kerr (1955)
Patricia Cutts (1955–1956)
Basil Davenport (1955)
Phyllis Cerf (1955)
Sherl Stern (1955)
John Kieran, Jr. (1955)
Arthur Treacher (1956)
Hildy Parks (1956)
Jimmy Nelson (1956)
Jayne Mansfield (1956)

Widely regarded as one of the wittiest, most intelligent panel shows on television, *Down You Go* was a deceptively simple word-game whose charm derived from its participants. The rules were simple: the panel was asked to guess a word or phrase that had been submitted by a viewer. A few cryptic clues were offered, and then the panelists filled in the words, letter by letter, on a "magic board." An incorrect guess by a panelist and "down you go," out of play until the next round. Viewers received $5 for submitting a phrase that was used, and $25 for one that stumped the panel (later these amounts were increased, but money was never the principal appeal of the show).

Dr. Bergen Evans, a witty and charming professor of English at Northwestern University, was the longtime host of *Down You Go*, which at first was telecast from Chicago over the DuMont network. The program became quite popular, and in 1954 a *Down You Go* game was being sold in stores, complete with tiles, board, and clock. In December 1954 the program moved to New York, with only Evans and Francis Coughlin, a Chicago radio editor, remaining from the original cast. During 1955 and 1956 a succession of regular and guest panelists appeared, but none of these later panels seemed to catch the flavor of the original. Nevertheless the program survived the end of the DuMont network, making a grand tour of the networks from CBS to ABC to NBC before it was canceled in September 1956.

The last version of *Down You Go* little resembled the original. Bergen Evans was replaced for the last two months of the show by Bill Cullen, and the panel was filled by such "literati" as Jimmy Nelson and his dummies, and Jayne Mansfield.

DRAGNET

Police Drama

FIRST TELECAST: *January 3, 1952*
LAST TELECAST: *September 10, 1970*
BROADCAST HISTORY:

Jan 1952–Dec 1955, NBC Thu 9:00–9:30
Jan 1956–Sep 1958, NBC Thu 8:30–9:00
Sep 1958–Jun 1959, NBC Tue 7:30–8:00
Jul 1959–Sep 1959, NBC Sun 8:30–9:00
Jan 1967–Sep 1970, NBC Thu 9:30–10:00

CAST:

Sgt. Joe Friday .... Jack Webb
Sgt. Ben Romero (1951) .... Barton Yarborough
Sgt. Ed Jacobs (1952) ...... Barney Phillips
Officer Frank Smith (1952) ...... Herb Ellis
Officer Frank Smith (1953–1959) .... Ben Alexander
Officer Bill Gannon (1967–1970) .... Harry Morgan

THEME:

"Dragnet" (also known as "Dragnet March" and "Danger Ahead"), by Walter Schumann

DIRECTOR:

Jack Webb

Dragnet was probably the most successful police series in the history of television. By providing the prototype of the realistic action series, it marked a major turning point for a medium that had, for its first few years, been dominated by comedy and vaudeville. *Dragnet*'s hallmark was its appearance of realism, from the documentary-style narration by Joe Friday, to the cases drawn from the files of a real police department (Los Angeles, which provided the locale), to its careful attention to the details of police work ("It was 3:55 . . . We were working the day watch out of homicide"). Viewers were reminded of the unglamorous dead ends and the constant interruptions of their private lives that plague real policemen, and this made the final shootout and capture of the criminal all the more exciting. At the end of each episode, after the criminal was apprehended, an announcer would describe what happened at the subsequent trial and the severity of the sentence.

The concept, as created by laconic actor-director Jack Webb, caught on immediately, perhaps because it stood out so sharply against the police-private eye caricatures then on the air. *Dragnet* became an enormous hit. Its catch phrases and devices became national bywords and were widely satirized. There was Webb's terse "My name's Friday—I'm a cop," and "Just the facts, ma'am"; the jargon—the criminal's "M.O.," "Book him on a 358"—and, of course, that arresting theme music, with possibly the most famous four-note introduction since Beethoven's Fifth Symphony ("Dum-de-dum-dum"). Music was an important part of *Dragnet*'s success, even aside from the theme. It was laced throughout every episode, dark and tension-filled, then erupting in a loud, sudden "stinger" after an especially significant revelation or denouement. In fact, *Dragnet* inspired two hit records in 1953: a recording of the theme music by Ray Anthony and His Orchestra, and the hilarious "St. George and the Dragonet" by Stan Freberg—probably the only parody of a current TV series ever to sell a million copies and reach number one on the hit parade. (The record's opening intoned, "The legend you are about to hear is true; only the needle should be changed to protect the record . . .")

Dragnet began on radio in 1949 and, after a special TV preview on *Chesterfield Sound Off Time* in December 1951, opened its official TV run on January 3, 1952. Friday's partner in the preview was played by Barton Yarborough, of the radio series. He died suddenly of a heart attack a few days after the telecast, and four actors subsequently portrayed Friday's sidekick: Barney Phillips in the spring of 1952, Herb Ellis in the fall, Ben Alexander for the remainder of the seven-and-a-half-year original run, and Harry Morgan for the revival in 1967–1970.

During most of its first 12 months on the air *Dragnet* ran every other Thursday, alternating with *Gangbusters*, another transplanted radio police show. From January of 1953 until 1959 it was a weekly series. In 1967, after a hiatus of more than seven years, it returned to the air under the slightly modified title *Dragnet '67*, to distinguish it from the reruns of the original series still being played on many stations. (Reruns were also known as *Badge 714*, after Friday's badge number.) Jack Webb returned to the role of Friday but with a new partner, Officer Bill Gannon. The format was essentially the same as the original *Dragnet* but there was somewhat stronger emphasis on the noncrime aspects of police work, such as community involvement and helping individuals in trouble. Today, more than a quarter century after its first telecast, reruns of *Dragnet* can still be seen on some local stations.

DRAMA AT EIGHT

Dramatic Anthology

FIRST TELECAST: *July 9, 1953*
LAST TELECAST: *July 30, 1953*
BROADCAST HISTORY:
Jul 1953, DUM Thu 8:00–8:30

This was a series of filmed dramas featuring lesser-known actors and actresses. The July 30 telecast, a comedy entitled "Uncle Charley," presented an early TV version of Cliff Arquette's Charley Weaver characterization. That was the last network airing of the program, though it continued locally in New York through October 1, 1953.

DRAW ME A LAUGH!

Cartoon Quiz/Panel

FIRST TELECAST: *January 15, 1949*
LAST TELECAST: *February 5, 1949*

BROADCAST HISTORY:

Jan 1949–Feb 1949, ABC Sat 8:30–9:00

EMCEE:

Walter Hurley
Patricia Bright

REGULARS:

Mel Casson
Jay Irving
Oscar Brand

The object of this show was for the participants, who were cartoonists, to draw cartoons based on ideas sent in by viewers. The show's regular cartoonist, Mel Casson, was given a description of the cartoon to be drawn but not the caption; simultaneously, the caption but not the description was given to another cartoonist, who made up his own illustration. The two cartoons were then compared and an audience panel voted on which was funnier. Other segments of the show included making cartoons out of scribbles, drawing blind, and "singing captions" by folk singer Oscar Brand.

The program lasted exactly four weeks.

DRAW TO WIN

Cartoon Quiz/Panel

FIRST TELECAST: *April 22, 1952*

LAST TELECAST: *June 10, 1952*

BROADCAST HISTORY:

Apr 1952–Jun 1952, CBS Tue 8:30–9:00

EMCEE:

Henry Morgan

PANELISTS:

Bill Holman
Abner Dean

Home viewers here were asked to send in slogans, names of objects, or anything else that could be described through a series of cartoon clues. The panel, composed of three cartoonists and a celebrity guest, would then try to guess the solution to the cartoon clues. Depending on how long it took them to identify correctly the meaning of the clues, the sender would receive a prize of up to $25.

DREAM HOUSE

Quiz

FIRST TELECAST: *March 27, 1968*

LAST TELECCAST: *September 19, 1968*

BROADCAST HISTORY:

Mar 1968–Aug 1968, ABC Wed 8:30–9:00
Sep 1968, ABC Thu 9:30–10:00

EMCEE:

Mike Darrow

Young married couples were offered a roomful of furniture for correct answers on this quiz show. Winners of four consecutive rounds (rooms) received a house worth up to $40,000 as well. The "dream house" might take several forms, a traditional house, mobile home, ski lodge, houseboat, or even a private island. *Dream House* was also seen in daytime.

DRESS REHEARSAL

Various

FIRST TELECAST: *March 21, 1948*

LAST TELECAST: *August 31, 1948*

BROADCAST HISTORY:

Mar 1948–Apr 1948, NBC Thu 8:00–8:30
Jul 1948–Aug 1948, NBC Mon 8:00–8:30
Aug 1948, NBC Tue 9:00–9:30

"DIRECTOR" (on camera):

Richard Goode

This was an umbrella title for a series of one-time and experimental programs that took the form of dress rehearsals. It included musical revues, quiz shows, and an occasional drama. Perhaps the best show was the last, entitled "Swap Night," which featured the first TV appearance of veteran radio commentator Norman Brokenshire, dressed as a rural Yankee trader and presiding over a swap session between cast members and viewers at home.

DREW PEARSON

Commentary

FIRST TELECAST: *May 4, 1952*

LAST TELECAST: *March 18, 1953*

BROADCAST HISTORY:

May 1952–Nov 1952, ABC Sun 11:00–11:15
Dec 1952–Mar 1953, DUM Wed 7:30–7:45

COMMENTATOR:

Drew Pearson

The famous columnist Drew Pearson, who covered the 1952 political conventions and the subsequent presidential election for ABC, presented commentary and his "Predictions of Things to Come" in these network telecasts in 1952–1953.

DROODLES

Cartoon Quiz/Audience Participation

FIRST TELECAST: *June 21, 1954*

LAST TELECAST: *September 17, 1954*

BROADCAST HISTORY:

Jun 1954–Sep 1954, NBC Mon 8:00–8:30
Sep 1954, NBC Fri 8:00–8:30

EMCEE:

Roger Price

PANELISTS:

Marc Connelly
Carl Reiner
Denise Lor

"Droodles" were simple line drawings that depicted an object or scene, often from a rather strange perspective. Roger Price, who had written a book called *Droodles*, was the emcee. The three regular panelists were joined by a fourth guest panelist, who started the show by drawing his or her own droodle for the other panelists to try to figure out. After this the guest joined the other panelists in guessing what was depicted in selected droodles submitted by home viewers (who won prizes if they stumped the panel) and some drawn by Price. In addition, there was a "Hundred Dollar Droodle" drawn by Price at the end of each show. Viewers were invited to send in postcards with possible titles for it, and the best title won the $100.

DUKE, THE

Situation Comedy

FIRST TELECAST: *July 2, 1954*

LAST TELECAST: *September 3, 1954*

BROADCAST HISTORY:

Jul 1954–Sep 1954, NBC Fri 8:00–8:30

CAST:

"The Duke" London ....Paul Gilbert
Johnny ....Allen Jenkins
Rudy Cromwell ....Claude Stroud
Sam Marco ....Sheldon Leonard
Gloria ....Phyllis Coates

The "Duke" in this comedy was a street-wise professional boxer who had, in his spare time, become an accomplished painter. Through that hobby he met Harvard graduate Rudy Cromwell, who offered to help him expand his intellectual and cultural horizons. Rudy was admirably suited to the purpose and enjoyed introducing Duke to "high-brow" forms of entertainment and diversion. The fighting side of the Duke's life kept intruding, however, in the persons of his trainer, Johnny, and fight promoter Sam Marco, both of whom wanted him to give up his pursuit of the finer things in life and return to what he knew best, boxing. Society blonde Gloria, the Duke's girl friend, also played a prominent part.

DUMONT ROYAL THEATER

Dramatic Anthology

FIRST TELECAST: *April 12, 1951*

LAST TELECAST: *June 26, 1952*

BROADCAST HISTORY:

Apr 1951–Jul 1951, DUM Thu 9:30–10:00
Apr 1952–Jun 1952, DUM Thu 9:00–9:30

This was a series of low-budget 30-minute dramatic films featuring an assortment of lesser-known talent, such as Edgar Barrier, Mary Sinclair, and Hugh O'Brien (later of *Wyatt Earp* fame). The 1952 version alternated with *Gruen Playhouse*. The series was also known as *Royal Playhouse*.

DUMPLINGS, THE

Situation Comedy

FIRST TELECAST: *January 28, 1976*

LAST TELECAST: *March 24, 1976*

BROADCAST HISTORY:

Jan 1976–Mar 1976, NBC Wed 9:30–10:00

CAST:

Joe Dumpling ....James Coco
Angela Dumpling ....Geraldine Brooks
Charles Sweetzer ....George S. Irving
Frederic Steele ....George Furth
Stephanie ....Marcia Rodd
Cully ....Mort Marshall
Bridget McKenna ....Jane Connell

There was a message in *The Dumplings*–fat people can be as kind, good, industrious, and lovable as anyone else. Joe and Angela were a chubby married couple running a lunch counter in a large office building in Manhattan. Among their regular customers were a city councilman, Mr. Steele; an executive of a large corporation with offices in the building, Mr. Sweetzer; his secretary, Bridget; and Angela's sister Stephanie. Joe and Angela were madly in love with life and each other, exuded good cheer and enthusiasm, and never had a bad word for each other.

DUNDEE AND THE CULHANE

Western

FIRST TELECAST: *September 6, 1967*

LAST TELECAST: *December 13, 1967*

BROADCAST HISTORY:

Sep 1967–Dec 1967, CBS Wed 10:00–11:00

CAST:

Dundee .... John Mills
Culhane .... Sean Garrison

Although their law offices were in Sausalito, across the bay from San Francisco, British attorney Dundee and his apprentice lawyer, The Culhane, traveled throughout the West to help their clients. Dealing with the sort of haphazard justice prevalent in much of the West during the latter part of the 19th century proved more of a problem than the actual courtroom defense. Judges were bribed, prisoners broke out of jails, and many citizens took the law into their own hands.

DUNNINGER SHOW, THE

see *Amazing Dunninger, The*

DUPONT CAVALCADE THEATER

see *Cavalcade of America*

DUPONT SHOW OF THE WEEK, THE

Various

FIRST TELECAST: *September 17, 1961*
LAST TELECAST: *September 6, 1964*
BROADCAST HISTORY:

Sep 1961–Sep 1964, NBC Sun 10:00–11:00

The DuPont Show of the Week presented a potpourri of various types of entertainment and informational programs. For three seasons it was NBC's late Sunday evening "class" showcase, with sponsor E.I. DuPont using the best available talent, both in front of and behind the cameras, to present everything from dramatic plays and documentaries to light comedies and musical revues. One of the aims of the series was to show the latitude and potential of the television medium as a means of communication. The format represented a change in the sponsor's philosophy. For the four years before the start of this weekly NBC series, DuPont had sponsored *DuPont Show of the Month*, an irregularly scheduled collection of culturally impressive 90-minute dramas on CBS. During the CBS period, adaptations of such classics as *Don Quixote, Hamlet, A Tale of Two Cities,* and *The Browning Version* had been aired. At the time, that was CBS's answer to NBC's *Hallmark Hall of Fame.*

The first telecast on NBC was the documentary "Hemingway," narrated by Chet Huntley, with Andrew Duggan providing Ernest Hemingway's voice. Later, retired actor Ken Murray presented his edited home movies of the stars at home in "Hollywood—My Home Town"; clown Emmett Kelly narrated a documentary on the universal appeal of the circus; and Peter Lind Hayes was narrator of a musical special, "Regards to George M. Cohan." Dramatic programs were not omitted; in fact, they became the primary staple of the series during its last two years. Starring were such people as Richard Conte, Claude Rains, Walter Matthau, Zachary Scott, Teresa Wright, Eddie Albert, Martha Scott, Lloyd Nolan, James Daly, Peter Falk, Arthur Kennedy, and Oscar Homolka. Documentaries also continued; one of the most interesting was "Comedian Backstage," a *cinéma-vérité* look at the real life of comedian Shelley Berman.

DUPONT SHOW WITH JUNE ALLYSON, THE

Dramatic Anthology

FIRST TELECAST: *September 21, 1959*
LAST TELECAST: *June 12, 1961*
BROADCAST HISTORY:

Sep 1959–Sep 1960, CBS Mon 10:30–11:00
Sep 1960–Dec 1960, CBS Thu 10:30–11:00
Jan 1961–Jun 1961, CBS Mon 10:30–11:00

HOSTESS/STAR:

June Allyson

Actress June Allyson was the regular hostess and occasional star of this filmed dramatic-anthology series. The plays, which ranged from light comedy to melodrama, told stories of contemporary American life. The budget for this show was lavish, and it attracted many Hollywood stars, including Ginger Rogers, Bette Davis, David Niven, Joseph Cotten, and Jane Powell. Among the telecasts were "A Summer's Ending," in which Miss Allyson and her husband Dick Powell made their first joint television appearance; "Slip of the Tongue," in which Italian actor Rossano Brazzi made his American television debut; and "Silent Panic," with Harpo Marx in a rare dramatic appearance as a deaf mute.

DUPONT THEATER

see *Cavalcade of America*

E.S.P.

Audience Participation/Anthology

FIRST TELECAST: *July 11, 1958*
LAST TELECAST: *August 22, 1958*
BROADCAST HISTORY:
Jul 1958–Aug 1958, ABC Fri 9:00–9:30
EMCEE/HOST:
Vincent Price

E.S.P. premiered as a contest show to determine the amount of extrasensory perception possessed by contestants, all of whom were first screened by a staff of psychologists. After only three telecasts the quiz format was replaced by dramas entitled *Tales of E.S.P.*, which depicted people with the abilities that the quiz show had been trying to find. Vincent Price was host of both programs.

EARL WRIGHTSON SHOW, THE

Music

FIRST TELECAST: *November 27, 1948*
LAST TELECAST: *February 21, 1952*
BROADCAST HISTORY:
Nov 1948–Jan 1949, ABC Sat 7:45–8:00
Jan 1949–Apr 1949, ABC Mon 7:15–7:30
Sep 1949–Jun 1950, CBS Wed 7:45–8:00
Sep 1950–Jun 1951, CBS Mon 11:00–11:15
Aug 1951–Feb 1952, ABC Thu 10:30–10:45
HOST:
Earl Wrightson
ACCOMPANIMENT:
Buddy Weed, piano and trio (1948–1949)
Norman Paris Trio and Orchestra (1949–1951)

Concert baritone Earl Wrightson was a familiar figure in the early days of television, appearing on his own 15-minute program of songs on both ABC and CBS. Wrightson's forte was Broadway show tunes and music from operettas such as *The Student Prince* and *H.M.S. Pinafore*, and he performed these in program segments called "Spotlight on Showtime" and "Masland Showtime." Guest stars were also featured.

The title of this program changed several times, from the original *Earl Wrightson Show* to *Earl Wrightson at Home* (September 1949), *At Home* (October 1949), *At Home Show* (September 1950), and finally, in honor of the sponsor, *Masland At Home Party* (August 1951).

In later years Wrightson made frequent guest appearances on other programs.

EARN YOUR VACATION

Quiz/Audience Participation

FIRST TELECAST: *May 23, 1954*
LAST TELECAST: *September 5, 1954*
BROADCAST HISTORY:
May 1954–Sep 1954, CBS Sun 7:00–7:30
EMCEE:
Johnny Carson

Young comedian Johnny Carson hosted this summer quiz show, which asked members of the studio audience where they would most like to go on a vacation and why. The people with the most interesting answers won the chance to become contestants and answer a series of four progressively more difficult questions, which could win them their dream vacation.

EAST SIDE/WEST SIDE

General Drama

FIRST TELECAST: *September 23, 1963*
LAST TELECAST: *September 14, 1964*
BROADCAST HISTORY:
Sep 1963–Sep 1964, CBS Mon 10:00–11:00
CAST:
Neil Brock ....George C. Scott
Frieda Hechlinger ....Elizabeth Wilson
Jane Foster ....Cicely Tyson

This dramatic series starred George C. Scott as Neil Brock, a young social worker in the New York slums. The stories involved child abuse, the welfare syndrome, problems of aging, drug addiction, and crime, situations all too familiar to Neil Brock in his daily routine. Frieda Hechlinger was the head of the welfare agency branch for which he worked, and Jane Foster was the office secretary. Critics appreciated the gritty realism of this series in the midst of TV's land of make-believe, but its downbeat subjects proved deadly with viewers and it was dropped after a single season.

EASY ACES

Humor

FIRST TELECAST: *May 10, 1950*
LAST TELECAST: *June 14, 1950*
BROADCAST HISTORY:
May 1950–Jun 1950, DUM Wed 7:45–8:00
REGULARS:
Goodman Ace
Jane Ace
Betty Garde

This was a video version of the longtime radio favorite, featuring Goodman and Jane

Ace in comedy chatter. As on radio, "Ace" was his witty, intelligent self, and his wife Jane was a charming bundle of malapropisms. After beginning as a local entry in New York, *Easy Aces* went on the DuMont network in May 1950, but lasted for only six weeks. Goodman Ace went on to make a much greater impression on the new medium as a top comedy writer for such stars as Perry Como.

EASY DOES IT . . . STARRING FRANKIE AVALON

Musical Variety

FIRST TELECAST: *August 25, 1976*
LAST TELECAST: *September 15, 1976*
BROADCAST HISTORY:

Aug 1976–Sep 1976, CBS Wed 8:30–9:00

REGULARS:

Frankie Avalon
Annette Funicello
The War Babies

Frankie Avalon, a pop singer and star of numerous "beach-party" movies in the early 1960s, was the star of this four-week mini-series. With him each week was Annette Funicello, his co-star in several of those movies. In addition to the musical numbers, the show featured blackouts and silly comedy sketches with an improvisational group, The War Babies.

ED SULLIVAN SHOW, THE

Variety

FIRST TELECAST: *June 20, 1948*
LAST TELECAST: *June 6, 1971*
BROADCAST HISTORY:

Jun 1948, CBS Sun 9:00–10:00
Jul 1948–Aug 1948, CBS Sun 9:30–10:30
Aug 1948–Mar 1949, CBS Sun 9:00–10:00
Mar 1949–Jun 1971, CBS Sun 8:00–9:00

REGULARS:

Ed Sullivan
Ray Bloch and His Orchestra
The June Taylor Dancers

If any program in the history of American television could be called an institution, it would probably be *The Ed Sullivan Show*. Every Sunday night for more than two decades this homely newspaper columnist with peculiar diction and awkward gestures brought an incredible variety of entertainment into American homes. No pandering to the lowest common denominator here—there was grand opera and the latest rock stars, classical ballet and leggy Broadway showgirls, slapstick comedy and recitations from great dramatic writings, often juxtaposed on a single telecast. Viewers loved it.

It began simply enough. Originally titled *Toast of the Town* (it was going to be called *You're the Top*, but that title was dropped before the first telecast), the program was one of many variety shows on early television—most of which had noticeably short lives. The first telecast, in the summer of 1948, was produced on a meager budget of $1,375. Only $375 was allocated for talent, and the two young stars of that show, Dean Martin and Jerry Lewis, split the lion's share of that—$200. But Ed had class. Also on that first telecast were concert pianist Eugene List, Richard Rodgers and Oscar Hammerstein II and the six original June Taylor Dancers (then called the Toastettes). The critics of the early Sullivan shows were not kind. They complained about his deadpan delivery, his lack of any noticeable talent as a performer, and the strange collections of acts he put together for a single program. That very variety, and a newspaperman's nose for "events," made Sullivan's show a resounding success. The format only seemed to be that of an old-fashioned vaudeville revue (Ed himself stoutly denied that it was "vaudeo"). Where in vaudeville would you have the Bolshoi Ballet one week, scenes from a hit Broadway show with the original cast on another, and dancing bears on a third?

Numerous performers made their American television debuts on the show, including Charles Laughton, Bob Hope, Lena Horne, Martin and Lewis, Dinah Shore, Eddie Fisher, the Beatles, and Walt Disney. Disney's appearance is ironic. He was featured in a full-hour special edition of *Toast of the Town* on February 8, 1953. The following year he began his own show, on ABC, and to date it is that program that has finally surpassed *Ed Sullivan* as the longest-running prime-time network show. It will be noted that Elvis Presley is missing from the above list of firsts. Although he is best remembered for his appearances on *The Ed Sullivan Show* in the fall of 1956, Elvis actually made his TV debut in January 1956, on Tommy and Jimmy Dorsey's *Stage Show*. No matter. To play Sullivan was to make headlines, and Presley's appearance just at the moment he was revolutionizing popular music did just that. So did the Beatles seven years later.

In addition to the firsts, virtually every "name" act in American music, comedy, theater, and film appeared over the years. There were also a few who never did make it out from under Ed's wing: Topo Gigio, the mechanical Italian mouse, and Señor Wences and his talking box (" 'S-all right? 'S-all right!") Those celebrities not appearing on the stage were in the audience. To be picked out by Ed from the stage and introduced on nationwide television was a high honor indeed.

Sullivan's mannerisms became legendary, the butt of a thousand comics. He himself participated in a parody record called "It's a Reeally Big SHEW Tonight!" in the mid-1950s, and his program was brilliantly satirized in the Broadway musical *Bye Bye Birdie* in the early 1960s—in which an all-American family reaches spiritual ecstasy when they learn, "We're going to be on . . . Ed Sullivan!"

The show itself changed little over the years, though its scope certainly widened. The title was changed officially to *The Ed Sullivan Show* on September 18, 1955. Some telecasts and segments originated from foreign countries, including Japan, the Soviet Union, Italy, France, England, Spain, Portugal, Ireland, Mexico, Israel, Cuba, and Hong Kong. Some shows were mini-spectaculars, such as the 90-minute tribute to songwriter Irving Berlin, which ended in true Sullivan fashion with a huge American flag in fireworks and the entire cast singing "God Bless America."

Sullivan's run finally ended in 1971, the victim not so much of falling ratings as of a desire by CBS to "modernize" its programming (Ed's appeal had increasingly been to older viewers). There followed some Ed Sullivan specials and a 25th-anniversary special in 1973, but shortly thereafter Sullivan was dead. He will not soon be forgotten.

ED WYNN SHOW, THE

Comedy Variety

FIRST TELECAST: *October 6, 1949*

LAST TELECAST: *July 4, 1950*

BROADCAST HISTORY:

Oct 1949–Dec 1949, CBS Thu 9:00–9:30
Jan 1950–Mar 1950, CBS Sat 9:00–9:30
Apr 1950–Jul 1950, CBS Tue 9:00–9:30

STAR:

Ed Wynn

ORCHESTRA:

Lud Gluskin

One year after being named by his fellow comedians as "the greatest visual comedian of our day," and more than 40 years after he began his career in vaudeville, Ed Wynn became a regular television performer with his own variety show. Although the show had guest stars, its main focus was Ed himself, in his giggling "Perfect Fool" characterization and in other roles he had created over the years on stage and radio. Ed's guests included many of the great names in film comedy. Ben Blue, Buster Keaton, Lucille Ball and Desi Arnaz (before *I Love Lucy*), Leon Errol, the Three Stooges (Moe Howard, Curly Howard, and Larry Fine), Joe E. Brown, Ben Wrigley, and Marie Wilson all made guest appearances on the show.

The Ed Wynn Show was the first regular show to originate from Hollywood, carried live on the West Coast and kinescoped for rebroadcast from New York to the CBS Eastern and Midwest networks. This was the reverse of the normal procedure of that day, in which live shows were aired from New York and had kinescoped repeats fed from Hollywood.

ED WYNN SHOW, THE

Situation Comedy

FIRST TELECAST: *September 25, 1958*

LAST TELECAST: *January 1, 1959*

BROADCAST HISTORY:

Sep 1958–Jan 1959, NBC Thu 8:00–8:30

CAST:

John Beamer . . . . Ed Wynn
Laurie . . . . Jacklyn O'Donnell
Midge . . . . Sherry Alberoni
Ernest Henshaw . . . . Herb Vigran

Ed Wynn came out of semi-retirement to make one final try at a regular series on television, and this short-lived situation comedy was the result. As John Beamer, he was an elderly widower whose children had also died, leaving him with the responsibility of raising his two granddaughters—Laurie, age 18, and Midge, age 9. With unbounded enthusiasm and optimism he helped not only his own family, but his friends, his neighbors, and anyone else he met. At one point he even got himself elected to the city council.

EDDIE CAPRA MYSTERIES, THE

Lawyer/Detective

FIRST TELECAST: *September 8, 1978*

LAST TELECAST:

BROADCAST HISTORY:

Sep 1978–   , NBC Fri 10:00–11:00

CAST:

Eddie Capra ....Vincent Baggetta
Lacey Brown ....Wendy Phillips
J. J. Devlin ....Ken Swofford
Harvey Winchell ....Michael Horton
Jennie Brown ....Seven Ann McDonald

Capra was introduced as a detective show in the "classic style." No fancy frills, just a straightforward homicide at the opening of each show, followed by an hour in which the viewer could watch the young lawyer-sleuth uncover clues one by one. Eddie Capra, the unconventional star, worked for the conventional, and very prestigeous, law firm of Devlin, Linkman and O'Brien. Lacey was his secretary, close to her boss both on the job and off; Harvey was his enthusiastic young legman; J. J. Devlin, the irascible senior partner in the firm; and Jennie was Lacey's precocious daughter.

EDDIE CONDON'S FLOOR SHOW

Music

FIRST TELECAST: *January 1, 1949*

LAST TELECAST: *June 24, 1950*

BROADCAST HISTORY

Jan 1949–Jul 1949, NBC Sat 8:30–9:00
Jul 1949–Sep 1949, NBC Sat 9:30–10:00
May 1950–Jun 1950, CBS Sat 7:30–8:00

HOST:

Eddie Condon
Carl Reiner (1950)

Guitarist Eddie Condon hosted this informal weekly jam session, one of the first network series devoted to jazz music. It had run previously on WPIX-TV, New York, and before that on WNBT-TV, New York, during the war, making it one of television's oldest features. Guests included many of the top names in jazz, such as Gene Krupa, Woody Herman, Sidney Bechet, Ella Fitzgerald, Louis Armstrong, and dozens of others, as well as such up-and-coming vocalists as Patti Page and Rosemary Clooney. A special feature during the summer of 1949 was a series of programs dramatizing—musically—great moments in jazz history. During the program's brief run on CBS, Condon was joined by Carl Reiner, who chatted with the guests about their careers.

EDDIE FISHER SHOW, THE

Musical Variety

FIRST TELECAST: *September 24, 1957*

LAST TELECAST: *March 17, 1959*

BROADCAST HISTORY:

Sep 1957–Mar 1959, NBC Tue 8:00–9:00 (OS)

REGULARS:

Eddie Fisher
George Gobel
Buddy Bregman and His Orchestra

After toiling in a limited-format 15-minute program for several years (see *Coke Time*), popular singer Eddie Fisher got his own full-hour variety show in the fall of 1957. It lasted for two seasons, alternating on Tuesdays with *The George Gobel Show.* Although there were no regulars on the show other than Fisher, George Gobel participated in comedy skits in most of the telecasts. To reciprocate, Eddie made frequent guest appearances on George's show.

EDDY ARNOLD SHOW, THE

Musical Variety

FIRST TELECAST: *July 14, 1952*

LAST TELECAST: *September 28, 1956*

BROADCAST HISTORY:

Jul 1952–Aug 1952, CBS Mon/Wed/Fri 7:45–8:00
Jul 1953–Oct 1953, NBC Tue/Thu 7:30–7:45
Apr 1956–Jun 1956, ABC Thu 8:00–8:30
Jun 1956–Sep 1956, ABC Wed 9:30–10:00

STAR:

Eddy Arnold

REGULARS:

The Russ Case Orchestra (1952)
The Dickens Sisters (1953)
Chet Atkins (1956)
The Paul Mitchell Quintet (1956)

Country and Western singer Eddy Arnold spent two summers filling in for vacationing singers with regularly scheduled song shows: Perry Como on CBS in 1952 and Dinah Shore on NBC in 1953. In both cases, these 15-minute programs, which filled the remainder of the half-hours in which the networks presented their news programs, provided little opportunity for anything but two or three songs. In the spring of 1956, with a full half-hour on ABC, Mr. Arnold could talk with special guest stars and do more involved production numbers as well as perform solos. Chet Atkins provided instrumental solos and the Paul Mitchell Quintet instrumental backup for this later series, which featured both popular and classical numbers, as well as the soft ballads for which Arnold was famous.

EDIE ADAMS SHOW, THE

Musical Variety

FIRST TELECAST: *September 26, 1963*

LAST TELECAST: *March 19, 1964*

BROADCAST HISTORY:

Sep 1963–Mar 1964, ABC Thu 10:00–10:30

STAR:

Edie Adams

Singer Edie Adams starred in this half-hour musical variety series that alternated with *The Sid Caesar Show* on Thursday nights during the 1963–1964 season. Edie and her guest stars sang, danced, and did comedy sketches. To start the season both Edie and Sid Caesar appeared together in a full-hour variety special that aired from 10:00–11:00 P.M. on September 19.

EDITOR'S CHOICE

News Analysis

FIRST TELECAST: *June 25, 1961*

LAST TELECAST: *September 24, 1961*

BROADCAST HISTORY:

Jun 1961–Sep 1961, ABC Sun 10:30–11:00

Each week, in either a filmed report, a filmed report with interviews, or interviews alone, members of the ABC News staff sought to treat a current news story or issue in greater depth than was possible within the framework of the regular nightly newscast.

EDWIN NEWMAN REPORTING

News/Documentary

FIRST TELECAST: *June 5, 1960*

LAST TELECAST: *September 4, 1960*

BROADCAST HISTORY:

Jun 1960–Sep 1960, NBC Sun 6:30–7:00

HOST/REPORTER:

Edwin Newman

This series was the 1960 summer replacement for *Time Present: Chet Huntley Reporting.* Edwin Newman, then chief of the NBC News Paris Bureau, filled in for Chet Huntley, focusing each week on one or two issues of current interest.

EIGHT IS ENOUGH

Comedy/Drama

FIRST TELECAST: *March 15, 1977*

LAST TELECAST:

BROADCAST HISTORY:

Mar 1977–May 1977, ABC Tue 9:00–10:00

Aug 1977– , ABC Wed 8:00–9:00

CAST:

Tom Bradford ....Dick Van Patten

Joan Bradford (1977) ....Diana Hyland

Sandra Sue Abbott ("Abby") (1977–) ....Betty Buckley

Nicholas Bradford (age 8) ......Adam Rich

Tommy Bradford (age 14) ....Willie Aames

Elizabeth Bradford (age 15) .... Connie Newton

Nancy Bradford (age 18) ......Dianne Kay

Susan Bradford (age 19) .... Susan Richardson

Joannie Bradford (age 20) ...Laurie Walters

Mary Bradford (age 21) ......Lani O'Grady

David Bradford (age 23) ....Grant Goodeve

Dr. Maxwell ....Michael Thoma

Daisy Maxwell ....Virginia Vincent

Donna (1978–) .... Jennifer Darling

This comedy-drama focused on a family with eight very independent children, aged 8 to 23. When the series began, Tom, the father, was a newspaper columnist for the Sacramento, California, *Register,* and Joan was his wife of 25 years. The death of actress Diana Hyland during production of the spring 1977 episodes of *Eight Is Enough* forced major changes, however. Hyland had completed only four shows and was written out of the remainder as being "away." When the series returned with new episodes that fall, Tom Bradford had become a widower, his wife having died, at least in the storyline, about "a year ago." With the help of his best friend Doc Maxwell, Tom set about keeping order among his large brood while re-entering, in middle age, the singles world. He soon found romance in the person of Abby, a pretty schoolteacher who came to the Bradford home to tutor one of the youngsters. Their romance blossomed, and on a special two hour telecast on November 9, 1977, Tom and Abby were married.

The series was based on the book *Eight Is Enough* by Thomas Braden.

87TH PRECINCT

Police Drama

FIRST TELECAST: *September 25, 1961*
LAST TELECAST: *September 10, 1962*
BROADCAST HISTORY:
Sep 1961–Sep 1962, NBC Mon 9:00–10:00
CAST:
Det. Steve Carella ....Robert Lansing
Det. Bert Kling ....Ron Harper
Det. Roger Havilland .....Gregory Walcott
Det. Meyer Meyer ....Norman Fell
Teddy Carella ....Gena Rowlands

Manhattan's 87th precinct was the base for the police detectives of this series. In addition to the various aspects of police work normally seen in action series of this type, the personal lives of the officers provided much of the side drama. Detective Steve Carella was married to a beautiful woman who unfortunately was a deaf mute. Bert Kling was the young detective learning the ropes, Roger Havilland the hardened old pro, and Meyer Meyer the older officer who, having "seen it all," often injected a dry humor into otherwise serious business. Most of the stories started in the precinct office where all of the detectives gathered to write up reports and wait for assignments.

ELDER MICHAUX

Religion

FIRST TELECAST: *October 31, 1948*
LAST TELECAST: *January 9, 1949*
BROADCAST HISTORY:
Oct 1948–Jan 1949, DUM Sun 6:00–6:30
PREACHER:
Elder Solomon Lightfoot Michaux

The black preacher Solomon Lightfoot Michaux (pronounced "Me-show") and his foot-stomping, hand-clapping revival meetings had been heard on radio since the very early days of that medium. The broadcasts emanated from his hometown of Washington, D.C., where he was pastor of the Church of God, and featured his Happy-Am-I Choir and an enthusiastic congregation that shouted ecstatic encouragement as the Elder preached. He became a regular feature on local Washington TV soon after the first station opened there, and his broadcasts were periodically fed over the DuMont network beginning in 1947. The network telecasts included a semi-regular run in 1948–1949, as shown above.

ELEVENTH HOUR, THE

Medical Drama

FIRST TELECAST: *October 3, 1962*
LAST TELECAST: *September 9, 1964*
BROADCAST HISTORY:
Oct 1962–Sep 1964, NBC Wed 10:00–11:00
CAST:
Dr. Theodore Bassett (1962–1963)
........................Wendell Corey
Dr. Paul Graham ....Jack Ging
Dr. L. Richard Starke (1963–1964)
........................Ralph Bellamy

The role of psychiatry in helping people cope with the world, as well as its use in law-enforcement areas, provided the grist for this dramatic series. Drs. Bassett and Graham were two psychiatrists sharing an office, and the patients who came to them "in the eleventh hour"—on the verge of some form of breakdown—provided the stories. Various forms of analysis and psychotherapy were used, and the two doctors often disagreed on the proper course to take with a specific patient. Dr. Bassett was also an advisor to the State Department of Correction and the police department and was often called upon to evaluate the mental competency of accused criminals.

During the first season the majority of stories dealt with Dr. Bassett's criminal cases. When Wendell Corey left the series, Ralph Bellamy took over his responsibilities, as Dr. Starke, and the emphasis was shifted to involve both of the doctors directly in more of the cases.

ELGIN TV HOUR, THE

Dramatic Anthology

FIRST TELECAST: *October 5, 1954*
LAST TELECAST: *June 14, 1955*
BROADCAST HISTORY:
Oct 1954–Jun 1955, ABC Tue 9:30–10:30

This one-hour Tuesday night series of dramatic presentations on ABC replaced the previous season's *Motorola TV Theatre*. The dramas were telecast live from New York and featured such top actors as Ralph Bellamy, Gertrude Berg, Franchot Tone, Boris Karloff, Polly Bergen, John Cassavetes, and John Forsythe, to name a few. The series alternated with *The U.S. Steel Hour.*

ELLERY QUEEN

see *Adventures of Ellery Queen, The*

EMERGENCY

General Drama

FIRST TELECAST: *January 22, 1972*
LAST TELECAST: *September 3, 1977*
BROADCAST HISTORY:
Jan 1972–Jul 1972, NBC Sat 8:00–9:00
Sep 1972–Sep 1977, NBC Sat 8:00–9:00
CAST:
Dr. Kelly Brackett .... Robert Fuller
Nurse Dixie McCall .... Julie London
Dr. Joe Early .... Bobby Troup
Paramedic Roy DeSoto .... Kevin Tighe
Paramedic John Gage .. Randolph Mantooth
Dr. Morton .... Ron Pinkhard
Captain Stanley (1973–1977)
.... Michael Norell
Fireman Chet Kelly (1973–1977)
.... Tim Donnelly
Fireman Lopez (1973–1977) .... Marco Lopez
Fireman Stoker (1973–1977) .... Mike Stoker
EXECUTIVE PRODUCER:
Jack Webb

Done in the semi-documentary style for which Jack Webb had become famous with *Dragnet*, *Emergency* followed the efforts of Squad 51 of the Los Angeles County Fire Department's Paramedical Rescue Service. Paramedics DeSoto and Gage were usually at the center of the action, while the emergency staff of Rampart Hospital provided backup assistance. Each telecast depicted several interwoven incidents, some humorous, some touching, others tragic. A typical night's work might have the paramedics called on to help an overweight woman who was having trouble breathing because her girdle was too tight, or aiding a maintenance worker who had broken his back in a 100-foot fall from a smokestack he was painting. Another night they might be saving children trapped in an abandoned building when a wrecking crew began demolishing the place, or rescuing a woman parachutist who had gotten caught in a tree. One of the specialties of the paramedics, in fact, seemed to be saving "danglers"—people trapped in precarious positions because of faulty rigging, collapsing scaffolding, or the like.

Former bandleader Bobby Troup, who played neurosurgeon Joe Early, was in real life married to Julie London, who played Rampart's head nurse. (She had previously been married to producer Jack Webb.) Squad 51's mascot was a dog named Boots.

Although *Emergency* ended its run as a series in 1977, special two hour movie versions, newly filmed, were periodically aired during the following season.

EMPIRE

Western

FIRST TELECAST: *September 25, 1962*
LAST TELECAST: *September 6, 1964*
BROADCAST HISTORY:
Sep 1962–Sep 1963, NBC Tue 8:30–9:30
Mar 1964–Sep 1964, ABC Sun 7:30–8:30
CAST:
Jim Redigo .... Richard Egan
Constance Garret .... Terry Moore
Lucia Garret .... Anne Seymour
Tal Garret .... Ryan O'Neal
Chuck .... Warren Vanders
Paul Moreno .... Charles Bronson

This drama was set on the sprawling Garret ranch in contemporary New Mexico. The ranch was indeed an empire, a multimillion-dollar operation covering half a million acres and including oil, mining, lumber, and crop-raising industries, plus cattle-, sheep-, and horse-breeding. All of these gave Jim Redigo, the foreman, plenty of opportunity for dramatic adventure.

Production of *Empire* ceased at the end of the 1962–1963 season, but ABC aired reruns of the original episodes during mid-1964. The main character, Jim Redigo, was saved by NBC for a shorter version of this series, simply titled *Redigo*, that was aired in the fall of 1963 but lasted only 13 weeks. (See *Redigo* for details.)

ENCORE PLAYHOUSE

see *Movies—Prior to 1961*

ENCORE THEATRE

Dramatic Anthology

FIRST TELECAST: *July 7, 1956*
LAST TELECAST: *September 14, 1957*
BROADCAST HISTORY:
Jul 1956–Sep 1956, NBC Sat 10:00–10:30
Jul 1957–Sep 1957, NBC Sat 10:00–10:30

Encore Theatre was the 1956 summer replacement for *The George Gobel Show* and ran in the summer of 1957 after Gobel left the Saturday schedule. The 1956 version consisted of reruns of episodes of *Pepsi-Cola Playhouse* and *Studio 57*. The 1957 version was made up of reruns of episodes of *Ford Theatre*.

ENCOUNTER

Dramatic Anthology

FIRST TELECAST: *October 5, 1958*
LAST TELECAST: *November 2, 1958*
BROADCAST HISTORY:
Oct 1958–Nov 1958, ABC Sun 9:30–10:30

Encounter was a live dramatic series, telecast from Toronto and produced by the Canadian Broadcasting Corporation. For a five-week period in the fall of 1958 these dramas were aired simultaneously by the CBC in Canada and by ABC in the United States, one of the few instances of a live "international network" involving the U.S.

The stories varied between romance, mystery and adventure, but all involved Canadians as characters and featured such Canadian and British actors as Patrick Macnee and Barry Morse.

END OF THE RAINBOW, THE

Audience Participation

FIRST TELECAST: *January 11, 1958*
LAST TELECAST: *February 15, 1958*
BROADCAST HISTORY:
Jan 1958–Feb 1958, NBC Sat 10:00–10:30
EMCEE:
Art Baker (Jan)
Bob Barker (Feb)
PRODUCER:
Ralph Edwards

End of the Rainbow was a poor man's traveling version of *This Is Your Life* and was produced by the same man, Ralph Edwards. Each week during its brief run, an unsuspecting person or couple would be surprised in their home town and honored for being good citizens who had made an outstanding contribution to the community. The chosen people were given "The Surprise of Their Lives," a gift, award, or opportunity that they could only have expected to find "at the end of the rainbow." As on *This Is Your Life*, the subjects were surprised by friends and relatives who were invited to participate in telling their story. The original emcee, Art Baker, left the show after three telecasts and was replaced by Bob Barker for the final three.

ENGELBERT HUMPERDINCK SHOW, THE

Musical Variety

FIRST TELECAST: *January 21, 1970*
LAST TELECAST: *September 19, 1970*
BROADCAST HISTORY:
Jan 1970–Jun 1970, ABC Wed 10:00–11:00
Jul 1970–Sep 1970, ABC Sat 9:30–10:30
REGULARS:
Engelbert Humperdinck
Irving Davies Dancers
The Jack Parnell Orchestra

ABC's success with *This Is Tom Jones*, an English musical variety hour, prompted the network to try this London-based revue starring another singer of similar background and musical style, Engelbert Humperdinck. The star (whose real name was Arnold George Dorsey) was a handsome, likable chap popular in both England and the United States. He had done well enough in an ABC special in December 1969, but his regular series failed to make the grade. It ceased production after six months, although reruns were aired on Saturday nights through the summer.

ENSIGN O'TOOLE

Situation Comedy

FIRST TELECAST: *September 23, 1962*
LAST TELECAST: *September 10, 1964*
BROADCAST HISTORY:
Sep 1962–Sep 1963, NBC Sun 7:00–7:30
Mar 1964–Sep 1964, ABC Thu 9:00–9:30
CAST:
Ensign O'Toole .... Dean Jones
Chief Petty Officer Homer Nelson .... Jay C. Flippen
Lt. (jg) Rex St. John .... Jack Mullaney
Seaman Gabby Di Julio ... Harvey Lembeck
Lt. Cdr. Virgil Stoner .... Jack Albertson
Seaman Howard Spicer ...... Beau Bridges
Seaman Claude White .... Bob Sorrells

This military comedy followed along the same lines as *McHale's Navy* (which also premiered in 1962), but it was set in peacetime. O'Toole was a junior officer aboard the destroyer *Appleby*, clever and an expert on almost everybody's subject, but seldom to be found when there was work to be done. His foils were the usual assortment of lunatic crew members and the overbearing and ambitious supply officer, Lt. Rex St. John. The ship's executive officer was Lt. Cdr. Virgil Stoner. He relayed orders from the captain, who was never seen but only heard, barking orders over the "squawk box."

Based on two books by Bill Lederer, *All the Ships at Sea* and *Ensign O'Toole and Me*. Lederer served as consultant for the series.

The ABC run consisted of reruns of episodes previously aired by NBC.

ENTERPRISE

Documentary

FIRST TELECAST: *October 19, 1952*
LAST TELECAST: *June 8, 1958*
BROADCAST HISTORY:

Oct 1952–Dec 1952, ABC Sun 7:30–8:00
Dec 1952–Mar 1953, ABC Sun 10:30–10:45
Jan 1954–Sep 1954, ABC Sat 8:00–8:30
Oct 1954–Jan 1955, ABC Wed 9:30–10:00
Jul 1957, ABC Thu 8:30–9:00
Aug 1957–Oct 1957, ABC Fri 9:00–9:30
Mar 1958–Apr 1958, ABC Sun 7:00–7:30
Apr 1958–Jun 1958, ABC Sun 9:30–10:00

These documentary films on American industry were run by ABC to fill various holes in the schedule. The original 1952–1953 series was billed in an interesting fashion: "These films, presented in cooperation with such industries as Bethlehem Steel and General Electric, will point out that America is out to prove democracy in industry and to fight communism in industry."

ENTERTAINERS, THE

Variety

FIRST TELECAST: *September 25, 1964*
LAST TELECAST: *March 27, 1965*
BROADCAST HISTORY:

Sep 1964–Dec 1964, CBS Fri 8:30–9:30
Jan 1965–Mar 1965, CBS Sat 9:00–10:00

REGULARS:

Carol Burnett
Caterina Valente
Bob Newhart (1964)
Tessie O'Shea (1964)
Art Buchwald (1964)
Don Crichton (1964)
John Davidson
Dom DeLuise
The Ernie Flatt Dancers (1964)
The Peter Gennaro Dancers (1965)
The Lee Hale Singers
The Harry Zimmerman Orchestra

The format of this variety series was designed to allow each of its three stars—Carol Burnett, Caterina Valente, and Bob Newhart—at least one week off each month. Sometimes all three of them were on a given episode, sometimes only two, and occasionally only one. There was no formal host; instead, each performer introduced the act to follow at the conclusion of his own act. In an effort to simulate a live show, the taping was done on the same evening that the program was actually aired. The regular repertory company of singers, dancers, and comedians was augmented by one or two guest stars each week.

By the end of 1964 one of the three co-stars, Bob Newhart, had left the series, along with several members of its regular cast, and Carol Burnett and Caterina Valente were seen together as co-stars on every episode in 1965. One interesting sidelight is that on November 13, 1964, *The Entertainers* presented a full-hour documentary on the Beatles' 1964 American tour.

ERN WESTMORE SHOW, THE

see *Hollywood Backstage*

ERNIE IN KOVACSLAND

Comedy Variety

FIRST TELECAST: *July 2, 1951*
LAST TELECAST: *August 24, 1951*
BROADCAST HISTORY:

Jul 1951–Aug 1951, NBC Mon–Fri 7:00–7:30

REGULARS:

Ernie Kovacs
Tony Di Simone Trio
Edith Adams

Emanating from Philadelphia during the summer of 1951, *Ernie in Kovacsland* was an unstructured live comedy show that highlighted its star's incredible repertoire of nutty characterizations. The humor was slapstick and almost entirely visual, and was a forerunner of the later Kovacs shows. Appearing as vocalist on *Ernie in Kovacsland* was one Edith Adams, who would later marry the star and shorten her first name to Edie.

ERNIE KOVACS SHOW, THE

Comedy Variety

FIRST TELECAST: *December 30, 1952*
LAST TELECAST: *September 10, 1956*
BROADCAST HISTORY:
Dec 1952–Apr 1953, CBS Tue 8:00–9:00
Jul 1956–Sep 1956, NBC Mon 8:00–9:00
REGULARS:
Ernie Kovacs
Edith Adams
Ernie Hatrak (1952–1953)
Trigger Lund (1952–1953)
Andy McKay (1952–1953)
Bill Wendell (1956)
Peter Hanley (1956)
Henry Lascoe (1956)
Al Kelly (1956)
Barbara Loden (1956)

Ernie Kovacs, one of the most original TV comedians of the 1950s, turned up on the CBS network for a few months in 1952–1953 with a live hour of comedy sketches (at first titled *Kovacs Unlimited,* the same as his local show). With him were many of the regulars from his local show, including singer Edith (not yet Edie) Adams, pianist Ernie Hatrak, and straight men Trigger Lund and Andy McKay. After an absence of three years Ernie returned in 1956, cigar in hand, as the summer replacement for *Caesar's Hour* on NBC. By then he and Edie were married. The supporting cast was different but the humor was the same, largely visual and always offbeat. Among the regular features were *You Asked to See It,* Percy Dovetonsils, the Nairobi Trio, Mr. Question Man, and Clowdy Faire, Your Weather Girl.

ESCAPE

Dramatic Anthology
FIRST TELECAST: *January 5, 1950*
LAST TELECAST: *March 30, 1950*
BROADCAST HISTORY:
Jan 1950–Mar 1950, CBS Thu 9:00–9:30

This live dramatic series was the television counterpart to a successful CBS radio series of the same name. The plays depicted people attempting to deal with danger, the supernatural, or some fantasized situation, allowing the viewer to escape from reality.

ESCAPE

Adventure Anthology
FIRST TELECAST: *February 11, 1973*
LAST TELECAST: *September 9, 1973*
BROADCAST HISTORY:
Feb 1973–Apr 1973, NBC Sun 10:00–10:30
Aug 1973–Sep 1973, NBC Sun 10:00–10:30
NARRATOR:
Jack Webb

Narrow escapes from danger, both natural and manmade, formed the subject matter of this brief semi-documentary adventure series narrated by Jack Webb. Only four original episodes were aired during February–April 1973, dealing with a submarine trapped on the ocean's floor, a demolition expert racing to avert disaster, two children lost in the woods, and an orphan who saves an American official during the Korean war. The four were repeated during the summer of 1973.

ESPIONAGE

Spy Drama
FIRST TELECAST: *October 2, 1963*
LAST TELECAST: *September 2, 1964*
BROADCAST HISTORY:
Oct 1963–Sep 1964, NBC Wed 9:00–10:00

Filmed on location throughout Europe, *Espionage* was an anthology of spy stories, all based on actual case histories. The periods ranged from World War I to the then-current cold war, and covered all forms of international intrigue, civil war, and underground resistance movements. Although most of the performers in these dramas were Europeans unfamiliar to American audiences, some fairly well-known names were also featured, such as Dennis Hopper, Patricia Neal, Arthur Kennedy, Jim Backus, Anthony Quayle, and, in a small supporting role in one episode, author Ian Fleming (of James Bond fame).

ETHEL AND ALBERT

Situation Comedy
FIRST TELECAST: *April 25, 1953*
LAST TELECAST: *July 6, 1956*
BROADCAST HISTORY:
Apr 1953–Dec 1954, NBC Sat 7:30–8:00 (OS)
Jun 1955–Sep 1955, CBS Mon 9:30–10:00
Oct 1955–Jul 1956, ABC Fri 10:00–10:30
CAST:
Ethel Arbuckle ....Peg Lynch
Albert Arbuckle ....Alan Bunce

Ethel and Albert was one of many popular radio shows of the 1940s that had a second life on television in the 1950s. The format was extremely simple and down-to-earth, following the middle-aged Ethel and Albert Arbuckle through the minor triumphs and crises of everyday life. A gentle realism was the keynote of this series, with blown fuses, burnt-out lightbulbs, and ruined dinners being about the worst things that happened in Sandy Harbor, where the couple lived. On radio the Arbuckles had generally been the only characters heard, but a few friends and neighbors wandered through the TV version from time to time.

Peggy Lynch, who had created the characters *Ethel and Albert* in the 1930s, played the role of Ethel on TV, and Alan Bunce, also a holdover from radio, was Albert. They first appeared on TV as a featured sketch on *The Kate Smith Hour*, before launching their own series.

EVE ARDEN SHOW, THE

Situation Comedy

FIRST TELECAST: *September 17, 1957*
LAST TELECAST: *March 25, 1958*
BROADCAST HISTORY:
Sep 1957–Mar 1958, CBS Tue 8:30–9:00
CAST:
Liza Hammond ....Eve Arden
George Howell ....Allyn Joslyn
Nora ....Frances Bavier
Jenny ....Gail Stone
Mary ....Karen Greene

Following Eve Arden's long association with *Our Miss Brooks*, which had ended the previous season, this comedy series cast the actress as novelist Liza Hammond. Liza was a widow who supplemented her writing income by giving lectures, and George Howell was the head of the lecture bureau that booked her tours. While Liza was out lecturing the population, her 12-year-old twin daughters, Jenny and Mary, were at home being looked after by her mother, Nora. The series was based on the autobiography of the writer Emily Kimbrough.

EVERYBODY'S BUSINESS

Documentary

FIRST TELECAST: *July 2, 1951*
LAST TELECAST: *September 28, 1952*
BROADCAST HISTORY:
Jul 1951–Aug 1951, ABC Sun 10:30–11:00
Jul 1952–Sep 1952, ABC Sun 7:30–8:00
HOST:
Oscar Ewing (1951)

This documentary film series on education, health, and social services was presented in cooperation with the Federal Security Agency during the summers of 1951 and 1952. The host was Oscar Ewing, Federal Security Administrator.

EXCLUSIVELY YOURS

see *Igor Cassini Show, The*

EXECUTIVE SUITE

General Drama

FIRST TELECAST: *September 20, 1976*
LAST TELECAST: *February 11, 1977*
BROADCAST HISTORY:
Sep 1976–Jan 1977, CBS Mon 10:00–11:00
Jan 1977–Feb 1977, CBS Fri 10:00–11:00
CAST:
Don Walling ....Mitchell Ryan
Howell Rutledge ....Stephen Elliott
Helen Walling ....Sharon Acker
Brian Walling ....Leigh McCloskey
Mark Desmond ....Richard Cox
Astrid Rutledge ....Gwyda DonHowe
Tom Dalessio ....Paul Lambert
Pearce Newberry ....Byron Morrow
Yvonne Holland ....Trisha Noble
Stacey Walling ....Wendy Phillips
Glory Dalessio ....Joan Prather
Hilary Madison ....Madlyn Rhue
Malcolm Gibson ....Percy Rodriguez
Anderson Galt ....William Smithers
Marge Newberry ....Maxine Stuart
Summer Johnson ....Brenda Sykes
Harry Ragin ....Carl Weintraub

Corporate intrigue, family problems, and all sorts of emotional involvements were part of the mix in this nighttime soap opera about the lives of people working for, and affected by, the huge Cardway Corporation. Don Walling was the president, Howell Rutledge the vice-president and chief rival to Walling, and their families, business associates, and personal entanglements all had their parts in this short-lived series.

EXPEDITION

Wildlife/Archeology

FIRST TELECAST: *September 20, 1960*
LAST TELECAST: *April 23, 1962*
BROADCAST HISTORY:
Sep 1960–Jun 1961, ABC Tue 7:00–7:30
Sep 1961–Apr 1962, ABC Mon 7:00–7:30
HOST:
Col. John D. Craig

Filmed accounts of safaris to Africa, meetings with remote and primitive tribes, archeological expeditions to ruined cities of antiquity, and studies of animals in their natural habitats were all part of this series. Col. Craig was widely seen in later years in a similar, syndicated series called *Of Lands and Seas*.

EYE WITNESS

Documentary

FIRST TELECAST: *November 6, 1947*
LAST TELECAST: *April 13, 1948*
BROADCAST HISTORY:
Nov 1947–Dec 1947, NBC Thu various times
Jan 1948–Apr 1948, NBC Thu 8:00–8:30
HOST:
Ben Grauer

One of the earliest regularly scheduled network programs was this behind-the-scenes introduction to the television medium itself. The program was telecast live with film inserts, and frequently went on location. Subjects included how a TV set works, how a TV studio operates, mobile units on location, and the problems of networking. One telecast, in February 1948, traced the history of television from Joseph May's experiments in 1873 to the present day.

EYE WITNESS

Dramatic Anthology

FIRST TELECAST: *March 30, 1953*
LAST TELECAST: *June 29, 1953*
BROADCAST HISTORY:
Mar 1953–Jun 1953, NBC Mon 9:00–9:30
PRODUCER:
Robert Montgomery

A live dramatic-anthology series produced by Robert Montgomery, with emphasis on the supernatural and strange twists of fate. Scripts were both originals written for TV and adaptations of stories. The guest host or hostess for each program, who was introduced at the start of the show by Mr. Montgomery, starred the following week on Montgomery's principal series, *Robert Montgomery Presents* (Monday 9:30–10:30 P.M.).

EYES HAVE IT, THE

See *Celebrity Time*

EYES HAVE IT, THE

Quiz/Panel

FIRST TELECAST: *November 20, 1948*
LAST TELECAST: *January 27, 1949*
BROADCAST HISTORY:
Nov 1948–Jan 1949, NBC Sat 8:00–8:30
MODERATOR:
Ralph McNair

This quiz program required panelists to identify a famous place or face from a portion of a picture—a picture in pieces, an unusual angle shot, extreme close-up, or a close shot of the eyes, gradually widening to reveal other parts of a face. The program emanated from NBC's station in Washington, D.C., where it had begun as a local show in September 1948. After its prime-time run it continued on the network on Sunday afternoons until June 1949.

EYEWITNESS TO HISTORY

News Analysis

FIRST TELECAST: *September 23, 1960*
LAST TELECAST: *August 2, 1963*
BROADCAST HISTORY:
Sep 1960, CBS Fri 9:00–9:30
Sep 1960–Jun 1961, CBS Fri 10:30–11:00
Sep 1961–Aug 1963, CBS Fri 10:30–11:00
ANCHORMAN:
Charles Kuralt (1960–1961)
Walter Cronkite (1961–1962)
Charles Collingwood (1962–1963)

An in-depth analysis of a major current news story was presented each Friday night on *Eyewitness to History*. The program was originally aired as a series of specials beginning in September 1959, then moved into a regular weekly time slot a year later. The title of the series was shortened to *Eyewitness* in September 1961.

F.B.I., THE

Police Drama

FIRST TELECAST: *September 19, 1965*
LAST TELECAST: *September 8, 1974*
BROADCAST HISTORY:
Sep 1965–Sep 1973, ABC Sun 8:00–9:00
Sep 1973–Sep 1974, ABC Sun 7:30–8:30
CAST:
Inspector Lewis Erskine .... Efrem Zimbalist, Jr.
Arthur Ward .... Philip Abbott
Barbara Erskine (1965–1966) .... Lynn Loring

Special Agent Jim Rhodes (1965–1967) ....Stephen Brooks
Special Agent Tom Colby (1967–1973) ....William Reynolds
Agent Chris Daniels (1973–1974) ....Shelly Novack

EXECUTIVE PRODUCER:
Quinn Martin

MUSICAL THEME:
"F.B.I. Theme," by Bronislaw Kaper

The Federal Bureau of Investigation has been the subject of several highly popular radio and TV shows (remember *The F.B.I. in Peace and War?*), but none portrayed the cool, professional operation of the agency so thoroughly as this long-running series starring Efrem Zimbalist, Jr., as Inspector Lewis Erskine. Despite a background more musical than dramatic (his father was a world-famous concert violinist, his mother the renowned opera star Alma Gluck), Zimbalist personified the calm, business-suited government agent who always tracked his quarry down, scientifically and methodically, and with virtually no emotion whatever.

The cases were supposedly based on real FBI files. They ranged across the United States and involved counterfeiters, extortionists, organized crime, Communist spies, and radical bombings (during the era of Vietnam dissent). Arthur Ward was the assistant to the FBI director and the man to whom Inspector Erskine reported, while several agents served as Erskine's sidekick over the years. Barbara Erskine, his daughter, appeared only during the first season, later being written out apparently because there was no room for anything so fallible as family ties in *The F.B.I.*

The program always portrayed the agency in a favorable light. It won the commendation of real-life FBI Director J. Edgar Hoover, who gave the show full government cooperation and even allowed filming of some background scenes at the FBI headquarters in Washington. Bringing the program even closer to real life, many telecasts closed with a short segment asking the audience for information on the FBI's most-wanted men (including, in April 1968, the fugitive James Earl Ray).

Associated with the program as sponsor throughout its run was the Ford Motor Company, which accounted for the fact that those agents were always seen driving Ford cars.

F.D.R.

Documentary

FIRST TELECAST: *January 8, 1965*
LAST TELECAST: *September 10, 1965*
BROADCAST HISTORY:
Jan 1965–Jun 1965, ABC Fri 9:30–10:00
Jun 1965–Sep 1965, ABC Fri 8:00–8:30

NARRATOR:
Arthur Kennedy
Charlton Heston

EXECUTIVE PRODUCER:
Robert D. Graff

PRODUCER:
Ben Feiner, Jr.

Created by the same team that had produced the acclaimed *Winston Churchill: The Valiant Years* several years before, *F.D.R.* was a presentation and analysis of the life of Franklin Delano Roosevelt. Eleanor Roosevelt, FDR's widow, acted as consultant during the development of the program and intended to appear on the telecasts, but she died before the series reached the air. Before her death she was filmed relating her reminiscences of FDR's early days, and these sequences were included in some of the early telecasts of the series. Arthur Kennedy was narrator of the series, and Charlton Heston read from the late president's writings.

F TROOP

Situation Comedy

FIRST TELECAST: *September 14, 1965*
LAST TELECAST: *August 31, 1967*
BROADCAST HISTORY:
Sep 1965–Aug 1966, ABC Tue 9:00–9:30
Sep 1966–Aug 1967, ABC Thu 8:00–8:30

CAST:
Capt. Wilton Parmenter ....Ken Berry
Sgt. Morgan O'Rourke ......Forrest Tucker
Cpl. Randolph Agarn ....Larry Storch
Wrangler Jane ....Melody Patterson
Chief Wild Eagle .... Frank deKova
Crazy Cat ....Don Diamond
Bugler Hannibal Dobbs ....James Hampton
Trooper Duffy ....Bob Steele
Trooper Vanderbilt ....Joe Brooks

CREATOR/PRODUCER:
Richard M. Bluel

The "stars" of this military farce were the gallant incompetents of F Troop at Fort

Courage, somewhere west of the Missouri, in post-Civil War days. The CO was the wide-eyed, bumbling Capt. Parmenter, who had been promoted from private during the closing days of the war when he accidentally led a charge in the wrong direction—toward the enemy. Unbeknownst to the captain, Sgt. O'Rourke had already negotiated a secret—and highly profitable—treaty with the Hekawi Indians, from whom he also had an exclusive franchise to sell their souvenirs to tourists. There was no peace treaty with the Shugs, however, and they sometimes caused trouble. Cpl. Agarn was O'Rourke's chief aide and assistant schemer, and Wrangler Jane the hard-riding, fast-shooting cowgirl who was out to marry Parmenter.

A lot of colorful Indians and others passed through this series in one-time special appearances, including Roaring Chicken (Edward Everett Horton); 147-year-old Flaming Arrow (Phil Harris); Bald Eagle (Don Rickles); Wise Owl (Milton Berle), an Indian detective; Sgt. Ramsden (Paul Lynde), a singing mountie; and Wrongo Starr (Henry Gibson), a jinxed cavalry trooper.

F.Y.I.

Public Affairs

FIRST TELECAST: *June 5, 1960*

LAST TELECAST: *September 25, 1960*

BROADCAST HISTORY:

Jun 1960–Sep 1960, CBS Sun 6:00–6:30

HOST:

Douglas Edwards

F.Y.I. (For Your Information) premiered as a Sunday morning informational program on CBS in January 1960. It moved to Sunday evenings for the summer of 1960, providing filmed reports and interviews covering such subjects as the political problems of shifting city populations, the pressures leading to mental breakdowns, and European attitudes toward the American way of electing political leaders.

FABLE FOR A SUMMER NIGHT

see *ABC Dramatic Shorts—1952–1953*

FACE IS FAMILIAR, THE

Quiz/Audience Participation

FIRST TELECAST: *May 7, 1966*

LAST TELECAST: *September 3, 1966*

BROADCAST HISTORY:

May 1966–Sep 1966, CBS Sat 9:30–10:00

EMCEE:

Jack Whitaker

This summer game show featured two teams of contestants, each consisting of a celebrity guest and a non-celebrity contestant. The teams competed to guess the identity of a familiar face from scrambled sections of a photograph of that face. As each team correctly answered questions from the emcee, increasing sections of the face were revealed. The first team to guess the correct identity won $200 and the chance to win an additional $500 by correctly identifying which sets of eyes, noses, and mouths belonged to specific predesignated celebrities.

FACE OF DANGER, THE

Dramatic Anthology

FIRST TELECAST: *April 18, 1959*

LAST TELECAST: *May 30, 1959*

BROADCAST HISTORY:

Apr 1959–May 1959, CBS Sat 9:00–9:30

The filmed dramas telecast in this short-lived series were all reruns of episodes previously aired in the series *Playhouse of Stars*.

FACE THE MUSIC

Music

FIRST TELECAST: May 2, 1948

LAST TELECAST: *May 19, 1949*

BROADCAST HISTORY:

May 1948, CBS Mon/Wed 7:15–7:30
May 1948, CBS Mon/Wed/Fri 7:15–7:30
May 1948–Jun 1948, CBS Mon/Wed/Thu/Fri 7:15–7:30
Jun 1948–Aug 1948, CBS Mon–Fri 7:15–7:30
Aug 1948–Feb 1949, CBS Mon–Fri 7:45–8:00
Feb 1949–Mar 1949, CBS Mon/Tue/Thu/Fri 7:45–8:00
Mar 1949–Apr 1949, CBS Tue/Thu 7:45–8:00
Apr 1949–May 1949, CBS Tue/Thu 7:15–7:30

REGULARS:

Johnny Desmond (1948)
Shaye Cogan (1948)
Carole Coleman
Tony Mottola Trio

This live musical show premiered as a twice-a-week feature starring vocalists Johnny Desmond and Shaye Cogan with music by the Tony Mottola Trio. Within six weeks of its premiere it had expanded to a five-day-a-week schedule. On December 13, 1948, the title was changed to *Make Mine Music* and Carole Coleman took over as featured singer.

FACE THE NATION

Interview

FIRST TELECAST: *October 2, 1960*
LAST TELECAST: *April 6, 1961*
BROADCAST HISTORY:

Oct 1960–Nov 1960, CBS Sun 6:00–6:30
Nov 1960–Dec 1960, CBS Mon 10:30–11:00
Jan 1961–Apr 1961, CBS Thu 10:00–1030

MODERATOR:

Stuart Novins

CBS' well-respected public-affairs program, in which leading politicians and other public figures were subjected to questioning by a panel of newsmen, premiered on Sunday afternoon, November 7, 1954. Though it has spent most of its long career as a Sunday daytime program, it was seen for short periods in the early 1960s as a nighttime show. Stuart Novins was the regular moderator during this period.

FACE TO FACE

Cartoon Quiz

FIRST TELECAST: *June 9, 1946*
LAST TELECAST: *January 26, 1947*
BROADCAST HISTORY:

Jun 1946–Jan 1947, NBC Sun 8:00–8:20

REGULARS:

Eddie Dunn
Bill Dunn
"Sugar"

The idea of this early game show was for an artist to draw a picture of an unseen person from verbal clues, then compare the results with the actual person, when he came into the studio. At first the subject was in a separate room, unseen by viewers and heard only over a telephone line; later he sat on the opposite side of a curtain from the artist, and viewers could compare the sketch as it progressed. There was also a quiz element, with prizes for identifying a celebrity from various clues. Bill Dunn did the sketching and Eddie Dunn the interviewing, with a woman named Sugar present on later telecasts as a kind of emcee.

As with some other early programs, it is not known whether this was carried over the NBC network from the start; however, it was a network feature by early November 1946 at the latest.

FACTS WE FACE, THE

Documentary

FIRST TELECAST: *August 27, 1950*
LAST TELECAST: *August 19, 1951*
BROADCAST HISTORY:

Aug 1950–Sep 1950, CBS Sun 9:30–10:00
Sep 1950, CBS Sun 10:15–11:00
Jul 1951–Aug 1951, CBS Sun 6:00–6:30

MODERATOR:

Bill Shadel (1950)
Walter Cronkite (1951)

The Facts We Face was originally a five-week series designed to inform the American public of the impact that the then-current Korean War mobilization would have on their lives. Through filmed reports and interviews the program covered the selective service, production and allocation of resources and manpower, rationing, economic prospects, and civil defense. Following its prime-time run the series moved to Sunday afternoons. It returned to nighttime television during the following summer, with Walter Cronkite as moderator and a new title, *Open Hearing*.

FAIR EXCHANGE

Situation Comedy

FIRST TELECAST: *September 21, 1962*
LAST TELECAST: *September 19, 1963*
BROADCAST HISTORY:

Sep 1962–Dec 1962, CBS Fri 9:30–10:30
Mar 1963–Sep 1963, CBS Thu 7:30–8:00

CAST:

Eddie Walker .... Eddie Foy, Jr.
Dorothy Walker .... Audrey Christie
Patty Walker .... Lynn Loring
Larry Walker .... Flip Mark
Tommy Finch .... Victor Maddern
Sybil Finch .... Diana Chesney
Heather Finch .... Judy Carne
Neville Finch .... Dennis Waterman

This hands-across-the-sea comedy concerned two middle-class families, the Eddie Walkers of New York City, U.S.A., and the Thomas Finches of London, England, who agreed to swap teenage daughters for a year. Eddie and Tommy had been wartime buddies, and now each had a lovely wife (Dorothy and Sybil), a son, and a daughter. The scene alternated between New York and London as the two daughters, Patty and Heather, explored their new surroundings.

Begun as an unusual experiment in full-hour comedy, *Fair Exchange* ran for only three months and was canceled. The unexpected volume of mail from the show's audience prompted CBS to give it another try. It was trimmed to half an hour and, after a three-month hiatus, returned in March 1963. The shorter format didn't work either, and the program left the air for good at the end of the season.

FAMILY

Drama

FIRST TELECAST: *March 9, 1976*

LAST TELECAST:

BROADCAST HISTORY:

Mar 1976–May 1978, ABC Tue 10:00–11:00 (OS)

Sep 1978–, ABC Thu 10:00–11:00

CAST:

Kate Lawrence .... Sada Thompson
Doug Lawrence .... James Broderick
Nancy Lawrence/Maitland (1976) .... Elayne Heilveil
Nancy Lawrence/Maitland (1976–) .... Meredith Baxter-Birney
Willie Lawrence .... Gary Frank
Letitia "Buddy" Lawrence .... Kristy McNichol
Jeff Maitland .... John Rubinstein
Mrs. Hanley .... Mary Grace Canfield
Salina Magee (1976–1977) .... Season Hubley
Annie Cooper (1978–) .... Quinn Cummings
Timmy Maitland (1978–) .... Michael David Schackelford.

Family was a prime-time soap opera that followed the travails of the middle-class Lawrence family in Pasadena, California. Doug was the father, a highly independent lawyer, and Kate his quiet, steadfast wife. The series opened with daughter Nancy discovering that her husband Jeff was untrue (she walked in on him making love to another woman!) and it was all downhill from there. Nancy had a baby (Timmy), divorced Jeff, then began having affairs of her own. Brother Willie, age 17, vulnerable and idealistic, was confronted with his first love, an unwed mother (Salina), then married a girl with a terminal illness (Lizzy). Little sister Buddy, age 13, feeling unwanted, ran away from home. Before Kate could worry about *that*, she discovered that she had breast cancer, after which Doug was temporarily blinded in an automobile accident. An eleven-year-old waif named Annie joined the household, only to reject everyone's affections. Then there was the dying grandmother, Doug's alcoholic sister, and so on, and on, and on . . .

FAMILY AFFAIR

Situation Comedy

FIRST TELECAST: *September 12, 1966*

LAST TELECAST: *September 9, 1971*

BROADCAST HISTORY:

Sep 1966–Sep 1969, CBS Mon 9:30–10:00

Sep 1969–Sep 1971, CBS Thu 7:30–8:00

CAST:

Bill Davis .... Brian Keith
Mr. (Giles) French .... Sebastian Cabot
Buffy .... Anissa Jones
Jody .... Johnnie Whitaker
Cissy .... Kathy Garver

Bill Davis's carefree existence as a swinging bachelor was just about perfect. A highly paid consulting engineer, he maintained an elegant apartment off Fifth Avenue in Manhattan and had his domestic needs cared for by a very English gentleman's gentleman, Mr. French. Into this life of independence came three young orphans, 6-year-old twins Buffy and Jody and 15-year-old Cissy. Their parents, Bill's brother and sister-in-law, had died in an accident, and other relatives felt that Bill could best provide for them. Despite initial misgivings, Bill and French became very attached to the children and learned to adjust their life-style to make room for the new members of the household. Mr. French, a stickler for neatness and order, had the toughest adjustment to make—he was with the children all the time while Bill was often out of town on assignments—but he and the children managed to compromise and learn to live with each other.

For a period during the show's first season, co-star Sebastian Cabot was taken ill and was replaced in nine episodes by John Williams. In the story line, Giles French was called away to special service of the

Queen of England and his brother Niles arrived at the Davis residence to serve the family during his absence. Although not a full-time member of the cast Nancy Walker appeared in the continuing role of Mr. Davis's part-time housekeeper, Emily, during the last season.

FAMILY HOLVAK, THE

General Drama

FIRST TELECAST: *September 7, 1975*

LAST TELECAST: *June 28, 1977*

BROADCAST HISTORY:

Sep 1975, NBC Sun 7:30–8:30
Sep 1975–Oct 1975, NBC Sun 8:00–9:00
Oct 1975, NBC Mon 8:00–9:00
Dec 1975, NBC Sun 8:00–9:00
May 1977–Jun 1977, CBS Tue 8:00–9:00

CAST:

Rev. Tom Holvak ....Glenn Ford
Elizabeth Holvak ....Julie Harris
Ramey Holvak ....Lance Kerwin
Julie Mae Holvak ......Elizabeth Cheshire

Life in the South during the Depression was hard on everyone, and a preacher was no exception. Rev. Tom Holvak was the poverty-stricken clergyman trying to scrape together enough money to support his wife Elizabeth and his two children, 13-year-old Ramey and 8-year-old Julie Mae. To add to his meager income, he sold produce grown on a small plot of land owned by the church. This unsuccessful series was, in many ways, patterned after the highly successful CBS series *The Waltons*, in that it stressed how love and understanding helped a Depression family survive, even though they lacked many of the comforts that most people now take for granted.

Reruns of *The Family Holvak* were aired briefly on CBS during the summer of 1977.

FAMOUS ADVENTURES OF MR. MAGOO, THE

Cartoon

FIRST TELECAST: *September 19, 1964*

LAST TELECAST: *August 7, 1965*

BROADCAST HISTORY:

Sep 1964–Dec 1964, NBC Sat 8:00–8:30
Jan 1965–Aug 1965, NBC Sat 8:30–9:00

VOICES:

Mr. Quincy Magoo ....Jim Backus
Various .... Marvin Miller, Howard Morris, Paul Frees

Mr. Magoo, that clumsy, crusty, near-sighted old man, has had a long history of success in theatrical cartoons and on TV. At Christmastime in 1962 and 1963, NBC aired a feature-length cartoon version of Dickens's *A Christmas Carol*, featuring Mr. Magoo as Ebeneezer Scrooge and retitled "Mr. Magoo's Christmas Carol." This prompted the development of a series in which Magoo played assorted characters of historic significance, both fictional and real. Long John Silver, Friar Tuck, William Tell, Dr. Watson (of the Sherlock Holmes stories), and Rip Van Winkle were among the characters played by Magoo in this humorous animated series.

FAMOUS FIGHTS

Sports

FIRST TELECAST: *September 15, 1952*

LAST TELECAST: *December 17, 1957*

BROADCAST HISTORY:

Sep 1952–Dec 1952, DUM Mon 9:45–10:00
Jul 1957–Dec 1957, ABC Wed 10:45–11:00

COMMENTATOR:

Jimmy Powers (1952)

Filmed highlights of outstanding boxing matches in the history of Madison Square Garden were shown preceding or following live fights in 1952 and 1957.

FAMOUS FILM FESTIVAL

see *Movies—Prior to 1961*

FAMOUS JURY TRIALS

Courtroom Drama

FIRST TELECAST: *October 12, 1949*

LAST TELECAST: *March 12, 1952*

BROADCAST HISTORY:

Oct 1949–May 1950, DUM Wed 9:30–10:00
May 1950–May 1951, DUM Wed 9:00–9:30
Nov 1951–Mar 1952, DUM Wed 9:00–9:30

This series presented re-enactments of real-life criminal trials and the crimes that led to them. Typically the story would open in the courtroom. While opposing witnesses related their versions of the events, the scene would shift to another set and re-enactments of the crime according to each witness' version. At the end the jury was given the case, and the viewer found out what really happened. Staged with little-known actors on a minuscule budget, this DuMont production nevertheless managed to survive off and on for two and a half years.

FANFARE

Dramatic Anthology

FIRST TELECAST: *July 7, 1959*
LAST TELECAST: *September 8, 1959*
BROADCAST HISTORY:
Jul 1959–Sep 1959, NBC Tue 9:00–9:30
HOST:
Richard Derr

This summer series consisted of repeats of *Loretta Young Show* plays in which Miss Young had not appeared. Actor Richard Derr was the host, introducing each play and giving a summary of the following week's offering at the conclusion of the telecast.

FANFARE

Musical Variety

FIRST TELECAST: *June 19, 1965*
LAST TELECAST: *September 11, 1965*
BROADCAST HISTORY:
Jun 1965–Sep 1965, CBS Sat 7:30–8:30
REGULARS:
Al Hirt

Al Hirt, the hefty, bearded New Orleans trumpet player, was the host and star of this summer musical variety series. In addition to his own flashy renditions of popular and classical trumpet pieces, Hirt presented various guest stars, all of whom participated in some type of musical number, whether or not they were themselves musicians.

FANTASTIC JOURNEY

Science Fiction

FIRST TELECAST: *February 3, 1977*
LAST TELECAST: *April 13, 1977*
BROADCAST HISTORY:
Feb 1977–Apr 1977, NBC Thu 8:00–9:00
CAST:
Varian .... Jared Martin
Dr. Fred Walters .... Carl Franklin
Scott Jordan .... Ike Eisenmann
Liana .... Katie Saylor
Dr. Jonathan Willaway ... Roddy McDowall

This science-fantasy series began with a group of university scientists exploring the area of the Bermuda Triangle. Their boat ran aground on an uncharted land mass, which turned out to be the source of a strange "time and space warp" in which past, present, and future were all intermingled. One of the scientists, Dr. Fred Walters, was drawn into the warp, where he met four people from various eras, each of whom was trying to find the way back to his or her own time. The four were Varian, a telepathic individual from the 23rd century; Liana, a survivor from the lost continent of Atlantis; Scott, a young boy from the present day who had occult abilities; and Dr. Jonathan Willaway, a scientist from the 1960s who was living with androids. The adventures of these wanderers in time and space, the bizarre creatures they encountered, and the conflicts between them were all interwoven in the series.

FANTASY ISLAND

Romantic Drama

FIRST TELECAST: *January 28, 1978*
LAST TELECAST:
BROADCAST HISTORY:
Jan 1978– , ABC Sat 10:00–11:00
CAST:
Mr. Roarke .... Ricardo Montalban
Tattoo .... Herve Villechaize

When ABC realized it had a major hit with *Love Boat*, it immediately began developing a second program using a similar theme. That program was *Fantasy Island*, and, scheduled right after *Love Boat* on Saturday night, it soon became an equally big hit.

Both programs were episodic, consisting of several different stories each week played out against a common background. The backdrop of *Fantasy Island* was romantic indeed; a remote island resort, where each visitor could have one lifelong dream come true. A homely young man wanted to become, during his stay, a sex symbol to beautiful girls (bikini-clad beauties abounded on *Fantasy Island*); a frustrated salesman whose career was going nowhere wanted to score the business coup of his life; a henpecked family man wanted a weekend of respect from his clan. Many of the stories involved glamour and excitement for ordinary people whose lives normally had none, and ABC obviously felt that viewers would relate this to their own lives. There was sometimes an element of danger, or a twist of fate, but everything always worked out for the best.

Overseeing the two or three little dramas

each week were the island's owner, the suave and slightly mysterious Mr. Roarke, and his midget-helper Tattoo. The visitors were played by guest stars, among them Henry Gibson, Georgia Engel, Christopher George, Marcia Strassman, Dennis James and others.

Fantasy Island was filmed at a real tropical paradise, a public park called the Arboretum, 25 miles from Los Angeles.

FARADAY AND COMPANY

Detective

FIRST TELECAST: *September 26, 1973*

LAST TELECAST: *August 13, 1974*

BROADCAST HISTORY:

Sep 1973–Jan 1974, NBC Wed 8:30–10:00
Apr 1974–Aug 1974, NBC Tue 8:30–10:00

CAST:

Frank Faraday ....Dan Dailey
Steve Faraday ....James Naughton
Holly Barrett ....Sharon Glass
Lou Carson ....Geraldine Brooks

Frank Faraday was a private detective who had served 25 years in a South American jail for a crime that he had not committed. When he was finally released he was forced to adjust to a world very much changed, including a son, Steve, he had never known (born to his secretary, Lou Carson, after his imprisonment). Steve had himself become a detective. After tracking down and bringing to justice the man who had actually committed the crime for which he had been imprisoned, Frank joined forces with his son in operating a Los Angeles detective agency that specialized in security investigations. The contrast in styles between the two men created constant tensions and strains in the relationship, for father Frank often resorted to old-style physical force against a new generation of technologically and legally astute criminals. *Faraday and Company* was one of the four rotating elements in the 1973–1974 version of the *NBC Wednesday Mystery Movie*. The others were *Banacek*, *The Snoop Sisters*, and *Tenafly*.

FARAWAY HILL

Romantic Drama

FIRST TELECAST: *October 2, 1946*

LAST TELECAST: *December 18, 1946*

BROADCAST HISTORY:

Oct 1946—Dec 1946, DUM Wed 9:00–9:30

CAST:

Karen St. John ....Flora Campbell

ALSO:

Mel Brandt
Ann Stell
Lorene Scott
Frederic Meyer
Melville Galliart
Jacqueline Waite
Jack Halloran
Ben Low
Bill Gale
Vivian King
Eve McVeagh
Julie Christy
Hal Studer
Barry Doig
Munroe Gabler

WRITER/DIRECTOR:

David P. Lewis

Faraway Hill was the first example on network television of a durable and tear-stained program type—the soap opera. The network wasn't very big (New York and Washington) and the program didn't last very long (12 weeks), but it had all the elements that today's serial viewers have come to know and love—two women after the same man, family jealousies, incredible complications, and the inevitable "tune in next time" to find out what happened.

Some of the specifics, such as character names, have been lost in the mists of history. The basic plot concerned a wealthy New York woman who, following the death of her husband, traveled to the country to visit relatives and get away from it all. The relatives, who lived on a farm, turned out to be a little more rural than she had expected, which resulted in conflict between her sophistication and their lack of it. Staying with them was an adopted farm boy, with whom the widow soon became romantically involved. Unfortunately, he was already promised to the farmer's daughter, which led to the inevitable romantic triangle. Widow St. John tried all her wiles to win him away, but—well, tune in next week.

Flora Campbell, a Broadway actress with numerous credits, played the leading role of Karen St. John, and Mel Brandt was the object of her affections.

Faraway Hill was an experiment to see how this kind of series would look on TV, and some of the devices used were interesting. On the initial episode the various characters were introduced with their names and relationships shown on the screen, so that viewers could keep everyone straight. Each subsequent episode began with a recap of what had gone before (illustrated by slides from the shows) and a reminder of who was who, narrated in emotional tones by Karen. Within the show an off-screen voice would relate Karen's thoughts, to serve as a bridge between scenes, and occasional film sequences were worked into the otherwise live show to depict such details as passing trains. The whole production was done on an absolutely minimal budget of $300 per week.

Though *Faraway Hill* was the first soap opera to be carried on a network, it was not the first one on television. During the summer of 1946 WRGB, the pioneering General Electric station in Schenectady, aired a 13-part serial called *War Bride*, about a GI returned from the war with a new love, much to the consternation of his mother and his former fiancée. There may have been a few others, also telecast on a local basis. In any event it was not until the networks moved into daytime telecasting in a big way in the 1950s that the TV soap opera really caught on, and the serialized grief has been endless ever since.

FARMER'S DAUGHTER, THE

Situation Comedy

FIRST TELECAST: *September 20, 1963*

LAST TELECAST: *September 2, 1966*

BROADCAST HISTORY:

Sep 1963–Nov 1963, ABC Fri 9:30–10:00
Dec 1963–Sep 1964, ABC Wed 8:30–9:00
Sep 1964–Jun 1965, ABC Fri 8:00–8:30
Jun 1965–Oct 1965, ABC Mon 9:30–10:00
Nov 1965–Sep 1966, ABC Fri 9:30–10:00

CAST:

Katrin "Katy" Holstrum ..... Inger Stevens
Congressman Glen Morley .... William Windom
Agatha Morley, Glen's Mother .... Cathleen Nesbitt
Steve Morley .... Mickey Sholdar
Danny Morley .... Rory O'Brien
Cooper, the Butler (1963–1964) .... Philip Coolidge

This comedy concerned Katy, a naive, sexy farm girl of Swedish descent, who came to Washington, D.C., to look for help from her congressman. Instead she wound up working for him, as governess of his two motherless boys, Danny (age 8) and Steve (age 14). Through simple charm and native intelligence Katy managed to loosen up the sometimes stuffy politicians around her and to further Glen's bumbling political career. On the telecast of November 5, 1965, Katy married Glen, but this failed to reverse the declining ratings, and the show concluded its run at the end of that season.

The program was based on the 1947 movie of the same name starring Loretta Young, for which Miss Young won an Oscar.

FASHION STORY, THE

Fashion/Comedy

FIRST TELECAST: *November 4, 1948*

LAST TELECAST: *March 1, 1949*

BROADCAST HISTORY:

Nov 1948–Jan 1949, ABC Thu 8:00–8:30
Jan 1949–Mar 1949, ABC Tue 7:30–8:00

REGULARS:

Marilyn Day
Carl Reiner
Don Saxon
Pamela O'Neill
Dennis Bohan
Doris Lane
Patsy Davis
Elaine Joyce
Aina Shields

PIANO:

Roger Stearns

This was a fashion show combined with a slight comedy story line to provide continuity. Marilyn Day was seen in the role of Lucky Marshall, a young model who hoped to break into show business as a singer (thus providing an excuse for periodic songs). Her young boss, who was forever causing problems, was played by Dennis Bohan. A bevy of fashion models paraded through each show, providing its main reason for being. Comic Carl Reiner was also a regular, but his talents were largely wasted, causing one reviewer to remark that he and Miss Day deserved "a good spot of their own on a variety show, without the drawback of tying together a fashion show." He soon got one. (See *Your Show of Shows*.)

FASHIONS ON PARADE

Fashion/Variety

FIRST TELECAST: *August 20, 1948*

LAST TELECAST: *January 7, 1949*

BROADCAST HISTORY:

Aug 1948–Jan 1949, DUM Fri 8:00–8:30

NARRATOR:

Adelaide Hawley

This combination fashion show and musical revue featured guest celebrities and the famous Conover (Modeling Agency) Cover Girls as models. A thin story line each week tied together the performances and the showing of the latest fashions. Among the guests were Vincent Lopez and Jerry Wayne.

The show was also seen locally in New York during various periods in 1948 and 1949.

FATHER KNOWS BEST

Situation Comedy

FIRST TELECAST: *October 3, 1954*

LAST TELECAST: *April 5, 1963*

BROADCAST HISTORY:

Oct 1954–Mar 1955, CBS Sun 10:00–10:30
Aug 1955–Sep 1958, NBC Wed 8:30–9:00
Sep 1958–Sep 1960, CBS Mon 8:30–9:00
Oct 1960–Sep 1961, CBS Tue 8:00–8:30
Oct 1961–Feb 1962, CBS Wed 8:00–8:30
Feb 1962–Sep 1962, CBS Mon 8:30–9:00
Sep 1962–Dec 1962, ABC Sun 7:00–7:30
Dec 1962–Apr 1963, ABC Fri 8:00–8:30

CAST:

Jim Anderson .... Robert Young
Margaret Anderson .... Jane Wyatt
Betty Anderson (Princess) .. Elinor Donahue
James Anderson, Jr. (Bud) .... Billy Gray
Kathy Anderson (Kitten) .... Lauren Chapin
Miss Thomas .... Sarah Selby
Ed Davis (1955–1959) .... Robert Foulk
Myrtle Davis (1955–1959) ...... Vivi Jannis
Dotty Snow (1954–1957) ..... Yvonne Lime
Kippy Watkins (1954–1959) .. Paul Wallace
Claude Messner (1954–1959)
.... Jimmy Bates
Doyle Hobbs (1957–1958) ..... Roger Smith
Ralph Little (1957–1958) .. Robert Chapman
April Adams (1957–1958) ..... Sue George
Joyce Kendall (1958–1959)
.... Jymme (Roberta) Shore

Father Knows Best was the classic wholesome family situation comedy. It was set in the typical Midwestern community of Springfield, where Jim Anderson was an agent for the General Insurance Company. Every evening he would come home from work, take off his sports jacket, put on his comfortable sweater, and deal with the everyday problems of a growing family. In contrast with most other family comedies of the period, in which one or the other of the parents was a blundering idiot, both Jim and his wife Margaret were portrayed as thoughtful, responsible adults. When a family crisis arose, Jim would calm the waters with a warm smile and some sensible advice.

When *Father Knows Best* went on television in 1954, the three children were aged 17 (Betty), 14 (Bud), and 9 (Kathy). As the seasons passed two of them graduated from high school, first Betty (1956) and then Bud (1959). Neither left home, however, both electing to go to Springfield's own State College.

The Andersons were truly an idealized family, the sort that viewers could relate to and wish to emulate. The children went through the normal problems of growing up, including those concerning school, friends, and members of the opposite sex. They didn't always agree with their parents and occasionally succeeded in asserting their independence (as when Jim and Margaret almost succeeded in pushing Betty into going to their alma mater, until they realized that she had to make her own decisions and let her choose State instead). But the bickering was minimal, and everything seemed to work out by the end of the half-hour.

Father Knows Best began as an NBC radio series in 1949, with Robert Young in the starring role. He was the only member of the radio cast who made the transition to TV in 1954. The TV series was not particularly successful at first, and CBS canceled it in March 1955. A flood of viewer protests demanding that the program be reinstated and moved to an earlier time slot so that the whole family could watch it, prompted NBC to pick it up for the following season with an 8:30 P.M. starting time. *Father Knows Best* prospered for the next five years.

The series became such a symbol of the "typical" American family that the U.S. Treasury Department commissioned the producers to film a special episode to help promote the 1959 U.S. Savings Bond Drive. The story, "24 Hours in Tyrant Land," told how the Anderson children attempted to live for a day under a make-believe dictatorship. Never aired on televison, this special episode was distributed to churches, schools, and civic organizations to show the importance of maintaining a strong American democracy.

During the 1959–1960 season, its last with original episodes, *Father Knows Best* had its most successful year, ranking sixth among all television programs. By the end of that season, however, star Robert Young had tired of the role, which he had been playing for 11 years, and decided it was time to move on to other things. This was one of the rare occasions in the history of television when production of a series ceased when it was at the peak of its popularity. CBS scheduled rerun episodes in prime time for another two years, also a rarity, and ABC reran them for another season after that. From November 1962 until February 1967, reruns were also seen on ABC in the daytime.

FATHER OF THE BRIDE

Situation Comedy

FIRST TELECAST: *September 29, 1961*

LAST TELECAST: *September 14, 1962*

BROADCAST HISTORY:

Sep 1961–Sep 1962, CBS Fri 9:30–10:00

CAST:

Stanley Banks .... Leon Ames
Ellie Banks .... Ruth Warrick
Kay Banks Dunston .... Myrna Fahey
Tommy Banks .... Rickie Sorensen
Buckley Dunston .... Burt Metcalfe
Herbert Dunston .... Ransom Sherman
Doris Dunston .... Lurene Tuttle
Delilah .... Ruby Dandridge

The adjustments parents must make when their children grow up and seek a life of their own were the subject of this comedy. Attorney Stanley Banks was not quite ready to accept his daughter Kay's decision when she announced that she was engaged to Buckley Dunston. Despite the enthusiasm of his wife Ellie, his son Tommy, his maid Delilah, and almost everyone else, Stanley was not happy about it at all. Episodes on the series involved Stanley's tribulations getting used to his prospective son-in-law and the son-in-law's parents, the planning and carrying out of the wedding, and learning to live without Kay around.

FAY

Situation Comedy

FIRST TELECAST: *September 4, 1975*

LAST TELECAST: *June 2, 1976*

BROADCAST HISTORY:

Sep 1975–Oct 1975, NBC Thu 8:30–9:00
May 1976–Jun 1976, NBC Wed 9:30–10:00

CAST:

Fay Stewart .... Lee Grant
Lillian .... Audra Lindley
Jack Stewart .... Joe Silver
Linda .... Margaret Willock
Elliott .... Stewart Moss
Danny Cassidy .... Bill Gerber
Letty .... Lillian Lehman
Al Messina .... Norman Alden

The exploits of an attractive, 40-ish divorcée who decides to become a swinging single were the subject of this short-lived and somewhat risqué comedy. After divorcing Jack, her philandering husband of 25 years, Fay first got herself a job as secretary to two off-the-wall attorneys, Danny Cassidy and Al Messina. She then moved into an apartment of her own and started dating. Onlookers to Fay's new life-style were Jack, who kept trying to get her back again, daughter Linda and son-in-law Elliott, who were appalled, and Fay's unhappily married friend Letty, who lived vicariously through Fay's affairs.

FAYE EMERSON SHOW, THE

Interview

FIRST TELECAST: *March 13, 1950*

LAST TELECAST: *December 23, 1950*

BROADCAST HISTORY:

Mar 1950–Apr 1950, CBS Mon 11:00–11:15
May 1950–Jul 1950, CBS Sun various 15 minute spots
Apr 1950–May 1950, NBC Sat 10:30–10:45
Jun 1950–Aug 1950, NBC Wed 8:00–8:15
Sep 1950–Dec 1950, CBS Tu/Th/Sat 7:45–8:00

HOSTESS:

Faye Emerson

Faye Emerson seemed to be everywhere on early television. In addition to numerous guest appearances on fashion, quiz, and dramatic shows, she hosted her own 15-minute "chat" on a variety of nights in 1950, sometimes appearing on two networks simultaneously. The format of *The Faye Emerson Show* was informal and gossipy, with Miss Emerson discussing fashions, the theater, and current celebrities and welcoming a guest from some area of show business. Perhaps her most widely publicized contribution to the new medium, however, were the gowns she wore—her trademark plunging neckline was the subject of considerable controversy during television's formative years.

From June to August 1950 Miss Emerson's NBC series was known as *Fifteen with Faye*. She also hosted several similarly formated local programs in New York, prior to and following her network run.

FAYE EMERSON'S WONDERFUL TOWN

Variety

FIRST TELECAST: *June 16, 1951*

LAST TELECAST: *April 12, 1952*

BROADCAST HISTORY:

Jun 1951–Apr 1952, CBS Sat 9:00–9:30

HOSTESS:

Faye Emerson

Each week Faye Emerson spotlighted a different city in America, using musical, dramatic, and narrative elements to convey the flavor of the city, both past and present. Guest stars for each telecast either were born in the city or had some strong association with it. In time, the scope of the show expanded to include interesting foreign cities, such as Paris and Mexico City.

FEAR AND FANCY

see *ABC Dramatic Shorts—1952–1953*

FEARLESS FOSDICK

Cartoon

FIRST TELECAST: *July 13, 1952*

LAST TELECAST: *September 28, 1952*

BROADCAST HISTORY:

Jul 1952–Sep 1952, NBC Sun 6:30–7:00

PUPPETS:

The Mary Chase Marionettes

Straight from Al Capp's comic strip "Li'l Abner" came this filmed summer series using puppets and animation. Fosdick—a parody of Dick Tracy—was Li'l Abner's favorite detective and, according to him, the world's greatest. The lantern-jawed Fosdick was abused by his boss on the police force and made barely enough money to live on, but he valiantly fought on against crime and evil. *Fearless Fosdick* premiered on June 15, 1952, on Sunday afternoon and later moved into an evening slot.

FEATHER AND FATHER GANG, THE

Crime Drama

FIRST TELECAST: *March 7, 1977*

LAST TELECAST: *August 6, 1977*

BROADCAST HISTORY:

Mar 1977–Apr 1977, ABC Mon 10:00–11:00
May 1977–Aug 1977, ABC Sat 10:00–11:00

CAST:

Toni "Feather" Danton .... Stephanie Powers
Harry Danton .... Harold J. Gould
Enzo .... Frank Delfino
Margo .... Joan Shawlee
Michael .... Monte Landis
Lou .... Lewis Charles

"Feather" was a beautiful young attorney, her father a suave, shrewd ex-con man. Together with their little band of grifters and bunco artists they comprised a crack investigative team, determined to "cheat the cheaters," the swindlers and murderers who were the targets of their investigations. Lots of disguises and elaborate ruses were used.

Harold Gould, the "father" in this show, was a rarity in show business—a Ph.D. and a former full professor of drama at UCLA who decided to practice what he taught.

FEATURE FILM

see *Movies—Prior to 1961*

FEATURE PLAYHOUSE

see *Movies—Prior to 1961*

FEATURE THEATRE

see *Movies—Prior to 1961*

FEDERAL MEN

syndicated title for *Treasury Men in Action*

FELONY SQUAD

Police Drama

FIRST TELECAST: *September 12, 1966*

LAST TELECAST: *January 31, 1969*

BROADCAST HISTORY:

Sep 1966–Sep 1968, ABC Mon 9:00–9:30
Sep 1968–Jan 1969, ABC Fri 8:30–9:00

CAST:

Det. Sgt. Sam Stone .... Howard Duff
Det. Jim Briggs .... Dennis Cole
Desk Sgt. Dan Briggs .... Ben Alexander
Capt. Nye .... Frank Maxwell
Capt. Franks (1967–1968) .... Barney Phillips

Det. Cliff Sims (1968–1969)
............................Robert DoQui

THEME:
"Felony Squad Theme," by Pete Rugulo

This police action drama was set in a large city in the West. The principals were 20-year veteran Sam Stone, his young partner Jim Briggs, and Briggs's father, Desk Sgt. Dan Briggs, a kind of paunchy house-mother to the younger cops in the station house. Capt. Nye was their commanding officer during the first and last seasons, temporarily replaced by Capt. Franks in 1967–1968. The series was filmed on location in the Los Angeles area.

FESTIVAL OF STARS

Dramatic Anthology

FIRST TELECAST: *June 30, 1956*
LAST TELECAST: *September 17, 1957*
BROADCAST HISTORY:
Jun 1956–Sep 1956, NBC Sat 9:30–10:00
Jul 1957–Sep 1957, NBC Tue 8:00–8:30
HOST:
Jim Ameche (1957)

The 1956 edition of this summer series of dramas was made up of reruns of episodes of *Ford Theatre.* When it returned the following summer, *Festival of Stars* consisted of reruns of episodes from *The Loretta Young Show* in which Miss Young had not appeared. Jim Ameche served as host of the latter series.

FIBBER MCGEE AND MOLLY

Situation Comedy

FIRST TELECAST: *September 15, 1959*
LAST TELECAST: *January 19, 1960*
BROADCAST HISTORY:
Sep 1959–Jan 1960, NBC Tue 8:30–9:00
CAST:
Fibber McGee ....Bob Sweeney
Molly McGee ....Cathy Lewis
Doc Gamble ....Addison Richards
Mayor La Trivia ....Harold Peary
Teeny ....Barbara Beaird

Fibber McGee and Molly was one of the most popular radio shows of all time, running from 1935 until 1957. In the fall of 1959 it came to television, but with much less success. The McGees were the residents of 79 Wistful Vista and, as on radio, had to cope with friends and neighbors who made life rather hilarious. Fibber's tendency to overstate—some people called it fibbing—constantly got him into trouble. Fortunately, Molly's common sense and talents as a peacemaker prevented most situations from getting out of hand. Symptomatic of the problems involved in bringing *Fibber McGee and Molly* to television was McGee's famous overcrowded hall closet, which always unleashed its contents in a crash whenever it was opened. Somehow this was not as funny seen on television as it had been when only heard on radio.

Most of the actors in the TV version had not been associated with the show on radio, but one did have an interesting connection with the earlier version. Harold Peary had created the role of Throckmorton P. Gildersleeve on *Fibber McGee and Molly* in 1939, later moving it to a series of his own as *The Great Gildersleeve.* When *Fibber McGee* came to TV, he returned as Mayor La Trivia.

FIFTEEN WITH FAYE

see *Faye Emerson Show, The*

FIFTY-FOURTH STREET REVUE, THE

Variety

FIRST TELECAST: *May 5, 1949*
LAST TELECAST: *March 25, 1950*
BROADCAST HISTORY:
May 1949–Sep 1949, CBS Thu 8:00–9:00
Sep 1949–Jan 1950, CBS Fri 9:00–10:00
Jan 1950–Mar 1950, CBS Sat 8:00–9:00
HOST:
Jack Sterling (1949)
Al Bernie (1949)
Billy Vine (1949–1950)
Joey Faye (1950)
REGULARS:
Russell Arms
Marilyn Day
Carl Reiner (1949)
Pat Bright (1949)
Cliff "Ukulele Ike" Edwards (1949)
Mort Marshall
Joe Silver
Joan Diener
Fosse and Niles
Virginia Gorski
Harry Sosnik Orchestra

This live musical and comedy revue derived its name from the street address of the New York studio in which is was produced. Its regular cast changed constantly, depending on what other jobs its members could find that were more substantial than employment in early television. Jack Sterling was the original host, soon replaced by Al Bernie. Bernie lasted until December 1949, to be replaced by Billy Vine, who lasted only two months, and finally by Joey Faye. Carl Reiner, Pat Bright, Cliff Edwards, and Marilyn Day were also early departures, with Miss Day returning for a second stint during Joey Faye's tenure as host.

FIGHT BEAT

Sports Commentary

FIRST TELECAST: *April 4, 1958*

LAST TELECAST: *December 26, 1958*

BROADCAST HISTORY:

Apr 1958–Dec 1958, NBC Fri 10:45–11:00

HOST:

Bud Palmer

Bud Palmer interviewed the winning fighters and other boxing celebrities in this short sports commentary program designed to fill the time remaining between the conclusion of the featured bout on *Cavalcade of Sports* and the 11 o'clock news. The title of the program was originally *Post Fight Beat,* but this was shortened to *Fight Beat* on May 23.

FIGHT OF THE WEEK, THE

see *Boxing*

FIGHT TALK

Sports Commentary

FIRST TELECAST: *January 24, 1953*

LAST TELECAST: *January 15, 1955*

BROADCAST HISTORY:

Jan 1953–Jan 1955, ABC Sat 9:45–10:00

COMMENTATORS:

Don Dunphy
Red Smith (1953–1954)
Bob Cook (1954–1955)

This show followed ABC's *Saturday Night Fights* and provided its two commentators with an opportunity to analyze the bout that had just been seen and make predictions and observations about other major fights that were coming up in the near future. Don Dunphy was with the show throughout its run, while Red Smith left and was replaced by Bob Cook.

FILM FAIR

see *Movies—Prior to 1961*

FILM FESTIVAL

see *ABC Dramatic Shorts—1952–1953*

FILM SHORTS

see *Movies—Prior to 1961*

FILM THEATRE OF THE AIR

see *Movies—Prior to 1961*

FIREBALL FUN-FOR-ALL

Comedy Variety

FIRST TELECAST: *June 28, 1949*

LAST TELECAST: *October 27, 1949*

BROADCAST HISTORY:

Jun 1949–Aug 1949, NBC Tue 8:00–9:00
Sep 1949–Oct 1949, NBC Thu 9:00–10:00

HOSTS:

Ole Olsen and Chick Johnson

REGULARS:

Bill Hayes
Marty May
June Johnson
J. C. Olsen
The Buick Belles

ORCHESTRA:

Al Goodman (Jun–Jul)
Charles Sanford (Jul–Oct)

This comedy free-for-all, hosted by old-time vaudevillians Olsen and Johnson, was based on their Broadway hit *Hellzapoppin'*. Gimmick props, midgets running frantically across the stage, leggy showgirls, seltzer water, and custard pies were all the stock-in-trade of this noisy and unpredictable revue, which generally resembled organized mayhem. At the beginning many of the gags took place in the studio audience, but when the show returned after a brief summer hiatus the action tended to be more confined to the stage.

The program was directed and staged by Ezra Stone, one of the stars of the *Henry Aldrich* series. June Johnson and J. C. Olsen were the daughter and son, respectively, of the show's hosts.

FIREHOUSE

Adventure

FIRST TELECAST: *January 17, 1974*

LAST TELECAST: *August 1, 1974*

BROADCAST HISTORY:

Jan 1974–Aug 1974, ABC Thu 8:30–9:00

CAST:

Capt. Spike Ryerson .... James Drury
Hank Myers .... Richard Jaeckel
Sonny Caputo .... Michael Delano
Billy Dalzell .... Brad David
Cal Dakin .... Bill Overton

In 1972 a crudely written but true-to-life book titled *Report from Engine Co. 82*, whose author was a real-life fireman, shot to the top of the bestseller list. About a year and a half later, a crudely produced but hopefully true-to-life television series called *Firehouse* premiered on the ABC network. Was it coincidence? Where do you suppose TV producers find their inspirations?

James Drury portrayed the father figure to the young smoke-eaters of Engine Co. 23 in this action drama. They encountered various disasters and performed various rescues each week; one of the more interesting of these was a man in traction whose house was about to slide off a hill. The firemen couldn't get into his room to maneuver him out without setting off the tilting house. How did they get him out? Sorry, series canceled.

FIRESIDE ARENA THEATRE

Dramatic Anthology

FIRST TELECAST: *July 3, 1951*

LAST TELECAST: *August 21, 1951*

BROADCAST HISTORY:

Jul 1951–Aug 1951, NBC Tue 9:00–9:30

PRODUCER/DIRECTOR:

Albert McCleery

This summer replacement for *Fireside Theater* was quite a different program, presenting eight weeks of live drama in a theater-in-the-round setting. A minimum of scenery and props was used, as the camera focused closely on the actors and the story.

FIRESIDE THEATRE

Dramatic Anthology

FIRST TELECAST: *April 5, 1949*

LAST TELECAST: *September 8, 1963*

BROADCAST HISTORY:

Apr 1949–Jun 1957, NBC Tue 9:00–9:30 (OS)

Sep 1957–May 1958, NBC Thu 10:30–11:00

Jun 1963–Sep 1963, ABC Sun 8:00–8:30

HOST:

Frank Wisbar (1952–1953)

Gene Raymond (1953–1955)

Jane Wyman (1955–1958)

Fireside Theatre was one of the earliest filmed dramatic shows produced especially for television. However, for its first three months this series was a showcase of new program ideas, some live and some on film, which were being tried out for possible inclusion on the network schedule. These included dramas, comedies, and musical revues. The very first episode was a situation comedy, "Friend of the Family," starring Virginia Gilmore, Yul Brynner, and Peter Barry. One of the musical revues was Leonard Sillman's "New Faces." Win Elliot was the original announcer for the show, but he left after eight telecasts, after which there was no regular announcer or host for the next few years.

In the fall of 1949 *Fireside Theatre* switched to filmed stories, mostly dramas, featuring a wide range of actors and actresses (generally not big names). According to *TV Guide* these were "quickie" films, each one ground out in two or three days at the Hal Roach studios in Hollywood. Most of them were produced by Frank Wisbar. During the 1949–1950 season the majority of these little dramas were 15 minutes long (there were two per week), but beginning in the fall of 1950 and for the rest of the series each telecast was a self-contained 30-minute presentation.

In the fall of 1952 producer Frank Wisbar began appearing at the start of each week's telecast, in an effort to give the series greater continuity. From 1953–1955 actor Gene Raymond was the host, in addition to appearing in many of the dramas. For the 1954–1955 season an effort was also made to develop a regular repertory company of actors and actresses, including William Bendix, George Brent, and Dorothy Malone.

The hostess who is most identified with the show in viewers' minds—Jane Wyman—made her first appearance in 1955. The movie actress also starred in many of the episodes during her association with the show. The program was renamed in her honor (eventually it became simply *The Jane Wyman Show*) and special theme music was written for her. Well-known actors and actresses were engaged for the weeks when Miss Wyman did not star, among them Keenan Wynn, Peter

Lawford, Dan Duryea, Ozzie Nelson, John Ireland, Gene Lockhart, Imogene Coca, Gene Barry, Joseph Cotten, and Vincent Price, plus many lesser-known Hollywood standbys. The program continued until the spring of 1958, when it was finally retired—to begin a very long run in syndication.

Reruns were shown on NBC as a summer replacement in 1954 and on the ABC network during the summer of 1963 (as *Jane Wyman Presents*).

Fireside Theatre, with and without Miss Wyman, was one of the most durable dramatic anthologies of the 1950s. Though generally not rising to the star-studded heights of *Studio One* or *Robert Montgomery Presents*, it did produce hundreds of fine dramas and also proved the practicality and value of a filmed series for the TV medium.

FIRST NIGHTER

see *Movies—Prior to 1961*

FIRST PERSON

see *Gulf Playhouse: 1st Person*

FISH

Situation Comedy

FIRST TELECAST: *February 5, 1977*
LAST TELECAST: *June 8, 1978*
BROADCAST HISTORY:
Feb 1977–May 1977, ABC Sat 8:30–9:00
Jun 1977–Aug 1977, ABC Thu 9:30–10:00
Aug 1977–Nov 1977, ABC Sat 8:00–8:30
Jan 1978–Apr 1978, ABC Thu 8:30–9:00
May 1978–Jun 1978, ABC Thu 9:30–10:00
CAST:
Det. Phil Fish .... Abe Vigoda
Bernice Fish .... Florence Stanley
Mike .... Lenny Bari
Loomis .... Todd Bridges
Victor Kreutzer .... John Cassisi
Jilly .... Denise Miller
Diane .... Sarah Natoli
Charlie Harrison .... Barry Gordon

Detective Fish, the dilapidated cop in the hit series *Barney Miller*, got his own show in 1977. It was unusual in that he not only remained in character, but for several months continued to appear in *Barney Miller* as well. *Fish* simply presented the domestic side of his life.

Fish and his wife Bernice had decided to move out of their New York apartment and into a run-down house, in order to become foster parents to five P.I.N.S.—the social workers' term for "Persons in Need of Supervision." The term was an understatement, for the five racially mixed street kids were constantly causing problems. Loomis was the cut-up of the lot, the preteen hipster who befriended the dead cat in Fish's basement. Mike was the oldest, charming but streetwise. Victor was the blustery tough guy, Jilly the angelic con artist, and Diane the young TV addict. Psychologist Charlie Harrison (played by onetime child star Barry Gordon) tended to be too impractical to help very much, leaving huffing, puffing Fish and chattering Bernice to quell each uproar and reestablish normalcy.

FISHING AND HUNTING CLUB

Sports

FIRST TELECAST: *September 30, 1949*
LAST TELECAST: *March 31, 1950*
BROADCAST HISTORY:
Sep 1949–Mar 1950, DUM Fri 9:00–9:30
HOST:
Bill Slater

This sports interview and demonstration program featured Bill Slater and experts from various fields. The title was changed on January 20, 1950, to *Sports for All*.

FITZPATRICKS, THE

General Drama

FIRST TELECAST: *September 5, 1977*
LAST TELECAST: *January 10, 1978*
BROADCAST HISTORY:
Sep 1977, CBS Mon 9:00–10:00
Sep 1977–Jan 1978, CBS Tue 8:00–9:00
CAST:
Mike Fitzpatrick .... Bert Kramer
Maggie Fitzpatrick ...... Mariclare Costello
Sean Fitzpatrick .... Clark Brandon
Jack Fitzpatrick .. James Vincent McNichol
Maureen (Mo) Fitzpatrick ... Michele Tobin
Max Fitzpatrick .... Sean Marshall
R. J. .... Derek Wells
Kerry .... Helen Hunt

Flint, Michigan, was the setting for this warm family drama about a middle-class Catholic family trying to make ends meet. The father, Mike Fitzpatrick, was a steelworker who put in lots of overtime, and mother Maggie worked part-time at a diner to help supplement the family income. The rest of the family consisted of four children—Sean (16), Jack (15), Mo (14), and Max (10)—and a mangy dog named Detroit. Seen regularly were Max's best friend R. J. and Kerry, the cute girl next door whose flirting with both of the older Fitzpatrick boys intensified their sibling rivalry. The stories were often little lessons in morality and growing up, making this series something like a modern-day *Waltons*. Previewed by CBS on a Monday night early in September, *The Fitzpatricks* moved into its regular Tuesday time slot two weeks later.

FIVE FINGERS

Spy Drama

FIRST TELECAST: *October 3, 1959*
LAST TELECAST: *January 9, 1960*
BROADCAST HISTORY:
Oct 1959–Jan 1960, NBC Sat 9:30–10:30
CAST:
Victor Sebastian .... David Hedison
Simone Genet .... Luciana Paluzzi
Robertson .... Paul Burke

Victor Sebastian was an American counterspy posing as a Communist agent in Europe. His code name was "Five Fingers," and his mission, to feed information on Communist activities to the United States government. Sebastian's public cover was that of a theatrical booking agent who placed musical talent in clubs and cafés all over the Continent. In this capacity he traveled with a beautiful young fashion model, Simone Genet, who aspired to become a singer. Romance blossomed between them, which complicated their relationship since she was not aware of his espionage activities. The only person who did know was Robertson, Sebastian's American contact. Victor and Simone's relationship provided both humorous and romantic counterpoint to the main theme of international intrigue.

The series was based, rather loosely, on a successful 1952 film of the same name directed by Joseph L. Mankiewiez and starring James Mason and Danielle Darrieux.

FIVE STAR JUBILEE

Musical Variety

FIRST TELECAST: *March 17, 1961*
LAST TELECAST: *September 22, 1961*
BROADCAST HISTORY:
Mar 1961–Apr 1961, NBC Fri 8:00–8:30
May 1961–Sep 1961, NBC Fri 8:30–9:00
STARS:
Snooky Lanson
Tex Ritter
Jimmy Wakely
Carl Smith
Rex Allen
REGULARS:
Slim Wilson and His Jubilee Band

The five stars of this Country music variety show appeared separately, on a rotating basis. The program featured square dancing as well as guest stars and originated from Springfield, Missouri. Although a network offering, *Five Star Jubilee* was never telecast in New York because of its primarily rural appeal.

FLIGHT #7

Travelogue

FIRST TELECAST: *June 14, 1954*
LAST TELECAST: *August 31, 1957*
BROADCAST HISTORY:
Jun 1954–Aug 1954, ABC Mon 7:30–7:45
Aug 1954–Feb 1955, ABC Sun 8:00–8:30
Jun 1955–Sep 1955, ABC Sat 7:00–7:30
Jun 1957–Aug 1957, ABC Sat 7:30–8:00

This summer series presented travel films, generally of areas outside the continental United States.

FLIGHT TO RHYTHM

Music

FIRST TELECAST: *May 15, 1949*
LAST TELECAST: *September 22, 1949*
BROADCAST HISTORY:
May 1949–Jul 1949, DUM Sun 6:30–7:00
Aug 1949–Sep 1949, DUM Thu 8:00–8:30
REGULARS:
Delora Bueno
Miguelito Valdez Orchestra

This 1949 summer series featured latin music, with vocalist Delora Bueno.

FLINTSTONES, THE

Cartoon

FIRST TELECAST: *September 30, 1960*
LAST TELECAST: *September 2, 1966*
BROADCAST HISTORY:
Sep 1960–Sep 1963, ABC Fri 8:30–9:00
Sep 1963–Dec 1964, ABC Thu 7:30–8:00
Dec 1964–Sep 1966, ABC Fri 7:30–8:00
VOICES:
Fred Flintstone .... Alan Reed

Wilma Flintstone ....Jean Vander Pyl
Barney Rubble ....Mel Blanc
Betty Rubble (1960–1964) ...Bea Benaderet
Betty Rubble (1964–1966) .....Gerry Johnson
Dino the Dinosaur ....Mel Blanc
Pebbles (1962–1966) ......Jean Vander Pyl
Bamm Bamm (1963–1966) ....Don Messick

CO-PRODUCERS:
Bill Hanna, Joe Barbera

The Flintstones was a parody on modern suburban life, set in the Stone Age. The characters in the cartoon series all behaved and spoke in a contemporary manner, though they lived in the prehistoric city of Bedrock. Fred worked as operator of a dinosaur-powered crane at the Rock Head & Quarry Cave Construction Co. (slogan: "Own Your Own Cave and Be Secure"). Around their split-level cave the Flintstones enjoyed such conveniences as Wilma's Stoneway piano, a hi-fi on which Fred could play his "rock" music (it consisted of a turntable and a bird with a long beak to serve as the needle), a vacuum cleaner (a baby elephant with a long trunk), and an automatic garbage-disposal unit (a famished buzzard stashed under the sink). Their car, which sported tail fins, also came equipped with steamroller wheels—to smooth out the rocky road.

At first the Flintstones had only Dino, their pet dinosaur, around the cave to play with. Then one day in 1962 they were blessed with a baby daughter, whom they named Pebbles. Not to be outdone, their neighbors the Rubbles adopted an orphan boy named Bamm Bamm. (The two kids later had a Saturday morning cartoon series of their own, *Pebbles and Bamm Bamm*.)

The Flintstones was always as much adult satire as children's fun. In many respects it resembled Jackie Gleason's popular *Honeymooners*, especially in the relationships of the principals. A wide range of caricatures passed through the stories: Lollobrickida, a pretty cook; Ann-Margrock, whose voice was supplied by Ann-Margret; attorney Perry Masonry (he never lost a case); Ed Sullyston, a TV host; Eddy Brianstone, a teenage impresario; and Weirdly and Creepella Gruesome, the strange couple who with their son Goblin moved into a cave nearby (this was a parody on *The Addams Family* and *The Munsters*, then popular). The Gruesomes thought that they were normal, and everyone *else* in Bedrock was odd.

In addition to being the longest-running animated series in prime-time history, *The Flintstones* and its spinoffs continued on Saturday mornings well into the 1970s.

FLIP WILSON SHOW, THE

Comedy Variety

FIRST TELECAST: *September 17, 1970*
LAST TELECAST: *June 27, 1974*
BROADCAST HISTORY:
Sep 1970–Jun 1971, NBC Thu 7:30–8:30
Sep 1971–Jun 1974, NBC Thu 8:00–9:00 (OS)

HOST:
Flip Wilson

Comic Flip Wilson was the first black performer to achieve major popularity as host of his own variety hour. *The Flip Wilson Show* was an enormous hit, placing number two among all programs on television during its first two seasons. Although music and guests were an important part of the format, Flip's comedy was the real focal point of the series. In various skits he played a collection of stock characters, which included: Geraldine Jones, sassy, swinging, liberated woman with a very jealous boy friend named "Killer"; Reverend LeRoy of the Church of What's Happening Now, a gospel preacher who seemed to be slightly less than honest and just a touch lecherous; Danny Danger, private detective; and Herbie, the Good Time Ice Cream Man. Flip's best known expression was a wide-eyed "The Devil made me do it!"

FLIPPER

Adventure

FIRST TELECAST: *September 19, 1964*
LAST TELECAST: *September 1, 1968*
BROADCAST HISTORY:
Sep 1964–Sep 1967, NBC Sat 7:30–8:00
Jan 1968–Jun 1968, NBC Sun 6:30–7:00
Jun 1968–Sep 1968, NBC Sun 7:00–7:30

CAST:
Porter Ricks ....Brian Kelly
Sandy Ricks ....Luke Halpin
Bud Ricks ....Tommy Norden
Hap Gorman (1964–1965) .....Andy Devine
Ulla Norstrand (1965–1966) .... Ulla Stromstedt

Porter "Po" Ricks was the chief ranger of Coral Key Park, Florida, responsible for protecting both the game fish and the skin divers in the park. A widower, he lived with his two children, 15-year-old Sandy and 10-year-old Bud, in a cottage near the shore. The real star of the series was the boys' pet dolphin, Flipper, who was both friend and helper in their weekly adventures. The stories generally revolved around Flipper and his two young companions, with Bud involved more often than Sandy. Also regularly seen during the first season was Hap Gorman, an old marine carpenter with endless numbers of stories about sea life and adventures. During the second season Ulla Norstrand, an attractive oceanographer, was a regular character.

The role of Flipper was played by a dolphin named Suzy.

FLOOR SHOW, THE

see *Eddie Condon's Floor Show*

FLYING HIGH

Adventure

FIRST TELECAST: *September 29, 1978*
LAST TELECAST:
BROADCAST HISTORY:

Sep 1978– , CBS Fri 10:00–11:00

CAST:

Marcy Bowers .... Pat Klous
Lisa Benton .... Connie Sellecca
Pam Bellagio .... Kathryn Witt
Capt. Doug March .... Howard Platt

Marcy, Lisa, and Pam were three sexy young girls who had just graduated from flight attendant school. As stewardesses for Sunwest Airlines, they had romantic, interesting and occasionally dangerous adventures. All three worked on the same jumbo jet, and reported to Captain Doug March. Sometimes the episodes centered on the girls' working hours and sometimes on their active social lives. The three actresses who played the leads in this series were all former New York City based models, with little previous acting experience. In an effort to make their roles more believeable, they met with groups of real flight attendants prior to starting production on the series, to hear about actual incidents that had occurred on real flights and the manner in which the stewardesses had handled them.

FLYING NUN, THE

Situation Comedy

FIRST TELECAST: *September 7, 1967*
LAST TELECAST: *September 18, 1970*
BROADCAST HISTORY:

Sep 1967–Jan 1969, ABC Thu 8:00–8:30
Feb 1969–Sep 1969, ABC Thu 7:30–8:00
Sep 1969–Jan 1970, ABC Wed 7:30–8:00
Jan 1970–Sep 1970, ABC Fri 7:30–8:00

CAST:

Sister Bertrille .... Sally Field
Sister Jacqueline .... Marge Redmond
Mother Superior ..... Madeleine Sherwood
Carlos Ramirez .... Alejandro Rey
Sister Sixto .... Shelly Morrison
Sister Ana .... Linda Dangcil
Police Capt. Gaspar Formento (1968–1969) .... Vito Scotti
Marcello, the orphan boy (1969–1970) .... Manuel Padilla, Jr.

The subject of this comedy was Sister Bertrille, a bright, effusive young novice—the former Elsie Ethington—who brightened the lives of all at the ancient Convent San Tanco, situated on a hilltop near San Juan, Puerto Rico. Not the least of Sister Bertrille's attributes was that she could fly. How? Well, "when lift plus thrust is greater than load plus drag," any object can fly, including sister Bertrille, who weighed only 90 pounds. Whenever a stiff wind caught the starched cornette worn by her order, off she went.

These aerodynamics were not always pleasant. Occasionally Sister Bertrille would get dunked in the ocean or be thrust in the midst of unlikely goings-on, and once she was almost shot down as an enemy aircraft (a pelican once fell in love with her, too). Least impressed was her staid, conservative Mother Superior. But Sister Bertrille got along well with the wise and humorous Sister Jacqueline, and with Sister Sixto, the Puerto Rican nun who fought a running battle with the English language. Sister Bertrille was also admired—from a distance—by Carlos Ramirez, the rich, handsome playboy owner of a discotheque in town who was a patron of the convent.

Believe it or not, *The Flying Nun* was commended by some religious orders—for "humanizing" nuns and their work. It was based on the book *The Fifteenth Pelican*, by Tere Rios.

FLYING TIGERS, THE

Wartime Adventure

FIRST TELECAST: *April 14, 1951*

LAST TELECAST: *May 26, 1951*

BROADCAST HISTORY:

Apr 1951–May 1951, DUM Sat 6:30–7:00

CAST:

Eric Fleming

Luis Van Rooten

This action-adventure series featured the famous United States flying squadron stationed in China during World War II. Lean, handsome Eric Fleming, the star of many Hollywood "B" films, played the lead. The series was later seen on Sunday afternoons with Ed Peck in the lead role.

FOCUS

Documentary

FIRST TELECAST: *March 18, 1952*

LAST TELECAST: *October 10, 1957*

This was a blanket title for documentary films carried by ABC in various 15-minute and half-hour time slots, usually for short periods of time, between 1952 and 1957.

FOCUS ON AMERICA

Documentary

FIRST TELECAST: *June 27, 1961*

LAST TELECAST: *September 10, 1963*

BROADCAST HISTORY:

Jun 1961–Sep 1961, ABC Tue 7:00–7:30

Jul 1962–Sep 1962, ABC Wed 8:00–8:30

Jul 1963–Sep 1963, ABC Tue 10:30–11:00

HOST:

Bill Shadel (1962)

Don Goddard (1963)

Documentaries that had originally been produced and aired by local ABC affiliates were telecast over the entire ABC network during three summers in the early 1960s. They were selected by members of the ABC News Department as examples of the best of locally originated informational programming, and ranged from "Clipper Ships and Paddle Wheels" (KGO-TV, San Francisco) to "Cows, Cowboys and Cow Country" (KOCO-TV, Oklahoma City) to "To The Moon and Beyond" (WTVN-TV, Columbus).

FOLLOW THAT MAN

syndicated title for *Man Against Crime*

FOLLOW THE LEADER

Quiz/Audience Participation

FIRST TELECAST: *July 7, 1953*

LAST TELECAST: *August 4, 1953*

BROADCAST HISTORY:

Jul 1953–Aug 1953, CBS Tue 9:00–9:30

HOSTESS:

Vera Vague

This live show, which was telecast from Hollywood, gave members of the studio audience the opportunity to see how well they could imitate a scene pantomimed by actress Vera Vague (whose real name was Barbara Jo Allen).

FOLLOW THE SUN

Adventure

FIRST TELECAST: *September 17, 1961*

LAST TELECAST: *September 9, 1962*

BROADCAST HISTORY:

Sep 1961–Sep 1962, ABC Sun 7:30–8:30

CAST:

Ben Gregory .... Barry Coe

Paul Templin .... Brett Halsey

Eric Jason .... Gary Lockwood

Katherine Ann Richards ...... Gigi Perreau

Lt. Frank Roper .... Jay Lanin

This adventure series focused on the exploits of two footloose, handsome, free-lance magazine writers living in Hawaii. Ben and Paul's bachelor pad was a plush penthouse in Honolulu, and they both led active social lives when not facing danger in pursuit of a story (their articles were not intended for the faint of heart). Helping them was Eric Jason, who did much of the legwork for their articles; Kathy Richards, who was a part-time secretary and full-time student at the University of Honolulu; and Lt. Roper of the Honolulu Police, who bailed them out whenever they got in over their heads.

FOOTBALL

Sports

FIRST TELECAST: *October 3, 1950*

LAST TELECAST:

BROADCAST HISTORY:

Oct 1950–Jan 1951, ABC Tue 8:00–8:30

Sep 1953–Dec 1953, ABC Sun 7:45–9:00

Oct 1953–Nov 1953, DUM Sat 8:00–Conclusion

Oct 1954–Nov 1954, DUM Sat 8:00–Conclusion

Oct 1957–Nov 1957, ABC Sun 10:00–10:30

Nov 1957–Dec 1957, ABC Sun 9:30–10:00
Aug 1959–Oct 1959, ABC Sat 11:0C–Conclusion
Sep 1970– , ABC Mon 9:00–Conclusion (Sep–Dec each year)

ANNOUNCERS:
Bill Fisher (1950–1951)
Harry Wismer (1953)
Ford Bond (1953)
Chuck Thompson (1954, 1959)
Chick Hearn (1957)
Howard Cosell (1959, 1970–)
Keith Jackson (1970)
Don Meredith (1970–1973, 1977–)
Frank Gifford (1971–)
Fred Williamson (1974)
Alex Karras (1974–1976)

The 1950–1951 season brought a weekly highlight film of a major college football game to ABC. Titled *The Game of the Week*, it was narrated by Bill Fisher. Three years later, ABC was back with a nighttime football series featuring the most popular college team in football history. *Notre Dame Football*, with Harry Wismer and Ford Bond doing the play-by-play, was still a highlight film, but a more extensive one than the half-hour series aired in 1950. It was edited to 75 minutes in length, leaving out only dull and uneventful plays. Wismer did double duty that fall, also announcing the weekly *Pro Football* game carried live by DuMont on Saturday nights. This was the same Harry Wismer who, a decade later, was the original owner of the New York Titans of the fledgling American Football League (later to become the New York Jets). DuMont was back with *Pro Football* in 1954, but Chuck Thompson had replaced Wismer at the mike. The year 1957 saw the revival of ABC's first football series, as *The All-American Football Game of the Week*, which highlighted a major college game of the weekend, this time narrated by Chick Hearn.

Professional football made its first appearance on ABC in the fall of 1959, but it wasn't until a decade later that it really became successful as a prime-time series. The 1959 series, which ran at 11:00 P.M. on Saturday nights, consisted of a full-length viedotape replay of a game that had been played earlier that day. Commentators were Chuck Thompson and Howard Cosell. When, in the spring of 1970, ABC secured the rights from the National Football League to carry a regularly scheduled *Monday Night Football* game that fall, it was around Cosell's caustic personality that the announcing team was organized. Whereas the traditional way of covering football was with two people, a play-by-play announcer and a color man to add insights and observations, ABC decided to put three people in the booth. Keith Jackson did the play-by-play during the first season, with Frank Gifford assuming that role in 1971. The other two commentators, Cosell and Don Meredith, were there to inform, observe, and entertain. It was this last aspect of their work that offended sports traditionalists. At times, especially during boring games, the men in the booth seemed to lose touch completely with what was happening on the field. They were accused of turning a sport into an entertainment show, but as long as the ratings were high enough (which they always were), they received full support from ABC's management. When Don Meredith left the show after the 1973 season, Fred Williamson was picked to replace him. The easy banter that had existed between Cosell and Meredith was absent; Fred was wooden and seemed intimidated on the air, and he lasted less than one month. Alex Karras, another former player who was more relaxed (he had announced Canadian football the previous season) and a natural clown, replaced Williamson, staying with the show until Meredith's return in 1977.

FOOTBALL NEWS

see *New York Giants Quarterback Huddle*

FOOTBALL SIDELINES

Sports

FIRST TELECAST: *October 6, 1952*
LAST TELECAST: *December 29, 1952*
BROADCAST HISTORY:
Oct 1952–Dec 1952, DUM Mon 9:30–9:45
HOST:
Harry Wismer

Football Sidelines filled half of a 30-minute sports block that preceded the Monday night fights on DuMont in 1952. (The second half consisted of film clips of *Famous Fights.*) Here Wismer commented on filmed highlights from the previous weekend's football action.

FOOTBALL THIS WEEK

Sports

FIRST TELECAST: *October 11, 1951*
LAST TELECAST: *December 6, 1951*
BROADCAST HISTORY:
Oct 1951–Dec 1951, DUM Thu 10:45–11:00

This program featured filmed highlights of the major college football games of the preceding weekend.

FOOTLIGHTS THEATER

Dramatic Anthology

FIRST TELECAST: *July 4, 1952*
LAST TELECAST: *September 11, 1953*
BROADCAST HISTORY:
Jul 1952–Sep 1952, CBS Fri 9:30–10:00
Jul 1953–Sep 1953, CBS Fri 9:30–10:00

For two summers this anthology series aired on CBS, presenting adaptations of plays and novels as well as original stories. The 1952 version was broadcast live from New York, while 1953 saw filmed dramas presented under the same title. Lesser-known and predominantly younger actors and actresses were featured in the plays, with various episodes starring Victor Jory, Gig Young, Lloyd Bridges, Gale Storm, Barbara Hale, and Lynn Bari.

FOR THE PEOPLE

Police Drama

FIRST TELECAST: *January 31, 1965*
LAST TELECAST: *May 9, 1965*
BROADCAST HISTORY:
Jan 1965–May 1965, CBS Sun 9:00–10:00
CAST:
David Koster ....William Shatner
Anthony Celese ....Howard Da Silva
Frank Malloy ....Lonny Chapman
Phyllis Koster ....Jessica Walter

William Shatner played David Koster, a strong-willed New York City assistant district attorney. David's passion for justice often brought him more trouble than he could handle, both from his superiors and from members of the criminal underground, who had little love for his obsessive dedication. Trying to keep David under tight rein, despite his admiration for the young prosecutor's zeal, was bureau chief Anthony Celese, his immediate boss. Helping David to ferret out criminals was detective Frank Malloy. David's wife, Phyllis, was a viola player in a classical string quartet, and had a life and priorities of her own that sometimes conflicted with his.

FOR YOUR PLEASURE

Music

FIRST TELECAST: *April 15, 1948*
LAST TELECAST: *September 10, 1949*
BROADCAST HISTORY:
Apr 1948–Jun 1948, NBC Thu 8:00–8:15
Jul 1948–Sep 1948, NBC Wed 8:00–8:15
Jul 1949–Sep 1949, NBC Sat 8:30–9:00
REGULARS:
Kyle MacDonnell
Norman Paris Trio
DANCERS:
Jack and Jill (Apr–Jun 1948);
Blaire and Deane (Jun–Sep 1948)
ORCHESTRA:
Conducted by Earl Shelton (Jun–Sep 1949)

This live studio musical program featured Kyle MacDonnell, the pretty singing star of Broadway's *Make Mine Manhattan* and one of the most frequently seen "personalities" on early TV screens. The program was set in a nightclub with Kyle strolling among the tables, chatting with guests and singing a song or two. TV-set owners in 1948 had to put up with a lot of inconveniences to watch the winsome Miss MacDonnell, however. A *New York Times* reviewer complained that "the lighting has been particularly erratic, at times almost blotting out Miss MacDonnell and the other artists in a haze of whiteness, and at other moments reflecting both skill and thought. More rehearsal . . . should correct such defects."

See *Girl about Town* for the continuation of this program in similar format.

FORD FESTIVAL

Musical Variety

FIRST TELECAST: *April 5, 1951*
LAST TELECAST: *June 26, 1952*
BROADCAST HISTORY:
Apr 1951–Dec 1951, NBC Thu 9:00–10:00
Jan 1952–Jun 1952, NBC Thu 9:30–10:30
REGULARS:
James Melton
Dorothy Warrenskjold
Vera Vague
The Wiere Brothers
Billy Barty

Ford Festival was originally a loosely structured "book" show in which a simple plot served to tie together performances by the singing star of the show, James Melton, and his semi-regulars, singer Dorothy Warrenskjold, comedienne Vera Vague (Barbara Jo Allen), and comedy singers The Wiere Brothers. On June 7, 1951, the format was changed to that of a straight revue, and all pretense of plot was dropped. Billy Barty was added to the cast of regulars the following week and The Wiere Brothers were dropped.

FORD SHOW, THE

Musical Variety

FIRST TELECAST: *October 4, 1956*

LAST TELECAST: *June 29, 1961*

BROADCAST HISTORY:

Oct 1956–Jun 1961, NBC Thu 9:30–10:00 (OS)

REGULARS:

Tennessee Ernie Ford
The Voices of Walter Schumann (1956–1957)
The Top Twenty (1957–1961)

Tennessee Ernie Ford was host, singer, comedian, and star of this variety show, whose title referred not to him, but to its sponsor, the Ford Motor Company. Ernie's informal, friendly quality set the tone for the program, which included his reminiscences about growing up in Bristol, Tennessee, and his homespun catch phrases ("Bless your pea-pickin' hearts!"). The musical portion of the program consisted mostly of Country and Western and gospel music, for which Ernie was famous, and the show generally ended with a hymn. The choral group "The Voices of Walter Schumann" backed Ernie during his first season; "The Top Twenty," a more contemporary mixed singing group, performed those duties for the remainder of the show's run.

FORD STAR REVUE

Comedy Variety

FIRST TELECAST: *July 6, 1950*

LAST TELECAST: *March 29, 1951*

BROADCAST HISTORY:

Jul 1950–Sep 1950, NBC Thu 9:00–10:00
Jan 1951–Mar 1951, NBC Thu 9:00–10:00

EMCEE:

Jack Haley

REGULARS:

Havel Brothers (Jul–Sep 1950)
Dr. Roy K. Marshall
Mindy Carson (Jan–Mar 1951)
Carl Hoff Orchestra (Jan–Mar 1951)
Ted Adolphus Dancers (Jan–Mar 1951)

This musical comedy–variety series began as a summer replacement for *Kay Kyser's Kollege of Musical Knowledge*, then was given its own regular season slot (briefly) in early 1951. Many famous guest stars and semi-regular performers came and went during the life of the show. Haley, who is perhaps best known for his role as the Tin Woodman in the 1939 movie classic *The Wizard of Oz*, failed to catch on as a TV host and the program was soon canceled.

Among the writers for the 1951 edition was Norman Lear.

FORD STARTIME

see *Startime*

FORD THEATRE

Dramatic Anthology

FIRST TELECAST: *October 7, 1949*

LAST TELECAST: *July 10, 1957*

BROADCAST HISTORY:

Oct 1949–Jun 1951, CBS Fri 9:00–10:00 (OS)
Oct 1952–Sep 1956, NBC Thu 9:30–10:00
Oct 1956–Jul 1957, ABC Wed 9:30–10:00

Ford Theatre began as a monthly series of live hour-long dramatic plays on CBS on October 17, 1948. It became a regular series a year later, airing on alternate Friday nights with other dramatic shows. The live CBS edition used New York-based actors and actresses, primarily those working on Broadway. Among the plays aired during this period were an adaptation of *Little Women*, with Peggy Ann Garner, Kim Hunter, and June Lockhart; *Twentieth Century*, with Fredric March and Lilli Palmer; and *One Sunday Afternoon*, with Hume Cronyn and Burgess Meredith.

After a season's absence, *Ford Theatre* returned to the air on NBC in October 1952, as a filmed series of half-hour plays. This version of the show remained on NBC for four years and then moved to ABC for a final season. With the shift to film, the production moved to Hollywood and the episodes starred motion-picture performers. The scope ranged from light comedy to heavy drama and consisted of adaptations of plays and novels as well as original stories. Such familiar names as Charles Coburn, Barry Sullivan, Peter Lawford, Thomas Mitchell, Ann Sheridan,

Claudette Colbert, Ida Lupino, and Teresa Wright starred in these shows. Ronald Reagan and his wife Nancy Davis made their first professional appearance together in this series, on February 5, 1953, in a teleplay titled "First Born."

FOREIGN LEGION

see *Assignment: Foreign Legion*

FOUR IN ONE

General Drama

FIRST TELECAST: *September 16, 1970*
LAST TELECAST: *September 8, 1971*
BROADCAST HISTORY:
Sep 1970–Sep 1971, NBC Wed 10:00–11:00

Four in One was an umbrella title for a group of four mini-series, each of which was aired for a period of six consecutive weeks and then was rerun on a rotating basis. See *McCloud, San Francisco International Airport, Night Gallery*, and *The Psychiatrist*.

FOUR SQUARE COURT

Discussion

FIRST TELECAST: *March 16, 1952*
LAST TELECAST: *June 29, 1952*
BROADCAST HISTORY:
Mar 1952–May 1952, ABC Sun 7:30–8:00
May 1952–Jun 1952, ABC Sun 9:00–9:30
MODERATOR:
Norman Brokenshire

Many TV entertainment series have dealt with criminals of various types. This was probably the only network series ever to star the real thing: masked ex-convicts out on parole, who appeared each week to discuss their crimes and rehabilitation. No doubt the parolees watched their language on this live, coast-to-coast show, as state parole board officials appeared on the panel with them. The program emanated from New York.

FOUR STAR PLAYHOUSE

Dramatic Anthology

FIRST TELECAST: *September 25, 1952*
LAST TELECAST: *September 27, 1956*
BROADCAST HISTORY:
Sep 1952–Sep 1954, CBS Thu 8:30–9:00
Oct 1954–Sep 1956, CBS Thu 9:30–10:00
REGULARS:
David Niven
Charles Boyer
Dick Powell
Ida Lupino

When *Four Star Playhouse* was announced, the four stars who were supposed to appear on a rotating basis were Charles Boyer, Dick Powell, Rosalind Russell, and Joel McCrea. Russell and McCrea never made it and were replaced by David Niven and Ida Lupino. Although *Four Star Playhouse* was essentially an anthology, one continuing character did make numerous appearances. That was nightclub owner Willie Dante, portrayed by Dick Powell. A later series based on Powell's characterization, *Dante's Inferno*, appeared on NBC in 1960 with Howard Duff in the title role.

The format of the individual episodes varied greatly, with the content ranging from comedy to drama. The four stars were not the only headliners, especially during the first two seasons. Others who were featured over the years were Ronald Colman, Merle Oberon, Joan Fontaine, Teresa Wright, and Frank Lovejoy.

Four Star Playhouse was originally an alternate-week series, expanding to a weekly basis in September 1953.

FOUR STAR REVUE

see *All Star Revue*

FRANK LEAHY SHOW, THE

Sports Commentary

FIRST TELECAST: *September 27, 1953*
LAST TELECAST: *December 6, 1953*
BROADCAST HISTORY:
Sep 1953–Dec 1953, ABC Sun 7:45–8:00
HOST:
Frank Leahy

The Frank Leahy Show was the pregame show leading up to *Notre Dame Football* in 1953. Notre Dame coach Frank Leahy would interview the coach of the team that Notre Dame had played the previous day. Following their discussion, the highlights of the game itself were shown on *Notre Dame Football*.

FRANK SINATRA SHOW, THE

Musical Variety

FIRST TELECAST: *October 7, 1950*
LAST TELECAST: *April 1, 1952*

BROADCAST HISTORY:

Oct 1950–Jun 1951, CBS Sat 9:00–10:00

Oct 1951–Apr 1952, CBS Tue 8:00–9:00

REGULARS:

Frank Sinatra

Ben Blue (1950–1951)

Joey Walsh (1950–1951)

Axel Stordahl and His Orchestra

Sid Fields (1950–1951)

Roberta Lee (1950–1951)

Pat Gaye (1950–1951)

A good deal of publicity attended Frank Sinatra's initial plunge into television in 1950. He certainly had superstar credentials from music, radio, and films (though his greatest films were still to come); would he make it in the new medium of TV? The answer was no, although there was never a clear reason why Sinatra didn't, when such other singers as Perry Como and Dinah Shore did. *The Frank Sinatra Show* was telecast live from New York and featured top-line guest stars and plenty of Frankie's singing, assisted and backed by an assortment of female vocalists and backup groups. There was also, at least for the first three months, a regular supporting cast of comedians to help provide variety.

One factor that certainly didn't help was the competition. Sinatra was first scheduled opposite Sid Caesar's *Your Show of Shows*, then a red-hot sensation. For the second season he was moved to Tuesday, against *The Texaco Star Theater* with Milton Berle—the number one show in television! Frank moved the show to Hollywood in November 1951, but it was hopeless.

There were no regulars other than host Sinatra during the second season.

FRANK SINATRA SHOW, THE

Variety/Drama

FIRST TELECAST: *October 18, 1957*

LAST TELECAST: *June 27, 1958*

BROADCAST HISTORY:

Oct 1957–Jun 1958, ABC Fri 9:00–9:30

HOST:

Frank Sinatra

REGULAR:

Nelson Riddle and His Orchestra

After his first, unsuccessful plunge into television in 1950–1952, singer-actor Frank Sinatra generally steered clear of the medium for several years. But despite the lack of success of his early variety show, he was considered a "hot property" and was actively sought for special appearances and another series of his own. His career in recording and movies had taken a considerable upturn in the mid-1950s, including his Academy Award for *From Here to Eternity*. Finally in 1957 he consented to do a regular weekly series for ABC, provided that he was given *carte blanche* to do it exactly as he wanted to. ABC paid $3 million for the honor of having him on its network.

What Sinatra had in mind was an unusual drama-plus-variety format, originally planned to include one-third variety shows, one-third dramas starring himself, and one-third dramas starring others, which he would host. Unfortunately he apparently approached the project with the attitude that all he had to do was appear, and TV success would be automatic. He rehearsed little, devoting most of his time to movie and other activities. The result was a disaster of the first magnitude, as *The Frank Sinatra Show* ran second or third in audience in its time period. Around December Sinatra buckled down to try to save the show. The number of musicals was increased, the show switched to filming before a live audience, and Sinatra himself began guesting on other shows to promote his program. Unfortunately it was too late.

Nelson Riddle, who had helped spark Sinatra's comeback on records with his imaginative arranging, was musical director on the variety episodes, whose guest stars included such names as Bob Hope, Peggy Lee, and the professional debut of Sinatra's daughter Nancy—aged 17—on November 1, 1957.

FRANKIE LAINE TIME

Musical Variety

FIRST TELECAST: *July 20, 1955*

LAST TELECAST: *September 19, 1956*

BROADCAST HISTORY:

Jul 1955–Sep 1955, CBS Wed 8:00–9:00

Aug 1956–Sep 1956, CBS Wed 8:00–9:00

REGULARS:

Frankie Laine

The Lynn Duddy Singers (1955)

The James Starbuck Dancers (1955)

The Jimmy Carroll Orchestra (1955)

The Mello Larks (1956)

The Edith Barstow Dancers (1956)

The Russ Case Orchestra (1956)

Popular singer Frankie Laine spent two summers on television as the replacement for *Arthur Godfrey and His Friends.* He sang, introduced and performed with assorted guest stars, and acted in comedy sketches.

FRED ASTAIRE PREMIERE THEATER
syndicated title for *Alcoa Premiere*

FRED WARING SHOW, THE
Musical Variety
FIRST TELECAST: *April 17, 1949*
LAST TELECAST: *May 30, 1954*
BROADCAST HISTORY:
Apr 1949–Jan 1952, CBS Sun 9:00–10:00 (OS)
Jan 1952–May 1954, CBS Sun 9:00–9:30 (OS)
REGULARS:
Fred Waring and His Pennsylvanians
THEME:
"Sleep," by Earl Lebieg

Fred Waring, and his orchestra and large chorus, had been an American institution for several decades when he first entered TV on a regular basis in 1949. Slotted right after the high-rated Ed Sullivan *Toast of the Town,* he quickly became a Sunday night standby. The entire Waring organization made up the regular TV cast of more than 60 members. In addition to standard instrumental and vocal numbers, the show included dancing (during the 1949–1950 season there was a dance contest titled "Video Ballroom" as a regular feature); sketch material that was musically related; and interpretations of fairy tales. Although all the members of the Pennsylvanians had solos at one time or another during the show's five-year run, those most frequently spotlighted were Jane Wilson, Joanne Wheatley, Joe Marine, Daisy Bernier, Keith and Sylvia Textor, Hugh "Uncle Lumpy" Brannum, Virginia Morley and Livingston Gearhart, and Poley McClintock (with whom Fred had founded his first band in 1915).

The Fred Waring Show was performed before a live studio audience during its first and last seasons, and without a live audience for the three seasons in between. In its last season it was cut back to alternate-week status, with *G.E. Theater* airing on the alternate Sundays.

FREDDY MARTIN SHOW, THE
Musical Variety
FIRST TELECAST: *July 12, 1951*
LAST TELECAST: *November 28, 1951*
BROADCAST HISTORY:
Jul 1951–Aug 1951, NBC Thu 10:00–10:30
Sep 1951–Nov 1951, NBC Wed 10:30–11:00
REGULARS:
Freddy Martin and His Orchestra
Merv Griffin
Murray Arnold
The Martin Men

Saxophone player and orchestra leader Freddy Martin was the star of this musical variety show, which featured, in addition to a guest female vocalist each week, the Freddy Martin Orchestra, a young male vocalist named Merv Griffin (later to have great success as a talk-show host), pianist Murray Arnold, and the Martin Men, a vocal quintet.

FREE COUNTRY
Situation Comedy
FIRST TELECAST: *June 24, 1978*
LAST TELECAST: *July 22, 1978*
BROADCAST HISTORY:
Jun 1978–Jul 1978, ABC Sat 8:00–8:30
CAST:
Joseph Bresner ....Rob Reiner
Anna Bresner ....Judy Kahan
Sidney Gewertzman ....Fred McCarren
Ida Gewertzman ....Renee Lippin
Leo Gold ....Larry Gelman
Louis Peschi ....Joe Pantoliano

Rob Reiner assumed the dual role of a young Lithuanian immigrant, and the same man at age 89, in this summer series. Reiner opened each episode as the elderly Joseph Bresner, reminiscing about the days when he was a young man newly arrived in the U.S.A. The scene then shifted to New York City's Lower East Side in the early 1900s, where Joseph and his bride Anna struggled to understand the customs of their adopted homeland. Ida and Sidney Gewertzman were their neighbors, Louis was a friend, and Leo Gold a border. Rob Reiner was co-writer and co-producer of this series, as well as its star.

FRIDAY COMEDY SPECIAL, THE
Comedy Anthology
FIRST TELECAST: *March 14, 1975*
LAST TELECAST: *May 23, 1975*
BROADCAST HISTORY:
Mar 1975–May 1975, CBS Fri 8:00–8:30

The situation comedies telecast in this series were a collection of unsold pilots for projected regular series.

FRIGIDAIRE SUMMER THEATER

Dramatic Anthology

FIRST TELECAST: *June 20, 1958*
LAST TELECAST: *August 1, 1958*
BROADCAST HISTORY:
Jun 1958–Aug 1958, ABC Fri 9:30–10:00

This program was a collection of filmed reruns of episodes from other anthology series.

FROM A BIRD'S EYE VIEW

Situation Comedy

FIRST TELECAST: *March 29, 1971*
LAST TELECAST: *August 16, 1971*
BROADCAST HISTORY:
Mar 1971–Aug 1971, NBC Mon 7:30–8:00
CAST:
Millie Grover .... Millicent Martin
Maggie Ralston .... Pat Finley
Mr. Clive Beauchamp .... Peter Jones

The misadventures of two young stewardesses for an international airline based in London, England. Britisher Millie was so good-natured and well-meaning that she could never resist helping people. Every time she tried to help, however, something went wrong, and the more she tried to straighten things out, the more complicated they became. Maggie, her level-headed American friend, spent most of her time trying to get Millie out of her predicaments. Also featured was the girls' boss, Mr. Beauchamp, a harassed middle-management executive for the airline.

FRONT PAGE, THE

Newspaper Drama

FIRST TELECAST: *September 29, 1949*
LAST TELECAST: *January 26, 1950*
BROADCAST HISTORY:
Sep 1949–Jan 1950, CBS Thu 8:00–8:30
CAST:
Walter Burns .... John Daly
Hildy Johnson .... Mark Roberts

Adapted from the famous Hecht-MacArthur play about a small-town newspaper editor and his star reporter, Hildy Johnson. The love-hate relationship between the two of them was the focal point of the story, as Hildy was always threatening to quit the *Center City Examiner* to find "a normal job." Despite what they said about each other, however, Walter and Hildy were loyal friends. The John Daly in this live series was the same person who worked for CBS and later ABC as a news correspondent. It was felt that his actual journalistic experience would give this dramatic role a sense of authenticity.

FRONT PAGE DETECTIVE

Newspaper Drama

FIRST TELECAST: *July 6, 1951*
LAST TELECAST: *November 13, 1953*
BROADCAST HISTORY:
Jul 1951–Feb 1952, DUM Fri 9:30–10:00
Oct 1953–Nov 1953, DUM Fri 8:00–8:30
CAST:
David Chase .... Edmund Lowe
David's Girlfriend .... Paula Drew

Movie actor Edmund Lowe, known both for his matinee-idol roles and his portrayal of the grimy Sgt. Quirt in *What Price Glory?*, starred in this early filmed series as David Chase, a newspaper columnist who "couldn't be bought." David's stories usually involved murders, which he was unusually good at solving. Paula Drew played his girl friend, a fashion designer.

Front Page Detective was primarily a syndicated series seen on local stations at various times, but it was carried on the DuMont network for two periods, as shown above.

FRONT ROW CENTER

Musical Variety

FIRST TELECAST: *March 25, 1949*
LAST TELECAST: *April 9, 1950*
BROADCAST HISTORY:
Mar 1949–Jun 1949, DUM Fri 9:00–9:30
Jun 1949–Sep 1949, DUM Fri 8:00–9:00
Oct 1949–Apr 1950, DUM Sun 7:00–8:00
REGULARS:
Phil Leeds
Monica Moore
Cass Franklin
Hal Loman
Bibi Osterwald
Joan Fields
Danny Shore

This was one of DuMont's early attempts to produce a big weekly variety show, and it starred numerous guests from Broadway and the nightclub circuit. Frank Fontaine hosted the first telecast, with special guest star Marilyn Maxwell in her TV debut. Various hosts appeared thereafter, along with a large and constantly changing supporting cast of regulars. Some of those with longer runs are listed above.

FRONT ROW CENTER

Dramatic Anthology

FIRST TELECAST: *June 1, 1955*

LAST TELECAST: *September 21, 1955*

BROADCAST HISTORY:

Jun 1955–Sep 1955, CBS Wed 10:00–11:00

Live full-hour adaptations of Broadway plays were presented under the title *Front Row Center* on CBS during the summer of 1955, starting with the acclaimed *Dinner at Eight*. The series aired weekly throughout June and then became an alternate-week program when *The U.S. Steel Hour* moved in to share its time slot in July.

FRONTIER

Western Anthology

FIRST TELECAST: *September 25, 1955*

LAST TELECAST: *September 9, 1956*

BROADCAST HISTORY:

Sep 1955–Sep 1956, NBC Sun 7:30–8:00

NARRATOR:

Walter Coy

Walter Coy's opening and closing lines, the same for each episode, were descriptive of this anthology series about the West: "This is the West. This is the land of beginning again. This is the story of men and women facing the frontier. This is the way it happened." And finally, "It happened that way . . . moving west."

There was no glamour in *Frontier*. It depicted real people with real problems moving into, and coping with, a new territory. Indians were not the only villains; roving criminals, rustlers, and the sometimes harsh environment also beset the settlers. In addition to serving as narrator, Walter Coy acted in some of the episodes.

FRONTIER CIRCUS

Circus Drama

FIRST TELECAST: *October 5, 1961*

LAST TELECAST: *September 20, 1962*

BROADCAST HISTORY:

Oct 1961–Jan 1962, CBS Thu 7:30–8:30
Feb 1962–Sep 1962, CBS Thu 8:00–9:00
Sep 1962, CBS Thu 7:30–8:30

CAST:

Col. Casey Thompson .... Chill Wills
Ben Travis .... John Derek
Tony Gentry .... Richard Jaeckel

Set in the Southwest during the late 1800s, *Frontier Circus* was a cross between a circus drama and a traditional Western. The T&T Circus, operated by Col. Casey Thompson, traveled from town to town in a wagon train. Two handsome hunks of masculinity typical of the TV West were at the center of much of the action: Ben Travis, the straw boss, who supervised the workmen, and Tony Gentry, the advance man, who scouted likely stopping places for the circus. The stories involved the relationships between the performers and workmen of the circus, and their encounters with assorted frontier types. Where did the name T&T come from? From Thompson and Travis, who were actually partners, despite their divergent functions.

FRONTIER JUSTICE

Western Anthology

FIRST TELECAST: *July 7, 1958*

LAST TELECAST: *September 28, 1961*

BROADCAST HISTORY:

Jul 1958–Sep 1958, CBS Mon 9:30–10:00
Jul 1959–Sep 1959, CBS Mon 9:00–9:30
Aug 1961–Sep 1961, CBS Thu 8:30–9:00

HOST:

Lew Ayres (1958)
Melvyn Douglas (1959)
Ralph Bellamy (1961)

For three summers, CBS aired reruns of episodes originally telecast on *Dick Powell's Zane Grey Theater*—in 1958 as the summer replacement for *December Bride*, in 1959 for *The Danny Thomas Show*, and in 1961 for the series from which they were taken, *Dick Powell's Zane Grey Theater*. Each season's host was a different actor.

FRONTIER THEATRE

see *Movies—Prior to 1961*

FROSTY FROLICS

Musical Variety

FIRST TELECAST: *September 19, 1951*

LAST TELECAST: *October 10, 1951*

BROADCAST HISTORY:

Sep 1951–Oct 1951, ABC Wed 8:00–9:00

This four-week series of musical variety shows on ice included the Ice Follies, Ice Capades, and Icelandia Skaters.

FUGITIVE, THE

General Drama

FIRST TELECAST: *September 17, 1963*

LAST TELECAST: *August 29, 1967*

BROADCAST HISTORY:

Sep 1963–Aug 1967, ABC Tue 10:00–11:00

CAST:

Dr. Richard Kimble ....David Janssen
Lt. Philip Gerard ....Barry Morse
Donna Taft ....Jacqueline Scott
Fred Johnson, the One-Armed Man
............................Bill Raisch

EXECUTIVE PRODUCER:

Quinn Martin

Dr. Richard Kimble had been accused, tried, convicted, and sentenced to die for a crime he did not commit—the murder of his wife. Kimble was being taken by Lt. Gerard to prison to be executed when the train in which they were riding was derailed and the lieutenant was knocked unconscious. Kimble escaped. For the next four highly successful seasons, while Gerard searched for Kimble, Kimble searched for the one-armed man he had seen actually murder his wife. Back and forth across the country, taking odd jobs and new identities, and constantly on the verge of being caught by the relentless Gerard, Kimble kept looking for the real killer. Only on rare occasions could the doctor return furtively to his former life (through contacts with his married sister Donna), and rarely did he glimpse his quarry, the one-armed man.

In a move unique among series of this type, *The Fugitive* actually resolved the situation that had sustained suspense throughout its run. In a special two-part story, aired on the last two Tuesdays that the show was seen on the network, Kimble found the one-armed man, Gerard found Kimble, and the doctor was exonerated of the crime—despite the death of the one-armed man. In a climactic chase scene, Kimble and the one-armed man cornered each other atop a water tower. Lt. Gerard, in hot pursuit on the ground, realized he had been wrong about Kimble and shot the one-armed man to save the doctor's life. The one-armed man plunged to his death before he could be captured.

This final episode of *The Fugitive*, which aired on August 29, 1967, was seen by more people than any single episode of a regular series in the history of television until that time, and its 72 percent share of all television viewers that night remains a regular-series standard to be reckoned with.

FUN FOR THE MONEY

Quiz/Audience Participation

FIRST TELECAST: *June 17, 1949*

LAST TELECAST: *December 9, 1949*

BROADCAST HISTORY:

Jun 1949–Dec 1949, ABC Fri 9:30–10:00

EMCEE:

Johnny Olsen

This audience-participation quiz show was modeled along the lines of baseball, with stunts and games.

FUNNY FACE

Situation Comedy

FIRST TELECAST: *September 18, 1971*

LAST TELECAST: *December 11, 1971*

BROADCAST HISTORY:

Sep 1971–Dec 1971, CBS Sat 8:30–9:00

CAST:

Sandy Stockton ....Sandy Duncan
Alice McRaven ....Valorie Armstrong
Kate Harwell ....Kathleen Freeman
Pat Harwell ....Henry Beckman

Sandy Duncan was considered one of the most promising new stars in television when this comedy series was launched in the fall of 1971. She was cast as Sandy Stockton, a pert young UCLA student majoring in education who made ends meet by working part-time as an actress in TV commercials. The big-city life of Los Angeles was a constant challenge for Sandy, who hailed from the small town of Taylorville, Illinois. Helping her cope were her next-door neighbor and best friend, Alice McRaven, and Mr. and Mrs. Harwell, the nosy landlords. *Funny Face* did not make the grade, but the character of Sandy Stockton was to return the following season in a similar venture called *The Sandy Duncan Show*.

FUNNY SIDE, THE

Comedy Variety

FIRST TELECAST: *September 14, 1971*

LAST TELECAST: *December 7, 1971*

BROADCAST HISTORY:

Sep 1971–Nov 1971, NBC Tue 9:30–10:30
Nov 1971–Dec 1971, NBC Tue 8:30–9:30

HOST:

Gene Kelly

REGULARS:

John Amos and Teresa Graves
Warren Berlinger and Pat Finley
Dick Clair and Jenna McMahon
Michael Lembeck and Cindy Williams
Burt Mustin and Queenie Smith

Comedy sketches, musical vignettes, and production numbers were the basic elements of this variety show, which each week looked at the funny side of a specific aspect of married life. Topics covered ranged from health to financial problems to sexual attitudes, and were seen from the perspectives of five married couples. John and Teresa were the minority couple, Warren and Pat represented blue-collar people, Dick and Jenna were wealthy, Michael and Cindy were counterculture teenagers, and Burt and Queenie were senior citizens. Gene Kelly was the regular host and participated in many of the sketches and production numbers.

FURTHER ADVENTURES OF ELLERY QUEEN, THE

see *Adventures of Ellery Queen, The*

G.E. COLLEGE BOWL, THE

Quiz/Audience Participation

FIRST TELECAST: *January 7, 1968*
LAST TELECAST: *June 14, 1970*
BROADCAST HISTORY:

Jan 1968–Jun 1968, NBC Sun 6:00–6:30
Jan 1969–Jun 1969, NBC Sun 6:00–6:30
Jan 1970–Jun 1970, NBC Sun 6:30–7:00

HOST/MODERATOR:

Robert Earle

G.E. College Bowl, one of the most intelligent of TV's many quiz shows, was seen through most of its long run as a Sunday afternoon program. However, on three occasions between 1968 and 1970 it was scheduled in the evening hours.

The format was simple, although the questions were not. Two teams of four scholars each, representing different colleges, were pitted against each other and the buzzer. Questions ranged across mathematics, science, engineering, literature, and philosophy and often sent viewers at home scurrying for their encyclopedias. The team amassing the most points won scholarship money for its college and the right to return the following week. A team winning for five consecutive weeks won a special trophy and was retired as an undefeated champion. Awards to a championship team could amount to as much as $19,500.

G.E. College Bowl premiered on Sunday afternoon, January 4, 1959, on CBS with Allen Ludden as host. He was succeeded by Robert Earle, who followed the program when it moved to NBC in 1963.

G.E. GUEST HOUSE

Quiz/Panel

FIRST TELECAST: *July 1, 1951*
LAST TELECAST: *August 26, 1951*
BROADCAST HISTORY:

Jul 1951–Aug 1951, CBS Sun 9:00–10:00

EMCEE:

Oscar Levant

A different panel of four celebrities from four areas of show business—a critic, a writer, a performer, and a producer—appeared each week to answer assorted questions on this live summer game show. The object of the game was to determine which of the four areas produced people most knowledgeable about show business. Emcee Oscar Levant, a pianist, played a number of musical selections and conducted a musical quiz during each show.

GABRIELLE

Music

FIRST TELECAST: *July 13, 1948*
LAST TELECAST: *August 12, 1948*
BROADCAST HISTORY:

Jul 1948–Aug 1948, ABC Tue/Thu 7:00–7:15

HOSTESS:

Gabrielle

This was a musical interlude with songs in the French style by Gabrielle.

GALE STORM SHOW, THE

Situation Comedy

FIRST TELECAST: *September 29, 1956*
LAST TELECAST: *March 24, 1960*
BROADCAST HISTORY:

Sep 1956–Apr 1959, CBS Sat 9:00–9:30
Oct 1959–Mar 1960, ABC Thu 7:30–8:00

CAST:

Susanna Pomeroy ....Gale Storm

Esmerelda Nugent ....ZaSu Pitts
Capt. Huxley ....Roy Roberts
Cedric (1956–1959) ....Jimmy Fairfax

Susanna Pomeroy was the social director of the luxury liner S.S. *Ocean Queen.* She spent much of her time in cahoots with her close friend Esmerelda "Nugey" Nugent, operator of the ship's beauty salon, and their alliance confounded the liner's rather stuffy Capt. Huxley. Adding to the captain's frustrations was the ship's steward, an impish little fellow named Cedric (who went overboard when the series moved to ABC). This filmed comedy was subtitled *Oh Susanna,* and that was the title it later adopted when it went into syndication.

GALEN DRAKE SHOW, THE

Children's Variety

FIRST TELECAST: *January 12, 1957*
LAST TELECAST: *May 11, 1957*
BROADCAST HISTORY:
Jan 1957–May 1957, ABC Sat 7:00–7:30
REGULARS:
Galen Drake
Stuart Foster
Rita Ellis

This unusual variety show was aimed directly at children. Galen Drake was a popular radio personality who was known for the pleasant way in which he told stories. Here he sang a little, interviewed guests, and introduced songs by the show's regular singers, Stuart Foster and Rita Ellis. Guests on this live series were people presumably of interest to youngsters, such as puppeteer Bil Baird, the president of an art school, and a young girl who had run away from home because she was in love with Elvis Presley.

GALLANT MEN, THE

War Drama

FIRST TELECAST: *October 5, 1962*
LAST TELECAST: *September 14, 1963*
BROADCAST HISTORY:
Oct 1962–Dec 1962, ABC Fri 7:30–8:30
Dec 1962–Sep 1963, ABC Sat 7:30–8:30
CAST:
Conley Wright ....Robert McQueeney
Capt. Jim Benedict ......William Reynolds
Lt. Frank Kimbro ....Robert Ridgely
1st Sgt. John McKenna
....................Richard X. Slattery
PFC Pete D'Angelo ....Eddie Fontaine
Private Ernie Lucavich ....Roland LaStarza
Private Sam Hanson ....Robert Gothie
Private Roger Gibson ....Roger Davis

One of the TV trends of the early 1960s that never really got off the ground was the wartime action drama. ABC premiered two such shows in 1962, *Combat* and *The Gallant Men.*

The Gallant Men was set in Italy during World War II and followed the progress of a front-line infantry company, part of the 36th Infantry ("Texas") Division, as it fought its way up the peninsula. The company was led by a determined young captain named Jim Benedict, and the action was seen through the eyes of a war correspondent, Conley Wright. Other principals included free-swinging 1st Sergeant McKenna; handsome, guitar-playing ladies' man D'Angelo (the company's "operator"); the inseparable Lucavich and Hanson; and the callow young driver, Gibson.

The Gallant Men offered action, heroics, and a kind of gritty realism, plus plenty of sexy Italian girls along the way, but it failed to establish a beachhead against either *Rawhide* on Friday night or *Jackie Gleason* on Saturday, and soon disappeared.

GALLERY OF MME. LUI-TSONG, THE

Crime Drama

FIRST TELECAST: *September 3, 1951*
LAST TELECAST: *November 21, 1951*
BROADCAST HISTORY:
Sep 1951–Oct 1951, DUM Mon 8:30–9:00
Oct 1951–Nov 1951, DUM Wed 9:00–9:30
CAST:
Mme. Lui-Tsong ....Anna May Wong

Chinese-American actress Anna May Wong portrayed the owner of a far-flung chain of art galleries who doubled as an exotic—and beautiful—sleuth in this short lived series. Stolen treasure, international intrigue, and shady operators all provided material for the stories. Effective October 10, 1951, the program's title was shortened to *Mme. Lui-Tsong.*

GAME OF THE WEEK, THE

See *Football*

GANGBUSTERS

Police Anthology

FIRST TELECAST: *March 20, 1952*
LAST TELECAST: *December 25, 1952*
BROADCAST HISTORY:
Mar 1952–Dec 1952, NBC Thu 9:00–9:30
CREATOR/WRITER/NARRATOR:
Phillips H. Lord

Gangbusters was one of the all-time classics of radio, running for some 21 years (1936–1957) on various networks. However, its history on television was short, for unusual reasons.

The format was the same as in the radio version. Action-packed stories on the apprehension of major criminals, taken from "actual police and FBI files," were presented in semi-documentary style. There was no continuing cast, but Phillips H. Lord, creator and writer of the show, appeared each week as narrator. At the end of each telecast a photo of one of the nation's most wanted criminals was shown, and anyone having knowledge of his whereabouts was asked to phone the local police, the FBI, or *Gangbusters*. (Over the years the "most wanted" feature of the radio *Gangbusters* resulted in the apprehension of several hundred criminals.)

Gangbusters premiered on TV in March 1952, alternating on Thursday nights with *Dragnet*. Both shows were phenomenally successful, completely overwhelming their competition. (In fact the other three networks virtually gave up trying to compete, and scheduled political-discussion programs opposite them.) During the fall of 1952 *Gangbusters* averaged a 42 rating, garnering virtually all of the audience available in its time slot and ranking number eight among all programs on TV. Nevertheless, it left the air in December—making it probably the highest-rated program ever to be canceled in the history of television.

The reason for the cancellation appears to be that *Gangbusters* was never intended to be a full-time TV series, but merely a stopgap provided by the sponsor to fill in the weeks when *Dragnet* wasn't on. Jack Webb even appeared at the end of each telecast to plug the next week's *Dragnet* episode. Webb could not at first provide a new *Dragnet* film every week, but when he could, *Dragnet* (which was even more popular than *Gangbusters*) went weekly and *Gangbusters* had to make way.

GARLUND TOUCH, THE

see *Mr. Garlund*

GARRISON'S GORILLAS

War Drama

FIRST TELECAST: *September 5, 1967*
LAST TELECAST: *September 17, 1968*
BROADCAST HISTORY:
Sep 1967–Sep 1968, ABC Tue 7:30–8:30
CAST:
Lt. Craig Garrison ....Ron Harper
Actor ....Cesare Danova
Casino ....Rudy Solari
Goniff ....Christopher Cary
Chief ....Brendon Boone

This action series focused on a motley group of commandos recruited from Stateside prisons to use their special skills against the Germans in World War II. They had been promised a presidential pardon at the end of the war if they worked out; if not, they could expect a firing squad. The four were Actor, a handsome, resonant-voiced con man; Casino, a tough, wiry safecracker; Goniff, a slender, likable cat burglar; and Chief, a rugged, somber American Indian proficient with a switchblade. Led by West Pointer Craig Garrison, and headquartered in a secluded spot in England, this slippery group ranged all over Europe in exploits that often took them behind enemy lines.

GARROWAY AT LARGE

Variety

FIRST TELECAST: *April 16, 1949*
LAST TELECAST: *June 25, 1954*
BROADCAST HISTORY:
Apr 1949–Jul 1949, NBC Sat 10:00–10:30
Jul 1949–Jun 1951, NBC Sun 10:00–10:30 (OS)
Oct 1953–Jun 1954, NBC Fri 8:00–8:30
HOST:
Dave Garroway
REGULARS:
Jack Haskell
Cliff Norton
Bette Chapel (1949–1951)
Carolyn Gilbert (1949)
Connie Russell (1949–1951)
Jill Corey (1953–1954)
Shirley Harmer (1953–1954)
Songsmiths Quartet (1949)
The Daydreamers (1950)
The Cheerleaders (1953–1954)

DANCERS:
Russell and Aura (1950–1951)
Ken Spaulding and Diane Sinclair (1953–1954)
ORCHESTRA:
Joseph Gallichio (1949–1951)
Skitch Henderson (1953–1954)
THEME:
"Sentimental Journey," by Bud Green, Les Brown, and Ben Homer

A former disc jockey and onetime NBC pageboy, Dave Garroway first brought his relaxed brand of humor to network audiences in 1949, with this easygoing musical revue. The program, which was telecast live from Chicago, had Garroway chatting with guests and casually strolling from set to set, past cameras, props, and technicians. No attempt was made at elaborate production. Entertainment was provided by guest stars and a regular supporting cast of singers and musicians. Sometimes the guest or setting was unusual, as in the 1950 New Year's Eve show when Dave's guests were the cleaning women of NBC's Chicago studios, "who work on New Year's Eve while others play"; and a May 1950 telecast that moved up onto the roof of the studio building for a view of the Chicago skyline at night.

Perhaps most evocative of Dave's sincere, straightforward style was his regular closing, when he would turn to the camera, raise his hand, and bid farewell with a simple, "Peace."

In January 1952 Garroway began his long run as host of NBC's pioneering *Today Show*. He returned to prime time for the 1953–1954 season, with a revue similar to his 1949–1951 series but this time emanating from New York and titled simply *The Dave Garroway Show*. Singer Jack Haskell and comedian Cliff Norton returned from the earlier show, but otherwise the supporting cast was new. Unfortunately this second series was faced with overwhelming competition from *Mama* and *Ozzie and Harriet*, which were running opposite on CBS and ABC, and it lasted only a single season.

GARRY MOORE SHOW, THE

Variety

FIRST TELECAST: *June 26, 1950*
LAST TELECAST: *December 27, 1951*
BROADCAST HISTORY:
Jun 1950–Jul 1950, CBS Mon–Fri 7:00–7:30
Jul 1950–Sep 1950, CBS Mon/Tue/Thu/Fri 7:00–7:30
Aug 1950–Sep 1950, CBS Wed 8:00–9:00
Oct 1951–Dec 1951, CBS Thu 8:00–8:30
REGULARS:
Garry Moore
Ken Carson
Denise Lor
Durward Kirby

The pace of the early, live *Garry Moore Show* was slow and relaxed, and very informal. Included were songs, poems, comedy sketches, chats with regulars and guests, and anything else that came to mind while the show was on the air. Ken Carson and Denise Lor were the featured vocalists while Durward Kirby doubled as announcer and comedian. The program was simulcast on television and radio, five days a week, during the summer of 1950. In August 1950 the Wednesday 7:00–7:30 P.M. telecast was moved (and expanded) to 8:00–9:00 P.M., to fill in for the vacationing Arthur Godfrey, who normally occupied that time slot.

The fall 1951 version of *The Garry Moore Show*, in the same format and with the same regulars, was aired once a week under the title *The Garry Moore Evening Show*, to distinguish it from Garry's highly successful daytime show on CBS.

GARRY MOORE SHOW, THE

Variety

FIRST TELECAST: *September 30, 1958*
LAST TELECAST: *January 8, 1967*
BROADCAST HISTORY:
Sep 1958–Jun 1964, CBS Tue 10:00–11:00 (OS)
Sep 1966–Jan 1967, CBS Sun 9:00–10:00
REGULARS:
Garry Moore
Durward Kirby
Marion Lorne (1958–1962)
Carol Burnett (1959–1962)
Dorothy Loudon (1962–1964)
Allen Funt (1959–1960)
John Byner (1966–1967)
Jackie Vernon (1966–1967)
Chuck McCann (1966–1967)
Pete Barbutti (1966–1967)

This Garry Moore variety series ran very successfully for six seasons in the late 1950s and early 1960s. Among other things, it made a star out of Carol Burnett, brought back Allen Funt's Candid Camera (as a regular feature), and showcased many fine musical and comedic talents. And then there was, of course, the friendly humor of the bow-tied, crewcut Moore himself. From 1958 to 1963 the highlight of the show was "That Wonderful Year," consisting of film clips, comedy sketches, and production numbers based on the events and styles of a given year. This often filled from one-third to one-half of the show.

The Garry Moore Show left the air in 1964, not because of low ratings but because Garry wanted to get away from the weekly grind and have some time to relax. After two years of well-earned rest (he had begun on network radio in 1939 and had been on television continuously since 1950) Garry returned in the fall of 1966 as host of a program featuring Durward Kirby and a rotating cast of comedians and guests. This was short-lived, however (partially due to the withering competition of *Bonanza*), and thereafter Garry was known primarily as a daytime TV personality.

GAS COMPANY PLAYHOUSE

Dramatic Anthology

FIRST TELECAST: *July 5, 1960*

LAST TELECAST: *September 13, 1960*

BROADCAST HISTORY:

Jul 1960–Sep 1960, NBC Tue 8:30–9:00

HOSTESS:

Julia Meade

This summer series was composed of reruns of *Goodyear TV Playhouse*, *The David Niven Show*, *Colgate Theatre*, and *Alcoa Theatre*. It was hosted by Julia Meade and alternated on Tuesday evenings with *NBC Playhouse*.

GAY NINETIES REVUE, THE

Musical Variety

FIRST TELECAST: *August 11, 1948*

LAST TELECAST: *January 14, 1949*

BROADCAST HISTORY:

Aug 1948–Oct 1948, ABC Wed 8:00–8:30
Nov 1948–Jan 1949, ABC Fri 8:30–9:00

EMCEE:

Joe Howard

REGULARS:

Lulu Bates
The Floradora Girls
Ray Bloch Orchestra

Joe Howard was about as authentic an old-timer as TV could get for a show like this. He had been in vaudeville throughout the 1890s and, as a songwriter, his biggest hits had been "Hello Ma Baby" (1899) and "I Wonder Who's Kissing Her Now" (1909). At 70 years of age he was still a spry performer (he lived to be 83), and he emceed this old-fashioned variety show with period style. Lulu Bates added boisterous Gay Nineties vocals, and the Floradora Girls (named after the hit 1900 Broadway show) provided female harmonizing. The setting was an old gaslight nightclub.

Howard starred in a radio version of *The Gay Nineties Revue* in the early 1940s. His life story was dramatized in the 1947 biographical film *I Wonder Who's Kissing Her Now*.

GEMINI MAN

Action/Adventure

FIRST TELECAST: *September 23, 1976*

LAST TELECAST: *October 28, 1976*

BROADCAST HISTORY:

Sep 1976–Oct 1976, NBC Thu 8:00–9:00

CAST:

Sam Casey ....Ben Murphy
Leonard Driscoll ....William Sylvester
Abby Lawrence ....Katherine Crawford

Sam Casey was an agent for INTERSECT, a government think-tank and operations center specializing in missions requiring the utmost secrecy. While on a diving assignment, Sam was affected by the radiation from an underwater explosion. The radiation rendered him invisible, and it was only through the combined efforts of computer expert Abby Lawrence and Leonard Driscoll, Sam's boss at INTERSECT, that a way was devised to control his invisibility. Sam was fitted with a computerized watchlike contraption that kept him visible. He could, however, switch it off and become invisible again, for short periods. If he did this for more than 15 minutes in any 24-hour period, he would die. Needless to say, the ability to become invisible, despite the time limits, made Sam a very effective agent indeed.

Unfortunately, stiff competition from ABC and CBS rendered the ratings for this program almost invisible, and it did a fast fade-out after only one month on the air.

GENE AUTRY SHOW, THE

Western

FIRST TELECAST: *July 23, 1950*

LAST TELECAST: *August 7, 1956*

BROADCAST HISTORY:

Jul 1950–Jul 1953, CBS Sun 7:00–7:30

Jul 1953–Sep 1954, CBS Tue 8:00–8:30

Sep 1954–Aug 1956, CBS Sat 7:00–7:30

REGULARS:

Gene Autry

Pat Buttram

THEME:

"Back in the Saddle Again," by Ray Whitley and Gene Autry.

Gene Autry, the singing cowboy, made the transition from feature-length movies to half-hour TV films in the early 1950s and became very wealthy doing it. For six seasons he and his sidekick, Pat Buttram, rode from town to town in the Southwest helping maintain law and order. Each episode provided opportunities for Gene to sing, his sidekick Pat to get into some silly predicament, and his horse Champion to show off the training that made him a very talented hunk of horseflesh.

GENERAL ELECTRIC SUMMER ORIGINALS

Dramatic Anthology

FIRST TELECAST: *July 3, 1956*

LAST TELECAST: *September 18, 1956*

BROADCAST HISTORY:

Jul 1956–Sep 1956, ABC Tue 9:00–9:30

This summer series consisted of 30-minute dramatic films never before seen on television, featuring such Hollywood standbys as Vivian Blaine, Joe E. Brown, Zachary Scott, and Ronald Reagan.

GENERAL ELECTRIC THEATER

Dramatic Anthology

FIRST TELECAST: *February 1, 1953*

LAST TELECAST: *September 16, 1962*

BROADCAST HISTORY:

Feb 1953–Sep 1962, CBS Sun 9:00–9:30

HOST/STAR:

Ronald Reagan (1954–1962)

This long-running filmed anthology series premiered in February 1953 as an alternate-week program with *The Fred Waring Show*. There was no host when it first went on the air, Ronald Reagan taking over that role at the start of the 1954–1955 season. He occasionally added the role of episode star to his regular function as host and commercial spokesman. At first, not all of the dramas were filmed, but, as Mr. Reagan said many years later, the problems inherent in live drama on television gave the live episodes a less finished look than the filmed ones. Eventually all of the shows were filmed in advance.

The range of material covered was vast, with one week's story a contemporary adventure, like "Ride the River" with Broderick Crawford and Neville Brand, and the next week's a period Biblical drama, like "The Stone" starring Tony Curtis. Everything from light bedroom comedy to heavy melodrama showed up on *General Electric Theater* and when Westerns became very popular in the late 1950s they were well represented too—"Saddle Tramp in the Old West" starring James Stewart and "Too Good with a Gun" starring Robert Cummings and young Michael Landon (pre-*Bonanza*) among them.

Although most of the stories used on *General Electric Theater* were either original teleplays or adaptations from lesser-known authors, there were occasional exceptions. Phyllis Thaxter and Patric Knowles starred in "Nora," based on Henrik Ibsen's *A Doll's House;* Burgess Meredith starred in a condensed version of the motion picture *Edison, the Man;* Teresa Wright and Richard Boone had the leads in "Love Is Eternal," based on Irving Stone's novel of the same name; and Ronald Reagan and his wife Nancy Davis starred in "Money and the Minister," written by Charlotte Armstrong.

In its eight-plus years, however, *General Electric Theater*'s emphasis was primarily on simple dramas and diversionary entertainment. It was there to entertain, not to preach or educate, and most of the stories were not memorable. However, the list of famous performers appearing was formidable. In addition to those mentioned above, such people as Sir Cedric Hardwicke, Ward Bond, June Havoc, Alan Ladd, Barry Fitzgerald, Jane Wyman, Cornel Wilde, Myrna Loy, Jack Benny, Bette Davis, Anne Baxter, and Barbara Stanwyck starred at one time or another.

GENERAL ELECTRIC TRUE

Dramatic Anthology

FIRST TELECAST: *September 30, 1962*

LAST TELECAST: *September 22, 1963*
BROADCAST HISTORY:
Sep 1962–Sep 1963, CBS Sun 9:30–10:00
HOST/NARRATOR:
Jack Webb

The distinction between this series and its predecessor, *General Electric Theater*, was that all of the stories presented in this series were based on actual incidents and were dramatized with as much fidelity to the original as possible. The stories tended to be in the adventure-suspense vein, and many had military themes. All were taken from the files of *True* magazine.

Jack Webb, who was the host and narrator for the entire series, was the closest thing to a major star to appear in *General Electric True*. In "Code-Name-Christopher," a two-part story which he also directed, Webb played an American agent planning the sabotage of a Nazi factory during World War II. Among the few other familiar names that appeared in these dramas were Jerry Van Dyke, Arte Johnson, Robert Vaughn, and Victor Buono.

GENERATION GAP, THE

Quiz
FIRST TELECAST: *February 7, 1969*
LAST TELECAST: *May 23, 1969*
BROADCAST HISTORY:
Feb 1969–May 1969, ABC Fri 8:30–9:00
EMCEE:
Dennis Wholey (Feb–Apr)
Jack Barry (Apr–May)

Quiz in which two teams, one composed of three teenagers and the other of three adults, were each asked questions about the other generation's life-styles and fads. The teenagers were quizzed about such things as the Edsel, Shirley Temple, Senator Claghorn, Carmen Miranda, and the like; the adults (all over 30) would have to answer questions about the boogaloo, current draft law, "hanging five," and so on. Film clips, photos, and recordings illustrated the questions. Celebrity parents and their offspring often appeared on opposing teams.

GENTLE BEN

Adventure
FIRST TELECAST: *September 10, 1967*
LAST TELECAST: *August 31, 1969*
BROADCAST HISTORY:
Sep 1967–Aug 1969, CBS Sun 7:30–8:00
CAST:
Tom Wedloe ....Dennis Weaver
Mark Wedloe ....Clint Howard
Ellen Wedloe ....Beth Brickell
Henry Boomhauer ....Rance Howard

Ben was a 650-pound American black bear who, fortunately, was as friendly and lovable as he was large. He lived in the Everglades of Florida with his "family," the Wedloes. Ben's constant companion was eight-year-old Mark Wedloe, whose father, Tom, was a wildlife officer. Henry Boomhauer, portrayed by young star Clint Howard's real father Rance, was a backwoodsman who was both friend and advisor to the Wedloes.

GEOGRAPHICALLY SPEAKING

Travelogue
FIRST TELECAST: *October 27, 1946*
LAST TELECAST: *December 1, 1946*
BROADCAST HISTORY:
Oct 1946–Dec 1946, NBC Sun 8:15–8:30
HOSTESS:
Mrs. Carveth Wells

This early series began locally on NBC's New York station on June 9, 1946, and was fed to the small NBC East Coast network in October, sponsored by Bristol-Myers. It consisted of travel films taken and narrated by Mrs. Carveth Wells, and it ended when she ran out of film.

GEORGE BURNS AND GRACIE ALLEN SHOW, THE

Situation Comedy
FIRST TELECAST: *October 12, 1950*
LAST TELECAST: *September 22, 1958*
BROADCAST HISTORY:
Oct 1950–Mar 1953, CBS Thu 8:00–8:30
Mar 1953–Sep 1958, CBS Mon 8:00–8:30
CAST:
George Burns ....Himself
Gracie Allen ....Herself
Blanche Morton ....Bea Benaderet
Harry Morton (1950–1951) ...... Hal March
Harry Morton (1951) ....John Brown
Harry Morton (1951–1953) ...... Fred Clark
Harry Morton (1953–1958)
.... Larry Keating
Bill Goodwin (1950–1951) ....Himself
Harry Von Zell (1951–1958) ......Himself
Mr. Beasley, the Mailman ... Ralph Seadan

Ronnie Burns (1955–1958) ....Himself
Bonnie Sue McAfee (1957–1958)
.... Judi Meredith

THEME:

"Love Nest," by Louis A. Hirsch and Otto Harbach

George Burns and Gracie Allen had one of the most enduring acts in the history of show business. They were headliners in vaudeville in the 1920s, on radio in the 1930s and 1940s, and for almost a full decade on television in the 1950s. The factor which finally terminated the act was not loss of audience appeal, but Gracie's decision to retire in 1958.

The format of the TV Burns & Allen show was simple enough. It was set in the Burns home, and cast George in the dual role of on-screen narrator of the proceedings and straight man for Gracie's scatterbrained but delightful involvements with various people and situations. Gracie's cohort in many of her predicaments was neighbor Blanche Morton, whose long-suffering accountant husband Harry was as infuriated by the girls' escapades as George was tolerant. George was unflappable. He would simply turn to the camera, cigar in hand, and philosophize to the audience.

When it first came to television in 1950 *The George Burns and Gracie Allen Show* was produced live in New York and aired every other Thursday night. Members of the radio cast who followed the show to television were Bill Goodwin, the commercial announcer who doubled as George and Gracie's friend; Bea Benaderet, as neighbor Blanche Morton; Hal March as Blanche's husband Harry; and Ralph Seadan as the mailman to whom Gracie gossiped. There was considerable turnover in the role of Harry Morton during the series' early years. March left the show in January 1951, to be replaced by John Brown. Brown lasted six months and was replaced in June by Fred Clark, who was in turn replaced in the fall of 1953 by Larry Keating. Harry Von Zell joined the cast at the start of the 1951–1952 season as replacement for Bill Goodwin, doing the commercials and playing a friend of the family. In the fall of 1952 the series became a weekly filmed feature originating from the West Coast.

GEORGE BURNS SHOW, THE

Situation Comedy

FIRST TELECAST: *October 21, 1958*

LAST TELECAST: *April 14, 1959*

BROADCAST HISTORY:

Oct 1958–Apr 1959, NBC Tue 9:00–9:30

CAST:

George Burns ....Himself
Blanche Morton ....Bea Benaderet
Harry Morton ....Larry Keating
Harry Von Zell ....Himself
Ronnie Burns ....Himself
Judi Meredith ....Herself
Miss Jenkins ....Lisa Davis

Following his wife Gracie's retirement from show business, George Burns attempted a series of his own, including most of the regulars from the highly successful *Burns and Allen Show.* George played a theatrical producer beset with the usual problems of casting, booking, eccentric stars, and a complement of helpful friends who tended to create more problems than they solved. Blanche was George's secretary; Harry, her husband; and Harry Von Zell, a bumbling friend. George's real-life son Ronnie also appeared in the series, while Judi Meredith portrayed an aspiring actress who was Ronnie's steady girl friend. Although Gracie Allen did not appear on this program, she was referred to. Blanche was a close friend of Gracie's, and as such was always trying to keep George from becoming involved with the attractive young starlets he constantly met—including a certain sexy secretary named Miss Jenkins.

Beginning in December and running through mid-February 1959, the format was altered to include a live variety show within almost every episode, featuring the regular cast and guest stars.

GEORGE GOBEL SHOW, THE

Comedy Variety

FIRST TELECAST: *October 2, 1954*

LAST TELECAST: *June 5, 1960*

BROADCAST HISTORY:

Oct 1954–Jun 1957, NBC Sat 10:00–10:30 (OS)

Sep 1957–Mar 1959, NBC Tue 8:00–9:00 (OS)

Oct 1959–June 1960, CBS Sun 10:00–10:30

HOST:

George Gobel

REGULARS:

Alice (1954–1958) ....Jeff Donnell
Alice (1958–1959) ....Phyllis Avery

Peggy King (1954–1956)
Johnnie Mann Singers (1957–1958)
Shirley Harmer (1957–1958)
John Scott Trotter Orchestra (1954–1958, 1959–1960)
Frank DeVol Orchestra (1958–1959)
Eddie Fisher (1957–1958)
The Kids Next Door (1958–1959)
Joe Flynn (1958–1959)
Anita Bryant (1959–1960)
The Modernaires (1959–1960)
Harry Von Zell (1959–1960)

THEME:
"Gobelues," by John Scott Trotter

Low-key comedian George Gobel, known affectionately as "Lonesome George," starred in his own live variety series for six years. It opened with George's monologue, included a sketch with or performance by the week's guest star, and always a sketch about George's family problems with his wife, Alice. Alice was his real-life wife's name, but on television she was portrayed first by Jeff Donnell and later by Phyllis Avery. (The Alice sketches were finally dropped when the series moved to CBS.)

For a time Gobel was one of TV's top hits, and his familiar sayings ("Well, I'll be a dirty bird!," "You don't hardly get those no more") became bywords. But then *Gunsmoke* came along, running opposite on CBS, and Gobel's star began to fade. During the two seasons that the show aired on Tuesday nights for a full hour, it alternated with *The Eddie Fisher Show*, and both stars were regular guests on each other's programs. When Gobel moved to CBS for a final season, he alternated with *The Jack Benny Show*.

GEORGE JESSEL SHOW, THE

Variety

FIRST TELECAST: *September 13, 1953*
LAST TELECAST: *April 11, 1954*
BROADCAST HISTORY:
Sep 1953–Apr 1954, ABC Sun 6:30–7:00
HOST:
George Jessel
WRITERS:
George Jessel, Sam Carlton

George Jessel's most famous act, which he used throughout his long career, was that of the after-dinner speaker, and it was in that role that he appeared here. Each week Jessel, the self-proclaimed "Toastmaster General of the United States," was seen in a mock testimonial dinner, paying comic homage to the assembled guests of honor. In most cases these were personalities from the field of entertainment, such as Sophie Tucker, Mitzi Gaynor, and Margaret O'Brien. Live from New York.

GEORGE SANDERS MYSTERY THEATER, THE

Dramatic Anthology

FIRST TELECAST: *June 22, 1957*
LAST TELECAST: *September 14, 1957*
BROADCAST HISTORY:
June 1957–Sep 1957, NBC Sat 9:00–9:30
HOST:
George Sanders

George Sanders served as host for all of these filmed dramas and appeared occasionally as an actor in them.

GEORGETOWN UNIVERSITY FORUM

Discussion

FIRST TELECAST: *July 3, 1951*
LAST TELECAST: *October 11, 1953*
BROADCAST HISTORY:
Jul 1951–Oct 1951, DUM Tue 8:00–8:30
Oct 1951–Nov 1951, DUM Thu 8:00–8:30
Dec 1951–Mar 1952, DUM Sun 6:30–7:00
Mar 1952–Oct 1953, DUM Sun 7:00–7:30
MODERATOR:
Frank Blair

Round-table discussions of topics of current interest, by members of the Georgetown University faculty and expert guests. At first the topics were political-social ("Is Our National Transportation Policy Outmoded?"), but later more popular subjects ("Flying Saucers") and descriptive programs on advances in medicine and daily living were featured as often as the debates. From Washington, D.C.

GEORGIA GIBBS AND HER MILLION RECORD SHOW

Music

FIRST TELECAST: *July 1, 1957*
LAST TELECAST: *September 2, 1957*
BROADCAST HISTORY:
Jul 1957–Sep 1957, NBC Mon 7:30–7:45
REGULARS:
Georgia Gibbs

"Her Nibs" Miss Georgia Gibbs (the nickname was given to her by Garry Moore) hosted this 15-minute summer show during 1957. In addition to introducing promising young singers, Georgia sang a number of popular songs, at least two of which were million sellers on record. Included, no doubt, were her own three gold records, "Kiss of Fire," "Tweedle Dee," and "Dance with Me, Henry." Occasionally, before doing her rendition of someone else's big hit, she would play an excerpt from the original recording which had sold a million.

GERTRUDE BERG SHOW, THE

Situation Comedy

FIRST TELECAST: *October 4, 1961*
LAST TELECAST: *April 5, 1962*
BROADCAST HISTORY:
Oct 1961–Jan 1962, CBS Wed 9:30–10:00
Jan 1962–Apr 1962, CBS Thu 9:30–10:00
CAST:
Sarah Green ....Gertrude Berg
Professor Crayton ....Sir Cedric Hardwicke
Maxfield ....Mary Wickes
Joe Caldwell ....Skip Ward

Gertrude Berg had become famous on radio and television in a series called *The Goldbergs*. Sarah Green, the character she played in this situation comedy, was in many ways an older version of her inimitable Molly Goldberg. Sarah was a matronly widow whose thirst for knowledge led her to enroll in college, despite her advancing years. Her English teacher, Professor Crayton, was an exchange teacher from Cambridge University. Maxfield ran the boardinghouse where Mrs. Green lived, and Joe Caldwell was an 18-year-old freshman in her class. The program was originally titled *Mrs. G. Goes to College*, but this was changed to *The Gertrude Berg Show* in January 1962.

GET CHRISTIE LOVE

Police

FIRST TELECAST: *September 11, 1974*
LAST TELECAST: *July 18, 1975*
BROADCAST HISTORY:
Sep 1974–Mar 1975, ABC Wed 10:00–11:00
Apr 1975–Jul 1975, ABC Fri 10:00–11:00
CAST:
Det. Christie Love ....Teresa Graves
Lt. Matt Reardon (1974) .....Charles Cioffi
Capt. Arthur P. Ryan (1975) ..... Jack Kelly
Det. Joe Caruso ....Andy Romano
Det. Steve Belmont ....Dennis Rucker
Det. Valencia ....Scott Peters
Sgt. Pete Gallagher (1975) .. Michael Pataki
TECHNICAL ADVISOR/SOMETIME WRITER:
Det. Olga Ford, NYPD

Action series with black, sexy Teresa Graves as supercop Christie Love of the Special Investigations Division, Los Angeles Police Department. Most of Christie's assignments were undercover jobs, giving her plenty of latitude for her slick, "with-it," rule-breaking style. Her hard-nosed boss was Lt. Matt Reardon, later replaced by Capt. Ryan, and her sidekick was Sgt. Pete Gallagher.

GET SMART

Situation Comedy

FIRST TELECAST: *September 18, 1965*
LAST TELECAST: *September 11, 1970*
BROADCAST HISTORY:
Sep 1965–Sep 1968, NBC Sat 8:30–9:00
Sep 1968–Sep 1969, NBC Sat 8:00–8:30
Sep 1969–Feb 1970, CBS Fri 7:30–8:00
Apr 1970–Sep 1970, CBS Fri 7:30–8:00
CAST:
Maxwell Smart, Agent 86 ......Don Adams
Agent 99 ....Barbara Feldon
Thaddeus, the Chief ....Edward Platt
Agent 13 (1966–1967) ......Dave Ketchum
Carlson (1966–1967) ....Stacy Keach
Conrad Siegfried (1966–1969) ....Bernie Kopell
Starker (1966–1969) ....King Moody
Hymie, the C.O.N.T.R.O.L. robot (1966–1969) ....Dick Gautier
Larrabee (1967–1970) ......Robert Karvelas
99's Mother (1968–1969) ....Jane Dulo
DEVELOPER/WRITERS:
Mel Brooks and Buck Henry

James Bond would have turned over in his grave. Here was secret agent Maxwell Smart, willing but inept, enthusiastic but confused, somehow stumbling through to defeat the evil agents of K.A.O.S. who, led by their mastermind Siegfried and his assistant Starker, planned to take over the world. Max worked for "The Chief," head of the Washington-based U.S. intelligence agency C.O.N.T.R.O.L., and had a beautiful and brilliant young partner known only as Agent 99. Love blossomed and this mismatched pair married during the 1968–1969 season. During the next season, after the show had moved from NBC to CBS, 99 gave birth to a baby boy.

Get Smart was a sophomoric, but highly successful, spoof of the secret-agent genre that had been spawned by James Bond movies in the 1960s, and was probably best typified by Max's pet expression "Would you believe?"—used whenever an agent of K.A.O.S. or someone on his own side didn't seem to accept one of his fabrications and he was trying to come up with a more acceptable alternative. That catchphrase became very popular with young people in the late 1960s.

GETTING TOGETHER

Situation Comedy

FIRST TELECAST: *September 18, 1971*

LAST TELECAST: *January 8, 1972*

BROADCAST HISTORY:

Sep 1971–Jan 1972, ABC Sat 8:00–8:30

CAST:

Bobby Conway .... Bobby Sherman
Lionel Poindexter .... Wes Stern
Jennifer Conway .... Susan Neher
Officer Rudy Colcheck .... Jack Burns
Rita Simon .... Pat Carroll

THEME:

"Getting Together," by Helen Miller and Roger Atkins

Recording star Bobby Sherman played a young songwriter struggling to make it in the popular music business in this youth-oriented comedy. Bobby had the melodies, and his tone-deaf, offbeat friend Lionel wrote the lyrics. Bobby's mod-rock world was not without responsibilities, however, as he was legal guardian of his freckle-faced, 12-year-old sister Jennifer. The three of them, Bobby, Lionel, and Jennifer, lived in an antique shop (it was cheap—but occasionally the furniture got sold out from under them) while Bobby worked as a recording engineer, and the boys tried to peddle their songs. Rita was their motherly landlady, and Rudy her policeman-boyfriend.

Getting Together would seem to have been a perfect vehicle for Sherman to use in launching new hits, but in fact his real-life recording career went into something of a slump when the series went on the air. He did have one moderately popular disc derived from the program, however—titled "Jennifer"—and an album named after the show.

Getting Together was previewed on a March 1971 telecast of *The Partridge Family,* in which the Partridges introduced Bobby and Lionel to each other.

GHOST AND MRS. MUIR, THE

Situation Comedy

FIRST TELECAST: *September 21, 1968*

LAST TELECAST: *September 18, 1970*

BROADCAST HISTORY:

Sep 1968–Sep 1969, NBC Sat 8:30–9:00
Sep 1969–Jan 1970, ABC Tue 7:30–8:00
Jan 1970–Sep 1970, ABC Fri 8:30–9:00

CAST:

Mrs. Carolyn Muir .... Hope Lange
Capt. Daniel Gregg .... Edward Mulhare
Martha Grant .... Reta Shaw
Candice Muir .... Kellie Flanagan
Jonathan Muir .... Harlen Carraher
Claymore Gregg ..... Charles Nelson Reilly

Somewhere along a desolate stretch of New England coastline, overlooking Schooner Bay, sat a charming little house known as Gull Cottage. It was charming except for one slight problem—it was haunted by the ghost of a previous owner, Capt. Daniel Gregg, a 19th-century sea captain. Every time his nephew Claymore, the current owner, tried to rent the cottage to someone, the captain scared them off. Into Gull Cottage moved attractive widow Carolyn Muir with her two young children (aged 8 and 9), their pet dog Scruffy, and Martha, a housekeeper. The captain resented the invasion—Carolyn was sleeping in *his* bedroom—and he tried to scare them off. Eventually, however, they established a truce, and even developed a fondness for each other. *The Ghost and Mrs. Muir* was picked up by ABC for a second season after being canceled by NBC.

GHOST STORY

Supernatural Anthology

FIRST TELECAST: *September 15, 1972*

LAST TELECAST: *June 22, 1973*

BROADCAST HISTORY:

Sep 1972–Jun 1973, NBC Fri 9:00–10:00

HOST:

Sebastian Cabot (as *Winston Essex;* 1972)

When *Ghost Story* premiered in September 1972 it dealt exclusively with tales of ghosts, vampires, witches, and various other aspects of the supernatural. It was hosted by Sebastian Cabot in the role of

Winston Essex. Essex would open the show by taking the audience to Essex House and introducing the story as something that could happen to anyone. As the story unfolded, however, it turned into a bizarre nightmare of one kind or another. On January 5, 1973, the title was changed to *Circle of Fear*. Under the new title stories of suspense could be included that did not have supernatural overtones. In addition, the narrator was no longer part of the program.

GIANT STEP

Quiz/Audience Participation

FIRST TELECAST: *November 7, 1956*

LAST TELECAST: *May 29, 1957*

BROADCAST HISTORY:

Nov 1956–May 1957, CBS Wed 7:30–8:00

EMCEE:

Bert Parks

Giant Step was somewhat different from the other big-money quiz shows of its time in that it restricted its contestants to students, mostly of high school age, who competed for a free college education. The students picked their topic and then tried to answer enough questions successfully to win a four-year scholarship, and an all-expense-paid vacation to Europe after graduation. There were eight steps involved in reaching the final victory. As with *The $64,000 Question*, suspense was built by having the contestants—after their initial appearance—answer only one big question per week.

GIBBSVILLE

Drama

FIRST TELECAST: *November 11, 1976*

LAST TELECAST: *December 30, 1976*

BROADCAST HISTORY:

Nov 1976–Dec 1976, NBC Thu 10:00–11:00

CAST:

Jim Malloy .... John Savage
Ray Whitehead .... Gig Young
Dr. Malloy .... Biff McGuire
Mrs. Malloy .... Peggy McCay
Pell .... Bert Remsen

This short-lived dramatic series centered around the activities of Jim Malloy in the small Pennsylvania town of Gibbsville, where he was cub reporter for the *Gibbsville Courier*, during the 1940s. Jim worked with senior reporter Ray Whitehead (both of them accountable to editor Pell) and made his home with his folks. Whitehead had started his career at the *Courier* and then moved on to more prestigious papers in larger cities. Unfortunately, he had lost a long bout with the bottle and was back in Gibbsville trying to salvage what was left of a once-promising career. Jim Malloy's father was the town physician. The stories and characters in this series were developed from the writings of John O'Hara.

GIDGET

Situation Comedy

FIRST TELECAST: *September 15, 1965*

LAST TELECAST: *September 1, 1966*

BROADCAST HISTORY:

Sep 1965–Jan 1966, ABC Wed 8:30–9:00
Jan 1966–Sep 1966, ABC Thu 8:00–8:30

CAST:

Francine "Gidget" Lawrence ... Sally Field
Professor Russ Lawrence .... Don Porter
Anne Cooper .... Betty Conner
John Cooper .... Peter Deuel
Larue .... Lynette Winter

There was lots of California sun and surf in this frothy comedy about the adventures of a bright, winsome teenager. Gidget was 15½, the daughter of Prof. Russ Lawrence, a widower. Despite the best efforts of her overly protective older sister, Anne, and Anne's husband John (a psychology student who practiced on the family), Gidget and her best friend Larue managed to find endless fun in the sun. Gidget's boy friend Jeff (Stephen Mines) was "off to college" and seldom seen.

Sally Field was plucked from obscurity for the starring role in this series. Only 18 when the show began, she had enrolled in a Columbia Pictures actor's workshop as a summertime lark after completing high school and before beginning college. It proved to be a direct path to TV stardom.

Based on the *Gidget* series of movies, the first of which (1959) starred Sandra Dee in the title role.

GILLETTE CAVALCADE OF SPORTS

see *Boxing*

GILLETTE SUMMER SPORTS REEL

Sports/Sports Commentary

FIRST TELECAST: *June 2, 1950*

LAST TELECAST: *August 19, 1955*

BROADCAST HISTORY:

Jun 1950–Aug 1955, NBC Fri 10:00–10:30 (summers only)

COMMENTATORS:

Don Dunphy (1950)
Jimmy Powers (1951)
Clem McCarthy (1953)
Ken Banghart (1953)
Ray Barrett (1953, 1955)
Jim Leaming (1954)
Bob Wilson (1953–1955)
Gene Kelly (1954)
Byrum Saam (1954)
Fred Caposella (1954–1955)
Lindsay Nelson (1955)
Radcliff Hall (1955)

For five years this series was the summer replacement for the Gillette *Cavalcade of Sports* Friday night boxing matches. There were very few live bouts scheduled during these summers and other sports programming was necessary to fill the time slot. The basic element of the show, and the one that was kept throughout its run, was the showing of newsreel highlights of major sports events from around the world.

In 1950, under the title *Cavalcade of Sports*, the show was hosted by Don Dunphy, who was the radio announcer for the boxing matches during the regular season. He made observations about the films shown as well as introducing the various events. This same format was used in 1951, under the title *Sports Newsreel*, when Jimmy Powers, the television announcer for winter boxing on Gillette *Cavalcade of Sports*, replaced Dunphy. In 1952 the stories stood on their own, with only the newsreel announcers providing explanations of the action and no commentary. The 1952 title was *Gillette Summer Sports Reel*, as it was the following summer when a regular group of commentators was used to discuss the various events shown on film. This same format with a group of commentators, not all of whom were seen every week, was used in 1954 and 1955 under the title *Sportsreel*.

GILLIGAN'S ISLAND

Situation Comedy

FIRST TELECAST: *September 26, 1964*

LAST TELECAST: *September 4, 1967*

BROADCAST HISTORY:

Sep 1964–Sep 1965, CBS Sat 8:30–9:00
Sep 1965–Sep 1966, CBS Thu 8:00–8:30
Sep 1966–Sep 1967, CBS Mon 7:30–8:00

CAST:

Gilligan .... Bob Denver
Jonas Grumby (The Skipper) .... Alan Hale, Jr.
Thurston Howell III .... Jim Backus
Mrs. Lovey Howell III ..... Natalie Schafer
Ginger Grant .... Tina Louise
Roy Hinkley (The Professor) .... Russell Johnson
Mary Ann Summers .... Dawn Wells

The small charter boat *Minnow* had been on a fishing party when it was caught in a storm and wrecked on the shore of an uncharted South Pacific island. Marooned together on the island were: the good-natured skipper; a somewhat blustery millionaire and his vacuous wife; a sexy movie star named Ginger; a high school science teacher known as The Professor; a sweet, naive country girl named Mary Ann; and Gilligan. Gilligan was the boat's sole crew member, aside from the skipper. He was well meaning but inept in his attempts to find a means of returning to civilization. That was perhaps unfortunate, as this exceedingly simple-minded comedy would have ended much sooner if he had found a way back.

GIRL ABOUT TOWN

Music

FIRST TELECAST: *September 8, 1948*

LAST TELECAST: *June 11, 1949*

BROADCAST HISTORY:

Sep 1948–Jan 1949, NBC Wed 8:00–8:30
Feb 1949–Jun 1949, NBC Sun 10:00–10:30

REGULARS:

Kyle MacDonnell
Johnny Downs (1948)
Earl Wrightson (1948–1949)
Norman Paris Trio

Live musical program built around singer Kyle MacDonnell. The songs and chatter were interspersed with films of Kyle as a glamorous New Yorker, visiting chic night spots and attending Broadway shows, sailing on Long Island Sound, etc. Johnny Downs was her first co-host, replaced by baritone Earl Wrightson about a month after the program began. During its final three months the program was known as *Around the Town*.

GIRL ALONE

see *Dotty Mack Show, The*

GIRL FROM U.N.C.L.E., THE

Spy Spoof

FIRST TELECAST: *September 13, 1966*
LAST TELECAST: *August 29, 1967*
BROADCAST HISTORY:
Sep 1966–Aug 1967, NBC Tue 7:30–8:30
CAST:
April Dancer ....Stefanie Powers
Mark Slate ....Noel Harrison
Alexander Waverly ....Leo G. Carroll
Randy Kovacs ....Randy Kirby

Following the success of *The Man from U.N.C.L.E.* (U.N.C.L.E. stood for the United Network Command for Law and Enforcement), NBC decided in the fall of 1966 to create *The Girl from U.N.C.L.E.*, a companion James Bond–type spy spoof. Organization head Alexander Waverly teamed American April Dancer, a young, attractive, and very resourceful agent, with Mark Slate, recently transferred from U.N.C.L.E.'s London office to its New York headquarters. In the fight against THRUSH and other enemies of the world community, this new team would add its skills and enthusiasm. If *The Man from U.N.C.L.E.* seemed rather far-fetched to fans of spy and espionage stories, *The Girl from U.N.C.L.E.* was even sillier and more implausible, and it soon disappeared.

GIRL OF THE WEEK

see *Sportswoman of the Week*

GIRL WITH SOMETHING EXTRA, THE

Situation Comedy

FIRST TELECAST: *September 14, 1973*
LAST TELECAST: *May 24, 1974*
BROADCAST HISTORY:
Sep 1973–Dec 1973, NBC Fri 8:30–9:00
Jan 1974–May 1974, NBC Fri 9:00–9:30
CAST:
John Burton ....John Davidson
Sally Burton ....Sally Field
Anne ....Zohra Lampert
Jerry Burton ....Jack Sheldon

Marriages often have rocky starts, but *The Girl with Something Extra* posed an unusual dilemma for her new spouse. On their wedding night Sally informed her husband John that she possessed E.S.P. and could read his mind. After deciding that their love was more important than the problems her mind reading might cause, John and Sally settled down to a decidedly abnormal marriage. Her ability to read minds, his as well as everyone else's, created embarrassing and amusing situations which formed the basis for most of the stories in this series. Featured were John's brother Jerry and Sally's friend Anne, both single, and platonic friends of each other.

GIRLS, THE

Situation Comedy

FIRST TELECAST: *January 1, 1950*
LAST TELECAST: *March 25, 1950*
BROADCAST HISTORY:
Jan 1950–Mar 1950, CBS Sun 7:00–7:30
CAST:
Cornelia Otis Skinner (Jan–Feb)
.... Bethel Leslie
Cornelia Otis Skinner (Feb–Mar)
.... Gloria Stroock
Emily Kimbrough ....Mary Malone

Based on the autobiographical novel *Our Hearts Were Young and Gay* by Cornelia Otis Skinner and Emily Kimbrough, this early live comedy series followed the adventures of the two young Bryn Mawr graduates as they returned to New York in search of their careers, following a post-graduate fling in Europe. They moved to Greenwich Village and started looking for work, Miss Skinner as an actress and Miss Kimbrough as a writer. Bethel Leslie left the series in February to accept a role in a new play (that was considered far better work than television!), and was replaced by Gloria Stroock, the sister of actress Geraldine Brooks. The original title of this series was *Young and Gay*, changed to *The Girls* after the first two episodes had aired.

GIRLS' BASEBALL

see *Baseball*

GISELE MACKENZIE SHOW, THE

Musical Variety

FIRST TELECAST: *September 28, 1957*
LAST TELECAST: *March 29, 1958*
BROADCAST HISTORY:
Sep 1957–Mar 1958, NBC Sat 9:30–10:00
REGULARS:
Gisele MacKenzie
The Curfew Boys
The Joe Pryor Group

ANNOUNCER:
Jack Narz (1957–1958)
Tom Kennedy (1958)

Canadian-born songstress Gisele MacKenzie made her starring debut in her own variety series in the fall of 1957, after being dropped from *Your Hit Parade* (along with the rest of the cast) in a "modernization" move. In addition to her singing and violin-playing, talents which she had regularly displayed in the past, she danced and acted with the guest stars who appeared each week. There was a small group of regular singers (The Joe Pryor Group) and dancers (The Curfew Boys) plus a regular announcer who was seen on camera. Initially the announcer was Jack Narz, who left the series on January 11, 1958, to be succeeded by his own brother, Tom Kennedy.

GLADYS KNIGHT & THE PIPS SHOW, THE

Musical Variety
FIRST TELECAST: *July 10, 1975*
LAST TELECAST: *July 31, 1975*
BROADCAST HISTORY:
Jul 1975, NBC Thu 8:00–9:00
HOSTS:
Gladys Knight & the Pips
(Merald Knight, William Guest, Edward Pattern)

Gladys Knight and the Pips had been one of the top rock recording groups for nearly 15 years when they were chosen to headline this four-week summer variety series in 1975. Miss Knight, a onetime child prizewinner on *Ted Mack's Original Amateur Hour,* was joined by the Pips (all relatives of hers) as hosts and singing stars of the show. Each week they sang a number of their record hits and joined guest stars in musical and comedy routines.

GLAMOUR-GO-ROUND

Interview
FIRST TELECAST: *February 16, 1950*
LAST TELECAST: *August 10, 1950*
BROADCAST HISTORY:
Feb 1950–Aug 1950, CBS Thu 9:30–9:45
HOSTS:
Ilka Chase
Durward Kirby
Bill Nalle

Ilka Chase, described in a CBS press release as "a recognized authority on style and beauty," hosted this informal talk show along with Durward Kirby. The setting was Miss Chase's drawing room where she and Durward, along with pianist Bill Nalle, welcomed distinguished visitors from New York's fashion world, show business, and various fields of cultural endeavors.

GLEN CAMPBELL GOODTIME HOUR, THE

Musical Variety
FIRST TELECAST: *January 29, 1969*
LAST TELECAST: *June 13, 1972*
BROADCAST HISTORY:
Jan 1969–Dec 1969, CBS Wed 7:30–8:30 (OS)
Dec 1969–Jun 1971, CBS Sun 9:00–10:00 (OS)
Sep 1971–Jun 1972, CBS Tue 7:30–8:30
REGULARS:
Glen Campbell
Ron Poindexter Dancers (1969–1971)
Danny Vaughn Singers (1969–1970)
Marty Paich Orchestra
Larry McNeeley (1970–1972)
Jerry Reed (1970–1972)
Mike Curb Congregation (1971–1972)
Dom DeLuise (1971–1972)
THEME:
"Gentle on My Mind," by John Hartford

Country-popular singer Glen Campbell looked like a potential successor to Perry Como when this weekly variety hour was launched in 1969. He had a long string of enormously successful records in the late 1960s (including his theme, "Gentle on My Mind"), was popular with both teenagers and adults, and had an easy, ingratiating style which had won him a wide TV following during his frequent appearances on *The Smothers Brothers Show.* His own show was reminiscent of Como's, too, in a contemporary way—relaxed, informal, and down-home friendly. In addition to hosting, he sang many of his hits (two of which, "Wichita Lineman" and "Galveston" were on the charts about the time this series began) and did instrumental solos (he was a first-rate guitarist). Guests on the show tended to be Country singers and sketch comedians. Although not usually credited as a regular, comedian Dom DeLuise appeared in more than half the show's telecasts during the final season. Composer-singer John Hartford, who had written Glen's theme song and was a close personal friend, was likewise not a regular but made frequent guest appearances throughout the show's run.

GLENN MILLER TIME

Music

FIRST TELECAST: *July 10, 1961*

LAST TELECAST: *September 11, 1961*

BROADCAST HISTORY:

Jul 1961–Sep 1961, CBS Mon 10:00–10:30

REGULARS:

Johnny Desmond
Ray McKinley
Patty Clark
The Castle Singers

THEME:

"Moonlight Serenade," by Glenn Miller and Mitchell Parish

Johnny Desmond and Ray McKinley were co-hosts of this summer music series that featured the style and sounds of the Glenn Miller Orchestra. Each telecast included a medley of something old–something new–something borrowed–something blue, a regular feature of the band during the days when it had a regularly scheduled radio series during World War II. In addition to starring in this live series, Ray McKinley was then touring with "The Original Glenn Miller Orchestra" (Miller himself had died in 1944).

GLYNIS

Situation Comedy

FIRST TELECAST: *September 25, 1963*

LAST TELECAST: *September 6, 1965*

BROADCAST HISTORY:

Sep 1963–Dec 1963, CBS Wed 8:30–9:00
Jul 1965–Sep 1965, CBS Mon 9:00–9:30

CAST:

Glynis Granville ....Glynis Johns
Keith Granville ....Keith Andes
Chick Rogers ....George Mathews

Keith Granville was a very successful attorney who had two problems, a scatter-brained wife and a penchant for getting involved in criminal cases as an amateur detective. With his wife joining him, they made a rather wacky pair of semipro sleuths who always managed to stumble onto the solution of whatever crime they were investigating. His wife's background as a mystery-story writer may have been of some help, but it was their incredible luck more than anything else that saved the day. Reruns of this series were aired by CBS during the summer of 1965.

GO LUCKY

Quiz/Audience Participation

FIRST TELECAST: *July 15, 1951*

LAST TELECAST: *September 2, 1951*

BROADCAST HISTORY:

Jul 1951–Sep 1951, CBS Sun 7:30–8:00

EMCEE:

Jan Murray

This comedy game show, the summer replacement in 1951 for *This Is Show Business*, gave contestants the challenge of identifying an activity—fishing, bowling, burping a baby, etc.—by asking questions of the host. The studio and home audience had seen what the activity was, and the host would only answer yes or no to the questions. Each contestant worked with a team of two celebrities, the three of them trying to narrow the subject down until they could identify the activity. Small prizes were awarded for guessing correctly within a short time limit.

GOING MY WAY

Situation Comedy

FIRST TELECAST: *October 3, 1962*

LAST TELECAST: *September 11, 1963*

BROADCAST HISTORY:

Oct 1962–Sep 1963, ABC Wed 8:30–9:30

CAST:

Father Chuck O'Malley ....Gene Kelly
Father Fitzgibbon ....Leo G. Carroll
Tom Colwell ....Dick York
Mrs. Featherstone ....Nydia Westman

Clerical comedy-drama based on the 1944 movie, with Gene Kelly assuming the role created in the film by Bing Crosby. Father O'Malley, a light-hearted, progressive young priest, was assigned to a parish in a lower-class New York City neighborhood to aid the crusty old pastor, Father Fitzgibbon. There he encountered boyhood friend Tom Colwell (who ran the local community center), humor, and a great deal of warmth. Mrs. Featherstone was the housekeeper at the rectory.

GOING PLACES WITH BETTY BETZ

Discussion

FIRST TELECAST: *February 20, 1951*

LAST TELECAST: *May 15, 1951*

BROADCAST HISTORY:

Feb 1951–May 1951, ABC Tue 7:15–7:30

MODERATOR:

Betty Betz

Teenage panel show in which panelists and guests discussed career opportunities and other topics of interest to young people. Betty Betz was a nationally syndicated columnist for the Hearst newspapers, and an "authority" on teenagers.

GOLD SEAL PLAYHOUSE

Dramatic Anthology

FIRST TELECAST: *September 17, 1953*

LAST TELECAST: *October 8, 1953*

BROADCAST HISTORY:

Sep 1953–Oct 1953, ABC Thu 10:00–10:30

This was a short series of filmed dramas.

GOLDBERGS, THE

Situation Comedy

FIRST TELECAST: *January 10, 1949*

LAST TELECAST: *October 19, 1954*

BROADCAST HISTORY:

Jan 1949–Feb 1949, CBS Mon 8:00–8:30
Mar 1949–Apr 1949 CBS Mon 9:00–9:30
Apr 1949–Jun 1951, CBS Mon 9:30–10:00
Feb 1952–Jul 1952, NBC Mon/Wed/Fri 7:15–7:30
Jul 1953–Sep 1953, NBC Fri 8:00–8:30
Apr 1954–Oct 1954, DUM Tue 8:00–8:30

CAST:

Molly Goldberg ....Gertrude Berg
Jake Goldberg (1948–1951) .... Philip Loeb
Jake Goldberg (1952) .... Harold J. Stone
Jake Goldberg (1953–1954) .... Robert H. Harris
Sammy Goldberg (1948–1952) .... Larry Robinson
Sammy Goldberg (1954) ....Tom Taylor
Rosalie Goldberg ....Arlene McQuade
Uncle David ....Eli Mintz
Mrs. Bloom (1953) ....Olga Fabian

Gertrude Berg had conceived the role of Molly Goldberg and made her a popular radio character for almost 20 years. In January 1949 the entire Goldberg clan moved to television. Living in an apartment house somewhere in the Bronx, they were a middle-class Jewish family with middle-class problems. Molly's husband Jake was in the clothing business, and their two children, Sammy and Rosalie, were active teenagers. Molly was a housewife, prone to gossip with her neighbors across the inside courtyard of the apartment building. Her call to her favorite cohort in gossip—"Yoo-hoo, Mrs. Bloom"—came whenever she had something juicy to spread, which was quite regularly. Also living with the family was the educated and philosophical Uncle David, patriarch of the family. Molly was a good soul and was constantly involved in trying to help everybody in the neighborhood solve their problems.

The Goldbergs was always a live series and spent time on three of the four networks. The program left CBS in 1951 after principal Philip Loeb was blacklisted for alleged left-wing political sympathies, causing sponsor General Foods to drop the show. It later reappeared briefly on NBC and finally on DuMont—without Loeb.

The charges against Loeb were never proven—indeed, he declared under oath that he was not a Communist Party member—but his career went into a sharp decline. He was now "controversial," and advertisers steered clear of him. He appealed to his union for help, but to no avail. His career in a shambles, Loeb became increasingly depressed and embittered. In 1955, alone in a hotel room, he took a fatal overdose of sleeping pills. Four years after he had been driven from TV, Philip Loeb was dead, a suicide.

GOLDDIGGERS, THE

see *Dean Martin Presents The Golddiggers*

GOLDEN GAME, THE

Religious

FIRST TELECAST: *April 9, 1950*

LAST TELECAST: *May 7, 1950*

BROADCAST HISTORY:

Apr 1950–May 1950, ABC Sun 6:30–7:00

Biblical charades. Two teams of laymen representing different nationalities and creeds acted out charades based on Biblical stories or proverbs. At the end they explained why they picked their subjects, and what these subjects meant to their lives.

GOLDEN TOUCH OF FRANKIE CARLE, THE

Music

FIRST TELECAST: *August 7, 1956*

LAST TELECAST: *October 29, 1956*

BROADCAST HISTORY:

Aug 1956, NBC Tue 7:30–7:45
Sep 1956, NBC Mon/Tue 7:30–7:45
Oct 1956, NBC Mon 7:30–7:45

REGULARS:

Frankie Carle

Pianist Frankie Carle starred in this live music show, originating from Hollywood, that filled the remainder of the half-hour in which NBC aired its network news program during the summer of 1956. Guest vocalists appeared on a regular basis and the selections of songs, both instrumental and vocal, ranged from standards to currently popular numbers.

GOMER PYLE, U.S.M.C.

Situation Comedy

FIRST TELECAST: *September 25, 1964*
LAST TELECAST: *September 9, 1970*
BROADCAST HISTORY:

Sep 1964–Jun 1965, CBS Fri 9:30–10:00
Sep 1965–Sep 1966, CBS Fri 9:00–9:30
Sep 1966–Aug 1967, CBS Wed 9:30–10:00
Sep 1967–Sep 1969, CBS Fri 8:30–9:00
Jul 1970–Sep 1970, CBS Wed 8:00–8:30

CAST:

Pvt. Gomer Pyle .... Jim Nabors
Sgt. Vince Carter .... Frank Sutton
Duke Slater .... Ronnie Schell
Corp. Boyle (1965–1968) .... Roy Stuart
Frankie (1965–1966) .... Ted Bessell
Bunny .... Barbara Stuart

After little more than a season playing Gomer Pyle on *The Andy Griffith Show*, Jim Nabors got his own series built around the same character. Gomer was a likable, naive, bumbling rural character who gave up his job as a gas station attendant in Mayberry to join the peacetime Marines. His nemesis in the Marine Corps was his immediate superior, Sgt. Carter, who tried hard to be a cynical, tough leatherneck, but was constantly confounded by Gomer's wide-eyed innocence and trust in practically everyone. At first Carter believed that Gomer was trying to make a fool out of him, but he later realized that it was just Gomer's nature to be the way he was. Sgt. Carter eventually became Gomer's friend and protector, a role belying his gruff exterior. That is not to say, however, that Gomer did not continue to drive him crazy on a relatively regular basis.

The episodes aired during the summer of 1970 in prime time and later in daytime were all reruns.

GOOD COMPANY

Interview

FIRST TELECAST: *September 7, 1967*
LAST TELECAST: *December 21, 1967*
BROADCAST HISTORY:

Sep 1967–Dec 1967, ABC Thu 10:00–10:30

HOST:

F. Lee Bailey

EXECUTIVE PRODUCER:

David Susskind

In a style reminiscent of Edward R. Murrow's *Person to Person*, famed criminal lawyer F. (for Francis) Lee Bailey visited the home of a different celebrity each week and chatted about his host's life and career. The principal difference was that Bailey was filmed at the home of the interviewee, rather than talking long-distance from the studio, as Murrow had done on his live program. Among those Bailey interviewed were actor Tony Curtis, publisher Hugh Hefner (at his million-dollar Chicago mansion), Senator Everett Dirksen, and Jack Paar (who was such a good talker that he required two telecasts).

GOOD GUYS, THE

Situation Comedy

FIRST TELECAST: *September 25, 1968*
LAST TELECAST: *January 23, 1970*
BROADCAST HISTORY:

Sep 1968–Sep 1969, CBS Wed 8:30–9:00
Sep 1969–Jan 1970, CBS Fri 8:00–8:30

CAST:

Rufus Butterworth .... Bob Denver
Bert Gramus .... Herb Edelman
Claudia Gramus .... Joyce Van Patten

Fresh from his success in *Gilligan's Island*, Bob Denver moved into the role of Rufus Butterworth in this 1968 comedy series. Rufus and Bert Gramus had been friends since they were children. Bert was married and ran a diner, "Bert's Place," while Rufus was single and worked as a cabdriver. Rufus also helped his friend out around the diner, and was constantly coming up with money-making schemes, none of which ever seemed to pan out—but all of which got the two of them into endless predicaments. Rufus gave up his cabdriving at the start of the second season to become a full-time partner in the diner, which closed its doors forever with the cancellation of the series in January 1970.

GOOD HEAVENS

Situation Comedy

FIRST TELECAST: *March 8, 1976*

LAST TELECAST: *June 26, 1976*

BROADCAST HISTORY:

Mar 1976–Apr 1976, ABC Mon 8:30–9:00

May 1976–Jun 1976, ABC Sat 8:00–8:30

CAST:

Mr. Angel .... Carl Reiner

EXECUTIVE PRODUCER:

Carl Reiner

Gentle comedy starring Carl Reiner as a warm and witty business-suited angel who descended to earth to bestow one wish on a different mortal each week—any wish except money. Thanks to Mr. Angel, and to themselves, a sporting-goods salesman got his long-dreamt-of tryout in the big leagues; a young woman who couldn't decide between two suitors got a new beau who combined the best qualities of each; and an unsuccessful author got an adventure to which everyone wanted the literary rights.

GOOD LIFE, THE

Situation Comedy

FIRST TELECAST: *September 18, 1971*

LAST TELECAST: *January 8, 1972*

BROADCAST HISTORY:

Sep 1971–Jan 1972, NBC Sat 8:30–9:00

CAST:

Albert Miller .... Larry Hagman
Jane Miller .... Donna Mills
Charles Dutton .... David Wayne
Grace Dutton .... Hermione Baddeley
Nick Dutton .... Danny Goldman

Albert and Jane Miller were a middle-class American couple who decided that the dull routine of their lives needed a change. Instead of dropping out, however, they contrived to "drop up"—obtaining work as butler and cook, respectively, for an extremely wealthy family. Amid the opulence of a millionaire's mansion, they hoped to share at least some of the benefits of "the good life." Their new employer, industrialist Charles Dutton, was unaware of their middle-class background. He recognized their inexperience but found them pleasant enough company. His stuck-up sister Grace was upset with their lack of proper training, however, and constantly looked for ways to get them fired. Dutton's teenage son Nick was the only member of the household who discovered the truth about the Millers, but he thought that their charade was great fun and helped them through the many catastrophes caused by their unfamiliarity with social etiquette among the wealthy.

GOOD MORNING, WORLD

Situation Comedy

FIRST TELECAST: *September 5, 1967*

LAST TELECAST: *September 17, 1968*

BROADCAST HISTORY:

Sep 1967–Sep 1968, CBS Tue 9:30–10:00

CAST:

Dave Lewis .... Joby Baker
Larry Clarke .... Ronnie Schell
Roland B. Hutton Jr. .... Billy De Wolfe
Linda Lewis .... Julie Parrish
Sandy Kramer .... Goldie Hawn

Comedy about "Lewis and Clarke," two early-morning radio disc jockeys who worked together as a team at a small Los Angeles station owned by the overbearing Roland B. Hutton, Jr. Their adventures both on and off the air were the subjects of stories in this series. Dave was happily married, while Larry, a single, fancied himself quite a swinger. Goldie Hawn, in her pre–*Laugh-In* days, played the Lewises' gossiping neighbor Sandy.

GOOD TIMES

Situation Comedy

FIRST TELECAST: *February 1, 1974*

LAST TELECAST:

BROADCAST HISTORY:

Feb 1974–Sept 1974, CBS Fri 8:30–9:00

Sep 1974–Mar 1976, CBS Tue 8:00–8:30

Mar 1976–Aug 1976, CBS Tue 8:30–9:00

Sep 1976–Jan 1978, CBS Wed 8:00–8:30

Jan 1978–May 1978, CBS Mon 8:00–8:30

Jun 1978–Sep 1978, CBS Mon 8:30–9:00

Sep 1978– , CBS Sat 8:30–9:00

CAST:

Florida Evans (1974–1977, 1978–)
.... Esther Rolle
James Evans (1974–1976) ...... John Amos
James Evans, Jr. (J.J.) .... Jimmie Walker
Willona Woods .... Ja'net DuBois
Michael Evans .... Ralph Carter
Thelma Evans Anderson
.... BernNadette Stanis
Carl Dixon (1977) .... Moses Gunn

Nathan Bookman (1977–) .... Johnny Brown
Penny Gordon Woods (1977–) .... Janet Jackson
Keith Anderson (1978–) ....Ben Powers

PRODUCER:
Norman Lear

Good Times was a spinoff from *Maude*, which in turn was a spinoff from *All in the Family*. Florida Evans was originally Maude Findlay's maid until, in the spring of 1974, she got a show of her own. Florida and James Evans were lower-middle-class blacks living with their three children in a high-rise ghetto on the South Side of Chicago. J.J. was the oldest (17 when the series started), Thelma was a year younger than him, and Michael was 10. Trying to make ends meet on the erratic income provided by James, who was always in and out of jobs, made life difficult, but there was plenty of love in the family. J.J. was an accomplished amateur painter who, though going to trade school, was always looking for some get-rich-quick scheme that would help get him and his family out of the ghetto. He formed a rock group, managed a young comic, and tried various other money making ideas after he got out of school. He did manage to earn money with his painting and was also quite popular with the girls, something his mother viewed with mixed emotions. His catchphrase "Dy-No-Mite" became very popular in the mid-1970s. Florida's neighbor and best friend was Willona Woods.

At the start of the 1976–1977 season there was a major change in the cast. James had found a job working as a partner in a garage in Mississippi when he was killed in an auto accident. The entire family, which had been planning to move to their new home and start a new life, was now fatherless. J.J. became the man of the house and was even more determined to find a way out of the ghetto for his family, whether by means that were entirely legal or not. Some of his schemes became decidedly shady. Meanwhile Florida found a new man in her life in the spring of 1977, in the person of Carl Dixon, the owner of a small appliance repair shop. They were married during the summer of 1977 (though the wedding was not seen) and in the fall were referred to on the show as being "on their honeymoon."

Series star Esther Rolle had become disenchanted with the role model for young blacks provided by J.J.'s "jive-talking," woman chasing, less-than-honest character and, on the pretense of illness, left the series prior to the start of the 1977–1978 season. In the story line, Florida became ill and was living with Carl Dixon in a Southern location that was better for her health. J.J. became the man of the house and friend and neighbor Willona became a surrogate mother to the Evans household. Little Penny Gordon, a victim of child abuse, became Willona's adopted daughter. J.J. was working full time at a small ad agency, a job he had gotten during the 1976–1977 season, and Bookman, the building superintendant, became a more prominent member of the cast. The following fall Esther Rolle returned to the cast, with the promise that J.J. would be a more respectable character, and daughter Thelma married football star Keith Anderson.

GOODRICH CELEBRITY TIME

see *Celebrity Time*

GOODYEAR SUMMERTIME REVUE

see *Paul Whiteman's Goodyear Revue*

GOODYEAR TV PLAYHOUSE

Dramatic Anthology

FIRST TELECAST: *October 14, 1951*
LAST TELECAST *September 12, 1960*
BROADCAST HISTORY:
Oct 1951–Sep 1957, NBC Sun 9:00–10:00
Sep 1957–Sep 1960, NBC Mon 9:30–10:00
PRODUCER:
Fred Coe (1951–1955)

For six years, from the fall of 1951 through the fall of 1957, *Goodyear TV Playhouse* presented full-hour live dramas, originating from New York, on Sunday evenings. Some were original plays for television and some were adapted from other media. The series ran on alternate weeks with *Philco Television Playhouse*. In the fall of 1955, the title was shortened to *Goodyear Playhouse* and a new sponsor took the alternate Sundays with *The Alcoa Hour*.

Young playwright Paddy Chayefsky wrote several original dramas for this series, two of which were later made into feature films. "The Catered Affair" appeared in 1955 as a TV drama with Thelma

Ritter, Pat Henning, and J. Pat O'Malley. The following year it was made into a movie with Bette Davis, Debbie Reynolds, and Ernest Borgnine. Chayefsky's other effort that became a successful theatrical feature was probably the single most acclaimed live drama in the history of television. It aired on May 24, 1953, with Rod Steiger in the title role of "Marty." There were no Emmy awards in 1953 for performances in a single telecast, only for series, so "Marty," ironically, won no TV awards. However, the 1955 movie version won Oscars for best picture and best performance by an actor (Ernest Borgnine). In addition to Rod Steiger, performers who starred in at least two *Goodyear TV Playhouse* productions during these live years included Roddy McDowall, Walter Matthau, Cyril Ritchard, Kim Stanley, Eva Marie Saint, Martin Balsam, Eli Wallach, Ralph Bellamy, Philip Abbott, and Tony Randall. Julie Harris, Paul Newman, Grace Kelly, Veronica Lake, and the Gish sisters (Lillian and Dorothy in separate but consecutive telecasts in 1953) also appeared.

In the fall of 1957, the series moved to Monday nights, was reduced to half an hour, and was on film rather than live. It was still alternating with Alcoa and, although the title of the Goodyear episodes was *Goodyear Theater*, the overall title for the series was *A Turn of Fate*, a designation that was dropped in February 1958. Initially there was to be a rotating roster of regular stars (David Niven, Robert Ryan, Jane Powell, Jack Lemmon, and Charles Boyer) but that concept petered out by the end of the first season. Stars featured during the last two seasons were Paul Douglas, Eddie Albert, Gig Young, Jackie Cooper, Ray Milland, James Mason, Edward G. Robinson, Peter Lawford, Errol Flynn, and Thomas Mitchell. In the spring of each of the last two seasons several of the episodes were pilots for proposed series. One of these was "Christobel" starring Arthur O'Connell as John Monroe, author James Thurber's harried hero. More than a decade later, the Thurber-based John Monroe character reappeared in the weekly series *My World and Welcome to It* starring William Windom.

GORDON MACRAE SHOW, THE

Music

FIRST TELECAST: *March 5, 1956*

LAST TELECAST: *August 27, 1956*

BROADCAST HISTORY:

Mar 1956–Aug 1956, NBC Mon 7:30–7:45

REGULARS:

Gordon MacRae
The Cheerleaders

The set used for this live musical program was a replica of Gordon MacRae's living room, with a large picture window looking out on a scene appropriate for the songs being performed on a given evening. Backing up MacRae, and occasionally with a featured number of their own, was a vocal group called the Cheerleaders. This show originated from Hollywood and was used to fill the remainder of the half-hour in which NBC aired its network news.

GOVERNOR & J.J., THE

Situation Comedy

FIRST TELECAST: *September 23, 1969*

LAST TELECAST: *August 11, 1972*

BROADCAST HISTORY:

Sep 1969–Sep 1970, CBS Tue 9:30–10:00
Sep 1970–Dec 1970, CBS Wed 8:30–9:00
Jun 1972–Aug 1972, CBS Fri 10:30–11:00

CAST:

Gov. William Drinkwater ....Dan Dailey
J.J. Drinkwater ....Julie Sommars
Maggie McLeod ....Neva Patterson
George Callison ....James Callahan
Sara Andrews ....Nora Marlowe

One of the needs of any man in high political office is someone to organize social functions and serve as first lady. For Governor William Drinkwater, the chief executive of a small Midwestern state, and a widower, that someone was his attractive young daughter Jennifer Jo. Despite the problems caused by their generation gap (J.J. was in her early 20s), J.J. served her father as a charming and efficient first lady. Bright and opinionated, she was always ready to debate issues with him, too. J.J. also had a regular job as assistant curator at a zoo, which presented a nice counterpoint to politics. Around the Executive Mansion she sought and received assistance from the governor's secretary Maggie, his press secretary George, and the housekeeper, Sara. During the summer of the 1972 presidential election year, CBS aired reruns of this series.

GRADY

Situation Comedy

FIRST TELECAST: *December 4, 1975*

LAST TELECAST: *March 4, 1976*

BROADCAST HISTORY:

Dec 1975, NBC Thu 8:00–8:30

Jan 1976–Mar 1976, NBC Thu 8:30–9:00

CAST:

Grady Wilson ....Whitman Mayo
Ellie Wilson Marshall ....Carol Cole
Hal Marshall ....Joe Morton
Laurie Marshall ....Roseanne Katan
Hayward Marshall ....Haywood Nelson

In this short-lived spinoff from *Sanford and Son,* Grady Wilson, one of Fred Sanford's friends, moved out of Watts and into a racially mixed middle-class neighborhood in Los Angeles to be with his daughter and her family. His daughter Ellie was married and had two children, Laurie and Hayward.

GRAND OLE OPRY

Country Music

FIRST TELECAST: *October 15, 1955*

LAST TELECAST: *September 15, 1956*

BROADCAST HISTORY:

Oct 1955–Sep 1956, ABC Sat 8:00–9:00

REGULARS:

Carl Smith
Ernest and Justin Tubb
Hank Snow
Minnie Pearl
Chet Atkins
Goldie Hill
Marty Robbins
Rod Brasfield
Cousin Jody
Roy Acuff
June Carter
Jimmy Dickens
Louvin Brothers

In the world of Country music an appearance on the *Grand Ole Opry* has long been considered a symbol of ultimate success. Oddly enough, the *Opry* has never become a regular feature on national TV although other, "lesser" Country music shows have had long runs (see for example *Ozark Jubilee*). During 1955–1956 ABC carried an hour of the *Opry* (it goes on all night) on a monthly basis, live from its longtime home in Nashville, Tennessee. The *Opry* troupe numbers in the dozens, and is constantly changing, and only those members most frequently seen during the ABC run are listed above.

The *Opry* began on radio in Nashville in 1925, was first heard on network radio in 1939, and is still going strong today. It will probably continue forever, with or without TV.

GRANDPA GOES TO WASHINGTON

Situation Comedy

FIRST TELECAST: *September 7, 1978*

LAST TELECAST:

BROADCAST HISTORY:

Sep 1978– , NBC Tue 8:00–9:00

CAST:

Senator Joe Kelley ....Jack Albertson
Major General Kevin Kelley . .Larry Linville
Rosie Kelley ....Sue Ane Langdon
Kathleen Kelley ....Michele Tobin
Kevin Kelley, Jr. ....Sparky Marcus
Madge ....Madge Sinclair
Tony De Luca ....Tom Mason

Jack Albertson portrayed a maverick freshman Senator in this hour long comedy series. Joe Kelley was a former political science professor who had been forcibly retired at age 66, and who promptly got himself elected to the U.S. Senate when the regular candidates were both exposed as crooks. Kelley's style was certainly unusual for Washington. He drove around in a Volkswagen, played drums for relaxation, and his campaign pledge was honesty in government (and he meant it!). His chief political asset was a network of "friends in low places," former students of his who regularly fed him inside political information. Kelley lived with his son, a bland, empty-headed Air Force general ("My son the fathead,") and his son's family, consisting of wife Rosie, daughter Kathleen, and son Kevin, Jr. Madge was the Senator's trusty secretary, and Tony his aide.

GREAT ADVENTURE, THE

Dramatic Anthology

FIRST TELECAST: *September 27, 1963*

LAST TELECAST: *April 23, 1965*

BROADCAST HISTORY:

Sep 1963–Sep 1964, CBS Fri 7:30–8:30

Mar 1965–Apr 1965, CBS Fri 8:30–9:30

NARRATOR:

Van Heflin

A great moment in American history was dramatized each week in this series. Careful attention was paid to the historical accuracy of each play, and all of them were produced with the cooperation and assistance of the National Education Association. Many well-known performers participated in the dramas—Joseph Cotten and Ricardo Montalban in "The Massacre at Wounded Knee," Lloyd Bridges in "Wild Bill Hickok—The Legend and the Man," Victor Jory and Robert Culp in "The Testing of Sam Houston," Jackie Cooper in "The Hunley" (the first submarine to sink an enemy warship), and Robert Cummings and Ron Howard in "The Plague" (about the discovery of anti-smallpox vaccine).

GREAT GHOST TALES

Occult Anthology

FIRST TELECAST: *July 6, 1961*

LAST TELECAST: *September 21, 1961*

BROADCAST HISTORY:

Jul 1961–Sep 1961, NBC Thu 9:30–10:00

This series of ghost stories was the 1961 summer replacement for *The Ford Show Starring Tennessee Ernie Ford*. Each of the plays was produced live in New York, something of a rarity for a dramatic show in the early 1960s. Among the actors who appeared were Robert Duvall, Arthur Hill, Lois Nettleton, Lee Grant, and a young Richard Thomas.

GREATEST FIGHTS OF THE CENTURY

Sports

FIRST TELECAST: *October 15, 1948*

LAST TELECAST: *July 23, 1954*

BROADCAST HISTORY:

Oct 1948–Jan 1949, NBC Fri 10:45–11:00

Apr 1949—Jun 1950, NBC Fri 10:45–11:00 (OS)

Sep 1950–Jul 1954, NBC Fri 10:45–11:00

NARRATOR:

Jim Stevenson

This program was used to fill the time between the conclusion of the boxing match on Gillette *Cavalcade of Sports* and the start of the 11:00 P.M. local news. Jim Stevenson narrated newsreel films of some of the major boxing matches of the 20th century.

GREATEST MAN ON EARTH, THE

Quiz/Audience Participation

FIRST TELECAST: *December 3, 1952*

LAST TELECAST: *February 19, 1953*

BROADCAST HISTORY:

Dec 1952–Feb 1953, ABC Thu 8:00–8:30

EMCEE:

Ted Brown (Dec–Jan)

Vera Vague (Jan–Feb)

Five men chosen from the studio audience competed for the title of *The Greatest Man on Earth* by performing stunts and answering questions, in this live, New York–based quiz show. Finalists and their wives were eligible for a new car, a trip to Europe, or other prizes. Ted Brown was the original emcee, replaced on January 22 by comedienne Vera Vague.

GREATEST MOMENTS IN SPORTS, THE

Sports Commentary

FIRST TELECAST: *July 30, 1954*

LAST TELECAST: *February 4, 1955*

BROADCAST HISTORY:

Jul 1954–Sep 1954, NBC Fri 10:30–10:45

Sep 1954–Feb 1955, NBC Fri 10:45–11:00

HOST:

Walter Kiernan

Greatest Moments in Sports was a 15-minute program comprised of interviews with famous sports personalities and film clips of memorable events in the world of sports. Walter Kiernan was the host to the various guests and served as narrator for the filmed portions of the program. It premiered on a regular basis at 10:30 P.M. and when the Gillette *Cavalcade of Sports* boxing bouts resumed in September was used to fill the time between the conclusion of the bout and 11:00 P.M.

GREATEST SHOW ON EARTH, THE

Circus Drama

FIRST TELECAST: *September 17, 1963*

LAST TELECAST: *September 8, 1964*

BROADCAST HISTORY:

Sep 1963–Sep 1964, ABC Tue 9:00–10:00

CAST:

Johnny Slate ....Jack Palance

Otto King ....Stu Erwin

THEME:

"March of the Clowns," by Richard Rodgers

The Ringling Brothers Barnum & Bailey Circus—"The Greatest Show on Earth"—provided the background for this behind-the-scenes drama of circus performers. Hard-driving Johnny Slate was the working boss of the circus, whose job included, among other things, maintaining peace among a large group of individualistic performers. Otto King was the circus' money man. Each week's story centered around the problems of a specific group—clowns, strongmen, aerialists, animal trainers, etc. Actual Ringling Brothers Barnum & Bailey performers were seen regularly in this series.

GREATEST SPORT THRILLS

Sports

FIRST TELECAST: *January 23, 1954*

LAST TELECAST: *September 27, 1956*

BROADCAST HISTORY:

Jan 1954–Sep 1954, ABC Sat 8:30–9:00
Jun 1955–Sep 1955, ABC Mon 7:30–8:00
Jul 1955–Sep 1955, ABC Thu 9:30–10:00
Jul 1955–Sep 1955, ABC Fri 8:00–8:30
Jul 1955–Aug 1955, ABC Fri 9:00–9:30
Jul 1955, ABC Sun 7:30–8:00
Nov 1955–Jan 1956, ABC Thu 10:00–10:30
Jun 1956–Sep 1956, ABC Thu 9:30–10:00

HOSTS:

Marty Glickman
Stan Lomax

Filmed highlights of sports events that had taken place at Madison Square Garden in New York City over the years were narrated and discussed by Marty Glickman and Stan Lomax on *Greatest Sport Thrills*. Used primarily as a filler program, during the summer of 1955 it was being offered as often as five times per week on the ABC network—often with the same episode repeated on different days. Many ABC stations, including the one in New York, often chose to carry other syndicated or local programming in its place.

GREEN ACRES

Situation Comedy

FIRST TELECAST: *September 15, 1965*

LAST TELECAST: *September 7, 1971*

BROADCAST HISTORY:

Sep 1965–Sep 1968, CBS Wed 9:00–9:30
Sep 1968–Sep 1969, CBS Wed 9:30–10:00
Sep 1969–Sep 1970, CBS Sat 9:00–9:30
Sep 1970–Sep 1971, CBS Tue 8:00–8:30

CAST:

Oliver Wendell Douglas ...... Eddie Albert
Lisa Douglas .... Eva Gabor
Mr. Haney .... Pat Buttram
Eb Dawson .... Tom Lester
Hank Kimball .... Alvy Moore
Fred Ziffel .... Hank Patterson
Doris Ziffel (1965–1969) .... Barbara Pepper
Doris Ziffel (1969–1970) .... Fran Ryan
Sam Drucker .... Frank Cady
Newt Kiley (1965–1970) ...... Kay E. Kuter
Alf Monroe (1966–1969) .... Sid Melton
Ralph Monroe (1966–1971)
.... Mary Grace Canfield
Darlene Wheeler (1970–1971)
.... Judy McConnell

One of the most successful of CBS's rural situation comedies of the 1960s, *Green Acres* was closely intertwined with *Petticoat Junction*, another show produced by the same people. Oliver Wendell Douglas was a highly successful Manhattan lawyer who, despite his good life in New York City, longed to get closer to nature. Ignoring the objections of his socialite wife Lisa, Oliver bought a 160-acre farm, sight unseen, from Mr. Haney. The farm was located outside the town of Hooterville (the setting for *Petticoat Junction*). It was in horrible shape. It had not been worked in years, the house was run-down, unfurnished, and in desperate need of major repairs.

Lisa wanted to turn right around and go back to their Park Avenue penthouse, but Oliver persisted in his determination to give it a chance. They found a shy, gawky handyman named Eb Dawson to help them get the place back into shape, and utilized the services of the Monroes, a sister-and-brother carpenter team, to rebuild the house and barn. Lisa never quite adjusted to the rural life. She kept applying the standards of sophisticated socialites to the ingenuous populace of Hooterville. Even her wardrobe, long flowing gowns and lots of jewelry, seemed out of place on Oliver's Green Acres. She did, however, grow quite fond of the animals they owned, giving names to all the chickens, cows, etc., on the farm. During the second season a pig, though not theirs, became a featured member of the cast. One of the Douglas' neighbors, pig farmer Fred Ziffel, had a pet pig named Arnold who watched television, could do various tricks on cue, and was so intelligent that Fred treated him like a son.

Until *Petticoat Junction* left the air in the fall of 1970, there was always a certain amount of interplay between it and *Green Acres*, with characters from one series making guest appearances on the other.

Green Acres itself, though still successful, was canceled in 1971 as part of CBS' general purging of rural comedies from its schedule.

GREEN HORNET, THE

Crime Drama

FIRST TELECAST: *September 9, 1966*

LAST TELECAST: *July 14, 1967*

BROADCAST HISTORY:

Sep 1966–Jul 1967, ABC Fri 7:30–8:00

CAST:

Britt Reid/The Green Hornet .... Van Williams
Kato .... Bruce Lee
Lenore "Casey" Case ...... Wende Wagner
Mike Axford .... Lloyd Gough
District Attorney F.P. Scanlon .... Walter Brooke

CREATED BY:

George W. Trendle (on radio, in 1936)

THEME:

An updated arrangement of Rimsky-Korsakov's "Flight of the Bumble Bee," played by Al Hirt.

"Faster, Kato!" Then, with a roar of Black Beauty's mighty engine, and the squeal of tires, *The Green Hornet* strikes again!

The TV version of this radio favorite of the 1930s and 1940s was launched close on the flying heels of *Batman,* in 1966, and was produced by the same production team. The plot outline was familiar: Britt Reid, crusading editor and publisher of *The Daily Sentinel,* fought crime in the secret guise of The Green Hornet. Only his faithful manservant Kato and the D.A. knew that Reid and the Hornet were one and the same. Even Reid's admiring secretary Casey and his hard-nosed crime reporter Mike never made the connection.

Some changes were made in adapting *The Green Hornet* to television, and to the 1960s. In addition to the *Daily Sentinel,* Britt owned a TV station. The evil he fought often involved organized crime (not the bizarre villains of *Batman*), and of course the crime-fighting gadgetry was brought up to date.

The chief piece of hardware was the Hornet's souped-up car, the Black Beauty (actually a 1966 Chrysler Imperial, rebuilt, at a cost of $50,000, by Hollywood customizer Dean Jeffries). Among its features were a built-in TV camera which could "see" four miles ahead, a kind of exhaust apparatus which spread ice over the road to foil pursuers, and brushes behind the rear wheels which lowered to sweep away tire tracks. For face-to-face combat, the Hornet had a special nonlethal gas gun which immobilized adversaries, and a sting gun which penetrated steel.

It is not generally known that *The Green Hornet* was directly related to George Trendle's other major hit, *The Lone Ranger,* whose plot line it closely paralleled. In fact, Britt Reid was originally introduced to radio audiences as the son of Dan Reid, the Lone Ranger's nephew.

GRIFF

Detective

FIRST TELECAST: *September 29, 1973*

LAST TELECAST: *January 5, 1974*

BROADCAST HISTORY:

Sep 1973–Jan 1974, ABC Sat 10:00–11:00

CAST:

Wade Griffin .... Lorne Greene
S. Michael (Mike) Murdoch ... Ben Murphy
Gracie Newcombe .... Patricia Stich
Capt. Barney Marcus .... Vic Tayback

Lorne Greene tried to discard his *Bonanza* image and shift to a more contemporary role in this short-lived detective series. He played Wade Griffin, a veteran police captain who had resigned from the force after 30 years—over a matter of principle—and gone into business on his own, as Wade Griffin Investigations. His home base was the swinging, youth-oriented Westwood section of Los Angeles, and his assistant was a young man named Mike Murdoch. Aided by their secretary Gracie, and Wade's many contacts in officialdom and in the streets, they tackled the usual array of murders, kidnappings, extortion schemes, etc.

GRINDL

Situation Comedy

FIRST TELECAST: *September 15, 1963*

LAST TELECAST: *September 13, 1964*

BROADCAST HISTORY:

Sep 1963–Sep 1964, NBC Sun 8:30–9:00

CAST:

Grindl .... Imogene Coca
Anson Foster .... James Millhollin

In this single-season comedy series Imogene Coca played Grindl, a highly efficient, well-organized domestic worker who was constantly put upon by a world that seemed determined to make life difficult for her. Grindl worked for Foster's Temporary Employment Service, and each week she found herself in a different job. She was, at one time or another, a maid, a laundress, a ticket-taker at a theater, a baby sitter, a cook, or anything else that Anson Foster could find for her to do.

GRIZZLY ADAMS

see *Life and Times of Grizzly Adams, The*

GROUCHO SHOW, THE

see *You Bet Your Life*

GROWING PAYNES, THE

Situation Comedy

FIRST TELECAST: *October 20, 1948*
LAST TELECAST: *August 3, 1949*
BROADCAST HISTORY:
Oct 1948–Aug 1949, DUM Wed 8:30–9:00
CAST:
Mr. Payne (1948–1949) ...... John Harvey*
Mr. Payne (1949) .... Ed Holmes
Mrs. Payne (1948–1949) ...... Judy Parrish
Mrs. Payne (1949) .... Elaine Stritch
ALSO:
David Anderson
Warren Parker
Lester Lonergan, Jr.
Ann Sullivan
ORIGINAL MUSIC:
Bill Wirges

This was an early live domestic comedy about the trials of an insurance salesman (John Harvey), his screwball wife (Judy Parrish), and young kids. Often it was Birdie, the maid, who saved the day. Plugs for the sponsor, Wanamaker's Department Store, were worked into the early stories, as was the custom at the time.

*Also given as John Henry

GRUEN GUILD THEATER

see *ABC Dramatic Shorts—1952–1953*

GRUEN PLAYHOUSE

Dramatic Anthology

FIRST TELECAST: *January 17, 1952*
LAST TELECAST: *July 3, 1952*
BROADCAST HISTORY:
Jan 1952–Jul 1952, DUM Thu 9:00–9:30

Filmed dramas featuring such talent as Patrick O'Neal, Elizabeth Fraser, and Bobby Jordan. At least some of these films also appeared on ABC at about the same time on the various series listed under *ABC Dramatic Shorts*. Seen on alternate weeks.

GUESS WHAT

Quiz/Panel

FIRST TELECAST: *July 8, 1952*
LAST TELECAST: *August 26, 1952*
BROADCAST HISTORY:
Jul 1952–Aug 1952, DUM Tue 9:00–9:30
EMCEE:
Dick Kollmar
PANELISTS:
Quentin Reynolds
Virginia Peine
Mark Hanna
Audrey Christie

Summer quiz show in which a panel of celebrities was given a series of cryptic quotations and asked to guess: "What is it?" Numerous personalities appeared on the panel during the short run of this show, of whom the above four were most frequently seen.

GUESTWARD HO!

Situation Comedy

FIRST TELECAST: *September 29, 1960*
LAST TELECAST: *September 21, 1961*
BROADCAST HISTORY:
Sep 1960–Sep 1961, ABC Thu 7:30–8:00
CAST:
Babs Hooten .... Joanne Dru
Hawkeye .... J. Carrol Naish
Bill Hooten .... Mark Miller
Brook Hooten .... Flip Mark

Fed up with the hustle and bustle of New York City, the Hootens decided to look for someplace else to live and work. Their dream house proved to be *Guestward Ho*, a dude ranch in New Mexico. They bought it, sight unseen, and moved west, only to find a rather run-down establishment in need of much work. The only source of supplies in the area was a store run by an Indian named Hawkeye. Hawkeye read the *Wall Street Journal*, sold Indian trinkets that had been made in Japan, and was bound and determined to find a way to return the country to its rightful owners, *his* people. He was not really militant, just industrious and conniving, and his relationship with the

Hootens, including their young son Brook, provided the basis for many amusing situations.

GUIDE RIGHT

Variety

FIRST TELECAST: *February 25, 1952*

LAST TELECAST: *October 30, 1953*

BROADCAST HISTORY:

Feb 1952–Dec 1952, DUM Mon 9:00–9:30
Dec 1952–Jul 1953, DUM Thu 8:00–8:30
Jul 1953–Oct 1953, DUM Fri 8:30–9:00

EMCEE:

Don Russell

CONDUCTOR:

Elliot Lawrence

Korean War era variety show designed to aid enlistments, and featuring both military and civilian talent. Some telecasts originated from military bases. Many of the Army and Air Force bands seen on *Guide Right* were unaccustomed to studio performances, and conductor Elliot Lawrence recalls that he was brought in after the first few telecasts specifically to rehearse the military musicians and direct them on the air. Among the civilian talent "doing their bit" for enlistments were Teresa Brewer, Denise Lor, Morey Amsterdam, Steve Lawrence and Eydie Gorme, Tony Bennett, and Chandu the Magician. Perhaps the hottest popular singer of the day came from the ranks, however—PFC Eddie Fisher, then serving his own enlistment, appeared in October 1952. Military talent such as The Airmen of Note and The Singing Sergeants were also seen.

GULF PLAYHOUSE: 1st PERSON

Dramatic Anthology

FIRST TELECAST: *October 3, 1952*

LAST TELECAST: *September 11, 1953*

BROADCAST HISTORY:

Oct 1952–Dec 1952, NBC Fri 8:30–9:00
Jul 1953–Sep 1953, NBC Fri 8:30–9:00

When *Gulf Playhouse* was originally aired in the fall of 1952 it was a conventional live dramatic anthology. It was replaced by *The Life of Riley* and was back again in the summer of 1953 as *Riley's* summer replacement. The format had changed, however. Although it was still a live anthology series, under the new title *Gulf Playhouse: 1st Person* the camera itself became one of the actors, through whose "eyes" all of the action was seen. It had a voice, and could have been a person or an object or an animal. The other actors addressed the camera as if it were a live member of the cast and gave the viewer a sense of participation in these plays.

GULF ROAD SHOW STARRING BOB SMITH, THE

Variety/Talent

FIRST TELECAST: *September 2, 1948*

LAST TELECAST: *June 30, 1949*

BROADCAST HISTORY:

Sep 1948–Jun 1949, NBC Thu 9:00–9:30

EMCEE:

Bob Smith

REGULARS:

Eve Young (1949)
Heathertones (1949)

ORCHESTRA:

Enoch Light (1948)
Johnny Guarnieri (1948–1949)
Bobby Wren (1949)

Bob Smith, originator (in 1947) of TV's long-running *Howdy Doody Show,* hosted this prime-time talent/variety series during the 1948–1949 season. The program was notable for its frequent changes of format. There were three such changes during the first month alone, and five in all. In order, viewers were treated to a straight musical variety revue (first two weeks), a musical quiz show (one week), a series subtitled *What's New* featuring new talent, inventions, movies, books, etc. (three months), a straight talent show (four and a half months), and finally back to the original musical revue, with guest stars and the audience-participation segment (last two months).

Howdy Doody made a couple of appearances on the show, singing "All I Want for Christmas Is My Two Front Teeth" on the Christmas show, and the new talent included such notable attractions as young songstress Patti Page and "Miss Television Tube of 1949" (comedienne Patricia Bright).

GUNS OF WILL SONNETT, THE

Western

FIRST TELECAST: *September 8, 1967*

LAST TELECAST: *September 15, 1969*

BROADCAST HISTORY:

Sep 1967–May 1969, ABC Fri 9:30–10:00
Jun 1969–Sep 1969, ABC Mon 8:30–9:00

CAST:

Will Sonnett ....Walter Brennan
Jeff Sonnett ....Dack Rambo

A grizzled old ex-cavalry scout and his grandson searched the West for the boy's father in this unusual Western, set in the 1870s. James Sonnett had disappeared 19 years before, leaving the infant Jeff in Will's care. As the years passed the boy had grown into manhood determined to find his father, who had meanwhile become a notorious, but elusive, gunfighter. The old man (played by character actor Walter Brennan, then 73) and his grandson followed James' trail, finding many who knew of him, some with bitterness and hatred, others with gratitude and awe. James Sonnett (played by Jason Evers) was seen fleetingly in a few episodes, but Will and Jeff never did catch up with him—although in the last original episode they met the man who claimed to have killed him. *Sic transit* gunfighters.

GUNSLINGER

Western

FIRST TELECAST: *February 9, 1961*
LAST TELECAST: *September 14, 1961*
BROADCAST HISTORY:

Feb 1961–Sep 1961, CBS Thu 9:00–10:00

CAST:

Cord ....Tony Young
Capt. Zachary Wingate .....Preston Foster
Pico McGuire ....Charles Gray
Billy Urchin ....Dee Pollock
Amby Hollister ....Midge Ware
Sgt. Major Murdock ....John Picard

Set in the Southwest in the decade following the conclusion of the Civil War, *Gunslinger* was the story of Cord, a fast gun who worked on undercover assignments for Capt. Zachary Wingate, the commandant of Fort Scott, New Mexico. Pico and Billy were Cord's two close friends, who often went with him on assignments, and Amby Hollister ran the general store at the fort.

GUNSMOKE

Western

FIRST TELECAST: *September 10, 1955*
LAST TELECAST: *September 1, 1975*
BROADCAST HISTORY:

Sep 1955–Sep 1961, CBS Sat 10:00–10:30
Sep 1961–Sep 1967, CBS Sat 10:00–11:00
Oct 1961–Jun 1964, CBS Tue 7:30–8:00
Sep 1967–Sep 1971, CBS Mon 7:30–8:30
Sep 1971–Sep 1975, CBS Mon 8:00–9:00

CAST:

Marshal Matt Dillon ....James Arness
Dr. Galen (Doc) Adams ..... Milburn Stone
Kitty Russell (1955–1974) ...Amanda Blake
Chester Goode (1955–1964) .... Dennis Weaver
Festus Haggen (1964–1975) ..... Ken Curtis
Quint Asper (1962–1965) ... Burt Reynolds
Sam, the bartender (1962–1974) .... Glenn Strange
Clayton Thaddeus (Thad) Greenwood (1966–1967) .... Roger Ewing
Newly O'Brien (1969–1975) ...Buck Taylor

MUSICAL THEME:

"Gunsmoke," by Richard Shores and John Parker

The few Westerns seen on television during the early 1950s starred old-style movie heroes such as the Lone Ranger and Hopalong Cassidy, and had little to do with the real West. Westerns were considered another form of obvious fantasy, strictly for the kids. Two shows, *Gunsmoke* and *The Life and Legend of Wyatt Earp*, changed all that. These two programs, which premiered during the same week in 1955, introduced the "adult Western" to TV, and began an enormous wave of Westerns on TV over the next ten years.

Gunsmoke had its genesis on CBS radio in the spring of 1952, with William Conrad in the role of the resolute, determined Marshal Matt Dillon. Conrad, who later became TV's *Cannon* in the 1970s, remained the radio voice of Matt Dillon for a total of nine years, but when CBS decided to add a video version of the series the first choice for the role was John Wayne. Wayne would probably have done very well in the role, but he did not want to commit himself to the rigors of a weekly television series and suggested James Arness, a young, relatively unknown actor friend of his. Wayne even offered to introduce the program's first episode, an offer which was quickly accepted by the CBS brass. James Arness, six feet seven inches in height, was even bigger physically than John Wayne, and he proved to be perfect casting for the role of the heroic marshal.

Gunsmoke was set in Dodge City, Kansas, around 1880. Crusty old Doc Adams, the only cast member besides Arness to stay with the show for its entire run, was the town's kindly, sympathetic physician. Doc spent most of his spare time, as did many of Dodge City's residents, at the Longbranch Saloon, which was owned and operated by Kitty Russell. Kitty was extremely soft-hearted, beneath what could be a very businesslike exterior, and would have willingly become romantically involved with Matt. In the radio version the implication was that she was a prostitute, but on TV Matt and Kitty exchanged no more than smiles. Matt's loyal, well-meaning deputy was Chester Goode, who walked with a pronounced limp, talked with a twang ("Misster Dillon!"), and "brewed a mean pot of coffee"—which was often seen behind the closing credits.

Gunsmoke was not an immediate hit. It premiered on Saturday night against the established *George Gobel Show* and did not make TV's top 15 during its first season. In its second year it jumped to No. 8, however, and for the next four years—1957 to 1961—it was the top-rated program in all of TV. *Gunsmoke* precipitated a deluge of Westerns in the late 1950s (at one time there were more than 30 prime-time network Westerns on in the same season), but it outlived them all. It went into a considerable decline in the mid-1960s, after being expanded to an hour, and was about to leave the air when CBS gave it one more chance, moving it to Monday night in 1967. The result was a stunning comeback that put the show in the top ten once again, where it stayed well into the 1970s. It is ironic that when it finally did leave the air in 1975, it was the last Western left on network television at that time. In all, *Gunsmoke* ran for 20 years, longer than any other series with continuing characters in the history of the medium.

Over the years there were changes in the supporting cast. Chester (Dennis Weaver) left in 1964 to be replaced by Festus Haggen, the scruffy hillbilly deputy who remained for the rest of the run. Half-breed Indian Quint Asper was featured for a while as the town blacksmith, as were gunsmith Newly O'Brien and Matt's friend Thad Greenwood. As the years passed, less and less was seen of Matt. Stories often revolved around other members of the cast while he was out of town, and, to some extent, *Gunsmoke* frequently resembled an anthology as stories often came to center on guest stars, using Dodge City simply as a background. "Hard" social issues of the 1960s, such as the rights of minorities, social protest, and crimes such as rape, began to be tackled in stories adapted to the Dodge City setting.

Matt Dillon set the tone of the show throughout its long life, however, standing for justice, sincerity, and truth. The opening of the show said it all. There was Matt in a fast-draw showdown in the main street of Dodge City. The other man fired a fraction of a second faster, but missed completely, while Matt's aim was true. Matt could be beaten up, shot, and ambushed, but that indomitable will would never be defeated.

For the first three seasons following the expansion of *Gunsmoke* from half an hour to a full hour on Saturday nights, CBS aired reruns of the original half-hour version on Tuesdays under the title *Marshal Dillon*.

GUY LOMBARDO'S DIAMOND JUBILEE

Musical Variety

FIRST TELECAST: *March 20, 1956*

LAST TELECAST: *June 19, 1956*

BROADCAST HISTORY:

Mar 1956–Jun 1956, CBS Tue 9:00–9:30

REGULAR:

Guy Lombardo and His Royal Canadians

Viewers of this series were asked to send in letters describing how a specific song had played an important role in their lives. Each week four of the people who had written in were selected to appear on the live show as Guy's guests and watch as their stories were dramatized. In addition to the viewer guests there was one celebrity guest who appeared on the show in connection with "the song of his life." The viewers who appeared on the show won, in addition to the free trip to New York, diamond jewelry and other gifts.

GUY MITCHELL SHOW, THE

Musical Variety

FIRST TELECAST: *October 7, 1957*

LAST TELECAST: *January 13, 1958*

BROADCAST HISTORY:

Oct 1957–Jan 1958, ABC Mon 8:00–8:30

REGULARS:

Guy Mitchell
Dolores Hawkins
The Van Alexander Orchestra

Singer Guy Mitchell hosted and starred in this short-lived musical variety series. Dolores Hawkins, not originally a cast regular, became one during the middle of the show's four-month run. Guest stars were featured and the focus of the show was on singing, which worked much better than the contrived comedy sketches that were also part of the format.

HAGGIS BAGGIS

Quiz/Audience Participation

FIRST TELECAST: *June 30, 1958*

LAST TELECAST: *September 29, 1958*

BROADCAST HISTORY:

Jun 1958–Sep 1958, NBC Mon 7:30–8:00

EMCEE:

Jack Linkletter

Contestants on *Haggis Baggis* faced a large game board consisting of 25 squares. The object was to guess the identity of the celebrity whose picture was revealed, bit by bit, as the squares were uncovered. The contestants picked questions corresponding to different squares, and upon answering correctly got to see what was behind that square. The winner (first to name the celebrity) had his choice of either of two groups of prizes, one labeled haggis (luxury items) and the other, baggis (utilitarian items). If the runner-up could guess which group the winner had taken, he got the other.

Haggis Baggis was also seen on NBC daytime, where it continued until June 1959.

HAIL THE CHAMP

Children's

FIRST TELECAST: *September 22, 1951*

LAST TELECAST: *June 14, 1952*

BROADCAST HISTORY:

Sep 1951–Dec 1951, ABC Sat 6:30–7:00

Dec 1951–Jun 1952, ABC Sat 6:00–6:30

EMCEE:

Herb Allen

Children's program in which six youngsters competed for prizes in games and stunts. Also seen on Saturday daytime from 1952–1953. From Chicago.

HAL IN HOLLYWOOD

see *Library of Comedy Films*

HALF HOUR THEATRE

see *ABC Dramatic Shorts—1952–1953*

HALLMARK SUMMER THEATRE

Dramatic Anthology

FIRST TELECAST: *July 6, 1952*

LAST TELECAST: *August 31, 1952*

BROADCAST HISTORY:

Jul 1952–Aug 1952, NBC Sun 10:00–10:30

PRODUCER/DIRECTOR:

Albert McCleery

The individual was the focus of this live summer drama series, which was sponsored by Hallmark Cards. The plays were produced using the theater-in-the-round technique, with a minimum of props to suggest time periods ranging from the American Revolution to the present day. Stories usually involved a crisis or act of courage in one person's life. The actors appearing were generally lesser-known performers from the Broadway stage.

HALLS OF IVY, THE

Situation Comedy

FIRST TELECAST: *October 19, 1954*

LAST TELECAST: *September 29, 1955*

BROADCAST HISTORY:

Oct 1954–Jul 1955, CBS Tue 8:30–9:00

Jul 1955–Sep 1955, CBS Thu 10:30–11:00

CAST:

Dr. William Todhunter Hall .... Ronald Colman

Vicky Hall .... Benita Hume

Alice .... Mary Wickes

Clarence Wellman .... Herb Butterfield

Dr. Merriweather .... James Todd

THEME:

"Halls of Ivy," by Henry Russell and Vick Knight

Dr. William Todhunter Hall was president of scenic Ivy College, somewhere in the Midwest, in this filmed comedy about a literate, witty college administrator. The school's students, its faculty, and its board of governors all figured in the stories, as did Dr. Hall's wife Vicky ("a former actress"), their housekeeper, Alice, and Chairman of the Board of Governors Clarence Wellman. *The Halls of Ivy* was adapted from the radio series of the same name (1950–1952), with Ronald Colman and his wife Benita Hume recreating their radio roles. However its very literacy and lack of physical action militated against it in the video medium, and it soon disappeared.

One of the more memorable elements of

the series was its theme ("We love the Halls of Ivy/That surround us here today . . ."), rendered in suitably collegiate fashion by a male chorus. The song achieved some popularity on records during the early 1950s.

HANDLE WITH CARE

see *Mail Story, The*

HANDS OF MYSTERY

Suspense Anthology

FIRST TELECAST: *September 30, 1949*
LAST TELECAST: *December 11, 1951*
BROADCAST HISTORY:

Sep 1949–Jul 1950, DUM Fri 8:00–8:30
Jul 1950–Sep 1951, DUM Fri 9:00–9:30
Sep 1951–Dec 1951, DUM Tue 10:00–10:30

The TV plays in this live series generally revolved around a theme of murder or suspense, with episode titles such as "Don't Go Out Alone" and "Vulture of the Waterfront." Included were some stories of the supernatural and stories based on true incidents, such as "The Man Who Killed Hitler." A novel aspect of the series, no doubt suggested to producer Larry Menkin by DuMont's minimal budget, was the almost complete absence of props and sets, with inventive camera angles and lighting used instead to suggest the locale. Lesser-known actors and actresses were featured.

The title of this series was changed twice, from the original *Hands of Murder* to *Hands of Destiny* in April 1950 and finally to *Hands of Mystery* in August 1950.

HANK

Situation Comedy

FIRST TELECAST: *September 17, 1965*
LAST TELECAST: *September 2, 1966*
BROADCAST HISTORY:

Sep 1965–Sep 1966, NBC Fri 8:00–8:30

CAST:

Hank Dearborn . . . . Dick Kallman
Doris Royal . . . . Linda Foster
Dr. Lewis Royal . . . . Howard St. John
Prof. McKillup . . . . Lloyd Corrigan
Tina Dearborn . . . . Katie Sweet
Franny . . . . Kelly Jean Peters
Ossie Weiss . . . . Dabbs Greer

Dick Kallman, a promising young Broadway and Hollywood comic of the 1950s and 1960s who never quite made it to major stardom, was showcased in this single-season campus comedy. He played Hank Dearborn, a resourceful young man determined to get a college education despite his lack of funds or family support (his parents had been killed in a car accident when he was 15, leaving him to support his baby sister, Tina). Hank simply "dropped in" to classes at Western State University, filling the seats of students he knew would be absent, and wearing a variety of ingenious disguises.

To support himself and Tina, he engaged in a number of moneymaking schemes, including running a campus laundry service, a watch and shoe repair shop, a dating agency, etc. He was always one step ahead of Dr. Royal, the registrar, who was bent on tracking down the campus phantom. Just about everyone else was in on the secret, however, including Doris, Hank's girl friend and Dr. Royal's daughter; Prof. McKillup; and Franny, Tina's baby sitter. The track coach, Ossie Weiss, after seeing Hank sprint to classes, wanted him to join the track team.

HANK MCCUNE SHOW, THE

Situation Comedy

FIRST TELECAST: *September 9, 1950*
LAST TELECAST: *December 2, 1950*
BROADCAST HISTORY:

Sep 1950–Dec 1950, NBC Sat 7:00–7:30

CAST:

Hank McCune
Larry Keating
Arthur Q. Bryan
Sara Berner
Frank Nelson
Tammy Kiper

This early filmed situation comedy starred "likable blunderer" Hank McCune, who was constantly getting himself into comic predicaments of his own making. For example, on the first telecast Hank attended a convention held by his sponsor, Peter Paul candy bars, in Atlantic City, where he proceeded to foul up the hotel reservations, infuriate lifeguards, and disrupt the neighboring convention of a mystic fraternal order. Larry Keating played Hank's sidekick. The program was filmed in Hollywood and first ran as a local series in the fall of 1949.

The comedy on *The Hank McCune Show* was slapstick, and the show quickly disappeared from the air. However one aspect of it has remained with us, with a vengeance. Toward the end of its review of the first telecast, *Variety* noted, almost incidentally, that the program

> . . . has an innovation in a sound track that contains audience laughter. Although the show is lensed on film without a studio audience, there are chuckles and yocks dubbed in. Whether this induces a jovial mood in home viewers is still to be determined, but the practice may have unlimited possibilities if it's spread to include canned peals of hilarity, thunderous ovations and gasps of sympathy.

HANNA-BARBERA HAPPY HOUR, THE

Comedy-Variety

FIRST TELECAST: *April 13, 1978*

LAST TELECAST: *May 4, 1978*

BROADCAST HISTORY:

Apr 1978–May 1978, NBC Thu 8:00–9:00

REGULARS:

Honey and Sis (puppets)
The Rudy Baga Band

PUPPETRY BY:

Twao Takamoto

EXECUTIVE PRODUCER:

Joseph Barbera

William Hanna and Joseph Barbera, famous for such cartoon creations as the Flintstones and Yogi Bear, tried their hands at a prime time variety hour with this short-lived series. The program was certainly unusual. Instead of a live host, it had as emcees two life-sized puppets, Honey (the flashy blonde) and Sis (the insecure redhead), who participated in skits and songs with such live guests as Tony Randall, Dan Haggerty, Twiggy and Leif Garrett. Regular features were "The Disco of Life," where puppets and stars swapped gags, and "The Truth Tub," where guests could confess their comic problems.

The appearance of the show was that of a normal, slicky-produced, live comedy-variety hour, and Honey and Sis appeared remarkably lifelike. (They were animated by a team of six men who stood behind them but who could not be seen on screen, due to an electronic masking technique called chroma-key.) However TV viewers apparently preferred human hosts, for this series attracted a small audience and was canceled after four weeks.

HAPPY

Situation Comedy

FIRST TELECAST: *June 8, 1960*

LAST TELECAST: *September 8, 1961*

BROADCAST HISTORY:

Jun 1960–Sep 1960, NBC Wed 9:00–9:30
Jan 1961–Sep 1961, NBC Fri 7:30–8:00

CAST:

Happy .... David/Steven Born
Sally Day .... Yvonne Lime
Chris Day .... Ronnie Burns
Charlie Dooley .... Lloyd Corrigan
Clara Mason .... Doris Packer

Sally and Chris Day were a young married couple who were managers and part-owners (with Clara Mason) of the Desert Palm Motel, a very posh resort. Their efforts to keep the hotel running smoothly were often complicated by the well-meaning but not always useful assistance of Uncle Charlie. The most novel aspect of this show revolved around the Days' infant son, Happy, who was played by the Born twins. All of the goings-on at the hotel, business and personal, were observed by Happy, who regularly voiced his reactions through facial expressions and an off-screen voice—a variation on the observer-speaking-to-the-camera device used by George Burns in the *Burns and Allen Show*, and elsewhere.

HAPPY DAYS

Variety

FIRST TELECAST: *June 25, 1970*

LAST TELECAST: *August 27, 1970*

BROADCAST HISTORY:

Jun 1970–Aug 1970, CBS Thu 8:00–9:00

HOST:

Louis Nye

REGULARS:

Bob Elliott
Ray Goulding
Chuck McCann
Julie McWhirter
Alan Copeland
The Happy Days Singers
The Wisa D'Orso Dancers
The Happy Days Band with Jack Elliott and Allyn Ferguson
Laara Lacey
Clive Clerk
Bill O'Berlin
Jim McGeorge
Jerry Dexter

Songs, dance numbers, and comedy blackouts and sketches were all part of this summer variety series hosted by comedian Louis Nye. All of the material, comedic and musical, was based on the 1930s and 1940s, the period referred to in the title as the "happy days." Sounds of the big bands—including appearances by Duke Ellington—Bob and Ray satirizing old radio shows, as well as real excerpts from actual shows of the era and parties hosted by such comic-strip characters as Mandrake the Magician and Little Orphan Annie were all woven into the show. There were even filmed interviews with major motion picture stars George Raft, Edward G. Robinson, and Charles Laughton talking about their memories of the period. Louis Nye had a regular spot as a song tester, trying to pick big potential hits; and Chuck McCann performed as The Great Voodini, the world's worst, and clumsiest, escape artist.

HAPPY DAYS

Situation Comedy

FIRST TELECAST: *January 15, 1974*

LAST TELECAST:

BROADCAST HISTORY:

Jan 1974– , ABC Tue 8:00–8:30

CAST:

Richie Cunningham .... Ron Howard
Arthur "Fonzie" Fonzarelli .... Henry Winkler
Howard Cunningham .... Tom Bosley
Marion Cunningham .... Marion Ross
Potsie Weber .... Anson Williams
Ralph Malph .... Donny Most
Joanie Cunningham .... Erin Moran
Chuck Cunningham (1974) .... Gavan O'Herlihy
Chuck Cunningham (1974–1975) .... Randolph Roberts
Marsha (1974–1976) .... Beatrice Colen
Gloria (1974–1975) .... Linda Purl
Wendy (1974–1975) .... Misty Rowe
Trudy (1974–1975) .... Tita Bell
Bill "Sticks" Downey (1975–1976) .... John Anthony Bailey
Arnold (1975–1976) .... Pat Morita
Alfred Delvecchio (1976–) .... Al Molinaro
Chachi Arcola (1977–) ...... Scott Baio
Lori Beth (1977–) .... Lynda Goodfriend

MUSIC:

"Happy Days"; "Rock Around the Clock," performed by Bill Haley & His Comets; also recordings by Fats Domino, Connie Francis, Johnnie Ray, Kay Starr, and other stars of the 1950s.

Nostalgia for the 1950s became big business in the mid-1970s, and leading the wave was this updated version of teenage life in the mid-1950s. It started modestly and built in popularity until in the 1976–1977 season *Happy Days* was the number one program in all of television. Along the way it made a major star out of one of its supporting actors.

Happy Days changed dramatically from the series that premiered in 1974. Originally it was the story of two high school kids, Richie Cunningham and his pal Potsie Weber, at Jefferson High in Milwaukee, Wisconsin. Howard Cunningham, Richie's father, ran a hardware store while Chuck was Richie's college-bound older brother and Joanie his 13-year-old kid sister. Richie and most of his friends hung out at Arnold's Drive-In, a malt shop near the school.

Richie was supposed to be the innocent teenager and Potsie his more worldly pal. So as not to make the show too much like *Ozzie & Harriet*, however, the producers added some slightly more extreme counterpoint in the person of the leather-jacketed, greasy-haired motorcycle kid, Fonzie. That was the move that made the show a hit. Instead of the fairly hackneyed Richie-Potsie relationship, the show came to center on the relationship between the "cool" dropout Fonz, and the "straight" kids represented by Richie. Henry Winkler made the character of Fonzie three-dimensional, vulnerable as well as hip. One of the classic episodes, which ran traditionally every Christmas, was the one that first showed the Fonz's own pad, a dingy, cluttered room with his motorcycle in the middle of the floor—and only a tiny, pathetic tree to indicate that it was Christmas. Too proud to admit to being alone for the holiday, the Fonz nevertheless allowed himself to be brought into the Cunningham's home to share in their celebration.

As Fonzie's popularity spread (his thumbs up gesture and "aaayyh!" became trademarks), the show became a bigger and bigger hit. Winkler moved from his original fifth billing to third, and then second behind Ronnie Howard. But ABC claimed that there would be no spinoff series, because without the Richie-Fonzie contrast there would be no *Happy Days*. Not only did Fonzie's billing change as the series grew, but so did his residence. To enable the Fonz to have more regular contact with the entire Cunningham household, he became one of the family, sort of. During the 1975–1976 season he moved into a small apartment over the Cunningham garage. He was thus always available to give Richie advice about life and girls (the Fonz made every girl in Milwaukee swoon).

Changes in the cast over the years were fairly minor. Dozens of high school kids came and went, and Richie's older brother disappeared from the family early on, never to be referred to again. Arnold, the Oriental who owned Arnold's, first showed his face in 1975 but was replaced by a new owner, Alfred, in 1976 (Pat Morita had gotten his own series that fall, *Mr. T. and Tina*). "Sticks" Downey, a black student whose nickname referred to his proficiency as a drummer, gave the series some ethnic counterpoint for a time, and two lower-middle-class girls who turned up briefly in late 1975—on a double date with Richie and Fonzie—quickly went on to a series of their own, *Laverne & Shirley*. Chachi arrived in 1977, as Fonzie's young cousin, the same season that Richie went steady with Lori Beth, with the performers who played both roles turning up together on an NBC series, *Who's Watching the Kids*, the following fall as well.

One of the most popular characters passing through was Pinky Tuscadero (played by Roz Kelly), the sexy motocycle queen who wrapped the Fonz around her little finger—as "cool" as he was, she was "cooler." An old girl friend of his, she roared into town in September 1976 with her Pinkettes (Tina and Lola, played by Doris Hess and Kelly Sanders) to join the Fonz in a demolition derby. A season later her sister Leather Tuscadero (played by rock star Suzi Quatro) turned up on a couple of episodes with her rock group, the Suedes. More nostalgic guests on the show ranged from Buffalo Bob Smith *(Howdy Doody)* to Jack Smith, onetime emcee of *You Asked For It*. Jack played the host of the mythical *You Wanted to See It* show in an episode where Fonzie tried to set a new world's record by leaping his motorcyle over 14 garbage cans behind Arnold's Drive-In, on live TV.

As the 1976–1977 season ended, Richie and the gang graduated from high school and it seemed that Fonzie, the dropout, might be left behind. But at the last minute it turned out that the Fonz, while working days at Happy's Garage, had been going to night school and would get his diploma too. Fonzie and his pals started the next season with a trip to Hollywood, where he tested for a movie career as the "new" James Dean. Then Richie, Potsie and Ralph enrolled at the University of Wisconsin at Milwaukee, with Fonzie still around (though not enrolled) to advise them on love and life. Richie enrolled as a journalism student and Potsie as a psychology major, while Ralph followed in his father's footsteps to become an eye doctor—though he really wanted to be a comedian.

The prototype for this immensely successful series was a skit which appeared on *Love, American Style* in February, 1972, titled "Love and the Happy Day" and which starred Ronnie Howard and Anson Williams. The theme song, an original song called "Happy Days," was on the hit parade in 1976.

HARBOURMASTER

Adventure

FIRST TELECAST: *September 26, 1957*

LAST TELECAST: *June 29, 1958*

BROADCAST HISTORY:

Sep 1957–Dec 1957, CBS Thu 8:00–8:30

Jan 1958–Jun 1958, ABC Sun 8:30–9:00

CAST:

Capt. David Scott .... Barry Sullivan

Jeff Kittridge .... Paul Burke

Anna Morrison .... Nina Wilcox

Off the New England coast lay Scott Island, an idyllic little place far removed from the hustle and bustle of the mainland. David Scott's family had settled the island generations ago and had lived there ever since. A bachelor, David was the "Harbourmaster" for the island, arranging dock space for boats, anchorages, and serving as a one-man rescue squad and police force.

His hobby, which he pursued between storms, fires and other problems, was running a boatyard. Here, with the help of young Jeff Kittridge, David repaired and rented small boats. Nearby was the Dolphin Restaurant, run by winsome Anna, a young woman whose interest in David was obvious to all but him. When the series moved to ABC in the middle of its one-season run, the title was changed to *Adventures at Scott Island.*

HARDY BOYS MYSTERIES, THE

Adventure

FIRST TELECAST: *January 30, 1977*

LAST TELECAST:

BROADCAST HISTORY:

Jan 1977– , ABC Sun 7:00–8:00

CAST:

Joe Hardy .... Shaun Cassidy
Frank Hardy .... Parker Stevenson
Fenton Hardy .... Edmund Gilbert
Callie Shaw (1977) .... Lisa Eilbacher
Aunt Gertrude .... Edith Atwater
Nancy Drew (1977–1978)
.... Pamela Sue Martin
Nancy Drew (1978) ... Janet Louise Johnson
Carson Drew (1977–1978)
.... William Schallert
George Fayne (1977–1978)
.... Susan Buckner
Bess (1977–1978) .... Ruth Cox
Harry Gibbon (1978–)
.... Phillip R. Allen

The adventures of 16-year-old Joe and 18-year-old Frank Hardy, the teenage detective sons of world famous investigator Fentor Hardy, were the basis of this series. Their exploits were usually on the nonviolent side, involving ghosts, missing persons, smugglers and other "mysteries" rather than violent action. Often they had a contemporary youth orientation, to appeal to the teenagers who made up much of the audience to this show, as when the boys traveled to Europe to Transylvania to attend a rock concert at Dracula's Castle, where they encountered strange goings-on. Helping out were Callie, who worked part time in Fenton Hardy's detective agency, and Aunt Gertrude. Added in 1978 was federal agent Harry Gibbon.

At first the series alternated on Sunday nights with *The Nancy Drew Mysteries*, which starred Pamela Sue Martin in the title role. In the fall of 1977 the Hardy Boys and Nancy Drew appeared jointly in some episodes, and then in February 1978, the two programs were combined into one, with the title changed to *Hardy Boys/Nancy Drew Mysteries* and all three leads appearing together regularly. Unhappy with the elimination of her separate series, Pamela Sue Martin left the program and was briefly replaced by 18-year-old Janet Louise Johnson. The character of Nancy Drew was dropped altogether in the fall of 1978.

In addition to his adventures, Shaun Cassidy found time to launch a singing career while on this program, much as his older brother David Cassidy had done while on another TV series, *The Partridge Family*, seven years earlier. Shaun sang "Da Do Ron Ron" on an April 1977 telecast, and saw it become a number one record hit.

The Hardy Boys was based on the Hardy Boys books by Franklin W. Dixon.

HARNESS RACING

Sports

FIRST TELECAST: *May 27, 1949*

LAST TELECAST: *August 19, 1958*

BROADCAST HISTORY:

May 1949–Sep 1949, NBC Fri 10:00–Conclusion
Jul 1949–Sep 1949, NBC Tue 9:30–Conclusion
Jun 1950–Aug 1950, NBC Thu 10:00–Conclusion
Jun 1950–Sep 1950, NBC Sat 10:00–Conclusion
Sep 1951–Nov 1951, ABC Sat Various (9:00, 9:30, 10:00 starts)
Jun 1958–Aug 1958, ABC Fri 10:00–10:30
Aug 1958, ABC Tue 10:00–10:30

Back in the relatively early days of network television, NBC aired live coverage of races from New York's Roosevelt Raceway, usually two or three races each night. Veteran horserace announcer Clem McCarthy called the races, described them prior to the start of each race, and talked about various horse owners and trainers. To keep viewers from being bored, there was a quiz game conducted between races with contestants from a studio audience. The quiz was conducted by Ray Barrett and Bill Stern, and was only used by NBC in the 1950 edition of *Trotting Races*, not the original in 1949.

ABC covered the trotters in 1951 and 1958 under the title *Harness Racing*. Races aired in 1951 originated from Maywood Park in Chicago until late October, and then shifted to Yonkers Raceway near New York City. The 1958 series, on ABC, originated only from the New York area, with individual telecasts aired from either Roosevelt Raceway or Yonkers Raceway.

HAROLD ROBBINS' "THE SURVIVORS"

see *Survivors, The*

HARRIGAN AND SON

Situation Comedy

FIRST TELECAST: *October 14, 1960*

LAST TELECAST: *September 29, 1961*

BROADCAST HISTORY:

Oct 1960–Sep 1961, ABC Fri 8:00–8:30

CAST:

James Harrigan Sr. .... Pat O'Brien
James Harrigan Jr. .... Roger Perry
Gypsy .... Georgine Darcy
Miss Claridge .... Helen Kleeb

James Harrigan, Sr., had been practicing law, as a criminal attorney, since before his son was born. Now his boy had just graduated from Harvard Law School and joined the firm as a junior partner. Junior's problem was that he tried to do everything by the book and was constantly at odds with his father who was not above playing angles that would help his case. The two lawyers had secretaries that matched their styles completely. Senior had fiery, flip, effervescent Gypsy and Junior had sedate, efficient Miss Claridge.

HARRIS AGAINST THE WORLD

Situation Comedy

FIRST TELECAST: *October 5, 1964*

LAST TELECAST: *January 4, 1965*

BROADCAST HISTORY:

Oct 1964–Jan 1965, NBC Mon 8:00–8:30

CAST:

Alan Harris .... Jack Klugman
Kate Harris .... Patricia Barry
Deedee Harris .... Claire Wilcox
Billy Harris .... David Macklin

Jack Klugman played Alan Harris, a plant superintendent at a huge movie studio who lived at 90 Bristol Court with his wife Kate and his two children, Deedee and Billy. Coping with life was a full-time job for Alan. His bosses, debts, taxes, and people in general always seemed to be one up on him. His wife was a champion spender who always managed to find him part-time jobs to work at in the spare time he didn't really have. But much as he complained about almost everything and everybody, Alan was really an old softie at heart.

Harris Against the World was the middle component of a series of three comedies that ran from 7:30–9:00 P.M. on Monday evenings under the blanket title *90 Bristol Court*, which referred to the fashionable apartment block where all three shows were set. *Karen* ran from 7:30–8:00 and *Tom, Dick and Mary* from 8:30–9:00.

HARRY'S GIRLS

Situation Comedy

FIRST TELECAST: *September 13, 1963*

LAST TELECAST: *January 3, 1964*

BROADCAST HISTORY:

Sep 1963–Jan 1964, NBC Fri 9:30–10:00

CAST:

Harry Burns .... Larry Blyden
Rusty .... Susan Silo
Lois .... Dawn Nickerson
Terry .... Diahn Williams

Harry Burns was a vaudeville entertainer with an act that featured three beautiful girl dancers, Rusty, Lois, and Terry. Although his act was much too old-fashioned to be successful in the United States, it was reasonably popular in Europe. Harry, in addition to being the star of the act, had to do the booking, handle finances, and try to keep tabs on the girls. The last was not always easy. Rusty was incredibly gullible and constantly falling in love, Lois was distressingly naive and often acted like a country girl on her first trip to the big city, and Terry was too sophisticated for her own good. Filmed on location throughout Europe, this series followed the travels of *Harry's Girls* as the act played in various continental cities. Occasional excerpts from the act were shown, but only as they fit into the story.

HARRY-O

Detective

FIRST TELECAST: *September 12, 1974*

LAST TELECAST: *August 12, 1976*

BROADCAST HISTORY:

Sep 1974–Aug 1976, ABC Thu 10:00–11:00

CAST:

Harry Orwell .... David Janssen
Det. Lt. Manuel (Manny) Quinlan (1974–1975) .... Henry Darrow
Lt. K.C. Trench (1975–1976) .... Anthony Zerbe
Lester Hodges (1975–1976) .... Les Lannom
Dr. Fong (1976) .... Keye Luke

Harry Orwell was one of TV's more bohemian private eyes, living in a beachfront cottage near San Diego and often using the city bus for transportation (his car didn't work). An ex-Marine and ex-cop pensioned from the force after being injured in the line of duty, he augmented his income by taking cases that especially interested him. These usually involved luscious girls—none of whom seemed to matter much to Harry, however.

Harry's sometime nemesis, sometime ally, was Lt. Manny Quinlan of the San Diego Police Department. Manny was killed off in a February 1975, telecast, after which Harry moved his base of operations to Santa Monica. There, he inherited a new official nemesis, Lt. Trench, plus occasional unsolicited help with his cases from amateur criminologists Lester Hodges and Dr. Fong.

Infrequently seen, but highly visible on those occasions when she did appear, was Harry's girl-next-door, Farrah Fawcett (in later years known as Farrah Fawcett-Majors).

HARTMANS, THE

Situation Comedy

FIRST TELECAST: *February 27, 1949*

LAST TELECAST: *May 22, 1949*

BROADCAST HISTORY:

Feb 1949–May 1949, NBC Sun 7:30–8:00

CAST:

Grace Hartman .... Herself
Paul Hartman .... Himself
The handyman .... Harold Stone
Their brother-in-law .... Loring Smith
Their nephew .... Bob Shawley
The man next door .... Gage Clark
Grace's sister .... Valerie Cossart

Grace and Paul Hartman, the famous dance satirists, played straight comedy in this early live series about the trials of a young married couple living in a suburb called Forest Heights.

HATHAWAYS, THE

Situation Comedy

FIRST TELECAST: *October 6, 1961*

LAST TELECAST: *August 31, 1962*

BROADCAST HISTORY:

Oct 1961–Aug 1962, ABC Fri 8:00–8:30

CAST:

Elinore Hathaway .... Peggy Cass
Walter Hathaway .... Jack Weston

The Hathaways were a family of five, all of them wearing normal clothes and eating together at the same table, but only two of them were people. Walter Hathaway was a real estate agent and Elinore was his wife. Charlie, Enoch, and Cindy were chimps—the Marquis Chimps—and very bright chimps at that. Elinore, besides treating them like her children, was booking agent for their show-business act, which included riding bicycles and making faces. Walter had mixed emotions about the whole arrangement, wondering if the chimps meant more to his wife than he did, and their suburban neighbors also had some difficulty adjusting to "the kids next door."

HAVE GUN WILL TRAVEL

Western

FIRST TELECAST: *September 14, 1957*

LAST TELECAST: *September 21, 1963*

BROADCAST HISTORY:

Sep 1957–Sep 1963, CBS Sat 9:30–10:00

CAST:

Paladin .... Richard Boone
Hey Boy (1957–1960; 1961–1963) .... Kam Tong
Hey Girl (1960–1961) .... Lisa Lu

THEME:

"The Ballad of Paladin," by Johnny Western, Richard Boone and Sam Rolfe, sung on the soundtrack by Johnny Western.

Have Gun Will Travel was one of the most popular programs of the late 1950s, and the chief prototype of a rash of dapper heroes invented by TV to populate the Old West. Paladin was certainly not your normal, everyday illiterate gunslinger. He was college-educated, having attended West Point in pursuit of a military career. Instead, after serving in the Civil War, he headed west to become a high-priced "gun for hire," a kind of Old West troubleshooter. He was based at the fancy Hotel Carlton in San Francisco and his calling card bore the figure of a paladin (the white chess knight) and the inscription, "Have Gun, Will Travel . . . Wire Paladin, San Francisco."

Paladin was a man of culture, enjoying the finest clothes, epicurean meals, and literate company—except when he was on assignment. Then, dressed all in black, he became a very intimidating figure indeed. Despite his somewhat violent profession, he had a sense of ethics that dictated what he would and would not do; it occasionally led him to seek out the very people who had hired him if they in fact were the guilty parties. Hey Boy, the Oriental working at the Hotel Carlton, was seen at the beginning of most episodes bringing a message to Paladin from a prospective client. (During the 1960–1961 season, while Kam Tong was involved in a more substantial role in another series, *The Garlund Touch*, he was replaced by Lisa Lu. He returned to *Have Gun Will Travel* after his new venture was canceled.)

Have Gun Will Travel was an overnight hit, ranking among the top five programs during its first season on the air. From 1958–1961 it was the number three program on television, behind two other Westerns—*Gunsmoke* and *Wagon Train*. Its theme song, "The Ballad of Paladin," was a hit single in the early 1960s.

HAVING BABIES

Medical Drama

FIRST TELECAST: *March 7, 1978*
LAST TELECAST: *April 18, 1978*
BROADCAST HISTORY:

Mar 1978–Apr 1978, ABC Tue 10:00–11:00

CAST:

Dr. Julie Farr .... Susan Sullivan
Dr. Blake Simmons .... Mitchell Ryan
Dr. Ron Danvers .... Dennis Howard
Kelly .... Beverly Todd

This medical drama was one of several new programs which got short run try-outs during the spring of 1978 to test their potential as regular fall series. Dr. Julie Farr was a dedicated physician at Lake General Hospital whose practice brought her into contact with couples from all walks of life, many of whom had one thing in common: the joy and pain of childbirth. Several stories were usually seen in each episode, at least one of which always dealt with childbirth: for example, the illegal alien who wanted her baby to be born in the United States, even though she was suffering from malaria; the "storybook marriage" that threatened to crumble with the prospect of pregnancy; the wealthy father who had never learned to enjoy his success.

Dr. Simmons was the experienced older doctor, and Dr. Danvers the eager intern.

Having Babies was first seen as a series of movie specials from 1976–1978. Effective with the March 28, 1978, episode its title was changed to *Julie Farr, M.D.*

HAWAII FIVE-O

Police

FIRST TELECAST: *September 26, 1968*
LAST TELECAST:
BROADCAST HISTORY:

Sep 1968–Dec 1968, CBS Thu 8:00–9:00
Dec 1968–Sep 1971, CBS Wed 10:00–11:00
Sep 1971–Sep 1974, CBS Tue 8:30–9:30
Sep 1974–Sep 1975, CBS Tue 9:00–10:00
Sep 1975–Nov 1975, CBS Fri 9:00–10:00
Dec 1975– , CBS Thu 9:00–10:00

CAST:

Det. Steve McGarrett .... Jack Lord
Det. Danny Williams ..... James MacArthur
Det. Chin Ho Kelly (1968–1978) .... Kam Fong
Det. Kono (1968–1972) .... Zulu
Governor Philip Grey .... Richard Denning
Det. Ben Kokua (1972–1974) .... Al Harrington
Coroner Che Fong (1970–1977) .... Harry Endo
Doc (1970–1976) .... Al Eban
May (1968–1969) .... Maggi Parker
Jenny (1969–1976) .... Peggy Ryan
Duke Lukela (1972–) .... Herman Wedemeyer
The Attorney General (1968–1969) .... Morgan White
Att. Gen. John Manicote (1975–1977) .... Glenn Cannon
Wo Fat (1968–1975) .... Khigh Dhiegh

Though based in the Iolani Palace in downtown Honolulu, the men of Hawaii's Five-O group were not members of the Honolulu Police Department. They worked instead as part of the Hawaiian State Police and were accountable directly to the governor. Stolid, unemotional Steve McGarrett was the head of Five-O, and worked with his own men and the local police in solving various individual crimes and fighting the organized forces of the Hawaiian underworld. Most hated of all the evil men in the islands was the criminal genius Wo Fat. He would pop up periodically to make life difficult for McGarrett, who was bound and determined to put him in jail. Though Steve did manage to interfere with Wo Fat's illegal operations, he never could piece together sufficient evidence to bring him to court.

Hawaii Five-O was filmed entirely on location and it may well have been the beautiful scenery as well as the action and adventure that made it so popular. Whatever the causes, *Hawaii Five-O* was immensely successful. It was the longest continuously running police show in the history of television. Surprisingly, there was practically no turnover among the leads. Steve did go through two secretaries, May being replaced by Jenny after the first season, and one of his assistants, Kono, left after four seasons, but for most of the cast the working conditions in Hawaii were too pleasant to give up. After ten seasons, however, Kam Fong tired of the role of Chin Ho Kelly and was written out of the show by having his character killed in the final episode of the 1977–1978 season.

The Iolani Palace which in this series was the seat of the Hawaiian government, had at one time housed the Hawaiian Legislature. That time was long gone, however, as it had been a museum for many years prior to the start of *Hawaii Five-O*.

HAWAIIAN EYE

Detective

FIRST TELECAST: *October 7, 1959*

LAST TELECAST: *September 10, 1963*

BROADCAST HISTORY:

Oct 1959–Sep 1962, ABC Wed 9:00–10:00
Oct 1962–Sep 1963, ABC Tue 8:30–9:30

CAST:

Tom Lopaka .... Bob Conrad
Tracy Steele (1959–1962) .. Anthony Eisley
Cricket Blake .... Connie Stevens
Kazuo Kim .... Poncie Ponce
Greg MacKenzie (1960–1963) .... Grant Williams
Quon (1960–1963) .... Mel Prestidge
Moke (1960–1963) .... Doug Mossman
Philip Barton (1962–1963) .. Troy Donahue

Hawaiian Eye has been called "*77 Sunset Strip* played in Hawaii." There certainly were similarities. Both shows were produced by the same studio (Warner Brothers), both featured two handsome, free-swinging young detectives as alternate leads, both had simple melodramatic plots set against glamorous backgrounds, and both made use of nutty sidekicks for comic relief.

Base of operations for Tom Lopaka and Tracy Steele was a swank, poolside office at the Hawaiian Village Hotel. Their sidekicks were a pert, somewhat addled young singer-photographer named Cricket, and a colorful cabbie named Kim. Kim, the operator of a one-man taxi service, was especially helpful as he had seemingly dozens of relatives scattered around the islands ready to help out if one of his employers needed some local assistance. Kim's trademarks were his *pupute* ("crazy") straw hat, dumb jokes, and ukulele.

A new detective named Greg MacKenzie arrived in December 1960, while Philip Barton joined the cast of characters in 1962 as the hotel's social director. Quon was the contact on the Honolulu police force. Fellow gumshoe Stu Bailey of *77 Sunset Strip* made an occasional visit from the mainland, possibly to get a closer look at some of the beautiful girls who peopled every *Hawaiian Eye* plot. But then, he had beautiful girls in *his* series, too.

HAWK

Police

FIRST TELECAST: *September 8, 1966*

LAST TELECAST: *August 11, 1976*

BROADCAST HISTORY:

Sep 1966–Dec 1966, ABC Thu 10:00–11:00
Apr 1976–Aug 1976, NBC Wed 10:00–11:00

CAST:

Lt. John Hawk .... Burt Reynolds
Det. Carter .... Wayne Grice

Hawk was a police story with a twist. John Hawk was a full-blooded Iroquois Indian working the night beat for the New York District Attorney's Office with his partner Det. Carter. Filmed on location in and around New York City at night, the cases in which he was involved sent him to the rich and the poor, from the exclusive penthouses along Park Avenue to the run-down tenements of the West Side. The star of this series, Burt Reynolds, was himself part Indian. *Hawk* was originally aired by ABC in the fall of 1966. Almost a decade later, hoping to capitalize on Burt Reynolds' later development into a celebrity, NBC aired reruns of the ABC series during the summer of 1976 (as CBS had done with *Dan August*, another ABC series in which Reynolds had starred).

HAWKINS

Lawyer

FIRST TELECAST: *October 2, 1973*

LAST TELECAST: *September 3, 1974*

BROADCAST HISTORY:

Oct 1973–Sep 1974, CBS Tue 9:30–11:00

CAST:

Billy Jim Hawkins .... James Stewart
R. J. Hawkins .... Strother Martin

Billy Jim Hawkins had given up his position as a deputy district attorney to enter private legal practice in rural West Virginia. His small-town location did not keep fancy clients away, however, as his fame as a specialist in murder cases attracted clients from far and wide. His pleasant, slow-talking, homespun qualities belied the shrewd, determined attorney that he really was, and he often traveled great distances with his cousin and investigative assistant R.J. in search of evidence that would clear his clients of guilt and lead to the apprehension of the real culprits.

Hawkins was one of the three rotating elements that filled the 9:30–11 P.M. time slot on Tuesday nights for CBS during the 1973–1974 season. The other two were *Shaft* and *The New CBS Tuesday Night Movies.*

HAWKINS FALLS, POPULATION 6,200

Comedy-Drama

FIRST TELECAST: *June 17, 1950*

LAST TELECAST: *October 12, 1950*

BROADCAST HISTORY:

Jun 1950–Aug 1950, NBC Sat 8:00–9:00
Aug 1950–Oct 1950, NBC Thu 8:30–9:00

CAST:

Clate Weathers .... Frank Dane
The Judge .... Phil Lord
Laif Flaigle .... Win Stracke
Mrs. Catherwood .... Hope Summers

This series, which later became a straightforward daytime soap opera, began as a prime-time summer replacement show containing an odd mixture of situation comedy, light drama, and musical entertainment. The setting was the "typical" small town of Hawkins Falls, U.S.A. (patterned after real-life Woodstock, Illinois). The format called for the local newspaper editor, Clate Weathers, to describe the latest events in town, which were then dramatized. Each weekly episode was complete in itself; for example, the uproar when the town loafer (Laif) was put forward as a candidate for mayor, and the events surrounding a typical country auction. Mrs. Catherwood was the president of the garden club.

Hawkins Falls returned to the air in April 1951, as a Monday–Friday daytime serial, retaining many of the same cast members. The daytime version lasted until July 1955.

HAYLOFT HOEDOWN

Country Music

FIRST TELECAST: *July 10, 1948*

LAST TELECAST: *September 18, 1948*

BROADCAST HISTORY:

Jul 1948–Sep 1948, ABC Sat 9:30–10:00

EMCEE:

Elmer Newman

WITH:

Jack Day
Murray Sisters
Jesse Rogers
Stuff Jumpers
Wesley Tuttle
Ranch Square Dancers
The Sleepy Hollow Gang (instrumental)

One of the earliest examples of Country music on network television, and one of ABC's first series, was this bush-league production from Town Hall in Philadelphia, telecast on Saturday nights during the summer of 1948. The talent was little known even in the Country field, but everyone pitched in with enthusiasm with square dancing, yodeling, comedy routines, and the like. Emcee Elmer Newman doubled as "Pancake Pete."

Previously heard on radio.

HAZEL

Situation Comedy

FIRST TELECAST: *September 28, 1961*

LAST TELECAST: *September 5, 1966*

BROADCAST HISTORY:

Sep 1961–Jul 1964, NBC Thu 9:30–10:00 (OS)
Sep 1964–Sep 1965, NBC Thu 9:30–10:00
Sep 1965–Sep 1966, CBS Mon 9:30–10:00

CAST:

Hazel .... Shirley Booth
George Baxter (1961–1965) .... Don DeFore
Dorothy Baxter (1961–1965)
.... Whitney Blake
Harold Baxter .... Bobby Buntrock
Mrs. Johnson (1961–1963) .. Norma Varden
Mr. Johnson (1961–1963) .... Donald Foster
Steve Baxter (1965–1966) ...... Ray Fulmer
Barbara Baxter (1965–1966) .. Lynn Borden
Susie Baxter (1965–1966) ... Julia Benjamin

George Baxter was a highly successful corporation lawyer who was always in control of everything at the office, but of almost nothing at home. When he returned from the office at day's end, to his wife Dorothy and his young son Harold, he entered the world of Hazel. Hazel was the maid/housekeeper who ran the Baxter household more efficiently than George ran his office. She was always right, knew exactly what needed doing, and preempted his authority with alarming, though justified, regularity. The Johnsons were the Baxters' nutty neighbors.

When this series moved to CBS in 1965, Hazel changed families. George and Dorothy had been "transferred" to the Middle East on an assignment, leaving Hazel and son Harold to live with George's brother's family—which consisted of brother Steve, his wife Barbara, and daughter Susie. Steve Baxter was a real estate agent who had never understood why George had let Hazel take over his home. He soon found out.

Hazel was based on the *Saturday Evening Post* cartoons of Ted Key.

HAZEL SCOTT

Music

FIRST TELECAST: *July 3, 1950*
LAST TELECAST: *September 29, 1950*
BROADCAST HISTORY:
Jul 1950–Sep 1950, DUM Mon/Wed/Fri 7:45–8:00
HOSTESS:
Hazel Scott

This summer music show was hosted by Trinidad-born singer and pianist Hazel Scott, who performed café favorites and show tunes. Miss Scott, a striking beauty who had appeared in nightclubs, on radio, and in a few movies and Broadway shows, was in private life the wife of New York Congressman Adam Clayton Powell, Jr. She also appeared on local television in New York for a time.

HE & SHE

Situation Comedy

FIRST TELECAST: *September 6, 1967*
LAST TELECAST: *September 11, 1970*
BROADCAST HISTORY:
Sep 1967–Sep 1968, CBS Wed 9:30–10:00
Jun 1970–Sep 1970, CBS Fri 8:00–8:30
CAST:
Paula Hollister ....Paula Prentiss
Dick Hollister ....Richard Benjamin
Oscar North ....Jack Cassidy
Harry Zarakardos ....Kenneth Mars
Andrew Hummel ....Hamilton Camp

Dick Hollister was a successful cartoonist whose creation, "Jetman," had been turned into a TV show starring Oscar North in the title role. Oscar was a bit on the arrogant, smug, egocentric side, and was constantly disagreeing with Dick about the proper interpretation of "Jetman." Paula, Dick's scatterbrained, social-worker wife, had problems of her own which always seemed to end up being shared by the two of them. Andrew Hummel was the fumbling superintendent of the New York apartment building in which Dick and Paula lived, and Harry was their fireman-friend.

Paula Prentiss and Richard Benjamin were husband and wife in real life. Reruns of this series, which bore more than a passing resemblance to the classic *Dick Van Dyke Show,* were aired by CBS in the summer of 1970.

HEADLINE

syndicated title for *Big Town*

HEADLINE CLUES

see *Broadway to Hollywood—Headline Clues*

HEADLINERS WITH DAVID FROST

Talk/Interview

FIRST TELECAST: *May 31, 1978*
LAST TELECAST: *July 5, 1978*
BROADCAST HISTORY:
May 1978–Jul 1978, NBC Wed 9:00–10:00
HOST:
David Frost
REGULARS:
Liz Smith
Kelly Garrett

Celebrity interviewer David Frost hosted this 1978 summer series, which originated live from the NBC studios in New York. Those interviewed were generally show business stars, with a few political figures thrown in, making the format an odd combination of superficial and serious subjects. Guests on the first show, for example, were the rock group the Bee Gees, actor John Travolta, and former C.I.A. chief Richard Helms. An additional feature was Headliners Forum, where Frost would pose a question such as "What is the secret of a happy marriage," and a succession of show business, literary, and political figures would be seen (on tape) giving short, humorous answers. Liz Smith contributed a weekly gossip segment and Kelly Garrett sang of recent events in a "That Was the Week That Was" segment.

HEADMASTER, THE

General Drama

FIRST TELECAST: *September 18, 1970*
LAST TELECAST: *September 10, 1971*
BROADCAST HISTORY:

Sep 1970–Jan 1971, CBS Fri 8:30–9:00
Jun 1971–Sep 1971, CBS Fri 8:30–9:00

CAST:

Andy Thompson ....Andy Griffith
Jerry Brownell ....Jerry Van Dyke
Mr. Purdy ....Parker Fennelly
Margaret Thompson .....Claudette Nevins

Andy Thompson was the headmaster of the Concord School, a private high school with high academic standards. His wife was one of the school's English teachers and his best friend, Jerry Brownell, was the physical education teacher and coach. Andy's professional life at the school, dealing with the problems of teachers and students, provided the central focus of this folksy series.

Andy Griffith's past television success had been in a very different, country-boy role, and the viewing public did not accept him in this more dignified dramatic setting. In January 1971 he tried to revert to his earlier type of portrayal on a series called *The New Andy Griffith Show*, but that too proved unsuccessful and reruns of *The Headmaster* returned to the time slot in June.

HEART OF THE CITY

syndicated title for *Big Town*

HEAVEN FOR BETSY

Situation Comedy

FIRST TELECAST: *September 30, 1952*
LAST TELECAST: *December 23, 1952*
BROADCAST HISTORY:

Sep 1952–Dec 1952, CBS Tue/Thu 7:45–8:00

CAST:

Pete Bell ....Jack Lemmon
Betsy Bell ....Cynthia Stone

This early live domestic comedy starred real-life newlyweds Jack Lemmon and Cynthia Stone as Pete and Betsy Bell, newlyweds who were adjusting to married life. Pete was assistant buyer in the toy department of a suburban New York department store. His biggest problem was his tendency to jump into a situation before realizing its ramifications. His wife Betsy, a secretary turned full-time homemaker, was not really occupied maintaining their two-room apartment, but had plenty to do getting Pete out of various scrapes. Lemmon and Stone worked together in several TV series in the early 1950s, before he began his highly successful movie career in 1954.

HEC RAMSEY

Western

FIRST TELECAST: *October 8, 1972*
LAST TELECAST: *August 25, 1974*
BROADCAST HISTORY:

Oct 1972–Aug 1974, NBC Sun 8:30–10:00

CAST:

Hec Ramsey ....Richard Boone
Sheriff Oliver B. Stamp ......Richard Lenz
Doc. Amos Coogan ....Harry Morgan
Arne Tornquist ....Dennis Rucker

Hec Ramsey was a grizzled old gunfighter, living around the turn of the century, who had become interested in the "newfangled" science of criminology and spent years learning all he could about it. He still carried a gun, but had come to rely on a trunk full of paraphernalia that included fingerprinting equipment, magnifying glasses, scales, and other odds and ends to track down culprits. As the series began Hec arrived in New Prospect, Oklahoma, to take a job as deputy sheriff. He soon discovered that the sheriff, Oliver B. Stamp, was very young and inexperienced. Stamp, fearing that Hec's legendary "fast gun" would attract trouble, was uncertain about his new partner, but young sheriff and old deputy eventually learned to make good use of Hec's novel methods.

Hec Ramsey spent two seasons as one of the four rotating elements of the *NBC Sunday Mystery Movie*. The other three elements were *Columbo*, *McCloud*, and *McMillan and Wife*.

HEE HAW

Variety

FIRST TELECAST: *June 15, 1969*
LAST TELECAST: *July 13, 1971*

BROADCAST HISTORY:

Jun 1969–Sep 1969, CBS Sun 9:00–10:00
Dec 1969–Jun 1970, CBS Wed 7:30–8:30
Sep 1970–Jul 1971, CBS Tue 8:30–9:30

REGULARS:

Buck Owens
Roy Clark
Grandpa Jones
Junior Samples
Cathy Baker
Jeannine Riley
Don Harron
The Hagers
Lisa Todd (1970–1971)
Archie Campbell
Stringbean
Sheb Wooley (1969)
Susan Raye (1969)
Lulu Roman
Gordie Tapp
Gunilla Hutton
Mary Taylor (1969–1970)

Hee Haw was Country music's answer to *Rowan & Martin's Laugh-In*. Blackouts, nutty running gags, cameos by assorted guest stars, and some of the worst "corny" one-liners imaginable, appropriately delivered from a cornfield, all contributed to the mix. An animated donkey was used on a regular basis to react to the humor, and to provide the "hee haw" of the title.

Although the humor was purposely cornball, the music on *Hee Haw* was first-rate Country and Western material. Co-hosts Buck Owens and Roy Clark were both major Country stars, Clark being one of the best banjoist-guitarists in the business. Other big names from the Country field, both current and long-established, were also featured regularly. *Hee Haw* was in the top 20 nationally when it was dropped from the network in 1971, a victim of CBS's decision to "de-ruralize" its programming (national advertisers want only young, urban audiences). Like *Lawrence Welk*, which was dropped by ABC for similar reasons, it promptly went into syndication with all new shows and has been a major hit ever since on a non-network basis.

HELEN O'CONNELL SHOW, THE

Music

FIRST TELECAST: *May 29, 1957*
LAST TELECAST: *September 6, 1957*
BROADCAST HISTORY:

May 1957–Sep 1957, NBC Wed/Fri 7:30–7:45

REGULAR:

Helen O'Connell

Big-band singer Helen O'Connell was on the air twice a week with this live musical show that occupied the remainder of the half-hour in which NBC telecast its network news program. The show originated from New York and gave Miss O'Connell the opportunity to sing several songs, occasionally with a guest star but more often without.

HELEN REDDY SHOW, THE

Musical Variety

FIRST TELECAST: *June 28, 1973*
LAST TELECAST: *August 16, 1973*
BROADCAST HISTORY:

Jun 1973–Aug 1973, NBC Thu 8:00–9:00

REGULAR:

Helen Reddy

THEME:

"I Am Woman," by Helen Reddy (lyrics) and Ray Burton (music)

Australian singer Helen Reddy, who became something of a symbol of the Women's Liberation movement through her best-selling recording "I Am Woman" ("I am strong, I am invincible . . ."), was the star and only regular on this 1973 summer series. The format of the show included comedy skits and musical numbers with guest stars. Each show closed with a question-and-answer session, with the questions coming from members of the studio audience.

HENNESEY

Comedy-Drama

FIRST TELECAST: *September 28, 1959*
LAST TELECAST: *September 17, 1962*
BROADCAST HISTORY:

Sep 1959–Sep 1962, CBS Mon 10:00–10:30 (OS)

CAST:

Chick Hennesey .... Jackie Cooper
Martha Hale .... Abby Dalton
Capt. Shafer .... Roscoe Karns
Max Bronski .... Henry Kulky
Harvey Spencer Blair III .... James Komack
Seaman Shatz .... Arte Johnson

Stationed at a naval base in San Diego, Lt. Chick Hennesey was a young medical officer who treated the base personnel and their families. He worked for crusty Capt.

Shafer (who during the course of the series would be promoted to admiral), and had attractive Martha Hale for an understanding and romantically interested nurse. Their romance blossomed and they became engaged, with the wedding taking place in the episode that aired on May 7, 1962. The biggest "character" in the entire medical department was Harvey Spencer Blair III, a young naval dentist whose society background and financial independence grated on all concerned. Blair was always looking for angles and gimmicks, much in the style of Ernie Bilko in *The Phil Silvers Show* but, unlike Bilko, fancied himself a real ladies' man.

HENNY AND ROCKY SHOW, THE

Comedy Variety

FIRST TELECAST: *June 1, 1955*

LAST TELECAST: *August 10, 1955*

BROADCAST HISTORY:

Jun 1955–Aug 1955, ABC Wed 10:45–11:00

REGULARS:

Rocky Graziano
Henny Youngman
Marion Colby
Bobby Hackett
Buddy Weed

Designed to fill the time slot between the end of *The Wednesday Night Fights* and the start of the eleven o'clock local news, *The Henny and Rocky Show* provided the singing of Marion Colby and the playing of a jazz combo featuring Bobby Hackett on trumpet and Buddy Weed on piano. Comedy was supplied by Henny Youngman and ex-middleweight boxing champion Rocky Graziano. Featured in the show was a recap of the night's fight and "Ribber's Digest" in which Henny satirized the current news. Henny left the show following the June 29 telecast and it was retitled *Rocky's Corner.*

HENRY MORGAN SHOW, THE

see *Henry Morgan's Great Talent Hunt*

HENRY MORGAN'S GREAT TALENT HUNT

Comedy Variety

FIRST TELECAST: *January 26, 1951*

LAST TELECAST: *June 1, 1951*

BROADCAST HISTORY:

Jan 1951–Mar 1951, NBC Fri 9:00–9:30
Mar 1951–Jun 1951, NBC Fri 9:30–10:00

REGULARS:

Henry Morgan
Dorothy Clair
Kay Ballard
Dorothy Jarnac
Arnold Stang
Art Carney
Pert Kelton

This program started as a satire on the *Original Amateur Hour*–type program with Henry Morgan introducing people with offbeat "talents"—a man who played the violin by picking the strings with his teeth, a girl who tap-danced while playing an instrument, a woman who had taught her dog to talk, etc. Arnold Stang was Henry's helper, supposedly tracking down all of the "talented" guests on the show. Morgan opened the show with a monologue and after the acts had performed, the winner was chosen by the applause level of the studio audience. On April 20, 1951, the title of this live program was shortened to *The Henry Morgan Show* and the format changed. It became a comedy variety show with the emphasis on satiric comedy skits. Singer Dorothy Clair and dancer Dorothy Jarnac provided musical numbers between the skits.

HERALD PLAYHOUSE

syndicated title for *Schlitz Playhouse of Stars*

HERB SHRINER SHOW, THE

Comedy Variety

FIRST TELECAST: *November 7, 1949*

LAST TELECAST: *December 4, 1956*

BROADCAST HISTORY:

Nov 1949–Feb 1950, CBS Mon/Tue/Thu/Fri/Sat 7:55–8:00
Oct 1951–Apr 1952, ABC Thu 9:00–9:30
Oct 1956–Dec 1956, CBS Tue 9:00–9:30

REGULARS:

Herb Shriner

Herb Shriner was a humorist who had become famous on radio in the late 1940s with his folksy monologues on rural life back home in Indiana, interspersed with harmonica solos. His homespun philosophy, and his disarming, ingenuous personality often led to comparisons with the late Will Rogers. During the 1948–1949 season Shriner had a Monday–Friday daytime show on CBS and in the fall of 1949 he moved into nighttime television with a five-a-week series of short monologues called *The Herb Shriner Show*. ABC brought him back in 1951 as the host of an evening half-hour entitled *Herb Shriner Time*. The longer format gave him a chance to play his harmonica and work in skits with guest stars, as well as deliver his tall tales. It was essentially this same format that was tried again in the fall of 1956 on CBS in *The Herb Shriner Show*.

HERE AND NOW

Documentary

FIRST TELECAST: *September 29, 1961*

LAST TELECAST: *December 29, 1961*

BROADCAST HISTORY:

Sep 1961–Dec 1961, NBC Fri 10:30–11:00

HOST:

Frank McGee

Frank McGee narrated the three or four stories that were covered in each telecast of this magazine-format news program. The subjects were people involved in major news stories in varied areas ranging from politics to medicine to the arts. Emphasis was placed on how the people involved were affected by the news events, not simply upon the events themselves.

HERE COME THE BRIDES

Comedy Adventure

FIRST TELECAST: *September 25, 1968*

LAST TELECAST: *September 18, 1970*

BROADCAST HISTORY:

Sep 1968–Sep 1969, ABC Wed 7:30–8:30
Sep 1969–Sep 1970, ABC Fri 9:00–10:00

CAST:

Jason Bolt .... Robert Brown
Jeremy Bolt .... Bobby Sherman
Joshua Bolt .... David Soul
Lottie .... Joan Blondell
Candy Pruitt .... Bridget Hanley
Aaron Stempel .... Mark Lenard
Big Swede .... Bo Svensen
Biddie Cloom .... Susan Tolsky
Capt. Charley Clancey .... Henry Beckman
Miss Essie Gillis .... Mitzi Hoag

THEME:

"Seattle," by Jack Keller, Hugo Montenegro, and Ernie Sheldon

Comedy-adventure set in boomtown Seattle (pop. 152) in the 1870s. Logging camp operator Jason Bolt and his young brothers Jeremy and Joshua were in danger of losing their timberland, at Bridal Veil Mountain, because their men were in near revolt—over the lack of women in Seattle. Jason contrived an ingenious scheme. Using funds borrowed from rival saw-mill operator Aaron Stempel, he sailed back to New Bedford, Massachusetts, and persuaded 100 prospective brides to return with him to the frontier. The girls, led by "straw boss" Candy Pruitt, returned with Jason aboard Capt. Clancey's decrepit ship, and Seattle was never the same again.

There was a catch, however. If any of the 100 girls left before a year was up, Jason would forfeit his land to Stempel. It was quite a year, but Jason won his wager.

Bobby Sherman and David Soul were both looked on as promising young singers when *Brides* was cast. Boosted by exposure on the series, Sherman went on to become a highly popular recording star beginning in 1969, and subsequently appeared in other TV series (see Index). Blond-haired David Soul, who had his first regular TV exposure as the hooded "mystery singer" on *The Merv Griffin Show* from 1966–1967, later became Hutch on the enormously popular *Starsky and Hutch*. He also married (in real life) one of the "brides" he met on this series' set, actress Karen Carlson.

HERE WE GO AGAIN

Situation Comedy

FIRST TELECAST: *January 20, 1973*

LAST TELECAST: *June 16, 1973*

BROADCAST HISTORY:

Jan 1973–Jun 1973, ABC Sat 8:00–8:30

CAST:

Richard Evans .... Larry Hagman
Susan Evans .... Diane Baker
Jerry Standish .... Dick Gautier
Judy Evans .... Nita Talbot
Jeff .... Chris Beaumont
Cindy .... Leslie Graves
Jan .... Kim Richards

Divorce-as-comedy; the trials of a newly married couple whose former mates lived nearby, and kept intruding on their connubial bliss. Susan's first husband was Jerry Standish, a free-swinging restauranteur, owner of Jerry's Polonesian Paradise. Richard's ex-wife was Judy, a rather domineering magazine editor. Adding to the general confusion were the children, Susan's two little girls, Cindy and Jan (who lived with the Evanses), and Richard's teenage son, Jeff (who lived with his mother, Judy).

HERE'S LUCY

see *Lucy Show, The*

HERITAGE

Music and Art

FIRST TELECAST: *August 1, 1951*
LAST TELECAST: *September 5, 1951*
BROADCAST HISTORY:
Aug 1951–Sep 1951, NBC Wed 8:00–9:00
HOST:
Frank Blair

The National Gallery of Art in Washington, D.C., was the setting for this cultural series telecast live during the summer of 1951. The program consisted primarily of classical selections played by the 30-piece National Gallery Orchestra, with commentary by one of its members, pianist Rose d'Amore. During the first intermission, chief curator of the museum John Walker or a member of his staff discussed the paintings currently on exhibit, while the camera gave viewers a chance to see them. During the second intermission Miss d'Amore interviewed one of the composers whose work was being performed that night.

HERMAN HICKMAN SHOW, THE

Sports Commentary

FIRST TELECAST: *October 3, 1952*
LAST TELECAST: *March 27, 1953*
BROADCAST HISTORY:
Oct 1952–Mar 1953, NBC Fri 7:00–7:15
REGULARS:
Herman Hickman
Rex Marshall

Herman Hickman was the star of this program which featured football predictions, reminiscences on his days as head football coach at Yale University, other stories in the sports vein, and an occasional poetic recitation. Actor Rex Marshall was a regular on the show and helped in its presentation. Sports and entertainment personalities served as guests, chatting with Herman on sports and other topics.

HERO, THE

Situation Comedy

FIRST TELECAST: *September 8, 1966*
LAST TELECAST: *January 5, 1967*
BROADCAST HISTORY:
Sep 1966–Jan 1967, NBC Thu 9:30–10:00
CAST:
Sam Garret ....Richard Mulligan
Ruth Garret ....Mariette Hartley
Paul Garret ....Bobby Horan
Fred Gilman ....Victor French
Burton Gilman ....Joey Baio
Dewey ....Marc London

The real world and the make-believe world of television are two completely different things. That was the message of this unusual TV self-satire. Sam Garret was a hugely popular TV star with his own (fictional) Western series, *Jed Clayton—U.S. Marshal*. The real Sam differed somewhat from the coolly imperturbable hero of the TV screen, however. To his wife Ruth and his son Paul, as well as to their neighbors, the Gilmans, Sam was a nice guy who, among other things, was afraid of horses, allergic to sagebrush, and all thumbs when it came to any activity requiring coordination.

HEY JEANNIE

Situation Comedy

FIRST TELECAST: *September 8, 1956*
LAST TELECAST: *September 30, 1960*
BROADCAST HISTORY:
Sep 1956–May 1957, CBS Sat 9:30–10:00
Jun 1960–Sep 1960, ABC Thu 9:00–9:30
CAST:
Jeannie MacLennan .... Jeannie Carson
Al Murray .... Allen Jenkins
Liz Murray .... Jane Dulo

Jeannie MacLennan was a sweet, naive young Scottish lass who had arrived in the United States with no job and no place to live. After clearing customs (which evidently didn't mind her lack of employment) she went on a tour of New York with cabdriver Al Murray. For reasons he never fully understood, he offered to become her sponsor. Jeannie moved in with Al and his sister Liz, and then set about learning about her adopted country, its strange customs and stranger people.

Three years after this filmed series ended its run on CBS it was brought back, in reruns, as an ABC summer series, under the title *The Jeannie Carson Show*.

HEY LANDLORD

Situation Comedy

FIRST TELECAST: *September 11, 1966*
LAST TELECAST: *May 14, 1967*
BROADCAST HISTORY:
Sep 1966–May 1967, NBC Sun 8:30–9:00
CAST:
Woody Banner .... Will Hutchins
Chuck Hookstratten .... Sandy Baron
Timothy Morgan .... Pamela Rodgers
Kyoko Mitsui .... Miko Mayama
Jack Ellenhorn .... Michael Constantine

Woody, the landlord in this comedy series, was not the usual bumbling old codger but a young, trusting Ohio lad fresh out of college, who had come to New York to find out more about life. His building, inherited from an uncle, was a brownstone in Manhattan's East 30s which was peopled with the usual assortment of lunatics generally found on TV comedies. Woody shared his own apartment with Chuck Hookstratten, an aspiring young comic who was born and raised in the city, and who was constantly amazed at Woody's blind faith in people. Woody planned to manage the building while living off the proceeds. Far from supporting him, however, he found that he had to go to work to support the brownstone—its condition and age caused constant and costly problems. Meanwhile his tenants, including photographer Jack, glamorous Timothy and her roommate Kyoko, yelled "Hey landlord!"

HEY MULLIGAN

see *Mickey Rooney Show, The*

HIGH ADVENTURE WITH LOWELL THOMAS

Adventure/Travelogue
FIRST TELECAST: *June 16, 1964*
LAST TELECAST: *September 15, 1964*
BROADCAST HISTORY:
Jun 1964–Sep 1964, CBS Tue 8:00–9:00
HOST:
Lowell Thomas

This summer series was a collection of reruns of selected specials, telecast under the same title, that had originally aired in the late 1950s. Lowell Thomas—newsman, adventurer, and explorer—had led these filmed expeditions to remote and exotic locations around the world. Among them were a visit to the capital of Tibet, a tour through the casbah of Morocco, and an expedition to the Australian Outback.

HIGH CHAPARRAL, THE

Western
FIRST TELECAST: *September 10, 1967*
LAST TELECAST: *September 10, 1971*
BROADCAST HISTORY:
Sep 1967–Sep 1968, NBC Sun 10:00–11:00
Sep 1968–Dec 1970, NBC Fri 7:30–8:30
Feb 1971–Sep 1971, NBC Fri 7:30–8:30
CAST:
Big John Cannon .... Leif Erickson
Buck Cannon .... Cameron Mitchell
Billy Blue Cannon (1967–1970) .... Mark Slade
Manolito Montoya .... Henry Darrow
Victoria Cannon .... Linda Cristal
Don Sebastian Montoya (1967–1970) .... Frank Silvera
Sam Butler .... Don Collier
Reno (1967–1970) .... Ted Markland
Pedro (1967–1970) ...... Roberto Contreras
Joe .... Robert Hoy
Wind (1970–1971) .... Rudy Ramos

High Chaparral was the name given to the ranch owned and operated by the Cannon family in the Arizona Territory during the 1870s. Stubborn, determined Big John Cannon was the patriarch of the family, and his driving ambition to establish a flourishing cattle empire in the rugged, Indian-infested, Arizona Territory was the thrust of the entire show. His younger brother Buck was a good-natured carouser who could outdrink, outshoot, outfight, and when properly motivated outwork any man alive—with the possible exception of his brother. John's son, Billy Blue, was a young man in his twenties whose mother was killed by an Apache arrow in the first episode of the series. After his first wife's death, Big John married Victoria, daughter of Don Sebastian Montoya and heiress to his extensive cattle holdings. Her brother Manolito accompanied her to the Cannon ranch and became a permanent member of the household. Sam was the foreman, while Reno, Pedro, and Joe were ranch hands.

The marriage of John and Victoria also united the Cannons and the Montoyas in their efforts to tame the land. Family differences, the conflicts between the Mexicans and the Americans, and the ever-present threats from rustlers and renegade Indians all provided material for the stories in this series.

A number of cast changes occurred in the

program's last season. The character of Billy Blue Cannon was dropped. Frank Silvera, who played Victoria's father, had died and his character was written out of the show by having Don Sebastian also pass away. Added to the cast was Wind, a half-breed youth who became a member of the Cannon household after helping Big John avoid a major disaster during a roundup.

HIGH FINANCE

Quiz/Audience Participation

FIRST TELECAST: *July 7, 1956*
LAST TELECAST: *December 15, 1956*
BROADCAST HISTORY:
Jul 1956–Dec 1956, CBS Sat 10:30–11:00
EMCEE:
Dennis James

Contestants on *High Finance* were asked questions based on news items that had appeared in their local papers during the preceding week. Each contestant was given a cash stake to start with and then invested part of it on the assumption that he could answer the questions correctly. Correct answers yielded high returns and the money could be invested again and again until the contestant had achieved his desired objective. There were pitfalls involved and contestants could lose everything by not "investing" wisely. There were prizes available as well as cash, and the ultimate amount that any one contestant could win was set at $110,000. Nobody ever came within $50,000 of the upper limit but there were many winners in the $10,000–$25,000 range.

HIGH ROAD, THE

see *John Gunther's High Road*

HIGH-LOW

Quiz/Audience Participation

FIRST TELECAST: *July 4, 1957*
LAST TELECAST: *September 19, 1957*
BROADCAST HISTORY:
Jul 1957–Sep 1957, NBC Thu 9:30–10:00
EMCEE:
Jack Barry
SEMI-REGULARS:
Burl Ives
John Van Doren
Patricia Medina
Walter Slezak
Hank Bloomgarden

This live quiz show was the 1957 summer replacement for *The Ford Show*. Contestants pitted their knowledge against that of the members of the panel, which consisted of three celebrities each week. The contestant was in an isolation booth and both he and the panelists were asked the same multi-part question. First the panelists each indicated how many parts of the question they could answer. Then the contestant could either attempt to answer as many parts as the "high" panelist, and triple his money, or answer as many parts as the "low" panelist, and double his money. If he failed to answer as many parts as the chosen panel member, however, he lost all but 10 percent of his previous winnings.

HIPPODROME

Circus Variety

FIRST TELECAST: *July 5, 1966*
LAST TELECAST: *September 6, 1966*
BROADCAST HISTORY:
Jul 1966–Sep 1966, CBS Tue 8:30–9:30

Filmed in England, this summer replacement for *The Red Skelton Hour* featured a different celebrity host each week who introduced an assortment of acts that included many circus stalwarts (animal acts, aerialists, clowns, etc.) as well as the more traditional variety-show staples (singers, dancers, and comedians). Hosts included Allan Sherman, Woody Allen, and Merv Griffin.

HIRAM HOLIDAY

see *Adventures of Hiram Holiday, The*

HOBBY LOBBY

Comedy

FIRST TELECAST: *September 30, 1959*
LAST TELECAST: *March 23, 1960*
BROADCAST HISTORY:
Sep 1959–Mar 1960, ABC Wed 8:00–8:30
STAR:
Cliff Arquette *(as Charley Weaver)*

Hobby Lobby gave Charley Weaver the opportunity to chat each week with two people, one a celebrity and one not, about their interesting or amusing hobbies. Zsa Zsa Gabor discussed her love of fencing on one telecast and Gypsy Rose Lee sang the praises of sport fishing on another. Charley also made joking references to the hobbies of residents of his fictional home town of Mount Idy, Ohio. The jokes were more interesting than the hobbies and the hobbies were eventually dropped. Effective with the November 25, 1959, telecast the title was changed to *The Charley Weaver Show*. Each week Charley had one or two guest celebrities come to visit with him in Mount Idy and chat about the activities of such local residents as Elsie Krack, Birdie Rudd, Wallace Swine, Clara Kimball Moots, and Grandpa Snider.

HOGAN'S HEROES

Situation Comedy

FIRST TELECAST: *September 17, 1965*
LAST TELECAST: *July 4, 1971*
BROADCAST HISTORY:

Sep 1965–Sep 1967, CBS Fri 8:30–9:00
Sep 1967–Sep 1969, CBS Sat 9:00–9:30
Sep 1969–Sep 1970, CBS Fri 8:30–9:00
Sep 1970–Jul 1971, CBS Sun 7:30–8:00

CAST:

Col. Robert Hogan .... Bob Crane
Col. Wilhelm Klink ..... Werner Klemperer
Sgt. Hans Schultz ....John Banner
Louis LeBeau ....Robert Clary
Peter Newkirk ....Richard Dawson
Sgt. Kinchloe ....Ivan Dixon
Lt. Carter ....Larry Hovis
Helga (1965–1967) ....Cynthia Lynn

Hogan's Heroes set out to prove that, at least in the world of televised situation comedies, life in a Nazi POW camp during World War II could be fun. Commandant of the camp was the incompetent, monocled Col. Klink, and guarding Stalag 13, where the American-led resistance forces were housed, was the equally inept Sgt. Schultz. Under the direction of Col. Robert Hogan, the prisoners were actually in complete control of the camp. They had rigged the barbed-wire fence so that it could be opened and closed like a garage door. They fed classified information to the Allied forces on the outside, helped fugitives escape from Germany, printed counterfeit money, and did anything else imaginable to confound the Germans. Their living conditions were more reminiscent of a fancy hotel than a POW camp. They had a French chef, a steam room, a barber shop, and more comforts than they would have had at home. Since they were more important to the Allied cause in the camp than out of it, they had no desire to escape, especially considering the fun and comforts they had there.

HOLD IT PLEASE

Quiz/Audience Participation

FIRST TELECAST: *May 8, 1949*
LAST TELECAST: *May 22, 1949*
BROADCAST HISTORY:

May 1949, CBS Sat 7:00–7:30

EMCEE:

Gil Fates

REGULARS:

Bill McGraw
Mort Marshall
Cloris Leachman

Contestants on this short-lived quiz program—it only lasted three weeks—were asked to answer questions that were acted out by the show's regulars. The questions might relate to events in history or be fictional in nature. The regulars often danced and sang, as well as acted, to illustrate the questions. The contestant who successfully answered the basic quiz questions won an opportunity to go for the $1,000 jackpot, as well as the prizes already won. If a contestant won the jackpot, he remained on the program as assistant emcee until there was a new jackpot winner.

HOLD THAT CAMERA

Game/Variety

FIRST TELECAST: *August 27, 1950*
LAST TELECAST: *December 15, 1950*
BROADCAST HISTORY:

Aug 1950–Sep 1950, DUM Sun 7:30–8:00
Sep 1950–Dec 1950, DUM Fri 8:30–9:00

EMCEE:

Jimmy Blaine
Kyle MacDonnell

ORCHESTRA:

Ving Merlin

Hold That Camera began as a game show in which viewers at home played an important role. A home viewer, contacted by telephone, would give directions over the phone to an on-camera contestant who performed stunts for prizes. The contestant completing the stunts in the least amount of time won for both himself and his telephone "partner." Interspersed with the games were songs by host Jimmy Blaine.

After only about a month, both Blaine and the game-show format were scrapped and *Hold That Camera* became a straight variety show, hosted by songstress Kyle MacDonnell. The setting was a nightclub called "The Camera Room," in which Miss MacDonnell and visiting guests stars performed.

HOLD THAT NOTE

Quiz/Audience Participation

FIRST TELECAST: *January 22, 1957*

LAST TELECAST: *April 2, 1957*

BROADCAST HISTORY:

Jan 1957–Apr 1957, NBC Tue 10:30–11:00

EMCEE:

Bert Parks

ANNOUNCER/HOST:

Johnny Olsen

Hold That Note appeared rather suddenly on January 22, 1957, as an unannounced and unexplained replacement for *Break the $250,000 Bank*, which had aired in the same time slot on the previous Tuesday. Bert Parks was the emcee of both programs, and informed viewers of the first telecast of *Hold That Note* that the contestants who were still on from last week's edition of *Break the $250,000 Bank* had been paid their winnings and given the opportunity to become contestants on the new show, which two of them did. There was really no mystery surrounding the sudden departure of *Break the $250,000 Bank*. It had been doing poorly in the ratings and seemed not to be working too well, so the producers decided to try another giveaway show in its place.

The object of *Hold That Note*, much like that of the somewhat similar but longer-lasting *Name That Tune*, was for the contestants to recognize a particular tune as soon as possible. The fewer notes played, the more the tune was worth. The first person to correctly identify three tunes was the winner of the round and the accumulated money in that round. There was a jackpot as an inducement for a winning contestant to keep playing, but also the possibility that he could lose some of his accumulated winnings. Bert Parks sang a song during each show and questions about the song he sang were worth extra money to the contestants.

HOLIDAY HANDBOOK

Travelogue

FIRST TELECAST: *April 4, 1958*

LAST TELECAST: *June 20, 1958*

BROADCAST HISTORY:

Apr 1958–Jun 1958, ABC Fri 10:00–10:30

Travel films, mostly of Western Europe, and keyed to what a visitor might find in local entertainment and culture.

HOLIDAY HOTEL

Musical Variety

FIRST TELECAST: *March 23, 1950*

LAST TELECAST: *October 4, 1951*

BROADCAST HISTORY:

Mar 1950–Jun 1950, ABC Thu 9:30–10:00
Sep 1950–Oct 1951, ABC Thu 9:00–9:30

EMCEE:

Edward Everett Horton (1950)
Don Ameche (1950–1951)

REGULARS:

Leonore Lonergan (1950)
Betty Brewer
Bill Harrington (1950)
Walter Dare Wahl (1950)
Don Sadler (1950)
June Graham Dancers
Bernie Green Orchestra
Don Craig's Chorus

Holiday Hotel premiered in the spring of 1950 as a musical variety show set in a Park Avenue hotel. Edward Everett Horton was the beleaguered manager of the hotel, running things for the absent Mr. Holiday, and trying to keep the bizarre tenants and guests under control. Leonore Lonergan provided comic counterpoint as the hotel's switchboard operator. After a comic sketch by the regulars the scene would shift to the ballroom for entertainment by the week's guest stars, and musical production numbers staged by Gordon Jenkins. Even the sponsor (Packard Motors) got into the act, with a Packard showroom conveniently located on the ground floor of the hotel.

Despite a big budget, the program received poor reviews, and for the fall Edward Everett Horton was replaced by Don Ameche as manager of the hotel. In July 1951 the hotel motif was dropped and the title changed to *Don Ameche's Musical Playhouse*. The setting became a playhouse run by "manager" Ameche, but otherwise format and cast were the same as for *Holiday Hotel*.

HOLIDAY LODGE

Situation Comedy

FIRST TELECAST: *June 25, 1961*
LAST TELECAST: *October 8, 1961*
BROADCAST HISTORY:
Jun 1961–Oct 1961, CBS Sun 9:30–10:00
CAST:
Johnny Miller ....Johnny Wayne
Frank Boone ....Frank Shuster
Dorothy Jackson ....Maureen Arthur
Woodrow ....Charles Smith
J. W. Harrington ....Justice Watson

The Canadian comedy team of Johnny Wayne and Frank Shuster starred as Johnny Miller and Frank Boone in this situation comedy about the adventures of two men working as social directors at a posh summer resort. All of the regulars in this series were employees of the hotel, with Dorothy Jackson the girl friend of Johnny Miller as well. The stories revolved around the wealthy, not-so-wealthy, and suspicious guests of the resort and the ways in which their activities involved them with the social directors.

HOLLYWOOD ADVENTURE TIME
see *Movies—Prior to 1961*

HOLLYWOOD AND THE STARS
Documentary
FIRST TELECAST: *September 30, 1963*
LAST TELECAST: *September 28, 1964*
BROADCAST HISTORY:
Sep 1963–Sep 1964, NBC Mon 9:30–10:00
HOST:
Joseph Cotten

Hollywood and the Stars looked at all aspects of the motion-picture industry, in documentary form. Each telecast surveyed a particular theme or subject, such as biographies of famous stars, specific types of films and film cycles, the people behind the scenes, and depictions of movies actually being made. Among the stars whose lives and careers were profiled were Rita Hayworth, Paul Newman, Natalie Wood, Bette Davis, and Humphrey Bogart. Other individual telecasts treated Westerns, musicals, gangster movies, war movies, teenage idols, great comedians, movie lovers, and glamour girls. One entire program was spent on location with Elizabeth Taylor and Richard Burton as Burton filmed *The Night of the Iguana*.

HOLLYWOOD BACKSTAGE
Beauty Tips
FIRST TELECAST: *August 7, 1955*
LAST TELECAST: *September 11, 1955*
BROADCAST HISTORY:
Aug 1955–Sep 1955, ABC Sun 7:30–8:00
HOST:
Ern Westmore

Ern Westmore, dean of Hollywood makeup artists, gave demonstrations and advice to women in this series, which was also seen in daytime at various times during the mid-1950s. A regular feature of the show called for a woman from the studio audience to be glamorized with the full Westmore Treatment. Ern would also demonstrate how a screen star was made up for a famous role.

The program was known in daytime as *The Ern Westmore Show*.

HOLLYWOOD FILM THEATRE
see *Movies—Prior to 1961*

HOLLYWOOD HOUSE
Variety
FIRST TELECAST: *December 4, 1949*
LAST TELECAST: *March 5, 1950*
BROADCAST HISTORY:
Dec 1949–Jan 1950, ABC Sun 7:30–8:00
Jan 1950–Mar 1950, ABC Sun 6:30–7:00
REGULARS:
Dick Wesson
Jim Backus

Comedy variety show set in a medium-sized Hollywood hotel, where anyone could wander in and anything could happen. Evidently not enough did, as the show was dropped after three months.

HOLLYWOOD MOVIE TIME
see *Movies—Prior to 1961*

HOLLYWOOD MYSTERY TIME
see *Movies—Prior to 1961*

HOLLYWOOD OFF BEAT
see *Steve Randall*

HOLLYWOOD OPENING NIGHT
Dramatic Anthology
FIRST TELECAST: *July 20, 1951*
LAST TELECAST: *March 23, 1953*

BROADCAST HISTORY:

Jul 1951–Mar 1952, CBS Fri 10:30–11:00
Oct 1952–Mar 1953, NBC Mon 9:00–9:30

HOST:

Jimmy Fiddler (1952–1953)

The dramas aired in this CBS series during the 1951–1952 season were half-hour films made especially for television. For the second season, however, the sponsor moved the show to NBC and the dramas became live productions. This was in fact the first live dramatic show to originate from the West Coast and the first program to make use of NBC's recently completed Burbank studios. Hollywood columnist Jimmy Fiddler opened each show in a "theater" lobby and invited the television audience to join him inside to see the play. At the end of each week's performance he gave a brief preview of the next week's offering.

The fare was quite varied, ranging from serious dramas such as "Delaying Action" starring John Hodiak, John Agar, and Tab Hunter, and "The Pattern" starring Gloria Swanson, to light comedies like "Uncle Fred Flits By" with David Niven and "Legal Affairs" with Franchot Tone. With the Hollywood talent pool to draw from, the casts in this series were generally quite impressive.

HOLLYWOOD PALACE, THE

Variety

FIRST TELECAST: *January 4, 1964*
LAST TELECAST: *February 7, 1970*
BROADCAST HISTORY:

Jan 1964–May 1967, ABC Sat 9:30–10:30
Sep 1967–Jan 1968, ABC Mon 10:00–11:00
Jan 1968–Feb 1970, ABC Sat 9:30–10:30 (OS)

ORCHESTRA:

Les Brown (1964)
Mitchell Ayres (1964–1970)

EXECUTIVE PRODUCER:

Nick Vanoff

The Hollywood Palace was a lavish, big-budget, big-name variety show of the 1960s which attempted to become to Saturday night what *The Ed Sullivan Show* was to Sunday. It premiered amid much hoopla in January 1964, live from the recently rebuilt ABC Palace Theater (formerly the El Capitan) in Hollywood. The first telecast headlined Bing Crosby as host, with Mickey Rooney, Bobby Van, Nancy Wilson, Bob Newhart, and Gary Crosby, as well as singers, dancers, magicians, balancing acts and even clowns.

A different host topped the bill each week, but some returned more ofen than others. Bing Crosby was most frequently seen (30-plus appearances), while Fred Astaire, Milton Berle, Jimmy Durante, Sid Caesar and Imogene Coca, Sammy Davis, Jr. and Don Adams also made multiple appearances as host. Other acts on the *Palace* bill ranged from old-timers Groucho Marx and Ed Wynn to Frank Sinatra with the Basie band, to Judy Garland, to the Rolling Stones. The strictly vaudeville acts (acrobats, etc.) were seen less often during later years, as the show became more of a straight musical-comedy variety hour. A highlight of every season was the Christmas holiday show, usually presided over by Bing Crosby (sometimes with his family), and also the glamorous billboard girls (at one time including the then-unknown Raquel Welch).

Though *The Hollywood Palace* featured top-line talent, and attracted a substantial audience, it never developed the loyal following of the other great variety hours, probably because of the lack of a central figure as continuing host.

The show was known during its first few weeks as *The Saturday Night Hollywood Palace.*

HOLLYWOOD PREMIERE

Variety

FIRST TELECAST: *September 22, 1949*
LAST TELECAST: *November 17, 1949*
BROADCAST HISTORY:

Sep 1949–Nov 1949, NBC Thu 8:00–8:30

A short-lived series of half-hour programs showcasing established talent in comedic and dramatic material. There was no continuing cast. Among those appearing were Pinky Lee, Howard da Silva, and Sterling Holloway. The programs were produced in Hollywood and shown via kinescope on the Eastern and Midwestern NBC networks.

HOLLYWOOD PREMIERE THEATRE

see *Hollywood Theatre Time*

HOLLYWOOD SCREEN TEST

Talent

FIRST TELECAST: *April 15, 1948*
LAST TELECAST: *May 18, 1953*

BROADCAST HISTORY:

Apr 1948–May 1948, ABC Thu 8:00–8:30
May 1948–Jun 1948, ABC Sun 6:30–7:00
Aug 1948–Sep 1948, ABC Sun 7:30–8:00
Oct 1948–May 1949, ABC Sun 8:00–8:30
May 1949–Sep 1950, ABC Sat 7:30–8:00
Sep 1950–May 1953, ABC Mon 7:30–8:00 (OS)

HOST:

Bert Lytell (1948)
Neil Hamilton (1948–1953)

ASSISTANT:

Robert Quarry (1949)

"You, the public, make the stars" was the oft-repeated slogan of this long-running talent show of TV's early years. Unlike many TV talent shows, the production values here were commendably high. The young talent appearing on *Hollywood Screen Test* all had previous professional experience, and were looking for the "big break" that would bring them stardom. They were paired with established stars in dramatic sketches and comedy skits written especially for the program, as well as scenes adapted from famous plays and novels. The behind-the-scenes ambience of the show was heightened by the setting, a Hollywood sound stage, with silent film actor Bert Lytell as the original "producer" and Neil Hamilton as his assistant. (Lytell left after a few months and Hamilton took over the show.)

While several newcomers got the break they were looking for, landing Hollywood contracts as a result of their appearance on the show, none developed into major stars. Among the program's Hollywood-bound alumni were Rita Colton, Susan Cabot, Joel Marston, and Robert Quarry (who also served as assistant on the show). Better known were the guest stars with whom they played their scenes, including Mercedes McCambridge, Jeff Morrow, Grace Kelly, Edward Everett Horton, and others.

HOLLYWOOD SQUARES

Quiz/Audience Participation

FIRST TELECAST: *January 12, 1968*
LAST TELECAST: *September 13, 1968*
BROADCAST HISTORY:

Jan 1968–Sep 1968, NBC Fri 9:30–10:00

EMCEE:

Peter Marshall

REGULARS:

Cliff Arquette *(Charley Weaver)*
Wally Cox

This nighttime version of the highly popular NBC daytime game show (which premiered in October 1966) was seen on the network in 1968. The host, as in the daytime version, was Peter Marshall.

The Hollywood Squares set resembled a huge tic-tac-toe board, with a different celebrity in each of the nine squares. Two contestants took turns choosing celebrities. The chosen celebrity would be asked a question—sometimes serious, sometimes strange, often ridiculous—by emcee Marshall, and would give an answer. The contestant would then have to state whether the answer given was right or wrong. If the contestant guessed correctly, he won that square. If not, his opponent won it, unless that square would give the opponent three squares in a row and a victory. The first contestant to win three squares in a row won the round. Often, however, nobody noticed who won, as the quiz element in *Hollywood Squares* was distinctly secondary to the quips and jokes of the celebrities. Paul Lynde, who was to become the star "center square" regular of the daytime version of *Hollywood Squares*, was not yet a regular when the nighttime version was on. He appeared only six times during its run and became a regular on the daytime show roughly one month after the nighttime show left the air.

HOLLYWOOD SUMMER THEATRE

Dramatic Anthology

FIRST TELECAST: *August 3, 1956*
LAST TELECAST: *September 28, 1956*
BROADCAST HISTORY:

Aug 1956–Sep 1956, CBS Fri 8:00–8:30

HOST:

Gene Raymond

This filmed summer anthology series was made up of original dramas, never before seen on television, and was hosted by Gene Raymond. Appearing were such performers as Merle Oberon, Laraine Day, Joanne Dru, Rod Cameron, Ricardo Montalban, and Preston Foster.

HOLLYWOOD TALENT SCOUTS

Variety

FIRST TELECAST: *June 22, 1965*

LAST TELECAST: *September 5, 1966*
BROADCAST HISTORY:
Jun 1965–Sep 1965, CBS Tue 8:30–9:30
Dec 1965–Sep 1966, CBS Mon 10:00–11:00
HOST:
Art Linkletter

The performers in this variety series were young unknowns who had been seen by celebrities and brought by those celebrities to *Hollywood Talent Scouts* to get their first national television exposure. Each week there were four or five guest celebrities who chatted briefly with host Art Linkletter and then introduced their discoveries.

During its initial summer run there were a few discoveries who actually became successful in future years, but not always doing what they did on this show. Tom Smothers brought a young comic named Pat Paulsen (later to work on the Smothers Brothers' variety show), actor Bob Crane presented a young singer named Marilyn McCoo (later the lead singer with The Fifth Dimension), and Carl Reiner brought one of the writers from his *Dick Van Dyke Show*, Gary Marshall. Marshall, who went on the show to try his luck as a comedian, later became the producer of *Happy Days* and *Laverne & Shirley*. Most of the young talents never made it, though, and some were not so young. Cliff Arquette, as Charley Weaver, introduced the Frivolous Five, a Dixieland jazz group composed entirely of women over sixty.

When this series returned in December, the title had been altered to *Art Linkletter's Hollywood Talent Scouts* and on-location interviews with celebrities were included in the format. Singer Donna Theodore was the most notable talent presented in this run. Virtually the same program, with different hosts, aired under the title *Celebrity Talent Scouts*.

HOLLYWOOD THEATRE TIME

Various
FIRST TELECAST: *October 8, 1950*
LAST TELECAST: *October 20, 1951*
BROADCAST HISTORY:
Oct 1950–Dec 1950, ABC Sun 8:00–8:30
Dec 1950–Oct 1951, ABC Sat 7:00–7:30

This series was a showcase for an assortment of variety shows, dramatic presentations, scenes from famous plays, and situation comedies, all produced in Hollywood. Frequently seen during the first few months was "The Gil Lamb Show," a half-hour musical variety show hosted by the screen comedian. Other presentations included "Mr. and Mrs. Detective" starring Gale Storm and Don Defore, and "The Spectre" starring Marjorie Reynolds.

During its first two months the series was known as *Hollywood Premiere Theatre*.

HOLMES AND YOYO

Situation Comedy
FIRST TELECAST: *September 25, 1976*
LAST TELECAST: *December 11, 1976*
BROADCAST HISTORY:
Sep 1976–Dec 1976, ABC Sat 8:00–8:30
CAST:
Det. Alexander Holmes . . . Richard B. Shull
Gregory "Yoyo" Yoyonovich . . . John Schuck
Capt. Harry Sedford . . . Bruce Kirby
Officer Maxine Moon . . . Andrea Howard

This was billed as the revival of the classic two-man comedy team. Said producer Leonard Stern, "For over thirty years we had the marvelous antics of Laurel & Hardy, Abbott & Costello, Hope & Crosby, Martin & Lewis, Gleason & Carney, and then suddenly came an unexplainable gap. But now, hopefully, Schuck & Shull will fill the comedy void."

Schuck & Shull did not become another Laurel & Hardy; their series *Holmes and Yoyo* lasted a brief three months. Holmes was an accident-prone cop who never got hurt himself, but kept sending partners to the hospital. So the department decided to try its latest development, a lifelike robot "computerperson" named Yoyo (after its inventor, Dr. Yoyonovich). Holmes was not supposed to know that his new partner was a robot. He did, secretly, but few others were aware of it, certainly not Officer Maxine Moon who kept making amorous advances to Yoyo. Yoyo did have his strong points, including a photographic memory, an independent power source, a silent trash compressor which permitted him to digest anything, and the ability to produce color prints. But there were drawbacks, too. Nobody could lift him because he weighed 427 pounds. And although he was uninjurable, an assailant's bullet once shorted out his rhythm system, causing him to tap-dance out of control during a chase.

HONDO

Western

FIRST TELECAST: *September 8, 1967*

LAST TELECAST: *December 29, 1967*

BROADCAST HISTORY:

Sep 1967–Dec 1967, ABC Fri 8:30–9:30

CAST:

Hondo Lane ....Ralph Taeger
Angie Dow ....Kathie Browne
Johnny Dow ....Buddy Foster
Buffalo Baker ....Noah Beery, Jr
Capt. Richards ....Gary Clarke
Chief Vittoro ....Michael Pate
Col. Crook ....William Bryant

Ralph Taeger played the title role of a cavalry scout in the Arizona Territory, *ca.* 1870, in this Western adventure. Hondo was an embittered loner. He had once been a Confederate Cavalry captain, and had lived with the Apaches for a time under the aegis of Chief Vittoro, only to see his Indian bride—Vittoro's daughter—slain by the army in a massacre. Now he traveled with a dog named Sam, troubleshooting for the army and trying to avert further bloodshed in the campaign against renegade Indians, land grabbers, gunmen, and bandits around Fort Lowell. Capt. Richards was the young martinet commander of the fort; Buffalo Baker, a colorful scout; Angie Dow, Hondo's romantic interest, and Johnny, her nine-year-old son.

Based on Louis L'Amour's story, and the 1953 John Wayne movie derived from it.

HONESTLY CELESTE

Situation Comedy

FIRST TELECAST: *October 10, 1954*

LAST TELECAST: *December 5, 1954*

BROADCAST HISTORY:

Oct 1954–Dec 1954, CBS Sun 9:30–10:00

CAST:

Celeste Anders ....Celeste Holm
Bob Wallace ....Scott McKay
Marty ....Mike Kellin
Mr. Wallace ....Geoffrey Lumb

Vivacious Celeste Anders had given up her position teaching journalism in the Midwest to come to New York and take a job as a reporter for *The New York Express*, to get some "real" experience. What she found was a new boy friend (Bob Wallace, the publisher's son), a friendly cabbie named Marty who took her to many of her reporting assignments, and all sorts of predicaments. Despite the attraction of film star Celeste Holm and much favorable pretelecast publicity, this filmed comedy series lasted less than three months.

HONEY WEST

Detective

FIRST TELECAST: *September 17, 1965*

LAST TELECAST: *September 2, 1966*

BROADCAST HISTORY:

Sep 1965–Sep 1966, ABC Fri 9:00–9:30

CAST:

Honey West ....Anne Francis
Sam Bolt ....John Ericson
Aunt Meg ....Irene Hervey

Honey West was a true rarity in 1965, a female private detective. She had inherited the family detective business and partner Sam Bolt from her late father, and she made quite a fetching female James Bond. Honey was skilled at judo, proficient at karate, owned a weapons arsenal full of the most amazing devices, and used a specially modified lipstick that contained a radio transmitter. Her traveling office was a specially equipped spy van labeled "H.W. Bolt & Co., TV Service." She had everything necessary to track down the bad guys—even a trench coat. The love of her life was her pet ocelot, Bruce, much to the consternation of partner Sam, who would willingly have married her.

Honey West was introduced to TV audiences in an April 1965 episode of *Burke's Law*, in which the sexy sleuth outwitted even that dapper investigator.

HONEYMOONERS, THE

Situation Comedy

FIRST TELECAST: *October 1, 1955*

LAST TELECAST: *May 9, 1971*

BROADCAST HISTORY:

Oct 1955–Feb 1956, CBS Sat 8:30–9:00
Feb 1956–Sep 1956, CBS Sat 8:00–8:30
Jan 1971–May 1971, CBS Sun 10:00–11:00

CAST:

Ralph Kramden ....Jackie Gleason
Ed Norton ....Art Carney
Alice Kramden (1955–1956)
.... Audrey Meadows
Trixie Norton (1955–1956)
.... Joyce Randolph

Alice Kramden (1971)	Sheila MacRae
Trixie Norton (1971)	Jane Kean

Although *The Honeymooners* is one of the best-remembered comedy highlights of TV's golden age, it was seen for most of its history as a segment within other programs. Oddly enough, on the few occasions when it was presented as an independent series, it was not successful. Yet practically anyone who has ever sat in front of a TV set has seen a bit of the saga of Ralph and Alice Kramden, the not-so-newlyweds living in a run-down apartment in Brooklyn. The surroundings were grimy and spartan, quite unlike the happy middle-class homes of most TV situation comedies. Ralph, a portly New York City bus driver, was one of life's colorful losers—blustery, ambitious, avaricious and constantly searching for the one great money-making scheme that would make him rich. Always willing to help was his best friend Ed Norton, who lived upstairs. Norton was no better off than "Ralphie-boy"—he worked in the city's sewers—but he was a veritable fountain of cheer and encouragement. Unfortunately Norton negated through incompetence and naïveté the benefits of his blind enthusiasm, and he was a constant source of grief and aggravation to Ralph. Their schemes never worked out, usually causing friction between Ralph and his more practical wife, Alice. Ralph's reaction, whenever Alice proved him wrong or disapproved of one of his great ideas, was to threaten to belt her, with such lines as "To the moon, Alice," or "One of these days, Alice, *one of these days* . . . Pow! Right in the kisser!" But Alice understood Ralph, and in the end, at the final curtain, he would beam and admit, "Alice . . . you're the greatest."

The Honeymooners was first seen in 1951 as a sketch within DuMont's *Cavalcade of Stars*, with Pert Kelton originating the role of Alice and Art Carney as Ed Norton. When the show moved to CBS as *The Jackie Gleason Show* Audrey Meadows assumed the role of Alice. *The Honeymooners* finally became a series in its own right in 1955. Jackie Gleason wanted a respite from the rigors of a full-hour live weekly variety show and was also interested in becoming a packager of other programs. It was decided to film a full season (39 episodes) of half-hour *Honeymooners* shows and fill the other half of what had been Gleason's regular hour in the CBS schedule with *Stage Show*, a program owned by Jackie. All of *The Honeymooners* episodes were filmed before a live audience, two episodes per week, using an advanced filming system called the Electronicam. This was one of the first examples of live audience, single-set filmed situation comedy, so prevalent today (though it was not *the* first—see *I Love Lucy*). In 1956, with the failure of *Stage Show*, the less-than-anticipated response to *The Honeymooners*, and the strong competition from *The Perry Como Show* on NBC, Gleason returned to a regular variety format.

In 1966 *The Honeymooners*, which had only been seen on a very occasional basis since Art Carney's departure as a regular on *The Jackie Gleason Show* in 1957, was revived in the form of full-hour episodes of Gleason's then-current variety series. Carney was back, with Sheila MacRae and Jane Kean playing the wives. These episodes, in which the Kramdens and the Nortons traveled together in addition to getting into trouble at home in New York, were done on a grander scale than the 1955–1956 series, complete with songs and production numbers. They accounted for roughly half the total output of *The Jackie Gleason Show* during its last four years on the air. A collection of reruns of these hour episodes was aired as another *Honeymooners* series in 1971. In addition, reruns of the original 39 half-hour episodes from the 1955–1956 season continue to be shown, and will probably run forever, on local stations.

HONG KONG

Adventure

FIRST TELECAST: *September 28, 1960*
LAST TELECAST: *September 20, 1961*
BROADCAST HISTORY:

Sep 1960–Sep 1961, ABC Wed 7:30–8:30

CAST:

Glenn Evans	Rod Taylor
Neil Campbell	Lloyd Bochner
Tully	Jack Kruschen
Fong (1960)	Harold Fong
Ying (1960–1961)	Gerald Jann

The British Crown Colony of Hong Kong was the locale for the adventures of Glenn Evans, an American journalist living and working amid the intrigue of that exotic city. His search for stories led him into encounters with smugglers, murderers, dope peddlers, and slinky women disappearing behind beaded curtains. A source of stories, as well as a friend, was Neil Campbell, chief of the Hong Kong Police. Tully ran the swank nightclub where Glenn spent much of his free time. Glenn's original houseboy was Fong, who was replaced by Ying within a month after the series premiered.

HOOTENANNY

Music

FIRST TELECAST: *April 6, 1963*

LAST TELECAST: *September 12, 1964*

BROADCAST HISTORY:

Apr 1963–Sep 1963, ABC Sat 8:30–9:00

Sep 1963–Sep 1964, ABC Sat 7:30–8:30

HOST:

Jack Linkletter

THEME:

"Hootenanny Saturday Night," by Alfred Uhry and Richard Lewine

A traveling musical jamboree, taped before a live audience at a different college campus each week, and featuring the popularized "folk music" of the early 1960s. Artists were generally commercial pop-folk groups such as the Limeliters, the Chad Mitchell Trio, and the Smothers Brothers, but also included some traditional performers such as Josh White and the Carter Family.

HOPALONG CASSIDY

Western

FIRST TELECAST: *June 24, 1949*

LAST TELECAST: *December 23, 1951*

BROADCAST HISTORY:

Jun 1949–Oct 1949, NBC Fri 8:00–9:00 (some telecasts local)

Apr 1950–Dec 1951, NBC Sun 6:00–7:00

CAST:

Hopalong Cassidy .... William Boyd

Red Connors .... Edgar Buchanan

Theatrical films of the adventures of Hopalong Cassidy had been shown on New York television at least as early as 1945, and became a regular local series in November 1948. The first films seen on TV were edited versions of his old "B" features, with Boyd adding narration and occasionally even a new scene or two (it is remarkable that a man of 50 could match scenes that he had filmed 15 years before, and look no different!). Then he made a new series of TV films, with Edgar Buchanan as his sidekick, which ran on NBC for a time and then went into syndication for many years thereafter.

The plots were the same as in the old "B" films, with Hoppy, silver-haired and dressed all in black, chasing villains to their doom on his faithful horse Topper.

William Boyd had been wise enough to buy the TV rights to his theatrical films during the 1940s, and it was television—not Hollywood features—that made him a millionaire. He died in 1972.

HORACE HEIDT SHOW, THE

Talent

FIRST TELECAST: *October 2, 1950*

LAST TELECAST: *September 24, 1951*

BROADCAST HISTORY:

Oct 1950–Sep 1951, CBS Mon 9:00–9:30

HOST:

Horace Heidt

This series, begun by the veteran bandleader on radio in 1947 as *Horace Heidt's Youth Opportunity Program,* added a television version in 1950. As with *The Original Amateur Hour,* the emphasis of the show was on finding young talent and exposing it to a national audience. At the end of each live show, the acts were voted upon by the studio audience, and the winner, as measured by applause meter, came back the following week to defend his championship.

HORIZONS

Discussion

FIRST TELECAST: *December 2, 1951*

LAST TELECAST: *March 6, 1955*

BROADCAST HISTORY:

Dec 1951, ABC Sun 6:00–6:30

May 1952–Jun 1952, ABC Sun 7:30–8:00

Dec 1954–Mar 1955, ABC Sun 9:15–9:30

HOST:

Dr. Louis H. Bauer (1954–1955)

PRODUCERS:

Erik Barnouw and Jack Pacey (1951–1952)

DIRECTOR:

Leslie Gorall (1951–1952)

Live lecture series in which prominent professors from Columbia University and occasional outside experts spoke on likely future developments in their specialties.

Included during the 1951–1952 season were Prof. Mark Van Doren on "The Future of Poetry," anthropologist Margaret Mead on "The Future of the Family," and Dr. Philip E. Mosley on "The Future of Soviet Diplomacy." For part of its run the 1951–1952 series aired on Sunday afternoons.

The title *Horizons* was revived in 1954 for a similarly erudite series of short talks on advances in medicine, presided over by Dr. Louis H. Bauer, past president of the American Medical Association and Secretary General of the World Medical Association.

HOT L BALTIMORE

Situation Comedy

FIRST TELECAST: *January 24, 1975*

LAST TELECAST: *June 6, 1975*

BROADCAST HISTORY:

Jan 1975–Jun 1975, ABC Fri 9:00–9:30

CAST:

Bill Lewis ....James Cromwell
Clifford Ainsley ....Richard Masur
April Green ....Conchata Ferrell
Charles Bingham ....Al Freeman, Jr
Suzy Marta Rocket ....Jeannie Linero
Millie ....Gloria Le Roy
Jackie ....Robin Wilson
Mr. Morse ....Stan Gottlieb
George ....Lee Bergere
Gordon ....Henry Calvert
Mrs. Bellotti ....Charlotte Rae

Hot L Baltimore was one of the most controversial comedies of recent years. Based on the award-winning off-Broadway play of the same name, and produced for TV by trendsetter Norman Lear (of *All in the Family* fame), it brought sexual innuendo and racy dialogue to the home screen. The setting was the lobby of the once grand but now dilapidated Hotel Baltimore (the "e" in the sign had burned out and never been replaced). Among its denizens were desk clerk Bill and his love, April; the harried manager, Clifford; the philosophical Charles; Suzy Marta Rocket, the Colombian prostitute; Millie, the unemployed waitress; Jackie, the tomboy; Mr. Morse, the septugenarian always on the brink of expiring; George and Gordon, the homosexual couple; and eccentric Mrs. Bellotti. Often heard but never seen onscreen was Mrs. Bellotti's 26-year-old prankster son Moose, who delighted in such escapades as buttering the hallways, staging *The Poseidon Adventure* in the bathtub, and collecting unlikely pets. Once when the lobby habitues protested a rent increase, Moose glued himself to the ceiling of his room in sympathy.

Despite the refusal of some affiliates to carry this show, ABC kept it on the air for four months before it was finally dropped due to viewer apathy.

HOT SEAT THE

Interview

FIRST TELECAST: *April 18, 1952*

LAST TELECAST: *December 29, 1952*

BROADCAST HISTORY:

Apr 1952–Jul 1952, ABC Fri 8:00–8:30
Oct 1952–Nov 1952, ABC Sun 7:30–8:00
Nov 1952–Dec 1952, ABC Mon 8:30–9:00

HOST:

Stuart Scheftel

Lively interview show in which public figures were grilled by ABC newsman Stuart Scheftel and a guest. Subjects ranged from radio-TV personality Tex McCrary to Senator Joseph McCarthy.

HOTEL BROADWAY

Variety

FIRST TELECAST: *January 20, 1949*

LAST TELECAST: *March 17, 1949*

BROADCAST HISTORY:

Jan 1949–Mar 1949, DUM Thu 8:30–9:00

REGULARS:

The Striders

Low-budget musical variety program featuring different singers and comedians each week, generally of less-than-top-name caliber. Among those who appeared were Johnny Desmond, Jean Darling, and Harry Ranch's orchestra. There was no host, but a quartet called the Striders was used to introduce each act.

HOTEL DE PAREE

Western

FIRST TELECAST: *October 2, 1959*

LAST TELECAST: *September 23, 1960*

BROADCAST HISTORY:

Oct 1959–Sep 1960, CBS Fri 8:30–9:00

CAST:

Sundance ....Earl Holliman
Monique ....Judi Meredith
Annette Deveraux ....Jeanette Nolan
Aaron Donager ....Strother Martin

Western centered in the Hotel de Paree, the fanciest (and only) lodging in Georgetown, Colorado, and its chief hero-in-residence, Sundance. Sundance had come to Georgetown via a rather circuitous route. After accidentally killing a man there, he had spent 17 years in prison. He nevertheless returned to the town upon his release, *ca.* 1870, to find the Hotel de Paree being operated by two rather attractive relatives of the dead man, Annette Deveraux and her niece, Monique. Their hotel was a little bit of European dignity in the midst of the Old West. They needed a strong arm (and fast gun) to keep things quiet, and Sundance was their man. Among his trademarks was a string of polished silver discs in the hatband of his black stetson, with which to blind his adversaries.

HOUR GLASS

see *ABC Dramatic Shorts—1952–1953*

HOUR GLASS

see *Movies–Prior to 1961*

HOUR GLASS

Variety

FIRST TELECAST: *May 9, 1946*
LAST TELECAST: *March 6, 1947*
BROADCAST HISTORY:
May 1946–Mar 1947, NBC Thu 8:00–9:00
EMCEE:
Helen Parrish (1946)
Eddie Mayehoff
PRODUCER:
Howard Reilly
DIRECTOR:
Ed Sobel

Hour Glass was one of the most important pioneers in the early history of television. Yet its very existence, much less its place in the development of the medium, has scarcely been acknowledged anywhere until now. It was the first hour-long entertainment series of any kind produced for network television, the first show to develop its own star, the first big variety series, and the most ambitious production by far ever attempted up to its time. Milton Berle, Ed Sullivan, *Your Show of Shows*, Carol Burnett, and dozens of others are all its lineal descendants, as is, in a sense, the whole concept of "big time" television.

To understand the breakthrough that *Hour Glass* represented we might first remember the other shows on the air in 1946. Commercial television was still in its infancy, with only a few thousand sets in use, mostly in New York and a few other large cities. New York was the only city with more than one station, and was the nation's TV "capital." The week in which *Hour Glass* premiered looked like this, in New York. Monday: one station on the air for one hour, with a 30-minute fashion show and a 30-minute excerpt from a grade-B Western film (*The Fighting Deputy* with Fred Scott). Tuesday: one station on for 90 minutes, 30 minutes of informal skits, 30 minutes of travel films and 30 minutes of a disc-jockey show called *King's Record Shop*. Wednesday: two stations on, one with film shorts and the other with 90 minutes of mixed films and studio chatter. Thursday: the other two channels offered a cartoonist, a newscast, and an adaptation of the radio show *Famous Jury Trials*. Friday: three stations on, with some very obscure grade-B films, a short studio game show, and boxing from St. Nicholas Arena. This, pretty much, had been the typical of TV programming up to that time.

Hour Glass was sponsored by a major company, Standard Brands (Chase & Sanborn Coffee, Tender Leaf Tea), which poured more money into it than TV had ever seen before—reportedly $200,000 over the show's ten-month run. For the first time there was money for elaborate sets, specially made films, and reasonably respectable talent. Of course everything they tried was an experiment, since no one had attempted such a show before. The premiere telecast, on May 9, 1946, opened with a song by recording star Evelyn Knight, followed by a seriocomic sketch starring actor Paul Douglas, set in a cabin. Next came a live commercial for Chase and Sanborn coffee—two and a half minutes long! Comedian Joe Besser then appeared with several supporting players in a hilarious take-off on the military entitled "The Rookie," followed in quick succession by a ballroom-dancing sequence, a brief talk about TV and a booklet available on the subject from NBC, another song by Evelyn Knight, a monologue by fast-talking comic Doodles Weaver (a well-known personality in the 1940s), and finally a film of South American dancing. The end commercial, which included film of coffee-growing country, ran for four and a half minutes.

Subsequent shows tightened up the commercials quite a bit, and also brought on such acts as Bert Lahr, the singing Merry Macs, Dennis Day, Jerry Colonna, Joey Faye, and Peggy Lee. In November the show added TV's first regular chorus line, a group of leggy beauties. Compared to the nightclub rejects generally seen on TV in the late 1940s this was big talent indeed. Perhaps the biggest coup was the TV debut, on November 14, 1946, of ventriloquist Edgar Bergen (and Charlie McCarthy). This was one of the earliest instances of a top radio star bringing his act to television, a practice which was to become quite prevalent in the years to come, until TV developed its own galaxy of stars.

The emcee on the first *Hour Glass* telecast was Evelyn Eaton, and guest hosts appeared thereafter until a pretty young actress named Helen Parrish was signed as permanent "femcee." She was bright, pixieish, and as fresh as the medium itself, and she made quite a hit with TV viewers of 1946 (just about all of whom watched *Hour Glass* on Thursday night). The sponsor gave her a substantial publicity build-up, and it was said that she became as well known, at least in the cities which had TV, as the top radio stars of the day. She left the show in November to have a baby, after which her co-host Eddie Mayehoff took over.

Standard Brands was well aware that the limited viewership of television at this time did not justify such a large investment on a purely financial basis. But they, and NBC, wanted to see what could be done with the new medium, and the lessons they learned have influenced what we see today. They learned, for example, not to let single commercials run for four to five minutes; that money is better spent on obtaining "star" talent than on fancy, highly visual sets; that viewers liked the idea of a regular host (or hostess) providing continuity from week to week; and that TV in general was a medium which demanded staging and pacing far different from movies, the stage, or radio.

The network history of *Hour Glass* is sketchy, due to incomplete records for this very early period. NBC's network consisted of three stations at the time, in New York, Philadelphia, and Schenectady, and while it is not known whether *Hour Glass* was being fed to all three at the start (it originated in New York) it definitely was on the network by early November at the latest.

More than a year was to pass after the demise of *Hour Glass* before another sponsor could be induced to put similar amounts of money into television for a big-time variety hour. That one, drawing on the lessons learned here, brought TV out of its infancy and produced its first superstar: Milton Berle. And what became of Helen Parrish? She returned to Hollywood, where she had been a child star in the 1930s, and made a few more films. She died in 1959 at the age of 35.

HOUR OF DECISION

Religion

FIRST TELECAST: *September 30, 1951*

LAST TELECAST: *February 28, 1954*

BROADCAST HISTORY:

Sep 1951–Mar 1952, ABC Sun 10:00–10:30
Jul 1952–Sep 1953, ABC Sun 10:00–10:15
Sep 1953–Feb 1954, ABC Sun 10:30–10:45

HOST:

Rev. Billy Graham

Almost from its inception as a mass medium, evangelist Billy Graham has made frequent use of television to publicize his religious crusades. During 1951–1954 the Billy Graham Evangelical Association sponsored regular weekly Sunday night talks by Dr. Graham on the ABC network.

HOW DID THEY GET THAT WAY

Discussion

FIRST TELECAST: *July 24, 1951*

LAST TELECAST: *March 10, 1952*

BROADCAST HISTORY:

Jul 1951–Sep 1951, ABC Tue 8:00–8:30
Sep 1951–Jan 1952, ABC Tue 8:30–9:00
Feb 1952–Mar 1952, ABC Mon 9:30–10:00

MODERATOR:

Isabelle Leighton

Public-service program dealing with emotional problems, utilizing medical films and discussions by psychiatrists and guests. Among the topics covered were "Gossip," "Hostility," "Feelings of Rejection," and "Why Tommy Won't Eat." During its first few months the program was known as *What's on Your Mind.*

HOW THE WEST WAS WON

Western

FIRST TELECAST: *February 12, 1978*
LAST TELECAST: *August 27, 1978*
BROADCAST HISTORY:
Feb 1978–May 1978, ABC Sun 8:00–9:00
Jul 1978–Aug 1978, ABC Sun 8:00–9:00
CAST:
Zeb Macahan .... James Arness
Aunt Molly Culhane .... Fionnula Flanagan
Luke Macahan .... Bruce Boxleitner
Laura Macahan .... Kathryn Holcomb
Josh Macahan .... William Kirby Cullen
Jessie Macahan .... Vicki Schreck

James Arness, the Marshal Dillon of the long running *Gunsmoke* series, returned to TV screens in 1978 in this mixture of western adventure and soap opera. Zeb Macahan was a rugged mountain man who had spent ten years in the Dakota Territory before returning to Virginia, where his brother's family was preparing to make the long trek west. No sooner had they set out than the Civil War broke out. Zeb's brother Timothy returned east and his wife Kate was subsequently killed in an accident, leaving the four Macahan children in Zeb's care. Luke, the eldest, had killed three men in self-defense, and was a fugitive from the law; Laura was pretty and ready for womanhood; Jessie was the tomboyish 12-year-old; and teenager Josh was exuberant and anxious to become the man of the family. Aunt Molly, Kate's widowed sister, came from Boston to help them on the long journey, through dangers and hardships caused by indians, renegades, nature and the other perils of an untamed West.

Adding to the epic scope of the series was the spectacular setting; the program was filmed on location in Utah, Colorado, Arizona and Southern California. The executive producer was John Mantley, who had also been producer of *Gunsmoke*. The series was based on the 1963 motion picture of the same name, which was directed by John Ford and featured an all star cast, including John Wayne.

HOW TO

Informational
FIRST TELECAST: *July 10, 1951*
LAST TELECAST: *September 11, 1951*
BROADCAST HISTORY:
Jul 1951–Sep 1951, CBS Tue 9:00–9:30
MODERATOR:
Roger Price
PANEL:
Leonard Stern
Stanley Adams
Anita Martell

The solutions that moderator Roger Price and his panel of experts had for the various questions that were asked of them were not the most sensible in the world. To the person who asked "How to" open a beer can with a thumbtack the response was "place the tack on top of the can and hit it with a large ax." The obvious way to keep a faucet from leaking was to turn it on. Such pearls of wisdom were dispensed weekly on both radio and television (though not simulcast) during the summer of 1951.

HOWARD K. SMITH—NEWS AND COMMENT

News Commentary
FIRST TELECAST: *February 14, 1962*
LAST TELECAST: *June 16, 1963*
BROADCAST HISTORY:
Feb 1962–Sep 1962, ABC Wed 7:30–8:00
Sep 1962–Jun 1963, ABC Sun 10:30–11:00
NEWSMAN:
Howard K. Smith

In his first regular television assignment for ABC, after severing a 20-year relationship with CBS News, Howard K. Smith presented this weekly news and commentary program. It featured a summary of the week's major news events, commentary and analysis by Mr. Smith, and interviews with prominent people in the news.

HUDSON BROTHERS SHOW, THE

Variety
FIRST TELECAST: *July 31, 1974*
LAST TELECAST: *August 28, 1974*
BROADCAST HISTORY:
Jul 1974–Aug 1974, CBS Wed 8:00–9:00
REGULARS:
The Hudson Brothers (Bill, Brett and Mark)
Ronny Graham
Gary Owens
Stephanie Edwards
Ron Hull

The Hudson Brothers were, according to series producer Alan Blye, "a cross between the Marx Brothers and the Beatles." They sang reasonably well and did sketch and monologue comedy in this short-lived summer variety series. They were all in their twenties and much of their material was aimed at the under-35 audience.

HULLABALOO

Music

FIRST TELECAST: *January 12, 1965*

LAST TELECAST: *August 29, 1966*

BROADCAST HISTORY:

Jan 1965–May 1965, NBC Tue 8:30–9:30
Jun 1965–Aug 1965, NBC Tue 10:00–11:00
Sep 1965–Aug 1966, NBC Mon 7:30–8:00

REGULARS:

The Hullabaloo Dancers (6 girls, 4 boys)

MUSIC DIRECTOR:

Peter Matz

PRODUCER:

Gary Smith

Hullabaloo was one of TV's few attempts to give rock 'n' roll a big-budget, top-quality showcase all its own in prime time. (Another, seen at about the same time, was *Shindig*.) Each week top popular recording artists performed their current hits, backed by elaborate production and the frenetic, miniskirted Hullabaloo Dancers. The whole affair was very youth-oriented, with a great deal of noise and motion, and the general atmosphere was that of a discotheque in full swing—in fact, one segment was called "Hullabaloo A-Go-Go." (Just for the record, the "girl in the cage" doing a perpetual frug was Lada Edmund, Jr.) A different host presided each week, including Paul Anka, Jack Jones, Frankie Avalon and Annette Funicello, and Jerry Lewis (with his rock-star son, Gary). Performing were such acts as the Supremes, the Ronettes, Sonny and Cher, and many others. A special feature during the first three months was a weekly segment taped in London, hosted by rock impresario Brian Epstein and presenting top English acts such as Gerry and the Pacemakers, Marianne Faithful, Herman's Hermits, and the Moody Blues. Brian never brought on the biggest English superstars of all, however—his own protégés, the Beatles. (They finally did appear after Brian had left the show, in a January 1966 telecast.)

HUMBLE REPORT, THE

Documentary

FIRST TELECAST: *March 1, 1964*

LAST TELECAST: *September 15, 1964*

BROADCAST HISTORY:

Mar 1964–May 1964, NBC Sun 10:00 –11:00
Jun 1964–Sep 1964, NBC Tue 10:00–11:00

This series of full-hour documentaries on various subjects, ranging from political issues to a profile of baseball player Willie Mays, aired on alternate weeks during the spring and summer of 1964. It was sponsored by the Humble Oil Company.

HUNTER

Foreign Intrigue

FIRST TELECAST: *February 18, 1977*

LAST TELECAST: *May 27, 1977*

BROADCAST HISTORY:

Feb 1977–May 1977, CBS Fri 10:00–11:00

CAST:

James Hunter .... James Franciscus
Marty Shaw .... Linda Evans
Gen. Baker .... Ralph Bellamy

Working for top Federal intelligence chief General Baker, James Hunter and his partner Marty Shaw were called upon to fight a multitude of international foes in their jobs as undercover counterespionage agents. Sometimes they fought with Communists, sometimes with underworld organizations, and occasionally with other U.S. intelligence agencies. Their assignments took them all over the world.

HUNTER, THE

International Intrigue

FIRST TELECAST: *July 3, 1952*

LAST TELECAST: *December 26, 1954*

BROADCAST HISTORY:

Jul 1952, CBS Thu 9:00–9:30
Jul 1952–Sep 1952, CBS Wed 9:30–10:00
Jul 1954–Dec 1954, NBC Sun 10:30–11:00

CAST:

Bart Adams (1952–1954) ..... Barry Nelson
Bart Adams (1954) .... Keith Larsen

Bart Adams was a wealthy, attractive young American businessman whose interests caused him to become involved in suspenseful adventures in exotic places all over the world. In order to move about unnoticed, he was a master of disguise, changing his appearance for each show. Most of the episodes in the series had Bart rescue someone who was in the clutches of Communist agents or thwart some evil plan that Communist agents had concocted to cause trouble for the Free World. The way he identified himself to friends in the European underground was by whistling "Frère Jacques," and ending it with a wolf whistle.

This filmed series was originally a CBS summer show, but films continued to be produced for syndication after the end of its network run. The episodes aired on NBC during the summer of 1954 were drawn from these syndicated films. Some new episodes were aired on NBC in the fall of 1954, with Keith Larsen replacing Barry Nelson in the role of Bart Adams.

HUSBANDS, WIVES & LOVERS

Situation Comedy

FIRST TELECAST: *March 10, 1978*

LAST TELECAST: *June 30, 1978*

BROADCAST HISTORY:

Mar 1978–Jun 1978, CBS Fri 10:00–11:00

CAST:

Helene Willis ....Jesse Welles
Ron Willis ....Ron Rifkin
Murray Zuckerman .....Stephen Pearlman
Paula Zuckerman ....Cynthia Harris
Harry Bellini ....Eddie Barth
Joy Bellini ....Lynne Marie Stewart
Lennie Bellini ....Mark Lonow
Rita DeLatorre ....Randee Heller
Dixon Carter Fielding ......Charles Siebert
Courtney Fielding ....Claudette Nevins

One format that has never worked in television, despite numerous attempts, has been the hour long situation comedy. This one followed the lives of five couples, all friends, who lived in the San Fernando Valley suburbs outside of Los Angeles. Murray Zuckerman was a traveling salesman for a pharmaceutical firm and spent much of his time out of town; Harry Bellini was a rough-hewn, self-taught garbage truck tycoon with a young, naive second wife; Lennie was Harry's younger brother who was living with Rita DeLatorre, with whom he ran a stylish jean boutique; Ron Willis was a dentist who had an amicable relationship with his wife Helene, from whom he was separated; and Dixon Carter Fielding was Ron's best friend, a corporate attorney who was also representing Helene in the separation proceedings. Carter's wife, Courtney, was a spendthrift who managed to go through even more money than his substantial income provided.

The series was created by comedienne Joan Rivers.

I COVER TIMES SQUARE

Newspaper

FIRST TELECAST: *October 5, 1950*

LAST TELECAST: *January 11, 1951*

BROADCAST HISTORY:

Oct 1950–Jan 1951, ABC Thu 10:00–10:30

CAST:

Johnny Warren ....Harold Huber

PRODUCER:

Harold Huber

Harold Huber, a veteran actor who had portrayed dozens of squint-eyed, scheming villains on radio and in films (including the Charlie Chan pictures), was cast as a crusading Broadway columnist in this early series. His favorite hangout was the out-of-town newspaper stand in Times Square, and his beat, the seamy side of show business. In the first episode, for example, he was out to break up a gambling syndicate that controlled the boxing business in New York. The real-life prototype for Huber's role was said to be Walter Winchell.

After its prime-time run *I Cover Times Square* moved to Saturday afternoon, where it continued until late 1951.

I DREAM OF JEANNIE

Situation Comedy

FIRST TELECAST: *September 18, 1965*

LAST TELECAST: *September 1, 1970*

BROADCAST HISTORY:

Sep 1965–Sep 1966, NBC Sat 8:00–8:30
Sep 1966–Aug 1967, NBC Mon 8:00–8:30
Sep 1967–Aug 1968, NBC Tue 7:30–8:00
Sep 1968–Aug 1969, NBC Mon 7:30–8:00
Sep 1969–Sep 1970, NBC Tue 7:30–8:00

CAST:

Jeannie ....Barbara Eden
Capt. Tony Nelson ....Larry Hagman
Capt. Roger Healey ....Bill Daily
Dr. Bellows ....Hayden Rorke
Gen. Wingard Stone (1965–1966) Philip Ober
Melissa Stone (1965–1966) ...Karen Sharpe
Gen. Peterson (1965–1969)
......................Barton MacLane
Amanda Bellows (1966–1970)
......................Emmaline Henry
Gen. Schaeffer (1969–1970)
......................Vinton Hayworth

Astronaut Tony Nelson was on a space mission that aborted, forcing him to parachute onto a desert island. While waiting for a rescue team he came across an old bottle that had apparently washed ashore. When he opened the bottle, out popped a 2,000-year-old (but remarkably well-preserved) genie, who promptly accepted him as her master, since he had set her free.

Returning to Cocoa Beach, Florida, with the rescue team, Tony found that nobody would believe that he had found a luscious, sexy genie. The base psychiatrist, Dr. Bellows, was convinced that Tony had suffered delusions caused by exposure. Complicating the matter, the genie, appropriately named Jeannie, refused to perform magic or ever appear for anyone but Tony. Her efforts to serve him often resulted in rather confusing situations, caused in part by her lack of familiarity with 20th-century American customs.

I Dream of Jeannie ran for five seasons. In its first year Tony was engaged to General Stone's daughter Melissa. Since Jeannie was in love with Tony she went out of her way to make his relationship with Melissa extremely difficult. By the second season, Melissa was gone, as was her father, and Tony had a new commanding officer in General Peterson. His social life was at this point involved with his girl-crazy buddy, and fellow astronaut, Roger Healey, the only person other than Tony who realized that Jeannie existed and had magical powers. Roger was always getting Tony into situations that aggravated the very jealous Jeannie. After four seasons of trying, Jeannie finally succeeded in convincing Tony that he loved her enough to marry her and they were wed in the episode telecast on December 2, 1969.

Roger and Tony, originally captains, were both promoted to Major during the run of the show.

I LOVE LUCY

Situation Comedy

FIRST TELECAST: *October 15, 1951*

LAST TELECAST: *September 24, 1961*

BROADCAST HISTORY:

Oct 1951–Jun 1957, CBS Mon 9:00–9:30 (OS)
Apr 1955–Oct 1955, CBS Sun 6:00–6:30
Oct 1955–Apr 1956, CBS Sat 6:30–7:00
Sep 1957–May 1958, CBS Wed 7:30–8:00
Jul 1958–Sep 1958, CBS Mon 9:00–9:30
Oct 1958–May 1959, CBS Thu 7:30–8:00
Jul 1959–Sep 1959, CBS Fri 8:30–9:00
Sep 1961, CBS Sun 6:30–7:00

CAST:

Lucy Ricardo .... Lucille Ball
Ricky Ricardo .... Desi Arnaz
Ethel Mertz .... Vivian Vance
Fred Mertz .... William Frawley
Little Ricky Ricardo (1956–1957) .... Richard Keith
Betty Ramsey (1957) ...... Mary Jane Croft
Ralph Ramsey (1957) .... Frank Nelson

THEME:

"I Love Lucy," by Harold Adamson and Eliot Daniel

Lucille Ball had spent three seasons on CBS radio as the female lead in the situation comedy *My Favorite Husband* when she decided to give the new medium, television, a try. In her radio role as Liz Cooper, she perfected many of the mannerisms that she would use in *I Love Lucy*, including the scatterbrained quality and the loud crying fits when things weren't going her way. CBS was enthusiastic about the concept of the show, but the network nabobs had two major objections—they were positive nobody would believe Desi was her husband (despite the fact that they were married in real life), and they wanted the show done live from New York, like all of the other early television comedies. Lucy was determined to use Desi and had no desire to commute from Hollywood to New York for the show. In the summer of 1950 the two of them went on tour performing before live audiences to prove that Desi was believable as her husband, and that summer they produced a film pilot for the series with $5,000 of their own money. The pilot convinced the CBS brass that they had something special and *I Love Lucy* was given a berth on the fall schedule.

The premise of *I Love Lucy* was not that much different from that of other family situation comedies on television and radio—a wacky wife making life difficult for a loving but perpetually irritated husband—but the people involved made it something very special. Lucy Ricardo was an American of Scottish ancestry (maiden name MacGillicuddy) married to a Cuban bandleader. Husband Ricky was employed at the Tropicana Club and since she was constantly trying to prove to him that she could be in show business too, he spent much of his time trying to keep Lucy off the nightclub's stage. Ricky just wanted her to be a simple housewife. Whenever he became particularly exasperated with one of her schemes, Ricky's already broken English would degenerate into a stream of Spanish epithets. The Tropicana Club was in Manhattan, and so was the Ricardo apartment, in a middle-class building in the East 60s where their neighbors, best friends, and landlords were Fred and Ethel Mertz. Lucy's partner in mischief was Ethel, and both Ricky and Fred had to endure the foolishness perpetrated by their wives.

I Love Lucy was an immediate smash hit and, during its six years in originals, never ranked lower than third in popularity among all television programs. The plots, by writers Madelyn Pugh and Bob Carroll, Jr., were superb, the gags were inventive, and Lucy's clowning the *pièce de résistance* that took *I Love Lucy* beyond the realm of other contemporary comedies. As wacky as she was, audiences could empathize and adore her. Watching *I Love Lucy* in the early 1950s became as much a part of life as watching Milton Berle's *Texaco Star Theater* had been in the late 1940s. It was a national event when, on January 19, 1953, Lucy Ricardo gave birth to Little Ricky on the air, the same night that Lucille Ball gave birth to her second child, Desiderio Alberto Arnaz IV.

Over the years, within the context of the show, Ricky became more successful. He got a movie offer that prompted a cross-country trip by car, with the Mertzes, during the 1954–1955 season. During the 1955–1956 season they took a trip to Europe, also with the Mertzes, and at the start of the 1956–1957 season Ricky opened his own club, the Ricky Ricardo Babaloo Club. He had also gotten a TV show and, with his good fortune, bought a country home in Connecticut early in 1957. (See *Lucy in Connecticut* for complete description.) It was also during the 1956–1957 season that Little Ricky was added to the regular cast. He had been played on a very occasional basis in the previous seasons by a pair of infant twins, Joseph David Mayer and Michael Lee Mayer.

Everyone has certain favorite episodes of *I Love Lucy*, and there were so many memorable ones that trying to cite the "best" is particularly difficult. Even CBS executives had problems doing it. During the summer of 1958 there was a collection of reruns titled *The Top Ten Lucy Shows*—there were 13 different episodes in that "top 10." There was the show in which Lucy maneuvered her way onto Ricky's TV show to do a cough medicine commercial, and got drunk sampling the high-alcohol-content medicine. There was the time she tried to bake her own bread, and was pinned to the far wall of her kitchen when the loaf—into which she had thrown two entire packages of yeast—was released from the oven. While looking for souvenirs to take back to New York from their trip to Hollywood, Lucy and Ethel tried to pry loose the block of cement with John Wayne's footprints from in front of Grauman's Chinese Theatre. There was the time Lucy tried to get into Ricky's nightclub show by impersonating a clown. When they were going to be interviewed on the TV show *Face to Face* they almost got into a fight with the Mertzes because Ricky's new agent wanted them to move into a classier apartment. The messiest episode, however, had to be one that was part of their trip to Europe. Lucy had been offered a minor role in a film by an Italian producer and, in an effort to absorb atmosphere, ended up in a vat of unpressed grapes fighting with a professional grape stomper.

The success of *I Love Lucy* is unparalleled in the history of television. The decision to film it, rather than do it live, made it possible to have a high-quality print of each episode available for endless rebroadcasts, as opposed to the poor-quality kinescopes of live shows. The reruns, sold to independent stations after *I Love Lucy* left the network, and translated into virtually every language for foreign distribution, made millions for Lucy and Desi, whose production company, Desilu, owned the series. This set the pattern for all of television. The appeal of reusable filmed programs, all started by *I Love Lucy*, eventually resulted in the shift of television production from New York, where it had all started, to Hollywood, where the film facilities were. *I Love Lucy* was practically unique in that it was filmed before a live audience, something that did not become widespread in the situation-comedy world until the 1970s, and the technique of simultaneously using three cameras during the filming to allow for editing of the finished product was also a *Lucy* first.

By the end of the 1956–1957 season, despite the fact it was still the number one program in all of television, *I Love Lucy* ceased production as a weekly series. For the two years prior to the suspension of production, both Lucy and Desi had been seeking to cut down on their workload. They finally succeeded. After the fall of 1957 there was no *I Love Lucy,* but there were a number of *Lucille Ball–Desi Arnaz Shows,* full-hour specials about the continuing travels and tribulations of the Richardos and the Mertzes. Reruns of *I Love Lucy* had aired during the summer of 1955 as *The Sunday Lucy Show* and during the 1955–1956 season on Saturdays as *The Lucy Show.* With the original show out of production, prime-time reruns of *I Love Lucy* were aired for another two years on CBS, showed up briefly in 1961, and ran in daytime on CBS until 1967. The syndicated reruns have been running continuously ever since, and there is no end in sight.

I LOVE TO EAT

Cooking

FIRST TELECAST: *August 30, 1946*

LAST TELECAST: *May 18, 1947*

BROADCAST HISTORY:

Aug 1946–Oct 1946, NBC Fri 8:15–8:30 (approximately)
Nov 1946–Mar 1947, NBC Fri 8:30–8:45
Apr 1947–May 1947, NBC Thu 8:30–9:00

HOST:

James Beard

This Borden-sponsored program opened with a sketch of Elsie, the famed Borden cow. Then James Beard took over to demonstrate the preparation of some of his unique dishes for the television audience. Beard's cooking demonstrations were seen earlier as a segment of NBC-TV's *Radio City Matinee.*

I MARRIED JOAN

Situation Comedy

FIRST TELECAST: *October 15, 1952*

LAST TELECAST: *April 6, 1955*

BROADCAST HISTORY:

Oct 1952–Apr 1955, NBC Wed 8:00–8:30

CAST:

Joan Stevens .... Joan Davis
Judge Bradley Stevens .... Jim Backus
Minerva Parker (1952–1953)
.... Hope Emerson
Beverly (1953–1955) .... Beverly Wills

Bradley Stevens served as a judge in domestic court. Each episode opened with Judge Stevens on the bench. In the course of trying to resolve the problems of those who came before him, he would explain to them how he had dealt with a similar type of problem with his own beloved but slightly wacky wife, Joan. As he started to tell the story, the courtroom scene would fade into his home and the situation would be enacted. During the first season, Joan's next-door neighbor and partner-in-mischief was Minerva Parker. The following two seasons Joan Davis' real daughter was the only other regular in the cast, playing the part of Joan Steven's much younger college-student sister, Beverly.

I REMEMBER MAMA

see *Mama*

I SPY

Adventure/Espionage

FIRST TELECAST: *September 15, 1965*

LAST TELECAST: *September 2, 1968*

BROADCAST HISTORY:

Sep 1965–Sep 1967, NBC Wed 10:00–11:00
Sep 1967–Sep 1968, NBC Mon 10:00–11:00

CAST:

Kelly Robinson .... Robert Culp
Alexander Scott .... Bill Cosby

I Spy was a departure from the traditional type of show about espionage. Both of its leads were realistically conceived characters and could see the humor in situations, enabling them to have fun with their work. It had its share of cloak-and-dagger action, but never took itself too seriously. Comedian Bill Cosby, who provided much of the subtle humor in the show, proved he was an accomplished serious actor and had the added distinction of being the first black performer to have a starring role in a regular dramatic series on American television.

Kelly Robinson and Alexander Scott were a team of American agents. The cover used by Kelly was that of a top-seeded tennis player traveling around the world for tournaments. A former law student at an Ivy League college, he had played on two Davis Cup teams. Alexander Scott's cover was as trainer and traveling companion to Robinson. A graduate of Temple and an Oxford scholar, his knowledge of languages was often useful in dealing with people all over the world. Both of them were dedicated to government service and America, but their dedication did not stop them from often questioning the motives and purposes behind some of the maneuvers in which they were involved. Their casual approach to life, and job, was a very refreshing contrast to the nature of their work.

ICE PALACE

Musical Variety

FIRST TELECAST: *May 23, 1971*

LAST TELECAST: *July 25, 1971*

BROADCAST HISTORY:

May 1971–Jul 1971, CBS Sun 10:00–11:00

Each week the cast was different but the format remained the same; a guest celebrity host, one or two featured musical or comedy acts, and a selection of performers from The Ice Capades. Everything was tied to and revolved around the skating acts, which made this variety series somewhat different from most.

ICHABOD AND ME

Situation Comedy

FIRST TELECAST: *September 26, 1961*

LAST TELECAST: *September 18, 1962*

BROADCAST HISTORY:

Sep 1961–Sep 1962, CBS Tue 9:30–10:00

CAST:

Robert Major .... Robert Sterling
Ichabod Adams .... George Chandler
Abigail Adams .... Christine White
Benjie Major .... Jimmy Mathers
Aunt Lavinia .... Reta Shaw

Tiring of the rat race of newspaper work in New York City, reporter Bob Major bought the only paper in a small rural town called Phippsboro, and moved there with his six-year-old son, Benjie. The man from whom Bob had purchased the paper, and who still owned most of the town, was Ichabod Adams. Ichabod still kept his finger in the operation of the paper, while his attractive young daughter Abigail kept her eye on the highly eligible Mr. Major. Bob, a widower, spent most of his time winding down to the snail's pace of Phippsboro and of the small *Phippsboro Bulletin.*

I'D LIKE TO SEE

Demonstration

FIRST TELECAST: *November 5, 1948*

LAST TELECAST: *March 29, 1949*

BROADCAST HISTORY:

Nov 1948–Dec 1948, NBC Fri 9:00–9:30
Dec 1948–Mar 1949, NBC Tue 9:00–9:30

HOST:

Ray Morgan

REGULAR:

Kuda Bux (Jan–Mar)

Viewer-participation program, which was the prototype for the long-running DuMont/ABC series *You Asked for It* (1950–1959). Viewers were asked to write in suggestions for unusual places or things they would like to see, and these were then presented via a combination of films and live studio demonstrations. The first show, for example, included scenes of the United Nations building, an Edgar Bergen–Charlie McCarthy routine, and film clips of presidents of the U.S. from McKinley to Truman. In January Indian performer Kuda Bux, "the man with the X-ray vision," was added as a regular and viewers were asked what feats they would like to see him perform blindfolded.

IDENTIFY

Quiz

FIRST TELECAST: *February 14, 1949*

LAST TELECAST: *May 9, 1949*

BROADCAST HISTORY:

Feb 1949–May 1949, ABC Mon 9:00–9:15

HOST:

Bob Elson

This short-lived sports picture quiz originated in Chicago.

IF YOU HAD A MILLION

syndicated title for *The Millionaire*

IGOR CASSINI SHOW, THE

Interview

FIRST TELECAST: *October 25, 1953*

LAST TELECAST: *March 3, 1954*

BROADCAST HISTORY:

Oct 1953–Jan 1954, DUM Sun 6:00–6:30
Jan 1954–Mar 1954, DUM Sun 6:15–6:30

HOST:

Igor Cassini

Igor Cassini, who as Cholly Knickerbocker wrote a society gossip column for the Hearst papers, hosted this interview program which was filmed in the homes of the guests. Typical of Cassini's guests was his first, Mrs. Gwen Cafritz, Washington's leading hostess. Society and literary types made up the bulk of the interviews. Cassini also reviewed current films and plays. The program was also known as *Exclusively Yours*.

ILONA MASSEY SHOW, THE

Music

FIRST TELECAST: *November 1, 1954*

LAST TELECAST: *January 3, 1955*

BROADCAST HISTORY:

Nov 1954–Jan 1955, DUM Mon 8:00–8:30

REGULARS:

Ilona Massey
Irving Fields Trio

Hungarian-born movie actress Ilona Massey sang sultry ballads in a nightclub atmosphere in this short-lived musical show. The Irving Fields trio provided instrumental backing to her intimate song styling.

I'M DICKENS—HE'S FENSTER

Situation Comedy

FIRST TELECAST: *September 28, 1962*

LAST TELECAST: *September 13, 1963*

BROADCAST HISTORY:

Sep 1962–Sep 1963, ABC Fri 9:00–9:30

CAST:

Arch Fenster ....Marty Ingels
Harry Dickens ....John Astin
Kate Dickens ....Emmaline Henry
Mel Warshaw ....Dave Ketchum
Mulligan ....Henry Beckman
Myron Bannister ....Frank DeVol

Comedy bordering on the slapstick with Dickens and Fenster, two carpenter-construction workers who were constantly getting into dangerous situations on and off the job. Single Arch Fenster was the more scatterbrained of the two, married Harry Dickens the responsible one. Warshaw and Mulligan were friends on the job. Bandleader Frank DeVol portrayed the balding building contractor in this series.

IMMORTAL, THE

Adventure

FIRST TELECAST: *September 24, 1970*

LAST TELECAST: *September 8, 1971*

BROADCAST HISTORY:

Sep 1970–Jan 1971, ABC Thu 10:00–11:00
May 1971–Sep 1971, ABC Wed 9:30–10:30

CAST:

Ben Richards ....Christopher George
Fletcher ....Don Knight
Arthur Maitland ....David Brian
Sylvia ....Carol Lynley

Handsome racing driver Ben Richards seemed to have everything in this adventure series, youth, health—and immortality. That last attribute was due to some peculiar antibodies in his blood which made him immune to disease or aging. Immortality was something that a lot of people wanted for their own purposes, however, so Richards was constantly pursued, principally by ruthless billionaire Arthur Maitland and his henchman Fletcher. Like *The Fugitive*, this was essentially a "chase" show, as Richards kept one step ahead of his relentless pursuers while living the life of a footloose young racing driver. Maitland and Ben's fiancée Sylvia were seen only occasionally in this series.

The Immortal was based on a TV movie aired in 1969, which had a somewhat different cast.

IMOGENE COCA SHOW, THE

Comedy Variety

FIRST TELECAST: *October 2, 1954*

LAST TELECAST: *June 25, 1955*

BROADCAST HISTORY:

Oct 1954–Jun 1955, NBC Sat 9:00–9:30

REGULARS:

Betty Crane ....Imogene Coca
Helen Milliken (1955) ......Bibi Osterwald
Jerry Crane (1955) ....Hal March
Harry Milliken (1955) ....David Burns

MUSIC:

The Carl Hoff Orchestra

The Imogene Coca Show never quite figured out what it wanted to be. Initially it went on the air as a situation comedy with Miss Coca essentially playing herself as an actress whose comic adventures in "real life," away from the TV cameras, formed the basis for stories. After only two weeks in this format, the show was altered to become a comedy variety show with sketches, production numbers, and guest stars. On February 19, 1955, the format was overhauled again. It was a situation comedy about a newlywed couple, the Cranes, and the adventures they had with their neighbors, the Millikens. All the changes and tinkering with format never gave the show a solid audience and it was canceled at the end of its first season.

IN RECORD TIME

see *Art Ford Show, The*

IN THE BEGINNING

Situation Comedy

FIRST TELECAST: *September 20, 1978*

LAST TELECAST: *October 18, 1978*

BROADCAST HISTORY:

Sep 1978–Oct 1978, CBS Wed 8:30–9:00

CAST:

Father Daniel M. Cleary .... McLean Stevenson
Sister Agnes .... Priscilla Lopez
Sister Lillian .... Priscilla Morrill
Willie .... Olivia Barash
Jerome Rockefeller .... Bobby Ellerbee
Msgr. Francis X. Barlow ...... Jack Dodson

This comedy was a kind of updated *Going My Way*, focusing on the conflict between the pompous, traditionalist and continually exasperated Father Cleary and the street-wise nun assigned to him, Sister Agnes. They worked in a storefront mission-community center in an inner-city section of Baltimore. It was Sister Aggie's home neighborhood, and she loved the assignment, but Father Cleary found both her and the neighborhood hookers, hustlers, and winos more than he could stand. He kept trying to get reassigned, hoping to get as far away as possible from the Sister he called "Attila the Nun."

IN THE FIRST PERSON

Interview

FIRST TELECAST: *January 29, 1949*

LAST TELECAST: *October 10, 1950*

BROADCAST HISTORY:

Jan 1949–Dec 1949, CBS Sat 7:30–7:45
Feb 1950–Mar 1950, CBS Sat 7:15–7:30
Mar 1950–Jun 1950, CBS Thu 10:30–10:45
Jun 1950–Jul 1950, CBS Sun 9:45–10:00
Jul 1950–Aug 1950, CBS Sun 9:15–9:30
Sep 1950–Oct 1950, CBS Tue 10:45–11:00

HOST:

Quincy Howe
Ned Calmer (1950)

Each week *In the First Person*'s host introduced and chatted informally with a celebrity or someone in the news. Entertainers, politicians, corporation heads, and others appeared on this live 15-minute program. Quincy Howe was the host from its inception through August 1950. He was replaced by Ned Calmer during the program's six-week run that fall.

IN THE KELVINATOR KITCHEN

Instruction

FIRST TELECAST: *May 21, 1947*

LAST TELECAST: *June 30, 1948*

BROADCAST HISTORY:

May 1947–Jun 1948, NBC Wed 8:30–8:45

HOSTESS:

Alma Kitchell

Cooking program seen during the very early days of network television.

IN THE MORGAN MANNER

Musical Variety

FIRST TELECAST: *March 1, 1950*

LAST TELECAST: *July 30, 1950*

BROADCAST HISTORY:

Mar 1950–Apr 1950, ABC Sun 10:00–10:30
Jul 1950, ABC Sun 8:00–8:30

HOST:

Russ Morgan and His Orchestra

THEME:

"Does Your Heart Beat for Me," by Mitchell Parish and Russ Morgan

This low-budget musical variety show originated in Chicago and featured Russ Morgan, who led one of the more popular dance bands of the late 1940s. Morgan was extremely big on the popular record charts at the time (at one point during 1949 he had six of the top 10 tunes, including the million-seller "Cruising Down the River"). That plus his easygoing personality made him a natural for television. This show was also seen on Sunday afternoons for a time.

Morgan's slogan was "Music in the Morgan Manner," hence the program's title.

INA RAY HUTTON SHOW, THE

Musical Variety

FIRST TELECAST: *July 4, 1956*

LAST TELECAST: *September 5, 1956*

BROADCAST HISTORY:

Jul 1956–Sep 1956, NBC Wed 10:30–11:00

REGULARS:

Ina Ray Hutton and Her All-Girl Band
Diane Brewster
Mickey Anderson

This may have been the first "Women's Lib" program on television. Ina Ray Hutton and Her All-Girl Band were the stars and principal performers. Miss Hutton, in addition to leading the band, sang and danced with guest stars in production numbers. Not only were the regulars on this show all women, but so were all of the guest stars, including Judy Canova, the King Sisters, Gogi Grant, Rose Marie, and Yma Sumac. Even the announcer was a woman, actress Diane Brewster. It was no wonder that the program was subtitled "No Men Allowed."

The most prominent member of Miss Hutton's 13-piece band was Mickey Anderson who, in addition to playing saxophone, clarinet, and flute, also did comic vocals. The remaining dozen members of the group were Dee Dee Ball, piano and organ; Helen Smith, bass; Margaret Rinker, drums; Jane Davies, guitar; Harriet Blackburn, saxophone and conga drums; Judy Von Euer, saxophone and clarinet; Evie Howeth, saxophone and clarinet; Helen Wooley, saxophone and clarinet; Lois Cronin, trombone and vibraphone; and trumpet players Peggy Fairbanks, Helen Hammond, and Zoe Ann Willy.

INCREDIBLE HULK, THE

Adventure Drama

FIRST TELECAST: *March 10, 1978*

LAST TELECAST:

BROADCAST HISTORY:

Mar 1978– , CBS Fri 9:00–10:00

CAST:

David Bruce Banner ....Bill Bixby
The Incredible Hulk ....Lou Ferrigno
Jack McGee ....Jack Colvin

David Banner was a research scientist who had been experimenting with various means of determining the effects of stress on physical strength. In a freak accident in his laboratory, David was exposed to a massive dosage of radiation that had a dramatic effect on his physiology. Normally a quiet, peaceful man, David now found that every time he became angered he turned into *The Incredible Hulk*, a huge, greenish, man-like monster of immense strength and primitive passions. David knew what was happening when the transformation started to take place but, when he calmed down and returned to normal, had no recollection of what he had done when he was the creature. Traveling around the country in search of a cure, and taking odd jobs to keep himself fed and clothed, David sought to avoid the pursuit of investigative reporter Jack McGee, who suspected his secret but who had no real proof.

The Incredible Hulk was a television adaptation of the Marvel Comic Book character of the same name.

INDUSTRIES FOR AMERICA

Documentary

FIRST TELECAST: *May 31, 1951*

LAST TELECAST: *September 19, 1957*

BROADCAST HISTORY:

May 1951–Jul 1951, ABC Thu 10:00–10:30
Jul 1951–Sep 1951, ABC Sun 10:00–10:30
Oct 1951–Dec 1951, ABC Fri 10:30–11:00
Feb 1952, ABC Thu 10:15–10:30
Jun 1957–Sep 1957, ABC Thu 9:30–10:00

Documentary films which ABC ran during the early and mid-1950s, mostly, it seems, to fill time. The central theme was American industry on parade, with such provocative titles as "The Magic of Lumber," "Drama of Portland Cement," and "The Cranberry Story."

INFORMATION PLEASE

Quiz/Audience Participation

FIRST TELECAST: *June 29, 1952*

LAST TELECAST: *September 21, 1952*

BROADCAST HISTORY:

Jun 1952–Sep 1952, CBS Sun 9:00–9:30

EMCEE:

Clifton Fadiman

PANELISTS:

Franklin P. Adams
John Kieran

Information Please had had a long and successful run on radio, but its only appearance on television was as the 1952 summer replacement for *The Fred Waring Show*. Viewers submitted questions to be answered by the members of the panel, two permanent and one guest. The viewer received a $10 certificate good for the purchase of books or magazines if his question was used, and a $50 certificate if it stumped the panel. Emcee/moderator Clifton Fadiman had long been associated with the radio version of this literate series, as had panelists Adams and Kieran.

INSIDE DETECTIVE

see *Rocky King—Inside Detective*

INSIDE PHOTOPLAY
see *Wendy Barrie Show, The*

INSIDE U.S.A. WITH CHEVROLET
Musical Variety
FIRST TELECAST: *September 29, 1949*
LAST TELECAST: *March 16, 1950*
BROADCAST HISTORY:
Sep 1949–Mar 1950, CBS Thu 8:30–9:00
HOST:
Peter Lind Hayes
REGULARS:
Mary Healy
Mary Wickes
Sheila Bond
Jay Blackton Orchestra
PRODUCER:
Arthur Schwartz

Songwriter and producer Arthur Schwartz brought his hit musical *Inside U.S.A.* to network television in the fall of 1949, as an alternate-week series. The program was done in revue style, with Peter Lind Hayes hosting in the role of a contemporary American minstrel, and each telecast included songs, comedy sketches, dance and lavish production numbers. As the minstrel, Hayes would travel across the country and provide background to the individual program elements as he observed the splendor of America's natural beauty and the diversity of its people. Featured in the regular cast was his wife, singer/actress Mary Healy. There was also a big-name "star of the week" for every show, with such varied talents as Lucille Ball, Boris Karloff, Ethel Merman, David Niven, and Oscar Levant starring in individual telecasts.

INSPECTOR MARK SABER—HOMICIDE SQUAD
see *Mark Saber*

INTERCOLLEGIATE BASKETBALL
see *Basketball*

INTERLUDE
see *Summer Theater*

INTERNATIONAL BOXING CLUB BOUTS
see *Boxing*

INTERNATIONAL PLAYHOUSE
see *Movies—Prior to 1961*

INTERNATIONAL SHOWTIME
Variety
FIRST TELECAST: *September 15, 1961*
LAST TELECAST: *September 10, 1965*
BROADCAST HISTORY:
Sep 1961–Sep 1965, NBC Fri 7:30–8:30
HOST:
Don Ameche

Circuses, ice shows, magic shows, and other similar types of spectaculars, from all over Europe, were shown each week on *International Showtime.* Some episodes focused on a specific talent—clowns, daredevils, etc.—and compiled the best examples from different performers into a single show. Don Ameche was the host of the series throughout its four-season run. He would introduce each act and then sit back as part of the audience to enjoy it. He traveled around Europe with the production crew and was actually present when each act was taped.

INTERNS, THE
Medical
FIRST TELECAST: *September 18, 1970*
LAST TELECAST: *September 10, 1971*
BROADCAST HISTORY;
Sep 1970–Sep 1971, CBS Fri 7:30–8:30
CAST:
Dr. Peter Goldstone ....Broderick Crawford
Dr. Greg Pettit ....Stephen Brooks
Dr. Pooch Hardin ....Christopher Stone
Dr. Cal Barrin ....Hal Frederick
Dr. Lydia Thorpe ....Sandra Smith
Dr. Sam Marsh ....Mike Farrell
Bobbe Marsh ....Elaine Giftos

Broderick Crawford starred in this medical series as the father figure to a nicely mixed group of five young interns (one black, one woman, one young married man, two swingers). New North Hospital was the setting, and the personal and professional lives of the young doctors provided the stories.

INVADERS, THE
Science Fiction
FIRST TELECAST: *January 10, 1967*
LAST TELECAST: *September 17, 1968*
BROADCAST HISTORY:
Jan 1967–Jan 1968, ABC Tue 8:30–9:30
Jan 1968–Sep 1968, ABC Tue 10:00–11:00

CAST:

David Vincent ....Roy Thinnes
Edgar Scoville ....Kent Smith

EXECUTIVE PRODUCER:

Quinn Martin

One of the most durable science-fiction ideas is the one that questions the very reality of what we see around us. Could there be aliens in our midst? Architect David Vincent certainly thought so. He had witnessed the landing of a flying saucer, and stumbled onto an incredible secret: that scattered throughout the world's population, disguised as humans, was an advance guard of alien creatures from a dying planet, who were preparing to conquer the earth!

Convincing his fellow citizens of this was of course no easy task, so Vincent went on a one-man crusade to obtain solid evidence and warn mankind of the dangers it faced—while trying not to fall into the clutches of the aliens. Identifying the enemy was tricky, but it could be done. Sometimes the invaders would have slightly mutated hands, such as a little finger jutting out awkwardly, sometimes, though rarely, they would begin to glow when they were in need of regeneration to retain their human form. And of course, they had no pulse or heartbeat—because they had no hearts.

For the first few months of the series Vincent fought a lonely, largely undercover battle. Eventually, feeling that he was a bit too lonely to be plausible, the producers gave him some allies, a group of seven others who also learned the secret and wanted to help. His chief confederate, who joined the show in December 1967, was Edgar Scoville, the head of an electronics firm.

Could it really happen? Well, you never know, but actor Roy Thinnes, in a bit of promotional hype released by the ABC press department, claimed that he had actually seen a UFO during the filming of the series. Then again, maybe *he* is one of *them*. . . .

INVESTIGATOR, THE

Detective

FIRST TELECAST: *June 3, 1958*

LAST TELECAST: *September 2, 1958*

BROADCAST HISTORY:

Jun 1958–Sep 1958, NBC Tue 8:00–9:00

CAST:

Jeff Prior ....Lonny Chapman
Lloyd Prior ....Howard St. John

Jeff Prior was a swinging private investigator in his early 30s whose ability to track down clues and resolve mysteries had made him very successful. He had learned his skills from his father, Lloyd, a retired newspaperman who had a reputation of his own for solving mysteries when he was a young reporter in the 1920s. Jeff dug up most of the facts in each case and, with his father's help, tied them all together to nail the culprits. This live detective series aired as a summer replacement in 1958.

INVESTIGATORS, THE

Detective

FIRST TELECAST: *October 5, 1961*

LAST TELECAST: *December 28, 1961*

BROADCAST HISTORY:

Oct 1961–Dec 1961, CBS Thu 9:00–10:00

CAST:

Russ Andrews ....James Franciscus
Steve Banks ....James Philbrook
Maggie Peters ....Mary Murphy
Bill Davis ....Al Austin

With offices on the fashionable East Side of New York, the firm of "Investigators, Inc." was a highly successful and highly specialized operation. The cases dealt with by its staff were all tied in to very large insurance claims. As a team of insurance investigators, Russ, Steve, and Bill became involved with the underworld, the police, and others as they tracked down clues to determine whether or not claims were legitimate. Helping back at the office, and occasionally as an undercover operative, was Maggie Peters, the girl Friday to the three investigators.

INVISIBLE MAN, THE

International Intrigue

FIRST TELECAST: *November 4, 1958*

LAST TELECAST: *September 22, 1960*

BROADCAST HISTORY:

Nov 1958–May 1959, CBS Tue 8:00–8:30
May 1959–Jul 1959, CBS Thu 7:30–8:00
Jul 1960–Sep 1960, CBS Thu 7:30–8:00

CAST:

Dr. Peter Brady ....Anonymous
Diane Brady ....Lisa Daniely
Sally Brady ....Deborah Watling

Dr. Peter Brady was an English scientist working with the principles that govern the refraction of light when he discovered a means of making himself invisible. The only problem was that after becoming invisible, he could not make himself visible again. Having decided to make the best of his handicap, Peter became an adventurer/agent, working with British Intelligence to thwart the efforts of evil organizations and their agents throughout Europe (he had no trouble getting through customs). Seen regularly were his sister Diane and his niece Sally.

The actor playing Peter was never seen at all, being concealed in bandages or only heard offscreen. His identity was kept a close secret by the producers and to this day no one has revealed his name (not that very many are asking anymore).

The episodes aired during the summer of 1960 were not repeats but an additional group of original episodes. The series was produced in England.

INVISIBLE MAN, THE

Adventure

FIRST TELECAST: *September 8, 1975*

LAST TELECAST: *January 19, 1976*

BROADCAST HISTORY:

Sep 1975–Jan 1976, NBC Mon 8:00–9:00

CAST:

Dr. Daniel Westin ....David McCallum
Walter Carlson ....Craig Stevens
Dr. Kate Westin ....Melinda Fee

In an attempt to update the classic H. G. Wells story, this series brought us Dr. Daniel Westin, a scientist who had discovered a means of making any object invisible—including himself. When he found out that the government planned to use his technique for military purposes, he memorized his secret formula, destroyed his equipment, and turned himself invisible to escape. Unfortunately his method for becoming visible again failed to work, and he was temporarily stuck in invisibility. Seeking the aid of a scientist friend, he had a wig, highly realistic face mask, and plastic hands made to conceal his invisibility, enabling him to resume a somewhat normal public life.

Daniel and his wife Kate then went to work for the KLAE Corporation, where he continued his experiments in order to find his way back. He also undertook an assortment of dangerous security missions for his boss, Walter Carlson. Whenever the situation got tight Daniel could take off his mask and clothes and "disappear." This did not always prove to be as helpful as it might seem, however, as when he was trapped in the house of a blind man, extraordinarily sensitive to sound, who was out to kill him.

IRON HORSE, THE

Western

FIRST TELECAST: *September 12, 1966*

LAST TELECAST: *January 6, 1968*

BROADCAST HISTORY:

Sep 1966–Sep 1967, ABC Mon 7:30–8:30
Sep 1967–Jan 1968, ABC Sat 9:30–10:30

CAST:

Ben Calhoun ....Dale Robertson
Dave Tarrant ....Gary Collins
Barnabas Rogers ....Bob Random
Nils Torvald (1966–1967) ....Roger Torrey
Julie Parsons (1967–1968) ....Ellen McRae

Ben Calhoun was a hard-driving ladies' man who had the good fortune to win a railroad in a poker game. Unfortunately, the Buffalo Pass, Scalplock and Defiance line was only half built and on the brink of bankruptcy, so it was up to Ben to finish the job. Helping him push the line to completion through the wild, untamed West of the 1880s were Dave, his young construction engineer; Nils, the giant crewman; and Barnabas, a young orphan who idolized Ben and served as his clerk. Julie Parsons arrived in the second season as the freight station operator and proprietor of the Scalplock General Store.

There was plenty of action in this epic of a railroad moving west, with crooked financiers, rampaging Indians, and assorted desperadoes peopling the stories.

IRONSIDE

Police

FIRST TELECAST: *September 14, 1967*

LAST TELECAST: *January 16, 1975*

BROADCAST HISTORY:

Sep 1967–Sep 1971, NBC Thu 8:30–9:30
Sep 1971–Nov 1971, NBC Tue 7:30–8:30
Nov 1971–Jan 1975, NBC Thu 9:00–10:00

CAST:

Robert Ironside ....Raymond Burr
Det. Sgt. Ed Brown ....Don Galloway
Eve Whitfield (1967–1971)
......................Barbara Anderson

Mark Sanger ....Don Mitchell
Fran Belding (1971–1975) . .Elizabeth Baur
Commissioner Randall ....Gene Lyons

Robert Ironside had been chief of detectives for the San Francisco Police Department for many years, and a member of the force for 25, when a would-be assassin's bullet grazed his spine and left him paralyzed from the waist down. Forced to leave the force as a regular member, he convinced Police Commissioner Randall to appoint him to a position as special consultant. Helping him wage his unrelenting war against crime were two former assistants, Sgt. Ed Brown and Policewoman Eve Whitfield, and an ex-delinquent (Mark Sanger) who became his aide and bodyguard. Confined to a wheelchair, Ironside made use of a specially equipped police van for transportation and some unused office space at police headquarters as a base of operations. When Barbara Anderson left the series at the end of the 1970–71 season over a contract dispute, she was replaced by Elizabeth Baur as Policewoman Fran Belding.

ISLANDERS, THE

Adventure

FIRST TELECAST: *October 2, 1960*

LAST TELECAST: *March 26, 1961*

BROADCAST HISTORY:

Oct 1960–Mar 1961, ABC Sun 9:30–10:30

CAST:

Sandy Wade ....William Reynolds
Zack Malloy ....James Philbrook
Wilhelmina Vandeveer .....Diane Brewster

Sandy and Zack were pilots flying for their own one-plane airline, based in the Spice Islands of the East Indies. Part of the spice was Wilhemina "Steamboat Willie" Vandeveer, their beautiful, blond, self-appointed business manager. Something of an operator herself, Willie was not above playing all the angles when it came to landing business for the boys. Unfortunately for Sandy and Zack, the results were designed more to benefit Willie than themselves. Whether flying passengers or cargo, the results were usually other than originally planned. Smugglers, escaped convicts, stolen goods, and mysterious, beautiful women were always keeping things busy.

IT COULD BE YOU

see *Bill Gwinn Show, The*

IT COULD BE YOU

Quiz/Audience Participation

FIRST TELECAST: *July 2, 1958*

LAST TELECAST: *September 27, 1961*

BROADCAST HISTORY:

Jul 1958–Sep 1958, NBC Wed 10:00–10:30
Nov 1958–Mar 1959, NBC Thu 8:30–9:00
Sep 1959–Jan 1960, NBC Sat 10:30–11:00
Jun 1961–Sep 1961, NBC Wed 10:00–10:30

EMCEE:

Bill Leyden

ASSISTANT:

Wendell Niles

Unsuspecting members of the studio audience were reunited with friends or relatives, called upon to perform stunts, or given the opportunity to meet guest celebrities on this program. As on *This Is Your Life*, research was done on the "victims" before the show, and anecdotes about their lives and pictures from their childhood were brought out. Being in the audience was always exciting, because you never knew when "It Could Be You." Bill Leyden was also the host of the daytime version of this show, which premiered in June 1956 and ran until December 1961.

IT HAPPENED IN SPORTS

Sports Commentary

FIRST TELECAST: *July 3, 1953*

LAST TELECAST: *January 19, 1954*

BROADCAST HISTORY:

Jul 1953–Aug 1953, NBC Fri 10:45–11:00
Sep 1953–Jan 1954, NBC Tue 10:45–11:00

HOST:

Bud Palmer

It Happened in Sports was used to fill the time between the conclusion of the boxing bout that started at 10 P.M. and the local news at 11 P.M. Bud Palmer was the host and presided over both live and filmed interviews with famous sports personalities as well as films of an historic event in the world of sport.

IT PAYS TO BE IGNORANT

Quiz/Audience Participation

FIRST TELECAST: *June 6, 1949*

LAST TELECAST: *September 27, 1951*

BROADCAST HISTORY:

Jun 1949–Sep 1949, CBS Mon 8:30–9:00
Jul 1951–Sep 1951, NBC Thu 8:00–8:30

EMCEE:

Tom Howard

PANELISTS:

Lulu McConnell
Harry McNaughton
George Shelton

It was appropriate that *It Pays to Be Ignorant* was the summer replacement for *You Bet Your Life* in 1951, for neither was really a quiz show—both were primarily vehicles for comedy. *It Pays to Be Ignorant* had started as a radio series in 1942 and aired on TV once before, in the summer of 1949. The four cheerful lunatics who comprised host and panel were the same on radio and TV. "Professor" Tom Howard, a spry, 65-year-old ex-vaudevillian, posed extremely simple questions to the panel and got replies that ranged from the ridiculous to the absurd. The frustrated emcee would watch as the "experts" stumbled through an improbable answer, interrupted each other, and found that they had changed the subject completely. Members of the studio audience were invited to pull questions out of a dunce cap for the experts. If the experts failed to answer the question correctly, and the studio contestant could squeeze the right answer into the mayhem, the contestant won a nominal award.

IT TAKES A THIEF

International Intrigue

FIRST TELECAST: *January 9, 1968*
LAST TELECAST: *September 14, 1970*
BROADCAST HISTORY:

Jan 1968–Aug 1969, ABC Tue 8:30–9:30
Aug 1969–Jan 1970, ABC Thu 10:00–11:00
Jan 1970–Sep 1970, ABC Mon 7:30–8:30

CAST:

Alexander Mundy ....Robert Wagner
Noah Bain (1968–1969) ...Malachi Throne
Wallie Powers (1969–1970) ..Edward Binns
Alister Mundy (1969–1970) ...Fred Astaire

Alexander Mundy was a cat burglar and professional thief who had style, class, and great talent. He had made only one mistake—getting caught. While serving a sentence in San Jobel Prison, he was contacted by representatives of U.S. Government spy agency, the SIA. They offered to get him out if he would put his talents to work stealing for the government. Accepting the offer, he worked closely with an SIA department head, Noah Bain, who was his boss, aide, associate, friend, and watchdog. Filmed throughout Europe, *It Takes a Thief* saw Al Mundy on various assignments as a master thief for the SIA, romancing beautiful women, and generally being his relaxed, handsome self.

At the start of the 1969–1970 season there were a few changes. Whereas previously Mundy had been under house confinement when not on an assignment, he was now a free agent. His SIA contact had become Wallie Powers, and his father, played by Fred Astaire, became a semi-regular. Al's father was the retired thief from whom he had learned all his skills, and who occasionally teamed with his son on special jobs.

IT WAS A VERY GOOD YEAR

Documentary

FIRST TELECAST: *May 10, 1971*
LAST TELECAST: *August 30, 1971*
BROADCAST HISTORY:

May 1971–Aug 1971, ABC Mon 8:30–9:00

HOST:

Mel Torme

An exercise in nostalgia. *It Was a Very Good Year* compiled old film clips, memorabilia, and interviews with famous personalities to provide a capsule summary of the news, fashions, and songs of a given year in the 20th century. Mel Torme was the host and, in addition to providing narration for some of the material and singing a song or two, he chatted with people who had been prominent in the year being covered. The years treated ranged from 1919 to 1964, but were mostly of the pre-rock 'n' roll era, so the show appealed primarily to older adults.

IT'S A BUSINESS?

Situation Comedy

FIRST TELECAST: *March 19, 1952*
LAST TELECAST: *May 21, 1952*
BROADCAST HISTORY:

Mar 1952–May 1952, DUM Wed 9:00–9:30

CAST:

Bob Haymes
Leo DeLyon
Dorothy Loudon

This situation comedy with music was set at the turn of the century and concerned the activities of a couple of Broadway song publishers. They had plenty of opportunities to demonstrate their wares (grand old favorites like "After the Ball"), as well as to welcome visiting vaudevillians to their offices. Bob Haymes, the brother of big-band singer Dick Haymes, and Leo DeLyon played the song-publisher partners and Dorothy Loudon played their secretary.

IT'S A GREAT LIFE

Situation Comedy

FIRST TELECAST: *September 7, 1954*

LAST TELECAST: *June 3, 1956*

BROADCAST HISTORY:

Sep 1954–Sep 1955, NBC Tue 10:30–11:00

Sep 1955–Jun 1956, NBC Sun 7:00–7:30

CAST:

Denny David ....Michael O'Shea
Steve Connors ....William Bishop
Uncle Earl ....James Dunn
Mrs. Amy Morgan ....Francis Bavier
Kathy Morgan ....Barbara Bates

Denny David and Steve Connors were two recently discharged GI's who decided to room together while trying to find civilian jobs. They headed for Southern California because Steve had been stationed there during World War II, and loved the weather. Once in California, they found lodgings in the home of widow Amy Morgan, whose household also included her daughter Kathy and her brother Earl. Stories revolved around Denny and Steve's problems in adjusting to civilian life, their problems with various jobs, and the trouble they got into by repeatedly letting the conniving Uncle Earl lure them into his money-making schemes.

IT'S A MAN'S WORLD

Situation Comedy

FIRST TELECAST: *September 17, 1962*

LAST TELECAST: *January 28, 1963*

BROADCAST HISTORY:

Sep 1962–Jan 1963, NBC Mon 7:30–8:30

CAST:

Wes Macauley ....Glenn Corbett
Howie Macauley ....Mike Burns
Tom-Tom DeWitt ....Ted Bessel
Vern Hodges ....Randy Boone
Houghton Stott ....Harry Harvey
Irene Hoff ....Jan Norris

Comedy set in a small Midwestern college town where two college students (Wes and Tom-Tom), one kid brother (Howie) and one footloose guitarist (Vern) lived together in a houseboat. The stories, which ranged from light comedy to drama, involved their problems with school, girls, jobs, and each other.

IT'S A SMALL WORLD

Travelogue

FIRST TELECAST: *June 27, 1953*

LAST TELECAST: *July 27, 1953*

BROADCAST HISTORY:

Jun 1953–Jul 1953, DUM Sat 7:30–8:00

Jul 1953, DUM Mon 8:00–8:30

HOST:

Dick Noel

Travel films narrated by Dick Noel. The program became a local New York presentation for the remainder of the summer.

IT'S ABOUT TIME

Quiz/Panel

FIRST TELECAST: *March 4, 1954*

LAST TELECAST: *May 2, 1954*

BROADCAST HISTORY:

Mar 1954, ABC Thu 8:00–8:30

Apr 1954–May 1954, ABC Sun 7:30–8:00

EMCEE:

Dr. Bergen Evans

PANEL:

Robert Pollack
Ruthie Duskin
Sherl Stern
Vim Gottschalk

Panelists on this quiz show were asked to identify well-known events of the past. Clues were given in the form of scrambled headlines, dramatic vignettes, old phonograph records, etc. There was also a mystery guest.

IT'S ABOUT TIME

Situation Comedy

FIRST TELECAST: *September 11, 1966*

LAST TELECAST: *August 27, 1967*

BROADCAST HISTORY:

Sep 1966–Aug 1967, CBS Sun 7:30–8:00

CAST:

Hector ....Jack Mullaney
Mac ....Frank Aletter
Shad ....Imogene Coca
Gronk ....Joe E. Ross
Boss ....Cliff Norton

Clon .... Mike Mazurki
Mlor .... Mary Grace
Breer .... Pat Cardi
Mr. Tyler .... Alan DeWitt

After their space capsule made a wrong turn somewhere, and cracked the time barrier, astronauts Hector and Mac discovered that they were headed back to a world quite different from the one they had left. They landed in a swamp smack in the middle of Earth's Stone Age, not far from a tribe of cave dwellers. Among their new prehistoric neighbors were a friendly couple, Shad and Gronk; their two children, Mlor and Breer; the tribal bully, Clon; and the suspicious chief, Boss. In the episode of January 22, the astronauts finally managed to repair their spaceship and return to the 20th century, bringing Shad, Gronk, and their children back with them. The cave people had even more trouble adjusting to modern-day Los Angeles than the astronauts did to the prehistoric world.

IT'S ALEC TEMPLETON TIME

Music

FIRST TELECAST: *June 10, 1955*
LAST TELECAST: *August 26, 1955*
BROADCAST HISTORY:
Jun 1955, DUM Fri 10:30–11:00
Jul 1955–Aug 1955, DUM Fri 10:00–10:30
HOST:
Alec Templeton

This summer musical series was hosted by Alec Templeton, the blind pianist-satirist, who introduced guest singers, dancers, and musicians, and chatted with them following their numbers.

IT'S ALWAYS JAN

Situation Comedy

FIRST TELECAST: *September 10, 1955*
LAST TELECAST: *June 30, 1956*
BROADCAST HISTORY:
Sep 1955–Jun 1956, CBS Sat 9:30–10:00
CAST:
Janis Stewart .... Janis Paige
Pat Murphy .... Patricia Bright
Val Marlowe .... Merry Anders
Josie Stewart .... Jeri Lou James
Stanley Schreiber .... Arte Johnson

Musical-comedy star Janis Paige starred in this comedy series about the problems of a single parent. Nightclub singer Janis Stewart had lost her husband during the war and had a 10-year-old daughter (Josie) to raise. Not possessed of very much money, Jan and Josie lived in a small apartment with two of Jan's friends. Pat was secretary to a theatrical producer and Val was an aspiring actress and model. Stanley Schreiber was the son of the man who owned the neighborhood delicatessen. The format of this series allowed Miss Paige the opportunity to sing a song in most episodes.

IT'S MAGIC

Magic

FIRST TELECAST: *July 31, 1955*
LAST TELECAST: *September 4, 1955*
BROADCAST HISTORY:
Jul 1955–Sep 1955, CBS Sun 7:00–7:30
HOST:
Paul Tripp

Each week on this summer series, three famous magicians appeared to perform some of their tricks before a studio audience. The host of the show, Paul Tripp, had been the producer and star of the popular children's program *Mr. I Magination.*

IT'S NEWS TO ME

Quiz/Audience Participation

FIRST TELECAST: *July 2, 1951*
LAST TELECAST: *August 27, 1954*
BROADCAST HISTORY:
Jul 1951–Mar 1952, CBS Mon 9:30–10:00
Apr 1952–Jun 1952, CBS Fri 9:30–10:00
Jul 1952–Aug 1952, CBS Sun 6:30–7:00
Sep 1952, CBS Fri 10:30–11:00
Sep 1952–Nov 1952, CBS Sat 6:30–7:00
Dec 1952–Sep 1953, CBS Sat 10:30–11:00
Jul 1954–Aug 1954, CBS Fri 10:30–11:00
MODERATOR:
John Daly (1951–1953)
Walter Cronkite (1954)
PANELISTS:
John Henry Faulk
Anna Lee
Quincy Howe (1951–1952)
Quentin Reynolds
Nina Foch (1954)

The object of this quiz show was for the celebrity panelists to describe what news story was represented by a visual or verbal clue. The stories were always current news items and members of the studio audience could win small amounts of money by determining whether or not the celebrity panelists were correct. John Daly was the original host/moderator and was succeeded by Walter Cronkite when the series was revived as a summer replacement for *Person to Person*.

IT'S POLKA TIME

see *Polka Time*

IVAN THE TERRIBLE

Situation Comedy

FIRST TELECAST: *August 21, 1976*
LAST TELECAST: *September 18, 1976*
BROADCAST HISTORY:

Aug 1976–Sep 1976, CBS Sat 8:30–9:00

CAST:

Ivan .... Lou Jacobi
Olga .... Maria Karnilova
Vladimir .... Phil Leeds
Tatiana .... Despo
Federov .... Christopher Hewett
Sascha .... Matthew Barry
Nikolai .... Alan Cauldwell
Sonya .... Caroline Kava
Raoul .... Manuel Martinez
Svetlana .... Nana Tucker

Ivan was the headwaiter at the Hotel Metropole in contemporary Moscow in this five-week summer mini-series. His biggest problem was the congestion in his 3½-room apartment, inhabited by nine people and a ferocious, but unseen, dog named Rasputin. Living with Ivan were his wife Olga; their children, Sonya, Nikolai, and Sascha; Olga's first husband, Vladimir, and her mother, Tatiana. Also in the household were Nikolai's wife Svetlana and a Cuban named Raoul. All of them except young Sascha and Raoul had various jobs in Moscow.

I'VE GOT A SECRET

Quiz/Audience Participation

FIRST TELECAST: *June 19, 1952*
LAST TELECAST: *July 5, 1976*
BROADCAST HISTORY:

Jun 1952–Jun 1953, CBS Thu 10:30–11:00
Jul 1953–Sep 1961, CBS Wed 9:30–10:00
Sep 1961–Sep 1962, CBS Mon 10:30–11:00
Sep 1962–Sep 1966, CBS Mon 8:00–8:30
Sep 1966–Apr 1967, CBS Mon 10:30–11:00
Jun 1976–Jul 1976, CBS Tue 8:00–8:30

MODERATOR:

Garry Moore (1952–1964)
Steve Allen (1964–1967)
Bill Cullen (1976)

PANELISTS:

Louise Allbritton (1952)
Laura Hobson (1952)
Walter Kieran (1952)
Orson Bean (1952)
Melville Cooper (1952)
Bill Cullen (1952–1967)
Kitty Carlisle (1952–1953)
Henry Morgan (1952–1976)
Laraine Day (1952)
Eddie Bracken (1952)
Faye Emerson (1952–1958)
Jayne Meadows (1952–1959)
Betsy Palmer (1957–1967)
Bess Myerson (1958–1967)
Pat Collins (1976)
Richard Dawson (1976)
Elaine Joyce (1976)

THEME:

"Plink, Plank, Plunk," by Leroy Anderson

PRODUCERS:

Mark Goodson and Bill Todman

The format of *I've Got a Secret* was both simple and durable. Four panelists took turns questioning the person with the secret to determine what the secret was. A nominal financial award was given to a contestant whose secret (flashed on the TV screen for the viewing audience) could not be guessed by the panel. Each show gave three regular contestants an opportunity to stump the panel, and also had one celebrity guest with his own secret to hide. *I've Got a Secret* ran on network television for fifteen years and was probably the most successful quiz show in the history of the medium—it placed in the top ten for four consecutive years during the late 1950s, and remained quite popular during the following decade as well, a record which no other quiz program has approached. Almost a decade after the final telecast of its original run, it was brought back for a short summer run in 1976, with Bill Cullen, one of the earliest regular panelists, in the role of moderator. It has also been seen in a syndicated version during the 1970s.

As with any panel show, the secret of *Secret*'s success lay with the chemistry of its regulars. After considerable turnover in 1952, the show settled down to a well-balanced and familiar crew. Through the 1950s it was grinning Bill Cullen and acerbic Henry Morgan, balanced on the female side by Faye Emerson and Jayne Meadows. In the 1960s the two men remained, but the girls were replaced by Betsy Palmer and Bess Myerson. The repartee was witty and spontaneous, although the unplanned quality was occasionally shattered, as on the occasion when Monty Woolley appeared as guest celebrity. His secret was that he slept with his beard inside the covers. When asked why, he replied, "As a matter of fact I don't. That's merely the secret they decided upon for me." Garry Moore, for once, was speechless.

JACK BENNY SHOW, THE

Comedy

FIRST TELECAST: *October 28, 1950*
LAST TELECAST: *August 30, 1977*
BROADCAST HISTORY:

Oct 1950–Jun 1959, CBS Sun 7:30–8:00 (OS)
Oct 1959–Jun 1960, CBS Sun 10:00–10:30
Oct 1960–Jun 1962, CBS Sun 9:30–10:00 (OS)
Sep 1962–Jun 1963, CBS Tue 9:30–10:00
Sep 1963–Sep 1964, CBS Tue 9:30–10:00
Sep 1964–Sep 1965, NBC Fri 9:30–10:00
Aug 1977, CBS Tue 8:00–8:30

REGULARS:

Jack Benny
Eddie "Rochester" Anderson
Don Wilson
Dennis Day
Mary Livingston
Frank Nelson
Artie Auerbach
Mel Blanc

THEME:

"Love in Bloom," by Leo Robin and Ralph Rainger

Jack Benny had been a regular network-radio personality since 1932. When he made his first tentative forays into television in 1950, it was with a series of specials that aired on an infrequent basis in what would eventually become his regular Sunday night time slot. Ten of them aired during the 1950–1951 and 1951–1952 seasons. From October 5, 1952, through the following January his show was televised once every four weeks, and when he returned again, on September 13, 1953, it was on an alternate-week basis that lasted through June of 1960. For his last five seasons, *The Jack Benny Show* aired every week.

The format of the show, and the personality of its star, so well honed in two decades on radio, made the transition to television almost intact. Jack's stinginess, vanity about his supposed age of 39, basement vault where he kept all his money, ancient Maxwell automobile, and feigned ineptness at playing the violin were all part of the act—and were, if anything, bolstered by their visibility on the TV show. Added to Jack's famous pregnant pause and exasperated "Well!" were a rather mincing walk, an affected hand to the cheek, and a pained look of disbelief when confronted by life's little tragedies.

The two regulars who were with Jack throughout his television run were Eddie "Rochester" Anderson as his valet and Don Wilson as his announcer and friend. Appearing on a more irregular basis were Dennis Day, Artie Auerbach, Frank Nelson, Mary Livingston (Mrs. Benny), and Mel Blanc, all veterans from the radio show. Blanc, the master of a thousand voices (including Bugs Bunny), was both heard as the engine of Jack's Maxwell and seen as Prof. Le Blanc, his long-suffering violin teacher.

Jack's underplayed comedy was as popular on television as it had been on radio. After fifteen years as a more or less regular television performer, he cut back his schedule to an occasional special and continued to appear until the year of his death, 1974. CBS brought back four episodes from *The Jack Benny Show*, originally filmed in the early 1960s, for a limited run in August 1977.

JACK CARTER SHOW, THE

Variety

FIRST TELECAST: *February 25, 1950*
LAST TELECAST: *June 2, 1951*
BROADCAST HISTORY:

Feb 1950–Jun 1951, NBC Sat 8:00–9:00 (OS)

EMCEE:

Jack Carter

REGULARS:

Don Richards
Bill Callahan

ORCHESTRA:

Lou Breese (1950)
Harry Sosnik (1950–1951)

NBC's innovative Vice President of Programs Pat Weaver introduced several novel concepts to television in the early 1950s, perhaps the best-remembered of which are the *Today* and *Tonight* shows. Another was the *Saturday Night Revue*, a package of two big-name variety shows on a single evening, one originating live from Chicago and the other live from New York. Comedian Jack Carter hosted the Chicago element from 8:00–9:00 P.M., while Sid Caesar and Imogene Coca starred from 9:00–10:30 P.M. in the New York segment, titled *Your Show of Shows.*

Jack Carter was a fast-rising young talent in 1950, having appeared on several programs, including his own series of specials on ABC in 1949. His element of the *Saturday Night Revue* was a music-comedy-variety hour, opening with a stand-up routine by Jack followed by guest stars and skits by a constantly changing supporting cast. Among the longer-lasting regulars were baritone Don Richards and dancer Bill Callahan. Memorable routines included a satire of current TV stars (Garroway, Godfrey, Berle, *et al.*) and elaborate musical productions such as "Gravediggers of 1950: A Musical Extravagangster" starring Carter, Cesar Romero, and the whole cast.

Both segments of the *Saturday Night Revue* were quite popular at the outset, blitzing the competition, but gradually the Caesar-Coca portion began to dominate. Carter's segment moved to New York at the start of the 1950–1951 season, but by the following summer it was dropped in favor of *The All Star Revue.*

JACK DREES SPORTS SHOW, THE

Sports News

FIRST TELECAST: *July 2, 1956*

LAST TELECAST: *August 24, 1956*

BROADCAST HISTORY:

Jul 1956–Aug 1956, ABC Mon–Fri 7:00–7:15

REPORTER:

Jack Drees

Jack Drees, who was also the announcer for ABC's *Wednesday Night Fights,* brought audiences up to date on the latest sports news with this nightly report. He also interviewed sports celebrities when they were available.

JACK LEONARD

Music

FIRST TELECAST: *March 10, 1949*

LAST TELECAST: *May 5, 1949*

BROADCAST HISTORY:

Mar 1949–May 1949, DUM Thu 7:15–7:30

HOST:

Jack Leonard

Songs by the former big-band singer.

JACK PAAR PROGRAM, THE

Variety

FIRST TELECAST: *September 21, 1962*

LAST TELECAST: *September 10, 1965*

BROADCAST HISTORY:

Sep 1962–Sep 1965, NBC Fri 10:00–11:00

HOST:

Jack Paar

ORCHESTRA:

Jose Melis

This was, in many respects, a prime-time version of Jack's earlier late-night talk show *(The Tonight Show),* which he had hosted from 1957–1962. It was somewhat more diversified, however, including topical films and recorded interviews, comedy sketches, musical segments, and home movies of Jack's travels with his wife Miriam and his teenage daughter Randy. Each telecast opened with a Paar monologue and then, depending on the guest stars, went to either sketches, songs, or chats. The films of the Paar family's various trips to Africa, Europe, and Russia were often shown, with daughter Randy present to help with the narration.

Among the more notable moments were Richard Nixon playing a composition of his own on the piano on March 8, 1963 (his first public appearance since losing the gubernatorial race in California in 1962); Barry Goldwater discussing his chances of defeating Lyndon Johnson in the 1964 presidential race, one month after having announced his candidacy; and a filmed interview in Africa with Dr. Albert Schweitzer. In a precursor of what would become one of the most popular television series of the 1970s, Paar presented a condensed 20-minute episode from the British comedy series *Steptoe and Son* on his April 24, 1964, telecast. That series was the basis for the American situation comedy *Sanford and Son.* Although not classified as a regular, Jonathan Winters was a frequent guest during *The Jack Paar Program*'s first two seasons.

JACK PAAR SHOW, THE

see *Tonight Show, The*

JACK PAAR SHOW, THE

Variety

FIRST TELECAST: *July 17, 1954*

LAST TELECAST: *September 4, 1954*

BROADCAST HISTORY:

Jul 1954–Sep 1954, CBS Sat 9:30–10:00

REGULARS:

Jack Paar
Betty Clooney
Johnny Desmond
Pupi Campo's Orchestra
Jose Melis

In addition to hosting a regular daytime series, which had started in November 1953, comedian Jack Paar served as host for this live summer replacement for *My Favorite Husband*. Jose Melis, who was to spend many years with Jack when he became host of *The Tonight Show* later in the 1950s, had started with him on the daytime show and appeared on this series. The format included monologues by Jack, appearances by guest stars, and songs by his regular singers.

JACKIE GLEASON SHOW, THE

Comedy Variety

FIRST TELECAST: *September 20, 1952*

LAST TELECAST: *September 12, 1970*

BROADCAST HISTORY:

Sep 1952–Jun 1955, CBS Sat 8:00–9:00 (OS)
Sep 1956–Jun 1957, CBS Sat 8:00–9:00
Oct 1958–Jan 1959, CBS Fri 8:30–9:00
Sep 1962–May 1968, CBS Sat 7:30–8:30 (OS)
Sep 1968–Sep 1970, CBS Sat 7:30–8:30

STAR:

Jackie Gleason

REGULARS:

Art Carney (1952–1957; 1966–1970)
Joyce Randolph (1952–1957)
Audrey Meadows (1952–1957)
Buddy Hackett (1958–1959)
Frank Fontaine (1962–1966)
Sue Ane Langdon (1962–1963)
Barbara Heller (1963–1965)
Horace McMahon (1963–1964)
Alice Ghostley (1962–1964)
Helen Curtis (1964–1966)
Sid Fields (1964–1966)
Phil Bruns (1964–1966)
George Jessel (1965–1966)
Sheila MacRae (1966–1970)
Jane Kean (1966–1970)
The June Taylor Dancers
The Glea-Girls (1956–1970)
Ray Bloch & His Orchestra (1952–1959)
Sammy Spear & His Orchestra (1962–1970)

ANNOUNCERS:

Jack Lescoulie (1952–1959)
Johnny Olsen (1962–1970)

THEME:

"Melancholy Serenade," by Jackie Gleason (written in 1953)

The lure of money brought *The Jackie Gleason Show* to CBS in the fall of 1952. The rotund comic had been starring in *The Cavalcade of Stars* on DuMont since the summer of 1950 and had developed into one of the few genuine successes on that money-poor network. When CBS offered him a staggering increase in weekly pay—reportedly $8,000 compared to the $1,600 that DuMont could afford—coupled with the funding to make his show a much more elaborate production, he could scarcely refuse.

Jackie's original CBS variety hour, done live from New York, bore a strong similarity to his previous show on DuMont, albeit with a much larger budget. His second banana, Art Carney, made the move with him, as did the June Taylor Dancers and Ray ("the Flower of the Musical World") Bloch's Orchestra. Audrey Meadows and Joyce Randolph were added to the cast of regulars, primarily in "The Honeymooners" sketches (see separate entry for details of *The Honeymooners*), and most of the characters that Gleason had developed on DuMont were honed to perfection on CBS. Among them, in addition to "The Honeymooners' " Ralph Kramden, were The Poor Soul, Joe the Bartender, The Loudmouth, Reggie Van Gleason III, Rudy the Repairman, and Fenwick Babbitt. The Great One, as Jackie was called, opened each telecast with a monologue and then led into the first sketch with "And awa-aaay we go," as he left the stage. His other catch-phrase, used in reaction to almost anything at all, was "How sweet it is!"

The original *Jackie Gleason Show* ran three seasons and was replaced, for the 1955–1956 season, with a half-hour situation comedy version of *The Honeymooners*. When the variety show returned the following fall, it was with the same basic cast and format, plus some decorative additions in "Glea-Girls," 16 young models who did little else than look beautiful and introduce various sketches. There was no

Gleason variety series during the 1957–1958 season, but Jackie was back in the fall of 1958 with a modified half-hour format. Gone were all the regular cast members from previous seasons and Buddy Hackett was added as Jackie's second banana. The chemistry wasn't there and, after only three months on the air, this short version of *The Jackie Gleason Show* expired.

In the fall of 1962, following an abortive failure with a quiz show (*You're in the Picture*) and the talk show (*The Jackie Gleason Show*) that replaced it in 1961, Jackie was back with a lavish full-scale variety show—*The Jackie Gleason Show: The American Scene Magazine*. His new second banana was Frank Fontaine (as Crazy Guggenheim in Joe the Bartender sketches), who could sing quite well when not in character and released a number of moderately successful record albums during his tenure with Gleason. Not only were most of Jackie's standard characters in evidence, but a new "Agnes and Arthur" sketch about two lovelorn tenement residents (with Alice Ghostley as Agnes) was added as a semi-regular feature. The beautiful "Glea-Girls," including Barbara Heller as "Christine Clam," were still in evidence introducing the segments of each show, but there was a considerable turnover in the supporting cast. There was more topical satire in this show than in Jackie's previous efforts, and more appearances by name guest stars. In keeping with the title, there were entire episodes that were done as musical comedies with book, lyrics, songs, dances, and sketches reflecting "the American Scene." At Jackie's insistence, the entire production moved from New York to Miami Beach before the start of the 1964–1965 season, and remained a Florida-based show throughout the remainder of its run. A feature added the following year was a nationwide talent hunt, in which George Jessel traveled around the country auditioning young performers who would get their first national exposure on Jackie's variety show.

The 1966–1967 season brought a basic change in format, a modified title, and a different supporting cast. The title was shortened to *The Jackie Gleason Show*, Art Carney was back with Gleason on a regular basis after a nine-year absence, and Sheila MacRae and Jane Kean were the only other cast regulars. "The Honeymooners" was brought back as the principal source of program material. There were still variety shows with sketches and guest stars, special shows devoted to single subjects like circuses or tributes to show-business greats, and book musicals, but throughout this last four-year run over half of the telecasts were full-hour "Honeymooners" episodes. Sometimes they were done without music and other times they were done as musical comedies with songs and production numbers. They took place in Brooklyn, around New York, and in different locations around the world. They were done with and without guest stars, but the constants were always there, the Kramdens (Jackie as Ralph and Sheila as Alice) and the Nortons (Art as Ed and Jane as Trixie), middle-class shleps bumbling their way through life.

JACKIE GLEASON SHOW, THE

Talk

FIRST TELECAST: *January 27, 1961*

LAST TELECAST: *March 24, 1961*

BROADCAST HISTORY:

Jan 1961–Mar 1961, CBS Fri 9:30–10:00

HOST:

Jackie Gleason

Jackie Gleason had been absent from network television for slightly over two years when he premiered a quiz show titled *You're in the Picture* on January 20, 1961. The program was a total failure and, on the following Friday, *The Jackie Gleason Show* was on in its place. The first telecast was simply a chat between Gleason and his television audience. It was an apology for *You're in the Picture*, made before a nationwide audience. For the next two months Gleason conducted an informal talk show in the time slot. Each telecast was devoted to a single guest who reminisced with Jackie about past experiences, both professional and personal. Among the guests were Mickey Rooney, Art Carney, Bobby Darin, and Jayne Mansfield.

JACKPOT BOWLING STARRING MILTON BERLE

Sports

FIRST TELECAST: *January 31, 1958*

LAST TELECAST: *March 13, 1961*

BROADCAST HISTORY:

Jan 1958–Jun 1960, NBC Fri 10:45–11:00

Sep 1960–Mar 1961, NBC Mon 10:30–11:00

HOSTS:

Leo Durocher (1958)
Mel Allen (1958–1959; 1959–1960)
Bud Palmer (1959)
Milton Berle (1960–1961)

Under its original title, *Phillies Jackpot Bowling,* this program was used to fill the time between the conclusion of the bout on *Cavalcade of Sports* and the start of the 11 P.M. local news. Top professional bowlers competed for a $1,000 weekly prize with a special bonus awarded to the bowler able to throw six strikes in a row. Leo Durocher was the host for the first two telecasts, and Mel Allen took over until April 10, 1959, when he was replaced by Bud Palmer. Palmer stayed though October 2, 1959, and Mel Allen returned the following week and continued as host throughout the remainder of its Friday night run, which ended on June 24, 1960.

On September 19, 1960, the program returned under the new title *Jackpot Bowling Starring Milton Berle,* essentially the same show moved to Monday nights. Funnyman Berle was the host and there were two matches each week instead of the single match played when the show had been on Friday nights. An added feature of the new version was the appearance of a show-business celebrity each week who bowled for his favorite charity between the two regular matches.

JACKSONS, THE

Musical Variety

FIRST TELECAST: *June 16, 1976*
LAST TELECAST: *March 9, 1977*
BROADCAST HISTORY:

Jun 1976–Jul 1976, CBS Wed 8:00–8:30
Jan 1977–Mar 1977, CBS Wed 8:30–9:00

REGULARS:

Michael Jackson
Jackie Jackson
Tito Jackson
Marlon Jackson
Randy Jackson
LaToya Jackson
Rebie (Maureen) Jackson
Janet Jackson
Jim Samuels (1976)
Marty Cohen (1976)

Five male members of the Jackson Family (aged 16–24) formed a rock combo called The Jackson Five, which had had numerous hit records. The boys were joined by three of their sisters in this four-week summer variety show. The emphasis was on comedy and popular music, with guest stars each week participating in both aspects of the show. When it returned for an additional run in the spring of 1977, Jim Samuels and Marty Cohen, who had acted in comedy sketches during the summer run, were no longer with the Jackson Family. The eight Jacksons were the only regulars, using each other and various guest stars in the comedy sketches.

JACQUES FRAY MUSIC ROOM, THE

Music/Talent

FIRST TELECAST: *February 19, 1949*
LAST TELECAST: *October 16, 1949*
BROADCAST HISTORY:

Feb 1949–Apr 1949, ABC Sat 8:00–8:30
May 1949–Aug 1949, ABC Sun 8:00–8:30
Sep 1949–Oct 1949, ABC Sun 9:30–10:00

REGULAR:

Jacques Fray

EMCEE:

Conrad Thibault

This unusual program was essentially a longhair vaudeville/talent show. Pianist Fray, who specialized in concert numbers and show tunes, would play a bit, but most of the program consisted of performances by aspiring "high-brow" talent, rated by two judges in the studio and one at home (by telephone). It was all very classy. In August Conrad Thibault was brought in as emcee. Among those guesting were Marguerite Piazza, Bess Myerson, and Russell & Aura.

Also known as *The Music Room.*

JAMES AT 15

Drama

FIRST TELECAST: *October 27, 1977*
LAST TELECAST: *July 27, 1978*
BROADCAST HISTORY:

Oct 1977–Mar 1978, NBC Thu 9:00–10:00
Jun 1978–Jul 1978, NBC Thu 9:00–10:00

CAST:

James Hunter .... Lance Kerwin
Mr. Hunter .... Linden Chiles
Mrs. Hunter .... Lynn Carlin
Sandy Hunter .... Kim Richards
Kathy Hunter .... Deirdre Berthrong
Sly Hazeltine .... David Hubbard
Marlene Mahoney .... Susan Myers
Mr. Shamley .... Jack Knight

James at 15 was one of TV's more honest attempts to portray the pains and joys of growing up in the 1970s. Fifteen-year-old James Hunter was a bright, sensitive boy who found his world completely disrupted when his father, a college professor, moved the family from Oregon to Boston, Mass., in order to accept a new teaching position. At first James tried to run away; then he began to learn how to cope with life in a new, city environment. Among his new friends at Bunker Hill High were a hip black named Sly, who always had a little sage advice, or "slychology," when James needed it; and Marlene, a plain but very intelligent girl who always took the intellectual point of view. Sandy was James' teenage sister, and Kathy their older sister.

James was an avid photographer and also a daydreamer. One of the novel elements of the series was his periodic lapses into day-dreaming of himself as he would like to be—heroic, suave, etc.—portrayed in special dreamlike sequences. Although there was comedy in *James at 15,* none of the main characters were caricatures, and likewise the subject matter was sometimes rather serious: a young friend who was dying of cancer, teenage alcoholism, venereal disease, the discovery that Kathy was having a pre-marital affair. Perhaps the most controversial episode was one in which James lost his own virginity in an affair with a Swedish exchange student, Christina Kollberg (portrayed by Kirsten Baker). Although the subject matter in the series was tastefully handled, and NBC had high hopes for the show, it did not attract a large audience and was canceled after a single season.

Effective February 9, 1978, the episode dealing with James' affair, the series' title was changed to *James at 16*.

JAMES GARNER AS NICHOLS

see *Nichols*

JAMES MICHENER'S ADVENTURES IN PARADISE

see *Adventures in Paradise*

JAMIE

Situation Comedy

FIRST TELECAST: *September 28, 1953*

LAST TELECAST: *October 4, 1954*

BROADCAST HISTORY:

Sep 1953–Oct 1954, ABC Mon 7:30–8:00 (OS)

CAST:

Jamison Francis McHummer (Jamie) .... Brandon De Wilde
Grandpa .... Ernest Truex
Aunt Laurie .... Polly Knowles
Cousin Liz .... Kathy Nolan
Annie .... Alice Pearce
Aunt Ella (occasional) .... Kathleen Comegys

Brandon De Wilde was one of the child-star discoveries of the 1950s. A sensitive lad, and a natural actor, he was signed by ABC for his own series three years after his professional debut (at age 8) in the hit Broadway play *A Member of the Wedding. Jamie,* which had previewed to rave reviews as an episode of *ABC Album* during the previous season, looked like a surefire winner as a series. De Wilde was cast as a likable orphan who had been shunted from one uncaring relative to another, until he landed in Aunt Laurie's household. There he met a kindred spirit in Grandpa (played to perfection by 63-year-old character actor Ernest Truex), who was similarly ignored by his kin. Grandpa, twinkle-eyed and with a zest for life, became Jamie's bosom buddy, sharing escapades, and the joys of growing up and of growing old. Others in the cast included Liz, Jamie's teenage cousin, and Annie, Aunt Laurie's helper in the catering business.

Jamie was a live weekly series and there was some publicity at the time about the problems of a youngster, however gifted, being so deeply involved in an adult profession during his formative years. De Wilde's parents had a special contract which allowed him to drop out of the series on short notice if he wanted to, or if his parents felt it was impairing his emotional growth. *Jamie* did indeed end abruptly two weeks into its second season, but it was not due to concern over Master De Wilde, but rather to a fight between network and sponsor over mundane business matters. An attempt was made to locate the popular program in another time slot or on another network, but this did not transpire.

The ending was unhappy in the long run for the tow-headed young star, as well. Never able to sustain the success of his youth into adulthood, Brandon De Wilde died in 1972, at the age of 30, in a traffic accident.

JAN MURRAY TIME

Variety

FIRST TELECAST: *February 11, 1955*

LAST TELECAST: *May 6, 1955*

BROADCAST HISTORY:

Feb 1955–May 1955, NBC Fri 10:45–11:00

REGULARS:

Jan Murray
Tina Louise
The Novelites
Fletcher Peck

This short and short-lived variety series was used to fill the time between the conclusion of the bout on *Cavalcade of Sports* and the start of the local 11 P.M. news, in the spring of 1955. It starred comedian Jan Murray and featured singer Tina Louise, the singing and instrumental group The Novelites, and pianist Fletcher Peck. There was no set format for this live show, since the length varied depending on how long the fight took. There were occasional guest stars and, time permitting, comedy sketches, in addition to Jan Murray's shorter comedy bits and musical numbers by his supporting cast.

JANE FROMAN SHOW, THE

see *Jane Froman's U.S.A. Canteen*

JANE FROMAN'S U.S.A. CANTEEN

Musical Variety

FIRST TELECAST: *October 18, 1952*

LAST TELECAST: *June 23, 1955*

BROADCAST HISTORY:

Oct 1952–Dec 1952, CBS Sat 9:00–9:30
Nov 1952–Jan 1954, CBS Tue/Thu 7:45–8:00 (OS)
Jan 1954–Jun 1955, CBS Thu 7:45–8:00 (OS)

HOST:

Jane Froman

Singer Jane Froman, who had worked long and hard entertaining the troops during the Second World War, featured men in uniform on her CBS network television series. In cooperation with the Department of Defense, the program sought out talented servicemen who competed for the opportunity to perform on this live program. The setting was a re-creation of a U.S.O. Canteen, and it was there that Miss Froman sang, chatted with her guests, and introduced young performing servicemen to the nation.

At the start of the 1953–1954 season the title of the program was shortened to *The Jane Froman Show*, the servicemen were dropped, and the emphasis shifted to a straight musical variety show.

Although Miss Froman was perhaps best known for her signature tune, "With a Song in My Heart" (which was also the title of her 1952 movie biography), this series was more notable for the introduction of another song—probably the first song to be made a hit by the new medium of television. It was "I Believe," a semi-religious number written especially for this series and sung incessantly on it by Miss Froman, which went on to become one of the top hits of 1953.

JANE PICKENS SHOW, THE

Music

FIRST TELECAST: *January 31, 1954*

LAST TELECAST: *September 12, 1954*

BROADCAST HISTORY:

Jan 1954–Apr 1954, ABC Sun 9:15–9:30
Apr 1954–Jul 1954, ABC Sun 6:30–6:45
Jul 1954–Sep 1954, ABC Sun 9:15–9:30

REGULARS:

Jane Pickens
The Vikings

Songstress Jane Pickens starred in this informal 15-minute musical show, backed by a male singing group called the Vikings.

JANE WYMAN PRESENTS

see *Fireside Theater*

JANE WYMAN SHOW, THE

see *Fireside Theater*

JAYE P. MORGAN SHOW, THE

Music

FIRST TELECAST: *June 13, 1956*

LAST TELECAST: *August 24, 1956*

BROADCAST HISTORY:

Jun 1956–Aug 1956, NBC Wed/Fri 7:30–7:45

REGULARS:

Jaye P. Morgan
The Morgan Brothers

Jaye P. Morgan starred in this 1956 summer replacement for *Coke Time*. The informal quarter-hour was filled with popular songs sung by Miss Morgan and a vocal quartet made up of her four brothers.

JEAN ARTHUR SHOW, THE

Situation Comedy

FIRST TELECAST: *September 12, 1966*
LAST TELECAST: *December 5, 1966*
BROADCAST HISTORY:

Sep 1966–Dec 1966, CBS Mon 10:00–10:30

CAST:

Patricia Marshall ....Jean Arthur
Paul Marshall ....Ron Harper
Morton ....Leonard Stone

Attractive Patricia Marshall was the best defense attorney in town and, as a widow, one of the most eligible women as well. Her 25-year-old son Paul had recently graduated from law school and returned home to practice law with her. Patricia's comic involvements with her clients and family provided the stories in this series. An almost silent member of the cast was her chauffeur, Morton, who would probably have had more to say if his boss had ever stopped talking long enough for him to get a word in.

JEAN CARROLL SHOW, THE

see *Take It from Me*

JEANNIE CARSON SHOW, THE

see *Hey Jeannie*

JEFFERSON DRUM

Western

FIRST TELECAST: *April 25, 1958*
LAST TELECAST: *April 23, 1959*
BROADCAST HISTORY:

Apr 1958–Sep 1958, NBC Fri 8:00–8:30
Sep 1958–Oct 1958, NBC Fri 7:30–8:00
Oct 1958–Apr 1959, NBC Thu 7:30–8:00

CAST:

Jefferson Drum ....Jeff Richards
Lucius Coin ....Cyril Delavanti
Joey Drum ....Eugene Martin
Big Ed ....Robert Stevenson

The lawless frontier town of Jubilee, a mining community somewhere in the West during the 1850s, was the setting for *Jefferson Drum*. Jefferson was the editor of the local newspaper who, although he believed that the pen was mightier than the sword, was quite a gunfighter when he had to be. A widower with a young son, Jefferson had a sense of great responsibility to his community and the law-abiding people who lived there. His efforts to maintain a decent town were aided by his printer, Lucius Coin, and by Big Ed, the bartender in the town saloon.

JEFFERSONS, THE

Situation Comedy

FIRST TELECAST: *January 18, 1975*
LAST TELECAST:
BROADCAST HISTORY:

Jan 1975–Aug 1975, CBS Sat 8:30–9:00
Sep 1975–Oct 1976, CBS Sat 8:00–8:30
Nov 1976–Jan 1977, CBS Wed 8:00–8:30
Jan 1977–Aug 1977, CBS Mon 8:00–8:30
Sep 1977–Mar 1978, CBS Sat 9:00–9:30
Apr 1978–May 1978, CBS Sat 8:00–8:30
Jun 1978–Sep 1978, CBS Mon 8:00–8:30
Sep 1978– , CBS Wed 8:00–8:30

CAST:

George Jefferson ....Sherman Hemsley
Louise Jefferson ....Isabel Sanford
Lionel Jefferson (1975) ....Mike Evans
Lionel Jefferson (1975–1978)
.... Damon Evans
Helen Willis ....Roxie Roker
Tom Willis ....Franklin Cover
Jenny Willis Jefferson ..... Berlinda Tolbert
Harry Bentley ....Paul Benedict
Mother Jefferson (1975–1978) ... Zara Cully
Ralph the Doorman ....Ned Wertimer
Florence ....Marla Gibbs
Marcus Garvey (1977–)
.... Ernest Harden, Jr.
Allan Willis (1978–) ..... Jay Hammer

PRODUCER:

Norman Lear

George Jefferson was the black Archie Bunker. In fact, he had been Archie's next-door neighbor in Queens for several years, a situation that created quite a turmoil between the two opinionated, blustery, bigoted individuals. George had started a small dry cleaning business and his success resulted in expansion to a small chain. It was at that point that this spinoff from *All in the Family* started, with George, his level-headed wife Louise, and their college-student son Lionel moving into a luxury high-rise apartment on Manhattan's East Side.

One of the Jeffersons' neighbors was an erudite Englishman, Harry Bentley; another was Tom Willis, a white man with a black wife (Helen). Their daughter Jenny became Lionel's girl friend, fiancée, and finally wife when they were married in the 1976 Christmas show. George's quickly acquired wealth enabled his natural snobbishness to assert itself, and he was often pretty intolerable. He resented Lionel's involvement with the child of a mixed marriage and was continually at odds with Tom and Helen. Adding to the general level of discord in the Jefferson apartment was their wise-cracking maid, Florence.

Mike Evans, who had played the role of Lionel on *All in the Family* and stayed with it when *The Jeffersons* first went on the air, left the show in the fall of 1975. He was replaced by Damon Evans, another young black actor, to whom he was not related. Early in the 1977–1978 season a young, street-wise black named Marcus Garvey was added to the cast as an employee of the branch of George Jefferson's chain of cleaning stores that was located in the lobby of the building in which the Jeffersons lived. The following fall brought Allan Willis, Jenny's white brother, back from a commune to become a regular member of the cast and source of irritation to both his own father and George Jefferson. Damon Evans had left the cast and, although Lionel was occasionally referred to in various episodes, he was no longer seen.

JEFF'S COLLIE

syndicated title for *Lassie*

JERICHO

War Drama

FIRST TELECAST: *September 15, 1966*
LAST TELECAST: *January 19, 1967*
BROADCAST HISTORY:
Sep 1966–Jan 1967, CBS Thu 7:30–8:30
CAST:
Franklin Sheppard .... Don Francks
Jean-Gaston André .... Marino Mase
Nicholas Gage .... John Leyton

Three undercover agents representing three countries worked together as Allied troubleshooters during the Second World War in this series. Their code name: *Jericho*. Franklin Sheppard was a captain in American Army Intelligence, Jean-Gaston André an officer in the Free French Air Force, and Nicholas Gage a lieutenant in the British Navy. Specially trained, and having worked together since early in the war, they tackled assignments that ranged from sabotage to espionage to intelligence-gathering.

JERRY COLONNA SHOW, THE

Comedy Variety

FIRST TELECAST: *May 28, 1951*
LAST TELECAST: *November 17, 1951*
BROADCAST HISTORY:
May 1951–Jun 1951, ABC Mon 8:00–8:30
Jun 1951–Aug 1951, ABC Fri 8:00–8:30
Aug 1951–Sep 1951, ABC Thu 10:00–10:30
Oct 1951–Nov 1951, ABC Sat 7:30–8:00
EMCEE:
Jerry Colonna
REGULARS:
Barbara Ruick
Gordon Polk
"Cookie" Fairchild's Band

A program of music, comedy and variety hosted by the famous comedian with the booming voice and the walrus mustache.

JERRY LEWIS SHOW, THE

Talk/Variety

FIRST TELECAST: *September 21, 1963*
LAST TELECAST: *December 21, 1963*
BROADCAST HISTORY:
Sep 1963–Dec 1963, ABC Sat 9:30–11:30
STAR:
Jerry Lewis
ANNOUNCER:
Del Moore
ORCHESTRA:
Lou Brown

This two-hour weekly marathon was possibly the most spectacular attempt at big-name variety programming in TV history—and also the most colossal flop. It was preceded by a greal deal of fanfare, including the revelation that ABC had committed $8,000,000 in production costs for the first year alone. Headlining was Jerry Lewis, long a TV series holdout, and guesting were all sorts of big names. The first telecast, live from Hollywood's El Capitan Theatre, co-starred Mort Sahl, Kay Stevens, Jack Jones, and Harry James. Later telecasts featured Sammy Davis, Jr., the Count Basie orchestra, heavyweight challenger Cassius Clay (discussing his upcoming title fight with the champ, Sonny Liston), and the all-star cast of the movie *It's A Mad, Mad, Mad, Mad World*.

Whether it was simply too big, whether the controversial Lewis grated on too many viewers, or whether the scheduling was bad (NBC and CBS viewers had to leave in the middle of *The Defenders* or the *Saturday Night Movie* to catch the beginning), the initial airings garnered terrible reviews and disastrously low ratings. A considerable uproar ensued, in which the president of ABC flew to the West Coast for intensive conferences with Lewis and his writers (who included the young Dick Cavett) on how to save the show. Subsequent telecasts improved, but the ratings did not and the colossus folded after 13 weeks.

Two weeks later, *The Hollywood Palace,* a similar show—but sans Lewis—took over the theater and the first half of the time slot, and ran for six years.

JERRY LEWIS SHOW, THE

Comedy Variety

FIRST TELECAST: *September 12, 1967*
LAST TELECAST: *May 27, 1969*
BROADCAST HISTORY:

Sep 1967–May 1968, NBC Tue 8:00–9:00
Sep 1968–May 1969, NBC Tue 7:30–8:30

REGULARS:

Jerry Lewis
Lou Brown & His Orchestra
The George Wyle Singers
The Nick Castle Dancers

Jerry Lewis starred in this comedy variety series that featured guest stars with primary appeal to young adults, teens, and children. The Osmond Brothers made a number of appearances on the show during its two seasons on the air and many other groups and individual performers popular with young people were occasional guests. Jerry's collection of comic characters, originally seen in his movies, all made their presence felt in short vignettes and longer comedy sketches. Among them were The Nutty Professor, The Poor Soul, The Shoeshine Boy, and, new for the TV series, Ralph Rotten. During the first season individual numbers and routines were recorded separately and pieced together to produce the hour-long show. In an attempt to generate a more spontaneous feeling, all shows for the second season were taped continuously in front of a live studio audience.

JERRY REED WHEN YOU'RE HOT YOU'RE HOT HOUR, THE

Comedy Variety

FIRST TELECAST: *June 20, 1972*
LAST TELECAST: *July 25, 1972*
BROADCAST HISTORY:

Jun 1972–Jul 1972, CBS Tue 7:30–8:30

REGULARS:

Jerry Reed
Spencer Quinn
Cal Wilson
Norman J. Andrews
Merie Earle
John Twomey

This five-week summer variety series starred the versatile Jerry Reed—comedian, singer, and songwriter. His musical success had been primarily in Country music and the entire show had a Country flavor. Comedy skits, songs, and production numbers were all part of the format. The most unusual regular on the show was John Twomey, a Chicago attorney who made music with his bare hands.

JESSE JAMES

see *Legend of Jesse James, The*

JETSONS, THE

Cartoon

FIRST TELECAST: *September 23, 1962*
LAST TELECAST: *September 8, 1963*
BROADCAST HISTORY:

Sep 1962–Sep 1963, ABC Sun 7:30–8:00

VOICES:

George Jetson ....George O'Hanlon
Jane Jetson ....Penny Singleton
Judy Jetson ....Janet Waldo
Elroy Jetson ....Daws Butler
Astro ....Don Messick

ALSO:

Mel Blanc, Howard Morris, Herschel Bernardi, Howard McNear, and Frank Nelson

PRODUCERS:

William Hanna and Joseph Barbera

This cartoon series about a middle-class family of the future was the twenty-first-century equivalent of *The Flintstones,* and was produced by the same people. George Jetson worked for Space Rockets, Inc., commuting to the job in an atomic-powered bubble. He lived with his wife Jane and their children in Skypad Apartments, which were raised and lowered on huge hydraulic lifts to stay clear of bad weather. A robot maid packed son Elroy off to school in a pneumatic tube each morning, while teenybopper daughter Judy spent her free time learning the latest dance, the Solar Swivel. Astro was the family dog. Appearing occasionally was George's boss, Cosmo G. Spacely, voiced by the versatile Mel Blanc.

The Jetsons continued as a Saturday

morning cartoon series for more than ten years after its prime-time run.

JIGSAW

Police

FIRST TELECAST: *September 21, 1972*

LAST TELECAST: *August 11, 1973*

BROADCAST HISTORY:

Sep 1972–Dec 1972, ABC Thu 9:00–10:00
Feb 1973–Aug 1973, ABC Sat 10:00–11:00

CAST:

Lt. Frank Dain .... James Wainwright

Frank Dain was a special investigator for the California State Police Department's Bureau of Missing Persons. A rebel who broke the rules when necessary, he was tough, dry, and sardonic. Naturally he got the most difficult and intriguing cases, and solved them all. *Jigsaw* was one of three rotating elements of *The Men*.

JIGSAW JOHN

Police

FIRST TELECAST: *February 2, 1976*

LAST TELECAST: *September 6, 1976*

BROADCAST HISTORY:

Feb 1976–Sep 1976, NBC Mon 10:00–11:00

CAST:

John St. John ("Jigsaw John")
.... Jack Warden
Sam Donner .... Alan Feinstein
Maggie Hearn .... Pippa Scott
Frank Chen .... James Hong

Filmed on location in Southern California, *Jigsaw John* dealt with the cases tackled by Los Angeles Police Department Special Investigator John St. John. He had received the nickname Jigsaw John because of the way in which he slowly, methodically, and precisely fitted together each of the seemingly unrelated pieces that collectively led to the determination of guilt in his homicide investigations. The highly individualistic way in which he and his partner, Sam Donner, worked did not always sit well with the police department bureaucracy, but the results could not be faulted. John's commitment to his job always took priority over the other things in his life, most noticeably his long-running romance with nursery-school teacher Maggie Hearn.

JIM BOWIE

see *Adventures of Jim Bowie, The*

JIM NABORS HOUR, THE

Comedy Variety

FIRST TELECAST: *September 25, 1969*

LAST TELECAST: *May 20, 1971*

BROADCAST HISTORY:

Sep 1969–May 1971, CBS Thu 8:00–9:00 (OS)

REGULARS:

Jim Nabors
Frank Sutton
Ronnie Schell
Karen Morrow
The Nabors Kids
The Tony Mordente Dancers
Paul Weston & His Orchestra

Jim Nabors, the twangy, rural comedian of *The Andy Griffith Show* and *Gomer Pyle—U.S.M.C.*, surprised everyone when in the mid-1960s he opened his mouth and began to sing. His voice was a rich baritone, and he proceeded to make quite a splash in the record field with several bestselling LP's. After *Gomer Pyle* had run its course, his versatility earned him his own Thursday night variety hour. With him were two of his former co-stars from *Gomer Pyle*, Frank Sutton and Ronnie Schell. There were also guest stars, comedy sketches, and musical numbers on the show. One continuing comedy sketch was "The Brother-in-Law," in which Karen Morrow played Jim's sister and Frank Sutton her husband. Frank's role was that of a self-centered, insecure neurotic trying to cope with what he perceived as a hostile world.

JIM STAFFORD SHOW, THE

Comedy Variety

FIRST TELECAST: *July 30, 1975*

LAST TELECAST: *September 3, 1975*

BROADCAST HISTORY:

Jul 1975–Sep 1975, ABC Wed 10:00–11:00

HOST:

Jim Stafford

REGULARS:

Valerie Curtin
Richard Stahl
Phil MacKenzie ("Adam")
Deborah Allen
Cyndi Wood
Jeanne Sheffield
Tom Biener
Jean Anne Chapman

Jim Stafford, an amiable, ingratiating young singer-composer with hits about such unlikely subjects as "My Girl Bill" and "Spiders and Snakes," hosted this summer variety hour. "Some people think I'm weird," he remarked. "I'm not really weird—unless you're picky." Rodney the robot, an insulting bag of transistors, also appeared on the show.

JIMMIE RODGERS SHOW, THE

Musical Variety

FIRST TELECAST: *March 31, 1959*
LAST TELECAST: *September 1, 1969*
BROADCAST HISTORY:
Mar 1959–Sep 1959, NBC Tue 8:30–9:00
Jun 1969–Sep 1969, CBS Mon 10:00–11:00
REGULARS:
Jimmie Rodgers
Connie Francis (1959)
Kirby Stone Four (1959)
The Clay Warnick Singers (1959)
Buddy Morrow Orchestra (1959)
Frank Comstock Orchestra (1969)
Burgundy Street Singers (1969)
Lyle Waggoner (1969)
Vicki Lawrence (1969)
Nancy Austin (1969)
Bill Fanning (1969)
Don Crichton (1969)

In 1959 folk-popular singer Jimmie Rodgers was riding the crest of a wave of success with a string of hit records, most notably "Honeycomb" and "Kisses Sweeter Than Wine." NBC signed him for a variety show in the hopes of making him a TV star as well, as ABC had done with Pat Boone. However, the show never caught on. By the summer, regulars Connie Francis and the Kirby Stone Four had abandoned ship, and the show was soon canceled.

A decade later, after recovering from a mysterious auto accident that almost cost him his life and which occasioned a long gap in his career, Rodgers returned to television as the summer replacement for Carol Burnett, with a new variety series called *Carol Burnett Presents the Jimmie Rodgers Show*. Two of the regulars from Carol's series, Lyle Waggoner and Vicki Lawrence, also served as regulars on the summer show.

JIMMY BLAINE'S JUNIOR EDITION

Music

FIRST TELECAST: *January 1, 1951*
LAST TELECAST: *August 31, 1951*
BROADCAST HISTORY:
Jan 1951–Feb 1951, ABC Mon/Wed/Fri 6:15–6:30
Jan 1951–Feb 1951, ABC Tue/Thu 6:15–6:45
Feb 1951–Jun 1951, ABC Mon–Fri 6:45–7:00
Jul 1951–Aug 1951, ABC Mon/Wed/Fri 6:45–7:00
HOST:
Jimmy Blaine

Jimmy Blaine, featured vocalist on *Stop the Music*, hosted this short musical program featuring songs for teenagers.

JIMMY DEAN SHOW, THE

Musical Variety

FIRST TELECAST: *June 22, 1957*
LAST TELECAST: *April 1, 1966*
BROADCAST HISTORY:
Jun 1957–Sep 1957, CBS Sat 10:30–11:00
Sep 1963–Mar 1964, ABC Thu 9:00–10:00
Mar 1964–Aug 1964, ABC Thu 9:30–10:30
Sep 1964–Sep 1965, ABC Thu 10:00–11:00
Sep 1965–Apr 1966, ABC Fri 10:00–11:00
HOST:
Jimmy Dean
REGULARS:
Texas Wildcats (1957)
The Country Lads (1957)
Jo Davis (1957)
Jan Crockett (1957)
Mary Klick (1957)
Chuck Cassey Singers (1963–1966)
Doerr-Hutchinson Dancers (1964–1965)
Tony Mordente Dancers (1965–1966)
ORCHESTRA:
Peter Matz (1963–1965)
Don Sebesky (1965–1966)

Country singer Jimmy Dean was frequently seen on daytime and nighttime television in the late 1950s and 1960s. A lanky, drawling Texan, he is best known for a Nashville-pop sound typified by his own most famous hit, "Big Bad John" (1961). Dean's first prime-time series was a summer variety show in 1957, which originated live from Washington, D.C. This was a low-budget affair which generally featured guest Country acts such as Johnny Cash and Jim Reeves, plus some rather out-of-date popular talent (the Andrews Sisters, Gene Austin).

Then from 1963–1966 Dean fronted his own big-league variety hour on ABC. Guests on this series also included Country and Western standbys such as Eddy Arnold, Homer and Jethro, and Molly Bee, but were more frequently popular talent. His first ABC telecast headlined comic Dick Shawn and cartoon character Fred Flintstone. A continuing character on the ABC series was Jim Henson's muppet hound, Rowlf, with whom Dean joked and bantered ("My ol' buddy"). Other semi-regulars included Ron Martin, the accident-prone singer who never seemed to finish a song, Lud and Lester (Roger Price and Mort Marshall) doing a Lum and Abner–type spot, and the Jubilee Four gospel quartet. The Chuck Cassey Singers, with their stetsons and guitars, provided vocal support.

In an effort to "jazz up" the show during its final season, special telecasts originated from the stage of the Grand Ole Opry (September), Miami Beach (November) and Carnegie Hall (December), while an October 1965 telecast played host to the first annual Country Music Awards presentations.

JIMMY DURANTE PRESENTS THE LENNON SISTERS

Musical Variety

FIRST TELECAST: *September 26, 1969*
LAST TELECAST: *July 4, 1970*
BROADCAST HISTORY:
Sep 1969–Jan 1970, ABC Fri 10:00–11:00
Feb 1970–Jul 1970, ABC Sat 9:30–10:30
STARS:
Jimmy Durante
Dianne Lennon
Peggy Lennon
Kathy Lennon
Janet Lennon

The year after they ended their long association with Lawrence Welk the four Lennon Sisters co-starred with veteran comedian Jimmy Durante in this weekly musical variety hour. The show normally opened with Durante at the piano, leading into a segment of friendly chatter and songs with the Lennons. Some big-name guests appeared, including Jack Benny, Glen Campbell, Bob Hope, and Phyllis Diller, but it didn't help much. The combination of old trooper and sweet young talent never quite worked and the show was canceled at the end of its first season.

JIMMY DURANTE SHOW, THE

Comedy Variety

FIRST TELECAST: *October 2, 1954*
LAST TELECAST: *September 21, 1957*
BROADCAST HISTORY:
Oct 1954–Jun 1956, NBC Sat 9:30–10:00
Jun 1957–Sep 1957, CBS Sat 8:00–8:30
Sep 1957, CBS Sat 8:30–9:00
REGULARS:
Jimmy Durante
Eddie Jackson
Jules Buffano
Jack Roth

The basic setting of *The Jimmy Durante Show* was a small nightclub, owned and operated by Jimmy and appropriately called the Club Durant. In the role of club operator, Jimmy interviewed and auditioned talent, coped with the headaches involved in dealing with his employees, and occasionally performed himself. His raspy voice and large "schnozzola" (nose, to the uninitiated) were his trademarks. With him were his long-time friend and partner from vaudeville days, Eddie Jackson, and two actor-musicians, Jules Buffano (piano) and Jack Roth (drums), along with a chorus line composed of The Durante Girls. At the end of each show, Jimmy would be seen walking off the stage, through a series of spotlights, after saying his perennial closing line: "And good night Mrs. Calabash, wherever you are."

During its first season *The Jimmy Durante Show* aired on alternate weeks with Donald O'Connor, under the umbrella title *Texaco Star Theatre.* Jimmy's shows were all live and Donald's were on film. The Durante show was seen weekly during 1955–1956. The CBS summer series in 1957 was made up of kinescopes from the live series on NBC.

JIMMY HUGHES, ROOKIE COP

Police

FIRST TELECAST: *May 8, 1953*
LAST TELECAST: *July 3, 1953*
BROADCAST HISTORY:
May 1953–Jul 1953, DUM Fri 8:30–9:00
CAST:
Officer Jimmy Hughes ....William Redfield
Inspector Ferguson ....Rusty Lane
Jimmy's sister ....Wendy Drew

In the opening telecast of this series Jimmy Hughes (William Redfield) was introduced as a young soldier just returned from Korea after his father, a policeman, was killed in a gun battle. Jimmy joined the police force to avenge his father's death, and won his father's badge. In the process of tracking down the killers he learned that teamwork is more important than individual action. In later episodes Jimmy tackled cases ranging from narcotics to teenage gangs to kidnaping. Rusty Lane played Inspector Ferguson, his hard-boiled mentor, and Wendy Drew played his sister.

JIMMY STEWART SHOW, THE

Situation Comedy

FIRST TELECAST: *September 19, 1971*
LAST TELECAST: *August 27, 1972*
BROADCAST HISTORY:

Sep 1971–Aug 1972, NBC Sun 8:30–9:00

CAST:

Prof. James K. Howard .....Jimmy Stewart
Martha Howard ....Julie Adams
Peter Howard ....Jonathan Daly
Wendy Howard ....Ellen Geer
Dr. Luther Quince ....John McGiver
Jake Howard ....Kirby Furlong
Teddy Howard ....Dennis Larson

Anthropology professor James Howard was a good-natured soul, but his home life became suddenly complicated when he offered to let his 29-year-old son Peter temporarily move his family in, after Peter's home had been destroyed by fire. Howard senior and junior coped as best they could with the conflicts arising in the somewhat overcrowded household, with three generations of the same family living under one roof. The fact that James and his wife Martha had a second son, Teddy, who was the same age (8) as their grandson Jake, only added to the complications. Teddy did, indeed, feel funny referring to Jake as his uncle.

The setting for *The Jimmy Stewart Show* was beautiful Easy Valley, California, home of Josiah Kessel College, founded by Prof. Howard's grandfather and the institution where both James and his good friend Dr. Quince taught.

JO STAFFORD SHOW, THE

Music

FIRST TELECAST: *February 2, 1954*
LAST TELECAST: *June 28, 1955*
BROADCAST HISTORY:

Feb 1954–Jun 1955, CBS Tue 7:45–8:00 (OS)

REGULARS:

Jo Stafford
The Starlighters
Paul Weston & His Orchestra

Singer Jo Stafford starred in this live 15-minute show that filled the remainder of the half-hour in which CBS aired its network news program. Miss Stafford sang, chatted with occasional guest stars, and performed with them. The orchestra was under the direction of her husband, Paul Weston.

JOAN EDWARDS SHOW, THE

Music

FIRST TELECAST: *July 4, 1950*
LAST TELECAST: *October 26, 1950*
BROADCAST HISTORY:

Jul 1950–Oct 1950, DUM Tue/Thu 7:45–8:00

HOSTESS:

Joan Edwards

Singer-pianist Joan Edwards, a familiar voice on radio and records during the 1940s (she had a long stint on *Your Hit Parade*), entertained on this 1950 musical interlude. She was actually something of a TV veteran, having starred on a local version of *Girl about Town* on New York television in 1941 during TV's early experimental period.

JOE & MABEL

Situation Comedy

FIRST TELECAST: *June 26, 1956*
LAST TELECAST: *September 25, 1956*
BROADCAST HISTORY:

Jun 1956–Sep 1956, CBS Tue 9:00–9:30

CAST:

Joe Sparton ....Larry Blyden
Mabel Spooner ....Nita Talbot
Mrs. Spooner ....Luella Gear
Sherman Spooner ....Michael Mann
Mike the Cabbie ....Norman Feld

The course of true love never quite ran smooth for Joe and Mabel. Joe was a big-city cabdriver and Mabel was his girl friend. Although he eventually planned to marry her, Joe's idea of when did not seem soon enough for Mabel. She was always trying to trap him into proposing and setting a date for the wedding. Mabel lived at home with her mother and her little brother, who helped her scheme to trap Joe. Joe's best friend was Mike, another cabdriver, who thought Joe was better off preventing the inevitable as long as possible.

JOE AND SONS
Situation Comedy

FIRST TELECAST: *September 9, 1975*

LAST TELECAST: *January 13, 1976*

BROADCAST HISTORY:

Sep 1975–Jan 1976, CBS Tue 8:30–9:00

CAST:

Joe Vitale ....Richard Castellano
Gus Duzik ....Jerry Stiller
Aunt Josephine ....Florence Stanley
Estelle ....Bobbi Jordan
Mark Vitale ....Barry Miller
Nick Vitale ....Jimmy Baio

Italian-American widower Joe Vitale lived in Hoboken, New Jersey, with two teenage sons. His best friend, Gus Duzik, worked with him at the Hoboken Sheet and Tube Company. As a typical middle class factory worker, Joe did the best he could to raise his boys, hold his job, and conduct some semblance of a social life, though the latter was rather limited. Helping him with the boys, and cooking an occasional meal for the entire family, was Estelle, the cocktail waitress who lived in the apartment across the hall.

JOE & VALERIE
Situation Comedy

FIRST TELECAST: *April 24, 1978*

LAST TELECAST: *May 10, 1978*

BROADCAST HISTORY:

Apr 1978–May 1978, NBC Mon 8:30–9:00
May 1978, NBC Wed 8:30–9:00

REGULARS:

Joe Pizo ....Paul Regina
Valerie Sweetzer ....Char Fontane
Frank Berganski ....Bill Beyers
Paulie Barone ....David Elliott
Thelma Medina ....Donna Ponterotto
Stella Sweetzer ....Pat Benson
Vincent Pizo ....Robert Costanzo

Young love and its pitfalls was the theme of this comedy series, which attempted to cash in on the disco craze of the late 1970s. Joe and Valerie had fallen in love at a New York City disco, but theirs was still a probing, tentative, teenage affair, which was constantly being upset by their nutty friends. Joe shared an apartment with the macho Frankie, who worked at a health spa, and simple-minded Paulie, who drove a hearse for a living. Valerie lived at home with her divorced mother, Stella. Thelma was Valerie's man-hungry best friend. By day Joe worked at his father Vincent Pizo's plumbing store, and Valerie was a clerk at a cosmetics counter, but by night, when they met on the disco's glittering dance floor, they were Cinderella and her Prince Charming.

JOE FORRESTER
Police

FIRST TELECAST: *September 9, 1975*

LAST TELECAST: *August 30, 1976*

BROADCAST HISTORY:

Sep 1975–Jan 1976, NBC Tue 10:00–11:00
Feb 1976–Aug 1976, NBC Mon 9:00–10:00

CAST:

Joe Forrester ....Lloyd Bridges
Georgia Cameron ....Patricia Crowley
Sgt. Bernie Vincent ....Eddie Egan
Jolene Jackson ....Dawn Smith
Det. Will Carson ....Taylor Lacher

Unlike most of the police series on television, *Joe Forrester* looked at the life of a regular cop on the beat, a patrolman who had been working the same district for many years. Joe felt that the friendships and information sources he had cultivated were worth much more than the comfort of a patrol car or the status of detective. He occasionally overlooked minor infractions of the law, but was known, respected, and trusted by everyone on his beat. When something serious took place, he could count on them for help in providing information. He had a girl friend, Georgia Cameron, a good buddy in watch commander Bernie Vincent (who was played by former New York policeman Eddie Egan), and had become friendly with members of the black community in his district, including young student Jolene Jackson. The locale of the series was never any more specific than "a large city in California."

JOEY & DAD
Musical Variety

FIRST TELECAST: *July 6, 1975*

LAST TELECAST: *July 27, 1975*

BROADCAST HISTORY:

Jul 1975, CBS Sun 7:30–8:30

REGULARS:

Joey Heatherton
Ray Heatherton
Pat Paulsen

Henny Youngman
Pat Proft

Sexy singer-dancer Joey Heatherton teamed with her father Ray in this short-lived summer variety series. Ray, who had been *The Merry Mailman* on television in the 1950s, was by this time more commonly known to TV viewers as the commercial spokesman for Tropicana Orange Juice. Father and daughter sang, danced, and did comedy sketches with the other regulars on the show and with their guest stars.

JOEY BISHOP SHOW, THE

Situation Comedy

FIRST TELECAST: *September 20, 1961*
LAST TELECAST: *September 7, 1965*
BROADCAST HISTORY:

Sep 1961–Jun 1962, NBC Wed 8:30–9:00
Sep 1962–Sep 1964, NBC Sat 8:30–9:00
Sep 1964–Dec 1964, CBS Sun 9:30–10:00
Dec 1964–Sep 1965, CBS Tue 8:00–8:30

CAST:

Joey Barnes .... Joey Bishop
J. P. Willoughby (1961–1962) .... John Griggs
Mrs. Barnes (1961–1962) ..... Madge Blake
Barbara Simpson (1961–1962) .... Nancy Hadley
Frank (1961–1962) .... Joe Flynn
Betty (1961–1962) .... Virginia Vincent
Larry Barnes (1961–1962) .... Warren Berlinger
Stella Barnes (1961–1962) .. Marlo Thomas
Ellie Barnes (1962–1965) ..... Abby Dalton
Mr. Jillson (1962–1965) .... Joe Besser
Freddie (1962) .... Guy Marks
Hilda (1962–1965) .... Mary Treen
Larry Corbett (1963–1965) .... Corbett Monica
Dr. Sam Nolan (1964–1965) ... Joey Forman

When it premiered in the fall of 1961, *The Joey Bishop Show* focused on Joey Barnes, a young assistant to Los Angeles press agent J. P. Willoughby. Barnes, as played by deadpan comic Joey Bishop, was a softhearted nice guy who had tried to build up his importance in the eyes of his family. Unfortunately, the members of that family often tried to take advantage of Joey's nonexistent influence with the big names of show business, and Joey spent much of his time getting into trouble while trying to help out his family. The program seemed to have too many regular characters, and by the middle of the first season, three of them were gone: Joey's older sister Betty, her husband Frank, an unsuccessful salesman, and Mr. Willoughby's secretary, Barbara. Joey's mother, stage-struck sister Stella, and kid brother Larry remained to the end of the first season.

At the start of the second season both the format and the supporting cast were changed completely. Joey Barnes was now the host of a *Tonight Show*–type talk program that originated in New York. Stories revolved around his personal and professional life as a TV celebrity, and many guest stars appeared, playing themselves. Joey was now married to a Texas girl named Ellie, had a manager named Freddie (later Larry Corbett became his manager), and lived in a fancy Manhattan apartment. In 1963 Ellie gave birth to a baby boy, who later was seen on the show, played by Abby Dalton's real-life infant son, Matthew Smith. Dr. Sam Nolan, a pediatrician neighbor, was added to the cast in 1964.

JOEY BISHOP SHOW, THE

Talk

FIRST TELECAST: *April 17, 1967*
LAST TELECAST: *December 26, 1969*
BROADCAST HISTORY:

Apr 1967–Dec 1969, ABC Mon–Fri 11:30–1:00 A.M.

HOST:

Joey Bishop

ANNOUNCER:

Regis Philbin

MUSICAL DIRECTOR:

Johnny Mann

The Joey Bishop Show was one of several attempts by ABC to establish a strong late-night talk show. Joey had been quite successful as a substitute host for Johnny Carson on NBC, and it was hoped that perhaps he could lure some of Carson's audience away permanently.

The beginning was not auspicious. The program was originally done live and, on premiere night, guest Governor Ronald Reagan showed up 14 minutes late. Petite actress Debbie Reynolds, demonstrating how to help someone on fire, tackled announcer Regis Philbin and threw him to the floor (to smother the "flames"). On the second night Joey gave a big introduction to guest Buddy Greco, only to be left gesturing toward an empty curtain—seems Buddy was still in the dressing room. Worse than the first-week gaffes, however, was a series of events on NBC. Just as Joey premiered Johnny Carson staged a dramatic walkout, garnering reams of publicity. A few weeks later he returned triumphantly, and of course all eyes were on NBC to see what would happen (nothing further did).

With his thunder thus stolen at the outset, Joey limped along for more than two years, never posing much of a threat to the mighty *Tonight Show*. In 1969 ABC finally gave up the ghost. For the last month guest hosts were used.

JOEY FAYE'S FROLICS

Comedy Variety

FIRST TELECAST: *April 5, 1950*
LAST TELECAST: *April 12, 1950*
BROADCAST HISTORY:
Apr 1950, CBS Wed 9:30–10:00
REGULARS:
Joey Faye
Audrey Christie
Mandy Kaye
Danny Dayton
Joe Silver

Comic Joey Faye starred in this comedy variety show that obviously did not work too well. It only lasted two weeks.

JOHN BYNER COMEDY HOUR, THE

Comedy Variety

FIRST TELECAST: *August 1, 1972*
LAST TELECAST: *August 29, 1972*
BROADCAST HISTORY:
Aug 1972, CBS Tue 7:30–8:30
REGULARS:
John Byner
Patty Deutsch
R. G. Brown
Linda Sublette
Gary Miller
Dennis Flannigan
The Ray Charles Orchestra

Comedian John Byner was the host and star of this short-lived summer variety series. In order to utilize his ability as an impressionist, the majority of comedy sketches were of the spoof variety. A continuing feature was "The Bland Family," satirizing situation comedies, while individual telecasts included takeoffs on *The Godfather*, soap operas, Fred Astaire–Ginger Rogers musicals (with Michele Lee as Ginger), Frank Sinatra, and George C. Scott's characterization of *Patton* shifted to the presidency of a toy company.

JOHN CONTE'S LITTLE SHOW

see *Van Camp's Little Show*

JOHN DAVIDSON SHOW, THE

Musical Variety

FIRST TELECAST: *May 30, 1969*
LAST TELECAST: *June 14, 1976*
BROADCAST HISTORY:
May 1969–Sep 1969, ABC Fri 8:00–9:00
May 1976–Jun 1976, NBC Mon 8:00–9:00
HOST:
John Davidson
REGULARS:
Rich Little (1969)
Mireille Mathieu (1969)
Jack Parnell Orchestra (1969)
Pete Barbutti (1976)
Lenny Stark Orchestra (1976)

Handsome singer John Davidson has starred in two summer variety series. The 1969 version originated in London and placed the accent on youth, with popular music stars and up-and-coming comedians as guests. In 1976, doing a four-week mini-series on NBC that originated from Los Angeles, Davidson added an element of audience participation to the traditional variety aspects of his show. He would wander into the audience and choose people at random to appear in small parts in comedy sketches and to help introduce his guest stars.

JOHN FORSYTHE SHOW, THE

Situation Comedy

FIRST TELECAST: *September 13, 1965*
LAST TELECAST: *August 29, 1966*
BROADCAST HISTORY:
Sep 1965–Aug 1966, NBC Mon 8:00–8:30
CAST:
Major John Foster ....John Forsythe
Miss Margaret Culver ......Elsa Lanchester
Miss Wilson ....Ann B. Davis
Ed Robbins ....Guy Marks
Joanna ....Peggy Lipton
Kathy ....Darleen Carr
Pamela ....Pamelyn Ferdin
Susan ....Tracy Stratford
Norma Jean ....Brooke Forsythe
Marcia ....Page Forsythe

Air Force Major John Foster had been a bachelor all his life and his dealings with women had been exclusively social. When he retired from the Air Force he became the headmaster of the Foster School, an exclusive San Francisco school for girls that he had recently inherited from his Aunt Victoria. Helping him run the school was a former Air Force sergeant and friend, Ed Robbins. The clash of these two men with an alien environment produced unexpected results. Misunderstandings between them and Miss Culver, the school principal, were frequent and often hilarious. John Forsythe's two daughters, Brooke (aged 11) and Page (aged 14) were among the young actresses portraying students at the school.

In the spring of 1966 there was a change in format. The Foster School was no longer the center of attention as John and Ed became world-traveling undercover agents for the U.S. government on a semi-regular basis, using the school only as a base from which to start, or end, their adventures. Their missions were not heavy cloak-and-dagger stuff, but were definitely more serious, and romantic, than anything that had happened at the school. No matter, the series never made it to a second season.

JOHN GARY SHOW, THE

Musical Variety

FIRST TELECAST: *June 22, 1966*
LAST TELECAST: *September 7, 1966*
BROADCAST HISTORY:
Jun 1966–Sep 1966, CBS Wed 10:00–11:00
REGULARS:
John Gary
Mitchell Ayres Orchestra
The Jimmy Joyce Singers
The Jack Regas Dancers

Singer John Gary was the star and host of this summer variety show that filled in for the vacationing Danny Kaye (who was Gary's special guest on both the first and last telecasts of this series). There was a pretty fair balance between music and comedy, with each week's guest stars encompassing both fields. The singers were generally middle-of-the-road (not rock 'n' roll), like Vikki Carr, Vic Damone, and Joanie Sommers, while several of the comedians were regulars in TV series of their own (Tim Conway, Bob Crane, and Morey Amsterdam).

JOHN GUNTHER'S HIGH ROAD

Travelogue

FIRST TELECAST: *September 7, 1959*
LAST TELECAST: *September 17, 1960*
BROADCAST HISTORY:
Sep 1959, ABC Mon 8:30–9:00
Sep 1959–Sep 1960, ABC Sat 8:00–8:30
HOST:
John Gunther

Noted author and world traveler John Gunther served as host and narrator for this series. The filmed trips to interesting places around the world were of two categories: those made specifically for the series and those that had been made by some other group but were purchased for use in the series. Gunther had been to many of the places shown, but very little of the film had been made on his own trips.

JOHNNY CARSON SHOW, THE

see *Tonight Show, The*

JOHNNY CARSON SHOW, THE

Comedy Variety

FIRST TELECAST: *June 30, 1955*
LAST TELECAST: *March 29, 1956*
BROADCAST HISTORY:
Jun 1955–Mar 1956, CBS Thu 10:00–10:30
REGULARS:
Johnny Carson
Virginia Gibson
Barbara Ruick
Jill Corey
Jack Prince
The Lud Gluskin Orchestra

In the mid-1950s the CBS Press Department was hailing Johnny Carson as "a bright young comic." He had begun his TV career in Omaha in 1948, then turned up in Los Angeles in 1951 with a well-received local show called *Carson's Cellar*. His big break came when he began writing monologues for Red Skelton. This led to a stint as host of the 1954 summer quiz show *Earn Your Vacation*, and a CBS daytime series titled *The Johnny Carson Show* early in 1955. By the spring of 1955 it was decided by the network that he was ready for prime time. The format of the nighttime *Johnny Carson Show* relied heavily on comedy sketches and singing, with more of the former than the latter. Johnny created many of the sketches himself and, in addition to his weekly guests, used comediennes Virginia Gibson and Barbara Ruick in them. Two sketches that kept popping up on a semi-regular basis were parodies of other successful TV shows (*You Are There, Person to Person,* and *What's My Line* among them) and his "catch up with the news" feature in which he acted as a roving reporter doing interviews. Whom did he interview? One week it was the inhabitants of a flying saucer, another week a man about to be shot out of a cannon, and yet a third such divergent subjects as a butcher trapped for two weeks in an icebox, a dentist trying to relieve a whale's toothache, and a dog being rescued from a 500-foot-deep well. Johnny's then-wife Jody was seen as the female singer for a few weeks at the beginning of the series, but Jill Corey took over that role. Jack Prince provided male vocals.

JOHNNY CASH PRESENTS THE EVERLY BROTHERS SHOW

Musical Variety

FIRST TELECAST: *July 8, 1970*

LAST TELECAST: *September 16, 1970*

BROADCAST HISTORY:

Jul 1970–Sep 1970, ABC Wed 9:00–10:00

REGULARS:

Don Everly
Phil Everly
Joe Higgins
Ruth McDevitt

Rock 'n' roll singers Don and Phil Everly spent the summer of 1970 as the replacement for *The Johnny Cash Show.* Although their songs were generally known as top-40 hits, the sources of much of their material were Country and gospel music and many of their guest stars were performers from that idiom. The emphasis of the series was on currently popular recordings, with Joe Higgins and Ruth McDevitt providing regular comic relief.

JOHNNY CASH SHOW, THE

Musical Variety

FIRST TELECAST: *June 7, 1969*

LAST TELECAST: *September 19, 1976*

BROADCAST HISTORY:

Jun 1969–Sep 1969, ABC Sat 9:30–10:30
Jan 1970–May 1971, ABC Wed 9:00–10:00 (OS)
Aug 1976–Sep 1976, CBS Sun 8:00–9:00

HOST:

Johnny Cash

REGULARS (1969–1971):

Mother Maybelle & The Carter Family (June, Helen, Anita)
Statler Brothers
Carl Perkins
The Tennessee Three (Marshall Grant, bass; W. S. Holland, drums; Bob Wootton, guitar)

REGULARS (1976):

June Carter Cash
Steve Martin
Jim Varney
Howard Mann

THEME:

"Folsom Prison Blues" (opening theme)
"I Walk the Line" (closing theme)

To date, one of the major attempts to bridge the gap between Country music and the mass audience was made by Johnny Cash in 1969–1971. Unlike such earlier efforts as *Ozark Jubilee* (strictly for the sticks) and *The Jimmy Dean Show* (more pop than Country), *The Johnny Cash Show* was true to its roots, yet packaged in a manner acceptable to most urban viewers. Part of its success lay with Cash himself, one of the few true superstars of both Country and popular music, and a dramatic figure in his Lincolnesque "man in black" outfit. His craggy-featured authenticity, honed in real-life hardship, made him believable in such segments as "Ride This Train." Backing him were the members of his regular road show, the Carter Family (one of the legendary groups in Country music history; Cash was married to one of the daughters, June), the Statler Brothers, Carl "Blue Suede Shoes" Perkins and the Tennessee Three. Guest stars included first-rate talent from almost every musical genre, ranging from Louis Armstrong to Arlo Guthrie, Jose Feliciano, Glen Campbell, Rod McKuen, Pete Seeger, Merle Haggard, James Taylor, and Minnie Pearl.

One of the highlights of the 1969–1971 series was a two-part telecast in January 1971 tracing the "Country Music Story." Practically everybody who was anybody in Country music appeared in this music-documentary, which included film clips of such stars of the past as the original Jimmie Rodgers, Hank Williams, and Jim Reeves, and live performances by others ranging across the generations from Roy Acuff to Tammy Wynette.

In 1976 Johnny returned with a four-week summer series originating from the Grand Ole Opry in Nashville, with guest stars almost exclusively from the Country field.

JOHNNY JUPITER

Children's

FIRST TELECAST: *March 21, 1953*
LAST TELECAST: *June 13, 1953*
BROADCAST HISTORY:
Mar 1953–Jun 1953, DUM Sat 7:30–8:00
REGULARS:
Ernest P. Duckweather ..... Vaughn Taylor
His Boss .... Gilbert Mack
PUPPETEER:
Carl Harms

This imaginative puppet show was produced by the company responsible for *Howdy Doody*, but it had a much shorter run. Its premise was a satirical view of our civilization as seen through the eyes of another planet's residents.

The initial setting was a TV studio, where E. P. Duckweather, an inquisitive janitor who liked to fiddle with the equipment, accidentally brought in Jupiter on one of the control-room consoles. He then talked with Johnny Jupiter and his friend B-12 (the puppets) and discovered that both Jupiterians were quite mystified about Earthling civilization—based on what they had seen on Earth's TV shows. Later the tables were turned and Duckweather became something of a personality on Jupiterian TV.

JOHNNY RINGO

Western

FIRST TELECAST: *October 1, 1959*
LAST TELECAST: *September 29, 1960*
BROADCAST HISTORY:
Oct 1959–Sep 1960, CBS Thu 8:30–9:00
CAST:
Johnny Ringo .... Don Durant
Laura Thomas .... Karen Sharpe
Cully .... Mark Goddard
Case Thomas .... Terence de Marney

Johnny Ringo was a gunfighter-turned-lawman. Folks around Velardi, Arizona, apparently didn't mind their sheriff's past, and in fact one of them—pretty young Laura—thought he was a right handsome hunk of man. Case Thomas, Laura's father, was an old drunk who also happened to own the general store. Helping Johnny protect the people of Velardi, and filling in for him when he was busy fending off Laura, was the young deputy, Cully.

There really was a gunfighter-turned-lawman named Johnny Ringo in the 1880s, though it is doubtful that his exploits resembled those portrayed in this series.

JOHNNY STACCATO

Detective

FIRST TELECAST: *September 10, 1959*
LAST TELECAST: *September 25, 1960*
BROADCAST HISTORY:
Sep 1959–Mar 1960, NBC Thu 8:30–9:00
Mar 1960–Sep 1960, ABC Sun 10:30–11:00
CAST:
Johnny Staccato .... John Cassavetes
Waldo .... Eduardo Ciannelli

When this series premiered in September 1959 its title was simply *Staccato*. Set in New York City, it centered on jazz pianist Johnny Staccato, who supplemented his meager income as a musician by working as a private detective. An important background for many episodes was "Waldo's," a small jazz club in Greenwich Village where Johnny Staccato spent much of his spare time and met most of his clients. Working at the club, and often featured in musical numbers, was the jazz combo of Pete Candoli which included Barney Kessel, Shelly Manne, Red Mitchell, Red Norvo, and Johnny Williams. After *Johnny Staccato* was canceled by NBC, ABC picked it up and aired reruns of the NBC episodes through September 1960.

JOHNS HOPKINS SCIENCE REVIEW, THE

Information

FIRST TELECAST: *December 31, 1948*
LAST TELECAST: *September 2, 1954*
BROADCAST HISTORY:
Dec 1948–May 1949, CBS Fri 9:00–9:30
Oct 1950–Oct 1951, DUM Tue 8:30–9:00
Oct 1951–Apr 1953, DUM Mon 8:30–9:00
Apr 1953–Apr 1954, DUM Wed 8:00–8:30
Apr 1954–Sep 1954, DUM Thu 9:00–9:30
HOST:
Lynn Poole (1948–1949)

This half-hour of learned scientific discussion and demonstrations was what is known in the trade as a "time-filler." During its long run on CBS and DuMont it was scheduled against such hit shows as *Break the Bank*, *Milton Berle*, *Arthur Godfrey* and

Dragnet, programs from which its network had little chance of luring away viewers.

Anyone who did happen to tune over from *Godfrey et al.* was treated to a genuinely worthwhile program, however. Conducted by members of the Johns Hopkins University faculty and other experts, and using films as well as discussions, it ranged across such topics as snails, TV, polio, X-rays, baby-feeding, cancer, human fear, transistors, sunburn, and "Electrons at Work in a Vacuum."

JOHNSON'S WAX THEATRE

Dramatic Anthology

FIRST TELECAST: *June 18, 1958*
LAST TELECAST: *September 17, 1958*
BROADCAST HISTORY:

Jun 1958–Sep 1958, CBS Wed 8:30–9:00

The filmed half-hour plays aired in this series were all repeats of episodes previously seen on *Schlitz Playhouse*.

JONATHAN WINTERS SHOW, THE

Comedy Variety

FIRST TELECAST: *October 2, 1956*
LAST TELECAST: *June 25, 1957*
BROADCAST HISTORY:

Oct 1956–Jun 1957, NBC Tue 7:30–7:45

REGULARS:

Jonathan Winters
Don Pardo (1956–1957)
Wayne Howell (1957)
The Eddie Safranski Orchestra

Comedian Jonathan Winters starred in this 15-minute series that occupied the remainder of the half-hour in which NBC aired its network news program. Assisting him in sketches and comedy blackouts was the announcer, Don Pardo, until March 1957, when Wayne Howell succeeded him. Jonathan also had guest stars, primarily singers and musicians, who both performed on their own and participated with him in assorted comedy bits. Most telecasts opened with a Winters monologue, contained a song by the evening's guest star, and closed with a sketch. Among the subjects that got the Winters treatment were Hollywood movie premieres, Robin Hood, and General Custer. Typical was an interview (in the *You Are There* tradition) between Edward R. Murrow and Napoleon, with Winters playing both parts.

JONATHAN WINTERS SHOW, THE

Comedy Variety

FIRST TELECAST: *December 27, 1967*
LAST TELECAST: *May 22, 1969*
BROADCAST HISTORY:

Dec 1967–Apr 1968, CBS Wed 10:00–11:00
Sep 1968–Dec 1968, CBS Wed 10:00–11:00
Dec 1968–May 1969, CBS Thu 8:00–9:00

REGULARS:

Jonathan Winters
Abby Dalton
Dick Curtis
Georgene Barnes (1968–1969)
Jerry Rannow (1968–1969)
Cliff Arquette (1968–1969)

Inventive sketch comedian Jonathan Winters was the star of his own one-hour variety show for two seasons. Regular characters portrayed by Jonathan included Maude Frickert, Willard (in the "Couple Up the Street" sketches with Abby Dalton as his wife Margaret), and various strange people he played in "Face the Folks" sketches. Another regular feature was a satire on a well-known movie. The addition of a new regular sketch in the second season, "Jack Armstrong—The All-American Boy," featuring Jonathan as Jack, brought three new regulars to the cast: Cliff Arquette as Uncle Charley Weaver, Jerry Rannow as Billy, and Georgene Barnes as Betty.

JONNY QUEST

Cartoon

FIRST TELECAST: *September 18, 1964*
LAST TELECAST: *September 9, 1965*
BROADCAST HISTORY:

Sep 1964–Dec 1964, ABC Fri 7:30–8:00
Dec 1964–Sep 1965, ABC Thu 7:30–8:00

VOICES:

Jonny Quest ....Tim Matthieson
Dr. Benton Quest (1964) .. John Stephenson
Dr. Benton Quest (1964–1965)
.... Don Messick
Race Bannon ....Mike Road
Hadji ....Danny Bravo

PRODUCERS:

William Hanna and Joseph Barbera

This rather realistic cartoon-adventure series, which later ran successfully as a Saturday morning children's show, spent one full season as a prime-time entry. The hero was 11-year old Jonny Quest, who traveled the world with his scientist father,

Dr. Benton Quest, on various missions. With them were Roger "Race" Bannon, their personal bodyguard; Hadji, a young Indian friend of Jonny's; and Bandit, the Quests' miniature bulldog.

JOSEPH COTTEN SHOW, THE

Dramatic Anthology

FIRST TELECAST: *September 14, 1956*

LAST TELECAST: *September 21, 1959*

BROADCAST HISTORY:

Sep 1956–Sep 1957, NBC Fri 9:00–9:30
Jun 1958–Aug 1958, NBC Sat 10:30–11:00
Jul 1959–Sep 1959, CBS Mon 9:30–10:00

HOST/STAR:

Joseph Cotten

The filmed half-hour plays in this anthology were all based on records of actual legal cases from various parts of the world, and various periods of history. The host and occasional star was Joseph Cotten. Others starring in individual episodes included Joan Fontaine, Keenan Wynn, Dane Clark, Kim Hunter, Hoagy Carmichael, June Lockhart, and MacDonald Carey

When this series first aired in the fall of 1956 its title was *On Trial.* Joseph Cotten became so identified with the series that its title was changed, effective February 1, 1957, to *The Joseph Cotten Show—On Trial.* NBC reran episodes from the series in the summer of 1958 as *The Joseph Cotten Show,* and CBS used that title again during the summer of 1959 for an anthology that included reruns from this series, *General Electric Theater,* and *Schlitz Playhouse.*

JOSEPH SCHILDKRAUT PRESENTS

Dramatic Anthology

FIRST TELECAST: *October 28, 1953*

LAST TELECAST: *January 21, 1954*

BROADCAST HISTORY:

Oct 1953–Dec 1953, DUM Wed 8:30–9:00
Jan 1954, DUM Thu 8:00–8:30

HOST/STAR:

Joseph Schildkraut

Joseph Schildkraut, an actor who had appeared in many prestigious Broadway and Hollywood productions over the years, hosted and sometimes starred in this dramatic anthology series during the fall of 1953. Schildkraut's stage and screen roles had ranged from comedy to romance to classical drama, and he displayed a fairly wide range of talents here as well. But DuMont, evidentally carried away with the very fact of his presence on its fledgling network (his name was always preceded by the glowing term "noted" or "distinguished"), failed to provide him with decent scripts, and the program folded after only three months.

Also known as *Personal Appearance Theatre.*

JOURNEY TO THE UNKNOWN

Suspense Anthology

FIRST TELECAST: *September 26, 1968*

LAST TELECAST: *January 30, 1969*

BROADCAST HISTORY:

Sep 1968–Jan 1969, ABC Thu 9:30–10:30

EXECUTIVE PRODUCER:

Joan Harrison

This series of melodramas focused on the psychological horrors experienced by warped and twisted minds, and the terrors that can confront people in situations that are all too real. The executive producer was a former aide to Alfred Hitchcock, and the producer of the Hitchcock television series, and she obviously tried to invoke the master's touch in this series—with only middling success. Among the stories: a mannequin comes to life for its loving admirer, but leads him into a nightmare; a mysterious man is seen in the crowd just before several disasters; and tales of witches, hallucinations and deserted islands.

Journey to the Unknown was produced in England.

JUBILEE U.S.A.

see *Ozark Jubilee*

JUDD, FOR THE DEFENSE

Lawyer

FIRST TELECAST: *September 8, 1967*

LAST TELECAST: *September 19, 1969*

BROADCAST HISTORY:

Sep 1967–May 1969, ABC Fri 10:00–11:00
May 1969–Sep 1969, ABC Fri 9:00–10:00

CAST:

Clinton Judd .... Carl Betz
Ben Caldwell .... Stephen Young

Clinton Judd was a high-priced, high-powered criminal attorney modeled along the lines of such real-life legal superstars as F. Lee Bailey and Percy Foreman. Based in Houston, Texas, he traveled all over the

U.S. with his young assistant Ben, defending wealthy tycoons and flower children. The series had a highly contemporary ring, as Judd was often involved in cases which mirrored recent headlines, such as draft evasion, Mexican-American labor activism, and civil rights murders.

JUDGE FOR YOURSELF

Quiz/Audience Participation

FIRST TELECAST: *August 18, 1953*
LAST TELECAST: *May 11, 1954*
BROADCAST HISTORY:
Aug 1953–May 1954, NBC Tue 10:00–10:30
EMCEE:
Fred Allen
ANNOUNCER:
Dennis James
REGULARS:
Bob Carroll (1954)
The Skylarks (1954)
Milton Delugg & His Orchestra
Kitty Kallen (1954)
Judy Johnson (1954)

Three professional acts—singers, dancers, musicians, comedians, etc.—performed on this show each week. The three acts were rated in 1-2-3 order by two panels of judges, one composed of three show-business personalities and the other made up of three members of the studio audience. If one of the amateur judges rated the acts in the same order as the professional (show-business) judges, he or she won $1,000. The only acts that performed on this show that also had some professional success were two instrumental jazz groups—vibraphonist Terry Gibbs and the Marian McPartland Trio.

On January 5, 1954, the format of the show was changed. Gone were the professional judges, and the amateur judges were now rating new songs to determine which would become big hits. The winning judge was determined by his or her agreement with applause voting by the studio audience. Songs were performed by a regular cast consisting of Bob Carroll, the Skylarks, and Kitty Kallen. Miss Kallen was only with the show for two weeks, leaving the female vocalist spot to guest singers until Judy Johnson joined the cast at the end of February.

JUDY GARLAND SHOW, THE

Musical Variety

FIRST TELECAST: *September 29, 1963*
LAST TELECAST: *March 29, 1964*
BROADCAST HISTORY:
Sep 1963–Mar 1964, CBS Sun 9:00–10:00
REGULARS:
Judy Garland
Jerry Van Dyke (1963)
Ken Murray (1964)
The Mort Lindsey Orchestra
The Ernie Flatt Dancers (1963)
The Nick Castle Dancers (1963)
The Peter Gennaro Dancers (1963–1964)

Throughout its short history, *The Judy Garland Show* was a series desperately looking for a format. When it first went into production under the guidance of young George Schlatter (who would later do *Rowan and Martin's Laugh-In*) it was to be modeled after Judy's highly successful special that had aired in the spring of 1963—glossy, full of big production numbers, with a brassy driving quality. Schlatter was relieved of the production responsibilities after five shows had been taped, and was replaced by Norman Jewison. His efforts were geared to make Judy's show more folksy, in the style of *The Garry Moore Show*, in the hope that that approach would attract some of the audience of its primary competition, NBC's top-rated *Bonanza*. By the time it left the air in March of 1964, *The Judy Garland Show* had gone through two more producers, still without making even a dent in *Bonanza*'s audience.

At the outset Judy was aided by comic Jerry Van Dyke, but he was gone by the end of 1963. For a while there was a regular "Tea for Two" segment in which Judy chatted with guests stars about show business and various personal experiences. Among the guests were her young daughter Liza Minnelli; her co-star from Andy Hardy days, Mickey Rooney; and Ray Bolger, who had played the scarecrow in *The Wizard of Oz*. Early in 1964 Ken Murray was a regular contributor, with his home movies of Hollywood stars. Nothing seemed to work. Judy was at her best just singing, and several of the shows during the last two months were just that—no guest stars, no regulars, but a full hour of Judy. That may have been the best format, but it was too little too late.

JUDY SPLINTERS

Children's

FIRST TELECAST: *June 13, 1949*
LAST TELECAST: *August 5, 1949*
BROADCAST HISTORY:
Jun 1949–Aug 1949, NBC Mon–Fri 7:00–7:15
HOST:
Shirley Dinsdale

Pretty 21-year-old ventriloquist Shirley Dinsdale and her saucy, pigtailed dummy Judy Splinters hosted this live program, which served as the 1949 summer replacement for *Kukla, Fran & Ollie*. The program was first seen in February 1949 as a local entry on KNBH, Los Angeles, moved to Chicago for its summer network run, and then to New York for nine months as a late afternoon show in 1949–1950.

JUKE BOX JURY
see *Peter Potter Show, The*

JULIA
Situation Comedy
FIRST TELECAST: *September 17, 1968*
LAST TELECAST: *May 25, 1971*
BROADCAST HISTORY:
Sep 1968–Jan 1971, NBC Tue 8:30–9:00
Jan 1971–May 1971, NBC Tue 7:30–8:00
CAST:
Julia Baker .... Diahann Carroll
Dr. Morton Chegley .... Lloyd Nolan
Marie Waggedorn .... Betty Beaird
Corey Baker .... Marc Copage
Earl J. Waggedorn .... Michael Link
Hannah Yarby .... Lurene Tuttle
Eddie Edson .... Eddie Quillan
Paul Cameron (1968–1970) .. Paul Winfield
Len Waggedorn .... Hank Brandt
Steve Bruce (1970–1971)
.... Fred Williamson

This comedy was more notable for its casting than its content. Singer Diahann Carroll became the first black female to star in her own comedy series in a "prestige" role (i.e., not as a domestic such as *Beulah*, or a second banana). Julia was an independent woman, a young, widowed nurse whose husband had been killed in Vietnam. After his death she moved to Los Angeles and found a job in the medical office of Astrospace Industries. There she met fellow nurse Hannah Yarby, and feisty Dr. Chegley, whose bark was much worse than his bite. Life at the office coupled with her home and social lives provided the material for the stories.

The show was thoroughly integrated, and after this attracted some initial attention as a novelty, it met with immediate acceptance—to the relief of nervous network executives. Julia lived in a modern, integrated apartment building with her little boy, Corey, whose best friend was white Earl J. Waggedorn, one of their neighbors. Paul Cameron was Julia's romantic interest for the first two seasons, and was replaced by Steve Bruce during the series' final year.

JULIE ANDREWS HOUR, THE
Musical Variety
FIRST TELECAST: *September 13, 1972*
LAST TELECAST: *April 28, 1973*
BROADCAST HISTORY:
Sep 1972–Jan 1973, ABC Wed 10:00–11:00
Jan 1973–Apr 1973, ABC Sat 9:00–10:00
HOSTESS:
Julie Andrews
REGULARS:
Rich Little
Alice Ghostley
Tony Charmoli Dancers
ORCHESTRA:
Nelson Riddle

British musical-comedy star Julie Andrews hosted this hour of sweetness-and-light which lasted for a single season on ABC. There were songs, skits, and blackouts, with Julie recreating some of her famous roles such as Eliza Doolittle (from *My Fair Lady*) and Mary Poppins. Comedians Rich Little and Alice Ghostley constituted a semi-regular comedy repertory company. Little's career received quite a boost on this series. Jack Benny so liked Rich's impersonation of him on the show that he sent the young comic an 18-carat-gold money clip and the message, "With Bob Hope doing my walk and you doing my voice, I can be a star and do nothing."

JULIE FARR, M.D.
see *Having Babies*

JULIUS LA ROSA SHOW, THE
Music
FIRST TELECAST: *June 27, 1955*
LAST TELECAST: *September 23, 1955*
BROADCAST HISTORY:
Jun 1955–Sep 1955, CBS Mon/Wed/Fri 7:45–8:00
REGULARS:
Julius La Rosa

The Debutones
The Russ Case Orchestra

Singer Julius La Rosa was the star of this thrice-weekly live summer music show that filled the remainder of the half-hour in which CBS aired its network news program. He sang, as did the female quartet, the Debutones, and introduced his guest stars.

JULIUS LA ROSA SHOW, THE

Musical Variety

FIRST TELECAST: *July 14, 1956*
LAST TELECAST: *September 7, 1957*
BROADCAST HISTORY:
Jul 1956–Aug 1956, NBC Sat 8:00–9:00
Jun 1957–Sep 1957, NBC Sat 8:00–9:00
REGULARS:
Julius La Rosa
Frank Lewis Dancers (1956)
The Spellbinders (1956)
Carl Hoff & His Orchestra (1956)
Louis DaPron Dancers (1957)
Artie Malvin Singers (1957)
Mitch Ayres & His Orchestra (1957)

Julius La Rosa spent two summers filling in for the vacationing Perry Como. During the summer of 1956, La Rosa, Patti Page, and Tony Bennett each spent about one month headlining a musical variety hour with the same supporting cast: the Spellbinders, the Frank Lewis Dancers, and Carl Hoff & His Orchestra. During the summer of 1957, La Rosa was the sole star and had Como's regular dancers and orchestra as part of his supporting cast.

JUNE ALLYSON SHOW, THE

see *DuPont Show with June Allyson, The*

JUNIOR PRESS CONFERENCE

Interview

FIRST TELECAST: *October 5, 1953*
LAST TELECAST: *December 13, 1954*
BROADCAST HISTORY:
Oct 1953–Dec 1954, ABC Mon 9:00–9:30
MODERATOR:
Ruth Geri Hagy

Public-service program in which politicians and other personalities in the news were interviewed by a panel of four college correspondents from various campus newspapers. *Junior Press Conference* was first seen in October 1952, as a Sunday daytime entry, and continued on Sundays after its prime-time run until November 1960. In October 1954 the title was changed to *College Press Conference.* From Philadelphia.

JUSTICE

Lawyer

FIRST TELECAST: *April 8, 1954*
LAST TELECAST: *March 25, 1956*
BROADCAST HISTORY:
Apr 1954–Jun 1955, NBC Thu 8:30–9:00
Oct 1955–Mar 1956, NBC Sun 10:30–11:00
CAST:
Jason Tyler (1954–1955) ......Gary Merrill
Richard Adams (1955–1956)
.... William Prince
PRODUCER:
David Susskind

Taken from the files of the National Legal Aid Society, the dramas presented in this live series were the stories of poor people in need of legal help, either criminal or civil in nature, with the emphasis on the former. There were no regulars in the cast when the series began but Legal Aid attorney Jason Tyler became the permanent lawyer on the series in the fall of 1954. He was replaced for the 1955–1956 season by a new attorney, Richard Adams.

A 1955 episode about song sharks in the music business, starring *Your Hit Parade* star Gisele MacKenzie, had an unexpected by-product. The song used in the drama, "Hard to Get," became quite a big seller on the real-life hit parade.

JUVENILE JURY

Quiz/Audience Participation

FIRST TELECAST: *April 3, 1947*
LAST TELECAST: *September 14, 1954*
BROADCAST HISTORY:
Apr 1947–Jul 1947, NBC Thu 8:00–8:30
Jun 1951–Sep 1951, NBC Tue 8:30–9:00
Jun 1952–Oct 1952, NBC Wed 8:00–8:30
Jul 1953–Sep 1953, NBC Mon 9:00–9:30
Jun 1954–Sep 1954, CBS Tue 8:30–9:00
EMCEE:
Jack Barry

Juvenile Jury was created by radio announcer Jack Barry, who served as its emcee on both radio and television. The format was simple and highly effective. A panel of five children, ranging in age from

3 to 12, was presented with "problems" sent in by viewers and asked to comment, or think up solutions. The kids were utterly uninhibited, and their answers were sometimes serious, sometimes funny, and always totally unpredictable. A typical exchange might go like this. A mother wrote in, "My little girl wakes up very early every morning so she won't be late for school. But school is only two blocks away and she awakens the whole family, then arrives at school so early she has to sit on the steps and wait for the doors to open." To which the "jury" replied:

Richard (10): "Well, there's one good thing about her getting up so early—the rest of the family won't have to get in line for the bathroom!"

Mai-Lan (7): "Instead of keeping everyone else awake, why doesn't she go out and walk around the block a few thousand times?"

Elberta (6½): "Her teacher must be Gregory Peck or something . . ."

David (6): "Maybe she gets ready fast and early now—but wait till she gets older. Wait till she starts putting lipstick on and wearing a girdle."

Barry picked his kids carefully, and the results were always entertaining. (A similar format was used for years by Art Linkletter on a segment of his *House Party* show.) Once a sweet young child told him that when she grew up she wanted to be a doctor. "Why?" asked Barry. "Because," she answered, full of sincerity, "I like to stick needles in people."

Perhaps the best exchange, though, came after Barry had just finished delivering a commercial for the sponsor's health tonic, in which he was obliged to take a couple swigs of the stuff. As he walked over to the panel to begin his next interview, the young subject eyed him suspiciously, sniffed the air, and piped up accusingly, "Have you been drinking?"

Juvenile Jury began on radio in 1946 and had a brief run on NBC's early East Coast TV network in mid-1947. It was seen again on network television, this time nationwide, for four summers from 1951–1954. It continued as a Sunday afternoon show until March 27, 1955.

KAISER ALUMINUM HOUR, THE

Dramatic Anthology

FIRST TELECAST: *July 3, 1956*

LAST TELECAST: *June 18, 1957*

BROADCAST HISTORY:

Jul 1956–Jun 1957, NBC Tue 9:30–10:30

Live hour-long dramas were presented every other week on *The Kaiser Aluminum Hour.* It alternated on Tuesday evenings with *The Armstrong Circle Theatre* prior to the latter program's move to CBS. The format was varied to include both serious and light subjects, with both well-known and lesser-known actors. The first production, "Army Game," was headlined by Paul Newman. Others who were featured in this series included Eli Wallach, Robert Culp, Natalie Wood, Forrest Tucker, Jack Warden, MacDonald Carey, Claude Rains, Henry Hull, Hume Cronyn, Franchot Tone, Geraldine Brooks, Kim Hunter, and Ralph Bellamy.

KALLIKAKS, THE

Situation Comedy

FIRST TELECAST: *August 3, 1977*

LAST TELECAST: *August 31, 1977*

BROADCAST HISTORY:

Aug 1977, NBC Wed 9:30–10:00

CAST:

Jasper T. Kallikak .... David Huddleston
Venus Kallikak .... Edie McClurg
Bobbi Lou Kallikak .... Bonnie Ebsen
Junior Kallikak .... Patrick J. Peterson
Oscar Heinz .... Peter Palmer

THEME:

"Beat the System," by Stanley Ralph Ross, sung by Roy Clark

In the hopes of finding his fortune out West, Jasper T. Kallikak had moved his family from their native Appalachia, where he had worked as a coal miner, to the small town of Nowhere, California. He had inherited a small two-pump gas station there and figured that, as his own boss, he would improve his lot. Conniving and avaricious, Jasper lived by the theme song of this mini-series, always looking for a way to beat the system. With his overly affectionate wife Venus, his social-climbing teenage daughter, and his mechanical genius preteen son, not to mention his German hired hand Oscar who could barely speak English, Jasper had quite a household. One member of the cast should have felt right at home with this hillbillies-move-west format. Bonnie Ebsen's father Buddy had spent most of the 1960s as Jed Clampett on *The Beverly Hillbillies.*

KAREN

Situation Comedy

FIRST TELECAST: *October 5, 1964*

LAST TELECAST: *August 30, 1965*

BROADCAST HISTORY:

Oct 1964–Aug 1965, NBC Mon 7:30–8:00

CAST:

Karen Scott ....Debbie Watson
Steve Scott ....Richard Denning
Barbara Scott ....Mary LaRoche
Mimi Scott ....Gina Gillespie

Karen was one of the three half-hour situation comedies that comprised the 90-minute *90 Bristol Court* series in the fall of 1964. The concept of *90 Bristol Court* was to link together three separate families living in the same Southern California apartment complex, each with their own story and own half-hour show each week. *Karen* was the only one of the three that made it through the entire 1964–65 season, however, the other two *(Harris Against the World* and *Tom, Dick and Mary)* being dropped in January.

Karen Scott was an energetic 16-year-old whose activities constantly confounded her tolerant parents, Steve and Barbara. Karen's tomboyish younger sister Mimi created a different set of problems for the elder Scotts, and the situations she became involved in functioned as counterpoint to those of her older sister. Handyman Cliff Murdock, the only character appearing in all three parts of *90 Bristol Court,* did not appear in *Karen* after the other two comedies were dropped.

KAREN

Situation Comedy

FIRST TELECAST: *January 30, 1975*

LAST TELECAST: *June 19, 1975*

BROADCAST HISTORY:

Jan 1975–Jun 1975, ABC Thu 8:30–9:00

CAST:

Karen Angelo ....Karen Valentine
Dale Busch (first telecast) ..... Denver Pyle
Dale Busch ....Charles Lane
Dena Madison ....Dena Dietrich
Cissy Peterson ....Aldine King
Adam Cooperman ....Will Seltzer
Jerry Siegel ....Oliver Clark
Cheryl Siegel ....Alix Elias

This contemporary situation comedy centered around Karen Angelo, a single, bright, involved young woman who worked for a citizen's action organization called Open America, headquartered in Washington, D.C. Helping Karen uncover crooked politicians and lobby for citizen's legislation were crusty Dale Busch, founder of Open America; Dena, the group's cynical office manager; Adam, a young student working for the organization, and Cissy, Karen's roommate. Jerry and Cheryl were Karen's neighbors in Georgetown.

KATE MCSHANE

Lawyer

FIRST TELECAST: *September 10, 1975*

LAST TELECAST: *November 12, 1975*

BROADCAST HISTORY:

Sep 1975–Nov 1975, CBS Wed 10:00–11:00

CAST:

Kate McShane ....Anne Meara
Pat McShane ....Sean McClory
Ed McShane ....Charles Haid

Kate McShane was the first network dramatic series to feature a woman lawyer in the lead role. As played by Anne Meara, Kate was single, independent, aggressive, and soft-hearted. She had a tendency to become emotionally involved with her clients, which was not always a good idea. When she encountered problems (which was every week) she could turn to her father, Pat, a former cop who served as her investigator, or to her brother Ed, a Jesuit priest and law professor who helped her with the stickier legal and moral questions.

Miss Meara was half of the husband-and-wife comedy team of Stiller and Meara, which appeared on many variety shows during the 1970s. This was her first dramatic series.

KATE SMITH EVENING HOUR, THE

Musical Variety

FIRST TELECAST: *September 19, 1951*

LAST TELECAST: *June 11, 1952*

BROADCAST HISTORY:

Sep 1951–Jun 1952, NBC Wed 8:00–9:00

REGULARS:

Kate Smith
Ted Collins
The Jack Allison Singers
The Johnny Butler Dancers
The Jack Miller Orchestra

Kate Smith, one of radio's favorite and most familiar personalities, made only two brief excursions into a nighttime television series (she also had a daytime show from 1950 to 1954). *The Kate Smith Evening Hour* was a live weekly variety show which featured Broadway and Hollywood stars in excerpts from famous plays, as well as musical numbers, comedy sketches, and the other traditional components of a variety show. Ted Collins, who was Miss Smith's manager and producer of this show, served as the host of the program. The semi-regular feature "Ethel and Albert," starring Peg Lynch and Alan Bunce, later became a series in its own right and ran for several seasons.

Two of Kate's guests on this series were making their television debuts: singer Josephine Baker and the Tommy Dorsey Orchestra. In contrast to her daytime theme, "When the Moon Comes Over the Mountain," Miss Smith opened her prime-time show with her stirring and familiar rendition of "God Bless America."

KATE SMITH SHOW, THE

Musical Variety

FIRST TELECAST: *January 25, 1960*

LAST TELECAST: *July 18, 1960*

BROADCAST HISTORY:

Jan 1960–Jul 1960, CBS Mon 7:30–8:00

REGULARS:

Kate Smith
Neil Hefti and His Orchestra
The Harry Simeone Chorus

Kate Smith returned to nighttime television, after an absence of almost a decade, with this musical variety show. She sang, introduced her guest stars, and participated with them in production numbers. Most of the guests were popular singers, dancers, or musicians.

KAY KYSER'S KOLLEGE OF MUSICAL KNOWLEDGE

Quiz/Audience Participation

FIRST TELECAST: *December 1, 1949*

LAST TELECAST: *September 12, 1954*

BROADCAST HISTORY:

Dec 1949–Dec 1950, NBC Thu 9:00–10:00 (OS)
Jul 1954–Sep 1954, NBC Sun 7:00–7:30

EMCEE:

Kay Kyser (1949–1950)
Tennessee Ernie Ford (1954)

REGULARS (1949–1950):

Ish Kabbible
Liza Palmer
Sue Bennett
Michael Douglas
Honeydreamers
Dr. Roy K. Marshall (announcer)
Ben Grauer (announcer)
Diane Sinclair
Ken Spaulding
Carl Hoff (orchestra director)

REGULARS (1954):

The Cheerleaders Quintet
Frank DeVol Orchestra
Jack Narz (announcer and "Dean")

THEME (1949–1950):

"Thinking of You," by Walter Donaldson and Paul Ash

Kay Kyser was one of several bandleaders who had developed an audience-involvement "gimmick" while touring dance halls across the country in the 1930s, and then brought his routine successfully to radio in the 1940s (another was Sammy Kaye with his *So You Want to Lead a Band* routine). When television came along, hungry for programming, the bandleaders were ready with their pretested and already successful entertainment packages.

The Kollege of Musical Knowledge was a musical quiz show. "Professor" Kay, garbed in cap and gown, recruited contestants from the studio audience and posed musical questions, which were performed or acted out by members of the band and special guests. Three bearded judges, dressed in tails and somewhat resembling the Smith Brothers, sat behind a long desk and comically "judged" the answers (all three speaking in perfect unison). The band was dressed in sweaters and beanies. Contestants were sometimes required to give a totally incorrect answer, upon which Kay would shout, "That's right, you're wrong," or "that's wrong, you're right," as might be the case. The whole atmosphere was somewhat antic, with Kay constantly mugging for the audience and comedy and musical routines interpolated.

Assisting with the musical questions were "dumb" comedian Ish Kabbible (real name: Merwyn Bogue) and several of the band's regular vocalists, including young Michael (Mike) Douglas—later of TV talk-show fame.

After a year's run the program was involved in a dispute between sponsor and network, which resulted in its cancellation. It probably could have been revived in another time slot or on another network, but Kyser, tired of years of the showbiz grind, threw in the towel and retired not only from TV but from the entertainment world entirely. He has since pursued religious activities.

The *Kollege of Musical Knowledge* idea was revived in 1954 as a summer show, with Tennessee Ernie Ford as host. Kay Kyser was listed as "consultant" for the 1954 revival, and even appeared as special guest on one telecast, but without the regular presence of Kay and his maniac crew the program had lost its spark, and was not renewed.

KAZ

Lawyer/Detective

FIRST TELECAST: *September 10, 1978*

LAST TELECAST:

BROADCAST HISTORY:

Sep 1978–Oct 1978, CBS Sun 10:00–11:00

Oct 1978– , CBS Sun 9:00–10:00

CAST:

Martin "Kaz" Kazinsky ...... Ron Leibman
Samuel Bennett ....Patrick O'Neal
Katie McKenna ....Linda Carlson
Mary Parnell ....Gloria LeRoy
Peter Colcourt ....Mark Withers
Illsa Fogel ....Edith Atwater
District Attorney Revko .....George Wyner
Malloy ....Dick O'Neill

Kaz had an unusual background for an attorney—he had earned his law degree while serving time in prison. Upon his release he had managed to secure a position as a junior partner with the prestigious Los Angeles law firm of Bennett, Rheinhart and Alquist. The pay wasn't very good (as he frequently reminded senior partner Samuel Bennett), but someone with his background and inexperience had little choice. Kaz did have one advantage, however. Having been on the other side of the law himself, he had an understanding of the criminal mind not usually found in attorneys. His girl friend was court reporter Katie McKenna, and his pad a small apartment over the Starting Gate, a jazz music nightclub owned by his friend Mary Parnell. Kaz often hung out at the Starting Gate, and sat in with the band as a drummer. Working with him at the law firm was another young attorney, Peter Colcourt.

KEANE BROTHERS SHOW, THE

Musical Variety

FIRST TELECAST: *August 12, 1977*

LAST TELECAST: *September 2, 1977*

BROADCAST HISTORY:

Aug 1977–Sep 1977, CBS Fri 8:30–9:00

REGULARS:

Tom Keane
John Keane
Jimmy Caesar
The Anita Mann Dancers
The Alan Copeland Orchestra

If ABC could make series stars out of teenagers Donny and Marie Osmond, CBS figured they could try a summer mini-series with two performers who were even younger. Probably the youngest co-stars ever on a network variety series, piano-playing Tom was 13, and his drummer brother John was only 12. They sang and played popular tunes and performed with assorted guest stars. Impressionist Jimmy Caesar provided comic relief.

KEEFE BRASSELLE SHOW, THE

Musicial Variety

FIRST TELECAST: *June 25, 1963*

LAST TELECAST: *September 17, 1963*

BROADCAST HISTORY:

Jun 1963–Sep 1963, CBS Tue 10:00–11:00

HOST:

Keefe Brasselle

REGULARS:

Noelle Adam
Anne B. Davis
Sammy Kaye
Rocky Graziano
Charles Sanford Orchestra

Keefe Brasselle was pushed hard as a "coming star" on television in the 1960s, but he never did seem to make the big time. In addition to producing programs and appearing in dramatic presentations, he starred in this summer variety series which was the summer replacement for *The Garry Moore Show*. Probably the highlight of the series was the premiere, on which a young guest named Barbra Streisand belted out "Soon It's Gonna Rain" from *The Fantastiks*.

Brasselle, who also worked in an executive capacity for CBS, later turned novelist and wrote a sex-and-scandal bestseller focusing on an unnamed TV network. The book was entitled *The CanniBalS*.

KEEP IT IN THE FAMILY

Quiz

FIRST TELECAST: *October 12, 1957*
LAST TELECAST: *February 8, 1958*
BROADCAST HISTORY:
Oct 1957–Feb 1958, ABC Sat 7:30–8:00
EMCEE:
Keefe Brasselle (1957)
Bill Nimmo
ANNOUNCER:
Johnny Olsen

This quiz show pitted two families against each other. Each team, which might comprise several generations within one family, was presented with a multi-part question. Each member of the family, starting with the youngest, then had to answer one part. Winning families continued on the program until defeated. Keefe Brasselle was the host on the first telecast of this show, but was replaced for the remainder of the run by Bill Nimmo.

KEEP ON TRUCKIN'

Comedy Variety

FIRST TELECAST: *July 12, 1975*
LAST TELECAST: *August 2, 1975*
BROADCAST HISTORY:
Jul 1975–Aug 1975, ABC Sat 8:00–9:00
CAST:
Franklyn Ajaye
Rhonda Bates
Kathrine Baumann
Jeannine Burnier
Didi Conn
Charles Fleischer
Wayland Flowers
Larry Ragland
Marion Ramsey
Rhilo Fahir
Jack Riley
Fred Travalena
Gailard Sartain
Richard Lee Sung

This four-week summer variety series featured a repertory company of 14 bright young comics, who did rapid-fire gags and satirical sketches, and indulged in general buffoonery. Each telecast was to be introduced by respected writer-actor Rod Serling, but Serling died two weeks before the premiere and his pretaped segments were omitted from the actual telecasts.

KEEP POSTED

Public Affairs

FIRST TELECAST: *October 9, 1951*
LAST TELECAST: *March 31, 1953*
BROADCAST HISTORY:
Oct 1951–Mar 1953, DUM Tue 8:30–9:00
MODERATOR:
Martha Rountree
REGULAR PANELIST:
Lawrence Spivak

Martha Rountree moderated this public-affairs program in which a panel of citizens, chaired by Lawrence Spivak, questioned a leading public figure. Among the guests was Rep. Richard M. Nixon (R-Calif), whose topic was "Fighting Communism." The program originated from Washington, D.C.

KEEP TALKING

Quiz/Audience Participation

FIRST TELECAST: *July 15, 1958*
LAST TELECAST: *May 3, 1960*
BROADCAST HISTORY:
Jul 1958–Sep 1958, CBS Tue 8:30–9:00
Sep 1958–Oct 1958, CBS Tue 8:00–8:30
Nov 1958–Feb 1959, CBS Sun 10:00–10:30
Feb 1959–Sep 1959, CBS Wed 8:00–8:30
Sep 1959–May 1960, ABC Tue 10:30–11:00
EMCEE:
Monty Hall (1958)
Carl Reiner (1958–1959)
Merv Griffin (1959–1960)
REGULARS:
Joey Bishop
Ilka Chase (1958–1959)
Audrey Meadows (1958–1959)
Elaine May (1958–1959)
Paul Winchell
Danny Dayton
Morey Amsterdam
Peggy Cass
Pat Carroll
Orson Bean (1959–1960)

The players on *Keep Talking* were divided into two teams of three each. The emcee gave each player a different secret phrase, which the player was then required to incorporate into a story. After the phrase had been used the emcee would stop the story and ask the other team what the phrase was. Guessing the phrase won the team a point and the team with the most points at the end of the show was the winner. The object, therefore, was to ad-lib so skillfully that the phrases were masked from the other team. Monty Hall was the original emcee but was replaced by Carl Reiner when the show moved to Sunday nights in November 1958. When the series moved to ABC in September 1959, Merv Griffin took over as emcee.

KELLY MONTEITH SHOW, THE

Comedy Variety

FIRST TELECAST: *June 16, 1976*

LAST TELECAST: *July 7, 1976*

BROADCAST HISTORY:

Jun 1976–Jul 1976, CBS Wed 8:30–9:00

REGULARS:

Kelly Monteith
Nellie Bellflower
Harry Corden

Kelly Monteith's forte was the comic monologue, with which he opened each episode of this four-week summer mini-series. Nellie Bellflower and Harry Corden, and a weekly guest star, also assisted Kelly in assorted sketches.

KEN BERRY "WOW" SHOW, THE

Musical Variety

FIRST TELECAST: *July 15, 1972*

LAST TELECAST: *August 12, 1972*

BROADCAST HISTORY:

Jul 1972–Aug 1972, ABC Sat 10:00–11:00

HOST:

Ken Berry

REGULARS:

Teri Garr
Bill Van
Carl Gottlieb
Don Lane
Steve Martin
Barbara Joyce
Laura Lacey
Cheryl Stoppelmoor (Cheryl Ladd)
Gene Merlino
Tom Kenny
Ted Ziegler
The New Seekers
Jaime Rogers Dancers
Jimmy Dale Orchestra

Ken Berry's previous exposure to a national television audience was almost exclusively as an actor in situation comedies, most notably *The Andy Griffith Show*, *Mayberry R.F.D.* and *F Troop*. This contemporary summer series gave him an opportunity to show off his skills as a dancer and singer as well. Satires and lampoons of movies and TV shows were frequent features.

KEN MURRAY SHOW, THE

Variety

FIRST TELECAST: *January 7, 1950*

LAST TELECAST: *June 21, 1953*

BROADCAST HISTORY:

Jan 1950–Jun 1952, CBS Sat 8:00–9:00 (OS)
Feb 1953–Jun 1953, CBS Sun 9:30–10:00

REGULARS:

Ken Murray
Darla Hood (1950–1951)
Joe Wong (1950–1951)
Tony Labriola (1950–1951)
Jack Mulhall (1950–1951)
Betty Lou Walters (1950–1951)
The Enchanters (1950–1951)
Joe Besser (1950–1951)
Art Lund (1951–1952)
Laurie Anders
Pat Conway (1951–1952)
Jane Bergmeier (1951–1952)
Lillian Farmer (1951–1952)
Anita Gordon (1951–1953)
Johnny Johnston (1953)

Old trooper Ken Murray, who had begun his career in vaudeville in the teens and who appeared on the first commercial program on television, in 1930, hosted his own comedy-variety series on CBS from 1950–1953. Murray was also a producer of some note, and his show featured top-name guest stars and elaborate sets—including his trademark Hollywood and Vine backdrop. He had a large cast of regular singers and dancers, including cowgirl Laurie "Ah love the wide open spaces" Anders and a bevy of long-stemmed "Glamourlovelies." Ken bridged the various acts with informal chatter and humor. The series began as an alternate-week entry, switched to weekly in the fall of 1950, and then back to alternate weeks in 1953. During the 1953 run it alternated with *The Alan Young Show* under the umbrella title *Time to Smile*.

KENTUCKY JONES

Comedy Drama

FIRST TELECAST: *September 19, 1964*

LAST TELECAST: *September 11, 1965*

BROADCAST HISTORY:

Sep 1964–Dec 1964, NBC Sat 8:30–9:00
Jan 1965–Sep 1965, NBC Sat 8:00–8:30

CAST:

"Kentucky" Jones .... Dennis Weaver
Ike Wong .... Ricky Der
Seldom Jackson .... Harry Morgan

Kenneth Yarborough Jones was a veterinarian and owner of a 40-acre ranch in Southern California. He had acquired the nickname Kentucky because of the way he signed his name: "K. Y. Jones." His wife had applied to adopt a nine-year-old Chinese orphan who arrived shortly after her sudden death. Kentucky's situation as a widower made him have second thoughts about taking the orphan, Dwight Eisenhower "Ike" Wong, into his household. Although reluctant to accept the responsibility, Kentucky came to love Ike. The only other regular in the series was the ranch handyman, Seldom Jackson.

KEY CLUB PLAYHOUSE

Dramatic Anthology

FIRST TELECAST: *May 31, 1957*
LAST TELECAST: *August 23, 1957*
BROADCAST HISTORY:

May 1957–Aug 1957, ABC Fri 9:00–9:30

The filmed dramas presented in this series were selected reruns of episodes from *Ford Theatre*.

KEY TO THE AGES

Discussion

FIRST TELECAST: *February 27, 1955*
LAST TELECAST: *May 22, 1955*
BROADCAST HISTORY:

Feb 1955–May 1955, ABC Sun 8:00–8:30

HOST:

Dr. Theodore Low

Ancient Greek poets, great novels, and other literary or cultural subjects were examined on this ABC program, which ran opposite Ed Sullivan for a few months in 1955. It originated from Baltimore and was produced in cooperation with the Enoch Pratt Free Library and the Walters Art Gallery.

KEY TO THE MISSING

Interview

FIRST TELECAST: *August 8, 1948*
LAST TELECAST: *September 16, 1949*
BROADCAST HISTORY:

Aug 1948–Oct 1948, DUM Sun 6:30–7:00
Oct 1948–Mar 1949, DUM Fri 7:00–7:30
Mar 1949–Apr 1949, DUM Thu 8:30–9:00
May 1949–Jun 1949, DUM Fri 9:30–10:00
Jun 1949–Sep 1949, DUM Fri 9:00–9:30

HOST:

Archdale J. Jones

This was a kind of missing persons bureau of the air. Archdale Jones interviewed relatives and friends and showed pictures, handwriting specimens, etc., of missing persons, and then appealed to viewers to call in any information they might have on the vanished person's whereabouts. Although some of the cases went back generations, quite a few long-lost kin were reunited this way. The wartime radio program upon which the show was based (called *Where Are They Now?*) claimed a success rate of 68 percent.

KHAN

Detective

FIRST TELECAST: *February 7, 1975*
LAST TELECAST: *February 28, 1975*
BROADCAST HISTORY:

Feb 1975, CBS Fri 8:00–9:00

CAST:

Khan .... Khigh Dhiegh
Anna Khan .... Irene Yah-Ling Sun
Kim Khan .... Evan Kim
Lt. Gubbins .... Vic Tayback

Based in San Francisco's Chinatown, private detective Khan, with the help of his two children, unraveled mysterious crimes in a style that could best be described as contemporary Charlie Chan. Daughter Anna was finishing a Ph.D. in criminology and son Kim was also a college grad. Using their mix of modern and traditional techniques, the three Khans made a highly efficient team. Unfortunately, they did not attract an audience and the show was canceled after only four weeks on the air.

KID GLOVES

Sports

FIRST TELECAST: *February 24, 1951*
LAST TELECAST: *August 4, 1951*
BROADCAST HISTORY:

Feb 1951–Mar 1951, CBS Sat 7:30–8:00
Mar 1951–Aug 1951, CBS Sat 6:30–7:00

REGULARS:

Frank Goodman

Bill Sears
John De Grosa

Originating live from Philadelphia, where it had been a successful local show for several months prior to its moving to the full CBS network, *Kid Gloves* gave young children an opportunity to display their skills as boxers. Contestants ranged in age from three to twelve and fought three-round matches. The length of each round was between 30 seconds and one minute, depending on the age of the contestants. Frank Goodman was the referee, the judge, and the matchmaker. Bill Sears was the ringside announcer, and John De Grosa of the Pennsylvania State Athletic Commission interviewed celebrities from the sports world between rounds.

KIERNAN'S CORNER

Interview

FIRST TELECAST: *August 16, 1948*
LAST TELECAST: *March 30, 1949*
BROADCAST HISTORY:

Aug 1948–Sep 1948, ABC Mon 8:00–8:30
Sep 1948–Jan 1949, ABC Mon 7:30–8:00
Jan 1949–Mar 1949, ABC Mon 8:00–8:30

HOST:

Walter Kiernan

Newspaperman Walter Kiernan, a familiar face on early television, conducted this talk show. He interviewed tourists in New York and visited interesting places around the city with the ABC cameras.

KING COLE'S BIRTHDAY PARTY

see *Birthday Party*

KING FAMILY SHOW, THE

Musical Variety

FIRST TELECAST: *January 23, 1965*
LAST TELECAST: *September 10, 1969*
BROADCAST HISTORY:

Jan 1965–Sep 1965, ABC Sat 7:30–8:30
Sep 1965–Jan 1966, ABC Sat 8:00–8:30
Mar 1969–Sep 1969, ABC Wed 8:30–9:00

CAST:

The King Sisters (Yvonne, Luise, Marilyn, Alyce, Maxine, Donna), *et al.*

ORCHESTRA:

Alvino Rey Orchestra directed by Mitchell Ayres (1965–1966)
Ralph Carmichael (1969)

EXECUTIVE PRODUCER:

Nick Vanoff (1965–1966)
Yvonne King Burch and Luise King Rey (1969)

Thirty-seven—count 'em—37 King family members all singing on one stage at one time! Or was it 36? Or 41? Whatever it was, there was a lot of kin in this wholesome family musical series, which was a spinoff from a special appearance the Kings had made on *The Hollywood Palace* in August 1964. That appearance had drawn a reported 53,000 letters and a King Family series was assured.

At the center of things were the six King Sisters, a singing group popular since the early 1940s, when they had been part of Alvino Rey's orchestra. (Alvino was in fact married to one of them, Luise.) Sisters, brothers, husbands, nephews, cousins, and masses of kids were featured on this series (each of the King Sisters had from two to five offspring). Ages ranged from seven months to 79 years. The oldster was William King Driggs, the father, an old-time vaudevillian who had begun the family's musical tradition in 1921. Music ranged from semi-classical to semi-rock, interspersed with lots of gentle family humor. Alvino Rey had a regular spot with his talking guitar. A "Family Circle" segment, exploring in verse and song the meaning of familial happiness, was a regular feature. Each telecast ended with the family *en masse* singing "Love at Home."

All this built up an intensely loyal following. One viewing family, knowing what would move a sponsor's cold heart, wrote in that "the King Family program was beautiful, talented, and completely entertaining. We are buying Clairol and Wisk tomorrow." Apparently not enough Clairol and Wisk was sold, however, for the show was canceled after only a year.

A brief revival in 1969 spotlighted a more contemporary sub-group, the King Cousins, along with the sisters, Alvino, and the rest of the family.

KING'S CROSSROADS

see *Movies—Prior to 1961*

KINGS ROW

Drama

FIRST TELECAST: *September 13, 1955*
LAST TELECAST: *January 17, 1956*

BROADCAST HISTORY:

Sep 1955–Jan 1956, ABC Tue 7:30–8:30

CAST:

Dr. Parris Mitchell .... Jack Kelly
Randy Monaghan .... Nan Leslie
Drake McHugh .... Robert Horton
Dr. Tower .... Victor Jory
Grandma .... Lillian Bronson
Dr. Gordon .... Robert Burton

Romantic drama (soap opera, if you prefer) about young Dr. Parris Mitchell, who returned to his home town at the turn of the century to set up a psychiatric practice. There he encountered considerable resistance to his new methods, due to the superstitious citizenry and the tradition-bound medical practices of the day. Based on the Henry Bellamann novel and 1941 movie classic.

Kings Row was seen approximately every third week, being one of three rotating elements of *Warner Brothers Presents*.

KINGSTON: CONFIDENTIAL

Newspaper

FIRST TELECAST: *March 23, 1977*
LAST TELECAST: *August 10, 1977*
BROADCAST HISTORY:

Mar 1977–Aug 1977, NBC Wed 10:00–11:00

CAST:

R. B. Kingston .... Raymond Burr
Tony Marino .... Art Hindle
Beth Kelly .... Pamela Hensley
Jessica Frazier .... Nancy Olson

San Francisco was the home base of the Frazier Group, a communications conglomerate that owned and operated 26 newspapers and nine radio and TV stations around the country. Jessica Frazier was the chief operating officer and R. B. Kingston was one of her top executives, with a long history as one of the finest investigative reporters in the country. Despite his high status, Kingston was more than willing to leave the office and do his own digging to help unearth a particularly difficult or juicy story. His two young assistants, Tony and Beth, often went undercover to help track down useful information.

KIRBY STONE QUINTET, THE

see *Strictly for Laughs*

KLEENEX SUMMER THEATRE

Dramatic Anthology

FIRST TELECAST: *July 5, 1955*
LAST TELECAST: *August 16, 1955*
BROADCAST HISTORY:

Jul 1955–Aug 1955, NBC Tue 9:00–9:30

Kleenex Summer Theatre alternated with *Clorets Summer Theatre* as a 1955 summer replacement series for *Fireside Theater*. The dramas shown were all reruns of episodes from *Four Star Playhouse*.

KLONDIKE

Adventure

FIRST TELECAST: *October 10, 1960*
LAST TELECAST: *February 6, 1961*
BROADCAST HISTORY:

Oct 1960–Feb 1961, NBC Mon 9:00–9:30

CAST:

Mike Halliday .... Ralph Taeger
Jeff Durain .... James Coburn
Kathy O'Hara .... Mari Blanchard
Goldie .... Joi Lansing

Skagway, Alaska, at the turn of the century, was the setting of this action-adventure series. In Alaska in search of gold and excitement during the famous gold rush of 1897–1899, rugged Mike Halliday spent much of his time trying to outwit Jeff Durain, a gambler and scoundrel whose efforts to make money often put him on the wrong side of the law. Durain owned and ran a hotel in Skagway that provided miners with a place to lose their earnings in games of chance that were not always on the up-and-up. The town's honest hotel was run by Kathy O'Hara, who often worked with Mike to foil Durain's illegal schemes. Mike was not quite ready to settle down with a good woman and raise a family and was involved with a number of ladies, including Durain's girl friend and accomplice in crime, the beautiful but greedy Goldie.

KOBB'S KORNER

Musical Variety

FIRST TELECAST: *September 29, 1948*
LAST TELECAST: *June 8, 1949*
BROADCAST HISTORY:

Sep 1948–Jan 1949, CBS Wed 8:00–8:30
Jan 1949–Feb 1949, CBS Thu 8:00–8:30
Feb 1949, CBS Wed 9:00–9:30
Mar 1949–Jun 1949, CBS Wed 9:30–10:00

REGULARS:

Stan Fritts and His Korn Kobblers

Hope Emerson
Jo Hurt

This live series originated from New York but, if you could believe it, was supposed to come from Shufflebottom's General Store, U.S.A. The Korn Kobblers were a group of accomplished musicians who, in addition to playing straight music, used mouth harps, whistles, sirens, cowbells, jugs, washboards, and anything else that would make a noise. Actress Hope Emerson played Maw Shufflebottom, the owner of the general store, and Jo Hurt played her daughter Josiebelle. It was a little bit like a cross between *Hee Haw* and *Spike Jones* although it preceded them both, at least on television.

KODAK REQUEST PERFORMANCE

Dramatic Anthology

FIRST TELECAST: *April 13, 1955*
LAST TELECAST: *September 28, 1955*
BROADCAST HISTORY:
Apr 1955–Sep 1955, NBC Wed 8:00–8:30
HOST:
Jack Clark

The dramas presented on *Kodak Request Performance* were all reruns of episodes of dramatic series that had aired originally during the 1954–1955 television season, primarily on *Ford Theatre* and *Fireside Theater*. Jack Clark provided live introductions to the filmed dramas.

KODIAK

Police

FIRST TELECAST: *September 13, 1974*
LAST TELECAST: *October 11, 1974*
BROADCAST HISTORY:
Sep 1974–Oct 1974, ABC Fri 8:00–8:30
CAST:
Kodiak ....Clint Walker
Abraham Lincoln Imhook
.... Abner Biberman

Clint Walker was a cop with an unusual beat in this short-lived series. Kodiak was a member of the Alaska State Patrol, responsible for 50,000 square miles of rugged country and all the criminals, avalanche victims, and squabbling miners contained therein. He worked alone most of the time, traveling by four-wheel-drive truck, snowmobile, on skis, or snowshoes, as appropriate. Abraham Lincoln Imhook was his Eskimo friend and confidant. Filmed on location in Alaska.

KOJAK

Police

FIRST TELECAST: *October 24, 1973*
LAST TELECAST: *April 15, 1978*
BROADCAST HISTORY:
Oct 1973–Sep 1974, CBS Wed 10:00–11:00
Sep 1974–Sep 1975, CBS Sun 8:30–9:30
Sep 1975–Jan 1977, CBS Sun 9:00–10:00
Jan 1977–Sep 1977, CBS Mon 10:00–11:00
Sep 1977–Dec 1977, CBS Sun 10:00–11:00
Dec 1977–Apr 1978, CBS Sat 10:00–11:00
CAST:
Lt. Theo Kojak ....Telly Savalas
Frank McNeil ....Dan Frazer
Lt. Bobby Crocker ....Kevin Dobson
Det. Stavros ....George Savalas
Det. Rizzo (1974–1977) ....Vince Conti
Det. Saperstein (1974–1977)
.... Mark Russell

When they started out together in the New York Police Department, Theo Kojak and Frank McNeil had worked closely together and, for a number of years, been partners. Over the years Frank had worked his way up the hierarchy to the point where he was now chief of detectives for the 13th Precinct in the Manhattan South district. Kojak, who had a cynical sense of humor and was determined to do things his way regardless of what his bosses thought, was now working for him. Kojak was outspoken and streetwise, and was not above stretching the literal interpretation of the law if it would help him crack a case. Working closely with him was plainclothes detective Bobby Crocker, as close to a regular partner as he had.

The supporting role of Detective Stavros was played by Telly Savalas' brother George who, during the first two seasons the show was on the air, was billed as Demosthenes in the credits rather than by his real name. Starting with the 1976–1977 season, considerable location filming was done in New York with Kojak seen all over the city licking his trademark lollipops. *Kojak* received much favorable publicity from police departments around the country for its realistic portrayal of police work.

KOLCHAK: THE NIGHT STALKER

Occult

FIRST TELECAST: *September 13, 1974*

LAST TELECAST: *August 30, 1975*
BROADCAST HISTORY:
Sep 1974–Dec 1974, ABC Fri 10:00–11:00
Jan 1975–Aug 1975, ABC Fri 8:00–9:00
CAST:
Carl Kolchak ....Darren McGavin
Tony Vincenzo ....Simon Oakland
Updike ....Jack Grinnage
Emily ....Ruth McDevitt

Stories of the bizarre and supernatural, seen through the eyes of Carl Kolchak, crime reporter for Chicago's Independent News Service. The series was an odd mixture of reality and fantasy, with wisecracking reporter Kolchak and his common-sense investigations juxtaposed with inexplicable happenings. Instead of the usual hoods, Kolchak kept running into vampires, werewolves, zombies, and other esoteric phenomena. If he was sent to cover a crooked politician, he would find that the man had sold his soul to the Devil—literally. If he was covering a museum opening, a 500-year-old Aztec mummy would come to life. Kolchak's main trouble was convincing his skeptical editor, Tony Vincenzo, to print his incredible revelations.

Kolchak was based on the highly successful TV movie of the same name. It premiered, appropriately enough, on Friday the 13th, but lasted for only a single season.

KOLLEGE OF MUSICAL KNOWLEDGE, THE

see *Kay Kyser's Kollege of Musical Knowledge*

KOPYCATS, THE

see *ABC Comedy Hour*

KOVACS UNLIMITED

see *Ernie Kovacs Show, The*

KRAFT MUSIC HALL, THE

Musical Variety
FIRST TELECAST: *September 13, 1967*
LAST TELECAST: *May 12, 1971*
BROADCAST HISTORY:
Sep 1967–May 1969, NBC Wed 9:00–10:00
Sep 1969–May 1971, NBC Wed 9:00–10:00
ANNOUNCER:
Ed Herlihy
ORCHESTRA:
Peter Matz
CHOREOGRAPHY:
Peter Gennaro

From 1933 to 1949 *The Kraft Music Hall* was one of the most popular variety shows on radio. Bing Crosby was probably its most famous host, at the helm from 1936–1946. When Kraft moved into television in 1947, it switched to weekly dramatic productions as *Kraft Television Theatre.* The music-hall format first appeared on television in the 1958–1959 season as *Milton Berle Starring in the Kraft Music Hall* and *Kraft Music Hall Presents the Dave King Show. Perry Como's Kraft Music Hall* filled the Wednesday 9:00–10:00 P.M. hour for the next four seasons and there was a *Kraft Summer Music Hall* in 1966.

All of the above variations of *The Kraft Music Hall* had regular hosts, but beginning in the fall of 1967 each program became self-contained and featured a different host. During its first season there were a number of "theme" programs. Rock Hudson narrated "The Hollywood Musical," Lorne Greene hosted the musical potpourri "How the West Was Swung," George Burns did "Tin Pan Alley Today," and Dinah Shore "The Nashville Sound." Although the title emphasized music, there were telecasts that were all comedy—"Woody Allen Looks at 1967" and Groucho Marx hosting "A Taste of Funny." In the spring and summer of 1968 there were periods when the same host appeared for a number of weeks—Eddy Arnold with the series subtitled "County Fair" from April 24–June 5; John Davidson for the next three weeks; and Ed McMahon from July 3–September 4. While Eddy Arnold was hosting there was one regular along with him, comic John Byner.

Several performers who starred during the series' first season appeared during each of the succeeding seasons. In addition to Eddy Arnold, Don Rickles, and Alan King—the three stars who would appear most often throughout *The Kraft Music Hall*'s run—Steve Lawrence and Eydie Gorme were annual visitors. Others with multiple telecasts were Mitzi Gaynor, Bobby Darin, Roy Rogers and Dale Evans, Wayne Newton, and Johnny Cash. The Country Music Association Awards were telecast each year on *The Kraft Music Hall* and it was on this series that the Friars Club Roasts (later to become a semi-regular series of specials as "The Dean Martin Celebrity Roasts") first had national exposure. Johnny Carson, Milton Berle, Jack Benny, Don Rickles, and Jerry Lewis were all "roasted" over the years. During the last season there were two appearances by the Kopycats, talented impressionists who were later featured on *The ABC Comedy Hour*.

Summer replacements for the 1967–1971 versions of the *Kraft Music Hall* were Sandler and Young, and Don Ho in 1969, and English star Des O'Connor in 1970 and 1971.

KRAFT MUSIC HALL PRESENTS SANDLER & YOUNG

Variety

FIRST TELECAST: *May 14, 1969*
LAST TELECAST: *August 13, 1969*
BROADCAST HISTORY:
May 1969–Aug 1969, NBC Wed 9:00–10:00
REGULARS:
Tony Sandler
Ralph Young
Jack Parnell and His Orchestra
Judy Carne
Norman Wisdom

The 1969 summer replacement for *The Kraft Music Hall* was this taped variety show from London, hosted by singers Tony Sandler and Ralph Young. A regular feature of the series was "Hands Across the Sea," a combination of messages to America from London and a salute to a foreign country. Des O'Connor was originally slated to host this series. He got his chance in a London-originated summer series of his own during the following two summers (see *Kraft Music Hall Presents the Des O'Connor Show*).

KRAFT MUSIC HALL PRESENTS: THE DAVE KING SHOW

Variety

FIRST TELECAST: *May 20, 1959*
LAST TELECAST: *September 23, 1959*
BROADCAST HISTORY:
May 1959–Sep 1959, NBC Wed 9:00–9:30
STAR:
Dave King
REGULARS:
Sid Greene
Dick Hills
Alan MacAteer
Jim Boles
Barney Martin
Bobby Gale
The Jerry Packer Singers
The Bill Foster Dancers

English comedian/singer Dave King made his American television debut in this summer variety series. The format varied from music to skit, comic monologues, and pantomime, depending on the talents of his weekly guest stars. The variety was reflected in the show's theme song—"Anything Goes." One unusual aspect of this series was that its two writers, Sid Greene and Dick Hills, were also regular members of the on-air cast.

KRAFT MUSIC HALL PRESENTS THE DES O'CONNOR SHOW

Variety

FIRST TELECAST: *May 20, 1970*
LAST TELECAST: *September 1, 1971*
BROADCAST HISTORY:
May 1970–Sep 1970, NBC Wed 9:00–10:00
Jun 1971–Sep 1971, NBC Wed 9:00–10:00
STAR:
Des O'Connor
REGULARS:
Jack D. Douglas
The MacGregor Brothers (1970)
Jim Coulton and Rex (1970)
Patrick Newell (1970)
The Mike Sammes Singers
Jack Parnell and His Orchestra
Joe Baker (1971)
Connie Stevens (1971)
The New Faces (1971)

British TV personality Des O'Connor was the host and star of this London-originated summer replacement for *The Kraft Music Hall*. With Des was his long-time partner, Jack D. Douglas, whose regular role on the series was that of Alf Ippittimus, a stage-struck buffoon. When the series returned for its second summer run in 1971, the title was shortened to *The Des O'Connor Show* and included two new recurring weekly features—"Dandy Sandy" and "I Say I Say." The former was a satire on a children's television show and the latter a situation in which members of the cast would interrupt Des' attempt to recite something with snappy one-line jokes.

KRAFT MYSTERY THEATER

Dramatic Anthology

FIRST TELECAST: *June 14, 1961*
LAST TELECAST: *September 25, 1963*
BROADCAST HISTORY:
Jun 1961–Sep 1961, NBC Wed 9:00–10:00
Jun 1962–Sep 1962, NBC Wed 9:00–10:00
Jun 1963–Sep 1963, NBC Wed 9:00–10:00
HOST:
Frank Gallop (1961)

Filmed dramatic-anthology series, which served as summer replacement for Perry Como's *Kraft Music Hall.* The 1961 version consisted of mystery-suspense dramas, most of them filmed in England, originally for English television and theatrical distribution. Frank Gallop was host for the series. In 1962 American films shot at the Desilu Studios in Hollywood were used, some of them originals and some having already been seen on CBS' *Westinghouse Desilu Playhouse* from 1958–1960. Many top Hollywood actors were seen. In 1963 the films were provided by Hollywood's Revue Studios, some of them having been aired previously on *Alcoa Playhouse* from 1961–1963.

KRAFT MYSTERY THEATRE

see *Kraft Television Theatre* for 1958 series

KRAFT SUMMER MUSIC HALL, THE

Variety
FIRST TELECAST: *June 6, 1966*
LAST TELECAST: *August 29, 1966*
BROADCAST HISTORY:
Jun 1966–Aug 1966, NBC Mon 9:00–10:00
STAR:
John Davidson
REGULARS:
George Carlin
Jackie and Gayle
The Five King Cousins
The Lively Set

Handsome young singer John Davidson was the host and star of this summer variety series which placed its emphasis on youth. Most of the guest stars, as well as the series regulars, were performers in their twenties. Comedian George Carlin, in addition to performing on the show himself, wrote all of the comedy material. The Five King Cousins were members of the huge King family, which had had its own series on ABC.

KRAFT SUSPENSE THEATER

Dramatic Anthology
FIRST TELECAST: *October 10, 1963*
LAST TELECAST: *September 9, 1965*
BROADCAST HISTORY:
Oct 1963–Sep 1965, NBC Thu 10:00–11:00

Kraft, which had used both dramatic and musical offerings to promote its products on TV over the years, mixed the two formats in the 1963 and 1964 seasons. The emphasis was on drama, preempted by a Perry Como *Kraft Music Hall* special approximately once a month, all in the Thursday 10:00–11:00 P.M. time period (this in itself was a major change, as Kraft had "owned" the Wednesday 9:00–10:00 P.M. hour on NBC for the previous 15 years).

The dramas, which were filmed in Hollywood, employed top-name talent, with Lee Marvin, Gig Young, and Lloyd Bridges headlining during the first month that the series was on the air. Most of the plots concerned murder, psychological terror, or other stories of danger and mystery. Among these was "Rapture at Two Forty," presented in April 1965, the pilot for the later series *Run For Your Life.*

KRAFT TELEVISION THEATRE

Dramatic Anthology
FIRST TELECAST: *May 7, 1947*
LAST TELECAST: *October 1, 1958*
BROADCAST HISTORY:
May 1947–Dec 1947, NBC Wed 7:30–8:30
Jan 1948–Oct 1958, NBC Wed 9:00–10:00 (OS)
Oct 1953–Jan 1955, ABC Thu 9:30–10:30
ANNOUNCER:
Ed Herlihy (1947–1955)
Charles Stark (1955)
REGULAR PRODUCER/DIRECTORS:
Stanley Quinn
Maury Holland
Harry Hermann
Richard Dunlap
Fielder Cook
William Graham
Norman Morgan
David Susskind
Robert Herridge
Alex March

Kraft Foods Co. was one of the major supporters of live television drama during the 1950s, before switching to musical offerings in 1958. The *Kraft Television Theatre* was one of television's most prestigious showcases, winning top ratings and many awards, and becoming a Wednesday night institution. By the end of its run, more than 650 plays, drama and comedy, both originals and adaptations for TV, had been presented. At one time *two* Kraft Theatre series were airing simultaneously on NBC and ABC. All of these plays were live (although kinescopes and a very few videotapes were made for delayed transmission purposes), so most of these dramatic presentations are lost to us today.

Kraft skimped on nothing. The casts were large, the sets often elaborate, and the playwrights and producers first-rate. One "event" production in 1956 about the sinking of the *Titanic* almost seemed to have an actor for each of the 1502 souls who went down with that ill-fated ship! (Actually there were 107 in the cast.) A brief sampling of the actors and actresses who starred over the years would include E. G. Marshall (frequently), Jack Lemmon, Cyril Ritchard (his first U.S. TV appearance, in 1951), Rod Steiger, James Dean, Lee Remick, Art Carney, Joanne Woodward, Grace Kelly, Anthony Perkins—and many, many more. A number of performers who would later become film and TV stars gained early exposure on *Kraft*, including Cloris Leachman (1949), Martin Milner (1949) and Paul Newman (1952).

Scripts ranged from the classics (Shakespeare, Ibsen) to Tennessee Williams, Agatha Christie, and Rod Serling. Many new or unknown writers were given exposure too, and during the 1955–1956 season Kraft offered a $50,000 prize for the best original play presented during the year. Judges were Helen Hayes, Walter Kerr, and Maxwell Anderson. The prize went to William Noble for "Snap Finger Creek," telecast on February 22, 1956.

During the mid-1950s quite a few youth-oriented episodes were presented, mostly dramas revolving around popular music. Among the popular singers playing dramatic (and singing) roles were Gisele MacKenzie (1955), Ferlin Husky (1957), and Julius La Rosa (1957). Even more rock-oriented were actor-singer Tommy Sands, who starred in an Elvis Presley–type role in "The Singing Idol" in January 1957 (the featured song on this telecast, "Teenage Crush," went on to become a million-selling record); and Sal Mineo, who introduced his biggest hit, "Start Movin'," on the Kraft dramatic presentation "Drummer Man" in May 1957.

Another notable landmark in the series' history was the use of color, which began intermittently in April 1954 and became permanent in July 1956.

In April 1958 *Kraft Television Theatre* was taken over by a new production company and its title was shortened to *Kraft Theatre*. In June 1958 the title was changed again to *Kraft Mystery Theatre* (not to be confused with the filmed series of the same name in the early 1960s).

At the end of Kraft's long run in live TV drama, *TV Guide* summoned up a few statistics. In 11½ years *Kraft* had presented 650 plays culled from 18,845 scripts, starred or featured 3,955 actors and actresses in 6,750 roles, used up 26,000 hours of rehearsal time and employed 5,236 sets. Costs had risen from $3,000 for the first production on May 7, 1947 (a play called "Double Door" starring John Baragrey) to $165,000 by 1958. Ed Rice, the script editor for *Kraft* throughout the program's run, observed that the entire studio facilities used in 1947 were half the size of the space used just to produce the commercials in 1958.

But *Kraft*'s contribution to television is not measured in statistics alone. Quite simply, the series presented superlative live drama throughout television's "Golden Age."

KREISLER BANDSTAND

Music

FIRST TELECAST: *March 21, 1951*

LAST TELECAST: *June 13, 1951*

BROADCAST HISTORY:

Mar 1951–Jun 1951, ABC Wed 8:30–9:00

EMCEE:

Fred Robbins

Big-name dance bands were featured each week on this program, hosted by New York disc jockey Fred Robbins. Among those appearing were Ralph Flanagan, Sammy Kaye, Duke Ellington, Benny Goodman, Art Mooney, and Cab Calloway, as well as such singers as Patti Page, Ella Fitzgerald, and Margaret Whiting.

KUDA BUX, HINDU MYSTIC

Magic

FIRST TELECAST: *March 25, 1950*

LAST TELECAST: *June 17, 1950*

BROADCAST HISTORY:

Mar 1950–Jun 1950, CBS Sat 6:30–6:45

REGULARS:

Kuda Bux (real name: Khudah Bukhsh)
Rex Marshall

Kuda Bux, "the man with the X-ray eyes," was one of the favorite novelty acts on early television. After appearing as a regular on several series (including the appropriately named *I'd Like to See*), he had his own 15-minute network show in the spring of 1950. Feats of magic, mind reading, and other illusions were performed weekly by the man from Kashmir, India (who had been plying his trade in Europe for years before coming to the U.S.). The highlight always came when Kuda Bux's eyes were wrapped in bandages, tin foil, lead, and just about anything one might conceive of. On one show, sponsored by a bakery, he had his eyes covered with baker's dough. He would then proceed to "see" through it all to thread needles, hit bull's-eyes, and perform other feats.

Every viewer had a theory about how he did it. One lad said it was obvious that Kuda saw through his nose. A lady said Kuda marked off places on the floor just before he was blindfolded, and then just felt his way around. A little boy wrote in to say he believed Kuda swiveled his head completely around, and then saw out the back. Kuda Bux just laughed, and looked mystifying.

Rex Marshall served as announcer and interpreter on this series.

KUKLA, FRAN & OLLIE

Children's

FIRST TELECAST: *November 29, 1948*

LAST TELECAST: *August 31, 1957*

BROADCAST HISTORY:

Nov 1948–Nov 1951, NBC Mon–Fri 7:00–7:30 (OS)
Nov 1951–Jun 1952, NBC Mon–Fri 7:00–7:15
Sep 1954–Aug 1957, ABC Mon–Fri 7:00–7:15 (OS)

HOSTESS:

Fran Allison

PUPPETEER:

Burr Tillstrom

MUSICAL DIRECTOR:

Jack Fascinato

PUPPETS:

Kukla
Ollie (Oliver J. Dragon)
Fletcher Rabbit
Mme. Ophelia Oglepuss
Buelah Witch
Cecil Bill
Col. Crackie
Mercedes
Dolores Dragon (1950–1957)
Olivia Dragon (1952–1957)

This whimsical puppet show was one of television's longest-running and most loved children's programs. It was always done live, and the dialogue was unscripted, with Fran and her little friends reacting to each other in an entirely spontaneous manner.

Burr Tillstrom created Kukla, the first of his "Kuklapolitan Players," in 1936. The name Kukla was supposedly bestowed by the famous Russian ballerina Tamara Toumanova when she first saw the puppet perform (it means "doll" in Russian). The Kuklapolitan troupe was seen on experimental television as early as 1939, and the *Kukla, Fran & Ollie* series (originally known as *Junior Jamboree*) began locally on Chicago's WBKB-TV on October 13, 1947. It was fed to NBC's newly established Midwest network beginning in November 1948, and as soon as coaxial cables were opened to the East Coast (1949) and West Coast (1951) it was seen live in those regions as well.

The members of the Kuklapolitan Players were as follows: Kukla, a solemn, bulb-nosed little fellow with a perpetually worried expression, who knew nothing of his own past; Fran, a Chicago actress and singer, and the only live character seen (the puppets performed on a miniature stage, with Fran standing in front of it); Oliver J. Dragon, a carefree, extroverted, one-toothed dragon who was born in Vermont, where his parents ran Dragon Retreat (there had been no fire-breathing dragons in Ollie's family since his great-great-great-great-grandfather swam the Hellespont, gulped some water, and doused the flame); Fletcher Rabbit, the mailman, whose ears drooped so badly they had to be starched for formal occasions; Ophelia Oglepuss, a haughty ex-opera star; Buelah Witch, who had studied electronics and who patrolled the coaxial cable, while not buzzing around on her jet-propelled broomstick; Cecil Bill, the stage manager who spoke a language all his own; Col. Crackie, the long-winded Southern-Gentleman emcee of the company, and Buelah's escort; Mercedes, the troupe's ingenue; Dolores Dragon, infant daughter of Ollie's long-lost Uncle Dorchester (Ollie considered her a horrible little monster); and Olivia Dragon, Ollie's elderly mother, who had hair 75 yards long, *two* fine teeth and a sharp New England accent.

In addition to episodes focusing on day-to-day experiences and songs, the Players sometimes presented full-dress productions, ranging from mild satires ("Martin Dragon, Private Tooth") to established operettas. *The Mikado,* with Kukla as Nanki Poo, Fran as Yum Yum, and Ollie as the Lord High Executioner, was an annual event for several years. There were also original musical plays, such as *St. George and the Dragon,* presented in June 1953, complete with musical accompaniment by Arthur Fiedler and the Boston Pops and Boston Mayor John B. Hines as special guest. This show was repeated in August 1953 as one of the first experimental telecasts in compatible color.

In addition to its prime-time telecasts, listed above, *Kukla, Fran & Ollie* appeared in weekend and late-afternoon time slots during various periods (including 1952–1954). It has been seen in numerous non-network revivals and special appearances in the 1960s and 1970s.

KUNG FU

Western

FIRST TELECAST: *October 14, 1972*
LAST TELECAST: *June 28, 1975*
BROADCAST HISTORY:

Oct 1972–Nov 1972, ABC Sat 8:00–9:00
Jan 1973–Aug 1974, ABC Thu 9:00–10:00
Sep 1974–Oct 1974, ABC Sat 9:00–10:00
Nov 1974–Jan 1975, ABC Fri 8:00–9:00
Jan 1975–Jun 1975, ABC Sat 8:00–9:00

CAST:

Kwai Chang Caine .... David Carradine
Master Po .... Keye Luke
Master Kan .... Philip Ahn
Caine (as a youth) .... Radames Pera
Margit McLean (occasional 1974–1975)
.... Season Hubley

Kung Fu could probably best be classified as a philosophical Western. It attracted quite a bit of notoriety and a cult following in the early 1970s, due to its unusual protagonist. Caine was a shaven-headed Buddhist monk, and a hunted man. He had been born in China in the mid-1800s of Chinese and American parents, and was raised as an orphan by the monks of Shaolin Temple. They tutored him in a mystic philosophy of internal harmony and the "oneness of all things," and a code of nonviolence. They also taught him the martial arts of kung fu—just in case.

Then one day young Caine was involved in an incident in which he was forced to kill a member of the Chinese royal family. Fleeing China, he landed in the American West where he began a search for a long-lost brother—while he himself was pursued by Chinese Imperial agents and American bounty hunters.

Besides his background, there were many other unusual things about this particular Western hero. He spoke very little, uttering occasional cryptic statements about the nature of being and universal harmony ("Remember," his teachers had said, "the wise man walks always with his head bowed, humble, like the dust"); his use, when cornered, of the ancient Chinese martial arts instead of a gun; his pariah status—a Chinaman, as well as a hunted man. *Kung Fu* used many gimmicks to lend it a surreal aspect, such as slow-motion photography, and included frequent flashbacks to Caine's days as a youth in China (in which his teachers, Master Po and Master Kan, appeared, as well as Caine as a young boy). Caine was usually a loner, although in the final season an American cousin, Margit, began to make occasional appearances.

The star, David Carradine, was responsible for much of the publicity surrounding this show. A member of a respected theatrical family (his father, John Carradine, had appeared in many famous movies of the 1930s and 1940s), David dropped out of Hollywood's glittering world and lived a decidedly unconventional life in a ramshackle old house in the hills, reflecting the same philosophy of mysticism and "oneness with nature" that Caine represented.

Kung Fu, incidentally, translates roughly as "accomplishment technique," and is China's ancient science of personal combat, from which karate and judo are derived. It enjoyed quite a vogue in the U.S. during the late 1960s and early 1970s as a result of the movies of Chinese-American actor Bruce Lee.

LADIES BE SEATED

Quiz/Audience Participation

FIRST TELECAST: *April 22, 1949*

LAST TELECAST: *June 10, 1949*

BROADCAST HISTORY:

Apr 1949–Jun 1949, ABC Fri 8:30–9:00

EMCEE:

Tom Moore

ASSISTANT:

Phil Patton

This TV version of the long-running radio show featured a quiz and penalty stunts for members of the studio audience. The stunts were similar to those generally found on such shows, such as a blindfolded couple after an apple on a string, a man racing to put on women's clothes, etc. From Chicago.

LAMB'S GAMBOL, THE

Musical Variety

FIRST TELECAST: *February 27, 1949*

LAST TELECAST: *May 22, 1949*

BROADCAST HISTORY:

Feb 1949–Mar 1949, NBC Sun 8:30–9:00
Mar 1949–May 1949, NBC Sun 8:00–8:30

Musical variety program using the resources of New York's famed theatrical association, the Lamb's Club. Broadway stars, old vaudevillians, and newcomers appeared each week to do their turns, or to reverse roles (such as a tragedian doing a song-and-dance routine). A different host presided each week, and there were no regulars.

LANCER

Western

FIRST TELECAST: *September 24, 1968*

LAST TELECAST: *September 9, 1971*

BROADCAST HISTORY:

Sep 1968–Jun 1970, CBS Tue 7:30–8:30
May 1971–Sep 1971, CBS Thu 8:00–9:00

CAST:

Johnny Madrid Lancer ....James Stacy
Scott Lancer ....Wayne Maunder
Murdoch Lancer ....Andrew Duggan
Teresa O'Brien ....Elizabeth Baur
Jelly Hoskins (1969–1970) ... Paul Brinegar

Set in California during the 1870s, *Lancer* was the story of the struggles of a landowner against locals who were trying to take over his property by force. Old Murdoch Lancer was no longer able to defend his cattle and sheep ranch in the San Joaquin Valley by himself, and even trying to run it with only the help of his attractive young ward, Teresa, had become difficult. At his behest his two sons (from different marriages) came to the ranch to help their father. The half brothers had never met each other and had widely divergent backgrounds. Johnny was a drifter/gunfighter who had spent most of his life wandering around the border towns of the Southwest. Scott was a sophisticated college graduate who had been living in Boston. Despite their differences, they learned to respect each other and help their father manage his vast real estate holdings. Jelly Hoskins, a crochety old ranch hand, became a regular member of the cast for the second season. The episodes telecast during the summer of 1971 were all reruns.

LAND OF THE GIANTS

Science Fiction

FIRST TELECAST: *September 22, 1968*

LAST TELECAST: *September 6, 1970*

BROADCAST HISTORY:

Sep 1968–Sep 1970, ABC Sun 7:00–8:00

CAST:

Capt. Steve Burton ....Gary Conway
Mark Wilson ....Don Matheson
Barry Lockridge ....Stefen Arngrim
Dan Erikson ....Don Marshall
Valerie Scott ....Deanna Lund
Betty Hamilton ....Heather Young
Cdr. Alexander Fitzhugh .....Kurt Kasznar
Inspector Kobrick ....Kevin Hagen

CREATOR/PRODUCER:

Irwin Allen

This science-fiction fantasy concerned seven very small people in a very large world. Seven Earthlings had been on a suborbital flight from the U.S. to London in the mid-1980s when their craft was drawn into a "space warp." They landed in a strange world, much like the Earth but with inhabitants 12 times their size. As the space castaways attempted to repair their rocketship in order to try and get home, they were continually menaced by giant children, huge pets and insects, and inhabitants who would exhibit them as freaks or experiment on them.

Capt. Steve Burton, his co-pilot Dan

Erikson, and stewardess Betty Hamilton made up the crew of the lost craft, while on the passenger roster were engineer-tycoon Mark Wilson, jet-set (rocket-set?) heiress Valerie Scott, 12-year-old Barry and his dog Chipper, and mystery passenger Cdr. Fitzhugh. Tracking the Earth people down in the giant world was the responsibility of Inspector Kobrick of S.I.B., a security agency.

LANIGAN'S RABBI

Police

FIRST TELECAST: *January 30, 1977*
LAST TELECAST: *July 3, 1977*
BROADCAST HISTORY:
Jan 1977–Jul 1977, NBC Sun Various
CAST:
Chief Paul Lanigan .... Art Carney
Rabbi David Small .... Bruce Solomon
Kate Lanigan .... Janis Paige
Miriam Small .... Janet Margolin
Bobbie Whittaker .... Barbara Carney
Lt. Osgood .... Robert Doyle

Paul Lanigan was the police chief of the small town of Cameron, California. A local rabbi and close personal friend of his was David Small. David was an amateur criminologist who had become quite good at analyzing clues and deducing the perpetrator of a crime. He had become so good, in fact, that his friend Paul had become somewhat dependent on his assistance in cracking tough cases. Not only did they work together, they spent many evenings socializing with their wives, who tended to get rather aggravated when the conversation inevitably turned to the latest case. The role of the persistent local reporter, Bobbie Whittaker, was played by Art Carney's daughter Barbara.

Lanigan's Rabbi was based on a series of novels by Harry Kemelman, the first of which was *Friday the Rabbi Slept Late*. In 1977 it aired in rotation with *Columbo*, *McCloud*, and *McMillan* under the umbrella title *The NBC Sunday Mystery Movie*.

LANNY ROSS SHOW, THE

see *Swift Show, The*

LARAMIE

Western

FIRST TELECAST: *September 15, 1959*
LAST TELECAST: *September 17, 1963*
BROADCAST HISTORY:
Sep 1959–Sep 1963, NBC Tue 7:30–8:30
CAST:
Slim Sherman .... John Smith
Jess Harper .... Robert Fuller
Jonesy (1959–1960) ..... Hoagy Carmichael
Andy Sherman (1959–1961) .... Bobby Crawford, Jr.
Mike Williams (1961–1963) .... Dennis Holmes
Daisy Cooper (1961–1963) .... Spring Byington
Mort Corey (1960–1963) .... Stuart Randall

Two brothers determined to maintain the family ranch after the death of their father were the central characters in this Western, which was set in the Wyoming Territory of the 1870s. After their father had been shot by a land-grabber, the responsibility of running the ranch had fallen to Slim and his 14-year-old brother Andy. Although possessed of great potential, the ranch had been barely able to provide a living for the Shermans before their father's death. Only Jonesy, a friend of their father who had helped raise them, was around to help run the ranch. In the first episode, however, a drifter named Jess Harper wandered in and was persuaded to settle down and throw in his lot with them. In addition to raising cattle, the Shermans used their ranch as a relay station for stagecoach traffic into and out of nearby Laramie, which accounted for many a desperado passing through.

There were cast changes. Jonesy, played by veteran singer-composer Hoagy Carmichael, left the show at the start of the second season while Sheriff Mort Corey of Laramie became a regular. Young Andy, who had previously left the ranch and appeared only occasionally, was gone entirely by 1961, at the same time that two new members were added to the household. Mike Williams, an orphan whose parents had been killed by Indians, joined the family, and Daisy Cooper took over the job of housekeeper and surrogate mother in the previously all-male household.

LAREDO

Western

FIRST TELECAST: *September 16, 1965*
LAST TELECAST: *September 1, 1967*
BROADCAST HISTORY:
Sep 1965–Sep 1966, NBC Thu 8:30–9:30
Sep 1966–Sep 1967, NBC Fri 10:00–11:00

CAST:

Reese Bennett .... Neville Brand
Chad Cooper .... Peter Brown
Joe Riley .... William Smith
Capt. Edward Parmalee .... Philip Carey
Erik Hunter (1966–1967) ... Robert Wolders

Stories of the Texas Rangers in the post–Civil War era were told with humor as well as action in this series. The stories centered around three members of Company B and their senior officer, Capt. Parmalee. Former Union Army officer Reese Bennett was already in his forties when he joined the Rangers, and his age was quite a source of amusement to the two much younger rangers who were his partners. Riley had been a gunfighter whose activities were not always completely legal, and he had joined the Rangers because he liked action but wanted sanctuary from lawmen in other territories who were after him. Cooper, a Boston native and wartime member of the Border Patrol, joined the Rangers after the war to continue his hunt for the American gunrunners who had sold arms to the Mexicans who had wiped out most of his comrades. All three retained a sense of humor about life, however, and Capt. Parmalee, a stern man who assigned them their missions, sometimes found their jokes and horseplay rather frustrating. Erik Hunter was added to the cast in the second season as a new Ranger.

LARRY STORCH SHOW, THE

Comedy Variety

FIRST TELECAST: *July 11, 1953*
LAST TELECAST: *September 12, 1953*
BROADCAST HISTORY:

Jul 1953–Sep 1953, CBS Sat 8:00–9:00

REGULARS:

Larry Storch
Ray Bloch and His Orchestra

Young nightclub comic Larry Storch was the star of this live 1953 summer replacement for *The Jackie Gleason Show.* Guest stars were featured along with Larry's odd assortment of sketch characters, built up from his club act. Among the characters were Victor, a 10-year-old troublemaking monster; Smilie Higgins, a TV cowboy; and Railroad Jack, a philosophical hobo.

LASH OF THE WEST

Children's

FIRST TELECAST: *January 4, 1953*
LAST TELECAST: *April 26, 1953*
BROADCAST HISTORY:

Jan 1953–Apr 1953, ABC Sun 6:30–6:45

HOST:

Lash La Rue

Lash La Rue, one of the popular movie cowboy stars of the 1940s, demonstrated "tricks of Western gunmen," "the bullwhip," and other skills on this short-lived network program.

LASSIE

Adventure

FIRST TELECAST: *September 12, 1954*
LAST TELECAST: *September 12, 1971*
BROADCAST HISTORY:

Sep 1954–Jun 1955, CBS Sun 7:00–7:30
Sep 1955–Sep 1971, CBS Sun 7:00–7:30

CAST:

Jeff Miller (1954–1957) .... Tommy Rettig
Ellen Miller (1954–1957) .... Jan Clayton
"Gramps" Miller (1954–1957)
.... George Cleveland
Sylvester "Porky" Brockway (1954–1957)
.... Donald Keeler
Timmy (1957–1964) .... Jon Provost
Doc Weaver (1957–1964) ..... Arthur Space
Ruth Martin (1957–1958)
.... Cloris Leachman
Paul Martin (1957–1958) ..... Jon Shepodd
Uncle Petrie Martin (1958–1959)
.... George Chandler
Ruth Martin (1958–1964) .... June Lockhart
Paul Martin (1958–1964) ...... Hugh Reilly
Boomer Bates (1958–1959) .... Todd Ferrell
Cully Wilson (1963–1964) ..... Andy Clyde
Corey Stuart (1964–1969) ...... Robert Bray
Scott Turner (1968–1970) .... Jed Allen
Bob Erickson (1968–1970) ... Jack De Mave

LASSIE'S TRAINER:

Rudd Weatherwax

The one constant in this favorite long-running children's adventure series was Lassie, a brave, loyal, and remarkably intelligent collie. Lassie was always alert, ready to help her masters and protect them from evil and adversity. In fact, her heroics were often incredible—leading lost persons to safety, warning of all sorts of impending disasters, tending the sick and manipulating various human devices with ease. Fortunately Lassie was able to shift her allegiances periodically, for she was required to go through several sets of owners during her long career.

As originally conceived, *Lassie* was the story of a young boy and his companion collie. The boy was Jeff Miller, who lived on a small modern farm outside the town of Calverton with his widowed mother and his grandfather. In the spring of 1957 a runaway orphan boy named Timmy was brought in by Lassie and joined the Miller household. That fall Gramps died suddenly (actor George Cleveland in fact died soon after the start of the season). Ellen Miller found that she and Jeff could not work the farm alone, so she sold it to the Martins and moved to the city. Lassie and the orphan Timmy remained behind in the care of the Martins, who were childless, and Timmy became Lassie's new companion in weekly adventures.

By 1964 the Martins decided to leave the farm, responding to an advertisement for free land in Australia. Timmy went with them but Lassie could not go—due to animal quarantine regulations. The collie was left for a time in the care of an elderly friend of the family, Cully Wilson, but he subsequently suffered a heart attack. Lassie trotted off to get help from forest ranger Corey Stuart, and soon found herself with a new master. By this time Lassie was beginning to get the feeling that human masters are a temporary thing. In her adventures with ranger Corey, the scope of her exploits widened considerably, as she traveled with him to various parts of the country and situations far more exotic than those encountered around the farm. The premise of a small boy and his dog was gone completely.

In the fall of 1968 Corey was seriously hurt fighting a forest fire, and the Forest Service chief assigned two other rangers, Scott Turner and Bob Erickson, to watch over Lassie. By this time, however, her exploits were often independent of human help, and her contact with the two new rangers was not as frequent as it had been with Corey. By the start of the final season Lassie had become a wanderer without any human companionship at all. The ultimate step in her progression to independence came in a special seven-part story that began the 1970–1971 season. Lassie met a male collie, fell in love, and bore him a litter of puppies. In reality that would have been quite a trick, for all of the many collies that had portrayed Lassie over the years were male.

LASSIE AND TIMMY

syndicated title for *Lassie*

LAST WORD, THE

Informational/Panel

FIRST TELECAST: *June 2, 1957*
LAST TELECAST: *May 25, 1958*
BROADCAST HISTORY:
Jun 1957–Sep 1957, CBS Sun 6:00–6:30
Mar 1958–May 1958, CBS Sun 6:00–6:30
HOST:
Dr. Bergen Evans

The wonderful world of grammar and language was explored each week in this series which requested viewers to send in questions to be discussed by Dr. Evans and a rotating panel of linguistic experts. As the CBS press release announcing its premiere said, the series would cover "... such things as euphemisms, regional dialects, occupational lingo, metaphors and similes, pronunciation, British versus American words and usage, clichés, figures of speech, slang, secret languages (like pig Latin), journalese ..." The series premiered in January as a Sunday afternoon entry but moved into evening hours for the summer of 1957 and the spring of 1958.

LATE SUMMER EARLY FALL BERT CONVY SHOW, THE

Musical Variety

FIRST TELECAST: *August 25, 1976*
LAST TELECAST: *September 15, 1976*
BROADCAST HISTORY:
Aug 1976–Sep 1976, CBS Wed 8:00–8:30
REGULARS:
Bert Convy
Henry Polic II
Sallie Janes
Marty Barris
Donna Ponterotto
Lenny Schultz

Bert Convy, who was the host of the CBS daytime game show *Tattletales*, was the singing and comedy star of this four-week summer mini-series. The only guest star to appear on the show was Don Knotts, on the premiere telecast. Bert and his comedy troupe, featuring Lenny Schultz as Lenny the Bionic Chicken, performed all of the musical and comedy numbers.

LAUGH-IN

see *Rowan and Martin's Laugh-In*

LAUGH LINE

Quiz/Audience Participation

FIRST TELECAST: *April 16, 1959*

LAST TELECAST: *June 11, 1959*

BROADCAST HISTORY:

Apr 1959–Jun 1959, NBC Thu 9:00–9:30

EMCEE:

Dick Van Dyke

REGULAR:

Dorothy Loudon

A changing group of comedians enacted a silent comedy routine submitted by a viewer in this short-lived show. The celebrity panel would then suggest punch lines for the routine. Prizes for the person submitting the routine were determined by which punch line was funnier, the one submitted with the sketch or the one supplied by the pros. The panelists were generally comedians or comedy writers, with Dorothy Loudon the only regular. The young comedy team of Mike Nichols and Elaine May, though not regulars, made several appearances.

LAUGHS FOR SALE

Comedy

FIRST TELECAST: *October 20, 1963*

LAST TELECAST: *December 22, 1963*

BROADCAST HISTORY:

Oct 1963–Dec 1963, ABC Sun 10:00–10:30

EMCEE:

Hal March

Each week a panel composed of prominent comics and comediennes participated in this series which sought to give young comedy writers exposure and help. The material that the writers submitted—sketches, monologues, routines, etc.—was performed by the members of the panel who then discussed the strong and weak points they perceived in it. Panel members changed each week, but Shecky Greene, Mickey Rooney, and Phil Foster appeared frequently.

LAVERNE & SHIRLEY

Situation Comedy

FIRST TELECAST: *January 27, 1976*

LAST TELECAST:

BROADCAST HISTORY:

Jan 1976– , ABC Tue 8:30–9:00

CAST:

Laverne De Fazio ....Penny Marshall
Shirley Feeney ....Cindy Williams
Carmine Ragusa ....Eddie Mekka
Frank De Fazio ....Phil Foster
Andrew "Squiggy" Squiggman
.....................David L. Lander
Lenny Kolowski ....Michael McKean
Mrs. Edna Babish ....Betty Garrett
Rosie Greenbaum (1976–1977)
.......................Carole Ita White

THEME:

"Making Our Dreams Come True," by Norman Gimbel and Charles Fox; sung by Cyndi Grecco.

This 1950s-era comedy was about two spunky girls from lower-class backgrounds, without much education, with no money, but with the determination to get ahead. They worked on an assembly line in the bottle-cap division of the Shotz Brewery in Milwaukee. Laverne was the quick-tempered, defensive one, always afraid of getting hurt (which she usually did)—a glib realist. Shirley was naive and trusting, a sucker for a sad story. Others in the cast included Lenny and Squiggy, the girls' screwball neighbors and truckdrivers at the plant; amorous Carmine, "The Big Ragu"; Laverne's father Frank, owner of the Pizza Bowl, a local hangout; Mrs. Babish, the sardonic landlady; and Rosie, an uppity friend.

Laverne & Shirley was a spinoff of sorts from *Happy Days* (in which the girls appeared only briefly), set in the same city and period, and the girls' friend Fonzie sometimes stopped by to say hello. With friends like that *Laverne & Shirley* shot to the top of the ratings. During the 1977–1978 season it was the number one program on television.

The theme song of this series was on the hit parade in 1976 in a recording by Cyndi Grecco, who was also heard on the show.

LAW AND MR. JONES, THE

Lawyer

FIRST TELECAST: *October 7, 1960*

LAST TELECAST: *October 4, 1962*

BROADCAST HISTORY:

Oct 1960–Sep 1961, ABC Fri 10:30–11:00
Apr 1962–Oct 1962, ABC Thu 9:30–10:00

CAST:

Abraham Lincoln Jones ...James Whitmore

Marsha Spear .... Janet De Gore
C. E. Carruthers .... Conlan Carter

That a man with a name like Abraham Lincoln Jones was honest was a foregone conclusion. This particular Abe was an attorney with great compassion for people, and a willingness to fight both literally and figuratively for his clients. His penchant for quoting Oliver Wendell Holmes did nothing to lessen his appeal. His cases rarely involved violence, however. Fraud, embezzlement, and jurisdictional disputes were the issues he most frequently addressed himself to. Abe's law clerk was young C. E. Carruthers, and his winsome secretary was Marsha Spear.

ABC canceled this series after its initial season, but viewer response, in the form of thousands of angry letters, was so strong that it was brought back the following April. Alas, the size of its audience did not increase and it was canceled again in October.

LAW OF THE PLAINSMAN

Western

FIRST TELECAST: *October 1, 1959*
LAST TELECAST: *September 24, 1962*
BROADCAST HISTORY:

Oct 1959–Sep 1960, NBC Thu 7:30–8:00
Jul 1962–Sep 1962, ABC Mon 8:30–9:00

CAST:

Deputy U.S. Marshal Sam Buckhart .... Michael Ansara
Marshal Andy Morrison ... Dayton Lummis
Tess Logan .... Gina Gillespie
Martha Commager .... Nora Marlowe

The struggle to reconcile Indian and white man in the wild New Mexico Territory of the 1880s was the subject of this series. The plainsman was Deputy U.S. Marshal Sam Buckhart, a lawman with a unique past. Born an Apache Indian, and known among the Indians as Buck Heart, he had befriended and nursed back to health a cavalry captain who had been wounded in an Indian ambush. When the captain died two years later, he left the youth money for an education at private schools and Harvard University.

Having acquired tremendous respect for the white man's laws and the U.S. Constitution, Sam returned to the troubled territory where he had spent his youth, determined to become a marshal. He served under Marshal Andy Morrison in Santa Fe, while living in a rooming house run by Martha Commager. The only other female in his life was eight-year-old Tess Logan, an orphan he had rescued from a stagecoach mishap. Martha served as a kind of surrogate mother for both Sam and his young ward.

Reruns of this NBC series were aired on ABC during the summer of 1962.

LAWLESS YEARS, THE

Police

FIRST TELECAST: *April 16, 1959*
LAST TELECAST: *September 22, 1961*
BROADCAST HISTORY:

Apr 1959–Jun 1959, NBC Thu 8:00–8:30
Jul 1959–Sep 1959, NBC Thu 8:30–9:00
Oct 1959–Mar 1960, NBC Thu 10:30–11:00
May 1961–Sep 1961, NBC Fri 9:00–9:30

CAST:

Barney Ruditsky .... James Gregory
Max .... Robert Karnes

The setting of this police drama was wide-open New York City in the Roaring Twenties, city of speakeasies, gangsters, bathtub gin, and flappers. The exploits of Police Detective Barney Ruditsky in his fight against organized crime were portrayed. *The Lawless Years* had a certain claim to authenticity, both in its meticulous attention to period detail and in the fact that it was based (loosely) on actual cases of a real-life New York cop named Barney Ruditsky. The careers of real gangsters of the period were depicted, although with fictitious names.

Six months after *The Lawless Years* premiered, *The Untouchables*, treating the same subject but with Chicago rather than New York as the background, began on ABC. *The Lawless Years* folded soon after, but the success of *The Untouchables* inspired a revival with new episodes in the summer of 1961.

The real Barney Ruditsky, who had retired from police work in 1941 and was running a West Coast detective agency, was the technical advisor for *The Lawless Years*.

LAWMAN, THE

Western

FIRST TELECAST: *October 5, 1958*
LAST TELECAST: *October 2, 1962*

BROADCAST HISTORY:

Oct 1958–Apr 1962, ABC Sun 8:30–9:00
Apr 1962–Oct 1962, ABC Sun 10:30–11:00

CAST:

Marshal Dan Troop ....John Russell
Deputy Johnny McKay ....Peter Brown
Lily Merrill (1959–1962) ......Peggy Castle
Jake (1961–1962) ....Dan Sheridan

The "lawman" in this straightforward Western was Marshal Dan Troop of Laramie, a granite-jawed, taciturn type. With his string tie and fatherly mustache, John Russell looked the part. There were no tricks or gimmicks in *Lawman*, just simple stories of desperadoes brought to justice by the long, stern arm of the law. Playing off Troop's fatherly image was his young deputy, Johnny McKay. Lily Merrill arrived in town during the second season to open the Birdcage Saloon and help the righteous marshal unbend a bit.

LAWRENCE WELK SHOW, THE

Music

FIRST TELECAST: *July 2, 1955*
LAST TELECAST: *September 4, 1971*
BROADCAST HISTORY:

Jul 1955–Sep 1963, ABC Sat 9:00–10:00
Sep 1963–Jan 1971, ABC Sat 8:30–9:30
Jan 1971–Sep 1971, ABC Sat 7:30–8:30

HOST:

Lawrence Welk

CHAMPAGNE LADY:

Alice Lon (1955–1959)
Norma Zimmer (1960–1971)

ORIGINAL REGULARS (1955):

Aladdin, violin (1955–1967)
Jerry Burke, piano-organ (1955–1965)
Dick Dale, saxophone, vocals (1955–1971)
Myron Floren, accordion (1955–1971)
Larry Hooper, piano, bass vocals (1955–1971)
Dick Kesner, violin (1955–1959)
Bob Lido, violin (1955–1971)
Tiny Little, Jr., piano (1955–1959)
Buddy Merrill, guitar (1955–1971)
Jim Roberts, vocals (1955–1971)
Rocky Rockwell, trumpet, gravel-voiced vocals (1955–1962)
Sparklers Quartet (1955–1957)

LATER REGULARS (in order they joined):

Lennon Sisters (Dianne, Peggy, Kathy, Janet) (1955–1968)
Larry Dean, vocals (1956–1960)
Frank Scott, piano, arranger (1956–1969)
Maurice Pearson, vocals (1957–1960)
Joe Feeney, Irish tenor (1957–1971)
Jack Imel, tap dancer (1957–1971)
Alvan Ashby, hymn singer (1957–1959)
Pete Fountain, Dixieland clarinet (1957–1959)
Jo Ann Castle, ragtime piano (1959–1969)
Jimmy Getzoff, violin (1960–1962)
Bobby Burgess and Barbara Boylan, dancers (1961–1967)
(Boylan replaced by Cissy King, 1967–1971)
Joe Livoti, violin (1962–1971)
Bob Ralston, piano-organ (1963–1971)
Art Duncan, dancer (1964–1971)
Steve Smith, vocals (1965–1969)
Natalie Nevins, vocals (1965–1969)
The Blenders, vocal quartet (1965–1967)
Lynn Anderson, vocals (1967–1968)
Andra Willis, vocals (1967–1969)
Tanya Falan, vocals (1968–1971)
Sandi Jensen and Salli Flynn, vocals (1968–1971)
Hotsy Totsy Boys (1969–1971)
Ralna English, vocals (1969–1971)
Clay Hart, vocals (1969–1971)
Guy Hovis, vocals (1970–1971)
Peanuts Hucko, clarinet (1970–1971)

THEME:

"Bubbles in the Wine," by Lawrence Welk, Frank Loesser, and Bob Calame

Lawrence Welk's Champagne Music was first heard on network television as a summer replacement program in 1955. The critics were not impressed. Reviewing the program at the end of the summer, *TV Guide* remarked smugly: "The program lacks the necessary sparkle and verve to give it a chance against any really strong competition. But it has been a satisfactory summertime entry. . . ." That proved to be the misjudgment of the year. Welk went on to a phenomenal 16-year network run on Saturday nights, and became one of the major musical success stories in all of TV history. From 1956 to 1959 he had *two* weekly hours on ABC, and he maintained good ratings throughout his run. In fact, when his program was finally canceled by ABC in 1971 it was primarily because his audience was "too old"—not too small. Welk then assembled a syndicated network of his own and even today continues to attract a bigger audience than most network shows.

The Welk formula was good, old-fashioned, melodic music, unadorned and straightforwardly presented. Old folks loved it. This was the one place on TV—probably in all of modern media—where "I Love You Truly" could be heard sung completely straight. Moreover, everyone on the show was completely good, clean, and wholesome (or else they were fired). Welk himself had about as much stage presence as Ed Sullivan, but that did not stop either of them. The maestro read stiffly through the brief introductions, and his thick accent was the butt of endless jokes. But when he played his accordion (which was rarely) or danced with one of the ladies in the audience, viewers loved it.

Much of the appeal of the program lay with its close-knit family of performers. Practically every player in the band was given a chance to solo from time to time, though some (listed above) were seen more often than others. Welk, who was highly sensitive to viewers' letters, kept a "fever chart" on which each comment on a performer, pro or con, was carefully tallied. Performers with a lot of favorable comments were featured more, and those in disfavor with the letter-writing public tended to disappear from view. The viewer, too, was part of the "family."

Probably the most famous of Welk's alumni were "da lovely Lennon Sisters," who were first brought to his attention in 1955 by his son, Lawrence, Jr., who was dating Dianne Lennon at the time. Lawrence, Sr., signed them immediately. They first appeared on his Christmas Eve 1955 broadcast, and stayed for more than 12 years. Dianne left to get married in 1960, and the quartet was only a trio until her return in 1964.

Other favorites included accordionist Myron Floren, who was also the assistant conductor; deep-voiced singer-pianist Larry Hooper (who was off the show from 1967–1971 due to heart trouble); dancers Bobby Burgess and Barbara Boylan; and Aladdin (real name: Aladdin Abdullah Achmed Anthony Pallante), the mustachioed violinist who also did dramatic readings. High point of the season was the annual Christmas show, when all the band members brought their children and Larry Hooper dressed up as Santa Claus for fun and gifts.

Most of Welk's musical family stayed with him for years, but there were a few highly publicized walkouts. Welk has always been a very strait-laced individual, and his moral as well as musical regimentation grated on some performers. Perhaps the most traumatic incident for Welk was his firing of Champagne Lady Alice Lon in July 1959, because she showed "too much knee" on camera. "Cheesecake does not fit our show," charged an angry Welk. "All I did was sit on a desk and cross my legs," replied Miss Lon. "That is the way a lady sits down." Welk got thousands of angry letters for his action, which evidently caused him second thoughts. He tried to get Alice back, but to no avail. After a year and a half of guest Champagne Ladies, soprano Norma Zimmer was hired on a permanent basis and has been with Welk ever since.

Hardly less painful was the departure of the Lennon Sisters in 1968, to build a career of their own. Dixieland clarinetist Pete Fountain, one of the most jazz-oriented musicians ever to star with Welk, quit when the maestro refused to let him jive up a carol on a Christmas show. He later built a successful career on his own, as have Jo Ann Castle and country singer Lynn Anderson.

During his later years Lawrence Welk made a conscious effort to add younger, reasonably contemporary performers to his troupe. The success of his record "Calcutta" in 1960 evidently convinced him that good music and something remotely resembling a contemporary beat were not necessarily incompatible. Dancers Burgess and Boylan joined after winning a "Calcutta" dance contest in 1961, and added later were Sandi and Salli, Tanya Falan (who married Welk's son), and tap dancer Art Duncan, the only black face in the crowd.

Though no longer carried on a network, *The Lawrence Welk Show* is now in syndication and is still one of the top-rated programs on American television—a tribute to the unwavering maestro of the "uh-one, uh-two" and his continued popularity with millions of viewers.

The Lawrence Welk Show was seen on local television in Los Angeles for two years before going on the network in 1955. It was known for a time in 1958 as *The Dodge Dancing Party*.

LAWRENCE WELK'S DODGE DANCING PARTY

see *Lawrence Welk Show, The*

LAWRENCE WELK'S TOP TUNES AND NEW TALENT

Talent

FIRST TELECAST: *October 8, 1956*

LAST TELECAST: *May 27, 1959*

BROADCAST HISTORY:

Oct 1956–Jun 1958, ABC Mon 9:30–10:30
Sep 1958–May 1959, ABC Wed 7:30–8:30

HOST:

Lawrence Welk

REGULARS:

The Lawrence Welk Orchestra
Lawrence Welk's Little Band (1958–1959)

In addition to his familiar Saturday night show, Lawrence Welk had a second hour on ABC between 1956 and 1959, featuring "top tunes and new talent." Some of the performers discovered in the talent-show portion of the series later became Welk regulars, among them Joe Feeney, Jack Imel, and Maurice Pearson. Also featured were Welk's regular orchestra and soloists.

In 1958 the title of the show was changed to *The Plymouth Show,* and the Lawrence Welk "Little Band" was added as a regular feature. This second band was composed of talented youngsters ranging in age from 12 to 20, and included such solo talent as drummer Cubby O'Brien (12), a former *Mickey Mouse Club* mousketeer.

LAWYERS, THE

Lawyer

FIRST TELECAST: *September 21, 1969*

LAST TELECAST: *August 20, 1972*

BROADCAST HISTORY:

Sep 1969–Sep 1972, NBC Sun 10:00–11:00

CAST:

Walter Nichols ....Burl Ives
Brian Darrell ....Joseph Campanella
Neil Darrell ....James Farentino

Three attorneys with different skills, interests, and approaches joined forces to form the law firm of Nichols, Darrell and Darrell. Walter Nichols had been practicing law since before either of his two young partners was born. His vast experience gave him a perspective and patience that neither of the Darrell brothers had. Shrewd and effective, Walter functioned as a stabilizing influence, consultant, and sometimes father figure to his partners. Brian, the older of the Darrell brothers, was a superb researcher and detail man who did everything by the book. Neil, the younger brother, was more sympathetic to unpopular causes and more unorthodox than either of his partners. He was not above stretching a law to achieve a desired end. The blending of these three diverse personalities caused occasional conflict among the attorneys but resulted in a very effective team. *The Lawyers* was one of the rotating elements that comprised *The Bold Ones.*

LAYTONS, THE

Situation Comedy

FIRST TELECAST: *August 11, 1948*

LAST TELECAST: *October 13, 1948*

BROADCAST HISTORY:

Aug 1948–Oct 1948, DUM Wed 8:30–9:00

CAST:

Amanda Randolph
Vera Tatum

Black actress Amanda Randolph, better known as Sapphire's Mama on both the radio and TV versions of *Amos 'n' Andy,* starred in this short-lived domestic comedy on DuMont. It had been previously seen as a local program in New York, in May–June 1948.

LEAVE IT TO BEAVER

Situation Comedy

FIRST TELECAST: *October 4, 1957*

LAST TELECAST: *September 12, 1963*

BROADCAST HISTORY:

Oct 1957–Mar 1958, CBS Fri 7:30–8:00
Mar 1958–Sep 1958, CBS Wed 8:00–8:30
Oct 1958–Jun 1959, ABC Thu 7:30–8:00
Jul 1959–Sep 1959, ABC Thu 9:00–9:30
Oct 1959–Sep 1962, ABC Sat 8:30–9:00
Sep 1962–Sep 1963, ABC Thu 8:30–9:00

CAST:

June Cleaver ....Barbara Billingsley
Ward Cleaver ....Hugh Beaumont
Beaver (Theodore) Cleaver ... Jerry Mathers
Wally Cleaver ....Tony Dow
Eddie Haskel ....Ken Osmond
Larry (1958–1959) .... Rusty Stevens
"Lumpy" Rutherford (1960–1963) .... Frank Bank
Mr. Fred Rutherford (1961–1963) .... Richard Deacon
Whitey (1960–1962) ....Stanley Fafara

Gilbert (1960–1963) ....Stephen Talbot
Miss Landers (1959–1962) .....Sue Randall

This family comedy focused on life through the eyes of a young boy. Beaver Cleaver was seven when the series began, and his brother Wally, 12. Beaver was a typically rambunctious youth, more interested in pet frogs than in girls, but Wally, just entering his teens, was beginning to discover other things in life. The counterpoint between the two, plus some good writing and acting, lent the series its charm. The boys' parents, June and Ward Cleaver, were one of those nice, middle-class couples so often seen in this kind of program. Larry, Whitey, and Gilbert (among others) were Beaver's pals, Eddie and Lumpy were Wally's buddies, and Miss Landers was Beaver's schoolteacher. The locale was the suburban town of Mayfield.

As the years passed and Beaver got older, the stories naturally moved away from the little-boy premise until, in the final season, Beaver was about to enter his teens and Wally was ready for college.

LEAVE IT TO LARRY

Situation Comedy

FIRST TELECAST: *October 14, 1952*
LAST TELECAST: *December 23, 1952*
BROADCAST HISTORY:
Oct 1952–Dec 1952, CBS Tue 8:00–8:30
CAST:
Larry Tucker ....Eddie Albert
Mr. Koppel ....Ed Begley
Amy Tucker ....Betty Kean
Stevie Tucker ....Glenn Walkin
Harriet Tucker ....Lydia Schaeffer

The problems of a young man working for his father-in-law formed the basis of this comedy. Larry Tucker, a pleasant enough fellow with a wife (Amy) and two children, faced Amy's father every morning in the shoe store where he worked. He faced Mr. Koppel every night, too, since Amy's father also owned and lived in the two-family house where Larry and his family lived. Too much family, all of the time, made Larry's life a bit hectic. Someone in the family always had it in for someone else, and he was always in the middle.

LEAVE IT TO THE GIRLS

Discussion

FIRST TELECAST: *April 27, 1949*
LAST TELECAST: *March 27, 1954*
BROADCAST HISTORY:
Apr 1949–May 1949, NBC Wed 8:00–8:30
May 1949–Aug 1949, NBC Sun 8:00–8:30
Aug 1949–Oct 1949, NBC Sun 8:30–9:00
Oct 1949–Sep 1951, NBC Sun 7:00–7:30
Oct 1951–Dec 1951, NBC Sun 10:30–11:00
Oct 1953–Mar 1954, ABC Sat 7:30–8:00
MODERATOR:
Maggi McNellis
PANELISTS:
Eloise ("The Mouth") McElhone
Vanessa Brown
Florence Pritchett
Lisa Ferraday
Ann Rutherford
Harriet Van Horne
Janet Blair
John Henry Faulk (1954)
CREATOR/PRODUCER:
Martha Rountree

This bit of piffle was created by Martha Rountree, the same woman responsible for *Meet the Press* and other deadly serious public-affairs shows. Indeed, when it was first heard on radio in 1945, *Leave It to the Girls* was conceived as a serious discussion of male-female problems by career women. However, it soon degenerated into a one-sided battle of the sexes, and by the time it got to TV the subject matter was mostly what was wrong with men, how to marry them, and clever jokes about their foibles. A lone male was generally present to "defend the honor of his sex," and he was given a toy horn with which to signal his intention to speak (which was often the only way to break in on the chatterbox panel).

The female panelists changed frequently. All were "of the Stork Club ilk," as *TV Guide* put it—glamorous, well-dressed, showbiz types. Eloise McElhone was the most constant panel member over the years, with Vanessa Brown and Florence Pritchett also closely associated with the show. Male guests were generally panel-show types, such as Henry Morgan, Morey Amsterdam, and George Jessel. A "permanent" male defender, John Henry Faulk, was added during the last months.

Leave It to the Girls was first seen on local television in New York in 1947, and moved to the network in 1949. Oddly enough, it was sponsored through part of its run by a tobacco company.

LEGEND OF CUSTER

see *Custer*

LEGEND OF JESSE JAMES, THE

Western

FIRST TELECAST: *September 13, 1965*
LAST TELECAST: *September 5, 1966*
BROADCAST HISTORY:
Sep 1965–Sep 1966, ABC Mon 8:30–9:00
CAST:
Jesse James ....Christopher Jones
Frank James ....Allen Case
Cole Younger ....John Milford
Bob Younger ....Tim McIntire
Marshal Sam Corbett ....Robert Wilke

Television is apparently capable of making a hero out of anyone. This Western sympathetically portrayed the murderous James brothers, notorious in the Old West as robbers and desperadoes, as latter-day Robin Hoods driven to violence against their will. Christopher Jones played young, handsome, romantic Jesse, while Allen Case played his steadier older brother Frank. Occasionally featured in stories were Cole and Bob Younger, another pleasant pair drawn from Western history, and Marshal Sam Corbett. The James' adventures, and attempts to show that they weren't all that bad, lasted for a single season on ABC.

LES CRANE SHOW, THE

see *ABC's Nightlife*

LESLIE UGGAMS SHOW, THE

Musical Variety

FIRST TELECAST: *September 28, 1969*
LAST TELECAST: *December 14, 1969*
BROADCAST HISTORY:
Sep 1969–Dec 1969, CBS Sun 9:00–10:00
REGULARS:
Leslie Uggams
Dennis Allen
Lillian Hayman
Lincoln Kilpatrick
Allison Mills
Johnny Brown
Nelson Riddle and His Orchestra

Singer Leslie Uggams was the star of this musical variety series. In addition to her singing and dancing, and turns by weekly guest stars, a regular feature of the program was a continuing comedy sketch called "Sugar Hill." It dealt with the lives of a middle-class black family in a large city. The family consisted of Henrietta (Leslie Uggams), her husband B.J. (Lincoln Kilpatrick), her mother (Lillian Hayman), her brother Lamar (Johnny Brown), and her sister Oletha (Allison Mills). The only white regular on the show was sketch comedian Dennis Allen.

LESSON IN SAFETY

Instruction

FIRST TELECAST: *September 8, 1951*
LAST TELECAST: *October 20, 1951*
BROADCAST HISTORY:
Sep 1951–Oct 1951, ABC Sat 9:00–9:30

Accident-prevention films, covering such subjects as fire safety, driving, bicycling, and freight handling.

LET THERE BE STARS

Musical Variety

FIRST TELECAST: *October 16, 1949*
LAST TELECAST: *November 27, 1949*
BROADCAST HISTORY:
Oct 1949–Nov 1949, ABC Sun 9:00–10:00

The premiere telecast of this hour-long musical revue was a producer's dream: big budget, cast of bright, talented young newcomers, top-notch production, and a rave review in the next morning's issue of *Variety* ("Here's a show to make the detractors of Hollywood's video entries eat their words"). The talent was rounded up by a Rodgers and Hammerstein talent scout in the process of casting R&H shows, and included Patti Brill, Jane Harvey, Tom Noonan, and Peter Marshall. One of the novel (for the time) production devices used on the program was "Teleparencies," a projected background effect that moved, dissolved, and faded in and out with the action.

Subsequent shows apparently did not live up to the premiere, and the series folded after a few weeks. It was seen in the East via kinescope, having premiered on West Coast television on September 21, 1949.

LET'S DANCE

Music

FIRST TELECAST: *September 11, 1954*

LAST TELECAST: *October 16, 1954*
BROADCAST HISTORY:
Sep 1954–Oct 1954, ABC Sat 8:00–9:00
REGULARS
(New York):
Ralph Flanagan Orchestra
Julius La Rosa
Martha Wright
(Chicago):
Art Mooney Orchestra
June Valli
Fran Allison

Short-lived dance-music series originating from both New York and Chicago. Featured bands were Ralph Flanagan from New York's Hotel New Yorker and Art Mooney from Chicago's Aragon Ballroom, with vocalists and guest celebrities. Celebrities, seated at a "VIP table" near the bandstand, were interviewed by Martha Wright in New York and Fran Allison (of *Kukla, Fran & Ollie* fame) in Chicago. Added features were a "Sing a Song for TV" segment in New York and a "Dance for TV" interlude in Chicago, in which a member of the audience was caught in the spotlight and invited to perform on live nationwide television. For the final telecast, Art Mooney was replaced on the Chicago end by Billy May's Orchestra.

LET'S MAKE A DEAL

Quiz/Audience Participation
FIRST TELECAST: *May 21, 1967*
LAST TELECAST: *August 30, 1971*
BROADCAST HISTORY:
May 1967–Sep 1967, NBC Sun 8:30–9:00
Feb 1969–May 1969, ABC Fri 9:00–9:30
May 1969–Jan 1970, ABC Fri 7:30–8:00
Jan 1970–Jan 1971, ABC Sat 7:30–8:00
Jan 1971–Aug 1971, ABC Mon 7:30–8:00
EMCEE:
Monty Hall
ANNOUNCER:
Jay Stewart

Let's Make a Deal premiered on the NBC daytime lineup in December 1963, and first moved to nighttime in 1967. The basic format had emcee Monty Hall open the show by choosing contestants from among members of the studio audience—who came dressed in outrageous costumes to attract his attention. The contestants chosen could trade something that they had brought with them for a first prize. They then had the opportunity to trade this first modest prize for objects hidden in boxes or behind curtains on the stage.

The hidden prizes could be trips, money, expensive jewelry, or other valuable merchandise—or they could be "zonks," worthless nonsense prizes. Many of the contestants were offered multiple options to test their greed in "trading" what they had already won for something possibly more expensive—or possibly a "zonk." At the end of the show the "Big Deal of the Day" gave two of the biggest winners the chance to trade their loot for whatever was behind one of three curtains. Although there was rarely a "zonk" at this point, a big winner could end up trading his current prizes for something worth much less.

Let's Make a Deal appeared in prime time as a summer replacement series on NBC in 1967, and as a regular series on ABC between 1969 and 1971. It continued as a daytime series until well into the 1970s, and is also in syndication.

LET'S PLAY THE GAME

see *Play the Game*

LET'S RHUMBA

Dance Instruction
FIRST TELECAST: *November 15, 1946*
LAST TELECAST: *January 17, 1947*
BROADCAST HISTORY:
Nov 1946–Jan 1947, NBC Fri 8:15–8:30 (approx.)
HOST:
D'Avalos

Dance-instruction program by D'Avalos, whose accent and oily good looks added a distinct Latin flavor to this early series. The featured dance was the "Ranchero."

LET'S SEE

Quiz
FIRST TELECAST: *July 14, 1955*
LAST TELECAST: *August 25, 1955*
BROADCAST HISTORY:
Jul 1955–Aug 1955, ABC Thu 10:00–10:30
EMCEE:
John Reed King

A short-lived, oddly-formatted quiz show filmed at Convention Hall in Atlantic City, New Jersey. Panelists attempted to discover through indirect questions what attractions contestants had seen in Atlantic

City. Sponsored by the Atlantic City Chamber of Commerce.

LETTER TO LORETTA, A

see *Loretta Young Show, The*

LEWISOHN STADIUM CONCERT

Music

FIRST TELECAST: *June 26, 1950*
LAST TELECAST: *August 7, 1950*
BROADCAST HISTORY:
Jun 1950–Aug 1950, NBC Mon 9:30–10:30

Live concerts from New York's Lewisohn Stadium, featuring the New York Philharmonic Orchestra (its first TV appearance) with various conductors and soloists.

LIBERACE SHOW, THE

Musical Variety

FIRST TELECAST: *July 1, 1952*
LAST TELECAST: *September 16, 1969*
BROADCAST HISTORY:
Jul 1952–Aug 1952, NBC Tue/Thu 7:30–7:45
Jul 1969–Sep 1969, CBS Tue 8:30–9:30
HOST:
Liberace
REGULARS:
George Liberace and Orchestra (1952)
Richard Wattis (1969)
Georgina Moon (1969)
Jack Parnell Orchestra (1969)

Flamboyant pianist "Lee" Liberace (real name: Wladziu Valentino Liberace) appeared frequently on television during the 1950s and 1960s. His trademarks were always the same, and always the butt of innumerable jokes: the outlandish and very expensive wardrobe, the curly hair and pearly-tooth smile, and a florid piano style. Atop his Steinway was always perched an ornate candelabra (imitation Louis XIV). Women, especially older ones, loved it. The critics were not kind, but Liberace did not mind. "I cried," he remarked in one of show business' more memorable quotes, "all the way to the bank."

Liberace's first television exposure was on a local program in Los Angeles in 1951, followed by a 15-minute network summer series in 1952. The following year he began a syndicated series which ran for several years and made him a great deal of money. He had another network summer show in 1969, this one a full hour in length. With him in the early years was violinist brother George, who led the orchestra. The 1969 variety show, which originated in London, featured guest stars and two regulars, Richard Wattis and Georgina Moon, who portrayed Liberace's butler and maid in a regular sketch sequence each week.

LIBRARY OF COMEDY FILMS

see *Movies—Prior to 1961*

LIEUTENANT, THE

Drama

FIRST TELECAST: *September 14, 1963*
LAST TELECAST: *September 5, 1964*
BROADCAST HISTORY:
Sep 1963–Sep 1964, NBC Sat 7:30–8:00
CAST:
Lt. William (Bill) Rice .....Gary Lockwood
Capt. Ray Rambridge ......Robert Vaughn
Lt. Samwell (Sanpan) Panosian (1963)
.... Steve Franken
Lt. Harris ....Don Penny
Lily ....Carmen Phillips
Various roles ....Chris Noel

The Lieutenant sought to convey what life was like for a newly commissioned officer in the peacetime Marine Corps. Bill Rice had graduated from Annapolis and gone through Marine Officers' Training School at Quantico, Virginia. After leaving Quantico, he was stationed as a second lieutenant at Camp Pendleton, California. Bill's friendly, easygoing manner made him popular with the recruits at Camp Pendleton and with the many girls he dated in an active off-duty social life. Bill's immediate superior was Capt. Ray Rambridge, who was harshly critical not because he disliked Bill, but because he wanted to make a good officer out of him. Also seen regularly was Lily, the owner of the nightclub frequented by Bill when he was off duty. Steve Franken was originally cast as one of Bill's fellow lieutenants, but left the show after five episodes were filmed and was replaced by Don Penny. Actress Chris Noel kept popping up as a recurring regular, but in a different role each time. In one episode she would be a nurse, in another a lady Marine, and in a third one of Bill's girl friends. Sometimes her role was substantial and sometimes she was only peripherally involved in the story.

LIFE AND LEGEND OF WYATT EARP, THE

Western

FIRST TELECAST: *September 6, 1955*
LAST TELECAST: *September 26, 1961*
BROADCAST HISTORY:

Sep 1955–Sep 1961, ABC Tue 8:30–9:00

CAST:

Wyatt Earp .... Hugh O'Brien
Bat Masterson (1955–1957) .... Mason Alan Dinehart III
Ben Thompson (1955–1956) ... Denver Pyle
Bill Thompson (1955–1956) ....Hal Baylor
Abbie Crandall (1955–1956) .... Gloria Talbot
Marsh Murdock (1955–1956) .... Don Haggerty
Doc Fabrique (1955–1956) .... Douglas Fowley
Ned Buntline (occasional) .... Lloyd Corrigan
Jim "Dog" Kelly (1956–1958) .... Paul Brinegar
Jim "Dog" Kelly (1958–1959) ....Ralph Sanford
Mayor Hoover (1956–1957) .... Selmer Jackson
Deputy Hal Norton (1957–1958) ....William Tannen
Doc Holliday (1957–1961) .... Douglas Fowley
Doc Holliday (temporary 1959) .... Myron Healy
Kate Holliday (1957–1958) .... Carol Stone
Shotgun Gibbs (1958–1961) .... Morgan Woodward
Morgan Earp (1959–1961) .....Dirk London
Virgil Earp (1959–1961) .... John Anderson
Nellie Cashman (1959–1960) .... Randy Stuart
Old Man Clanton (1959–1961) .... Trevor Bardette
Emma Clanton (1959–1960) .... Carol Thurston
Sheriff Johnny Behan (1959) .... Lash La Rue
Sheriff Johnny Behan (1959–1961) .... Steve Brodie
Curley Bill Brocius (1959–1961) .... William Phipps
Johnny Ringo (1960–1961) ... Britt Lomond
Mayor Clum (1960–1961) ..... Stacy Harris
Doc Goodfellow (1959–1961) .... Damian O'Flynn

In the make-believe world of TV Westerns, *Wyatt Earp* was unique. Not only was it based on fact (more or less—there was a real Marshal Wyatt Earp, and he did have a very colorful life), but it developed its characters over a period of six years in a continuing story involving politics and family relationships as well as standard Western action. It was in many respects a serial drama. Part of the reason for this orientation was no doubt author-playwright Frederick Hazlitt Brennan, who wrote the scripts from the start.

The series began in 1955 with an episode titled "Mr. Earp Becomes a Marshal," in which Wyatt's friend, Marshal Whitney of Ellsworth, Kansas, was killed by a gunman. Wyatt accepted his badge and avenged his death. Wyatt's friend, famed showman and writer Ned Buntline, then provided him with his trademark, two "Buntline Special" pistols—.45s with extra long barrels—with which to keep the peace. (The first time Wyatt saw them he locked Buntline in the pokey for carrying "oversized pistols.") Their recoil was pretty ferocious, but their extra range allowed the marshal to drop an opponent from the other side of town. They proved handy, for during the rest of the first season Wyatt faced an array of foes in and around Ellsworth, including the murderous John Wesley Hardin and—most frequently—the outlaw Thompson brothers.

But Ellsworth was too small for Wyatt's talents, and for the second season he moved on to Dodge City to become marshal there (with no reference made to the fact that Matt Dillon already had that job, at least on Saturday nights). Young Bat Masterson joined him as deputy for a while, before becoming a county sheriff in his own right. Wyatt then tried out Bat's brother Ed Masterson as a sidekick, but finally settled on Hal Norton as his deputy. Another character introduced in the 1956–1957 season was Wyatt's pal Jim "Dog" Kelly, who eventually got himself elected Mayor of Dodge City, replacing Mayor Hoover. The 1957–1958 season brought an even more colorful real-life character to Dodge, the notorious Doc Holliday, a physician turned gambler and schemer (played by the same actor who had previously been Ellsworth's Doc Fabrique). Wyatt's brothers Virgil and Morgan Earp began to turn up in occasional episodes, usually requiring a steadying hand from their older brother.

In the 1959–1960 season Wyatt moved again, this time to Tombstone, Arizona, and the greatest battle of his career. Tombstone was a rough-and-ready town run by Old Man Clanton, leader of the "Ten Percent Gang." Clanton ruled the territory with an iron hand, exacting tribute from citizens and masterminding gunrunning schemes across the Mexican border. Johnny Behan was his handpicked sheriff in Tombstone, and he had a private army of gunslingers to enforce his will. For two years, Earp, as marshall, battled the Clanton gang through political and legal means. Shotgun Gibbs, a peace-loving frontiersman, followed Wyatt from Dodge City to Tombstone to become his deputy. Some of Dodge's less respectable citizens showed up too, including Doc Holliday and gunslinger Curley Bill Brocius. Nellie Cashman provided some love interest for a season (Wyatt was always handy with the womenfolk) as the operator of the Birdcage Saloon.

The final showdown, again based on fact, came at the end of the last season, in 1961. In a five-part story that concluded *Wyatt Earp*'s original run, Wyatt discovered that the Clanton gang was using the O.K. corral as a center and fortress for their illegal activities. Wyatt tried to prevent bloodshed, but events moved rapidly toward a climactic shootout in which Wyatt, his brothers Morgan and Virgil, and Doc Holliday broke the power of the Clanton gang in the famous gunfight at the O.K. corral.

LIFE AND TIMES OF GRIZZLY ADAMS, THE

Adventure

FIRST TELECAST: *February 9, 1977*

LAST TELECAST: *July 26, 1978*

BROADCAST HISTORY:

Feb 1977–Jul 1978, NBC Wed 8:00–9:00

CAST:

James "Grizzly" Adams .....Dan Haggerty
Mad Jack ....Denver Pyle
Nakuma ....Don Shanks
Robbie Cartman ....John Bishop

Set in the Western United States during the late 1800s, *The Life and Times of Grizzly Adams* was the story of a man accused of a crime he had not committed, who sought refuge in the wilderness and discovered that life there suited him better than life in the city. With the help of a friend named Mad Jack and an Indian blood brother, Nakuma, Grizzly built a sturdy cabin and determined to live in harmony with nature. A grizzly bear cub that he had rescued from a ledge became his roommate. The bear was christened Ben, and though he grew to be an imposing animal weighing several hundred pounds, he remained as friendly as a child. With Ben as his constant companion, the bearded Grizzly Adams found wilderness adventure in dealing with nature, the elements, and strangers passing through. A frequent visitor was young Robbie Cartman, the son of a farmer living in the area, who loved to listen to Grizzly's tales.

Dan Haggerty, who starred in this series, played the same role in the movie *The Life and Times of Grizzly Adams*, and a similar role in another film, *The Adventures of Frontier Freemont*. Haggerty was originally an animal trainer rather than an actor, and was chosen for the film roles partly because of his remarkable rapport with bears. Denver Pyle appeared as his costar in both films.

There was a real Grizzly Adams, upon whom this series was loosely based. He was born in Massachusetts in 1812, and spent many years in the Sierra Nevada after having gone bankrupt through a series of unfortunate business deals. The real Grizzly was a bit less altruistic than his TV counterpart. Having deserted his wife and children, he spent much of his time hunting and killing animals and capturing others for zoos (a few of the larger beasts almost killed *him* on one occasion or another). The real Ben died in a zoo that Adams himself opened in San Francisco in the 1850s. But Adams also loved animals and cared for many of them throughout his wilderness days. He died while on tour with P.T. Barnum in 1860.

LIFE BEGINS AT EIGHTY

Discussion

FIRST TELECAST: *January 13, 1950*

LAST TELECAST: *February 25, 1956*

BROADCAST HISTORY:

Jan 1950–Mar 1950, NBC Fri 9:30–10:00
Apr 1950–Jul 1950, NBC Sat 7:30–8:00
Jul 1950–Aug 1950, NBC Fri 9:00–9:30
Oct 1950–Dec 1950, ABC Tue 10:00–10:30
Dec 1950–Sep 1951, ABC Tue 9:30–10:00
Oct 1951–Mar 1952, ABC Mon 8:30–9:00

Mar 1952–Jun 1952, DUM Fri 8:30–9:00
Jul 1952–Jun 1954, DUM Fri 9:00–9:30
Sep 1954–Jul 1955, DUM Sun 9:30–10:00
Aug 1955–Oct 1955, ABC Sun 9:30–10:00
Oct 1955–Dec 1955, ABC Sun 10:00–10:30
Jan 1956–Feb 1956, ABC Sat 10:00–10:30

EMCEE:
Jack Barry

REGULAR PANELISTS:
Mrs. Georgiana Carhart
Fred Stein

Jack Barry created a radio version of *Life Begins at 80* in 1948, as a copy of his successful *Juvenile Jury*—substituting octogenarians for the youngsters. A panel of oldsters was posed questions submitted by viewers, and given the opportunity to expound on life from the vantage point of their years. They often provided hilarious quips and insights, and needed little prompting from Barry. An additional highlight of the show, which became more prominent toward the later years of the TV run, was the "Footlight Favorite." This was a show-business personality who performed for the audience. Some of these guests were themselves old-timers, like vaudevillians Joe Howard and Smith & Dale, singer Morton Downey and cornetist Vincent Buono (who performed with other original members of the Sousa Band); others, such as Lanny Ross and Faye Emerson, were younger.

Much of the appeal of *Life Begins at 80* lay in the chemistry of its panelists, the most delightful of whom were Mrs. Georgiana Carhart, an engaging flirt who told stories with an Irish brogue ("Why worry," she quipped, "you'll never get out of life alive anyway"), and Fred Stein, an active realtor who viewed life with similar enthusiasm. The two of them were with the show throughout its history, though both were nearing ninety by the end of the run. (The ages given for individual panelists vary somewhat, according to the source!) Oddly enough, continuity of panel members was less a problem on this show than on those with younger panels. The panelists might eventually die off, but none seemed to give up voluntarily. Among those appearing for extended periods were Joseph Rosenthal (85), John Draney (89), pianist Paolo Gallico (82), vaudevillian Lorna Standish (80) and Thomas Clark (81).

Emcee Barry (32) sometimes closed the show with a quote from Julia Ward Howe, who said of old age that "all the sugar is at the bottom of the cup."

LIFE IS WORTH LIVING

Religious Talk

FIRST TELECAST: *February 12, 1952*
LAST TELECAST: *April 8, 1957*
BROADCAST HISTORY:
Feb 1952–Apr 1955, DUM Tue 8:00–8:30 (OS)
Oct 1955–Apr 1956, ABC Thu 8:00–8:30
Oct 1956–Apr 1957, ABC Mon 9:00–9:30

HOST:
Bishop Fulton J. Sheen

There was a time when anything was possible in prime-time television, even a weekly half-hour featuring a charming, well-spoken Catholic bishop offering anecdotes and little lessons in morality ("sermons" would be too stuffy a word) for a large and devoted following. *Life Is Worth Living* was probably the most widely viewed religious series in TV history, and sponsors often paid a premium to have their commercials next to it (since they couldn't get *in* it). Its "star" and only "regular" was the Most Reverend Fulton J. Sheen, Auxiliary Bishop of New York, a modest, middle-level cleric who had long been heard on radio. On TV he was seen in a simulated study, punctuating his points with drawings scrawled on a blackboard. (One of his "angels," his TV crew, would slip in when he moved away, to clean off the board; the identity of this unseen hand was a great source of speculation among viewers). The bishop's famous sign-off: "God love you."

Many of Bishop Sheen's talks revolved around the evils of world communism, and perhaps the series' most dramatic incident came in early 1953 when he delivered a hair-raising reading of the burial scene from *Julius Caesar*, with the names of Caesar, Cassius, Marc Antony, and Brutus replaced by Stalin, Beria, Malenkov, and Vishinsky. "Stalin," Sheen intoned, with hypnotic forcefulness, "must one day meet his judgment." A few days later the Russian dictator suffered a sudden stroke, and a week later he was dead. There was never any comment from Sheen's office on this remarkable coincidence, which was widely reported in the press.

LIFE OF LEONARDO DA VINCI, THE

Historical Drama

FIRST TELECAST: *August 13, 1972*

LAST TELECAST: *September 10, 1972*

BROADCAST HISTORY:

Aug 1972–Sep 1972, CBS Sun 9:30–10:30

CAST:

Leonardo Da Vinci ....Philippe Leroy

This five-part dramatization of the life, achievements, and explorations of one of the greatest geniuses the world has ever known was originally produced in Italy. It was the Grand Prize winner at the 1972 Monte Carlo International Television Festival and was brought to American television by CBS in the summer of 1972.

LIFE OF RILEY, THE

Situation Comedy

FIRST TELECAST: *October 4, 1949*

LAST TELECAST: *August 22, 1958*

BROADCAST HISTORY:

Oct 1949–Mar 1950, NBC Tue 9:30–10:00
Jan 1953–Sep 1956, NBC Fri 8:30–9:00 (OS)
Oct 1956–Dec 1956, NBC Fri 8:00–8:30
Jan 1957–Aug 1958, NBC Fri 8:30–9:00

CAST (1949–1950):

Chester A. Riley ....Jackie Gleason
Peg Riley ....Rosemary DeCamp
Junior ....Lanny Rees
Babs ....Gloria Winters
Jim Gillis ....Sid Tomack
Digby "Digger" O'Dell ....John Brown

CAST (1953–1958):

Chester A. Riley ....William Bendix
Peg Riley ....Marjorie Reynolds
Junior ....Wesley Morgan
Babs Riley Marshall ......Lugene Sanders
Jim Gillis (1953–1955, 1956–1958)
.... Tom D'Andrea
Honeybee Gillis (1953–1955, 1956–1958)
.... Gloria Blondell
Cunningham ....Douglas Dumbrille
Dangle ....Robert Sweeney
Riley's boss ....Emory Parnell
Waldo Binney ....Sterling Holloway
Calvin Dudley (1955–1956)
.... George O'Hanlon
Belle Dudley (1955–1956)
.... Florence Sundstrom
Don Marshall (1957–1958)
.... Martin Milner

Television's original lovable bumbler was Chester A. Riley, a hardhat with a soft heart and a genius for unwittingly turning order into chaos. The role had been created on radio in 1943 by William Bendix. However, when the time came for the move to television, Bendix was tied up with movie commitments, and the opportunity went to young Jackie Gleason—his first TV series.

Riley worked in an aircraft plant in California, but viewers usually saw him at home, cheerfully disrupting life with his malapropisms and ill-timed intervention into minor problems. His stock answer to every turn of fate became a catch phrase: "What a revoltin' development this is!" Riley's long-suffering wife Peg and their children, Babs and Junior, somehow saw that it always came out all right in the end. Others seen were Gillis, Riley's sarcastic friend, and "Digger" O'Dell, the smiling undertaker ("Guess I'd better be shoveling off . . ."), played by John Brown, the only member of the radio cast to make the transition to TV.

Jackie Gleason's bug-eyed portrayal of Riley did not catch on, and the program was canceled after only one season. Three years later it returned with an entirely new cast, headed by William Bendix, and ran for five years. The cast was relatively stable through the second run, although a few neighbors came and went and Babs eventually left to get married and Junior to go to college. Both kids returned occasionally to visit.

The show was filmed in Hollywood.

LIFE WITH FATHER

Situation Comedy

FIRST TELECAST: *November 22, 1953*

LAST TELECAST: *July 5, 1955*

BROADCAST HISTORY:

Nov 1953–May 1954, CBS Sun 7:00–7:30
Aug 1954–Dec 1954, CBS Tue 10:00–10:30
Jan 1955–Jul 1955, CBS Tue 8:00–8:30

CAST:

Clarence Day, Sr. ....Leon Ames
Vinnie Day ....Lurene Tuttle
Clarence Day, Jr. (1953–1954)
.... Ralph Reed
Clarence Day, Jr. (1954–1955)
.... Steven Terrell
Whitney Day (1953–1954) .... Ronald Keith
Whitney Day (1954–1955) ... B. G. Norman
Whitney Day (1955) ..... Freddy Ridgeway
Harlan Day ....Harvey Grant
John Day (1953–1954) ..... Freddie Leiston
John Day (1954–1955) .... Malcolm Cassell

Margaret	Dorothy Bernard
Nora	Marion Ross

Clarence Day, Jr.'s nostalgic autobiographical articles in *The New Yorker* were very successful in the 1920s. They later led to a bestselling novel, hit play, Hollywood movie, and in 1953 to this live television series. Set in New York City in the 1880s, *Life With Father* was the story of Clarence Day, Sr., a stern but loving Victorian father, his wife Vinnie, and their four red-headed sons. Despite the fact that he ruled with an iron hand, and was a staunch traditionalist, Father Day dealt fairly with his family and earned their lifelong respect.

The turnover in actors playing the Day children in this series was rather high, although the adult members of the cast lasted longer. This was the first live color series for network TV originating in Hollywood.

LIFE WITH LINKLETTER

Variety/Audience Participation

FIRST TELECAST: *October 6, 1950*

LAST TELECAST: *April 25, 1952*

BROADCAST HISTORY:

Oct 1950–Apr 1952, ABC Fri 7:30–8:00 (OS)

EMCEE:

Art Linkletter

This was a nighttime version of Linkletter's long-running *House Party* show, a daytime standby on radio and television from 1945 until 1970. All of the familiar Linkletter elements were present, including the mad stunts performed by members of the studio audience for prizes, and the interviews with children. Guest stars also appeared, but the center of attraction was always Art himself, one of broadcasting's all-time favorite personalities. The program originated in Hollywood, and for a time in 1951–1952 alternated with *Say It with Acting.*

LIFE WITH LUIGI

Situation Comedy

FIRST TELECAST: *September 22, 1952*

LAST TELECAST: *December 22, 1952*

BROADCAST HISTORY:

Sep 1952–Dec 1952, CBS Mon 9:30–10:00

CAST:

Luigi Basco	J. Carrol Naish
Pasquale	Alan Reed
Rosa	Jody Gilbert
Miss Spalding	Mary Shipp
Schultz	Sig Ruman
Olson	Ken Peters
Horwitz	Joe Forte

Irish-American actor J. Carroll Naish became typecast as an Italian after playing the role of Luigi Basco for several years, first on CBS radio starting in 1948, and for a short period on a live TV series in 1952. Luigi was a newly arrived Italian immigrant who was learning to love his new homeland. He did not always understand what everything meant, and often took things too literally, but his sweet, gentle nature won everyone over. The setting alternated between Luigi's antique shop and his friend Pasquale's restaurant. Pasquale, a fellow immigrant who had been in this country for several years, had paid Luigi's boat fare to America in hopes that he might be able to marry off his fat daughter Rosa to his impressionable countryman.

Despite its popularity on radio, *Life with Luigi* had only a short career on TV. Its extreme ethnic stereotyping was found offensive by some, and sponsor troubles provided the *coup de grâce.*

LIFE WITH SNARKY PARKER

Children's

FIRST TELECAST: *January 9, 1950*

LAST TELECAST: *August 30, 1950*

BROADCAST HISTORY:

Jan 1950–Mar 1950, CBS Mon/Tue/Thu/Fri 7:45–8:00

Apr 1950–Aug 1950, CBS Mon–Fri 6:15–6:30

PUPPETEERS:

Bil Baird

Cora Baird

PRODUCER/DIRECTOR:

Yul Brynner

The marionettes of puppeteers Bil and Cora Baird performed in this "saga" of life in the Old West. Snarky Parker was the deputy sheriff of the town of Hot Rock. He was in love with the local schoolteacher, rode a horse named Heathcliffe, and fought with Ronald Rodent, the local villain. Also seen regularly in this live series were Slugger, the piano player in the Bent Elbow Saloon, and Paw, the father of the schoolteacher. Yul Brynner, later more successful as a performer, was the producer and director of this show. After leaving evening hours in August, it remained on the air for another month as a late-afternoon weekday entry.

LIFE WITH THE ERWINS

see *Stu Erwin Show, The*

LIFELINE

Medical Anthology

FIRST TELECAST: *September 9, 1978*

LAST TELECAST:

BROADCAST HISTORY:

Sep 1978, NBC Thu 10:00–11:00
Oct 1978–, NBC Sun 10:00–11:00

PRODUCER:

Alfred Kelman

DIRECTOR OF PHOTOGRAPHY:

Robert Elfstrom

This unusual program used no actors. It was essentially a medical documentary, focusing on a different real-life doctor in a different city each week, as he met one medical emergency after another. To produce the programs a camera crew followed each doctor for several months, filming him with his family and at work, including actual operating room and emergency room scenes where lives often hung in the balance. Viewers got to know the doctor and his patients, heightening the sense of real-life drama. *Lifeline* was produced by the company which had earlier produced the highly acclaimed "Body Human" specials, during the 1977–1978 season.

LIGHTS, CAMERA, ACTION

Talent

FIRST TELECAST: *July 4, 1950*

LAST TELECAST: *August 20, 1950*

BROADCAST HISTORY:

Jul 1950–Aug 1950, NBC Sun 10:00–10:30

EMCEE:

Walter Woolf King

Summer talent show originating in Hollywood and shown via kinescope over the NBC East and Midwest networks. Professional young talent and a panel of "name" judges were featured. Walter Woolf King, a matinee idol of the 1930s, emceed.

LIGHTS OUT

Suspense Anthology

FIRST TELECAST: *July 19, 1949*

LAST TELECAST: *September 29, 1952*

BROADCAST HISTORY:

Jul 1949–Aug 1949, NBC Tue 9:00–9:30
Nov 1949–Sep 1952, NBC Mon 9:00–9:30

NARRATOR:

Jack LaRue (1949–1950)
Frank Gallop (1950–1952)

SPECIAL MUSICAL EFFECTS:

Paul Lipman, theremin (1949)
Arlo Hults, organ (1949–1952)
Doris Johnson, harp (1950–1952)

Live dramatic show featuring stories of mystery, suspense, and the supernatural. At the beginning of each episode viewers would see only a close shot of a pair of eyes, then a bloody hand reaching to turn out the lights, followed by an eerie laugh and the words, "Lights out, everybody . . ."

The plays themselves were a combination of adaptations and dramas written especially for TV. Spooky houses, loved ones returned from the dead, and lonely country roads were frequent elements of *Lights Out*. At first lesser-known actors and actresses were featured, but beginning in 1950 a "guest star" policy brought in such names as Boris Karloff, Burgess Meredith, Billie Burke, Leslie Nielsen, Basil Rathbone, Eddie Albert, Raymond Massey, and Yvonne DeCarlo.

Lights Out began on radio in 1934 and had been seen on television in 1946 as a series of four specials produced by Fred Coe.

LINEUP, THE

Police

FIRST TELECAST: *October 1, 1954*

LAST TELECAST: *January 20, 1960*

BROADCAST HISTORY:

Oct 1954–Jun 1958, CBS Fri 10:00–10:30 (OS)
Sep 1958–Sep 1959, CBS Fri 10:00–10:30
Sep 1959–Jan 1960, CBS Wed 7:30–8:30

CAST:

Det. Lt. Ben Guthrie . . . Warner Anderson
Inspector Matt Grebb (1954–1959) . . . Tom Tully
Inspector Fred Asher (1955–1959) . . . Marshall Reed
Inspector Dan Delaney (1959–1960) . . . William Leslie
Inspector Charlie Summers (1959–1960) . . . Tod Barton
Officer Pete Larkin (1959–1960) . . . Skip Ward
Policewoman Sandy McAllister (1959–1960) . . . Rachel Ames

Produced in cooperation with the San Francisco Police Department, *The Lineup* sought to give realistic semi-documentary portrayals of the work of law officers in the beautiful Bay City. Ben Guthrie and Matt Grebb were the officers who tracked down criminals throughout most of the series' run. The stories were all based on actual cases from the files of the S.F.P.D., and generally included a police lineup where the victims of the crime attempted to pick out the perpetrators.

When the series expanded to an hour in the fall of 1959, there were a number of changes in the cast. Matt Grebb and Fred Asher were gone, replaced by two new inspectors. In addition, Officer Pete Larkin and Policewoman Sandy McAllister became regulars.

LITTLE HOUSE ON THE PRAIRIE

Adventure/Drama

FIRST TELECAST: *September 11, 1974*

LAST TELECAST:

BROADCAST HISTORY:

Sep 1974–Sep 1976, NBC Wed 8:00–9:00

Sep 1976– , NBC Mon 8:00–9:00

CAST:

Charles Ingalls .... Michael Landon
Caroline Ingalls .... Karen Grassle
Laura Ingalls .... Melissa Gilbert
Mary Ingalls .... Melissa Sue Anderson
Carrie Ingalls (alternating)
.... Lindsay Greenbush
Carrie Ingalls (alternating)
.... Sidney Greenbush
Lars Hanson (1974–1978) .... Karl Swenson
Nels Oleson .... Richard Bull
Harriet Oleson .... Katherine MacGregor
Nellie Oleson .... Alison Arngrim
Willie Oleson (1975–)
.... Jonathan Gilbert
Dr. Baker (1974–1978) .... Kevin Hagen
Rev. Alden (1974–1978) .... Dabbs Greer
Eva Beadle Simms (1974–1978)
.... Charlotte Gilbert
Mr. Edwards (1974–1977) .... Victor French
Grace Edwards (1976–1977)
.... Bonnie Bartlett
Jonathan Garvey (1977–)
.... Merlin Olsen
Andy Garvey (1977–)
.... Patrick Laborteaux
Alice Garvey (1977–)
.... Hersha Parady
Albert (1978–) .... Matthew Laborteaux
Adam Kendall (1978–)
.... Linwood Boomer
Grace Ingalls (alternating) (1978–)
.... Wendy Turnbeaugh
Grace Ingalls (alternating) (1978–)
.... Brenda Turnbeaugh

The time was the late 1870s, and the location was the American West, but *Little House on the Prairie* was not a Western in the usual sense. There were no cowboys, Indians or cowtown saloons in this version of frontier life—it was more like *The Waltons* in a different setting, the story of a loving family in trying times.

Charles Ingalls was a homesteader struggling to make a living for his family on a small farm near the town of Walnut Grove, Plum Creek, Minnesota. The Ingalls had moved from the great plains of Kansas to Walnut Grove in search of a future in a young and growing community. With Charles were his wife Caroline and their three daughters, teenagers Mary and Laura, and little Carrie (played alternately by a pair of identical twins). Stories related the experiences of family life and growing children, the constant struggle against natural disasters and ruined crops, and the dealings with other members of the little community in which they lived. Among the Ingalls' new friends were Mr. Hanson, the mill owner; Nels Oleson, the proprietor of the general store; and Mr. Edwards, a nearby farmer who became a good friend, despite his rather harsh exterior.

Mr. Edwards departed at the start of the 1977–1978 season, when actor Victor French left the series to star in his own show, *Carter Country*. He was replaced by Jonathan Garvey (played by former Los Angeles Rams football star Merlin Olsen), another neighborly farmer, who had a wife named Alice and a young son named Andy. Andy became a good friend of the Ingalls girls.

Some major developments took place in 1978. Caroline gave birth to her fourth daughter, Grace (portrayed by another set of identical twins). The eldest daughter, Mary, who had once had scarlet fever, lost her eyesight and was sent to a school for the blind in Iowa. Mary eventually decided to become a teacher of the blind herself, and moved to the Dakotas with Adam Kendall, her instructor from the school in Iowa. Then the town of Walnut Grove suffered an economic collapse, brought on by problems with the railroad upon which it was dependent for supplies. In the fall of 1978 Charles packed up his family and moved to the bustling frontier city of Winoka, in the Dakota Territory, where they were united with Mary and Adam. Moving with them were some of their friends from Walnut Grove, including the Garveys and the Olesons. Joining the household was a young orphan, Albert, whom they adopted. Faced with the necessity of supporting their family in the alien environment of a city, Charles and Caroline took on jobs at a hotel, but the city life proved so distasteful that they soon were on their way back to Walnut Grove.

The stories told on *Little House on the Prairie* were based on the "Little House" books by Laura Ingalls Wilder, which contained her recollections of growing up on the American frontier. On the TV series the actress playing Laura functioned as the narrator, in much the same manner as Katrin on the *Mama* series 25 years earlier. Michael Landon, who starred in this series, was also its executive producer.

LITTLE PEOPLE, THE

see *Brian Keith Show, The*

LITTLE REVUE, THE

Music

FIRST TELECAST: *September 4, 1949*
LAST TELECAST: *April 21, 1950*
BROADCAST HISTORY:

Sep 1949–Mar 1950, ABC Sun 8:30–9:00
Mar 1950–Apr 1950, ABC Fri 9:30–10:00

REGULARS:

Nancy Evans
Dick Larkin
Bill Sherry
Gloria Van
Billy Johnson
Nancy Doran and Dick France, dancers
Bill Weber Marionettes
Rex Maupin's Orchestra

A program of smooth, relaxed music and assorted variety-show elements from Chicago.

LITTLE SHOW, THE

see *Van Camp's Little Show*

LITTLE THEATRE

see *ABC Dramatic Shorts—1952–1953*

LIVE LIKE A MILLIONAIRE

Talent/Variety

FIRST TELECAST: *January 5, 1951*
LAST TELECAST: *February 7, 1953*
BROADCAST HISTORY:

Jan 1951–Apr 1951, CBS Fri 9:30–10:00
Apr 1951–Jun 1951, CBS Fri 9:00–9:30
Jul 1951–Mar 1952, CBS Fri 10:00–10:30
Oct 1952–Feb 1953, ABC Sat 7:30–8:00

EMCEE:

Jack McCoy (1951)
John Nelson

ASSISTANT:

Michael O'Halloran (1951)
Connie Clawson (1951–1952)

The format of *Live Like a Millionaire* was a variation on *Arthur Godfrey's Talent Scouts*. Each week three or four sets of talented parents performed on the show, after being introduced by their children. The winning parent or parents won the chance to live "like a millionaire" for an entire week. They were waited on, sent on trips, provided with expensive cars, or whatever else they might desire.

Jack McCoy was the original emcee and, when he left at the end of March 1951, he was replaced by the show's announcer, John Nelson. At the outset, Michael O'Halloran played Merton the Butler, waiting on the winners, but he was soon replaced by hostess Connie Clawson. When ABC picked up *Live Like a Millionaire* in the fall of 1952, only emcee Nelson was with the show. The basic format was retained but the prize became purely monetary. The winning parents received one week's interest on $1,000,000.

LIVELY ONES, THE

Musical Variety

FIRST TELECAST: *July 26, 1962*
LAST TELECAST: *September 12, 1963*
BROADCAST HISTORY:

Jul 1962–Sep 1962, NBC Thu 9:30–10:00
Jul 1963–Sep 1963, NBC Thu 9:30–10:00

HOST:

Vic Damone

HOSTESSES:

Joan Staley ("Tiger," 1962)
Shirley Yelm ("Charley," 1962)
Quinn O'Hara ("Smitty," 1963)
Gloria Neil ("Melvin," 1963)

ORCHESTRA:

Jerry Fielding

Vic Damone was host of this big, brash, swinging musical variety show which aired during the summers of 1962 and 1963. Each show presented established stars and new talent, appearing in different, often offbeat locations around the country. The only regulars on the series, other than Vic Damone, were his two "dates," Tiger and Charley in 1962 and Smitty and Melvin in 1963.

LLOYD BRIDGES SHOW, THE

Dramatic Anthology

FIRST TELECAST: *September 11, 1962*
LAST TELECAST: *August 27, 1963*
BROADCAST HISTORY:
Sep 1962–Aug 1963, CBS Tue 8:00–8:30
CAST:
Adam Shepherd and various others .... Lloyd Bridges

Lloyd Bridges narrated and starred in this dramatic-anthology series. Each episode began with freelance journalist Adam Shepherd digging into a story, sometimes current and sometimes historical. Shepherd then imagined himself as the primary protagonist (also played by Bridges), and the drama unfolded.

LOGAN'S RUN

Science Fiction

FIRST TELECAST: *September 16, 1977*
LAST TELECAST: *January 16, 1978*
BROADCAST HISTORY:
Sep 1977, CBS Fri 9:00–10:00
Oct 1977–Jan 1978, CBS Mon 8:00–9:00
CAST:
Logan .... Gregory Harrison
Jessica .... Heather Menzies
Rem .... Donald Moffat
Francis .... Randy Powell

The Earth of 2319 was radically different from that of the 20th century. There had been a nuclear holocaust that had devastated much of the planet. The remnants of civilization were living in isolated cities, each with its own life-style, separated from each other by vast stretches of wasteland and ruins. One of the surviving communities was the City of Domes, where all residents lived entirely for their own pleasure. It would have been idyllic were it not mandated that nobody could live past his 30th birthday. Logan was one of the city's citizens, a Sandman (elite policeman) who had fled as his 30th birthday approached. Together with a young girl named Jessica, who had helped him escape from the city, and an android (humanlike robot) named Rem, Logan searched for a purported utopia called Sanctuary. Pursuing them was a dedicated Sandman (Francis) who wanted to take them back to the City of Domes to die in the ritual ceremony known as Carousel. The chase of the fugitives by their pursuer, and their encounters with the diverse and strange remnants of human civilization, both in modern cities and in the wilds between them, provided the subject matter for this series.

It was based on a novel by William F. Nolan and George Clayton Johnson and a feature-length movie, both also titled *Logan's Run*.

LONE RANGER, THE

Western

FIRST TELECAST: *September 15, 1949*
LAST TELECAST: *September 12, 1957*
BROADCAST HISTORY:
Sep 1949–Sep 1957, ABC Thu 7:30–8:00
Jun 1950–Sep 1950, ABC Fri 10:00–10:30
CAST:
The Lone Ranger (1949–1952, 1954–1957) .... Clayton Moore
The Lone Ranger (1952–1954) ... John Hart
Tonto .... Jay Silverheels
THEME:
"William Tell Overture," by G. Rossini (composed 1829)

The Lone Ranger was typical of the first wave of Westerns to hit TV, in the early 1950s. Characters and plots were simple—good guys *vs.* bad guys—and there was none of the character development that marked the later "adult" Westerns.

The Lone Ranger had begun as a local radio show in 1933, and had quickly spread to a nationwide hookup (it was, in fact, the cornerstone of the then new Mutual Radio Network). In 1949 it was brought to TV in a series of half-hour films, made in Hollywood especially for the new medium. The opening episode, on September 15, 1949, told the familiar story of how the Lone Ranger got his name and his mission in life. He had been one of a posse of six Texas Rangers tracking a gang of desperadoes. The Rangers were lured into an ambush in a canyon, and five of them were slaughtered. The sixth, young John

Reid, was left for dead. But Reid managed to crawl to safety in a water hole, where he was found and nursed back to health by a friendly Indian named Tonto. Reid had once helped Tonto and the Indian now vowed to stay with him as the "lone" Ranger sought to avenge the deaths of his comrades. "You kemo sabe," said Tonto; "that mean 'faithful friend'."

Avenge they did, cornering the outlaw Cavendish in a dramatic battle on a canyon cliff.

Reid buried his past at the graves of the five dead Rangers, donned a mask, and set out with Tonto to avenge wrongs throughout the Old West. He had no visible means of support (he never accepted payment for his good deeds), but subsisted on the income from a silver mine that he and his brother—who was one of the deceased Rangers—had discovered. Periodically he returned to the mine, which was run for him by an honest old man, to collect the proceeds and stock up on silver bullets. Then, with a hearty "Hi-yo Silver, away!" he would sally forth once again, like some idealized Don Quixote, with faithful Tonto at his side and their faithful mounts Silver and Scout.

Although the Lone Ranger never killed anyone (sometimes his adversaries killed themselves and each other), there was plenty of action, and the show was a great favorite with the younger audience. Parents liked it too, because of the lack of overt killing and the hero's faultless grammar—which in itself was unique for the Old West. *The Lone Ranger* was in fact the biggest hit ABC had in its early years, and when the A. C. Nielsen Company first began compiling national ratings for network programs in 1950 it was the only ABC program to rank in the top 15. Everything else was on NBC or CBS. The program continued in prime time until 1957, on Sunday afternoons until 1961, and was seen in reruns and a cartoon version after that.

The Lone Ranger was created by George W. Trendle and Fran Striker, who were also responsible for *The Green Hornet*, and there was an unusual link between the two programs. John Reid's nephew Dan was supposed to be the father of Britt Reid, who became the avenger of crime in another era as *The Green Hornet*.

Clayton Moore was the best known TV Lone Ranger (he also filled the role in two feature films made in the late 1950s), but the character was also played by veteran actor John Hart for a couple of seasons. Tonto was always played to poker-faced perfection by Jay Silverheels, a mixed-blood Mohawk Indian who in later years became quite successful as a horse breeder and racer. Asked once if he would consider racing Scout, he smiled and replied, "Heck, *I* can beat Scout."

LONER, THE

Western

FIRST TELECAST: *September 18, 1965*
LAST TELECAST: *April 30, 1966*
BROADCAST HISTORY:
Sep 1965–Apr 1966, CBS Sat 9:30–10:00
CAST:
William Colton ....Lloyd Bridges

At the conclusion of the Civil War, ex-Union cavalry officer William Colton decided to head west in search of adventure and a new life. As he wandered the frontier, looking for something that would give his life meaning, his encounters with people both honest and dishonest, hardworking and fast-buck, gave him an expanded understanding of himself and of human beings in general.

LONG, HOT SUMMER, THE

Drama

FIRST TELECAST: *September 16, 1965*
LAST TELECAST: *July 13, 1966*
BROADCAST HISTORY:
Sep 1965–Jan 1966, ABC Thu 10:00–11:00
Jan 1966–Jul 1966, ABC Wed 10:00–11:00
CAST:
"Boss" Will Varner (1965) .... Edmond O'Brien
"Boss" Will Varner (1966) .... Dan O'Herlihy
Ben Quick ....Roy Thinnes
Clara Varner ....Nancy Malone
Jody Varner ....Paul Geary
Minnie Littlejohn .... Ruth Roman
Eula Harker ....Lana Wood

Adult drama set in small, Deep South community of Frenchman's Bend, dominated by aging, tyrannical Will Varner, who owned the town, and young Ben Quick, who had returned after 13 years to reclaim his father's farm and challenge Varner's absolute authority. Ben's father had been "destroyed" by Varner, but Ben was determined to settle the fight from which his father ran. Also featured were Varner's troubled, sensitive daughter Clara, his weak, immature son Jody, his mistress Minnie, and Eula, the sexy young daughter of the local postmaster.

The Long, Hot Summer was based on material by William Faulkner, primarily the novel *The Hamlet* and the short story "Barn Burning," which were adapted for a hit movie in 1958.

LONGSTREET

Detective

FIRST TELECAST: *September 9, 1971*

LAST TELECAST: *August 10, 1972*

BROADCAST HISTORY:

Sep 1971–Aug 1972, ABC Thu 9:00–10:00

CAST:

Mike Longstreet ....James Franciscus

Nikki Bell ....Marlyn Mason

Duke Paige ....Peter Mark Richman

Mike Longstreet was a New Orleans insurance-company investigator. While on a case he had the double misfortune of having his wife killed and his eyesight destroyed by people determined that he not solve the case. Despite his injury, Mike refused to quit the business. With his German shepherd guide dog Pax to help him get around, and an electronic cane to judge distances, Longstreet remained a remarkably successful investigator. If anything, blindness sharpened his other senses and analytical skills. Mike's girl Friday, Nikki, was his biggest booster; his insurance-company friend Duke Paige worked with him on many cases.

Kung Fu expert Bruce Lee appeared in this series as Longstreet's self-defense instructor.

LOOK MA, I'M ACTING

see *Say It with Acting*

LOOK PHOTOCRIME

see *Photocrime*

LORETTA YOUNG SHOW, THE

Dramatic Anthology

FIRST TELECAST: *September 20, 1953*

LAST TELECAST: *September 10, 1961*

BROADCAST HISTORY:

Sep 1953–Jun 1958, NBC Sun 10:00–10:30 (OS)

Oct 1958–Sep 1961, NBC Sun 10:00–10:30

HOSTESS/STAR:

Loretta Young

The Loretta Young Show's trademark, one that was often lampooned by comedians, was the dramatic entrance Miss Young made at the beginning of each episode. She would come sweeping through a doorway with her full-skirted dress swirling around her and move into the center of the room to introduce the evening's play. Equally distinctive was the program's close, when she would return and read a few lines of poetry or a passage from the Bible that amplified or restated the message of the play just telecast. Miss Young starred in over half the plays aired during this filmed series' eight-season run, playing everything from nuns to housewives. The periods and locations varied, the story may have been serious, amusing, or touching, but all of the tales told on *The Loretta Young Show* were uplifting. They portrayed the nobler side of the human spirit and were designed to teach as well as entertain. Episodes in which Miss Young had not starred were rerun under various titles as summer series with other performers functioning as host. When *The Loretta Young Show* went into syndication, the introductions were deleted in compliance with Miss Young's wishes. She was concerned that the dresses she had worn for them had become dated with the passage of time.

When this series premiered in September 1953 it was titled *Letter to Loretta*. All of the stories were done as responses to letters that she had received from her fans during the years she had been a motion-picture star. She would read a letter at the beginning of each show and then star in the dramatized answer. Although the title was changed to *The Loretta Young Show* on February 14, 1954, this format was retained through the first two seasons of the series, with Miss Young starring in every episode. At the start of the 1955–1956 season there were a number of changes. The series became a straight dramatic show and the letter concept was dropped. Miss Young, who was recovering from an operation when filming had started in June, was replaced by a succession of guest hosts and stars until her return on Christmas night. After her return, however, she cut back her starring appearances to roughly half of each year's episodes.

Over the years many performers starred, with or without Miss Young, in episodes of this series. Those who had the leads in at least three stories were Eddie Albert, George Nader, Hugh O'Brien, Beverly Washburn, Jock Mahoney, Craig Stevens, Ralph Meeker, James Daly, James Philbrook, Stephen McNally, Pat Crowley, Claude Akins, Barry Atwater, Regis Toomey, Everett Sloane, Ricardo Montalban, and John Newland. The latter two deserve special mention. Ricardo Montalban starred on nine different occasions and John Newland on thirteen. Mr. Newland, in addition to being Loretta's most frequent co-star, from 1957–1959 directed numerous episodes in which he was not acting.

LOST IN SPACE

Science Fiction

FIRST TELECAST: *September 15, 1965*

LAST TELECAST: *September 11, 1968*

BROADCAST HISTORY:

Sep 1965–Sep 1968, CBS Wed 7:30–8:30

CAST:

Prof. John Robinson ....Guy Williams
Maureen Robinson ....June Lockhart
Don West ....Mark Goddard
Judy Robinson ....Marta Kristen
Will Robinson ....Billy Mumy
Penny Robinson ....Angela Cartwright
Dr. Zachary Smith ....Jonathan Harris

The spaceship *Jupiter II* was supposed to take the Robinson family—Professor John, wife Maureen, and their three children—on a five-year voyage of exploration to a planet in the Alpha Centauri star system. It was, that is, until Dr. Zachary Smith sabotaged the control system so that it could not function properly. The control system was tied into the programming of the robot that went along as part of the exploration team, a friendly, logical, ambulatory machine that was strongly reminiscent of Robby the Robot in the movie *Forbidden Planet*. Smith, apparently in the employ of some foreign government, found himself trapped aboard the ship when it took off, leaving him hopelessly "lost in space" with the Robinsons and the ship's pilot, Major Donald West. An uneasy truce was made between all parties, for none of the scheduled passengers particularly trusted Dr. Smith, knowing what he had done. For three seasons the Robinsons and their unwanted guest wandered from planet to planet, trying to find their way home. The stories were fanciful and rather childish, full of monsters and strange intelligent life forms that were a constant threat, and an endless series of cliff-hanger endings designed to bring viewers back the following week. Dr. Smith was always trying to make a deal with some form of extraterrestrial intelligence to get him back without the others, but his plans never worked out. If he wasn't thwarted by the adults in the party, resourceful little Will Robinson, or the Robot, he managed to botch it up all by himself. He was a rather pompous, cowardly, and inept character.

LOTSA LUCK

Situation Comedy

FIRST TELECAST: *September 10, 1973*

LAST TELECAST: *May 24, 1974*

BROADCAST HISTORY:

Sep 1973–Jan 1974, NBC Mon 8:00–8:30
Jan 1974–May 1974, NBC Fri 8:30–9:00

CAST:

Stanley Belmont ....Dom DeLuise
Mrs. Belmont ....Kathleen Freeman
Arthur Swann ....Wynn Irwin
Olive Swann ....Beverly Sanders
Bummy ....Jack Knight

Bachelor Stanley Belmont was the custodian of the New York City bus company's lost-and-found department. But it was his home life and not his job that was the source of most of his problems and aggravations. Living with him was his bossy, autocratic mother, his klutzy sister Olive, and Olive's unemployed husband Arthur. The fact that Arthur was perfectly content to live off Stanley's earnings, and did not seem particularly interested in finding a job and moving out of Stanley's home, did not endear him to his brother-in-law. One of Stanley's co-workers, his good friend Bummy, was the only other regular in the cast. Based on the British series *On the Busses*.

LOU GRANT

Newspaper

FIRST TELECAST: *September 20, 1977*

LAST TELECAST:

BROADCAST HISTORY:

Sep 1977–Jan 1978, CBS Tue 10:00–11:00
Jan 1978– , CBS Mon 10:00–11:00

CAST:

Lou Grant .... Edward Asner
Charlie Hume .... Mason Adams
Joe Rossi .... Robert Walden
Billie Newman .... Linda Kelsey
Margaret Pynchon .... Nancy Marchand
Art Donovan .... Jack Bannon
Animal .... Darryl Anderson
National Editor .... Sidney Clute
Foreign Editor .... Laurence Haddon
Carla Mardigian (1977) ... Rebecca Balding

In the final episode of *The Mary Tyler Moore Show,* Lou Grant and most of the news staff of WJM-TV in Minneapolis were all fired. Fifty years old, and out of work, Lou moved to Los Angeles where, next season, he got a new job. No longer involved with television news, he became city editor of the *Los Angeles Tribune,* a struggling newspaper under the autocratic rule of its owner-publisher, Margaret Pynchon. Though he officially worked for managing editor Charlie Hume, an old friend, Lou often found himself in a battle of wills with the widowed Mrs. Pynchon, a woman with personality traits—stubbornness, toughness, and determination—very similar to his own. Despite the fireworks that usually erupted when they disagreed, there was an underlying mutual respect between them. Other principals included Joe Rossi, the hotshot, talented young investigative reporter; Carla Mardigian, an ambitious young girl reporter (who lasted only a few weeks, to be replaced by Billie Newman, another young reporter with similar aspirations); Art Donovan, the assistant city editor; and Animal, the staff photographer. Although essentially a dramatic series, *Lou Grant* did have its lighter moments, usually revolving around the interplay between the members of the paper's staff.

LOVE, AMERICAN STYLE

Comedy Anthology

FIRST TELECAST: *September 29, 1969*
LAST TELECAST: *January 11, 1974*
BROADCAST HISTORY:

Sep 1969–Jan 1970, ABC Mon 10:00–11:00
Jan 1970–Sep 1970, ABC Fri 10:00–11:00
Sep 1970–Jan 1971, ABC Fri 9:30–10:00
Jan 1971–Jan 1974, ABC Fri 10:00–11:00

REPERTORY COMPANY:

Mary Grover (1969–1970)
Stuart Margolin (1969–1973)
Buzz Cooper (1969–1970)
Barbara Minkus
Bill Callaway (1969–1971)
Lynne Marta (1969–1970)
Tracy Reed (1969–1970, 1972–1974)
Phyllis Elizabeth Davis (1970–1974)
Jaki De Mar (1970–1972)
Richard Williams (1970–1972)
Jim Hampton (1971–1974)
Clifton Davis (1971)
James A. Watson, Jr. (1972–1974)
Jed Allen (1973–1974)

This imaginative anthology was a collection of short comedy playlets, starring all sorts of big names, and dealing with the all-important subject of love. Love was seen from all sides, young and old, rich and poor, unmarried, just married, long married, and multi-married. Generally three or four playlets were presented on each episode, interspersed with short comic "blackouts" by a repertory company of six or seven young performers. In 1972 a tasteful "Lovemate of the Week" centerfold was also added, featuring a different girl each week.

A short list of those appearing in *Love, American Style* reads like a Who's Who of Hollywood: Phyllis Diller, Nanette Fabray, Tammy Grimes, Ann Sothern, Paul Ford, Pat Paulsen, Milton Berle, Sonny & Cher, the Lennon Sisters, George Gobel, Dorothy Lamour, Wally Cox, Tony Randall, Paul Lynde, Burt Reynolds, Harry Morgan, Rich Little, Ozzie & Harriet, Tiny Tim (as a suspected vampire), Sid Caesar, Imogene Coca, Jacqueline Susann, and Martha Raye. Ronnie Howard and Anson Williams appeared in a skit entitled "Love and the Happy Day," which served as the pilot for the hit series, *Happy Days.*

The first telecast, on September 29, 1969, was typical of the show's format. Act I, "Love and a Couple of Couples": Michael Callan is a suitor about to propose when his ex-wife turns up, spies the ring, tries it on—and can't get it off. Act II, "Love and the Hustler": Flip Wilson is pool shark "Big Red," who undertakes to instruct a young lady in the fine points of the game. Act III, "Love and the Pill": Bob Cummings and Jane Wyatt are parents worried about their daughter's plans to embark on a "swinger's tour" of Europe with her boy friend.

Love, American Style reruns were seen in ABC daytime for several years.

LOVE & MARRIAGE

Situation Comedy

FIRST TELECAST: *September 21, 1959*

LAST TELECAST: *January 25, 1960*

BROADCAST HISTORY:

Sep 1959–Jan 1960, NBC Mon 8:00–8:30

CAST:

William Harris .... William Demarest
Pat Baker .... Jeanne Bal
Steve Baker .... Murray Hamilton
Sophie .... Kay Armen
Stubby Wilson .... Stubby Kaye
Susan Baker .... Susan Reilly
Jennie Baker .... Jennie Lynn

William Harris was an old-time music publisher whose hatred for the currently popular rock'n'roll music was hurting his business and his health. He loved melodious music and refused to deal with most of the popular songs submitted to him. His progressive son-in-law Steve was a constant source of irritation and his daughter Pat was often left in the role of mediator between her father and her husband. Pat had inveigled herself into partnership with her father so that she could keep an eye on him. Featured in the show were William Harris' secretary, Sophie, and song-plugger Stubby Wilson, who performed many of the songs submitted to the publisher and spent a lot of time reminiscing about the "good old days" in the music-publishing business.

LOVE BOAT, THE

Situation Comedy

FIRST TELECAST: *September 24, 1977*

LAST TELECAST:

BROADCAST HISTORY:

Sep 1977–Jan 1978, ABC Sat 10:00–11:00
Jan 1978– , ABC Sat 9:00–10:00

CAST:

Captain Merrill Stubing ... Gavin MacLeod
Ship's Doctor Adam Bricker .... Bernie Kopell
Yeoman-Purser Burl "Gopher" Smith .... Fred Grandy
Bartender Isaac Washington .... Ted Lange
Cruise Director Julie McCoy .... Lauren Tewes

Love Boat was closely patterned after ABC's hit series *Love, American Style,* which ran from 1969 to 1974. Both programs consisted each week of several short comic sketches dealing with love of all types, young and old, married and unmarried, and both featured famous guest stars in the sketches. The difference was that all of *Love Boat's* stories were set aboard the Pacific Princess, a luxury cruise ship which embarked each week on a romantic, sentimental and often hilarious voyage across tropic seas. The three or four stories told on each telecast were thus interwoven and often involved the ship's crew, who were seen on the show every week.

Based on Jeraldine Saunders' *The Love Boats,* and previously seen as a series of specials during the 1976–1977 season.

LOVE ON A ROOFTOP

Situation Comedy

FIRST TELECAST: *September 6, 1966*

LAST TELECAST: *September 8, 1971*

BROADCAST HISTORY:

Sep 1966–Jan 1967, ABC Tue 9:30–10:00
Jan 1967–Apr 1967, ABC Thu 9:00–9:30
Apr 1967–Aug 1967, ABC Thu 9:30–10:00
May 1971–Sep 1971, ABC Wed 9:00–9:30

CAST:

David Willis .... Peter Deuel
Julie Willis .... Judy Carne
Stan Parker .... Rich Little
Carol Parker .... Barbara Bostock
Phyllis Hammond .... Edith Atwater
Fred Hammond .... Herbert Voland
Jim Lucas .... Sandy Kenyon

The joys of young love between a young married couple from different social backgrounds was the theme of this comedy. Art student Julie came from a wealthy family, but when she met $85-a-week apprentice architect David it was love at first sight. They married and moved into a small, windowless, top-floor walkup apartment. Its only asset was an adjacent stairway which led to the roof, and a spectacular view of the San Francisco Bay Area. Also seen were the neighbors, the Parkers (Stan was an "idea" man who composed menus for a living), Julie's unsympathetic parents, the Hammonds, and David's co-worker, Jim.

Reruns of the 1966–1967 series were aired during the summer of 1971.

LOVE STORY

Anthology

FIRST TELECAST: *April 20, 1954*

LAST TELECAST: *June 29, 1954*

BROADCAST HISTORY:

Apr 1954–Jun 1954, DUM Tue 8:30–9:00

The teleplays that were aired in this live anthology were all stories that showed the better side of human nature—the affection and concern people could have for one another. Lesser-known actors and actresses were starred.

LOVE STORY

Dramatic Anthology

FIRST TELECAST: *October 3, 1973*

LAST TELECAST: *January 2, 1974*

BROADCAST HISTORY:

Oct 1973–Jan 1974, NBC Wed 10:00–11:00

THEME:

"Love Story (Where Do I Begin)," by Francis Lai

In the wake of the bestselling novel and smash-hit 1970 movie starring Ryan O'Neal and Ali MacGraw, NBC felt that *Love Story* was just what was needed for prime time. Unfortunately, the TV series had nothing to do with the book or movie, sharing only the name and that pretty theme song. That may have accounted for its short tenure on the air.

The stories were about people in love, young and old, rich and poor, married and single, and were set in various locations across the U.S. Generally, lesser-known actors and actresses appeared.

LOVE THAT BOB

syndicated title for *Bob Cummings Show, The*

LOVE THAT JILL

Situation Comedy

FIRST TELECAST: *January 20, 1958*

LAST TELECAST: *April 28, 1958*

BROADCAST HISTORY:

Jan 1958–Apr 1958, ABC Mon 8:00–8:30

CAST:

Jill Johnson ....Anne Jeffreys
Jack Gibson ....Robert Sterling
Richard ....James Lydon
Pearl ....Betty Lynn

Real-life husband-and-wife team Robert Sterling and Anne Jeffreys played the heads of rival Manhattan model agencies in this short-lived comedy. Jill was always after one of Jack's clients or models, and vice versa, and Jack would not have minded landing Jill as well. Also seen regularly were Jill's male secretary Richard, Jack's secretary Pearl, and a bevy of beautiful models with names such as Melody, Ginger, and Peaches.

LOVE THY NEIGHBOR

Situation Comedy

FIRST TELECAST: *June 15, 1973*

LAST TELECAST: *September 19, 1973*

BROADCAST HISTORY:

Jun 1973–Jul 1973, ABC Fri 9:30–10:00
Aug 1973–Sep 1973, ABC Wed 8:00–8:30

CAST:

Ferguson Bruce ....Harrison Page
Jackie Bruce ....Janet MacLachlan
Charlie Wilson ....Ron Masak
Peggy Wilson ....Joyce Bulifant
Murray Bronson ....Milt Kamen
Harry Mulligan ....Herbie Faye

This integrated comedy revolved around the friendship between a Caucasian family and a young black couple who had just moved into their previously all-white neighborhood. Charlie Wilson was somewhat nonplused when he first discovered that his new neighbor on Friar Tuck Lane in suburban Sherwood Forest Estates (near Los Angeles) was not only black, but was the new efficiency expert at Turner Electronics, the company where he was a union shop steward.

Based on the English TV hit, *Love Thy Neighbor*.

LOVES ME, LOVES ME NOT

Situation Comedy

FIRST TELECAST: *March 20, 1977*

LAST TELECAST: *April 27, 1977*

BROADCAST HISTORY:

Mar 1977, CBS Sun 10:30–11:00
Mar 1977–Apr 1977, CBS Wed 8:30–9:00

CAST:

Jane ....Susan Dey
Dick ....Kenneth Gilman
Tom ....Art Metrano
Sue ....Phyllis Glick

This short romantic-comedy mini-series was about two young single people who were dating each other. Dick and Jane had their ups and their downs and, since their relationship was just getting off the ground, were unsure of their feelings for each other. He was a newspaper reporter and she was a teacher. Tom was Dick's best friend and his editor at the newspaper, and Sue was Tom's wife.

LUCAN

Adventure

FIRST TELECAST: *December 26, 1977*

LAST TELECAST:

BROADCAST HISTORY:

Dec 1977–Jan 1978, ABC Mon 8:00–9:00
Jun 1978–Jul 1978, ABC Sun 8:00–9:00
Nov 1978– , ABC Mon 8:00–9:00

CAST:

Lucan .... Kevin Brophy
Dr. Hoagland .... John Randolph
Prentiss .... Don Gordan

Lucan was the story of a young man of 20 who had been raised in the forest, by wolves. For his first ten years he had never known another human being, and now, though acclimated to the ways of civilization, he still found himself ill at ease in cities. His search for his parents and for his own identity formed the basis for most of the stories. The series was seen briefly during the winter of 1977–1978, with reruns the following summer.

LUCAS TANNER

School Drama

FIRST TELECAST: *September 11, 1974*

LAST TELECAST: *August 20, 1975*

BROADCAST HISTORY:

Sep 1974–Aug 1975, NBC Wed 9:00–10:00

CAST:

Lucas Tanner .... David Hartman
Margaret Blumenthal ... Rosemary Murphy
Glendon Farrell .... Robbie Rist
Jaytee Drumm .... Alan Abelew
Cindy Damon .... Trish Soodik
Terry Klitsner .... Kimberly Beck
Wally Moore ...... Michael Dwight-Smith
John Hamilton (1975) ...... John Randolph

Lucas Tanner had been both a baseball player and a sportswriter but had given up both after the death of his wife and son in an auto accident. Wanting to start a new life, he moved to St. Louis and obtained a job as an English teacher at Harry S Truman Memorial High School in suburban Webster Groves, Mo. There he encountered frustrating resistance to his down-to-earth teaching style, primarily from the more tradition-bound teachers. The support of principal Margaret Blumenthal, who was replaced in January by John Hamilton, and the gratitude of his students were often the only things that kept him from "throwing in the towel." Lucas' warm and understanding nature made him a favorite of the students, who appreciated his ability to treat them as individuals. A special friend was little Glendon, a small boy who was one of Lucas's neighbors and who would often come over to visit and talk.

LUCILLE BALL SHOW, THE

see *Lucy Show, The*

LUCKY PUP

Children's

FIRST TELECAST: *August 23, 1948*

LAST TELECAST: *June 23, 1951*

BROADCAST HISTORY:

Aug 1948–Sep 1948, CBS Mon/Wed/Fri Various
Sep 1948–Sep 1950, CBS Mon–Fri 6:30–6:45
Jan 1949–Jun 1951, CBS Sat Various half hours between 6:00–7:15

HOSTESS:

Doris Brown

PUPPETEERS:

Hope and Morey Bunin

Lucky Pup was one of the more popular puppet shows on early television. It was first previewed between 8:00 P.M. and 9:00 P.M. on two consecutive weeks in 1948 to let parents see what their children would have available to them at an earlier hour, and then began a three-year run in the early evening.

With the exception of hostess and narrator Doris Brown, all of the characters on *Lucky Pup* were puppets. Lucky Pup was a little dog that had inherited $5 million from a recently deceased circus queen. Foodini was the magician who was trying to use his black arts to steal the treasure, Pinhead was Foodini's dumb but friendly stooge, and Jolo was the resident clown. All of the action took place in a circus setting. Gradually Foodini and Pinhead came to dominate the stories, and Lucky Pup himself was seldom seen.

The series ended in June 1951, when Doris Brown married and left television. A charming, modest woman, she later recalled of those early days: "I can't honestly say I miss performing. I never was a real professional at it; just enjoyed myself and often wondered why they ever let me get away with it." The Bunins later returned with a spinoff series called *Foodini the Great*.

LUCY-DESI COMEDY HOUR, THE

Situation Comedy

FIRST TELECAST: *July 2, 1962*

LAST TELECAST: *August 31, 1967*

BROADCAST HISTORY:

Jul 1962–Sep 1962, CBS Mon 9:00–10:00
Jun 1963–Sep 1963, CBS Sat 7:30–8:30
Jun 1964–Sep 1964, CBS Sat 7:30–8:30
Jun 1965–Sep 1965, CBS Wed 10:00–11:00
Jun 1967–Aug 1967, CBS Thu 7:30–8:30

CAST:

Lucy Ricardo .... Lucille Ball
Ricky Ricardo .... Desi Arnaz
Ethel Mertz .... Vivian Vance
Fred Mertz .... William Frawley
Little Ricky .... Richard Keith

At the end of the 1956–1957 season of *I Love Lucy*, the show's stars decided that they wanted to experiment with a longer form of program. Starting on November 14, 1957, and over the course of the next few seasons, all of the *I Love Lucy* regulars starred in a number of full-hour specials. In the specials they traveled to different places and became involved with various guest stars. Collections of these specials were aired as summer series for five years by CBS under the title *The Lucy-Desi Comedy Hour*.

LUCY IN CONNECTICUT

Situation Comedy

FIRST TELECAST: *July 3, 1960*

LAST TELECAST: *September 25, 1960*

BROADCAST HISTORY:

Jul 1960–Sep 1960, CBS Sun 10:00–10:30

CAST:

Lucy Ricardo .... Lucille Ball
Ricky Ricardo .... Desi Arnaz
Ethel Mertz .... Vivian Vance
Fred Mertz .... William Frawley
Betty Ramsey .... Mary Jane Croft
Ralph Ramsey .... Frank Nelson

The episodes that made up this summer series were all reruns of episodes of *I Love Lucy* that covered the period in which Lucy had convinced Ricky that it would be a great idea to move to the country. She got him to make a large down payment on a big home in Westport, Connecticut, and they spent the next several weeks learning about the advantages and disadvantages of suburban living. Mary Jane Croft, who would later replace Vivian Vance as Lucy's friend and companion in mischief on *The Lucy Show*, was showcased here as the Ricardos' next-door neighbor in Westport.

LUCY SHOW, THE

see *I Love Lucy*

LUCY SHOW, THE

Situation Comedy

FIRST TELECAST: *October 1, 1962*

LAST TELECAST: *September 2, 1974*

BROADCAST HISTORY:

Oct 1962–Jun 1964, CBS Mon 8:30–9:00 (OS)
Sep 1964–Jul 1965, CBS Mon 9:00–9:30
Sep 1965–Jun 1967, CBS Mon 8:30–9:00 (OS)
Sep 1967–Sep 1971, CBS Mon 8:30–9:00
Sep 1971–Sep 1974, CBS Mon 9:00–9:30

CAST:

Lucy Carmichael/Carter .... Lucille Ball
Vivian Bagley (1962–1965) ... Vivian Vance
Theodore J. Mooney/Harrison Otis Carter (1963–1974) .... Gale Gordon
Harry Conners (1962–1964) ... Dick Martin
Chris Carmichael (1962–1965) .... Candy Moore
Jerry Carmichael (1962–1966) .... Jimmy Garrett
Sherman Bagley (1962–1965) ... Ralph Hart
Harrison Cheever (1965–1968) .... Roy Roberts
Mary Jane Lewis (1965–1974) .... Mary Jane Croft
Kim Carter (1968–1974) ...... Lucie Arnaz
Craig Carter (1968–1971) ... Desi Arnaz, Jr.

Tackling a series on her own, without husband Desi Arnaz, Lucille Ball firmly established herself as the first lady of American television with this long-running series. With one exception, the supporting cast underwent numerous changes over the years, and at one time included both of Miss Ball's real-life children. The one exception was Gale Gordon, who provided Lucy with a stubborn, stuffy foil for most of the show's run. The real constant, however, was Lucy and her special brand of slapstick humor, played off of all sorts of guests and regulars. Such was her fame by this time that she could attract Richard Burton and Elizabeth Taylor (and their well-publicized diamond ring) as special guests to open one season (1971), as well as many other stars who normally shunned television.

When it appeared in the fall of 1962, *The Lucy Show* cast its star as a widow with two children, Chris and Jerry, living in suburban Danfield, Connecticut, and sharing her home with a divorced friend, Vivian Bagley, and Vivian's son, Sherman. Both women were desperately looking to snag new husbands and Lucy, in an effort to keep busy and meet eligible men, eventually went to work part-time for Mr. Mooney at the Danfield First National Bank. In September 1965, Lucy moved to San Francisco, as coincidentally did banker Mooney, and again she was working as his secretary, this time at the Westland Bank. Mooney, who had been president of the bank in Connecticut, was a vice-president at the bank in San Francisco, which was run by Harrison Cheever. Lucy's daughter Chris was no longer with the cast and Vivian Bagley, no longer a series regular, appeared only occasionally as a visitor from the East. Lucy's new cohort was friend Mary Jane Lewis. The last episode under this title aired on September 16, 1968.

In September 1968 the show returned with a new title (*Here's Lucy*), a couple of major cast changes, and a modified story line. Lucy had moved to Los Angeles and her last name was now Carter. She was still a widow with two children, but they were now named Kim and Craig (played by her real-life children, Lucie and Desi). She worked for the Unique Employment Agency, which was owned by her brother-in-law, Harrison "Uncle Harry" Carter. Gale Gordon was thus retained as her blustery, ever-suffering foil. During the summers of 1968–1971 reruns of the earlier *Lucy Shows* were aired (prior to 1968 the series was replaced by various other programs during the summer months).

The program was initially titled *The Lucille Ball Show* when it went on the air in 1962, shortened to *The Lucy Show* after only one month, and then retitled *Here's Lucy* in the fall of 1968.

LUX PLAYHOUSE

Dramatic Anthology

FIRST TELECAST: *October 3, 1958*

LAST TELECAST: *September 18, 1959*

BROADCAST HISTORY:

Oct 1958–Sep 1959, CBS Fri 9:30–10:00

This filmed dramatic-anthology series aired on alternate Fridays with *Schlitz Playhouse*. Content ranged from light comedies, to romance, to melodrama. Generally, better-known performers participated, with Polly Bergen and Rod Taylor in "The Best House in the Valley," Barry Nelson and Audrey Totter in "Drive a Desert Road," Jan Sterling in "Stand-in for Murder," and Gisele MacKenzie and John Forsythe in "The Miss and Missiles" among the presentations.

LUX SHOW STARRING ROSEMARY CLOONEY, THE

Musical Variety

FIRST TELECAST: *September 26, 1957*

LAST TELECAST: *June 19, 1958*

BROADCAST HISTORY:

Sep 1957–Jun 1958, NBC Thu 10:00–10:30

REGULARS:

Rosemary Clooney
Paula Kelly & the Modernaires
Frank DeVol and His Orchestra
The Jones Boys (1958)

Rosemary Clooney starred in this variety series that included comedy skits as well as musical numbers. Regulars on the series were the vocal group of Paula Kelly & the Modernaires, who left in March 1958 and were replaced by an all-male group, the Jones Boys.

LUX VIDEO THEATRE

Dramatic Anthology

FIRST TELECAST: *October 2, 1950*

LAST TELECAST: *September 12, 1957*

BROADCAST HISTORY:

Oct 1950–Jun 1951, CBS Mon 8:00–8:30
Aug 1951–Mar 1953, CBS Mon 8:00–8:30
Apr 1953–Jun 1954, CBS Thu 9:00–9:30
Aug 1954–Sep 1957, NBC Thu 10:00–11:00

HOST:

James Mason (1954–1955)
Otto Kruger (1955–1956)
Gordon MacRae (1956–1957)
Ken Carpenter (summers 1955–1957)

After 16 years on radio as a weekly dramatic series, *Lux Radio Theatre* became *Lux Video Theatre* on October 2, 1950. The first live play, from New York, was an adaptation of Maxwell Anderson's *Saturday's Children*, starring Joan Caulfield. For three seasons this live dramatic series originated from New York, finally moving to Hollywood with the September 2, 1953, telecast. Major motion-picture stars and Broadway actors performed on the show. Some of the names to appear during this period were Veronica Lake, Zachary Scott, Franchot Tone, Nina Foch, Celeste Holm, Broderick Crawford, Dennis O'Keefe, and young Charlton Heston. The subject matter ranged from contemporary to period, serious to light. On the more literary side, William Faulkner adapted two of his short stories—"The Brooch" and "Shall Not Perish"—for presentation on *Lux Video Theatre* in 1953 and 1954.

When the series moved to NBC in the fall of 1954, there were a number of changes in the format. The length of each telecast was expanded to a full hour, a regular host was added to the program, and adaptations of theatrical films became the principal type of material presented. The host introduced each act and, at the end of the show, conducted short interviews with the stars (female stars always gave plugs for their "Lux Complexion"). When the show had been adapted from a movie, the host also interviewed a principal from the studio whose film had been adapted to plug a current film from that studio. Film clips from the current film were shown as part of the interview.

A preview of this adaptation of feature films had actually occurred in 1954 while *Lux Video Theatre* was still on CBS. On January 28, 1954, John Derek, Ann Blyth, and Marilyn Erskine had starred in a television version of *A Place in the Sun*, with Ronald Reagan hosting. The first NBC telecast was an abridgement of *To Each His Own*, starring Dorothy Malone and Gene Barry. At the end of the show, Alfred Hitchcock was interviewed about his current film, *Rear Window*. Popular movies that aired in abbreviated versions over the years were *Double Indemnity*, with Laraine Day and Frank Lovejoy; *Sunset Boulevard*, with Miriam Hopkins and James Daly; *Casablanca*, with Paul Douglas, Arlene Dahl, and Hoagy Carmichael; *Mildred Pierce*, with Virginia Bruce and Zachary Scott; *Jezebel*, with Martha Hyer, Charles Drake, and Jack Lord; and *To Have and Have Not*, with Edmond O'Brien and Beverly Garland.

During the summers Ken Carpenter, the regular announcer for the series, doubled as host and the plays presented were short versions of scripts that were under consideration by the studios as possible full-length features. None of them were subsequently produced as feature films.

M*A*S*H

Situation Comedy

FIRST TELECAST: *September 17, 1972*

LAST TELECAST:

BROADCAST HISTORY:

Sep 1972–Sep 1973, CBS Sun 8:00–8:30
Sep 1973–Sep 1974, CBS Sat 8:30–9:00
Sep 1974–Sep 1975, CBS Tue 8:30–9:00
Sep 1975–Nov 1975, CBS Fri 8:30–9:00
Dec 1975–Jan 1978, CBS Tue 9:00–9:30
Jan 1978– , CBS Mon 9:00–9:30

CAST:

Capt. Benjamin Franklin Pierce (Hawkeye) .... Alan Alda
Capt. John McIntyre (Trapper John) (1972–1975) .... Wayne Rogers
Maj. Margaret Houlihan (Hot Lips) .... Loretta Swit
Maj. Frank Burns (1972–1977) .... Larry Linville
Cpl. Radar O'Reilly .... Gary Burghoff
Lt. Col. Henry Blake (1972–1975) .... McLean Stevenson
Father John Mulcahy .... William Christopher
Corp. Maxwell Klinger (1973–) .... Jamie Farr
Col. Sherman Potter (1975–) .... Harry Morgan
Capt. B. J. Hunnicut (1975–) .... Mike Farrell
Maj. Charles Emerson Winchester (1977–) .... David Ogden Stiers
Lt. Maggie Dish (1972) .... Karen Philipp
Spearchucker Jones (1972) .... Timothy Brown
Ho-John (1972) .... Patrick Adiarte
Ugly John (1972–1973) .... John Orchard
Lt. Leslie Scorch (1972–1973) .... Linda Meiklejohn
Gen. Brandon Clayton (1972–1973) .... Herb Voland
Lt. Ginger Ballis (1972–1974) .... Odessa Cleveland
Nurse Margie Cutler (1972–1973) .... Marcia Strassman

Nurse Louise Anderson (1973)
.... Kelly Jean Peters
Lt. Nancy Griffin (1973) .... Lynette Mettey
Various nurses (1973–1977)
.... Bobbie Mitchell
Gen. Mitchell (1973–1974)
.... Robert F. Simon
Nurse Kelly (1974–)
.... Kellye Nakahara
Various nurses (1974–)
.... Patricia Stevens
Various nurses (1976–) ... Judy Farrell
Igor (1976–1977) ....Jeff Mitchell
Nurse Bigelow (1977–) ..... Enid Kent
Sgt. Zale (1977–1978) ..... Johnny Haymer

THEME:

"Suicide Is Painless," by Johnny Mandel

In 1972 America was still embroiled in a lingering war in Vietnam, a war that had polarized the population. The climate created by an unpopular war was the perfect environment for an antiwar comedy like *M*A*S*H*. The setting was different, Korea in the early 1950s, but the stories and situations could just as easily have been from Vietnam in the 1970s.

The cast of characters in *M*A*S*H* were all members of the 4077th *M*obile *A*rmy *S*urgical *H*ospital, stationed behind the lines during the Korean War. Their job was to treat the wounded being sent to them from the front lines and to try to save as many lives as possible. The environment was depressing; many of the doctors (who had all been drafted) could not really believe they were living under the conditions to which they were being subjected. There was an overwhelming sense of the futility and insanity of war that permeated their daily lives. A certain sense of humor was necessary for survival.

Most of the senior members of the M.A.S.H. unit had wives and families back home, but that never stopped them from propositioning every good-looking nurse they could con into their quarters. After all, they did need something to alleviate the depression that resulted from contact with a constant stream of maimed and dying young G.I.'s. Two of the surgeons were Hawkeye Pierce and Trapper John McIntyre. Like virtually everyone else, they were always breaking regulations. Hawkeye, despite his escapades, was probably the most intellectual of the doctors and was sometimes seen musing on the dehumanizing nature of war and questioning its moral validity.

Among others who were featured was Frank Burns, who was possibly the worst doctor in the unit, and the constant butt of practical jokes perpetrated by Hawkeye and Trapper because of his arrogance and his feigned adherence to military regulations. Hot Lips Houlihan was the head nurse who, despite her admonitions to both her nurses and the doctors about fooling around with each other, had been having an affair with Frank Burns for an extended period. Henry Blake, the commanding officer whose prime concern was the work of the doctors in the operating room, couldn't care less about what they did during their free time. Radar O'Reilly was the extremely shy and bumbling young aide to Col. Blake. There were also numerous nurses who came and went, with the same actress being referred to in different episodes by different names—a large number of actresses were collectively called Nurse Able and Nurse Baker.

There were changes in the cast over the years. The most significant addition was that of Cpl. Maxwell Klinger, an aide to the doctors in the operating room. There was nothing really wrong with him; it was just that he always dressed in women's clothing in a desperate, though futile, attempt to get himself discharged as mentally unfit. McLean Stevenson left the series in the spring of 1975, to sign a long term contract with NBC, and his character, Col. Blake, was written out of the show by having him die in a helicopter crash in the last episode of the 1974–1975 season. He was replaced by Col. Potter, who was somewhat more sardonic and definitely less silly than his predecessor. In the summer of 1975 Wayne Rogers also left the series, in a contract dispute; his character, Trapper, got a discharge and returned home at the beginning of the 1975–1976 season. B.J. Hunnicut replaced Trapper as Hawkeye's roommate and co-conspirator.

At the beginning of the 1977–1978 season Larry Linville left, and so Major Burns was written out of the series. Having seen his love affair with Hot Lips end when she married Lt. Col. Donald Penobscott, Frank abruptly went AWOL and was permanently transferred. Replacing him was an aristocratic Bostonian, Maj. Charles Emerson Winchester. Hot Lips' marriage to Col.

Penobscott, who was not stationed with the 4077th and who was virtually never seen with his wife after the honeymoon, ended in divorce during the 1978–1979 season.

*M*A*S*H* was based on the hit motion picture of the same name, which in turn was taken from the novel. The novel had been written by a doctor who had actually served in one of the Korean War M.A.S.H. units, but who used a pseudonym—Richard Hooker—in writing, so as not to compromise his medical standing by his revelations.

MGM PARADE

Documentary

FIRST TELECAST: *September 14, 1955*
LAST TELECAST: *May 2, 1956*
BROADCAST HISTORY:

Sep 1955–May 1956, ABC Wed 8:30–9:00

HOST:

George Murphy (1955–1956)
Walter Pidgeon (1956)

Originally conceived as an opportunity for the viewer to see the workings of a major motion-picture studio, this series was hosted by actor (eventually to become Senator) George Murphy. Segments included interviews with stars, explanations and demonstrations of technical aspects of production, excerpts from current and past MGM productions, and special entertainment featurettes produced specifically for this series. Due to weak ratings, in the spring of 1956 the format was revised to serialize classic MGM films. Walter Pidgeon took over as host to present *Captains Courageous*, highlights of the work of Greta Garbo, and *The Pirate*.

M SQUAD

Police

FIRST TELECAST: *September 20, 1957*
LAST TELECAST: *September 13, 1960*
BROADCAST HISTORY:

Sep 1957–Sep 1959, NBC Fri 9:00–9:30
Sep 1959–Jan 1960, NBC Fri 9:30–10:00
Jan 1960–Sep 1960, NBC Tue 10:00–10:30

CAST:

Lt. Frank Ballinger .... Lee Marvin
Capt. Grey .... Paul Newlan

The M Squad was an elite group of plainclothes detectives working to fight organized crime in Chicago. Lt. Frank Ballinger was one of these top detectives who worked, as did most of the other members of M Squad, by himself. Ballinger was a hard-nosed cop with no romantic interests. His commanding officer, and the man who assigned him to most of his cases, was Capt. Grey. Lee Marvin starred as Ballinger and also served as narrator of the series.

The original *M Squad* theme had been composed by the show's music director, Stanley Wilson. At the start of *M Squad*'s second season, however, the original theme was replaced by a more jazz-oriented tune composed by Count Basie, which was also known as the "Theme from *M Squad*."

MAC DAVIS SHOW, THE

Musical Variety

FIRST TELECAST: *July 11, 1974*
LAST TELECAST: *June 17, 1976*
BROADCAST HISTORY:

Jul 1974–Aug 1974, NBC Thu 8:00–9:00
Dec 1974–Feb 1975, NBC Thu 8:00–9:00
Mar 1975–May 1975, NBC Thu 9:00–10:00
Mar 1976–Jun 1976, NBC Thu 8:00–9:00

REGULARS:

Mac Davis
Robert Shields and Lorene Yarnell (1976)
Strutt (1976)
Ron Silver (1976)

Country-oriented singer and composer Mac Davis had three tries as host of his own variety series, in the summer of 1974, early 1975, and the spring of 1976. None of the three attempts attracted sufficient audience to stay on the schedule more than a few months. Regular features on all three shows were Mac's singing of his own songs, reminiscing about his growing-up years in Texas, and informal chats with the audience. In fact, he was often seen seated with the audience during part of the show, while he answered questions or sang and played his guitar. He would also improvise songs from title suggestions submitted by the audience. The 1976 edition had, in addition to Mac and his guest stars, three regulars: the mime team of Shields and Yarnell, comedian Ron Silver, and a group of singers and dancers known collectively as Strutt.

MME LIU TSONG

see *Gallery Of Madame Liu Tsong, The*

MADE IN AMERICA

Quiz/Audience Participation

FIRST TELECAST: *April 5, 1964*
LAST TELECAST: *May 3, 1964*
BROADCAST HISTORY:
Apr 1964–May 1964, CBS Sun 9:30–10:00
EMCEE:
Hans Conried
PANELISTS:
Jan Sterling
Walter Slezak
Don Murray

The object of the panel on this show was to guess in what manner each of the contestants had made their fortunes. All of the contestants were millionaires and they donated their winnings to charity. The amount they won, up to $600, was dependent on how long it took the panel to identify the source of their incomes. Three contestants appeared on each show.

MADISON SQUARE GARDEN

see *Saturday Night at the Garden*

MADISON SQUARE GARDEN HIGHLIGHTS

Sports Commentary

FIRST TELECAST: *June 25, 1953*
LAST TELECAST: *April 15, 1954*
BROADCAST HISTORY:
Jun 1953–Sep 1953, ABC Thu 9:00–9:30
Sep 1953–Oct 1953, ABC Sat 8:30–9:00
Oct 1953–Dec 1953, ABC Sat 10:00–10:30
Jan 1954, ABC Sat 8:30–9:00
Feb 1954–Apr 1954, DUM Thu 8:00–8:30
HOSTS:
Marty Glickman
Stan Lomax

Sportscasters Marty Glickman and Stan Lomax narrated this weekly collection of filmed highlights of sports events that had taken place the previous week at Madison Square Garden in New York. There was some analysis and commentary mixed in with their narration of the events.

MAGGI'S PRIVATE WIRE

Interview

FIRST TELECAST: *April 12, 1949*
LAST TELECAST: *July 2, 1949*
BROADCAST HISTORY:
Apr 1949, NBC Tue 7:30–7:45
May 1949–Jul 1949, NBC Sat 7:30–7:45
HOSTESS:
Maggi McNellis

Radio and TV personality Maggi McNellis hosted this weekly talk show, interviewing celebrities from show business and other fields.

MAGIC COTTAGE

Children's

FIRST TELECAST: *July 18, 1949*
LAST TELECAST: *February 9, 1951*
BROADCAST HISTORY:
Jul 1949–Feb 1951, DUM Mon–Fri 6:30–7:00
HOSTESS:
Pat Meikle

Pat Meikle, who earlier had a daytime program billed as "The TV Babysitter," hosted this storytelling session in 1949–1951. Her cottage had a drawing board, and from the board stepped children's characters from "Jack and the Beanstalk" and "Goldilocks," among other sources, to relate their famous tales, much to the delight of the youthful studio audience. Original stories such as "Oogie the Ogre's Christmas" and the continuing adventures of Wilmer the Pigeon were also presented, and there were games and contests for the kids. *Magic Cottage* was also seen as a daytime program and as a local series in New York.

MAGIC SLATE, THE

Children's

FIRST TELECAST: *June 2, 1950*
LAST TELECAST: *August 25, 1950*
BROADCAST HISTORY:
Jun 1950–Aug 1950, NBC Fri 8:00–8:30
PRODUCER:
Norman Gant

These dramatizations of classic and original children's stories were produced under the supervision of Charlotte Chorpenning of the Goodman Children's Theater in Chicago. *The Magic Slate* alternated with *Quiz Kids* on Friday nights in 1950, and then returned in the summer of 1951 as a Sunday afternoon series. Telecast from Chicago.

MAGICIAN, THE

Adventure

FIRST TELECAST: *October 2, 1973*
LAST TELECAST: *May 20, 1974*

BROADCAST HISTORY:

Oct 1973–Jan 1974, NBC Tue 9:00–10:00
Jan 1974–May 1974, NBC Mon 8:00–9:00

CAST:

Anthony Blake .... Bill Bixby
Max Pomeroy .... Keene Curtis
Dennis Pomeroy .... Todd Crespi
Jerry Wallace .... Jim Watkins
Dominick .... Joseph Sirola

Earlier in his life, stage magician Tony Blake had spent time in prison for a crime he had not committed. Prison had been a particularly distasteful experience for a man of his background, and had left him with a strong sense of concern for personal freedom and individual rights. Once released, he put his talents as an illusionist and escape artist to use helping people in danger and preventing crimes. Syndicated columnist and novelist Max Pomeroy was a close friend of Tony's and was often responsible for bringing him cases. Max's paraplegic son Dennis, although confined to a wheelchair, also became involved in the cases, as did Jerry Wallace, the pilot of Tony's private airliner, *The Spirit*.

When this series moved to Monday nights in January 1974, Tony had taken up residence at Hollywood's famous Magic Castle, where many of the most renowned magicians in the world performed, and some of them were seen on this show. The magic acts performed by Blake were also genuine: Bill Bixby was himself an amateur magician.

MAGNAVOX THEATER

Dramatic Anthology

FIRST TELECAST: *September 15, 1950*
LAST TELECAST: *December 8, 1950*
BROADCAST HISTORY:

Sep 1950–Dec 1950, CBS Fri 9:00–10:00

The first few dramas presented on this series were produced live in New York and aired on alternate Fridays with *Ford Theatre*. Content ranged from serious dramas starring Dane Clark and Geraldine Brooks, to light comedy with Edward Everett Horton. The most notable telecast in *Magnavox Theater*'s short run aired on November 24, 1950. There was nothing spectacular about Magnavox's adaptation of *The Three Musketeers*—which starred "fast-rising" young movie actor Robert Clarke (he had been trying to crash the big time since 1944) and such obscure supporting players as Mel Archer and Marjorie Lord. But this was, according to CBS, the first hour-long film made in Hollywood especially for television. It took just four and a half days to film, and was produced at the Hal Roach Studios, as were the two films which were aired as the last two telecasts of *Magnavox Theater*.

MAIL STORY, THE

Dramatic Anthology

FIRST TELECAST: *October 7, 1954*
LAST TELECAST: *December 30, 1954*
BROADCAST HISTORY:

Oct 1954–Dec 1954, ABC Thu 8:00–8:30

There were two completely different types of stories presented on *The Mail Story*: those that dealt with the good and varied services provided by the U.S. Postal Service, which were often in quasi-documentary form; and those that were dramas of people attempting to misuse the postal system and the efforts made by postal authorities to apprehend them. The latter were all based on actual case histories from the Postal Service's files and ranged from stagecoach robbing in the middle 1850s to contemporary mail fraud. This series was subtitled *Handle With Care*.

MAJOR ADAMS, TRAILMASTER

syndicated title for *Wagon Train*

MAJORITY RULES

Quiz/Panel

FIRST TELECAST: *September 2, 1949*
LAST TELECAST: *July 30, 1950*
BROADCAST HISTORY:

Sep 1949–Jan 1950, ABC Fri 8:00–8:30
Feb 1950–Mar 1950, ABC Fri 9:30–10:00
Mar 1950–Jul 1950, ABC Sun 8:30–9:00

EMCEE:

Ed Prentiss
Tom Moore
Myron Wallace

A panel of three contestants was posed questions in this Chicago-originated quiz show, with the "right" answer being determined by the majority of two. Several hosts came and went during the run of the series, and a telephone gimmick involving celebrities was also introduced.

MAKE ME LAUGH

Quiz/Audience Participation

FIRST TELECAST: *March 20, 1958*

LAST TELECAST: *June 12, 1958*

BROADCAST HISTORY:

Mar 1958–Jun 1958, ABC Thu 10:00–10:30

EMCEE:

Robert Q. Lewis

The object of this game show was for contestants to refrain from laughing. Each week three different comedians participated in trying to make contestants laugh. One minute was allotted to each comedian. The contestants could win up to $180, one dollar for every second they refrained from laughter.

MAKE MINE MUSIC

see *Face the Music*

MAKE ROOM FOR DADDY

see *Danny Thomas Show, The*

MAKE ROOM FOR GRANDDADDY

see *Danny Thomas Show, The*

MAKE THAT SPARE

Sports

FIRST TELECAST: *October 8, 1960*

LAST TELECAST: *September 11, 1964*

BROADCAST HISTORY:

Oct 1960–Sep 1963, ABC Sat 10:45–11:00 (OS)

Sep 1963–Sep 1964, ABC Fri 10:45–11:00

COMMENTATOR:

Johnny Johnston (1960–1961, 1962–1964)

Win Elliot (1961–1962)

In this post-fight feature, a top professional bowler, or amateur, had the chance to win up to $5,000 with one roll of the ball by making a hard spare (two or more pins separated in such a way as to require great precision if all were to be knocked down with a single ball). The winner returned the following week—there were usually two bowlers competing each night—to defend his title of "King of the Hill," and individual champions collected as much as $38,000 competing on this show. *Make That Spare* was telecast live from Paramus, New Jersey.

MAKE THE CONNECTION

Quiz/Audience Participation

FIRST TELECAST: *July 7, 1955*

LAST TELECAST: *September 29, 1955*

BROADCAST HISTORY:

Jul 1955–Sep 1955, NBC Thu 8:30–9:00

MODERATOR:

Jim McKay

Gene Rayburn

PANELISTS:

Betty White

Gloria DeHaven

Gene Klavan

Eddie Bracken

The object of this live summer game show was for the panelists to guess the circumstances (when, where, how, and why) that caused the paths of the guests on the program to cross. They tried to *Make the Connection* between the guests. It was a variation on the successful formats of *What's My Line* and *I've Got a Secret*. Jim McKay was the moderator of the show until early in September, when he was replaced by Gene Rayburn.

MAKE YOUR OWN KIND OF MUSIC

Musical Variety

FIRST TELECAST: *July 20, 1971*

LAST TELECAST: *September 7, 1971*

BROADCAST HISTORY:

Jul 1971–Sep 1971, NBC Tue 8:00–9:00

REGULARS:

The Carpenters

Al Hirt

Mark Lindsay

The New Doodletown Pipers

Tom Patchett and Jay Tarses

This summer musical variety series featured popular singers Richard and Karen Carpenter, trumpet player Al Hirt, singer Mark Lindsay (formerly lead singer of the rock group Paul Revere and the Raiders), the New Doodletown Pipers (16-person singing group), and the comedy team of Patchett and Tarses.

The title for this show was taken from a popular song of 1969.

MALIBU RUN

see *Aquanauts, The*

MALIBU U

Music

FIRST TELECAST: *July 21, 1967*

LAST TELECAST: *September 1, 1967*

BROADCAST HISTORY:

Jul 1967–Sep 1967, ABC Fri 8:30–9:00

REGULARS:

Rick Nelson
Robie Porter
The Bob Banas Dancers

Popular singer Rick Nelson was the host of this summer music show which originated from the famous Malibu Beach area in Southern California. As "Dean of the Drop-Ins" at this mythical college, Rick invited guest professors—all popular singers—to lecture (sing their hits) to the student body. There was a lot of body to lecture, mostly bikini-clad young girls ("Malibeauties"), and the curriculum for the summer school included such subjects as surfing, sunbathing, girl-watching, and a field trip to a bikini factory (not much going on there). Australian singer Robie Porter was a featured regular.

MAMA

Comedy/Drama

FIRST TELECAST: *July 1, 1949*

LAST TELECAST: *July 27, 1956*

BROADCAST HISTORY:

Jul 1949–Jul 1956, CBS Fri 8:00–8:30 (OS)

CAST:

"Mama" Marta Hansen .... Peggy Wood
"Papa" Lars Hansen .... Judson Laire
Nels .... Dick Van Patten
Katrin .... Rosemary Rice
Dagmar (1949) .... Iris Mann
Dagmar (1950–1956) .... Robin Morgan
Aunt Jenny .... Ruth Gates
T. R. Ryan (1952–1956) .... Kevin Coughlin

THEME MUSIC:

"Holverg Suite" (open), "The Last Spring" (close), by Edvard Grieg

Mama was one of the best-loved of the early family comedies, and was in many ways the prototype of the "growing family" series which later proliferated on television (*Ozzie and Harriet, Danny Thomas, et al*). There were no cheap gags or bumbling parents in *Mama*, but rather a warm-hearted, humorous, true-to-life account of a Norwegian-American family of five making their way in turn-of-the-century San Francisco.

The opening each week was in the style of a reminiscence by Katrin, leafing through the pages of the family album, past the pictures she knew so well—"I remember my brother Nels . . . and my little sister Dagmar . . . and of course, Papa. But most of all, I remember Mama."

Mama herself was played to perfection by the noted stage actress, Peggy Wood. Strict yet loving, she epitomized the gentleness which endeared the series to viewers for so many years. Papa was a carpenter who made just enough money to support his family decently, if not richly. Nels, Katrin, and Dagmar were the children. Any member of the family might be the subject of a week's story—Papa's new invention, Dagmar's braces, Mama's attempts to brighten the household—but all shared in the resolution. Each week's episode ended with the family seated around a pot of the sponsor's Maxwell House coffee, sharing the lessons learned.

One of the classic stories, presented each year, was the Christmas episode in which Papa told Dagmar how the animals were given the gift of speech for a few hours each Christmas Eve, as a reward for their protection of the Christ child in Bethlehem. When the rest of the family was asleep, Dagmar slipped out to the stable, to await the special moment.

Other regulars who passed through the Hansens' proper Victorian household on Steiner Street were Aunt Jenny ("Yenny" to all), T. R. Ryan, and Willie, the family dog.

So popular was *Mama* that when CBS announced that it was finally canceling the show, in 1956, the outcry was sufficient to bring the program back for a short additional run on Sunday afternoons. These episodes, aired from December 1956 through March 1957, were on film and featured the same cast as the prime-time series, except that Toni Campbell took over the role of Dagmar.

Mama was based on a book, *Mama's Bank Account*, which was written by a real-life Kathryn (Forbes). The book had subsequently become a highly successful play (1944) and movie (1948), both of which were titled *I Remember Mama*. Unlike some other early TV comedies such as *The Life of Riley* and *I Love Lucy*, *Mama* was telecast live rather than filmed. So while Lucy will be with us forever, the weekly dramas of life in the big white house on Steiner Street are, for the most part, gone forever. Like Katrin turning the pages of the album, we can only remember.

MAMA ROSA

Situation Comedy

FIRST TELECAST: *May 21, 1950*
LAST TELECAST: *June 11, 1950*
BROADCAST HISTORY:
May 1950–Jun 1950, ABC Sun 9:30–10:00

This was a short-lived Italian-American situation comedy, but no other information about it seems to have survived.

MAN AGAINST CRIME

Detective

FIRST TELECAST: *October 7, 1949*
LAST TELECAST: *August 19, 1956*
BROADCAST HISTORY:
Oct 1949–Mar 1952, CBS Fri 8:30–9:00 (OS)
Apr 1952–Jun 1952, CBS Thu 9:00–9:30
Oct 1952–Jun 1953, CBS Wed 9:30–10:00
Jul 1953–Oct 1953, CBS Fri 8:30–9:00
Oct 1953–Apr 1954, DUM Sun 10:30–11:00
Oct 1953–Jul 1954, NBC Sun 10:30–11:00
Jul 1956–Aug 1956, NBC Sun 10:00–10:30
CAST:
Mike Barnett (1949–1954) .. Ralph Bellamy
Mike Barnett (1956) .... Frank Lovejoy

The "man" was hard-boiled private detective Mike Barnett, who made his first appearance on CBS in the fall of 1949. Mike was a loner who used his brains and especially his fists to solve crimes in this rather violent show. The setting was the New York City area. The show was done live until the fall of 1952, when it went to film. The filmed episodes were all made at the Thomas A. Edison Studios in the Bronx and on location around New York.

When it left CBS in 1953 *Man Against Crime* did something almost unique—it became a regularly scheduled series on two different networks, NBC and DuMont, airing at the same time on both (Sunday, 10:30 P.M.). The program left the air in 1954 but returned in the summer of 1956 as a live program, with Frank Lovejoy in the lead role.

MAN AND THE CHALLENGE

Adventure

FIRST TELECAST: *September 12, 1959*
LAST TELECAST: *September 3, 1960*
BROADCAST HISTORY:
Sep 1959–Sep 1960, NBC Sat 8:30–9:00
CAST:
Dr. Glenn Barton ....George Nader

Dr. Glenn Barton was an athlete, doctor, and research scientist who worked for the government. Each week he was assigned to help others test the limits of their equipment and themselves under conditions of extreme stress. Barton's curiosity about his varied subjects and the fields with which he became involved occasionally resulted in his subjecting himself to the stresses in question before he would test their effects on others. He helped explorers test advanced jungle-survival techniques, he subjected two volunteers to an extended period in a small capsule to simulate the period in which astronauts await retrieval after returning from space, and he subjected other volunteers to the psychological torture and stress of brainwashing. In many of the episodes an emergency occurred, and Dr. Barton would have to push his own or others' endurance to limits not previously reached to try to save the situation—not always with positive results.

MAN AND THE CITY, THE

Drama

FIRST TELECAST: *September 15, 1971*
LAST TELECAST: *January 5, 1972*
BROADCAST HISTORY:
Sep 1971–Jan 1972, ABC Wed 10:00–11:00
CAST:
Mayor Thomas Jefferson Alcala
.... Anthony Quinn
Andy Hays ....Mike Farrell
Marian Crane ....Mala Powers

Academy Award winner Anthony Quinn starred as the ruggedly independent mayor of a fast-growing contemporary city in the Southwest. Mayor Alcala was no youngster, having been in office for 16 years. His longevity was assured by a constant and personal attention to the needs of individual constituents, whose stories made up this series. The mayor's sensible, button-down aide Andy tried to keep Hizzoner from becoming completely engrossed in individual people's problems, to the detriment of citywide affairs. Marian was the mayor's secretary.

Although the locale of *Man and the City* was not explicitly identified, the program was filmed on location in Albuquerque, New Mexico.

MAN BEHIND THE BADGE, THE

Police Anthology

FIRST TELECAST: *October 11, 1953*

LAST TELECAST: *October 3, 1954*

BROADCAST HISTORY:

Oct 1953–Oct 1954, CBS Sun 9:30–10:00

HOST/NARRATOR:

Charles Bickford

Each of the stories told in this live semi-documentary anthology series was a reenactment of an actual case from the files of a law enforcement agency. Although many of the stories were about police officers, they were not the only persons who fell into the category of "man behind the badge." Parole officers, park rangers, public defenders, U.S. Army MP's in Europe, and judges also appeared as leading characters in stories. Crime was not always the theme, either, as rehabilitation, life in a home for boys, and divorce were all touched upon at one time or another. On occasion the "man" behind the badge turned out to be a woman, such as a lady judge or a policewoman in a large city. Lesser-known talent was featured, although some of the actors (Jack Warden, Joey Faye, Bruce Gordon, and young Leslie Nielsen among them) later became well known.

MAN CALLED SHENANDOAH, A

Western

FIRST TELECAST: *September 13, 1965*

LAST TELECAST: *September 5, 1966*

BROADCAST HISTORY:

Sep 1965–Sep 1966, ABC Mon 9:00–9:30

CAST:

Shenandoah .... Robert Horton

In the opening episode of this series two buffalo hunters out on the prairie stumbled upon a stranger who had been shot in a gunfight and left to die. Assuming that he might be an outlaw with a price on his head, they hauled the half-dead man into the nearest town. It turned out that he wasn't wanted, but when he recovered from the wound he couldn't remember who he was or why he had been shot. Taking the name Shenandoah, the stranger spent the rest of the season wandering from town to town in search of clues to his real identity. Robert Horton had left *Wagon Train* with the vow never to do another Western, but he relented long enough to play the lead in this single-season series.

MAN FROM ATLANTIS

Adventure

FIRST TELECAST: *September 22, 1977*

LAST TELECAST: *July 25, 1978*

BROADCAST HISTORY:

Sep 1977, NBC Thu 9:00–10:00

Oct 1977–Jan 1978, NBC Tue 8:00–9:00

Apr 1978–Jul 1978, NBC Tue 8:00–9:00

CAST:

Mark Harris .... Patrick Duffy

Dr. Elizabeth Merrill .... Belinda Montgomery

C. W. Crawford .... Alan Fudge

Mr. Schubert .... Victor Buono

Brent .... Robert Lussier

Jomo .... Richard Williams

Chuey .... J. Victor Lopez

Jane .... Jean Marie Hon

Mark Harris was the last survivor of the lost continent of Atlantis. Though he appeared to be human, there were distinct differences between Mark and his air-breathing brethren. Having grown up under the sea, Mark possessed gill tissue rather than lungs, which meant that he could survive for only about twelve hours before he had to return to the sea to "breathe." His hands and feet were webbed, he could swim faster than a dolphin, and he had superhuman strength and superacute senses.

Despite his powers Mark had been washed ashore unconscious, where he was discovered by Dr. Elizabeth Merrill, who nursed him back to health. He then agreed to join her and a team of scientists from the Foundation for Oceanic Research in a project to learn more about life undersea. They traveled about in the "Getacean," a special submersible vehicle, and their adventures included confrontations with extraterrestrial life and numerous evil scientists, notably the diabolical Mr. Schubert and his assistant, Brent. The Foundation's director, preoccupied with budget problems, was C. W. Crawford.

Man from Atlantis was first seen in a series of four pilots that aired during the spring and summer of 1977 on varying days of the week. The first of these was telecast on March 4, 1977.

MAN FROM BLACKHAWK, THE

Western

FIRST TELECAST: *October 9, 1959*
LAST TELECAST: *September 23, 1960*
BROADCAST HISTORY:
Oct 1959–Sep 1960, ABC Fri 8:30–9:00
CAST:
Sam Logan ....Robert Rockwell

This was a Western with a twist. Its hero was neither a gunfighter nor a lawman; he was an insurance investigator. Sam Logan, Chicago-based investigator for the Blackhawk Insurance Company, wore a city-slicker outfit complete with string tie and briefcase. He almost never used a gun but often had to resort to his fists as he traveled from place to place investigating attempts to defraud the company and settling claims. In addition to visiting many typical Western frontier towns, Logan also frequently turned up in cities like New Orleans and San Francisco.

MAN FROM INTERPOL

Police
FIRST TELECAST: *January 30, 1960*
LAST TELECAST: *October 22, 1960*
BROADCAST HISTORY:
Jan 1960–Oct 1960, NBC Sat 10:30–11:00
CAST:
Anthony Smith ....Richard Wyler

Filmed in England, *Man from Interpol* told of the adventures of Anthony Smith, a special agent for the Scotland Yard division of "Interpol," the International Police Force. The crimes he investigated were therefore generally international in scope, sending him trotting around Europe in pursuit of smugglers, counterfeiters, and other border-crossing culprits.

MAN FROM U.N.C.L.E., THE

Spy Spoof
FIRST TELECAST: *September 22, 1964*
LAST TELECAST: *January 15, 1968*
BROADCAST HISTORY:
Sep 1964–Dec 1964, NBC Tue 8:30–9:30
Jan 1965–Sep 1965, NBC Mon 8:00–9:00
Sep 1965–Sep 1966, NBC Fri 10:00–11:00
Sep 1966–Sep 1967, NBC Fri 8:30–9:30
Sep 1967–Jan 1968, NBC Mon 8:00–9:00
CAST:
Napoleon Solo ....Robert Vaughn
Illya Kuryakin ....David McCallum
Mr. Waverly ....Leo G. Carroll
Lisa Rogers (1967–1968) .... Barbara Moore

The Man from U.N.C.L.E. was American television's answer to the very popular James Bond movies. Two superagents, Napoleon Solo and Illya Kuryakin, were teamed to fight the international crime syndicate THRUSH. U.N.C.L.E. (which stood for United Network Command for Law and Enforcement) had its secret American headquarters in New York. Running the office was Mr. Waverly, whose function was to assign agents to cases and coordinate their efforts. The suave, urbane American Solo and the blond, introverted Russian Kuryakin spent most of their time saving the world from THRUSH and, as the series wore on, the plots became more and more farfetched. The pinnacle of silliness was reached in the 1966–1967 season when *The Girl from U.N.C.L.E.* was created, bringing to television two hours of U.N.C.L.E. per week, with plots that were closer to ABC's *Batman* than to any sort of believable spy thriller.

At the end of the 1966–1967 season, *The Girl from U.N.C.L.E.* was dead and *The Man from U.N.C.L.E.* was dying. A transfusion of reality was tried at the start of the 1967–1968 season, with new sets for U.N.C.L.E.'s New York offices and stories that were more traditionally suspenseful, with danger that no longer seemed as if it had just come off the comic-book pages, and with a new regular cast member in Mr. Waverly's secretary Lisa Rogers. Unfortunately it was too late, and the series ended on the evening of January 15, 1968, to be replaced by the biggest hit of the late 1960s, *Laugh-In.*

MAN IN A SUITCASE

Detective
FIRST TELECAST: *May 3, 1968*
LAST TELECAST: *September 20, 1968*
BROADCAST HISTORY:
May 1968–Sep 1968, ABC Fri 8:30–9:30
CAST:
McGill ....Richard Bradford

Filmed in England, as were most of the series about "loners" in the 1960s, *Man in a Suitcase* was the story of a private detective who had once been an American intelligence agent. McGill had been falsely accused of failing to prevent a noted scientist from defecting to Russia, a treasonous offense. The series followed McGill through the European underworld as he searched for the evidence and people that could prove his innocence.

MAN OF THE WEEK

Interview

FIRST TELECAST: *April 20, 1952*
LAST TELECAST: *August 22, 1954*
BROADCAST HISTORY:
Apr 1952–Jan 1953, CBS Sun 6:00–6:30
Jul 1954–Aug 1954, CBS Sun 6:30–7:00
MODERATOR:
Walter Cronkite (1952–1953)
Ron Cochran (1954)

Each week on *Man of the Week*, a prominent public figure was interviewed about subjects of general interest. The program premiered as a Sunday afternoon entry in August 1951, and ran continuously until October 1954, alternating between nighttime and afternoon time slots. The nighttime telecasts are indicated above. This series was the forerunner of *Face the Nation*.

MAN WHO NEVER WAS, THE

International Intrigue

FIRST TELECAST: *September 7, 1966*
LAST TELECAST: *January 4, 1967*
BROADCAST HISTORY:
Sep 1966–Jan 1967, ABC Wed 9:00–9:30
CAST:
Peter Murphy/Mark Wainwright .... Robert Lansing
Eva Wainwright ....Dana Wynter
Col. Jack Forbes ....Murray Hamilton
Roger Barry ....Alex Davion

This spy thriller starred Robert Lansing as an American espionage agent who took another man's identity—and wife, fortune, and life-style. As the series opened Peter Murphy was fleeing from East Berlin with enemy agents in hot pursuit. Taking refuge in a bar, he came upon his exact look-alike, millionaire playboy Mark Wainwright, who was later mistaken for him by the enemy and killed. Sensing an opportunity, Peter assumed Wainwright's identity, his wealth, and his aristocratic wife as a perfect cover for his undercover activities in the glamorous capitals of Europe.

Wainwright's wife Eva knew that Murphy was an impostor, but she went along with him to keep the family fortune, which would have otherwise fallen into the hands of grasping half-brother Roger. Eva even taught Murphy her late husband's habits, so the "cover" would be perfect. Eventually Eva fell in love with her new "husband"—but Peter remained wary. The only other person who knew Murphy's new identity was his boss, Chief of Intelligence Col. Forbes.

Filmed on location in Berlin, Munich, London, Athens, and other cities of Europe.

MAN WITH A CAMERA

General Drama

FIRST TELECAST: *October 10, 1958*
LAST TELECAST: *February 29, 1960*
BROADCAST HISTORY:
Oct 1958–Mar 1959, ABC Fri 9:00–9:30
Oct 1959–Feb 1960, ABC Mon 10:30–11:00
CAST:
Mike Kovac ....Charles Bronson

During World War II Mike Kovac had been a combat photographer. Now he was making his living as a freelance professional lensman. At times it seemed as if he were still in combat. Mike took assignments from newspapers, insurance companies, the police, private individuals, and anyone else who wanted a filmed record of an event. The nature of his assignments often made Mike more private detective than photographer, a situation which was most likely planned by the producers of this series to capitalize on the popularity of detective shows at the time.

MANHATTAN MAHARAJA

Variety

FIRST TELECAST: *October 4, 1950*
LAST TELECAST: *February 26, 1951*
BROADCAST HISTORY:
Oct 1950–Nov 1950, ABC Wed 9:30–10:00
Nov 1950–Feb 1951, ABC Mon 9:15–9:30
HOST:
George Ansbro
REGULARS:
Joseph Biviano
Ralph Norman

In this odd series, George Ansbro donned the guise of a maharaja in the Arabian Nights vein and in tongue-in-cheek verse touched upon modern topics as they would be seen through the eyes of an Eastern potentate. "Pasha" Joseph Biviano and his Snake Charmers provided upbeat music, while "Sahib" Ralph Norman and his string group played for the maharaja's favorite dancing girls. Seen only on a limited number of ABC network stations during its prime-time run, *Manhattan Maharaja* continued in daytime until 1952.

MANHATTAN SHOWCASE

Musical Variety

FIRST TELECAST: *February 28, 1949*
LAST TELECAST: *June 16, 1949*
BROADCAST HISTORY:
Feb 1949–Apr 1949, CBS Various, 7:15–7:30
Apr 1949–May 1949, CBS Mon/Tue/Thu/Fri 7:45–8:00
May 1949–Jun 1949, CBS Mon/Wed/Thu 7:15–7:30
HOSTS:
Johnny Downs
Helen Gallagher
Virginia Gorski
Evelyn Ward
MUSIC:
The Tony Mottola Trio

Manhattan Showcase provided young entertainers with the opportunity to perform before a nationwide audience in the early days of live television. Johnny Downs was the one host who stayed with the show from beginning to end. His female helper was originally Helen Gallagher, who was joined by Virginia Gorski in April; the two of them left in June, to be replaced by Evelyn Ward. The series was initially aired on Mondays, Wednesdays, and Fridays, but later shifted to various combinations of weeknights.

MANHATTAN SPOTLIGHT

Interview

FIRST TELECAST: *January 24, 1949*
LAST TELECAST: *April 20, 1951*
BROADCAST HISTORY:
Jan 1949–Apr 1951, DUM Mon–Fri Various 15 minute
Apr 1950–May 1950, DUM Wed 10:00–10:15
May 1950–Jun 1950, DUM Wed 10:30–10:45
HOST:
Chuck Tranum

DuMont Chief Announcer Chuck Tranum was primarily responsible for the station breaks and other announcements made over the fledgling network from its flagship station in New York. He also hosted this nightly 15-minute interview program, which featured ordinary citizens and small-time entertainers with interesting hobbies and talents. Among those appearing were a Mr. Bimstein, who sculpted the Empire State Building in ice, the city's leading umbrella collector, a custom shoe manufacturer, a team of calypso dancers, the head of a lonely hearts club, and a man with a collection of electric eels.

Manhattan Spotlight began in daytime before moving to the nighttime schedule, where it was seen between 7:30 and 8:00 P.M. on various weeknights. There was also a late-night run during April–June 1950. During some periods the show was only seen locally in New York.

MANHATTAN TRANSFER

Variety

FIRST TELECAST: *August 10, 1975*
LAST TELECAST: *August 31, 1975*
BROADCAST HISTORY:
Aug 1975, CBS Sun 7:30–8:30
REGULARS:
Laurel Masse
Tim Hauser
Janis Seigel
Alan Paul

The Manhattan Transfer was a popular recording group whose material was impossible to type. Their routines, both musical and comic, spanned the entire 20th century and ran the gamut from semi-classical to rock. This potpourri of songs and humor aired for four weeks in the summer of 1975.

MANHUNT

Dramatic Anthology

FIRST TELECAST: *July 14, 1951*
LAST TELECAST: *August 23, 1952*
BROADCAST HISTORY:
Jul 1951–Sep 1951, NBC Sat 10:30–11:00
Jul 1952–Aug 1952, NBC Sat 10:30–11:00

Also known as *Assignment Manhunt,* this live dramatic series spent two years as the summer replacement for *Your Hit Parade.* The plays were all adaptations of suspense and adventure stories that had appeared previously in magazines or as books or movies.

MANHUNTER, THE

Detective

FIRST TELECAST: *September 11, 1974*
LAST TELECAST: *April 9, 1975*
BROADCAST HISTORY:
Sep 1974–Apr 1975, CBS Wed 10:00–11:00
CAST:
Dave Barrett ....Ken Howard
Sheriff Paul Tate ....Robert Hogan
Lizabeth Barrett ....Hilary Thompson
James Barrett ....Ford Rainey
Mary Barrett ....Claudia Bryar
PRODUCER:
Quinn Martin

The Manhunter was a detective series set in the United States during the depression years of the 1930s. Dave Barrett was an ex-Marine whose best friend had been killed by bank robbers during a holdup. Following his friend's death, Dave gave up his Idaho farm and became a private investigator with a mission: to bring to justice as many gangsters of the type that had killed his friend as possible. Tracking down these criminals sent him back and forth across the country, never staying in one place for long, except when he returned home to see his sister Liz and his folks.

MANNIX

Detective

FIRST TELECAST: *September 16, 1967*
LAST TELECAST: *August 27, 1975*
BROADCAST HISTORY:
Sep 1967–Sep 1971, CBS Sat 10:00–11:00
Sep 1971–Sep 1972, CBS Wed 10:00–11:00
Sep 1972–Dec 1972, CBS Sun 9:30–10:30
Jan 1973–Sep 1974, CBS Sun 8:30–9:30
Sep 1974–Jun 1975, CBS Sun 9:30–10:30
Jul 1975–Aug 1975, CBS Wed 10:00–11:00
CAST:
Joe Mannix ....Mike Connors
Lou Wickersham (1967–1968)
....................Joseph Campanella
Peggy Fair (1968–1975) ....Gail Fisher
Lt. Adam Tobias (1969–1975)
..........................Robert Reed

Mannix was one of the most violent detective shows of recent years, and also one of the longest-running. The original format had Joe Mannix, a Los Angeles–based private detective, employed by a sophisticated detective firm called Intertect. Despite the fact that the company was dedicated to the use of computers and other advanced scientific detection aids, Mannix seemed happiest when working with no implements other than his own intuition and fists. At the start of the second season he had struck out on his own, taking a small office on the first floor of the building in which he lived. Helping him in his new role as an independent investigator was his secretary and girl Friday, Peggy Fair. Her husband, a friend of Mannix's and a former police officer, had been killed in the line of duty. Lou Wickersham, Joe's old boss from Intertect, was also seen occasionally during the second season. Lt. Adam Tobias joined the cast as Joe's friend and contact on the police force at the start of the 1969–1970 season.

The high point of every episode seemed to be a wild brawl, and the body count even in the first few minutes of the show was sometimes appalling. On their radio show, Bob and Ray ran a continuing parody on the series called *Bummix*, in which the hero always held a polite conversation with some suspect, calmly agreed that mayhem was the only answer, and then was invariably beaten to a pulp.

MANY HAPPY RETURNS

Situation Comedy

FIRST TELECAST: *September 21, 1964*
LAST TELECAST: *April 12, 1965*
BROADCAST HISTORY:
Sep 1964–Apr 1965, CBS Mon 9:30–10:00
CAST:
Walter Burnley ....John McGiver
Harry Price ....Richard Collier
Joan Randall ....Elinor Donahue
Wilma Fritter ....Jesslyn Fax
Bob Randall ....Mark Goddard
Joe Foley ....Mickey Manners
Laurie Randall ....Andrea Sacino
Lynn Hall ....Elena Verdugo

Life was not peaceful for Walter Burnley. He had one of the most thankless jobs in the world, managing the complaint desk at Krockmeyer's department store. Working with him was a staff of four harried souls (Harry, Wilma, Joe, and Lynn), not all of whom managed to maintain their composure under the constant abuse of irate shoppers. Walter was a widower who made his home with his daughter Joan, Joan's husband Bob, and his four-year-old granddaughter Laurie.

MANY LOVES OF DOBIE GILLIS, THE

Situation Comedy

FIRST TELECAST: *September 29, 1959*
LAST TELECAST: *September 18, 1963*
BROADCAST HISTORY:

Sep 1959–Sep 1962, CBS Tue 8:30–9:00
Sep 1962–Sep 1963, CBS Wed 8:30–9:00

CAST:

Dobie Gillis ....Dwayne Hickman
Maynard G. Krebs ....Bob Denver
Herbert T. Gillis ....Frank Faylen
Winifred (Winnie) Gillis ...Florida Friebus
Zelda Gilroy ....Sheila James
Thalia Menninger (1959–1960)
.... Tuesday Weld
Milton Armitage (1959–1960)
.... Warren Beatty
Riff Ryan (1959–1960) ......Tommy Farrell
Melissa Frome (1959–1960) .. Yvonne Lime
Davey Gillis (1959–1960) .. Darryl Hickman
Mr. Pomfritt ....William Schallert
Clarice Armitage (1959–1960)
.... Doris Packer
Mrs. Chatsworth Osborne Sr. (1960–1963)
.... Doris Packer
Chatsworth Osborne Jr. (1960–1963)
.... Stephen Franken
Mrs. Ruth Adams (1959–1960)
.... Jean Byron
Dr. Burkhart (1961–1963) ...... Jean Byron
Mrs. Blossom Kenney (1959–1961)
.... Marjorie Bennett
Lt. Merriweather (1961) ...... Richard Clair
Dean Magruder (1961–1963)
.... Raymond Bailey
Duncan Gillis (1962–1963)
.... Bobby Diamond

Dobie Gillis was a "typical" American teenager, with three primary interests in life: beautiful women, fancy cars, and money. Unfortunately he was the son of a grocer and not the most attractive of boys, which put a certain crimp in his aspirations. Dobie and his beatnik buddy Maynard—to whom work was a dirty word—did their best to get by with a minimum of effort. Dobie had two real nemeses in his life. The first was intelligent but unattractive Zelda Gilroy, who was constantly trying to get herself married to Dobie. The second, through most of the series, was millionaire Chatsworth Osborne, Jr., a spoiled young man who flaunted his social status, not to mention his money, to snare the attractive girls who eluded Dobie.

When the series premiered in 1959, Dobie had to contend with handsome Milton Armitage for the attention of his favorite girl, the aristocratic (despite her rather modest means) and mercenary Thalia Menninger. She was interested mostly in acquiring "oodles and oodles" of money. To this end she was constantly looking to better Dobie's prospects for supporting her in the style to which she would like to become accustomed. Dobie was also much concerned about his future, and was seen at the beginning and end of each episode in Central City's park next to a statue of *The Thinker,* assuming the same pose while pondering his fate.

In February of 1960, Milton Armitage was replaced by Chatsworth Osborne, Jr., with Doris Packer assuming the role of his snobbish, overbearing mother, essentially the same part she had played as Milton's mother when the series began. In March 1961, Dobie and Maynard enlisted in the army, thinking that would help them find themselves. The army hitch lasted only until the first episode of the 1961–1962 season, when they resigned from the service and enrolled in S. Peter Prior Junior College. It was there that they remained, Maynard still fighting the system in his nonconformist way and his "good buddy" Dobie chasing women and trying to find himself, for the last two seasons that *The Many Loves of Dobie Gillis* was on the air.

Based on characters created by author Max Shulman.

MARCH OF MEDICINE, THE

Documentary

FIRST TELECAST: *July 8, 1958*
LAST TELECAST: *July 29, 1958*
BROADCAST HISTORY:

Jul 1958, ABC Tue 10:00–10:30

NARRATORS:

Ben Grauer
Eric Sevareid

Public-service films about the mental-health field made up this series.

MARCUS WELBY, M.D.

Medical Drama

FIRST TELECAST: *September 23, 1969*
LAST TELECAST: *May 11, 1976*
BROADCAST HISTORY:

Sep 1969–May 1976, ABC Tue 10:00–11:00

CAST:

Dr. Marcus Welby ....Robert Young
Dr. Steven Kiley ....James Brolin

Consuelo Lopez .... Elena Verdugo
Myra Sherwood (1969–1970)
.... Anne Baxter
Kathleen Faverty (1974–1976)
.... Sharon Gless
Sandy Porter (1975–1976) .. Ann Schedeen
Phil Porter (1975–1976) .... Gavin Brendan
Janet Blake (1975–1976) ... Pamela Hensley

MEDICAL ADVISOR:
Dr. Robert Forten

CREATOR/PRODUCER:
David Victor

Robert Young was one of the few actors in television history to be closely identified with two highly successful and long running roles—that of kindly family man Jim Anderson on *Father Knows Best* in the 1950s (8 years) and that of kindly Dr. Marcus Welby in the 1970s (7 years). The 62-year-old Young came out of a seven-year retirement to originate the role of Welby.

Marcus Welby, M.D. portrayed the cases of a veteran general practitioner in Santa Monica, California, whose thoroughness and dedication involved him in the lives of all sorts of patients. Assisting him was young Dr. Steven Kiley, who during the first season contracted to work with Welby for one year before resuming his training as a neurologist (he stayed). Thus the inevitable tension between youth and experience was established, but in this case Welby tended to be the more unorthodox of the two, often confounding the dedicated but textbook-oriented Kiley with his psychiatric approach to medicine. Welby treated the whole patient, his temperament, fears and family environment, as well as his physical ailments. The ailments were certainly varied for a suburban GP: during the first season alone there were tumors, autistic children, strokes, pernicious anemia, blindness, emphysema, LSD side effects, leukemia, diabetes, Huntington's Chorea, faith healing, dope addiction, an overweight racing jockey, and a diver who kept getting the bends.

A love interest was provided for Dr. Welby during the first season by Myra Sherwood, but this role was soon dropped. The only other suggestion that Welby might have a life of his own came in the last season, when his married daughter (Sandy) and six-year-old grandson (Phil) were occasionally seen. There was no Mrs. Welby. The only other regulars over the years, in fact, were nurses Consuelo Lopez and Kathleen Faverty.

Although romance eluded Dr. Welby it did finally come to young Dr. Kiley, in the person of Janet Blake, public relations director of Hope Memorial Hospital. They were married on the telecast of October 21, 1975.

Marcus Welby premiered in 1969 and soon became the biggest hit in the history of the ABC network to that time—it was the first ABC series ever to rank number one among all TV programs for a full season (1970–1971). Part of its success, truth to tell, was in scheduling; for its first two years it ran against a CBS news documentary hour and frequently against documentaries on NBC as well (*First Tuesday*). The limited appeal of these shows practically forfeited the audience to ABC. But once viewers had gotten used to Welby they stayed, against competition soft and strong. The program also won an Emmy and was held in very high esteem by medical groups, with Young serving offscreen as honorary chairman of numerous national fund drives and observances.

MARGE AND GOWER CHAMPION SHOW, THE

Situation Comedy

FIRST TELECAST: *March 31, 1957*
LAST TELECAST: *June 9, 1957*
BROADCAST HISTORY:
Mar 1957–Jun 1957, CBS Sun 7:30–8:00

CAST:
Marge Champion .... Herself
Gower Champion .... Himself
Marge's Father .... Jack Whiting
Cozy .... Buddy Rich
Amanda .... Peg La Centra
Miss Weatherly .... Barbara Perry

ORCHESTRA:
Richard Pribor

The format of this comedy series was designed to give the Champions at least one opportunity to dance each week. Gower played a choreographer and Marge his dancing partner, as they were in real life, and the situations used in the series were based on their actual experiences. Drummer Buddy Rich, appropriately, played their drummer and accompanist, and actress/singer Peg La Centra was cast as Marge's close friend and interior decorator.

The program aired on alternate Sundays with *The Jack Benny Show.*

MARGE AND JEFF

Situation Comedy

FIRST TELECAST: *September 21, 1953*

LAST TELECAST: *September 24, 1954*

BROADCAST HISTORY:

Sep 1953–Sep 1954, DUM Mon–Fri 7:15–7:30

CAST:

Marge .... Marge Greene
Jeff .... Jess/Jeff Cain

Pleasant 15-minute domestic comedy, presented five nights a week, concerned the day-to-day life of newlyweds Marge and Jeff, starting life together in a big-city apartment. Sharing in their little adventures were occasional neighbors and their cocker spaniel, Paisley. The program was written by Miss Greene, who previously produced a similar local program (called *Marge and Fred*) in Philadelphia.

Because of the confusing similarity of actor Jess Cain's name to that of his character Jeff, the actor had his name legally changed to Jeff shortly after the series began.

MARGIE

Situation Comedy

FIRST TELECAST: *October 12, 1961*

LAST TELECAST: *August 31, 1962*

BROADCAST HISTORY:

Oct 1961–Apr 1962, ABC Thu 9:30–10:00
Apr 1962–Aug 1962, ABC Fri 7:30–8:00

CAST:

Margie Clayton .... Cynthia Pepper
Maybelle Jackson .... Penney Parker
Nora Clayton .... Wesley Tackitt
Aunt Phoebe .... Hollis Irving
Harvey Clayton .... Dave Willock
Heywood Botts .... Tommy Ivo
Johnny Green .... Richard Gering

Growing up in the Roaring Twenties didn't seem to be radically different from growing up in the 1960s, as this series pointed out. The superficial things were different: flappers, bathtub gin, rumble seats, prohibition, raccoon coats, and the Charleston. The real issues were the same: conflicts with parents, troubled love affairs, the hassle of school, and maintaining "true" friends. Margie lived with her parents and her aunt Phoebe. Her best friend, Maybelle Jackson, was a flapper, and Heywood and Johnny were the two boys fighting for her affection. To add to the period flavor of the show, *Margie*'s producers intermixed silent movie slides that told the audience "Please Pay Attention," "The Plot Thickens," etc., at critical points in the action.

MARILYN MCCOO AND BILLY DAVIS, JR. SHOW, THE

Musical Variety

FIRST TELECAST: *June 15, 1977*

LAST TELECAST: *July 20, 1977*

BROADCAST HISTORY:

Jun 1977–Jul 1977, CBS Wed 8:30–9:00

REGULARS:

Marilyn McCoo
Billy Davis, Jr.
Jay Leno

Summer variety series featuring the husband-and-wife team of McCoo and Davis, who were members of the original Fifth Dimension pop group. This series, with music, comedy, and guest stars, came on the heels of their Grammy Award–winning record "You Don't Have to Be a Star to Be in My Show."

MARK SABER

Detective

FIRST TELECAST: *October 5, 1951*

LAST TELECAST: *May 15, 1960*

BROADCAST HISTORY:

Oct 1951–Apr 1952, ABC Fri 8:00–8:30
Apr 1952–Jun 1952, ABC Wed 9:30–10:00
Oct 1952–Jun 1953, ABC Mon 8:00–8:30
Oct 1953–Jun 1954, ABC Wed 7:30–8:00
Dec 1955–Jun 1957, ABC Fri 9:30–10:00
Sep 1957–Dec 1957, NBC Fri 7:30–8:00
Oct 1958–May 1959, NBC Sun 7:00–7:30
Oct 1959–May 1960, NBC Sun 6:30–7:00

CAST:

Mark Saber (1951–1954) ..... Tom Conway
Mark Saber (1955–1960) ...... Donald Gray
Sgt. Tim Maloney (1951–1954)
.... James Burke
Barney O'Keefe (1955–1956)
.... Michael Balfour
Judy (1956) .... Teresa Thorne
Stephanie Ames (1956–1957)
.... Diana Decker
Pete Paulson (1957–1958)
.... Neil McCallum
Pete Paulson (1958) .... Gordon Tanner
Bob Page (1958–1960) .... Robert Arden

Inspector Parker (1957–1960) .... Colin Tapley

Mark Saber was an American cop show with an international flavor. Saber was British, though he worked on the homicide squad of a big-city American police department. Dapper in appearance (with pencil-thin mustache and pinstriped suits) and elegant in speech, he tracked down villains by leaps of brilliant deduction as much as by routine police work. His assistant was a more familiar TV type, the loyal but somewhat thick-headed Sgt. Maloney.

After a three-year run Saber left the air in June 1954, only to return a year and a half later in a series called *The Vise*. This time he was cast as a one-armed private detective in London. The settings were exclusively European, as Saber tracked assorted blackmailers, murderers, and other crooks through London, Paris, along the Riviera, and in other glamorous locales. The cast was all new, with Donald Gray taking the role of Saber and a succession of actors playing his sidekicks, Barney O'Keefe, Judy, Stephanie Ames, Pete Paulson, and Bob Page. Numerous Scotland Yard inspectors came and went as his "official" foil, with Colin Tapley, as Inspector Parker, seen most often.

When first seen in 1951, the program was known as *Mystery Theater*. It was later retitled *Inspector Mark Saber—Homicide Squad* in 1952, *The Vise* in December 1955 (see also under that title for another series by the same name), and *Saber of London* in 1957. It was called *Detective's Diary* in syndication.

MARKHAM

Detective

FIRST TELECAST: *May 2, 1959*

LAST TELECAST: *September 22, 1960*

BROADCAST HISTORY:

May 1959–Jan 1960, CBS Sat 10:30–11:00
Jan 1960–Sep 1960, CBS Thu 9:30–10:00

CAST:

Roy Markham .... Ray Milland
John Riggs (1959) .... Simon Scott

Movie star Ray Milland turned private eye for this series. Roy Markham was wealthy, well educated, and a very successful attorney. After spending many years trying cases, he had decided to attempt unraveling them, becoming a private investigator mainly for the excitement of it. Although he was based in New York, his cases took him all over the world on assignments ranging from murder to corporate fraud. Since he had other sources of income, Roy's fees were flexible, sometimes exorbitant and sometimes free, depending on the client. When this series first went on the air, Markham had an assistant named John Riggs who traveled with him and did much of the legwork, but less than two months after the show's premiere, Markham was doing it all by himself.

MARRIAGE, THE

Situation Comedy

FIRST TELECAST: *July 8, 1954*

LAST TELECAST: *August 19, 1954*

BROADCAST HISTORY:

Jul 1954–Aug 1954, NBC Thu 10:00–10:30

CAST:

Ben Marriott .... Hume Cronyn
Liz Marriott .... Jessica Tandy
Pete Marriott .... Malcolm Broderick
Emily Marriott .... Susan Strasberg

To this obscure comedy belongs the distinction of having been the first network series to be regularly telecast in color. *The Marriage* was a live comedy dealing with the home life of New York lawyer Ben Marriott. Ben's practice was moderately successful, allowing his wife Liz, who had been employed previously as a buyer for a department store, to stay home and run the household. Liz's need to keep occupied got her involved in all sorts of community, organizational, and personal projects. The Marriotts had two children, Pete, aged 10, and Emily, aged 15. Cronyn and Tandy had starred in the NBC radio version of this series, which had left the air in the spring of 1954.

MARSHAL DILLON

see *Gunsmoke*

MARSHAL OF GUNSIGHT PASS, THE

Western

FIRST TELECAST: *March 12, 1950*

LAST TELECAST: *September 30, 1950*

BROADCAST HISTORY:

Mar 1950–Sep 1950, ABC Sat 6:30–7:00

CAST:

Russell "Lucky" Hayden
Roscoe Ates

Two veterans of Hollywood's Western "B" film factories starred in this obscure TV oater in 1950. Hayden had been in dozens of Hopalong Cassidy features, and Ates was usually seen as a dopey-faced, bug-eyed sidekick.

MARSHALL PLAN IN ACTION, THE

Documentary

FIRST TELECAST: *June 24, 1950*
LAST TELECAST: *February 22, 1953*
BROADCAST HISTORY:

Jun 1950–Jul 1950, ABC Sat 9:00–9:30
Jul 1950–Oct 1950, ABC Sun 10:00–10:30
Oct 1950–Mar 1952, ABC Sun 9:30–10:00
Jan 1951–Jun 1951, ABC Fri 10:00–10:30 (reruns)
Jul 1951–Oct 1951, ABC Mon 8:30–9:00 (reruns)
Apr 1952–Jun 1952, ABC Tue 8:00–8:30
Jul 1952–Aug 1952, ABC Thu 9:00–9:30
Sep 1952–Feb 1953, ABC Sun 6:00–6:30

Documentary films prepared by the U.S. government showing the results of Marshall Plan aid to war-ravaged Europe. Each film opened with a statement from Federal Administrator Paul G. Hoffman describing the films as "the story of one successful battle in the series of struggles now going on that have become known as the Cold War."

Improverished ABC (which could have used some economic aid itself at this time) was sufficiently desperate for inexpensive programming to schedule two showings a week of these films during much of 1951. Effective December 30, 1951, the series' title was changed to *Strength for a Free World.*

MARTHA RAYE SHOW, THE

Comedy Variety

FIRST TELECAST: *September 20, 1955*
LAST TELECAST: *May 29, 1956*
BROADCAST HISTORY:

Sep 1955–May 1956, NBC Tue 8:00–9:00

STAR:

Martha Raye

REGULARS:

Rocky Graziano
Carl Hoff and His Orchestra
The Danny Daniels Dancers

Loud-voiced comedienne and singer Martha Raye first brought her slapstick comedy to TV as one of the stars of NBC's *All Star Revue* in 1951. Between 1953 and 1955 she was seen in a series of specials entitled *The Martha Raye Show,* which served as a periodic replacement for *Your Show of Shows* and *The Milton Berle Show.* Finally, in 1955, she got her own weekly series.

The earlier specials had been relatively unstructured variety shows, with Rocky Graziano regularly appearing as her boy friend in comedy skits. The 1955–1956 series attempted to tell a complete story each week, in musical variety format. Rocky was once again her boy friend in each story, and the night's theme was developed in integrated comedy, singing, and musical production numbers. Guest stars also appeared.

MARTHA WRIGHT SHOW, THE

Music

FIRST TELECAST: *April 18, 1954*
LAST TELECAST: *December 5, 1954*
BROADCAST HISTORY:

Apr 1954–Jul 1954, ABC Sun 9:15–9:30
Sep 1954–Dec 1954, ABC Sun 9:15–9:30

REGULARS:

Martha Wright
Norman Paris
Bobby Hackett and His Band

Songstress Martha Wright was the star of this live music show. Featured with her were pianist Norman Paris and trumpet player Bobby Hackett and his band. Miss Wright, whose show was the replacement for *The Jane Pickens Show* in April, was herself replaced on Miss Pickens' return in July, and replaced Miss Pickens again in September. Also known as *The Packard Showroom.*

MARTIN KANE, PRIVATE EYE

Detective

FIRST TELECAST: *September 1, 1949*
LAST TELECAST: *June 17, 1954*
BROADCAST HISTORY:

Sep 1949–Jun 1954, NBC Thu 10:00–10:30 (OS)

CAST:

Martin Kane (1949–1951) .. William Gargan
Martin Kane (1951–1952) ..... Lloyd Nolan
Martin Kane (1952–1953) .... Lee Tracy
Martin Kane (1953–1954) .... Mark Stevens
Happy McMann ....Walter Kinsella
Don Morrow (1954) ....Himself
Lt. Bender (1949–1950) .... Fred Hillebrand

Capt. Willis (1950–1951) .... Horace McMahon
Sgt. Ross (1950–1952) .. Nicholas Saunders
Capt. Leonard (1951) .... Walter Greaza
Capt. Burke (1951–1952) .... Frank Thomas
Lt. Grey (1952–1954) .... King Calder

This popular, live detective series, which was also heard on radio for several years, underwent several changes of emphasis as well as of cast during its run. William Gargan's original Martin Kane was a smooth, wisecracking operator who worked in close cooperation with the police, an unusual arrangement for TV sleuths. His base of operation was New York, and the crime was usually murder. Later Kanes projected more of a tough-guy image and got less cooperation from the cops, as Lt. Bender gave way to other, more antagonistic officers. In August 1953 the title of the series was shortened to *Martin Kane* and the emphasis shifted to greater mystery and suspense, with less reliance on the somewhat stereotyped situations of earlier seasons.

Throughout most of the run Happy McMann's tobacco shop served as Kane's hangout, and gave him the opportunity to slip in plugs for the sponsor's tobacco products (which included Sano and Encore cigarettes, and Old Briar pipe tobacco). After August 1953 Kane no longer frequented the store, but it remained the setting for the commercials, first by Happy and later (January 1954) by "new owner" Don Morrow.

There was in fact a real Martin Kane. The man who lent his name for use in the show was no sleuth, but an executive with J. Walter Thompson & Co., the advertising agency which produced this series. The real-life Kane later became a senior editor of *Sports Illustrated* magazine and died at the age of 70, in 1977.

Three years after it left the network *Martin Kane* was revived in a syndicated series called *The New Adventures of Martin Kane*, which was sold individually to local stations. In this version Kane was doing his sleuthing in London and sometimes Paris. The title role, ironically enough, was played by William Gargan—the original 1949 Martin Kane.

MARTY FELDMAN COMEDY MACHINE, THE

Comedy Variety

FIRST TELECAST: *April 12, 1972*
LAST TELECAST: *August 16, 1972*
BROADCAST HISTORY:
Apr 1972–Aug 1972, ABC Wed 9:00–9:30
HOST:
Marty Feldman

Bug-eyed, shaggy-haired British comedian Marty Feldman starred in this fast-paced half-hour of comedy sketches, blackouts, and music.

MARY

Comedy Variety

FIRST TELECAST: *September 24, 1978*
LAST TELECAST: *October 8, 1978*
BROADCAST HISTORY:
Sep 1978–Oct 1978, CBS Sun 8:00–9:00
REGULARS:
Mary Tyler Moore
Dick Shawn
James Hampton
Swoosie Kurtz
David Letterman
Judy Kahan
Michael Keaton

After starring in two highly successful situation comedies, *The Dick Van Dyke Show* in the 1960s and *The Mary Tyler Moore Show* in the 1970s, Miss Moore branched out as star of this comedy variety hour. Relying primarily on a group of repertory players rather than guest stars, much in the manner of the highly successful *Carol Burnett Show* which had ended its long run the previous season, *Mary* placed strong emphasis on topical sketch comedy. Frequently referred to, but not seen, was Mary's husband, Grant Tinker, who was also producer of this show.

MARY KAY AND JOHNNY

Situation Comedy

FIRST TELECAST: *November 18, 1947*
LAST TELECAST: *March 11, 1950*
BROADCAST HISTORY:
Nov 1947–Dec 1947, DUM Tues 9:00–9:15
Jan 1948–Aug 1948, DUM Tue 7:15–7:30
Oct 1948–Feb 1949, NBC Sun 7:00–7:30
Mar 1949–Jun 1949, CBS Wed 9:00–9:30
Jun 1949–Aug 1949, NBC Mon–Fri 7:15–7:30
Aug 1949–Dec 1949, NBC Thu 8:30–9:00
Jan 1950–Feb 1950, NBC Sat 9:00–9:30
Feb 1950–Mar 1950, NBC Sat 7:30–8:00
CAST:
Mary Kay Stearns .... Herself

Johnny Stearns ....Himself
Howie ....Howard Thomas
Mary Kay's mother .... Nydia Westman
Christopher William Stearns
....................Himself (1949–1950)

WRITER:
Johnny Stearns

Live domestic comedy, revolving around young New York newlyweds Mary Kay and Johnny Stearns. She was pretty, pert, and something of a screwball, while he was more serious and always getting her out of various dilemmas. Johnny worked in a bank, but the setting for the action was usually the couple's apartment in Greenwich Village. The Stearns, who were also married in real life, had a baby boy in December 1948, whom they named Christopher. The blessed event was worked into the script and infant Chris was added to the cast less than a month after his birth, appearing in his bassinet. He was surely one of the youngest regular cast members on any show in TV history. Howie was Johnny's best friend, while Nydia Westman played Mary Kay's mother.

In addition to being one of the earliest network situation comedies, the series was notable for its longtime sponsor Anacin, which even in 1948 was using an outline chart of a human figure with flashing lights to show the product bringing fast, fast relief to every corner of the body.

That sponsors were quite uncertain of the effectiveness of TV at this early stage, however, is illustrated by the following. A few weeks after the program premiered, the sponsor, who had no way of knowing whether anyone was watching (there were no audience ratings), decided to conduct a test by offering a free mirror to the first 200 viewers who wrote in their comments on the program. Just to be safe, the company ordered an extra 200 mirrors so as not to disappoint anyone. 8,960 letters were received!

MARY MARGARET MCBRIDE

Interview

FIRST TELECAST: *September 21, 1948*
LAST TELECAST: *December 14, 1948*
BROADCAST HISTORY:
Sep 1948–Dec 1948, NBC Tue 9:00–9:30
HOSTESS:
Mary Margaret McBride

Interview program featuring the popular radio personality.

MARY TYLER MOORE SHOW, THE

Situation Comedy

FIRST TELECAST: *September 19, 1970*
LAST TELECAST: *September 3, 1977*
BROADCAST HISTORY:
Sep 1970–Dec 1971, CBS Sat 9:30–10:00
Dec 1971–Sep 1972, CBS Sat 8:30–9:00
Sep 1972–Oct 1976, CBS Sat 9:00–9:30
Nov 1976–Sep 1977, CBS Sat 8:00–8:30
CAST:
Mary Richards ....Mary Tyler Moore
Lou Grant ....Edward Asner
Ted Baxter ....Ted Knight
Murray Slaughter ....Gavin MacLeod
Rhoda Morgenstern (1970–1974)
.... Valerie Harper
Phyllis Lindstrom (1970–1975)
.... Cloris Leachman
Bess Lindstrom (1970–1975)
........................Lisa Gerritsen
Gordon (Gordy) Howard (1970–1973)
.... John Amos
Georgette Franklin Baxter (1973–1977)
........................Georgia Engel
Sue Ann Nivens (1973–1977)
..........................Betty White
Marie Slaughter (1971–1977)
........................Joyce Bulifant
Edie Grant (1973–1974) ....Priscilla Morrill
David Baxter (1976–1977) ..... Robbie Rist

The Mary Tyler Moore Show was one of the most literate, realistic, and enduring situation comedies of the 1970s. Unlike the efforts generated by producer Norman Lear, typified by *All in the Family* and *Maude*, there was never a conscious attempt to humiliate or ridicule. Mary Richards was the idealized single career woman. She had come to Minneapolis after breaking up with a man she had been dating for four years. Ambitious, and looking for new friends, she moved into an older apartment building and went to work as an assistant producer of the local news show on television station WJM-TV. In her early 30s, Mary symbolized the independent woman of the 1970s. She would like to find a man and settle down to raise a family, but was not desperately grabbing at any chance for marriage. She would get married, but only if it was to the right man. She was warm, loving, and vulnerable, and although it was never bluntly thrown out at the audience, could spend the night with a man she was not madly in love with.

Mary worked for WJM-TV News producer Lou Grant, an irascible, cantankerous, blustery man whose bark was much worse than his bite. Underneath that harsh exterior beat the heart of a pussycat. Lou had problems with his home life as well as his job. During the 1973–1974 season he separated from his wife Edie and they were later divorced. Though it never developed, there was an underlying feeling that he and Mary might have had a serious relationship, if they could have ever really gotten together.

Murray Slaughter was the head newswriter at the station. He was happily married, had a positive outlook no matter what happened, and was a good friend to all. Anchorman on the WJM-TV News was Ted Baxter, not too bright, prone to put his foot in his mouth both on and off the air, and possessor of such a misplaced sense of his own wonderfulness that he was the butt of everyone's jokes. Ted's long courtship of bland, emptyheaded but well-meaning Georgette Franklin culminated in a marriage he was not quite ready to commit himself to in November 1975. The following spring he and Georgette adopted eight-year-old David, and in the fall of 1976 had a baby of their own.

Mary's closest friend was one of her neighbors, Rhoda Morgenstern, an interior decorator for a local department store who, like Mary, was still single though in her 30s. Unlike Mary, however, Rhoda was desperately looking for a husband. Unable to find one in Minneapolis, she moved back home to New York City, and to her own series, *Rhoda*, in the fall of 1974. The other neighbor seen frequently in Mary's apartment was Phyllis Lindstrom. Phyllis was the building's resident busybody, and though it took quite a while to find out, also its landlady (her husband Lars, who was talked about but never seen, actually owned the building). Phyllis was oblivious to everyone else's feelings and had an extremely flaky personality. She, too, got her own series when, following Lars' death, she and her daughter Bess moved to San Francisco in the fall of 1975 (see *Phyllis*).

As some of the regulars left the series, including WJM-TV's weatherman Gordy Howard, others took up the slack. Sue Ann Nivens arrived at the station in 1973 with her "Happy Homemaker Show," and Georgette's role was expanded. Sue Ann was in her late 40s and extremely manhungry. She was constantly trying to get every male in sight into the sack, but primarily Lou Grant. Mary eventually was promoted from associate producer to producer as Lou moved to the job of news director.

Mary Tyler Moore, who, with her husband Grant Tinker, produced *The Mary Tyler Moore Show*, decided that the series would end in 1977, despite its still large audience. In the last episode new management took over the station and, in an effort to bolster its weak news ratings, fired virtually the entire staff. Ironically, the one survivor was anchorman Ted Baxter, probably the primary cause for the news' low ratings. There were tearful farewells and everyone went their separate ways.

MASK, THE

Crime Drama

FIRST TELECAST: *January 10, 1954*

LAST TELECAST: *May 16, 1954*

BROADCAST HISTORY:

Jan 1954–May 1954, ABC Sun 8:00–9:00

Mar 1954–Apr 1954, ABC Tue/Wed 8:00–9:00

CAST:

Walter Guilfoyle .... Gary Merrill

Peter Guilfoyle .... William Prince

Though short-lived, this program was a pioneer in several ways. It was the first hour-long mystery series to feature a continuing cast of characters—and as such was the father of one of the predominant forms on TV today. It was also, during part of its run, repeated twice a week in prime time, in order that viewers who had missed the original live telecast on Sunday night might see the kinescope repeat on Tuesday or Wednesday (at least on those stations which carried all three).

Unfortunately, the content was not as innovative as the format and scheduling. *The Mask* was a routine crime show centering on two brothers who were attorneys and partners in the firm of Guilfoyle & Guilfoyle. Each week they tackled another case, somewhat in the manner of modern Robin Hoods, unmasking assorted gangsters and rescuing helpless victims. Unable to find a sponsor, and quite expensive to produce, *The Mask* was canceled after four months.

MASLAND AT HOME PARTY
see *Earl Wrightson Show, The*

MASQUERADE PARTY
Quiz/Audience Participation
FIRST TELECAST: *July 14, 1952*
LAST TELECAST: *September 16, 1960*
BROADCAST HISTORY:
Jul 1952–Aug 1952, NBC Mon 8:00–8:30
Jun 1953–Sep 1953, CBS Mon 9:30–10:00
Jun 1954–Sep 1954, CBS Mon 9:30–10:00
Sep 1954–Jun 1956, ABC Wed 9:00–9:30
Jun 1956–Dec 1956, ABC Sat 10:00–10:30
Mar 1957–Sep 1957, NBC Wed 8:00–8:30
Aug 1958–Sep 1958, CBS Mon 8:30–9:00
Oct 1958–Sep 1959, NBC Thu 10:30–11:00
Oct 1959–Jan 1960, CBS Mon 7:30–8:00
Jan 1960–Sep 1960, NBC Fri 9:30–10:00
MODERATOR:
Bud Collyer (1952)
Douglas Edwards (1953)
Peter Donald (1954–1956)
Eddie Bracken (1957)
Robert Q. Lewis (1958)
Bert Parks (1958–1960)
PANELISTS:
Peter Donald (1952–1953)
Ilka Chase (1952–1957)
John S. Young (1952)
Madge Evans (1952)
Buff Cobb (1953–1955)
Ogden Nash (1953–1957)
Bobby Sherwood (1954–1957)
Dagmar (1955–1956)
Mary Healy (1955–1956)
Betsy Palmer (1956–1957)
Frank Parker (1957)
Johnny Johnston (1957–1958)
Jonathan Winters (1958)
Jinx Falkenberg (1958)
Pat Carroll (1958)
Audrey Meadows (1958–1960)
Lee Bowman (1958–1960)
Faye Emerson (1958–1960)
Sam Levenson (1958–1960)

Well-known celebrities were disguised in elaborate costumes and makeup when they appeared as contestants on *Masquerade Party*. The costume was designed to serve as a clue to the panelists, who questioned the contestants in an attempt to determine their real identities. Any prize money won by contestants was donated to their favorite charities. When contestants answered the panelists' questions, they did so through a special microphone which also disguised their voices. On the air through nine seasons, *Masquerade Party* went through six moderators and a total of 19 regular panelists.

MASTERPIECE PLAYHOUSE
Dramatic Anthology
FIRST TELECAST: *July 23, 1950*
LAST TELECAST: *September 3, 1950*
BROADCAST HISTORY:
Jul 1950–Sep 1950, NBC Sun 9:00–10:00

Live productions of seven great classics (Ibsen's *Hedda Gabler*, Shakespeare's *Richard III*, etc.), telecast during the summer of 1950. The plays were immaculately produced and used the top talent available to television in those days. Among those appearing were Jessica Tandy, William Windom, and Boris Karloff.

MASTERS OF MAGIC
Magic
FIRST TELECAST: *February 16, 1949*
LAST TELECAST: *May 11, 1949*
BROADCAST HISTORY:
Feb 1949–May 1949, CBS Wed 7:45–8:00
HOST:
André Baruch

This live series, which filled the remainder of the half-hour in which CBS aired its network news program, gave famous magicians the opportunity to dazzle the viewing audience, and host André Baruch, with their feats of magic.

MATT DENNIS SHOW, THE
Music
FIRST TELECAST: *June 27, 1955*
LAST TELECAST: *August 29, 1955*
BROADCAST HISTORY:
Jun 1955—Aug 1955, NBC Mon/Wed/Fri 7:30–7:45
REGULAR:
Matt Dennis

Versatile singer, composer, and pianist Matt Dennis was the host and star of this summertime musical interlude. Backing Dennis on many of his own hits ("Let's Get Away From It All," "Angel Eyes") was a small, jazz-flavored combo. Guest stars were featured occasionally.

MATT HELM
Detective

FIRST TELECAST: *September 20, 1975*
LAST TELECAST: *January 3, 1976*
BROADCAST HISTORY:
Sep 1975–Jan 1976, ABC Sat 10:00–11:00
CAST:
Matt Helm ....Anthony Franciosa
Claire Kronski ....Laraine Stephens
Sgt. Hanrahan ....Gene Evans
Ethel ....Jeff Donnell

Matt Helm was another of the swinging, wisecracking detectives who proliferated during TV's second and third decades. This one was based in Los Angeles (where else?), lived the good life with a fancy foreign sports car and a sexy girlfriend-attorney (Claire), and took on only "high-level" cases around the world. The series certainly had an opulent look, with a posh bachelor pad provided for Matt and much of the outside filming done at private estates around Southern California. Sgt. Hanrahan was the somewhat less highly paid police contact (who nevertheless dined with Matt at the best restaurants), and Ethel the answering-service operator. It was, according to the producer, pure escapist fare.

Based on an extensive collection of detective novels by Donald Hamilton and several movies with Dean Martin in the title role.

MATT LINCOLN

Medical Drama

FIRST TELECAST: *September 24, 1970*
LAST TELECAST: *January 14, 1971*
BROADCAST HISTORY:
Sep 1970–Jan 1971, ABC Thu 7:30–8:30
CAST:
Dr. Matt Lincoln ....Vince Edwards
Tag ....Chelsea Brown
Kevin ....Michael Larrain
Jimmy ....Felton Perry
Ann .... June Harding

Matt Lincoln was one of the youthful "relevance" dramas of the early 1970s. Vince Edwards (ex-*Ben Casey*) starred as a hip young psychiatrist who founded and ran a center-city telephone-assistance service for troubled teenagers. His helpers at Hotline were Tag and Jimmy, two equally hip young blacks; Ann; and Kevin, a cynical cop. As if Hotline didn't get him enough points, Matt also headed a walk-in clinic for those too poor to pay. His own life completed the picture: sports car, bachelor pad at the beach, and a small sailboat. The stories of these beautiful young people, and those they tried to help, formed the plots.

MATTY'S FUNDAY FUNNIES

Cartoon

FIRST TELECAST: *September 30, 1960*
LAST TELECAST: *December 29, 1962*
BROADCAST HISTORY:
Sep 1960–Sep 1961, ABC Fri 7:30–8:00
Oct 1961–Dec 1962, ABC Sat 7:00–7:30
CARTOONIST:
Bob Clampett (for *Beany and Cecil*)

Matty's Funday Funnies was first seen on Sunday afternoons in October 1959, sponsored by the Mattel Toy Co. and "hosted" by cartoon characters Matty and Sisterbelle. The cartoons most frequently seen were those featuring Casper the Friendly Ghost, Little Audrey, Herman the Mouse, Catnip, Tommy the Tortoise, and Buzzy the Crow. Generally two or three cartoons were seen in each half-hour program.

In 1960 the series moved to nighttime television. Then in January 1962 the early characters were dropped and the series became *Matty's Funnies with Beany and Cecil*, starring the familiar characters of Bob Clampett's *Time for Beany* puppet show (which had been in syndication since the early 1950s). This time Beany and his friends were in cartoon form. Beany was the little boy with a big grin and a cap with a propeller on top. He sailed the seven seas with Capt. Huffenpuff on the *Leakin' Lena*, and his best friend was Cecil the Seasick Sea Serpent. Together they had adventures all over the world (and sometimes out of it), encountering such characters as the villainous Dishonest John, Homer the Octopus, Tear-a-Long the Dotted Lion (get it?), Careless the Mexican Hairless, and many others. Cartoonist Clampett always was fond of puns! He also developed his characters with an intelligence and wit that had made *Beany and Cecil* a favorite of many adults, including such diverse fans as Lionel Barrymore and Groucho Marx.

After the first three months the program's title was shortened to simply *Beany and Cecil*. Following its prime-time run during 1962 the show continued on ABC at other times of the day until 1967.

MAUDE

Situation Comedy

FIRST TELECAST: *September 12, 1972*

LAST TELECAST: *April 29, 1978*

BROADCAST HISTORY:

Sep 1972–Sep 1974, CBS Tue 8:00–8:30
Sep 1974–Sep 1975, CBS Mon 9:00–9:30
Sep 1975–Sep 1976, CBS Mon 9:30–10:00
Sep 1976–Sep 1977, CBS Mon 9:00–9:30
Sep 1977–Nov 1977, CBS Mon 9:30–10:00
Dec 1977–Jan 1978, CBS Mon 9:00–9:30
Jan 1978–Apr 1978, CBS Sat 9:30–10:00

CAST:

Maude Findlay ....Beatrice Arthur
Walter Findlay ....Bill Macy
Carol ....Adrienne Barbeau
Phillip (1972–1977) .... Brian Morrison
Phillip (1977–1978) .... Kraig Metzinger
Dr. Arthur Harmon ....Conrad Bain
Vivian Cavender Harmon
.... Rue McClanahan
Florida Evans (1972–1974) .... Esther Rolle
Henry Evans (1973–1974) ...... John Amos
Chris (1973–1974) ....Fred Grandy
Mrs. Naugatuck (1974–1977)
.... Hermione Baddeley
Bert Beasley (1975–1977) ... J. Pat O'Malley
Victoria Butterfield (1977–1978)
.... Marlene Warfield

PRODUCER:

Norman Lear

Maude was the first spinoff from producer Norman Lear's enormously successful comedy, *All in the Family*. Edith Bunker's cousin Maude was upper-middle-class, liberal and extremely outspoken—a perfect counterpoint to Archie Bunker's blustering, hard-hat bigotry. The character became so popular that in the fall of 1972 Maude was given a series of her own—and it soon became almost as big a hit as *All in the Family* itself.

Maude lived in suburban Tuckahoe, New York, with her fourth husband, Walter, owner of Findlay's Friendly Appliances. Living with them was Carol, Maude's divorced, 27-year-old daughter, and Carol's nine-year-old son Phillip.

Even though much of the comedy centered on Maude's determination to represent the independent, even dominant, woman, she herself always had a female servant in the house. In fact, during the course of the series, she ran through three of them. Maude's first maid was Florida, a bright, witty black woman who left early in 1974 to star in her own program, *Good Times*. (Her husband, Henry, was renamed James in *Good Times*, even though the same actor continued in the role.) Florida was succeeded by a cynical, hard-drinking Englishwoman, Mrs. Naugatuck. Mrs. Naugatuck was never as popular with viewers as Florida had been, and after marrying Bert Beasley in November 1976 she left the show, ostensibly to return to the British Isles. Her replacement was Victoria Butterfield, who joined the Findlay household in the fall of 1977.

The Findlays' next-door neighbor, and Walter's best friend, was Dr. Arthur Harmon. When the series began Arthur was a widower, but he subsequently began dating Maude's best friend, Vivian (who had just been divorced), and in February 1974 they were married. Everyone on this show seemed to be either married or getting married, except for Maude's daughter Carol. She came close with boyfriend Chris in 1974, but that didn't work out and he soon disappeared from the cast.

Although this was a comedy show, the subject matter was often on the serious side. During the run, Maude became involved in politics, had a face lift, had an abortion (which drew heavy viewer protest mail) and went through menopause. Walter went through a severe bout with alcoholism, saw his store go bankrupt, and had a nervous breakdown. *Maude* could be very funny, but in its efforts to be realistic, it could also be controversial and sometimes depressing. Yet for several seasons viewers made it one of the top programs on television.

Finally in 1977–1978 the audience began to decline, and some major cast changes were planned for the next season. The Harmons and Carol were to move out of town, and Walter was to retire from the appliance business. Maude would begin a career in politics, with a new supporting cast. But early in 1978 Bea Arthur announced that she was leaving the series. The producers candidly admitted that no one else could play the role as she had, and so after six years *Maude* ended its run.

MAVERICK

Western

FIRST TELECAST: *September 22, 1957*

LAST TELECAST: *July 8, 1962*

BROADCAST HISTORY:

Sep 1957–Sep 1961, ABC Sun 7:30–8:30
Sep 1961–Jul 1962, ABC Sun 6:30–7:30

CAST:

Bret Maverick (1957–1960) .... James Garner
Bart Maverick .... Jack Kelly
Samantha Crawford (1958–1959) .... Diane Brewster
Cousin Beauregard Maverick (1960–1961) .... Roger Moore
Brent Maverick (1961) ...... Robert Colbert

In the days when dozens of staunch TV heroes were chasing lawbreakers in every corner of the Old West, this program was indeed a maverick—a Western with a sense of humor. It didn't start out that way. For the first few episodes *Maverick* was a fairly straight series about a dapper cardsharp and his adventures on the frontier. Then a bored scriptwriter slipped in some stage directions for star James Garner to look at someone "with his beady little eyes." Garner thought this great fun, and played the scene for laughs. It worked, and soon the whole series was moving toward a satirical orientation. Wisecracking ladies' man Bret was joined by a fairly straight brother, Bart, in November 1957, to keep the series from straying too far from the traditional Western mold (and indeed the series could always be enjoyed as a straight Western). But neither of the Brothers Maverick was really a hero in the usual sense. They would just as soon slip quietly out of town as face a gunman in an impending showdown; they were usually honest in poker (unless they were dealing); and Bret, in particular, handled a gun rather ineptly.

Bret and Bart alternated as leads, and sometimes appeared together, but Bret clearly had the juicier role and was more visible. Their exploits took them to frontier towns like Hounddog, Apocalypse, and Oblivion, and sometimes out of the country entirely, as when Bret sailed to the South Pacific to inspect an island. Occasionally appearing were Bart's friend Dandy Jim Buckley (played by Efrem Zimbalist, Jr.) and Gentleman Jack Darby (Richard Long). During the second season Bret had a running feud with Samantha Crawford, a pretty slick operator in her own right, to see who could out-con whom. And he would always remind listeners of the advice given him by his "pappy," who said that in the face of overwhelming odds, run. (Pappy, often referred to, actually showed up in one episode, played by Garner!)

Among the high points of *Maverick* were the periodic satires of other TV shows, Western and non-Western alike, such as a takeoff on *Gunsmoke* and another on *Dragnet* (in which Bret intoned a narration in deadpan Joe Friday style). Perhaps the best was a wild parody on *Bonanza*, in which Bart encountered a ranching baron named Joe Wheelwright (played by Jim Backus), owner of the vast Subrosa Ranch, who was trying to marry off his three idiot sons Moose (Hoss), Henry (Adam), and Small Paul (Little Joe). On still another show Bart, in trouble as usual, ran into Clint (*Cheyenne*) Walker, John Russell and his deputy Peter Brown (*Lawman*), Will (*Sugarfoot*) Hutchins, Ty (*Bronco*) Hardin, and Edd "Kookie" Byrnes, all in one episode. None of them were of any help whatever!

James Garner was a maverick offscreen as well as on. In 1960 he walked out on Warner Brothers Studios, demanding a better contract. In a virtual replay of the confrontation between Warner Brothers and Clint Walker two years before (see *Cheyenne*), the studio refused to give in, and instead hired a new actor to replace him. Enter Cousin Beau Maverick, who was introduced as an expatriate Texan who had fought with valor in the Civil War (unusual behavior for a Maverick), then moved to England, and now returned as a cultured Englishman to further the family fortunes in America.

Unlike the situation in *Cheyenne*, James Garner never did return to *Maverick*. In December 1960 a court ruled that he could not be held to his contract, and he left Warner Brothers (and TV). Cousin Beau and Bart alternated for the rest of the 1960–1961 season, and in the spring of 1961 still another brother, Brent Maverick, was tried out to see if he could fill Garner's shoes. None of this worked out very well, so in 1961–1962, the final season, Bart was seen alone, together with a healthy quantity of reruns of earlier episodes starring Bret and the two brothers together.

MAXINE BARRAT

see *And Everything Nice*

MAYA

Adventure

FIRST TELECAST: *September 16, 1967*

LAST TELECAST: *February 10, 1968*

BROADCAST HISTORY:

Sep 1967–Feb 1968, NBC Sat 7:30–8:30

CAST:

Terry Bowen .... Jay North
Raji .... Sajid Khan

Filmed in India, *Maya* was the story of two teenage boys who traveled around that country on the back of an elephant. American Terry Bowen had come to India to be with his father, a professional hunter, only to learn that his father was missing and presumed dead following an attack by a man-eating tiger. Terry refused to accept his father's death and, with the help of Raji, an orphan about his own age, set out to look for the missing man. Raji's faithful elephant Maya was their source of transportation and of much help during their jungle adventures in search of Mr. Bowen, whom the boys never found.

MAYBERRY R.F.D.

Situation Comedy

FIRST TELECAST: *September 23, 1968*

LAST TELECAST: *September 6, 1971*

BROADCAST HISTORY:

Sep 1968–Sep 1971, CBS Mon 9:00–9:30

CAST:

Sam Jones .... Ken Berry
Aunt Bee (1968–1970) ...... Frances Bavier
Goober Pyle .... George Lindsey
Howard Sprague .... Jack Dodson
Emmett Clark .... Paul Hartman
Millie Swanson .... Arlene Golonka
Mike Jones .... Buddy Foster
Alice (1970–1971) .... Alice Ghostley

This was the successor to *The Andy Griffith Show,* in which Andy had starred for eight years as the sheriff of quiet, rural Mayberry, North Carolina. When Griffith decided to call it quits in 1968, CBS kept most of the rest of the cast together, added a new lead in the person of Ken Berry, and continued the show under the title *Mayberry, R.F.D.*

Like Griffith's Andy, Berry's Sam Jones was a young widower with a small son, Mike. Sam was a gentleman farmer who had recently taken up residence near Mayberry. Not long after his arrival he found himself elected to the Mayberry Town Council, a position for which he had no prior experience. That hardly mattered in Mayberry, however, as in his friendly, bumbling way he attempted to perform his new duties and tend to the simple needs of the townsfolk. Aunt Bee moved in with him as his housekeeper for two years, then was replaced by Aunt Alice for the 1970–1971 season. Millie Swanson was Sam's romantic interest.

For a couple of years *Mayberry R.F.D.* was virtually as popular as *The Andy Griffith Show* had been. The new program was one of the top four shows on television during its first two years (*Andy Griffith* had reached number one in its final season). It was still in the top 20 when CBS canceled it in 1971, as part of an extensive cutback in "rural"-oriented programming.

MAYOR OF HOLLYWOOD

Variety

FIRST TELECAST: *July 29, 1952*

LAST TELECAST: *September 18, 1952*

BROADCAST HISTORY:

Jul 1952–Sep 1952, NBC Tue/Thu 7:00–7:30

CAST:

Walter O'Keefe .... Himself
Secretary .... Jeanne Dyer
Campaign Manager .... Lou Crosby
Campaign Manager .... Bill Baldwin
Secretary .... Lina Romay

Walter O'Keefe, a well-known radio personality of the 1930s and 1940s, starred as himself in this live series. In his fictional quest to be elected mayor of Hollywood, he took viewers on a tour around the Hollywood area of Los Angeles while trying to drum up support for his campaign. As part of the "tour" he interviewed numerous famous personalities. His original secretary, Jeanne Dyer, was replaced by Lina Romay on August 14, and his campaign manager Lou Crosby, who was also the show's announcer, was replaced by Bill Baldwin on August 7.

MCCLOUD

Police

FIRST TELECAST: *September 16, 1970*

LAST TELECAST: *August 28, 1977*

BROADCAST HISTORY:

Sep 1970–Oct 1970, NBC Wed 9:00–10:00
Mar 1971–Aug 1971, NBC Wed 9:00–10:00
Sep 1971–Aug 1972, NBC Wed 8:30–10:00
Sep 1972–Aug 1975, NBC Sun 8:30–10:00

Sep 1975–Aug 1976, NBC Sun 9:00–11:00
Oct 1976–Aug 1977, NBC Sun Various

CAST:

Sam McCloud .... Dennis Weaver
Peter B. Clifford .... J. D. Cannon
Sgt. Joe Broadhurst .... Terry Carter
Chris Coughlin .... Diana Muldaur

McCloud was one of television's more tongue-in-cheek police series. Here was Deputy Marshal Sam McCloud from Taos, New Mexico, driving the New York City Police crazy. He had originally arrived in New York to chase a prisoner who had escaped from him, and his direct, rather strong-arm methods were hard for the big-city police to cope with. After capturing his man, McCloud somehow found himself on temporary assignment in Manhattan's 27th Precinct under Chief Peter B. Clifford. Although he was ostensibly there to learn the methods employed by a large metropolitan police department, McCloud usually took things into his own hands and reverted to type, much to the chagrin and frustration of Chief Clifford. Whenever McCloud went on a case he dragged Sgt. Joe Broadhurst with him and, though they usually solved the crime and got along well with each other, Broadhurst's association with McCloud didn't seem to be doing him much good with their mutual superior Clifford. McCloud really looked out of place on the streets of New York, with his cowboy hat, sheepskin jacket, and matching accent. He was full of Western homilies and used the catch phrase "There you go" quite regularly. His romantic interest, not seen in every episode, was writer Chris Coughlin, who was working on a book that related to the fugitive he had chased to New York in the pilot for this series.

McCloud premiered in 1970 as the first of four mini-series aired under the collective title *Four in One*—The others being *San Francisco International Airport*, *Night Gallery*, and *The Psychiatrist*. The following fall it became, along with *Columbo* and *McMillan and Wife*, one of the three original elements in the *NBC Mystery Movie* rotation. It remained with that series throughout the rest of its run.

MCCOY

Detective

FIRST TELECAST: *October 5, 1975*
LAST TELECAST: *March 28, 1976*
BROADCAST HISTORY:

Oct 1975–Mar 1976, NBC Sun 9:00–11:00

CAST:

McCoy .... Tony Curtis
Gideon Gibbs .... Roscoe Lee Browne

The combination of an addiction to gambling, at which he was not particularly successful, and a very expensive life-style prompted McCoy to make a living as a sophisticated con man. He was something of a latter-day Robin Hood, finding ways to relieve wealthy criminals of their ill-gotten gains, then returning most of the loot to those who had been bilked of it, while retaining a healthy fee for his services. He would work elaborate cons on the con men themselves, and would usually take them for so much that after expenses, paying off the many accomplices who worked with him, and reimbursing the original victim, there was still a tidy sum left over for himself. McCoy's principal aide was a nightclub comedian named Gideon Gibbs.

McCoy was seen briefly as one of four rotating elements that made up the 1975–1976 edition of the *NBC Sunday Mystery Movie*. Its resemblance to the hit movie *The Sting* may or may not have been coincidental, but in any event did not help as only four episodes of *McCoy* were actually telecast before the program was canceled.

MCCOYS, THE

syndicated title for *Real McCoys, The*

MCGRAW

see *Meet McGraw*

MCHALE'S NAVY

Situation Comedy

FIRST TELECAST: *October 11, 1962*
LAST TELECAST: *August 30, 1966*
BROADCAST HISTORY:

Oct 1962–Sep 1963, ABC Thu 9:30–10:00
Sep 1963–Aug 1966, ABC Tue 8:30–9:00

CAST:

Lt. Cdr. Quinton McHale .. Ernest Borgnine
Capt. Wallace B. Binghamton .... Joe Flynn
Ensign Charles Parker .... Tim Conway
Lester Gruber .... Carl Ballantine
Christy .... Gary Vinson
Harrison "Tinker" Bell .... Billy Sands
Virgil Farrell .... Edson Stroll
Happy Haines (1962–1964)
.... Gavin MacLeod
Willy Moss (1964–1966) ...... John Wright

Fuji Kobiaji .... Yoshio Yoda
Lt. Elroy Carpenter .... Bob Hastings
Col. Harrington (1965–1966)
.... Henry Beckman
Gen. Bronson (1965–1966) .... Simon Scott
Mayor Mario Lugatto (1965–1966)
.... Jay Novello
Rosa Giovanni (1965–1966)
.... Peggy Mondo

The U.S. Navy was never like this. Lt. Commander Quinton McHale was the commander of a World War II P.T. boat with one of the strangest, most outrageous crews ever assembled. The program was in many respects a copy of Phil Silvers' classic Sgt. Bilko show, its broad humor built on the conflict between the easygoing, regulation-ignoring, conartist McHale and his long-suffering superior, Capt. Binghamton (known behind his back as "Old Lead Bottom"). The men loved McHale, Binghamton hated him, and the Navy put up with him because, in the South Seas where P.T. 73 was based at the island of Taratupa, McHale knew the territory "like the back of his hand."

At the start of *McHale's Navy*'s last season, the entire crew, including Capt. Binghamton, were transferred to Italy, where they helped maintain the occupation of the small town of Voltafiore against the possible incursion of German troups. Not only did Binghamton still have to deal with the incorrigible McHale, but he was now saddled with a conniving Italian mayor, Mario Lugatto, who was almost as adept a con man as McHale himself. Nothing changed but the environment. The gambling that had run rampant in the Pacific now included local residents as well as military personnel.

MCKEEVER & THE COLONEL

Situation Comedy

FIRST TELECAST: *September 23, 1962*
LAST TELECAST: *June 16, 1963*
BROADCAST HISTORY:
Sep 1962–Jun 1963, NBC Sun 6:30–7:00
CAST:
Cadet Gary McKeever .... Scott Lane
Col. Harvey Blackwell .... Allyn Joslyn
Sgt. Barnes .... Jackie Coogan
Mrs. Warner .... Elizabeth Fraser
Tubby .... Keith Taylor
Monk .... Johnny Eimen

Comedy about life in a military school. The cadets—McKeever abetted by his pals Tubby and Monk—were constantly getting into trouble and making it virtually impossible for Col. Blackwell to maintain any semblance of order, decorum, or discipline. Sgt. Barnes was the colonel's aide, Mrs. Warner the head of the school cafeteria.

MCLEAN STEVENSON SHOW, THE

Situation Comedy

FIRST TELECAST: *December 1, 1976*
LAST TELECAST: *March 3, 1977*
BROADCAST HISTORY:
Dec 1976–Jan 1977, NBC Wed 8:30–9:00
Feb 1977–Mar 1977, NBC Wed 9:30–10:00
CAST:
Mac Ferguson .... McLean Stevenson
Peggy Ferguson .... Barbara Stuart
Grandma .... Madge West
Janet .... Ayn Ruymen
Chris .... Steve Nevil
David .... David Hollander
Jason .... Jason Whitney

Mac Ferguson was a typical middle-class family man, owner of a hardware store in his home town of Evanston, Illinois. He and his wife had two grown children who, through circumstances that could not possibly have been anticipated by their parents, were living with them. Janet had separated from her husband and moved in along with her two young children, David and Jason. Chris, after several years of trying to "find" himself, principally spent bumming around in Hawaii, returned home to go back to college part time, taking up residence in the basement and setting it up as a bachelor pad. If this didn't create enough congestion, Peggy's mother was also a member of the household.

MCMILLAN AND WIFE

Police

FIRST TELECAST: *September 29, 1971*
LAST TELECAST: *August 21, 1977*
BROADCAST HISTORY:
Sep 1971–Aug 1972, NBC Wed 8:30–10:00
Sep 1972–Jul 1974, NBC Sun 8:30–10:00
Sep 1974–Jul 1975, NBC Sun 8:30–10:30
Sep 1975–Aug 1976, NBC Sun 9:00–11:00
Dec 1976–Aug 1977, NBC Sun 8:00–9:30
CAST:
Commissioner Stewart McMillan
.... Rock Hudson

Sally McMillan (1971–1976)
.... Susan Saint James
Sgt. Charles Enright ....John Schuck
Mildred (1971–1976) ....Nancy Walker
Agatha (1976–1977) ....Martha Raye
Sgt. Steve DiMaggio (1976–1977)
.... Richard Gilliland
Maggie (1976–1977) ....Gloria Strook

San Francisco Police Commissioner Stewart McMillan had a beautiful wife who had a penchant for getting both of them involved in criminal cases which she inadvertently stumbled upon. Mac was very supportive, though occasionally bewildered by the situations Sally got them into, and was often called upon to help solve the cases. This mystery/comedy police series was patterned after the relationship between Nick and Nora Charles in *The Thin Man* movies and TV series of the 1940s and 1950s. There were elements of romance and comedy thrown in with the actual case being solved. Mac's aide was plodding but enthusiastic Sgt. Enright, and Mildred was the McMillans' sarcastic, sharp-tongued maid.

McMillan and Wife was one of the three original rotating elements in the *NBC Mystery Movie*—the other two were *McCloud* and *Columbo*–and remained with the series throughout its long run. When Nancy Walker and Susan Saint James left the series at the end of the 1975–1976 season, the former to star in her own series on ABC and the latter in a contract dispute, the title was shortened to *McMillan* and cast changes were made. Sally was written out of the series by having her die in a plane crash, and Mac, now a widower, had a new maid/housekeeper named Agatha, who happened to be Mildred's sister. Mac also acquired a second assistant in Sgt. Dimaggio (the dimwitted Enright had been promoted to lieutenant) and a new secretary named Maggie.

ME AND THE CHIMP

Situation Comedy

FIRST TELECAST: *January 13, 1972*

LAST TELECAST: *May 18, 1972*

BROADCAST HISTORY:

Jan 1972–May 1972, CBS Thu 8:00–8:30

CAST:

Mike Reynolds ....Ted Bessell
Liz Reynolds ....Anita Gillette
Scott Reynolds ....Scott Kolden
Kitty Reynolds ....Kami Cotler

Mike Reynolds was a happily married dentist living in the suburban Southern California community of San Pascal. He and his wife Liz had two young children and a small chimpanzee named Buttons. Buttons had been found in a local park by the two Reynolds children, Scott and Kitty, and been brought home as a pet. Despite Mike's objections, Buttons became a regular member of the household, having been given that name because of his infatuation with pushing any and all buttons he found on appliances, radios, cars, dental equipment, or anything else he got his little hands onto. Though very friendly and affectionate, Buttons caused all sorts of problems with his curiosity about almost everything and managed to get the entire household into difficult situations. It always seemed to be Mike's responsibility to get them out.

MEDALLION THEATER

Dramatic Anthology

FIRST TELECAST: *July 11, 1953*

LAST TELECAST: *April 3, 1954*

BROADCAST HISTORY:

Jul 1953–Apr 1954, CBS Sat 10:00–10:30

This series of adaptations of plays and works from other media was aired live from New York with a different cast each week. The premiere telecast starred Henry Fonda in "The Decision of Arrowsmith," adapted from Sinclair Lewis' novel. Cast in the leads of other presentations were generally well-known performers, including Ronald Reagan, Jack Lemmon, Claude Rains, Robert Preston, Dane Clark, Martha Scott, and Jan Sterling.

MEDIC

Medical

FIRST TELECAST: *September 13, 1954*

LAST TELECAST: *November 19, 1956*

BROADCAST HISTORY:

Sep 1954–Nov 1956, NBC Mon 9:00–9:30

CAST:

Dr. Konrad Styner ....Richard Boone

THEME:

"Blue Star," by Edward Heyman and Victor Young

Case histories from the files of the Los Angeles County Medical Association were dramatized in this filmed series. In its efforts to present the practice of medicine realistically, *Medic* was shot at real hospitals and clinics, and often used real doctors and nurses as part of the cast. Dr. Styner was the host and narrator of the series, as well as a frequent participant in the cases. His introduction to each episode always included this description of the doctor: ". . . guardian of birth, healer of the sick, and comforter of the aged." The dramas generally centered around the struggle to preserve life, and the tragedies and triumphs that resulted.

Medic was a pioneer in TV realism, and was the first starring vehicle for actor Richard Boone. Its pretty theme song, "Blue Star," was quite popular during 1955.

MEDICAL CENTER

Medical

FIRST TELECAST: *September 24, 1969*

LAST TELECAST: *September 6, 1976*

BROADCAST HISTORY:

Sep 1969–May 1973, CBS Wed 9:00–10:00
May 1973–Sep 1976, CBS Mon 10:00–11:00

CAST:

Dr. Paul Lochner .... James Daly
Dr. Joe Gannon .... Chad Everett
Nurse Chambers (1969–1972) .... Jayne Meadows
Dr. Jeanne Bartlett (1969–1971) .... Corinne Camacho
Nurse Courtland .... Chris Hutson
Nurse Wilcox (1972–1976) .... Audrey Totter
Dr. Barnes (1970–1971) ..... Fred Holliday
Nurse Murphy (1971–1972) ...... Jane Dulo
Nurse Holmby (1971–1976) .... Barbara Baldavin
Nurse Canford (1975–1976) .... Virginia Hawkins
Lt. Samuels (1971–1976) .... Martin E. Brooks

Located in the Los Angeles area, Medical Center was an otherwise unnamed hospital complex that was part of a large university campus. Dr. Paul Lochner was the chief of staff, an experienced, professional, compassionate man. Dr. Joe Gannon was a young associate professor of surgery and close friend and colleague of Dr. Lochner. At the start of the show's second season, Dr. Gannon took on the added responsibilities of director of the student health service, an appropriate post for a young physician who could identify closely with the students. A number of other doctors and nurses came and went in the cast; Miss Wilcox, the extremely efficient head nurse, achieved co-star billing in 1972.

The personal and medical stories of the doctors and their patients, as well as others with whom they came into contact, provided the drama in this series. Gannon and Lochner embodied the youth *vs.* experience tension which seems to be a necessary element of every medical show. The elements certainly worked here, as *Medical Center*, with its seven-year run, was the longest-lasting medical series in the history of prime-time television.

MEDICAL HORIZONS

Public Affairs

FIRST TELECAST: *September 12, 1955*

LAST TELECAST: *March 5, 1956*

BROADCAST HISTORY:

Sep 1955–Mar 1956, ABC Mon 9:30–10:00

HOST:

Quincy Howe (1955)
Don Goddard (1955–1956)

During the 1955–1956 season ABC attempted to bring the television viewer an insight into the advances being made in medicine and an introduction to the people who were responsible for them. Quincy Howe was the original host/narrator, but other commitments forced him to leave this live series after a month. He was replaced by Don Goddard. Each week a different discovery, program of research, or branch of medicine was discussed, with interviews with doctors, technicians, researchers, etc., supplemented by actual scenes of the technique, equipment, or operation.

MEDICAL STORY

Medical Anthology

FIRST TELECAST: *September 4, 1975*

LAST TELECAST: *January 8, 1976*

BROADCAST HISTORY:

Sep 1975–Jan 1976, NBC Thu 10:00–11:00

Medical Story attempted to remove the mantle of sainthood from doctors. It dealt with the personal problems and human failings of members of the medical profession, as well as with their skills. Stories confronted many sensitive issues, most notably the mistakes made in hospitals and the selfishness and insensitivity of many doctors. Such a critical view of a profession whose practitioners people want to trust apparently did not sit well with viewers, and the program was dropped after a few months.

MEET CORLISS ARCHER

Situation Comedy

FIRST TELECAST: *July 12, 1951*

LAST TELECAST: *March 29, 1952*

BROADCAST HISTORY:

Jul 1951–Sep 1951, CBS Thu 9:00–9:30
Jul 1951–Sep 1951, CBS Fri 10:00–10:30
Jan 1952–Mar 1952, CBS Sat 6:30–7:00

CAST:

Corliss Archer ....Lugene Sanders
Mr. Harry Archer ....Fred Shields
Dexter Franklin ....Bobby Ellis
Mrs. Janet Archer (1951) ... Frieda Inescort
Mrs. Janet Archer (1952) ..... Irene Tedrow

Meet Corliss Archer had been on CBS radio since 1943 and was still being aired in the early 1950s when this television version was added in 1951. It was the story of a typical high school girl, her boy friend Dexter, and her parents. The stories revolved around the energetic and vivacious Corliss as she made the transition from little girl to young woman. Fred Shields, who had played Mr. Archer through most of the radio run, recreated his role for the new medium, as did Irene Tedrow as Mrs. Archer in part of the television run.

This series was fed to different parts of the country on different days during the summer of 1951. The Thursday shows were seen in the Midwest while the rest of the country was seeing *Your Esso Reporter*. On Friday nights *Meet Corliss Archer* was available to those stations that did not carry it on Thursdays. Since it was done live from New York, the cast did the same show on consecutive nights.

MEET McGRAW

Detective

FIRST TELECAST: *July 2, 1957*

LAST TELECAST: *October 8, 1959*

BROADCAST HISTORY:

Jul 1957–Jun 1958, NBC Tue 9:00–9:30
Nov 1958–Dec 1958, ABC Sun 10:00–10:30
Jan 1959, ABC Sun 9:30–10:00
Feb 1959–Sep 1959, ABC Sun 10:30–11:00
Oct 1959, ABC Thu 9:00–9:30

CAST:

McGraw ....Frank Lovejoy

Although McGraw (that was the only name he used) was not officially a private detective, for all intents and purposes he might as well have been. Tough, willing to get into a fight, but never carrying a gun, he accepted all sorts of dangerous jobs for pay. In most of the episodes he regretfully had to leave a pretty woman behind but, as a loner, he just couldn't let himself get tied down. This series premiered on NBC, as *Meet McGraw*, on December 31, 1957, changed its title to *The Adventures of McGraw*, and was rerun on ABC in 1958–1959.

MEET MILLIE

Situation Comedy

FIRST TELECAST: *October 25, 1952*

LAST TELECAST: *March 6, 1956*

BROADCAST HISTORY:

Oct 1952–Jun 1953, CBS Sat 9:30–10:00
Jun 1953–Aug 1953, CBS Sat 9:00–9:30
Aug 1953–Sep 1953, CBS Sat 9:30–10:00
Oct 1953–Feb 1954, CBS Sat 7:00–7:30
Mar 1954–Mar 1956, CBS Tue 9:00–9:30

CAST:

Millie Bronson ....Elena Verdugo
"Mama" Bronson ....Florence Halop
Mr. Boone (1952–1953) ....Earl Ross
Johnny Boone, Jr. (1952–1955) ...Ross Ford
Alfred Prinzmetal ....Marvin Kaplan
Mr. Boone (1953–1956) ....Roland Winters
Mrs. Boone (1953–1955) ... Isabel Randolph
Gladys (1956) .... Virginia Vincent

Millie Bronson was a young, attractive, middle-class secretary working in Manhattan. She lived in a brownstone apartment with her mother, who was always promoting Millie to eligible men as a potential spouse. Millie's boy friend through most of the series' run was Johnny Boone, Jr., the son of her boss. A close friend of the Bronsons, who managed to get involved in most everything, was Alfred Prinzmetal. Alfred was an aspiring author-poet-composer.

Meet Millie had originated on CBS radio in July 1951 with Audrey Totter in the starring role. When her movie studio refused to let her do the TV version, Elena Verdugo took it over and eventually replaced Miss Totter in the radio edition before it expired in 1954. Earl Ross, as her boss, made the transition from radio to TV but was replaced by Roland Winters in June 1953.

MEET MR. McNUTLEY

see *Ray Milland Show, The*

MEET THE BOSS

Interview

FIRST TELECAST: *June 10, 1952*

LAST TELECAST: *August 26, 1952*

BROADCAST HISTORY:

Jun 1952–Aug 1952, DUM Tue 10:30–11:00

HOST:

Bill Cunningham

Newsman Bill Cunningham interviewed top American executives on their careers and their industries in general, in this paean to big business.

MEET THE CHAMP

see *Boxing*

MEET THE CHAMPIONS

Sports Interview

FIRST TELECAST: *July 21, 1956*

LAST TELECAST: *January 12, 1957*

BROADCAST HISTORY:

Jul 1956–Jan 1957, NBC Sat 6:45–7:00

HOST:

Jack Lescoulie

Each episode of this live program gave viewers the opportunity to see a sports celebrity interviewed by Jack Lescoulie, as well as a second sports world figure (not necessarily an athlete) making predictions about the outcome of an upcoming athletic event.

MEET THE PRESS

Interview

FIRST TELECAST: *November 20, 1947*

LAST TELECAST: *August 29, 1965*

BROADCAST HISTORY:

Nov 1947–Dec 1947, NBC Thu 8:00–8:30
Sep 1948–Feb 1949, NBC Sun 8:30–9:00
Feb 1949–Jul 1949, NBC Wed 10:00–10:30
Jul 1949–Sep 1949, NBC Mon 10:00–10:30
Sep 1949–Feb 1950, NBC Sat various
Oct 1950–May 1952, NBC Sun various
Jun 1951–Sep 1951, NBC Tue 8:00–8:30
May 1952–Sep 1952, NBC Sun 7:30–8:00
Oct 1952–Aug 1965, NBC Sun 6:00–6:30

REGULAR MODERATOR:

Martha Rountree (1947–1953)
Ned Brooks (1953–1965)

REGULAR PANELISTS:

Lawrence Spivak
Bill Monroe

This NBC public affairs program, which styles itself "America's Press Conference of the Air," is as of this writing the longest-running series on network television. Part of its career (as noted above) has been in prime time, while during other periods it has been telecast on Sunday afternoons.

Meet the Press usually originates from NBC's Washington, D.C., studios. It was created by Martha Rountree and Lawrence Spivak in 1945 as a radio promotion for the *American Mercury Magazine*, of which Spivak was then editor. It started on local television on November 6, 1947, and was first fed over the network (then consisting of two stations) on November 20 of that year. The format has always remained the same: a panel of reporters questions a leading public figure. Over the years virtually every major political figure in the United States has occupied the *Meet the Press* hot seat, and many foreign dignitaries as well. Martha Rountree was the original TV moderator. NBC newsman Ned Brooks took over in 1953, while Spivak remained a regular panelist and occasional moderator. Since 1965 moderating chores have alternated among various newsmen, with Spivak, Bill Monroe, and Edwin Newman frequently at the helm.

During the summer of 1951, in a move unique to political interview shows of this type, *Meet the Press* aired two times per week, with different guests on each Sunday and Tuesday telecast. Following the end of its nighttime run, in August of 1965, *Meet the Press* became a regular fixture on the NBC Sunday afternoon lineup, where it remains to this day.

MEET THE VEEP

Discussion

FIRST TELECAST: *June 30, 1953*

LAST TELECAST: *August 25, 1953*

BROADCAST HISTORY:

Jun 1953–Aug 1953, NBC Tue 10:45–11:00

REGULARS:

Alben W. Barkley
Earl Godwin

Originating live from Washington, D.C., this discussion show featured former Vice President Alben W. Barkley, who had acquired the affectionate nickname "The Veep" during his tenure with Truman and NBC news commentator Earl Godwin. They would discuss various political issues, reminisce about Mr. Barkley's career, or chat about current nonpolitical issues. On occasion guests appeared on the show to discuss their points of view, be they similar to or different from Mr. Barkley's.

MEET YOUR CONGRESS

Debate

FIRST TELECAST: *July 1, 1949*

LAST TELECAST: *July 4, 1954*

BROADCAST HISTORY:

Jul 1949–Aug 1949, NBC Fri 9:00–9:30
Aug 1949–Oct 1949, NBC Sat 8:00–8:30
Jul 1953–Sep 1953, DUM Wed 9:30–10:00
Oct 1953–Jul 1954, DUM Sun 6:30–7:00

MODERATOR:

Sen. Blair Moody

Public-affairs debate show, in which two Republican and two Democratic Congressmen gave their views on an issue of national importance. The program originated in NBC's Washington, D.C., studios and was first seen as a Sunday afternoon program (March–June 1949). In 1953–1954, it turned up on DuMont. Former Senator Blair Moody of Michigan was the moderator.

MELBA MOORE–CLIFTON DAVIS SHOW, THE

Musical Variety

FIRST TELECAST: *June 7, 1972*

LAST TELECAST: *July 5, 1972*

BROADCAST HISTORY:

Jun 1972–Jul 1972, CBS Wed 8:00–9:00

REGULARS:

Melba Moore
Clifton Davis
Timmy Rogers
Ron Carey
Dick Libertini
Liz Torres

Young Broadway stars Melba Moore and Clifton Davis were starred in this summer variety series. With the help of their regular supporting cast and special guest stars they performed skits and did musical numbers. The set for the show was designed to look like the side of an apartment building with the various acts taking place in different apartments.

MELODY, HARMONY & RHYTHM

Music

FIRST TELECAST: *December 13, 1949*

LAST TELECAST: *February 16, 1950*

BROADCAST HISTORY:

Dec 1949–Feb 1950, NBC Tue/Thu 7:30–7:45

REGULARS:

Lynne Barrett
Carol Reed
Charlie Dobson
Tony DeSimone Trio

This musical interlude featured three vocalists and an instrumental trio. It originated from WPTZ, Philadelphia.

MELODY STREET

Music

FIRST TELECAST: *September 23, 1953*

LAST TELECAST: *February 5, 1954*

BROADCAST HISTORY:

Sep 1953–Oct 1953, DUM Wed 8:30–9:00
Nov 1953–Feb 1954, DUM Fri 8:30–9:00

HOST:

Elliot Lawrence (1953)
Tony Mottola (1954)

REGULARS:

Lyn Gibbs
Joe Buwen
Roberta McDonald

Another stop in DuMont's never-ending search for low-cost programming was this "musical stroll down Tin Pan Alley," in which a cast of regulars and guests lip-synced (mouthed) the words to a song while a phonograph record was played. The original host was noted orchestra leader Elliot Lawrence, who was seen sitting at a piano with a cigarette dangling from his mouth, Hoagy Carmichael-style, commenting on the music. "I was awful," he frankly admits today, "I don't even smoke!" Lawrence soon returned to what he does very well, conducting an orchestra, and guitarist Tony Mottola took over the host's spot for the show's last month.

MELODY TOUR

Musical Variety

FIRST TELECAST: *July 8, 1954*

LAST TELECAST: *September 30, 1954*

BROADCAST HISTORY:

Jul 1954–Sep 1954, ABC Thu 8:00–9:00

REGULARS:

Stan Freeman
Norman Scott
Neil Fisher
Jorie Remeus
Nancy Kenyon

Interesting summer musical series built around the concept of a vacation trip. The premiere took place mostly in a pier setting, as the cast prepared to embark, and subsequent programs highlighted various foreign ports of call. Guests were featured in addition to the regular cast.

MEN, THE

Adventure

FIRST TELECAST: *September 21, 1972*
LAST TELECAST: *September 1, 1973*
BROADCAST HISTORY:

Sep 1972–Jan 1973, ABC Thu 9:00–10:00
Jan 1973–Sep 1973, ABC Sat 10:00–11:00

THEME MUSIC (overall):

Isaac Hayes

This was the umbrella title for three rotating series, *Assignment Vienna, Delphi Bureau*, and *Jigsaw*. At first these elements rotated in normal fashion, each one appearing every third week. However, in January 1973, when *The Men* moved to Saturdays, the rotation scheme was changed and each element appeared for several weeks in a row, as follows:

Jan 13–Feb 10: *Assignment Vienna*
Feb 17–Mar 3: *Jigsaw*
Mar 17–Apr 7: *Delphi Bureau*
Apr 14–Jun 9: *Assignment Vienna*
Jun 16–Aug 11: *Jigsaw*
Aug 18–Sep 1: *Delphi Bureau*

See individual element titles for more complete program information.

MEN AT LAW

see *Storefront Lawyers*

MEN FROM SHILOH, THE

see *Virginian, The*

MEN INTO SPACE

Science Fiction

FIRST TELECAST: *September 30, 1959*
LAST TELECAST: *September 7, 1960*
BROADCAST HISTORY:

Sep 1959–Sep 1960, CBS Wed 8:30–9:00

CAST:

Col. Edward McCauley . . . William Lundigan

On October 4, 1957, Russia launched the world's first manmade earth satellite. It was too late to get a show about it on television that season, or even the next, but in 1959 CBS was ready to capitalize on the high public interest in and concern about the "space race" with this realistic dramatization of space exploration. *Men into Space* was produced with the cooperation and assistance of the Army, Navy, Air Force, and numerous scientific organizations, and every attempt was made to present an accurate picture of man's likely experiences and problems away from Earth. Col. Edward McCauley was the only regular member of the cast. His adventures on the moon base, the space station, other planets within the solar system, and on rocketships in transit provided the stories. Problems with equipment, the environment, and the people involved in the space program all created crisis situations for the indomitable Col. McCauley.

MEN OF TOMORROW

Documentary

FIRST TELECAST: *June 29, 1954*
LAST TELECAST: *September 21, 1954*
BROADCAST HISTORY:

Jun 1954–Sep 1954, ABC Tue 7:30–8:00

This filmed series was devoted to the Boy Scouts of America. Each episode explored some aspect of the Boy Scout movement, such as the training of young scouts and trips taken by them.

MENASHA THE MAGNIFICENT

Situation Comedy

FIRST TELECAST: *July 3, 1950*
LAST TELECAST: *September 11, 1950*
BROADCAST HISTORY:

Jul 1950–Sep 1950, NBC Mon 8:00–8:30

CAST:

Menasha . . . . .Menasha Skulnik
Mrs. Davis . . . . .Zanah Cunningham

Short-lived situation comedy starring Yiddish comedian Menasha Skulnik, who began each day singing "Oh, What a Beautiful Morning," but usually wound up in trouble. Menasha, a little fellow with a hoplike walk and a tragicomic mien, was cast as the meek manager of a restaurant owned by the domineering, Amazon-like Mrs. Davis. His fate was to be pushed around constantly. Jean Cleveland appeared as Mrs. Davis in the first telecast, but was replaced by Zanah Cunningham the following week.

MEREDITH WILLSON SHOW, THE

Music

FIRST TELECAST: *July 31, 1949*
LAST TELECAST: *August 21, 1949*
BROADCAST HISTORY:
Jul 1949–Aug 1949, NBC Sun 8:30–9:00
HOST:
Meredith Willson
REGULAR:
Norma Zimmer

Four-week summer musical series, hosted by famed composer and orchestra leader Meredith Willson. The regulars included Norma Zimmer, later to become Lawrence Welk's "Champagne Lady."

MERV GRIFFIN SHOW, THE

Talk

FIRST TELECAST: *August 18, 1969*
LAST TELECAST: *February 11, 1972*
BROADCAST HISTORY:
Aug 1969–Feb 1972, CBS Mon–Fri 11:30–1:00 A.M.
HOST:
Merv Griffin
ANNOUNCER:
Arthur Treacher
ORCHESTRA:
Mort Lindsey

Merv Griffin had had a highly successful syndicated talk show for several years when CBS chose him to wage war on a network scale with Johnny Carson's *Tonight Show* in 1969. His arrival meant that there were competing late-night talk shows on all three networks, Joey Bishop having started one on ABC in the summer of 1967. A cherubic folksy individual, Merv was a former band singer and veteran of several network daytime talk and game shows, in addition to his syndicated show. His ingratiating manner and aversion to virtually anything that might be considered radical, offensive, or controversial made his show rather bland. It did force Joey Bishop off the air, to be replaced by the dry, intellectual wit of Dick Cavett, but it could never make a dent in Carson's late-night audience. As CBS's first regular late-night entry since *Chronoscope* in the mid-1950s, *The Merv Griffin Show* was never as big an audience-grabber as CBS had hoped and was canceled two and one-half years after its premiere. It was replaced by late-night movies, while Merv returned to the syndicated talk-show world.

METROPOLITAN OPERA AUDITIONS OF THE AIR

Talent

FIRST TELECAST: *January 15, 1952*
LAST TELECAST: *April 1, 1952*
BROADCAST HISTORY:
Jan 1952–Apr 1952, ABC Tue 8:30–9:00
COMMENTATOR:
Milton J. Cross

This must have been one of the classiest talent shows in the history of network television, as newcomers competed for a place at the fabled "Met." Similar operatic auditions had been telecast by ABC on a specials basis as early as 1948.

MICHAEL SHAYNE

Detective

FIRST TELECAST: *September 30, 1960*
LAST TELECAST: *September 22, 1961*
BROADCAST HISTORY:
Sep 1960–Sep 1961, NBC Fri 10:00–11:00
CAST
Michael Shayne ....Richard Denning
Tim Rourke ....Jerry Paris
Lucy Hamilton ....Patricia Donahue
Will Gentry ....Herbert Rudley
Dick Hamilton ....Gary Clarke

Michael Shayne was a suave, debonaire Miami-based private detective whose cases tended to revolve around bizarre murders. Helping him solve the cases were Tim Rourke, a young newspaper-reporter friend; Will Gentry, the chief of the Miami police department; and Dick Hamilton, the younger brother of Shayne's secretary-girl friend Lucy. Lucy was not the only love of his life, however, and his fondness for beautiful women often got him into sticky situations. The character of Michael Shayne had been established in a series of detective novels written by Brett Halliday, as well as in a radio series, a dozen movies, and a monthly mystery magazine. Mr. Halliday acted as technical consultant for the series.

MICKEY

Situation Comedy

FIRST TELECAST: *September 16, 1964*

LAST TELECAST: *January 13, 1965*

BROADCAST HISTORY:

Sep 1964–Jan 1965, ABC Wed 9:00–9:30

CAST:

Mickey Grady .... Mickey Rooney
Nora Grady .... Emmaline Henry
Sammy Ling .... Sammee Tong
Timmy Grady .... Tim Rooney
Buddy Grady .... Brian Nash

At the outset of this comedy series Mickey Rooney was cast as a Coast Guard recruiter in landlocked Omaha, who dreamt of a life on the open sea. He got his wish—or at least got close to it—when he inherited a luxurious beachfront hotel in Newport Harbor, California. When the Gradys moved from Omaha to take over the Marina Palms, they thought their money worries and other troubles would be over. Little did they realize that Sammy Ling, the hotel's manager (with a "lifetime contract"), had let it go deeply into debt by letting too many of his relatives in on the operation. The legal work was being done by Ling's shyster cousin and the mortgage was held by the Ling Savings & Loan at an annual rate of 17 percent. Mickey and family set out to straighten things out, in their own comedic way. Mickey Rooney's real-life son Tim played his 16-year-old son Timmy, and Brian Nash played the 8-year-old, Buddy.

MICKEY ROONEY SHOW, THE

Situation Comedy

FIRST TELECAST: *September 4, 1954*

LAST TELECAST: *June 4, 1955*

BROADCAST HISTORY:

Sep 1954–Jun 1955, NBC Sat 8:00–8:30

CAST:

Mickey Mulligan .... Mickey Rooney
Mrs. Mulligan .... Claire Carleton
Mr. Mulligan .... Regis Toomey
Pat .... Carla Balenda
Mr. Brown .... John Hubbard
Freddie .... Joey Forman
The Drama Instructor ...... Alan Mowbray

Mickey Mulligan was a young man working as a page at the NBC Studios in Hollywood. His aspirations, however, went far beyond his lowly position. He really wanted to be a serious dramatic actor, and was only using the page job as a springboard to bigger things. At night Mickey attended dramatic school, with less-than-spectacular results. By day his thespian ambitions were not encouraged by either his peers or superiors at NBC. But there was no keeping Mickey down. The only people who did encourage him were his father and his girl friend Pat, who worked as a secretary at the studios. Mickey lived with his mother, a one-time star in burlesque, and his father, a life-long cop.

Ironically, in real life the position of page at NBC is widely regarded as an excellent starting job in the broadcasting industry, and many former pages have gone on to become stars or top-level executives.

The official title of this series was *The Mickey Rooney Show;* however, it was also known by its subtitle, *Hey Mulligan.*

MICKIE FINN'S

Musical Variety

FIRST TELECAST: *April 21, 1966*

LAST TELECAST: *September 1, 1966*

BROADCAST HISTORY:

Apr 1966–Sep 1966, NBC Thu 9:30–10:00

REGULARS:

Fred E. Finn
Mickie Finn
The Fred Finn Band
The Mickie Finn Dancers
The Dapper Dans
Harold "Hoot" Connors
Mickey Manners

The set on which this variety series was taped was a replica of the warehouse in San Diego that Fred and Mickie Finn had converted into a "Gay '90s" nightclub. The music played by the band ranged from current hits to ragtime and Dixieland jazz. In addition to the guest stars, the regular cast included Fred, as the proprietor who played piano and led the band, and his wife Mickie, who played banjo. Harold Connors and Mickey Manners were the bartenders who often provided comic relief.

MIDNIGHT SPECIAL, THE

Music

FIRST TELECAST: *February 2, 1973*

LAST TELECAST:

BROADCAST HISTORY:

Feb 1973– , NBC Fri 1:00–2:30 A.M.

HOSTESS:
Helen Reddy (1975–1976)
ANNOUNCER:
Wolfman Jack

For young people coming home from a Friday night date, or for those who were still up after *The Tonight Show, The Midnight Special* provided 90 minutes of taped in-concert popular music. The emphasis was on rock and, when the series first went on the air, everyone was a guest star—there was no regular host. Among the popular stars who hosted the show were Johnny Rivers, Mac Davis, Paul Anka, Lou Rawls, Ray Charles, Jerry Lee Lewis, Chubby Checker, Al Green, Curtis Mayfield, David Bowie, and Charlie Rich. It was Helen Reddy, the hostess of the premiere telecast, however, who finally became permanent host, two years later—in July, 1975. Less than a year later she gave up that role and weekly guest hosts returned.

Beginning in the summer of 1975, a regular feature of The Midnight Special was "Rock Tribute," a segment that profiled a different rock star each week. Included were scenes of the star in concert, interviews, and various other insights into the star's life.

MIDWESTERN HAYRIDE
Musical Variety
FIRST TELECAST: *June 16, 1951*
LAST TELECAST: *September 6, 1959*
BROADCAST HISTORY:
Jun 1951–Sep 1951, NBC Sat 9:00–10:00
Jun 1952–Sep 1952, NBC Tue 8:00–9:00
Jun 1954–Sep 1954, NBC Tue 8:00–8:30
May 1955–Sep 1955, NBC Fri 8:00–8:30
Sep 1955–Jun 1956, NBC Wed 10:00–10:30
Jul 1957–Oct 1957, ABC Sun 9:30–10:00
Jun 1958–Sep 1958, ABC Sat 10:00–10:30
May 1959–Sep 1959, NBC Sun 7:00–7:30
EMCEE:
Bill Thall (1951–1954)
Bob Shrede (1951)
Hugh Cherry (1955–1956)
Paul Dixon (1957–1958)
Dean Richards (1959)
REGULARS:
The County Briar Hoppers (1951–1952)
Slim King & the Pine Mountain Boys
Zeke Turner
Bonnie Lou Ewins (1952–1959)
The Midwesterners (1954–1959)
The Hometowners (1957–1959)

This Country music hoedown was a nighttime summer standby during the 1950s. Originating from the NBC affiliate in Dayton or Cincinnati, Ohio, it featured such talent as a square-dance ensemble (the County Briar Hoppers, later the Midwesterners), yodlers, guitarists, string bands, country comedy acts, etc. Many performers came and went over the years, among them guitarist Jerry Byrd, Ernie Lee, Charlie Gore & the Rangers, Lee Jones, Buddy Ross, the Kentucky Boys, Salty and Mattie (later Billy) Holmes, Freddy Langdon, Tommy Watson, Bobby Bobo, Penny West, Kenny Price, Helen and Billy Scott, and the Lucky Pennies.

Midwestern Hayride was also frequently seen on the network in non-evening hours during the regular season.

MIKE WALLACE INTERVIEWS
Interview
FIRST TELECAST: *April 28, 1957*
LAST TELECAST: *September 14, 1958*
BROADCAST HISTORY:
Apr 1957–Sep 1957, ABC Sun 10:00–10:30
Sep 1957–Apr 1958, ABC Sat 10:00–10:30
Apr 1958–Sep 1958, ABC Sun 10:00–10:30
HOST:
Mike Wallace

Newsman Mike Wallace conducted this ABC interview program in the aggressive style for which he was to become famous. Among the guests undergoing his grilling were Gloria Swanson, the Imperial Wizard of the Ku Klux Klan, Mickey Cohen, Steve Allen, Arkansas Governor Faubus, stripper Lili St. Cyr, Tennessee Williams, and Major Donald Kehoe, an Air Force expert on Unidentified Flying Objects.

MILLIONAIRE, THE
Dramatic Anthology
FIRST TELECAST: *January 19, 1955*
LAST TELECAST: *September 28, 1960*
BROADCAST HISTORY:
Jan 1955–Sep 1960, CBS Wed 9:00–9:30
CAST:
Michael Anthony ....Marvin Miller

Each week eccentric multibillionaire John Beresford Tipton (whose face was never seen on the series) would instruct his personal secretary, Michael Anthony, to present some unsuspecting individual with a cashier's check for one million dollars, tax free. The object was to see how this newfound wealth would change the lives of its recipients. The answers to the question "What would you do if you had a million dollars?" intrigued and entertained audiences for more than five years. Michael Anthony was the only regular member of the cast and functioned more as a host than as a participant in the dramas. The one stipulation that Mr. Anthony made when he presented the checks to their recipients was that they make no attempt to find out who their mysterious benefactor was. If they did, they would have to forfeit the money.

Viewers never found out who he was, either. Each program opened with Tipton seated in the study of his huge estate, Silverstone, toying with his chessmen. He would call in his faithful secretary, deliver a few philosophical words of wisdom, and hand over the name of the latest recipient. Only the back of Tipton's head or his hand on the arm of a chair was ever seen on camera, and the files do not record who that hand or head belonged to (probably to several people over the years). The deep, authoritative voice of Mr. Tipton was that of a well-known Hollywood announcer, Paul Frees.

MILTON BERLE SHOW, THE

Comedy Variety

FIRST TELECAST: *June 8, 1948*

LAST TELECAST: *January 6, 1967*

BROADCAST HISTORY:

Jun 1948–Jun 1956, NBC Tue 8:00–9:00 (OS)
Oct 1958–May 1959, NBC Wed 9:00–9:30
Sep 1966–Jan 1967, ABC Fri 9:00–10:00

EMCEE:

Milton Berle

REGULARS:

Fatso Marco (1948–1952; as *Marko Marcelle* from 1951)
Ruth Gilbert (1952–1955)
Bobby Sherwood (1952–1953)
Arnold Stang (1953–1955)
Jack Collins (1953–1955)
Milton Frome (1953–1955)
Irving Benson (*Sidney Sphritzer*; 1966–1967)

COMMERCIAL ANNOUNCER:

Sid Stone (1948–1951)
Jimmy Nelson (1952–1953)
Jack Lescoulie (1954–1955)

ORCHESTRA:

Alan Roth (1948–1955)
Victor Young (1955–1956)
Billy May (1958–1959)

THEME:

"Near You," by Kermit Goell and Francis Craig

The most popular hour of the week during the early years of TV was Milton Berle's, on Tuesday night. Although Berle was the host on the very first telecast of *Texaco Star Theater*, June 8, 1948, he was not at that time considered the permanent emcee. During the summer of 1948 Harry Richman, Georgie Price, Henny Youngman, Morey Amsterdam, Jack Carter, and Peter Donald rotated in the host's spot. Berle won the "competition" and was made permanent emcee in September 1948.

Milton Berle was not unknown at the time, but he could hardly have been called a big name. He had been on radio since the 1930s, and even in a few films, but hadn't scored a big hit in either medium. On TV, however, he fast developed into something of a national institution—"Mr. Television"—and it is said that he sold more TV sets than any advertising campaign. People bought the newfangled thing just to see this crazy comedian everyone was talking about.

The original *Texaco Star Theater* was built along the lines of an old-fashioned vaudeville variety hour, with half a dozen guests each week, including singers, comedians, ventriloquists, acrobats—you name it. But the star was Berle, and he involved himself in many of the acts, adding comedy counterpoint. Soon the basic format was set. Each show opened with the four Texaco Service Men, singing the Texaco jingle ("Oh, we're the men of Texaco, we work from Maine to Mexico . . .") and then working into a musical introduction of Berle, who came on dressed in some outlandish costume. "And now the man with jokes from the Stone Age," and Berle came on dressed as a caveman. "The man who just paid his taxes . . . ," and Berle arrived wearing a barrel. For the sponsor's commercials, old-fashioned pitchman Sid Stone ("Awright, I'll tell ya what I'm gonna do!") would come on stage, set up his sample case, and launch into his spiel—until chased off by a whistle-blowing policeman. And each show would end with Berle singing his theme song, "Near You."

This format changed little during the first four seasons, although the accent was gradually placed more on Berle himself, his sight gags, outlandish costumes and props. In 1952 young ventriloquist Jimmy Nelson and his dummy Danny O'Day replaced Sid Stone as the commercial announcer. In the fall of 1952 Berle returned with a somewhat different format. There were fewer guest acts, and each show was built around a central theme or comedy plot (often it was the rehearsal for the show itself), involving Berle, his guests, and several regulars. Ruth Gilbert joined the cast as Max, his secretary, and in 1953 Arnold Stang joined as Francis, an NBC stagehand and Max's secret love. In the fall of 1955 the regulars were dropped and an entirely new production staff was hired. The program's format was freer, alternating between straight variety hours, satires, and book musicals (including "State of Confusion" on October 18, 1955, a satirical comedy written for Berle by Gore Vidal). One of the guests during the last few months was Elvis Presley, making two appearances in early 1956.

Title and scheduling underwent several changes in the 1950s. After 1953 Texaco shifted its sponsorship to another night (see the *Jimmy Durante* and *Donald O'Connor* shows) and Berle's hour became the *Buick-Berle Show*. Then from 1954–1956 it was simply *The Milton Berle Show*, which alternated variously with Martha Raye, Bob Hope, and Steve Allen.

By 1956 the steam had run out for "Mr. Television." TV was by then becoming dominated by dramatic-anthology shows, Westerns, and private eyes, and the sight of a grinning comic jumping around in crazy costumes no longer had the appeal it did in 1948, when things were simpler.

Two years after his departure from the Tuesday lineup, Berle returned to prime time with a half-hour variety series on NBC, for Kraft (called *Milton Berle Starring in The Kraft Music Hall*). He was a more restrained performer this time—no slapstick or outrageous costumes—attempting to function more as a host than as the central focus of the show. Each telecast began with an opening monologue, often including informal patter with the evening's guest stars. Later, Berle might perform in skits with his guests. With the exception of the interplay between Milton and bandleader Billy May, the show was a somewhat refined version of *The Red Skelton Show*. Berle's new image did not, however, attract sufficient viewers to warrant renewal for a second season.

After his Kraft show was canceled Berle continued to show up as a guest on other programs, increasingly a nostalgic figure. Then in 1966 he was signed for a new variety hour of his own on ABC, and columnists made a great deal of his "comeback." "Can he grab the new generation?" headlined one. To give the show a youthful image singers Bobby Rydell and Donna Loren were signed as regulars (but they soon disappeared), while Irving Benson played the heckler in the audience. The producer was comic Bill Dana, who also appeared periodically as Jose Jiminez. Despite an infusion of top-name guests, Lucille Ball and Bob Hope among them, the program was massacred in the ratings by *The Man from U.N.C.L.E.* and was soon dropped.

MILTON BERLE STARRING IN THE KRAFT MUSIC HALL

see *Milton Berle Show, The*

MRS. G GOES TO COLLEGE

see *Gertrude Berg Show, The*

MISSION: IMPOSSIBLE

International Intrigue

FIRST TELECAST: *September 17, 1966*
LAST TELECAST: *September 8, 1973*
BROADCAST HISTORY:

Sep 1966–Jan 1967, CBS Sat 9:00–10:00
Jan 1967–Sep 1967, CBS Sat 8:30–9:30
Sep 1967–Sep 1970, CBS Sun 10:00–11:00
Sep 1970–Sep 1971, CBS Sat 7:30–8:30
Sep 1971–Dec 1972, CBS Sat 10:00–11:00
Dec 1972–May 1973, CBS Fri 8:00–9:00
May 1973–Sep 1973, CBS Sat 10:00–11:00

CAST:

Daniel Briggs (1966–1967) ..... Steven Hill
Cinnamon Carter (1966–1969) .... Barbara Bain
Rollin Hand (1966–1969) ... Martin Landau
Barney Collier ....Greg Morris
Willie Armitage ....Peter Lupus
James Phelps (1967–1973) .... Peter Graves
Paris (1969–1971) ....Leonard Nimoy

Dana Lambert (1970–1971)
.... Lesley Ann Warren
Casey (1971–1973) ......Lynda Day George

THEME:
"Mission: Impossible," by Lalo Schifrin

At the opening of each episode of *Mission: Impossible,* the leader of the Impossible Missions Force, a group of highly specialized government agents, would receive a tape-recorded message outlining instructions for an assignment he was to consider taking. The voice on the tape would give him some background information, usually tied to the pictures of adversaries that were included with the tape, and conclude with "Your mission, Dan, should you decide to accept it, is . . . As always, should you or any member of your I.M. Force be caught or killed, the secretary will disavow any knowledge of your actions. This tape will self-destruct in five seconds." On cue, five seconds later, the tape, and often the small portable recorder that had contained it, went up in a puff of smoke and flame. The leader would then leaf through the dossiers of the various operatives who might be utilized on the mission and pull out the appropriate ones. Except for an occasional guest star, however, he always picked out exactly the same team to work with, which made the entire selection process seem rather superfluous. This opening was so stylized that it was parodied on virtually every comedy show on the air during the period, from *The Carol Burnett Show* to *The Tonight Show.* Over the years it was modified and toward the end of the series' run the process of leafing through dossiers was dropped completely.

The top-secret assignments taken on by this elite group of agents usually involved disrupting the activities of various small foreign powers seeking to create problems for America or the Free World. By the last season the agents had begun to run out of little Communist countries and obscure principalities, so they concentrated their efforts more on dealing with organized crime within the United States. All of the plans executed by the Impossible Missions Force were incredibly complex and depended on split-second timing and an astounding array of sophisticated electronic gadgetry. The leader of the group, Daniel Briggs during the first season and Jim Phelps through the rest of *Mission: Impossible*'s seven seasons, devised the complex plans used to accomplish the team's missions. Barney Collier was the electronics expert and Willie Armitage provided muscle throughout the series' run. Rollin Hand was an expert at disguise and Cinnamon Carter was the versatile, beautiful female member of the team. Martin Landau and Barbara Bain, husband and wife in real life, left the show at the end of the 1968–1969 season in a contract dispute and were replaced by other performers filling their respective functions.

The music for *Mission: Impossible* was written by Lalo Schifrin and had a pulsating, jazz-oriented urgency. The show's theme, which typified the music of the show, was released as a single and was on *Billboard*'s "Hot 100" chart for 14 weeks in 1968. There were also two albums of *Mission: Impossible* music released in the late 1960s.

MR. ADAMS AND EVE

Situation Comedy

FIRST TELECAST: *January 4, 1957*
LAST TELECAST: *September 23, 1958*
BROADCAST HISTORY:
Jan 1957–Feb 1958, CBS Fri 9:00–9:30
Feb 1958–Sep 1958, CBS Tue 8:00–8:30

CAST:
Eve Drake ....Ida Lupino
Howard Adams ....Howard Duff
Steve ....Hayden Rorke
Elsie ....Olive Carey
J. B. Hafter ....Alan Reed

Movie stars Howard Duff and Ida Lupino were married to each other in real life at the time they played husband-and-wife film stars in this series. Happenings at the studio, fights with the studio boss J. B. Hafter, negotiations and dealings with their agent Steve, and the good and troublesome sides of their home life were all shown in *Mr. Adams and Eve.* Though exaggerated for comic effect, many of the stories were based on actual situations that had happened to Duff and Lupino.

MR. & MRS. CARROLL

see *Most Important People, The*

MR. & MRS. NORTH

Comedy Mystery

FIRST TELECAST: *October 3, 1952*
LAST TELECAST: *July 20, 1954*

BROADCAST HISTORY:

Oct 1952–Sep 1953, CBS Fri 10:00–10:30
Jan 1954–Jul 1954, NBC Tue 10:30–11:00

CAST:

Pamela North ....Barbara Britton
Jerry North ....Richard Denning
Lt. Bill Weigand ....Francis De Sales

Jerry North was a publisher of mystery stories who fancied himself a fairly adept amateur detective. However, his wife Pamela, an attractive, pleasant, rather naïve woman, somehow always seemed to be one step ahead of both him and the police when it came to solving mysterious crimes. The Norths were supposed to be entirely normal Greenwich Village residents, but they seemed to stumble across bodies at every turn. *Mr. & Mrs. North* had long been a favorite on radio, and was also produced as a Broadway play and a movie. The characters were conceived by Richard and Frances Lockridge for a series of stories for *The New Yorker* magazine.

MR. ARSENIC

Talk

FIRST TELECAST: *May 8, 1952*
LAST TELECAST: *June 26, 1952*
BROADCAST HISTORY:

May 1952–Jun 1952, ABC Thu 9:00–9:30

HOST:

Burton Turkus

Burton Turkus, co-author of *Murder, Incorporated* and prosecutor of Murder, Inc. during William O'Dwyer's terms of office as mayor of New York, hosted this program of factual information on current political personalities and gangsters. Mr. Turkus answered questions from an off-camera voice and gave detailed insights into headliners in crime and politics. Definitely not for the squeamish.

MR. BLACK

Mystery Anthology

FIRST TELECAST: *September 19, 1949*
LAST TELECAST: *November 7, 1949*
BROADCAST HISTORY:

Sep 1949–Oct 1949, ABC Mon 9:30–10:00
Oct 1949–Nov 1949, ABC Mon 9:00–9:30

CAST:

Mr. Black ....Andy Christopher

This spooky series always saw that the bad guys got their due. That was taken care of by Mr. Black—Lucifer's representative on Earth—who appeared at the open and close of each show amid cobwebs and flickering lights. Stories were standard suspense yarns. From Chicago.

MR. BROADWAY

Drama

FIRST TELECAST: *September 26, 1964*
LAST TELECAST: *December 26, 1964*
BROADCAST HISTORY:

Sep 1964–Dec 1964, CBS Sat 9:00–9:30

CAST:

Mike Bell ....Craig Stevens
Hank McClure ....Horace McMahon
Toki ....Lani Miyazaki

Michael Bell Associates—Public Relations, was a highly successful venture that numbered among its clients movie stars, politicians, businessmen, philanthropists, and even phonies. All of them had one thing in common, a willingness to pay well for the creation and maintenance of their desired public image. That was Mike Bell's job and it got him into many an exciting, romantic, dangerous, and frequently amusing situation as he worked to protect his clients' images. Helping him were his assistant, ex-newspaperman Hank McClure, and his attractive and highly efficient girl Friday, Toki.

MR. CITIZEN

Dramatic Anthology

FIRST TELECAST: *April 20, 1955*
LAST TELECAST: *July 13, 1955*
BROADCAST HISTORY:

Apr 1955–Jul 1955, ABC Wed 8:30–9:00

HOST:

Allyn Edwards

Dramatizations of acts of heroism by real people were presented each week in this series. Allyn Edwards introduced the show by providing background on the incident being dramatized. At the end of each episode, the person whose act of heroism had just been shown appeared in person to receive the "Mr. Citizen" award for the week. Each show had a different person in public life (senators, military personnel, etc.) present the award.

MR. DEEDS GOES TO TOWN

Situation Comedy

FIRST TELECAST: *September 26, 1969*

LAST TELECAST: *January 16, 1970*

BROADCAST HISTORY:

Sep 1969–Jan 1970, ABC Fri 8:30–9:00

CAST:

Longfellow Deeds ....Monte Markham
Tony Lawrence ....Pat Harrington, Jr.
Mr. Masterson ....Herb Voland

Longfellow Deeds, a young newspaper editor in the small town of Mandrake Falls, suddenly inherited the multimillion-dollar corporation founded by his uncle, the unscrupulous Alonzo P. Deeds. Young Mr. Deeds promptly moved to New York to take over the corporation, and use the money to right the wrongs his uncle had perpetrated. His country naïveté and extreme honesty almost brought him down in the cutthroat world of big business. Tony Lawrence was Uncle Alonzo's former public-relations man who became Longfellow Deeds' best friend and confidant, and Mr. Masterson was the continually infuriated Chairman of the Board of Deeds Enterprises.

Based rather loosely on the 1936 Gary Cooper movie of the same name.

MR. DISTRICT ATTORNEY

Police

FIRST TELECAST: *October 1, 1951*

LAST TELECAST: *June 23, 1952*

BROADCAST HISTORY:

Oct 1951–Jun 1952, ABC Mon 8:00–8:30

CAST:

District Attorney Paul Garrett ... Jay Jostyn
Harrington ....Len Doyle
Miss Miller ....Vicki Vola

Mr. District Attorney was one of the most popular radio crime shows of the 1940s, largely because of its uncanny realism. It was often based on real headlines, and in some cases actually anticipated them. In addition, the lead character was based on a real, and very famous, D.A.—New York's crime-busting Thomas E. Dewey, who later became governor of the state and a two-time candidate for President of the U.S.

The leads in the TV version were the same as those through most of the radio run, Jay Jostyn as the relentless D.A., Len Doyle as an ex-cop who was his investigator, and Vicki Vola as his secretary. Producer Edward C. Byron, who had created the radio show in 1939, also supervised the TV series. The opening lines will be remembered by any fan of either the radio or TV show: "Mister District Attorney! Champion of the people! Guardian of our fundamental rights to life, liberty and the pursuit of happiness!"

Mr. District Attorney was produced live and alternated with *The Amazing Mr. Malone* during the 1951–1952 season. It was later seen in a syndicated version with David Brian in the lead role.

MR. ED

Situation Comedy

FIRST TELECAST: *October 1, 1961*

LAST TELECAST: *September 8, 1965*

BROADCAST HISTORY:

Oct 1961–Sep 1962, CBS Sun 6:30–7:00
Sep 1962–Mar 1963, CBS Thu 7:30–8:00
Mar 1963–Oct 1964, CBS Sun 6:30–7:00
Dec 1964–Sep 1965, CBS Wed 7:30–8:00

CAST:

Wilbur Post ....Alan Young
Carol Post ....Connie Hines
Roger Addison (1961–1963) .. Larry Keating
Kay Addison (1961–1964) ... Edna Skinner
Gordon Kirkwood (1963–1965)
.... Leon Ames
Winnie Kirkwood (1963–1965)
.... Florence MacMichael

One of the more nonsensical TV comedies was this series about a talking horse. Ed belonged to Wilbur Post, a young architect who had decided to move out of the city and get a little closer to nature. The rambling country home Wilbur and his wife bought was everything they had imagined, except for one thing—with it came a palomino that could talk. Mr. Ed didn't talk to everybody; in fact he would only talk to Wilbur, because Wilbur was the first person worth talking to he had met. The confusion caused by a talking horse, and the situations Ed got Wilbur into, and occasionally out of, formed the stories. Larry Keating was featured as the Post's next-door neighbor. Unfortunately he passed away shortly after the start of the 1963–1964 season. Edna Skinner, as his wife, remained a while longer but was phased out as the Posts got new neighbors that December. After leaving the nighttime schedule in 1965, *Mr. Ed* continued for one more season, airing on Sundays from 5:30–6:00 P.M. The only regular cast members during the 1965–1966 season were Ed and the Posts.

MR. GARLUND

Adventure

FIRST TELECAST: *October 7, 1960*

LAST TELECAST: *January 13, 1961*

BROADCAST HISTORY:

Oct 1960–Jan 1961, CBS Fri 9:30–10:00

CAST:

Frank Garlund ....Charles Quinlivan
Kam Chang ....Kam Tong

At the age of 30, Frank Garlund had already amassed a considerable fortune. He was a financial wizard whose skill and conspicuous success had brought him into contact with a myriad of people, both honest and dishonest, none of whom were quite the same after their association with him. The young Mr. Garlund had a mysterious background and few close associates. The one person in whom he did confide, and from whom he sought counsel, was his foster brother Kam Chang. Stories revolved around Garlund's rise in the world of international business and intrigue. The title of this series was changed to *The Garlund Touch* on November 11, 1960.

MR. I MAGINATION

Children's

FIRST TELECAST: *May 29, 1949*

LAST TELECAST: *April 13, 1952*

BROADCAST HISTORY:

May 1949–Jul 1949, CBS Sun 7:00–7:30
Jul 1949, CBS Sun 7:30–8:00
Aug 1949–Sep 1949, CBS Sun 7:30–7:55
Oct 1949–Jun 1951, CBS Sun 6:30–7:00 (OS)
Jan 1952–Feb 1952, CBS Sun 6:30–7:00
Feb 1952–Apr 1952, CBS Sun 6:00–6:30

REGULARS:

Paul Tripp
Ruth Enders
Ted Tiller
Joe Silver

The title role of *Mr. I Magination* was played by the versatile Paul Tripp, author of *Tubby the Tuba* and other stories for children. Not only did he star in the show, but he created it and wrote many of the fantasies which were presented. Children who viewed this live series were asked to send in letters describing something that they wished could happen. Tripp and his fellow regulars would then transform the wishes into television playlets. Each show opened with Tripp in candy-striped overalls, as the engineer of a train carrying children to Imaginationland. The passengers got off at places like Ambitionville, Inventorsville, Seaport City, and "I Wish I Were" Town. That last stop was the point from which plays based on the life of various historical figures were done, with a young (9–12) actor as the historical figure. *Mr. I Magination* began as a local show in New York, and expanded to a four-station network on May 29, 1949, five weeks after its premiere.

MR. LUCKY

Adventure

FIRST TELECAST: *October 24, 1959*

LAST TELECAST: *September 3, 1960*

BROADCAST HISTORY:

Oct 1959–Sep 1960, CBS Sat 9:00–9:30

CAST:

Mr. Lucky ....John Vivyan
Andamo ....Ross Martin
Lt. Rovacs ....Tom Brown

THEME:

"Mr. Lucky," by Henry Mancini

Mr. Lucky was an honest professional gambler who had won a plush floating casino, the ship *Fortuna*, and made it his base of operations. Staying beyond the 12-mile limit, where he could operate a gambling ship legally, Mr. Lucky played host to a wide variety of people, all of whom came to make use of his sumptuous facility. Helping him run the casino was his good friend Andamo. When he got into scrapes that required police assistance, Lt. Rovacs usually provided it. The music from this series, composed by Henry Mancini, produced two successful albums, *The Music from Mr. Lucky* and *Mr. Lucky Goes Latin*.

MR. MAGOO

see *Famous Adventures of Mr. Magoo, The*

MR. NOVAK

Drama

FIRST TELECAST: *September 24, 1963*

LAST TELECAST: *August 31, 1965*

BROADCAST HISTORY:

Sep 1963–Aug 1965, NBC Tue 7:30–8:30

CAST:

John Novak ....James Franciscus
Albert Vane ....Dean Jagger
Jean Pagano (1963–1964) ......Jeanne Bal

Martin Woodridge (1964–1965)
.... Burgess Meredith

The challenges, accomplishments, and frustrations of a young high school English teacher on his first job provided the stories in this series. John Novak started his career at Jefferson High School in Los Angeles under Principal Albert Vane who, although not in complete agreement with Mr. Novak's approach to teaching, took a strong liking to him as a dedicated teacher. When Vane was elected to the post of State Superintendent of Schools, he chose Martin Woodridge, another English teacher at Jefferson High, to replace him as principal.

MR. PEEPERS

Situation Comedy

FIRST TELECAST: *July 3, 1952*

LAST TELECAST: *June 12, 1955*

BROADCAST HISTORY:

Jul 1952–Sep 1952, NBC Thu 9:30–10:00
Oct 1952–Jul 1953, NBC Sun 7:30–8:00
Sep 1953–Jun 1955, NBC Sun 7:30–8:00

CAST:

Robinson Peepers .... Wally Cox
Rayola Dean (1952) .... Norma Crane
Charlie Burr (1952) .... David Tyrell
Mr. Gabriel Gurney (1952–1953)
.... Joseph Foley
Mrs. Gurney .... Marion Lorne
Superintendent Bascom .... Gage Clark
Nancy Remington .... Patricia Benoit
Harvey Weskit .... Tony Randall
Mr. Remington .... Ernest Truex
Marge Weskit .... Georgiann Johnson
Mr. Hansen (1953–1954)
.... Arthur O'Connell
Mrs. Remington (1953–1955)
.... Sylvia Field
Frank Whip (1953–1955) ..... Jack Warden
Mom Peepers (1953–1955) .. Ruth McDevitt
Agnes Peepers (1953–1955) .... Jenny Egan

Jefferson High School, located in the small Midwestern town of Jefferson City, was the setting for this live situation comedy. The central character was Robinson Peepers, a shy, quiet, slow-moving science teacher whose efforts to do the right thing always seemed to backfire. He was such a nice guy that everyone on the staff tried to mother him and the students all thought he was great, despite being laughable at times. His best friend was history teacher Harvey Weskit, whose brash self-confidence contrasted with Robinson's low-key personality. Other regulars in the cast were the school nurse Nancy Remington, English teacher Mrs. Gurney (whose husband was the principal for the first season), and their families.

Mr. Peepers went on the air in the summer of 1952 with a scheduled eight-week run and was slotted for oblivion when the regular fall season began. At the start of the season, however, an NBC filmed series called *Doc Corkle* met with such overwhelming critical and public castigation that it was canceled after only three episodes had been aired. *Mr. Peepers* was rushed back into production and returned on the last Sunday in October. The one major change was in Robinson's romantic interest. During the summer it had been music appreciation teacher Rayola Dean. Nurse Nancy Remington became his girl friend that fall. Almost as quiet and unassuming as Robinson, she just seemed "right" for him. Their romance blossomed and at the end of the 1953–1954 season they were married on the air, an event that excited viewers at the time in much the same way that Rhoda's TV marriage would do more than twenty years later.

MR. ROBERTS

Comedy Adventure

FIRST TELECAST: *September 17, 1965*

LAST TELECAST: *September 2, 1966*

BROADCAST HISTORY:

Sep 1965–Sep 1966, NBC Fri 9:30–10:00

CAST:

Lt. (j.g.) Douglas Roberts ...... Roger Smith
Ensign Frank Pulver .... Steve Harmon
Captain John Morton ... Richard X. Slattery
Doc .... George Ives
Seaman D'Angelo .... Richard Sinatra
Seaman Mannion .... Ronald Starr
Seaman Reber .... Roy Reese

The adventures of the crew of the *U.S.S. Reluctant*, a cargo ship operating far behind the lines in the South Pacific during World War II, provided the stories for this comedy. Life on board was incredibly dull and monotonous, especially for young Mr. Roberts. He wanted the opportunity to really participate in the war effort, not slosh around in the middle of nowhere on a mangy old tub, and was desperately trying to get transferred to another ship. Ensign Pulver was the crewman who was always scheming to find ways of livening up the otherwise boring existence of the crew—as long as no real work was involved. Stern old Captain Morton was the major concern of most of the crew—they were preoccupied with finding ways to drive him slowly out of his mind.

Based on the book by Thomas Heggen, which was subsequently made into a hit play (1948) and movie (1955).

MR. SMITH GOES TO WASHINGTON

Situation Comedy

FIRST TELECAST: *September 29, 1962*

LAST TELECAST: *March 30, 1963*

BROADCAST HISTORY:

Sep 1962–Mar 1963, ABC Sat 8:30–9:00

CAST:

Sen. Eugene Smith ....Fess Parker
Pat Smith ....Sandra Warner
Uncle Cooter ....Red Foley
Arnie ....Stan Irwin
Miss Kelly ....Rita Lynn

While starring as Davy Crockett in the mid-1950s, Fess Parker was at one point called upon to portray Crockett as a rustic representative to the United States Congress. In this series Parker once again headed for Washington, this time in contemporary garb, but with the same low-keyed, homespun approach to national—and family—politics and problems. Freshman Senator Eugene Smith and his wife Pat were from a small town, and they used the homilies of Middle America to cope with urban, political Washington. Arnie was Senator Smith's chauffeur, Uncle Cooter his philosophical, guitar-strumming uncle, and Miss Kelly his secretary.

Based on the 1939 movie starring James Stewart.

MR. T. AND TINA

Situation Comedy

FIRST TELECAST: *September 25, 1976*

LAST TELECAST: *October 30, 1976*

BROADCAST HISTORY:

Sep 1976–Oct 1976, ABC Sat 8:30–9:00

CAST:

Taro Takahashi ("Mr. T.") ...... Pat Morita
Tina Kelly ....Susan Blanchard
Michi ....Pat Suzuki
Harvard ....Ted Lange
Miss Llewellyn ......Miriam Byrd-Nethery
Uncle Matsu ......"Jerry" Hatsuo Fujikawa
Sachi ....June Angela
Aki ....Gene Profanato

A comedy of clashing cultures. Mr. T. was a brilliant Japanese inventor who had been transferred by his firm from Tokyo to Chicago. There, he had to cope with the Americanization of his household by a nutty, effervescent Nebraska-born housekeeper named Tina. Tina was well-intentioned but sometimes her ideas of a happy home were at fearful odds with the traditional, male-dominated society from which the Takahashis had so recently come. Michi was Mr. T.'s sister-in-law, Uncle Matsu the staunch traditionalist, and Sachi and Aki the two children. On the American side was Harvard, the hip handyman, and Miss Llewellyn, the landlady.

MR. TERRIFIC

Situation Comedy

FIRST TELECAST: *January 9, 1967*

LAST TELECAST: *August 28, 1967*

BROADCAST HISTORY:

Jan 1967–Aug 1967, CBS Mon 8:00–8:30

CAST:

Stanley Beamish (Mr. Terrific)
.... Stephen Strimpell
Barton J. Reed ....John McGiver
Hal Walters ....Dick Gautier
Harley Trent ....Paul Smith

Stanley Beamish was a young gas station operator whose partner in the service station, as well as his best friend and roommate, was Hal Walters. Stanley did have one secret that he kept from his buddy—with the aid of special top-secret power pills he could become that caped crime fighter, Mr. Terrific. The pills had been developed by the Bureau of Secret Projects, a special government agency. BSP chief Barton J. Reed sent Stanley on his missions and supplied him with the pills. A power pill would give him extraordinary abilities for only one hour. In emergencies he could take two booster pills, each good for an extra 20 minutes, but after that he reverted to normal. He was a nice, soft-spoken, naïve guy who, unfortunately for the BSP, was the only person on whom the pills worked. His efforts to serve his government were noble, but not always what Mr. Reed would have liked. Stanley was too gullible, too considerate, and frequently to preoccupied to pay attention to the time limits of his powers. He had a disturbing propensity for returning to normal at the most inopportune times.

MR. WIZARD

see *Watch Mr. Wizard*

MIXED DOUBLES

Drama

FIRST TELECAST: *August 5, 1949*
LAST TELECAST: *October 29, 1949*
BROADCAST HISTORY:
Aug 1949–Sep 1949, NBC Fri 9:00–9:30
Sep 1949–Oct 1949, NBC Sat 8:30–9:00
CAST:
Elaine Coleman (first 2 weeks) .... Rhoda Williams
Elaine Coleman ....Bonnie Baken
Eddy Coleman ....Eddy Firestone
Ada Abbott ....Ada Friedman
Bill Abbott ....Billy Idelson

This early prime-time soap opera was about two newly married couples living side by side in one-room apartments, trying to build their lives on the husbands' meager incomes. Eddy and Bill were both copywriters at large advertising agencies. The program was created by Carleton E. Morse *(One Man's Family)* and first seen locally on the West Coast.

MOBILE ONE

Adventure

FIRST TELECAST: *September 12, 1975*
LAST TELECAST: *December 29, 1975*
BROADCAST HISTORY:
Sep 1975–Oct 1975, ABC Fri 8:00–9:00
Oct 1975–Dec 1975, ABC Mon 8:00–9:00
CAST:
Peter Campbell ....Jackie Cooper
Maggie Spencer ....Julie Gregg
Doug McKnight ....Mark Wheeler
EXECUTIVE PRODUCER:
Jack Webb

Jackie Cooper, whose first acting experience was as a member of the *Our Gang* comedies in 1925 (at age 3), played a veteran TV news reporter in this 1975 series. Together with his producer Maggie, cameraman Doug, and the mobile unit from station KONE, he covered hard news and human interest stories in a large city (not named, but the series was filmed in and around Los Angeles).

MOD SQUAD, THE

Police

FIRST TELECAST: *September 24, 1968*
LAST TELECAST: *August 23, 1973*
BROADCAST HISTORY:
Sep 1968–Aug 1972, ABC Tue 7:30–8:30
Sep 1972–Aug 1973, ABC Thu 8:00–9:00
CAST:
Pete Cochran ....Michael Cole
Linc Hayes ....Clarence Williams III
Julie Barnes ....Peggy Lipton
Capt. Adam Greer ....Tige Andrews
CREATOR:
Bud Ruskin

The Mod Squad was probably the ultimate example of the establishment co-opting the youth movement of the late 1960s. Its three members were "hippie cops," each of them a drop-out from straight society who had had his own brush with the law. Pete was a longhaired youth who had been kicked out by his wealthy Beverly Hills parents and stolen a car; Linc was the Afro-ed son of a ghetto family of 13, raised in Watts and arrested in the Watts rioting; Julie was the daughter of a San Francisco prostitute who had run away from home and been arrested for vagrancy. All three were on probation and looking for some way to make sense out of their lives when they were approached by Capt. Adam Greer, who recruited them for a special "youth squad." Their purpose was to infiltrate the counterculture and ferret out the adult criminals who preyed upon the young in Southern California (no finking on their own generation, thank you).

A contentious trio, always questioning their own motives and their differing cultural backgrounds, the *Mod Squad* nevertheless proved an effective undercover task force against adult crime. For the first season they rattled around in a battered old 1950 station wagon named "Woody," but this was killed off early in the second season (driven over a cliff).

Strangely enough, *The Mod Squad* was based on the true experiences of creator Bud Ruskin, a former police officer and later private detective. While a member of the Los Angeles Sheriff's Department in the 1950s he was a member of an undercover narcotics squad composed of young officers, which served as the inspiration for *The Mod Squad*. He first wrote a pilot script for the series in 1960, but it took nine more years before it reached the air in this highly successful ABC program.

MODERN SCIENCE THEATER

Documentary

FIRST TELECAST: *January 30, 1958*

LAST TELECAST: *March 13, 1958*

BROADCAST HISTORY:

Jan 1958–Mar 1958, ABC Thu 10:00–10:30

Documentary films on science and industry.

MOHAWK SHOWROOM

Music

FIRST TELECAST: *May 2, 1949*

LAST TELECAST: *November 23, 1951*

BROADCAST HISTORY:

May 1949–Dec 1949, NBC Mon–Fri 7:30–7:45
Dec 1949–Jul 1951, NBC Mon/Wed/Fri 7:30–7:45
Sep 1951–Nov 1951, NBC Mon/Wed/Fri 7:30–7:45

REGULARS:

Morton Downey (1949)
Trio (Carmen Mastren, Jim Ruhl, Trigger Alpert) (1949)
Roberta Quinlan
Harry Clark Trio

ANNOUNCER:

Bob Stanton

Live musical program with guest stars. For the first few months Morton Downey was featured on Monday, Wednesday, and Friday, while Roberta Quinlan appeared on Tuesday and Thursday. Beginning in December 1949 Miss Quinlan was the sole host. Sometimes announcer Bob Stanton also took part in the proceedings.

MOMENT OF DECISION

Dramatic Anthology

FIRST TELECAST: *July 3, 1957*

LAST TELECAST: *September 25, 1957*

BROADCAST HISTORY:

Jul 1957–Sep 1957, ABC Wed 9:30–10:00

The dramas that made up this 1957 summer series consisted of reruns of episodes previously aired on *Ford Theatre*.

MOMENT OF FEAR

Dramatic Anthology

FIRST TELECAST: *July 1, 1960*

LAST TELECAST: *August 10, 1965*

BROADCAST HISTORY:

Jul 1960–Sep 1960, NBC Fri 10:00–11:00
May 1964–Sep 1964, NBC Tue 8:30–9:00
May 1965–Aug 1965, NBC Tue 8:30–9:00

The 1960 version of *Moment of Fear* consisted of live dramas dealing with individuals who reached emotional crises in their lives. In the summers of 1964 and 1965 *Moment of Fear* was made up of filmed reruns of episodes from other anthology series. In 1964 the reruns were from *G.E. Theater, Schlitz Playhouse, Lux Video Theatre,* and *Studio 57*. In 1965 they came from the above four shows plus *Pepsi-Cola Playhouse*.

MOMENTS OF MUSIC

Music

FIRST TELECAST: *July 24, 1951*

LAST TELECAST: *September 11, 1951*

BROADCAST HISTORY:

Jul 1951–Sep 1951, ABC Tue 8:30–8:45

A short, and short-lived filmed program of music.

MONA McCLUSKEY

Situation Comedy

FIRST TELECAST: *September 16, 1965*

LAST TELECAST: *April 14, 1966*

BROADCAST HISTORY:

Sep 1965–Apr 1966, NBC Thu 9:30–10:00

CAST:

Mona McCluskey .... Juliet Prowse
Mike McCluskey ...... Denny (Scott) Miller
Gen. Crone .... Herb Rudley
Frank Caldwell .... Bartlett Robinson
Sgt. Gruzewsky .... Robert Strauss
Alice Henderson .... Elena Verdugo

Mona Carroll was a beautiful Hollywood star who made the astronomical salary of $5,000 per week. She was married to Mike McCluskey, a sergeant in the Air Force whose salary was $500 per month. In order to let her husband prove that he could support her, Mona lived with him in a two-room apartment and promised not to use any of her money to supplement his income. Her tastes, coupled with the knowledge that she really had much more money than she could spend, prompted Mona to try all sorts of schemes to improve her husband's financial situation.

MONDAY NIGHT BASEBALL

see *Baseball*

MONDAY NIGHT FOOTBALL

see *Football*

MONDAY NIGHT SPECIAL

Varied Format

FIRST TELECAST: *January 10, 1972*
LAST TELECAST: *August 14, 1972*
BROADCAST HISTORY:
Jan 1972–Aug 1972, ABC Mon 8:00–9:00

Throughout most of 1972, ABC set aside the 8:00–9:00 P.M. hour on Monday nights as a place for regular "specials." The programs telecast in this time slot varied greatly in format. Included were Jacques Cousteau nature programs, documentaries on athletics, an occasional circus, and Danny Kaye starring in "The Emperor's New Clothes."

MONDAY THEATRE

Anthology

FIRST TELECAST: *July 21, 1969*
LAST TELECAST: *August 10, 1970*
BROADCAST HISTORY:
Jul 1969–Sep 1969, NBC Mon 8:00–8:30
Jul 1970–Aug 1970, NBC Mon 8:00–8:30

Monday Theatre spent two summers as a partial replacement for *Rowan & Martin's Laugh-In.* It was comprised of pilots for projected situation-comedy series in 1969 and projected adventure and drama series in 1970. None of them ever made the jump from pilot to regular series.

MONKEES, THE

Situation Comedy

FIRST TELECAST: *September 12, 1966*
LAST TELECAST: *August 19, 1968*
BROADCAST HISTORY:
Sep 1966–Aug 1968, NBC Mon 7:30–8:00
CAST:
Davy (guitar) .... David Jones
Peter (guitar) .... Peter Tork
Micky (drums) .... Micky Dolenz
Mike (guitar)
.... Mike Nesmith ("Wool Hat")
MUSIC SUPERVISION:
Don Kirshner

This was a free-form youth-oriented comedy series, inspired by the Beatles' film *A Hard Day's Night* (1964). *The Monkees* was similarly unconventional, utilizing surrealistic film techniques (fast and slow motion, distorted focus, comic film inserts), one-liners, non sequiturs, etc., all delivered at a very fast pace. The Monkees played a rock quartet that got into all sorts of bizarre scrapes as they rescued maidens, ran afoul of dastardly villains, and generally played pranks on the world.

The Monkees simultaneously had a highly successful career on records, a fact which has driven some rock critics into paroxysms of fury since they were so obviously a "manufactured" group. The four members were carefully picked from among nearly 500 applicants in auditions held during the fall of 1965, then drilled and rehearsed until they could pass as reasonably competent musicians (Dolenz and Jones were actors, Tork and Nesmith had some previous musical experience). They were not allowed to play their instruments on their early records, supplying only the vocals, a fact which led to some embarrassment when they went on tour and could not recreate their recorded sound. It also led to dissension among the boys, some of whom had real musical ambitions. Nevertheless their discs, heavily promoted and carefully coordinated with the TV series, sold in the millions. (These included "Last Train to Clarksville," "I'm a Believer" and "Words.") Finally there was a showdown with the program's producers, following a rather remarkable 1967 press conference in which Nesmith bitterly complained that "we're being passed off as something we aren't." The boys were later allowed to "do their own thing" musically. Despite its commercial success, however, the group broke up shortly after the series left the air in 1968.

The Monkees was later seen on CBS in reruns on Saturday mornings.

MONROES, THE

Western

FIRST TELECAST: *September 7, 1966*
LAST TELECAST: *August 30, 1967*
BROADCAST HISTORY:
Sep 1966–Aug 1967, ABC Wed 8:00–8:30
CAST:
Clayt Monroe .... Michael Anderson, Jr.
Kathy Monroe .... Barbara Hershey
Jefferson Monroe .... Keith Schultz
Fennimore Monroe .... Kevin Schultz
Amy Monroe .... Tammy Locke

Major Mapoy .... Liam Sullivan
Dirty Jim .... Ron Soble
Sleeve .... Ben Johnson
Ruel Jaxon .... Jim Westmoreland
Barney Wales .... Robert Middleton

The story of five orphaned youngsters, aged 6 to 18, who fought to establish a homestead in the rugged Wyoming Territory of 1876, after their parents had drowned. Leaders of the crew were Clayt (18) and Kathy (16), who looked after the 13-year-old twins Jeff ("Big Twin") and Fenn ("Little Twin"), 6-year-old Amy, and a dog named Snow. Their ally was the renegade Indian Dirty Jim, and the villain in the piece was wicked British cattle baron Major Mapoy, who wanted their land (heh-heh!). Jaxon was one of Mapoy's cowboys.

Filmed on location in the rugged Grand Teton National Park area of Wyoming.

MONTEFUSCOS, THE

Situation Comedy

FIRST TELECAST: *September 4, 1975*

LAST TELECAST: *October 16, 1975*

BROADCAST HISTORY:

Sep 1975–Oct 1975, NBC Thu 8:00–8:30

CAST:

Tony Montefusco .... Joe Sirola
Rose Montefusco .... Naomi Stevens
Frank Montefusco .... Ron Carey
Joseph Montefusco .... John Aprea
Theresa Montefusco .... Phoebe Dorin
Angela Montefusco Cooney .... Linda Dano
Jim Cooney .... Bill Cort
Nunzio Montefusco .... Sal Viscuso

This short-lived series was about Tony Montefusco, a boisterous, middle-class Italian, living in Connecticut, who had his entire family over for dinner every Sunday night. The subjects that came up and situations that developed at, prior to, and following Sunday dinner provided the stories of the series. Tony's wife Rose, his three sons and one daughter, and their families made up the entire cast. Frankie was a dentist, Joseph a priest, Nunzio an unemployed actor, and son-in-law Jim Cooney the token WASP. Theresa was Frankie's wife.

MONTGOMERY'S SUMMER STOCK

see *Robert Montgomery Presents*

MOREY AMSTERDAM SHOW, THE

Comedy Variety

FIRST TELECAST: *December 17, 1948*

LAST TELECAST: *October 12, 1950*

BROADCAST HISTORY:

Dec 1948–Jan 1949, CBS Fri 8:30–9:00
Jan 1949–Mar 1949, CBS Mon Various
Apr 1949–Oct 1950, DUM Thu 9:00–9:30

REGULARS:

Morey Amsterdam
Art Carney
Jacqueline Susann

In June 1948 Morey Amsterdam premiered a series on the CBS radio network in which he was the emcee of a small fictional nightclub located in Times Square in New York City. The club was the Golden Goose Cafe and the only other regulars in the series were Art Carney as Charlie the Doorman (later as Newton the Waiter), and Jacqueline Susann as Lola, the wide-eyed cigarette girl. Morey told jokes, played his cello, and introduced guest acts on the show. In December 1948 the show moved to CBS television, while a separate radio version continued to be aired. The producer was Irving Mansfield—Miss Susann's husband.

Then in early 1949 CBS canceled the show, ostensibly not because of low ratings but because the network already had too many big names to promote. CBS's loss was DuMont's gain, because Morey was back a month later with his "yuk-a-puk" jokes on a Thursday night DuMont variety show which ran for a year and a half. The setting changed to the Silver Swan Cafe, but Carney and Susann remained.

MORK & MINDY

Situation Comedy

FIRST TELECAST: *September 14, 1978*

LAST TELECAST:

BROADCAST HISTORY:

Sep 1978– , ABC Thu 8:00–8:30

CAST:

Mork .... Robin Williams
Mindy McConnell .... Pam Dawber
Frederick McConnell .... Conrad Janis
Cora Hudson .... Elizabeth Kerr
Eugene .... Jeffrey Jacquet

Mork & Mindy was a spin-off from an episode of *Happy Days* seen in February, 1978, in which an alien from the planet Ork landed on earth and attempted to kidnap

Richie. So popular was the nutty character created by Robin Williams that Williams was given his own series in the fall of 1978, and it became an instant hit.

Mork was a misfit on his own planet because of his sense of humor (he was heard to call the Orkan leader, Orson, "cosmic breath"). So the humorless Orkans sent him off to study Earthlings, whose "crazy" customs they had never been able to understand. Mork landed, in a giant eggshell, near Boulder, Colorado. There he was befriended by pretty Mindy McConnell, a clerk at the music store run by her father, Frederick. Mork looked human, but his strange mixture of Orkan and Earthling customs—such as wearing a suit, but putting it on backwards, or sitting in a chair, but upside down—led most people to think of him as just some kind of nut. Mindy knew where he came from, and helped him adjust to Earth's strange ways. She also let him stay in her apartment, which scandalized her conservative father, but not her swinging grandmother, Cora.

Mork & Mindy succeeded due to the versatile talents of Detroit-born Robin Williams, who mugged, mimicked and delivered torrents of one-liners and Orkan gibberish. His weekly sign-off was "Na nu, na nu," meaning goodbye in Orkan.

MORTON DOWNEY SHOW, THE

see *Mohawk Showroom, The*

MOSES—THE LAWGIVER

Historical Drama

FIRST TELECAST: *June 21, 1975*
LAST TELECAST: *August 2, 1975*
BROADCAST HISTORY:
Jun 1975–Aug 1975, CBS Sat 10:00–11:00
CAST:
Moses .... Burt Lancaster
Aaron .... Anthony Quayle
Miriam .... Ingrid Thulin
Zipporah .... Irene Papas

The story of the book of Exodus had been told twice by Cecil D. DeMille in spectacular feature films, in a silent and a sound version of *The Ten Commandments*. This series of six one-hour programs retold the story of the enslavement of the Jewish people at the hands of the Egyptians, their release by the pharaoh, and the long, arduous journey to the Promised Land. Filmed on location in Italy and Israel, this series was later re-edited and released as a theatrical feature.

MOST DEADLY GAME, THE

Detective

FIRST TELECAST: *October 10, 1970*
LAST TELECAST: *January 16, 1971*
BROADCAST HISTORY:
Oct 1970–Jan 1971, ABC Sat 9:30–10:30
CAST:
Jonathan Croft .... George Maharis
Vanessa Smith .... Yvette Mimieux
Mr. Arcane .... Ralph Bellamy

A series in the classic whodunit tradition, involving a trio of highly trained criminologists who dealt only in unusual murders ("the most dangerous game"). This elite, and expensive, team was composed of Mr. Arcane, the urbane, cerebral leader; Jonathan, a ruggedly handsome, ex-military intelligence officer; and Vanessa, a beautiful, college-trained criminologist (formerly Mr. Arcane's ward).

MOST IMPORTANT PEOPLE, THE

Musical Variety

FIRST TELECAST: *October 18, 1950*
LAST TELECAST: *April 13, 1951*
BROADCAST HISTORY:
Oct 1950–Apr 1951, DUM Wed/Fri 7:30–7:45
REGULARS:
Jimmy Carroll
Rita Carroll

This was a 15-minute program of songs and chatter by singer-pianist Jimmy Carroll and his wife Rita, plus guest performers.

The title *The Most Important People* referred to babies, who were indeed important to the sponsor, Gerber's baby food, but had little to do with this show. In December the title was changed to *Mr. and Mrs. Carroll*.

MOST WANTED

Police

FIRST TELECAST: *October 16, 1976*
LAST TELECAST: *April 25, 1977*
BROADCAST HISTORY:
Oct 1976–Feb 1977, ABC Sat 10:00–11:00
Mar 1977–Apr 1977, ABC Mon 9:00–10:00
CAST:
Capt. Linc Evers .... Robert Stack
Sgt. Charlie Benson .... Shelly Novack

Officer Kate Manners .... Jo An Harris
Mayor Dan Stoddard .... Harry Rhodes

PRODUCER:

Quinn Martin

The "Most Wanted" unit was an elite task force of the Los Angeles Police Department, concentrating exclusively on criminals on the mayor's most-wanted list. By taking on one case at a time, and cutting through normal red tape, Capt. Linc Evers and his two assistants were able to track down the city's most dangerous criminals, often by use of daring undercover work.

MOTHERS-IN-LAW, THE

Situation Comedy

FIRST TELECAST: *September 10, 1967*
LAST TELECAST: *September 7, 1969*
BROADCAST HISTORY:

Sep 1967–Sep 1969, NBC Sun 8:30–9:00

CAST:

Eve Hubbard ....Eve Arden
Kaye Buell ....Kaye Ballard
Roger Buell (1967–1968) .....Roger Carmel
Roger Buell (1968–1969) ... Richard Deacon
Herb Hubbard ....Herbert Rudley
Jerry Buell ....Jerry Fogel
Susie Hubbard Buell ......Deborah Walley

The Hubbards and the Buells had been neighbors in suburban Los Angeles for 15 years. Herb Hubbard was a successful lawyer and a member of the board of trustees of his alma mater. His wife Eve was a great cook, former champion golfer, terrific gardener, and supporter of all the right causes. They were very straight. The Buells, on the other hand, were extremely unconventional. Roger Buell was a television writer who did most of his work at home and would test his scripts on anyone who happened to be available as a sounding board. His wife Kaye was not a particularly enthusiastic housekeeper and rather overbearing on occasion. Despite their differences, the Hubbards and the Buells were the best of friends and their children had gotten married to each other. The children, Jerry and Susie, were both in college and had to cope with in-laws who had very different ideas on how they should live. Roger Carmel left the series after the first season, in a contract dispute, and was replaced by Richard Deacon.

MOTOR CITY BOXING

see *Boxing*

MOTOROLA TV THEATRE

Dramatic Anthology

FIRST TELECAST: *December 1, 1953*
LAST TELECAST: *May 18, 1954*
BROADCAST HISTORY:

Dec 1953–May 1954, ABC Tue 9:30–10:30

Live dramas from New York featuring such first-rate talent as Jack Palance, Brian Donlevy, and Sir Cedric Hardwicke in the first three presentations. Later telecasts starred Helen Hayes, Charlie Ruggles, Walter Matthau, and many others. The program alternated with *The U.S. Steel Hour* in the Tuesday 9:30–10:30 P.M. time slot.

MOVIELAND QUIZ

Quiz/Audience Participation

FIRST TELECAST: *August 15, 1948*
LAST TELECAST: *November 9, 1948*
BROADCAST HISTORY:

Aug 1948–Nov 1948, ABC Tue 7:30–8:00

EMCEE:

Arthur Q. Bryan
Ralph Dumke
Patricia Bright

Studio contestants were asked to identify titles and stars of old-time movies from selected scenes shown on this 1948 quiz show, which was first seen locally in Philadelphia. The set depicted a theater front, with Patricia Bright as ticket seller and Arthur Q. Bryan (later replaced by Ralph Dumke) as emcee.

MOVIES—PRIOR TO 1961

The arrival of commercial television in the mid-1940s was not greeted with much enthusiasm by the major American movie studios. At first they considered television a passing fad that would have no long-range effects on their audience. Then, by the early 1950s, television had become their mortal enemy. Theater owners could not do what some had done in the heyday of radio—stop the film and let the audience listen to *Amos 'n' Andy* over the theater's sound system—all they could do was look at the dwindling attendance figures. On Mondays people stayed home to watch *I Love Lucy*, on Tuesday to watch Milton Berle, on Saturday to watch *The Jackie*

Gleason Show and *Your Show of Shows*, and on Sunday to watch *The Toast of the Town*.

In this climate of life-and-death competition, it was no surprise that the motion-picture studios were not willing to provide television with recently released major films. Nor did they look favorably on actors who wanted to try the new medium. Many stars' contracts expressly forbade their appearance on television. Despite the efforts of the studios to restrict the availability of motion pictures for television, there *were* movies all over the home screen in the early days. They may not have been recent (most were made in the 1930s) or big hits (many were strictly "B" grade), but they filled time. Independent producers and suppliers of B films, such as Monogram, Republic, and RKO, provided television with many of its early movies.

Aged Westerns, including some that had been released as silent films but had sound tracks added, low-budget second features, and imported films (primarily from England) were seen locally, as network fillers, and as network series in the late 1940s and early 1950s. Some were so dreadful that in one city passersby seeing TV for the first time in a shop window were reportedly laughing out loud at the antique two-reelers being aired. One of the earliest network movie series was titled simply *Western Movie*, and aired on the fledgling DuMont network beginning in late 1946. Ironically, the first attempt to get quality films on TV was made not by a network but by an independent station, WPIX-TV in New York. In the spring of 1948 that station signed an agreement with Sir Alexander Korda, the English producer, for the rights to 24 major British films featuring such stars as Vivien Leigh, Laurence Olivier, and Charles Laughton.

Even when major films started becoming available to television, there was a tacit agreement among the producers to limit television films to features released no later than 1948. In this era of old and/or minor films, ABC's package during the summer of 1957, *Hollywood Film Theater*, was the most ambitious effort to date. Among the films aired in that series were *Gunga Din* starring Gary Cooper, *Mr. Blandings Builds His Dream House* and *Bringing Up Baby*, both with Cary Grant, *Top Hat* with Fred Astaire and Ginger Rogers, and the original 1933 version of *King Kong*. Most of television's early efforts at showing theatrical films were not nearly so memorable. It was not until the advent of *Saturday Night at the Movies* on NBC in 1961 that major contemporary films would become part of the television scene (See *Movies—1961 to Date*). Summarized below by title are most of the nighttime network movie series aired between 1948 and 1960. Some were full-length features, some were shorts, and some were serials, but they all had one thing in common—despite their age and/or quality they had all been released theatrically.

ABC FEATURE FILM

Oct 1948–Apr 1949, ABC Thu 9:00–10:00
May 1949–Jun 1949, ABC Fri 7:30–8:30
May 1949–Sep 1949, ABC Wed 8:00–9:00

ADMISSION FREE

May 1951–Aug 1951, ABC Mon 10:00–11:00
Aug 1951–Dec 1951, ABC Sun 8:00–9:00

ADVENTURE PLAYHOUSE

Apr 1950–May 1950, DUM Wed 8:00–9:00

BUDWEISER SUMMER THEATRE

Jun 1951–Sep 1951, CBS Sat 8:00–9:00

CINEMA-SCOPE

Apr 1952–May 1952, ABC Sun 9:30–10:30
Jun 1952, ABC Sun 10:00–11:00

CINEMA VARIETIES

Sep 1949–Nov 1949, DUM Sun 8:30–9:00

COMEDY PARADE

Apr 1951–May 1951, ABC Mon 8:00–8:30

CURTAIN UP

May 1951–Sep 1951, ABC Tue 10:00–11:00
Oct 1951–Dec 1951, ABC Mon 9:00–10:00
Nov 1951–Dec 1951, ABC Sat 9:00–10:00

ENCORE PLAYHOUSE

May 1952–Oct 1952, ABC Fri 8:30–9:00

FAMOUS FILM FESTIVAL

Sep 1955–Sep 1956, ABC Sun 7:30–9:00
Oct 1956–May 1957, ABC Sat 7:30–9:00
Jun 1957–Jul 1957, ABC Sat 7:30–8:00
Sep 1957, ABC Sat 7:30–8:30

FEATURE FILM

Oct 1950–Jan 1951, ABC Mon 10:00–11:00
Apr 1951, ABC Mon 10:00–11:00

FEATURE PLAYHOUSE

Jun 1952–Aug 1952, ABC Sat 8:30–10:30
Sep 1952–Jan 1953, ABC Sat 8:00–10:00
Feb 1953–Sep 1953, ABC Sat 8:00–9:00

FEATURE THEATRE

Mar 1949–Jun 1949, DUM Tue 8:00–9:00
Aug 1949–Jan 1950, DUM Tue 9:30–10:30
Jan 1950–Aug 1950, DUM Tue 10:00–11:00
Mar 1950–Apr 1950, DUM Thu 8:00–9:00

FILM SHORTS
Dec 1950–Jan 1951, ABC Sun 8:00–8:30
FILM FAIR
Mar 1956–Jul 1956, ABC Mon 9:00–11:00
Jul 1956–Oct 1956, ABC Mon 9:00–10:30
FILM THEATRE OF THE AIR
Mar 1949–Jul 1949, CBS Sat 8:00–9:30
Apr 1951–Oct 1951, CBS Tue 8:00–9:00
Apr 1953–Jun 1953, CBS Tue 8:00–9:00
FIRST NIGHTER
Oct 1950–Jan 1951, ABC Wed 8:00–9:00
FRONTIER THEATRE
May 1950–Sep 1950, Dum Sat 6:30–7:30
HOLLYWOOD ADVENTURE TIME
Jan 1951–Aug 1951, ABC Sun 8:00–9:00
HOLLYWOOD FILM THEATRE
Apr 1957–Sep 1957, ABC Sun 7:30–9:00
HOLLYWOOD MOVIE TIME
Jan 1951–May 1951, ABC Wed 8:00–9:00
Mar 1952–May 1952, ABC Sat 9:00–11:00
HOLLYWOOD MYSTERY TIME
Feb 1951–Jul 1951, ABC Tue 8:00–9:00
HOUR GLASS
Jun 1956–Sep 1956, ABC Thu 8:00–9:00
INTERNATIONAL PLAYHOUSE
Apr 1951–May 1951, DUM Mon 7:30–9:00
KING'S CROSSROADS
Oct 1951–Dec 1951, ABC Wed 10:00–11:00
Dec 1951–Oct 1952, ABC Sun 8:00–9:00
LIBRARY OF COMEDY FILMS
see *Comedy Parade*
MYSTERY THEATRE
Sep 1949–Mar 1950, DUM Thu 8:00–9:00
NBC CINEMA PLAYHOUSE
Jun 1950–Sep 1950, NBC Tue 8:00–9:00
NBC PRESENTS
Jun 1948–Aug 1948, NBC Tue 9:00–9:30
Sep 1948–Oct 1948, NBC Fri 8:00–8:30
Oct 1948–Dec 1948, NBC Thu 7:30–7:45
NORTHWEST PATROL
Jun 1951–Aug 1951, ABC Wed 8:00–9:00
PREMIERE PLAYHOUSE
Mar 1949–Jul 1949, CBS Fri 9:30–10:45
Jul 1949–Dec 1949, CBS Sat 9:00–10:00
May 1950–Jul 1950, CBS Sat 10:00–11:00
SADDLE PAL CLUB
Dec 1951–May 1952, ABC Sat 7:00–7:30
May 1952–Jun 1952, ABC Sat 6:30–7:30
Jun 1952–Aug 1952, ABC Sat 7:00–8:00
SCHLITZ FILM FIRSTS
Jul 1951–Sep 1951, CBS Fri 9:00–10:00
SCREEN MYSTERY
Apr 1950–Oct 1950, DUM Thu 8:00–9:00
SCREEN SHORTS
May 1951–Jul 1951, ABC Sun 10:30–11:00
SUMMER CINEMA
Jun 1952–Oct 1952, CBS Sat 8:00–Conclusion
WASHDAY THEATRE
Apr 1952–Aug 1952, ABC Mon 8:30–9:30
Sep 1952–Oct 1952, ABC Mon 9:00–10:00

MOVIES—1961 TO DATE

The evening of September 23, 1961, ushered in a new era in network-television programming. On that night NBC aired the movie *How to Marry a Millionaire* starring Marilyn Monroe, Lauren Bacall, and Betty Grable. It was the premiere telecast of a new series, *Saturday Night at the Movies*, the first movie series composed of films released by major studios after 1948. The war that had existed between the motion-picture community and the television community was finally over. The studios, which had initially feared that television would drive them out of business, were now thriving as the principal suppliers of filmed weekly TV series. It had been only a matter of time before they made the decision to release relatively current theatrical films for network showing.

Unlike previous efforts to program movies on television (ABC's *Hollywood Film Theater* in 1957 had been the most recent), *Saturday Night at the Movies* was very successful. It did, admittedly, have certain advantages over earlier movie series. For one thing, *Saturday Night at the Movies* was the first movie series that could air color movies in color. But its primary advantage was that it had access to recent movies showcasing currently popular stars, not the poor grade-B films, imports, and dated films previously seen. The popularity of good-quality movies on TV was demonstrated by the rapid growth of such programming. Within a year of the premiere of *Saturday Night at the Movies*, ABC was carrying theatrical films on Sundays and NBC had added a Monday movie to its schedule. By the end of the decade their were as many as nine network movies on each week.

The increased demand for movies on television eventually led to another major development, the made-for-television film. Universal was the first major studio to attempt producing a film expressly for television, during the 1963–1964 season. Their first effort, however, was a brutal film called *The Killers* with Lee Marvin and Angie Dickinson that was deemed too violent for television and went into theatrical release instead.

The distinction of being the first made-for-television film aired goes to *See How They Run* starring John Forsythe and Senta Berger, originally telecast on October 7, 1964. Many of the early made-for-TV films (and a substantial quantity of those currently being made) were pilots for proposed TV series, one of the most successful being *Fame Is the Name of the Game,* which became the series *Name of the Game.* It was common practice for motion-picture companies to release these tele-features theatrically outside the U.S.

The acceptance of made-for-television films, which had originally been dropped into series that were made up primarily of theatrically released films, resulted in the first series of made-for-television films only, *The ABC Movie of the Week,* in the fall of 1969. The attraction was that every week would be a "world premiere" of a new motion picture. Over the years, the number of series relying on these new films has fluctuated under titles such as *World Premiere Movie* and *Movie of the Week,* with recent trends tending to minimize the distinction between theatrical and made-for-TV films.

The highest-rated movies since the advent of *Saturday Night at the Movies* in 1961 (up to the start of the 1978–1979 season) are ranked in the table below. Following the table is a chronology of network movie series by night of the week. In cases where a series consisted primarily of made-for-television films, it has been indicated by (TV).

HIGHEST RATED MOVIES ON TELEVISION

	Title	Rating
1.	*Gone with the Wind*	47.6
2.	*Airport*	42.3
3.	*Love Story*	42.3
4.	*The Poseidon Adventure*	39.0
5.	*True Grit*	38.9
6.	*The Birds*	38.9
7.	*Patton*	38.5
8.	*The Bridge on the River Kwai*	38.3
9.	*The Godfather*	38.2
10.	*Jeremiah Johnson*	37.5
11.	*Ben-Hur*	37.1
12.	*Little Ladies of the Night (TV)*	36.9
13.	*Helter Skelter (TV)*	36.4
14.	*Planet of the Apes*	35.2
15.	*Born Free*	34.2
16.	*The Sound of Music*	33.6
17.	*Bonnie and Clyde*	33.4
18.	*The Ten Commandments*	33.2
19.	*A Case of Rape (TV)*	33.1
20.	*The Longest Yard*	33.1

In addition to the various prime-time movie series, CBS premiered *The CBS Late Night Movie,* a Monday–Friday 11:30 P.M. collection of theatrical and made-for-television reruns, on February 14, 1972, replacing the canceled *Merv Griffin Show.*

CHRONOLOGY OF NETWORK MOVIES BY NIGHT OF THE WEEK

SUNDAY

Apr 1962–Sep 1963 ABC
Sep 1964– ABC
Jun 1971–Sep 1972 CBS
May 1977–Sep 1977 NBC (TV)
Jul 1977–Sep 1977 CBS

MONDAY

Feb 1963–Sep 1964 NBC
Sep 1968–Dec 1970 NBC
Jan 1970–Aug 1974 ABC (Jan–Aug Each Year)
Jan 1971–Aug 1971 NBC (TV)
Sep 1971–May 1975 NBC (Sep–May Each Year)
Jan 1975–Feb 1975 ABC
Sep 1975–Jan 1976 NBC
Feb 1976–May 1976 ABC
Sep 1976– NBC
Dec 1976–Feb 1977 ABC

TUESDAY

Sep 1965–Aug 1971 NBC
Sep 1969–Aug 1975 ABC (TV)
Jun 1970–Sep 1970 CBS
Sep 1972–Sep 1974 CBS (TV)
Jan 1973–Aug 1973 NBC
Sep 1974–Sep 1975 NBC (TV)
Jun 1977–Aug 1977 ABC
Jan 1978– CBS

WEDNESDAY

Sep 1964–Sep 1965 NBC
Jul 1966–Aug 1966 ABC
Jan 1967–Jan 1970 ABC
Sep 1972–Sep 1975 ABC (TV)
Jan 1974–Aug 1974 NBC
Sep 1976–Nov 1976 NBC (TV)
Nov 1976– CBS
Mar 1978–May 1978 NBC
Aug 1978– NBC

THURSDAY

Sep 1965–Nov 1975 CBS
May 1975–Sep 1975 NBC
Jan 1976–Sep 1976 NBC
Apr 1977–Sep 1977 NBC
Jun 1978–Aug 1978 ABC

FRIDAY

Sep 1966–Sep 1971 CBS
Sep 1971–Aug 1972 CBS (TV)
Sep 1971–Dec 1971 NBC (TV)
Jan 1972–Sep 1972 NBC
Sep 1972–Sep 1975 CBS
Jun 1973–Sep 1973 NBC
May 1974–Aug 1974 NBC
Jul 1975– ABC
Dec 1975–Jan 1977 CBS
Apr 1977–Mar 1978 CBS

SATURDAY

Sep 1961–Sep 1978 NBC
Sep 1971–May 1972 ABC (TV)
Jun 1972–Aug 1972 ABC
Sep 1973–Aug 1974 ABC (TV)
Jan 1975–Aug 1975 ABC
Apr 1976–Aug 1976 ABC
May 1978– CBS

MOVIN' ON

Adventure

FIRST TELECAST: *September 12, 1974*
LAST TELECAST: *September 14, 1976*
BROADCAST HISTORY:
Sep 1974—May 1975, NBC Thu 10:00–11:00
Sep 1975–Sep 1976, NBC Tue 8:00–9:00
CAST:
Sonny Pruitt ....Claude Akins
Will Chandler ....Frank Converse
Moose (1975–1976) ....Rosey Grier
Benjy (1975–1976) ....Art Metrano
THEME:
"Movin' On," written and performed by Merle Haggard

Sonny and Will were two gypsy truckdrivers who came from radically different backgrounds. Sonny was a burly veteran trucker, owner of the giant rig that they operated, and prone to settle most of his arguments with his fists. Will was much younger, a law school graduate who had turned to trucking as a means of learning more about himself. His legal training and quick mind often prevented disagreements from turning into brawls. They were good for each other; Sonny's outgoing gregariousness counterbalanced Will's quiet, reserved personality, while Will's rational approach to problems counteracted Sonny's sucker-prone willingness to help anyone at any time. Together they traveled back and forth across the country in search of adventure and freight to haul. During the second season another pair of truckers, Moose and Benjy, were seen frequently. Less than completely ethical, they were two of the most mobile con men ever seen on television. *Movin' On* was filmed on location in a different part of the country each week.

One of the fans of this program was President Gerald Ford. Once, when *Movin' On* was filming in Atlanta, Claude Akins happened to be staying at the same hotel as the President. Approached in the hotel dining room by a Secret Service agent, the actor was invited to the President's suite, where he and Ford chatted about the show for half an hour. "Now," remarked the President, "I can tell Betty I know more about *Movin' On* than she does."

MULLIGAN'S STEW

Comedy Drama

FIRST TELECAST: *October 25, 1977*
LAST TELECAST: *December 13, 1977*
BROADCAST HISTORY:
Oct 1977–Dec 1977, NBC Tue 9:00–10:00
CAST:
Michael Mulligan .....Lawrence Pressman
Jane Mulligan ....Elinor Donahue
Mark Mulligan ....Johnny Doran
Melinda Mulligan .....Julie Anne Haddock
Jimmy Mulligan ....K. C. Martel
Adam Friedman ....Chris Ciampa
Stevie Friedman ....Suzanne Crough
Kimmy Friedman ....Sunshine Lee
Polly Friedman ....Lory Kochheim
Polo Polocheck ....Jaime Alba

Set in the fictitious Southern California suburban community of Birchfield, *Mulligan's Stew* was the story of Michael and Jane Mulligan and their extended family. The Mulligans had three children of their own, and were managing reasonably well, when Michael's sister and her husband were killed, leaving them with four more children, including a recently adopted five-year-old Vietnamese orphan named Kimmy. The Mulligan home, barely comfortable with its original family of five, was severely overcrowded with nine. The Mulligan children and the Friedman children had been raised with different life-styles and had considerable problems adjusting to each other. Michael's income as a high school teacher/football coach was enough to get by on, but with nine mouths to feed very little was left for luxuries.

MUNSTERS, THE

Situation Comedy

FIRST TELECAST: *September 24, 1964*

LAST TELECAST: *September 1, 1966*

BROADCAST HISTORY:

Sep 1964–Sep 1966, CBS Thu 7:30–8:00

CAST:

Herman Munster ....Fred Gwynne
Lily Munster ....Yvonne DeCarlo
Grandpa Munster ....Al Lewis
Edward Wolfgang (Eddie) Munster .... Butch Patrick
Marilyn Munster (1964) ..... Beverly Owen
Marilyn Munster (1964–1966) .... Pat Priest

At 1313 Mockingbird Lane in Mockingbird Heights stood a musty, cobweb-covered gothic mansion. The residents considered themselves just a normal, everyday American family, but to neighbors—and viewers—they were a bit unusual. Herman, the man of the house, was seven feet tall and bore a striking resemblance to the Frankenstein monster. His wife Lily looked very much like a lady vampire; son Eddie looked like he was in the midst of changing from boy to wolf, or vice versa, take your pick; and Grandpa could have passed for an aging, 350-year-old Count Dracula. They all had their idiosyncracies. Grandpa was not above changing into a bat when the situation warranted it. Not only did this family look like monsters, they were monsters—albeit friendly, unassuming ones. They were concerned about their niece Marilyn, who looked somewhat strange to them (to an outsider she was the only normal-looking one of the lot). The effect their physical appearance had on the rest of the world was always predictable, often hilarious, and occasionally poignant. Herman, appropriately, worked in a menial capacity for the funeral home of Gateman, Goodbury & Graves, and was always on the lookout for a better job. Beverly Owen, who originated the role of Marilyn, left the series in December 1964 to get married, and was replaced by Pat Priest.

MUSEUM OF SCIENCE AND INDUSTRY

Instruction

FIRST TELECAST: *July 30, 1948*

LAST TELECAST: *September 24, 1948*

BROADCAST HISTORY:

Jul 1948–Sep 1948, NBC Fri 8:00–8:30

A live and film program featuring exhibits at a New York City museum.

MUSIC AT THE MEADOWBROOK

Musical Variety

FIRST TELECAST: *May 23, 1953*

LAST TELECAST: *April 19, 1956*

BROADCAST HISTORY:

May 1953–Sep 1953, ABC Sat 7:00–8:00
Oct 1953–Dec 1953, ABC Sat 8:00–9:00
Jan 1956–Apr 1956, ABC Thu 10:00–10:30

HOSTS:

Jimmy Blaine
Bill Williams
Walter Herlihy, and others

REGULAR:

Frank Dailey

This series of band remotes from Frank Dailey's famous Meadowbrook Night Club in Cedar Grove, New Jersey, was reminiscent of radio in the 1930s. In those days the Meadowbrook was one of the chief points of origination for live, nationwide broadcasts by the traveling big bands. In the TV era, however, it—and the big bands—were anachronisms and were televised only briefly, in the 1950s.

In addition to music by a different guest band each week (sometimes one stayed for several weeks) the 1953 series featured a regular college salute, in which students were interviewed and campus talent, such as the glee club, performed. Premiere-night guests in 1953 were Ralph Marterie and His Orchestra, Richard Hayman, and the Douglas Duke Trio. Seen later were such bands as those of Sauter-Finegan, Neal Hefti, Ray McKinley, the Korn Kobblers, Art Mooney, Ralph Flanagan, and King Guion and His Double Rhythm Orchestra, as well as assorted singers, dancers and other acts.

Jimmy Blaine was the most frequent host in both 1953 and 1956, though others did appear and club owner Frank Dailey also wandered on and off the set.

MUSIC BINGO

Quiz/Audience Participation

FIRST TELECAST: *May 29, 1958*

LAST TELECAST: *September 11, 1958*

BROADCAST HISTORY:

May 1958–Sep 1958, NBC Thu 10:30–11:00

EMCEE:

Johnny Gilbert

Music Bingo was a variation on the highly successful *Name That Tune*. Two contestants would listen to a tune being played and, when the tune was abruptly stopped, would run to an assigned place and push a buzzer. The first one to push the buzzer got the opportunity to identify the song. If correct, the contestant could place his mark—a musical sharp or flat symbol—anyplace on the music bingo board he chose. The first person to successfully complete a bingo, five in a line, was the winner of $500 and would keep facing new contestants until defeated.

MUSIC COUNTRY

see *Dean Martin Presents Music Country*

MUSIC COUNTRY USA

Musical Variety

FIRST TELECAST: *January 17, 1974*
LAST TELECAST: *May 16, 1974*
BROADCAST HISTORY:
Jan 1974–May 1974, NBC Thu 10:00–11:00

The concept of *Music Country USA* was essentially the same as that of *Dean Martin Presents Music Country*, a summer replacement for *The Dean Martin Show*. Country and Western acts performed on the show, which was taped on location in various places around the country. There was a different host each week, including Jerry Reed, Lynn Anderson, Marty Robbins, Donna Fargo, Tom T. Hall, Mac Davis, Buck Owens, Wayne Newton, Dionne Warwicke, Doug Kershaw, and Charlie Rich. All of them also made frequent appearances as performers on the show.

MUSIC 55

Music

FIRST TELECAST: *July 12, 1955*
LAST TELECAST: *September 13, 1955*
BROADCAST HISTORY:
Jul 1955–Sep 1955, CBS Tue 8:30–9:00
REGULAR:
Stan Kenton

This live weekly summer music series featured the sounds of Stan Kenton and his band. The repertoire included jazz, standards, and contemporary hits. Stan also played host to weekly guest stars.

MUSIC FOR A SUMMER NIGHT

Music

FIRST TELECAST: *June 3, 1959*
LAST TELECAST: *September 21, 1960*
BROADCAST HISTORY:
Jun 1959–Aug 1959, ABC Wed 7:30–8:30
Feb 1960–Mar 1960, ABC Wed 7:30–8:00
Mar 1960–Sep 1960, ABC Wed 7:30–8:30
REGULAR:
Glenn Osser and His Orchestra

ABC salvaged a bit of the prestige it had lost by canceling the *Voice of Firestone* with this replacement program, produced by the same man (Fred Heidler) and containing approximately the same musical ingredients—but on a much lower budget. Like *Voice*, *Music for a Summer Night* ranged across the "better" musical idioms, principally Broadway show tunes and the classics. Good but not top-name singers were used, such as Betty Ann Grove, Bill Hayes, and Dorothy Collins. Complete productions of *Madame Butterfly*, *La Traviata*, and *Tosca* (set in Mussolini's Italy) were aired, along with lighter fare such as a visit to summer theaters and musical festivals around the country. A novel touch was the use of John Hoppe's Mobilux creations to introduce numbers.

When the program returned in February 1960, too early to be classified as a summer show, it was titled *Music for a Spring Night*, reverting to its original title in May. ABC documentary news specials preempted this series on an irregular but frequent basis.

MUSIC FROM CHICAGO

Music

FIRST TELECAST: *April 15, 1951*
LAST TELECAST: *June 17, 1951*
BROADCAST HISTORY:
Apr 1951–Jun 1951, DUM Sun 9:30–10:00

A short-lived music series originating in Chicago, which at the time was a fairly important production center for network programs.

MUSIC FROM MANHATTAN

see *Sammy Kaye Show, The*

MUSIC FROM THE MEADOWBROOK

see *Music at the Meadowbrook*

MUSIC HALL

Music

FIRST TELECAST: *July 1, 1952*

LAST TELECAST: *September 25, 1952*
BROADCAST HISTORY:
Jul 1952–Sep 1952, CBS Tue/Thu 7:45–8:00
REGULARS:
Patti Page
Carl Hoff and His Orchestra

Patti Page was the singing star of this twice-weekly 15-minute music show that filled the remainder of the half-hour in which CBS aired its nightly network news program. The show originated from New York and was telecast live.

MUSIC IN VELVET

Music
FIRST TELECAST: *January 16, 1949*
LAST TELECAST: *October 28, 1951*
BROADCAST HISTORY:
Jan 1949–Apr 1949, ABC Sun 9:30–10:00
Jul 1951–Oct 1951, ABC Sun 7:30–8:00
REGULARS:
Johnny Hill (1949)
The Velveteers (1949)
Don Lindley Orchestra (1949)
Rex Maupin (1951)

This was another of the easygoing song-and-dance programs that originated from Chicago during TV's early years, when that city was an important network production center. Baritone Johnny Hill was featured during the 1949 run, and Rex Maupin in 1951.

MUSIC ON ICE

Musical Variety
FIRST TELECAST: *May 8, 1960*
LAST TELECAST: *September 11, 1960*
BROADCAST HISTORY:
May 1960–Sep 1960, NBC Sun 8:00–9:00
HOST:
Johnny Desmond
REGULARS:
The Skip Jacks
The Dancing Blades

The melding of a musical variety hour with an ice show in a weekly series was unique. Not all of the numbers in the series were performed on ice, but there were a number of ice-skating features in each program. Johnny Desmond was the host, the Skip Jacks were the regular vocalists, and the Dancing Blades provided regular precision group skating. Guest singers and ice performers were on each show. Perfect for a warm summer's evening.

MUSIC ROOM, THE

see *Jacques Fray Music Room*

MUSIC SCENE, THE

Music
FIRST TELECAST: *September 22, 1969*
LAST TELECAST: *January 12, 1970*
BROADCAST HISTORY:
Sep 1969–Jan 1970, ABC Mon 7:30–8:15
HOSTS:
David Steinberg
Larry Hankin
Christopher Ross
Paul Reid Roman
Chris Bokeno
Lily Tomlin

A contemporary popular music program, at first utilizing six rotating hosts, but beginning in November hosted by David Steinberg (and guests) only. Practically every big name in rock music appeared on this short-lived show, with the first telecast alone featuring the Beatles, James Brown, Crosby, Stills, Nash & Young, Buck Owens, Three Dog Night, Oliver, and Tom Jones. Seen in later telecasts were Janis Joplin, Bobby Sherman, Sly & the Family Stone, Isaac Hayes, Stevie Wonder, Mama Cass, and even Groucho Marx, among others. A special feature was performances of the latest hit songs in various fields, such as rock, rhythm & blues, Country & Western, and comedy, based on *Billboard* magazine's record popularity charts. An improvisational comedy group was also seen.

MUSIC SHOP, THE

Musical Variety
FIRST TELECAST: *January 11, 1959*
LAST TELECAST: *March 8, 1959*
BROADCAST HISTORY:
Jan 1959–Mar 1959, NBC Sun 7:30–8:00
HOST:
Buddy Bregman

Most of the singers who appeared on this series had currently popular hit songs, with the emphasis on young performers on the way up. In addition to serving as host, Buddy Bregman accompanied on piano those who performed live. However, the majority lip-synced to their hit records. Among those who appeared were Bobby

Darin, Ritchie Valens, the Platters, the Teddy Bears, and Annette Funicello, along with an established, older star each week (Milton Berle, Jerry Lewis, etc.) who would chat and perhaps perform. At the end of each show, Buddy announced the top five records of the week.

MUSIC SHOW, THE

Music

FIRST TELECAST: *May 19, 1953*
LAST TELECAST: *October 17, 1954*
BROADCAST HISTORY:

May 1953–Jun 1953, DUM Tue 9:00–9:30
Jul 1953–Oct 1953, DUM Tue 8:30–9:00
Oct 1953–Jan 1954, DUM Wed 10:30–11:00
Jan 1954–Sep 1954, DUM Wed 10:00–10:30
Sep 1954–Oct 1954, DUM Sun 10:00–10:30

REGULARS:

Mike Douglas
Jackie Van
Henri Noel
Eleanor Warner (1953–1954)
Dolores Peterson (1954)
Robert Trendler Orchestra

This Chicago-originated program was exactly as billed—just music, with no frills, no fancy production, and no gimmicks. Four pleasant-voiced singers shared the vocal honors, with Mike Douglas and Jackie Van handling the more popular tunes and Henri Noel and Eleanor Warner (later replaced by Dolores Peterson) the meatier stuff. Repertoire was primarily standards, including medleys from *Carousel, South Pacific,* and other Broadway shows. Robert Trendler's 34-piece orchestra provided lush accompaniment.

MUSICAL ALMANAC

Music

FIRST TELECAST: *May 10, 1948*
LAST TELECAST: *April 30, 1949*
BROADCAST HISTORY:

May 1948–Dec 1948, NBC Mon–Thurs various nights and times between 7:30–8:00
May 1948–Aug 1948, NBC Fri 9:00–9:15
Oct 1948–Dec 1948, NBC Fri 8:00–8:30
Feb 1949–Apr 1949, NBC various nights 10:00–10:30

EMCEE:

Harvey Harding

For the first few weeks pianist-singer Harvey Harding "and his musical nostalgia" were featured exclusively on this 15–30-minute musical interlude, but later a variety of cabaret talent appeared from night to night. Among those seen were Ted Steele (from WPTZ, Philadelphia), Barbara Marshall, Verle Mills, and Roberta Quinlan. The program wandered all over the prime-time schedule for about a year in 1948–1949. The title was changed to *Musical Miniatures* in August 1948.

Harding was one of TV's pioneers, having had a similar regular weekly series on New York local television from July 1941 to May 1942.

MUSICAL CHAIRS

Quiz/Audience Participation

FIRST TELECAST: *July 9, 1955*
LAST TELECAST: *September 17, 1955*
BROADCAST HISTORY:

Jul 1955–Sep 1955, NBC Sat 9:00–9:30

MODERATOR:

Bill Leyden

PANELISTS:

Mel Blanc
Johnny Mercer
Bobby Troup

SINGERS:

The Cheerleaders

After two years as a local show in Los Angeles, *Musical Chairs* moved to the NBC network for a summer run in 1955. Viewers of this musical quiz show were encouraged to send in questions to test the knowledge of the panel. Those who submitted questions that stumped the panel won a 21-inch RCA TV. There were four panel members: Mel Blanc, actor and impressionist who was most famous for his work as the voice of Bugs Bunny; composer Johnny Mercer; pianist-orchestra leader Bobby Troup (whose band, the Troup Group, provided the music for this series); and a guest panelist. The questions could have anything to do with music, from arranging, to composing, to performing. Members of the panel were often called on to imitate the singing or playing styles of well-known performers and occasionally collaborated on individual answers.

MUSICAL COMEDY TIME

Musical Comedy

FIRST TELECAST: *October 2, 1950*
LAST TELECAST: *March 19, 1951*

BROADCAST HISTORY:

Oct 1950–Mar 1951, NBC Mon 9:30–10:30

Musical Comedy Time aired on alternate Monday evenings with *Robert Montgomery Presents*. Broadway musical comedies and standard operettas were adapted for presentation as live hour-long TV programs. Among the adaptations were such musical comedies as *Anything Goes* and *No No Nanette*, and such operettas as *The Merry Widow*.

MUSICAL MERRY-GO-ROUND

Music

FIRST TELECAST: *July 25, 1947*

LAST TELECAST: *March 11, 1949*

BROADCAST HISTORY:

Jul 1947–Sep 1947, NBC Fri 8:00–8:30
Oct 1947–Jan 1948, NBC Thu 8:00–8:30
Jan 1948–Feb 1948, NBC Fri 7:45–8:00
Feb 1948–Mar 1949, NBC Fri 7:30–7:50

HOST:

Jack Kilty

REGULARS:

Frederic (Fritz) DeWilde
Eve Young (1947)
Penny Gerard (1948–1949)

One of the earliest regular musical programs on network TV, this extremely simple series was at first called *Disc Magic* and was essentially a disc-jockey show. Viewers watched d.j. Kilty play popular records and occasionally introduce some live entertainment. In 1947, *anything* on the flickering screen seemed interesting to watch. Then in October 1947 the title was changed to *Musical Merry-Go-Round* and the format shifted to live entertainment exclusively, with songs by Kilty, Eve Young (and, later, Penny Gerard), bits by actor Fritz DeWilde, and guest performers. Most of the guests were unknown cabaret talent rather than established stars.

MUSICAL MINIATURES

see *Musical Almanac*

MY FAVORITE HUSBAND

Situation Comedy

FIRST TELECAST: *September 12, 1953*

LAST TELECAST: *September 8, 1957*

BROADCAST HISTORY:

Sep 1953–Jun 1955, CBS Sat 9:30–10:00 (OS)
Oct 1955–Dec 1955, CBS Tue 10:30–11:00
Jun 1957–Sep 1957, CBS Sun 7:30–8:00

CAST:

George Cooper .... Barry Nelson
Liz Cooper (1953–1955) ..... Joan Caulfield
Liz Cooper (1955) .... Vanessa Brown
Myra Cobb/Myra Shepard ...... Alix Talton
Gillmore Cobb (1953–1955)
.... Bob Sweeney
Oliver Shepard (1955) .... Dan Tobin

George Cooper was a successful bank executive with a fancy suburban home and a beautiful but scatterbrained wife. Living next door were the Cobbs, Gillmore, the peanut magnate, and Myra, the social snob. The Coopers, though wealthy, were rather unpretentious, and the Cobbs were always trying to get them to improve their social image.

Several changes took place at the start of the third season. Vanessa Brown replaced Joan Caulfield in the role of Liz, the next-door neighbors became the Shepards (with Alix Talton still playing the wife), and there was less emphasis on social status. Despite the changes, the program folded three months later. Reruns of this last group of episodes were aired during the summer of 1957.

My Favorite Husband was based on the 1948 radio series of the same name, which starred Lucille Ball as the nutty housewife Liz (the prototype for her long-running Lucy characterization on TV).

MY FAVORITE MARTIAN

Situation Comedy

FIRST TELECAST: *September 29, 1963*

LAST TELECAST: *September 4, 1966*

BROADCAST HISTORY:

Sep 1963–Sep 1966, CBS Sun 7:30–8:00

CAST:

Uncle Martin (The Martian)
.... Ray Walston
Tim O'Hara .... Bill Bixby
Mrs. Lorelei Brown .... Pamela Britton
Angela Brown (1963–1964)
.... Ann Marshall
Mr. Harry Burns (1963–1964)
.... J. Pat O'Malley
Det. Bill Brennan (1964–1966)
.... Alan Hewitt
The Police Chief (1965–1966) ... Roy Engle

On his way to cover an assignment for his paper, *The Los Angeles Sun*, reporter Tim O'Hara stumbled upon a Martian whose one-man ship had crashed on Earth. Tim took the dazed Martian back to his rooming house to help him recuperate, while thinking of the fantastic story he would be able to present to his boss, Mr. Burns, about his find. The Martian, however, looked human, spoke English, and refused to admit to anyone but Tim what he was. Tim befriended him, passed him off as his uncle, and had many an interesting adventure with the stranded alien. Uncle Martin had little retractable antennae, could make himself invisible, was telepathic, could move objects just by pointing at them, and had a vast storehouse of advanced technological knowledge. While he was trying to fix his ship he stayed with Tim in Mrs. Brown's rooming house. During the first season, Mrs. Brown's teenage daughter Angela was a cast regular. The following year policeman Bill Brennan joined the cast as Mrs. Brown's boy friend, a threat to Uncle Martin on two counts—not only was he always a potential discoverer of the Martian's true identity, but Uncle Martin had become romantically interested in Mrs. Brown himself and looked upon Brennan as a rival for her affections.

MY FRIEND FLICKA

Adventure

FIRST TELECAST: *February 10, 1956*

LAST TELECAST: *May 18, 1958*

BROADCAST HISTORY:

Feb 1956–Feb 1957, CBS Fri 7:30–8:00
Mar 1957, CBS Sat 7:00–7:30
Apr 1957–May 1957, CBS Sun 6:00–6:30
Jun 1957–Aug 1957, CBS Wed 7:30–8:00
Sep 1957–Dec 1957, NBC Sun 6:30–7:00
Jan 1958–May 1958, NBC Sun 7:00–7:30

CAST:

Rob McLaughlin .... Gene Evans
Nell McLaughlin .... Anita Louise
Ken McLaughlin ...... Johnny Washbrook
Gus Broeberg .... Frank Ferguson
Hildy Broeberg (1956) ...... Pamela Beaird

Set in the ranchlands of Montana around the turn of the century, *My Friend Flicka* was the story of a boy and his horse. Young Ken McLaughlin's best friend was his beloved horse, Flicka. Ken, Flicka, Ken's parents, and ranch hand Gus encountered assorted adventures while struggling to make a living from the land and dealing with their neighbors and friends. Originally aired as a black-and-white series on CBS, this program, which had been filmed in color, was rerun as a color entry on NBC during the following season.

Based on the 1943 movie, which had been adapted from the stories of Mary O'Hara.

MY FRIEND IRMA

Situation Comedy

FIRST TELECAST: *January 8, 1952*

LAST TELECAST: *June 25, 1954*

BROADCAST HISTORY:

Jan 1952–Mar 1952, CBS Tue 10:30–11:00
Apr 1952–Jun 1953, CBS Fri 8:30–9:00 (OS)
Oct 1953–Jun 1954, CBS Fri 10:00–10:30

CAST:

Irma Peterson .... Marie Wilson
Jane Stacy (1952–1953) .... Cathy Lewis
Mrs. O'Reilly .... Gloria Gordon
Professor Kropotkin (1952–1953) .... Sig Arno
Al (1952–1953) .... Sid Tomack
Richard Rhinelander III (1952–1953) .... Brooks West
Mrs. Rhinelander (1952–1953) .... Margaret Dumont
Mr. Clyde .... Don McBride
Joe Vance (1953–1954) .... Hal March
Bobby Peterson (1953–1954) .... Richard Eyer
Kay Foster (1953–1954) .... Mary Shipp
Mr. Corday (1953–1954) .... John Carradine

Marie Wilson was TV's—and radio's, and Hollywood's—favorite dumb blonde. She played many similar characters, but her most famous was the title role in *My Friend Irma*, which she created on radio in 1947. Irma Peterson was possibly the kookiest secretary in the entire world. She was friendly, enthusiastic, sexy—and very wacky. She just had no sense of logic. Her roommate was level-headed Jane Stacy, whose affection for Irma usually overcame the frustrations she met coping with Irma's predicaments. Irma and Jane shared an apartment in Mrs. O'Reilly's run-down Manhattan boardinghouse, where much of the action took place in this live series. Jane's boy friend was Richard Rhinelander III, her millionaire boss, while Irma's was an impoverished con artist named Al.

When the TV version was added to radio's *My Friend Irma* in 1952, the three female principals—Marie Wilson, Gloria Gordon, and Cathy Lewis—made the transition, with Miss Lewis talking to the audience in the manner of a narrator to set up the scenes as well as participating in them, as she had done on radio. However, the 1953–1954 season brought a number of cast changes. Irma had a new roommate in newspaper reporter Kay Foster (Jane had moved to Panama), her seven-year-old nephew Bobby had come to live with her, and she had a new boy friend named Joe Vance. Her original nutty neighbor Professor Kropotkin, the violinist at the Paradise Burlesque, was also gone, replaced by an eccentric actor, Mr. Corday. The only original regulars left in the cast were Irma, her landlady Mrs. O'Reilly, and Mr. Clyde, the blustery, cranky attorney for whom she worked.

MY FRIEND TONY

Detective

FIRST TELECAST: *January 5, 1969*
LAST TELECAST: *September 31, 1969*
BROADCAST HISTORY:
Jan 1969–Sep 1969, NBC Sun 10:00–11:00
CAST:
Prof. John Woodruff ...... James Whitmore
Tony Novello .... Enzo Cerusico

When he was in Italy shortly after the end of World War II, John Woodruff almost had his wallet stolen by a street urchin named Tony. Years later, a fully grown Tony arrived in America to join John as half of a private-investigation team. Professor Woodruff, whose academic career in criminology had given him the ability to analyze the most obscure clues to resolve cases, needed Tony to do his legwork and handle the physical side of the business. As they traveled around the country on various assignments the contrast between Woodruff's stolid, conservative, analytical approach and Tony's carefree romanticism provided a contentious but productive relationship.

MY HERO

Situation Comedy

FIRST TELECAST: *November 8, 1952*
LAST TELECAST: *August 1, 1953*
BROADCAST HISTORY:
Nov 1952–Apr 1953, NBC Sat 7:30–8:00
Apr 1953–Aug 1953, NBC Sat 8:00–8:30
CAST:
Robert S. Beanblossom .. Robert Cummings
Julie Marshall .... Julie Bishop
Willis Thackery .... John Litel

Robert S. Beanblossom was a real estate salesman for the Thackery Realty Company. He was not a particularly good salesman, and his carefree attitude tended to create problems, but he was very lucky. In each episode of this filmed series he somehow managed to stumble through a proposed real estate deal and come out a winner. His luck was helped along by the office secretary, Julie Marshall, who went out of her way to straighten out his mistakes and protect him from the wrath of the boss, Willis Thackery.

MY LITTLE MARGIE

Situation Comedy

FIRST TELECAST: *June 16, 1952*
LAST TELECAST: *August 24, 1955*
BROADCAST HISTORY:
Jun 1952–Sep 1952, CBS Mon 9:00–9:30
Oct 1952–Nov 1952, NBC Sat 7:30–8:00
Jan 1953–July 1953, CBS Thu 10:00–10:30
Sep 1953–Aug 1955, NBC Wed 8:30–9:00
CAST:
Margie Albright .... Gale Storm
Vernon Albright .... Charles Farrell
Roberta Townsend .... Hillary Brooke
Freddie Wilson .... Don Hayden
Mr. Honeywell .... Clarence Kolb
Mrs. Odetts .... Gertrude Hoffman
Charlie .... Willie Best

Vern Albright was a very eligible widower whose 21-year-old daughter was determined to save him from the machinations of various women. An executive with the investment-counseling firm of Honeywell and Todd, Vern was trimly athletic at age 50, and was most often romantically linked with Roberta Townsend. Margie, who shared her father's Fifth Avenue apartment, was always scheming with old Mrs. Odetts, the next-door neighbor, to make Dad more sedate, as well as to circumvent the parental control he vainly tried to maintain over her. Also recruited to help with various subterfuges were Margie's boy friend Freddie, and Charlie, the combination handyman and elevator operator in the Albrights' apartment building.

In a somewhat unusual move, *My Little Margie* went from TV to radio in December 1952, airing concurrently on the CBS radio network for the rest of its TV run (not in simulcasts, but in different original episodes). Gale Storm and Charles Farrell also played the leads in the radio version.

MY LIVING DOLL

Situation Comedy

FIRST TELECAST: *September 27, 1964*

LAST TELECAST: *September 8, 1965*

BROADCAST HISTORY:

Sep 1964–Dec 1964, CBS Sun 9:00–9:30
Dec 1964–Sep 1965, CBS Wed 8:00–8:30

CAST:

Dr. Robert McDonald ....Robert Cummings
Rhoda Miller ....Julie Newmar
Peter Robinson ....Jack Mullaney
Irene Adams ....Doris Dowling

This comedy introduced the ultimate in male fantasy, a sexy, curvaceous, female robot programmed to do anything she was told—absolutely anything. AF 709 was the secret project number that designated this ultimate achievement in space-age technology, a robot that could think on its own and function like a man—well, like a woman. Statuesque Julie Newmar played the robot. She wandered into the office of base psychiatrist Robert McDonald one day and had a pleasant chat with him. Only later did he find out that she was a robot designed by Dr. Carl Miller. When Dr. Miller was called away on assignment to Pakistan he left the robot in Bob's care. Bob named her Rhoda and passed her off as Dr. Miller's niece. She moved into his home, where Bob took on the task of training her to be the "perfect" woman—one that only talked when spoken to, and did what was asked of her. To complicate things, Bob's neighbor Peter fell in love with Rhoda and had to be fended off lest he discover her secret.

MY MOTHER THE CAR

Situation Comedy

FIRST TELECAST: *September 14, 1965*

LAST BROADCAST: *September 6, 1966*

BROADCAST HISTORY:

Sep 1965–Sep 1966, NBC Tue 7:30–8:00

CAST:

Dave Crabtree ....Jerry Van Dyke
His Mother's Voice ....Ann Sothern
Barbara Crabtree ....Maggie Pierce
Cindy Crabtree ....Cindy Eilbacher
Randy Crabtree ....Randy Whipple
Capt. Mancini ....Avery Schreiber

In what was surely one of her more unusual roles, Ann Sothern played a talking car in this 1965 comedy. Dave Crabtree was a small-town lawyer of modest means with a wife (Barbara), two children (Cindy and Randy), and a small dog. On a visit to a used-car lot in search of an inexpensive secondhand car he found himself strangely attracted to an ancient 1928 Porter. When he got behind the wheel, the car talked to him, informing him that it was the reincarnation of his mother. Against the advice of family and friends he bought the car, because he didn't want to lose "Mother." Dave was the only one whom the car would talk to, or who could really hear what it had to say. The "villain" in the series was Capt. Mancini, an antique car collector who was constantly trying to find a way to get the Porter away from Dave.

MY SISTER EILEEN

Situation Comedy

FIRST TELECAST: *October 5, 1960*

LAST TELECAST: *April 12, 1961*

BROADCAST HISTORY:

Oct 1960–Apr 1961, CBS Wed 9:00–9:30

CAST:

Ruth Sherwood ....Elaine Stritch
Eileen Sherwood ....Shirley Bonne
Mr. Appopoplous ....Leon Belasco
Chick Adams ....Jack Weston
Bertha ....Rose Marie
Mr. Beaumont ....Raymond Bailey

Ruth and Eileen Sherwood moved to New York from Ohio in order to further their careers, Ruth as a writer and her younger sister as an aspiring actress. They moved into a Manhattan brownstone, found an agent named Chick Adams to help them get work, and tried to adjust to life in the big city. Ruth was more serious, more ambitious, and much more sensible than her beautiful younger sister. She got a job working for Mr. Beaumont, a publisher, and made a good friend of her co-worker Bertha. Eileen, on the other hand, was a sucker for every con man and would-be boy friend who came along. Her life was full of all kinds of propositions, but few real jobs. Ruth spent much of her time trying to watch over her kid sister.

Based on a book by Ruth McKinley and two movies (1942 and 1955) derived from it.

MY SON JEEP

Situation Comedy

FIRST TELECAST: *July 4, 1953*

LAST TELECAST: *September 22, 1953*

BROADCAST HISTORY:

Jul 1953–Aug 1953, NBC Sat 7:30–8:00
Sep 1953, NBC Tue 8:00–8:30

CAST:

Dr. Robert Allison .... Jeffrey Lynn
Jeep Allison .... Martin Huston
Peggy Allison .... Betty Lou Keim
Barbara Miller .... Anne Sargent
Mrs. Bixby .... Leona Powers
Tommy Clifford .... William Lally
Boots .... Richard Wiggington

Grove Falls, U.S.A., was the setting for this live situation comedy that aired during the summer of 1953. "Jeep" Allison was ten years old and lived with his 13-year-old sister Peggy and their widowed father, Robert. Robert, a physician, tried to be both mother and father to his two children but found them, particularly Jeep, almost too much to handle. The housekeeper, Mrs. Bixby, attempted to maintain some semblance of order at home while Dr. Allison was at the office. Beautiful Barbara Miller, a substitute teacher who also worked part time as receptionist for Dr. Allison, was the romantic interest, primarily because Jeep liked her and tried to get his father interested in her in more than just a professional manner.

MY THREE SONS

Situation Comedy

FIRST TELECAST: *September 29, 1960*
LAST TELECAST: *August 24, 1972*
BROADCAST HISTORY:

Sep 1960–Sep 1963, ABC Thu 9:00–9:30
Sep 1963–Sep 1965, ABC Thu 8:30–9:00
Sep 1965–Aug 1967, CBS Thu 8:30–9:00
Sep 1967–Sep 1971, CBS Sat 8:30–9:00
Sep 1971–Dec 1971, CBS Mon 10:00–10:30
Jan 1972–Aug 1972, CBS Thu 8:30–9:00

CAST:

Steve Douglas .... Fred MacMurray
Mike Douglas (1960–1965) .... Tim Considine
Robbie Douglas .... Don Grady
Chip Douglas .... Stanley Livingston
Michael Francis "Bub" O'Casey (1960–1964) .... William Frawley
Uncle Charley O'Casey (1965–1972) .... William Demarest
Sally Ann Morrison Douglas (1963–1965) .... Meredith MacRae
Ernie Thompson Douglas (1963–1972) .... Barry Livingston
Katie Miller Douglas (1967–1972) .... Tina Cole
Dave Welch (1965–1967) ..... John Howard
Dodie Harper Douglas (1969–1972) .... Dawn Lyn
Barbara Harper Douglas (1969–1972) .... Beverly Garland
Steve Douglas Jr. (1970–1972) .... Joseph Todd
Charley Douglas (1970–1972) .... Michael Todd
Robbie Douglas II (1970–1972) .... Daniel Todd
Fergus McBain Douglas (1971–1972) .... Fred MacMurray
Terri Dowling (1971–1972) .... Anne Francis
Polly Williams Douglas (1970–1972) .... Ronne Troup

THEME:

"Theme from *My Three Sons*," by Frank DeVol

This long-running family comedy had a Disney flavor to it. Fred MacMurray and Tim Considine had starred together in the hit Disney movie *The Shaggy Dog,* and Don Grady was a former *Mickey Mouse Club* mouseketeer. Even little Stanley Livingston was a show-business veteran, having appeared in several episodes of *The Adventures of Ozzie & Harriet.*

The "family" in this case was all-male. Steve Douglas, a consulting aviation engineer, lived in a medium-sized Midwestern city with his children. A widower, he seemed to spend more time raising his three sons than he did at his job, what with the usual growing pains of boys just beginning to date, going on camping trips, and the other "adventures" of middle-class suburbia. Steve also spent a good deal of time fending off attractive women, who wanted to marry him and take over that lovable, readymade family. Steve's father-in-law was "Bub" O'Casey, a lovable old coot who lived with them and served as a kind of housekeeper to the clan. When he left after five seasons to take a trip to Iceland (William Frawley had passed away during production), he was replaced by his brother, Uncle Charley, a retired sailor whose crusty disposition masked a soft heart. Others joining the cast in the early years were Sally, as Mike's fiancée, and Ernie, as the boy next door and Chip's pal. Tramp was the family dog.

When the series began in 1960, the boys were aged 18 (Mike), 14 (Robbie), and 7 (Chip). By the start of the 1965–1966 season, when the show moved from ABC to CBS, Tim Considine had grown out of the role as oldest son and wanted out of the series. In the first CBS episode, Mike and Sally got married and moved east so that he might accept a job teaching psychology on the college level. To reestablish the "three sons," Steve subsequently adopted the orphaned Ernie. Things went along much as before for the next two seasons.

In the fall of 1967, Steve moved the family from the Midwest to North Hollywood, California, where his job had taken him. Although the adjustment was not completely pleasant—many of the Douglases' new acquaintances were not too friendly at first—there were good sides to the move. Robbie fell in love with Katie Miller, one of his fellow students at college, and their romance blossomed into marriage before the end of the season. In the fall of 1968, the newlyweds discovered that Katie was pregnant and during that season she gave birth to triplets, Steve, Jr., Charley, and Robbie II—three sons, of course. 1969 finally brought new love to father Steve in the person of widow Barbara Harper, one of Ernie's teachers. They were married during the season and Barbara's young daughter Dodie joined the family. Even Chip (who was by now 17) got into the act, eloping with his college girl friend Polly Williams in the fall of 1970.

As if the sprawling family had not gotten big enough already, Steve's cousin, Fergus McBain Douglas, arrived in the fall of 1971 in search of a wife to take back home to Scotland. A nobleman in his native land, Lord Fergus fell in love with cocktail waitress Terri Dowling. She felt inadequate to go back to Scotland as royalty, but was eventually persuaded.

In its later years, as the size of the family on *My Three Sons* grew and separated into individual households, episodes could no longer include the entire group. More and more often, they dealt with the specific problems of only a part of the large cast of regulars, with different members taking the spotlight from week to week.

MY TRUE STORY

Dramatic Anthology

FIRST TELECAST: *May 5, 1950*

LAST TELECAST: *September 22, 1950*

BROADCAST HISTORY:

May 1950–Jun 1950, ABC Fri 8:30–9:00
Jun 1950–Sep 1950, ABC Fri 8:00–8:30

Early television, hungry for inexpensive material, tapped many sources. These romantic dramas were based on first-person stories from the pages of *My True Story* magazine. Examples: the conflict in a woman's mind when she must decide whether to marry for money or love; a forgotten actress makes a comeback and then dies; a man-hungry blonde's predicament.

MY WORLD AND WELCOME TO IT

Situation Comedy

FIRST TELECAST: *September 15, 1969*

LAST TELECAST: *September 7, 1972*

BROADCAST HISTORY:

Sep 1969–Sep 1970, NBC Mon 7:30–8:00
Jun 1972–Sep 1972, CBS Thu 8:00–8:30

CAST:

John Monroe .... William Windom
Ellen Monroe .... Joan Hotchkis
Lydia Monroe .... Lisa Gerritsen
Hamilton Greeley .... Harold J. Stone
Philip Jensen .... Henry Morgan

My World and Welcome To It was loosely based on the works of the late James Thurber. John Monroe was a writer and cartoonist whose overly active imagination was often as much of a problem as a blessing. As with most Thurber men, John was vaguely unsatisfied with his work, concerned about the direction his life was taking, and mortified by women. In his imaginary secret world he was king, but in real life he was somewhat dominated by his wife and terrified by his daughter. He would constantly muse about the predatory nature of women and was convinced that their sole function was to make his life miserable. Each episode opened with John making observations on a given situation before walking into an animated Thurber-like home in which his wife was reaching around to devour him. The use of Thurber-like cartoons to picture John's fears, as well as his dream world, gave this series a pleasant aspect of fantasy. Other than John's wife Ellen and daughter Lydia, the only two regulars were his publisher Hamilton Greeley and cynical fellow writer Philip Jensen. In the summer of 1972

CBS reran episodes of the original NBC series.

MYSTERIES OF CHINATOWN

Crime Drama

FIRST TELECAST: *December 4, 1949*

LAST TELECAST: *October 23, 1950*

BROADCAST HISTORY:

Dec 1949–May 1950, ABC Sun 9:30–10:00
May 1950–Sep 1950, ABC Sun 9:00–9:30
Sep 1950, ABC Tue 8:30–9:00
Oct 1950, ABC Mon 8:30–9:00

CAST:

Dr. Yat Fu ....Marvin Miller

ALSO:

Robert Bice

Marvin Miller portrayed Dr. Yat Fu, proprietor of an herb and curio shop in San Francisco's Chinatown, and an amateur sleuth of some note. The program originated in Hollywood and was seen in the East via kinescope.

MYSTERY IS MY BUSINESS

syndicated title for *Ellery Queen* (1954 edition)

MYSTERY PLAYHOUSE

see *Danger*

MYSTERY PLAYHOUSE STARRING BORIS KARLOFF

see *Starring Boris Karloff*

MYSTERY THEATER

see *Mark Saber*

MYSTERY THEATRE

see *Movies—Prior to 1961*

NBC ACTION PLAYHOUSE

Dramatic Anthology

FIRST TELECAST: *June 24, 1971*

LAST TELECAST: *September 5, 1972*

BROADCAST HISTORY:

Jun 1971–Sep 1971, NBC Thu 7:30–8:30
May 1972–Sep 1972, NBC Tue 8:30–9:30

HOST:

Peter Marshall

The filmed dramas presented as *NBC Action Playhouse* were reruns of former episodes of *Bob Hope Presents the Chrysler Theatre*. Peter Marshall taped new introductions for the episodes, to replace the original introductions done by Hope. In 1971 this series was the summer replacement for *The Flip Wilson Show*. In 1972 some of the 1971 episodes were aired again with the same Peter Marshall introductions they had had the previous summer.

NBC ADVENTURE THEATRE

Dramatic Anthology

FIRST TELECAST: *July 24, 1971*

LAST TELECAST: *September 7, 1972*

BROADCAST HISTORY:

Jul 1971–Sep 1971, NBC Sat 7:30–8:30
Jun 1972–Sep 1972, NBC Thu 8:00–9:00

HOST:

Art Fleming (1971)
Ed McMahon (1972)

NBC Adventure Theatre consisted of reruns of episodes of *Bob Hope Presents the Chrysler Theatre*. Art Fleming was the host in 1971 and Ed McMahon in 1972. The introductions that they provided to the filmed dramas replaced the original ones that had been done by Bob Hope. Some of the shows aired in 1972 were repeats of episodes aired in 1971.

NBC CINEMA PLAYHOUSE

see *Movies—Prior to 1961*

NBC COMEDY HOUR

Comedy Variety

FIRST TELECAST: *January 8, 1956*

LAST TELECAST: *June 10, 1956*

BROADCAST HISTORY:

Jan 1956–Jun 1956, NBC Sun 8:00–9:00

REGULARS:

Jonathan Winters
Hy Averback
Gale Storm

When *NBC Comedy Hour* premiered in January of 1956, the network envisioned it as a showcase for new comedy talent. It was a rather unstructured vaudevillian collection of skits, monologues, song-and-dance numbers, one-liners, blackouts, pantomime, etc. There was to be no regular headliner and new young performers were to work with veterans. Initial reaction from both critics and viewers was extremely negative and the concept was altered drastically. The enormous writing staff was reduced substantially, musical production numbers were added, and each show was designed to have more of a sense of continuity than the disorganized, fragmented original. Gale Storm became the regular hostess at the start of February and remained for two months, to be replaced by a succession of weekly hosts. The only two other regular performers were comedian Jonathan Winters and actor-announcer Hy Averback.

NBC COMEDY PLAYHOUSE

Comedy Anthology

FIRST TELECAST: *June 24, 1968*

LAST TELECAST: *September 5, 1970*

BROADCAST HISTORY:

Jun 1968–Aug 1968, NBC Mon 9:00–10:00
Aug 1970–Sep 1970, NBC Sat 7:30–8:30

HOST:

Monty Hall (1968)
Jack Kelly (1970)

The full-hour light comedies presented as *NBC Comedy Playhouse* were reruns of episodes of *Bob Hope Presents the Chrysler Theatre.* Monty Hall was the host of the 1968 edition and Jack Kelly was the host in 1970. They provided introductions to replace the originals that had been done by Bob Hope.

NBC COMEDY THEATER

Comedy Anthology

FIRST TELECAST: *June 7, 1971*

LAST TELECAST: *September 2, 1972*

BROADCAST HISTORY:

Jun 1971–Aug 1971, NBC Mon 8:00–9:00
Jul 1972–Sep 1972, NBC Sat 8:00–9:00

HOST:

Jack Kelly

The light romantic comedies that comprised *NBC Comedy Theater* were filmed reruns of episodes of *Bob Hope Presents the Chrysler Theatre.* Jack Kelly was the host and provided introductions to replace the originals done by Hope. In 1971 this was the summer replacement for *Laugh-In* and in 1972 for *Emergency.*

NBC CONCERT HALL

Music

FIRST TELECAST: *August 29, 1948*

LAST TELECAST: *September 26, 1948*

BROADCAST HISTORY:

Aug 1948–Sep 1948, NBC Sun 9:00–9:30

A brief summer series of excerpts from classical music and ballet, live and on film.

NBC FOLLIES

Comedy Variety

FIRST TELECAST: *September 13, 1973*

LAST TELECAST: *December 27, 1973*

BROADCAST HISTORY:

Sep 1973–Dec 1973, NBC Thu 10:00–11:00

REGULARS:

Sammy Davis Jr.
Mickey Rooney

Although there was no host on *NBC Follies,* Sammy Davis Jr. and Mickey Rooney were two performers who appeared in virtually every episode. Without a host, the various acts—sketches, comedy monologues, musical numbers, etc.—were arranged to flow in much the same manner that a vaudeville show did, with one turn leading into the next. Guest talent was featured in each show.

NBC MYSTERY MOVIE, THE

Police/Detective

FIRST TELECAST: *September 15, 1971*

LAST TELECAST: *September 4, 1977*

BROADCAST HISTORY:

Sep 1971–Jan 1974, NBC Wed 8:30–10:00
Sep 1972–Sep 1974, NBC Sun 8:30–10:00
Jan 1974–Sep 1974, NBC Tue 8:30–10:00
Sep 1974–Sep 1975, NBC Sun 8:30–10:30
Sep 1975–Sep 1976, NBC Sun 9:00–11:00
Oct 1976–Apr 1977, NBC Sun Various
May 1977–Sep 1977, NBC Sun 8:00–9:30

The NBC Mystery Movie was an umbrella title used to cover a number of rotating series that appeared in the same time slot on different weeks. The first *Mystery Movie* series premiered in 1971 on Wednesday nights, and included *Columbo, McCloud,* and *McMillan and Wife,* three series that had considerable success over the years.

Due to the popularity of the *Mystery Movie* concept in the 1971–1972 season NBC decided to try another one. The three original elements were moved to Sunday night (retitled *The NBC Sunday Mystery Movie*) and three new ones were introduced on Wednesday, under the new blanket title *The NBC Wednesday Mystery Movie.* However, *Madigan, Cool Million,* and *Banacek* were not as successful as their predecessors, nor were any of the elements that were subsequently tried. Following is a listing of all the various *Mystery Movie* elements aired over the years. Details on each will be found under their separate title headings.

1971–1972: *Mystery Movie* (Wed.): *Columbo, McCloud, McMillan and Wife*

1972–1973: *Sunday Mystery Movie: Columbo, McCloud, McMillan, Hec Ramsey*

Wednesday Mystery Movie: Madigan, Cool Million, Banacek

1973–1974: *Sunday Mystery Movie: Columbo, McCloud, McMillan, Hec Ramsey*

Wednesday Mystery Movie: Madigan, Tenafly, Faraday & Company, The Snoop Sisters. (Series moved to Tuesday effective January 1972, retitled *NBC Tuesday Mystery Movie.*)

1974–1975: *Sunday Mystery Movie: Columbo, McCloud, McMillan, Amy Prentiss*

1975–1976: *Sunday Mystery Movie: Columbo, McCloud, McMillan, McCoy*

1976–1977: *Sunday Mystery Movie: Columbo, McCloud, McMillan, Quincy M.E.* (to December 1976); *Lanigan's Rabbi* (effective January 1977).

NBC NEWS ENCORE

Documentary

FIRST TELECAST: *June 26, 1966*
LAST TELECAST: *August 21, 1966*
BROADCAST HISTORY:
Jun 1966–Aug 1966, NBC Sun 6:30–7:30
HOST:
Robert Abernathy

Host Robert Abernathy introduced and concluded each of the episodes of *NBC News Encore,* a series of rebroadcasts of selected NBC news documentaries, the bulk of which had originally aired as *NBC News Actuality Specials.*

NBC PLAYHOUSE

see *Variety*

NBC PLAYHOUSE

Dramatic Anthology

FIRST TELECAST: *June 28, 1960*
LAST TELECAST: *September 6, 1960*
BROADCAST HISTORY:
Jun 1960–Sep 1960, NBC Tue 8:30–9:00
HOSTESS:
Jeanne Bal

Actress Jeanne Bal hosted this summer series composed of reruns of episodes of *The Loretta Young Show* in which Miss Young had not starred. *NBC Playhouse* alternated with *The Gas Company Playhouse.*

NBC PRESENTS

see *Movies—Prior to 1961*

NBC REPERTORY THEATRE

Dramatic Anthology

FIRST TELECAST: *April 17, 1949*
LAST TELECAST: *July 10, 1949*
BROADCAST HISTORY:
Apr 1949–Jul 1949, NBC Sun 9:00–10:00
PRODUCER:
Owen Davis, Jr.

Early live dramatic program, presenting an original TV play or adaptation each week. Many noted stars appeared during the course of the series, which did not utilize a repertory company (despite the title) but had a new cast for each telecast. Perhaps the most notable single production was *Macbeth,* the annual Shakespearean production of The Players, a New York theatrical association. Among those appearing during the course of the series were Walter Hampden, Joyce Redman, Leo G. Carroll, Ralph Bellamy, John Carradine, David Wayne, and many others.

NBC REPORTS

Documentary

FIRST TELECAST: *September 12, 1972*
LAST TELECAST: *September 4, 1973*
BROADCAST HISTORY:
Sep 1972–Sep 1973, NBC Tue 10:00–11:00

NBC Reports aired on a regular basis during the 1972–1973 season, presenting news documentaries on various subjects of current interest. It had no permanent host or narrator. Some of the subjects covered were "Pensions: The Broken Promise," "What Price Health," "And When the War Is Over . . . The American Military in the '70s," "The Meaning of Watergate" (on May 22, 1973, five days after the start of the hearings which ran all that summer), "American Communism Today," and, in a special three-hour final telecast, "The Energy Crisis—An American White Paper." The title *NBC Reports* has also frequently been used for irregularly scheduled documentaries.

NBC SPORTS IN ACTION

Sports

FIRST TELECAST: *May 23, 1965*

LAST TELECAST: *September 5, 1965*

BROADCAST HISTORY:

May 1965–Sep 1965, NBC Sun 6:30–7:30

HOST:

Jim Simpson

NBC Sports in Action was an early attempt to compete with *ABC's Wide World of Sports*. Jim Simpson was the regular host and narrator of the series, which covered various types of sporting events in depth, with action footage of the event in progress, as well as interviews with and profiles of sports celebrities. Such sports as surfing, skiing, auto racing, rugby, sailing, and lacrosse—none of them seen on a regular basis on American TV—were featured in all or part of various episodes of this show. Although it aired in the evening only from May to August, *NBC Sports in Action* had actually premiered in January 1965 and ran until June 1966, usually airing on Sunday afternoons.

NBC SPORTS SPOT

Sports Commentary

FIRST TELECAST: *January 10, 1958*

LAST TELECAST: *January 24, 1958*

BROADCAST HISTORY:

Jan 1958, NBC Fri 10:45–11:00

NBC Sports Spot replaced *Fight Beat* as the show filling the time between the end of the bout on *The Gillette Cavalcade of Sports* and the start of the 11:00 P.M. local news. Each week an outstanding nationally known sportswriter was to be host to a famous sports personality whom he would interview. Red Barber served as host for the first two weeks and Bud Palmer was the host on the third. After only three weeks on the air, however, *NBC Sports Spot* was replaced by *Phillies Jackpot Bowling*.

NBC SUNDAY MYSTERY MOVIE, THE

see *NBC Mystery Movie, The*

NBC TUESDAY MYSTERY MOVIE, THE

see *NBC Mystery Movie, The*

NBC WEDNESDAY MYSTERY MOVIE, THE

see *NBC Mystery Movie, The*

NBC'S BEST SELLERS

Drama

FIRST TELECAST: *September 30, 1976*

LAST TELECAST: *April 25, 1977*

BROADCAST HISTORY:

Sep 1976–Jan 1977, NBC Thu 9:00–10:00
Jan 1977–Apr 1977, NBC Thu 9:00–11:00
Apr 1977, NBC Mon 9:00–11:00

NBC's Best Sellers was the umbrella title used to describe a collection of four novels which were serialized in consecutive installments. In order of their showing they were: *Captains and the Kings* (September 30–November 25), *Once an Eagle* (December 2–January 13), *Seventh Avenue* (February 10–24), and *The Rhinemann Exchange* (March 10–24). The first two were aired primarily in one-hour installments, except for the first and last chapters which ran two hours in length, while the latter two ran in two-hour segments. Of the four, only *Captains and the Kings* was repeated, all in two-hour segments, with its concluding chapter running on *NBC's Monday Night at the Movies*. See under individual titles for specific details.

NBC'S SATURDAY NIGHT LIVE

Comedy/Variety

FIRST TELECAST: *October 11, 1975*

LAST TELECAST:

BROADCAST HISTORY:

Oct 1975– , NBC Sat 11:30–1:00 A.M.

REGULARS:

Gilda Radner
Garrett Morris
Jane Curtin
Laraine Newman
John Belushi
Jim Henson's Muppets (1975–1976)
Chevy Chase (1975–1976)
Dan Aykroyd
Albert Brooks (1975–1976)
Gary Weis (1976–1977)
Bill Murray (1977–)

NBC's Saturday Night was an attempt to bring young, innovative comedy and the excitement of live television to late night viewers (practically everything else on TV is now on film or tape). It featured "The Not Ready for Prime Time Players," a repertory company of wacky comics who presented 90 minutes of topical satire, straight comedy, and music. Each week a different guest star served as the host and the person around whom many of the sketches were written. Those who starred more than once during the first two seasons were Candice Bergen, Buck Henry, Elliott Gould, Lily Tomlin, Dick Cavett, Steve Martin, Eric Idle and Paul Simon. Presidential Press Secretary Ron Nessen made a controversial (but good humored) appearance, as did consumer advocate Ralph Nader.

The chief "discovery" of *Saturday Night* during its initial season was comic Chevy Chase, famous for his opening pratfall and his role as the straight-faced young newsman reporting preposterous headlines on "Weekend Update." His trademark line was, "Good evening. I'm Chevy Chase and you're not." Jane Curtin took over the role as newscaster after Chevy left in November 1976. Other frequent bits included Chevy as bumbling President Ford, Dan Aykroyd as candidate, and later President, Jimmy Carter, Gilda Radner as a lisping Barbara Walters (Ba Ba Wawa), and, later, Gilda as rambling, loudmouthed newscaster Rosanne Rosanna-Dana. Originally Jim Henson's Muppets were a regular feature, as was a short, offbeat film produced each week by Albert Brooks (later the films were by Gary Weis). Also seen on virtually every telecast were satiric "commercials" for everything from the telephone company to milk. A continuing domestic comedy, "The Coneheads" (yes, they had cones for heads), was also added.

Despite the departure of its brightest star, Chevy Chase, *Saturday Night* became more and more popular in succeeding years, and by 1977–1978 it was by far the most popular program in late night television, surpassing the longtime champ *The Tonight Show* (which aired on different nights of the week). Steve Martin was especially popular as host, but an all time audience record was set when a "nobody" hosted the show—80-year-old Mrs. Miskel Spillman, who had won an "Anyone Can Host" write-in contest.

NFL ACTION

Sports

FIRST TELECAST: *May 12, 1971*
LAST TELECAST: *September 8, 1971*
BROADCAST HISTORY:
May 1971–Sep 1971, ABC Wed 10:30–11:00
NARRATOR:
John Facenda (and others)

Football films focusing on various players, teams, and big games.

N.Y.P.D.

Police

FIRST TELECAST: *September 5, 1967*
LAST TELECAST: *September 16, 1969*
BROADCAST HISTORY:
Sep 1967–Sep 1969, ABC Tue 9:30–10:00
CAST:
Det. Lt. Mike Haines ....Jack Warden
Det. Jeff Ward ....Robert Hooks
Det. Johnny Corso ....Frank Converse

New York City was the real star of this police series. Much of the filming was done on location there, and the city's underworld denizens were realistically portrayed. The three N.Y.P.D. plainclothes detectives were experienced Mike Haines, 18 years on the force, the younger Johnny Corso, and black officer Jeff Ward. Together they tracked murderers, extortionists, drug pushers, bombers, rapists, and other thugs around the bustling city. Locales varied from the Bowery to Wall Street, the Empire State Building to Shubert Alley, Greenwich Village to Times Square. The program was commended by real-life Mayor John Lindsay, who permitted filming of some scenes in City Hall. *N.Y.P.D.* was produced with the cooperation of the New York Police Department, with episodes based on actual cases.

NAKED CITY

Police

FIRST TELECAST: *September 30, 1958*
LAST TELECAST: *September 11, 1963*
BROADCAST HISTORY:
Sep 1958–Sep 1959, ABC Tue 9:30–10:00
Oct 1960–Sep 1963, ABC Wed 10:00–11:00
CAST:
Det. Lt. Dan Muldoon (1958–1959)
.... John McIntire
Det. Jim Halloran (1958–1959)
.......................James Franciscus
Janet Halloran (1958–1959)
.... Suzanne Storrs
Ptlm./Sgt. Frank Arcaro ..... Harry Bellaver
Lt. Mike Parker (1959–1963)
.... Horace McMahon

Det. Adam Flint (1960–1963) . . . Paul Burke
Libby (1960–1963) . . . . .Nancy Malone

THEME (1960–1963):

"Naked City Theme" ("Somewhere in the Night"), by Billy May and Milton Raskin

This popular series was shot on location all over the New York City metropolis, from the Staten Island Ferry to Times Square. A feeling of gritty reality pervaded the stories as veteran cop Dan Muldoon and his young sidekick Jim Halloran ran down the murderers and muggers, petty thieves and swindlers who inhabited the city's seamy side.

The program began undergoing cast changes even in its first season. Det. Muldoon was killed in a spectacular chase sequence seen in a March 1959 episode, when his squad car plowed into a gasoline tank truck (stunt men were often used in *Naked City* for such effects). Lt. Mike Parker became the wizened old pro for the remainder of that season, and also returned when the series came back in hour-long form after a year's layoff. With him in the 1960–1963 run was a new young partner, Det. Adam Flint, Flint's girl friend Libby, and Sgt. Frank Arcaro (who had been a patrolman from 1958–1959).

Parker, portrayed by steely-eyed Horace McMahon, was the perfect hard-nosed cop for a hard city, and his portrayal helped make the series a success. Added, too, was some dramatic city-at-dawn theme music by Billy May. But the star was New York itself, where, as the narrator intoned, "There are eight million stories in the Naked City . . ."

Based on a story by Mark Hellinger, which was made into a 1948 movie titled *Naked City*.

NAKIA

Police

FIRST TELECAST: *September 21, 1974*
LAST TELECAST: *December 28, 1974*
BROADCAST HISTORY:

Sep 1974–Dec 1974, ABC Sat 10:00–11:00

CAST:

Deputy Nakia Parker . . . . . . .Robert Forster
Sheriff Sam Jericho . . . . . . .Arthur Kennedy
Irene James . . . . .Gloria DeHaven
Deputy Hubbel Martin . . . . . .Taylor Lacher

This action series was about a modern-day deputy sheriff in a New Mexico city. Nakia was of Indian heritage, and he frequently found his loyalties divided between ancient tribal customs and modern police methods. Symbolic was his transportation, which alternated between pickup truck and horse rather than a squad car. His cases involved everything from violent demonstrations on the reservation to inflammatory political scheming on the town council. Irene James was the secretary in the sheriff's office.

Filmed in and around Albuquerque, New Mexico.

NAME OF THE GAME, THE

Adventure

FIRST TELECAST: *September 20, 1968*
LAST TELECAST: *September 10, 1971*
BROADCAST HISTORY:

Sep 1968–Sep 1971, NBC Fri 8:30–10:00

CAST:

Glenn Howard . . . . .Gene Barry
Jeff Dillon . . . . .Tony Franciosa
Dan Farrell . . . . .Robert Stack
Peggy Maxwell . . . . .Susan Saint James
Joe Sample . . . . .Ben Murphy
Andy Hill .Cliff Potter
Ross Craig . . . . .Mark Miller

The Name of the Game was actually three series under one title. Each of the three stars of the show, Robert Stack, Tony Franciosa, and Gene Barry, was featured in his own self-contained episodes. The connection between them was Howard Publications, a Los Angeles–based publishing empire that had been built up from scratch by its dynamic owner, Glenn Howard. Glenn's position of power, his confrontations with business and political enemies, and his own flamboyant life-style were portrayed in his portion of *The Name of the Game*. Within the Howard empire were investigative correspondent Jeff Dillon and editor Dan Farrell. Dillon was a super-aggressive former newsboy who had clawed his way up to a position of power and respect working for Howard's *People Magazine*. Farrell was a former FBI agent (possibly type-casting for Robert Stack, Eliot Ness in *The Untouchables*) who had gone into the publishing business because it provided a position from which to make the public aware of the threats posed by organized crime. He was the senior editor of *Crime Magazine*. Common to all three elements of *The Name of the Game* was

Peggy Maxwell, the bright, ambitious, and occasionally somewhat kooky editorial assistant to all three men. Joe, Andy, and Ross were reporters with recurring, but not weekly, roles. What was "The Name of the Game"? Well, the title of the 1966 TV movie on which this series was based was more explicit. It was called *Fame Is the Name of the Game.*

NAME THAT TUNE

Quiz/Audience Participation

FIRST TELECAST: *June 29, 1953*

LAST TELECAST: *October 19, 1959*

BROADCAST HISTORY:

Jun 1953–Jun 1954, NBC Mon 8:00–8:30
Sep 1954–Mar 1955, CBS Thu 10:30–11:00
Sep 1955–Sep 1958, CBS Tue 7:30–8:00
Sep 1958–Oct 1959, CBS Mon 7:30–8:00

EMCEE:

Red Benson (1953–1954)
Bill Cullen (1954–1955)
George de Witt (1955–1959)

Contestants on *Name That Tune* competed with each other to identify the title of a song being played by the Harry Salter Orchestra. When a contestant thought he knew the title, he would race his competitor to ring a bell that was 25 feet away to have the opportunity to guess the title. The biggest winner at the end of each show had the opportunity to win a $1,600 jackpot by correctly identifying seven songs in 30 seconds. Viewers submitted the songs used in this "Golden Medley" and won as much money as the contestants if their song list was used. As the era of the big-money quiz show arrived, a variation in this jackpot system was devised. People working in teams could return each week and try to build their winnings up to a possible $25,000 in the renamed "Golden Medley Marathon." They could win $5,000 per week for a maximum of five weeks.

NAME'S THE SAME, THE

Quiz/Panel

FIRST TELECAST: *December 5, 1951*

LAST TELECAST: *October 7, 1955*

BROADCAST HISTORY:

Dec 1951–Nov 1952, ABC Wed 7:30–8:00
Dec 1952–Aug 1954, ABC Tue 10:30–11:00
Oct 1954–Jun 1955, ABC Mon 7:30–8:00
Jun 1955–Sep 1955, ABC Tue 10:00–10:30
Sep 1955–Oct 1955, ABC Fri 10:00–10:30

EMCEE:

Robert Q. Lewis (1951–1954)
Dennis James (1954–1955)
Bob Elliott and Ray Goulding (1955)
Clifton Fadiman (1955)

PANELISTS:

Abe Burrows (1951–1952)
Joan Alexander
Meredith Willson (1951–1953)
Bill Stern (1953–1954)
Gene Rayburn (1953–1955)
Bess Myerson (1954–1955)
Roger Price (1954–1955)
Audrey Meadows (1955)

PRODUCERS:

Mark Goodson and Bill Todman

This simple variation on *What's My Line* (produced by the same company) could well have been called *What's My Name.* The gimmick was that each of the contestants appearing on the show, whose names the panel had to guess, had the same name as a famous person or an object. Thus ordinary folks who happened to be named A. Garter, A. Beard, Abraham Lincoln, Mona Lisa, or Napoleon Bonaparte tried to stump the panel.

The regular panel was fairly stable during the program's first two years, but then considerable turnover began to take place. In addition to those listed above (who lasted six months or more), such celebrities as Jerry Lester, Carl Reiner, Basil Rathbone, and Mike Wallace appeared for shorter runs.

NANCY

Situation Comedy

FIRST TELECAST: *September 17, 1970*

LAST TELECAST: *January 7, 1971*

BROADCAST HISTORY:

Sep 1970–Jan 1971, NBC Thu 9:30–10:00

CAST:

Nancy Smith ....Renne Jarrett
Dr. Adam Hudson ....John Fink
Uncle Everett ....Robert F. Simon
Abigail Townsend ....Celeste Holm
Turner ....William Bassett
Rodriguez ....Ernesto Macias

Nancy was the attractive young daughter of the President of the United States. She met a young veterinarian from Center City, Iowa, and they fell in love. Unfortunately, being under constant surveillance by secret service agents Turner and Rodriguez did nothing to promote the romance, and Nancy's chaperone Abigail and Adam's Uncle Everett also seemed constantly to get in the way, not to mention the press. The President was never shown on camera, but his aides were, and his voice was heard on occasion. The couple got married in the November 5, 1970, episode, but even that could not save the series from cancellation.

NANCY DREW MYSTERIES, THE

Adventure

FIRST TELECAST: *February 6, 1977*

LAST TELECAST: *January 1, 1978*

BROADCAST HISTORY:

Feb 1977–Jan 1978, ABC Sun 7:00–8:00

CAST:

Nancy Drew ....Pamela Sue Martin
Carson Drew ....William Schallert
Ned Nickerson (1977) .... George O'Hanlon
George Fayne (1977) .... Jean Rasey
George Fayne (1977–1978)
.... Susan Buckner
Bess ....Ruth Cox

Nancy Drew was the girls' equivalent of *The Hardy Boys Mysteries*, with which it alternated on Sunday nights. Both programs featured teenage sleuths helping adults solve exciting (but not usually violent) mysteries, such as robberies, haunted houses, blackmail attempts on a college football star, etc.

Nancy was 18 and the daughter of famed criminal lawyer Carson Drew, a widower. George (a girl) was her buddy, not particularly brave but willing to stick by Nancy through thick and thin. Ned was her father's law-student assistant, always willing to help (later he became an investigator for the district attorney's office, and more anxious to keep Nancy out of cases than in them). The Drews' home base was River Heights, a suburb of New York, but the mysteries took them far and wide.

In the fall of 1977 Nancy Drew appeared in several joint episodes with the Hardy Boys. Then in February 1978 the two series were combined under the title *Hardy Boys/Nancy Drew Mysteries*, at which time Pamela Sue Martin left the program. See *Hardy Boys Mysteries* for further details.

Based on the Nancy Drew books by Carolyn Keene.

NANCY WALKER SHOW, THE

Situation Comedy

FIRST TELECAST: *September 30, 1976*

LAST TELECAST: *December 23, 1976*

BROADCAST HISTORY:

Sep 1976–Dec 1976, ABC Thu 9:30–10:00

CAST:

Nancy Kitteridge ....Nancy Walker
Lt. Cdr. Kenneth Kitteridge
.... William Daniels
Terry Folson ....Ken Olfson
Lorraine ....Beverly Archer
Glen ....James Cromwell
Michael Futterman ....Sparky Marcus
Teddy Futterman ....William Shallert

EXECUTIVE PRODUCER:

Norman Lear

THEME:

"Nancy's Blues," by Marilyn & Alan Bergman and Marvin Hamlisch

Sarcastic, wisecracking Nancy Kitteridge had an ideal life. Ten months of the year she was an active career woman, head of the Nancy Kitteridge Talent Agency which she ran from her Hollywood apartment. Two months of the year, when her Navy husband of 29 years returned for his annual shore leave, she was a newlywed, madly in love. Then disaster struck. Hubby came home to stay, and he seemed intent on both bringing Navy-style order to her chaotic life and making up for 29 years of lost time romantically. Ken didn't see why that gay, unemployed actor named Terry should be kept around the house (Terry earned his room and board by serving as Nancy's secretary), and in fact he thought she should close down the talent agency entirely. Adding to the confusion was Nancy's hand-wringing, hypochondriac daughter Lorraine, son-in-law Glen, and Michael, the precocious, six-year-old son of boy-wonder TV network executive Teddy Futterman.

NANETTE FABRAY SHOW, THE

see *Westinghouse Playhouse*

NANNY AND THE PROFESSOR

Situation Comedy

FIRST TELECAST: *January 21, 1970*

LAST TELECAST: *December 27, 1971*

BROADCAST HISTORY:

Jan 1970–Aug 1970, ABC Wed 7:30–8:00
Sep 1970–Sep 1971, ABC Fri 8:00–8:30
Sep 1971–Dec 1971, ABC Mon 8:00–8:30

CAST:

Phoebe Figalilly ....Juliet Mills

Prof. Harold Everett ....Richard Long
Hal Everett ....David Doremus
Butch Everett ....Trent Lehman
Prudence Everett ....Kim Richards

Phoebe was an uncanny young nanny who breezed in unannounced from England and captivated the Everett household. She arrived just at the right time, as Miss Dunbar, Prof. Everett's fifth housekeeper in a year, had just quit in utter frustration at trying to keep order in the chaotic household. That left the widowed mathematics professor in charge of Hal, a 12-year-old with a fascination for scientific experiments; eight-year-old Butch, who was into everything; and five-year-old Prudence, a musical prodigy who practiced the same piano piece incessantly; plus Waldo, the family sheepdog, Myrtle, the guinea pig, and other pets. Nanny's sunny disposition and apparently psychic abilities (could she really talk to the animals?) won everybody's heart in this relentlessly cute comedy.

NASH AIRFLYTE THEATER

Dramatic Anthology

FIRST TELECAST: *September 21, 1950*

LAST TELECAST: *March 15, 1951*

BROADCAST HISTORY:

Sep 1950–Mar 1951, CBS Thu 10:30–11:00

HOST:

William Gaxton

This live New York–originated anthology series aired during the 1950–1951 season and was hosted by William Gaxton. The range of material was extremely varied. John Payne starred in the premiere telecast, a Western adapted from the O. Henry story "A Double-Dyed Deceiver." Metropolitan Opera soprano Marguerite Piazza starred in an original musical comedy called "The Box Supper," and Patricia Morison was featured in an adaptation of the Gilbert and Sullivan operetta *Trial by Jury.* On the more serious dramatic side, Barbara Bel Geddes starred in the first televised adaptation of a John Steinbeck story, "Molly Morgan." Grace Kelly, Otto Kruger, Fredric March, and Lee Bowman also starred in straight plays on this series.

NASHVILLE 99

Police

FIRST TELECAST: *April 1, 1977*

LAST TELECAST: *April 22, 1977*

BROADCAST HISTORY:

Apr 1977, CBS Fri 8:00–9:00

CAST:

Det. Lt. Stonewall Jackson "Stoney" Huff .... Claude Akins
Det. Trace Mayne ....Jerry Reed
Birdie Huff ....Lucille Benson

Filmed on location in Nashville, and utilizing many Country music performers as guest stars playing themselves, *Nashville 99* was the story of a Southern lawman fighting crime in the C & W capital of the world. Stoney Huff was a veteran cop who, with the aid of his partner Trace (played by Country music star Jerry Reed), fought organized crime, chased down kidnappers, and performed other law-enforcement duties in this short-lived series.

NAT "KING" COLE SHOW, THE

Musical Variety

FIRST TELECAST: *November 5, 1956*

LAST TELECAST: *December 17, 1957*

BROADCAST HISTORY:

Nov 1956–Jun 1957, NBC Mon 7:30–7:45
Jul 1957–Sep 1957, NBC Tue 10:00–10:30
Sep 1957–Dec 1957, NBC Tue 7:30–8:00

REGULARS:

Nat "King" Cole
The Boataneers (1956)
The Herman McCoy Singers
The Randy Van Horne Singers (1957)
The Jerry Graff Singers (1957)
The Cheerleaders (1957)
Nelson Riddle and His Orchestra

Nat "King" Cole was a man ahead of his time, and that fact cost him his network series. When his 15-minute show premiered in 1956, he became the first major black performer to headline a network variety series. There had been previous attempts at black series, but they were either short-lived fill-ins with lesser-known talent such as *Sugar Hill Times* in 1949 and *Hazel Scott* in 1950, or rather degrading parodies such as *Beulah* or *Amos 'n' Andy.* Nat's short Monday evening show, which filled the remainder of the half-hour in which NBC aired its nightly news program, allowed him little more than the opportunity to sing a couple of songs and occasionally welcome a guest vocalist. The following July, Nat moved to Tuesdays with an expanded half-hour show, allowing time for more variety and guests.

Throughout its run, however, *The Nat "King" Cole Show* was plagued with problems. It failed to attract a significant audience, and therefore sponsors were reluctant to underwrite the show. From 1956–1957 Nat averaged only 19 percent of the viewing audience, compared to the 50 percent who were watching *Robin Hood* on CBS. Nat even trailed a documentary-travelogue on ABC, called *Bold Journey*, which got 21 percent of the audience (the remaining 10 percent were watching non-network programs).

Despite widespread apathy on the part of viewers and sponsors, NBC did not give up on the show, keeping it on the air, at a loss, through the fall of 1957. The performing community was well aware of Nat's sponsor problems, and many stars appeared on the show for minimum fees as personal favors to him, in an effort to save the show. Virtually every black musical star showed up at one time or another, including Count Basie, Mahalia Jackson, Pearl Bailey, Billy Eckstine, Sammy Davis Jr., the Mills Brothers, Cab Calloway, Ella Fitzgerald, and Harry Belafonte. Nat had his white supporters too, among them Stan Kenton, Frankie Laine, Mel Torme, Peggy Lee, Gogi Grant, Tony Martin, and Tony Bennett. But the effort was in vain. It would be another decade before black entertainers could begin to make a significant dent in the mass medium of television.

NATIONAL BARN DANCE, THE

see *ABC Barn Dance*

NATIONAL BOWLING CHAMPIONS

Sports

FIRST TELECAST: *April 8, 1956*

LAST TELECAST: *December 29, 1957*

BROADCAST HISTORY:

Apr 1956–Dec 1956, NBC Sun 10:30–11:00
Sep 1957–Dec 1957, ABC Sun 8:30–9:00

COMMENTATOR:

"Whispering" Joe Wilson

In 1956 *National Bowling Champions* was telecast live from Chicago. Two professional bowlers competed in a three-game match, the last game and a half telecast on the air. The winner received $1 for every pin knocked down, $10 for every pin in excess of 700 for the series, and $10,000 for a perfect "300" game.

Essentially the same show, with some minor changes, returned on ABC in the fall of 1957, under the title *Bowling Stars*. Also originating from Chicago, the ABC show was filmed in advance, and the winner who, as on NBC, would return the following week to defend his "King of the Hill" title, won a minimum of $1,000. The bonuses for scores in excess of 700 applied to both bowlers, with the loser taking home $1 for every pin knocked down (instead of the flat $500 on NBC), and the $10,000 bonus for a "300" game was still in effect. *Bowling Stars* moved to Sunday afternoons in 1958.

NATIONAL VELVET

Adventure

FIRST TELECAST: *September 18, 1960*

LAST TELECAST: *September 10, 1962*

BROADCAST HISTORY:

Sep 1960–Sep 1961, NBC Sun 8:00–8:30
Sep 1961–Sep 1962, NBC Mon 8:00–8:30

CAST:

Velvet Brown ....Lori Martin
Martha Brown ....Ann Doran
Mi Taylor ....James McCallion
Herbert Brown ....Arthur Space
Edwina Brown ....Carole Wells
Donald Brown ....Joseph Scott
Teddy ....Carl Crow
John Hadley (1961–1962) .... Ricky Kelman

National Velvet, with its story of a girl and her dreams to run her horse in a championship race, is a classic young people's novel. The movie version (1944) had propelled child actress Elizabeth Taylor to stardom. For TV the setting was changed from England to a Midwestern American dairy farm. Twelve-year-old Velvet had a beautiful chestnut thoroughbred named King, and her greatest dream in the whole world was to train King well enough to run in the Grand National Steeplechase. Velvet's parent's, Herbert and Martha, who ran the small diary farm, shared her love and hopes. Helping her train King was Mi Taylor, an ex-jockey who worked around the farm as a handyman. Also in the cast were Velvet's teenage sister Winna, her younger brother Donald, Winna's boy friend Teddy, and Donald's friend John. The episodes dealt with the other members of the family on occasion, but centered mostly on Velvet and King.

NATIONAL WOMEN'S PROFESSIONAL BASEBALL LEAGUE GAMES

see *Baseball*

NATION'S FUTURE, THE

Debate

FIRST TELECAST: *November 12, 1960*

LAST TELECAST: *September 16, 1961*

BROADCAST HISTORY:

Nov 1960–Sep 1961, NBC Sat 9:30–10:30

MODERATOR:

John K. M. McCaffery (1960–1961)
Edwin Newman (1961)

The Nation's Future was a live weekly debate series in which two internationally known public figures, often politicians, expressed their opposing views on a specific issue of national interest. Topics covered ranged from foreign policy and social services to censorship and birth control. On occasion the first half-hour of the show was national with local stations filling the second half-hour with their own discussion of the issue being covered. John K. M. McCaffery was the moderator through May 27, 1961, and was replaced on June 10, 1961, by Edwin Newman.

NATURE OF THINGS, THE

Instruction

FIRST TELECAST: *February 5, 1948*

LAST TELECAST: *August 29, 1952*

BROADCAST HISTORY:

Feb 1948–Mar 1948, NBC Thu 9:45–10:00
Apr 1948–Dec 1948, NBC Thu 8:15–8:30
Dec 1948–May 1949, NBC Mon various 15 minute
Jul 1949–Aug 1949, NBC Mon 9:30–9:45
Sep 1949–Feb 1950, NBC Sat 7:30–7:45
Mar 1950–Jun 1950, NBC Sat 6:45–7:00
Jun 1950–Sep 1950, NBC Wed 8:15–8:30
Jun 1951–Aug 1951, NBC Fri 10:45–11:00
Jul 1952–Aug 1952, NBC Fri 10:45–11:00

HOST:

Dr. Roy K. Marshall

Dr. Roy K. Marshall of the Fels Planetarium was one of early TV's favorite scientists. His live science program, which was telecast from Philadelphia, featured illustrated talks and interviews on many subjects, including physics, astronomy, and the weather. One early 1948 telecast originated from an observatory, where the camera gave a live telescope's-eye view of the moon and Saturn. Such subjects as the possibility of future space travel were also discussed.

After two and a half years in prime time the program left the air in September 1950. It returned the following January as a Saturday afternoon show, and remained a Saturday/Sunday fixture (aside from some prime-time telecasts in the summers) until 1954.

NAVY LOG

Military Anthology

FIRST TELECAST: *September 20, 1955*

LAST TELECAST: *September 25, 1958*

BROADCAST HISTORY:

Sep 1955–Sep 1956, CBS Tue 8:30–9:00
Oct 1956–Oct 1957, ABC Wed 8:30–9:00
Oct 1957–Jan 1958, ABC Thu 10:00–10:30
Jan 1958–Sep 1958, ABC Thu 9:30–10:00

The filmed dramas aired in this series were all re-enactments of incidents that had actually happened to U.S. Navy personnel.

The focus was on individual sailors and airmen, often in a battle setting but sometimes in their private lives, as in the story of a mentally disturbed veteran, or a romance disrupted by a sailor's transfer. Most of the subjects were ordinary servicemen, but some famous incidents were dramatized, such as the plan to ambush the plane carrying Admiral Yamamoto, the Japanese commander during World War II, and the sinking of John F. Kennedy's PT-109 in the South Pacific (Kennedy, then a Senator, appeared as a special guest on this telecast). Lesser known actors and actresses were featured, although famous personalities sometimes served as host. The stories were all based on official Navy files, and produced with the cooperation of the Navy Department.

NEEDLES AND PINS

Situation Comedy

FIRST TELECAST: *September 21, 1973*

LAST TELECAST: *December 28, 1973*

BROADCAST HISTORY:

Sep 1973–Dec 1973, NBC Fri 9:00–9:30

CAST:

Nathan Davidson .... Norman Fell
Harry Karp .... Louis Nye
Wendy Nelson .... Deirdre Lenihan
Sonia Baker .... Sandra Deel

Charlie Miller .... Bernie Kopell
Max .... Larry Gelman
Myron Russo .... Alex Henteloff
Julius Singer .... Milton Seltzer

New York City's famous garment district was the setting for this situation comedy about Nathan Davidson, owner of the Lorelei Fashion House, a manufacturer of women's clothing. Also prominent were Nathan's brother and partner Harry, and his new designer Wendy, a Nebraska girl adjusting both to life in the big city and the hectic pace of the fashion industry. Featured in the series were Sonia, the bookkeeper and secretary; Charlie, the firm's salesman; Max, the fabric cutter; Myron, the pattern maker; and Singer, Nathan's principal competitor.

NEW ADVENTURES OF HUCK FINN, THE

Adventure

FIRST TELECAST: *September 15, 1968*
LAST TELECAST: *September 7, 1969*
BROADCAST HISTORY:
Sep 1968–Sep 1969, NBC Sun 7:00–7:30
CAST:
Huck Finn .... Michael Shea
Becky Thatcher .... Lu Ann Haslam
Tom Sawyer .... Kevin Schultz
Injun Joe .... Ted Cassidy

Much in the style of the highly successful Disney movie *Mary Poppins, The New Adventures of Huck Finn* combined live actors with animated settings. The three young principals, Huck, Becky, and Tom, were confronted with Injun Joe at the start of the first episode. He had sworn to get even with Huck for testifying against him in court and the three boys, fearing for their lives, ran away to escape him. As they ran, they began an adventure in which the villain was an animated version of Injun Joe. From episode to episode, the settings varied between contemporary and historical, domestic and foreign. The youngsters were always the only live characters in an otherwise animated adventure series.

NEW ADVENTURES OF MARTIN KANE, THE

see *Martin Kane, Private Eye*

NEW ADVENTURES OF PERRY MASON, THE

see *Perry Mason*

NEW ADVENTURES OF WONDER WOMAN, THE

see *Wonder Woman*

NEW ANDY GRIFFITH SHOW, THE

Situation Comedy

FIRST TELECAST: *January 8, 1971*
LAST TELECAST: *May 21, 1971*
BROADCAST HISTORY:
Jan 1971–May 1971, CBS Fri 8:30–9:00
CAST:
Andy Sawyer .... Andy Griffith
Lee Sawyer .... Lee Meriwether
Nora .... Ann Morgan Guilbert
Lori Sawyer .... Lori Rutherford
T. J. Sawyer .... Marty McCall
Buff MacKnight .... Glen Ash

Andy Sawyer had been working in a government capacity in the state capital when he was informed that the mayor of his home town of Greenwood was retiring and looking for someone to take over the unexpired portion of his current term. Andy moved home, with his wife Lee and his two children, to take the job. Greenwood was a small, rural Southern town and the role of mayor gave star Andy Griffith the opportunity to return to the type of gentle, homespun comedy that had made the original *Andy Griffith Show* so popular. This was on the heels of his failure in the much different title role in *The Headmaster,* but it lasted little longer.

NEW BILL COSBY SHOW, THE

Comedy Variety

FIRST TELECAST: *September 11, 1972*
LAST TELECAST: *May 7, 1973*
BROADCAST HISTORY:
Sep 1972–May 1973, CBS Mon 10:00–11:00
REGULARS:
Bill Cosby
Lola Falana
Susan Tolsky
Foster Brooks
Frank Shaw
Quincy Jones Orchestra
Oscar DeGruy
Pat McCormick
Mike Elias
Ronny Graham
Stan Ross
Ray Jessel

Comedian Bill Cosby was the star and host of this variety series that showcased guest stars in addition to its regulars. Each episode included a Cosby monologue, several comedy sketches, and one or two musical numbers. Two regular sketches were "The Wife of the Week" and vigenettes about "The Dude," a character who was so cool that nothing fazed him. Dancer Lola Falana also functioned as the announcer on this series.

NEW BREED, THE

Police

FIRST TELECAST: *October 3, 1961*

LAST TELECAST: *September 25, 1962*

BROADCAST HISTORY:

Oct 1961–Nov 1961, ABC Tue 9:00–10:00
Nov 1961–Sep 1962, ABC Tue 8:30–9:30

CAST:

Lt. Price Adams ....Leslie Nielsen
Sgt. Vince Cavelli ....John Beradino
Ptlmn. Joe Huddleston ....John Clarke
Ptlmn. Pete Garcia ....Greg Roman
Capt. Keith Gregory ....Byron Morrow

These men were a "new breed" of policeman. They were trained in the use of sophisticated electronic gadgetry to track down criminals who were uncapturable by traditional police methods. As members of the elite Metropolitan Squad of the Los Angeles Police Department, they were under the immediate supervision of Lt. Price Adams. Price was both their superior and leader as they assaulted the underworld in the Southern California area.

NEW CHRISTY MINSTRELS, THE

Musical Variety

FIRST TELECAST: *August 6, 1964*

LAST TELECAST: *September 10, 1964*

BROADCAST HISTORY:

Aug 1964–Sep 1964, NBC Thu 9:30–10:00

REGULARS:

The New Christy Minstrels

This five-week summer replacement for *Hazel* was actually titled *Ford Presents the New Christy Minstrels*, in deference to its sponsor. The nine-member folk-singing group was led by Randy Sparks and was quite popular during the mid-1960s. Lead singer was Barry McGuire. Sparks and his group were joined each week by a guest comedian and the shows all had outdoor settings, including two from the New York World's Fair and three from locations in the Los Angeles area. The original Christy Minstrels was a famous minstrel troupe of the mid-1800s which popularized many of Stephen Foster's songs.

NEW COMEDY SHOWCASE

Comedy Anthology

FIRST TELECAST: *August 1, 1960*

LAST TELECAST: *September 19, 1960*

BROADCAST HISTORY:

Aug 1960–Sep 1960, CBS Mon 10:00–10:30

The situation comedies that were aired in this anthology series were unsold pilots for projected regular series, including one starring Johnny Carson called *Johnny Come Lately* and another with Dick Van Dyke titled *The Trouble with Richard*.

NEW DICK VAN DKYE SHOW, THE

Situation Comedy

FIRST TELECAST: *September 18, 1971*

LAST TELECAST: *September 2, 1974*

BROADCAST HISTORY:

Sep 1971–Sep 1972, CBS Sat 9:00–9:30
Sep 1972–Dec 1972, CBS Sun 9:00–9:30
Jan 1972–Sep 1973, CBS Sun 7:30–8:00
Sep 1973–Sep 1974, CBS Mon 9:30–10:00

CAST:

Dick Preston ....Dick Van Dyke
Jenny Preston ....Hope Lange
Bernie Davis (1971–1973) ...... Marty Brill
"Mike" Preston (1971–1973) .. Fannie Flagg
Carol Davis (1971–1973) ... Nancy Dussault
Annie Preston .... Angela Powell
Max Mathias (1973–1974)
.... Dick Van Patten
Dennis Whitehead (1973–1974)
.... Barry Gordon
Alex Montenez (1973–1974) . . .Henry Darrow

During its first two seasons on the air, *The New Dick Van Dyke Show* was filmed on location at Carefree, Arizona. Dick Preston was the host of a local talk show on KXIV-TV, a mythical Phoenix, Arizona, television station. The series revolved around his personal life with his wife Jenny and their nine-year-old daughter, and his professional life with the talk show. His manager, Bernie, and Bernie's wife were personal friends and his sister Mike doubled as his secretary.

For the third season, the setting of the show moved to Hollywood, and so did its production. Dick moved his family there so that he could take advantage of an opportunity to star in a daytime soap opera,

Those Who Care. New series regulars were the soap opera's writer, Dennie Whitehead; its producer, Max Mathias; and its stage manager, Alex Montenez.

NEW DOCTORS, THE

Medical

FIRST TELECAST: *September 14, 1969*
LAST TELECAST: *June 23, 1973*
BROADCAST HISTORY:

Sep 1969–Sep 1972, NBC Sun 10:00–11:00
Sep 1972–Jan 1973, NBC Tue 9:00–10:00
May 1973–Jun 1973, NBC Fri 10:00–11:00

CAST:

Dr. David Craig .... E. G. Marshall
Dr. Paul Hunter .... David Hartman
Dr. Ted Stuart (1969–1972) .... John Saxon
Dr. Martin Cohen (1972–1973) .... Robert Walden

The stories told on *The New Doctors* took place at the fictional David Craig Institute of New Medicine. The institute was a combination hospital and research center, founded, named after, and run by Dr. David Craig, and dedicated to perfecting new medical techniques. Dr. Craig's expertise in the field had earned him the respect of the profession and had made it possible for him to obtain the funding to pursue new medical breakthroughs. His chief of surgery was brilliant young heart-transplant specialist Dr. Ted Stuart, while Dr. Paul Hunter worked on nonsurgical techniques for treating disease. Dr. Martin Cohen became a regular at the start of the final season, replacing the departed Dr. Stuart. Incidents involving these dedicated men and their patients were dramatized on *The New Doctors*.

This program was an element of *The Bold Ones*. It was the only *Bold Ones* element to be aired throughout that series' entire four-season run, and was, in fact, the only element left in the series during the final season, all of the others having been dropped.

NEW LAND, THE

Adventure

FIRST TELECAST: *September 14, 1974*
LAST TELECAST: *October 19, 1974*
BROADCAST HISTORY:

Sep 1974–Oct 1974, ABC Sat 8:00–9:00

CAST:

Anna Larsen .... Bonnie Bedelia
Christian Larsen .... Scott Thomas
Tuliff Larsen .... Todd Lookinland
Anneliese Larsen .... Debbie Lytton
Bo .... Kurt Russell
Rev. Lundstrom .... Donald Moffat
Molly Lundstrom .... Gwen Arner
Murdock .... Lou Frizzel

The hardships and triumphs of a courageous family of young Scandinavian immigrants struggling to carve out a life in the hostile wilderness near Solna, Minnesota, in 1858. Anna and Christian were the parents, Tuliff (aged nine) and Anneliese (eight) their children, and Bo their best friend. Rev. Lundstrom and his wife and Murdock, the owner of the general store, also pitched in, but the Larsens' travails lasted for only six weeks before the series was canceled.

Filmed on location in Oregon and California, and based (loosely) on two Swedish movies, *The Emigrants* (1972) and *The New Land* (1973).

NEW LORETTA YOUNG SHOW, THE

General Drama

FIRST TELECAST: *September 24, 1962*
LAST TELECAST: *March 18, 1963*
BROADCAST HISTORY:

Sep 1962–Mar 1963, CBS Mon 10:00–10:30

CAST:

Christine Massey .... Loretta Young
Paul Belzer .... James Philbrook
Marnie Massey .... Celia Kaye
Vickie Massey .... Beverly Washburn
Judy Massey .... Sandy Descher
Binkie Massey .... Carol Sydes
Dirk Massey .... Dirk Rambo
Dack Massey .... Dack Rambo
Maria Massey .... Tracy Stratford

Christine Massey was a widowed mother of seven children, living in the suburban community of Ellendale, Connecticut. Her children ranged in age from 6 to 18 and were typical of other youngsters of their respective ages in terms of attitudes, wants, and conflicts with each other and with their mother. Christine made her living as a magazine writer, selling stories to various publications. One of those publications, *Belzer's Woman's Journal*, was edited and owned by Paul Belzer, the mature bachelor who was Christine's love interest. They met when she was working on her first assignment for his magazine and their romance continued throughout the six-month run of this series, culminating in marriage on the last telecast, March 18, 1963.

This was Miss Young's sole venture in a continuing role on television. Her previous series, *The Loretta Young Show*, gave her the freedom of playing different people on the occasions in which she starred as well as hosted the show. On this show, she was the center of action in roughly every other episode, with stories centering around individuals in the family on alternate weeks.

NEW PEOPLE, THE

Drama

FIRST TELECAST: *September 22, 1969*

LAST TELECAST: *January 12, 1970*

BROADCAST HISTORY:

Sep 1969–Jan 1970, ABC Mon 8:15–9:00

CAST:

Susan Bradley ....Tiffany Bolling
Bob Lee .... Zooey Hall
Ginny Loomis ....Jill Jaress
Gene Washington ....David Moses
Stanley Gabriel ....Dennis Olivieri
George Potter ....Peter Ratray

CREATOR:

Rod Serling

This fantasy drama centered on a heterogeneous group of 40 young Americans stranded on a South Pacific atoll after a plane crash. The island just happened to be an abandoned U.S. atomic test site, which meant that, though safe, it came complete with buildings, provisions, and all the other physical appurtenances of a modern society—but no people. Inhabiting this eerie world, the young folks, with their differing ethnic and social backgrounds (they were returning from a cultural exchange tour of Southeast Asia), set about organizing their own "new" society, sans adults. A few guest stars did wander on and off their "lost" island, however.

NEW PHIL SILVERS SHOW, THE

Situation Comedy

FIRST TELECAST: *September 28, 1963*

LAST TELECAST: *June 27, 1964*

BROADCAST HISTORY:

Sep 1963–Nov 1963, CBS Sat 8:30–9:00
Nov 1963–Jun 1964, CBS Sat 9:30–10:00

CAST:

Harry Grafton ....Phil Silvers
Brink ....Stafford Repp
Waluska ....Herbie Faye
Roxy ....Pat Renella
Lester ....Jim Shane

The character played by Phil Silvers in his second series was similar to Sgt. Ernie Bilko in the original *Phil Silvers Show*, with one exception—Harry was a civilian. He was the maintenance superintendent of Osborne Industries, a small manufacturing company whose products changed from episode to episode, to suit the plot. Harry was a small-time swindler and office con artist. He would do almost anything to avoid real work, and managed to find angles to provide himself with a little something extra from each job that he and his crew worked on. The boss, Mr. Brink, could only look on helplessly.

NEW TEMPERATURES RISING SHOW, THE

see *Temperatures Rising*

NEW YORK GIANTS QUARTERBACK HUDDLE

Sports Commentary

FIRST TELECAST: *September 15, 1950*

LAST TELECAST: *November 12, 1953*

BROADCAST HISTORY:

Sep 1950–Dec 1950, ABC Fri 8:30–9:00
Sep 1952–Dec 1952, DUM Wed 7:30–8:00
Oct 1953–Nov 1953, DUM Thu 8:00–8:30

HOST:

Joe Hasel (1950)
Steve Owen (1952–1953)

Highlight films of the New York Giants' game of the previous week, interviews with players, and discussions of more general National Football League news and issues were all included in this weekly show. Sportscaster Joe Hasel hosted the ABC version in 1950, while Steve Owen, coach of the New York Giants team, hosted on DuMont. The 1953 DuMont version continued as a local show until the season ended. Also known as *Pro Football Highlights*, *Football News*, and *New York Giants Football Huddle*.

NEW YORK TIMES YOUTH FORUM

Discussion

FIRST TELECAST: *October 5, 1952*

LAST TELECAST: *June 21, 1953*

BROADCAST HISTORY:

Oct 1952–Jun 1953, DUM Sun 6:00–7:00

Discussion of topics of importance to young people, by politicians, scientists, and other authorities, including writers from *The New York Times*. Subjects included "Do We Learn Only at School?," "How Does Soviet Policy Affect Us?," "Music: Jazz *vs.* Classics," and "Are Mothers Necessary?"

NEWLYWED GAME, THE

Quiz/Audience Participation

FIRST TELECAST: *January 7, 1967*

LAST TELECAST: *August 30, 1971*

BROADCAST HISTORY:

Jan 1967–Jan 1971, ABC Sat 8:00–8:30

Jan 1971–Aug 1971, ABC Mon 8:00–8:30

EMCEE:

Bob Eubanks

EXECUTIVE PRODUCER:

Chuck Barris

Each week on *The Newlywed Game* four couples, all married less than one year, competed with each other to win their own special "dream gift," usually appliances or furniture. The emcee asked the wives questions about their husbands, and the husbands questions about their wives, each while the other mate was out of earshot. The couple that correctly guessed the greatest number of each other's answers was the winner. Questions were usually designed to produce embarrassing situations and disagreements between husbands and wives, much to the delight of the audience. For example, "What animal would you compare your mother-in-law to?" or "Would your wife say she sleeps with her toes pointing toward the wall, the ceiling, or the floor?" Bob Eubanks hosted both the nighttime and the long-running daytime version of this series.

NEWS—ABC

FIRST TELECAST: *August 11, 1948*

LAST TELECAST:

BROADCAST HISTORY:

Aug 1948–Oct 1952, ABC Mon–Sat 7:00–7:15

Oct 1952–Dec 1952, ABC Mon 9:00–10:00

Oct 1952–Dec 1952, ABC Wed 8:00–9:00

Oct 1952–Dec 1952, ABC Thu 8:00–8:30

Oct 1952–Jan 1953, ABC Fri 8:30–9:30

Oct 1952–Aug 1953, ABC Sun 8:00–9:00

Oct 1953–May 1959, ABC Mon–Fri 7:15–7:30

May 1959–Jan 1967, ABC Mon–Fri Various (15 min.)

Sep 1958–May 1959, ABC Mon–Fri 10:30–10:45

Oct 1961–Jan 1965, ABC Mon–Fri 11:00–11:10

Jan 1965– , ABC Sat/Sun 11:00–11:15

Jan 1967– , ABC Mon–Fri Various (30 min.)

Feb 1973– , ABC Sat 6:30–7:00

ABC's first regularly scheduled nightly newscast was *News and Views*, which premiered in August 1948 with H. R. Baughage and Jim Gibbons sharing the anchor position. Aired six nights each week, it lasted three years, and was succeeded by *After the Deadlines* in April 1951.

The program that succeeded *After the Deadlines* was the most ambitious news show in the early days of television. In an attempt to offer news as an alternative to prime time entertainment, ABC introduced *All Star News* in October 1952. This offered four and one-half hours of national news coverage per week, a full hour on some nights, all running in the middle of the evening against NBC's and CBS' top entertainment shows. Featured were Bryson Rash, Pauline Frederick, Gordon Fraser and Leo Cherne. In addition to straight headline reporting, *All Star News* provided analysis and interviews with newsmakers, and had a documentary quality to much of its coverage. It was a noble effort, but it attracted few viewers against *Ed Sullivan, Arthur Godfrey* and *I Love Lucy*, and by early 1953 only the Sunday night edition remained on the air.

Smarting from this expensive disaster, ABC reverted to a 15-minute early evening news in October 1953. The anchor was veteran newsman John Daly, who was brought over from CBS. An interesting sidelight is that even while Daly was anchoring ABC's nightly news, he remained moderator of CBS' top-rated quiz show, *What's My Line*. Daly remained in the ABC anchor seat for more than seven years, except for one short stint from 1958–1959 when he anchored a short-lived 10:30 P.M. newscast, and Don Goddard filled in at 7:15 P.M. When Daly left ABC in December 1960, a trio of anchormen took over the early news, Bill Lawrence, Al Mann and former NBC anchorman John Cameron Swayze.

In the fall of 1961 ABC introduced its first 11:00 P.M. newscast, running from Monday to Friday. The first anchor was

Ron Cochran, succeeded by Murphy Martin in 1963 and Bob Young in 1964. In January 1965 ABC dropped this newscast and substituted an 11 P.M. Saturday/Sunday news instead. Called *The ABC Weekend News,* this has remained on the air ever since, although after a short tenure by Bob Young (1965–1966) there was no regular anchor. Weekends also saw the addition of an early evening news on Saturday in 1973. At first called *The Reasoner Report,* this was taken over by Ted Koppel in the summer of 1975.

There has been, over the years, considerable turnover in anchormen on ABC's traditionally last place early evening news. Ron Cochran took over in January 1963. He was replaced by youthful Peter Jennings in February 1965, and Jennings was still with the newscast when it expanded from 15 minutes to a half hour on January 9, 1967. Bob Young replaced Jennings in January 1968, and Frank Reynolds took over in May 1968. A year later ABC decided to try two anchors, and Howard K. Smith joined Reynolds. In December 1970 it became *The ABC Evening News with Howard K. Smith and Harry Reasoner,* Reasoner having been hired away from CBS (where, it seemed, he was never going to get the chance to succeed the venerable Walter Cronkite). The Smith-Reasoner team lasted almost five years, with Reasoner going it alone in September 1975. In October 1976 he was joined, amid a blaze of publicity, by former NBC newswoman Barbara Walters, who reportedly got an annual salary of $1,000,000 to make the switch. Reasoner and Walters did not work well together, however, and in the summer of 1978 the network decided to try a *four* person arrangement, originating from four different cities each night: Barbara Walters from New York, Max Robinson from Chicago, Frank Reynolds from Washington, and Peter Jennings (remember him?) from London. Regardless of all the changes and publicity, and the network's spectacular success in other parts of the schedule, ABC news remained mired in third place among the evening network newscasts.

NEWS—CBS

FIRST TELECAST: *May 3, 1948*
LAST TELECAST:
BROADCAST HISTORY:

May 1948–Sep 1955, CBS Mon–Fri 7:30–7:45
Aug 1948–Dec 1948, CBS Sun Various (15 min) 7:00–8:00
Jan 1949–Jun 1950, CBS Sun Various (15 min) 10:00–11:00
Jan 1949–Mar 1950, CBS Sat 7:30–7:45
Jun 1950–Sep 1950, CBS Sat 6:15–6:30
Aug 1950–Sept 1950, CBS Sun 10:00–10:15
Sep 1950–Jan 1951, CBS Sat 7:30–7:45
Jan 1951– , CBS Sun 11:00–11:15
Oct 1951–Nov 1951, CBS Sat 6:30–6:45
Nov 1951–Jan 1952, CBS Sat 6:45–7:00
Sep 1955–Aug 1963, CBS Mon–Fri 7:15–7:30
Sep 1963– , CBS Mon–Fri Various (30 min)
Jan 1966– , CBS Sat 6:30–7:00
Jan 1970–Sep 1972, CBS Sun 6:00–6:30 (Jan–Sep each year)
Jan 1976– , CBS Sun 6:00–6:30

Doug Edwards had been doing television news for the CBS station in New York since the mid-1940s and, when it was decided to produce a nightly network newscast, his local show became CBS's first network news show. Edwards remained with the weekday evening news until 1962. One month short of Edwards' 14th anniversary with the series Walter Cronkite took over, on April 16, 1962. In more than 30 years on the air, *The CBS Evening News* has had only these two men at its helm (as this book goes to press).

The show expanded to a full half hour on September 2, 1963.

Compared to the extreme stability of the weekday news, CBS' weekend shows have gone through many more changes of personnel. The Saturday early news debuted in January 1949 with Quincy Howe reporting. *Quincy Howe with the News* lasted 15 months and was replaced in the summer of 1950 by *The Week in Review,* a filmed newsreel summary of the happenings of the past week. That September *The Saturday News Special,* anchored by Don Hollenbeck, replaced the newsreels for slightly over three months. *Up to the Minute* arrived in October 1951, with Edward P. Morgan anchoring for the first three weeks and Walter Cronkite for the last two months. After no Saturday news program for 14 years, *The CBS Saturday News* arrived on January 12, 1966. Roger Mudd was the original anchor of this show, replaced in July 1973 by Dan Rather, who was in turn replaced by Bob Schieffer in November 1976.

CBS's initial news offering on Sundays, running from August 1948 to June 1950, was the filmed newsreel *The Week in Review*. John Daly had a brief turn with a Sunday weekly news summary show that fall, but the long lasting 11:00 P.M. Sunday news did not actually start until January 1951. It has been in that time slot ever since. Walter Cronkite was at the helm for more than 11 years, leaving to take over *The CBS Evening News* in April 1962. Cronkite has, therefore, been on continuous view as a CBS anchorman since he started on *Up to the Minute* in 1951. None of the Sunday anchormen who succeeded Cronkite had his endurance. Eric Sevareid was his initial replacement (lasting only nine months), followed by Harry Reasoner (February 1963–November 1970), Dan Rather (November 1970–July 1973), Bob Schieffer (July 1973–August 1974), Rather again (September 1974–December 1975), Morton Dean (December 1975–December 1976), and Ed Bradley. In addition to the late Sunday news, there was an early evening version for parts of 1970 and 1971 with Roger Mudd anchoring, and in 1976 with Bob Schieffer. Schieffer departed in November of that year, with Morton Dean moving over from the late Sunday news to the earlier edition.

NEWS—DUMONT

FIRST TELECAST: *August 25, 1947*
LAST TELECAST: *April 1, 1955*
BROADCAST HISTORY:

Aug 1947–May 1948, DUM Mon–Fri 6:45–7:00
Jan 1948–Jan 1949, DUM Mon–Fri 7:30–7:45
Jan 1948–Jan 1949, DUM Tue 7:45–8:00
Nov 1948–Feb 1949, DUM Sun 6:30–7:00
Feb 1949–May 1950, DUM Mon 8:00–8:30
Sep 1954–Apr 1955, DUM Mon–Fri 7:15–7:30

DuMont never had the financial resources of the other television networks and, though it was second only to NBC with a regularly scheduled evening news program, the DuMont news never developed into the complex and comprehensive effort that its competitors were to become by the early 1950s. The first DuMont network news show, carried on a two-station network, was 1947's *Walter Compton News*. The first network news series to originate from Washington, D.C., where it had been seen since June 1947, *Walter Compton News* became a network program when it was seen simultaneously in New York starting in August. The production was minimal, with Compton reading from a script and only occasional slides being shown.

In January 1948 *Camera Headlines*, a filmed 15-minute newsreel, was added to the DuMont schedule at 7:30 P.M. Since *Camera Headlines* dealt only with domestic stories, *INS Telenews* followed it on Tuesday nights to provide world news coverage. The *INS Telenews* newsreel was a wrap-up of the major world news stories of the week, provided to DuMont by Hearst's International News Service, essentially a print service similar to U.P.I. and A.P.

Not precisely a hard news show, *Newsweek Analysis* premiered in November 1948. Moderated by senior *Newsweek* editor Ernest K. Lindley, it was an interview program in which various editors of the magazine chatted with personalities in the news. When the series moved from Sundays to Mondays the following February, the title was changed to *Newsweek Views the News*.

In the fall of 1954, after an absence of almost five years, regularly scheduled nightly news returned to the DuMont network. Anchored by Morgan Beatty, this show remained on the air until the crumbling DuMont network virtually ceased functioning the following April.

NEWS—NBC

FIRST TELECAST: *February 17, 1946*
LAST TELECAST:
BROADCAST HISTORY:

Feb 1946–Jun 1946, NBC Sun 8:00–8:15
Apr 1946–Dec 1946, NBC Mon/Thu 7:50–8:00
Dec 1946–Oct 1947, NBC Mon 9:00–9:10
Dec 1946–Oct 1947, NBC Thu 7:50–8:00
Nov 1947–Dec 1947, NBC Wed 8:45–9:00
Feb 1948–Feb 1949, NBC Mon–Fri 7:50–8:00
Jun 1948–Sep 1948, NBC Sun 7:50–8:00
Sep 1948–Feb 1949, NBC Sun 7:20–7:30
Feb 1949–Sep 1957, NBC Mon–Fri 7:45–8:00
Apr 1949–Feb 1950, NBC Sat 7:45–8:00
Jul 1949–Oct 1949, NBC Sun 7:00–7:30
Sep 1957–Sep 1963, NBC Mon–Fri 6:45–7:00
Oct 1961–Oct 1965, NBC Sat 6:00–6:15
Sep 1963– , NBC Mon–Fri Various (30 min.)
Sep 1965–Aug 1967, NBC Sun 6:00–6:30

Oct 1965– , NBC Sat 6:30–7:00
Sep 1967– , NBC Sun 6:30–7:00

NBC was the first television network to broadcast a regular news program, beginning early in 1946. Called variously *The Esso Newsreel* and *The Esso Reporter* in its early days, it was a thrice-weekly (Monday, Thursday, Sunday) 10- or 15-minute show consisting primarily of filmed coverage and some commentary by Paul Alley, whose presence on the show in 1946 must place him as one of television's first anchormen. Alley stayed with the Sunday show until its cancellation in 1949, but other things began happening during the rest of the week.

November 1947 brought *Current Opinion* to the NBC Wednesday night schedule for a one month run. Hosted by Robert McCormick from Washington, D.C., it was one of the earliest examples of a news commentary program, with opinions rather than fact taking the spotlight. In February 1948, NBC began a Monday–Friday evening news show called the *Camel Newsreel Theatre*. It was only 10 minutes long, and was not much different from *Esso Newsreel*, which it succeeded, but it was the genesis of the *Camel News Caravan* which took its place a year later. When that happened, John Cameron Swayze, one of the announcers behind the newsreels, moved in front of the camera and became the anchorman, a position he held for more than eight years. Swayze was replaced in 1956 by the charismatic team of Chet Huntley and David Brinkley, whose performance during the political conventions of 1956 earned them a shot at the nightly news that October.

The Huntley-Brinkley Report was to be NBC's news showcase for almost 14 years, through the expansion from 15 minutes to a half-hour (on September 9, 1963, one week after CBS had done the same thing), and an expansion from five to six days a week in January 1969. When Chet Huntley left the show in July 1970, it was retitled *The NBC Nightly News* with Brinkley, John Chancellor, and Frank McGee rotating as anchormen seven days a week for slightly over a year. In August 1971, John Chancellor became the sole anchor on *The NBC Nightly News*, with his duties restricted to Monday through Friday. He remained the only person at the helm until Brinkley (who had contributed pieces to the show over the years as a commentator) returned to make it a team again in June 1976.

There had been an early NBC effort at a Saturday newscast—*Leon Pearson and the News*—in 1949 and 1950, but it would be another decade before news became a regular feature on NBC's Saturday schedule. It occurred in October 1961, with *The Sandor Vanocur Saturday Report*. Vanocur lasted three years, then was replaced by a succession of people during the 1964–1965 season when the show was simply *The NBC Saturday Report*. The show got a new title, *The Scherer-MacNeil Report*, when Ray Scherer and Robert MacNeil became its regular team in October 1965. It was at about that time that Frank McGee began hosting the first regular NBC Sunday evening news show since 1949, a post he held until he joined the rotation on *The NBC Nightly News* in 1970. There was also a period, from May 1967 to December 1968, when McGee was doing both the Saturday and Sunday news shows. Since 1971 a succession of people have helmed the weekends. Garrick Utley did both Saturday and Sunday for two years (until August 1973), but ever since they have had separate anchors. Tom Brokaw took Saturdays for a year and John Hart has been doing it since August 1976. *The NBC Sunday Night News* was picked up by Floyd Kalber from August 1973 to December 1974, by Tom Snyder for the next year, by John Hart until he took over Saturdays, by an assortment of people from August 1976 until the end of that year, by Catherine Mackin until July 1977, and by Jessica Savitch in late 1977.

NEWSSTAND THEATRE

Dramatic Anthology

FIRST TELECAST: *January 16, 1952*
LAST TELECAST: *February 6, 1952*
BROADCAST HISTORY:

Jan 1952–Feb 1952, ABC Wed 9:30–10:00

Four-week series of dramatizations of short stories from national magazines. Included was "Size 12 Tantrum," starring Jack Lemmon and his then wife, Cynthia Stone.

NICHOLS

Western

FIRST TELECAST: *September 16, 1971*
LAST TELECAST: *August 1, 1972*

BROADCAST HISTORY:

Sep 1971–Nov 1971, NBC Thu 9:00–10:00
Nov 1971–Aug 1972, NBC Tue 9:30–10:30

CAST:

Nichols .... James Garner
Ma Ketcham .... Neva Patterson
Ketcham .... John Beck
Mitch .... Stuart Margolin
Ruth .... Margot Kidder
Bertha .... Alice Ghostley

This was one TV series in which the hero really was shot because of low ratings—as in the movie *Network*. The setting was Nichols, Arizona, in 1914. Nichols (he never did have a first name) returned to the town his family had founded only to discover that it had been taken over by the powerful Ketcham family, dominated by matriarchal Ma Ketcham. He was promptly blackmailed by Ma into serving as sheriff, a powerless but hazardous position where she could keep an eye on him. Although Nichols had spent 18 years in the army, he really hated violence and didn't even carry a gun. His real aim in life was to find a means to get rich, and he concocted all sorts of schemes toward that end. Mitch was the town bully, Ma Ketcham's son, and Nichols' not-too-honest deputy; Ruth, the barmaid, was Nichols' girl friend; and Bertha was the proprietor of the saloon where Ruth worked. The program had an interesting early-20th-century Western background, with Nichols using an auto and motorcycle rather than the traditional horse.

In the last episode Nichols was shot down, only to be avenged by his identical twin brother Jim Nichols (yes, *he* had a first name) also played by James Garner. At the time that the last episode was filmed it was assumed that, despite marginal ratings, the series would be renewed. By replacing the avaricious Nichols with his stronger, more traditionally heroic twin brother, it was felt that the next season's program would be more successful. By the time the episode actually aired, however, establishing a real hero for the series had become a moot point—*Nichols* had been given the ax.

Effective with the October 25, 1971, telecast, the official title of the series became *James Garner as Nichols*, in the hopes that the drawing power of its star would boost ratings.

NICK KENNY SHOW, THE

Talk/Music

FIRST TELECAST: *July 18, 1951*
LAST TELECAST: *January 1, 1952*
BROADCAST HISTORY:

Jul 1951–Aug 1951, NBC Wed 11:00–11:15
Aug 1951–Jan 1952, NBC Tue 11:00–11:15

REGULARS:

Nick Kenny
Irene Walsh
Don Tippen

Nick Kenny was a columnist for the *New York Daily Mirror* and this series was set in a replica of his newspaper office. Each week he read some of his original poetry, sang, chatted with guests from the worlds of theater and sports, and philosophized about life. Irene Walsh was his secretary and assistant while Don Tippen provided piano background and accompaniment for singers. The show returned for a couple of months in the spring of 1952 on Saturday afternoons.

NIGHT EDITOR

Dramatic Anthology

FIRST TELECAST: *March 14, 1954*
LAST TELECAST: *September 8, 1954*
BROADCAST HISTORY:

Mar 1954–Jul 1954, DUM Sun 10:45–11:00
Jul 1954–Sep 1954, DUM Wed 10:30–10:45

HOST:

Hal Burdick

This was one of many attempts by DuMont to devise low-cost TV programming. In this case there was one actor and one set. Hal Burdick, the night editor of an unidentified newspaper, was seen in his office narrating a short crime or human interest story. As he spoke he would sit at his desk or walk around the room, changing his voice to differentiate between characters. The stories ranged across many periods and subjects, including an old policeman on school-crossing duty who had an adventure on his last day on the force; a Korean War veteran who got a medal undeservedly; and a Civil War sentry who fell asleep at his post.

Films of *Night Editor* had been seen locally and in late night for several years before this prime-time network run.

NIGHT GALLERY

Supernatural Anthology

FIRST TELECAST: *December 16, 1970*
LAST TELECAST: *August 12, 1973*
BROADCAST HISTORY:
Dec 1970–Sep 1972, NBC Wed 10:00–11:00
Sep 1972–Jan 1973, NBC Sun 10:00–10:30
May 1973–Aug 1973, NBC Sun 10:00–10:30
HOST:
Rod Serling

Night Gallery was one of the original elements in the 1970–1971 NBC series *Four in One*. It aired for six weeks from December 16, 1970, to January 20, 1971, and was rerun on a rotating basis with the other three elements of the series—*McCloud, San Francisco International Airport*, and *The Psychiatrist*—from April through the end of the season. It remained in the Wednesday time slot by itself during the 1971–1972 season and was then moved to Sunday nights.

Night Gallery was a weekly collection of short, supernatural vignettes. Rod Serling introduced each one from a bizarre gallery, in which grotesque paintings foreshadowed the stories to follow. Not all of the stories were frightening, and many times humorous blackouts were used between more serious stories. In many respects, *Night Gallery* was the supernatural equivalent of *Love, American Style*.

NINE THIRTY CURTAIN

Dramatic Anthology
FIRST TELECAST: *October 13, 1953*
LAST TELECAST: *January 1, 1954*
BROADCAST HISTORY:
Oct 1953–Jan 1954, DUM Fri 9:30–10:00

A series of 30-minute filmed dramas starring lesser-known actors and actresses. After its network run *Nine Thirty Curtain* was seen for a time as a local show in New York.

90 BRISTOL COURT

Situation Comedy
FIRST TELECAST: *October 5, 1964*
LAST TELECAST: *January 4, 1965*
BROADCAST HISTORY:
Oct 1964–Jan 1965, NBC Mon 7:30–9:00

90 Bristol Court was actually three situation comedies airing in consecutive half-hours. They were tied together by the fact that the principal characters in each lived in the same apartment complex at 90 Bristol Court. For specific information see the titles of the individual situation comedies—*Karen, Harris against the World*, and *Tom, Dick and Mary*. Although the overall series failed, one of the three parts—*Karen*—was successful enough to finish out the season after the other two elements were canceled in January. A thread of continuity between the three individual comedies was provided in the person of the complex's handyman Cliff Murdoch, portrayed by Guy Raymond. He was generally seen greeting the residents of the three focal apartments and working around the complex.

NO TIME FOR SERGEANTS

Situation Comedy
FIRST TELECAST: *September 14, 1964*
LAST TELECAST: *September 6, 1965*
BROADCAST HISTORY:
Sep 1964–Sep 1965, ABC Mon 8:30–9:00
CAST:
Airman Will Stockdale ....Sammy Jackson
Sgt. King ....Harry Hickox
Airman Ben Whitledge ......Kevin O'Neal
Millie Anderson ....Laurie Sibbald
Capt. Martin ....Paul Smith

Comedy about a simpleminded but resourceful hillbilly who found new worlds to conquer in the Air Force. Airman Will Stockdale didn't have much in the way of rank, but he always seemed to be "improving" things around Oliver Air Force Base, usually to the exasperation of the brass. In the opening episode, for example, he was assigned to permanent K.P., whereupon the food in the mess hall improved so much that the officers began eating there along with the enlisted men. When the colonel inspected the kitchen he discovered that Will had been trading with the local farmers for choice meat and produce—but it was *what* Will had been trading away that upset the colonel when he discovered equipment missing. Sgt. King was Will's incredulous NCO, while Ben was his buddy and Millie his sexy girl friend.

Based on the novel by Mac Hyman, which was subsequently made into a hit play (1955) and movie (1958), both starring Andy Griffith.

NO WARNING

Dramatic Anthology
FIRST TELECAST: *April 6, 1958*

LAST TELECAST: *September 7, 1958*
BROADCAST HISTORY:
Apr 1958–Sep 1958, NBC Sun 7:30–8:00

People involved in sudden, unanticipated crisis situations were the protagonists in *No Warning.* At the start of each story the focal character was established, along with the crisis that was thrust upon him. The remainder of the story presented the resolution of the crisis. All of the episodes dealt with personal and emotional crises, rather than with the threat of violence.

NOAH'S ARK

Medical

FIRST TELECAST: *September 18, 1956*
LAST TELECAST: *October 5, 1958*
BROADCAST HISTORY:
Sep 1956–Feb 1957, NBC Tue 8:30–9:00
Jun 1958–Oct 1958, NBC Sun 7:00–7:30
CAST:
Dr. Noah McCann ....Paul Burke
Dr. Sam Rinehart ....Vic Rodman
Liz Clark ....May Wynn
PRODUCER/DIRECTOR:
Jack Webb

Produced in cooperation with the Southern California Veterinary Medical Association and the American Humane Association, *Noah's Ark* was the story of two veterinarians, the veterinary hospital where they worked, and the animals they treated. Dr. Sam Rinehart was an older man confined to a wheelchair. His young assistant and partner was Dr. Noah McCann. Their secretary and all-purpose assistant was Liz Clark. The relationships that developed between the regulars were as much a part of the story as the collection of animals that they treated. Reruns of the series were aired in the summer of 1958.

NORBY

Situation Comedy

FIRST TELECAST: *January 5, 1955*
LAST TELECAST: *April 6, 1955*
BROADCAST HISTORY:
Jan 1955–Apr 1955, NBC Wed 7:00–7:30
CAST:
Pearson Norby ....David Wayne
Helen Norby ....Joan Lorring
Diane Norby ....Susan Hallaran
Hank Norby ....Evan Elliot
Wahleen Johnson ....Janice Mars
Mr. Rudge ....Ralph Dunn
Mrs. Maude Endles ....Carol Veazie

Pearson Norby was vice-president in charge of small loans at the Pearl River First National Bank, in Pearl River, a small town in upstate New York. He lived there with his wife Helen and his two children, Diane and Hank. The problems Pearson had on the job and situations involving his wife and his children were subjects for episodes. Featured were three of the bank's employees, president Maud Endles, vice-president and efficiency expert Mr. Rudge, and switchboard operator Wahleen Johnson. *Norby* was the first television series to be filmed in color and was, appropriately, sponsored by the Eastman Kodak Company.

NORTHWEST PASSAGE

Adventure

FIRST TELECAST: *September 14, 1958*
LAST TELECAST: *September 8, 1959*
BROADCAST HISTORY:
Sep 1958–Jan 1959, NBC Sun 7:30–8:00
Jan 1959–Jul 1959, NBC Fri 7:30–8:00
Jul 1959–Sep 1959, NBC Tue 7:30–8:00
CAST:
Major Robert Rogers ....Keith Larsen
Sgt. Hunk Marriner ....Buddy Ebsen
Ensign Langdon Towne ....Don Burnett
Gen. Amherst ....Philip Tonge

The actual historical search for an inland waterway that would enable boat traffic to cross the breadth of America was the focal point of *Northwest Passage,* which was set during the French and Indian War (1754–1759). Major Robert Rogers, an experienced explorer and Indian fighter, had organized Rogers' Rangers to help him search for that mythical route. The adventures of these men, exploring, fighting Indians, and battling the American wilderness, provided the stories. Chief among the troops were veteran Indian fighter and long-time friend Hunk Marriner, and Langdon Towne, a Harvard graduate from a well-to-do Eastern family who had become the company mapmaker. They never found the Northwest Passage, but did do a lot of fighting with both the French and the Indians in the course of helping settlers in the area now known as New York State and Eastern Canada.

NORTHWEST PATROL

see *Movies–Prior To 1961*

NOT FOR PUBLICATION

Newspaper Drama

FIRST TELECAST: *May 1, 1951*
LAST TELECAST: *May 27, 1952*
BROADCAST HISTORY:

May 1951–Sep 1951, DUM Mon/Thu 7:45–8:00
Dec 1951–Mar 1952, DUM Fri 8:30–9:00
Mar 1952–May 1952, DUM Tue 10:00–10:30

CAST:

Collins (May–Sep 1951) ..... William Adler
Collins (Dec 1951–May 1952) .... Jerome Cowan

Human-interest stories and adventures in the lives of ordinary people as seen through the eyes of kind-hearted reporter Collins of the big-city newspaper, *The Ledger*. Among the stories were those of an actor who agreed to impersonate an ambassador whose life was in danger; a baseball player who set out to clear his father's name; and a doctor who faced conflict in the operating room. Generally lesser-known actors and actresses appeared in these short dramas, although one February 1952 telecast was billed as the dramatic acting debut of Morey Amsterdam.

NOTHING BUT THE BEST

Musical Variety

FIRST TELECAST: *July 7, 1953*
LAST TELECAST: *September 13, 1953*
BROADCAST HISTORY:

Jul 1953–Aug 1953, NBC Tue 9:00–9:30
Aug 1953–Sep 1953, NBC Sun 10:00–10:30

REGULARS:

Eddie Albert
Skitch Henderson & His Orchestra

Eddie Albert was the star and emcee of this live musical variety show that started out on Tuesday evenings as the summer replacement for *Fireside Theater* and then moved to Sundays.

The acts, each billed as the best in their field, were introduced by Mr. Albert, who chatted with the performers and then left them to perform. As he had said on his opening show: "I have the dream spot on TV this season for the sponsor told me to go out and get my favorite talent and to let them do on the show what they feel is the best of their career—for the show is *Nothing but the Best.*"

NOTHING BUT THE TRUTH

see *To Tell the Truth*

NOTRE DAME FOOTBALL

see *Football*

NOW

Documentary

FIRST TELECAST: *May 9, 1954*
LAST TELECAST: *September 14, 1970*
BROADCAST HISTORY:

May 1954–Jun 1954, ABC Sun 7:30–8:00
Mar 1970–Sep 1970, ABC Mon 10:30–11:00

EXECUTIVE PRODUCER:

Arthur Holch (1970)

Two unrelated summer documentary series were aired under the title *Now*. The 1954 version consisted of assorted documentary films. The 1970 series was produced by ABC News and hosted by a different ABC newsman each week. It covered such subjects as communes, Women's Liberation, and "A Black Mayor in Dixie."

NURSES, THE

Medical

FIRST TELECAST: *September 27, 1962*
LAST TELECAST: *September 7, 1965*
BROADCAST HISTORY:

Sep 1962–Dec 1962, CBS Thu 9:00–10:00
Jan 1963–Sep 1964, CBS Thu 10:00–11:00
Sep 1964–Sep 1965, CBS Tue 10:00–11:00

CAST:

Liz Thorpe .... Shirl Conway
Gail Lucas .... Zina Bethune
Dr. Alex Tazinski (1964–1965) .... Michael Tolan
Dr. Ted Steffen (1964–1965) .... Joseph Campanella

Filmed on location in New York, *The Nurses* dealt primarily with the personal and professional lives of two nurses working in a large metropolitan hospital. Liz Thorpe was the older, more experienced head nurse and Gail Lucas (played by 17-year-old Zina Bethune) was the somewhat naive student nurse. Two doctors, one older (Steffen) and one a young resident (Tazinski), joined the program when it moved to Tuesday nights in the fall of 1964. They made efforts to help the nurses with their medical and moral problems and the series title was changed to *The Doctors and the Nurses* to include them.

The Nurses was seen as a daytime serial following its nighttime run. The cast changed but the setting (New York City's Alden General Hospital) remained the same.

O.K. CRACKERBY

Situation Comedy

FIRST TELECAST: *September 16, 1965*

LAST TELECAST: *January 6, 1966*

BROADCAST HISTORY:

Sep 1965–Jan 1966, ABC Thu 8:30–9:00

CAST:

O.K. Crackerby .... Burl Ives
St. John Quincy .... Hal Buckley
O.K., Jr. .... Brian Corcoran
Cynthia Crackerby .... Brooke Adams
Hobart Crackerby .... Joel Davison
Susan Wentworth .... Laraine Stephens
Slim .... Dick Foran

CREATED BY:

Cleveland Amory and Abe Burrows

Widower O.K. Crackerby was the richest man in the world, but he lacked the one thing he wanted above all else—acceptance in the world of high society. A rough-and-tumble Oklahoman, he lacked certain qualities that the refined snobs who controlled the Social Register deemed necessary. To help his kids "get into polite society," O.K. hired an unemployed Harvard graduate, St. John Quincy, as a tutor. Traveling from one society playground to another, the two men split their time fighting with each other on an intellectual level and banding together to battle the social snobs on a personal level. Susan was St. John's girl friend, and Slim was O.K.'s business pal.

Although they would probably rather not be reminded of it, this short-lived comedy was the creation of Cleveland Amory, who skewered many a TV series in print during his long tenure as *TV Guide*'s chief critic and reviewer, and noted playwright Abe Burrows.

O.S.S.

War Drama

FIRST TELECAST: *September 26, 1957*

LAST TELECAST: *March 17, 1958*

BROADCAST HISTORY:

Sep 1957–Jan 1958, ABC Thu 9:30–10:00
Jan 1958–Mar 1958, ABC Mon 7:30–8:00

CAST:

Capt. Frank Hawthorn .... Ron Randall
The Chief .... Lionel Murton
Sgt. O'Brien .... Robert Gallico

After just about every police file in the country had been raided for "true stories," ABC came up with an obvious source of true-life high adventure: the Office of Strategic Services (OSS), America's World War II superspy agency. Since the OSS had been dissolved by executive order after the war, to be replaced by the CIA, its files were open to the public. Authenticity was insured by co-producer Colonel William Eliscu, who had been real-life aide to OSS Chief General "Wild Bill" Donovan during the war.

In this series, agent Frank Hawthorn engaged in considerable derring-do behind German lines, often in cohoots with the French Resistance. Sgt. O'Brien was his assistant. Filmed in England and France.

OBOLER COMEDY THEATRE

Comedy Anthology

FIRST TELECAST: *October 11, 1949*

LAST TELECAST: *November 20, 1949*

BROADCAST HISTORY:

Oct 1949, ABC Tue 9:00–9:30
Nov 1949, ABC Sun 7:30–8:00

A short series of original stories by Arch Oboler, the noted radio writer.

OCCASIONAL WIFE

Situation Comedy

FIRST TELECAST: *September 13, 1966*

LAST TELECAST: *August 29, 1967*

BROADCAST HISTORY:

Sep 1966–Aug 1967, NBC Tue 8:30–9:00

CAST:

Peter Christopher .... Michael Callan
Greta Patterson .... Patricia Harty
Max Brahms .... Jack Collins
Mrs. Brahms .... Joan Tompkins

Peter Christopher was a young executive at the Brahms Baby Food Company whose single status had prevented him from getting numerous promotions. Due to the nature of its product, the Brahms Company was a strong believer in marriage and family. Peter hit upon the idea of having someone pose as his wife, whenever his boss was around, so that he could move up in the company and still retain his bachelor status. To that end, he convinced Greta Patterson, an aspiring young painter who was temporarily working as a hat-check girl, to take the "job" of his "occasional wife." In return, he set her up in an apartment two floors above his and agreed to pay for her art lessons and a pair of contact lenses. She had to be in his apartment whenever his boss dropped by and appear at his office from time to time, as well as attend company functions with him. The problems caused by this arrangement, which often saw one or both of them on the fire escape between their apartments, provided most of the material for episodes.

ODD COUPLE, THE

Situation Comedy

FIRST TELECAST: *September 24, 1970*

LAST TELECAST: *July 4, 1975*

BROADCAST HISTORY:

Sep 1970–Jan 1971, ABC Thu 9:30–10:00
Jan 1971–Jun 1973, ABC Fri 9:30–10:00
Jun 1973–Jan 1974, ABC Fri 8:30–9:00
Jan 1974–Sep 1974, ABC Fri 9:30–10:00
Sep 1974–Jan 1975, ABC Thu 8:00–8:30
Jan 1975–Jul 1975, ABC Fri 9:30–10:00

CAST:

Felix Unger .... Tony Randall
Oscar Madison .... Jack Klugman
Murray .... Al Molinaro
Speed (1970–1974) .... Garry Walberg
Vinnie .... Larry Gelman
Roger (1973–1974) .... Archie Hahn
Roy (1970–1971) .... Ryan McDonald
Cecily Pigeon (1970–1971) ... Monica Evans
Gwendolyn Pigeon (1970–1971)
.... Carol Shelly
Dr. Nancy Cunningham
(1970–1972) .... Joan Hotchkiss
Gloria Unger (1971–1975) ... Janice Hansen
Blanche Madison (occasional)
.... Brett Somers
Myrna (1971–1975) .... Penny Marshall
Miriam (1972–1974) .... Elinor Donahue

If comedy thrives on contrasts, *The Odd Couple* offered a perfect situation. Felix was a prim, fastidious photographer, a compulsive cleaner; Oscar was a gruff, sloppy sportswriter for the fictional *New York Herald,* to whom a floor was a place to toss things. Both were divorced, and only a mutual need for companionship and a place to stay brought them together to live in the same apartment. Well, co-exist in the same apartment. The conflicts were obvious and endless, as each upset the other's way of life and attempted to mix with the other's friends. Frequently seen were Oscar's poker partners, notably Murray the cop, Speed the compulsive gambler, and meek Vinnie. Nancy Cunningham was Oscar's girl friend during the first season, and Myrna his secretary. The Pigeon Sisters were two nutty English girls who lived upstairs, and Christopher Shea for a time played the obnoxious kid next door. Oscar's ex-wife Blanche was played by Jack Klugman's real-life wife Brett Somers, in occasional appearances.

For a couple of seasons Miriam served as Felix's girl friend, but by the final season he had reconciled with his ex-wife Gloria. The situation on which the series had been built was neatly resolved in the final episode when Felix moved out to remarry Gloria. Oscar returned to the apartment alone, looked around, and exploded into noisy, messy celebration at the prospect of uninhibited chaos—at last!

The Odd Couple was based on Neil Simon's hit Broadway play (1965), which was made into a movie (1968) starring Walter Matthau and Jack Lemmon.

OF MANY THINGS

Discussion

FIRST TELECAST: *October 5, 1953*

LAST TELECAST: *January 11, 1954*

BROADCAST HISTORY:

Oct 1953–Jan 1954, ABC Mon 8:30–9:00

HOST:

Dr. Bergen Evans

Discussion program that ranged over many subjects, from the capture of the German submarine *U-505* on the high seas during World War II (with a Navy admiral as guest), to American popular music (with Mitch Miller), to the art of practical joking. From WBKB-TV, Chicago.

OFF TO SEE THE WIZARD

Children's Films

FIRST TELECAST: *September 8, 1967*

LAST TELECAST: *September 20, 1968*

BROADCAST HISTORY:

Sep 1967–Sep 1968, ABC Fri 7:30–8:30

This series was a collection of films, geared specifically to appeal to children. Among the movies aired, often in two parts if they were full-length theatrical features, were

Flipper, Clarence, the Cross-eyed Lion, and *The Adventures of Huckleberry Finn.* In addition, a number of films were made especially for this series. Most of these were nature documentaries, but one was an engaging hour entitled "Who's Afraid of Mother Goose," featuring such stars as Frankie Avalon and Nancy Sinatra as Jack and Jill, Rowan & Martin as Simple Simon and the Pieman, the Three Stooges as Three Men in a Tub, and other major names in storybook roles.

The title *Off to See the Wizard* derived from the use of animated characters from *The Wizard of Oz* to host each telecast—Dorothy, the Tin Woodman, the Cowardly Lion, the Scarecrow, Toto, the Wicked Witch of the West, the Wizard, and others.

OH, BOY

Music

FIRST TELECAST: *July 16, 1959*

LAST TELECAST: *September 3, 1959*

BROADCAST HISTORY:

Jul 1959–Sep 1959, ABC Thu 7:30–8:00

HOST:

Tony Hall

Filmed in England, and featuring popular vocal groups from Great Britain plus American guest stars, this series of half-hour musical programs aired on ABC for an eight-week period during the summer of 1959. Among those most frequently featured were Cliff Richard and the Drifters, the Dallas Boys, Marty Wilde, Cherry Wainer, and Dickie Pride. Jimmy Henny was co-host of the program for the last few weeks.

OH, SUSANNA

syndicated title for *Gale Storm Show, The*

OH, THOSE BELLS

Comedy

FIRST TELECAST: *March 8, 1962*

LAST TELECAST: *May 31, 1962*

BROADCAST HISTORY:

Mar 1962–May 1962, CBS Thu 7:30–8:00

CAST:

Herbie Bell .... Herbert Wiere
Harry Bell .... Harry Wiere
Sylvie Bell .... Sylvester Wiere
Henry Slocum .... Henry Norell
Kitty Mathews .... Carol Byron

This series was a loosely structured attempt to bring contemporary slapstick humor to television. The Wiere Brothers, an internationally known trio of slapstick comedians, portrayed the last living members of a family with a long history as theatrical prop, costume, and wig makers. They worked in a Hollywood prop shop, run by irascible Henry Slocum with the help of his sweet, understanding secretary, Kitty. Despite their gentle natures, the brothers managed to turn simple everyday situations into frenetic disasters. When things started to go wrong their world looked like it had been taken over by The Three Stooges in their prime.

O'HARA, U.S. TREASURY

Police

FIRST TELECAST: *September 17, 1971*

LAST TELECAST: *September 8, 1972*

BROADCAST HISTORY:

Sep 1971–Dec 1971, CBS Fri 8:30–9:30
Jan 1972–Sep 1972, CBS Fri 8:00–9:00

CAST:

Jim O'Hara .... David Janssen

Produced with the approval and cooperation of all of the various branches of the Department of the Treasury, this series followed the adventures of special agent Jim O'Hara. Working in pursuit of violators of federal laws, sometimes undercover, Jim served all five of the enforcement agencies of the Department: Bureau of Customs, Secret Service, Internal Revenue Service Intelligence Division, Internal Revenue Service Inspection Division, and Internal Revenue Service, Alcohol, Tobacco, and Firearms Division.

OKY DOKY RANCH

see *Adventures of Oky Doky*

OLD AMERICAN BARN DANCE

Music

FIRST TELECAST: *July 5, 1953*

LAST TELECAST: *August 9, 1953*

BROADCAST HISTORY:

Jul 1953–Aug 1953, DUM Sun 10:30–11:00

EMCEE:

Bill Bailey

Filmed summertime Country music show, featuring Pee Wee King, Tennessee Ernie Ford, and others.

OLD FASHIONED MEETING

Religion

FIRST TELECAST: *October 8, 1950*

LAST TELECAST: *April 1, 1951*

BROADCAST HISTORY:

Oct 1950–Apr 1951, ABC Sun 10:00–10:30

An old-fashioned religious revival hour, sponsored by the Gospel Broadcasting Association.

OLDSMOBILE MUSIC THEATRE

Anthology with Music

FIRST TELECAST: *March 26, 1959*

LAST TELECAST: *May 7, 1959*

BROADCAST HISTORY:

Mar 1959–May 1959, NBC Thu 8:30–9:00

HOSTS:

Bill Hayes
Florence Henderson

This anthology series presented live plays in which a musical element was woven into the storyline, as in musical comedies or dramas with incidental songs. None of the music used was original, however. Hosts Bill Hayes and Florence Henderson appeared in some presentations, along with such stars as Carol Lawrence and Roddy McDowall. The series premiered as *Oldsmobile Music Theatre,* had a single telecast on April 16 as *Oldsmobile Theatre,* and on April 23 became *Oldsmobile Presents.*

OMNIBUS

Culture

FIRST TELECAST: *October 4, 1953*

LAST TELECAST: *March 31, 1957*

BROADCAST HISTORY:

Oct 1953–Apr 1956, CBS Sun 5:00–6:30 (OS)
Oct 1956–Mar 1957, ABC Sun 9:00–10:30

HOST:

Alistair Cooke

Omnibus was the most outstanding and longest-running cultural series in the history of commercial network television. It premiered on November 9, 1952, as a late Sunday afternoon offering on CBS, running from 4:30–6:00 P.M. for its first season. That premiere telecast set the tone for the diversity that would make *Omnibus* a unique program throughout its run. William Saroyan narrated an adaptation of his short story "The Bad Men," there were excerpts from Gilbert and Sullivan's *The Mikado,* and Rex Harrison and his then wife Lilli Palmer starred in Maxwell Anderson's "The Trial of Anne Boleyn"—all in one 90-minute program.

As in that first telecast, the range of subject matter presented on *Omnibus* was quite impressive. Opera, symphony, ballet, dramatic plays, and true-life adventure films prepared by the New York Zoological Society and the American Museum of Natural History were but a few of the offerings of this award-winning show. The financing came from the Ford Foundation TV-Radio Workshop, and enabled the producers to devote the full 90 minutes of each show to program content—there were no commercials on *Omnibus,* a rarity in commercial television.

In the fall of 1953, the start time of *Omnibus* was moved up to 5:00 P.M. and, since it ran until 6:30 P.M. it is eligible for inclusion in this book as an evening program. That first evening season presented dramas based on the works of William Inge, James Thurber, Stephen Vincent Benét, Ernest Hemingway, Carson McCullers, John Steinbeck, and T. S. Eliot. Performing were such talents as Hume Cronyn, Jessica Tandy, Carol Channing, Yul Brynner, Walter Slezak, Elsa Lanchester, Anne Bancroft, Mel Ferrer, Helen Hayes, Claude Rains, E. G. Marshall, John Cassavetes, Susan Strasberg, and Thomas Mitchell. But there was much, much more that season. Orson Welles starred in *King Lear,* Jack Benny in a full 90-minute recreation of his film role in *The Horn Blows at Midnight,* and Victor Borge in a solo segment showing his piano and comedic mastery. Jacques Cousteau, who would have many popular documentaries aired on television in the 1970s, had his first network exposure in January 1954 with "Undersea Archaeology." There were excerpts from the musical *Oklahoma!,* a performance by the Azumi Kabuki Dancers from Japan, a demonstration of the recording techniques used by popular performers Les Paul and Mary Ford, and the ballet *Billy the Kid* with music by Aaron Copland performed by the Ballet Theatre Company. Informational pieces included discussions of the medical uses of X-ray photography and new techniques for determining art forgeries.

Omnibus had a little bit of everything. In subsequent seasons Leonard Bernstein made his television debut with a technical explanation of Beethoven's *Fifth Symphony*, George C. Scott played Robespierre, Peter Ustinov played Samuel Johnson, and Kim Stanley played Joan of Arc. When it left the evening hours in the spring of 1957, it was only to return on Sunday afternoons that fall on NBC, where it remained until its final telecast on May 10, 1959. When it left the air, something wonderful about television went with it, creating a void that was not to be filled until the emergence of network Public Television a decade later.

ON BROADWAY TONIGHT

Talent/Variety

FIRST TELECAST: *July 8, 1964*

LAST TELECAST: *March 12, 1965*

BROADCAST HISTORY:

Jul 1964–Sep 1964, CBS Wed 10:00–11:00
Jan 1965–Mar 1965, CBS Fri 8:30–9:30

EMCEE:

Rudy Vallee

Many talented young performers were given their first national television exposure on this show. Host Rudy Vallee would interview each of the six acts that were performing on a given week's telecast, and then let them do their routines. A special feature of each show was the appearance of a well-known celebrity who would chat with Mr. Vallee about his or her big break in show business. Interestingly, most of the young performers on this series who later became successful were comedians. Among them were Rich Little, Richard Pryor, Marilyn Michaels, Rodney Dangerfield, George Carlin, Jo Anne Worley, and Renee Taylor. Singer Adam Wade, however, made more appearances on the show than anyone else.

ON GUARD

Documentary

FIRST TELECAST: *April 28, 1952*

LAST TELECAST: *May 29, 1954*

BROADCAST HISTORY:

Apr 1952–Aug 1952, ABC Mon 9:30–10:00
Sep 1952–Dec 1952, ABC Thu 9:30–10:00
Dec 1952–Apr 1953, ABC Sun 6:00–6:30
Dec 1953–May 1954, ABC Sat 10:00–10:30

This program consisted of documentary films about the military, produced by the Army, Navy, and Air Force.

ON OUR OWN

Situation Comedy

FIRST TELECAST: *October 9, 1977*

LAST TELECAST: *August 20, 1978*

BROADCAST HISTORY:

Oct 1977–Aug 1978, CBS Sun 8:30–9:00

CAST:

Maria Teresa Bonino ....Lynnie Greene
Julia Peters ....Bess Armstrong
Toni McBain ....Gretchen Wyler
April Baxter ....Dixie Carter
Craig Boatwright ....Dan Resin
Eddie Barnes ...... John Christopher Jones
J. M. Bedford ....Bob Randall

On Our Own, the story of two young women trying to make it in the New York advertising world, was the only prime time series actually being produced in New York as of the start of the 1977–1978 season. Maria and Julia had both just been promoted from the secretarial positions they had previously held at the Bedford Advertising Agency, Maria to art director and Julia to copywriter. They were enthusiastic and energetic, if a bit naive and inexperienced, and wanted desperately to take full advantage of their first big step up the corporate ladder. Others in the agency were copywriter April Baxter, beautiful, sexy, and worldly wise with all sorts of advice about men; Eddie Barnes, creative producer of television commercials; and salesman Craig Boatwright. Running the whole operation was sophisticated, slogan-making Toni McBain, the head of the agency. The only person she had to please was board chairman J. M. Bedford.

ON PARADE

Musical Variety

FIRST TELECAST: *July 17, 1964*

LAST TELECAST: *September 18, 1964*

BROADCAST HISTORY:

Jul 1964–Sep 1964, NBC Fri 9:30–10:00

On Parade was originally produced by the Canadian Broadcasting Company. Each telecast spotlighted a particular performer or group of performers from the American musical world such as Rosemary Clooney, Henry Mancini, Diahann Carroll, and the Limeliters. Production numbers, comedy sketches, and interviews were all part of the regular format.

ON THE BOARDWALK WITH PAUL WHITEMAN

Variety

FIRST TELECAST: *May 30, 1954*

LAST TELECAST: *August 1, 1954*

BROADCAST HISTORY:

May 1954–Aug 1954, ABC Sun 8:00–9:00

EMCEE:

Paul Whiteman

Telecast live from the famous Steel Pier in Atlantic City, New Jersey, this program was a variation on *The Original Amateur Hour.* During the first half-hour of each show, eight young acts auditioned briefly and were rated by a panel of four people from show business. The four acts with the greatest potential would then return the following week to perform again after they had had a full week of professional coaching.

ON THE CORNER

Variety

FIRST TELECAST: *April 18, 1948*

LAST TELECAST: *May 16, 1948*

BROADCAST HISTORY:

Apr 1948–May 1948, ABC Sun 6:30–7:00

HOST:

Henry Morgan

A modest variety program which is said by ABC to have been the first ABC network series. The network at the time consisted of four stations: WFIL in Philadelphia (where *On the Corner* originated); WMAR, Baltimore; WMAL, Washington; and WABD, New York. The latter was a DuMont station, since ABC's own New York outlet was not yet on the air.

Henry Morgan was a major radio star in the 1940s, and was one of the first performers to try the new medium of television on a regular basis. *On the Corner* showed him thumbing the pages of *Variety,* turning up the names of his guests—who generally turned out to be little-known, and sometimes second-rate, nightclub performers. Appearing on the first telecast were George Guest with his marionettes, puppeteer Virginia Austin, impersonator Roy Davis, and the Clark Sisters singing quartet. Laced through it all was Morgan's sardonic wit, which included jibes at the sponsor's commercials. Apparently Admiral Corporation was not amused, as *On the Corner* was canceled after only five weeks of its projected 13-week run.

ON THE LINE WITH CONSIDINE

News Interview

FIRST TELECAST: *January 8, 1952*

LAST TELECAST: *August 29, 1954*

BROADCAST HISTORY:

Jan 1952–Jun 1953, NBC Tue 10:45–11:00
Jun 1953–Jan 1954, NBC Tue 10:30–10:45
Jul 1954–Aug 1954, ABC Sun 9:00–9:15

HOST:

Bob Considine

After a long career as a journalist, both in print and on radio, Bob Considine came to television. His show, *On the Line with Considine,* actually premiered on Saturday, January 20, 1951, at 5:45 P.M. After a year in that time slot, it moved to Tuesday evening where it remained on NBC for two years. After the show was canceled, it returned for the summer of 1954 on ABC. The format of the show consisted of Bob Considine reading the current news headlines, with occasional comment, and then conducting a short interview with a prominent figure about a pertinent issue of current interest.

ON THE ROCKS

Situation Comedy

FIRST TELECAST: *September 11, 1975*

LAST TELECAST: *May 17, 1976*

BROADCAST HISTORY:

Sep 1975–Jan 1976, ABC Thu 8:30–9:00
Jan 1976–May 1976, ABC Mon 8:00–8:30

CAST:

Hector Fuentes .... Jose Perez
DeMott .... Hal Williams
Cleaver .... Rick Hurst
Nicky Palik .... Bobby Sandler
Mr. Gibson .... Mel Stewart
Mr. Sullivan .... Tom Poston
Gabby .... Pat Cranshaw

Comedy centering on the inmates of Alamesa Minimum Security Prison, a "low risk" institution apparently run as much by the prisoners as by the authorities. The usual setting was the cell containing Hector, the resourceful Latin; his friend DeMott; Cleaver, the eternal optimist; and Nicky, a juvenile offender. Nearby was Gabby, a toothless elderly inmate. Mr Gibson was the hard-nosed corrections officer, whose attempts at keeping the boys in line were often unintentionally thwarted by Mr. Sullivan, a mild-mannered guard.

Taped before a live audience and originally telecast immediately following TV's leading cop comedy, *Barney Miller*.

ON TRIAL

see *Joseph Cotten Show, The*

ON TRIAL

Debate

FIRST TELECAST: *November 22, 1948*

LAST TELECAST: *August 12, 1952*

BROADCAST HISTORY:

Nov 1948–Feb 1950, ABC Various nights and times, 30 minutes

Mar 1950–Sep 1950, ABC Wed 8:00–8:30

Oct 1950–Sep 1951, ABC Mon 9:30–10:00

Oct 1951–Jun 1952, ABC Tue 9:30–10:00

Jun 1952–Aug 1952, ABC Tue 8:00–8:30

MODERATOR:

David Levitan

Public-affairs debate in the manner of a courtroom trial, with a real-life judge presiding; affirmative and negative counsel and expert witnesses (guest authorities) argued the various points of an issue. Later the format was altered slightly to provide for affirmative arguments one week followed by negative arguments the next. The first issue "on trial" in November 1948 was "Should Wiretapping Be Prohibited?"

For its first fifteen months *On Trial* was shifted all over the ABC schedule, seldom spending more than two months in any one time slot. Beginning in early 1950 it settled down to longer runs on various weeknights.

ON YOUR WAY

Quiz/Talent

FIRST TELECAST: *September 9, 1953*

LAST TELECAST: *April 17, 1954*

BROADCAST HISTORY:

Sep 1953–Jan 1954, DUM Wed 9:30–10:00

Jan 1954–Apr 1954, ABC Sat 7:00–7:30

EMCEE:

Bud Collyer (1953–1954)

Kathy Godfrey (1954)

John Reed King (1954)

On Your Way began as an audience-participation quiz show in which contestants were given the opportunity to win free transportation to a destination of their choice (thus sending them "on their way"). Bud Collyer was the original host. On January 23, 1954, the program moved to ABC, with new hosts and (two weeks later) a new format. Kathy Godfrey, Arthur Godfrey's younger sister, interviewed four aspiring young performers who then competed in a talent show, under the supervision of emcee John Reed King. In its talent-show format the program was supposed to send winners "on their way" in show business. Unfortunately, not many of them ever gained any sort of fame, although one contestant—a 16-year-old guitarist named Charlie Gracie—later became an important rock star in the late 1950s.

ONCE AN EAGLE

Military Drama

FIRST TELECAST: *December 2, 1976*

LAST TELECAST: *January 13, 1977*

BROADCAST HISTORY:

Dec 1976–Jan 1977, NBC Tue 9:00–10:00

CAST:

Sam Damon .... Sam Elliott
Courtney Massengale .... Cliff Potts
Tommy Caldwell Damon ..... Darleen Carr
George Caldwell .... Glenn Ford
Lt. Merrick .... Clu Gulager
Emily Massengale .... Amy Irving
Jinny Massengale .... Melanie Griffith
Donny Damon .... Andrew Damon

Adapted from Anton Myrer's novel, *Once an Eagle* was the story of two men's careers in the military over a 30-year period. Sam Damon was a dedicated soldier who cared little for the comforts of home, prestige, power, and the other affectations of rank. Relishing front-line combat, he was a soldier who regarded the military life as a profession to be handled to the best of his ability. Courtney Massengale, on the other hand, was a conniver and maneuverer. More concerned about appearance than substance, he was always on the lookout for a contact to help boost him further up on the ladder to power and prestige. The two men had started out in similar situations as young officers in World War I and individual chapters of *Once an Eagle* showed how their respective lives changed and developed during the intervening period to, and through, World War II.

Once an Eagle was one of four novels dramatized under the collective title *NBC's Best Sellers*. Although individual chapters generally ran only one hour, as indicated in the broadcast history above, the first and last chapters ran from 9:00–11:00 P.M.

ONCE UPON A FENCE

Children's

FIRST TELECAST: *April 13, 1952*

LAST TELECAST: *July 20, 1952*

BROADCAST HISTORY:

Apr 1952–Jul 1952, NBC Sun 6:30–7:00

REGULARS:

Dave Kaigler
Katherine Heger

Music, stories, and magical adventures were all part of this live children's show that originated from Philadelphia during the summer of 1952. The show starred Dave Kaigler, a singer and guitar player who was aided by Eric the Bluebird, an imaginary pet, and Princess Katherine of Storyland, played by Katherine Heger. Miss Heger was a dancer and actress who told stories to the children by acting out all the parts.

ONCE UPON A TUNE

Musical Anthology

FIRST TELECAST: *March 6, 1951*

LAST TELECAST: *May 15, 1951*

BROADCAST HISTORY:

Mar 1951–May 1951, DUM Tue 10:00–11:00

REGULARS:

Phil Hanna
Holly Harris
Reginald Beane
Bernice Parks
Ed Holmes

This bright, though somewhat amateurish program presented a complete musical every week, usually a takeoff on a current Broadway show or a famous story (for instance, "Little Red Riding Hood"). Various young performers were seen, in addition to the regulars listed above. The program was previously seen locally in New York.

ONE DAY AT A TIME

Situation Comedy

FIRST TELECAST: *December 16, 1975*

LAST TELECAST:

BROADCAST HISTORY:

Dec 1975–Jul 1976, CBS Tue 9:30–10:00
Sep 1976–Jan 1978, CBS Tue 9:30–10:00
Jan 1978– , CBS Mon 9:30–10:00

CAST:

Ann Romano .... Bonnie Franklin
Julie Cooper .... Mackenzie Phillips
Barbara Cooper .... Valerie Bertinelli
Dwayne Schneider ...... Pat Harrington, Jr.
David Kane (1975–1976) .... Richard Masur
Ginny Wrobliki (1976–1977)
.... Mary Louise Wilson
Mr. Davenport (1976–)
.... Charles Siebert

After seventeen years of marriage, Ann Romano found herself divorced and living with her two teenage daughters in an apartment building in her home town of Indianapolis. The problems of trying to keep a job and be an understanding mother to two headstrong girls provided the plots for most episodes of this series. Ann resumed use of her maiden name while both 17-year-old Julie and 15-year-old Barbara kept their father's. The building's super, who regarded himself as the Rudolph Valentino of Indianapolis, was Dwayne Schneider. His first name was virtually never used—all the tenants referred to him only as Schneider. David Kane was Ann's romantic interest during the first season, and at one point they did almost get married, but he departed early in the fall of 1976. Not long after his departure, Ann acquired an outspoken, brassy new neighbor in Ginny Wrobliki, but she only lasted one season in the cast. It was during that season, however, that Ann found herself a substantial job working as an account executive for the advertising agency of Connors and Davenport. Although not a regular in the series, Joseph Campanella made occasional appearances as Ann's ex-husband, Ed Cooper.

ONE HAPPY FAMILY

Situation Comedy

FIRST TELECAST: *January 13, 1961*

LAST TELECAST: *September 8, 1961*

BROADCAST HISTORY:

Jan 1961–Mar 1961, NBC Fri 8:00–8:30
May 1961–Sep 1961, NBC Fri 8:00–8:30

CAST:

Dick Cooper .... Dick Sargent
Penny Cooper .... Jody Warner
Barney Hogan .... Chick Chandler
Mildred Hogan .... Elisabeth Fraser
Charlie Hackett .... Jack Kirkwood
Lovey Hackett .... Cheerio Meredith

Newlyweds Dick and Penny Cooper moved in with Penny's family for a night and somehow ended up as permanent residents. Also part of the household were Penny's grandparents, the Hacketts. Dick was a meteorologist whose good nature was often strained by the efforts of his assembled in-laws to be "helpful," despite their protestations that they would let the young couple lead their own lives. Penny's father, Barney Hogan, was a successful plumbing contractor with an extremely energetic wife, Mildred. Grandfather Charlie Hackett was a strong-willed old coot with a nutty, fun-loving wife named Lovey. The conflicts between the three generations making up *One Happy Family* generated most of the humor in this series.

100 GRAND

Quiz/Audience Participation

FIRST TELECAST: *September 15, 1963*

LAST TELECAST: *September 29, 1963*

BROADCAST HISTORY:

Sep 1963, ABC Sun 10:00–10:30

EMCEE:

Jack Clark

Promoted by ABC as the return of the "big money" quiz show (none had been aired since the 1958 quiz show scandals), this program offered contestants the chance to win up to $100,000. Each contestant challenged a panel of five professional authorities in his particular field of knowledge and, if successful, was to contend with five questions submitted by viewers to the show. The concept didn't work very well and the ratings were so low that the show was canceled after only three weeks on the air.

ONE MAN'S FAMILY

Soap Opera

FIRST TELECAST: *November 4, 1949*

LAST TELECAST: *June 21, 1952*

BROADCAST HISTORY:

Nov 1949–Jan 1950, NBC Fri 8:00–8:30
Jan 1950–May 1950, NBC Thu 8:30–9:00
Jul 1950–Jun 1952, NBC Sat 7:30–8:00 (OS)

CAST:

Henry Barbour .... Bert Lytell
Fanny Barbour .... Marjorie Gateson
Paul Barbour .... Russell Thorson
Hazel Barbour/Herbert ...... Lillian Schaaf
Claudia Barbour (1949–1950) .... Nancy Franklin
Claudia Barbour/Roberts (1950–1952) .... Eva Marie Saint
Cliff Barbour (1949) ..... Frank Thomas, Jr.
Cliff Barbour (1949) .... Billy Idelson
Cliff Barbour (1949–1952) .... James Lee
Jack Barbour (1949–1950) ... Arthur Cassell
Jack Barbour (1951–1952) .... Richard Wigginton
Judge Hunter (1949) .... Calvin Thomas
Dr. Thompson (1949–1950) .... Luis Van Rooten
Johnny Roberts (1949–1951) .... Michael Higgins
Beth Holly (1949–1950) .... Mercedes McCambridge
Beth Holly (1950–1952) .... Susan Shaw
Mrs. Roberts (1950–1951) ..... Mona Bruns
Mr. Roberts (1950–1952) ...... Ralph Locke
Judith Richardson (1950) .... Athena Lorde
Danny Frank (1950) .... John Newland
Mac (1950–1952) .... Tony Randall
Joe Yarbourogh (1950–1952) ..... Jim Boles
Bill Herbert (1950) .... Les Treymaine
Bill Herbert (1950–1952) ..... Walter Brooke
Teddy Lawton (1951–1952) .... Madeline Belgard
Ann Waite (1951–1952) .... Nancy Franklin
Burton (1951–1952) .... Billy Greene
Capt. Nicholas Lacey (1952) .... Lloyd Bochner
Sgt. Tony Adams (1952) .... Michael McAloney
Sir Guy Vane (1952) ...... Maurice Manson
Jo Collier (1952) .... Gina Holland

CREATOR/WRITER:

Carleton E. Morse

THEME:

"Deserted Mansion"

Television version of the favorite radio serial, which began in 1932. None of the radio cast initially carried over into the TV version, but the story remained essentially the same. It was the saga of San Francisco banker Henry Barbour and his clan, set at the Barbours' suburban home in Sea Cliff, overlooking the Golden Gate Bridge. Paul, the eldest son, was the philosophical member of the family, serving as confidant for the other children and the person they turned to when in trouble (which was often). He was single and a pilot by profession (he had been wounded in World War II). Hazel, the eldest daughter, was 28 when the TV series began and rather anxious to find a husband—which she finally did, in Bill Herbert. Claudia and Cliff were the twins, students at Stanford University, and somewhat rebellious against their father's old-fashioned ways. Jack was the youngest child, aged 10, mischievous and loved by all.

Among the central plot developments during the program's three-year run in prime time were the stormy marriages of Hazel and Claudia, Paul's adopting the orphan Teddy Lawson, Claudia's adventures in Paris where she met the sinister Sir Guy Vane, and assorted illnesses, family feuds, and intrigues. Longtime fans of the radio *One Man's Family* must have had the strange feeling that they were going back in time when watching the TV version—for the action was a full generation behind the continuing radio serial. Ten-year-old Jack was 32 years old on radio, and had six children; the college-age twins were 37 on radio, each having had been through two marriages and endless traumas; Paul had been a pilot in World War I on radio—and so on.

The TV version was also seen as a daytime serial from 1954–1955. The program continued on radio until 1959.

ONE MINUTE PLEASE

Quiz/Audience Participation

FIRST TELECAST: *July 6, 1954*

LAST TELECAST: *February 17, 1955*

BROADCAST HISTORY:

Jul 1954–Oct 1954, DUM Tue 8:30–9:00
Oct 1954, DUM Tue 9:00–9:30
Nov 1954–Jan 1955, DUM Fri 9:30–10:00
Jan 1955–Feb 1955, DUM Thu 9:30–10:00

MODERATOR:

John K. M. McCaffery (1954)
Allyn Edwards

REGULAR PANELISTS:

Hermione Gingold
Alice Pearce
Cleveland Amory
Ernie Kovacs
Marc Connelly

The object of *One Minute Please* was to see how well the panelists could do at talking nonstop for a full minute on subjects of which they had little knowledge. Such topics as "How to Make Glue," "Breeding Guppies," "Whale Blubber," and "Why I Ride Sidesaddle" were representative of the nonsense talked about. The panelist who managed to say the most in one minute was the winner for the week. Effective November 19, 1954, Allyn Edwards replaced John K. M. McCaffrey as permanent moderator.

ONE STEP BEYOND

syndicated title for *Alcoa Presents*

1, 2, 3 GO

Educational Children's

FIRST TELECAST: *October 8, 1961*

LAST TELECAST: *May 27, 1962*

BROADCAST HISTORY:

Oct 1961–May 1962, NBC Sun 6:30–7:00

REGULARS:

Richard Thomas
Jack Lescoulie

Hosts of this educational program for children were 10-year-old Richard and his adult friend Jack, who traveled around the country learning about our society and the people who comprise it. Trips were taken to such diverse places as NASA headquarters in Houston, the Treasury Department in Washington, D.C., and an Eskimo village in Alaska. Although informative to viewers of all ages, the emphasis of the show was on professions, skills, and environments that would be of particular interest to young children. Young Richard later went on to fame as John-Boy on *The Waltons.*

O'NEILLS, THE

Drama

FIRST TELECAST: *September 6, 1949*

LAST TELECAST: *January 10, 1950*

BROADCAST HISTORY:

Sep 1949–Jan 1950, DUM Tue 9:00–9:30

CAST:

Peggy O'Neill .... Vera Allen
Janice O'Neill .... Janice Gilbert
Eddie O'Neill .... Michael Lawson
Uncle Bill .... Ian Martin
Mrs. Bailey .... Jane West
Morris Levy .... Ben Fishbein
Mrs. Levy .... Celia Budkin

The O'Neills was an attempt to recreate on television one of the most popular radio serials of the 1930s. Although the radio version had been off the air since 1943, TV brought back many of the characters, including dress designer Peggy O'Neill, who was struggling to raise two fatherless children, cantankerous Uncle Bill, nosy Mrs. Bailey, and the next-door neighbors, the Levys. Actresses Janice Gilbert and Jane

West were veterans of the radio show, but their presence was not enough to save the video version of it, which folded after a few months.

OPEN HEARING

Public Affairs

FIRST TELECAST: *February 1, 1954*
LAST TELECAST: *September 28, 1958*
BROADCAST HISTORY:
Feb 1954–Jul 1954, ABC Thu 9:00–9:30
Feb 1957–Mar 1957, ABC Sun 8:30–9:00
Nov 1957–Jan 1958, ABC Sun 9:00–9:30
Jan 1958–Mar 1958, ABC Sun 7:00–7:30
Jun 1958–Sep 1958, ABC Sun 9:30–10:00
HOST/MODERATOR:
John Daly (1954)
John Secondari (1957–1958)

The first ABC program called *Open Hearing* consisted of filmed documentaries and commentary on various topics of general interest, such as the Army-McCarthy controversy, corporate stockholders' meetings, and Alcholics Anonymous. The 1957–1958 version was a live interview program in which public figures were either interviewed by ABC newsmen, or participated in debates on subjects of current interest. Among the non-politicians appearing were disc jockey Dick Clark, commenting on teenagers and rock 'n' roll, and academician Dr. Henry Kissinger on the state of the nation in 1958. In addition to the prime-time telecasts listed above, this latter version was frequently seen on Sunday afternoons, where it continued until 1960.

For an earlier series on CBS called *Open Hearing* see *The Facts We Face*.

OPENING NIGHT

Dramatic Anthology

FIRST TELECAST: *June 14, 1958*
LAST TELECAST: *September 8, 1958*
BROADCAST HISTORY:
Jun 1958–Sep 1958, NBC Sat 9:00–9:30
HOSTESS:
Arlene Dahl

The filmed dramas presented on *Opening Night* were reruns of episodes of the ABC series *Ford Theatre*. Arlene Dahl introduced the plays, which aired on alternate Saturdays with *Club Oasis*.

OPERA CAMEOS

Music

FIRST TELECAST: *January 10, 1954*
LAST TELECAST: *November 21, 1954*
BROADCAST HISTORY:
Jan 1954–Nov 1954, DUM Sun 7:30–8:00 (OS)
COMMENTATOR:
Giovanni Martinelli
CONDUCTOR:
Maestro Guiseppe Bamboschek (and others)

Grand opera has been a rare commodity on American television, but this program of excerpts from famous operas was a fixture on New York TV for many years beginning in 1950. For several months in 1954 (and perhaps for other short periods as well) it was also fed out on the DuMont network. The host, retired Metropolitan Opera star tenor Giovanni Martinelli, introduced the presentations, describing the plot and setting. A mixture of established and younger, lesser-known operatic talent was featured, including some who were billed as future superstars (whatever *did* happen to Gianni Iaia, "the next Caruso"?), some who later did have important careers (such as Beverly Sills), and some whose connection with grand opera was tenuous at best (such as movie vocalist Marni Nixon). Martinelli himself did not appear in the productions, which generally included standard repertoire such as *Tosca, Cavalleria Rusticana, Madame Butterfly, Carmen*, and the like.

OPERA VS. JAZZ

Music

FIRST TELECAST: *May 25, 1953*
LAST TELECAST: *September 21, 1953*
BROADCAST HISTORY:
May 1953–Sep 1953, ABC Mon 7:30–8:00
HOSTESS:
Nancy Kenyon
REGULAR:
ABC Piano Quartet

This was not really a competition, but simply a mixed presentation of popular tunes (not "jazz") and standard operatic arias, performed by a different pair of guests each week. Nancy Kenyon gave the musical introductions, and accompaniment was by the ABC Piano Quartet, four pianos on a revolving stage. Among those representing the popular field were Alan Dale, Don Cornell, Karen Chandler, and Jerry Vale; the operatic, Jan Peerce, Thomas Hayward, Robert Merrill, and Virginia MacWatters.

OPERATION: ENTERTAINMENT

Variety

FIRST TELECAST: *January 5, 1968*
LAST TELECAST: *January 31, 1969*
BROADCAST HISTORY:
Jan 1968–Apr 1968, ABC Fri 8:30–9:30
Sep 1968–Jan 1969, ABC Fri 7:30–8:30
REGULARS:
The Operation Entertainment Girls
The Terry Gibbs Band
EXECUTIVE PRODUCER:
Chuck Barris

With a different guest host and new guest stars each week, this series of filmed variety shows traveled around the world to entertain U.S. military personnel at Army, Navy and Air Force bases, much in the manner of the Bob Hope Christmas Shows. Rich Little was host of the first telecast, from Camp Pendleton, California, and such top-name stars as Tim Conway, Jimmy Dean, and Ed Ames appeared on subsequent telecasts.

OPERATION INFORMATION

Instruction

FIRST TELECAST: *July 17, 1952*
LAST TELECAST: *September 18, 1952*
BROADCAST HISTORY:
Jul 1952–Sep 1952, DUM Thu 8:00–8:30

Korean War era informational program for veterans, designed to acquaint them with their benefit rights.

OPERATION NEPTUNE

Science Fiction

FIRST TELECAST: *June 28, 1953*
LAST TELECAST: *August 16, 1953*
BROADCAST HISTORY:
Jun 1953–Aug 1953, NBC Sun 7:00–7:30
CAST:
Commander Bill Hollister .. Todd Griffin
Dink Melvin ....Richard Holland
Kebeda ....Harold Conklin
Mersennus ....Del Berti
Admiral Bigelow ....Rusty Lane

Operation Neptune was a live science-fiction series with a strong children's orientation. After the disappearance of a number of ships, the Navy concluded that certain evil forces were operating from under the seas to destroy the people living on the surface of Earth. Bill Hollister, who had the nickname "Captain Neptune" for his extensive undersea survey work, was called upon by the Navy to track down the source of the trouble, which turned out to be the evil Kebeda and his henchman Mersennus. Helping Captain Neptune was his young assistant and protégé, Dink Melvin.

OPERATION PETTICOAT

Situation Comedy

FIRST TELECAST: *September 17, 1977*
LAST TELECAST: *October 19, 1978*
BROADCAST HISTORY:
Sep 1977–May 1978, ABC Sat 8:30–9:00
May 1978–Jun 1978, ABC Thu 8:30–9:00
Jun 1978–Aug 1978, ABC Fri 8:30–9:00
Sep 1978–Oct 1978, ABC Mon 8:30–9:00
CAST:
Lt. Comdr. Matthew Sherman (1977–1978) ....John Astin
Lt. Nick Holden (1977–1978) ....Richard Gilliland
Major Edna Howard (1977–1978) ....Yvonne Wilder
Lt. Dolores Crandall ....Melinda Naud
Lt. Barbara Duran (1977–1978) ....Jamie Lee Curtis
Lt. Ruth Colfax (1977–1978) ....Dorrie Thomson
Lt. Claire Reid (1977–1978) ....Bond Gideon
Yeoman Hunkle ....Richard Brestoff
Ensign Stovall (1977–1978) ....Christopher J. Brown
Seaman Dooley (1977–1978) ....Kraig Cassity
Ramon Gallardo (1977–1978) ....Jesse Dixon
Chief of Boat Herbert Molumphrey (1977–1978) ....Wayne Long
Pharmacist's Mate Williams (1977–1978) ....Richard Marion
Radioman Gossett (1977–1978) ....Michael Mazes
Chief Machinist's Mate Tostin (1977–1978) ....Jack Murdock
Seaman Horwich (1977–1978) ....Peter Schuck
Lt. Watson (1977–1978) ...Raymond Singer
Seaman Broom ....Jim Varney
Lt. Mike Bender (1978) Randolph Mantooth
Lt. Comdr. Haller (1978) ..... Robert Hogan
Lt. Katherine O'Hara (1978) ... JoAnn Pflug
Lt. Betty Wheeler (1978 .. Hilary Thompson

Chief Engineer Dobritch (1978)
.... Warren Berlinger
Seaman Horner (1978) ....Don Sparks
Doplos (1978) ....Fred Kareman
Seaman Dixon (1978) ...... Scott McGinnis

This was a World War II comedy set in the Pacific. Lt. Comdr. Matthew Sherman was a Navy career officer anxious to see action before the war was over. When he finally was assigned to command the submarine *Sea Tiger*, however, he arrived to find the craft sunk at dockside. No sooner did he get it patched up and half painted, with pink undercoating, than he had to put to sea quickly to avoid another air raid—hence the Navy's first pink submarine. Compounding his problems on board were five Army nurses, whom he had rescued, and a wheeler-dealer supply officer, Lt. Holden, who wanted to avoid combat as much as Sherman wanted to find it.

Operation Petticoat was as leaky in the ratings as it was at sea, and when it returned for a second season virtually the entire cast had been changed. Lt. Comdr. Haller was the new skipper, and Lt. Bender his wheeler-dealer executive officer. There were new nurses, led by Lt. O'Hara, new crew members, and also a new mission. The *Sea Tiger* was now assigned to patrol the Pacific for downed airmen and sailors. It didn't help. The series was cancelled after only four episodes with the new crew.

Based on the 1959 movie starring Cary Grant and Tony Curtis, whose daughter, Jamie Lee Curtis, played one of the nurses in this series during the 1977–1978 season.

OPERATION: RUNAWAY

Drama

FIRST TELECAST: *April 27, 1978*
LAST TELECAST: *August 31, 1978*
BROADCAST HISTORY:
Apr 1978–May 1978, NBC Thu 9:00–10:00
Aug 1978, NBC Thu 10:00–11:00
CAST:
David McKay ....Robert Reed
Karen Wingate ....Karen Machon
Mark Johnson ....Michael Biehn
Susan Donovan ....Ruth Cox

Each year in the U.S. between one and two million teenagers run away from home. This program dramatized that phenomenon, through the fictional stories of youngsters trying to escape from the demands of insensitive parents, broken homes, the shame of unwanted pregnancies, or other problems which were more than they could face. The central character was David McKay, a psychologist who maintained an office on the campus of a large Los Angeles college, but whose travels in search of runaway youngsters took him up and down the West Coast. David's girl friend, Karen Wingate, was Dean of Women at the college. Mark and Susan were his two wards, one time runaways who had built lives of their own under David's care. Both were now college students nearing graduation.

OPERATION SUCCESS

Information

FIRST TELECAST: *January 27, 1949*
LAST TELECAST: *June 23, 1949*
BROADCAST HISTORY:
Jan 1949–Jun 1949, DUM Thu 8:00–8:30

Veteran's show.

ORCHID AWARD, THE

Musical Variety

FIRST TELECAST: *May 24, 1953*
LAST TELECAST: *January 24, 1954*
BROADCAST HISTORY:
May 1953–Jul 1953, ABC Sun 6:45–7:00
Jul 1953–Jan 1954, ABC Sun 9:15–9:30
EMCEE:
Bert Lytell (1953)
Ronald Reagan (1953–1954)
Donald Woods (1953–1954)

This musical variety show formed a half-hour block with Walter Winchell's news and gossip program. After Winchell had finished "throwing orchids" (i.e., brickbats) at leading entertainers in his commentary, *The Orchid Award* presented one with a real orchid and had him or her perform. Originally *The Orchid Award* presented a performer's biography in music, with Rosemary Clooney being the first guest. Later it became a straight (though short) variety show, with such guests as Rex Harrison, Teresa Brewer, Victor Borge, Lauritz Melchior, Eddie Fisher, and others. Bert Lytell was the original host, replaced in July by alternating hosts Ronald Reagan from Hollywood and Donald Woods from New York. Also known as *The Orchid Room*.

OREGON TRAIL, THE

Western

FIRST TELECAST: *September 21, 1977*

LAST TELECAST: *October 26, 1977*

BROADCAST HISTORY:

Sep 1977–Oct 1977, NBC Wed 9:00–10:00

CAST:

Evan Thorpe .... Rod Taylor
Margaret Devlin .... Darleen Carr
Luther Sprague .... Charles Napier
Andrew Thorpe .... Andrew Stevens
William Thorpe .... Tony Becker
Rachel Thorpe .... Gina Marie Smika

In 1842 widower Evan Thorpe decided to leave his native Illinois with his three children—Andy, aged 17; William, aged 12; and Rachel, aged 10—in search of a new life in the Oregon Territory. He joined a wagon train heading west, was soon elected its captain when the original leader proved to be unreliable, and found a new romantic interest in fellow traveler Margaret Devlin. As the train moved west it was beset with all the traditional enemies—bad weather, unfriendly Indians, rough terrain, and dishonest con men. Luther Sprague was the hardened scout who had little tolerance for the citified travelers' lack of preparedness for the rigors of the trip.

ORIGINAL AMATEUR HOUR, THE

Talent

FIRST TELECAST: *January 18, 1948*

LAST TELECAST: *September 26, 1960*

BROADCAST HISTORY:

Jan 1948–Sep 1949, DUM Sun 7:00–8:00
Oct 1949–Jan 1952, NBC Tue 10:00–11:00
Jan 1952–Sep 1952, NBC Tue 10:00–10:45
Apr 1953–Sep 1954, NBC Sat 8:30–9:00
Oct 1955–Dec 1955, ABC Sun 9:30–10:00
Jan 1956–Feb 1956, ABC Sun 9:30–10:30
Mar 1956–Sep 1956, ABC Sun 9:00–10:00
Oct 1956–Mar 1957, ABC Sun 7:30–8:30
Apr 1957–Jun 1957, ABC Sun 9:00–10:00
Jul 1957–Sep 1957, NBC Mon 10:00–10:30
Sep 1957–Dec 1957, NBC Sun 7:00–7:30
Feb 1958–Oct 1958, NBC Sat 10:00–10:30
May 1959–Jun 1959, CBS Fri 8:30–9:00
Jul 1959–Oct 1959, CBS Fri 10:30–11:00
Mar 1960–Sep 1960, ABC Mon 10:30–11:00

EMCEE:

Ted Mack

Ted Mack's durable talent show made the rounds of all four networks during its 22 sporadic years on television, including ten (1960–1970) on Sunday afternoons. It was first brought to television on the DuMont network in 1948, a year and a half after the radio version had ended due to the death of Major Bowes, the founder and original host. It quickly became a Sunday night institution. The *Amateur Hour* was DuMont's most popular program, and one of the few that was competitive with NBC and CBS—so it was soon stolen away by NBC, in 1949. (This was a pattern which was often repeated during the existence of the DuMont network—whenever a successful program was developed, one of the major networks lured it away with the promise of much more money.)

The format was taken directly from radio's *Major Bowes' Amateur Hour*, on which Mack had been an assistant. Mack, in fact, used the same booking staff and even the same Wheel of Fortune ("Round and around she goes, and where she stops, nobody knows"). He presided over the weekly parade of mimics, kazoo players, and one-man bands with genial good humor. Viewers voted for their favorites by telephone or postcard, and the finalists were awarded scholarships.

Although thousands of hopefuls appeared on the *Original Amateur Hour* over the years and hundreds were winners, surprisingly few ever went on to major or even minor stardom in show business. Probably the most famous "find" of radio days was Frank Sinatra, in 1937. On TV, 18-year-old college sophomore Pat Boone was among the three-time winners. On August 10, 1954, the program celebrated its 1,001st broadcast with a lineup of all-time talent who had graduated from the show.

A familiar feature during the early TV days (1948–1952) was the dancing Old Gold cigarette pack and matchbook (with very shapely legs!) of sponsor P. Lorillard Tobacco Company.

OTHER LANDS, OTHER PLACES

Travelogue

FIRST TELECAST: *July 24, 1951*

LAST TELECAST: *May 17, 1953*

BROADCAST HISTORY:

Jul 1951–Sep 1951, ABC Tue 8:45–9:00
Nov 1951–Dec 1951, ABC Sun 9:00–9:30
Apr 1953–May 1953, ABC Sun 7:30–7:45

Documentary travel films. Also known as *Others Lands, Other People,* and also seen locally in New York at various times.

OUR MAN HIGGINS

Situation Comedy

FIRST TELECAST: *October 3, 1962*

LAST TELECAST: *September 11, 1963*

BROADCAST HISTORY:

Oct 1962–Sep 1963, ABC Wed 9:30–10:00

CAST:

Higgins ....Stanley Holloway
Alice MacRoberts ....Audrey Totter
Duncan MacRoberts ....Frank Maxwell
Tommy MacRoberts ....Ricky Kelman
Dinghy MacRoberts ....K. C. Butts
Joanie MacRoberts ....Regina Groves

Stanley Holloway, the veteran British music-hall comic who achieved fame in America in the role of Eliza's Doolittle's father in *My Fair Lady,* was the star of this comedy. He played Higgins, a gentleman butler from Scotland who found himself sent to America to serve a suburban couple, the MacRoberts. They had "inherited" him as part of an ancestral bequest. The couple and their three children, Tommy, Dinghy, and Joanie, were constantly being saved from various predicaments by the ever-resourceful Higgins.

OUR MISS BROOKS

Situation Comedy

FIRST TELECAST: *October 3, 1952*

LAST TELECAST: *September 21, 1956*

BROADCAST HISTORY:

Oct 1952–Jun 1953, CBS Fri 9:30–10:00
Oct 1953–Jun 1955, CBS Fri 9:30–10:00
Oct 1955–Sep 1956, CBS Fri 8:30–9:00

CAST:

Connie Brooks ....Eve Arden
Osgood Conklin ....Gale Gordon
Philip Boynton ....Robert Rockwell
Walter Denton ....Dick Crenna
Mrs. Davis ....Jane Morgan
Harriet Conklin ....Gloria McMillan
Mr. Munsey (1955–1956) .....Bob Sweeney
Mrs. Nestor (1955–1956) ......Nana Bryant
Gene Talbot (1955–1956) ......Gene Barry
Benny Romero (1955–1956) ....Ricky Vera

Our Miss Brooks had originated on CBS radio in 1948, and was heard on both radio and TV throughout the mid-1950s with essentially the same cast. It was one of the period's most popular and loved comedies, and gave Eve Arden a role with which she will forever be identified. She played Connie Brooks, the wisecracking English teacher at Madison High. Her nemesis was crusty, blustery principal Osgood P. Conklin, who was constantly blowing his stack at her for something. Mr. Boynton, the handsome but incredibly shy biology teacher, was the potential husband she was always trying to snag—without success. Connie rented a room from kindly old Mrs. Davis and rode to school each morning with one of her students, the somewhat dimwitted Walter Denton. Her interaction with these varied regulars, played by an excellent supporting cast, comprised the stories. No one in *Our Miss Brooks* was an out-and-out lunatic, as is so often the case in TV comedies, but everyone had some pronounced but realistic idiosyncrasy that viewers could identify with, thus making the show's principals a perfect TV "family." Eve Arden herself was much in demand to speak to educational groups and at PTA meetings, and even received a dozen offers of positions as an English teacher at real high schools. They could hardly have afforded her, as she was by then making $200,000 per year!

By the start of the 1955–1956 season the ratings were beginning to slip and the setting was changed. Madison High was razed for a highway project and Miss Brooks found a new job at Mrs. Nestor's Private Elementary School nearby. For some reason, Mr. Conklin had acquired the job of principal there, and he and other cast members remained on the show to harass her. Connie's new love interest was the young physical education teacher, Gene Talbot, who was chasing her, quite a turnaround from Mr. Boynton's shy indifference. Somehow the revised format seemed to limp along and Mr. Boynton was brought back in the spring of 1956. His return did not help, however, and the show ended its run shortly thereafter.

OUR NEIGHBORS TO THE NORTH

Documentary

FIRST TELECAST: *June 15, 1952*

LAST TELECAST: *August 29, 1952*

BROADCAST HISTORY:

Jun 1952, ABC Sun 10:00–10:30
Aug 1952, ABC Fri 8:00–8:30

This was a series of film shorts about Canada, produced by the Canadian Government.

OUR PLACE

Musical Variety

FIRST TELECAST: *July 2, 1967*

LAST TELECAST: *September 3, 1967*

BROADCAST HISTORY:

Jul 1967–Sep 1967, CBS Sun 9:00–10:00

REGULARS:

The Doodletown Pipers
Jack Burns
Avery Schreiber

Narrated by a huge puppet dog named Rowlf, one of Jim Henson's Muppets, this musical and comedy variety series was the 1967 summer replacement for *The Smothers Brothers Comedy Hour.* It featured the singing of the Doodletown Pipers and the comic antics of the team of Burns & Schreiber.

OUR PRIVATE WORLD

Soap Opera

FIRST TELECAST: *May 5, 1965*

LAST TELECAST: *September 10, 1965*

BROADCAST HISTORY:

May 1965–Sep 1965, CBS Wed 9:30–10:00
May 1965–Sep 1965, CBS Fri 9:00–9:30

CAST:

Lisa Hughes .... Eileen Fulton
Helen Eldredge .... Geraldine Fitzgerald
John Eldredge .... Nicolas Coster
Eve Eldredge .... Julienne Marie
Tom Eldredge .... Sam Groom
Brad Robinson .... Robert Drivas
Dr. Tony Larson .... David O'Brien
Sandy Larson .... Sandy Smith
Franny Martin .... Pamela Murphy

In the wake of ABC's great success with its prime-time soap opera *Peyton Place,* CBS decided to try its own version of the form during the summer of 1965. This series was a spinoff from the highly successful daytime serial *As the World Turns,* and focused on Lisa Hughes, one of *World*'s leading characters. Young divorcee Lisa decided to find a new life for herself by leaving her small home town and moving to Chicago, where she found a job in the admitting room of a hospital. The two major plot lines involved her life and associations at the hospital and the machinations of the Eldredges, a socially prominent and extremely wealthy family living in the exclusive suburb of Lake Forest. The CBS experiment proved not to be very successful and the series was canceled at the end of the summer, leaving actress Eileen Fulton to her daytime role only.

OUR SECRET WEAPON—THE TRUTH

Discussion

FIRST TELECAST: *February 6, 1951*

LAST TELECAST: *April 17, 1951*

BROADCAST HISTORY:

Feb 1951–Apr 1951, DUM Tue 7:30–8:00

PANELISTS:

Leo Cherne
Ralph de Toledano

This propaganda program had been presented on CBS radio during World War II as a forum for debunking Nazi claims against America. It was revived during the Korean War for use against a new enemy, with regulars Leo Cherne and Ralph de Toledano on hand each week to "answer Communist lies about us" with facts and testimony from special guests. Previously a local program in New York.

OUT OF THE FOG

Drama

FIRST TELECAST: *April 7, 1952*

LAST TELECAST: *September 22, 1952*

BROADCAST HISTORY:

Apr 1952–Sep 1952, ABC Mon 8:00–8:30

This was a short-lived series of mystery films, which alternated with *Mr. District Attorney* from April through June, then was seen weekly.

OUT THERE

Science Fiction

FIRST TELECAST: *October 28, 1951*

LAST TELECAST: *January 13, 1952*

BROADCAST HISTORY:

Oct 1951–Jan 1952, CBS Sun 6:00–6:30

A live anthology series which used filmed special effects, *Out There* sought to bridge the gap between serious drama and the juvenile science fiction of such shows as *Captain Video* and *Tom Corbet—Space Cadet.* All of the episodes were adapted from stories by prominent science-fiction writers and were presented in such a way as to attract an adult audience but still be exciting enough to hold the attention of children.

OUTCASTS, THE

Western

FIRST TELECAST: *September 23, 1968*
LAST TELECAST: *September 15, 1969*
BROADCAST HISTORY:
Sep 1968–Sep 1969, ABC Mon 9:00–10:00
CAST:
Earl Corey .... Don Murray
Jemal David .... Otis Young

This violent Western teamed a Virginia aristocrat-turned-gunman-and-drifter with a freed slave-turned-bounty hunter, in the years after the Civil War. The two of them had an uneasy relationship at best, often erupting into fights and arguments, as they pursued a common goal of making money by tracking down wanted criminals. Corey was the white man, and David the black.

OUTER LIMITS, THE

Science Fiction Anthology

FIRST TELECAST: *September 16, 1963*
LAST TELECAST: *January 16, 1965*
BROADCAST HISTORY:
Sep 1963–Sep 1964, ABC Mon 7:30–8:30
Sep 1964–Jan 1965, ABC Sat 7:30–8:30
CREATOR/EXECUTIVE PRODUCER:
Leslie Stevens

At the opening of each episode in this anthology series the picture on the TV screen started to do funny things and a deep voice intoned: "There is nothing wrong with your TV set. We are controlling transmission. We can control the vertical. We can control the horizontal. For the next hour we will control all that you see and hear and think. You are watching a drama that reaches from the inner mind to . . . *The Outer Limits.*" The special effects were good, the alien costumes interesting, and the plots tolerable. Unfortunately, at the end of each episode, before the control voice returned your television set to you, it felt compelled to end the story with a moral, often ruining the effect of the whole show.

OUTLAWS, THE

Western

FIRST TELECAST: *September 29, 1960*
LAST TELECAST: *September 13, 1962*
BROADCAST HISTORY:
Sep 1960–Sep 1962, NBC Thu 7:30–8:30
CAST:
U.S. Marshal Frank Caine (1960–1961) .... Barton MacLane
Deputy Marshal Will Forman .... Don Collier
Deputy Marshal Heck Martin (1960–1961) .... Jock Gaynor
Deputy Marshal Chalk Breeson (1961–1962) .... Bruce Yarnell
Slim (1961–1962) .... Slim Pickens
Connie Masters (1961–1962) ... Judy Lewis

In its first season, *The Outlaws* approached the struggle between law officers of the Old West and the desperadoes they chased from a novel point of view. Although Marshal Frank Caine and his two deputies, Will Forman and Heck Martin, were the series regulars, each episode was seen through the eyes of the outlaws they were pursuing. The setting for the series was the Oklahoma Territory in the 1890s, when the Dalton Boys, the Jennings Gang, and other outlaws made it one of the most lawless of all the West's frontiers.

When *The Outlaws* returned in the fall of 1961 there were a number of changes. Gone were Caine and Martin, and Will Forman was a full marshal with his own deputy. The perspective of the series was now from the side of the marshals and the honest citizens rather than the criminals. The action was based in the town of Stillwater, Oklahoma, where the marshals were headquartered. Connie Masters worked at the Wells Fargo office, and Slim was the town character.

OUTLOOK

see *Chet Huntley Reporting*

OUTSIDE U.S.A.

Documentary

FIRST TELECAST: *September 1, 1955*
LAST TELECAST: *June 3, 1956*
BROADCAST HISTORY:
Sep 1955–Oct 1955, ABC Thu 10:00–10:30
Nov 1955–Jan 1956, ABC Tue 10:00–10:30
Jan 1956–Mar 1956, ABC Mon 10:00–10:30
Apr 1956–Jun 1956, ABC Sun 10:00–10:30
NARRATOR/COMMENTATOR:
Quincy Howe

Each week Mr. Howe introduced filmed coverage of an event or issue in world politics. Following the film he would analyze or evaluate the situation being covered.

OUTSIDER, THE

Detective

FIRST TELECAST: *September 18, 1968*
LAST TELECAST: *September 3, 1969*
BROADCAST HISTORY:

Sep 1968–Sep 1969, NBC Wed 10:00–11:00

CAST:

David Ross ....Darren McGavin

David Ross was not the stereotyped glamorous private detective. He did not make much money, lived in a run-down Los Angeles apartment building, drove a beat-up 10-year-old car, and often got beat up himself while on cases. Ross was a loner who had never finished high school and had been orphaned when a small child. As an adult, he had served six years in prison on a trumped-up murder charge, before being pardoned. In short Ross had found the world a very unfriendly place—he was an "outsider." Nevertheless he turned private eye to tackle other people's problems, and proved an extremely thorough and productive investigator.

OVERLAND TRAIL, THE

Western

FIRST TELECAST: *February 7, 1960*
LAST TELECAST: *September 11, 1960*
BROADCAST HISTORY:

Feb 1960–Sep 1960, NBC Sun 7:00–8:00

CAST:

Frederick Thomas Kelly ...William Bendix
Frank "Flip" Flippen ....Doug McClure

The opening of the Overland Trail, one of the major stage routes to the West, and the effort to push that route all the way to the Pacific Ocean served as the backdrop for this series. The two men charged with moving the stage line from Missouri, over the Rockies, and through to California were Frederick Thomas Kelly and Frank Flippen. Kelly was a crusty former civil engineer and Union Army guerrilla who found getting the Overland Stage Line into operation the most exciting challenge of his life. His young friend and aide, nicknamed Flip, had been brought up by Indians and was full of an adventurous enthusiasm that complemented Kelly's cautious nature. Their adventures and the adventures of their passengers provided the stories for this series.

OWEN MARSHALL, COUNSELOR AT LAW

Lawyer

FIRST TELECAST: *September 16, 1971*
LAST TELECAST: *August 24, 1974*
BROADCAST HISTORY:

Sep 1971–Jan 1973, ABC Thu 10:00–11:00
Jan 1973–Jan 1974, ABC Wed 10:00–11:00
Jan 1974–Aug 1974, ABC Sat 10:00–11:00

CAST:

Owen Marshall ....Arthur Hill
Jess Brandon ....Lee Majors
Danny Paterno (1973–1974)
..........................Reni Santoni
Ted Warrick (1974) ....David Soul
Melissa Marshall ....Christine Matchett
Frieda Krause ....Joan Darling

This popular lawyer drama depicted the life and trails of Owen Marshall, a compassionate defense attorney practicing in a small town in California. Marshall's cases ranged from civil suits to murder, but were always marked by a warmth and consideration for the accused. In a way, *Owen Marshal* was the courtroom equivalent of medicine's kindly *Marcus Welby*, and, in fact, the two series sometimes had joint episodes. In 1972 Marshall found himself defending the father of one of Dr. Welby's patients against a murder charge, and in 1974 he defended Dr. Kiley, Welby's associate, against a paternity suit.

Owen Marshall had several young law partners during his run, the first of whom was Jess Brandon. For a time in 1973–1974 Lee Majors, the actor portraying Brandon, was starring in two ABC series, this one and *The Six Million Dollar Man*. He was finally replaced in February 1974 by another future superstar, David Soul, in the role of Ted Warrick. In addition, Danny Paterno was seen as a partner during the final season. Melissa was widower Marshall's 12-year-old daughter, and Frieda his loyal law clerk.

Owen Marshall was well regarded by real-life legal associations, and won several public-service awards. Its co-creators were David Victor and University of Wisconsin Law Professor Jerry McNeely.

OZARK JUBILEE

Country Music

FIRST TELECAST: *January 22, 1955*
LAST TELECAST: *September 24, 1960*
BROADCAST HISTORY:

Jan 1955–Jun 1955, ABC Sat 9:00–10:00
Jul 1955–Sep 1956, ABC Sat 7:30–9:00
Oct 1956–Dec 1956, ABC Thu 10:00–11:00
Dec 1956–Jun 1957, ABC Sat 10:00–11:00
Jun 1957–Sep 1957, ABC Sat 10:00–10:30
Sep 1957–Sep 1959, ABC Sat 8:00–9:00
Oct 1959–Sep 1960, ABC Sat 10:00–11:00

EMCEE:

Red Foley
Webb Pierce (occasional 1955–1956)

REGULARS:

Jean Shepard (1955)
Hawkshaw Hawkins (1955)
Tommy Sosebee (1955)
Porter Wagoner (1955–1956)
Foggy River Boys/Marksmen (1955–1959)
Pete Stamper (1956)
Oklahoma Wranglers (1955)
Bud Isaac (1955)
Uncle Cyp & Aunt Sap Brasfield (1956–1960)
Flash & Whistler (1956–1957)
Tadpoles (1956)
Bobby Lord (1957–1960)
Jim Wilson (1957)
Marvin Rainwater (1957)
Bill Wimberly's Country Rhythm Boys (1956–1957)
Slim Wilson's Jubilee Band (1958–1960)
Wanda Jackson (1957–1960)
Billy Walker (1957)
Tall Timber Trio (1957–1960)
Bill McMain (1957)
Norma Jean (1958)
Leroy Van Dyke (1958)
Suzi Arden (1958–1959)
Smiley Burnette (1959)
The Promenaders (1959–1960)
Shug Fisher (1960)
Lew Childre (1960)

THEME:

"Sugarfoot Rag," by Hank Garland

Country and Western music had a major showcase on network television in the late 1950s in this weekly hoedown from Springfield, Missouri. The host was genial country singer Red Foley, a veteran of the *Grand Ole Opry,* who projected a good-natured warmth and sincerity which characterized the whole proceedings. Appearing on *Jubilee* were many of the top names in Country music, including regulars Webb Pierce (who was once-a-month host for a time in 1955–1956), the Foggy River Boys vocal quartet (renamed the Marksmen in 1957), comic Pete Stamper, and Porter Wagoner. Among the regular features were square dancing by the Tadpoles, a group of two-to-ten year olds, and the cornpone comedy act of Uncle Cyp and Aunt Sap, who portrayed an elderly married couple who were always throwing ancient jokes at one another. The "Junior Jubilee" portion of the show gave exposure to younger talent. Perhaps its biggest discovery was a sweet-as-peaches little 11-year-old with a booming voice, named Brenda Lee. She made her first appearance in March 1956, quickly became a *Jubilee* favorite, and later went on to stardom in both the Country and popular music fields.

Jubilee ran until 1960, when it was abruptly canceled by ABC. The official reason was that the network had acquired the Gillette fights and wanted to carry them in *Jubilee*'s time slot. The real reason, however, was that host Red Foley had been indicted for tax fraud and was about to stand trial—a situation hardly consonant with the down-home sincerity he projected on the show (Foley's first trial ended in a hung jury, and a second, in 1961, in acquittal).

Ozark Jubilee underwent two name changes during its run, becoming *Country Music Jubilee* in July 1957 and *Jubilee U.S.A.* in August 1958.

PABST BLUE RIBBON BOUTS

see *Boxing*

PACKARD SHOWROOM, THE

see *Martha Wright Show, The*

PALL MALL PLAYHOUSE

Western Anthology

FIRST TELECAST: *July 20, 1955*
LAST TELECAST: *September 7, 1955*
BROADCAST HISTORY:

Jul 1955–Sep 1955, ABC Wed 8:30–9:00

This summer series was comprised of a collection of unsold pilots for dramatic Westerns. Among those starring were John Ireland, Carolyn Jones, and Will Rogers, Jr.

PANIC

Dramatic Anthology

FIRST TELECAST: *March 5, 1957*
LAST TELECAST: *September 17, 1957*

BROADCAST HISTORY:

Mar 1957–Sep 1957, NBC Tue 8:30–9:00

NARRATOR:

Westbrook Van Voorhees

At the outset of each episode of *Panic* an individual was put into a sudden crisis situation which posed threats of an emotional or physical nature to him. The remainder of each episode delineated how well he reacted to and coped with the crisis. For example, a young man found himself on the brink of suicide; a vaudeville dancer was stalked by a murderer; and a family was trapped in their home. Appearing were such stars as June Havoc, Darryl Hickman, and James and Pamela Mason.

PANTOMIME QUIZ

Quiz/Audience Participation

FIRST TELECAST: *July 3, 1950*

LAST TELECAST: *September 16, 1963*

BROADCAST HISTORY:

Jul 1950, CBS Mon 9:30–10:00
Jul 1950–Sep 1950, CBS Mon 8:00–8:30
Jul 1951–Aug 1951, CBS Mon 8:00–8:30
Jan 1952, NBC Wed 10:30–11:00
Jan 1952–Mar 1952, NBC Wed 10:00–10:30
Jul 1952–Sep 1952, CBS Fri 8:30–9:00
Jul 1953–Aug 1953, CBS Fri 8:00–8:30
Oct 1953–Apr 1954, DUM Tue 8:30–9:00
Jul 1954–Aug 1954, CBS Fri 8:00–8:30
Jan 1955–Mar 1955, ABC Sun 9:30–10:00
Jul 1955–Sep 1955, CBS Fri 8:00–8:30
Jul 1956–Sep 1956, CBS Fri 10:30–11:00
Jul 1957–Sep 1957, CBS Fri 10:30–11:00
Apr 1958–Sep 1958, ABC Tue 9:30–10:00
Jun 1959–Sep 1959, ABC Mon 9:00–9:30
Sep 1962–Sep 1963, CBS Mon 10:30–11:00

HOST:

Mike Stokey
Pat Harrington, Jr. (1962)

REGULARS:

Hans Conried (1950–1952, 1955–1957, 1962–1963)
Vincent Price (1950–1952)
Adele Jergens (1950–1952)
Jackie Coogan (1950–1955)
John Barrymore, Jr. (1953–1954)
Dave Willock (1953–1954)
Rocky Graziano (1954–1956)
Dorothy Hart (1953–1958)
Robert Clary (1954–1957)
Peter Donald (1953–1955, 1957)
Carol Haney (1955–1956)
Milt Kamen (1957–1959)
Jan Clayton (1953–1954, 1962–1963)
Elaine Stritch (1953–1955, 1958)
Jerry Lester (1953–1955)
Carol Burnett (1958–1959)
Stubby Kaye (1958–1959, 1962–1963)
Dick Van Dyke (1958–1959)

Pantomime Quiz was the perennial summer-replacement series. Created by Mike Stokey, who was its producer and host, it had premiered as a local show in Los Angeles in 1947. The game itself was a variation on the parlor game of charades. Two teams of four members each, three regulars and one guest, competed with each other in attempting to act out famous phrases, mottos, literary quotes, etc. The team that took the least amount of time solving the total of four or five phrases that each team was given during a telecast was declared the winner. Home viewers were asked to send in suggestions for phrases to be used on the show and won cash if their submissions were used, and a bonus if the team trying to solve it could not do so within the two-minute time limit.

The durability of *Pantomime Quiz* is evident in its survival on network television for more than a decade, generally running during the summers. It was one of only four series to have aired on all four networks. When it was revived for the last time, for a full-season run on CBS in 1962–1963, the title was changed to *Stump the Stars* and Pat Harrington, Jr., became the host. He lasted less than three months in that role, however, being replaced by program producer Mike Stokey on December 10, 1962.

The turnover among regular charaders on *Pantomime Quiz* was extremely high. The list of regulars shown above only includes those who were with the show for at least two different runs. Among the other personalities who were regulars for a single season were Fred Clark, Robert Stack, Angela Lansbury, Orson Bean, Rose Marie, John Carradine, Howard Morris, Tom Poston, Beverly Garland, Sebastian Cabot, Ross Martin, Diana Dors, Mickey Manners, and Ruta Lee.

PAPER CHASE, THE

General Drama

FIRST TELECAST: *September 9, 1978*

LAST TELECAST:

BROADCAST HISTORY:

Sep 1978, CBS Sat 8:00–9:00

Sep 1978– , CBS Tue 8:00–9:00

CAST:

Professor Charles W. Kingsfield, Jr. .... John Houseman

James T. Hart .... James Stephens

Franklin Ford III .... Tom Fitzsimmons

Thomas Craig Anderson ...... Robert Ginty

Willis Bell .... James Keane

Jonathan Brooks .... Jonathan Segal

Elizabeth Logan .... Francine Tacker

Asheley Brooks .... Deka Beaudine

James T. Hart was a first-year law student whose upbringing in rural Iowa had not prepared him for the intensity and ruthlessness that he found at a highly competitive law school. His nemesis was Professor Charles Kingsfield, the world's leading authority on contract law, who inspired both awe and terror in his students with his imperious and authoritarian manner. To help cope with the heavy work load, Hart joined a study group consisting of other students who were working together sharing notes and assignments. The group had been organized by Franklin Ford III, a would-be third generation lawyer from a socially prominent family. Others in the group were Anderson, Bell, Brooks and Logan. Brooks, also from a wealthy family, was the only married member of the group.

John Houseman won an Academy Award for his role in the movie *The Paper Chase*, on which this series was based. Although the movie took place at Harvard, no mention was made of a specific university in the television series.

PAPER MOON

Situation Comedy

FIRST TELECAST: *September 12, 1974*

LAST TELECAST: *January 2, 1975*

BROADCAST HISTORY:

Sep 1974–Jan 1975, ABC Thu 8:30–9:00

CAST:

Moses (Moze) Pray ... Christopher Connelly

Addie Pray .... Jodie Foster

THEME:

"It's Only a Paper Moon," by Harold Arlen, Yip Harburg, and Billy Rose

This was a gentle comedy about an itinerant Bible salesman/con artist and his precocious eleven-year-old daughter, traveling across Kansas during the Depression years. If Moze and Addie never had much money, it wasn't for lack of trying every fast-buck scheme in the book. Though they just "got by," and were often only one step ahead of the law, they at least had each other. Much period flavor was featured in this series, including an authentic 1933 theme song. The series was filmed on location in Kansas.

Based on the 1973 hit movie starring Ryan and Tatum O'Neal, which had in turn been taken from the novel *Addie Pray* by Joe David Brown.

PARIS CAVALCADE OF FASHIONS

Fashion Show

FIRST TELECAST: *November 11, 1948*

LAST TELECAST: *January 20, 1949*

BROADCAST HISTORY:

Nov 1948–Jan 1949, NBC Thu 7:15–7:30

NARRATOR:

Faye Emerson (Nov–Dec 1948)

Julie Gibson (Dec 1948–Jan 1949)

Films of the latest Paris creations. The series was formerly seen locally on WNBT, New York.

PARIS 7000

Adventure

FIRST TELECAST: *January 22, 1970*

LAST TELECAST: *June 4, 1970*

BROADCAST HISTORY:

Jan 1970–Jun 1970, ABC Thu 10:00–11:00

CAST:

Jack Brennan .... George Hamilton

Robert Stevens .... Gene Raymond

Jules Maurois .... Jacques Aubuchon

Movie star George Hamilton starred in this series as a State Department employee attached to the U.S. Embassy in Paris, whose job it was to help Americans in trouble. The number to call for help: Paris 7000. Robert Stevens was his aide, and Maurois the contact on the local gendarmerie.

PARTNERS, THE

Situation Comedy

FIRST TELECAST: *September 18, 1971*

LAST TELECAST: *September 8, 1972*

BROADCAST HISTORY:

Sep 1971–Jan 1972, NBC Sat 8:00–8:30

Jul 1972–Sep 1972, NBC Fri 8:00–8:30

CAST:

Det. Lennie Crooke .... Don Adams

Det. George Robinson ....Rupert Crosse
Capt. Andrews ....John Doucette
Sgt. Higgenbottom ....Dick Van Patten

Lennie Crooke and George Robinson were a pair of police detectives who were always getting into crazy situations while investigating crimes. In their enthusiasm, they would occasionally get themselves into more trouble than did the criminals they were after. Their boss, Captain Andrews, was constantly frustrated and confounded by their activities which, despite all, somehow resulted in their solving the crimes. Sgt. Higgenbottom, who was trying to ingratiate himself with the captain, spent much of his time belittling Lennie and George.

PARTRIDGE FAMILY, THE

Situation Comedy

FIRST TELECAST: *September 25, 1970*

LAST TELECAST: *August 31, 1974*

BROADCAST HISTORY:

Sep 1970–Jun 1973, ABC Fri 8:30–9:00
Jun 1973–Aug 1974, ABC Sat 8:00–8:30

CAST:

Shirley Partridge ....Shirley Jones
Keith Partridge ....David Cassidy
Laurie Partridge ....Susan Dey
Danny Partridge ....Danny Bonaduce
Christopher Partridge (1970–1971)
......................Jeremy Gelbwaks
Christopher Partridge (1971–1974)
..........................Brian Forster
Tracy Partridge ....Suzanne Crough
Reuben Kinkaid ....David Madden
Ricky Stevens (1973–1974) .... Ricky Segall

THEME:

"Come On, Get Happy," by Wes Farrell and Danny Janssen

Oscar-winner Shirley Jones and her stepson David Cassidy starred in this comedy about a family that hit the big time in the music business. Shirley Partridge was just another widowed suburban mother with a houseful of rambunctious kids, until one day the kids asked her to take part in an impromptu recording session they were holding in the garage. Seems they needed a vocalist. The song they were recording was "I Think I Love You," and to everyone's surprise they sold it to a record company, the record became a smash hit, and the Partridges were soon setting off in a wildly painted old school bus to perform around the country. They were authentic members of the rock generation. Stories depicted their exploits on the road, and in their California home town.

Besides Shirley and 16-year-old Keith (Cassidy), the band included Laurie (15), Danny (10, and the freckle-faced con man of the family), Christopher (7), and Tracy (5). Reuben Kinkaid was their fast-talking, child-hating agent—and perpetual foil for Danny. During the 1973–1974 season a neighbor's son, four-year-old Ricky, joined the cast, and he sang too. Simone was the family pooch.

The Partridges were heavily promoted in the real-life music business, and they caught on with several hit singles, including "I Think I Love You," which sold four million copies, as well as albums. David Cassidy became the hero of the subteen set and had considerable success as a single act. Unlike the Monkees, the Partridges had no artistic pretensions—none of them were professional musicians—and the backgrounds on their records were in fact done by professional studio musicians, with Shirley and David providing the vocals. Their success was as spectacular on the record charts as on TV, but it did not last long in either case.

The Partridge Family was loosely based on the experiences of a real-life popular recording family, the Cowsills.

PARTY LINE

Quiz/Audience Participation

FIRST TELECAST: *June 8, 1947*

LAST TELECAST: *August 31, 1947*

BROADCAST HISTORY:

Jun 1947–Aug 1947, NBC Sun 8:30–9:00

EMCEE:

Bert Parks

Bert Parks, one of the most familiar faces on early TV, hosted this primitive phone-in quiz show which occupied half of the Sunday 8:00–9:00 P.M. Bristol-Myers hour during the summer of 1947. (For the other half, see *Tex and Jinx*.) Bert would ask a question, sometimes illustrated with a short film or performed by actors in the studio, and then would call a number at random from among the cards sent in by viewers. If the person called was watching and could answer the question, he won a prize of $5 and a box of Bristol-Myers products.

The program was sponsored on a two-station network consisting of WNBT, New York, and WPTZ, Philadelphia.

PARTY TIME AT CLUB ROMA

Variety

FIRST TELECAST: *October 14, 1950*

LAST TELECAST: *January 6, 1951*

BROADCAST HISTORY:

Oct 1950–Jan 1951, NBC Sat 11:00–11:30

EMCEE:

Ben Alexander

REGULARS:

Pat Emery
Chris Emery
Camille Leong
Doodles and Spicer
The Cheerleaders

Set in the mythical Club Roma in San Francisco, where this series was actually filmed, *Party Time at Club Roma* started out as a variation on *Beat the Clock*, with emcee Alexander inviting guests at the club to join in attempting various stunts or playing games in which they might win small merchandise prizes. His assistants included a pair of identical twins (Pat and Chris), a beautiful girl from San Francisco's Chinatown (Camille), and the pantomime team of Doodles and Spicer. The format was soon changed to a talent contest with emcee Alexander picking acts out of the audience to perform for the crowd at the club. The winners were chosen by applause meter.

An interesting sidelight to this series is that it was also produced by Ben Alexander. He was an account executive with Foote, Cone & Belding, the advertising agency for the sponsor, Roma Wines, and this was his first exposure to network television. He subsequently left the agency and played Jack Webb's partner on *Dragnet*.

PASSWORD

Quiz/Audience Participation

FIRST TELECAST: *January 2, 1962*

LAST TELECAST: *May 22, 1967*

BROADCAST HISTORY:

Jan 1962–Sep 1962, CBS Tue 8:00–8:30
Sep 1962–Mar 1963, CBS Sun 6:30–7:00
Mar 1963–Sep 1963, CBS Mon 10:00–10:30
Sep 1963–Sep 1964, CBS Thu 7:30–8:00
Sep 1964–Sep 1965, CBS Thu 9:00–9:30
Apr 1967–May 1967, CBS Mon 10:30–11:00

EMCEE:

Allen Ludden

Password was a word-association game. Two teams, each composed of one celebrity and one non-celebrity contestant, competed in trying to identify the "password" with the least number of clues. The "password," usually a common word, was handed to one member of each team and these two people would then take turns giving their partners one-word clues to make them guess the word. After the first clue a correct response was worth ten points, after the second clue, nine points, and so forth. The first team to accumulate 25 points won the round. In the "Lightning Round" one member of each team would have 60 seconds to get his partner to properly associate a total of five "passwords." Winners got cash prizes and the chance to return to face a new challenging team.

The daytime version of *Password* premiered in October 1961 and remained on the air until September 1967. It was revived in ABC daytime in 1971. Allen Ludden was the series' sole host.

PAT BOONE–CHEVY SHOWROOM, THE

Musical Variety

FIRST TELECAST: *October 3, 1957*

LAST TELECAST: *June 23, 1960*

BROADCAST HISTORY:

Oct 1957–Jun 1960, ABC Thu 9:00–9:30 (OS)

HOST:

Pat Boone

REGULARS:

Louise O'Brien (1959)
Artie Malvin Chorus (1958–1960)
Mort Lindsay Orchestra

Pat Boone was one of the fastest rising stars in show business when this series went on the air. He had just completed a long stint with Arthur Godfrey, his records were selling in the millions ("Love Letters in the Sand" was riding high on the charts just as the show premiered), and his movies were box-office hits. The publicity about him was enormous. Kids loved him and so did adults, for his smooth, super-wholesome appearance and that deep, rich voice. A somewhat jaded *TV Guide* reviewer called his new ABC show "about as exciting as a milkshake with two straws," but that didn't matter to viewers. The show continued for three seasons, without the benefit of a large supporting cast or fancy production.

Guests tended to the "nicer" popular singers, such as the Four Lads, Johnny Mathis, Nat "King" Cole, and Gogi Grant (though Danny and the Juniors did slip in), together with such well-scrubbed acts as the Texas Boys' Choir. Most shows ended with an inspirational tune. In 1959 a regular was added in the person of singer Louise O'Brien, a former Miss Oklahoma, but Pat really needed no supporting cast and she soon became an occasional guest.

PAT PAULSEN'S HALF A COMEDY HOUR

Comedy Variety

FIRST TELECAST: *January 22, 1970*
LAST TELECAST: *April 16, 1970*
BROADCAST HISTORY:
Jan 1970–Apr 1970, ABC Thu 7:30–8:00
HOST:
Pat Paulsen
REGULARS:
Hal Smith
Bob Einstein
Sherry Miles
Jean Byron
Joan Gerber
Pepe Brown
Pedro Regas
Vanetta Rogers

Comedian Pat Paulsen's *Half a Comedy Hour* lasted for less than half a season in early 1970. Pat and his cast of youthful comics were seen in skits such as "Children's Letters to the Devil," and with guest stars. Guesting on the first telecast were Debbie Reynolds, former Vice President Hubert H. Humphrey, and Daffy Duck.

PATRICE MUNSEL SHOW, THE

Musical Variety

FIRST TELECAST: *October 18, 1957*
LAST TELECAST: *June 13, 1958*
BROADCAST HISTORY:
Oct 1957–Dec 1957, ABC Fri 8:30–9:00
Jan 1958–Jun 1958, ABC Fri 9:30–10:00
REGULARS:
Patrice Munsel
The Martins Quartet
The Charles Sanford Orchestra

Metropolitan Opera soprano Patrice Munsel demonstrated her versatility as a singer in this live variety show. Show tunes, popular songs, and operatic excerpts were all part of her repertoire in addition to comedy sketches with her weekly guest stars.

PATRICIA BOWMAN SHOW, THE

Dance/Music

FIRST TELECAST: *August 11, 1951*
LAST TELECAST: *November 3, 1951*
BROADCAST HISTORY:
Aug 1951–Nov 1951, CBS Sat 6:45–7:00
STAR:
Patricia Bowman

This live dance-and-music show was hosted by famous American ballerina Patricia Bowman. Each show featured Miss Bowman and her guest stars performing various types of dances, from ballroom, to jazz, to modern, to ballet.

PATTI PAGE OLDS SHOW, THE

Musical Variety

FIRST TELECAST: *September 24, 1958*
LAST TELECAST: *March 16, 1959*
BROADCAST HISTORY:
Sep 1958–Nov 1958, ABC Wed 9:30–10:00
Dec 1958–Mar 1959, ABC Mon 10:00–10:30
REGULARS:
Patti Page
The Matt Mattox Dancers
The Vic Schoen Orchestra

Popular singer Patti Page was the hostess and star of this live musical variety show that featured her singing, regular guest stars, and the dance numbers of the Matt Mattox Dancers.

PATTI PAGE SHOW, THE

Musical Variety

FIRST TELECAST: *June 16, 1956*
LAST TELECAST: *July 7, 1956*
BROADCAST HISTORY:
Jun 1956–Jul 1956, NBC Sat 8:00–9:00
REGULARS:
Patti Page
The Frank Lewis Dancers
The Spellbinders
The Carl Hoff Orchestra

Patti Page was one of three stars who filled in for *The Perry Como Show* during the summer of 1956, the other two being Julius La Rosa and Tony Bennett. They shared the services of the Frank Lewis Dancers and the vocal group the Spellbinders. Each star had his/her own guest stars and the show included production numbers, songs by the star, and performances by each week's guests.

PATTY DUKE SHOW, THE

Situation Comedy

FIRST TELECAST: *September 18, 1963*

LAST TELECAST: *August 31, 1966*

BROADCAST HISTORY:

Sep 1963–Aug 1966, ABC Wed 8:00–8:30

CAST:

Patty/Cathy Lane ....Patty Duke
Martin Lane ....William Schallert
Natalie Masters ....Jean Byron
Ross Lane ....Paul O'Keefe
Richard ....Eddie Applegate

Teenage actress Patty Duke, fresh from her motion-picture triumph in *The Miracle Worker* (for which she won an Academy Award), starred in a dual role in this light family comedy. As Patty Lane she was a perky, bubble-gum-chewing teenager who dug Paul Anka records and "slumber parties" with her girl friends. As Cathy, she was Patty's intellectual Scottish cousin, newly arrived from overseas to live with the Lanes, complete with bagpipes and burr. The girls confused everybody in their middle-class Brooklyn Heights, New York, neighborhood by mischievously switching personalities at critical moments. Since they were exact look-alikes, no one could tell them apart. Martin Lane was Patty's harried father, a newspaper editor; Natalie the mother; and 12-year-old Ross the younger brother, who was constantly at war with the girls. Richard was Patty's boy friend, a part-time Western Union messenger (she liked men in uniform).

Guest appearances by popular singing stars such as Bobby Vinton, Chad and Jeremy, and Frankie Avalon helped boost this series' popularity among teenagers.

PAUL ARNOLD SHOW, THE

Music

FIRST TELECAST: *October 24, 1949*

LAST TELECAST: *June 23, 1950*

BROADCAST HISTORY:

Oct 1949–Dec 1949, CBS Mon/Wed/Fri 7:15–7:30
Jan 1950, CBS Mon/Wed/Thu/Fri 7:15–7:30
Jan 1950–Jun 1950, CBS Mon–Fri 7:15–7:30

STAR:

Paul Arnold

This thrice-weekly 15-minute program gave Mr. Arnold an opportunity to sing a few Country and Western and rural songs, play his guitar, relate a little homespun philosophy, and chat with an occasional guest. Originating live from New York, it added a fourth day of the week the first week in January and became a five-day-a-week series three weeks later.

PAUL DIXON SHOW, THE

Variety

FIRST TELECAST: *August 8, 1951*

LAST TELECAST: *September 24, 1952*

BROADCAST HISTORY:

Aug 1951–Sep 1951, ABC Wed 8:00–9:00
Sep 1951–Oct 1951, ABC Mon 9:00–10:00
Oct 1951–Jan 1952, ABC Thu 10:00–10:30
Oct 1951–Sep 1952, ABC Wed 8:00–9:00

EMCEE:

Paul Dixon

REGULARS:

Dottie Mack
Wanda Lewis

Paul Dixon, one of the most popular radio and TV personalities in the Midwest, was brought to network television by ABC for a prime-time run from 1951–1952. His program was similar in format to his long-running local variety show in Cincinnati, which began in 1949: fun and games with the audience, occasional guests, and his specialty, pantomiming to popular records. Paul contorted his face and mouthed the words as the top singers of the day sang their big hits, on record. Dottie Mack also did musical pantomimes (she later had her own network series doing this), and Wanda Lewis drew pictures as the records were played. Other features in this folksy show included "Visits for Interviews," both light and serious, and "People in Your Life"—the mailman, milkman, policeman, etc. At one time Paul was on two nights a week, for a total of two hours, with this potpourri.

PAUL HARVEY NEWS

News and Comment

FIRST TELECAST: *November 16, 1952*

LAST TELECAST: *August 9, 1953*

BROADCAST HISTORY:

Nov 1952–Aug 1953, ABC Sun 11:00–11:15

NEWSCASTER:

Paul Harvey

Famed radio commentator Paul Harvey presented news and his own highly individual opinions on current events in this 1952–1953 ABC series, which originated live from Chicago. Harvey always ended his newscasts with an upbeat "Good . . . day!"

PAUL LYNDE SHOW, THE

Situation Comedy

FIRST TELECAST: *September 13, 1972*

LAST TELECAST: *September 8, 1973*

BROADCAST HISTORY:

Sep 1972–May 1973, ABC Wed 8:00–8:30
Jun 1973–Sep 1973, ABC Sat 8:30–9:00

CAST:

Paul Simms . . . . Paul Lynde
Martha Simms . . . . Elizabeth Allen
Sally Simms . . . . Pamelyn Ferdin
Barbara Simms/Dickerson . . . . Jane Actman
Howie Dickerson . . . . John Calvin
Barney Dickerson . . . . Jerry Stiller
Grace Dickerson . . . . Anne Meara

Comedian Paul Lynde, a familiar face on TV for many years in guest-star and supporting roles, starred in this situation comedy. He portrayed Paul Simms, a quiet, respectable attorney living with his wife Martha and two daughters in Ocean Grove, California. Quiet—until one day the household was invaded by Howie, a blond, shaggy-haired, blue-jeaned, eccentric university student with an IQ of 185—Paul's new son-in-law. Howie and his bride Barbara took up residence in the Simms home, for while the new family genius was a whiz at just about anything he tried—and he tried to offer advice on everything—he couldn't seem to hold a job. All of this drove Paul to distraction, and gave Mr. Lynde plenty of opportunities to do that slow burn for which he was so famous.

Jerry Stiller and Anne Meara were seen occasionally as Howie's parents, the Dickersons.

PAUL SAND IN FRIENDS AND LOVERS

Situation Comedy

FIRST TELECAST: *September 14, 1974*

LAST TELECAST: *January 4, 1975*

BROADCAST HISTORY:

Sep 1974–Jan 1975, CBS Sat 8:30–9:00

CAST:

Robert Dreyfuss . . . . Paul Sand
Charlie Dreyfuss . . . . Michael Pataki
Janice Dreyfuss . . . . Penny Marshall
Jack Riordan . . . . Dick Wesson
Fred Meyerbach . . . . Steve Landesberg
Mason Woodruff . . . . . Craig Richard Nelson
Ben Dreyfuss . . . . Jack Gilford

Robert Dreyfuss was a bass violinist with the Boston Symphony Orchestra. A young, unaggressive, incurable romantic whose shyness always made success with women difficult, Robert was nevertheless constantly falling in love with just about every pretty girl he met. His emotional opposite was his older brother Charlie—aggressive, loud, and overprotective of Robert. Charlie's wife Janice was forever making fun of Robert's girl problems.

PAUL WHITEMAN'S GOODYEAR REVUE

Musical Variety

FIRST TELECAST: *November 6, 1949*

LAST TELECAST: *March 30, 1952*

BROADCAST HISTORY:

Nov 1949–Mar 1952, ABC Sun 7:00–7:30 (OS 1950)

EMCEE:

Paul Whiteman

REGULARS:

Earl Wrightson (1950–1952)
Maureen Cannon (1951–1952)
Glenn Osser conducting the Paul Whiteman Orchestra (summer 1951)

At the same time that *Paul Whiteman's TV Teen Club* was a Saturday night fixture during the early 1950s, the bandleader was also seen on Sunday nights with his *Goodyear Revue.* The format was that of a standard musical variety show, with guests such as Victor Borge, Jane Froman, Mel Torme, Charles Laughton, Mindy Carson, and numerous others. Eleven-year-old Junie Keegan of the *TV Teen Club* was a semi-regular at the outset of the show, and vocalists Earl Wrightson and Maureen Cannon later became regulars. Dancers and choral groups were also featured.

During the summer of 1951, while Whiteman was on vacation, the program was hosted by regulars Earl Wrightson and Maureen Cannon and renamed *The Goodyear Summertime Revue.*

PAUL WHITEMAN'S TV TEEN CLUB

Talent

FIRST TELECAST: *April 2, 1949*

LAST TELECAST: *March 28, 1954*

BROADCAST HISTORY:

Apr 1949–Aug 1949, ABC Sat 9:00–10:00
Sep 1949–Dec 1951, ABC Sat 8:00–9:00
Dec 1951–Aug 1952, ABC Sat 8:00–8:30
Sep 1952–Oct 1952, ABC Sat 7:30–8:00

Oct 1952–Dec 1953, ABC Sat 7:00–7:30 (OS)
Dec 1953–Mar 1954, ABC Sun 7:30–8:00

EMCEE:
Paul Whiteman

CO-EMCEE:
Margo Whiteman (1949)
Nancy Lewis (1949–1953)

REGULARS:
Junie Keegan (1949–1953)
Stanley Klet (1950–1953)
Andrea McLaughlin

PRODUCER/DIRECTOR:
Skipper Dawes

Paul Whiteman, one of the great innovators in American popular music, was something of a musical institution by the time television came along in the late 1940s. During the 1920s he had led a fabulously successful dance and concert band, which had been a veritable hotbed of new talent and musical innovation. He was dubbed, with some poetic license, "The King of Jazz." In the 1930s and 1940s he appeared regularly on radio and in films, and when TV came along he plunged enthusiastically into that medium too. From 1949 until the mid-1950s he was frequently seen on the new ABC-TV network, as host of several programs, and he was also ABC's vice president in charge of music.

Paul Whiteman's TV Teen Club provided a second childhood for the rotund, gregarious bandleader. The idea for a teenage talent contest had originated in an antidelinquency program he had begun in his home town of Lambertville, Pennsylvania. In 1949 he moved the talent show to the ABC network, live from Philadelphia. Each week a series of youthful singers, tap dancers, and instrumentalists would perform, with the winners being given professional coaching and returning for subsequent appearances. Special contests were also held, such as a *TV Guide*–Paul Whiteman Talent Search in 1952 which brought in 1,500 applications.

Youngsters not only performed on the *TV Teen Club,* but helped run it as well. Whiteman's daughter Margo was the original co-emcee, later replaced by 14-year-old Nancy Lewis. Singer Stan Klet (also 14) became a regular, as did "Pop's" youngest protégé, 4-year-old Andrea McLaughlin. Whiteman's most famous discovery in the 1920s had been young Bing Crosby, and while no one on the TV show equalled that "find" he did have one youngster of whom he was particularly proud: 11-year-old singer Junie Keegan. A notable moment in Junie's career came in June 1950 when she was honored on the show by the National Confectioners' Association as their "Crown Princess of Candyland." She received from Pops "a crown of gumdrops, an all-day sucker, and a giant peppermint-stick scepter as the fitting symbols of her installation as The Sweetest Girl in America"—an auspicious, if somewhat gooey beginning to any girl's career. Junie later made guest appearances on other TV shows, had her own show in New York, and a Decca recording contract.

The dynamo who kept things rolling on the *Teen Club,* however, was Pops himself. Dressed in a flamboyant shirt and an even louder sports jacket, he delighted in using the kids' own catch phrases ("Real gone!") and dispensing the sponsor's Tootsie Rolls and chewing gum from a paper bag. Since he couldn't remember all the kids' names, they variously became "Junior," "Brains," "Pardner," or "Squidgage." One day when he overdid it a bit, little Andrea shot back, "Oh Pops, how corny can we get!"

But Pops didn't mind. "The way to feel young," he confided to a reporter, "is to stay around young people."

During its last few months on the air the show's format was altered to include "at home" and "on camera" guest celebrities who judged the performances (previously this had been done by audience applause). The *TV Teen Club* finally left the air in early 1954, after a five-year run. The concept was revived during the following summer for Whiteman's *On the Boardwalk.*

PAUL WINCHELL–JERRY MAHONEY SHOW, THE

Comedy Variety

FIRST TELECAST: *September 18, 1950*
LAST TELECAST: *May 23, 1954*
BROADCAST HISTORY:
Sep 1950–Jun 1953, NBC Mon 8:00–8:30 (OS)
Aug 1953–May 1954, NBC Sun 7:00–7:30

EMCEE:
Paul Winchell

REGULARS:
Dorothy Claire (1951–1952)
Diane Sinclair and Ken Spaulding (1951–1953)
Mary Ellen Terry (1953–1954)

Margaret Hamilton (1953–1954)
John Gart Orchestra

Ventriloquist Paul Winchell and his dummy Jerry Mahoney were the stars of this variety series, which mixed comedy, music, quiz show, and even dramatic elements during its four-year run. At first the program opened with a comedy routine by Winchell and Mahoney, followed by a quiz segment called "What's My Name?", which they emceed. The questions all had to do with famous personalities, and guest stars appeared to act out or sing the clues. Contestants were drawn from the studio audience and viewers could also be called at home if they had sent in their name and phone number.

Gradually the entertainment element took over an increasing portion of the show, and the quiz portion was dropped altogether by 1953. Featured in the variety segments were Winchell and his dummies Jerry, Knucklehead, Oswald, and others, plus vocalist Dorothy Claire, dancers Sinclair and Spaulding, other regulars and guests.

During the fall of 1953 the program added a filmed dramatic vignette of approximately 10 minutes' duration, starring a well-known actor or actress in a serious short story (Winchell was often seen in a supporting role). This odd insertion lasted until November, when the show returned to a straight comedy-variety format for the rest of its run.

The annual *Look* Magazine TV Awards were presented on special telecasts of this series in December 1952 and December 1953, with many top names appearing.

The *Winchell-Mahoney* show was known as the *Speidel Show* during its first year and a half on the air (until December 1951), and was also sometimes referred to by the quiz element, *What's My Name?*

PAULINE FREDERICK'S GUESTBOOK

Interviews

FIRST TELECAST: *January 12, 1949*
LAST TELECAST: *April 13, 1949*
BROADCAST HISTORY:
Jan 1949–Apr 1949, ABC Wed 9:15–9:30
HOSTESS:
Pauline Frederick

Interviews with guests from business, political, and cultural life. The program had been seen locally in New York since August 1948.

PEAK OF THE SPORTS NEWS, THE

see *Red Barber's Corner*

PEARL BAILEY SHOW, THE

Musical Variety

FIRST TELECAST: *January 23, 1971*
LAST TELECAST: *May 8, 1971*
BROADCAST HISTORY:
Jan 1971–May 1971, ABC Sat 8:30–9:30
REGULARS:
Pearl Bailey
The Allan Davies Singers
The Robert Sidney Dancers
Louis Bellson & His Orchestra

Pearl Bailey's sole venture into series television was this musical variety series in which she starred during early 1971. Her husband, drummer Louis Bellson, directed the orchestra and Pearlie Mae entertained with an assortment of celebrity guest stars, including Bing Crosby, Louis Armstrong, Andy Williams, Kate Smith, and B. B. King.

PECK'S BAD GIRL

Situation Comedy

FIRST TELECAST: *May 5, 1959*
LAST TELECAST: *September 29, 1960*
BROADCAST HISTORY:
May 1959–Aug 1959, CBS Tue 9:00–9:30
Jun 1960–Sep 1960, CBS Tue 8:00–8:30
Sep 1960, CBS Thu 9:30–10:00
CAST:
Steve Peck .... Wendell Corey
Jennifer Peck .... Marsha Hunt
Torey Peck .... Patty McCormack
Roger Peck .... Ray Ferrell

Research physicist Steve Peck was a typical middle-class American with a typical middle-class family. He had a charming wife, two children, and a home in the suburbs. Torey, his 12 year-old, was at that awkward age. She wasn't quite sure whether she was going to become a young lady or stay an aggressive tomboy. Her indecision and inconsistency were very trying on her parents, who tried to understand and give useful advice, and completely mind-boggling to her little brother, who never quite figured out what was going on. The episodes telecast by CBS during the summer of 1960 were all reruns.

The title and format were a variation on the *Peck's Bad Boy* movies of the 1920s and 1930s starring Jackie Cooper.

PEE WEE KING SHOW

Musical Variety

FIRST TELECAST: *May 23, 1955*

LAST TELECAST: *September 5, 1955*

BROADCAST HISTORY:

May 1955–Sep 1955, ABC Mon 9:00–10:30

REGULARS:

Pee Wee King and His Golden West Cowboys
Redd Stewart
Little Eller Long
Neal Burris

Ninety-minute Country Music–variety show from WEWS, Cleveland, Ohio, featuring best-selling Country bandleader King ("Tennessee Waltz," "Slow Poke"), his vocalist Redd Stewart, six-foot-five comedienne Little Eller Long, "shuffling cowboy singer" Neal Burris, and a square-dance unit, among others.

PENDULUM, THE

syndicated title for *Vise, The*

PENNY TO A MILLION

Quiz

FIRST TELECAST: *May 4, 1955*

LAST TELECAST: *October 5, 1955*

BROADCAST HISTORY:

May 1955–Oct 1955, ABC Wed 9:30–10:00

EMCEE:

Bill Goodwin

The first question in the playoff round of this summer quiz show was worth exactly one cent. However, each subsequent question doubled in value until a contestant could win as much as a million pennies ($10,000). Contestants were chosen in a preliminary round from two teams drawn from the studio audience.

PENTAGON

Interview

FIRST TELECAST: *May 13, 1951*

LAST TELECAST: *November 24, 1952*

BROADCAST HISTORY:

May 1951–Nov 1951, DUM Sun 8:30–9:00
Dec 1951–Nov 1952, DUM Mon 8:00–8:30

Korean War era interview program in which top Pentagon brass and other officials discussed the war effort.

PENTAGON U.S.A.

Dramatic Anthology

FIRST TELECAST: *August 6, 1953*

LAST TELECAST: *September 24, 1953*

BROADCAST HISTORY:

Aug 1953–Sep 1953, CBS Thu 10:00–10:30

CAST:

The Colonel ....Addison Richards

The dramas presented in this live summer anthology series were adaptations of cases from the criminal investigation files of the U.S. Army. At the beginning of each episode, the Colonel assigned the investigators who were to handle that week's case and gave them a rundown on what or who they were looking for. His office was located in the Pentagon, in Washington.

PENTHOUSE PARTY

Variety

FIRST TELECAST: *September 15, 1950*

LAST TELECAST: *June 8, 1951*

BROADCAST HISTORY:

Sep 1950–Dec 1950, ABC Fri 10:00–10:30
Jan 1951–Jun 1951, ABC Fri 8:30–9:00

HOSTESS:

Betty Furness

REGULARS:

Don Cherry
Buddy Weed Trio

Betty Furness opened this weekly gathering with the words, "Come on inside and meet all the folks." The "folks," her guests, were generally celebrities from the New York music and theater world who, with little coaxing, would demonstrate unsuspected talents for the viewing audience. Matinee idol Hurd Hatfield did a Hindu dance, British actor Arthur Treacher sang "Ragtime Cowboy Joe," and actress Joan Blondell, famous for her wisecracking blond chorine characterization in films, whipped up a casserole. It all took place in the styles of a swell party in Betty's New York penthouse.

PEOPLE

News Magazine

FIRST TELECAST: *September 18, 1978*

LAST TELECAST: *November 6, 1978*

BROADCAST HISTORY:

Sep 1978–Nov 1978, CBS Mon 8:30–9:00

STAR:

Phyllis George

REGULAR CONTRIBUTOR:
Mark Shaw

People was a televised version of the magazine of the same name and, in fact, was produced by the television production arm of Time, Inc., the publishers of the magazine. Hosted by former Miss America Phyllis George, *People* provided short interviews and profiles of people in the news, especially show business personalities. Despite its half hour length, *People* offered fleeting glimpses of many celebrities in each episode. One telecast included Jimmy Durante, Carroll O'Connor, Bette Midler, Francesco Scavullo, Cheryl Tiegs, Kristy McNichol, Bill Cosby, Merv Griffin, Rob Reiner, and several lesser known folk. As with the magazine, the coverage here tended to be fast, flashy and without much substance. Mark Shaw was a regular contributor, travelling around the country to visit interesting places and interview subjects.

PEOPLE ARE FUNNY

Quiz/Audience Participation

FIRST TELECAST: *September 19, 1954*
LAST TELECAST: *April 2, 1961*
BROADCAST HISTORY:
Sep 1954–Sep 1955, NBC Sun 7:00–7:30
Sep 1955–Sep 1956, NBC Sat 9:00–9:30
Sep 1956–Sep 1959, NBC Sat 7:30–8:00
Sep 1959–Apr 1960, NBC Fri 7:30–8:00
Apr 1960–Sep 1960, NBC Wed 10:30–11:00
Sep 1960–Apr 1961, NBC Sun 6:30–7:00
EMCEE:
Art Linkletter

Contestants on *People Are Funny* were picked from the studio audience by host Art Linkletter prior to the filming of each week's episode. On the air they would be interviewed by Art and then asked to get involved in some stunt that would prove that "people are funny." Some stunts, including tests of memory, greed, decision-making or some other trait took place in the studio—and often ended in pie-throwing, water-dousing or the like as the penalty. In others, contestants were given an assignment to complete before the next week's telecast, usually a trick on or test of unsuspecting outsiders—for example, trying to cash a check written on a 40-pound watermelon, or simply trying to give away money to passersby (that can be surprisingly hard). On the next show the contestant would report back with the often hilarious results.

People Are Funny began on radio in 1942. During its first three seasons on TV the radio broadcasts continued, consisting of the sound track from the TV version. Later the TV version was a film of the previously aired radio show. In the 1956–1957 season a computer-dating feature was added, in which a couple, matched by Univac computer, got to know each other while answering questions in a quiz-show segment of the program.

PEOPLE'S CHOICE, THE

Situation Comedy

FIRST TELECAST: *October 6, 1955*
LAST TELECAST: *September 25, 1958*
BROADCAST HISTORY:
Oct 1955–Dec 1955, NBC Thu 8:30–9:00
Jan 1956–Sep 1958, NBC Thu 9:00–9:30
CAST:
Sock Miller .... Jackie Cooper
Mandy Peoples .... Pat Breslin
Aunt Gus .... Margaret Irving
Mayor Peoples .... Paul Maxey
Roger (1955–1957) .... John Stephenson
Rollo (1956–1958) .... Dick Wesson
Cleo .... Herself (voice: Mary Jane Croft)

Socrates (Sock) Miller was a government naturalist who had been elected to the city council, a job he took with great seriousness. His interest in helping the community occasionally got him in trouble with Mayor Peoples, a problem that was compounded by the fact that the mayor's daughter Mandy was Sock's girl friend. Making numerous observations to the audience, although no one in the cast could hear her, was Cleo, Sock's pet basset hound. At the end of the 1956–1957 season Sock and Mandy were secretly married. They made it public early in the 1957–1958 season, following his graduation from law school. He got a job selling homes in the neighboring community of Barkerville, for the developer Mr. Barker, and he and Mandy were given one of the homes to live in. Moving in with them was Sock's freeloading friend Rollo. After the move, neither the mayor nor Sock's Aunt Gus were seen on a weekly basis.

PEOPLE'S PLATFORM

Discussion

FIRST TELECAST: *August 17, 1948*
LAST TELECAST: *August 11, 1950*
BROADCAST HISTORY:
Aug 1948–Dec 1948, CBS Tue 9:30–10:00
Jan 1949–Sep 1949, CBS Mon Various
Oct 1949–Aug 1950, CBS Fri 10:00–10:30

This long-running public-affairs program was begun by the noted educator Dr. Lyman Bryson on CBS radio in 1938, and continued on radio until 1952. It was first seen on TV as a local New York program in May 1948, and moved to the network three months later.

The format was that of a simple debate between major political or other public figures on an important issue of the day. Each side stated its opening arguments, followed by rebuttals. The program was seen on Mondays during most of 1949, but the time varied from week to week (usually between 8:30 and 10:00 P.M.). It continued on TV as a Sunday afternoon feature until July 1951.

PEPSI-COLA PLAYHOUSE

Dramatic Anthology
FIRST TELECAST: *October 2, 1953*
LAST TELECAST: *June 26, 1955*
BROADCAST HISTORY:
Oct 1953–Jun 1954, ABC Fri 8:30–9:00
Jul 1954–Jun 1955, ABC Sun 7:30–8:00
HOSTESS:
Arlene Dahl (1953–1954)
Anita Colby (1954)
Polly Bergen (1954–1955)

Arlene Dahl was the original hostess of this dramatic series which began as a live show and switched to film in the middle of its first season. Miss Colby took over the hostess function in April 1954 and was in turn superceded by Polly Bergen in October 1954.

The stories ranged from melodrama to comedy, and generally featured lesser-known (and thus inexpensive) actors and actresses. Such stars as Craig Stevens, Lee Marvin, Vera Miles, Hans Conried, and Charles Bronson made early TV appearances here.

PERFECT CRIME, THE

see *Telltale Clue, The*

PERRY COMO SHOW, THE

Musical Variety
FIRST TELECAST: *December 24, 1948*
LAST TELECAST: *June 12, 1963*
BROADCAST HISTORY:
Dec 1948–Jan 1949, NBC Fri 7:00–7:15
Jan 1949–Jun 1949, NBC Fri 11:00–11:15
Oct 1949–Jun 1950, NBC Sun 8:00–8:30
Oct 1950–Jun 1955, CBS Mon/Wed/Fri 7:45–8:00 (OS)
Sep 1955–Jun 1959, NBC Sat 8:00–9:00 (OS)
Sep 1959–Jun 1963, NBC Wed 9:00–10:00 (OS)
HOST:
Perry Como
REGULARS:
Fontane Sisters (1948–1954)
Ray Charles Singers (1950–1963)
Louis Da Pron Dancers (1955–1960)
Peter Gennaro Dancers (1960–1963)
KRAFT MUSIC HALL PLAYERS:
Kaye Ballard (1961–1963)
Don Adams (1961–1963)
Sandy Stewart (1961–1963)
Jack Duffy (1961–1963)
Paul Lynde (1961–1962)
Pierre Olaf (1962–1963)
ANNOUNCER:
Martin Block (1948–1950)
Durward Kirby (1950–1951)
Dick Stark (1951–1955)
Frank Gallop (1955–1963)
Ed Herlihy (1959–1963)
ORCHESTRA:
Mitchell Ayres
THEME (1955–1963):
"Dream along with Me (I'm on My Way to a Star)," by Carl Sigman

Perry Como was one of the hottest properties in show business, with a four-year string of hit records and an NBC radio series already to his credit, when his first TV series began in 1948. The *Chesterfield Supper Club* premiered in the Friday 7:00–7:15 P.M. time slot on December 24, 1948, but stayed there only three weeks before moving to 11:00 P.M. on January 14, 1949. It was at first a simulcast of Perry's popular radio show and made few concessions to the new medium. Cameras were simply brought into the radio studio and Como and his guests were seen in front of a radio microphone, with scripts and music stands in full view. In succeeding months this was gradually modified, with simple backdrops and props being added. The basic format remained Perry's easygoing crooning, often of his latest hit record, with interludes by regulars the Fontane Sisters (Marge, Bea, and Geri) and assorted guest stars. The guest on the very first show, Christmas Eve 1948, was a boys' choir, which included Perry's eight-year-old son Ronnie. Subsequent guest spots tended also to be filled by singers, some headliners such as Nat "King" Cole, Burl Ives, Patti Page, etc., and some less well known, including an early appearance by the black rhythm and blues group, the Ravens. Personalities from other areas of show business, such as comedians and actors, were also seen.

In 1950 Perry moved to CBS with a three-a-week 15-minute program called *The Perry Como Show*. Then in 1955 he finally graduated to a full prime-time variety hour on Saturday nights, on NBC. The basic format remained unchanged for the next eight years. Perry opened with his new theme, "Dream along with me, I'm on my way to a star . . . ," there was a request spot introduced by girls singing "Letters, we get letters, we get stacks and stacks of letters!", and top-name guest stars engaging in easy banter with the relaxed Mr. C. The show would frequently close with Perry singing a religious or serious number, blending into the closing theme, "You are never far away from me . . ." In 1961 Kraft took over sponsorship and a group of young players was added, backing Perry and his guests in regular comedy skits. Announcer Frank Gallop also assumed a regular role on the show over the years, as a comic foil to Perry. Gallop was generally heard off camera, his voice booming as if in an echo chamber.

Although Perry's regular weekly series ended in 1963, he remained popular with TV viewers and was seen every five or six weeks in Kraft Music Hall specials from 1963 to 1967. Since then his specials have been somewhat less frequent.

PERRY MASON

Lawyer

FIRST TELECAST: *September 21, 1957*

LAST TELECAST: *January 27, 1974*

BROADCAST HISTORY:

Sep 1957–Sep 1962, CBS Sat 7:30–8:30
Sep 1962–Sep 1963, CBS Thu 8:00–9:00
Sep 1963–Sep 1964, CBS Thu 9:00–10:00
Sep 1964–Sep 1965, CBS Thu 8:00–9:00
Sep 1965–Sep 1966, CBS Sun 9:00–10:00
Sep 1973–Jan 1974, CBS Sun 7:30–8:30

CAST (1957–1966):

Perry Mason . . . . Raymond Burr
Della Street . . . . Barbara Hale
Paul Drake . . . . William Hopper
Lt. Tragg (1957–1964) . . . . Ray Collins
Lt. Anderson (1964–1965) . . . . . Wesley Lau
Lt. Drum (1965–1966) . . . Richard Anderson
Hamilton Burger . . . . William Talman

CAST (1973–1974):

Perry Mason . . . . Monte Markham
Della Street . . . . Sharon Acker
Paul Drake . . . . Albert Stratton
Lt. Arthur Tragg . . . . Dane Clark
Hamilton Burger . . . . Harry Guardino
Gertrude Lade . . . . Brett Somers

CREATED BY:

Erle Stanley Gardner

Perry Mason was television's most successful and longest-running lawyer series. For nine seasons during the 1950s and 1960s Erle Stanley Gardner's famous defense attorney solved murder mysteries in the courtroom. With the aid of his personal investigator Paul Drake and his devoted secretary Della Street, Perry always managed to piece together the puzzle just in time to thwart District Attorney Hamilton Burger, his perpetual adversary. The format was certainly predictable, which may have accounted for much of its appeal. Every case culminated in a courtroom trial, and every trial culminated in the guilty party taking the witness stand, only to break down in a dramatic confession under Mason's battering cross-examination ("But if you were at home on the night of the murder, Mr. Jones, then *how could you have known that* . . ." To which the shell-shocked culprit could only sob, "I didn't mean to kill her"). Judges never seemed to object to these histrionics, and in fact looked on with as much fascination as the viewing audience. Often the deciding clue would be rushed into the courtroom at the last moment by Paul Drake. At the end of every episode, Perry, Della, and Paul would gather to recap and explain what had led to the solution, a neat little coda which often sorted things out for confused viewers.

Mason never lost a case and it seemed that the accumulated frustrations made D.A. Burger determined to convict at least one of Perry's clients. Once actor Raymond Burr was confronted by a fan who demanded to know how it was that he won every case. "But madam," he replied smoothly, "You only see the cases I try on Saturday." Actually, Perry did lose one trial, in 1963, when his client refused to reveal the evidence that would save her. Mason found the real culprit anyway, and eventually exonerated his client, despite herself.

Perry Mason was revived in 1973 with an all new cast (Burr was by that time sleuthing around in a wheelchair on *Ironside*). A new regular was his receptionist, Gertie. However *The New Adventures of Perry Mason* could not recapture the magic of the old, and the revival soon folded.

The Perry Mason character has an interesting background. The fictional alter ego of lawyer-novelist Erle Stanley Gardner, he first became famous in a series of best-selling novels, then in a CBS radio series which ran from 1953 to 1955. The radio series was part soap opera and part detective story (it ran five days a week), and when the time came to move to TV Gardner opted to shift the emphasis to pure sleuthing. The original format also went on TV, in 1956, as *The Edge of Night* (complete with the *Perry Mason* radio production staff and most of the cast, who were given new names). This has continued ever since in daytime. The name Perry Mason was used for the Raymond Burr series, which had a whole new cast and which dropped the soap-opera elements.

PERRY PRESENTS

Musical Variety

FIRST TELECAST: *June 13, 1959*

LAST TELECAST: *September 5, 1959*

BROADCAST HISTORY:

Jun 1959–Sep 1959, NBC Sat 8:00–9:00

REGULARS:

Teresa Brewer
Tony Bennett
The Four Lads
J. P. Morgan
The Modernaires
The Mel Pahl Chorus
The Louis Da Pron Dancers
Mitchell Ayres Orchestra

Following *The Perry Como Show*'s last season on Saturday nights, *Perry Presents* aired as the summer replacement. It was a musical variety show starring Teresa Brewer and Tony Bennett, who also acted as hosts, and the Four Lads. Miss Brewer left the show on July 4 and the Four Lads departed on July 25. On August 1, J. P. Morgan and the Modernaires were added to the regular cast. Each show attempted to treat events in history and issues of current interest musically, with songs and production numbers as well as comedy skits.

PERSON TO PERSON

Interview

FIRST TELECAST: *October 2, 1953*

LAST TELECAST: *September 15, 1961*

BROADCAST HISTORY:

Oct 1953–Jun 1959, CBS Fri 10:30–11:00 (OS)
Oct 1959–Sep 1960, CBS Fri 10:30–11:00
Sep 1960–Dec 1960, CBS Thu 10:00–10:30
Jun 1961–Sep 1961, CBS Fri 10:30–11:00

HOST:

Edward R. Murrow (1953–1959)
Charles Collingwood (1959–1961)

Being chosen as one of Ed Murrow's subjects on *Person to Person* was both an honor and an ordeal. Each Friday night Ed would "visit" with two celebrities at their homes. The interviews were all done live, with Ed seated in a comfortable chair in the studio while the subject showed him around his or her home—via the immediacy of live television. At the midpoint of the show Ed would shift to a different personality, who could well be in a different part of the country entirely. TV cameras were bulky and inconvenient to move around those days, meaning that a technical crew virtually had to take over the home of the subject several days in advance, running heavy cables from room to room and carefully mapping out every movement to be used on the night of the broadcast, to avoid tangles and confusion.

Among the people who chatted informally with Murrow were Marilyn Monroe, Zsa Zsa Gabor, A. C. Nielsen of the ratings company, Fidel Castro, Margaret Mead, John Steinbeck, Sam Rayburn, Tom Dewey, and then Senator John F. Kennedy. Actors and actresses, politicians, diplomats, heads of state, inventors, scientists, musicians, and high church officials were all "visited" on the series. When Charles Collingwood took over for Murrow at the start of the 1959–1960 season, enabling Ed to ease off on his busy schedule, the show did more world traveling and many of the interviews were filmed or taped on location.

PERSONAL APPEARANCE

Dramatic Anthology

FIRST TELECAST: *July 4, 1958*

LAST TELECAST: *September 19, 1958*

BROADCAST HISTORY:

Jul 1958–Sep 1958, CBS Fri 10:30–11:00

The filmed dramas telecast in this summer replacement for *Person to Person* were all reruns of shows that had originally aired as episodes of *Schlitz Playhouse* and *Screen Director's Playhouse*.

PERSONAL APPEARANCE THEATER

Dramatic Anthology

FIRST TELECAST: *October 27, 1951*

LAST TELECAST: *May 23, 1952*

BROADCAST HISTORY:

Oct 1951–Nov 1951, ABC Sat 7:00–7:30
Dec 1951–Jan 1952, ABC Fri 9:30–10:00
May 1952, ABC Fri 8:30–9:00

A collection of 30-minute comedy and mystery films starring lesser-known actors and actresses, such as Franklin Pangborn, Jane Darwell, Robert Clarke, and Anita Louise.

PERSONAL APPEARANCE THEATRE

see *Joseph Schildkraut Presents*

PERSONALITY PUZZLE

Quiz/Panel

FIRST TELECAST: *March 19, 1953*

LAST TELECAST: *June 25, 1953*

BROADCAST HISTORY:

Mar 1953–Jun 1953, ABC Thu 10:30–11:00

EMCEE:

Robert Alda

REGULAR PANELIST:

Lisa Ferraday

Quiz in which the panelists were given personal possessions of a famous celebrity, who was seated behind them, and then had to guess who the celebrity was. Various guests appeared on the panel from week to week along with regular Lisa Ferraday. The program alternated with the similar *Quick as a Flash*.

PERSPECTIVE

Discussion

FIRST TELECAST: *November 13, 1952*

LAST TELECAST: *April 6, 1953*

BROADCAST HISTORY:

Nov 1952–Jan 1953, ABC Thu 9:00–9:30
Jan 1953–Apr 1953, ABC Mon 9:00–9:30

Live public-affairs program produced in cooperation with the Bar Association of the City of New York, and featuring experts from politics, education, science, and industry discussing how their fields could benefit society.

PERSUADERS, THE

Adventure

FIRST TELECAST: *September 18, 1971*

LAST TELECAST: *June 14, 1972*

BROADCAST HISTORY:

Sep 1971–Jan 1972, ABC Sat 10:00–11:00
Jan 1972–Jun 1972, ABC Wed 9:30–10:30

CAST:

Danny Wilde ....Tony Curtis
Lord Brett Sinclair ....Roger Moore
Judge Fulton ....Laurence Naismith

THEME:

"The Persuaders," by John Barry

Danny and Brett were two wealthy playboys who had attained their wealth in very different ways. Danny Wilde was an American, born and raised in Brooklyn, who was a self-made man. Although he had made a great deal of money in the stock market, he was still a "poor kid" underneath. As a member of the British aristocracy, Brett Sinclair was born to great wealth. They were brought together at a Riviera party by retired Judge Fulton, who persuaded them to tackle criminal cases which the legal authorities couldn't handle. So they set out, half serious and half on a lark, traveling around Europe looking for romance, adventure, and wrongs to right. The contrast in their styles and backgrounds was always apparent, as when they went camping out. There was Danny, under the stars with nothing but a blanket for protection, while Brett had a deluxe tent, complete with bar and freezer.

The show was produced in England.

PET SHOP

Animals

FIRST TELECAST: *December 1, 1951*

LAST TELECAST: *March 14, 1953*

BROADCAST HISTORY:

Dec 1951–Mar 1953, DUM Sat 7:30–8:00

REGULARS:

Gail Compton
Gay Compton
George Menard (1953)

This gentle pet show was presided over by Gail Compton and her young daughter Gay. They exhibited a variety of domestic animals, welcomed guests with their performing pets, and encouraged adoptions (more than 3,000 homeless dogs were placed during the first nine months alone). Among the regulars were Sissie the poodle, Snooky the squirrel monkey, Mac the macaw, and Tin Can the goat.

George Menard was host for the show's last four weeks on the network. From Chicago.

PETE AND GLADYS

Situation Comedy

FIRST TELECAST: *September 19, 1960*
LAST TELECAST: *September 10, 1962*
BROADCAST HISTORY:

Sep 1960–Sep 1962, CBS Mon 8:00–8:30

CAST:

Pete Porter ....Harry Morgan
Gladys Porter ....Cara Williams
Hilda Crocker (1960–1961) ... Verna Felton
Peggy Briggs (1961–1962) ....Mina Kolb
Ernie Briggs (1961–1962) ......Joe Mantell
Uncle Paul ....Gale Gordon
Nancy (1961–1962) ....Frances Rafferty

During his years as the sardonic next-door neighbor on *December Bride,* Pete Porter was always complaining about his scatter-brained, ineffectual wife Gladys. She was never seen on that series but became the co-star, in the person of Cara Williams, in this successor to *December Bride.* Along from the original series was Hilda Crocker, the nosy older woman friend who had tried to defend Gladys when Pete made some nasty comment about his wife. Gladys' Uncle Paul was seen occasionally during the first season and became a regular the second, as did the Porters' next-door neighbors and Gladys' friend Nancy (played by *December Bride* regular Frances Rafferty, in a different role). The conflict between the sincere, ingenuous, and often confused Gladys and sarcastic, deprecating Pete formed the crux of the stories in this series.

PETE KELLY'S BLUES

Drama

FIRST TELECAST: *April 5, 1959*
LAST TELECAST: *September 4, 1959*
BROADCAST HISTORY:

Apr 1959–Jul 1959, NBC Sun 8:30–9:00
Jul 1959–Sep 1959, NBC Fri 7:30–8:00

CAST:

Pete Kelly ....William Reynolds
Savannah Brown ....Connee Boswell
George Lupo ....Than Wyenn
Fred ....Phil Gordon

PRODUCER:

Jack Webb

Life in Kansas City during the Roaring Twenties, from the standpoint of a musician working in a speakeasy, was the subject of *Pete Kelly's Blues.* Pete was a trumpet player and the leader of Pete Kelly's Original Big Seven Band. His best friend was the band's pianist, Fred, and his closest female friend was Savannah Brown, a blues singer at another speakeasy. Pete worked for George Lupo, who was essentially a nice guy but had become rather jaded since opening his own place on Cherry Street. The stories revolved around the adventures Pete had as he ran into people who got him involved in murder, tracking down missing people, and other non-musical exploits.

Jack Webb, who produced this series, had been the original Pete Kelly in the radio series of the same name, which ran for six months in 1951, and also starred in the movie version which was released in 1955. The offscreen trumpet player who dubbed in Pete's solos was Dick Cathcart, a well-regarded jazz performer of the period. He had originally been picked by Webb for the radio series and also appeared with him in the movie.

PETER AND MARY SHOW, THE

see *Peter Lind Hayes Show, The*

PETER GUNN

Detective

FIRST TELECAST: *September 22, 1958*
LAST TELECAST: *September 25, 1961*
BROADCAST HISTORY:

Sep 1958–Sep 1960, NBC Mon 9:00–9:30
Oct 1960–Sep 1961, ABC Mon 10:30–11:00

CAST:

Peter Gunn ....Craig Stevens
Edie Hart ....Lola Albright

Lt. Jacoby .... Herschel Bernardi
"Mother" (1958–1959) ...... Hope Emerson
"Mother" (1959–1961) ..... Minerva Urecal

THEME:

"Peter Gunn," by Henry Mancini

Peter Gunn was one of the first suave, aggressive, lady-killer private detectives to be seen on television. Working to get his clients out of trouble, and to solve crimes, he often found himself on the short end of a fight but somehow managed to come out on top, often through the intervention of his friend, police lieutenant Jacoby. Gunn spent much of his free time at a jazz nightclub called "Mother's," where his girl friend Edie was the featured singer.

Original jazz themes by Henry Mancini punctuated the action and conveyed mood in this detective series, setting a pattern that was followed by many of the other detective shows of the late 1950s and early 1960s. RCA released two very successful albums of music from this series, *The Music of Peter Gunn* and *More Music from Peter Gunn.*

PETER LIND HAYES SHOW, THE

Situation Comedy

FIRST TELECAST: *November 23, 1950*
LAST TELECAST: *March 29, 1951*
BROADCAST HISTORY:

Nov 1950–Mar 1951, NBC Thu 8:30–9:00

REGULARS:

Peter Lind Hayes
Mary Healy
Mary Wickes (1950)
Claude Stroud (1950)

The set for this live series was a replica of the New Rochelle, New York, home of its stars, Peter Lind Hayes and Mary Healy. At the start of each episode, a guest star would be seen apologizing over the phone to someone with whom he could not have dinner that evening because of a previous commitment to have dinner with Peter and Mary. The guest star(s) then went to Peter and Mary's "house" for dinner where the talents they possessed—singing, dancing, comedy, etc.—were worked into the script. The series had actually premiered as *The Peter and Mary Show* but was changed to *The Peter Lind Hayes Show* on December 14. Mary Wickes was their housekeeper and Claude Stroud an unemployed comedian who had come for a visit and become a permanent member of the household. Both of them were last seen in the December 28 telecast.

PETER LOVES MARY

Situation Comedy

FIRST TELECAST: *October 12, 1960*
LAST TELECAST: *May 31, 1961*
BROADCAST HISTORY:

Oct 1960–May 1961, NBC Wed 10:00–10:30

CAST:

Peter Lindsey .... Peter Lind Hayes
Mary Lindsey .... Mary Healy
Wilma .... Bea Benaderet
Leslie Lindsey .... Merry Martin
Steve Lindsey .... Gil Smith

Peter Lind Hayes and Mary Healy, husband and wife in real life, here played a show-business couple adjusting to a move to the suburbs. The move from Manhattan to Oakdale affected the members of the household in different ways. Peter longed for the exciting life of the city, where all the show-business people with whom they were friendly congregated in such hangouts as Lindy's. Mary wanted to become involved in all the traditional suburban activities—local government, P.T.A., social causes, etc. The conflicts between their work in the city and their suburban life with housekeeper Wilma and their two children, Leslie and Steve, provided the material for the stories in this series.

PETER POTTER SHOW, THE

Music/Discussion

FIRST TELECAST: *September 13, 1953*
LAST TELECAST: *March 28, 1954*
BROADCAST HISTORY:

Sep 1953–Jan 1954, ABC Sun 9:30–10:30
Jan 1954–Mar 1954, ABC Sun 9:30–10:00

HOST:

Peter Potter

Hollywood disc jockey Peter Potter brought his *Juke Box Jury* to national television in 1953. It consisted of the playing of new records, with ensuing discussion by a panel of celebrities from movies, theater, TV, and the recording industry. The studio audience also participated in the voting on each new record—"Will it be a hit (bong!) . . . or a miss (clunk!)?" Some live performances were also included.

The program was known during its first

month by the familiar title *Juke Box Jury*, then switched to *The Peter Potter Show*.

PETROCELLI

Lawyer

FIRST TELECAST: *September 11, 1974*

LAST TELECAST: *March 3, 1976*

BROADCAST HISTORY:

Sep 1974–Mar 1976, NBC Wed 10:00–11:00

CAST:

Tony Petrocelli ....Barry Newman
Maggie Petrocelli ....Susan Howard
Pete Ritter ....Albert Salmi
Lt. Ponce ....David Huddleston

Set in the fictional Southwestern town of San Remo, *Petrocelli* was not quite a typical legal series. Harvard-educated Tony Petrocelli had decided to practice law in a part of the country that was not always receptive to big-city, Eastern ways. He and his wife moved to the Southwest, set up housekeeping in a camper-trailer, and opened up his law practice in the middle of wide-open cattle country. Tony hired Pete Ritter, a local cowboy, as his investigator. Tony's propensity for taking on cases whether or not his clients could really afford his services often made it rather hard for him and his wife to make ends meet. Lt. Ponce of the local police, a good friend of Tony's despite the fact that they found themselves in adversary positions in the courtroom, was often involved in investigating the cases Tony was working on. An interesting technique used in this series was showing the actual crime in flashbacks from the perspective of various people involved. The flashbacks, naturally, differed depending on whose recollections were being shown.

Barry Newman created the role of Petrocelli in a 1970 movie called *The Lawyer*, which was loosely based on the Sam Sheppard murder case.

PETTICOAT JUNCTION

Situation Comedy

FIRST TELECAST: *September 24, 1963*

LAST TELECAST: *September 12, 1970*

BROADCAST HISTORY:

Sep 1963–Sep 1964, CBS Tue 9:00–9:30
Sep 1964–Aug 1967, CBS Tue 9:30–10:00
Sep 1967–Sep 1970, CBS Sat 9:30–10:00

CAST:

Kate Bradley (1963–1969)
.... Bea Benaderet
Uncle Joe Carson ....Edgar Buchanan
Billie Jo Bradley (1963–1965)
.... Jeannine Riley
Billie Jo Bradley (1965–1966)
.... Gunilla Hutton
Billie Jo Bradley (1966–1970)
.... Meredith MacRae
Bobbie Jo Bradley (1963–1965)
.... Pat Woodell
Bobbie Jo Bradley (1965–1970)
.... Lori Saunders
Betty Jo Bradley ....Linda Kaye
Charlie Pratt (1963–1967)
.... Smiley Burnette
Floyd Smoot (1963–1968) ......Rufe Davis
Homer Bedloe (1963–1966) ... Charles Lane
Sam Drucker ....Frank Cady
Steve Elliott (1967–1970) ......Mike Minor
Dr. Janet Craig (1969–1970)
.... June Lockhart
Wendell Gibbs (1969–1970)
.... Byron Foulger

The small farming community of Hooterville provided the setting for this highly successful rural situation comedy. Kate Bradley was the widowed owner of the only transient housing in town, the Shady Rest Hotel. Helping her run the hotel were her three beautiful daughters, Billie Jo, Bobbie Jo, and Betty Jo. Also assisting was the girls' Uncle Joe, who had assumed the title of manager. In addition to her involvement with the hotel, the romantic lives of her daughters, and her associations with the townspeople, Kate was constantly at odds with Homer Bedloe, vice president of the C.F. & W. Railroad. Homer was determined to close down the steam-driven branch of the railroad that ran through Hooterville, scrap its lone engine (the Cannonball), and put its two engineers (Charlie Pratt and Floyd Smoot) out of jobs.

Two years after the premiere of *Petticoat Junction*, CBS added *Green Acres* to its lineup. This situation comedy was the story of a Manhattan businessman who gave up big-city life and bought a farm near Hooterville. For the remainder of their existences there was a certain interplay between the characters of the two shows.

In the fall of 1967 pilot Steve Elliott crashed outside Hooterville and was nursed back to health by the Bradley girls. He later became romantically involved with Betty Jo and eventually married her and set up housekeeping not far from the hotel.

Bea Benaderet passed away during the 1968–1969 production season and her absence left the show without a unifying center of attention. To fill the void, the role of Dr. Janet Craig, a mature woman doctor who assumed the role of town physician, was added for the 1969–1970 season. The chemistry was not there anymore, however, and the show was canceled at the end of the year.

PEYTON PLACE

Romantic Drama

FIRST TELECAST: *September 15, 1964*

LAST TELECAST: *June 2, 1969*

BROADCAST HISTORY:

Sep 1964–Jun 1965, ABC Tue/Thu 9:30–10:00
Jun 1965–Oct 1965, ABC Tue/Thu/Fri 9:30–10:00
Nov 1965–Aug 1966, ABC Mon/Tue/Thu 9:30–10:00
Sep 1966–Jan 1967, ABC Mon/Wed 9:30–10:00
Jan 1967–Aug 1967, ABC Mon/Tue 9:30–10:00
Sep 1967–Sep 1968, ABC Mon/Thu 9:30–10:00
Sep 1968–Jan 1969, ABC Mon 9:00–9:30/Wed 8:30–9:00
Feb 1969–Jun 1969, ABC Mon 9:00–9:30

CAST:

Constance Mackenzie/Carson (1964–1968) .... Dorothy Malone
Allison Mackenzie/Harrington (1964–1966) .... Mia Farrow
Dr. Michael Rossi .... Ed Nelson
Matthew Swain, editor of The Clarion *(1964–1965)* .... Warner Anderson
Leslie Harrington (1964–1968) .... Paul Langton
Rodney Harrington, Leslie's oldest son .... Ryan O'Neal
Norman Harrington, Leslie's younger son .... Christopher Connelly
Betty Anderson/Harrington/Cord/Harrington .... Barbara Parkins
Julie Anderson, Betty's mother .... Kasey Rogers
George Anderson, her father (1964–1965) .... Henry Beckman
Dr. Robert Morton (1964–1965) .... Kent Smith
Steven Cord .... James Douglas
Hannah Cord, Steven's mother (1965–1967) .... Ruth Warrick
Paul Hanley (1965) .... Richard Evans
Elliott Carson (1965–1968) .... Tim O'Connor
Eli Carson, Elliott's father .... Frank Ferguson
Nurse Choate (1965–1968) .... Erin O'Brien-Moore
Dr. Claire Morton (1965) .... Mariette Hartley
Dr. Vincent Markham (1965) .... Leslie Nielsen
Rita Jacks/Harrington (1965–1969) .... Patricia Morrow
Ada Jacks, Rita's mother (1965–1969) .... Evelyn Scott
David Schuster (1965–1966) .... William Smithers
Doris Schuster, his wife (1965) .... Gail Kobe
Kim Schuster, his deaf, 6-year old child (1965) .... Kimberly Beck
Theodore Dowell, attorney (1965) .... Patrick Whyte
Stella Chernak (1965–1966) .... Lee Grant
Joe Chernak (1965) .... Don Quine
Gus Chernak (1965–1966) .... Bruce Gordon
Dr. Russ Gehring (1965–1966) .... David Canary
District Attorney John Fowler (1965–1966) .... John Kerr
Marian Fowler, his wife (1965–1966) .... Joan Blackman
Martin Peyton (1965–1968) .... George Macready
Martin Peyton (temporary replacement, 1967) .... Wilfred Hyde-White
Sandy Webber (1966–1967) .... Lana Wood
Chris Webber (1966–1967) .... Gary Haynes
Lee Webber (1966–1968) .... Steven Oliver
Ann Howard (1966) .... Susan Oliver
Rachael Welles (1966–1967) .... Leigh Taylor-Young
Jack Chandler (1966–1967) .... John Kellogg
Adrienne Van Leyden (1967) .... Gena Rowlands
Eddie Jacks, Rita's father (1967–1968) .... Dan Duryea
Carolyn Russell (1968–1969) .... Elizabeth Walker
Fred Russell (1968–1969) .... Joe Maross
Marsha Russell (1968–1969) .... Barbara Rush
Rev. Tom Winter (1968–1969) .... Bob Hogan
Susan Winter, his wife (1968–1969) .... Diana Hyland
Dr. Harry Miles (1968–1969) .... Percy Rodriguez

Alma Miles, Harry's wife (1968–1969)
. . . . .Ruby Dee
Lew Miles, Harry's teenage son (1968–1969)
. . . . Glynn Turman
Jill Smith/Rossi (1968) . . . . .Joyce Jillson
Joe Rossi, Dr. Rossi's brother (1968)
. . . . Michael Christian

EXECUTIVE PRODUCER:
Paul Monash

Based on the novel *Peyton Place,* by Grace Metalious, this continuing romantic drama was set in the small New England town of Peyton Place, a community that was apparently seething with extramarital affairs, dark secrets, and assorted skulduggery. *Peyton Place* was the most successful soap opera in the history of prime time. It aired up to three times per week, and every telecast during its five-year run was an original episode.

At the center of much of the drama was bookshop proprietress Constance Mackenzie, whose own dark secret involved the circumstances surrounding the birth of her daughter Allison 18 years earlier. In May 1965 Constance was finally able to marry Allison's real father, Elliott Carson, upon his release from prison. Meanwhile Allison experienced her own romantic entanglements, leading to her marriage to wealthy Rodney Harrington in April 1966. A few months later Allison mysteriously "disappeared" (Mia Farrow having decided to leave the series). Her character was not soon forgotten, however. First a young girl named Rachael turned up with a clue to Allison's disappearance (a bracelet), setting off a long investigation. Then in 1968 another girl, Jill, arrived in town with what she claimed was Allison's baby.

Other major stories revolved around Rodney Harrington, who was tried for murder in an extended story from 1965–1966. Rodney's lawyer was Steven Cord, another young man with a past, who soon found himself embroiled in the town's active romantic life. So did Dr. Michael Rossi, a young physician who had arrived in Peyton Place on the first telecast in 1964, and who was facing his own murder trial when the series ended in 1969.

And there were many, many more: loose-living Betty Anderson, who was married successively to Rodney Harrington (October 1964), Steven Cord (April 1966), and then Rodney Harrington again (June 1968); tavernkeeper's daughter Rita Jacks, who married Normam Harrington (January 1966); David Schuster, who took over the management of the Peyton Mills when Leslie Harrington, Rodney and Norman's father, was sacked by owner Martin Peyton; Rev. Tom Winter, whose affairs were more than clerical; and, toward the end, in a bow to relevance, Dr. Harry Miles, a black neurosurgeon with *his* family and problems.

Aging Martin Peyton, the town's patriarch, was not seen at first. He first appeared in November 1965, as his grandson Rodney Harrington was about to go on trial for murder. Over the next two years Peyton was an important character. An extended story in late 1967 had newcomer Adrienne Van Leyden all set to marry the old codger and collect his loot, until she was murdered (December 1967), resulting in another trial with multiple consequences. Shortly thereafter Martin Peyton departed for a Boston clinic, where he died in November 1968, and was buried in a funeral attended by most of the town. (Notwithstanding this fact, he was brought back to life when *Peyton Place* was revived as a daytime serial in the early 1970s.)

The regular cast of *Peyton Place* would fill a telephone book. One ABC cast credits card lists over 100 "regulars." Those shown above figured most prominently in the various continuing stories. At the outset of the series Dorothy Malone, in the role of Constance Mackenzie, received top billing. A year later, in September 1965, Miss Malone suddenly fell ill and the role was taken over temporarily by Lola Albright. Miss Malone returned in January 1966 and continued for another two and a half years. After she left in June 1968, Ed Nelson, as heartthrob Dr. Michael Rossi, was given top billing.

Probably the two most famous discoveries of *Peyton Place,* however, were Mia Farrow and Ryan O'Neal. Miss Farrow, as the alluring Allison, was seen only during the first two seasons, but O'Neal, as Rodney, continued for the full run of the series.

PHIL HANNA SINGS

see *Starlit Time*

PHIL SILVERS SHOW, THE

Situation Comedy

FIRST TELECAST: *September 20, 1955*
LAST TELECAST: *September 11, 1959*
BROADCAST HISTORY:

Sep 1955–Oct 1955, CBS Tue 8:30–9:00
Nov 1955–Feb 1958, CBS Tue 8:00–8:30
Feb 1958–Sep 1959, CBS Fri 9:00–9:30

CAST:

Sgt. Ernie Bilko .... Phil Silvers
Rocco Barbella .... Harvey Lembeck
Fender .... Herbie Faye
Col. Hall .... Paul Ford
Doberman .... Maurice Gosfield
Sgt. Ritzik .... Joe E. Ross
Henshaw .... Alan Melvin
Sgt. Joan Hogan (1955–1958)
.... Elisabeth Fraser

Mythical Fort Baxter, Kansas, was the setting for this outrageous satire on military life. Master Sergeant Ernie Bilko was the biggest con man on the post. With little to do in the wilds of Middle America, Bilko spent most of his time gambling, conjuring up assorted money-making schemes, and outmaneuvering his immediate superior, Colonel Hall. Loud, brash, and highly resourceful, Ernie could talk his way out of almost any situation. His attitude and approach filtered down to most of the members of his platoon, and collectively they ran roughshod over the rest of the men stationed at Fort Baxter. WAC Joan Hogan, who worked in the base's office, was Bilko's mild romantic interest during the first three seasons, but was phased out. The original title of the series was *You'll Never Get Rich,* which remained as the subtitle when the series became *The Phil Silvers Show* less than two months after its premiere.

PHILCO TV PLAYHOUSE

Dramatic Anthology

FIRST TELECAST: *October 3, 1948*
LAST TELECAST: *October 2, 1955*
BROADCAST HISTORY:

Oct 1948–Oct 1955, NBC Sun 9:00–10:00

HOST:

Bert Lytell (1948–1949)

This live dramatic-anthology series featured top-name actors and actresses in original TV plays and adaptations of novels, short stories, and plays. The first season was produced under the aegis of the Actor's Equity Association, and concentrated on TV adaptations of Broadway dramas and musicals, often with original cast members appearing. Former Equity president Bert Lytell was the host. Perhaps the most elaborate production during the firt season was an adaptation of *Cyrano de Bergerac* with Jose Ferrer and a large supporting cast, which used seven sets (including street scenes) to recreate 17th-century Paris. This, remember, was on *live* television. Other first-season productions included adaptations of *Dinner at Eight* with Peggy Wood and Dennis King, and *Counsellor at Law* starring Paul Muni (his TV debut, recreating the role that had brought him fame on Broadway 17 years earlier).

During the second season Equity was no longer involved, but instead an arrangement was made with the Book of the Month Club to present each week a dramatization of a different novel, usually one which was currently popular. After 1950 this theme was dropped and offerings ran the gamut between original and adapted plays, musicals and occasional true-life documentaries, always meticulously produced. Among the many top stars who appeared on *Philco* were Anthony Quinn, Grace Kelly, young Brandon De Wilde, Lillian Gish (narrating "The Birth of the Movies," a documentary), Walter Matthau, Julie Harris, Rod Steiger, Paul Newman (as Billy the Kid), and Charlton Heston. The last *Philco* telecast was a rough waterfront drama called "A Man Is Ten Feet Tall" with Sidney Poitier, one of the few instances of a black actor appearing in a starring role in a 1950s drama.

From 1951–1955 *Philco TV Playhouse* alternated with *Goodyear TV Playhouse* which presented similar productions.

PHILIP MARLOWE

Detective

FIRST TELECAST: *October 6, 1959*
LAST TELECAST: *March 29, 1960*
BROADCAST HISTORY:

Oct 1959–Mar 1960, ABC Tue 9:30–10:00

CAST:

Philip Marlowe .... Philip Carey

When author Raymond Chandler wrote his first Philip Marlowe stories in the late 1930s, the detective hero was a hard-bitten loner, rough around the edges, and particularly aggressive. When Philip Marlowe reached television in 1959 he had been laundered considerably. He was still a rather independent loner but had become a much more gentlemanly sort than on the printed page. Working to protect people, solve crimes, and track down missing persons, he moved freely from place to place without getting entangled in any lasting personal relationships.

PHILIP MORRIS PLAYHOUSE

Dramatic Anthology

FIRST TELECAST: *October 8, 1953*

LAST TELECAST: *March 4, 1954*

BROADCAST HISTORY:

Oct 1953–Mar 1954, CBS Thu 10:00–10:30

This live dramatic series, with individual plays ranging in tone from comedies to melodramas, was aired from New York. Lorne Greene, Eddie Albert, and Constance Ford starred in the premiere telecast, titled "Journey to Nowhere," and Nina Foch, Franchot Tone, Sterling Hayden, Vincent Price, and Otto Kruger appeared in subsequent episodes.

PHILLIES JACKPOT BOWLING

see *Jackpot Bowling Starring Milton Berle*

PHOTOCRIME

Crime Drama

FIRST TELECAST: *September 21, 1949*

LAST TELECAST: *December 14, 1949*

BROADCAST HISTORY:

Sep 1949–Dec 1949, ABC Wed 8:30–9:00

CAST:

Inspector Hannibal Cobb . . .Chuck Webster

Easygoing Inspector Hannibal Cobb was the long arm of the law in this mystery series, which was produced in cooperation with *Look* magazine. Also known as *Look Photocrime*.

PHOTOGRAPHIC HORIZONS

Instruction

FIRST TELECAST: *January 12, 1949*

LAST TELECAST: *March 7, 1949*

BROADCAST HISTORY:

Jan 1949–Mar 1949, DUM Mon 8:00–8:30

HOST:

Joe Costa

REGULARS:

Peggy Corday

Many unusual program formats were tried in the early days of television, including that of the TV camera club. It seemed like a natural for the new medium. Not only could expert photographers describe picture-taking techniques, home-darkroom procedures, etc., they could actually show the results. *Photographic Horizons* began as a local show on DuMont's New York station in December 1947, and was quite popular with early set owners. Not only were there interviews and demonstrations, but the succession of lovely models didn't hurt viewership. The models posed before special backgrounds and viewers at home were encouraged to take pictures of them off the TV screen. Joe Costa, president of the National Press Photographers Association, was host, and 23-year-old Peggy Corday his chief model. Maxine Barrat also frequently modeled for home shutterbugs.

PHOTOPLAY TIME

see *Wendy Barrie Show, The*

PHYLLIS

Situation Comedy

FIRST TELECAST: *September 8, 1975*

LAST TELECAST: *August 30, 1977*

BROADCAST HISTORY:

Sep 1975–Jan 1977, CBS Mon 8:30–9:00
Jan 1977–Jul 1977, CBS Sun 8:30–9:00
Aug 1977, CBS Tue 8:30–9:00

CAST:

Phyllis Lindstrom ....Cloris Leachman
Bess Lindstrom ....Lisa Gerritsen
Julie Erskine (1975–1976) ......Liz Torres
Leo Heatherton (1975–1976)
.... Richard Schaal
Audrey Dexter ....Jane Rose
Judge Jonathan Dexter ....Henry Jones
Mother Dexter ....Judith Lowry
Leonard Marsh (1976–1977) ... John Lawlor
Harriet Hastings (1976–1977)
.... Garn Stephens
Dan Valenti (1976–1977) ... Carmini Caridi
Arthur Lanson (1976) ....Burt Mustin
Mark Valenti (1977) ....Craig Wasson

After five years playing Mary Richards' neighbor, friend, and landlady on *The Mary Tyler Moore Show*, Cloris Leachman began her own spinoff series. Phyllis Lindstrom returned to her home town of San Francisco following the death of her husband Lars. In her mid-40s, and with a teenage daughter to support, Phyllis moved in with her scatterbrained mother, Audrey, and Audrey's second husband, Judge Jonathan Dexter. Though not a member of the household when the series started, Judge Dexter's mother was also living with them before the first season's end.

Phyllis found a job working as assistant to Julie Erskine at Erskine's Commercial Photography Studio. Also working as a photographer for Julie was Leo Heatherton. Barbara Colby was the actress originally signed for the role of Julie Erskine but only appeared in the first episode of the series. She had died unexpectedly soon after production had started and was replaced by Liz Torres. This job, with Phyllis being her busybody, self-centered, oblivious self, lasted only one season.

At the start of the 1976–1977 season, in an effort to improve upon the mediocre ratings of the first season, Phyllis was given a new job as administrative assistant to Dan Valenti, a member of the San Francisco Board of Supervisors. She worked in an office with another supervisor, Leonard Marsh, and his assistant Harriet. On the home front things were also changing. Witty, sharp-tongued Mother Dexter, far and away the best member of the family when it came to putting down Phyllis, had become involved with a man. She was 87 and Arthur was 92, but love flowered and they were married in December 1976. Ironically, elderly actress Judith Lowry had died while on vacation in New York during a break in production early in December, before the episode aired, and Bert Mustin, who was too ill to see it, died not long after. Bess also found a man, in the person of Phyllis' boss' nephew Mark. They sneaked off to Las Vegas and were married in the spring. The changes in cast and multiple marriages didn't help the ratings enough to save the series. It was canceled at the end of the 1976–1977 season.

PHYLLIS DILLER SHOW, THE

see *Pruitts of Southampton, The*

PICCADILLY PALACE, THE

Musical Variety

FIRST TELECAST: *May 20, 1967*
LAST TELECAST: *September 9, 1967*
BROADCAST HISTORY:
May 1967–Sep 1967, ABC Sat 9:30–10:30
HOSTS:
Millicent Martin
Eric Morecambe
Ernie Wise
REGULARS:
The Paddy Stone Dancers
The Michael Sammes Singers
The Jack Parnell Orchestra

The Piccadilly Palace was produced in London and was the 1967 summer replacement for *The Hollywood Palace.* It followed a similar format, but with regular hosts—who also performed—and with young popular singers (primarily) as guests. The hosts were singer Millicent Martin and the comedy team of Morecambe and Wise, who were seen each week introducing the guests, performing with them, and performing on their own.

PICK THE WINNER

Political

FIRST TELECAST: *August 14, 1952*
LAST TELECAST: *October 31, 1956*
BROADCAST HISTORY:
Aug 1952–Oct 1952, CBS/DUM Thu 9:00–9:30
Nov 1952, CBS/DUM Mon 10:00–10:30
Sep 1956–Oct 1956, CBS Wed 7:30–8:00
HOST:
Walter Cronkite

In both the 1952 and 1956 Presidential election years, CBS newsman Walter Cronkite hosted a series of political telecasts that enabled the candidates and various spokesmen for the parties to discuss the issues and explain their respective positions. The 1952 edition, which was sponsored by Westinghouse Electric as a public service, was carried simultaneously on both the CBS and DuMont networks. After the conclusion of the regular 1956 series, a special telecast was aired from 10:45–11:00 P.M. on the night before the election in which CBS correspondents made analyses of various races and predicted winners.

PICTURE THIS

Cartoons

FIRST TELECAST: *November 17, 1948*
LAST TELECAST: *February 9, 1949*
BROADCAST HISTORY:
Nov 1948–Feb 1949, NBC Wed 8:20–8:30
HOSTESS:
Wendy Barrie

This was a live program, each week featuring a different guest cartoonist who would draw sketches to accompany stories or jokes, some of them submitted by the viewing audience.

PICTURE THIS

Quiz/Audience Participation

FIRST TELECAST: *June 25, 1963*

LAST TELECAST: *September 17, 1963*

BROADCAST HISTORY:

Jun 1963–Sep 1963, CBS Tue 9:30–10:00

EMCEE:

Jerry Van Dyke

This summer game show featured two teams, each composed of a celebrity and noncelebrity contestant. One member of each team was given a secret phrase, then had to direct the drawing of a picture which was supposed to provide his partner with a clue to the phrase. The first partner to guess the phrase won for his team, while the emerging picture and the byplay between contestants provided the laughs.

This was the first regular series for Jerry Van Dyke, who had previously appeared in a few episodes of his brother's popular series, *The Dick Van Dyke Show*.

PINKY LEE SHOW, THE

Situation Comedy

FIRST TELECAST: *April 5, 1950*

LAST TELECAST: *November 9, 1950*

BROADCAST HISTORY:

Apr 1950–May 1950, NBC Wed 8:30–9:00
Jun 1950–Aug 1950, NBC Wed 10:30–11:00
Sep 1950–Oct 1950, NBC Sat 6:30–7:00
Oct 1950–Nov 1950, NBC Thu 8:30–9:00

CAST:

The Stagehand ....Pinky Lee
The Stage Manager ......William Bakewell

Pinky Lee (real name: Pincus Leff) first came to network TV in 1950. This series was a loosely structured situation comedy, set in a vaudeville theater. Pinky appeared as a stagehand, dressed in baggy clothes, who usually managed to fumble every assignment, but who was nevertheless called upon to fill in for singers and comedians who couldn't make it—thus giving him the opportunity to appear on stage in a variety of roles.

The program originated in Hollywood and was seen in the rest of the country via kinescope. Pinky later starred in the comedy *Those Two* from 1951 to 1953 and in various weekday afternoon and Saturday morning children's shows in 1954–1957.

PISTOLS 'N' PETTICOATS

Situation Comedy

FIRST TELECAST: *September 17, 1966*

LAST TELECAST: *August 19, 1967*

BROADCAST HISTORY:

Sep 1966–Jan 1967, CBS Sat 8:30–9:00
Jan 1967–Aug 1967, CBS Sat 9:30–10:00

CAST:

Henrietta Hanks ....Ann Sheridan
Grandpa ....Douglas Fowley
Grandma ....Ruth McDevitt
Lucy Hanks ....Carole Wells
Sheriff Harold Sikes ....Gary Vinson

Set in and around the town of Wretched, Colorado, in the 1870s, this Western situation comedy told the story of the Hanks family, three generations strong. Despite their respective ages and sex, all the members of the Hanks family, with the exception of Henrietta's city-bred daughter Lucy, were remarkably adept with guns. They could outdraw and outshoot any desperadoes and hotshot gunslingers within 500 miles of their home. It was extremely embarrassing for a reputedly dangerous outlaw to be subdued by an attractive woman and her grandparents, but that was a common occurrence around Wretched, especially since inept and bumbling young Sheriff Sikes offered little resistance.

PLACE THE FACE

Quiz/Audience Participation

FIRST TELECAST: *July 2, 1953*

LAST TELECAST: *September 13, 1955*

BROADCAST HISTORY:

Jul 1953–Aug 1953, NBC Tue 8:30–9:00
Aug 1953–Aug 1954, CBS Thu 10:30–11:00
Sep 1954–Dec 1954, NBC Sat 8:00–8:30
Jun 1955–Sep 1955, NBC Tue 8:00–8:30

EMCEE:

Jack Smith (1953)
Jack Bailey (1953–1954)
Bill Cullen (1954–1955)

Contestants on *Place the Face* were confronted with an individual from their past, who had encountered them in a specific situation, and asked to identify the face within a short time limit. The associations were such things as the person who had walked next to the contestant at his high school graduation, a policeman who had given him or her a ticket, a former teacher, etc. Clues were given by the emcee and the contestant could ask questions requiring only a yes or no answer of the individual. When Jack Smith was the emcee, the majority of the contestants were not celebrities and won prizes dependent on how quickly they made the identification. Jack Bailey took over as interim host in November 1953 and Bill Cullen became the permanent emcee the following February. By the time Cullen took over most of the contestants were celebrities, the prize aspect was minimized, and the emcee chatted at length with each contestant before the game began.

PLACES PLEASE

Talent Variety

FIRST TELECAST: *August 16, 1948*

LAST TELECAST: *February 25, 1949*

BROADCAST HISTORY:

Aug 1948–Feb 1949, CBS Mon/Wed/Fri 7:15–7:30

HOST:

Barry Wood

This live talent show was produced and emceed by Barry Wood. Each week he would introduce a number of young performers who were then given the opportunity to do their acts on network television. The show had originated as a local show in New York during early July 1948. It had three network telecasts at different times during the week of July 13–16 and then reverted to local status for another month before becoming a regular network feature.

PLAINCLOTHESMAN, THE

Police

FIRST TELECAST: *October 12, 1949*

LAST TELECAST: *September 19, 1954*

BROADCAST HISTORY:

Oct 1949–May 1950, DUM Wed 9:00–9:30

May 1950–May 1951, DUM Wed 9:30–10:00

Jun 1951–Sep 1954, DUM Sun 9:30–10:00

CAST:

The Lieutenant .... Ken Lynch

Sgt. Brady .... Jack Orrison

A number of series over the years have featured an unseen character—Bracken in *Bracken's World*, Charlie in *Charlie's Angels*—but this was one of the few series in which the lead role went to someone who was never seen on screen. The technique was camera-as-actor, in which the viewer saw everything exactly as the Lieutenant would. If he lit his cigar, a hand (his) came toward the camera with a lighted match (even the tip of his cigar could be seen jutting out at the bottom of the screen); if he was knocked down, the viewer looked up from floor level; if he got something in his eye, the camera blinked, flickered and winked clear again. A punch in the nose provided the most spectacular effect for home viewers.

Aside from the novel effects, *The Plainclothesman* was a straightforward big-city crime drama, with the unnamed Lieutenant and his sidekick Sgt. Brady working out of homicide to solve assorted murders. Scientific crime-detection techniques were used.

Oh yes, the unseen Lieutenant, in reality a handsome actor named Ken Lynch, *was* seen at least once—in a July 1952 episode which featured a series of flashbacks.

PLANET OF THE APES, THE

Science Fiction

FIRST TELECAST: *September 13, 1974*

LAST TELECAST: *December 27, 1974*

BROADCAST HISTORY:

Sep 1974–Dec 1974, CBS Fri 8:00–9:00

CAST:

Galen .... Roddy McDowall

Alan Virdon .... Ron Harper

Ted Burke .... James Naughton

Urko .... Mark Lenard

Zaius .... Booth Colman

Astronauts Alan Virdon and Ted Burke, hurled through the time barrier by some unexplained force, found themselves crash-landed on an Earth of the far future. This future Earth was ruled by apes who regarded humans as representatives of a destructive and dangerous past civilization. In the ape civilization, gorillas like Urko comprised the military class and orangutangs like Zaius were the ruling class. Befriended by a curious chimpanzee named Galen, the astronauts sought to find acceptance in their strange new world. The threat they posed to the ape civilization made them hunted quarry and forced them into the life of fugitives. Roddy McDowall recreated the role he had played in a number of the highly successful *Planet of the Apes* theatrical films, upon which this rather less successful television series was based. The movie, in turn, was adopted from a novel by Pierre Boulle.

PLAY THE GAME

Charades

FIRST TELECAST: *September 24, 1946*

LAST TELECAST: *December 17, 1946*

BROADCAST HISTORY:

Sep 1946–Dec 1946, DUM Tue 8:00–8:30

HOST:

Dr. Harvey Zorbaugh

Dr. Harvey Zorbaugh, Professor of Educational Sociology at New York University, was something of a minor celebrity among the small band of TV-set owners during the early and mid-1940s. His charade show was seen locally on the NBC station in New York as early as 1941, had a 13-week run on DuMont in 1946, and was seen locally again on ABC in 1948. It was charades, pure and simple, with celebrity guests such as Ireene Wicker, Ray Knight, and Will Mullin performing. Viewers were invited to phone in their guesses to certain charades.

Although seen over DuMont's two-station network, this version was produced by ABC. That network did not yet have any stations of its own on the air, and so bought time on other stations in order to allow its production crews to gain experience against the day when ABC's own facilities would open.

Also known as *Let's Play the Game.*

PLAY YOUR HUNCH

Quiz/Audience Participation

FIRST TELECAST: *April 15, 1960*

LAST TELECAST: *September 26, 1962*

BROADCAST HISTORY:

Apr 1960–Jun 1960, NBC Fri 7:30–8:00
Jun 1960–Sep 1960, NBC Fri 9:00–9:30
Jun 1962–Sep 1962, NBC Wed 10:00–10:30

EMCEE:

Merv Griffin

ANNOUNCER:

Johnny Olsen

Two teams of related contestants—father and son, husband and wife, etc.—competed in this game. Various problems were presented to them and they pooled their knowledge to try to come up with the solutions. Each correct solution was worth a point and the first team to score three points won the game. The winners kept playing until they lost a game. Each point was worth $100 and the losers kept whatever money they had won. Merv Griffin was also the host of the daytime version of this show, which ran from 1958 through 1963. When he left the daytime version in November 1962, he was replaced by Robert Q. Lewis.

PLAYERS, THE

see Variety

PLAYHOUSE, THE

syndicated title for *Schlitz Playhouse of Stars*

PLAYHOUSE, THE

Dramatic Anthology

FIRST TELECAST: *September 3, 1957*

LAST TELECAST: *September 24, 1959*

BROADCAST HISTORY:

Sep 1957, CBS Tue 10:30–11:00
Jul 1959–Sep 1959, CBS Wed/Thu 7:30–8:00

The films aired on this summer anthology series were all reruns of episodes previously seen on other anthology programs, primarily *Schlitz Playhouse of Stars.* The 1957 edition lasted only four weeks. When *The Playhouse* returned as a summer series two years later, it was aired on Wednesdays and Thursdays. To distinguish between the days, the Wednesday episodes were titled *Wednesday Playhouse* while the Thursday films went under the generic title *The Playhouse.*

PLAYHOUSE 90

Dramatic Anthology

FIRST TELECAST: *October 4, 1956*

LAST TELECAST: *September 19, 1961*

BROADCAST HISTORY:

Oct 1956–Jan 1960, CBS Thu 9:30–11:00
Jul 1961–Sep 1961, CBS Tue 9:30–11:00

Of all the fine live dramatic-anthology series to grace television in the 1950s, *Playhouse 90* was the most ambitious and remains the standard against which all the others are judged. Each week this series aired a complete 90-minute live drama. Blessed with a very high budget, *Playhouse 90* could afford to hire the best actors, producers, directors, and writers that money could buy. The logistics of doing such a long show live every week (before it switched to videotape in the fall of 1957) gave the series' principal director, John Frankenheimer, a task worthy of a military strategist. The sets, the camera movements, the action, the timing were all planned so precisely that even the slightest slip could mean disaster. Yet there were few disasters, and the very first season produced such classics as "Requiem for a Heavyweight" starring Jack Palance (the series' second telecast), "The Miracle Worker" with young Patty McCormack, "The Comedian" with Mickey Rooney, "Charley's Aunt" with Art Carney, and "The Helen Morgan Story" with Polly Bergen. Directors for these and later telecasts included Fred Coe, Franklin Schaffner, George Roy Hill, Alex Segal, and Robert Stevens. Plays included adaptations from Hemingway, Shaw, Faulkner, and Saroyan and originals by Rod Serling (who wrote "Requiem"), Reginald Rose, and others.

In succeeding seasons there were "Points of No Return," "Bitter Heritage," "The Plot to Kill Stalin," "The Days of Wine and Roses," "Judgment at Nuremberg," and a two-part "For Whom the Bell Tolls." Aired weekly for three seasons, *Playhouse 90* was cut back to alternate-week status in the fall of 1959, sharing the time period with *The Big Party*. Its last telecast as a regular series was on January 21, 1960. A total of eight more shows aired on an irregular basis in different time slots through May 18, 1960, and a series of reruns was presented weekly during the summer of 1961.

PLAYHOUSE #7

see *ABC Dramatic Shorts—1952–1953*

PLAYHOUSE OF MYSTERY

see *Johnson's Wax Theater*

PLAYHOUSE OF MYSTERY

Dramatic Anthology

FIRST TELECAST: *February 10, 1959*
LAST TELECAST: *September 15, 1959*
BROADCAST HISTORY:
Feb 1959–Mar 1959, CBS Tue 8:00–8:30
May 1959–Sep 1959, CBS Tue 8:00–8:30

The dramas telecast in this filmed anthology series were all reruns of previously aired episodes from other anthology series. They all had one element in common—the plot was designed to keep viewers in suspense until the action resolved itself.

PLAYHOUSE OF STARS

Dramatic Anthology

FIRST TELECAST: *July 21, 1960*
LAST TELECAST: *September 1, 1960*
BROADCAST HISTORY:
Jul 1960–Sep 1960, CBS Thu 8:00–8:30

The filmed episodes of this summer anthology series were made up of reruns of episodes from other series.

PLAYROOM

Children's

FIRST TELECAST: *January 9, 1948*
LAST TELECAST: *May 28, 1948*
BROADCAST HISTORY:
Jan 1948–May 1948, DUM Fri 7:00–7:30

This was an early children's program, about which no specific information is available.

PLAY'S THE THING, THE

see *Actors Studio*

PLEASE DON'T EAT THE DAISIES

Situation Comedy

FIRST TELECAST: *September 14, 1965*
LAST TELECAST: *September 2, 1967*
BROADCAST HISTORY:
Sep 1965–Aug 1966, NBC Tue 8:00–8:30
Sep 1966–Sep 1967, NBC Sat 8:00–8:30
CAST:
Joan Nash .... Patricia Crowley
James (Jim) Nash ....Mark Miller
Kyle Nash ....Kim Tyler
Joel Nash ....Brian Nash
Tracey Nash ....Joe Fithian
Trevor Nash ....Jeff Fithian
Marge Thornton ....Shirley Mitchell
Herb Thornton (1966–1967) .... King Donovan
Ed Hewley (1965–1966) ....Dub Taylor
Martha O'Reilly ....Ellen Corby

Based on the best-selling book and popular Doris Day movie of the same title, *Please Don't Eat the Daisies* was author Jean Kerr's story of an unusual suburban family. Jim Nash was a professor of English at Ridgemont College in Ridgemont, New

York, the community in which he lived with his family. Wife Joan was a newspaper columnist who hated housework, didn't like to cook, and was totally unconcerned about how her traditional suburban housewife neighbors felt about it. She got up at noon and did whatever moved her at the moment. Completing the household were the four Nash children, all boys, including mischievous seven-year-old twins; Martha, the family maid; and a huge 150-pound sheep dog named Ladadog. The Thorntons were next-door neighbors of the Nashes.

PLYMOUTH PLAYHOUSE

Various

FIRST TELECAST: *April 12, 1953*

LAST TELECAST: *June 21, 1953*

BROADCAST HISTORY:

Apr 1953–Jun 1953, ABC Sun 7:30–8:00

HOST:

Donald Cook

This series of auditions for possible series was presented by ABC in hopes of attracting sponsor interest for the fall 1953 season. The productions used top-named talent and expensive budgets (ABC wanted to show that it could produce "big-time programming," just like CBS and NBC) and, indeed, three of the efforts became series. Unfortunately, only one of them aired on ABC—*Jamie,* starring child actor Brandon De Wilde. DuMont picked up *Colonel Humphrey Flack* with Alan Mowbray for its fall lineup, and *Justice,* based on the files of the Legal Aid Society and starring Paul Douglas and Lee Grant, turned up on NBC for a two-year run in the fall of 1954. (See those titles for details.)

Other productions included an elaborate, live, two-part adaptation of *A Tale of Two Cities* starring John Ireland, Wendell Corey, and Joanne Dru, with original music by Dmitri Tiomkin; "Mr. Glencannon Takes All," directed by Sir Cedric Hardwicke and starring Robert Newton; and a series of four classic short stories produced by Hardwicke. Other stars appearing included Robert Preston, Janis Paige, and Walter Matthau. Some productions were live, others on film.

The series was first known as *ABC Album,* but switched to *Plymouth Playhouse* when a sponsor came aboard beginning with the third telecast.

PLYMOUTH SHOW, THE

see *Lawrence Welk's Top Tunes and New Talent*

POLICE STORY

Police Anthology

FIRST TELECAST: *April 4, 1952*

LAST TELECAST: *September 26, 1952*

BROADCAST HISTORY:

Apr 1952–Sep 1952, CBS Fri 10:00–10:30

NARRATOR:

Norman Rose

Case histories were drawn from the files of various law-enforcement agencies and adapted for television presentation in this live dramatic series that originated from New York. Not only were crime-detection stories presented but episodes devoted to crime prevention were included as well. The actors playing lead roles were chosen for their resemblance to the actual officers who had been involved in the cases and used the officers' real names. Settings were various big cities and rural areas around the country with both local and state police operations shown. Generally lesser-known performers participated, with James Gregory, Edward Binns, and E. G. Marshall the most familiar.

POLICE STORY

Police Anthology

FIRST TELECAST: *September 25, 1973*

LAST TELECAST: *August 23, 1977*

BROADCAST HISTORY:

Oct 1973–Sep 1975, NBC Tue 10:00–11:00
Sep 1975–Oct 1975, NBC Tue 9:00–10:00
Nov 1975–Aug 1976, NBC Fri 10:00–11:00
Aug 1976–Aug 1977, NBC Tue 10:00–11:00

CREATOR:

Joseph Wambaugh

One of the more realistic police series to be seen on television was *Police Story,* created by former Los Angeles policeman Joseph Wambaugh. After retiring from the force, Wambaugh had written two highly successful novels about police operations, *The New Centurions* and *The Blue Knight* (the latter also became a TV series in its own right). Wambaugh served as a consultant to this series, insuring that everything was treated with utmost authenticity. Stories covered the more mundane aspects of police work as well as the excitement. They probed the psychology of individual police officers and even dealt with their home lives, how their jobs affected their families, and personal problems such as drinking, injuries, and forced retirement.

Two episodes from *Police Story* went on to become series of their own. "The Gamble" was aired on March 26, 1974, with Angie Dickinson in the role of policewoman Lisa Beaumont. That fall, with her name changed to Pepper Anderson, she became *Police Woman*. "The Return of Joe Forrester," aired as a special 90-minute episode on May 6, 1975, became *Joe Forrester* that fall, with Lloyd Bridges recreating his role. Although *Police Story* was an anthology, characters occasionally made return appearances. The most notable examples were Tony Lo Bianco (as Tony Calabrese) and Don Meredith (as Bert Jameson). During its first two seasons on the air, these two appeared four times as partners and once each separately as detectives on various cases. Despite the frequency of their visits, they never got a series of their own. NBC aired occasional two hour *Police Story* specials after the series ceased weekly production.

POLICE WOMAN

Police

FIRST TELECAST: *September 13, 1974*
LAST TELECAST: *August 30, 1978*
BROADCAST HISTORY:

Sep 1974–Oct 1975, NBC Fri 10:00–11:00
Nov 1975–Aug 1977, NBC Tue 9:00–10:00
Oct 1977–Dec 1977, NBC Tue 10:00–11:00
Dec 1977–Mar 1978, NBC Wed 10:00–11:00
Mar 1978–May 1978, NBC Thu 10:00–11:00
Jun 1978–Aug 1978, NBC Wed 10:00–11:00

CAST:

Sgt. Suzanne "Pepper" Anderson .... Angie Dickinson
Lt. Bill Crowley ....Earl Holliman
Det. Joe Styles ....Ed Bernard
Det. Pete Royster ....Charles Dierkop
Lt. Paul Marsh (1974–1976) ... Val Bisoglio

Sexy Sgt. Pepper Anderson was an undercover agent for the criminal conspiracy department of the Los Angeles Police Department. Working on a vice-squad team that included Joe Styles and Pete Royster, two other undercover cops, she was called on to pose as everything from a prostitute to a gangster's girl friend. The team reported directly to Lt. Bill Crowley, who was the coordinator of its operations. Although not seen on a regular basis, Pepper's autistic younger sister Cheryl, played by Nichole Kallis, was visited occasionally at the Austin School for the Handicapped during the first season of *Police Woman*. Her role was dropped in the fall of 1975.

The pilot for *Police Woman*, which also starred Angie Dickinson but none of the other series regulars, aired as an episode of *Police Story* titled "The Gamble."

POLITICS ON TRIAL

Debate

FIRST TELECAST: *September 4, 1952*
LAST TELECAST: *October 30, 1952*
BROADCAST HISTORY:

Sep 1952–Oct 1952, ABC Thu 9:00–9:30

This was a public-affairs debate in the style of a courtroom trial, and was presented in the weeks leading up to the 1952 Presidential election. A prominent Republican or Democrat presented his party's position on a major issue, which was then attacked by "opposing counsel" and defended by his own "counsel." A real-life judge presided.

POLKA-GO-ROUND

Music

FIRST TELECAST: *June 23, 1958*
LAST TELECAST: *September 28, 1959*
BROADCAST HISTORY:

Jun 1958–Sep 1958, ABC Mon 9:30–10:30
Oct 1958–Dec 1958, ABC Mon 7:30–8:30
Dec 1958–May 1959, ABC Mon 8:00–8:30
Jun 1959–Sep 1959, ABC Mon 7:30–8:30

EMCEE:

Bob Lewandowski

REGULARS:

Carolyn DeZurik
Lou Prohut
The Polka Rounders
Caine Dancers
Tom "Stubby" Fouts
The Singing Waiters
Georgia Drake

A full hour of polka music in network prime time every week? That's what this program provided throughout most of its run. The colorfully costumed singers and dancers performed in an outdoor cafe setting. Telecast from Chicago.

POLKA TIME

Music

FIRST TELECAST: *July 13, 1956*

LAST TELECAST: *September 24, 1957*
BROADCAST HISTORY:
Jul 1956–Oct 1956, ABC Fri 10:00–10:30
Oct 1956–Sep 1957, ABC Tue 10:00–10:30
EMCEE:
Bruno (Junior) Zielinski
REGULARS:
Carolyn DeZurik
Richard (Hodyl) and Mildred (Lawnik)
Wally Moore and Chick Hurt
Rusty Gill
Stan Wolowic's Polka Chips

A half-hour of authentic Polish music and dancing, telecast from Chicago. Also known as *It's Polka Time.*

POLLY BERGEN SHOW, THE

Musical Variety
FIRST TELECAST: *September 21, 1957*
LAST TELECAST: *May 31, 1958*
BROADCAST HISTORY:
Sep 1957–May 1958, NBC Sat 9:00–9:30
REGULARS:
Polly Bergen
Peter Gennaro Dancers
Bill Bergen
The Luther Henderson, Jr. Orchestra

Singer Polly Bergen starred in this musical variety series which featured Peter Gennaro and his dancers, special guest stars, and, from November through February, her father Bill Bergen. Each show was tailored to the talents of the gest stars, be they singers, dancers, comedians, etc., but always included some songs by Miss Bergen.

PONDEROSA

see *Bonanza*

PONDS THEATER

Dramatic Anthology
FIRST TELECAST: *January 13, 1955*
LAST TELECAST: *July 7, 1955*
BROADCAST HISTORY:
Jan 1955–Jul 1955, ABC Thu 9:30–10:30

For fifteen months, the Kraft Corporation had been sponsoring two live plays a week, both titled *Kraft Television Theater*. The NBC version, which aired on Wednesday nights at 9:00 P.M. and had been in that time period since the late 1940s, was by far the more successful. When Kraft decided to drop the Thursday night version on ABC, Ponds took over sponsorship and retitled the series *Ponds Theater*. The dramas continued to be produced live in New York, and included such leading talent as Joanne Woodward, E. G. Marshall, Ed Begley, Roddy McDowall, Eva Gabor, Lee Grant, and Ernest Truex.

PONTIAC PRESENTS PLAYWRIGHTS 56

Dramatic Anthology
FIRST TELECAST: *October 4, 1955*
LAST TELECAST: *June 19, 1956*
BROADCAST HISTORY:
Oct 1955–Jun 1956, NBC Tue 9:30–10:30

During the 1955–1956 season *Pontiac Presents Playwrights 56* aired live plays on alternate Tuesdays with *Armstrong Circle Theatre*. The plays in this series were all adapted from the works of such famous writers as Irwin Shaw, Ernest Hemingway, and F. Scott Fitzgerald, and were somewhat more traditional in form than the documentary-dramas presented on *Armstrong Circle Theatre*.

POPI

Situation Comedy
FIRST TELECAST: *January 20, 1976*
LAST TELECAST: *August 24, 1976*
BROADCAST HISTORY:
Jan 1976–Feb 1976, CBS Tue 8:30–9:00
Jul 1976–Aug 1976, CBS Tue 8:00–8:30
CAST:
Abraham Rodriguez ......Hector Elizondo
Lupe ....Edith Diaz
Junior Rodriguez ....Anthony Perez
Luis Rodriguez ....Dennis Vasquez
Maggio ....Lou Criscuolo

Abraham Rodriguez was a poor Puerto Rican immigrant who held three part-time jobs to make enough money to support his family. A widower with two young sons, he lived in a small apartment. One of his neighbors in the building was Lupe, the woman he was dating. Life in New York City was not easy for him, but he managed somehow to survive and maintain his self-respect and dignity. The first five episodes of this series aired early in 1976 but did so poorly that the show was canceled. During the following summer the remaining original episodes were aired, along with a few reruns.

POPSICLE PARADE OF STARS, THE

Variety

FIRST TELECAST: *May 15, 1950*
LAST TELECAST: *July 17, 1950*
BROADCAST HISTORY:
May 1950–Jul 1950, CBS Mon 7:45–8:00

A different guest star appeared every week on this short-lived, 15-minute variety show sponsored by the Popsicle company. Each star performed his own specialty, whether it was singing, dancing, playing an instrument, or doing comedy sketches, aiming his material at both adults and children—both, hopefully, being consumers of the sponsor's product.

PORTRAIT
Interview
FIRST TELECAST: *August 9, 1963*
LAST TELECAST: *September 6, 1963*
BROADCAST HISTORY:
Aug 1963–Sep 1963, CBS Fri 10:30–11:00
HOST:
Charles Collingwood

Host Charles Collingwood interviewed guests from many walks of life in this series, including comedian Peter Sellers, commentator H. V. Kaltenborn, General Curtis E. LeMay, Oregon Governor Mark Hatfield, and actor Jimmy Stewart. The program was first seen in February 1963, and continued irregularly until the end of September. For five weeks during August and September, however, it was seen as a regular weekly feature.

PORTRAIT OF AMERICA
Interview
FIRST TELECAST: *December 8, 1949*
LAST TELECAST: *December 29, 1949*
BROADCAST HISTORY:
Dec 1949, NBC Thu 8:00–8:30
HOST:
Norman Barry

Four-week documentary series in which NBC's cameras visited a different "typical American family" at home each week.

POST FIGHT BEAT
see *Fight Beat*

POWER OF WOMEN, THE
Discussion
FIRST TELECAST: *July 1, 1952*
LAST TELECAST: *November 11, 1952*
BROADCAST HISTORY:
Jul 1952–Nov 1952, DUM Tue 8:00–8:30
Sep 1952–Oct 1952, DUM Mon 8:00–8:30
HOSTESS:
Vivien Kellems
Mrs. John G. Lee

Discussion of politics and social problems from the woman's point of view, by Vivien Kellems, president of the Liberty Belles. Sometimes guests appeared, sometimes it was a one-woman show. In October Mrs. John G. Lee, president of the League of Woman Voters, took over as moderator. The final telecast, on the week after the 1952 Presidential election, the topic was "Who Cares?"

PRACTICE, THE
Situation Comedy
FIRST TELECAST: *January 30, 1976*
LAST TELECAST: *January 26, 1977*
BROADCAST HISTORY:
Jan 1976–Jul 1976, NBC Fri 8:30–9:00
Oct 1976–Nov 1976, NBC Wed 8:00–8:30
Dec 1976–Jan 1977, NBC Wed 9:30–10:00
CAST:
Dr. Jules Bedford .... Danny Thomas
Molly Gibbons .... Dena Dietrich
Jenny Bedford .... Shelley Fabares
Dr. David Bedford .... David Spielberg
Helen .... Didi Conn
Paul Bedford .... Allen Price
Tony Bedford .... Damon Raskin
Dr. Roland Caine .... John Byner
Nate .... Sam Laws
Lenny .... Mike Evans

There were two doctors in the Bedford family, but they had radically different approaches to the practice of medicine. The elder Bedford, Jules, was really from the old school. He was a little absentminded, could be grouchy and preoccupied, but was a warm, concerned individual with a love of people and a willingness to help, whether or not there was money to be made. Jules' office was on Manhattan's middle-class West Side. His nurse, Molly, had been with him for years and had an obvious crush on the widowed doctor; the outer office was "run" by a young, slightly daft receptionist named Helen. Son David Bedford, on the other hand, had set up practice on exclusive Park Avenue, was making money hand over fist, and was always after his dad to move in and share office space with him. Completing the cast were David's wife Jenny and his two young boys.

PRACTICE TEE
Golf Lesson
FIRST TELECAST: *August 5, 1949*
LAST TELECAST: *September 9, 1949*
BROADCAST HISTORY:
Aug 1949–Sep 1949, NBC Fri 7:30–7:45
HOST:
William P. Barbour

Fifteen-minute golf lesson, notable mostly for being the first regular network TV series to originate from Cleveland. Host William P. Barbour served as golf pro.

PREMIERE
Dramatic Anthology
FIRST TELECAST: *July 1, 1968*
LAST TELECAST: *September 9, 1968*
BROADCAST HISTORY:
Jul 1968–Sep 1968, CBS Mon 10:00–11:00

The full-hour dramas that were aired in this summer replacement for *The Carol Burnett Show* were all pilots for dramatic series that had not been bought by any of the networks. Among the stars who did not make it, this time around, were Burt Reynolds in "Lassiter," Carl Betz and Susan Strasberg in "Crisis," and Sally Kellerman and John McMartin in "Higher and Higher." "Call to Danger," made some years earlier as the pilot film for *Mission: Impossible,* was also included.

PREMIERE PLAYHOUSE
see *Movies—Prior to 1961*

PRESIDENT EISENHOWER'S NEWS CONFERENCE
News
FIRST TELECAST: *February 2, 1955*
LAST TELECAST: *September 11, 1955*
BROADCAST HISTORY:
Feb 1955–May 1955, ABC Wed 10:00–10:30
Feb 1955–Sep 1955, ABC Sun 8:30–9:00

Coverage of President Eisenhower's weekly news conferences was provided by ABC during most of 1955. On weeks when there was no news conference a half-hour filmed drama was presented. From the latter part of February through the end of May these filmed news conferences were offered on both Wednesdays and Sundays, after which they were telecast on Sundays only.

PRESIDENTIAL COUNTDOWN
Political
FIRST TELECAST: *September 12, 1960*
LAST TELECAST: *October 31, 1960*
BROADCAST HISTORY:
Sep 1960–Oct 1960, CBS Mon 10:30–11:00
ANCHORMAN:
Walter Cronkite

As the 1960 Presidential campaign moved toward its conclusion in September and October, CBS aired a weekly summary program that covered candidates Nixon and Kennedy. Results of CBS News polls on the mood of the voters in various parts of the country were also part of the show. Walter Cronkite anchored the series with regular contributions from other CBS News correspondents. On Friday November 4, a final telecast was aired in which the contributing reporters summed up what they had seen and felt throughout the campaign.

PRESIDENTIAL STRAWS IN THE WIND
Political
FIRST TELECAST: *August 24, 1948*
LAST TELECAST: *October 5, 1948*
BROADCAST HISTORY:
Aug 1948–Oct 1948, CBS Tue 9:30–10:00
FEATURED:
Elmo Roper
HOST:
Lyman Bryson

Pollster Elmo Roper was the star of this pre-election series that broadcast the results of public-opinion polls his organization had taken on various issues, and on the popularity of the candidates themselves. Four members of the studio audience were brought on stage and asked the same questions that had been asked in the poll, so that viewers could see how the poll had been taken, and the results of the actual poll were then analyzed by Mr. Roper. The first telecast of this series had aired as a local program in New York on August 10, then it expanded to the full network for the four succeeding biweekly telecasts.

PRESIDENTIAL TIMBER
Public Affairs
FIRST TELECAST: *May 27, 1948*

LAST TELECAST: *June 20, 1952*
BROADCAST HISTORY:
May 1948–Jul 1948, CBS Thu 9:00–9:30
Apr 1952–Jun 1952, CBS Fri 10:30–11:00

Presidential Timber gave candidates for the nation's highest office, or their authorized representatives, the opportunity to present their platforms and programs to a nationwide television audience. This live program did not air each week, only when there was a candidate who wanted to speak. The series was patterned after the CBS radio program of the same name that had been aired during previous Presidential election years.

PRESS CONFERENCE

Interview
FIRST TELECAST: *July 4, 1956*
LAST TELECAST: *July 15, 1957*
BROADCAST HISTORY:
Jul 1956–Sep 1956, NBC Wed 8:00–8:30
Oct 1956–Dec 1956, ABC Sun 8:30–9:00
Apr 1957–Jul 1957, ABC Mon 9:00–9:30
MODERATOR:
Martha Rountree

In a format similar to that of *Meet the Press*, this series brought people in the news, generally the political news, to a weekly news conference. Some of them made opening statements and others simply began by asking for the first question. Martha Rountree was the moderator and called on various members of the press for questions. At the end of each program, she summed up the key points for the viewing audience. The series moved from NBC to ABC in the fall of 1956, moved from prime time to Sunday afternoons for three months at the beginning of 1957, and returned to prime time in April with the title changed to *Martha Rountree's Press Conference*.

PRESS CORRESPONDENTS PANEL

Discussion
FIRST TELECAST: *April 10, 1949*
LAST TELECAST: *May 22, 1949*
BROADCAST HISTORY:
Apr 1949, CBS Sun 6:30–7:00
Apr 1949–May 1949, CBS Sun 6:00–6:30

This live weekly program gave news correspondents an opportunity to discuss the events of the week in a round-table discussion fashion.

PREVIEW TONIGHT

Dramatic Anthology
FIRST TELECAST: *August 14, 1966*
LAST TELECAST: *September 11, 1966*
BROADCAST HISTORY:
Aug 1966–Sep 1966, ABC Sun 8:00–9:00

This was a collection of unsold pilots for proposed series which never made the network's schedule. It was, in other words, a "preview" of series which never happened. Perhaps the most unusual was *Great Bible Adventures*, starring Hugh O'Brien as Joseph leading the Jews in Egypt.

PRICE IS RIGHT, THE

Quiz/Audience Participation
FIRST TELECAST: *September 23, 1957*
LAST TELECAST: *September 11, 1964*
BROADCAST HISTORY:
Sep 1957–Jun 1958, NBC Mon 7:30–8:00
Jun 1958–Sep 1958, NBC Thu 10:00–10:30
Sep 1958–Sep 1961, NBC Wed 8:30–9:00
Sep 1961–Sep 1962, NBC Mon 8:30–9:00
Sep 1962–Jan 1963, NBC Mon 9:30–10:00
Feb 1963–Sep 1963, NBC Fri 9:30–10:00
Sep 1963–Nov 1963, ABC Wed 8:30–9:00
Dec 1963–Sep 1964, ABC Fri 9:30–10:00
EMCEE:
Bill Cullen
PRODUCERS:
Mark Goodson and Bill Todman

Four contestants competed with each other on *The Price Is Right*. They tried to guess the retail price of merchandise prizes, which were displayed by two beautiful models. The contestant who came closest to the retail price, without going over it, won the merchandise. Most prizes were open to continuously rising price guesses until either the contestants decided to stop, or an undefined time limit forced them to make final bids. If a contestant wanted to hold at a final bid, he could "freeze" at that level and wait until the bidding was over to see if he had won. An added attraction was a home-viewer game in which TV watchers sent in their to-the-nearest-penny price estimates for a group of prizes, which they might then win. The daytime version of this show ran from 1956 until 1969, and was revived with a modified format as *The New Price Is Right* in daytime in 1972.

PRIDE OF THE FAMILY, THE

Situation Comedy

FIRST TELECAST: *October 2, 1953*

LAST TELECAST: *July 10, 1955*

BROADCAST HISTORY:

Oct 1953–Sep 1954, ABC Fri 9:00–9:30
Jun 1955–Jul 1955, CBS Sun 7:00–7:30

CAST:

Albie Morrison ....Paul Hartman
Catherine Morrison ....Fay Wray
Ann Morrison ....Natalie Wood
Junior Morrison ....Bobby Hyatt

Albie Morrison worked in the advertising department of the newspaper in the small town in which he lived. He was married and had two teenage children, Ann and Junior. Despite the best of intentions, Albie somehow managed to ruin almost everything he tried to do, whether it was something industrious at the office or an attempt to prove how handy he was around the house. His wife still loved him and, except for the occasions when they resented his attempts to prevent them from being as independent as they would have liked, so did his children. Reruns of this filmed ABC series were aired on CBS for a short time during the summer of 1955.

PRINCESS SAGAPHI

Travelogue

FIRST TELECAST: *September 6, 1948*

LAST TELECAST: *January 7, 1949*

BROADCAST HISTORY:

Sep 1948, NBC Mon 8:00–8:15
Sep 1948–Dec 1948, NBC Thu 8:00–8:15
Dec 1948–Jan 1949, NBC Mon 8:45–9:00

HOSTESS:

Princess Annette Sagaphi

Princess Sagaphi, an authority on the Far East, narrated these travelogue films of faraway places.

PRISONER, THE

Mystery Adventure

FIRST TELECAST: *June 1, 1968*

LAST TELECAST: *September 11, 1969*

BROADCAST HISTORY:

Jun 1968–Sep 1968, CBS Sat 7:30–8:30
May 1969–Sep 1969, CBS Thu 8:00–9:00

CAST:

The Prisoner (Number 6)
.... Patrick McGoohan
The Butler ....Angelo Muscat

The Prisoner was one of the most original dramas seen on U.S. television. Perhaps it was too original, for it lasted for only two summers. Filmed in England, it was the story of a former government agent who was abducted and imprisoned in a strange, Kafkaesque community. His mind held top-secret information which somebody obviously wanted—but who? Or was he simply being tested? His captors were nowhere in sight. The village itself was a beautiful little hamlet, set on a hilly peninsula, ringed by mountains, forest, and the sea. But there was no leaving. Anyone who got close to the perimeter was set upon by a strange, glowing sphere that floated overhead and kept an eye on everyone in the village.

The inhabitants were enigmas too. Some, like the hero (who was known only as "Number 6"), were prisoners, resisting the brainwashing attempts of their captors. Others had already been brainwashed of their secrets and were condemned to spend the rest of their days in the comfortable and peaceful, but eerie village. Others might be spies. Which was which? Standing alone in a clearing was the Castle, used both as a hospital and interrogation center by the mysterious "Number 1" and his chief agent (played by different actors in different episodes, but invariably designated "Number 2").

Number 6, though he could not escape, outwitted his captors at every turn. Finally, in the last episode, they not only admitted defeat but made an astonishing offer: they wanted him to be their leader. Skeptical, he was at last led into the Castle to meet Number 1—and into a trap. With his ally, the silent Butler (the only other regular in the series), and two other rebels, he managed to escape as the Castle and its inhabitants and their mysterious world were destroyed.

The Prisoner was created and produced by its star, Patrick McGoohan, who also wrote some episodes. The series was rerun during the summer of 1969.

PRIVATE SECRETARY

Situation Comedy

FIRST TELECAST: *February 1, 1953*

LAST TELECAST: *September 10, 1957*

BROADCAST HISTORY:

Feb 1953–Jun 1953, CBS Sun 7:30–8:00
Jun 1953–Sep 1953, NBC Sat 10:30–11:00

Sep 1953–Jun 1954, CBS Sun 7:30–8:00
Jun 1954–Sep 1954, NBC Sat 10:30–11:00
Sep 1954–Mar 1957, CBS Sun 7:30–8:00
Apr 1957–Sep 1957, CBS Tue 8:30–9:00

CAST:

Susie McNamera ....Ann Sothern
Peter Sands ....Don Porter
Vi Praskins ....Ann Tyrrell
Cagey Calhoun ....Jesse White
Sylvia ....Joan Banks

Susie McNamera was private secretary to Peter Sands, a very successful New York talent agent. She was attractive, efficient, and conscientious, but she also had one serious failing. Susie couldn't tell when her responsibilities to her boss ended, and, as a result, kept getting mixed up in his personal life. Her efforts to help him with personal problems usually led to confusion and misunderstanding, despite their good intent. Vi Praskins, the agency's receptionist/switchboard operator, was Susie's friend, as was Sylvia, although the latter was often vying with Susie for the affections of a particularly attractive man. Peter's chief competition in the talent business was fast-talking, loudmouthed, cigar-smoking Cagey Calhoun.

The CBS episodes aired during the winter season were rerun by NBC during the summers of 1953 and 1954. During the winter seasons from the fall of 1954 through the spring of 1957, *Private Secretary* aired on alternate Sundays with *The Jack Benny Show*. While Benny was on vacation during the summers, *Private Secretary* played every week.

PRIZE PERFORMANCE

Talent Variety

FIRST TELECAST: *July 3, 1950*
LAST TELECAST: *September 12, 1950*
BROADCAST HISTORY:

Jul 1950–Aug 1950, CBS Mon 8:30–9:00
Aug 1950–Sep 1950, CBS Tue 10:00–10:30

HOST:

Cedric Adams

PANELISTS:

Arlene Francis
Peter Donald

Each week four professional child entertainers competed on this live talent show. Arlene Francis and Peter Donald were the judges, evaluating the talent and picking the week's winner. Every five weeks a grand prize of a $500 scholarship was awarded after a special competition among the weekly winners from the four preceding weeks.

PRO FOOTBALL HIGHLIGHTS

see *New York Giants Quarterback Huddle*

PRODUCER'S CHOICE

Dramatic Anthology

FIRST TELECAST: *March 31, 1960*
LAST TELECAST: *September 15, 1960*
BROADCAST HISTORY:

Mar 1960–Sep 1960, NBC Thu 8:30–9:00

The filmed dramas shown on this summer series consisted of reruns of former episodes of *G.E. Theater*, *Lux Playhouse*, *Schlitz Playhouse*, and *Lux Video Theatre*.

PRODUCERS' SHOWCASE

Anthology

FIRST TELECAST: *October 18, 1954*
LAST TELECAST: *May 27, 1957*
BROADCAST HISTORY:

Oct 1954–May 1957, NBC Mon 8:00–9:30

Live 90-minute productions were aired under this title every fourth Monday on NBC for three seasons. The productions were lavish and included many memorable performances by top stars. *Peter Pan* was presented on this series on March 7, 1955, with Mary Martin and Cyril Ritchard in the lead roles. So popular was this family show, that it was repeated live on the same series less than a year later (January 9, 1956), with Miss Martin and Ritchard repeating their roles. Humphrey Bogart and Lauren Bacall made their TV dramatic debuts in an adaptation of *The Petrified Forest*, which also starred Henry Fonda. Bogie's role was the same one that had propelled him to stardom on Broadway more than twenty years previously, and one that he had played on the silver screen as well.

Thornton Wilder's *Our Town* had been adapted for television on *Robert Montgomery Presents* in 1950, but the musical version of the play that aired on *Producer's Showcase* in 1955 is the best-remembered TV version of this classic. It starred Paul Newman and Eva Marie Saint, with Frank Sinatra (as the stage manager) singing most of the songs, including "Love and Marriage," which became a major hit record for him.

The range of material was vast. Margot Fonteyn and Michael Somes starred in two ballets, *Sleeping Beauty* and *Cinderella*. *Romeo and Juliet* was presented with Claire Bloom, Paul Rogers, and John Neville heading the cast. Fredric March, Claire Trevor, and Geraldine Fitzgerald starred in an adaptation of *Dodsworth*. The most unusual telecast in the series, because of its contrast to the general tone of the show, was probably the premiere of *Wide Wide World*. The conceptualization of dynamic NBC President Pat Weaver, *Wide Wide World* sought to take full advantage of the technical marvel of live television. Hosted by Dave Garroway, who would remain with it during its run as a late Sunday afternoon series during the latter half of the 1950s, this premiere telecast of *Wide Wide World* enabled the audience to see live entertainment from three countries—the United States, Canada, and Mexico—on the same show, the first inter-American telecast in the history of television.

PRODUCTION FOR FREEDOM

Documentary

FIRST TELECAST: *June 22, 1952*
LAST TELECAST: *September 21, 1952*
BROADCAST HISTORY:
Jun 1952–Jul 1952, ABC Sun 9:30–10:00
Jul 1952–Sep 1952, ABC Sun 10:30–11:00

Documentary films about leading power companies and industries of America.

PROFESSIONAL FATHER

Situation Comedy

FIRST TELECAST: *January 8, 1955*
LAST TELECAST: *July 2, 1955*
BROADCAST HISTORY:
Jan 1955–Jul 1955, CBS Sat 10:00–10:30
CAST:
Thomas Wilson, M.D. ....Steve Dunne
Helen Wilson ....Barbara Billingsley
Thomas (Twig) Wilson, Jr. ....Ted Marc
Kathryn (Kit) Wilson ....Beverly Washburn

Tom Wilson was a highly successful child psychologist. At the office he spoke with the wisdom of Solomon as he resolved family problems that were causing aggravation and suffering to the many parents who sought his services. At home, however, it was a completely different story. All the good judgment and analytical skills that had made him so proficient at his profession deserted him when he tried to cope with his own family.

PROFILES IN COURAGE

Biography

FIRST TELECAST: *November 8, 1964*
LAST TELECAST: *May 9, 1965*
BROADCAST HISTORY:
Nov 1964–May 1965, NBC Sun 6:30–7:30

This program marked the first time that a President of the United States was directly involved in the production of a television dramatic series. John F. Kennedy's Pulitzer Prize–winning book *Profiles in Courage* was first adapted for TV in 1956, in a special based on the chapter concerning the senator who cast the deciding vote against the impeachment of President Andrew Johnson. Kennedy, then a U.S. Senator, served as a consultant for the broadcast. Eight years later, after Kennedy's death, this anthology series dramatized additional chapters from the book, as well as the stories of other Americans who had also displayed extraordinary personal courage. Prior to his death, President Kennedy himself had stipulated that more biographies be afded to those in his book so that the scope of the series would be broader than politics. He had approved of all the additions and read all of the scripts to make sure that they conformed to the Kennedy definition of a "Profile in Courage."

PROGRAM PLAYHOUSE

Various

FIRST TELECAST: *June 22, 1949*
LAST TELECAST: *September 14, 1949*
BROADCAST HISTORY:
Jun 1949–Sep 1949, DUM Wed 9:00–9:30

This was a series of tryouts for potential series on the DuMont network. At least one of them, *The Hands of Murder*, later became reasonably successful as an independent series. Among the others were "Trouble, Inc." starring Earl Hammond as an amateur private eye, Ernest Truex in a live comedy called "The Timid Soul," and Roscoe Karns in his first TV effort (before *Rocky King*), playing comedy in "Roscoe Karns and Inky Poo." This family comedy had Karns being followed around by his conscience, which was dressed in a clown suit and called "Inky Poo."

PROJECT: ADVENTURE

syndicated title for *Adventure Theater*

PROJECT U.F.O.

Drama

FIRST TELECAST: *February 19, 1978*
LAST TELECAST:
BROADCAST HISTORY:
Feb 1978–Sep 1978, NBC Sun 8:00–9:00
Sep 1978–, NBC Thu 8:00–9:00
CAST:
Maj. Jake Gatlin (1978) ..... William Jordan
Capt. Ben Ryan .... Edward Winter
Staff Sgt. Harry Fitz .... Caskey Swaim
Libby Virdon .... Aldine King
EXECUTIVE PRODUCER:
Jack Webb
PRODUCER:
Col. William T. Coleman

Jack Webb applied his highly successful drama-documentary technique to the unlikely subject of unidentified flying objects (i.e., flying saucers) in this 1978 series. To prepare the series Webb spent eight months pouring over the files of the real-life U.S. Air Force investigation into U.F.O.'s, Project Blue Book, which had been disbanded in 1969. Many of the sightings had turned out to be mistaken or simply fraudulent, but about 30 percent remained unexplained—and it was those that Webb dramatized in this series.

Regulars were Maj. Jake Gatlin and S/Sgt. Harry Fitz, Project Blue Book's stolid investigators, who travelled around the country interviewing people who had reported seeing a U.F.O. Some of the stories verged on character studies of these people, but there was always a certain amount of hardware seen, including vivid recreations of the flying saucers and spacemen that the people had claimed seeing. Off-screen narration reinforced the series' appearance of authenticity.

Maj. Gatlin was replaced in the fall of 1978 by Capt. Ben Ryan as Project Bluebook's chief. Libby was Gatlin's, and later Ryan's, secretary. Colonel William T. Coleman, who had headed the real life Project Bluebook, was producer of the series.

PROTECTORS, THE

Police

FIRST TELECAST: *September 28, 1969*
LAST TELECAST: *September 6, 1970*
BROADCAST HISTORY:
Sep 1969–Sep 1970, NBC Sun 10:00–11:00
CAST:
Sam Danforth .... Leslie Nielsen
William Washburn .... Hari Rhodes

Deputy Police Chief Sam Danforth and District Attorney William Washburn were both committed to enforcing the law, but approached that enforcement from very different positions. Chief Danforth followed the rules that had always worked in the past, though they were being sorely tested in the changing moral climate of a modern big city. D.A. Washburn, a black who had used his political savvy to reach his current post, dealt with issues on a more human basis, as objectively and honestly as he could. Each of these men believed that his way of handling situations was right, and they were often in conflict with each other. Each, in his own way, was a dedicated public servant attempting to protect the society he served.

The Protectors was one of three rotating elements that comprised *The Bold Ones* during the 1969–1970 season. The other two were *The New Doctors* and *The Lawyers*.

PRUDENTIAL FAMILY PLAYHOUSE, THE

Dramatic Anthology

FIRST TELECAST: *October 10, 1950*
LAST TELECAST: *March 27, 1951*
BROADCAST HISTORY:
Oct 1950–Mar 1951, CBS Tue 8:00–9:00

This live hour-long dramatic presentation aired on alternate Tuesdays with *Sure as Fate*. The policy was to present top stars in outstanding dramas. Among the stars who appeared were Gertrude Lawrence, Ruth Chatterton, Helen Hayes, Walter Abel, Bert Lahr, and Grace Kelly.

PRUITTS OF SOUTHAMPTON, THE

Situation Comedy

FIRST TELECAST: *September 6, 1966*
LAST TELECAST: *September 1, 1967*
BROADCAST HISTORY:
Sep 1966–Jan 1967, ABC Tue 9:00–9:30
Jan 1967–Sep 1967, ABC Fri 9:30–10:00

CAST:

Phyllis (Mrs. Poindexter) Pruitt .... Phyllis Diller
Uncle Ned Pruitt ....Reginald Gardiner
Stephanie Pruitt ....Pam Freeman
Regina Wentworth ....Gypsy Rose Lee
Sturgis ....Grady Sutton
Norman Krump (1967) ....Marty Ingels
Harvey (1967) ....Paul Lynde
Mr. Baldwin (1967) ....Richard Deacon
Vernon Bradley (1967) ......Billy DeWolfe

Phyllis Diller, whose trademarks were a fright wig and an uproarious cackle, was cast as the widowed matriarch of a down-on-their-luck Long Island society family in this frantic comedy. The Pruitts could live life to the hilt in their 60-room Southampton mansion, despite the fact that they were $10 million in debt to the government, so long as they kept the secret. Seems an unusually understanding I.R.S. would rather let them maintain the fiction that they were fabulously wealthy than risk a stock-market tumble with news of the Pruitts' bankruptcy. Phyllis spent most of her time on harebrained schemes to keep the family afloat, and keep the secret. Ned was her octogenarian uncle, Regina Wentworth her nosy neighbor and archrival, Sturgis the butler, and Stephanie her 22-year-old daughter.

In January 1967 the program title was changed to *The Phyllis Diller Show*, and the mansion became an elegant boardinghouse in an attempt to raise money to pay off the government. Neighborhood Mr. Fixit Norman Krump was a boarder, while Harvey was introduced as Phyllis' ne'er-do-well brother. Occasional roles were star boarder Vernon Bradley, an author; Mr. Baldwin of the I.R.S.; and assorted relatives played by such guest stars as Louis Nye and John Astin.

Based on the novel *House Party* by Patrick Dennis.

PSYCHIATRIST, THE

Medical

FIRST TELECAST: *February 3, 1971*
LAST TELECAST: *September 1, 1971*
BROADCAST HISTORY:

Feb 1971–Sep 1971, NBC Wed 10:00–11:00

CAST:

Dr. James Whitman ....Roy Thinnes
Dr. Bernard Altman ....Luther Adler

Jim Whitman was a young psychiatrist working in association with a Los Angeles–based institute. His use of modern techniques to help emotionally troubled people, through personal and group therapy, were explored in this series. His older colleague, Dr. Bernard Altman, worked with Jim in evaluating procedures and the progress of various patients. *The Psychiatrist* was one of the four elements that were all aired under the overall title *Four in One*.

PUBLIC DEFENDER, THE

Lawyer

FIRST TELECAST: *March 11, 1954*
LAST TELECAST: *June 23, 1955*
BROADCAST HISTORY:

Mar 1954–Jul 1954, CBS Thu 10:00–10:30
Jul 1954–Sep 1954, CBS Mon 9:00–9:30
Sep 1954–Jun 1955, CBS Thu 10:00–10:30

CAST:

Bart Matthews ....Reed Hadley

Actor Reed Hadley had most recently been seen in the role of a police officer who tracked down confidence men in *Racket Squad*. Here, he portrayed another side of the law—an attorney defending destitute individuals who had been charged with a crime and could not afford their own legal counsel. As a public defender he tried to help these people prove their innocence. The cases adapted for this series were all based on files from public-defender agencies throughout the country and a feature of each episode was a salute to a real public defender who had made some outstanding effort to exonerate a falsely accused person.

PUBLIC LIFE OF CLIFF NORTON, THE

Comedy

FIRST TELECAST: *January 7, 1952*
LAST TELECAST: *February 29, 1952*
BROADCAST HISTORY:

Jan 1952–Feb 1952, NBC Mon–Fri 11:10–11:15

REGULAR:

Cliff Norton

Veteran comic Cliff Norton appeared five times per week, giving short, humorous talks about the problems of everyday life.

PUBLIC PROSECUTOR

see *Crawford Mystery Theatre*

PULITZER PRIZE PLAYHOUSE

Dramatic Anthology

FIRST TELECAST: *October 6, 1950*

LAST TELECAST: *June 4, 1952*

BROADCAST HISTORY:

Oct 1950–Jun 1951, ABC Fri 9:00–10:00
Dec 1951–Jun 1952, ABC Wed 10:00–10:30

This was one of ABC's most prestigious programming efforts in the early 1950s, presenting top-quality dramas written or adapted for television and starring first-rate talent. Among those appearing were Helen Hayes in her TV debut, Melvyn Douglas, Raymond Massey, Edmond O'Brien, Peggy Wood, and Mildred Natwick. The first telecast was an adaptation of the Moss Hart–George S. Kaufman classic *You Can't Take It with You.* Equally famous writers (many of them Pulitzer Prize winners) such as Maxwell Anderson, Thornton Wilder, Marc Connelly, Edna Ferber, and James A. Michener were later represented. There were also original TV plays by Budd Schulberg and Lawrence Hazard, among others.

During its second season *Pulitzer Prize Playhouse* alternated with *Celanese Theatre* on Wednesday nights.

PUREX SUMMER SPECIALS

Anthology

FIRST TELECAST: *July 11, 1961*

LAST TELECAST: *September 12, 1963*

BROADCAST HISTORY:

Jul 1961–Sep 1961, NBC Tue 10:00–11:00
Jul 1962–Sep 1962, NBC Fri 9:30–10:30
Jun 1963–Sep 1963, NBC Thu 10:00–11:00

For three summers, NBC aired a series comprised of reruns of special programs that the Purex Corporation had originally sponsored. During 1961 and 1962 approximately half of the shows were reruns of various *Purex Special for Women* telecasts, and the remainder were profiles of famous people, some historical and some current show-business personalities. In 1963 the majority of the shows were profiles, and aired under the general title *The World of . . . .*

PURSUIT

Dramatic Anthology

FIRST TELECAST: *October 22, 1958*

LAST TELECAST: *January 14, 1959*

BROADCAST HISTORY:

Oct 1958–Jan 1959, CBS Wed 8:00–9:00

The plays that were aired on this live dramatic series had one element in common—they all told in some way the story of a man, or group, being pursued. The circumstances varied from show to show, but the element of the hunter and the hunted was present in each episode. The casting was strong and several of the authors were well known. A Daphne duMaurier story, "Kiss Me Again, Stranger," featured Jeffrey Hunter, Margaret O'Brien, and Mort Sahl; a Ross MacDonald thriller entitled "Epitaph for a Golden Girl" starred Michael Rennie, Rick Jason, Rip Torn, Sally Forrest, and Joan Bennett; and Rod Serling provided "The Last Night of August" with Franchot Tone, Dennis Hopper, and Cameron Mitchell.

Q.E.D.

Quiz/Panel

FIRST TELECAST: *April 3, 1951*

LAST TELECAST: *October 9, 1951*

BROADCAST HISTORY:

Apr 1951–Sep 1951, ABC Tue 9:00–9:30
Oct 1951, ABC Tue 10:00–10:30

MODERATOR:

Doug Browning
Fred Uttal

REGULAR PANELISTS:

Hy Brown
Nina Foch
Harold Hoffman

This show presented its panel with a short mystery story, sketch, or playlet, submitted by a viewer, which stopped just before the solution to the mystery was revealed. The panel was then supposed to guess the outcome, based on the clues within the story and a limited number of questions which could be answered with a yes or no. *Q.E.D.* stands for *quod erat demonstrandum* in Latin, or, in English, "which was to be proved."

Doug Browning was moderator for the first telecast only, replaced on April 10 by Fred Uttal. The program was also known as *Mystery File.*

QUADRANGLE, THE

see *Campus Corner*

QUARK

Situation Comedy

FIRST TELECAST: *February 24, 1978*

LAST TELECAST: *April 14, 1978*

BROADCAST HISTORY:

Feb 1978–Apr 1978, NBC Fri 8:00–8:30

CAST:

Adam Quark ....Richard Benjamin
Gene/Jean ....Tim Thomerson
Ficus ....Richard Kelton
Betty I ....Tricia Barnstable
Betty II ....Cyb Barnstable
Andy the Robot ....Bobby Porter
Otto Palindrome ....Conrad Janis
The Head ....Alan Caillou

Quark was a parody on space adventure epics, which were highly popular at this time due to the success of the movie *Star Wars.* The setting was the year 2222 A.D. on the giant space station Perma One, where Adam Quark had been given command of a vital, though not necessarily romantic, mission: to clean up the garbage in outer space. His assignments came from The Head, a disembodied head who governed the universe, and who was seen only on a TV screen; and from Otto Palindrome, the fussy chief architect of Perma One. Quark's crew included first officer Gene/Jean, a transmute with both male and female characteristics; science officer Ficus, a kind of humanoid vegetable; copilots Betty I and Betty II, two sexy and identical girls, one of whom was a clone of the other (nobody knew which was which); and Andy the Robot, a walking junkpile.

Though Quark was supposed to stick to his sanitation patrols, he often met adventure with such colorful space denizens as the evil High Gorgon, Zoltar the Magnificent, and Zorgon the Malevolent. A strange mixture of sex, intellectual jokes, and basic slapstick comedy, *Quark* failed to attract a substantial audience and was soon canceled.

QUEEN AND I, THE

Situation Comedy

FIRST TELECAST: *January 16, 1969*

LAST TELECAST: *May 1, 1969*

BROADCAST HISTORY:

Jan 1969–May 1969, CBS Thu 7:30–8:00

CAST:

Charles Duffy ....Larry Storch
Oliver Nelson ....Billy DeWolfe
Becker ....Carl Ballantine
Barney ....Pat Morita
Wilma Winslow ....Barbara Stuart
Max ....Dave Morick
Capt. Washburn ....Liam Dunn

The *Amsterdam Queen* was an aging ocean liner whose owners had decided to retire and sell her for scrap. Fighting the inevitable was the ship's purser, Charles Duffy, who was not above trying anything to save the boat and his job. The various ways in which he had been able to supplement his income with the ship—making it available for weddings and bar mitzvahs when it was in port, shaming the passengers into giving bigger tips, etc.—made him particulary desperate to save it. Most of the crew members were enthusiastic about his efforts, with the exception of First Mate Nelson, who had never been able to catch Charlie at any of his shenanigans but who would be happy to see him out of a job.

QUEST, THE

Western

FIRST TELECAST: *September 22, 1976*

LAST TELECAST: *December 29, 1976*

BROADCAST HISTORY:

Sep 1976–Dec 1976, NBC Wed 10:00–11:00

CAST:

Morgan Beaudine ....Kurt Russell
Quentin Beaudine ....Tim Matheson

Set in the West during the 1890s, *The Quest* was the story of two young brothers in search of their long-lost sister. Several years before, Morgan Beaudine and his sister Patricia had been captured by Cheyenne Indians and become separated. Morgan had been raised by the Cheyenne but was now living in the white man's world, though he actually trusted the Indians more than he did the whites. His brother Quentin, meanwhile, was educated in San Francisco and planned to be a doctor. Together these two young men set out in search of their sister. Morgan affected Indian dress, spoke fluent Cheyenne, and understood Indian customs well enough to get them out of dangerous situations when they encountered unfriendly red men. He even had an Indian name, Two Persons.

The time seemed ripe for a successful Western when this series premiered. The season before had seen not a single Western on prime time network television, for the first time in more than 20 years. There was plenty of action and violence on *The Quest*, but it could not compete with the pulchritude on ABC's new entry opposite it, *Charlie's Angels*.

QUEST FOR ADVENTURE

see *ABC Presents*

QUICK AS A FLASH

Quiz/Panel

FIRST TELECAST: *March 12, 1953*

LAST TELECAST: *February 25, 1954*

BROADCAST HISTORY:

Mar 1953–Jul 1953, ABC Thu 10:30–11:00
Sep 1953–Feb 1954, ABC Thu 8:00–8:30

MODERATOR:

Bobby Sherwood
Bud Collyer

REGULAR PANELISTS:

Jimmy Nelson
Faye Emerson

Quick as a Flash was designed to test the panel's speed in guessing the significance or outcome of a short, specially prepared film. The film might depict a person, event, or a mystery playlet. The program was based on the long-running (1944–1951) radio quiz of the same name, but unlike the radio version it utilized celebrity panelists. Many guest panelists appeared, in addition to the regulars shown above. Bud Collyer replaced Bobby Sherwood as host in May.

The program was telecast live from New York, and alternated with *Personality Puzzle*.

QUICK ON THE DRAW

Quiz/Panel

FIRST TELECAST: *January 15, 1952*

LAST TELECAST: *December 9, 1952*

BROADCAST HISTORY:

Jan 1952–Dec 1952, DUM Tue 9:30–10:00

HOSTESS:

Robin Chandler

CARTOONIST:

Bob Dunn

This panel show used cartoons suggested by viewers and drawn by cartoonist Bob Dunn to provide pictorial clues to familiar words and phrases. The clues were usually in the form of puns or plays on words, for example a comedian on a stage taking off his clothes (representing "a newspaper term"); a baseball player about to swing a rolled-up venetian blind (for "a well-known expression"); or a man putting a tuxedo on a rabbit (for "an occupation"). (See below for the correct answers.) A different panel of celebrities appeared each week.

Quick on the Draw had been seen locally in New York since 1950.

Answers: (1) comic strip; (2) "blind as a bat"; (3) hair (hare) dresser.

QUINCY, M.E.

Police

FIRST TELECAST: *October 3, 1976*

LAST TELECAST:

BROADCAST HISTORY:

Oct 1976–Nov 1976, NBC Sun 9:30–11:00
Feb 1977–May 1977, NBC Fri 10:00–11:00
Jun 1977–Jul 1977, NBC Fri 9:30–11:00
Jul 1977–Aug 1978, NBC Fri 10:00–11:00
Sep 1978–, NBC Thu 9:00–10:00

CAST:

Quincy, M.E. .... Jack Klugman
Lt. Frank Monahan .... Garry Walberg
Sam Fujiyama .... Robert Ito
Lee (1976–1977) .... Lynette Mettey
Danny .... Val Bisoglio
Dr. Robert Astin .... John S. Ragin
Sgt. Brill .... Joseph Roman

Quincy was a man with a strong sense of principle. He had given up a lucrative private medical practice to join the Los Angeles County Coroner's Office as a medical examiner ("M.E."). His understanding of forensic medicine led him to conclude that many of the supposed "normal" deaths that he was assigned to investigate were actually murders. Whenever this happened, Quincy tended to resemble a detective more than a pathologist, as he sought evidence to prove his contentions. These wanderings out of his field into the province of the police did not endear Quincy to Dr. Astin, his vacuous, pompous, and insecure superior in the Coroner's Office. It also alienated many of the police officers who were involved in the investigations and got in the way of his social life, much to the consternation of his girl friend Lee. None of this seemed to bother Quincy, however, as he and his young assistant Sam plugged away at solving the cases. Quincy lived on a boat and spent much of his free time at Danny's Place, the bar adjacent to the marina where the boat was docked.

Quincy was one of the four rotating elements in the 1976–1977 edition of *The NBC Sunday Mystery Movie*—the others being *Columbo, McCloud*, and *McMillan*. It proved so popular during the fall of 1976, however, that after the first of the year it moved to Friday nights as a weekly series.

QUIZ KIDS

Quiz/Panel

FIRST TELECAST: *March 1, 1949*

LAST TELECAST: *September 27, 1956*

BROADCAST HISTORY:

Mar 1949–May 1949, NBC Tue 8:00–8:30 (Midwest net only)
Jun 1949–Sep 1949, NBC Wed 8:00–8:30
Sep 1949–Jan 1950, NBC Mon 10:00–10:30
Jan 1950–Oct 1951, NBC Fri 8:00–8:30
Jul 1952–Sep 1952, NBC Mon 8:00–8:30
Jan 1953–Jul 1953, CBS Sat 10:00–10:30
Jul 1953–Nov 1953, CBS Sun 7:00–7:30
Jan 1956–Sep 1956, CBS Thu 10:30–11:00

EMCEE:

Joe Kelly (1949–1953)
Clifton Fadiman (1956)

This popular series had started on radio in 1940 and was brought intact to television, first as a local program on WNBQ, Chicago (January 1949) and later as a network entry (March 1949). The format was simple: a panel of four or five youngsters, chosen through a battery of tests, answered difficult questions requiring both general and specific knowledge. One youngster might be an "arithmetic expert," another a "music expert," etc. Panelists were as young as six, and a child could remain on the show as long as his answering rank remained high or until he or she reached 16. Celebrity guests sometimes appeared, and periodic contests were held for viewers (e.g., describe your "teacher of the year"). Viewers also submitted questions for the panel and received cash prizes if the young intellects failed to come up with the correct answers. *Quiz Kids* was sometimes scheduled in afternoon time slots during its long run; only the prime time telecasts are reflected above.

One of the great ironies of the show was that Joe Kelly, who was quizmaster from the early 1940s until 1953, had only a third-grade education himself.

Possibly the most famous of the gifted children who appeared as panelists on *Quiz Kids* was young Robert Strom, who became a regular on the show in March 1956 when he was nine years old. His specialty on *Quiz Kids* was astronomy, but during the next two years his general knowledge of mathematics and physics won him huge sums of money on *The $64,000 Question, The $64,000 Challenge*, and other big-money quiz shows.

QUIZZING THE NEWS

Quiz/Panel

FIRST TELECAST: *August 16, 1948*

LAST TELECAST: *March 5, 1949*

BROADCAST HISTORY:

Aug 1948–Sep 1948, ABC Mon 7:30–8:00
Sep 1948–Oct 1948, ABC Mon 8:00–8:30
Nov 1948–Jan 1949, ABC Wed 8:30–9:00
Jan 1949–Mar 1949, ABC Sat 8:30–9:00

EMCEE:

Allan Prescott

A panel of guest celebrities attempted to identify news events from cartoon clues in this early ABC quiz show. Viewers could also participate, and win prizes. *Quizzing the News* was one of the programs produced locally in New York by ABC production crews, using the facilities of an independent station, so that the ABC personnel could gain working experience in TV prior to the opening of ABC's own flagship station. As soon as ABC's own station opened on August 10, 1948, the program moved over intact and was fed to the newly established network.

RCA VICTOR SHOW, THE

Various

FIRST TELECAST: *November 23, 1951*

LAST TELECAST: *August 2, 1954*

BROADCAST HISTORY:

Nov 1951–Jun 1953, NBC Fri 8:00–8:30 (OS)
Oct 1953–Aug 1954, NBC Mon 9:00–9:30

CAST:

Ezio Pinza (1951–1952) ....Himself
Dennis Day (1952–1954) ....Himself
Mrs. Day (1952) ....Verna Felton
Kathy (1952) ....Kathy Phillips
Charley Weaver (1952–1954)
........................Cliff Arquette
Lois Sterling (1952–1953) ......Lois Butler
Mrs. Pratt (1952–1953) .....Minerva Urecal
Hal March (1952–1953) ....Himself
Susan Sterling (1952–1954)
........................Jeri Lou James
Lavinia (1953–1954) ....Ida Moore

Marian (1953–1954) ....Carol Richards
Peggy (1953–1954) ....Barbara Ruick

When *The RCA Victor Show* premiered, its sole star was singer Ezio Pinza. Each episode of the loosely formatted show opened with urbane bachelor Pinza in his luxurious penthouse apartment, from which he would chat with the audience and sing a song or two. He would then leave the apartment, encounter the evening's guest star, and the two would return to his home. Pinza and guest would perform musical numbers separately and together, and the show closed with Mr. Pinza alone at home singing a last song.

On February 8, 1952, Dennis Day made his first appearance as the alternate-week star of *The RCA Victor Show*. His shows were more traditional situation comedies. Dennis played himself as a singer whose mother felt that he had been underpaid working on Jack Benny's radio program and should look for a career of his own. The only person who had real love and faith in him was his girl friend Kathy.

On April 11, 1952, the format of the Ezio Pinza part of the show was changed. Each episode starred Mr. Pinza in a dramatic story with guest stars and appropriate songs woven into the general plot line. When *The RCA Victor Show* returned in the fall of 1952, after a summer hiatus, Dennis Day was its sole star, the Ezio Pinza episodes having been dropped.

The format for the Dennis Day situation comedy had also changed. He played himself again, but was a young bachelor living in a luxurious apartment building in Hollywood. He couldn't really afford it, but felt that it was necessary for his image in the quest to get ahead in show business. Charley Weaver was the janitor, Mrs. Pratt his landlady, Hal March a girl-crazy neighbor, and Lois Sterling his girl friend who lived with her little sister.

In the fall of 1953, the show returned with essentially the same format under the new title *The Dennis Day Show*. Previously live, it was now filmed. Charley Weaver had acquired a girl friend named Lavinia, and Dennis went through two new girl friends, Marian and Peggy. Although Lois Sterling was gone, her little sister Susan was still in the cast as Dennis' youngest fan.

R.F.D. AMERICA

Instruction

FIRST TELECAST: *May 26, 1949*
LAST TELECAST: *September 15, 1949*
BROADCAST HISTORY:
May 1949–Sep 1949, NBC Thu 8:00–8:30
EMCEE:
Bob Murphy

A "how to" program dealing with plants and animals, and originating from Chicago (where it began as a local show in January 1949). Host Murphy interviewed various guest experts on raising cattle, watering plants, carving meat, etc., and occasionally displayed live examples of the animal subject at hand. For example, the premiere telecast was said to be the first time in history that an entire herd of cattle was driven into a studio to be seen on live television.

RACKET SQUAD

Police

FIRST TELECAST: *June 7, 1951*
LAST TELECAST: *September 28, 1953*
BROADCAST HISTORY:
Jun 1951–Dec 1952, CBS Thu 10:00–10:30
Jan 1953–Jul 1953, CBS Thu 10:30–11:00
Jul 1953–Sep 1953, CBS Mon 9:00–9:30
CAST:
Capt. John Braddock ....Reed Hadley

Capt. John Braddock worked in the racket squad of a large metropolitan police department. He did not deal with crimes of violence but instead sought to protect the public from the various confidence rackets that were a more direct threat to them than outright robbery. The series was based on actual case records from police departments around the country and described in detail the means by which shady characters fleeced unsuspecting people of their money. Reed Hadley, in addition to his role as star, provided the narration for each episode.

RAFFERTY

Medical

FIRST TELECAST: *September 5, 1977*
LAST TELECAST: *November 28, 1977*
BROADCAST HISTORY:
Sep 1977–Nov 1977, CBS Mon 10:00–11:00
CAST:
Sid Rafferty, M.D. ......Patrick McGoohan
Nurse Vera Wales ....Millie Slavin
Daniel Gentry, M.D. ....John Getz

Dr. Calvin ....David Clemmon
Nurse Keynes ....Joan Pringle
Nurse Koscinski ....Eddie Benton

After 23 years as a doctor in the U.S. Army, Sid Rafferty had retired from the service to open a private practice. Used to military discipline, and possessed of a very short temper, the idealistic and stubborn Rafferty was not the easiest person to get along with. He did things his way, resented the clubbiness of other doctors—particularly their tendency to cover up for each other's shortcomings and mistakes—and was often at odds with the staff of City General Hospital, where he performed surgery. Rafferty's young associate in his private practice was Daniel Gentry, whose free-wheeling personal life was in marked contrast to Rafferty's more conservative approach. Their nurse/receptionist was Vera Wales, thoroughly professional in the office but also madly in love with widower Rafferty.

RANGO

Situation Comedy

FIRST TELECAST: *January 13, 1967*
LAST TELECAST: *September 1, 1967*
BROADCAST HISTORY:
Jan 1967–Sep 1967, ABC Fri 9:00–9:30
CAST:
Rango ....Tim Conway
Pink Cloud ....Guy Marks
Capt. Horton ....Norman Alden
THEME:
"Rango," by Earle Hagen, sung by Frankie Laine

Rango was a Western comedy about the Texas Ranger that legends don't talk about. He was an inept, bumbling lawman who had been assigned to Deep Wells Ranger Station, the quietest post in the state, in an attempt to keep him out of trouble. But trouble came with him. Criminal activity sprouted in a town which had been quiet for 20 years. Rango's assistant in the post supply room was Pink Cloud, a "chicken" Indian who had discovered that the white man's ways were much to his liking—an interesting book in a comfortable bed was much better than sulking around the plains. "Rango say him return when sun high over teepee," grunted the red man. "By that, I presume he meant he would be back by noon."

Rango's nemesis was Captain Horton, the post commander, who would have dearly loved to have him transferred, but couldn't, because Rango's father happened to be head of the Texas Rangers.

RANSOM SHERMAN SHOW, THE

Comedy Variety

FIRST TELECAST: *July 3, 1950*
LAST TELECAST: *August 25, 1950*
BROADCAST HISTORY:
Jul 1950–Aug 1950, NBC Mon–Fri 7:00–7:30
HOST:
Ransom Sherman
REGULARS:
Nancy Wright
Art Van Damme Quintet

Radio emcee and comic Ransom Sherman brought his wide-ranging monologues to television in 1950, as summer replacement for *Kukla, Fran & Ollie*. A variety of vocalists provided musical entertainment, including Nancy Wright and four different vocal groups who rotated from night to night. One of these groups, the Four Lads, later became famous in their own right.

Sherman was later seen in an afternoon series on NBC.

RAT PATROL, THE

War Drama

FIRST TELECAST: *September 12, 1966*
LAST TELECAST: *September 16, 1968*
BROADCAST HISTORY:
Sep 1966–Sep 1968, ABC Mon 8:30–9:00
CAST:
Sgt. Sam Troy ....Chris George
Sgt. Jack Moffitt ....Gary Raymond
Pvt. Mark Hitchcock ......Lawrence Casey
Pvt. Tully Pettigrew ....Justin Tarr
Capt. Hauptman Hans Dietrich
.......................Hans Gudegast

"Leapin' jeeps!" *The Rat Patrol* came roaring onto TV screens in 1966 as a wartime action-adventure series with a touch of humor. The Rat Patrollers were four young commandoes, three Americans and one Englishman, fighting General Rommel's elite Afrika Korps in the North African desert early in World War II. Sam Troy was the head rat, Jack Moffitt his very British demolitions expert (and there was a lot of demolition in *Rat Patrol*), Mark Hitchcock the young private trying to live down a "sissy" reputation, and Tully Pettigrew the charming con man of the group. They traveled over the burning sands in two machine-gun-mounted jeeps, working as an independent team because no organized unit could hold them. Capt. Dietrich, C.O. of a German armored unit, was their usual enemy, though sometimes the two sides had to join forces to fight off the Arabs.

The Rat Patrol was filmed in part on the deserts of Spain, where a great deal of war materiel left over from the filming of the movies *Battle of the Bulge* and *The Great Escape* was used for backdrop.

RAWHIDE

Western

FIRST TELECAST: *January 9, 1959*
LAST TELECAST: *January 4, 1966*
BROADCAST HISTORY:

Jan 1959–Apr 1959, CBS Fri 8:00–9:00
May 1959–Sep 1963, CBS Fri 7:30–8:30
Sep 1963–Sep 1964, CBS Thu 8:00–9:00
Sep 1964–Sep 1965, CBS Fri 7:30–8:30
Sep 1965–Jan 1966, CBS Tue 7:30–8:30

CAST:

Rowdy Yates .... Clint Eastwood
Gil Favor (1959–1965) .... Eric Fleming
Pete Nolan (1959–1965) ...... Sheb Wooley
Wishbone .... Paul Brinegar
Jim Quince .... Steve Raines
Joe Scarlett (1959–1964) .... Rocky Shahan
Mushy (1959–1965) .... James Murdock
Hey Soos Patines (1961–1964)
.... Robert Cabal
Clay Forrester (1962–1963) ... Charles Gray
Ian Cabot (1965–1966) ...... David Watson
Solomon King (1965–1966)
.... Raymond St. Jacques

THEME:

"Rawhide," by Ned Washington and Dmitri Tiomkin, sung over credits by Frankie Laine

Rawhide was the cattleman's answer to *Wagon Train*. Whereas *Wagon Train* told of the adventures of people traveling across the Great Plains in wagons, *Rawhide* took its regular performers back and forth across the country as organizers and runners of communal cattle drives. The constant traveling allowed both series to tell stories of people met along the way and those who joined the regulars in transit. Gil Favor was the trail boss, the supervisor of the entire cattle-drive operation. His right-hand man, and second-in-command, was Rowdy Yates. Other regulars were the cooks, drovers, and scouts who helped the cattle drive stay together and avoid possible dangers. In the fall of 1965 Rowdy Yates took over as trail boss and organized his own team to start another drive. This last one, however, only made it part way, or wherever it was when it was canceled in January 1966.

RAY ANTHONY SHOW, THE

Musical Variety

FIRST TELECAST: *October 12, 1956*
LAST TELECAST: *May 3, 1957*
BROADCAST HISTORY:

Oct 1956–Apr 1957, ABC Fri 10:00–11:00
Apr 1957–May 1957, ABC Fri 10:00–10:30

REGULARS:

Ray Anthony and His Orchestra
Frank Leahy
The Four Freshmen
Don Durant
Med Flory
Gene Merlino
Belvederes
Leroy Anthony
The Savoys

ABC, which had struck gold with bandleader Lawrence Welk the previous summer, was reportedly trying to repeat its success by signing up Ray Anthony in 1956. Unfortunately Anthony did not possess quite the same magic, but he did provide a season's worth of pleasing entertainment with a somewhat more sophisticated brand of music than Welk's. A few guests were seen, but mostly it was just Anthony, his trumpet, orchestra, and regulars. Former Notre Dame coach Frank Leahy added an unusual touch with a regular sports feature. Live from Hollywood.

RAY BOLGER SHOW, THE

Situation Comedy

FIRST TELECAST: *October 8, 1953*
LAST TELECAST: *June 10, 1955*
BROADCAST HISTORY:

Oct 1953–Jul 1954, ABC Thu 8:30–9:00
Sep 1954–Jun 1955, ABC Fri 8:30–9:00

CAST:

Raymond Wallace .... Ray Bolger
Jonathan (1953–1954) .... Allyn Joslyn
Pete Morrisey .... Richard Erdman
June (1953–1954) .... Betty Lynn
Susan (1954–1955) .... Marjie Millar
Katie Jones (1954–1955)
.... Christine Nelson
Artie Herman (1954–1955)
.... Charlie Cantor

Ray's dancing partner (1954–1955)
.... Sylvia Lewis

Singer-dancer Ray Bolger tried two situation-comedy formats in two successive years in the mid-1950s, and had little luck with either. The 1953–1954 edition, called *Where's Raymond,* cast him as a musical-comedy star with a bright, infectious personality but an unfortunate tendency to arrive at the theater at the last possible moment before the show began—causing constant pandemonium. Jonathan was his meticulous agent (and brother), Pete his pal, and June a friend who ran a restaurant near the theater. This format was little more than an excuse to get Ray into one of his dance routines in each show, often employing one of his famous characterizations such as his role in the Broadway show *Where's Charley* (where he introduced "Once in Love with Amy") or the scarecrow from *The Wizard of Oz.*

In the fall of 1954 the program became *The Ray Bolger Show.* It still had Ray cast as a Broadway star, but this time he was in love with a young lass from Iowa (Susan) who was trying to achieve fame in the big city as a writer. His attempts to help her inevitably backfired. Of the previous year's supporting cast, only Pete returned, being joined by Susan, her roommate Katie, Ray's new friend Artie, and Sylvia Lewis, who served as Ray's dancing partners in the big production numbers.

RAY MILLAND SHOW, THE

Situation Comedy

FIRST TELECAST: *September 17, 1953*
LAST TELECAST: *September 30, 1955*
BROADCAST HISTORY:
Sep 1953–Jun 1955, CBS Thu 8:00–8:30 (OS)
Jul 1955–Sep 1955, CBS Fri 9:30–10:00
CAST:
Prof. Ray McNutley/McNulty
.... Ray Milland
Peggy McNutley/McNulty .... Phyllis Avery
Dean Josephine Bradley (1953–1954)
.... Minerva Urecal
Pete Thompson (1953–1954)
.... Gordon Jones

During its first season the title of this series was *Meet Mr. McNutley.* Ray McNutley was the married, but very attractive, head of the English Department of Lynnhaven College, an exclusive women's school. In fact, the only female on campus who was not distracted by his suave manners was stern, matronly Dean Bradley. Constantly getting McNutley into trouble was his hulking friend, Pete Thompson.

When the show returned in the fall of 1954, a number of changes had been made. Ray's last name was now McNulty, he was now teaching at coeducational Comstock University, and he was now a drama professor rather than an English teacher. The show's title had also been changed, to *The Ray Milland Show.* The basic plot, however, remained the same. He was still an attractive professor whose female acquaintances were somewhat infatuated with him, he still had the same loving and supportive wife, and still had his problems with other members of the faculty.

RAY SCHERER'S SUNDAY REPORT

News/Documentary

FIRST TELECAST: *June 23, 1963*
LAST TELECAST: *August 25, 1963*
BROADCAST HISTORY:
Jun 1963–Aug 1963, NBC Sun 6:30–7:00
HOST:
Ray Scherer

NBC White House correspondent Ray Scherer opened each show with about five minutes of hard news and spent the rest of the half-hour reviewing in detail the major event, or events, of the past week. Subject matter of these expanded stories ranged from politics to science to international affairs.

RAY STEVENS SHOW, THE

see *Andy Williams Presents Ray Stevens*

RAYMOND BURR SHOW, THE

syndicated title for *Ironside*

REAL McCOYS, THE

Situation Comedy

FIRST TELECAST: *October 3, 1957*
LAST TELECAST: *September 22, 1963*
BROADCAST HISTORY:
Oct 1957–Sep 1962, ABC Thu 8:30–9:00
Sep 1962–Sep 1963, CBS Sun 9:00–9:30
CAST:
Grandpa Amos McCoy .... Walter Brennan
Luke McCoy .... Richard Crenna
Kate McCoy (1957–1962) ..... Kathy Nolan
"Aunt" Hassie .... Lydia Reed

Little Luke (1957–1962)
. . . . Michael Winkleman
Pepino . . . . Tony Martinez
George MacMichael . . . . Andy Clyde
Flora MacMichael . . . . Madge Blake
Aggie Larkin (1959–1960) . . . . . Betty Garde

When this rural comedy was first proposed to the networks by writers Irving and Norman Pincus, the experts said it would never work. Okay for the sticks, maybe, but no good for city viewers. NBC, at first interested, finally turned the series down cold. Walter Brennan, their intended star, wanted nothing to do with it. But the Pincus brothers persevered. Brennan was finally won over, financing was obtained from Danny Thomas Productions, and a spot was found on ABC's impoverished schedule. The two New York–bred Pincuses had the last laugh, as *The Real McCoys* became one of the biggest hits on TV for the next six years, and started a major trend toward rural comedy shows which lasted through the 1960s. This was the inspiration for *The Andy Griffith Show, Beverly Hillbillies, Petticoat Junction, Green Acres,* and several others.

The premise was simple: a happy-go-lucky West Virginia mountain family picks up stakes and moves to a ranch in California's San Fernando Valley. Center of the action, and undisputed star of the show, was Grandpa, a porch-rockin', gol-darnin', consarnin' old codger with a wheezy voice who liked to meddle in practically everybody's affairs, neighbors and kin alike. Three-time Academy Award–winner Walter Brennan (who was 63 when the series began) played the role to perfection. His kin were grandson Luke and his new bride Kate; Luke's teenage sister "Aunt" Hassie; and Luke's 11-year-old brother Little Luke (their parents were deceased). Completing the regular cast were Pepino, the musically inclined farm hand, and George MacMichael, their argumentative neighbor. George's spinster sister Flora had eyes for Grandpa, but she never did snare him.

In 1962, when the series moved to CBS, Luke became a widower and many of the plots began to revolve around Grandpa's attempts to match him up with a new wife. The series ended its run in 1963.

REBEL, THE

Western

FIRST TELECAST: *October 4, 1959*
LAST TELECAST: *September 12, 1962*
BROADCAST HISTORY:

Oct 1959–Sep 1961, ABC Sun 9:00–9:30
Jun 1962–Sep 1962, NBC Wed 8:30–9:00

CAST:

Johnny Yuma . . . . Nick Adams

THEME:

"The Ballad of Johnny Yuma," by Andrew J. Fenady and Dick Markowitz

Johnny Yuma was an ex-Confederate soldier whose adventures on the Western frontier, following the end of the Civil War, were the basis of the stories in this series. As the only regular in the series, he traveled from town to town, getting involved with people and functioning, in an unofficial way, as an arbiter of justice. Not only did he get involved in criminal issues, but moral ones as well. The theme song was sung over the opening credits of each episode by popular singer Johnny Cash. In the summer of 1962, NBC aired reruns of episodes that had previously been seen on ABC.

REBOUND

Dramatic Anthology

FIRST TELECAST: *February 8, 1952*
LAST TELECAST: *January 16, 1953*
BROADCAST HISTORY:

Feb 1952–Jun 1952, ABC Fri 9:00–9:30
Nov 1952–Jan 1953, DUM Fri 8:30–9:00

This filmed anthology series presented short stories of mystery and suspense, always with a trick O. Henry-type ending. The films were made in Hollywood by Bing Crosby Enterprises, and featured lesser-known (at the time) talent such as Onslow Stevens, Lee Marvin, John Doucette, and Rita Johnson.

RECKONING

Dramatic Anthology

FIRST TELECAST: *July 11, 1959*
LAST TELECAST: *September 18, 1963*
BROADCAST HISTORY:

Jul 1959–Sep 1959, CBS Sat 7:30–8:30
Jun 1960–Aug 1960, CBS Wed 7:30–8:30
Jun 1963–Sep 1963, CBS Wed 10:00–11:00

The dramas presented in this summer series were all reruns of episodes previously shown on *Pursuit, Climax!,* and

Studio One in Hollywood. All of the originals had aired in 1958.

RED BARBER'S CORNER

Sports Commentary

FIRST TELECAST: *July 2, 1949*

LAST TELECAST: *January 3, 1958*

BROADCAST HISTORY:

Jul 1949–Feb 1950, CBS Sat 6:30–6:45
Sep 1950–Oct 1950, CBS Tue 10:30–10:45
Sep 1953–Dec 1953, CBS Sat 6:45–7:00
Dec 1954–May 1955, CBS Wed 10:45–11:00
May 1955–Jun 1955, NBC Fri 10:45–11:00
Sep 1955–Jan 1958, NBC Fri 10:45–11:00

REPORTER:

Red Barber

Sportscaster Red Barber, "the Old Redhead," was reporter, interviewer, and analyst on this weekly sports news program. In 1949 and 1950 it went under the title *Red Barber's Clubhouse*, and in the fall of 1953 it was *The Peak of the Sports News*. During that period Red was director of sports for CBS. From the fall of 1954 on CBS, then on NBC through the winter of 1958, under the title *Red Barber's Corner*, this series was used to fill the time between the conclusion of the boxing match and the start of the local 11:00 P.M. news. The format remained relatively constant. There were feature pieces on sports or individual athletes, interviews with sports figures, and bulletins on and scores of current contests.

RED BUTTONS SHOW, THE

Comedy Variety

FIRST TELECAST: *October 14, 1952*

LAST TELECAST: *May 13, 1955*

BROADCAST HISTORY:

Oct 1952–Dec 1952, CBS Tue 8:30–9:00
Dec 1952–Jan 1953, CBS Sat 9:00–9:30
Jan 1953–Jun 1954, CBS Mon 9:30–10:00 (OS)
Oct 1954–May 1955, NBC Fri 8:00–8:30

REGULARS:

Red Buttons
Dorothy Jolliffe (1952)
Pat Carroll (1952–1953)
Beverly Dennis (1952–1953)
Allan Walker (1952–1953)
Joe Silver
Betty Ann Grove (1953–1954)
Phyllis Kirk (1955)
Paul Lynde (1955)
Bobby Sherwood (1955)
The Elliot Lawrence Orchestra

The most memorable thing about *The Red Buttons Show* was an inane little song that Red sang called the "Ho-Ho" song. He would put his hands together in what appeared to be a gesture of supplication, lean his head against them at a funny angle, and hop around the stage singing "Ho! Ho! . . . He! He! . . . Ha! Ha! . . . Strange things are happening." For a time that song became a national craze that infected millions of children around the country. The show itself featured monologues and dance numbers by Red, and sketches with his regulars and any guest stars. Some of the recurring characters portrayed by Red were Rocky Buttons, a punchy boxer; the Kupke Kid, a lovable little boy; the Sad Sack; and Keeglefarven, a dumb, blundering German. There were also regular sketches about Red and his wife (in a style that was to be imitated by George Gobel later in the 1950's) with Dorothy Jolliffe as his wife when the show first started. She was replaced in October by Beverly Dennis, and Miss Dennis gave way to Betty Ann Grove at the start of the 1953–1954 season.

A smash hit in its first season, *The Red Buttons Show* began to fade in its second year on CBS and was picked up by NBC after it had been canceled. The NBC series started as a variety show with guests but no regulars other than Red. That didn't seem to work so the format was changed to a situation comedy at the end of January. Red played himself as a TV comic who was always getting into troubles of one sort or another. Phyllis Kirk was his new wife, Bobby Sherwood his pal and director of the TV show, and Paul Lynde played Mr. Standish, a network vice president with whom Red had constant run-ins. Nothing seemed to help and Red, who had gone through literally dozens of writers in his quest to find a workable format, left the air that spring.

RED SKELTON SHOW, THE

Comedy Variety

FIRST TELECAST: *September 30, 1951*

LAST TELECAST: *August 29, 1971*

BROADCAST HISTORY:

Sep 1951–Jun 1952, NBC Sun 10:00–10:30
Sep 1952–Jun 1953, NBC Sun 7:00–7:30
Sep 1953–Jun 1954, CBS Tue 8:30–9:00

Jul 1954–Sep 1954, CBS Wed 8:00–9:00
Sep 1954–Dec 1954, CBS Tue 8:00–8:30
Jan 1955–Jun 1961, CBS Tue 9:30–10:00 (OS)
Sep 1961–Jun 1962, CBS Tue 9:00–9:30
Sep 1962–Jun 1963, CBS Tue 8:30–9:30
Sep 1963–Jun 1964, CBS Tue 8:00–9:00
Sep 1964–Jun 1970, CBS Tue 8:30–9:30
Sep 1970–Mar 1971, NBC Mon 7:30–8:00
Jun 1971–Aug 1971, NBC Sun 8:30–9:00

REGULARS:
Red Skelton
David Rose and His Orchestra

THEMES:
"Holiday for Strings" (main); "Lovable Clown" (Freeloader skits); "Our Waltz" (intermittent), all by David Rose

Comedian Red Skelton, son of a circus clown, was one of the brightest young stars in radio during the 1940s. While many of radio's big names never fully made the transition to television, Red did. He had been essentially a visual comedian all along. In September 1951, almost ten years to the day after he had first appeared with his own show on network radio, he arrived on TV, and remained a TV superstar for the next 20 years.

Most of Red's repertoire of regular characters had been developed on radio, before a live audience, and they worked just as well on television. Among the best known were The Mean Widdle Kid, who left chaos wherever he went (his favorite expression: "I dood it!"); Clem Kadiddlehopper, the befuddled rustic; Sheriff Deadeye, the scourge of the West; boxer Cauliflower McPugg; Willie Lump-Lump, the drunk; San Fernando Red, the con man; and Bolivar Shagnasty. The one major addition to Red's character list for the TV show was Freddie the Freeloader, a hobo who never spoke. The sketches with Freddie were always pantomimed, and would, therefore, have been completely lost on a radio audience.

The format of the show consisted of an opening monologue by Red, performances by his guest stars, and comedy sketches with them. The only other regular on the show was orchestra leader David Rose, who had been with Red on radio and stayed with him throughout his 20 years on television. In general the humor was broad, but occasionally it could be touching and warm, particularly in the mime sketches with Freddie the Freeloader. These were often included in the completely pantomimed "Silent Spot," which for years was written for Red by Mort Greene.

Skelton was a warm, human performer who loved his audience as much as they loved him. His closing line was always a sincere, "God bless."

REDD FOXX

Comedy Variety

FIRST TELECAST: *September 15, 1977*
LAST TELECAST: *January 26, 1978*
BROADCAST HISTORY:
Sep 1977–Jan 1978, ABC Thur 10:00–11:00

EMCEE:
Redd Foxx

MUSICAL DIRECTOR:
Gerald Wilson

Old trouper Redd Foxx had been an obscure standup comic for decades before he got his first big break as the star of *Sanford and Son* in 1972. He had to clean up his act considerably for the television medium, as he had previously been known for his off-color humor and "party" albums, but the public loved his crochety old Fred Sanford characterization and the show became a major hit.

In 1977 Foxx left that series and turned up on ABC in the kind of program he had wanted to do all along, his own comedy variety hour with a strong black orientation. Among the regular features were "Redd's Corner," in which he spotlighted old show-business friends who had not had much TV exposure (usually for good reason—they were awful) and "The History of the Black in America," Redd's view of how things *really* happened. Among Redd's semi-regular guests were comedian Slappy White, songstress Damita Jo, and Redd's comic partner from *Sanford and Son*, LaWanda Page. Gravel-voiced Redd also frequently offered a song or two.

REDIGO

Western

FIRST TELECAST: *September 24, 1963*
LAST TELECAST: *December 31, 1963*
BROADCAST HISTORY:
Sep 1963–Dec 1963, NBC Tue 8:30–9:00

CAST:
Jim Redigo ....Richard Egan
Mike ....Roger Davis
Frank Martinez ....Rudy Solari
Gerry ....Elena Verdugo

Empire had failed during the 1962–1963 season but its focal character, Jim Redigo, survived to try it on his own. In *Empire* he had been the manager of the vast Garret ranch in the contemporary Southwest. Now he was the owner and operator of his own small ranch in the same area at roughly the same time. The problems of making the ranch profitable and the relationships between people on it provided the story material. The two most prominent employees on the Redigo ranch were Mike and Frank, and Jim's casual romantic interest (despite the fact that she was seriously in love with him) was Gerry, manager of the Gran Quivera Hotel in the nearby town of Mesa.

REEL GAME, THE

Quiz/Audience Participation

FIRST TELECAST: *January 18, 1971*

LAST TELECAST: *May 3, 1971*

BROADCAST HISTORY:

Jan 1971–May 1971, ABC Mon 8:30–9:00

EMCEE:

Jack Barry

Each of the three contestants in this quiz show was given a sum of money and then asked to bet portions of it on his knowledge of famous people and events. The answers were then compared with newsreels or film clips of the right answers.

The program was created by Jack Barry, who was said to have been involved in the creation and production of 30 different quiz, game, and audience-participation shows up to this time.

REHEARSAL CALL

Variety

FIRST TELECAST: *March 20, 1949*

LAST TELECAST: *April 24, 1949*

BROADCAST HISTORY:

Mar 1949–Apr 1949, ABC Sun 9:15–9:30

HOSTESS:

Dee Parker

Short-lived 15-minute variety program originating from Detroit.

RENDEZVOUS

International Intrigue

FIRST TELECAST: *February 13, 1952*

LAST TELECAST: *March 5, 1952*

BROADCAST HISTORY:

Feb 1952–Mar 1952, ABC Wed 9:30–10:00

CAST:

Ilona Massey

David McKay

This short-lived series starred gorgeous Hungarian-born film star Ilona Massey as the owner and chief attraction at Chez Nikki, a posh nightclub in Paris. She had been a French underground agent during World War II, and was now engaged in international espionage on the Continent, foiling Communist agents and incidentally romancing newspaperman David McKay. Miss Massey also had an opportunity to sing one or two songs in each episode, in her sultry style.

RENDEZVOUS WITH MUSIC

Music

FIRST TELECAST: *July 11, 1950*

LAST TELECAST: *August 8, 1950*

BROADCAST HISTORY:

Jul 1950–Aug 1950, NBC Tue 9:00–9:30

EMCEE:

Carol Reed

REGULARS:

Don Gallagher

Tony DeSimone Trio

This was a musical interlude, reflecting "the varied tempos of summertime." Emcee Carol Reed was also featured as a singer on the show.

REPORT CARD FOR PARENTS

Discussion

FIRST TELECAST: *December 1, 1952*

LAST TELECAST: *February 2, 1953*

BROADCAST HISTORY:

Dec 1952–Feb 1953, DUM Mon 8:00–8:30

Panel-discussion program on the problems of bringing up children, with different guests each week.

REPORT FROM . . .

News/Travelogue

FIRST TELECAST: *July 9, 1963*

LAST TELECAST: *September 10, 1963*

BROADCAST HISTORY:

Jul 1963–Sep 1963, NBC Tue 10:30–11:00

Film portraits of 11 cities around the world, hosted by the NBC News correspondent in each city.

REPORT ON . . .

Documentary

FIRST TELECAST: *March 13, 1949*
LAST TELECAST: *April 3, 1949*
BROADCAST HISTORY:
Mar 1949–Apr 1949, CBS Sun 6:30–7:00
NARRATOR:
Charles Hodges

This four-week documentary series, hosted and narrated by CBS News correspondent Charles Hodges, analyzed the current world political situation. The reports were on Moscow, the North Atlantic Pact, Italy, and a United Nations press conference.

REPORTER, THE

Newspaper Drama

FIRST TELECAST: *September 25, 1964*
LAST TELECAST: *December 18, 1964*
BROADCAST HISTORY:
Sep 1964–Dec 1964, CBS Fri 10:00–11:00
CAST:
Danny Taylor ....Harry Guardino
Lou Sheldon ....Gary Merrill
Artie Burns ....George O'Hanlon
Ike Dawson ....Remo Pisani

Danny Taylor was a reporter for *The New York Globe,* a Manhattan daily. He was young, tough, and determined, all qualities necessary for a newsman in "The Big Apple." City editor Lou Sheldon was Danny's boss. He was also the father figure who understood what made Danny tick and could use his knowledge of the workings of the younger man's mind to drive him to dig deeper and harder into a story. Artie Burns was the friendly cabbie who was always available to take Danny off on a story, and Ike Dawson ran the Press Box, a bar where newspaper people gathered in their off hours.

REPORTER COLLINS

see *Not for Publication*

RESTLESS GUN, THE

Western

FIRST TELECAST: *September 23, 1957*
LAST TELECAST: *September 14, 1959*
BROADCAST HISTORY:
Sep 1957–Sep 1959, NBC Mon 8:00–8:30
CAST:
Vint Bonner ....John Payne

The adventures of a loner traveling through the post–Civil War Southwest provided the stories told in *The Restless Gun.* Vint Bonner was a cowboy who just couldn't seem to stay in one place too long. Although he was a very proficient gunfighter, Vint was basically a quiet, idealistic individual who preferred not to fight if there was an acceptable alternative. Unfortunately, there often was no alternative.

RETURN ENGAGEMENT

see *ABC Dramatic Shorts—1952–1953*

RETURN ENGAGEMENT

syndicated title for *Fireside Theater*

REVLON MIRROR THEATRE

Dramatic Anthology

FIRST TELECAST: *June 23, 1953*
LAST TELECAST: *December 12, 1953*
BROADCAST HISTORY:
Jun 1953–Sep 1953, NBC Tue 8:00–8:30
Sep 1953–Dec 1953, CBS Sat 10:30–11:00
HOSTESS:
Robin Chandler

During the summer of 1953, Revlon sponsored a series of live dramas that aired on NBC on Tuesday nights. When the series moved to CBS in September, the plays shown were on film. During the NBC run, Eddie Albert, Martha Scott, Jackie Cooper, and Peggy Ann Garner appeared. Joan Crawford made her TV dramatic debut in the first CBS episode, and subsequent telecasts featured such stars as Agnes Moorehead, Dane Clark, Angela Lansbury, and Charles Bickford. Hostess Robin Chandler was also the commercial spokeswoman for Revlon Cosmetics, the show's sponsor.

REVLON REVUE, THE

Variety

FIRST TELECAST: *January 28, 1960*
LAST TELECAST: *June 16, 1960*
BROADCAST HISTORY:
Jan 1960–Jun 1960, CBS Thu 10:00–11:00

This series was a collection of variety specials, each of which starred different performers. It presented both comedy and music with the emphasis of a particular show depending on the makeup of its cast. Among the stars of individual telecasts were Mickey Rooney, Maurice Chevalier,

Jackie Cooper, Gordon and Sheila MacRae, and Peggy Lee. Miss Lee starred in several shows, while the others were in only one each. On March 24 the show's title was changed to *Revlon Presents* and, effective May 12, when it began a series of musical specials, to *Revlon Spring Music Festival.*

RHINEMANN EXCHANGE, THE

Foreign Intrigue

FIRST TELECAST: *March 10, 1977*
LAST TELECAST: *March 24, 1977*
BROADCAST HISTORY:

Mar 1977, NBC Tue 9:00–11:00

CAST:

David Spaulding .... Stephen Collins
Leslie Hawkewood .... Lauren Hutton
Bobby Ballard .... Roddy McDowall
Walter Kendall .... Claude Akins
Geoffrey Moore .... Jeremy Kemp
Ambassador Granville .... John Huston
Gen. Swanson .... Vince Edwards
Erich Rhinemann .... Jose Ferrer
Heinrik Stoltz .... Bo Brundin

Adapted from Robert Ludlam's best-selling novel of World War II espionage, *The Rhinemann Exchange* was the story of the exploits of David Spaulding, a young intelligence officer who had covered Europe on concert tours with his late father prior to the start of the war. His familiarity with the Continent and knowledge of many European tongues made him an invaluable wartime agent for the U.S. His biggest assignment developed when he was sent to Argentina to set up a deal between the Americans and certain dissident elements in Hitler's Germany for the exchange of material desperately needed to facilitate the successful conduct of the war by the Allies.

The Rhinemann Exchange was one of four novels dramatized under the collective title *NBC's Best Sellers.*

RHODA

Situation Comedy

FIRST TELECAST: *September 9, 1974*
LAST TELECAST:
BROADCAST HISTORY:

Sep 1974–Sep 1975, CBS Mon 9:30–10:00
Sep 1975–Jan 1977, CBS Mon 8:00–8:30
Jan 1977–Sep 1978, CBS Sun 8:00–8:30
Sep 1978– , CBS Sat 8:00–8:30

CAST:

Rhoda Morgenstern Gerard
.... Valeria Harper
Brenda Morgenstern .... Julie Kavner
Joe Gerard (1974–1977) .... David Groh
Ida Morgenstern (1974–1976, 1977–)
.... Nancy Walker
Martin Morgenstern (1974–1976, 1977–)
.... Harold J. Gould
Carlton the Doorman (voice only)
.... Lorenzo Music
Mae (1974–1975) .... Cara Williams
Alice Barth (1974–1975) ..... Candy Azzara
Donny Gerard (1974) ...... Todd Turquand
Myrna Morgenstern (1974–1976)
.... Barbara Sharma
Justin Culp (1975–1976) .... Scoey Mitchlll
Gary Levy (1976–1978) .... Ron Silver
Sally Gallagher (1976–1977)
.... Anne Meara
Johnny Venture (1977–1978)
.... Michael Delano
Benny Goodwin (1977–)
.... Ray Buktenica
Jack Doyle (1977–) ..... Ken McMillan
Ramón Diaz, Jr. (1977–1978)
.... Rafael Campos
Tina (1978–) .... Nancy Lane

As Mary Richards' friend and neighbor on *The Mary Tyler Moore Show,* Rhoda had been somewhat overweight, insecure in her relationships with men, and jealous of the trim Mary. Over the years, however, she had slimmed down, and when she returned home to New York for a visit at the start of *Rhoda* in the fall of 1974, she was a more attractive and self-confident person. The visit turned into a permanent change of residence when she met and fell in love with Joe Gerard. Joe was the owner of the New York Wrecking Company, divorced, and the father of a 10-year-old son. Rhoda moved in with her sister Brenda, since living with her parents Ida and Martin was just not working out, and got a job as a window dresser for a department store. The romance blossomed and, in a special full-hour telecast on October 28, 1974, Rhoda Morgenstern the husband-hunter became Rhoda Gerard.

The newlyweds moved out of Joe's bachelor apartment (too many of his old girl friends had keys) and into the same building in which Brenda and Rhoda had been living. Joe went off every day to the office to deal with his partner Justin and other concerns of his business, while Rhoda was a relatively unoccupied housewife, having given up her job. Her inactivity didn't last too long, however, as boredom precipitated her decision to start her own window-dressing business with a high school friend, shy Myrna Morgenstern (no relation), as a partner. With Rhoda happily married, the comedy shifted to her chubby sister Brenda, a bank teller with constant problems trying to get a boy friend, sort of a younger version of the Rhoda who started on *The Mary Tyler Moore Show* in 1970.

After two years of stories about wedded bliss the producers of *Rhoda* decided that a happily married couple was just not as funny as two single people trying to cope with the world. In order to create more flexibility in Rhoda's role, she and Joe separated soon after the start of the 1976–1977 season. Now they were able to make new friends, suffer the adjustments of living apart, and again deal with the world of the lonely "single." Joe was gradually phased out of the show, preparatory to the inevitable divorce, and Rhoda joined her sister at mixers and singles bars. She found a new friend in 39-year-old divorced airline stewardess Sally Gallagher, and both she and Brenda were frequently escorted by platonic friend Gary Levy. In the middle of that season Rhoda began an off-again on-again romance with egocentric Las Vegas–based entertainer Johnny Venture.

The 1977–1978 season brought another raft of changes. Rhoda was now a divorced woman (David Groh was gone completely from the cast) and early on she found a new job working at the Doyle Costume Company, a rundown business struggling to survive. Jack Doyle was the owner of the company and his assistant was Ramón. Brenda had a new boy friend in Benny Goodwin, and mother Ida had just returned from a year's traveling around the country (Nancy Walker had been away during the 1976–1977 season starring in two short-lived series of her own—*The Nancy Walker Show* and *Blansky's Beauties*).

RHYTHM RODEO

Music

FIRST TELECAST: *August 6, 1950*

LAST TELECAST: *January 7, 1951*

BROADCAST HISTORY:

Aug 1950–Jan 1951, DUM Sun 8:00–8:30

HOST:

Art Jarrett

REGULARS:

Paula Wray
The Star Noters

Art Jarrett, a band singer with a career stretching back into the 1920s, hosted this early, low-budget musical program from Chicago. Although the motif was supposed to be "Western," all types of songs were featured. Running opposite Ed Sullivan's *Toast of the Town*, it didn't really matter what they did.

RICH LITTLE SHOW, THE

Comedy Variety

FIRST TELECAST: *February 2, 1976*

LAST TELECAST: *July 19, 1976*

BROADCAST HISTORY:

Feb 1976–May 1976, NBC Mon 8:00–9:00
Jun 1976–Jul 1976, NBC Mon 8:00–9:00

REGULARS:

Rich Little
Charlotte Rae
Julie McWhirter
R. G. Brown
Mel Bishop
Joe Baker

Impressionist Rich Little was the host and star of this comedy variety series. Each episode contained a monologue, a number of comedy sketches, and performances by the week's guest stars. The one running character that appeared on each episode was Julie McWhirter's Family Hour Good Fairy (a satire on the TV networks' recently announced policy of reserving 8:00–9:00 P.M. each night for wholesome "family entertainment" rather than violence). For a four-week period in the middle of this show's run, from May 24 to June 14, it was replaced by a mini-series, *The John Davidson Show*.

RICH MAN, POOR MAN—BOOK I

Drama

FIRST TELECAST: *February 1, 1976*

LAST TELECAST: *June 21, 1977*

BROADCAST HISTORY:

Feb 1976–Mar 1976, ABC Mon 10:00–11:00
May 1977–Jun 1977, ABC Tue 9:00–11:00

CAST:

Rudy Jordache .... Peter Strauss
Tom Jordache .... Nick Nolte

Julie Prescott/Abbott/Jordache .... Susan Blakely
Axel Jordache .... Edward Asner
Mary Jordache .... Dorothy McGuire
Willie Abbott .... Bill Bixby
Duncan Calderwood .... Ray Milland
Teddy Boylan .... Robert Reed
Virginia Calderwood .... Kim Darby
Sue Prescott .... Gloria Grahame
Asher Berg .... Craig Stevens
Joey Quales .... George Maharis
Linda Quales .... Lynda Day George
Nichols .... Steve Allen
Smitty .... Norman Fell
Teresa Sanjoro .... Talia Shire
Marsh Goodwin .... Van Johnson
Irene Goodwin .... Dorothy Malone
Kate Jordache .... Kay Lenz
Sid Gossett .... Murray Hamilton
Arnold Simms .... Mike Evans
Al Fanducci .... Dick Butkus
Clothilde .... Fionnula Flanagan
Brad Knight .... Tim McIntire
Bill Denton .... Lawrence Pressman
Claude Tinker .... Dennis Dugan
Gloria Bartley .... Jo Ann Harris
Pete Tierney .... Roy Jenson
Lou Martin .... Anthony Carbone
Papadakis .... Ed Barth
Ray Dwyer .... Herbert Jefferson, Jr.
Arthur Falconetti .... William Smith
Col. Deiner .... Andrew Duggan
Pinky .... Harvey Jason
Martha .... Helen Craig
Phil McGee .... Gavan O'Herlihy
Billy .... Leigh McCloskey
Wesley .... Michael Morgan

MUSIC:
Alex North

If it had not been overshadowed so quickly by *Roots, Rich Man, Poor Man* would probably be ranked today as the biggest dramatic spectacular in the history of television. It was an enormous hit, not only spawning a separate series the following season (see *Rich Man, Poor Man—Book II*) but also stimulating a rash of novels-for-television.

The source was Irwin Shaw's sprawling (720-page) 1970 best-seller about the divergent careers of two brothers in the years from 1945 to the 1960s. Rudy Jordache was the "rich man," the ambitious, educated entrepreneur who triumphed over his impoverished immigrant background to build a business and political empire. Tom was the "poor man," the trouble-prone rebel who turned boxer for a time, and was eventually murdered in the last episode by the vicious Falconetti. Axel and Mary were the parents, and Julie, Rudy's lifelong love. An enormous, all-star cast paraded through the 12-hour presentation as lovers, enemies, scoundrels, and friends. The entire 12 hours was repeated in May–June 1977.

RICH MAN, POOR MAN—BOOK II

Drama

FIRST TELECAST: *September 21, 1976*
LAST TELECAST: *March 8, 1977*
BROADCAST HISTORY:
Sep 1976–Mar 1977, ABC Tue 9:00–10:00
CAST:
Senator Rudy Jordache .... Peter Strauss
Wesley Jordache .... Gregg Henry
Billy Abbott .... James Carroll Jordan
Maggie Porter .... Susan Sullivan
Arthur Falconetti .... William Smith
Marie Falconetti .... Dimitra Arliss
Ramona Scott .... Penny Peyser
Scotty .... John Anderson
Charles Estep .... Peter Haskell
Phil Greenberg .... Sorrell Brooke
Annie Adams .... Cassie Yates
Diane Porter .... Kimberly Beck
Arthur Raymond .... Peter Donat
Claire Estep .... Laraine Stephens
Senator Paxton .... Barry Sullivan
Kate Jordache .... Kay Lenz
John Franklin .... Philip Abbott
Max Vincent .... George Gaynes
Al Barber .... Ken Swofford
Senator Dillon .... G. D. Spradlin

This sequel to the 1976 mini-series began in the year 1965, after the death of Tom Jordache, and followed brother Rudy's further career as a U.S. Senator. Rudy was now surrogate father to a family consisting of Wesley (Tom's boy) and Billy (Julie's boy, by one of her marriages), two young men ambitious for futures of their own. Much of the action in Book II involved their entanglements, and Senator Rudy's protracted battle against the greedy, power-hungry, and mysterious billionaire Estep, owner of Tricorp. Falconetti was back, apparently intent on killing off *all* the Jordaches. Backgrounds of Las Vegas, Aspen, and other haunts of the rich gave this melodrama a lavish appearance, but it was soap opera nevertheless.

In the last original episode, Rudy and Falconetti faced each other with guns in hand and shot it out, apparently leaving the two of them lying bleeding to death on a sidewalk.

RICHARD BOONE SHOW, THE

Dramatic Anthology

FIRST TELECAST: *September 24, 1963*

LAST TELECAST: *September 15, 1964*

BROADCAST HISTORY:

Sep 1963–Sep 1964, NBC Tue 9:00–10:00

HOST:

Richard Boone

REGULARS:

Robert Blake
Lloyd Bochner
Laura Devon
June Harding
Bethel Leslie
Harry Morgan
Jeanette Nolan
Ford Rainey
Warren Stevens
Guy Stockwell

The Richard Boone Show was television's equivalent of repertory theater. Although there were no continuing roles in this anthology series, the same group of actors and actresses played parts in almost all the plays. Richard Boone was the host for all episodes and starred in roughly half of the shows. Each of the regulars had an opportunity to star in at least one of the episodes, in addition to having supporting roles in many of them.

RICHARD DIAMOND, PRIVATE DETECTIVE

Detective

FIRST TELECAST: *July 1, 1957*

LAST TELECAST: *September 6, 1960*

BROADCAST HISTORY:

Jul 1957–Sep 1957, CBS Mon 9:30–10:00
Jan 1958–Sep 1958, CBS Thu 8:00–8:30
Feb. 1959–Sep 1959, CBS Sun 10:00–10:30
Oct 1959–Jan 1960, NBC Mon 7:30–8:00
Jun 1960–Sep 1960, NBC Tue 9:00–9:30

CAST:

Richard Diamond ....David Janssen
Lt. McGough (1957–1958) ...Regis Toomey
Karen Wells (1959) ....Barbara Bain
Lt. Kile (1959–1960) ....Russ Conway
"Sam" (1959) ....Mary Tyler Moore
"Sam" (1959–1960) ....Roxanne Brooks

Richard Diamond was an ex–New York City policeman who had turned in his badge to go into private practice as a detective. His familiarity with the force and his friends on it, most notably Lt. McGough, gave him access to information and help not normally afforded private detectives. In February 1959 he relocated to Hollywood, acquired a semi-regular girl friend in Karen Wells, and began using an answering service to get his messages. His contact at the answering service was a sultry-voiced woman whom he called "Sam." Her voice was heard and her body was seen from the waist down, to show off her legs, but her identity was not revealed in the screen credits at the end of each episode. The first actress to play "Sam" was young Mary Tyler Moore, a fact that was revealed to readers of *TV Guide* when an article appeared in May 1959 in which she modeled the latest in women's hosiery. It was in the middle of that month that she left the series to be replaced by another unbilled leggy actress. "Sam" was important to Richard Diamond since she often reached him in his car, which had a built-in phone, to warn of impending danger.

Dick Powell, whose Four Star Productions produced this series, had starred as Richard Diamond on radio from 1949–1952.

RICHARD PRYOR SHOW, THE

Comedy Variety

FIRST TELECAST: *September 13, 1977*

LAST TELECAST: *October 20, 1977*

BROADCAST HISTORY:

Sep 1977–Oct 1977, NBC Tue 8:00–9:00
Oct 1977, NBC Thu 9:00–10:00

STAR:

Richard Pryor

The career of young black comic Richard Pryor was definitely on the rise when production started on his first regular television series during the summer of 1977. He had become successful as a nightclub performer, was seen regularly on television's talk shows, and had begun a career in motion pictures. His original commitment had been to do a minimum of ten variety shows for the series but, with the demands for his time growing after the success of two 1977 films, *Silver Streak* and *Greased Lightning*, coupled with censorship problems he had with NBC management, it was mutually agreed that he would do only five shows.

Although considered one of the most inventive, offbeat, and satirical performers around, Pryor's background as a nightclub comic led him to try material that might be considered in questionable taste for television. There were constant disagreements on what material was acceptable, and the opening sequence from his first show—in which he was shown nude from the waist up commenting that he had lost nothing in his battles with the network censors, followed by a pan down his body in which he appeared to be both completely nude and emasculated (he was actually wearing a body stocking)—was censored before the show was aired. His feud with NBC was highly publicized in the press but did little to attract viewers from ABC's *Happy Days*, his prime competition, which had twice as large an audience as *The Richard Pryor Show*.

RICHIE BROCKELMAN, PRIVATE EYE

Detective

FIRST TELECAST: *March 17, 1978*

LAST TELECAST: *August 24, 1978*

BROADCAST HISTORY:

Mar 1978–Apr 1978, NBC Fri 9:00–10:00

Aug 1978, NBC Thu 9:00–10:00

CAST:

Richie Brockelman ....Dennis Dugan

Sgt. Coopersmith ....Robert Hogan

Sharon ....Barbara Bosson

Richie Brockelman didn't look like a detective and that, as he put it, was his "trump card." Since almost no one, criminal or police, took the youthful looking sleuth seriously, he was able to talk his way into and out of all sorts of dangerous situations in the course of his investigations. But Brockelman was indeed for real, a glib, 23-year-old college educated private investigator with his own, admittedly small, agency. Sharon was his trusted secretary and Sgt. Coppersmith his skeptical police contact.

The series was a spin-off of *The Rockford Files*, on which Brockelman had appeared on occasion to help out Jim Rockford.

RIDDLE ME THIS

see *Celebrity Time*

RIFLEMAN, THE

Western

FIRST TELECAST: *September 30, 1958*

LAST TELECAST: *July 1, 1963*

BROADCAST HISTORY:

Sep 1958–Sep 1960, ABC Tue 9:00–9:30

Sep 1960–Sep 1961, ABC Tue 8:00–8:30

Oct 1961–Jul 1963, ABC Mon 8:30–9:00 (OS)

CAST:

Lucas McCain ....Chuck Connors

Mark McCain ....Johnny Crawford

Marshal Micah Torrance ....Paul Fix

Miss Milly Scott (1960–1962) ....Joan Taylor

Lou Mallory (1962–1963) ..... Patricia Blair

The Rifleman was the saga of Lucas McCain, a homesteader in the Old West struggling to make a living off his ranch and make a man out of his motherless son, Mark. Chuck Connors, a former professional baseball player, won critical acclaim for his portrayal of Lucas, and young Johnny Crawford was also started on a successful career by this series. The setting was the town of North Fork, New Mexico, whose marshal seemed incapable of handling any of the numerous desperadoes who infested the series (as they did all Western series) without the help of Lucas. Helpful, too, was the trick rifle that Lucas always carried, a modified Winchester with a large ring which cocked it as he drew. Supposedly, he could fire off his first round in three-tenths of a second, which certainly helped in a showdown.

Though quite successful at first, the series began to slip in its third season, due to a number of reasons including Lucas' rather righteous tone. To "humanize" him the producers brought Miss Milly to North Fork, to serve as storekeeper and McCain's love interest. In 1962 a somewhat pushier female arrived: Lou Mallory, a kind of con-artist-with-a-heart-of-gold hotel-keeper who began buying up the property around town and took out a lease on Lucas as well. In addition, Mark began to experience problems associated with adolescence (he had been "12" when the series started).

RIVERBOAT

Adventure

FIRST TELECAST: *September 13, 1959*

LAST TELECAST: *January 16, 1961*

BROADCAST HISTORY:

Sep 1959–Jan 1960, NBC Sun 7:00–8:00
Feb 1960–Jan 1961, NBC Mon 7:30–8:30

CAST:

Grey Holden ....Darren McGavin
Ben Frazer (1959–1960) ..... Burt Reynolds
Travis (1959–1960) ..... William D. Gordon
Carney ....Richard Wessell
Joshua ....Jack Lambert
Chip (1959–1960) .... Mike McGreevey
Pickalong (1959–1960) ...... Jack Mitchum
Terry Blake (1959–1960) .... Bart Patten
Bill Blake (1960–1961) .... Noah Beery

The *Enterprise* was a 100-foot-long sternwheeler that churned up and down the Mississippi, Missouri, and Ohio rivers during the 1840s. The captain and owner of the boat was Grey Holden, a former fighter, rumrunner, swordsman, dock foreman, and soldier. A fun-loving romantic, he had won the boat in a poker game and was determined to make it a profitable venture, carrying passengers, hauling freight, and doing anything else it could to generate revenue. Boat pilot Ben Frazer was the co-lead when *Riverboat* first aired, an orphan whose entire life had been spent along the Mississippi. Both he and crew member Travis were written out of the series in the middle of its first season. When it returned in the fall of 1960, *Riverboat* had a new co-lead in Bill Blake, as a pilot who had bought 49 percent of the *Enterprise* and was constantly seeking to take controlling interest. First mate Joshua and crew member Carney were still in the cast, but gone were cabin boy Chip; Pickalong, the ballad singing cook; and Terry Blake, the cub-pilot who had replaced Ben Frazer. Captain Holden spent more time away from the boat and got involved in more romantic entanglements than during the first season.

ROAD WEST, THE

Western

FIRST TELECAST: *September 12, 1966*
LAST TELECAST: *August 28, 1967*
BROADCAST HISTORY:

Sep 1966–Aug 1967, NBC Mon 9:00–10:00

CAST:

Benjamin Pride ....Barry Sullivan
Timothy Pride ....Andrew Prine
Midge Pride ....Brenda Scott
Kip Pride ....Kelly Corcoran
Grandpa Pride ....Charles Seel
Chance Reynolds ....Glenn Corbett
Elizabeth Reynolds ....Kathryn Hays

Benjamin Pride was a widower who had taken his family from Springfield, Ohio, where they had lived for generations, and moved them to the Kansas Territory shortly after the end of the Civil War. The problems encountered by this pioneering family in the fertile but lawless West provided the stories in this series. Benjamin's family consisted of his 24-year-old son Timothy, his daughters Midge (18) and Kip (8), Elizabeth Reynolds, and her younger brother Chance. Elizabeth, the daughter of a doctor, had become Benjamin's second wife just prior to his move to Kansas. Her brother had gone with the Prides in search of excitement and adventure.

ROAR OF THE RAILS, THE

Adventure

FIRST TELECAST: *October 26, 1948*
LAST TELECAST: *December 12, 1949*
BROADCAST HISTORY:

Oct 1948–Dec 1948, CBS Tue 7:00–7:15
Oct 1949–Dec 1949, CBS Mon 7:00–7:15

The object of this live adventure/documentary series was to dramatize the events that had made railroad history. Veteran railroad men appeared to explain what their jobs were like and the dramatizations were carried out with model trains and a miniature set that included mountains and tunnels. Not coincidentally, the program's sponsor was the A.C. Gilbert Company, manufacturer of American Flyer model trains. The sponsor had created the miniature set that was used in the series.

ROARING TWENTIES, THE

Newspaper

FIRST TELECAST: *October 15, 1960*
LAST TELECAST: *September 21, 1962*
BROADCAST HISTORY:

Oct 1960–Jan 1962, ABC Sat 7:30–8:30
Sep 1962, ABC Fri 7:30–8:30

CAST:

Scott Norris ....Rex Reason
Pat Garrison ....Donald May
Pinky Pinkham ....Dorothy Provine
Chris Higbee ....Gary Vinson
Jim Duke Williams ....John Dehner
Lt. Joe Switolski ....Mike Road

This adventure series was set in New York City in the 1920s and, in an attempt at documentary-style authenticity, included newsreel footage of events that had actually happened during that period. Pat and Scott were investigative reporters for the *New York Record* who, with the assistance of their young copy boy and friend Chris, sought big scoops by infiltrating the underworld and exposing the hoods who were controlling the city during the Prohibition Era. They were often seen at the Charleston Club, a posh speakeasy where the leading attraction was beautiful songstress Pinky Pinkham. Working in a club that was frequented by mobsters, Pinky often had tips that would help the reporters break their cases. Whenever they got in over their heads, Lt. Switolski of the N.Y.P.D. would bail them out.

If this format sounds slightly familiar don't be surprised. Except for the fact that the leads in the series were reporters rather than detectives, *The Roaring Twenties* was interchangeable with any of the other formula series Warner Brothers produced for ABC in the late 1950s and early 1960s, the most successful of which were *77 Sunset Strip*, *Hawaiian Eye*, and *Surfside Six*. Canceled early in 1962, *The Roaring Twenties* returned for a few weeks that September with reruns.

ROBBINS NEST, THE

Comedy Variety

FIRST TELECAST: *September 29, 1950*
LAST TELECAST: *December 22, 1950*
BROADCAST HISTORY:
Sep 1950–Dec 1950, ABC Fri 11:00–11:15
REGULARS:
Fred Robbins
Nate Cantor
Fran Gregory

New York disc jockey Fred Robbins, known for his hip slang, tried TV comedy in this late-night program. Robbins and his supporting players appeared in various skits, and he also sang (passably), but the humor was rather weak. A typical gag had Robbins telling his secretary Fran to file a letter, whereupon she pulled out a metal file and began honing away. The program lasted three months.

ROBERT MONTGOMERY PRESENTS

Dramatic Anthology

FIRST TELECAST: *January 30, 1950*
LAST TELECAST: *June 24, 1957*
BROADCAST HISTORY:
Jan 1950–Jun 1957, NBC Mon 9:30–10:30
HOST/EXECUTIVE PRODUCER:
Robert Montgomery
SUMMER REPERTORY PLAYERS:
John Newland (1952–1954)
Vaughn Taylor (1952–1954)
Margaret Hayes (1952–1953)
Elizabeth Montgomery (1953–1954, 1956)
Jan Miner (1954–1956)
Anne Seymour (1954)
Cliff Robertson (1954)
Charles Drake (1955–1956)
Augusta Dabney (1955)
House Jameson (1955)
Dorothy Blackburn (1955)
Eric Sinclair (1955)
Mary K. Wells (1956)
John Gibson (1956)
Tom Middleton (1956)

One of the best-remembered big-budget live dramatic series of TV's golden age. Hollywood actor-director-producer Robert Montgomery introduced each telecast, sometimes interviewing one of the stars and sometimes appearing in the play himself. The series had a Hollywood flavor, with many familiar names from the screen appearing in leading roles. At first it presented adaptations of classic motion pictures, such as *Rebecca*, *A Star Is Born* and *Dark Victory*, all of which were done within the first few months. Later original TV plays and adaptations of stage plays, books and short stories were used due to copyright rules which prevented the kinescoping of any production based on a motion picture—these could be telecast on a live basis only. (Kinescopes were needed so that the program could be seen on some non-interconnected affiliates.)

The first telecast was an adaptation of W. Somerset Maugham's classic *The Letter*, and the quality of the scripts remained similarly high throughout the run of the series. The program won many awards. Jane Wyatt, Zachary Scott, and Montgomery's daughter Elizabeth (later of *Bewitched* fame) made their TV debuts on this program. Claudette Colbert made one of her rare appearances in the medium, as did James Cagney. Helen Hayes and other famous stars, as well as newer talent, were also featured.

Some of the productions were truly spectacular for live television, such as a drama built around the destruction of the great dirigible Hindenburg, followed by interviews with some of the actual survivors.

Beginning in 1952, during the summers, *Robert Montgomery Presents* adopted a summer-stock format, with a repertory company of regulars appearing in starring or supporting roles in each production. Among these regulars were both newcomers such as Elizabeth Montgomery, Cliff Robertson, and John Newland, and some old-timers as well.

While the series was generally known as *Robert Montgomery Presents* the actual title varied from week to week according to the sponsor: *Robert Montgomery Presents Your Lucky Strike Theater, . . . the Johnson's Wax Program, . . . the Richard Hudnut Summer Theater*, etc. It alternated with various other programs during its first two years on the air, then became a weekly series in December 1951.

ROBERT Q. LEWIS SHOW, THE

Comedy/Talk

FIRST TELECAST: *July 16, 1950*

LAST TELECAST: *January 7, 1951*

BROADCAST HISTORY:

Jul 1950–Sep 1950, CBS Sun 9:00–9:15
Sep 1950–Jan 1951, CBS Sun 11:00–11:15

HOST:

Robert Q. Lewis

While still functioning as emcee on *The Show Goes On*, comedian Robert Q. Lewis added this informal show to his list of television credits. The live 15-minute show gave him the opportunity to chat with guest stars and introduce the weekly "Breadwinner of the Week," an individual performing an unusual job somewhere in the New York City area.

ROBERT TAYLOR'S DETECTIVES

see *Detectives, Starring Robert Taylor, The*

ROBERT YOUNG, FAMILY DOCTOR

syndicated title for *Marcus Welby, M.D.*

ROBIN HOOD

see *Adventures of Robin Hood, The*

ROCK AND ROLL YEARS, THE

see *Dick Clark Presents The Rock and Roll Years*

ROCKFORD FILES, THE

Detective

FIRST TELECAST: *September 13, 1974*

LAST TELECAST:

BROADCAST HISTORY:

Sep 1974–May 1977, NBC Fri 9:00–10:00
Jun 1977, NBC Fri 8:30–9:30
Jul 1977–   , NBC Fri 9:00–10:00

CAST:

Jim Rockford . . . . .James Garner
Joseph "Rocky" Rockford . . . . . .Noah Beery
Det. Dennis Becker . . . . .Joe Santos
Beth Davenport (1974–1978) . . . . .Gretchen Corbett
Angel Martin . . . . .Stuart Margolin
John Cooper (1978–   ) . . . . . . Bo Hopkins

THEME:

"The Rockford Files"

Jim Rockford was a private detective with a difference. He was an ex-convict. Once imprisoned for a crime he had not committed, but eventually exonerated when new evidence turned up to prove his innocence, Jim had a penchant for taking cases that were closed—those the police were sure had been resolved. His knack for turning up information that might reverse the already established verdict did not endear him to the police, particularly to Det. Dennis Becker with whom he had a love-hate relationship. Jim was always getting Dennis involved in situations he would have preferred to avoid, aggravating the cop who, despite it all, had a personal affection for him. Jim lived in, and worked out of, a house trailer in the Los Angeles area and was not the cheapest detective available, charging $200 per day plus expenses. His father, a retired trucker, helped him on occasions and his girl friend/attorney Beth Davenport was always around to bail him out when he ran afoul of the law. Having been in prison, Jim had many ex-con friends. One of them, his former cellmate Angel Martin, was constantly in need of Jim's help because of his tendency to get involved with his former criminal associates. Another friend was John Cooper, a disbarred lawyer whose ties to the Corporation for Legal Research proved useful.

The theme song from this series was on the hit parade in mid-1975.

ROCKY KING, INSIDE DETECTIVE

Police

FIRST TELECAST: *January 14, 1950*

LAST TELECAST: *December 26, 1954*

BROADCAST HISTORY:

Jan 1950–Jul 1950, DUM Sat 8:30–9:00

Jul 1950–Mar 1951, DUM Fri 9:30–10:00

Mar 1951–Dec 1954, DUM Sun 9:00–9:30

CAST:

Det. Rocky King ....Roscoe Karns

Mabel King ....Grace Carney

Sgt. Lane (1950–1953) ......Earl Hammond

Det. Hart (1953–1954) ....Todd Karns

Rocky King was probably the most popular continuing dramatic show to come out of the DuMont network. It never had the opportunity to attain top nationwide ratings, due to DuMont's limited station lineup and severely restricted production budgets (you never saw a big-name guest star acting in a *Rocky King* episode!), but it did attract a loyal and enthusiastic following which kept it on the air for five years, nearly until the end of DuMont operations.

The program centered on hard-working Rocky King, a detective on the New York City Homicide Squad, and was in most respects a standard low-budget cops-and-robbers show. What set it apart were its lead, Roscoe Karns; its sense of believability; and its touches of humor. Those who think that *Dragnet* brought realism to TV cop shows obviously never saw *Rocky King*. Rocky had no flashes of brilliant deduction or unbelieveably lucky breaks, nor did he tackle impossibly convoluted cases. He simply tracked down the facts, doggedly, and pieced them together until they made sense—and pointed to the culprit. There was plenty of action in *Rocky King* too, but it usually came after some good, hard work.

Rocky also had a family, which generated a good deal of interest, because they were heard but never seen on camera. This began as an economy measure (typical of DuMont), when an actress who was playing a role in a mystery was asked to double as Rocky's wife at home. Since there was no time to change clothes or makeup (the show was live), she spoke from offscreen. Viewers liked the touch and Grace Carney became a permanent feature, her off-camera presence always bringing Rocky back to earth with her problems around the house. For a time there was also an unseen son, named Junior.

Roscoe Karns, who had had a long career in Hollywood as a second banana, was appreciative of the opportunity to extend his career via TV (he frankly said that *Rocky King* had "rescued" him from enforced retirement) and stayed with the show until its demise. During the final year of its run, his son, Todd Karns, played his sidekick, Det. Hart. Roscoe Karns later had a leading role in *Hennessey*. He died in 1970.

ROCKY'S CORNER

see *Henny & Rocky Show, The*

ROD SERLING'S NIGHT GALLERY

see *Night Gallery*

ROGER MILLER SHOW, THE

Musical Variety

FIRST TELECAST: *September 12, 1966*

LAST TELECAST: *December 26, 1966*

BROADCAST HISTORY:

Sep 1966–Dec 1966, NBC Mon 8:30–9:00

REGULAR:

Roger Miller

Singer-composer Roger Miller, who had won five 1965 Grammy Awards for his recordings, starred in this short-lived variety show. In addition to singing popular songs and the Country and Western tunes which had made him so popular, he introduced and performed with one or two guests stars each week. There were no other regulars, but the Doodletown Pipers made a number of appearances during the less than four months the show was on the air.

ROGUES, THE

Comedy Drama

FIRST TELECAST: *September 13, 1964*

LAST TELECAST: *September 5, 1965*

BROADCAST HISTORY:

Sep 1964–Sep 1965, NBC Sun 10:00–11:00

CAST:

Tony Fleming ....Gig Young

Alec Fleming ....David Niven

Marcel St. Clair ....Charles Boyer

Timmy St. Clair ....Robert Coote

Margaret St. Clair ....Gladys Cooper

"Honor before Honesty" was the credo of the Flemings and the St. Clairs, the two most successful families of scoundrels the civilized world had every known. Their lines had been forever crossed when Sir Giles Fleming and la Comtesse Juliette St. Clair had met and fallen in love while both were independently trying to lift a jewel box from Marie Antoinette of France in 1789. The modern descendants of these aristocratic jewel thieves and con men, whose primary activity was relieving the rich of their wealth, were spread all over the world. Tony was the dashing young American member of the family, who worked out of New York and had been hand-picked to take over the family "throne" from his English cousin Alec when the latter went into semi-retirement. Alec had moved to Montego Bay but was still active for special deals. Marcel was the head of the French branch of the family and Timmy, a master of disguises, was on hand to help each of the principals. His mother, Aunt Margaret, was the planner and coordinator of most of the heists and cons, all of which were finalized at her home across from Buckingham Palace.

ROLL OUT

Situation Comedy

FIRST TELECAST: *October 5, 1973*

LAST TELECAST: *January 4, 1974*

BROADCAST HISTORY:

Oct 1973–Dec 1973, CBS Fri 8:30–9:00
Jan 1974, CBS Fri 8:00–8:30

CAST:

Cpl. "Sweet" Williams	Stu Gilliam
Pfc. Jed Brooks	Hilly Hicks
Sgt. B. J. Bryant	Mel Stewart
Capt Rocco Calvelli	Val Bisoglio
Lt. Robert W. Chapman	Ed Begley, Jr.
"Wheels"	Garrett Morris
Madam Delacort	Penny Santon

Set in France during World War II, *Roll Out* was the story of the men of the 5050th Trucking Company, the "Red Ball Express," an Army trucking unit that managed to get supplies through to troops at the front despite any and all problems. Military discipline meant little to these rowdy men, whose prime purpose was to move war supplies no matter how they did it. Capt. Calvelli was the leader of the unit, which was mostly black, Sweet and Jed were two of his best drivers, and Sgt. Bryant the tough, crusty career military man. When not on assignment, the men of the 5050th sought recreation at the nightclub adjacent to their base camp, run by Madame Delacort.

Based on the story of an actual World War II transportation unit.

ROLLER DERBY

Sports

FIRST TELECAST: *March 24, 1949*

LAST TELECAST: *August 16, 1951*

BROADCAST HISTORY:

Mar 1949–Jun 1949, ABC Thu 10:00–11:15
Mar 1949–May 1949, ABC Sat 10:00–11:00
May 1949–Jun 1949, ABC Mon 9:30–Conclusion
May 1949–Jul 1949, ABC Fri 10:00–Conclusion
Sep 1949–Nov 1949, ABC Mon/Fri 10:00–Conclusion
Sep 1949–Sep 1950, ABC Thu 10:00–Conclusion
Nov 1949–May 1951, ABC Sat 9:00–Conclusion
Jun 1950–Sep 1950, ABC Fri 8:30–9:30
Sep 1950–May 1951, ABC Tue/Thu 10:00–11:15
Jul 1951–Aug 1951, ABC Thu 10:00–11:15

ANNOUNCER:

Ken Nydell
Joe Hasel (1949–1950)
Howard Myles (1950–1951)
Ed Begley (1951)

Roller Derby was at one time the most popular program on the ABC schedule, that is if amount of air time occupied is a measure of popularity. The sport, which sometimes seemed more like a head-bashing free-for-all than a test of athletic skill, combined elements of skating, football, rugby, and wrestling, aired as often as three times a week. The show originated from such exotic locations as the 14th Regiment Armory in Brooklyn, and other similar places around New York City and adjacent areas of Long Island and New Jersey. The resident announcer was Ken Nydell, who did the play by play throughout the run, sometimes by himself and sometimes with an assistant. The New York Chiefs were always the home team, playing the San Francisco Bay Bombers, the Midwest Pioneers, and others.

ROLLER GIRLS, THE

Situation Comedy

FIRST TELECAST: *April 24, 1978*

LAST TELECAST: *May 10, 1978*

BROADCAST HISTORY:

Apr 1978–May 1978, NBC Mon 8:00–8:30
May 1978, NBC Wed 8:00–8:30

CAST:

Don Mitchell .... Terry Kiser
Mongo Sue Lampert .... Rhonda Bates
J.B. Johnson .... Candy Ann Brown
Selma "Books" Cassidy .... Joanna Cassidy
Honey Bee Novak .... Marcy Hanson
Shana "Pipeline" Akira
.... Marilyn Tokuda
Howie Devine .... James Murtaugh

The Pittsburgh Pitts were an all girl roller derby team, owned and managed by conniving Don Mitchell, who was constantly looking for ways to save the foundering team—and his investment. The Pitts were a sexy, but sometimes inept crew: towering Mongo, feisty J.B. (the token black), sophisticated "Books," dizzy blonde Honey Bee, and innocent "Pipeline," an Eskimo-American. Announcer for the team's raucous games was the snobbish Howie Devine, a down-on-his-luck former opera commentator who would do anything for a buck.

ROMANCE

Dramatic Anthology

FIRST TELECAST: *November 3, 1949*

LAST TELECAST: *December 29, 1949*

BROADCAST HISTORY:

Nov 1949–Dec 1949, CBS Thu 8:30–9:00

Premiering with an updated version of *Camille,* this live anthology series presented television adaptations of famous love stories. *Romance* aired on alternate Thursdays with *Inside U.S.A. with Chevrolet.*

ROOKIES, THE

Police

FIRST TELECAST: *September 11, 1972*

LAST TELECAST: *June 29, 1976*

BROADCAST HISTORY:

Sep 1972–Sep 1975, ABC Mon 8:00–9:00
Sep 1975–Apr 1976, ABC Tue 9:00–10:00
May 1976–Jul 1976, ABC Tue 10:00–11:00

CAST:

Officer Terry Webster
.... Georg Stanford Brown
Officer Willie Gillis (1972–1974)
.... Michael Ontkean
Officer Mike Danko .... Sam Melville
Jill Danko .... Kate Jackson
Lt. Eddie Ryker ...... Gerald S. O'Loughlin
Officer Chris Owens (1974–1976)
.... Bruce Fairbairn

Three wet-behind-the-ears rookies cops in a large Southern California city provided the focus on this series. The trio, variously fresh out of college, a government social program, and the Army, were dedicated to the new, more humane methods of law enforcement, which often put them at odds with their hard-nosed mentor, Lt. Ryker. The combination of their youthful enthusiasm and Ryker's experienced guidance helped mold them into effective officers. The only married one of the three was Mike, whose wife Jill was a registered nurse. In 1974 a cast change occurred when Willie was replaced by Chris Owens, a new recruit.

ROOM FOR ONE MORE

Situation Comedy

FIRST TELECAST: *January 27, 1962*

LAST TELECAST: *September 22, 1962*

BROADCAST HISTORY:

Jan 1962–Sep 1962, ABC Sat 8:00–8:30

CAST:

George Rose .... Andrew Duggan
Anna Rose .... Peggy McCay
Flip Rose .... Ronnie Dapo
Laurie Rose .... Carol Nicholson
Mary Rose .... Anna Carri
Jeff Rose .... Timmy Rooney
Ruth .... Maxine Stuart

This family comedy was about a middle-class couple, George and Anna Rose, their two natural children, Flip and Laurie, and their adopted children Mary and Jeff (the latter played by Mickey Rooney's son Timmy). The Roses' easygoing ways and sympathy for children in general kept bringing other homeless waifs in and out of the household as well—they always had "room for one more." Tramp was the family dog, and Ruth a family friend (Jack Albertson appeared briefly as her husband).

Adapted from the autobiography of Anna Perrott Rose, which was also made into a 1952 movie (originally titled *Room for One More,* later retitled *The Easy Way*) starring Cary Grant.

ROOM 222

School Drama

FIRST TELECAST: *September 17, 1969*

LAST TELECAST: *January 11, 1974*

BROADCAST HISTORY:

Sep 1969–Jan 1971, ABC Wed 8:30–9:00
Jan 1971–Sep 1971, ABC Wed 8:00–8:30
Sep 1971–Jan 1974, ABC Fri 9:00–9:30

CAST:

Pete Dixon .... Lloyd Haynes
Liz McIntyre .... Denise Nicholas
Seymour Kaufman .... Michael Constantine
Alice Johnson .... Karen Valentine
Richie Lane (1969–1971) ..... Howard Rice
Helen Loomis .... Judy Strangis
Jason Allen .... Heshimu
Al Cowley (1969–1971) . Pendrant Netherly
Bernie (1970–1974) .... David Jolliffe
Pam (1970–1972) .... Ta-Tanisha
Larry (1971–1973) .... Eric Laneuville

Schoolroom drama about Pete Dixon, a black history teacher in an integrated big-city high school. An idealist, Pete instilled his students at Walt Whitman High with gentle lessons in tolerance and understanding. The number of his home room was 222, but wherever he went he was surrounded by a cluster of kids. They loved him for his easygoing manner and willingness to side with them when he knew they were being short-changed by the system. Seymour Kaufman was the cool, slightly sarcastic principal, Liz McIntyre Pete's girl friend and a school counselor, and Alice Johnson an exuberant student teacher (in the second season she was promoted to full-fledged English teacher). The rest of the regulars were students.

The program was highly regarded for tackling current problems relevant to today's youth (prejudice, drugs, dropping out, etc.) and it received many awards and commendations from educational and civil rights groups. Its sense of reality was heightened by the fact that it was based on, and partially filmed at, 3000-student Los Angeles High School.

ROOTS

Drama

FIRST TELECAST: *January 23, 1977*

LAST TELECAST: *September 10, 1978*

BROADCAST HISTORY:

Jan 1977, ABC 9:00–11:00 or 10:00–11:00 each night for eight days
Sep 1978, ABC 8:00–11:00 or 9:00–11:00 each night for five days

CAST:

Kunta Kinte (as a boy) .... LeVar Burton
Kunta Kinte (Toby; adult) ...... John Amos
Binta .... Cecily Tyson
Omoro .... Thalmus Rasulala
Nyo Boto .... Maya Angelou
Kadi Touray .... O. J. Simpson
the wrestler .... Ji-Tu Cumbuka
Kintango .... Moses Gunn
Brima Cesay .... Harry Rhodes
Fanta .... Ren Woods
Fanta (later) .... Beverly Todd
Capt. Davies .... Edward Asner
Third Mate Slater .... Ralph Waite
Gardner .... William Watson
Fiddler .... Louis Gossett, Jr.
John Reynolds .... Lorne Greene
Mrs. Reynolds .... Lynda Day George
Ames .... Vic Morrow
Carrington .... Paul Shenar
Dr. William Reynolds .... Robert Reed
Bell .... Madge Sinclair
Grill .... Gary Collins
The Drummer .... Raymond St. Jacques
Tom Moore .... Chuck Connors
Missy Anne .... Sandy Duncan
Noah .... Lawrence-Hilton Jacobs
Ordell .... John Schuck
Kizzy .... Leslie Uggams
Squire James .... Macdonald Carey
Mathilda .... Olivia Cole
Mingo .... Scatman Crothers
Stephen Bennett .... George Hamilton
Mrs. Moore .... Carolyn Jones
Sir Eric Russell .... Ian McShane
Sister Sara .... Lillian Randolph
Sam Bennett .... Richard Roundtree
Chicken George .... Ben Vereen
Evan Brent .... Lloyd Bridges
Tom .... Georg Stanford Brown
Ol' George Johnson .... Brad Davis
Lewis .... Billy Hicks
Jemmy Brent .... Doug McClure
Irene .... Lynne Moody
Martha .... Lane Binkley
Justin .... Burl Ives

PRODUCER:

Stan Margulies

ADAPTED FOR TV BY:

William Blinn

Under the usual definition of a "series," *Roots* would not be included in this book—it was really an extended special. But the fact that it was the most-watched dramatic show in TV history, and its considerable impact on viewers, warrant an exception.

Roots' success was unprecedented. Approximately 100-million viewers saw the concluding installment, and it must be considered an event of considerable magnitude when nearly half the entire population of the U.S. can be assembled in front of its TV sets to watch a single dramatic presentation. No one, not even ABC, was prepared for anything that big. In fact, one of the reasons given for scheduling *Roots* on eight consecutive nights was that if it were a flop it would be over with quickly.

Alex Haley's novel of his own roots was 12 years in the writing. Its story began in 1750 in Gambia, West Africa, with the birth of Kunta Kinte to Binta and Omoro. Kunta grew up free and happy until, at the age of 17, he was taken prisoner by white slave catchers and shipped to America on a vessel commanded by the conscience-stricken Capt. Davies and his cruel third mate, Slater. Kunta remained rebellious for the rest of his life, making several attempts to escape and eventually losing a foot in the process. Then his daughter Kizzy was born. She grew to womanhood and bore a son (after she was raped by her owner), later to be named Chicken George. Chicken George was sent into servitude in England in the 1820s, as rumors of slave rebellions swept the American South. Thirty years later he returned, an old but free man, only to find America on the brink of Civil War. George's son Tom, a blacksmith, was recruited into the Army, but after emancipation found that freedom meant little in a land of hooded nightriders and economic exploitation. As the series ended, Tom—the great-grandson of Kunta Kinte—struck out to start a new life in Tennessee, and sow the roots for a better life for his free descendants.

The TV *Roots* was daring in many ways, including its massive historical sweep, its often mature content (including bare breasts in the early African segments), and its scheduling over a full week. However, it was not for rape or nudity that *Roots* received most of its criticism, but for distortion of history, particularly its sensationalized version of black-white relations in the slave era (one critic called it ABC's "shackles, whips and lust" view of slavery). It was pointed out that much of cruelty attributed to racism was in reality the cruelty of the 18th and 19th centuries, which affected whites fully as much as it did blacks; and that the slave trade rested largely on African blacks selling their own brothers into slavery, not on "white slave parties."

Whether or not the TV *Roots* was pseudo-history, it reached and affected an unprecedented audience, and its effect on future TV programming is likely to be profound. That kind of success is not ignored by TV's programmers.

Roots was repeated in September 1978, again as a one week special.

ROSCOE KARNS, INSIDE DETECTIVE

see *Rocky King, Inside Detective*

ROSEMARY CLOONEY LUX SHOW, THE

see *Lux Show Starring Rosemary Clooney, The*

ROSETTI AND RYAN

Lawyer

FIRST TELECAST: *September 22, 1977*
LAST TELECAST: *November 10, 1977*
BROADCAST HISTORY:

Sep 1977–Nov 1977, NBC Thu 10:00–11:00

CAST:

Joseph Rosetti .... Tony Roberts
Frank Ryan .... Squire Fridell
Jessica Hornesby .... Jane Elliott
Judge Hardcastle .... Dick O'Neill
Judge Black .... William Marshall

They were both single and good-looking, they were both attorneys (in fact, partners), but they had very different personalities. Rosetti had been born to the comfortable life of an upper-middle-class family. He wore the finest clothes, considered himself a gourmet, and was a smooth operator around attractive women. He was also brash, arrogant, and egocentric. Ryan was a former cop who had worked his way through law school at night. He was introspective, modest, and a dogged, persistent researcher—the perfect complement to his glib, impulsive partner. The combination was highly successful, usually to the consternation of Assistant District Attorney Jessica Hornesby, their frequent opponent in the courtroom.

ROUGH RIDERS, THE

Western

FIRST TELECAST: *October 2, 1958*
LAST TELECAST: *September 24, 1959*
BROADCAST HISTORY:
Oct 1958–Sep 1959, ABC Thu 9:30–10:00
CAST:
Capt. Jim Flagg .... Kent Taylor
Lt. Kirby .... Jan Merlin
Sgt. Buck Sinclair .... Peter Whitney

At the end of the Civil War three soldiers, each of whom planned to move west in search of a new life, joined forces for mutual companionship and protection on the trip. Jim Flagg and Buck Sinclair were veterans of the Union Army, and Lt. Kirby had served the Confederacy. As they crossed the country they encountered numerous bands of outlaws, renegade Indians, and deserters from both armies.

ROUNDERS, THE

Comedy Western
FIRST TELECAST: *September 6, 1966*
LAST TELECAST: *January 3, 1967*
BROADCAST HISTORY:
Sep 1966–Jan 1967, ABC Tue 8:30–9:00
CAST:
Ben Jones .... Ron Hayes
Howdy Lewis .... Patrick Wayne
Jim Ed Love .... Chill Wills
Ada .... Bobbi Jordan
Sally .... Janis Hansen

Robust comedy, set in the contemporary West. Ben Jones and Howdy Lewis were two rowdy, fun-loving cowpokes who found themselves hogtied and in debt to unscrupulous Jim Ed Love, owner of a vast ranch and reputedly the second richest man in Texas (Andy Devine made a single guest appearance as Honest John Denton, the first richest man). Jim Ed, a fast-talking wheeler-dealer, dressed in custom-tailored white cowboy suits and rode the range in a souped-up station wagon, while Ben and Howdy had to put up with a mean old roan named Old Fooler. They got some relief at the Longhorn Cafe in the nearby town of Hi Lo, which they tore up every Saturday night, with the assistance of their girl friends Ada and Sally.

Based on the novel by Max Evans, which was made into a 1965 movie co-starring Chill Wills in the same role he played on TV.

ROUTE 66

Adventure
FIRST TELECAST: *October 7, 1960*
LAST TELECAST: *September 18, 1964*
BROADCAST HISTORY:
Oct 1960–Sep 1964, CBS Fri 8:30–9:30
CAST:
Tod Stiles .... Martin Milner
Buz Murdock (1960–1963) . George Maharis
Linc Case (1963–1964) ...... Glenn Corbett

Tod Stiles and Buz Murdock were two young men who traveled around the country together in Tod's Corvette in search of adventure. They came from radically different backgrounds but had become good friends. Tod was born to wealth, but when his father had died unexpectedly, he discovered that most of the money was gone. Buz had grown up in the jungle of New York's Hell's Kitchen and had been employed by Tod's father prior to his death. The series was filmed on location as they crisscrossed the United States in their destinationless travels, meeting all sorts of people and getting into all kinds of situations; romantic, dangerous, amusing, etc. George Maharis left the series in November 1962, while production was still in progress for the 1962–1963 season, because of the lingering effects of a case of hepatitis. He was seen intermittently in episodes aired through March 1963. In the episode aired on March 22, 1963, Linc Case, who was to take over as Tod's traveling companion, was introduced. He was a Vietnam War hero from Houston who returned to the United States unsure of what he was looking for in life. He joined Tod while trying to find himself and stayed with him throughout the remainder of the series.

Nelson Riddle's recording of his theme music for the show, a driving jazz melody which sounded like the open road, was on the hit parade in 1962.

ROWAN AND MARTIN SHOW, THE

see *Dean Martin Summer Show, The*

ROWAN & MARTIN'S LAUGH-IN

Comedy Variety
FIRST TELECAST: *January 22, 1968*
LAST TELECAST: *May 14, 1973*
BROADCAST HISTORY:
Jan 1968–May 1973, NBC Mon 8:00–9:00 (OS)
REGULARS:
Dan Rowan

Dick Martin
Gary Owens
Ruth Buzzi
Judy Carne (1968–1970)
Eileen Brennan (1968)
Goldie Hawn (1968–1970)
Arte Johnson (1968–1971)
Henry Gibson (1968–1971)
Roddy-Maude Roxby (1968)
Jo Anne Worley (1968–1970)
Larry Hovis (1968, 1971–1972)
Pigmeat Markham (1968–1969)
Charlie Brill (1968–1969)
Dick Whittington (1968–1969)
Mitzi McCall (1968–1969)
Chelsea Brown (1968–1969)
Alan Sues (1968–1972)
Dave Madden (1968–1969)
Teresa Graves (1969–1970)
Jeremy Lloyd (1969–1970)
Pamela Rodgers (1969–1970)
Byron Gilliam (1969–1970)
Ann Elder (1970–1972)
Lily Tomlin (1970–1973)
Johnny Brown (1970–1972)
Dennis Allen (1970–1973)
Nancy Phillips (1970–1971)
Barbara Sharma (1970–1972)
Harvey Jason (1970–1971)
Richard Dawson (1971–1973)
Moosie Drier (1971–1973)
Patti Deutsch (1972–1973)
Jud Strunk (1972–1973)
Brian Bressler (1972–1973)
Sarah Kennedy (1972–1973)
Donna Jean Young (1972–1973)
Tod Bass (1972–1973)
Lisa Farringer (1972–1973)
Willie Tyler & Lester (1972–1973)

Rowan & Martin's Laugh-In was one of TV's classics, one of those rare programs which was not only an overnight sensation, but was highly innovative, created a raft of new stars, and started trends in comedy which other programs would follow. In some ways, it was not original at all, being a cross between Olsen & Johnson's *Helzapoppin'* (which in turn traced its lineage to the frantic, knockabout comedy of the Keystone Cops) and the highly topical satire of *That Was the Week That Was*. But *Laugh-In* crystallized a kind of contemporary, fast-paced, unstructured comedy "happening" that was exactly what an agitated America wanted in 1968.

Laugh-In was first seen as a one-time special on September 9, 1967. It was such an enormous hit that it inevitably led to a series premiering the following January. Its lightning-fast pace took full advantage of the technical capabilities of television and videotape. Blackouts, sketches, one-liners, and cameo appearances by famous show-business celebrities and even national politicians were all edited into a frenetic whole. The regular cast was large and the turnover high, and of the 40 regulars who appeared in the series only four were with it from beginning to end—the two hosts, announcer Gary Owens, and Ruth Buzzi.

The essence of *Laugh-In* was *shtick*, a comic routine or trademark repeated over and over until it was closely associated with a performer. People love it, come to expect it, and talk about it the next morning after the show. All great comedians have at least one, but what was remarkable about *Laugh-In* was that it developed a whole repertoire of sight gags and catch phrases using little-known talent exclusively (though some of them became quite famous later). Among the favorites: Arte Johnson as the German soldier, peering out from behind a potted palm and murmuring, "Verrry interesting!"; Ruth Buzzi as the little old lady with an umbrella, forever wacking the equally decrepit old man who snuggled up beside her on a park bench; Lily Tomlin as the sarcastic, nasal telephone operator (even the phone company wanted to hire her to do commercials using that routine—she wouldn't); Gary Owens as the outrageously overmodulated announcer, facing the microphone, hand cupped to ear; Alan Sues as the grinning moron of a sports announcer; Goldie Hawn as the giggling dumb blonde, and so on.

Some of the devices of the show were the Cocktail Party, Letters to Laugh-In, The Flying Fickle Finger of Fate Award, Laugh-In Looks at the News (of the past, present, and future), Hollywood News with Ruth Buzzi, the gags written on the undulating body of a girl in a bikini, and the joke wall at the close of each show, in which cast members kept popping out of windows to throw each other one-liners—or a bucket of water.

Many catch phrases came out of the sketches and blackouts on *Laugh-In*, and some became national bywords. It is said that a foreign delegate at the United Nations once approached an American member of that organization to ask, in all seriousness, "I have heard a phrase in your country that I do not understand. What is it you mean by 'bippy'?" Besides "You bet your bippy," there were: "Sock it to me" (splash!), "Look that up in your Funk and Wagnalls," "Beautiful Downtown Burbank," and even "Here come de judge!"

The pace never let up. If it wasn't a short clip of a raincoated adult falling off a tricycle, it was a shot of Richard M. Nixon solemnly declaring "Sock it to me." It didn't even end at the closing credits, as jokes kept flying and, finally, one pair of hands was heard clapping until a station break forcibly took over.

Laugh-In went straight to the top of the TV ratings and was the number one program on the air for its first two full seasons, 1968–1970. It then began to drop off as the best talent left to pursue newfound careers, and finally ended its run in 1973.

ROY ROGERS & DALE EVANS SHOW, THE

Musical Variety

FIRST TELECAST: *September 29, 1962*

LAST TELECAST: *December 29, 1962*

BROADCAST HISTORY:

Sep 1962–Dec 1962, ABC Sat 7:30–8:30

HOSTS:

Roy Rogers & Dale Evans

REGULARS:

Pat Brady
Sons of the Pioneers
Kirby Buchanon
Kathy Taylor
Cliff Arquette (as Charley Weaver)
Ralph Carmichael Orchestra

This short-lived series featured "The King of the Cowboys" with his wife Dale Evans, plus regulars and guests in a very wholesome musical variety hour. Regulars included Roy's old sidekick Pat Brady, rodeo-rider-turned-singer Kirby Buchanon, folk singer Kathy Taylor, and comic Cliff Arquette. Circus and horseshow acts were also included.

ROY ROGERS SHOW, THE

Western

FIRST TELECAST: *December 30, 1951*

LAST TELECAST: *June 23, 1957*

BROADCAST HISTORY:

Dec 1951–Jun 1952, NBC Sun 6:30–7:00
Aug 1952–Jun 1957, NBC Sun 6:30–7:00

REGULARS:

Roy Rogers
Dale Evans
Pat Brady

THEME:

"Happy Trails to You," by Dale Evans

Singing Western movie actor Roy Rogers, who, ironically, was born and raised in Cincinnati, Ohio, struck gold as the most popular television cowboy of the early and mid-1950s. The "King of the Cowboys" was joined by his wife Dale Evans and bumbling sidekick Pat Brady in his fight for law and order in the contemporary West. In addition to the people, Roy's horse Trigger, dog Bullet, and Pat's cantankerous jeep Nellybelle were regular members of the cast around the ol' Double R Bar Ranch.

ROYAL PLAYHOUSE

see *DuMont Royal Theater*

ROYAL PLAYHOUSE

syndicated title for *Fireside Theater*

RUGGLES, THE

Situation Comedy

FIRST TELECAST: *November 3, 1949*

LAST TELECAST: *June 19, 1952*

BROADCAST HISTORY:

Nov 1949–Dec 1949, ABC Thu 9:30–10:00
Dec 1949–Mar 1950, ABC Fri 8:30–9:00
Apr 1950–Jun 1950, ABC Sun 10:00–10:30
Jun 1950–Aug 1950, ABC Thu 9:30–10:00
Sep 1950–Dec 1950, ABC Sun 6:30–7:00
Jan 1951–Mar 1951, ABC Mon 8:30–9:00
Mar 1951–Jun 1951, ABC Wed 8:00–8:30
Jun 1951–Sep 1951, ABC Fri 8:30–9:00
Oct 1951–Nov 1951, ABC Sat 7:00–7:30
Dec 1951–Jan 1952, ABC Sun 6:30–7:00
Jan 1952–Apr 1952, ABC Wed 9:00–9:30
Apr 1952–Jun 1952, ABC Thu 8:00–8:30

CAST:

Charlie Ruggles .... Himself
Mrs. Ruggles (early episodes)
.... Irene Tedrow
Mrs. Ruggles (later episodes)
.... Erin O'Brien-Moore

ALSO:

Margaret Kerry
Tommy Bernard
Judy Nugent
Jimmy Hawkins

Veteran Hollywood character actor Charlie Ruggles portrayed the harassed hubby in this early family comedy. His family, which was the source of Charlie's dilemma around the house, consisted of his wife, two teenagers (Sharon and Chuck), and two sub-teeners. The program originated from Hollywood and was seen in the East and Midwest via poor-quality kinescopes. That, plus the series' constant movement all over the ABC schedule, may have contributed to its failure to catch on.

RUN BUDDY RUN

Situation Comedy

FIRST TELECAST: *September 12, 1966*

LAST TELECAST: *January 2, 1967*

BROADCAST HISTORY:

Sep 1966–Jan 1967, CBS Mon 8:00–8:30

CAST:

Buddy Overstreet .... Jack Sheldon
Devere (Mr. D.) .... Bruce Gordon
Junior .... Jim Connell
Wendell .... Nick Georgiade
Harry .... Gregg Palmer

Buddy Overstreet was a very average person. He had made one mistake, however, which altered his entire life. While relaxing at a Turkish bath he accidentally overheard syndicate gangsters discussing a proposed rub-out. They realized that he had heard them and spent the rest of the season trying to capture him because he knew too much. They were not particularly adept at this and kept fouling it up. The front for their organization was Devere Enterprises, where Mr. Devere's son, Junior, proved to be inept at running either the legitimate or criminal side of the business.

RUN FOR YOUR LIFE

Adventure

FIRT TELECAST: *September 13, 1965*

LAST TELECAST: *September 11, 1968*

BROADCAST HISTORY:

Sep 1965–Sep 1967, NBC Mon 10:00–11:00
Sep 1967–Sep 1968, NBC Wed 10:00–11:00

CAST:

Paul Bryan .... Ben Gazzara

Paul Bryan was a very successful 35-year-old lawyer who had everything a man could want—intelligence, good looks, popularity, and money. He also had something that nobody wants—an incurable disease. Told by doctors that he had, at most, two years to live, Paul closed down his law practice and started traveling around the world in the hope of cramming a lifetime of adventure and excitement into the limited time he had left. With money no problem, he went from one exotic and fascinating place to another and encountered all sorts of people. He had come to terms with his problem and, rather than running away from life, he ran toward it. The show ran three years, even though he supposedly had only two years to live, and he was still running when it faded from the screen in 1968. The series was based on an episode of *Kraft Suspense Theater*, which was telecast in April 1965.

RUSS HODGES' SCOREBOARD

Sports News

FIRST TELECAST: *April 14, 1948*

LAST TELECAST: *May 22, 1949*

BROADCAST HISTORY:

Apr 1948–Jan 1949, DUM Mon–Fri 6:30–6:45
Jan 1949–Mar 1949, DUM Mon–Fri 6:45–7:00
Mar 1949–May 1949, DUM Mon–Fri 7:45–8:00

REPORTER:

Russ Hodges

Latest news from the world of sports. Game scores, observations and commentary by Russ Hodges, and his interviews with sports celebrities were all part of this nightly show.

RUSS MORGAN SHOW, THE

Music

FIRST TELECAST: *July 7, 1956*

LAST TELECAST: *September 1, 1956*

BROADCAST HISTORY:

Jul 1956–Sep 1956, CBS Sat 9:30–10:00

REGULARS:

Russ Morgan
Helen O'Connell

Bandleader Russ Morgan was the host and star of this live summer music show that featured the singing of Helen O'Connell.

RUTHIE ON THE TELEPHONE

Comedy

FIRST TELECAST: *August 7, 1949*

LAST TELECAST: *November 5, 1949*

BROADCAST HISTORY:

Aug 1949–Sep 1949, CBS Mon/Tue/Thu/Sat/Sun 7:55–8:00
Sep 1949–Nov 1949, CBS Mon/Tue/Thu/Sat 7:55–8:00

CAST:

Ruthie .... Ruth Gilbert
Richard .... Philip Reed

Ruthie was a young lady much in love with Richard, a man she had never met and who was not interested in meeting her. Regardless, every night for five minutes she tried to inspire Richard over the phone while he tried to avoid her. Split-screen technique was used in this live show, enabling the viewer to see both Ruthie at home and Richard at his desk at the advertising agency where he worked. The idea for this series originated on the Robert Q. Lewis radio program, on which Ruthie's telephone adventures had been featured for about a year.

S.R.O. PLAYHOUSE

Dramatic Anthology

FIRST TELECAST: *May 11, 1957*
LAST TELECAST: *September 7, 1957*
BROADCAST HISTORY:

May 1957–Sep 1957, CBS Sat 9:30–10:00

The dramas telecast in this summer series were all reruns of episodes that had originally aired on *Schlitz Playhouse.*

S.S. HOLIDAY

see *Starlit Time*

S.W.A.T.

Police

FIRST TELECAST: *February 24, 1975*
LAST TELECAST: *June 29, 1976*
BROADCAST HISTORY:

Feb 1975–Aug 1975, ABC Mon 9:00–10:00
Aug 1975–Apr 1976, ABC Sat 9:00–10:00
Apr 1976–Jul 1976, ABC Tue 9:00–10:00

CAST:

Lt. Dan "Hondo" Harrelson
.... Steve Forrest
Sgt. David "Deacon" Kay .... Rod Perry
Officer Jim Street .... Robert Urich
Officer Dominic Luca .... Mark Shera
Officer T. J. McCabe .... James Coleman
Betty Harrelson .... Ellen Weston
Matt Harrelson .... Michael Harland
Kevin Harrelson .... David Adams

THEME:

"Theme from 'S.W.A.T.'," by Barry DeVorzon

This series brought army-style warfare to big-city police work. S.W.A.T. stood for *S*pecial *W*eapons *A*nd *T*actics, whose job it was to tackle situations—usually violent ones—that line police couldn't handle, with whatever weaponry was necessary. Vietnam veterans all, the S.W.A.T. squad dressed in semi-military attire, and were organized along the lines of a front-line patrol. Capt. Harrelson was the C.O., Sgt. Kay the observer and communicator, Jim the team scout, Dominic the marksman, and T.J. the backup. Often the young junior officers were a bit too eager to use their firepower, and Capt. Harrelson had to hold them back. But as often as not, it was blast away. The team traveled in a specially equipped van, since tanks don't work too well in urban locales.

Filmed in Southern California, and based, loosely at least, on real-life S.W.A.T. teams formed in several large American cities following the disturbances of the late 1960s.

SABER OF LONDON

see *Mark Saber*

SADDLE PAL CLUB

see *Movies—Prior to 1961*

SAINT, THE

Mystery Adventure

FIRST TELECAST: *May 21, 1967*
LAST TELECAST: *September 12, 1969*
BROADCAST HISTORY:

May 1967–Sep 1967, NBC Sun 10:00–11:00
Feb 1968–Sep 1968, NBC Sat 7:30–8:30
Apr 1969–Sep 1969, NBC Fri 10:00–11:00

CAST:

Simon Templar (The Saint)
.... Roger Moore

Simon Templar was a dashing figure, urbane, sophisticated, and independently wealthy. He was also a crook, but a gentlemanly, modern-day Robin Hood–type crook who took on the causes of those who had been robbed, swindled, or in other ways taken advantage of by their fellow man. He pursued his quest for adventure throughout Europe and the world. His calling card, a stick figure with a halo (representing a "saint"), was equally well known in society circles and among the police of six continents. The police generally regarded him as a mixed blessing, for although he was dedicated to justice, he often used extralegal means to achieve his ends.

The Saint had long been a popular character in fiction, first in the best-selling mystery novels of Leslie Charteris and later in a series of movies and a radio show in the 1930s and 1940s. This television version was produced in England and was first seen in syndication in the U.S. in the early 1960s. It made its network television debut, with all new episodes, in 1967.

SAINTS AND SINNERS

Newspaper Drama

FIRST TELECAST: *September 17, 1962*

LAST TELECAST: *January 28, 1963*

BROADCAST HISTORY:

Sep 1962–Jan 1963, NBC Mon 8:30–9:30

CAST:

Nick Alexander .... Nick Adams
Mark Grainger .... John Larkin
Lizzie Hogan .... Barbara Rush
Klugie .... Richard Erdman
Dave Tabak .... Robert F. Simon
Polly .... Sharon Farrell
Charlie .... Nicky Blair

Newspaper action-drama centering on Nick Alexander, crusading reporter for the *New York Bulletin.* Also seen were editor Mark Grainger, staff photographer Klugie, copyeditor Dave Tabak, and Washington correspondent Lizzie Hogan.

SALLY

Situation Comedy

FIRST TELECAST: *September 15, 1957*

LAST TELECAST: *March 30, 1958*

BROADCAST HISTORY:

Sep 1957–Mar 1958, NBC Sun 7:30–8:00

CAST:

Sally Truesdale .... Joan Caulfield
Mrs. Myrtle Banford .... Marion Lorne
Bascomb Bleacher (1958) ..... Gale Gordon
Jim Kendall (1958) .... Johnny Desmond
Bascomb Bleacher, Jr. (1958)
.... Arte Johnson

When this series premiered, Sally Truesdale was a former department store salesgirl who had become the traveling companion of a wealthy widow named Myrtle Banford. The matronly Mrs. Banford was slightly wacky and always getting into scrapes of one sort or another as she and Sally moved from city to city around the world. When they returned home, in the February 16, 1958, episode, the format changed. Sally and Mrs. Banford spent most of their time helping to run the Banford-Bleacher Department Store, of which Mrs Banford was part owner. Added to the cast were Mr. Bleacher and his incompetent but lovable son, and Jim Kendall, an artist in the store's advertising department who became Sally's love interest.

SAM

Police Drama

FIRST TELECAST: *March 14, 1978*

LAST TELECAST: *April 18, 1978*

BROADCAST HISTORY:

Mar 1978–Apr 1978, CBS Tue 8:00–8:30

CAST:

Officer Mike Breen .... Mark Harmon
Captain Tom Clagett .... Len Wayland

An unusual variation on police series, *Sam* dealt with the exploits of a man-and-dog patrol car team of the Los Angeles Police Department. Mike Breen was the human half of the team and Sam was the yellow Labrador retriever police dog with which he was partnered. They patrolled in a police car designated Two-Henry-Six and made much use of Sam's uncommon skills in detection (his speed, maneuverability, and keen senses of smell and hearing) in their pursuit of criminals. Despite their record of performance, Mike's boss Capt. Clagett had his doubts about Sam's abilities as a crime fighter.

SAM BENEDICT

Lawyer

FIRST TELECAST: *September 15, 1962*

LAST TELECAST: *September 7, 1963*

BROADCAST HISTORY:

Sep 1962–Sep 1963, NBC Sat 7:30–8:30

CAST:

Sam Benedict .... Edmond O'Brien
Hank Tabor .... Richard Rust
Trudy Wagner .... Joan Tompkins

Courtroom drama series loosely based on the career of famed real-life trial lawyer Jacob W. "Jake" Erlich. Set in San Francisco, the program was notable for its intermixing of human-interest and comic elements with the standard lawyer-as-sleuth format. Hank was Sam's assistant, and Trudy his secretary.

The real Erlich served as "technical consultant" for the show.

SAM LEVENSON SHOW, THE

Comedy

FIRST TELECAST: *January 27, 1951*

LAST TELECAST: *June 10, 1952*

BROADCAST HISTORY:

Jan 1951–Jun 1951, CBS Sat 7:00–7:30
Feb 1952–Apr 1952, CBS Sun 6:30–7:00
Apr 1952–Jun 1952, CBS Tue 8:00–8:30

REGULAR:

Sam Levenson

Former schoolteacher Sam Levenson was the star and only regular performer in this informal comedy series aired live from New York. His gentle humor manifested itself in monologues about his growing up in New York, family life in general, and the experiences he had had as a teacher. A regular feature of the program was a visit by a guest celebrity and his or her child.

SAMMY DAVIS JR. SHOW, THE

Musical Variety

FIRST TELECAST: *January 7, 1966*

LAST TELECAST: *April 22, 1966*

BROADCAST HISTORY:

Jan 1966–Apr 1966, NBC Fri 8:30–9:30

REGULAR:

Sammy Davis Jr.

The multi-talented Sammy Davis Jr. starred in this short-lived musical variety series. In addition to regular guest stars, the series was a showcase for Mr. Davis as singer, dancer, comedian, musician, and impressionist. An unusual situation occurred at the start of this series. Mr. Davis had a prior commitment to do a special on ABC with the stipulation that he could not appear on television during the three weeks preceding the special. For that reason, he was seen on the premiere of *The Sammy Davis Jr. Show,* had substitute hosts for the three succeeding telecasts, and returned to the show on February 11. The substitute hosts were Johnny Carson, Sean Connery, and Jerry Lewis.

SAMMY KAYE SHOW, THE

Musical Variety

FIRST TELECAST: *June 11, 1950*

LAST TELECAST: *June 13, 1959*

BROADCAST HISTORY:

Jun 1950–Jul 1950, NBC Sun 8:00–8:30
Jul 1951–Jul 1952, CBS Sat 7:00–7:30
Aug 1953–Sep 1953, NBC Sat 8:00–8:30
Aug 1954–Jan 1955, ABC Thu 9:00–9:30
Sep 1958–Feb 1959, ABC Sat 10:00–10:30
Feb 1959–Apr 1959, ABC Thu 10:00–10:30
Apr 1959–Jun 1959, ABC Sat 10:00–10:30

HOST:

Sammy Kaye

REGULARS:

Tony Alamo (1950–1955)
Judy Johnson (1950)
Barbara Benson (1951–1952)
Peggy Powers (1953)
Ray Michaels (1958–1959)
Lynn Roberts (1958–1959)
Susan Silo (1958–1959)
J. Blasingame Bond & the Dixieland Quartet (1958–1959)
Larry Ellis (1958–1959)
Hank Kanui (1958–1959)
Johnny McAfee (1958–1959)
Harry Reser (1958–1959)
The Kaydets
Sammy Kaye Choir

Bandleader Sammy Kaye first brought his swing-and-sway music to television in 1949, with two specials. He later appeared in several series during the 1950s, on various networks. Kaye's most famous trademark was his "So You Want to Lead a Band" audience-participation routine, which he had used for years in personal appearances and on radio, and it was also featured in most of his TV series. In it, Kaye chose half a dozen members of the studio audience to try their hands at bandleading. The band did exactly what the "leader's" baton indicated, sometimes with hilarious effect. The best bandleader was chosen by audience applause and awarded a prize. Kaye also provided straight entertainment with his orchestra, vocalists, and guests, and often led a community sing. He ended each program with an inspirational poem.

The various Sammy Kaye series, though essentially similar in format, went under a number of titles over the years. The 1950 edition was called *So You Want to Lead a Band.* In 1951–1952 it was *The Sammy Kaye Variety Show,* in 1953 *The Sammy Kaye Show* and in 1954–1955 *So You Want to Lead a Band.* The 1958 series was first called *Sammy Kaye's Music from Manhattan* (the sponsor was Manhattan shirts), then in January 1959 switched to *The Sammy Kaye Show* and in April 1959 to *Music from Manhattan.* You would never have known the difference by watching them.

SAN FRANCISCO BEAT

syndicated title for *Lineup, The*

SAN FRANCISCO INTERNATIONAL AIRPORT

Suspense Drama

FIRST TELECAST: *October 28, 1970*

LAST TELECAST: *August 25, 1971*

BROADCAST HISTORY:

Oct 1970–Dec 1970, NBC Wed 10:00–11:00

Mar 1971–Aug 1971, NBC Wed 10:00–11:00

CAST:

Jim Conrad ....Lloyd Bridges
Bob Hatten ....Clu Gulager
June ....Barbara Werle

San Francisco International Airport attempted to portray the problems and challenges involved in running one of the larger airports in the nation, and probably the world. "SFX" employed 35,000 workers, and 15 million passengers used it annually. Jim Conrad was the airport manager, Bob Hatten its chief of security, and June was Mr. Conrad's secretary. Real problems in airport life were depicted—mechanical crises, demonstrations, security issues, etc. *San Francisco International Airport* was one of four elements in the NBC series *Four in One*. Each of the elements aired for a six-week period in the first part of the 1970–1971 TV season and the reruns were aired on a rotating basis.

SAN PEDRO BEACH BUMS, THE

Situation Comedy

FIRST TELECAST: *September 19, 1977*

LAST TELECAST: *December 19, 1977*

BROADCAST HISTORY:

Sep 1977–Dec 1977, ABC Mon 8:00–9:00

CAST:

Buddy ....Christopher Murney
Stuf ....Stuart Pankin
Dancer ....John Mark Robinson
Moose ....Darryl McCullough
Boychick ....Chris De Rose
Louise ....Louise Hoven
Suzi ....Susan Mullen
Margie ....Lisa Reeves
Ralphie ....Christoff St. John
Julie ....Nancy Morgan

Knockabout comedy about five carefree young "beach bums" in sunny California, living on a houseboat called "Our Boat." The five boys, who had been buddies since their high school days, were the ever-confident Buddy, self-proclaimed leader of the group; the shy and nervous Dancer (so named because he couldn't sit still); Stuf, a compulsive eater who believed that heavy is beautiful; the muscular but very gentle Moose; and Boychick, the beach bums' answer to Clark Gable.

SANDY DREAMS

Children's Variety

FIRST TELECAST: *October 7, 1950*

LAST TELECAST: *December 2, 1950*

BROADCAST HISTORY:

Oct 1950–Dec 1950, ABC Sat 7:00–7:30

A musical fantasy in which Sandy, an eight-year-old girl, dreamt of adventure and travel. As she drifted off to sleep viewers were transported along with her to a program of sketches and songs and dances, performed by a changing cast of youngsters. Previously seen as a local program in Los Angeles.

SANDY DUNCAN SHOW, THE

Situation Comedy

FIRST TELECAST: *September 17, 1972*

LAST TELECAST: *December 31, 1972*

BROADCAST HISTORY:

Sep 1972–Dec 1972, CBS Sun 8:30–9:00

CAST:

Sandy Stockton ....Sandy Duncan
Bert Quinn ....Tom Bosley
Kay Fox ....Marian Mercer
Alex Lembeck ....M. Emmet Walsh
Hilary ....Pam Zarit
Ben Hampton ....Eric Christmas

Sandy Stockton was a cute young woman working for Quinn & Cohen, a small advertising agency. She lived in an apartment building where two of her neighbors, Kay and Alex, were also close friends. Alex was a somewhat overprotective motorcycle cop who was worried about what could happen to a young single girl living alone. Sandy was always trying to help people out and frequently got into trouble because of it.

The character of Sandy Stockton had previously appeared in Miss Duncan's 1971 series *Funny Face*, which was no more successful than this attempt.

SANDY STRONG

Children's

FIRST TELECAST: *September 25, 1950*

LAST TELECAST: *March 23, 1951*

BROADCAST HISTORY:

Sep 1950–Mar 1951, ABC Mon–Fri 6:15–6:30

CAST:

Sandy Strong and:
Mr. Mack (1950) ....Ray Suber
Mr. Mack (1950–1951) ....Forrest Lewis

Children's program from Chicago.

SANFORD AND SON

Situation Comedy

FIRST TELECAST: *January 14, 1972*
LAST TELECAST: *September 2, 1977*
BROADCAST HISTORY:

Jan 1972–Sep 1977, NBC Fri 8:00–8:30
Apr 1976–Aug 1976, NBC Wed 9:00–9:30

CAST:

Fred Sanford ....Redd Foxx
Lamont Sanford ....Demond Wilson
Melvin (1972) ....Slappy White
Bubba ....Don Bexley
Officer Swanhauser (1972) ....Noam Pitlik
Officer Smith (Smitty) (1972–1976) .... Hal Williams
Julio Fuentes (1972–1975) .... Gregory Sierra
Rollo Larson ....Nathaniel Taylor
Aunt Esther (1973–1977) ...LaWanda Page
Grady Wilson (1973–1977) .... Whitman Mayo
Donna Harris ....Lynn Hamilton
Officer Hoppy (1974–1976) ... Howard Platt
Ah Chew (1974–1975) ....Pat Morita
Janet (1976–1977) ....Marlene Clark
Woody (1976–1977) ....Raymond Allen

PRODUCER:

Norman Lear

Fred Sanford was a 65-year-old Los Angeles junk dealer whose 34-year-old son Lamont was his partner, a situation that Lamont was not always happy with. At his advanced age, Fred was very happy with his little business and the marginal income it provided him. Lamont, on the other hand, was looking to better himself by getting out of the junk business and trying something more challenging and, hopefully, more lucrative. Fred, whose wife Elizabeth had died some years before, would do anything to keep his son from deserting him and the business. Every time Lamont threatened to leave, Fred would fake a heart attack and start moaning, "I'm coming, Elizabeth, I'm coming." Lamont wasn't really fooled by his father's machinations but did love him and, despite what he said about his future, really wouldn't have left the old man or the business.

Sanford and Son was producer Norman Lear's second major hit (*All in the Family*, was the first) and, like *All in the Family*, was based on a successful British TV comedy. *Sanford and Son's* source was called *Steptoe and Son*. *Sanford and Son* was an instantaneous hit and ranked among the top ten programs throughout its run. Fred had a steady girl friend in Nurse Donna Harris, whom he was always promising to marry, and was constantly at odds with Aunt Esther, who ran the Sanford Arms, a run-down rooming house that was located next to the junkyard. Early in 1976 Lamont found a serious romantic interest in Janet, a divorcee with a young son, and they became engaged at the end of the 1975–1976 season. The marriage never took place, however, as the series left the air in the fall of 1977. Redd Foxx had committed himself to do a variety show for ABC and co-star Demond Wilson left the series in a dispute over his remuneration as the sole star of the series after Foxx's departure. With the two stars gone, NBC premiered *The Sanford Arms* (named after Aunt Esther's rooming house) in the fall of 1977, which featured most of the supporting players from *Sanford and Son*.

For a three-month period during the summer of 1976, a second episode of *Sanford and Son* was seen each week on Wednesday nights. The second episodes were reruns from previous seasons and titled *The Best of Sanford and Son*.

SANFORD ARMS, THE

Situation Comedy

FIRST TELECAST: *September 16, 1977*
LAST TELECAST: *October 14, 1977*
BROADCAST HISTORY:

Sep 1977–Oct 1977, NBC Fri 8:00–8:30

CAST:

Phil Wheeler ....Theodore Wilson
Aunt Esther ....LaWanda Page
Jeannie ....Bebe Drake-Hooks
Grady Wilson ....Whitman Mayo
Dolly Wilson ....Norma Miller
Bubba ....Don Bexley
Woody ....Raymond Allen
Angie Wheeler ....Tina Andrews
Nat Wheeler ....John Earl

In 1977 NBC's highly successful comedy *Sanford and Son* lost both of its stars—

Redd Foxx to a variety series of his own on ABC, and Demond Wilson because the producers would not meet his salary demands. With most of the supporting players still around, however, *The Sanford Arms* took its place. The new lead character was Phil Wheeler, a widower with two teenage children. He had made a down payment on the entire Sanford property—house, junkyard, and rooming house—and attempted to turn the latter into a successful residential hotel. With Fred and Lamont Sanford having moved to Arizona, Fred's sister-in-law Esther was left to watch over the property and collect the monthly mortgage payments. Also carried over from the *Sanford and Son* cast of characters were Esther's husband Woody, Fred's friend Grady (who had married Dolly), and Bubba, who worked at the Sanford Arms as both bellboy and maintenance man. Newcomers to the cast in addition to Phil Wheeler were his children Angie and Nat, and his girl friend Jeannie.

If anything proved more difficult than getting customers for the hotel, it was finding an audience for the series. The attempt to salvage the series without its two departed stars was a total failure and it lasted less than a month.

SARA

Western

FIRST TELECAST: *February 13, 1976*

LAST TELECAST: *July 30, 1976*

BROADCAST HISTORY:

Feb 1976–Jul 1976, CBS Fri 8:00–9:00

CAST:

Sara Yarnell ....Brenda Vaccaro
Emmet Ferguson ....Bert Kramer
Martin Pope ....Albert Stratton
Claude Barstow ....William Phipps
George Bailey ....William Wintersole
Julia Bailey ....Mariclare Costello
Martha Higgins ....Louise Latham
Georgie Bailey ....Kraig Metzinger
Debbie Higgins ....Debbie Lytton
Emma Higgins ....Hallie Morgan

Set in the frontier town of Independence, Colorado, in the 1870s, *Sara* was the story of a strong-willed young schoolteacher who had given up a dull, predictable existence in the East for the challenge of the West. A fighter, Sara battled ignorance and prejudice, to the horror of many of the more conservative townspeople who had expected a passive "schoolmarm" for their children. Her actions drew mixed reviews from the school board members Emmett Ferguson, Claude Barstow, and George Bailey; the approval of newspaper editor Martin Pope and her friend Julia Bailey; and the disapproval of her landlady, Martha Higgins. Most important to Sara, however, was the fact that she had the endorsement and enthusiastic interest of her students in the one-room school where she was the only teacher.

SARGE

Drama

FIRST TELECAST: *September 21, 1971*

LAST TELECAST: *January 11, 1972*

BROADCAST HISTORY:

Sep 1971–Nov 1971, NBC Tue 8:30–9:30
Nov 1971–Jan 1972, NBC Tue 7:30–8:30

CAST:

Father Samuel Cavanaugh (Sarge)
.......................George Kennedy
Valerie ....Sallie Shockley
Kenji Takichi ....Harold Sakata
Barney Verick ....Ramon Bieri

Set in San Diego, *Sarge* was the story of Father Samuel Cavanaugh, a priest at St. Aloysius Parish. Father Cavanaugh had spent nine years as a member of the San Diego Police Department, part of the time as a homicide detective in the same area in which he was now a priest. He was known as "Sarge" because of his police background, which often helped him provide guidance to his parishioners in their struggle to cope with the problems of a metropolitan environment. The other members of the parish staff seen regularly were Kenji, the rectory cook, and Valerie, the parish secretary. Barney Berick, chief of detectives and long-time friend of Father Cavanaugh, often sought the priest's help when members of the parish were involved in criminal cases.

SATURDAY NIGHT AT THE GARDEN

Sports

FIRST TELECAST: *October 7, 1950*

LAST TELECAST: *March 31, 1951*

BROADCAST HISTORY:

Oct 1950–Mar 1951, DUM Sat 8:30–11:00

Back when Saturday night viewing was dominated by Sid Caesar and Imogene Coca's *Your Show of Shows* on NBC, DuMont offered this weekly program as an alternative to those who preferred sports. Aired live from New York City's Madison Square Garden, *Saturday Night at the Garden* presented whatever event was being staged there, in its entirety. The first three telecasts consisted of a rodeo at which Gene Autry was the guest star, with Don Russell functioning as emcee, and there was one week devoted to a horse show, but most of the remaining telecasts were of more conventional sporting contests. The majority of the broadcasts were basketball games, both professional and college, including the then prestigious NIT College Basketball Tournament, with Curt Gowdy and Don Dunphy doing the commentary. Several track meets were also aired in the spring.

Originally titled *Madison Square Garden*, the series' name was changed to *Saturday Night at the Garden* in November.

SATURDAY NIGHT DANCE PARTY

Variety

FIRST TELECAST: *June 7, 1952*
LAST TELECAST: *August 30, 1952*
BROADCAST HISTORY:
Jun 1952–Jul 1952, NBC Sat 9:30–10:30
Jul 1952–Aug 1952, NBC Sat 9:00–10:30
HOST:
Jerry Lester

This series was the 1952 summer replacement for *Your Show of Shows*. It was a comedy and music variety show that was hosted by comedian Jerry Lester. Each week his guests included a different name band and a number of variety acts.

SATURDAY NIGHT FIGHTS, THE

see *Boxing*

SATURDAY NIGHT HOLLYWOOD PALACE, THE

see *Hollywood Palace, The*

SATURDAY NIGHT JAMBOREE

Country Music

FIRST TELECAST: *December 4, 1948*
LAST TELECAST: *July 2, 1949*
BROADCAST HISTORY:
Dec 1948–Jan 1949, NBC Sat 8:00–9:00
Jan 1949–Apr 1949, NBC Sat 8:00–8:30
Apr 1949–Jul 1949, NBC Sat 9:30–10:00
EMCEE:
Elton Britt (1948)
Boyd Heath (1949)
REGULARS:
Chubby Chuck Roe, comic
Sophrony Garen, vocals
Ted Grant, violin
Eddie Howard, banjo
John Havens, guitar
Edwin Smith, accordion
Gabe Drake, bass

Country music program, with a heavy leavening of cornpone humor. Yodler Elton Britt was the original host, but he skedaddled after three telecasts and no other major stars from the Country field associated themselves with this New York–based program during its brief run.

SATURDAY NIGHT LIVE

see *NBC's Saturday Night Live*

SATURDAY NIGHT LIVE WITH HOWARD COSELL

Variety

FIRST TELECAST: *September 20, 1975*
LAST TELECAST: *January 17, 1976*
BROADCAST HISTORY:
Sep 1975–Jan 1976, ABC Sat 8:00–9:00
EMCEE:
Howard Cosell
ORCHESTRA:
Conducted by Elliot Lawrence
"EXECUTIVE IN CHARGE OF COMEDY":
Alan King

This is the kind of program ABC used to put on before it became a big-league network. Howard Cosell, the acerbic sportscaster who had been a regular for years on *Monday Night Football*, was chosen as host apparently on the dubious premise that familiarity equals popularity. Polls showed him to be one of the best-known personalities in all of television. More people also said that they couldn't stand him than practically anyone else in TV.

He presided over this variety hour with awkward unease and, despite the presence of all sorts of top-name talent, the whole affair had a very amateurish air to it (Ed Sullivan, from whose old theater *Saturday Night Live* originated, was awkward too, but at least he sounded like he knew show business inside out—as indeed he did.)

The program was produced by the head of ABC Sports, and was telecast live, which was highly unusual for TV at the time. This was supposed to give it a greater "immediacy," but apparently viewers didn't notice the difference.

The premiere featured the U.S. TV debut of one of the hottest groups in popular music, the Bay City Rollers, live via satellite, who drove a teenybopper audience to frenzy. Frank Sinatra, John Denver, and John Wayne showed up, as did such sports stars as Evel Knievel, Alex Karras, Jimmy Connors, and Muhammad Ali and Joe Frazier, live by satellite from Manila on the eve of their championship fight. Cosell even offered Shamu the 5,000-pound killer whale, in a pickup from San Diego's Seaworld Oceanarium.

Howard tried hard—he even sang on one telecast, coached by Andy Williams—but bad is not good, and the show folded after half a season.

SATURDAY NIGHT REVUE

Variety

FIRST TELECAST: *June 6, 1953*
LAST TELECAST: *September 18, 1954*
BROADCAST HISTORY:
Jun 1953–Sep 1953, NBC Sat 9:00–10:30
Jun 1954–Sep 1954, NBC Sat 9:00–10:30
REGULARS:
Hoagy Carmichael (1953)
Eddie Albert (1954)
Ben Blue (1954)
Alan Young (1954)
Pat Carroll (1954)

This live series was the summer replacement for *Your Show of Shows* in 1953 and 1954. The 1953 edition starred Hoagy Carmichael, who opened the show from his penthouse apartment (a set) where he informally entertained his friends. In the same building was a nightclub called the Sky Room, to which Hoagy invited his guests to see the dinner show. The locale then switched to the nightclub set where the various acts on the evening's program performed. Emphasis was on introducing and showcasing new talent.

The 1954 version starred Eddie Albert and was more a straight revue. Albert would introduce the acts, sing, dance, and act in sketches himself. The guest artists, in addition to solo performances, also participated in sketches and production members with regular members of the cast. As in 1953, the focus was on showcasing new talent.

SATURDAY NIGHT REVUE, THE

see *Jack Carter Show, The* and *Your Show of Shows*

SATURDAY ROUNDUP

Western Anthology

FIRST TELECAST: *June 10, 1951*
LAST TELECAST: *September 1, 1951*
BROADCAST HISTORY:
Jun 1951–Sep 1951, NBC Sat 8:00–9:00
REGULAR:
Kermit Maynard

The stories of James Oliver Curwood were dramatized in this filmed Western anthology. Although Kermit Maynard starred in all of them, the character that he played varied from show to show.

Maynard was a onetime world's champion rodeo rider, and had appeared in many B-grade Westerns in the 1930s. He was the younger brother of cowboy star Ken Maynard.

SATURDAY SPORTS FINAL, THE

Sports News

FIRST TELECAST: *July 7, 1962*
LAST TELECAST: *October 6, 1962*
BROADCAST HISTORY:
Jul 1962–Oct 1962, ABC Sat 10:45–11:00
SPORTSCASTER:
Merle Harmon

Weekly wrap-up of news from the world of sports, including filmed highlights of major events. Harmon also interviewed guest sports celebrities.

SATURDAY SPORTS MIRROR

Sports News

FIRST TELECAST: *July 14, 1956*
LAST TELECAST: *September 15, 1956*
BROADCAST HISTORY:
Jul 1956–Sep 1956, CBS Sat 7:00–7:30
REGULARS:
Jack Drees
Bill Hickey

This summer sports series featured sportscasters Drees and Hickey with a summary of the week's sports news, interviews with sports celebrities, and occasional coverage of events in progress on the day of the telecast.

SATURDAY SQUARE

Variety

FIRST TELECAST: *January 7, 1950*
LAST TELECAST: *February 18, 1950*
BROADCAST HISTORY:
Jan 1950–Feb 1950, NBC Sat 8:00–9:00

Short-lived musical variety program which originated from Chicago and incorporated elements from *Chicago Jazz* and *Stud's Place,* which it replaced. In *Saturday Square,* a central figure, at first a policeman but in later telecasts a street-corner loafer, directed the viewer to different spots around the square where entertainment was being offered. The viewer was then transported to one of those spots: a musical rehearsal hall where a jam session was in progress, a stylish penthouse party, to Studs Terkel's pub, etc. Various talent appeared as guests.

SAWYER VIEWS HOLLYWOOD

Musical Variety

FIRST TELECAST: *June 29, 1951*
LAST TELECAST: *August 31, 1951*
BROADCAST HISTORY:
Jun 1951–Aug 1951, ABC Fri 10:00–10:30
EMCEE:
Hal Sawyer
REGULAR:
Gaylord Carter Trio

Musical variety program, featuring Hal Sawyer's interviews with Hollywood stars. Previously seen in daytime as *Hal in Hollywood.*

SAY IT WITH ACTING

Charades

FIRST TELECAST: *January 6, 1951*
LAST TELECAST: *February 22, 1952*
BROADCAST HISTORY:
Jan 1951–May 1951, NBC Sat 6:30–7:00
Aug 1951–Feb 1952, ABC Fri 7:30–8:00
TEAM CAPTAINS:
Maggi McNellis (1951)
Bud Collyer (1951)

Celebrity charades, featuring two teams of actors and actresses from current Broadway productions. Team captains for the NBC series were Maggi McNellis and Bud Collyer, while team members varied. Formerly a local program in New York, where it began in January 1949 under the title *Look Ma, I'm Acting,* then became *Act It Out,* and finally *Say It with Acting.*

SCHLITZ FILM FIRSTS

see *Movies—Prior to 1961*

SCHLITZ PLAYHOUSE OF STARS

Dramatic Anthology

FIRST TELECAST: *October 5, 1951*
LAST TELECAST: *March 27, 1959*
BROADCAST HISTORY:
Oct 1951–Mar 1952, CBS Fri 9:00–10:00
Apr 1952–Sep 1955, CBS Fri 9:00–9:30
Oct 1955–Mar 1959, CBS Fri 9:30–10:00
HOSTESS:
Irene Dunne (1952)

For eight seasons, the Schlitz Brewing Company sponsored a regular Friday night dramatic-anthology series on CBS. When it premiered in October 1951, under the title *Schlitz Playhouse of Stars,* it was an hour-long live drama from New York. The premiere telecast starred Helen Hayes and David Niven in "Not a Chance," and CBS heavily promoted the fact that Miss Hayes had signed an exclusive contract to perform only for this series. She did make two other appearances during 1951, but was never seen again on this show. The hour version produced some substantial dramas. Walter Hampden and Chester Morris starred in an adaptation of Herman Melville's *Billy Budd,* Dane Clark in Ernest Hemingway's "Fifty Grand," and Margaret Sullavan and Wendell Corey in a version of *Still Life,* the first Noel Coward play adapted for television.

In April 1952 the length of the plays presented was cut from an hour to 30 minutes and the literary merit of the material started to slip. There were still occasional plays like W. Somerset Maugham's "A String of Beads" starring Joan Caulfield and Tom Drake; and experiments like "Autumn in New York," a musical love story with Polly Bergen and Skip Homeier; but potboilers like "The Ordeal of Dr. Sutton" with Raymond Burr and Marilyn Erskine became progressively more common. For roughly six months, in the second half of 1952, Irene Dunne was on hand as a regular hostess, but that function was dropped in favor of letting one of the week's stars introduce the play, and then that too was phased out.

Although this was essentially a live series, filmed episodes started showing up in the summer of 1953, at first on an infrequent basis, then for the entire summer of 1954, and accounting for more than half of the telecasts during the 1954–1955 season. By the fall of 1956 there were no live episodes at all, and that November the title was shortened to *Schlitz Playhouse.* It remained weekly until the start of its last season, when it aired on an alternate-week basis with *Lux Playhouse.*

With a run of almost eight years, countless stars appeared on *Schlitz Playhouse of Stars.* Young James Dean made one of his rare television appearances as the star of "The Unlighted Road" in 1955, and in 1957 Gene Kelly made his television dramatic debut in "The Life You Save" with Agnes Moorehead and Janice Rule. Two episodes were turned into series—"The Restless Gun" starring John Payne and "A Tale of Wells Fargo" starring Dale Robertson—both Westerns aired during the 1956–1957 season. They turned up on NBC's lineup in the fall of 1957.

SCHOOL HOUSE

Comedy Variety

FIRST TELECAST: *January 18, 1949*

LAST TELECAST: *April 19, 1949*

BROADCAST HISTORY:

Jan 1949–Apr 1949, DUM Tue 9:00–9:30

EMCEE ("Teacher"):

Kenny Delmar

APPEARING:

Arnold Stang
Wally Cox
Tommy Dix
Betty Anne Nyman
Kenny Bowers
Maureen Cannon
Roger Price
Wendy Drew
Mary Ann Reeve
Aileen Stanley, Jr.
Russell Arms
Beverly Fite
Patty Adair
Buddy Hackett

Early television sometimes looked back into show-business history—*way* back—for material. Gus Edwards' "School Days" routine had been a sensation in vaudeville just after the turn of the century, producing such future stars as Georgie Jessel, Groucho Marx, Eleanor Powell, Walter Winchell, Eddie Cantor, Ray Bolger, and Mae Murray. Evidently DuMont felt that it might be a hit all over again for video viewers in 1949. The format was a comedy variety show set in a schoolhouse, with a constantly beset "teacher" as emcee and a class full of talented youngsters as "students" (plus some older acts). Arnold Stang and Wally Cox were among the comical students on this TV version, and such notable performers as Buddy Hackett and Russell Arms also appeared. Except for "teacher" Kenny Delmar, the cast was constantly changing and those listed above are a sampling of the talent that performed.

Also seen as a local New York program during 1948, under the title *School Days,* with Happy Felton as "teacher."

SCIENCE CIRCUS

Instruction

FIRST TELECAST: *July 4, 1949*

LAST TELECAST: *September 12, 1949*

BROADCAST HISTORY:

Jul 1949–Sep 1949, ABC Mon 8:30–9:00

HOST:

Bob Brown

Children's instructional program featuring Bob Brown in the role of an absent-minded science professor presenting scientific stunts and experiments in front of a studio audience. From Chicago.

SCOTLAND YARD

Police Anthology

FIRST TELECAST: *November 17, 1957*

LAST TELECAST: *October 3, 1958*

BROADCAST HISTORY:

Nov 1957–Mar 1958, ABC Sun 10:00–10:30
May 1958–Jun 1958, ABC Wed 9:30–10:00
Aug 1958–Oct 1958, ABC Fri 10:00–10:30

HOST:

Edgar Lustgarten

Filmed in England, this series presented dramas based on actual cases from the files of Scotland Yard, Britain's world-renowned crime investigation unit. Series host Edgar Lustgarten was a noted English criminologist. No regular characters appeared in this series—there seemed to be a different superintendent, inspector, or sergeant on the case every week—but one role, that of Inspector Duggan (played by Russell Napier), did recur in about half a dozen episodes.

SCOTT ISLAND

see *Harbourmaster*

SCOTT MUSIC HALL

Musical Variety

FIRST TELECAST: *October 8, 1952*
LAST TELECAST: *August 26, 1953*
BROADCAST HISTORY:
Oct 1952–Aug 1953, NBC Wed 8:30–9:00
REGULARS:
Patti Page
Frank Fontaine

Patti Page had come to prominence in the late 1940s singing Country-flavored tunes and employing an unusual recording technique which allowed her to sing in harmony with herself, or even in whole choruses of her own voice. Her biggest hit, from 1950–1951, was "The Tennessee Waltz." Her first network TV series was this variety program in which she initially co-starred with Frank Fontaine, Fontaine providing the comedy and Miss Page ("The Singing Rage") the songs. Guests were also seen. In February 1953 Fontaine was phased out of the show and Miss Page became the only regular.

SCRAPBOOK JUNIOR EDITION

Children's

FIRST TELECAST: *June 27, 1948*
LAST TELECAST: *November 14, 1948*
BROADCAST HISTORY:
Jun 1948–Nov 1948, CBS Sun 6:00–6:30
HOSTS:
Jini Boyd O'Conner
Scotty MacGregor

This children's show invited viewers to send in information or examples of their hobbies and interests so that the TV audience could learn from them. The show started as a local program in October 1947 and remained on the air until May 1949 at an earlier time on Sunday afternoons. A feature which enabled viewers to win prizes was the puzzle tune contest. A child was called on the phone and asked to identify what was wrong with a picture that represented a nursery rhyme. If he or she identified the flaw it was worth anything from a pet dog, to a camping set, to a new bicycle.

SCREEN DIRECTOR'S PLAYHOUSE

Anthology

FIRST TELECAST: *October 5, 1955*
LAST TELECAST: *September 26, 1956*
BROADCAST HISTORY:
Oct 1955–Jun 1956, NBC Wed 8:00–8:30
Jul 1956–Sep 1956, ABC Wed 9:00–9:30

The one distinguishing characteristic of this filmed anthology series was that each of the dramatizations was directed by an outstanding director of Hollywood motion pictures. Among the participating directors were John Ford, Alfred Hitchcock, Fred Zinnemann, and Rouben Mamoulian. The scope of the series ranged from serious dramas to Westerns to comedies, and the players from relative newcomers such as Cloris Leachman, Alan Young, and Pat Hitchcock (Alfred's daughter) to such old-timers as Walter Brennan and Edgar Buchanan.

SCREEN MYSTERY

see *Movies—Prior to 1961*

SCREEN SHORTS

see *Movies—Prior to 1961*

SEARCH

Adventure

FIRST TELECAST: *September 13, 1972*
LAST TELECAST: *August 29, 1973*
BROADCAST HISTORY:
Sep 1972–Aug 1973, NBC Wed 10:00–11:00
CAST:
Hugh Lockwood ....Hugh O'Brien
Nick Bianco ....Tony Franciosa
C. R. Grover ....Doug McClure
Cameron ....Burgess Meredith
Gloria Haring ....Angel Tompkins

The Probe Division of World Securities had reached the ultimate in sophistication and technological development in equipping its agents as they traveled around the world on missions. Each agent had a transmitter and earphone implanted in one ear, enabling him to keep in constant contact with mission control. He also carried a miniaturized scanning device, in a ring or tie clip, that provided visual contact as well. The staff at mission control could maintain complete surveillance on whatever was happening to any of the agents. Hugh Lockwood, Nick Bianco, and C. R. Grover were the three agents whose exploits were shown, on a rotating basis, from week to week. Their assignments usually involved finding and/or protecting some valuable object or person, often with political implications. The control staff was headed by Cameron and included Gloria Harding, a telemetry specialist. Her function was to monitor the agents' vital signs. Mission control also provided the agents with computer support, status reports, warnings of impending danger, and the advice of the many experts on its permanent staff who were on hand to assist them.

SEARCH, THE

Documentary

FIRST TELECAST: *July 12, 1955*

LAST TELECAST: *October 5, 1958*

BROADCAST HISTORY:

Jul 1955–Sep 1955, CBS Tue 10:30–11:00

Jun 1958–Oct 1958, CBS Sun 6:00–6:30

NARRATOR:

Charles Romine

Produced in cooperation with a number of American universities, this series spotlighted the research projects that were being carried out in such diverse fields as speech therapy, marriage counseling, automobile safety, and robotics. All of the episodes were filmed at the respective schools where the research was in progress. The series had actually premiered in October 1954 on Sunday afternoons before moving into prime time for the summer of 1955. All of the episodes aired in 1958 were reruns of the earlier series.

SECOND HUNDRED YEARS, THE

Situation Comedy

FIRST TELECAST: *September 6, 1967*

LAST TELECAST: *September 19, 1968*

BROADCAST HISTORY:

Sep 1967–Feb 1968, ABC Wed 8:30–9:00

Mar 1968–Sep 1968, ABC Thu 7:30–8:00

CAST:

Luke Carpenter/Ken Carpenter .... Monte Markham

Edwin Carpenter ....Arthur O'Connell

Col. Garroway ....Frank Maxwell

In the year 1900 Luke Carpenter, 33, bid farewell to his wife and his infant son Edwin and set out to prospect for gold in Alaska. He was lost in a glacier slide. Sixty-seven years later, by some freak of nature, Luke thawed out, revived, and was brought to the home of his now-aging son in Woodland Oaks, California. Chronologically Luke was 101, but he hadn't aged while in deep freeze and was physiologically still 33—younger than his own son.

In fact, he was younger in spirit, at least, than his 33-year-old grandson Ken, who was his exact lookalike (both parts were played by Monte Markham). Ken was stuffy and conservative, while Luke was ebullient, full of fun, and a rugged individualist.

The comedy centered both on the contrast between them and on Luke's problems in adapting to the modern world, while his origin was kept a military secret (Col. Garroway, an Army doctor, was assigned to look after him). The first thing Luke had seen on awakening in Edwin's home was a 1967 TV set with what appeared to be little people aiming guns at him. He applied his simple, individualistic ways to the problems of the 20th century with some success, though he never could get used to a modern job.

SECRET AGENT

International Intrigue

FIRST TELECAST: *April 3, 1965*

LAST TELECAST: *September 10, 1966*

BROADCAST HISTORY:

Apr 1965–Sep 1965, CBS Sat 9:00–10:00

Dec 1965–Sep 1966, CBS Sat 8:30–9:30

CAST:

John Drake ....Patrick McGoohan

THEME:

"Secret Agent Man," by Phil Sloan and Steve Barri

John Drake was a special security agent working for the British government as a professional spy. He traveled throughout Europe on various cases and had the usual confrontations with enemy agents and beautiful women. His supposed function was to "preserve world peace and promote brotherhood and better understanding between people and nations." He was one of the more violent "peaceful" people seen on television during the 1960s. Somehow, preserving peace always demanded beating people up and shooting them. This series was produced in England and had been popular in Europe before its importation by CBS. Popular singer Johnny Rivers had a highly successful recording of "Secret Agent Man," the theme song which he sang over the opening titles of this series. *Secret Agent* was actually an expanded version of *Danger Man*, another British series. Patrick McGoohan played the same character in both.

SECRET FILES OF CAPTAIN VIDEO, THE

see *Captain Video and His Video Rangers*

SEE IT NOW

Documentary

FIRST TELECAST: *April 20, 1952*
LAST TELECAST: *July 5, 1955*
BROADCAST HISTORY:

Apr 1952–Jun 1953, CBS Sun 6:30–7:00 (OS)
Sep 1953–Jul 1955, CBS Tue 10:30–11:00 (OS)

HOST:

Edward R. Murrow

See It Now was the prototype of the in-depth quality television documentary. It had started as a Sunday afternoon program on November 18, 1951. On that first telecast, Edward R. Murrow showed a live camera shot of the Atlantic Ocean, followed by a live shot of the Pacific Ocean, and then commented: "We are impressed by a medium through which a man sitting in his living room has been able for the first time to look at two oceans at once." The subject matter could be as serious as his famous essay on Senator Joe McCarthy or as light as an interview with painter Grandma Moses. Despite the fact that many of the personalities covered in this series could also have been on his other weekly series, *Person to Person*, the tone of *See It Now* was more serious and informative. The thing that distinguished *See It Now* was its penchant for taking controversial positions and dealing directly with major, and often unpopular, issues. In addition to his attacks on McCarthyism and the threat it posed in a free society, Murrow's documentaries detailed the recriminations of atomic scientist J. Robert Oppenheimer over the course of nuclear technology, and the relationship between cigarette smoking and cancer (despite the fact that Murrow himself was a chain smoker). His in-person visit to GI's on the front lines in Korea was a memorable telecast. Each broadcast ended with "Good night . . . and good luck."

Six months after its premiere, *See It Now* moved into the evening lineup, where it remained for more than three years. When it returned in the fall of 1955 it was no longer a weekly half-hour, but had become an irregularly scheduled hour. The longer format enabled more complete coverage of an issue. The last telecast of *See It Now* was on July 7, 1958. Murrow made occasional appearances on its successor, *CBS Reports*.

SENATOR, THE

Political Drama

FIRST TELECAST: *September 13, 1970*
LAST TELECAST: *August 22, 1971*
BROADCAST HISTORY:

Sep 1970–Aug 1971, NBC Sun 10:00–11:00

CAST:

Sen. Hayes Stowe . . . . Hal Holbrook
Jordan Boyle . . . . Michael Tolan
Erin Stowe . . . . Sharon Acker
Norma Stowe . . . . Cindy Eilbacher

Junior Senator Hayes Stowe was a very idealistic politician. His goals were the betterment of society and the environment in which we live. His affinity for getting involved with causes and issues of public concern did not endear him to the old-line professional politicians he had to deal with in Washington. In trying to resolve problems he often stepped on the toes of entrenched business interests with impressive political connections. With the help of Jordan Boyle, his administrative aide, and the support of his wife (Erin) and his daughter (Norma), Hayes relentlessly fought for what he believed was right and just.

The Senator was one of the three rotating elements that comprised *The Bold Ones* during the 1970–1971 season. The other two were *The New Doctors* and *The Lawyers*.

SERENADE

see *Sing-O-Pation*

SERGEANT BILKO

syndicated title for *Phil Silvers Show, The*

SERGEANT PRESTON OF THE YUKON

Police/Adventure

FIRST TELECAST: *September 29, 1955*

LAST TELECAST: *September 25, 1958*

BROADCAST HISTORY:

Sep 1955–Sep 1958, CBS Thu 7:30–8:00

CAST:

Sgt. Preston ....Richard Simmons

This series told stories of an officer of the Royal Northwest Mounted Police who dealt single-handedly with lawbreakers in the Klondike territory at the turn of the century. Sgt. Preston, aided only by his faithful Malemute dog Yukon King, and his trusty horse Rex, chased and caught almost every renegade and outlaw that crossed the frozen territory that he patrolled. Filmed in mountainous sections of California and Colorado, the stories centered around adventurers trying to take advantage of others during the Gold Rush period at the end of the 19th century.

SERPICO

Police

FIRST TELECAST: *September 24, 1976*

LAST TELECAST: *January 28, 1977*

BROADCAST HISTORY:

Sep 1976–Jan 1977, NBC Fri 10:00–11:00

CAST:

Frank Serpico ....David Birney
Tom Sullivan ....Tom Atkins

Frank Serpico was a New York City cop who may have been too idealistic for the system through which he had to work. He often went undercover to track down drug dealers, break up numbers racket operations, and cut down the illegal traffic in weapons. He was also very involved in efforts to prove that various police officers and officials, some in very high places, were on the take from organized crime. Tom Sullivan was a full-time undercover agent who worked with Frank and was his contact with the police when he was on an undercover assignment.

There was a real Frank Serpico, on whose career this series was based. His search for, and exposure of, corruption in the New York City Police Department did not endear him to his fellow officers, many of whom expressed their hatred of him as a "troublemaker." On February 3, 1971 he was shot in the face by a dope pusher, and he subsequently retired from the force on a disability pension. He left with a profound sense of disillusionment and a permit to carry a gun for his own protection, possibly from other police personnel. He later was the subject of a book titled *Serpico* which was the story of his experiences as a police officer. The book was made into a movie of the same name, starring Al Pacino, and that in turn, was the basis for this series.

SERVING THROUGH SCIENCE

Instructional

FIRST TELECAST: *June 18, 1946*

LAST TELECAST: *May 27, 1947*

BROADCAST HISTORY:

Jun 1946–May 1947, DUM Tue 9:00–9:30 (approx.)

HOST:

Dr. Guthrie McClintock (also given as Dr. Miller McClintock)

This was an early experiment in educational programming, consisting of short films from the Encyclopedia Britannica with discussion by Dr. McClintock and guests. The setting was Dr. McClintock's study. Shortly after the program began *Television* magazine conducted a poll of its readers that indicated that while everyone thought the presentation worthwhile, some found it to be rather boring ("It made us very sleepy," wrote one respondent). So the sponsor added a musical segment with performances by promising young artists, which had nothing whatever to do with the subject at hand but was supposed to "liven things up." This mishmash lasted only a few weeks before the program was finally dropped.

As with some other early programs, it is not known whether *Serving through Science* was fed over the network from the beginning, though it was on the network by the beginning of 1947 at the latest. Sponsor U.S. Rubber had presented similar educational TV shows locally in New York in 1945 and perhaps earlier.

SESSIONS

see *Chicago Jazz*

SEVEN AT ELEVEN

Comedy Variety

FIRST TELECAST: *May 28, 1951*

LAST TELECAST: *June 27, 1951*

BROADCAST HISTORY:

May 1951–Jun 1951, NBC Mon/Wed 11:00–Midnight

HOST:

George de Witt

REGULARS:
Sid Gould
George Freems
Sammy Petrillo
Dorothy Keller
Jane Scott
Denise Lor
Betty Luster & Jack Stanton
Jackie Loughery
Herbie Faye
Milton Delugg & His Sextet

Short-lived live comedy variety series originating from New York.

SEVENTH AVENUE

Drama

FIRST TELECAST: *February 10, 1977*
LAST TELECAST: *February 24, 1977*
BROADCAST HISTORY:
Feb 1977, NBC Thu 9:00–11:00
CAST:
Jay Blackman .... Steven Keats
Rhoda Gold .... Dori Brenner
Myrna Gold .... Anne Archer
Joe Vitelli .... Herschel Bernardi
Harry Lee .... Alan King
Marty Cass .... John Pleshette
Eva Meyers .... Jane Seymour
Al Blackman .... Kristoffer Tabori
Celia Blackman .... Anna Berger
Morris Blackman .... Mike Kellin
Frank Topo .... Richard Dimitri

Adapted from Norman Bogner's novel, *Seventh Avenue* was the story of Jay Blackman, a poor young man from New York's Lower East Side who succeeded in becoming a major force in the garment industry in the 1940 and 1950s. His rise to power from humble beginnings and involvements with organized crime as well as his marital problems and affairs were all chronicled.

Seventh Avenue was one of four novels dramatized under the collective title *NBC's Best Sellers*.

77 SUNSET STRIP

Detective

FIRST TELECAST: *October 10, 1958*
LAST TELECAST: *September 9, 1964*
BROADCAST HISTORY:
Oct 1958–Oct 1959, ABC Fri 9:30–10:30
Oct 1959–Sep 1962, ABC Fri 9:00–10:00
Sep 1962–Sep 1963, ABC Fri 9:30–10:30
Sep 1963–Feb 1964, ABC Fri 7:30–8:30
Apr 1964–Sep 1964, ABC Wed 10:00–11:00
CAST:
Stuart Bailey .... Efrem Zimbalist, Jr.
Jeff Spencer (1958–1963) ..... Roger Smith
Gerald Lloyd Kookson III ("Kookie") (1958–1963) .... Edd Byrnes
Roscoe (1958–1963) .... Louis Quinn
Suzanne (1958–1963) ...... Jacqueline Beer
Rex Randolph (1960–1961) .... Richard Long
J. R. Hale (1961–1963) .... Robert Logan
THEME:
"77 Sunset Strip," by Mack David and Jerry Livingston

77 Sunset Strip was the prototype for a rash of glamorous private-detective teams in the late 1950s and early 1960s. Half the team was Stu Bailey, a suave, cultured former OSS officer who was an expert in languages. An Ivy League Ph.D., he had intended to become a college professor but turned private investigator instead. The other half was Jeff Spencer, also a former government undercover agent, who had a degree in law. Both of them were judo experts. They worked out of an office at No. 77 Sunset Strip, in Hollywood, though their cases took them to glamour spots all over the world.

Next door to No. 77 was Dino's, a posh restaurant whose *maître d'*, Mario, was seen occasionally in the series. Seen often was Dino's parking lot attendant, a gangling, jive-talking youth named Kookie, who longed to be a private detective himself and who often helped Stu and Jeff on their cases. Kookie provided comic relief for the series, and his "Kookie-isms" became a trademark. For example: "the ginchiest" (the greatest); "piling up the Z's" (sleeping); "keep the eyeballs rolling" (be on the lookout); "play like a pigeon" (deliver a message); "a dark seven" (a depressing week); and "headache grapplers" (aspirin).

Other regulars included Roscoe the racetrack tout and Suzanne the beautiful French switchboard operator. But it was Kookie who caught the public's fancy and propelled the show into the top ten. In the first telecast of the 1959–1960 season he helped Stu Bailey catch a jewel thief by staging a revue, in which he sang a novelty song called "Kookie, Kookie, Lend Me Your Comb" (after his habit of constantly combing his hair). The song was released on record as a duet between Byrnes and Connie Stevens, and became a smash hit. Byrnes soon began to overshadow the series' principals as a popular celebrity, a kind of "Fonzie" of the 1950s.

Unsatisfied with his secondary role in the show, the young actor demanded a bigger part and eventually walked out. Warner Brothers at first replaced him with Troy Donahue as a long-haired bookworm, about as far from the Kookie character as you could get. But Brynes came back a few months later and was promoted to a full-fledged partner in the detective firm at the start of the 1961–1962 season. His permanent replacement at the parking lot was J. R. Hale. Previously, for a single season, Rex Randolph had been seen as a third partner in the firm.

Kookie was not the only one who tried parlaying the show's success into a hit record. Following his example, actor Roger Smith put out an album called *Beach Romance* (which bombed), and even Efrem Zimbalist, Jr., who was no singer but who had perhaps the best musical background of the lot (he was the son of a famous concert violinist and a famous opera singer), was lured into a studio to record "Adeste Fideles" in English and Latin. Also, the finger-snapping theme music from the series was made into a best-selling album.

By 1963 the novelty had worn off and the show was in decline. In an attempt to save it, Jack Webb was brought in as producer and drastic changes were made. The entire cast was dropped with the exception of Efrem Zimbalist, Jr., who became a freelance investigator traveling around the world on cases. Lavish production values were featured. The season opened with a five-part chase-thriller featuring two dozen big-name guest stars and written by eight top writers. Stu Bailey was seen pursuing operatives of a gigantic smuggling ring across two continents. The rest of the season was spent on the road as well, but it didn't help.

Reruns of *77 Sunset Strip* were seen during the summer of 1964.

77TH BENGAL LANCERS, THE

see *Tales of the 77th Bengal Lancers*

SHADOW OF THE CLOAK

International Intrigue

FIRST TELECAST: *June 6, 1951*
LAST TELECAST: *April 3, 1952*
BROADCAST HISTORY:
Jun 1951–Nov 1951, DUM Wed 9:30–10:00
Dec 1951–Apr 1952, DUM Thu 9:00–9:30
CAST:
Peter House ....Helmut Dantine

Helmut Dantine, who played the arrogant Nazi in many Hollywood films during the 1940s, starred as the chief agent of International Security Intelligence in this espionage series. He tangled with an assortment of spies, traitors, and other international villains. Despite scripts by a number of notable writers, including Mel London and a young Rod Serling, the series disappeared in less than a year. During its last three months it alternated with *Gruen Playhouse*.

SHAFT

Detective

FIRST TELECAST: *October 9, 1973*
LAST TELECAST: *August 20, 1974*
BROADCAST HISTORY:
Oct 1973–Aug 1974, CBS Tue 9:30–11:00
CAST:
John Shaft ....Richard Roundtree
Lt. Al Rossi ....Ed Barth
THEME:
"Theme from 'Shaft'," by Isaac Hayes

John Shaft was a flamboyant, streetwise black private detective working in New York City, although his cases often took him far from the "Big Apple." Smooth, imperturbable, and deadly efficient, he was sought out by all sorts of people when they needed help. His source of information, when he needed it, was police lieutenant Al Rossi, with whom he had a friendly working relationship.

Shaft was one of three elements that rotated in the Tuesday 9:30–11:00 P.M. time period on CBS during the 1973–1974 season. The other two were *Hawkins* and *The New CBS Tuesday Night Movies*. Richard Roundtree brought John Shaft to television after a series of highly successful theatrical features in which he had played the part. The theme for the television series was written for the first *Shaft* movie, and had won composer Hayes an Academy Award.

SHANE

Western

FIRST TELECAST: *September 10, 1966*
LAST TELECAST: *December 31, 1966*
BROADCAST HISTORY:
Sep 1966–Dec 1966, ABC Sat 7:30–8:30
CAST:
Shane ....David Carradine
Marian Starett ....Jill Ireland
Tom Starett ....Tom Tully
Joey Starett ....Christopher Shea
Rufe Ryker ....Bert Freed
Sam Grafton ....Sam Gilman

The 1953 Western movie *Shane* is considered one of the classics of the cinema. It was the story of a young boy's idolization of a wandering gunfighter who stops to help the boy's family but who must, in time, move on. In the poignant final scene he did, as the boy (played by Brandon De Wilde) cried out, "Shane . . . come back!"

Shane did come back, for a few months anyway, in this 1966 TV version starring David Carradine as the silent, brooding gunfighter and Christopher Shea as the eight-year-old rancher's son, Joey. Marian Starett was recently widowed and was having a difficult time protecting her homestead against the ravages of nature and of the vicious rancher Ryker. It was the classic confrontation between the cattle ranchers who first claimed the land (Ryker) and the homesteaders who followed (the Staretts). Though Shane was there to help them in their battle, the Staretts knew that he might at any time move on. Tom, Marian's father-in-law, and Sam Grafton, the saloonkeeper, were the only other regulars.

SHEILAH GRAHAM IN HOLLYWOOD
Talk
FIRST TELECAST: *January 20, 1951*
LAST TELECAST: *July 14, 1951*
BROADCAST HISTORY:
Jan 1951–Jul 1951, NBC Sat 11:00–11:15
HOSTESS:
Sheilah Graham

Syndicated Hollywood gossip columnist Sheilah Graham had been doing a weekly live show in Los Angeles for several months before NBC decided it would be interesting to give it a try on the network. The show combined straight movie news, gossip, fashion information, and chats with visiting stars. Aired live in Los Angeles on Tuesday evenings, with a kinescope made and flown to New York for telecast by NBC on the following Saturday at 11:00 P.M.

SHIELDS AND YARNELL
Variety
FIRST TELECAST: *June 13, 1977*
LAST TELECAST: *March 28, 1978*
BROADCAST HISTORY:
Jun 1977–Jul 1977, CBS Mon 8:30–9:00
Jan 1978–Mar 1978, CBS Tue 8:30–9:00
REGULARS:
Robert Shields
Lorene Yarnell
Ted Zeigler (1977)
Joanna Cassidy (1977)
Gailard Sartain (1978)

The talented young mime team of Shields and Yarnell first starred in a brief summer series which featured, in addition to mime, dancing and comedy sketches. A recurring sketch concerned the adventures of the Clinkers, a pair of clumsy robots adjusting to life in their new suburban home. The show was one of the major hits of the summer of 1977, and promised a bright future in TV for the young performers. That future was temporarily dimmed when they returned in January 1978 opposite ABC's top-rated *Laverne & Shirley* and lasted only two months before being replaced.

SHINDIG
Music
FIRST TELECAST: *September 16, 1964*
LAST TELECAST: *January 8, 1966*
BROADCAST HISTORY:
Sep 1964–Jan 1965, ABC Wed 8:30–9:00
Jan 1965–Sep 1965, ABC Wed 8:30–9:30
Sep 1965–Jan 1966, ABC Thu/Sat 7:30–8:00
HOST:
Jimmy O'Neill
REGULARS:
The Shindig Dancers
FREQUENTLY SEEN:
Bobby Sherman
Righteous Brothers
The Wellingtons
Everly Brothers
Donna Loren
Glen Campbell
Sonny & Cher

Shindig was one of two rock 'n' roll shows seen on TV during the mid-1960s (the other: NBC's *Hullabaloo*). It was a fast-paced, youthful program and, like its NBC counterpart, featured many of the top names in popular music performing their latest hits, while platoons of dancers staged elaborate production numbers. There was also a "disc pick of the week" feature.

The premiere telecast starred Sam Cooke and featured such acts as the Everly Brothers, Righteous Brothers, the Wellingtons, Bobby Sherman (a *Shindig* "discovery"), and comic Alan Sues. The second season had an even bigger opening, as the show expanded to two nights a week and opened with the Rolling Stones. Although none of the rock stars seen on *Shindig* were weekly regulars, some (noted above) returned many times. Others appearing included such superstars as the Beatles, the Beach Boys, Chuck Berry, Neil Sedaka, and even old-timer Louis Armstrong. They couldn't get the biggest rock star of all, however—nobody could get Elvis—so in May 1965 *Shindig* devoted an entire telecast to his songs, as a tribute to Elvis' tenth anniversary in show business.

During the 1965–1966 season guest stars from other areas of show business also began to appear, such as Mickey Rooney, Zsa Zsa Gabor, Ed Wynn and, on Halloween, Boris Karloff.

SHIRLEY TEMPLE'S STORYBOOK

Children's Anthology

FIRST TELECAST: *January 12, 1959*

LAST TELECAST: *September 10, 1961*

BROADCAST HISTORY:

Jan 1959–Dec 1959, ABC Mon 7:30–8:30 (OS)
Sep 1960–Sep 1961, NBC Sun 7:00–8:00

HOSTESS/OCCASIONAL STAR:

Shirley Temple

Shirley Temple, the popular child star of movies in the 1930s, came to television as narrator, hostess, and sometimes star of this series of dramatized fairy tales. Among the stories adapted (often in musical form) for this family entertainment program were "Winnie the Pooh," "The Prince and the Pauper," "Babes in Toyland," and "The Reluctant Dragon." Many famous stars appeared in the productions, including Claire Bloom, Charlton Heston, Jonathan Winters, and Agnes Moorehead.

The show was first seen as a series of sixteen specials which aired on ABC on various nights between January and December 1958. In January 1959 the program began to run regularly every third Monday night, alternating with *Cheyenne.* When it moved to NBC in 1960 it was a weekly series and was renamed *The Shirley Temple Show.*

SHIRLEY'S WORLD

Situation Comedy

FIRST TELECAST: *September 15, 1971*

LAST TELECAST: *January 5, 1972*

BROADCAST HISTORY:

Sep 1971–Jan 1972, ABC Wed 9:30–10:00

CAST:

Shirley Logan .... Shirley MacLaine
Dennis Croft .... John Gregson

Movie actress Shirley MacLaine starred as a mod young reporter-photographer in this, her first TV series. Shirley Logan was based in London, but her assignments for *World Illustrated* magazine took her all over the world. She was saucy, bubbly, and impulsive, and her knack for getting involved with her subjects, be they spies or movie queens, often led to hilarious results, much to the despair of her editor, Dennis Croft.

Filmed in England, Scotland, Tokyo, Hong Kong, and other locales.

SHORT SHORT DRAMAS

Dramatic Anthology

FIRST TELECAST: *September 30, 1952*

LAST TELECAST: *April 9, 1953*

BROADCAST HISTORY:

Sep 1952–Apr 1953, NBC Tue/Thu 7:15–7:30

HOSTESS:

Ruth Woods

Model and cover girl Ruth Woods hosted this filmed series of one-act plays that aired twice weekly during the 1952–1953 season. At the start of each episode she would introduce a different storyteller, who would set the scene for the play to follow. By establishing the background in this way the producer hoped to compress into a short time period a story that would otherwise require at least half an hour to do. Once the background had been set the storyteller, who was one of the stars in the short drama, joined the rest of the cast and the play began. Some of the stories were serious and others light, but none of them particularly memorable. Among the stars performing in this series were Leslie Nielsen, Neva Patterson, E. G. Marshall,

Cliff Robertson, Tony Randall, and Bethel Leslie.

SHORT STORY PLAYHOUSE

Dramatic Anthology

FIRST TELECAST: *July 5, 1951*

LAST TELECAST: *August 23, 1951*

BROADCAST HISTORY:

Jul 1951–Aug 1951, NBC Thu 10:30–11:00

NARRATOR:

Robert Breen

Originating live from Chicago, this was aired only on the NBC Midwest network, as a summer replacement for *The Wayne King Show*. The off-screen voice of Robert Breen was heard throughout the productions, serving to add story elements and to tie together loose ends. The performers were not well known, but many of the stories were adapted from works by major authors—Sinclair Lewis' "The Good Sport," James Thurber's "My Life and Hard Times," and Pearl Buck's "Ransom" being the most noteworthy.

SHOW BUSINESS, INC.

Variety

FIRST TELECAST: *March 20, 1947*

LAST TELECAST: *May 4, 1947*

BROADCAST HISTORY:

Mar 1947, NBC Thu 8:00–8:30

Apr 1947–May 1947, NBC Sun 8:00–8:30

REGULARS:

Helen V. Parrish

John Graham

Early music and variety show, telecast only four times in early 1947 over NBC's fledgling East Coast network. There was apparently no regular host, but the performers listed above appeared on all four telecasts.

The title was also used briefly for a series hosted by columnist Danton Walker in 1949 (see *Broadway Spotlight*).

SHOW FOR A SUMMER EVENING

Dramatic Anthology

FIRST TELECAST: *July 16, 1957*

LAST TELECAST: *September 10, 1957*

BROADCAST HISTORY:

Jul 1957–Sep 1957, NBC Tue 9:30–10:00

Show for a Summer Evening alternated with *Armstrong Summer Playhouse* on Tuesday nights during the summer of 1957. All of the dramas shown on it were filmed reruns of episodes from a syndicated series, *Heinz Playhouse*.

SHOW GOES ON, THE

Variety

FIRST TELECAST: *January 19, 1950*

LAST TELECAST: *February 16, 1952*

BROADCAST HISTORY:

Jan 1950–Mar 1950, CBS Thu Various

Mar 1950–Nov 1950, CBS Thu 8:00–9:00

Nov 1950–Jun 1951, CBS Thu 8:30–9:00

Jun 1951–Feb 1952, CBS Sat 9:30–10:00

HOST:

Robert Q. Lewis

The format of this talent show had young hopefuls performing their acts for a group of interested talent "buyers," who were on hand to appraise the acts and sign up the best ones for actual theater and nightclub bookings. Impresario Max Gordon and bandleader Guy Lombardo were among those who appeared on the show in that capacity. Talent ranged from acrobats, to singers, to comics.

Robert Q. Lewis, who had substituted for Arthur Godfrey on *Arthur Godfrey's Talent Scouts* during the summertime, had his own first starring role with this series. When it first went on the air in January 1950, *The Show Goes On* wandered all over the CBS Thursday night schedule in 30- and 60-minute versions. It finally stabilized in March at a full hour from 8:00 P.M. to 9:00 P.M., and was cut back to a half-hour the following fall.

SHOWCASE '68

Variety

FIRST TELECAST: *June 11, 1968*

LAST TELECAST: *September 3, 1968*

BROADCAST HISTORY:

Jun 1968–Sep 1968, NBC Tue 8:00–8:30

HOST:

Lloyd Thaxton

Each week *Showcase '68* originated from a different city in the United States, introducing talented young performers to the viewing audience. All of them were under 22 years of age and made their television debuts on the show. In addition to the young performers, an established star appeared on each telecast. At the end of each show a panel of judges selected the performer with the greatest potential for success. On its last telecast *Showcase '68* expanded to a full hour (8:00–9:00 P.M.) and the ten weekly winners competed for a final $10,000 prize. The winner of the grand prize was rock group Sly and the Family Stone (which already had its first hit on the record charts while this show was on the air). Among the runners-up were Julie Budd, the Chambers Brothers, and the American Breed.

SHOWCASE THEATER

Dramatic Anthology

FIRST TELECAST: *September 12, 1953*
LAST TELECAST: *November 20, 1953*
BROADCAST HISTORY:

Sep 1953–Oct 1953, ABC Sat 8:00–8:30
Oct 1953–Nov 1953, ABC Fri 10:00–10:30

This was a filmed anthology series.

SHOWTIME

Variety

FIRST TELECAST: *June 11, 1968*
LAST TELECAST: *September 17, 1968*
BROADCAST HISTORY:

Jun 1968–Sep 1968, CBS Tue 8:30–9:30

REGULARS:

The Mike Sammes Singers
The London Line Dancers
Jack Parnell and his Orchestra

This 1968 summer replacement for *The Red Skelton Hour* was produced in London and featured a different roster of guest performers each week. Most of the headliners, with the exceptions of Englishmen Terry-Thomas and Dave Allen and South African–born Juliet Prowse, were Americans. Of the Americans, most were comics—Don Knotts, Phyllis Diller, Godfrey Cambridge, Steve Allen, and George Gobel among them.

SHOWTIME, U.S.A.

Variety

FIRST TELECAST: *October 1, 1950*
LAST TELECAST: *June 24, 1951*
BROADCAST HISTORY:

Oct 1950–Jun 1951, ABC Sun 7:30–8:00

PRODUCER/EMCEE:

Vinton Freedley

This weekly variety show was a plug for Broadway. Produced and co-hosted by Vinton Freedley, president of the American National Theatre Academy, it featured scenes from top (and usually current) Broadway productions performed by the original stars. One of the stars would serve as co-host each week. The first telecast had Helen Hayes, Carol Channing, Alec Templeton, Grace and Paul Hartman, Henry Fonda, and the chorus from the currently running *Kiss Me Kate*. Later shows presented Gertrude Lawrence in scenes from *Susan and God*, Fonda in *Mr. Roberts*, and a host of others.

SID CAESAR INVITES YOU

Comedy Variety

FIRST TELECAST: *January 26, 1958*
LAST TELECAST: *May 25, 1958*
BROADCAST HISTORY:

Jan 1958–May 1958, ABC Sun 9:00–9:30

REGULARS:

Sid Caesar
Imogene Coca
Carl Reiner
Paul Reed
Milt Kamen
Bernie Green Orchestra

Sid Caesar and Imogene Coca had become two of the most famous comedians in America, thanks to *Your Show of Shows* in the early 1950s. When that series ended its run in 1954 Caesar and Coca went separate ways, hoping to build independent careers with separate series. But alone, neither one could capture the magic they had created together, and so in 1958 they were briefly reunited in this live comedy program. As in the days of old, they appeared in sketches and pantomime, with excellent support from regulars, including Carl Reiner, and writers, including Neil Simon and Mel Brooks. But classic comedy is a fragile commodity which cannot easily be revived, and this attempt ended in failure after only a four-month run.

SID CAESAR SHOW, THE

see *Caesar's Hour*

SID CAESAR SHOW, THE

Comedy Variety

FIRST TELECAST: *October 3, 1963*
LAST TELECAST: *March 12, 1964*
BROADCAST HISTORY:

Oct 1963–Mar 1964, ABC Thu 10:00–10:30

REGULARS:

Sid Caesar
Joey Forman

Gisele MacKenzie
Marilyn Hanold

Sid Caesar's inventive sketch comedy filled this Thursday night half-hour on alternate weeks during the 1963–1964 TV season. Singer Edie Adams starred in a musical variety half-hour on the alternate weeks. To start the season they both starred together in a full-hour variety special that ran from 10:00 to 11:00 P.M. on September 19. Sid's regulars included comic Joey Forman and singer Gisele MacKenzie, with frequent visits by a gorgeous lass named Marilyn Hanold—who never spoke, only looked beautiful. Although the production team was first-rate (including head writer Goodman Ace and producer-director Greg Garrison), the program failed to catch on and ended after a single season.

SIERRA

Dramatic Adventure

FIRST TELECAST: *September 12, 1974*
LAST TELECAST: *December 12, 1974*
BROADCAST HISTORY:
Sep 1974–Dec 1974, NBC Thu 8:00–9:00
CAST:
Ranger Tim Cassidy .... James G. Richardson
Ranger Matt Harper .....Ernest Thompson
Chief Ranger Jack Moore ....Jack Hogan
Ranger P. J. Lewis ....Mike Warren
Ranger Julie Beck ....Susan Foster

The work of rangers employed by the National Park Service at fictitious Sierra National Park was dramatized in this series. The problems and satisfactions of supervisor Jack Moore and his staff, consisting of rangers Cassidy, Harper, Lewis, and Beck, were shown. Their problems stemmed from the conflict between trying to preserve the natural beauty of the wilderness and accommodating the flood of tourists wanting to utilize the resources of the park. The campers, skiers, hikers, and climbers came in all shapes and sizes. Some were friendly, some stubborn, and some nasty and cruel. Tracking people who had gotten lost, coping with the visitor who got into a situation he couldn't really handle, and enforcing park regulations were all part of the job. *Sierra* was filmed on location, primarily at Yosemite National Park, in cooperation with the National Park Service. Cruncher was the Park's troublemaking bear.

SILENT FORCE, THE

Police

FIRST TELECAST: *September 21, 1970*
LAST TELECAST: *January 11, 1971*
BROADCAST HISTORY:
Sep 1970–Jan 1971, ABC Mon 8:30–9:00
CAST:
Ward Fuller ....Ed Nelson
Jason Hart ....Percy Rodriguez
Amelia Cole ....Lynda Day

The Silent Force was a strike force of government agents assigned to fight organized crime. Ward, Jason, and Amelia were the agents, working mostly undercover to infiltrate "the mob" and expose its operations which preyed on innocent citizens. On several occasions they became involved with companies or individuals who were being pressured by the syndicate, and in the first telecast they exposed a candidate for governor who was actually a member of the syndicate.

Set in Southern California.

SILENTS PLEASE

Silent Movies

FIRST TELECAST: *August 4, 1960*
LAST TELECAST: *October 5, 1961*
BROADCAST HISTORY:
Aug 1960–Oct 1960, ABC Thu 10:30–11:00
Mar 1961–Oct 1961, ABC Thu 10:30–11:00
HOST:
Ernie Kovacs (1961)

Classic silent films, some in their entirety, some condensed to fit the confines of a half-hour time slot, were aired in this series. The films included the work of Buster Keaton, Charlie Chaplin, Laurel & Hardy, Lillian Gish, and Douglas Fairbanks, Sr. When it was first telecast in the summer of 1960 there was no host. Ernie Kovacs, whose show *Take a Good Look* had aired in this time slot from October 1960 until *Silents Please* returned the following March, became the host of the show during its second run.

SILVER THEATER, THE

Dramatic Anthology

FIRST TELECAST: *October 3, 1949*
LAST TELECAST: *June 26, 1950*

BROADCAST HISTORY:

Oct 1949–June 1950, CBS Mon 8:00–8:30

HOST:

Conrad Nagel

The teleplays in this series, most of which were aired live, emphasized romance—the humorous, silly, frustrating, futile, and rewarding aspects of it. Famous stars such as Burgess Meredith, Paul Lucas, Glenda Farrell, and Geraldine Brooks appeared in the dramas and Conrad Nagel was the host. The sponsor, the International Silver Company, whence came the title, had also sponsored a radio version of this show during the 1930s and 1940s. A special feature of this program was the monthly "Silver Award" presented to the most deserving supporting performer in the dramas aired in the series during the month. A panel of drama critics determined the monthly winner.

SING ALONG

Music

FIRST TELECAST: *June 4, 1958*

LAST TELECAST: *July 9, 1958*

BROADCAST HISTORY:

Jun 1958–Jul 1958, CBS Wed 7:30–8:00

REGULARS:

Jim Lowe
Tina Robin
Florence Henderson
Somethin' Smith
The Redheads
Harry Sosnick Orchestra

Jim Lowe, a radio personality whose one hit record was a novelty item called "The Green Door," was the host of this live weekly music show. The regular singers were joined by guest stars and the studio and home audience was invited to "sing along." The lyrics were provided by various forms of cue cards so that everyone would know what to sing. Apparently Lowe was a few years ahead of his time. This show had a mere six-week run and then disappeared forever, but while it was on the air an obscure Columbia record album by Mitch Miller called "Sing Along with Mitch" first began attracting attention. Three years and several million records later, Miller brought the idea back to television, and was a national sensation.

SING ALONG WITH MITCH

Musical Variety

FIRST TELECAST: *January 27, 1961*

LAST TELECAST: *September 2, 1966*

BROADCAST HISTORY:

Jan 1961–Apr 1961, NBC Fri 9:00–10:00
Sep 1961–Sep 1962, NBC Thu 10:00–11:00
Sep 1962–Sep 1963, NBC Fri 8:30–9:30
Sep 1963–Sep 1964, NBC Mon 10:00–11:00
Apr 1966–Sep 1966, NBC Fri 8:30–9:30

REGULARS:

Mitch Miller
The Sing Along Gang
The Sing Along Kids
Leslie Uggams
Diana Trask (1960–1962)
Gloria Lambert
Louise O'Brien
Sandy Stewart (1963–1964)

THEME:

"Sing Along," by Robert Allen

Bearded record producer Mitch Miller was responsible for a large proportion of America's popular music during the 1950s. As head of recording for mighty Columbia Records, he launched literally dozens of stars and trends in music, and even had a choral hit under his own name ("The Yellow Rose of Texas" in 1955). But Mitch didn't like rock 'n' roll, and when the teen beat began swamping the business in the late 1950s *his* kind of music—melodic and stylish—went into a severe decline. In 1958 he conceived the idea of packaging "Singalong" LPs consisting of old favorites with the words printed on the album cover so the listener could sing along with the chorus. This ran contrary to everything that was happening in popular music, but it found a large, obviously frustrated audience, and the albums became enormous sellers. In 1961 Miller tried the idea on television. Overnight, Mitch Miller, who had for decades been a behind-the-scenes man, became a national celebrity. During the first season his show alternated with *The Bell Telephone Hour*. It became such a large ratings success that when it returned in the fall of 1961 it was a weekly show. Old favorites and some currently popular songs were sung by Mitch's Sing Along Gang, the preteenaged Sing Along Kids, and by featured vocalists doing solos. Mitch himself said very little, simply standing there waving his baton. For all the group songs, the lyrics would be flashed on the screen so that the home audience could also sing along. In addition to the regulars, occasional guest stars and lavish production numbers were a part of the show. Three of Mitch's "discoveries," Leslie Uggams, Diana Trask, and Sandy Stewart, went on to considerable success in the music business.

The 1966 summer series was made up entirely of reruns.

SING IT AGAIN

Quiz/Audience Participation

FIRST TELECAST: *September 2, 1950*

LAST TELECAST: *June 23, 1951*

BROADCAST HISTORY:

Sep 1950, CBS Sat 10:00–10:30

Oct 1950–Jun 1951, CBS Sat 10:00–11:00

EMCEE:

Dan Seymour (1950–1951)

Jan Murray (1951)

REGULARS:

Alan Dale

Judy Lynn

Bob Howard

Ray Bloch Orchestra

The Riddlers

Betty Luster

Jack Stanton

This musical quiz show was simulcast on the CBS Radio and Television networks. Dan Seymour was the host when the radio show expanded to both media and was replaced in February by Jan Murray. The regulars, both singers and dancers, stayed with the show throughout most of its TV run. Musical questions were asked of studio audience members and viewers at home. A special feature was the Phantom Voice, in which home viewers attempted to guess the identity of a celebrity, not known as a singer, when they were called. Correct identification could be worth a $15,000 jackpot. Each week a new clue to the identity of the Phantom Voice was given by the emcee.

SINGING LADY, THE

Children's

FIRST TELECAST: *November 7, 1948*

LAST TELECAST: *August 6, 1950*

BROADCAST HISTORY:

Nov 1948–Sep 1949, ABC Sun 6:30–7:00

Oct 1949–Aug 1950, ABC Sun 6:00–6:30

HOSTESS:

Ireene Wicker

REGULARS:

The Suzari Marionettes

Ireene Wicker was one of the most famous—and least likely—victims of the political blacklisting which disgraced television in the early 1950s. She had been a radio favorite for nearly 20 years with her gentle children's stories and lessons in good behavior when she first appeared on the ABC-TV network in 1948. Her program, as on radio, consisted of songs and fairy tales, acted out with the aid of the Suzari Marionettes. Some were true stories of American history, such as Betsy Ross and the flag.

In February 1950 her program was renewed for another year. Then in June a right-wing publication called *Red Channels* listed her among a large group of actors and actresses who had allegedly been associated with left-wing causes. In August, her program was abruptly canceled.

The principal charge, that she had in 1945 signed a petition for the election of Communist candidate Benjamin J. Davis to the New York City Council, turned out to be totally erroneous. An investigation was made of the 30,000 signatures on his petitions and her name was not there (Miss Wicker herself said that she had never heard of Benjamin Davis). Another citation, that she had sided with leftist causes in the Spanish Civil War, turned out to refer to her support of a fund-raising drive for Spanish refugee children. In Miss Wicker's defense, it was pointed out that she had performed playlets emphasizing good citizenship, had conducted an "I'm glad I'm an American because . . ." contest for children, and even recorded a series of records based on American history. Her accusers reluctantly admitted that *perhaps* a mistake had been made.

But the damage had been done. Advertisers and their agencies did not want to be associated with anyone "controversial." No network could find a spot for her. Her only work in this period was at a small radio station in western Massachusetts, and a couple of guest appearances. Finally from 1953–1954 ABC found a sponsor for a Sunday morning show for her, which lasted a single year. A bright and worthwhile career, built laboriously over two decades, had been destroyed by innuendo.

SING-O-PATION

Music

FIRST TELECAST: *January 23, 1949*

LAST TELECAST: *October 30, 1949*

BROADCAST HISTORY:

Jan 1949–Mar 1949, ABC Sun 7:45–8:00
Mar 1949–Aug 1949, ABC Sun 9:00–9:15
Sep 1949–Oct 1949, ABC Sun 6:45–7:00

REGULARS:

Dolores Marshall
George Barnes Trio

Musical interlude from Chicago, featuring vocalist Dolores Marshall. During the program's final month the title was changed to *Serenade*.

SIR FRANCIS DRAKE

see *Adventures of Sir Francis Drake, The*

SIR LANCELOT

see *Adventures of Sir Lancelot, The*

SIROTA'S COURT

Situation Comedy

FIRST TELECAST: *December 1, 1976*

LAST TELECAST: *April 13, 1977*

BROADCAST HISTORY:

Dec 1976–Jan 1977, NBC Wed 9:00–9:30
Apr 1977, NBC Wed 9:30–10:00

CAST:

Matthew J. Sirota .....Michael Constantine
Maureen O'Connor ....Cynthia Harris
Gail Goodman ....Kathleen Miller
Bud Nugent ....Fred Willard
Sawyer Dabney ....Ted Ross
Bailiff John ....Owen Bush

Matthew J. Sirota was a night-court judge in a large metropolitan city, and far from the traditional serious, austere justices of most TV series. He had a sense of humor, was often more concerned with the practical rather than strictly legal resolution of cases, and was considered a character by many of his associates. For years he had been having an on-again off-again affair with court clerk Maureen O'Connor, and periodically seemed on the verge of marriage. Others seen regularly in his court were super-liberal public defender Gail Goodman, forever the idealist but lacking the skills to be really successful; District Attorney Bud Nugent, whose incredible ambition and vanity blinded him to his own incompetence; Sawyer Dabney, an attorney who would handle any case if the price were right; and John, Sirota's bailiff, who treated the judge with the adoration of one who believed him to be Solomon.

SIT OR MISS

Quiz/Audience Participation

FIRST TELECAST: *August 6, 1950*

LAST TELECAST: *October 29, 1950*

BROADCAST HISTORY:

Aug 1950–Oct 1950, ABC Sun 8:30–9:00

EMCEES:

Kay Westfall
George Sotos

MUSICAL ACCOMPANIMENT:

Porter Heaps

This was a TV variation on the old parlor game of musical chairs. Five contestants competed. Each time one of them missed a chair, he was faced with a question, and if he missed the question he had to perform a stunt to win a $10 prize. At the end of the game all five contestants had a chance at a $75 jackpot by guessing, from a verbal clue, the contents of a mystery box. From Chicago.

SIX MILLION DOLLAR MAN, THE

Adventure

FIRST TELECAST: *January 18, 1974*

LAST TELECAST: *March 6, 1978*

BROADCAST HISTORY:

Jan 1974–Oct 1974, ABC Fri 8:30–9:30
Nov 1974–Jan 1975, ABC Fri 9:00–10:00
Jan 1975–Aug 1975, ABC Sun 7:30–8:30
Sep 1975–Jan 1978, ABC Sun 8:00–9:00
Jan 1978–Mar 1978, ABC Mon 8:00–9:00

CAST:

Col. Steve Austin ....Lee Majors
Oscar Goldman ....Richard Anderson
Dr. Rudy Wells (1974–1975)
.... Alan Oppenheimer
Dr. Rudy Wells (1975–1978)
.... Martin E. Brooks

The Six Million Dollar Man touched off a wave of superheroes on TV in the mid-1970s. It was first seen as a series of 90-minute movies run on ABC in March, October, and November 1973 (part of the *ABC Suspense Movie* package), then became a regular weekly series in January 1974. At first the ratings were mediocre, but the program grew steadily until by 1975 it was one of TV's biggest hits.

Handsome, athletic Steve Austin was a

U.S. astronaut who had been critically injured when the moon-landing craft he was testing over a Southwestern desert crashed to the ground. Fighting to save his life, government doctors decided to try a new type of operation devised by Dr. Rudy Wells—the replavement of certain human parts by atomic-powered electromechanical devices, capable of superhuman performance. Steve lived and became a cyborg—part human, part machine, endowed with powerful legs that permitted him great speed, a right arm of incredible strength, and a left eye of penetrating vision (it even had a built-in grid screen!). Armed with these weapons, Steve set out on dangerous missions for the Office of Scientific Information, battling international villains, mad scientists, and even a few alien monsters such as Bigfoot.

Early in the series Steve learned that he was not the only bionic wonder around. It seemed that Dr. Wells had built a *seven*-million-dollar man as backup for Steve, using an injured racecar driver named Barney Miller (played by Monte Markham). Unfortunately the other superman ran amok, and Steve had to find a way to dispatch him, in a battle of the bionic men. A few months later, in January 1975, Jaime Sommers (Lindsay Wagner) was introduced as Steve's love interest and a former tennis pro who had been grievously injured in a sky-diving accident. She was reconstructed into the Bionic Woman. Unfortunately her body rejected its bionic parts, and she died—at least Steve (and viewers) thought she did, until she was brought back ("out of a coma") for several more episodes in the fall. Then she got her own spinoff series called *The Bionic Woman*.

Steve and Jaime's romance seemed destined never to be fulfilled, but nevertheless in November 1976 the series did produce a bionic boy—not theirs, but 16-year-old athlete Andy Sheffield (played by Vincent Van Patten), whose paralyzed legs were replaced by Dr. Wells. Using his new powers the boy promptly set out on a crusade to clear his dead father's name.

Oscar Goldman appeared as Steve's government boss, and Peggy Callahan (Jennifer Darling) was seen occasionally as his secretary. The role of Dr. Rudy Wells was played by a number of actors, including Martin Balsam in the movie pilot and Alan Oppenheimer and Martin E. Brooks in the series.

Based on the novel *Cyborg*, by Martin Caidin.

SIX WIVES OF HENRY VIII, THE

Historical Drama

FIRST TELECAST: *August 1, 1971*

LAST TELECAST: *September 5, 1971*

BROADCAST HISTORY:

Aug 1971–Sep 1971, CBS Sun 9:30–11:00

CAST:

Henry VIII .... Keith Michell
Catherine of Aragon (divorced)
.... Annette Crosbie
Anne Boleyn (beheaded) .... Dorothy Tutin
Jane Seymour (natural death)
.... Anne Stallybrass
Anne of Cleves (divorced) .... Elvi Hale
Catherine Howard (beheaded)
.... Angela Pleasence
Catherine Parr (outlived him)
.... Rosalie Crutchley
Duke of Norfolk .... Patrick Troughton
Oliver Cromwell .... Wolfe Morris
Archbishop Cranmer ...... Bernard Hepton

NARRATOR:

Anthony Quayle

This series of six 90-minute programs had been produced in England by the BBC and won the British equivalent of the Emmy award in five categories. CBS brought it to American television in the summer of 1971. The one addition to the American version was narrator Anthony Quayle. He introduced and concluded each telecast and provided historical background. During his reign as English monarch, Henry VIII had two wives beheaded for adultery, saw one die of natural causes, was divorced from two others and, when he died in 1547 at the age of 56, was survived by his sixth, Catherine Parr.

SIXTH SENSE, THE

Occult

FIRST TELECAST: *January 15, 1972*

LAST TELECAST: *December 30, 1972*

BROADCAST HISTORY:

Jan 1972–Dec 1972, ABC Sat 10:00–11:00 (OS)

CAST:

Dr. Michael Rhodes .... Gary Collins
Nancy Murphy (Jan–May)
.... Catherine Ferrar

"You enter a strange room for the first time, yet you know you've been there before. You dream about an event that happens some days later. Someone begins to talk, and you already know what they're going to say. A coincidence? Maybe. But more than likely it's extrasensory perception, a sixth sense that many scientists believe we all possess, but rarely use."

That quotation from a press release pretty well sums up the kind of stories told on *The Sixth Sense*. Dr. Michael Rhodes' studies in parapsychology at a major university took him into the uncharted world of ESP, telepathy, and other psychic phenomena every week, sometimes leading to eerie adventures. Perhaps his most useful exploit was communicating an escape plan to an American prisoner of war in Vietnam, by thought transference. Nancy Murphy was his research assistant during the series' first few months.

$64,000 CHALLENGE, THE

Quiz/Audience Participation

FIRST TELECAST: *April 8, 1956*

LAST TELECAST: *September 7, 1958*

BROADCAST HISTORY:

Apr 1956–Sep 1958, CBS Sun 10:00–10:30

EMCEE:

Sonny Fox (1956)
Ralph Story (1956–1958)

This was a highly successful spinoff of CBS's popular big-money quiz show *The $64,000 Question*. Any of the winners from the original show whose earnings had been at least $8,000 were eligible to be challenged on this series, in the field of knowledge in which they had already demonstrated their skill. The same questions were asked of champion and challenger, each in a separate isolation booth. If one of them missed a question at any level, and the other answered it correctly, the loser was then eliminated. The contestant who had answered correctly continued alone until he also missed a question, quit, or reached the $64,000 question. In any event, he was guaranteed no less than the amount at which he had defeated his opponent. A successful challenger could be challenged by others. On occasion a defeated champion returned as a challenger and won. Through this format, contestants could multiply their winnings from a prior round several times over.

The biggest winner in the era of big-money quiz shows became a regular on this show. Teddy Nadler was a $70-per-week civil service clerk from St. Louis who happened to have a photographic memory. He had, apparently, memorized a complete encyclopedia and could dredge up the most obscure information. By the time *The $64,000 Challenge* left the air in 1958, he had won $252,000 and was still going strong. He became such a celebrity on the show that he was often competing with two or three different people, on totally unrelated topics, all at the same time.

$64,000 QUESTION, THE

Quiz/Audience Participation

FIRST TELECAST: *June 7, 1955*

LAST TELECAST: *November 2, 1958*

BROADCAST HISTORY:

Jun 1955–Jun 1958, CBS Tue 10:00–10:30
Sep 1958–Nov 1958, CBS Sun 10:00–10:30

EMCEE:

Hal March

ASSISTANT:

Lynn Dollar

QUESTION AUTHORITY:

Dr. Bergen Evans

The era of the big-money quiz show arrived during the summer of 1955 in the form of *The $64,000 Question*. A much-inflated variation on radio's *$64 Question*, it offered contestants the opportunity to win vast sums of money by answering extremely complex questions on whatever subject they professed to be experts. A contestant first went through preliminary rounds up to the $4,000 level, with each question, starting at $64, worth twice as much as the preceding question. At that point the contestant would go home and return to answer one question a week until missing or reaching $64,000. The consolation prize for missing after reaching the $8,000 plateau was a new Cadillac. Contestants could quit at any time and leave with their winnings. In order to enable the contestants to concentrate completely, and to avoid any possible answers shouted from the studio audience, all questions from $8,000 on up were asked while contestants were sealed inside a Revlon isolation booth (named for the sponsor).

The appeal of seeing ordinary people sweating through complex questions to reach huge sums of money was enormous, and *The $64,000 Question* became an overnight sensation. It shot to number one among all programs on TV in its first season on the air, displacing *I Love Lucy*, and it spawned many imitators in the big-money sweepstakes. Among them were *Twenty-One* and, from Louis G. Cowan, the man who had started it all here, *The Big Surprise* and *The $64,000 Challenge*.

Many of the contestants were interesting people and generated tremendous empathy from the audience. One of the early winners was New York City policeman Redmond O'Hanlon, an expert on Shakespeare, who took home $16,000. Gino Prato, a shoemaker from the Bronx, took home $32,000 for his knowledge of opera. Catherine Kreitzer was a housewife who won $32,000 on the subject of the Bible, and was then signed to do a series of Bible readings on *The Ed Sullivan Show*. Jockey Billy Pearson was an early winner of $64,000—his subject was art. Many of the winners on *The $64,000 Question* went on to make extra money on its companion show, *The $64,000 Challenge*. One of those was a young psychologist, Dr. Joyce Brothers, who parlayed her knowledge of boxing to the grand prize of $64,000 here, another $70,000 on *Challenge*, and a long and successful career as a radio and television personality. The biggest winner on *The $64,000 Question*, however, was young Robert Strom, an 11-year-old genius who amassed $192,000 during a period when, in order to hold onto its audience amid the competing shows, three new plateaus were added to *The $64,000 Question* making the maximum possible winnings $256,000. Strom's total quiz-show winnings, $224,000 including money won on other shows, made him the second biggest winner of the big-money quiz-show era. Only Teddy Nadler's $252,000 on *The $64,000 Challenge* was higher.

The money angle was a magic attraction, especially during the early days of the giant giveaway shows. *TV Guide* kept a running total of the amount given away on this show—$750,000 and 10 Cadillacs in the first year and $1,000,000 by November 1956—and published numerous articles about the show and its contestants. There were always rumors that the series was rigged, that the desire to put interesting personalities on the air, rather than brilliant but dull geniuses, resulted in the producers providing answers in advance to some, but not all, of the contestants. As early as September 1956 there was a lengthy article in *TV Guide* in which the producers of *Question*, *Challenge*, and *The Big Surprise* adamantly denied that there was anything misleading or dishonest about the shows, but in the fall of 1958 the bubble burst. A disgruntled loser on *Dotto*, another giveaway show, announced that the show was rigged, and precipitated the quiz-show scandal that eventually forced all of them off the air. No longer would contestants sweat and ponder in the "isolation booths" that kept them from hearing what was going on in the outside world while searching for answers to incredibly complicated questions.

60 MINUTES

News Magazine

FIRST TELECAST: *September 24, 1968*
LAST TELECAST:
BROADCAST HISTORY:

Sep 1968–Jun 1971, CBS Tue 10:00–11:00 (OS)
Jan 1972–Jun 1972, CBS Sun 6:00–7:00
Jan 1973–Jun 1973, CBS Sun 6:00–7:00
Jun 1973–Sep 1973, CBS Fri 8:00–9:00
Jan 1974–Jun 1974, CBS Sun 6:00–7:00
Jul 1974–Sep 1974, CBS Sun 9:30–10:30
Jan 1975–Jun 1975, CBS Sun 6:00–7:00
Jul 1975–Sep 1975, CBS Sun 9:30–10:30
Dec 1975– , CBS Sun 7:00–8:00

CORRESPONDENTS:

Mike Wallace
Harry Reasoner (1968–1970, 1978–)
Morley Safer (1970–)
Dan Rather (1975–)
Andrew Rooney (1978–)

DEBATERS:

James J. Kilpatrick (1971–)
Nicholas Von Hoffman (1971–1974)
Shana Alexander (1975–)

60 Minutes was the *Time* magazine of the air. Each telecast opened with a "table of contents" (brief excerpts from the three or more stories that would be covered on that episode) superimposed on what appeared to be a magazine cover. Also superimposed at various times, usually between stories, was a moving stopwatch letting viewers know precisely how much of that night's "60 Minutes" was left. Within the magazine trappings lay a documentary series with remarkable scope. There were pieces on politics and politicians; the workings of governments, both domestic and foreign; personality profiles on artists, athletes, and citizens whose stories had mass appeal; and light feature pieces on everything from trade shows, to new inventions, to the shopping phenomenon that was Bloomingdale's department store. Indeed, *60 Minutes* was sufficiently diversified so that, like each issue of a successful magazine, it had something to appeal to, concern, or interest almost everybody.

Among the more provocative stories featured in segments of *60 Minutes* were numerous items on politics in the Middle East; a 1971 feature on the situation in the Gulf of Tonkin; "The Poppy Fields of Turkey—The Heroin Labs of Marseilles—The N.Y. Connection" (1972); "The Selling of Colonel Herbert" (1973); "The End of a Salesman" (1974); "Local News and the Ratings War" (1974); several items on, and interviews with, participants in the Watergate scandal during 1974–1976; a controversial story on the plight of Jordanian Jews (1976); and a feature on the brain damage suffered by workers in a chemical plant manufacturing Kepone (1976).

60 Minutes spent its first three seasons on an alternate-week schedule with *CBS News Hour*. It was during this period that one of the original two correspondents, Harry Reasoner, left the show to join ABC News. His last appearance was on November 24, 1970. Two weeks later, Morley Safer joined Mike Wallace. When it moved into its own weekly time slot on Sunday evenings, a new regular feature called "Point Counterpoint" was added. Each week two columnists at opposite ends of the ideological spectrum—conservative James J. Kilpatrick and liberal Nicholas Von Hoffman (replaced by Shana Alexander in 1975)—would debate a current issue. They have yet to be in agreement about anything. Dan Rather joined the show in December 1975, when it moved into the prime 7:00–8:00 P.M. hour, expanding the correspondent team from a duet to a trio. It was here that *60 Minutes* became a major hit, violating the traditional role of information programs as marginal, at best, audience attractions. The summer of 1978 saw the addition of "Three Minutes or So with Andy Rooney" as a weekly feature filling in for the vacationing debaters from "Point Counterpoint". At the start of the 1978–1979 season Mr. Rooney's musings shared time with "Point Counterpoint," each feature airing on alternate weeks. It was also that fall that Harry Reasoner returned to *60 Minutes*, bringing the number of correspondents to four.

The conclusion of *60 Minutes* telecasts, in true magazine fashion, consisted of one of the correspondents reading a collection of letters to the editors, followed by that ever-moving stopwatch signalling the end of the hour while the closing credits rolled.

SKIP FARRELL SHOW, THE

Music

FIRST TELECAST: *January 17, 1949*
LAST TELECAST: *August 28, 1949*
BROADCAST HISTORY:

Jan 1949–Feb 1949, ABC Mon 9:00–9:30
Feb 1949–May 1949, ABC Mon 9:15–9:30
May 1949–Jun 1949, ABC Mon 9:00–9:30
Jul 1949–Aug 1949, ABC Sun 9:30–10:00

HOST:

Skip Farrell

REGULARS:

The Honeydreamers
Adele Scott Trio
Bill Moss Orchestra

Musical program from Chicago, starring singer Skip Farrell.

SKY KING

Western

FIRST TELECAST: *September 21, 1953*
LAST TELECAST: *September 12, 1954*
BROADCAST HISTORY:

Sep 1953–Sep 1954, ABC Mon 8:00–8:30
Aug 1954–Sep 1954, ABC Sun 6:00–6:30

CAST:

Sky King .... Kirby Grant
Penny .... Gloria Winters
Clipper .... Ron Haggerty

Sky King was a contemporary Western, starring Kirby Grant as an Arizona pilot-rancher who used an airplane instead of a horse to fight wrongdoers. With him on the Flying Crown Ranch were his teenage niece Penny and nephew Clipper. Sky's twin-engine Cessna was called *The Songbird*.

Sky King wandered all over the weekend daytime schedule before touching down in prime time in 1953. It was seen Sunday afternoons on NBC from 1951–1952 and Saturday afternoons on ABC from 1952–

1953. Later, from 1959–1966, the same films showed up Saturday afternoons on CBS. The program was also heard on radio from 1946–1954.

SLATTERY'S PEOPLE

Political Drama

FIRST TELECAST: *September 21, 1964*

LAST TELECAST: *November 26, 1965*

BROADCAST HISTORY:

Sep 1964–Dec 1964, CBS Mon 10:00–11:00

Dec 1964–Nov 1965, CBS Fri 10:00–11:00

CAST:

James Slattery .... Richard Crenna

Frank Radcliff .... Edward Asner

Johnny Ramos .... Paul Geary

B.J. Clawson .... Maxine Stuart

Speaker Bert Metcalf .... Tol Avery

Liz Andrews (1965) .... Kathie Browne

Mike Valera (1965) .... Alejandro Rey

Wendy Wendkowski (1965) .. Francine York

The professional and personal conflicts and activities of the minority leader in a fictional state legislature were depicted in *Slattery's People*. James Slattery was an idealistic, concerned state representative who was very interested in governmental reforms and constantly found himself involved in causes. With the help of his aide, Johnny Ramos, and his secretary, B.J., he attempted to push legislation that would better the lot of his constituents. House Speaker Bert Metcalf of the stronger opposition party, was his friendly enemy. When this series returned for an abbreviated second season, Slattery had a new aide (Mike Valera), a new secretary (Wendy Wendkowski), and a regular girl friend in Liz Andrews.

SLEEPY JOE

Children's

FIRST TELECAST: *October 3, 1949*

LAST TELECAST: *October 28, 1949*

BROADCAST HISTORY:

Oct 1949, ABC Mon–Fri 6:45–7:00

Short-lived children's puppet show. A filmed version was later produced for syndication.

SMALL FRY CLUB

Children's

FIRST TELECAST: *March 11, 1947*

LAST TELECAST: *June 15, 1951*

BROADCAST HISTORY:

Mar 1947–Apr 1947, DUM Tue 7:00–8:00

Apr 1947–Jan 1948, DUM Mon–Fri 7:00–7:30

Jan 1948–Apr 1948, DUM Mon–Fri 6:15–6:45

Apr 1948–Jun 1951, DUM Mon–Fri 6:00–6:30

HOST:

Bob Emery

DuMont's *Small Fry Club* was one of the gentlest and most widely lauded children's shows of TV's early days. To an adult viewer it might be pure corn: letters from the little tykes read over the air, with their pictures shown; lessons on good behavior, safety, drinking more milk, etc.; and sketches by a studio cast of actors representing different animals. For the kindergarten set, however, it was *their* show. Its host, a remarkable man who went by the name of "Big Brother" Bob Emery, had spent his whole life entertaining youngsters while imparting lessons of good behavior. From the time he began his "club" on a radio station in Medford, Massachusetts, in 1921, he stressed involvement rather than one-way entertainment, and his young listeners flocked to obtain official membership cards, wrote him letters, sent in pictures and drawings, and joined in contests.

Emery (he then spelled it Emory) later came to New York and got into television on the ground floor, as announcer and producer at DuMont's WABD. He assumed his radio role of "Big Brother" on the station's Christmas show in 1946, and in March 1947 began his first video series, called *Movies for Small Fry*. At first it was just that, cartoons and other children's films, with voiceover narration by Bob—he was not even seen. But soon the program expanded to five days a week (possibly the first ever to do so) and a regular studio setting was developed. Membership cards were offered and letters came pouring in. If anyone doubted the effectiveness of the new medium in reaching an audience, they had only to look at the figures for the *Small Fry Club*: 1,200 cards sent out by May 1947, 15,000 by January 1948, 150,000 "active" members by 1950. Some of these were the children of parents who had themselves been *Small Fry Club* members in the 1920s. Contests drew enormous responses, including 150 returns a week for a jingle contest in 1947, 10,000 drawings by 1948 (these were regularly shown on the air) and

24,000 letters to name a new member of the cast in 1951. (She became Trina the Kitten.)

Other regulars with Bob were Honey the Bunny, Mr. Mischief the Panda, Willy the Wiz, and Peggy the Penguin. Big Brother himself always appeared in a business suit, with heavy, dark-rimmed glasses—the picture of a kindly uncle. In addition to skits such as "Columbus and Isabella" and "Washington at Mr. Vernon," educational films and advice for kids were offered.

As with some other early shows, it is not known whether the *Small Fry Club* was fed over the network from the start; in any event, it was on the network (i.e., two stations) by late 1947. Bob Emery left DuMont in 1951 to return to Boston, where he later was seen in a series of local programs.

SMALL WORLD

Discussion

FIRST TELECAST: *October 12, 1958*
LAST TELECAST: *May 29, 1960*
BROADCAST HISTORY:
Oct 1958–May 1960, CBS Sun 6:00–6:30 (OS)
MODERATOR:
Edward R. Murrow

Each week on this filmed series, moderator Edward R. Murrow conducted an informal, unrehearsed discussion with three or four world celebrities. The celebrities were located at widely divergent places around the world and it was only through the use of advanced electronic technology that these people could get together "face to face." Serious discussions on world politics might include Thomas E. Dewey, Jawaharlal Nehru, and writer Aldous Huxley, as on the premiere telecast. Lighter shows might involve actress Ingrid Bergman, *New York Times* film critic Bosley Crowther, and producer Darryl F. Zanuck chatting about the state of the motion-picture industry.

SMILIN' ED McCONNELL AND HIS BUSTER BROWN GANG

Children's

FIRST TELECAST: *August 26, 1950*
LAST TELECAST: *May 19, 1951*
BROADCAST HISTORY:
Aug 1950–May 1951, NBC Sat 6:30–7:00
HOST:
Ed McConnell

Children's program, based on McConnell's radio show, which featured him playing the piano, singing and telling stories from his storybook—sometimes in the form of films, always with a moral. In the cast were Midnight the tabby cat, Squeaky the mouse, Old Grandie the talking piano, and Uncle Fishface, the world's greatest storyteller. After its prime-time run the series returned to television on Saturday mornings from 1953–1955, with Andy Devine replacing McConnell upon the latter's death in 1954.

SMITH FAMILY, THE

Drama

FIRST TELECAST: *January 20, 1971*
LAST TELECAST: *June 14, 1972*
BROADCAST HISTORY:
Jan 1971–Sep 1971, ABC Wed 8:30–9:00
Sep 1971–Jan 1972, ABC Wed 9:00–9:30
Apr 1972–Jun 1972, ABC Wed 8:30–9:00
CAST:
Det. Sgt. Chad Smith ....Henry Fonda
Betty Smith ....Janet Blair
Cindy Smith ....Darleen Carr
Bob Smith ....Ronny Howard
Brian Smith ....Michael-James Wixted
Capt. Hughes ....Charles McGraw
Sgt. Ray Martin ....John Carter

Henry Fonda starred in this family drama about the home life of a big-city cop. Det. Sgt. Chad Smith was a Los Angeles plainclothesman, 25 years on the force, who worked on burglaries, drug busts, runaway children, bomb threats and, occasionally, homicides. His suburban family consisted of wife Betty; 18-year-old daughter Cindy, an L.A. City College student with marriage on her mind; 15-year-old son Bob; and 7-year-old son Brian. Stories touched on the generation gap and the problems of youth as much as on Chad's police work, which did include some dangerous situations but not really much hard action. His captain and partner, Sgt. Martin, were only seen occasionally.

SMITHSONIAN, THE

Documentary

FIRST TELECAST: *June 25, 1967*
LAST TELECAST: *August 27, 1967*
BROADCAST HISTORY:
Jun 1967–Aug 1967, NBC Sun 6:30–7:00

HOST:
Bill Ryan

The vast Smithsonian Museum complex in Washington, D.C., was the starting point for this series. Each week a specific exhibit in one of the Smithsonian buildings opened a filmed exploratory journey into history or some field of scientific endeavor. NBC newsman Bill Ryan narrated the background material with on-location film footage, stills, and animation. The series had originally aired from October 1966 to April 1967 on Saturdays at 12:30 P.M. The episodes seen on Sunday evenings during the summer of 1967 were all reruns.

SMOTHERS BROTHERS COMEDY HOUR, THE

Comedy Variety

FIRST TELECAST: *February 5, 1967*
LAST TELECAST: *May 26, 1975*
BROADCAST HISTORY:
Feb 1967–Jun 1969, CBS Sun 9:00–10:00 (OS)
Jul 1970–Sep 1970, ABC Wed 10:00–11:00
Jan 1975–May 1975, NBC Mon 8:00–9:00

REGULARS:
Tom Smothers
Dick Smothers
Pat Paulsen
Leigh French (1967–1969, 1975)
Bob Einstein (as *Officer Judy*) (1967–1969, 1975)
The Louis DaPron Dancers (1967–1968)
The Ron Poindexter Dancers (1968–1969)
The Anita Kerr Singers (1967)
The Jimmy Joyce Singers (1967–1969)
Nelson Riddle and His Orchestra (1967–1969)
The Denny Vaughn Orchestra (1970)
Mason Williams (1967–1969)
Jennifer Warren (1967–1969)
John Hartford (1968–1969)
Sally Struthers (1970)
Spencer Quinn (1970)
Betty Aberlin (1975)
Don Novello (1975)
Steve Martin (1975)
Nino Senporty (1975)
The Marty Paich Orchestra (1975)

Tom and Dick Smothers had been a very popular comedy/singing team in the early and mid-1960s with a number of successful offbeat comedy albums. Tom, who played the guitar, acted the role of the dullard, unable to think logically, making all sorts of inane remarks, and being generally impossible to deal with. Dick, who played bass, was, by contrast, calm, reasonable, and hard pressed to retain his composure when confronted by his brother's stupidity and silliness. Extremely popular with young people, they were an immediate hit with their irreverent variety series on CBS in 1967. Abetted by Pat Paulsen's low-keyed "editorials" and other material, which at times rivaled Tom for the evening's silliest moments, and a large supporting cast, *The Smothers Brothers Comedy Hour* poked fun at virtually all the hallowed institutions of American society—motherhood, church, politics, government, etc. It was topical, it was funny, and occasionally it was in bad taste.

There were always problems getting program material cleared with the CBS censors, and the adamant position taken by the show's stars over what they considered was acceptable did not endear them to CBS management. First there were minor skirmishes. Pat Paulsen had started a campaign for President on their summer series in 1968 (*The Summer Brothers Smothers Show*) with the slogan "If nominated I will not run, and if elected I will not serve." It was a joke but CBS, fearing demands for equal time from real candidates, kept him off the show until after the election. Pete Seeger, a controversial folk singer long blacklisted on television, made several appearances on the show and got them into trouble with his Vietnam protest song "Knee Deep in the Big Muddy." Early in 1969 they did a comedy sketch making fun of religion that outraged the clergy and forced an on-air apology.

CBS had had enough. The ratings were still high, but CBS management finally concluded that *The Smothers Brothers Comedy Hour* was just not worth the trouble. The brothers' choice of guests, predominantly antiwar, left-wing, and outspoken; their fights over material; and their repeated failure to deliver finished programs early enough in the week for the censors to get them edited by air time on Sunday were all advanced as reasons when the series was abruptly canceled. There was a good deal of furor over freedom of speech and the like, but the CBS decision stuck. The Smothers Brothers were replaced by *Hee Haw*.

Thirteen months later, *The Smothers Summer Show* turned up on ABC. Apparently their time had passed, and the show (which included three repeats of episodes from the original CBS series) did not make it to the ABC fall schedule. In 1975 NBC gave Tom and Dick yet another chance, with a new variety series simply titled *The Smothers Brothers Show*. There were no real problems with the NBC censors, probably because the biting edge was gone from their material. The closest they came to anything controversial on the premiere telecast was when Tom announced that they had an "iron-clad" 13-week contract. It got off to a strong start, due more to audience curiosity about what had happened to Tom and Dick in the five years since they had last been on network television than to the merits of the program, but quickly sank into obscurity.

SMOTHERS BROTHERS SHOW, THE

Situation Comedy

FIRST TELECAST: *September 17, 1965*
LAST TELECAST: *September 9, 1966*
BROADCAST HISTORY:
Sep 1965–Sep 1966, CBS Fri 9:30–10:00
CAST:
Tom Smothers ....Himself
Dick Smothers ....Himself
Leonard J. Costello ....Roland Winters

As a rising young executive at Pandora Publications, working for publisher Leonard J. Costello, Dick Smothers should have been enjoying the life of a prosperous bachelor. But one little thing kept getting in the way—his brother Tom. Not in ordinary ways, either. Tom had been lost at sea and two years later showed up as an apprentice angel, assigned to do good works on Earth to become a full-fledged regular angel. His efforts to help people did not always seem to work out the way he had planned, and he was forever seeking the aid of his earthly brother to help bail him out of some blunder he had created.

SNEAK PREVIEW

Anthology

FIRST TELECAST: *July 3, 1956*
LAST TELECAST: *August 7, 1956*
BROADCAST HISTORY:
Jul 1956–Aug 1956, NBC Tue 9:00–9:30
HOST:
Nelson Case

The implication of this series was that the viewer would be seeing pilot films for series which might turn up on the fall schedule. None of them made it, however. Included were half-hour comedies starring Zsa Zsa Gabor, Ann Sheridan, and Celeste Holm. *Sneak Preview* was the 1956 summer replacement for *Jane Wyman's Fireside Theater*.

SNOOP SISTERS, THE

Detective

FIRST TELECAST: *December 19, 1973*
LAST TELECAST: *August 20, 1974*
BROADCAST HISTORY:
Dec 1973, NBC Wed 8:30–10:00
Jan 1974–Aug 1974, NBC Tue 8:30–10:00
CAST:
Ernesta Snoop ....Helen Hayes
Gwen Snoop ....Mildred Natwick
Barney ....Lou Antonio
Lt. Ostrowski ....Bert Convy

Ernesta and Gwen Snoop were two elderly sisters who were well named. Despite the fact that they were very successful mystery writers, or possibly because of it, they could not resist getting involved in real mysteries. Their experience working with clues in the fictitious stories they wrote for a living stood them in good stead when they were confronted with the urge to try to solve real crimes. All the physical work was handled for them by Barney, their combination chauffeur and bodyguard, and their nephew, police lieutenant Ostrowski. *The Snoop Sisters* was one of the four rotating elements in the 1973–1974 version of *The NBC Wednesday/Tuesday Mystery Movie*. The others were *Banacek*, *Faraday and Company*, and *Tenafly*.

SO THIS IS HOLLYWOOD

Situation Comedy

FIRST TELECAST: *January 1, 1955*
LAST TELECAST: *August 19, 1955*
BROADCAST HISTORY:
Jan 1955–Jun 1955, NBC Sat 8:30–9:00
Jul 1955–Aug 1955, NBC Fri 10:30–11:00
CAST:
Queenie Dugan ....Mitzi Green
Kim Tracy ....Virginia Gibson
Andy Boone ....Jimmy Lydon
Hubie Dodd ....Gordon Jones

So This Is Hollywood was the story of two young women trying to make it in show business. Queenie Dugan was a stunt woman who had been around Hollywood long enough to know how to avoid being hustled and to realize that she wasn't ever going to be a star herself. Her roommate, Kim Tracy, was a young starlet and movie extra who, despite the efforts of her agent, Andy, seemed unable to get the one big break that would make her a star. Queenie was always trying to find ways to promote Kim's career, as were both Andy and Queenie's stunt-man boy friend Hubie.

SO YOU WANT TO LEAD A BAND

see *Sammy Kaye Show, The*

SOAP

Situation Comedy

FIRST TELECAST: *September 13, 1977*

LAST TELECAST:

BROADCAST HISTORY:

Sep 1977–Mar 1978, ABC Tue 9:30–10:00

Jun 1978–Sep 1978, ABC Mon/Tue 11:30–12:00 Midnight

Sep 1978– , ABC Thu 9:30–10:00

CAST:

Chester Tate .... Robert Mandan
Jessica Tate .... Katherine Helmond
Corrine Tate .... Diana Canova
Eunice Tate .... Jennifer Salt
Billy Tate .... Jimmy Baio
Benson .... Robert Guillaume
The Major .... Arthur Peterson
Mary Dallas Campbell ..... Cathryn Damon
Burt Campbell .... Richard Mulligan
Jodie Dallas .... Billy Crystal
Danny Dallas .... Ted Wass
The Godfather (1977–1978)
.... Richard Libertini
Claire (1977–1978) ...... Kathryn Reynolds
Peter Campbell (1977) .... Robert Urich
Chuck/Bob Campbell .... Jay Johnson
Dennis Phillips .... Bob Seagren
Father Timothy Flotsky (1978–)
.... Sal Viscuso
Carol David (1978–)
.... Rebecca Balding
Elaine Lefkowitz (1978–)
.... Dinah Manoff

Soap was undoubtedly the most controversial new series of the 1977–1978 "season of sex." Even before it went on the air ABC had received 22,000 letters about the show—all but four of them against it—ABC affiliates had been picketed for planning to air it, and sponsors had been urged to boycott the show (which a few did). Some ABC affiliates refused to carry it, and many who did ran it late at night.

The object of all this ire was a half-hour comedy which was billed as a satire on soap operas. It had a continuing story line of sorts, but was populated by a cast such as was seldom seen on any serious dramatic show. Stories centered on the wealthy Tates and the blue-collar Campbells. Chester Tate was a pompous businessman with an affinity for extramarital affairs; no wonder, since his wife, Jessica, was an empty-headed, fluttery idiot. Of their three children, sexy Corrine was always putting her best attributes forward; Eunice was quieter and more conservative; and Billy, 14, was a wisecracking brat. Living with the Tates was Jessica's father, "the Major," who crawled around the floor in his old Army uniform, still fighting World War II; and Benson, the insolent and obnoxious black servant and cook, who commented on the proceedings.

Across town lived Jessica's sister, Mary Campbell. Her husband, Burt, was a "working stiff" whose main problem lay in dealing with stepsons Jodie (who was gay) and Danny (who was involved with organized crime). Surreptitious sex was on practically everyone's mind, and formed the basis of many of the stories.

The major development during the first season was the murder of Peter, the handsome tennis pro (and Burt's son), who had been luring most of his female students into bed with him. First Corrine was accused, but then Jessica was arrested and subsequently convicted of the crime. In the last episode of the 1977–1978 season, an off-screen narrator informed viewers that she didn't really do it, and as the following season opened, Chester confessed to the crime.

Soap attracted a large and loyal audience, but nevertheless the controversy continued. ABC intimated that the program represented a major breakthrough in TV comedy, and claimed that "through the Campbells and the Tates many of today's social concerns will be dealt with in a comedic manner." Others considered *Soap* nothing more than an extended dirty joke being piped into America's living rooms. Much of the opposition to the program was led by religious groups, including the National Council of Churches. Rev. Everett

Parker, a longtime critic of TV, called *Soap* "a deliberate effort to break down any resistance to whatever the industry wants to put into prime time. . . . Who else besides the churches is going to stand against the effort of television to tear down our moral values and make all of us into mere consumers?"

SOAP BOX THEATRE

Dramatic Anthology

FIRST TELECAST: *June 24, 1950*

LAST TELECAST: *December 3, 1950*

BROADCAST HISTORY:

Jun 1950–Oct 1950, ABC Sun 9:30–10:00
Oct 1950–Dec 1950, ABC Sun 9:00–9:30

This was a series of filmed dramas.

SOLDIER PARADE

see *Talent Patrol*

SOLDIERS, THE

Situation Comedy

FIRST TELECAST: *June 25, 1955*

LAST TELECAST: *September 3, 1955*

BROADCAST HISTORY:

Jun 1955–Sep 1955, NBC Sat 8:00–8:30

CAST:

Hal ....Hal March
Tom ....Tom D'Andrea

This live summer comedy series, originating from Hollywood, starred Hal March and Tom D'Andrea in the roles they had played over the years on numerous variety shows. As two typical GI's who found nothing but trouble in the Army, Tom and Hal complained about almost everything—the regimentation, the food, their superior officers, etc. Each episode contained one or more vignettes about a specific aspect of life in the Army: getting letters from home, trying to get passes, being sent to an isolated location for a special assignment, and the problems of adjusting to civilian life after getting discharged.

SOMERSET MAUGHAM TV THEATRE

Dramatic Anthology

FIRST TELECAST: *October 18, 1950*

LAST TELECAST: *December 10, 1951*

BROADCAST HISTORY:

Oct 1950–Mar 1951, CBS Wed 9:00–9:30
Apr 1951–Jun 1951, NBC Mon 9:30–10:30
Jul 1951–Aug 1951, NBC Mon 9:30–10:00
Sep 1951–Dec 1951, NBC Mon 9:30–10:30

HOST:

W. Somerset Maugham

This anthology series had the distinction of having as host the author of the novels and short stories that had been adapted for television presentation. The plays themselves were live, originating from New York, but the opening and closing remarks by the author had all been filmed prior to the start of the season at his home on the French Riviera. He would introduce each play and return at the end to thank the audience for watching and to announce the title of the next week's production. When it premiered on CBS as a half-hour series, its title was *Teller of Tales*. After three telecasts the title was changed to *Somerset Maugham TV Theatre*. On NBC during the spring and fall of 1951, a full-hour version of the show aired on alternate weeks with *Robert Montgomery Presents*. It ran during the summer of 1951 as a half-hour show every week.

SONG AND DANCE

Music

FIRST TELECAST: *December 17, 1948*

LAST TELECAST: *June 21, 1949*

BROADCAST HISTORY:

Dec 1948–Jan 1949, NBC Fri 8:00–8:30
Jan 1949–Mar 1949, NBC Mon 8:00–8:30
Mar 1949–Apr 1949, NBC Mon 8:15–8:30
May 1949–Jun 1949, NBC Various nights and times

EMCEE:

Roberta Quinlan (1948–1949)
Barbara Marshall (1949)

DANCERS:

Ellsworth & Fairchild

Live musical interlude featuring songs and dancing. Quite a number of "regular" singers and dancers came and went during the program's short run. Roberta Quinlan was the original hostess, replaced by Barbara Marshall in April 1949.

SONG SNAPSHOTS ON A SUMMER HOLIDAY

see *Summer Holiday*

SONGS AT TWILIGHT

Music

FIRST TELECAST: *July 3, 1951*

LAST TELECAST: *August 31, 1951*

BROADCAST HISTORY:

Jul 1951–Aug 1951, NBC Mon–Fri 7:30–7:45

REGULARS:

Bob Carroll
Buddy Greco
Johnny Andrews

Songs at Twilight was a live informal 15 minutes of song and talk by its host and his guest star of the evening. It spent the summer of 1951 filling the remainder of the half-hour in which NBC aired its network news program. Holding on to a host was a problem for this series. When it premiered, singer Bob Carroll had the job. On July 16 he was replaced by singer-pianist Buddy Greco, who was replaced on July 30 by singer Johnny Andrews. Andrews somehow managed to last until the program went off the air.

SONGS FOR SALE

Music

FIRST TELECAST: *July 7, 1950*
LAST TELECAST: *June 28, 1952*
BROADCAST HISTORY:

Jul 1950–Sep 1950, CBS Fri 9:00–10:00
Feb 1951, CBS Sat 7:30–8:00
Jun 1951–Feb 1952, CBS Sat 10:00–11:00
Mar 1952–Jun 1952, CBS Sat 9:30–11:00
Jun 1952, CBS Sat 8:00–9:00

EMCEE:

Jan Murray (1950–1951)
Steve Allen (1951–1952)

REGULARS:

Rosemary Clooney (1950–1951)
Tony Bennett (1950)
Richard Hayes (1950–1951)
Ray Bloch and His Orchestra
Mitch Miller (1951)
Peggy Lee (1951–1952)
Barry Gray (1952)

Songs for Sale was a showcase for the efforts of aspiring amateur songwriters. Each week a number of them (usually three) had their songs performed by professional singers and rated by a panel of judges. The winning song was guaranteed to be published, and the runners-up might be if a publisher who was listening liked them. The show, needless to say, was swamped with submissions. Originally there were two permanent singers on the show, and a rotating panel of judges. Rosemary Clooney and Tony Bennett were relatively unknown when the series began, but both immediately attracted considerable attention and went on to become major stars—they were probably more important "discoveries" of this show than any of the songs. (Both had previously been winners on *Arthur Godfrey's Talent Scouts.*) Bennett left the show after a month, but Rosemary Clooney continued, joined by Richard Hayes. Both of them remained until the show was temporarily shelved in the fall of 1950.

When it returned in 1951 singers were generally rotated, though Peggy Lee became a regular in December 1951 and remained for several months. Panelists changed too. For a period in the spring of 1951 Mitch Miller was a regular panelist, and Barry Gray served in a similar capacity in the spring of 1952. From its inception until September 1951, *Songs for Sale* was simulcast on radio and TV.

During its last season there were cash awards, up to $1,000, available to weekly winners whose songs also won a special runoff held once every five or six weeks, before an enlarged panel of judges.

SONGTIME

Religion

FIRST TELECAST: *October 6, 1951*
LAST TELECAST: *May 17, 1952*
BROADCAST HISTORY:

Oct 1951–May 1952, ABC Sat 11:00–11:30

HOST:

Jack Wyrtzen

Hymns, gospel songs, and inspirational talks by youth leader Jack Wyrtzen. The program began locally in New York in November 1950, and was seen live over the network during the 1951–1952 season. Also known as *The Word of Life Songtime.*

SONNY AND CHER COMEDY HOUR, THE

Musical Variety

FIRST TELECAST: *August 1, 1971*
LAST TELECAST: *August 29, 1977*
BROADCAST HISTORY:

Aug 1971–Sep 1971, CBS Sun 8:30–9:30
Dec 1971–Jun 1972, CBS Mon 10:00–11:00
Sep 1972–Dec 1972, CBS Fri 8:00–9:00
Dec 1972–May 1974, CBS Wed 8:00–9:00
Feb 1976–Jan 1977, CBS Sun 8:00–9:00
Jan 1977–Mar 1977, CBS Fri 9:00–10:00
May 1977–Aug 1977, CBS Mon 10:00–11:00

REGULARS:

Sonny Bono

Cher Bono Allman
Ted Zeigler
Chastity Bono (1973–1977)
Tom Solari (1971–1972)
Clark Carr (1971–1972)
Murray Langston (1971–1974)
Freeman King (1971–1974)
Peter Cullen (1971–1974)
The Jimmy Dale Orchestra (1971–1973)
The Marty Paich Orchestra (1973–1974)
Steve Martin (1972–1973)
Teri Garr (1973–1974)
Billy Van (1973–1976)
Bob Einstein (1973–1974)
Gailard Sartain (1976)
Jack Harrell (1976)
Robert Shields and Lorene Yarnell (1976–1977)
The Tony Mordente Dancers (1971–1974)
The Earl Brown Singers (1971–1974)
The Harold Battiste Orchestra (1976–1977)

THEME:

"The Beat Goes On"

After almost a decade performing in clubs and auditoriums, Sonny and Cher were given their own summer variety series on CBS. The interplay between the two stars—Sonny's ebullient enthusiasm and Cher's sardonic wit and continual put-downs of her husband—was one of the strong points of the program. The summer show did well and returned that December to become a hit regular series. During its initial run, *The Sonny and Cher Comedy Hour* utilized several recurring comedy sketches. There was a "Vamp" segment in which Cher would portray several of the more notorious women throughout history; a "Sonny's Pizza" segment featuring Sonny as the dumb owner of a pizzeria and Cher as his sexy, beautiful waitress Rosa; the "Dirty Linen" segment with housewife Laverne (Cher) giving her views on men to her friend Olivia (Teri Garr) at the laundromat; and a segment in which news headlines, both current and past, were treated in blackouts. Frequently seen were full-scale operettas based on legitimate operas, television commercials, types of TV programs, and almost anything else that could be spoofed.

All was going well, the ratings were good, the couple seemed to be the picture of happiness (they had even made their daughter a semi-regular at the show's close when they would sing their record hit "I've Got You Babe"). Unfortunately, reality and appearances were two dfferent things. The Bonos were having marital problems, and it was announced in the spring of 1974 that they were getting divorced and would give up the series. They went their separate ways. Sonny failed with *The Sonny Comedy Revue,* his own show on ABC that fall, and Cher had only middling success with *Cher,* her solo effort that began on CBS the following January. With her solo venture limping along after less than a year on the air, a professional reconciliation was arranged with Sonny so that they might work together again. Cher had since married rock singer Greg Allman and given birth to a son. The new venture was titled *The Sonny and Cher Show,* but it could never regain the magic of the original. Cher's putdowns of Sonny, which seemed funny when they were married, just didn't work as well after they were divorced. The new series limped along for two seasons and was canceled in the summer of 1977.

SONNY COMEDY REVUE, THE

Comedy Variety

FIRST TELECAST: *September 22, 1974*

LAST TELECAST: *December 29, 1974*

BROADCAST HISTORY:

Sep 1974–Dec 1974, ABC Sun 8:00–9:00

HOST:

Sonny Bono

REGULARS:

Ted Zeigler
Billy Van
Peter Cullen
Freeman King
Murray Langston
Teri Garr

After Sonny and Cher broke up their successful act, and marriage, in 1974, each of them tried continuing on their own. Sonny's effort was this short-lived comedy variety show in which he was supposed to play the Chaplinesque "little man," always beset by troubles, and always the underdog. A repertory company of young comedians appeared with him in sketches, as did assorted guests.

SONNY KENDIS SHOW, THE

Music

FIRST TELECAST: *April 18, 1949*

LAST TELECAST: *January 6, 1950*

BROADCAST HISTORY:

Apr 1949–May 1949, CBS Mon/Wed 7:15–7:30

May 1949–Sep 1949, CBS Tue/Thu 7:45–7:55

Sep 1949–Jan 1950, CBS Mon/Tue/Thu/Fri 7:45–7:55

REGULARS:

Sonny Kendis

Gigi Durston

Pianist Sonny Kendis starred in this twice- to four-times-per-week live musical series. His featured vocalist was Gigi Durston. Sonny was reputed to have such fast hands that they appeared to be a blur on the television screen when he played piano rapidly.

SONS AND DAUGHTERS

General Drama

FIRST TELECAST: *September 11, 1974*

LAST TELECAST: *November 6, 1974*

BROADCAST HISTORY:

Sep 1974–Nov 1974, CBS Wed 8:00–9:00

CAST:

Jeff Reed .... Gary Frank

Anita Cramer .... Glynnis O'Connor

Lucille Reed .... Jay W. Macintosh

Walter Cramer .... John S. Ragin

Ruth Cramer .... Jan Shutan

Danny Reed .... Michael Morgan

Stash .... Scott Colomby

Moose .... Barry Livingston

Mary Anne .... Laura Siegel

Charlie .... Lionel Johnston

Evie .... Debralee Scott

Cody .... Christopher Nelson

In almost soap-opera fashion, *Sons and Daughters* attempted to portray what it was like to be teenagers in love in the mid-1950s. The two in love were Jeff and Anita, 16-year-old sweethearts and students at Southwest High School in Stockton, California. Jeff's dad had recently passed away and Anita's mother had just left her husband and moved in with another man. Their adjustments to the sudden changes in their home lives and the good and bad times they had with each other, with their friends, and with their families were told in the series. The peripheral relationships and involvements of the other cast members, despite the central focus on Jeff and Anita, gave *Sons and Daughters* an almost *Peyton Place* quality.

SOUND OFF TIME

see *Chesterfield Sound Off Time*

SOUPY SALES

Children's

FIRST TELECAST: *July 4, 1955*

LAST TELECAST: *April 13, 1962*

BROADCAST HISTORY:

Jul 1955–Aug 1955, ABC Mon–Fri 7:00–7:15

Jan 1962–Apr 1962, ABC Fri 7:30–8:00

HOST:

Soupy Sales

ASSISTANT:

Clyde Adler

Soupy Sales, the world's leading authority on pie-throwing, has been seen in a number of local and network series over the years, including two which ran in nighttime hours. His comedy featured outrageous puns, slapstick sketches, and a regular cast of puppet characters including White Fang, the giant dog (only his paw was seen); Black Tooth, the kindest dog in the U.S.; Marilyn Monwolf, a curvaceous friend of White Fang and Black Tooth; Herman the Flea; Willie the Worm; Pookie the Lion; and Hippy the Hippo. The 1955 series originated live from Soupy's home base of Detroit, Michigan, and the 1962 version live from Hollywood. In between, from 1959 to 1961, he was seen on the ABC network on Saturday afternoons in *Lunch with Soupy Sales.*

SOUTHERNAIRES QUARTET

Music

FIRST TELECAST: *September 19, 1948*

LAST TELECAST: *November 21, 1948*

BROADCAST HISTORY:

Sep 1948–Oct 1948, ABC Sun 9:00–9:30

Oct 1948–Nov 1948, ABC Sun 7:30–8:00

REGULARS:

The Southernaires

Musical interlude.

SPACE CADET

see *Tom Corbett—Space Cadet*

SPACE PATROL

Children's

FIRST TELECAST: *June 9, 1951*

LAST TELECAST: *June 1, 1952*

BROADCAST HISTORY:

Jun 1951–Sep 1951, ABC Sat 6:00–6:30

Dec 1951–Jun 1952, ABC Sun 6:00–6:30

CAST:

Commander Buzz Corey ....Ed Kemmer
Cadet Happy ....Lyn Osborn
Carol Karlyle ....Virginia Hewitt
Tonga ....Nina Bara
Major Robbie Robertson ....Ken Mayer
Secretary General of the United Planets .... Norman Jolley
Mr. Proteus ....Marvin Miller
Prince Baccarratti, alias the Black Falcon .... Bella Kovacs

CREATED BY:

Mike Moser

Space Patrol began in early 1950 as a local program on the West Coast, and was seen until 1955. During most of its run it was an ABC network Saturday or Sunday daytime series. However, during the two periods shown above it was run at 6:00 P.M., and thus qualifies as a "nighttime" series.

Set in the 30th century A.D., *Space Patrol* made much use of time travel. depositing its heroes in various historical periods. Commander of the Space Patrol was Buzz Corey (played by real-life World War II flying hero Ed Kemmer), who battled assorted villains in the name of the United Planets of the Universe. His youthful sidekick, Cadet Happy, was always ready with a colorful rejoinder ("Smokin' rockets, Commander!") or a simplistic question to allow Buzz to explain some obvious truth to home viewers. Other leading characters were Carol, pretty daughter of the Secretary General of the United Planets, who had romantic designs on Buzz; Tonga, a beautiful villainess-turned-heroine; and frequent villains Mr. Proteus (played by Marvin Miller, later of *The Millionaire* fame), and Prince Baccarratti.

No one ever got killed on *Space Patrol*. The worst fate was to be rendered inanimate by Buzz's Paralyzer Ray Gun, and then shown the path of truth and justice by the Brainograph. Replicas of these and other devices were available to viewers as premiums. In what was perhaps the most spectacular of all the space-opera promotions, in 1954 a 30-foot model of Buzz's spaceship, the *Terra*, toured the U.S. (on the ground) and then was given away to a lucky viewer.

SPARRING PARTNERS WITH WALTER KIERNAN

Quiz

FIRST TELECAST: *April 8, 1949*
LAST TELECAST: *May 6, 1949*
BROADCAST HISTORY:

Apr 1949–May 1949, ABC Fri 9:30–10:00

EMCEE:

Walter Kiernan

This short-lived quiz show pitted a team of men against a team of women, with Walter Kiernan as the quizmaster.

SPEIDEL SHOW, THE

see *Paul Winchell–Jerry Mahoney Show*

SPENCER'S PILOTS

Adventure

FIRST TELECAST: *September 17, 1976*
LAST TELECAST: *November 19, 1976*
BROADCAST HISTORY:

Sep 1976–Nov 1976, CBS Fri 8:00–9:00

CAST:

Cass Garrett ....Christopher Stone
Stan Lewis ....Todd Susman
Spencer Parish ....Gene Evans
Linda Dann ....Margaret Impert
Mickey Wiggins ....Britt Leach

Spencer Aviation was a small charter airline service located in Southern California that would do everything from cropdusting to transporting convicted criminals from one location to another for the police. Spencer Parish was the owner, Cass and Stan his two pilots, Linda the office manager, and Mickey the company's mechanic. This series never got off the ground, and was canceled after only two months on the air.

SPIKE JONES SHOW, THE

Comedy Variety

FIRST TELECAST: *January 2, 1954*
LAST TELECAST: *September 25, 1961*
BROADCAST HISTORY:

Jan 1954–May 1954, NBC Sat 8:00–8:30
Apr 1957–Aug 1957, CBS Tue 10:30–11:00
Aug 1960–Sep 1960, CBS Mon 9:30–10:00
Jul 1961–Sep 1961, CBS Mon 9:00–9:30

REGULARS:

Spike Jones
Helen Grayco
Bill Dana (1960)
Joyce Jameson (1960)
Len Weinrib (1960)

Spike Jones and his singer wife Helen Grayco, along with Spike's City Slicker

Band, starred in this weekly fill-in series that appeared in four different seasons. Cowbells, foghorns, slide whistles, and other paraphernalia were the featured instruments in Spike's band, as virtually every type of music was reduced to mayhem. Spike, in his striped suit, presided over the merry band of musical lunatics. The nature of their work could probably best be described by one of their album titles—*Dinner Music for People Who Aren't Very Hungry*. The series included, along with the outrageous musical numbers, straight singing by Helen Grayco, appearances by guest stars, and comedy sketches. During the summer of 1960 there was a regular group of supporting comedians, the most famous being Bill Dana in his role as Jose Jimenez. The members of the band all participated in the comedy skits and in general contributed to the frenetic nuttiness of the show.

SPIN THE PICTURE

Quiz/Audience Participation

FIRST TELECAST: *June 18, 1949*

LAST TELECAST: *February 4, 1950*

BROADCAST HISTORY:

Jun 1949–Jan 1950, DUM Sat 8:00–9:00
Jan 1950–Feb 1950, DUM Sat 8:00–8:30

EMCEE:

Carl Caruso (1949)
Eddie Dunn (1949)
Kathi Norris

REGULARS:

Gordon Dillworth
Shaye Cogan
Bob Dunn
Jerry Shad's Quartet

This was one early quiz show that gave away fairly large prizes. The first jackpot winner, who identified a "spinning picture" of lyricist Richard Rodgers, took home a cool $7,635. The bulk of the hour-long show consisted of dramatic sketches, songs, and other entertainment, with each act providing a clue to the name of a famous person, event, movie, etc. After each segment the host would call a viewer and ask if they could identify the name (viewers were asked to send in their phone numbers on postcards, and more than 25,000 did during the first weeks alone). The jackpot round presented a quickly flashed picture of a mystery celebrity, along with verbal clues to his identity.

Carl Caruso was the original emcee, replaced after about a month by the team of Kathi Norris and Eddie Dunn. Later Miss Norris alone was the principal emcee.

SPORTS CAMERA

Sports Anthology

FIRST TELECAST: *September 12, 1950*

LAST TELECAST: *May 24, 1952*

BROADCAST HISTORY:

Sep 1950, ABC Tue 9:30–10:00
Sep 1951, ABC Thu 10:45–11:00
Dec 1951–May 1952, ABC Sat 8:30–9:00
May 1952, ABC Sat 10:30–11:00

A collection of filmed short subjects on various sports and sports personalities. Known from December 1951 to March 1952 as *Sports on Parade*.

SPORTS FOCUS

Sports News/Commentary

FIRST TELECAST: *June 3, 1957*

LAST TELECAST: *September 12, 1958*

BROADCAST HISTORY:

Jun 1957–Jul 1957, ABC Mon–Fri 7:00–7:15
Sep 1957–Sep 1958, ABC Mon–Fri 7:00–7:15

REPORTER:

Howard Cosell

Broadcast live from New York, this was Howard Cosell's first foray into the world of network television sports. Each night he summed up the day's news in the sports world, provided personal commentary on any currently controversial issues, and conducted interviews with sports personalities.

SPORTS FOR ALL

see *Fishing and Hunting Club*

SPORTS NEWSREEL

see *Gillette Summer Sports Reel*

SPORTS ON PARADE

see *Sports Camera*

SPORTS SPOT

Sports Commentary

FIRST TELECAST: *June 13, 1951*

LAST TELECAST: *November 24, 1954*

BROADCAST HISTORY:

Jun 1951–Nov 1954, CBS Wed 10:45–11:00

HOST:

Jim McKay (1951)
Mel Allen (1951–1954)

This short live sports program filled the time between the end of *Pabst Blue Ribbon Bouts* and the start of the local 11:00 P.M. news. It was primarily an interview show in which a sports celebrity chatted with the host about his career or sports in general. Jim McKay was the original host, and was succeeded by Mel Allen in October 1951.

SPORTS WITH JOE HASEL

Sports News

FIRST TELECAST: *August 21, 1948*

LAST TELECAST: *April 26, 1949*

BROADCAST HISTORY:

Aug 1948–Jan 1949, ABC Sat 7:30–7:45
Jan 1949–Mar 1949, ABC Fri 9:30–9:45
Mar 1949–Apr 1949, ABC Tue 7:15–7:30

COMMENTATOR:

Joe Hasel

Weekly summary of the news from the world of sports—scores, commentary, and interviews with celebrities from various games.

SPORTSMAN'S QUIZ

Sports Information

FIRST TELECAST: *April 26, 1948*

LAST TELECAST: *April 25, 1949*

BROADCAST HISTORY:

Apr 1948–Aug 1948, CBS Mon 8:00–8:05
Aug 1948–Dec 1948, CBS Fri 8:00–8:05
Dec 1948–Jan 1949, CBS Fri 8:30–8:35
Jan 1949–Apr 1949, CBS Mon 7:10–7:15

REGULARS:

Don Baker
Bernard Dudley

With the cooperation and assistance of the staff of *Sports Afield* magazine, the program's sponsor, this short weekly series posed questions about hunting, fishing, conservation, and wild life, and then answered them with drawings, pictures, diagrams, or other visual aids. Bernard Dudley asked the questions and Don Baker provided the answers. Viewers were invited to send in questions of their own.

SPORTSREEL

see *Gillette Summer Sports Reel*

SPORTSWOMAN OF THE WEEK

Interview

FIRST TELECAST: *September 9, 1948*

LAST TELECAST: *December 2, 1948*

BROADCAST HISTORY:

Sep 1948–Dec 1948, NBC Thu 7:45–7:50

HOSTESS:

Sarah Palfrey Cooke

This brief program was originally a documentary about a different notable woman each week, but soon changed to a straight interview show with tennis champion Sarah Cooke playing host to an outstanding woman guest from the world of sports. It was at first called *Girl of the Week.*

SPOTLIGHT

Comedy Variety

FIRST TELECAST: *July 4, 1967*

LAST TELECAST: *August 29, 1967*

BROADCAST HISTORY:

Jul 1967–Aug 1967, CBS Tue 8:30–9:30

REGULARS:

The Mike Sammes Singers
The Lionel Blair Dancers
Jack Parnell and His Orchestra

Produced in London, this 1967 summer replacement for *The Red Skelton Show* each week featured a different cast of stars in a variety format. At least one of the stars was a singer and at least one of them was a comic. The emphasis shifted depending on the talents of the performers, from music to comedy, with the majority of the shows highlighting the latter. Although the supporting acts were from all over the world, most of the stars were from America, especially the comics. Phil Silvers, Shelley Berman, Jack Carter, Frank Gorshin, and Bill Dana were among them. The singers included Barbara McNair, Paul Anka, Trini Lopez, Vikki Carr, Robert Goulet, Lainie Kazan, and then husband and wife Eddie Fisher and Connie Stevens. Welsh singer Tom Jones appeared as one of the stars, sharing that function with American Fran Jeffries, and eventually got a series of his own, *This Is Tom Jones,* on ABC.

SPOTLIGHT ON SPORTS

Sports

FIRST TELECAST: *July 8, 1950*

LAST TELECAST: *September 3, 1950*

BROADCAST HISTORY:

Jul 1950, NBC Sat 7:30–8:00
Aug 1950–Sep 1950, NBC Sun 8:30–9:00

HOST:

Bill Stern

An interview and discussion program with various celebrities from the sports world. Bill Stern, NBC Sports Director, appeared on many telecasts on the network, including pre- and postgame shows and regular nightly reports, from 1949 through the 1950s. See the performer index for his other series.

SPOTLIGHT PLAYHOUSE

Dramatic Anthology

FIRST TELECAST: *June 21, 1955*
LAST TELECAST: *September 22, 1959*
BROADCAST HISTORY:

Jun 1955–Sep 1955, CBS Tue 9:30–10:00
Jun 1956–Sep 1956, CBS Tue 9:30–10:00
Jul 1957–Sep 1957, CBS Tue 9:30–10:00
Jul 1958–Sep 1958, CBS Tue 9:30–10:00
Jun 1959–Sep 1959, CBS Tue 9:30–10:00

HOST:

Anita Louise (1958)
Julia Meade (1959)
Zachary Scott (1959)

For five summers *Spotlight Playhouse* filled in for the vacationing Red Skelton. All of the episodes telecast in the series were filmed reruns from other anthology series. During the first two seasons most of the plays came from *Schlitz Playhouse of Stars.* When reruns from *The Loretta Young Show* were used in 1958 Anita Louise was on hand to host the series. The following summer, with episodes coming from *G.E. Theater, Schlitz Playhouse,* and *The Jane Wyman Show,* Julia Meade and Zachary Scott served as hosts on alternate weeks.

STACCATO

see *Johnny Staccato*

STAGE A NUMBER

Talent

FIRST TELECAST: *September 17, 1952*
LAST TELECAST: *May 20, 1953*
BROADCAST HISTORY:

Sep 1952–Apr 1953, DUM Wed 9:00–10:00
Apr 1953–May 1953, DUM Wed 8:30–9:00

EMCEE:

Bill Wendell

This was one of many low-budget talent shows on TV during the early years. The acts presented were young professionals, or aspiring professionals, who were introduced by a "sponsor" and then "staged their number" before a panel of show-business judges (producers, actors, etc.). Backdrops were simple, and accompaniment was usually just a piano or organ. The acts tended to be theatrical, such as dramatic acting or ballet, with several appearances by the Nina Youshkevitch Ballet Workshop, among others.

STAGE DOOR, THE

General Drama

FIRST TELECAST: *February 7, 1950*
LAST TELECAST: *March 28, 1950*
BROADCAST HISTORY:

Feb 1950–Mar 1950, CBS Tue 9:00–9:30

CAST:

Celia Knox ....Louise Allbritton
Hank Merlin ....Scott McKay
Rocco ....Tom Pedi

Life in and around the Broadway theater, as seen through the eyes of two young and aspiring performers, was the subject of this live dramatic series. It was based on the play *Stage Door* by Edna Ferber and George S. Kaufman. In addition to being struggling young performers, Celia and Hank, the two principals, were also madly in love with each other. The problems they had, both on and off stage, were portrayed each week.

STAGE ENTRANCE

Interview

FIRST TELECAST: *May 2, 1951*
LAST TELECAST: *March 9, 1952*
BROACAST HISTORY:

May 1951–Aug 1951, DUM Wed 7:45–8:00
Sep 1951–Dec 1951, DUM Mon 8:00–8:30
Dec 1951–Mar 1952, DUM Sun 7:00–7:30

HOST:

Earl Wilson

Broadway columnist Earl Wilson ("The Midnight Earl") interviewed established stars and young hopefuls, and gave news of show business in this 1951–1952 TV version of his *New York Post* newspaper column.

STAGE 7

Dramatic Anthology

FIRST TELECAST: *December 12, 1954*
LAST TELECAST: *September 25, 1955*
BROADCAST HISTORY:

Dec 1954–Sep 1955, CBS Sun 9:30–10:00

This filmed anthology series featured Hollywood stars and a varied format that ranged from comedy, to Westerns, to melodrama. When it premiered in December 1954, its title was *Your Favorite Playhouse* and it was composed of reruns from other anthologies. Effective with the play that aired on January 30, 1955, the title changed to *Stage 7* and the plays were new ones created for this series. The best-known leading players that appeared were Frank Lovejoy, Vanessa Brown, Pat O'Brien, Dennis Morgan, Regis Toomey, George Brent, Alexis Smith, and Angela Lansbury.

STAGE SHOW

Musical Variety

FIRST TELECAST: *July 3, 1954*

LAST TELECAST: *September 22, 1956*

BROADCAST HISTORY:

Jul 1954–Sep 1954, CBS Sat 8:00–9:00
Oct 1955–Feb 1956, CBS Sat 8:00–8:30
Feb 1956–Sep 1956, CBS Sat 8:30–9:00

REGULARS:

Tommy Dorsey
Jimmy Dorsey
The June Taylor Dancers

THEME:

"I'm Getting Sentimental over You"

The opening of *Stage Show* was done with the camera used as the eyes of the home viewer. It entered the theater, moved down the aisle to their seats, and then awaited the start of the show. The theme song was "I'm Getting Sentimental over You," long identified with the Dorsey Brothers. Tommy and Jimmy alternated as hosts and the show featured various guest stars. At the end of the program, the camera again became the eyes of the viewer, rising from his seat, leaving the theater, and moving out into the bustle of Manhattan on a Saturday night.

Stage Show was produced under the supervision of Jackie Gleason, and was the 1954 summer replacement for Gleason's Saturday night show. It aired intermittently in the Gleason time slot as a special during the 1954–1955 season, and when the half-hour *Honeymooners* became Gleason's regular series in the fall of 1955, *Stage Show* was used to fill the remainder of the hour every week. Gleason himself did the booking for the show.

Probably the most memorable night in the entire run was January 28, 1956, when the guest was a young County-rock singer from Memphis who was just beginning to attract national attention. This was the TV debut of Elvis Presley, the first time he had been seen or heard by most Americans, and he created pandemonium. He sang "Heartbreak Hotel" on that first telecast; released as a single record, it quickly became a multimillion seller. Elvis was booked for a total of six consecutive appearances on *Stage Show,* then went on to a career that dwarfed even that of the fabulous Dorseys. Ironically, the biggest superstar in the history of rock was introduced by two greats of the big-band swing era, in one of their last professional appearances.

Both Tommy and Jimmy Dorsey passed away shortly after this series ended its run, Tommy in November 1956 and brother Jimmy in June 1957.

STAGE 13

Dramatic Anthology

FIRST TELECAST: *April 19, 1950*

LAST TELECAST: *June 28, 1950*

BROADCAST HISTORY:

Apr 1950–Jun 1950, CBS Wed 9:30–10:00

Tales of mystery and suspense were told in this live anthology series that originated from New York. The title was supposed to convey the general feeling of the show, since 13 is an unlucky number and was avoided in numbering building floors, rooms, and the stages on movie lots. It was not particularly lucky for this series, either, which did not last even 13 weeks.

STAGE TWO REVUE

Musical Variety

FIRST TELECAST: *July 30, 1950*

LAST TELECAST: *September 24, 1950*

BROADCAST HISTORY:

Jul 1950–Sep 1950, ABC Sun 8:00–8:30

REGULARS:

Georgia Lee
Buzz Adlam's Orchestra
Arlene Harris
Bob Carroll

Summer variety show, featuring Buzz Adlam's Orchestra, vocals by Georgia Lee, and guest acts.

STAGECOACH WEST

Western

FIRST TELECAST: *October 4, 1960*
LAST TELECAST: *September 26, 1961*
BROADCAST HISTORY:
Oct 1960–Sep 1961, ABC Tue 9:00–10:00
CAST:
Luke Perry .... Wayne Rogers
Simon Kane .... Robert Bray
David Kane .... Richard Eyer

There were very few Western series that paid any attention at all to the people who drove the stagecoaches back and forth from Missouri to California, in the days before the expanding railroad system made their jobs obsolete. This series focused on three. Luke Perry and Simon Kane were a team of drivers and Simon's son David went along to keep them company. The passengers they carried, the people they met, and the things that happened to them en route provided the stories told in this series.

STAINED GLASS WINDOWS

Religion
FIRST TELECAST: *September 26, 1948*
LAST TELECAST: *October 16, 1949*
BROADCAST HISTORY:
Sep 1948–Nov 1948, ABC Sun 6:30–7:00
Jan 1949–Mar 1949, ABC Sun 7:15–7:45
Mar 1949–Oct 1949, ABC Sun 7:00–7:30

This early religious program included dramatizations, and discussions dealing with viewers' moral problems.

STAND BY FOR CRIME

Police
FIRST TELECAST: *January 11, 1949*
LAST TELECAST: *August 27, 1949*
BROADCAST HISTORY:
Jan 1949–Apr 1949, ABC Sat 9:30–10:00
May 1949–Aug 1949, ABC Sat 8:00–8:30
CAST:
Inspector Webb (Jan–Apr) ..... Boris Aplon
Lt. Anthony Kidd (May–Aug)
.... Myron Wallace
Sgt. Kramer (May–Aug) .... George Cisar

On January 11, 1949, New York and Chicago were first linked by television and this was the first program transmitted to Eastern audiences from Chicago. Though it was popular enough in the Midwest, Eastern reviewers found it rather crudely produced, and it did not last long.

It was a crime show with a novel twist. The drama was seen up to the point of the murder, with Inspector Webb (later Lt. Kidd of the homicide squad, whose assistant was Sgt. Kramer) sifting through the clues. Before the culprit was revealed, however, the action stopped and viewers were invited to phone in their guesses as to whodunit.

For a time guest "detectives" (celebrities) also appeared to offer their guesses as to who the guilty party might be.

STANLEY

Situation Comedy
FIRST TELECAST: *September 24, 1956*
LAST TELECAST: *March 11, 1957*
BROADCAST HISTORY:
Sep 1956–Mar 1957, NBC Mon 8:30–9:00
CAST:
Stanley Peck .... Buddy Hackett
Horace Fenton .... Paul Lynde
Celia .... Carol Burnett
Marvin .... Reedy Talton
Mr. Phillips .... Frederic Tozere

Stanley Peck was the outgoing proprietor of a newsstand in a fancy New York hotel, the Sussex-Fenton. Because of his friendly nature he was also the hotel guests' source of all sorts of inside information on what to do and where to go in New York, and a confidant to his co-workers. Despite being short and fat, his personality made him very popular, and he was constantly involved in trying to help other people. The degree of this involvement often got him in trouble with his girl friend Celia and with Mr. Phillips, the hotel's manager. Horace Fenton, the owner of the hotel chain, although never seen on camera, was heard regularly giving orders to members of the staff. *Stanley* was aired live from New York.

STAR OF THE FAMILY

Comedy Variety
FIRST TELECAST: *September 22, 1950*
LAST TELECAST: *June 26, 1952*
BROADCAST HISTORY:
Sep 1950–Jun 1951, CBS Fri 10:00–10:30
Jul 1951–Jan 1952, CBS Sun 6:30–7:00
Jan 1952–Jun 1952, CBS Thu 8:00–8:30
HOSTS:
Morton Downey (1950–1951)
Peter Lind Hayes (1951–1952)
Mary Healy (1951–1952)
ORCHESTRA:
Carl Hoff

The gimmick in this variety show was unique. The host of the show interviewed people who were related to famous celebrities without disclosing who the celebrities were. After the family members had chatted with the host, the "star of their family" was introduced, joined the conversation, and performed for the audience. Singer Morton Downey was the host during the first season, adding his songs to provide a change of pace from the interviews. He was replaced by Peter Lind Hayes and Mary Healy in the summer of 1951, and the emphasis shifted from music to comedy, depending of course on the talents of the celebrities whose relatives appeared on each week's telecast.

STAR STAGE

Dramatic Anthology

FIRST TELECAST: *September 9, 1955*

LAST TELECAST: *September 7, 1956*

BROADCAST HISTORY:

Sep 1955–Aug 1956, NBC Fri 9:30–10:00

Sep 1956, NBC Fri 9:00–9:30

HOST:

Jeffrey Lynn

Approximately two-thirds of the two-act plays aired on *Star Stage* were live and the remainder were filmed. The live dramas originated from both Hollywood and New York. Initially, there was no host, until Jeffrey Lynn assumed that post on November 18, 1955. One of the early telecasts was "On Trial" starring Joseph Cotten. He later hosted and starred in a courtroom series of the same name. Others who were seen on *Star Stage* included Sylvia Sidney, Alan Young, Lorne Greene, Jeanne Crain, Dan Duryea, Ward Bond, Wendell Corey, and Polly Bergen.

STAR TIME

Musical Variety

FIRST TELECAST: *September 5, 1950*

LAST TELECAST: *February 27, 1951*

BROADCAST HISTORY:

Sep 1950–Feb 1951, DUM Tue 10:00–11:00

REGULARS:

Frances Langford
Benny Goodman Sextet
Lew Parker
Kathryn Lee

In the fall of 1950 DuMont made another of its feeble efforts to launch a full-fledged prime-time variety hour with this series. Like most of the other attempts, it lacked the lure of a big-name (or rising) star who could attract viewers, and soon folded.

Star Time did have some good talent, however, including singer Frances Langford and the Benny Goodman Sextet as regulars. Comic Lew Parker and dancer Kathryn Lee also contributed, along with assorted, but not usually top-name, guests.

STAR TIME PLAYHOUSE

Dramatic Anthology

FIRST TELECAST: *July 12, 1955*

LAST TELECAST: *September 13, 1955*

BROADCAST HISTORY:

Jul 1955–Sep 1955, CBS Tue 8:00–8:30

The filmed dramas in this series had never before been aired on television, tended to be on the serious side, and were headlined by well-known performers. Victor Jory starred in "The Man Who Escaped Devil's Island," and Ronald Reagan and Neville Brand in "Edge of Battle." Others appearing were Peter Lorre, Basil Rathbone, Broderick Crawford, and Angela Lansbury—she being the only woman to have star billing throughout *Star Time Playhouse*'s summer run.

STAR TONIGHT

Dramatic Anthology

FIRST TELECAST: *February 3, 1955*

LAST TELECAST: *August 9, 1956*

BROADCAST HISTORY:

Feb 1955–Aug 1956, ABC Thu 9:00–9:30

Star Tonight was designed as a showcase for young actors and actresses working in New York. Each week a live play was telecast with a relative unknown in the lead, hopefully as a springboard to future stardom. The plays were chosen specifically for the individual young "stars" or written to suit their talents. Some of those who went on to greater things were Bruce Gordon, Joanne Woodward, Theodore Bikel, Neva Patterson, Kay Medford, and Robert Culp.

STAR TREK

Science Fiction

FIRST TELECAST: *September 8, 1966*

LAST TELECAST: *September 2, 1969*

BROADCAST HISTORY:

Sep 1966–Aug 1967, NBC Thu 8:30–9:30

Sep 1967–Aug 1968, NBC Fri 8:30–9:30
Sep 1968–Apr 1969, NBC Fri 10:00–11:00
Jun 1969–Sep 1969, NBC Tue 7:30–8:30

CAST:

Capt. James T. Kirk ....William Shatner
Mr. Spock ....Leonard Nimoy
Dr. Leonard McCoy ....DeForest Kelly
Yeoman Janice Rand (1966–1967) .... Grace Lee Whitney
Sulu ....George Takei
Uhura ....Nichelle Nichols
Engineer Montgomery Scott .. James Doohan
Nurse Christine Chapel .... Majel Barrett
Ensign Chekov (1967–1969) .. Walter Koenig

Set 200 years in the future, *Star Trek* followed the adventures of the starship *U.S.S. Enterprise*, a cruiser-sized spacecraft whose mission included reconnaissance of previously unexplored worlds and transporting supplies to Earth colonies in space. Confrontations with two alien races, Klingons and Romulans, provided recurring conflicts and there were numerous encounters with other "strange" forms of alien life as well. *Star Trek* differed from previous series such as *Captain Video* in that stories were often well written, serious science-fiction short stories, dealing with current social issues thinly disguised in extraterrestrial settings.

The program was canceled by NBC in 1969 due to gradually declining audiences and the heavy proportion of teenagers and children in its viewership, which made it unattractive to network advertisers. Since then, however, the program has been very successful in syndication, and developed a fanatical cult following in the 1970s. This cult organized itself, lobbied to get the series brought back to network television, and has even sponsored annual conventions in the U.S. and England. Probably no prime-time program has had such a well-publicized "life after death" as *Star Trek*. *Star Trek* did return to the network—in modified form—as an animated cartoon series on Saturday morning, from 1973 to 1975.

STARLAND VOCAL BAND SHOW, THE

Variety

FIRST TELECAST: *July 31, 1977*
LAST TELECAST: *September 2, 1977*
BROADCAST HISTORY:

Jul 1977–Aug 1977, CBS Sun 8:30–9:00
Aug 1977–Sep 1977, CBS Fri 8:30–9:00

REGULARS:

Bill Danoff
Taffy Danoff
Margot Chapman
Jon Caroll
Mark Russell
Dave Letterman
Jeff Altman
Phil Proctor
Peter Bergman
Milt Okun and His Orchestra

The four members of the popular music group The Starland Vocal Band (Bill, Taffy, Margot, and Jon) starred in this whimsical variety show which featured music and satirical comedy sketches. Political satirist Mark Russell was also a cast regular in this series, which was filmed on locations in such diverse places as a concert at Georgetown University in Washington, D.C., and at an outdoor picnic in Great Falls, Virginia. The group's main claim to fame, and the reason they got this summer series, was a 1976 hit record called "Afternoon Delight." Featured regularly in comedy sketches were three of the show's writers—Dave Letterman, Phil Proctor, and Peter Bergman.

STARLIGHT THEATRE

Dramatic Anthology

FIRST TELECAST: *April 2, 1950*
LAST TELECAST: *October 4, 1951*
BROADCAST HISTORY:

Apr 1950–Jun 1950, CBS Sun 7:00–7:30
Jul 1950, CBS Mon 8:00–8:30
Jul 1950–Sep 1950, CBS Thu 9:00–9:30
Sep 1950, CBS Thu 9:30–10:00
Oct 1950, CBS Wed 9:00–9:30
Nov 1950–Oct 1951, CBS Thu 8:00–8:30

Stories of romance were presented on this live anthology series that bounced all over the CBS schedule during the 18 months it was on. The players came from both the legitimate theater and the motion-picture world. During its longest run in a single time slot, from November 1950 through October 1951, *Starlight Theatre* was reduced from a weekly to a biweekly series, alternating with *The George Burns and Gracie Allen Show*. Among the more familiar faces that showed up during the run were Barry Nelson, Mary Sinclair, Ernest Truex, Melvyn Douglas, Eve Arden, Julie Harris, Wally Cox, and John Forsythe.

STARLIT TIME

Musical Variety

FIRST TELECAST: *April 9, 1950*

LAST TELECAST: *November 26, 1950*

BROADCAST HISTORY:

Apr 1950, DUM Sun 6:00–8:00

Apr 1950–Nov 1950, DUM Sun 7:00–8:00

EMCEES:

Bill Williams

Phil Hanna

REGULARS:

Minnie Jo Curtis

Gordon Dilworth

Bibi Osterwald

Holly Harris

Alan Prescott

Ralph Stantley

Sondra Lee & Sam Steen

Roberto & Alicia

Eddie Holmes

Reggie Beane Trio

Cy Coleman Trio

Starlit Time was an early attempt by DuMont to compete in the Sunday night variety-show sweepstakes. Unfortunately a severe lack of budget, and therefore of big-name stars, hampered the show considerably. It premiered as an ambitious, two-hour affair consisting of two one-hour segments, "Welcome Mat," emceed by disc jockey Bill Williams, and "Phil Hanna Sings," emceed by vocalist Hanna. The two parts were linked together by Minnie Jo Curtis, who did a running bit as a celestial switchboard operator and who introduced some of the acts. Two hours proved unwieldy for such lightweight talent, and *Starlit Time* was soon reduced to a one-hour variety show co-hosted by Williams and Hanna. Among the regulars were folk singer Gordon Dilworth, dance teams Sondra Lee & Sam Steen and Roberto & Alicia, and assorted comics and vocalists.

During the summer months *Starlit Time* was known as *S.S. Holiday*.

STARRING BORIS KARLOFF

Suspense Anthology

FIRST TELECAST: *September 22, 1949*

LAST TELECAST: *December 15, 1949*

BROADCAST HISTORY:

Sep 1949–Oct 1949, ABC Thu 9:30–10:00

Nov 1949–Dec 1949, ABC Thu 9:00–9:30

STAR:

Boris Karloff

ORGANIST:

George Henniger

Tales of horror, starring Hollywood's best-known practitioner of that genre. The first telecast, titled "Five Golden Guineas," is illustrative. An English hangman unduly enjoys his work, which brings him payment of five guineas per hanging. He revels in the snap of the victim's neck, and the dangling arms. When his pregnant wife discovers his true occupation she leaves him. Twenty years later the hangman is called upon to execute a young man, which he does with pleasure, despite the fact that he has secret evidence that the youth is in fact innocent. Only then is he confronted by his ex-wife, who tells him that he has just hung his own son. Enraged, he strangles his wife—and is subsequently sent to the gallows himself. Another hangman collects five golden guineas.

The title of this anthology series was changed to *Mystery Playhouse Starring Boris Karloff* effective with the October 27 telecast.

STARS IN ACTION

Dramatic Anthology

FIRST TELECAST: *September 30, 1958*

LAST TELECAST: *September 29, 1959*

BROADCAST HISTORY:

Sep 1958–Sep 1959, CBS Tue 7:30–8:00

The filmed plays that were aired in this anthology series were reruns of episodes originally telecast on *Schlitz Playhouse*, an unusual practice for the start of a season. Reruns were frequently repackaged and retitled for use in the summer but rarely to fill a time slot for an entire season.

STARS OF JAZZ

Music

FIRST TELECAST: *April 18, 1958*

LAST TELECAST: *November 30, 1958*

BROADCAST HISTORY:

Apr 1958–Jun 1958, ABC Fri 8:30–9:00

Jun 1958–Sep 1958, ABC Mon 9:00–9:30

Sep 1958–Oct 1958, ABC Thu 10:00–10:30

Nov 1958, ABC Sun 9:30–10:00

HOST:

Bobby Troup

Each week a different jazz musician or group was featured on this music series. Host Bobby Troup, himself a jazz musician, would introduce the week's guests, chat with them about their work, and sit back while they played for the audience.

STARS ON PARADE

Musical Variety

FIRST TELECAST: *November 4, 1953*

LAST TELECAST: *June 30, 1954*

BROADCAST HISTORY:

Nov 1953–Jan 1954, DUM Wed 10:00–10:30
Jan 1954–May 1954, DUM Wed 9:30–10:00
May 1954–Jun 1954, DUM Wed 9:00–9:30

EMCEE:

Don Russell (1953)
Bobby Sherwood (1953–1954)

REGULAR:

Elliot Lawrence

Another of the military variety shows on television in the early 1950s. In addition to military bands, which were rehearsed for the occasion by civilian bandleader Elliot Lawrence, the talent included such stars as Perry Como, June Valli, Sarah Vaughan, and Errol Garner. The Glenn Miller Army Air Force Band also made an appearance. Don Russell was host for the first two telecasts only, being replaced on November 18 by Bobby Sherwood.

STARS OVER HOLLYWOOD

Anthology

FIRST TELECAST: *September 6, 1950*

LAST TELECAST: *August 29, 1951*

BROADCAST HISTORY:

Sep 1950–Aug 1951, NBC Wed 10:30–11:00

Early filmed dramatic series, produced in Hollywood and generally featuring lesser-known actors and actresses. The star of the first presentation ("Beauty Is a Joy") was Mary Stuart, later to become the central character in CBS's long-running daytime serial *As the World Turns*. Future star Raymond Burr was seen in two 1951 productions.

STARSKY AND HUTCH

Police

FIRST TELECAST: *September 3, 1975*

LAST TELECAST:

BROADCAST HISTORY:

Sep 1975–Sep 1976, ABC Wed 10:00–11:00
Sep 1976–Jan 1978, ABC Sat 9:00–10:00
Jan 1978–Aug 1978, ABC Wed 10:00–11:00
Sep 1978–, ABC Tue 10:00–11:00

CAST:

Det. Dave Starsky .....Paul Michael Glaser
Det. Ken Hutchinson ("Hutch") .... David Soul
Capt. Harold Dobey ......Bernie Hamilton
Huggy Bear ....Antonio Fargas

MUSIC:

Lalo Schifrin; Mark Snow

Starsky and Hutch was one of the light, youth-oriented police-action shows that populated TV in the 1970s. The two young plainclothes cops were both swinging bachelors, and their personalities fit each other perfectly—they almost seemed to operate as one. Starsky was the streetwise member of the team, and Hutch the better-educated, soft-spoken one. Together they tackled cases in the roughest neighborhood in town (presumably Los Angeles), full of pimps, muggers, dope pushers, and big-time hoodlums. Sometimes they went undercover, but often they were highly visible, racing around the city, tires squealing, in Starsky's bright red hot rod (a 1974 Ford Torino). Capt. Dobey was their quick-tempered but understanding boss, and Huggy Bear their flamboyant informant.

STARTIME

Variety

FIRST TELECAST: *October 6, 1959*

LAST TELECAST: *May 31, 1960*

BROADCAST HISTORY:

Oct 1959–Jan 1960, NBC Tue 9:30–10:30
Jan 1960–May 1960, NBC Tue 8:30–9:30

PRODUCER:

Hubbell Robinson

The Ford Motor Company was the sponsor of this potpourri of hour-long specials that ran as a series during the 1959–1960 season. When it was sponsored by the Ford Division its full title was *Ford Startime—TV's Finest Hour*. When it was sponsored by the Lincoln-Mercury Division the title became *Lincoln-Mercury Startime*.

Serious dramatic presentations, musical comedies, and musical variety shows were all presented under the generic title *Startime*. One of the specials in this series that eventually became a series on its own was "Sing Along with Mitch," telecast on May 24, 1960, and back as a series the following January. Dean Martin, who would also eventually have a variety series on NBC, starred twice with variety specials. His former partner, Jerry Lewis, was also on *Startime*, but in the dramatic role of "The Jazz Singer," a version of Al Jolson's classic film. Ingrid Bergman made her American TV dramatic debut in "The Turn of the Screw" and so did Alec Guinness in "The Wicked Scheme of Jebal Deeks." The list of top-rank stars on this series was almost endless. Jimmy Stewart starred in "Cindy's Fella," a Western musical based loosely on "Cinderella," and Ed Wynn and Bert Lahr were featured in a straight comedy, "The Greatest Man Alive." Three of the most popular comedians of the century—Jack Benny, George Burns, and Eddie Cantor—starred together in a musical comedy revue.

STEVE ALLEN COMEDY HOUR, THE

Comedy Variety

FIRST TELECAST: *June 14, 1967*
LAST TELECAST: *August 16, 1967*
BROADCAST HISTORY:
Jun 1967–Aug 1967, CBS Wed 10:00–11:00
REGULARS:
Steve Allen
Jayne Meadows
Louis Nye
Ruth Buzzi
David Winters Dancers
John Byner

After an absence of several seasons, Steve Allen returned to prime time television with this summer comedy variety series. With him were his wife, Jayne Meadows, comedian Louis Nye, comedienne Ruth Buzzi, and the David Winters Dancers. Although there was music in the series, the emphasis, regardless of who the week's guest stars were, was on comedy. Among the featured routines used regularly was the "Man on the Street Interview" in which Louis Nye played the suave, smug Gordon Hathaway. Although not listed by CBS as a regular, John Byner appeared in most of the episodes.

STEVE ALLEN SHOW, THE

Comedy Variety

FIRST TELECAST: *December 25, 1950*
LAST TELECAST: *September 11, 1952*
BROADCAST HISTORY:
Dec 1950–Mar 1951, CBS Mon–Fri 7:00–7:30
Jul 1952–Sep 1952, CBS Thu 8:30–9:00
REGULAR:
Steve Allen

Steve Allen got his first network exposure on CBS with a live series that aired Monday–Friday at 7:00 P.M. and premiered on Christmas Day 1950. He played the piano, chatted with one or two guest stars, and had funny ad-lib interviews with both the guests and random members of the studio audience. When it left the early evening at the start of March 1951, the series was expanded to a full hour from 11:30 A.M. to 12:30 P.M. weekdays. He returned to CBS's nighttime lineup during the summer of 1952 on Thursday nights, running on alternate weeks with *Amos 'n' Andy*.

STEVE ALLEN SHOW, THE

Comedy Variety

FIRST TELECAST: *June 24, 1956*
LAST TELECAST: *December 27, 1961*
BROADCAST HISTORY:
Jun 1956–Jun 1958, NBC Sun 8:00–9:00
Sep 1958–Mar 1959, NBC Sun 8:00–9:00
Mar 1959, NBC Sun 7:30–9:00
Apr 1959–Jun 1959, NBC Sun 7:30–8:30
Sep 1959–Jun 1960, NBC Mon 10:00–11:00
Sep 1961–Dec 1961, ABC Wed 7:30–8:30
REGULARS:
Steve Allen
Louis Nye
Gene Rayburn (1956–1959)
Skitch Henderson (1956–1959)
Marilyn Jacobs (1956–1957)
Tom Poston (1956–1959, 1961)
Gabe Dell (1956–1957, 1958–1961)
Don Knotts (1956–1960)
Dayton Allen (1958–1961)
Pat Harrington, Jr. (1958–1961)
Cal Howard (1959–1960)
Bill Dana (1959–1960)
Joey Forman (1961)
Buck Henry (1961)
Jayne Meadows (1961)
John Cameron Swayze (1957–1958)

The multi-talented Steve Allen—musician, composer, singer, comedian, author—was the star of this live weekly variety series that bore a strong resemblance to his informal late-night *Tonight Show*. Although the program had elements of music and serious aspects, comedy was far and away its major component. Steve had with him one of the most versatile and talented collections of improvisational comics ever assembled. Among the features that were used at one time or another on a semi-regular basis were: "Letters to the Editor," "The Allen Report to the Nation," "Mad-Libs," "Crazy Shots," "Where Are They Now," "The Question Man," "The Allen Bureau of Standards," and "The Allen All Stars."

The most frequently used feature, and by far the most memorable, was the "Man on the Street Interview." It was here that the comics on the show developed their best-remembered characters; Louis Nye as suave, smug Gordon Hathaway, Tom Poston as the man who can't remember his name, Skitch Henderson as Sidney Ferguson, Don Knotts as the extremely nervous and fidgety Mr. Morrison, Pat Harrington as Italian golf pro Guido Panzini, and Bill Dana as shy Jose Jimenez.

The Steve Allen Show spent three years on Sunday evenings in head-to-head competition with *The Ed Sullivan Show*. On its second telecast, as a matter of fact, one of the guest stars was young rock 'n' roll singer Elvis Presley, a performer whose three appearances later that fall on Sullivan's show are better remembered than his stint with Steve Allen. In the fall of 1959, when the show moved to Monday evenings, it was retitled *The Steve Allen Plymouth Show*, a sop to its new full sponsor. When ABC picked up the show for a short run on Wednesdays in the fall of 1961, the title reverted to *The Steve Allen Show*. The series had originated from New York throughout its Sunday evening run but moved to Hollywood when it shifted to Mondays in the fall of 1959.

STEVE CANYON

Adventure

FIRST TELECAST: *September 13, 1958*

LAST TELECAST: *September 8, 1960*

BROADCAST HISTORY:

Sep 1958–Jan 1959, NBC Sat 9:00–9:30
Jan 1959–Mar 1959, NBC Thu 8:00–8:30
Mar 1959–Sep 1959, NBC Tue 8:00–8:30
Apr 1960–Sep 1960, ABC Thu 7:30–8:00

CAST:

Lt. Col. Stevenson B. Canyon .... Dean Fredericks
Police Chief Hagedorn (1959–1960) .... Ted DeCorsia
Major "Willie" Williston (1959–1960) .... Jerry Paris
Airman Abel Featherstone (1959–1960) .... Abel Fernandez
Sgt. Charley Berger (1959–1960) .... Robert Hoy
Ingrid (1959–1960) .... Ingrid Goude

Milton Caniff's popular comic strip *Steve Canyon* was already 11 years old when this filmed series went on the air in the fall of 1958. Steve Canyon was a command pilot and troubleshooter for the Air Force and traveled from base to base around the country in the course of his work. Actual on-location footage of Air Force bases was used in the series, which had government approval and was considered a possible aid in recruiting drives. On January 3, 1959, Steve settled down as commanding officer of Big Thunder Air Force Base and acquired a regular supporting cast. Although based at Big Thunder in California, he still flew all over the world on special assignments. ABC aired reruns of the NBC series during the summer of 1960.

STEVE LAWRENCE–EYDIE GORME SHOW, THE

Musical Variety

FIRST TELECAST: *June 13, 1958*

LAST TELECAST: *August 31, 1958*

BROADCAST HISTORY:

Jun 1958–Aug 1958, NBC Sun 8:00–9:00

REGULARS:

Steve Lawrence
Eydie Gorme
Gene Rayburn

The husband-and-wife singing team of Steve Lawrence and Eydie Gorme starred in this 1958 summer replacement for *The Steve Allen Show*. They sang separately and together, introduced and participated with their various guest stars in song, and occasionally acted in comedy skits. Gene Rayburn was the show's announcer.

The full title was *Steve Allen Presents the Steve Lawrence–Eydie Gorme Show*.

STEVE LAWRENCE SHOW, THE

Musical Variety

FIRST TELECAST: *September 13, 1965*

LAST TELECAST: *December 13, 1965*

BROADCAST HISTORY:

Sep 1965–Dec 1965, CBS Mon 10:00–11:00

REGULARS:

Steve Lawrence

Charles Nelson Reilly
Betty Walker

Singer Steve Lawrence was the host and star of this musical variety series. It featured appearances by name guest stars, songs, comedy sketches, and production numbers. Comics Charles Nelson Reilly and Betty Walker were originally supposed to be featured regulars in the show, but were both gone by the end of September, leaving Steve and his guest stars to fend for themselves.

STEVE RANDALL

Detective

FIRST TELECAST: *November 7, 1952*
LAST TELECAST: *January 30, 1953*
BROADCAST HISTORY:
Nov 1952–Jan 1953, DUM Fri 8:00–8:30
CAST:
Steve Randall ....Melvyn Douglas

In this filmed series screen star Melvyn Douglas appeared as a disbarred lawyer who had turned sleuth in an attempt to regain his right to practice law. A suave, mustachioed detective, he greased his way through assorted cases of blackmail and murder before finally reaching his goal—reinstatement as a lawyer—in the final episode. There this short series ended.

Prior to the network run, some episodes of *Steve Randall* were seen locally under the title *Hollywood Off Beat*.

STOCK CAR RACES

Sports

FIRST TELECAST: *June 24, 1952*
LAST TELECAST: *August 26, 1952*
BROADCAST HISTORY:
Jun 1952–Aug 1952, ABC Tue 9:00–10:30
ANNOUNCER:
Chick Hearn

Live coverage of weekly late-model automobile racing from the 87th Street Speedway in Chicago.

STONEY BURKE

Western

FIRSH TELECAST: *October 1, 1962*
LAST TELECAST: *September 2, 1963*
BROADCAST HISTORY:
Oct 1962–Sep 1963, ABC Mon 9:00–10:00
CAST:
Stoney Burke ....Jack Lord
Cody Bristol ....Robert Dowdell
E. J. Stocker ....Bruce Dern
Ves Painter ....Warren Oates
Red ....Bill Hart

Professional rodeo rider Stoney Burke was after one thing—the Golden Buckle, the award given to the world's champion saddle bronco rider. Unfortunately he didn't make it during the first season, which is as long as this contemporary Western series lasted, although he did survive a considerable array of violence and villainy along the way. Filmed in the Southwest.

STOP, LOOK AND LISTEN

see *Celebrity Time*

STOP ME IF YOU'VE HEARD THIS ONE

Quiz/Panel

FIRST TELECAST: *March 4, 1948*
LAST TELECAST: *April 22, 1949*
BROADCAST HISTORY:
Mar 1948–Dec 1948, NBC Fri 8:30–9:00
Jan 1949–Apr 1949, NBC Fri 9:00–9:30
EMCEE:
Roger Bower (1948)
Leon Janney (1948–1949)
REGULAR PANELISTS:
Cal Tinney
Lew Lehr (1948)
Morey Amsterdam (1948)
Benny Rubin
George Givot (1949)

Live comedy game show in which the emcee read jokes sent in by viewers to a panel of three comedians. If one of the comics recognized the joke he would immediately shout "Stop!," and continue the story himself up to the punch line. For every wrong ending supplied by the comedians the viewer won a prize. Guest comedians were also sometimes seen on the panel of "gag-busters."

Based on the radio program of the same name, which was first heard in 1939 with Milton Berle as its star gagster.

STOP THE MUSIC

Quiz/Audience Participation

FIRST TELECAST: *May 5, 1949*
LAST TELECAST: *June 14, 1956*
BROADCAST HISTORY:
May 1949–Apr 1952, ABC Thu 8:00–9:00
Sep 1954–May 1955, ABC Tue 10:30–11:00
Sep 1955–Jun 1956, ABC Thu 8:30–9:00

EMCEE:
Bert Parks
VOCALISTS:
Estelle Loring (1949–1950)
Jimmy Blaine (1949–1952)
Betty Ann Grove (1949–1955)
Marion Morgan (1950–1951)
June Valli (1952)
Jaye P. Morgan (1954–1955)
ORCHESTRA:
Harry Salter

Stop the Music was introduced on radio in 1948, where it was an overnight sensation. The following year ABC brought it to TV, complete with Bert Parks and Harry Salter's orchestra, and it was a major hit there. It continued on radio as well.

The format was a mixture of musical entertainment and quiz. Bert, a cast of regular singers, and the orchestra would perform parts of songs, which contestants from the audience would be asked to identify for cash prizes. Viewers at home could get into the act by sending in official entry blanks with their names and phone numbers. Three lovely operators on stage would begin placing calls as Bert crooned a tune, and as soon as a connection was made, someone would yell "stop the music!" The home viewer would then be given a chance to identify the tune. It could be worth knowing, too, as a correct answer might be worth a jackpot of $20,000 or more. Mink coats and trips to Paris were also frequent prizes.

Various modifications in the basic format took place from time to time, such as a "mystery medley" and a competition between a contestant in the studio and a viewer at home on the telephone. There was also a good deal of turnover among vocalists on the show, with Betty Ann Grove having the longest run. Guest singers also appeared, and there were segments with straight musical entertainment and comedy sketches and interviews.

STOREFRONT LAWYERS

Lawyer

FIRST TELECAST: *September 16, 1970*
LAST TELECAST: *September 1, 1971*
BROADCAST HISTORY:
Sep 1970–Sep 1971, CBS Wed 7:30–8:30
CAST:
David Hansen ....Robert Foxworth
Deborah Sullivan ....Sheila Larkin
Gabriel Kaye ....David Arkin
Roberto Alvarez ....A. Martinez
Gloria Byrd ....Pauline Myers
Devlin McNeil ......Gerald S. O'Loughlin

1970 was the year of relevance, and no series tried to be more relevant than *Storefront Lawyers*. In its premiere episode, young lawyer David Hansen gave up his position with the prestigious law firm of Horton, Troy, McNeil, Carroll and Clark, in plush Century City, California, to join two other young attorneys in a nonprofit practice. He, Deborah Sullivan, and Gabriel Kaye set up an office in a small store in a poor section of Los Angeles and offered their services to poor people who needed legal help but could not afford an expensive attorney. Following an unsuccessful fall, and a three-week hiatus in January, the series returned on February 3, 1971, with a new title, *Men at Law*, and a new format. The three young attorneys were now working for the fancy law firm that Hansen had left in the fall, under the guidance of senior partner Devlin McNeil, and the cases were more conventional. They still worked on cases involving the underprivileged, but also took on those of more affluent members of the community. At this point, the amount of each episode that actually took place in the courtroom also increased substantially.

STORK CLUB, THE

Talk

FIRST TELECAST: *July 7, 1950*
LAST TELECAST: *July 24, 1955*
BROADCAST HISTORY:
Jul 1950, CBS Wed/Fri 7:45–8:00
Jul 1950–Sep 1950, CBS Mon/Wed/Fri 7:45–8:00
Sep 1950–Dec 1950, CBS Mon-Fri 7:00–7:30
Dec 1950–Jan 1951, CBS Tue/Thu/Sat 7:45–8:00
Jan 1951–Jun 1952, CBS Tue/Thu 7:45–8:00
Jul 1952–Oct 1953, CBS Sat 7:00–7:30
Sep 1954–Mar 1955, ABC Sat 10:00–10:30
Mar 1955–Jun 1955, ABC Sun 9:15–10:00
Jul 1955, ABC Sun 9:30–10:00
REGULARS:
Sherman Billingsley
Peter Lind Hayes (1950)
Mary Healy (1950)
Johnny Johnston (1950–1951)
Virginia Peine (1950–1951)

Stork Club owner Sherman Billingsley became a television celebrity through this series. It was unique in that it was broadcast live from a specially designed permanent set at the club itself. Guest celebrities were informally interviewed at the special "Table 50" and were often given Welsh terriers and boxers as gifts for appearing. Home viewers could also receive one of the pets by sending in particularly interesting questions to be asked of a specific guest. When the series began Peter Lind Hayes and Mary Healy were regulars. They left in the fall of 1950, around the time Johnny Johnston and Virginia Peine (wife of writer Quentin Reynolds) were added. Johnny lasted only a couple of months and Miss Peine was on until the following June. At that point Sherman Billingsley decided to become the sole host of the show.

STORY OF THE WEEK

Interview

FIRST TELECAST: *January 7, 1948*

LAST TELECAST: *January 5, 1949*

BROADCAST HISTORY:

Jan 1948–Nov 1948, NBC Wed 8:45–9:00

Nov 1948–Jan 1949, NBC Wed 7:15–7:30

HOST:

Richard Harkness

Public-affairs program from Washington, D.C. NBC political analyst Richard Harkness interviewed prominent public figures and commented on the latest events in the capital. Among the many notable guests was freshman Congressman Richard M. Nixon (Rep—Calif.), who commented on his solution to the problem of Communism.

STRAIGHTAWAY

Adventure

FIRST TELECAST: *October 6, 1961*

LAST TELECAST: *July 4, 1962*

BROADCAST HISTORY:

Oct 1961–Dec 1961, ABC Fri 7:30–8:00

Jan 1962–Jul 1962, ABC Wed 8:00–8:30

CAST:

Scott Ross ....Brian Kelly

Clipper Hamilton ....John Ashley

Scott and Clipper were partners in the Straightaway Garage, where they designed, built, and serviced racing cars. Scott was primarily a designer, and Clipper was the better mechanic. Their involvement with lovers of speed and racing led to the adventures depicted in this series. Originally, the title was to be *The Racers*, but it had to be changed because of sponsor problems. Autolite, the maker of spark plugs, loved racing. But the Ford Motor Company bought up Autolite between the commitment for the series and its actual premiere date. Ford makes cars and loved safety. The title had to be changed and many racing clips in the ten already finished episodes deleted before broadcast, due to Ford's objections.

STRANGE REPORT

Detective

FIRST TELECAST: *January 8, 1971*

LAST TELECAST: *September 10, 1971*

BROADCAST HISTORY:

Jan 1971–Sep 1971, NBC Fri 10:00–11:00

CAST:

Adam Strange ....Anthony Quayle

Hamlyn Gynt ....Kaz Garas

Evelyn McLean ....Anneke Wills

Strange Report showcased the use of advanced scientific analytic methods as aids in the solution of complex crimes. Adam Strange was renowned as being the foremost authority on the workings of the criminal mind in the entire Western world. Operating out of his flat in the Paddington section of London, he handled special "problem" cases that the British government could not afford to be officially involved in. Adam and Hamlyn "Ham" Gynt, his American companion and assistant, traveled around town in Adam's unlicensed English taxicab working on cases. Gynt was a former Rhodes scholar whose formal job was in the research department of a London museum. Evelyn McLean, one of Adam's neighbors, was a model and aspiring artist whose friendship with him got her involved in many of his bizarre cases.

STRANGER, THE

Crime Drama

FIRST TELECAST: *June 25, 1954*

LAST TELECAST: *February 11, 1955*

BROADCAST HISTORY:

Jun 1954–Feb 1955, DUM Fri 9:00–9:30

CAST:

The Stranger ....Robert Carroll

Mystery series dramatizing the adventures of a benevolent stranger who entered into the lives of people threatened by evildoers. The first episode told of a member of a ship's crew pursued by thieves who wanted his collection of beer steins from various ports. The sailor didn't know why they were after him, but "the stranger" did. Later episodes dealt with murder, kidnapping, etc., and at one point "the stranger" even went behind the Iron Curtain. He never accepted payment for his services, and disappeared as mysteriously as he had come after each case was solved.

STRAUSS FAMILY, THE

Romantic Drama

FIRST TELECAST: *May 5, 1973*

LAST TELECAST: *June 16, 1973*

BROADCAST HISTORY:

May 1973–Jun 1973, ABC Sat 9:00–10:00

CAST:

Johann Strauss, Sr. .... Eric Woolfe
Johann Strauss, Jr. .... Stuart Wilson
Anna Strauss .... Anne Stallybrass
Emilie Trampusch .... Barbara Ferris
Lanner .... Derek Jacobi
Josef .... Nicholas Simmonds
Hetti .... Margaret Whiting
Edi .... Tony Anholt
Annele .... Hilary Hardiman
Theresa .... Amanda Walker

True saga of the fabulous "waltz kings" of 19th-century Vienna, produced in England and aired in the U.S. as a seven part miniseries. The family's history was certainly the stuff of good soap opera. Johann, Sr., was a famous composer and the toast of Vienna, but he was gradually being overshadowed by his amibitious son, who wrote such immortal melodies as "The Blue Danube Waltz" and "Tales From the Vienna Woods." Father and son clashed not only over musical prestige but over politics, women, and just about everything else, and Johann, Sr.'s wife Anna was torn between the two. Eventually she left Sr. to his mistress, Emilie, and devoted her full attention to aiding Jr.'s growing career. Romance, death, unfaithful lovers, and great political struggles swept through this epic, along with dozens of cast members, the most prominent of whom are listed above. Music was provided by members of the London Symphony Orchestra.

STRAW HAT THEATRE

see *ABC Dramatic Shorts—1952–1953*

STRAWHATTERS, THE

Variety

FIRST TELECAST: *May 27, 1953*

LAST TELECAST: *September 8, 1954*

BROADCAST HISTORY:

May 1953–Sep 1953, DUM Wed 8:30–9:30
Jun 1954–Sep 1954, DUM Wed 9:00–10:00

EMCEE:

Johnny Olsen (1953)
Virginia Graham (1954)

This was essentially an hour-long advertisement for Palisades Amusement Park, located in New Jersey, across the Hudson River from New York City. It was (and looked like) a super-cheap production, consisting of a talent show, diving exhibitions in the park's big pool, musical entertainment in the ballroom, and pickups from other locations around the park. Much of the show was done outdoors.

The program was seen locally in New York in 1952 and went out over the full DuMont network (such as it was) from 1953–1954. The 1954 version was called *Summer in the Park.*

STREETS OF SAN FRANCISCO, THE

Police

FIRST TELECAST: *September 16, 1972*

LAST TELECAST: *June 23, 1977*

BROADCAST HISTORY:

Sep 1972–Jan 1973, ABC Sat 9:00–10:00
Jan 1973–Aug 1974, ABC Thu 10:00–11:00
Sep 1974–Sep 1976, ABC Thu 9:00–10:00
Sep 1976–Jun 1977, ABC Thu 10:00–11:00

CAST:

Det. Lt. Mike Stone .... Karl Malden
Inspector Steve Keller (1972–1976) .... Michael Douglas
Inspector Dan Robbins (1976–1977) .... Richard Hatch

EXECUTIVE PRODUCER:

Quinn Martin

There always seems to be room on TV for a police show set in San Francisco (remember *The Lineup?*). *The Streets of San Francisco* was such a show for the 1970s, following the cases of Lt. Mike Stone and his young partner as they used modern police methods to track down criminals, against the backdrop of the Bay Area. Mike was a 23-year veteran of the force, a widower, assigned to the Bureau of Inspectors Division of the San Francisco Police Department. His original partner was 28-year-old Steve Keller, a smart, college-educated man who rose from assistant inspector tb inspector during his tenure on the show. In 1976 he left ("to enter teaching") and was replaced by the athletic Dan Robbins.

Mike's co-ed daughter was seen occasionally during the early years (played by Darleen Carr), but later the emphasis was shifted to the cases, rather than the home lives, of the principals. Some scenes in the series were filmed in actual San Francisco police buildings, such as the communications center, the morgue, etc.

Based on characters from the novel *Poor, Poor Ophelia*, by Carolyn Weston.

STRENGTH FOR A FREE WORLD

see *Marshall Plan in Action, The*

STRICTLY FOR LAUGHS

Music

FIRST TELECAST: *November 22, 1949*
LAST TELECAST: *June 23, 1950*
BROADCAST HISTORY:
Nov 1949–Dec 1949, CBS Tue/Wed/Fri 7:00–7:15
Dec 1949, CBS Mon/Tue/Wed/Fri 7:00–7:15
Jan 1950, CBS Mon/Wed/Thu/Fri 7:00–7:15
Jan 1950–Jun 1950, CBS Mon–Fri 7:00–7:15
REGULARS:
The Kirby Stone Quintet

The light-hearted harmonizing of the Kirby Stone Quintet was featured in this live 15-minute musical program. Their songs were often pleasantly amusing, though not up to the level of silliness attained by the likes of Spike Jones. Rather, the lyrics tended to have subtle twists. Occasionally they were joined by guest performers. Effective with the telecast of April 3, 1950, the title of the series was changed to *The Kirby Stone Quintet*.

STRIKE IT RICH

Quiz/Audience Participation

FIRST TELECAST: *July 4, 1951*
LAST TELECAST: *January 12, 1955*
BROADCAST HISTORY:
Jul 1951–Jan 1955, CBS Wed 9:00–9:30
EMCEE:
Warren Hull

Strike It Rich was one of the most hotly debated programs on television during the 1950s. To some it was TV's noblest hour, helping those less fortunate than most through the charity and good will of viewers. To others it was one of the most sickening spectacles ever seen on a TV screen, exploiting those same unfortunates for the vicarious thrill of viewers and the selfish gain of advertisers, a kind of video "kick the cripple." It was investigated by governmental bodies, limned by charitable organizations, and defended by others. Whichever way you looked at it, though, it was certainly popular, and perhaps the ultimate example of viewer-participation television.

Strike It Rich was created by producer Walt Framer and was first heard on CBS radio in 1947. It consisted of a quiz show whose contestants were exclusively people in need of money—for medical treatment, for a destitute family, for a crippled children's hospital, for a little girl who had lost her dog. About a quarter of the contestants were actually representing someone else who was in need. The questions were easy and most contestants were winners—if you could classify anyone on a show like this a "winner"—but even if they lost, there was always the "Heart Line." After they told their tale of woe, emcee Hull would open up the telephone lines and ask viewers to pitch in what they could. And they did, thousands of dollars every broadcast, expensive therapeutic equipment, clothes and furniture for those who had none, an endless stream of gifts from all over America to help ease the contestant's suffering.

The problem, besides the obvious ethical one, was that the program seemed to promise more than it could deliver. For every charity case that got on the air, hundreds were turned away (only "appealing" or "interesting" cases were wanted). From 3,000 to 5,000 letters a week poured in from desperate people, and despite the program's repeated advice to the contrary, dozens of them journeyed to New York in hopes of being picked out of the studio audience. Most of these wound up stranded in the city, and were forced to go to welfare agencies or the Salvation Army—which complained bitterly about the effect the show was having. The New York City Commissioner of Welfare called

Strike It Rich "a disgusting spectacle and a national disgrace," and demanded that it be investigated. The supervisor of the Travelers Aid Society said, "We don't know if the successes on the show balance off against the human misery caused by it. But from what we see, I'd say they didn't. . . . Putting human misery on display can hardly be called right." The General Director of the Family Service Association of America said flatly, "Victims of poverty, illness, and everyday misfortune should not be made a public spectacle or seemingly be put in the position of begging for charity." A New York State legislative committee did look into the controversy, but then washed its hands of the affair, claiming that it did not have jurisdiction. As for CBS and NBC, the networks that carried the show in daytime and nighttime versions, they were unconcerned. "We don't want to do anything that would antagonize the sponsor," said NBC.

And so the program which *TV Guide* called "a despicable travesty on the very nature of charity" continued untouched until it ended its normal run.

STU ERWIN SHOW, THE

Situation Comedy

FIRST TELECAST: *October 21, 1950*

LAST TELECAST: *April 13, 1955*

BROADCAST HISTORY:

Oct 1950–Sep 1951, ABC Sat 7:30–8:00
Oct 1951–Apr 1952, ABC Fri 8:30–9:00
May 1952–Oct 1954, ABC Fri 7:30–8:00
Oct 1954–Apr 1955, ABC Wed 8:30–9:00

CAST:

Stu Erwin .... Himself
June Erwin .... June Collyer
Jackie Erwin .... Sheila James
Joyce Erwin (1950–1954) .... Ann Todd
Joyce Erwin (1954–1955) .... Merry Anders
Willie .... Willie Best
Harry (1954–1955) .... Harry Hayden
Jimmy Clark (1954–1955) ... Martin Milner

This was perhaps TV's leading bumbling-father series in the 1950s. Stu Erwin had made a long career of similar roles in movies and on radio before he came to TV in 1950. He was perfect for the role: he looked and acted like a well-meaning, folksy but completely incompetent middle-aged suburban parent.

Stu was principal of Hamilton High School, which often served to get him involved in various civic activities. But most of the action was around the Erwins' own home, where Stu's every attempt to fix or improve things, surprise someone, or bring up the kids turned to disaster. Wife June (played by Erwin's real-life wife, June Collyer) generally came to the rescue. Teenage Joyce and tomboy Jackie rounded out the family, while Willie was the handyman and various neighbors came and went.

In 1954 Joyce began going steady with Jimmy Clark, and in a December telecast they were married. Also in the 1954–1955 season the producers made an effort to portray Stu as a little less blundering than he had been—something devoutly wished for by actor Erwin—but the series had run its course by early 1955.

The series was first known as *Life with the Erwins,* and later *The Trouble with Father* (which continued as its subtitle). During the final season, to emphasize the changes, it became *The New Stu Erwin Show.*

STUDIO 57

Dramatic Anthology

FIRST TELECAST: *September 21, 1954*

LAST TELECAST: *September 6, 1955*

BROADCAST HISTORY:

Sep 1954–Oct 1954, DUM Tue 9:00–9:30
Oct 1954–Sep 1955, DUM Tue 8:30–9:00

This filmed dramatic series had few distinctions—the scripts were weak, the actors generally lesser known (at the time)—except that it was one of the last regularly scheduled series ever carried on the crumbling DuMont network. Only *What's the Story,* among non-sports series, lasted a few weeks longer. The title derived from the sponsor, "Heinz 57 Varieties."

Stories on *Studio 57* were generally mysteries or melodramas, set in various historical periods. Among the actors and actresses appearing were Craig Stevens, Natalie Wood, Hugh O'Brien, Pat Carroll, Peter Graves, Charles Coburn, and Brian Keith.

STUDIO ONE

Dramatic Anthology

FIRST TELECAST: *November 7, 1948*

LAST TELECAST: *September 29, 1958*

BROADCAST HISTORY:

Nov 1948–Mar 1949, CBS Sun 7:30–8:30
Mar 1949–May 1949, CBS Sun 7:00–8:00
May 1949–Sep 1949, CBS Wed 10:00–11:00
Sep 1949–Sep 1958, CBS Mon 10:00–11:00

COMMERCIAL SPOKESPERSON:

Betty Furness (1949–1958)

When *Studio One* premiered on CBS radio in the spring of 1947, there was little immediate concern at the network over the possible incursion of television as a competing medium. Little priority was given to TV, as CBS did not yet have a TV network. All that changed after the success of NBC's video coverage of the 1947 World Series. There was a crash development program at CBS and one of the principal components in that development was to be a live dramatic-anthology series. The radio version of *Studio One* lasted less than a year, but under the dynamic early leadership of producer Worthington Miner the new TV version became a major success, lasting for almost a full decade.

Miner's approach to television was somewhat different from that of many of the other producers of early dramatic shows. His concern was with the visual impact of the stories, for television was a visual medium, and he placed a greater emphasis on that than on the literary merit of the story. It was not that he produced second rate plays—to the contrary, many of them were adaptations of classics and from the best young writers available (Miner personally did many of the adaptations during his tenure with *Studio One*)—but Miner's major contribution to television drama was more in his experimentation with camera techniques and other innovations in whaz the viewer saw, rather than in what was heard.

The premiere telecast of *Studio One*, on November 7, 1948, was an adaptation of the mystery play *The Storm*, starring stage and screen actress Margaret Sullavan, one of the few established stars who was willing to perform on the new medium, especially considering the lowly pay (a maximum of $500 was budgeted for talent on early telecasts). The budgetary problems resulted in other interesting innovations. *Julius Caesar* was done twice in the spring of 1949, with Robert Keith in the lead and young Charlton Heston in a minor role, but lack of money forced the producers to stage it in modern dress. In 1955, with more cash available, *Julius Caesar* was done for a third time, in traditional period costumes, with Theodore Bikel starring.

Studio One had gone on the air without a sponsor, but it gained one in Westinghouse Electric in early 1949. On Westinghouse's third telecast the commercials were done by an actress named Betty Furness. She went on to become the most recognized and famous commercial spokesperson in the history of television. She would remain with the series until its cancellation in 1958 and continued with its successor, *Westinghouse Desilu Playhouse*. The picture of her demonstrating a range or opening a refrigerator and the slogan "You Can Be Sure If It's Westinghouse" were ingrained with a generation of Americans.

In the early years of *Studio One*, three performers were seen far more often than any others—Charlton Heston, Mary Sinclair, and Maria Riva—each with the lead roles in at least a dozen plays. Heston starred in adaptations of *Of Human Bondage*, *Jane Eyre* with Miss Sinclair, *The Taming of the Shrew* with Phyllis Kirk, and *Wuthering Heights*, again with Miss Sinclair, and many lesser-known plays. Many of the better plays were repeated. The premiere presentation, *The Storm*, was redone in 1949 with Marsha Hunt in the lead role, *Jane Eyre* was done again in 1952, "Flowers from a Stranger" starred Yul Brynner in both 1949 and 1950, and *Julius Caesar*, as mentioned above, was done three times.

Doing live shows often presented problems. In a 1953 story, "Dry Run," whole sections of a submarine were built in the studio and the entire cast was almost electrocuted when the water that was used for special effects got very close to the power cables. Many young directors, such as Frank Schaffner, George Roy Hill, Sidney Lumet, and Paul Nickell got their baptism under fire with this hectic live series. Authors like Rod Serling, Gore Vidal, Paul Monash, and Reginald Rose contributed teleplays for *Studio One* and it was Rose's "The Twelve Angry Men" in 1954 that won Emmys for writing (Rose), direction (Frank Schaffner), and performance by an actor in a drama (Bob Cummings).

Two months after "The Twelve Angry Men," another episode of *Studio One* aired that is remembered not for its dramatic merit, but for a song. The producers were planning to do a drama about skulduggery in the record industry and they needed a song, so they turned to Mitch Miller, head of recording for CBS' subsidiary, Columbia Records. Miller gave them an obscure ballad called "Let Me Go, Devil," and urged that it be sung on the soundtrack by an unknown songstress rather than to an established star, to heighten the dramatic impact. With remarkable foresight he then saw to it that, prior to the telecast, record stores were well stocked with her Columbia recording of the song.

There was little demand for the record until the night of the telecast (November 15, 1954). Now called "Let Me Go, Lover," and emotionally sung by Joan Weber, it was woven skillfully throughout the drama. The next morning record stores were deluged with customers wanting "that song that was on TV last night"—and "Let Me Go, Lover" became a phenomenal hit, selling more than 500,000 copies in the next five days (it eventually sold over one million). It was one of the few times in the history of television that a single telecast was directly responsible for a major song hit.

People appeared on *Studio One* who may now seem to have been somewhat out of place. Newsman Mike Wallace appeared in two dramas. Jackie Gleason and Art Carney, while still doing their live variety show, took time to star in a serious drama called "The Laugh Maker" in the spring of 1953, and later made other occasional appearances on the show separately. Ironically, Elizabeth Montgomery showed up on *Studio One* a few times in the mid-1950s. Her father was the host of *Robert Montgomery Presents*, the NBC Monday night dramatic showcase that was in direct competition with *Studio One* for most of its run. Even Edward R. Murrow was featured on the series, though not as an actor. He was the narrator of a 1957 documentary-drama, "The Night America Trembled," about Orson Welles' 1938 broadcast of "War of the Worlds."

With the first telecast in January 1958, *Studio One* moved to Hollywood, with the title appropriately changed to *Studio One in Hollywood*. It had moved because that was where the talent was, and the facilities for production were better than in New York. It was still done live, but only remained on the air for another nine months. Live drama was dying, as was New York origination of TV series.

In its decade on the air, *Studio One* presented nearly 500 plays. Literally thousands of actors and actresses appeared, but only a few of them were featured in at least half a dozen plays. Other than those already mentioned above they were Katherine Bard, Richard Kiley, Priscilla Gillette, Judson Laire, Harry Townes, John Forsythe, Nina Foch, Hildy Parks, Sheppard Strudwick, Leslie Nielsen, James Daly, Everett Sloane, Betsy Palmer, Skip Homeier, James Gregory, Cathleen Nesbitt, Edward Andrews, Barbara O'Neill, Burt Brinckerhoff, Cliff Norton, Stanley Ridges, and Felicia Montealegre.

During the summers, when the regular *Studio One* production team was vacationing, the series was variously titled *Summer Theatre*, *Westinghouse Summer Theatre*, and *Studio One Summer Theatre*.

STUD'S PLACE

Variety

FIRST TELECAST: *November 26, 1949*

LAST TELECAST: *January 28, 1952*

BR&ADCAST HISTORY:

Nov 1949–Dec 1949, NBC Sat 8:45–9:00
Apr 1950–May 1950, NBC Thu 8:00–8:30
May 1950–Aug 1950, NBC Thu 8:30–9:00
Oct 1950–Aug 1951, ABC Fri 10:30–11:00
Aug 1951–Jan 1952, ABC Mon 10:30–11:00

CAST:

Studs Terkel .... Himself
The Waitress (1950) ...... Beverly Younger
Wynn (1950–1952) .... Win Strache
Mr. Lord (1950) .... Phil Lord
Mr. Denby (1950) .... Jonathan Hole
Pianist (1950–1952) .... Chet Roble

Studs Terkel presided over this affable program of songs and stories, which was at first set in Stud's bar in New York, with Studs as the bartender. This version ran only about a month, and was then incorporated as a regular segment in the Saturday night series *Saturday Square*. When *Saturday Square* was canceled Studs returned again with his own series, this time cast as the proprietor of a Chicago barbecue restaurant frequented by a number of regulars. Among them were Wynn the folk-singing handyman, and Chet the jazz pianist. Both series were loosely plotted, with Studs' garrulous, philosophical ramblings the center of attention.

Telecast from Chicago.

STUMP THE AUTHORS

Stories

FIRST TELECAST: *January 15, 1949*
LAST TELECAST: *April 2, 1949*
BROADCAST HISTORY:
Jan 1949–Apr 1949, ABC Sat 9:00–9:30
EDITOR:
Syd Breeze

Ad-lib storytelling session in which three or four authors tried to spin yarns based on props given to them, which they had never seen before. From Chicago.

STUMP THE STARS

see *Pantomime Quiz*

SUGAR HILL TIMES

Musical Variety

FIRST TELECAST: *September 13, 1949*
LAST TELECAST: *October 20, 1949*
BROADCAST HISTORY:
Sep 1949, CBS Tue 8:00–9:00
Oct 1949, CBS Thu 8:30–9:00
REGULARS:
Willie Bryant
Harry Bellafonte
Timmy Rogers
The Jubileers
Don Redman and His Orchestra

Sugar Hill Times was one of network television's first, short-lived attempts at showcasing black talent. All of the performers in the live weekly musical variety show were black. It aired three times as a full-hour show, and each time had a different title; premiering as *Uptown Jubilee*, changing to *Harlem Jubilee*, and finally settling on *Sugar Hill Times*, the title it also used during its two half-hour telecasts on October 6 and 20. It may have been an unintentional oversight on the part of the CBS press department at the time, but every press release for the show spelled singer Harry Belafonte's name as it's listed above, with two *l*'s.

SUGAR TIME!

Situation Comedy

FIRST TELECAST: *August 13, 1977*
LAST TELECAST: *May 29, 1978*
BROADCAST HISTORY:
Aug 1977–Sep 1977, ABC Sat 8:30–9:00
Apr 1978–May 1978, ABC Mon 8:00–8:30
CAST:
Maxx .... Barbi Benton
Maggie .... Marianne Black
Diane .... Didi Carr
Al Marks .... Wynn Irwin
Paul Landson .... Mark Winkworth

Popular singer/composer Paul Williams wrote original songs and was musical supervisor for this summer comedy series about three beautiful young girls who were aspiring rock singers. The talented trio called themselves Sugar, and shared an apartment in California where they were attempting to launch their act, without pay, at Al Marks' Tryout Room. Maxx, beautiful and naive, worked as a hat-check girl; Diane, a wisecracking native of the Bronx, was a dental hygienist; and Maggie, the practical one, taught dancing to children. A constant threat to the group's success was Diane's indecision over whether she should marry her favorite dentist.

SUGARFOOT

Western

FIRST TELECAST: *September 17, 1957*
LAST TELECAST: *July 3, 1961*
BROADCAST HISTORY:
Sep 1957–Sep 1960, ABC Tue 7:30–8:30
Oct 1960–Jul 1961, ABC Mon 7:30–8:30
CAST:
Tom "Sugarfoot" Brewster ... Will Hutchins

Western about the exploits of a young correspondence-school law student who rode west in search of adventure. Unfortunately, Tom Brewster was somewhat inept as a cowboy, and he promptly earned the nickname "Sugarfoot"—one grade lower than a tenderfoot—in the first episode. Undeterred, and with a redeeming sense of humor, he set out to lasso some outlaws and round up a few pretty girls, if possible.

Although it was a Western in the traditional sense, with plenty of action, *Sugarfoot* always had a light touch which set it apart from most examples of the genre. It ran on an alternate-week basis with *Cheyenne* from 1957–1959, with *Bronco* from 1959–1960, and then became one of three rotating elements of the *Cheyenne* anthology for its final season.

SUMMER BROTHERS SMOTHERS SHOW, THE

Comedy Variety

FIRST TELECAST: *June 23, 1968*

LAST TELECAST: *September 8, 1968*

BROADCAST HISTORY:

Jun 1968–Sep 1968, CBS Sun 9:00–10:00

REGULARS:

Glen Campbell
Pat Paulsen
Leigh French
The Jimmy Joyce Singers
Nelson Riddle & His Orchestra

This 1968 summer replacement for *The Smothers Brothers Comedy Hour* starred Country singer Glen Campbell, who was later to get a regular series of his own, and two of the regulars from the Smothers Brothers group, comics Pat Paulsen and Leigh French. Regular features of the show were comedy sketches featuring Leigh French as a hippie, and Pat Paulsen doing improbable editorials and campaigning for President.

SUMMER CINEMA

see *Movies—Prior to 1961*

SUMMER FAIR

see *ABC Dramatic Shorts—1952–1953*

SUMMER FOCUS

Documentary

FIRST TELECAST: *May 18, 1967*

LAST TELECAST: *August 31, 1967*

BROADCAST HISTORY:

May 1967–Aug 1967, ABC Thu 10:00–11:00

This series of documentaries included an examination of political protest in America, a debate on the limits of free speech in a democracy, a pictorial study of the paintings of Leonardo Da Vinci, an examination of health-care problems in America, and a look at the pollution problems facing both small and large cities.

SUMMER FUN

Comedy Anthology

FIRST TELECAST: *July 22, 1966*

LAST TELECAST: *September 2, 1966*

BROADCAST HISTORY:

Jul 1966–Sep 1966, ABC Fri 8:00–8:30

ABC aired a collection of unsold pilots for projected situation comedy series on for seven consecutive Fridays during the summer of 1966. Among them were shows starring Cliff Arquette, Bert Lahr, and Shelley Fabares.

SUMMER HOLIDAY

Music

FIRST TELECAST: *June 24, 1954*

LAST TELECAST: *September 9, 1954*

BROADCAST HISTORY:

Jun 1954–Sep 1954, CBS Thu 7:45–8:00
Jul 1954–Aug 1954, CBS Tue 7:45–8:00

REGULARS:

Merv Griffin
Betty Ann Grove

This twice-weekly summer replacement for both *The Jo Stafford Show* and *The Jane Froman Show* was a live musical interlude that filled the remainder of the half-hour in which CBS aired its network news program. The Tuesday edition was titled *Summer Holiday* and the Thursday edition *Song Snapshots on a Summer Holiday.* The format had the two singing stars portray camera bugs on an around the world tour, with sets and costumes of an appropriate nature, all to serve as a backdrop for their solos and duets.

SUMMER IN THE PARK

see *Strawhatters, The*

SUMMER NIGHT THEATER

Anthology

FIRST TELECAST: *July 7, 1953*

LAST TELECAST: *July 28, 1953*

BROADCAST HISTORY:

Jul 1953, DUM Tue 10:00–10:30

A four-week series of filmed dramas, starring Gale Storm, Lloyd Bridges, and others. The series continued to be seen locally in New York for the remainder of the summer.

SUMMER PLAYHOUSE

Anthology

FIRST TELECAST: *July 6, 1954*

LAST TELECAST: *September 6, 1965*

BROADCAST HISTORY:

Jul 1954–Aug 1954, NBC Tue 9:00–9:30
Jul 1957–Sep 1957, NBC Tue 9:30–10:00
Jul 1964–Sep 1964, CBS Sat 9:30–10:00
Jun 1965–Sep 1965, CBS Mon 8:30–9:00

HOST:

Nelson Case (1954)
Jane Wyman (1957)

These were all summer anthology series used to fill time until the fall season started. On the two occasions a program with the title *Summer Playhouse* aired on NBC, the episodes were reruns from other anthology series. The two CBS versions in the 1960s were made up of unsold pilots for projected regular series.

SUMMER SPORTS SPECTACULAR, THE

Sports Anthology

FIRST TELECAST: *April 27, 1961*
LAST TELECAST: *September 28, 1961*
BROADCAST HISTORY:
Apr 1961–Sep 1961, CBS Thu 7:30–8:30
HOST:
Bud Palmer

CBS had premiered a weekly sports anthology on Sunday afternoons in January 1960 titled *The Sunday Sports Spectacular.* During the summer of 1961 it moved to Thursday evenings as *The Summer Sports Spectacular.* Host Bud Palmer covered a different type of sporting event each week. The premiere telecast was a figure-skating memorial tribute to the members of the 1960 U.S. Olympic Figure Skating team who had died tragically in an airplane crash. Subsequent episodes covered spring training with one of the two brand-new American League Baseball teams—Gene Autry's Los Angeles Angels—coverage of the European soccer championships, the Army-Navy lacrosse game, a gymnastics meet between the U.S. and Japan, and a motorcycle rally. In addition to actual event coverage, each telecast included background on the sport and interviews with participants.

The Sunday Sports Spectacular, which changed its name to *The CBS Sports Spectacular* in January 1963, is still carried as a daytime feature on that network.

SUMMER THEATRE

see *Studio One*

SUMMER THEATRE

Dramatic Anthology

FIRST TELECAST: *July 10, 1953*
LAST TELECAST: *September 11, 1953*
BROADCAST HISTORY:
Jul 1953–Sep 1953, ABC Fri 8:00–8:30

This filmed anthology series aired on ABC during the summer of 1953 as the replacement for *The Adventures of Ozzie & Harriet.* The title alternated from week to week because of sponsorship. One week it was *Summer Theatre* and on the alternate week it was *Interlude.* Among the presentations were "Myrt and Marge" with Franklyn Pangborn and Lyle Talbot and "Foo Young" with Richard Loo.

SUMMERTIME U.S.A.

Music

FIRST TELECAST: *July 7, 1953*
LAST TELECAST: *August 27, 1953*
BROADCAST HISTORY:
Jul 1953–Aug 1953, CBS Tue/Thu 7:45–8:00
REGULARS:
Teresa Brewer
Mel Torme
The Honeydreamers
Ray Bloch & His Orchestra

This series was the 1953 summer replacement for another music series, *Jane Froman's U.S.A. Canteen.* The two stars, Teresa Brewer and Mel Torme, were seen in a different resort setting for each of the live telecasts. The scenic backgrounds ranged from Atlantic City and Niagara Falls on the domestic side, to Rio, Havana, and the Casbah on the international side.

SUNDAY AT HOME

Music

FIRST TELECAST: *July 3, 1949*
LAST TELECAST: *July 31, 1949*
BROADCAST HISTORY:
Jul 1949, NBC Sun 7:15–7:30
FEATURED:
The Pickard Family

Short-lived summer show which presented the Pickard family (Mom, Dad, and four children) singing hymns and old favorite songs. Filmed in Hollywood.

SUNDAY DATE

Music

FIRST TELECAST: *August 21, 1949*
LAST TELECAST: *October 9, 1949*
BROADCAST HISTORY:
Aug 1949–Oct 1949, NBC Sun 7:15–7:30

Live musical interlude featuring an assortment of young, lesser-known singers and instrumentalists, and set in an imaginary sidewalk cafe just off New York's Central Park.

SUNDAY LUCY SHOW, THE

see *I Love Lucy*

SUNDAY MYSTERY HOUR, THE

see *Chevy Mystery Show, The*

SUNDAY SHOWCASE

Variety

FIRST TELECAST: *September 20, 1959*

LAST TELECAST: *May 1, 1960*

BROADCAST HISTORY:

Sep 1959–May 1960, NBC Sun 8:00–9:00

Sunday Showcase was actually a varied series of specials that aired in the 8:00 P.M—9:00 P.M. hour on Sunday evenings during the 1959–1960 season. Some of them were dramatic plays, some were comedy variety shows (such as "The Milton Berle Show"), some were musical comedies, and some were historical dramas (such as "Our American Heritage"). Among the other notable telecasts were a two-part version of Budd Schulberg's novel *What Makes Sammy Run* and the premiere offering, a "poetic drama" by S. Lee Pogostin called "People Kill People Sometimes," starring George C. Scott, Geraldine Page, and Jason Robards, Jr.

SUNSHINE

Situation Comedy

FIRST TELECAST: *March 6, 1975*

LAST TELECAST: *June 19, 1975*

BROADCAST HISTORY:

Mar 1975–Jun 1975, NBC Thu 8:00–8:30

CAST:

Sam Hayden .... Cliff DeYoung
Jill .... Elizabeth Cheshire
Weaver .... Bill Mumy
Givits .... Corey Fischer
Nora .... Meg Foster

THEME:

"Sunshine on My Shoulder," by John Denver, Dick Kniss, and Mike Taylor

Set in Vancouver, British Columbia, *Sunshine* was the story of a young widower and his daughter trying to make ends meet. Sam Hayden's wife had died of cancer, leaving him to care for Jill, her five-year-old daughter by a previous marriage. Sam was a composer and, along with his two friends, Weaver and Givits, a member of a singing trio. With his musical career not generating much money, Sam sought all sorts of odd jobs to help support Jill and himself. He also tried to be both mother and father to Jill, who was always on the lookout for a likely candidate to marry her father. Helping Sam out, in addition to his two long-haired partners, was his neighbor and friend Nora. The easy and contemporary lifestyle led by Sam and Jill was cheered by some and condemned by others, and caused concern among those who felt it was not good for Jill's welfare. The title of the series referred to Jill's mother's favorite song.

SUPER, THE

Situation Comedy

FIRST TELECAST: *June 21, 1972*

LAST TELECAST: *August 23, 1972*

BROADCAST HISTORY:

Jun 1972–Aug 1972, ABC Wed 8:00–8:30

CAST:

Joe Girelli .... Richard Castellano
Francesca Girelli .... Ardell Sheridan
Joanne Girelli .... Margaret Castellano
Anthony Girelli .... Bruce Kirby, Jr.
Frankie .... Phil Mishkin

All Joe wanted was a cold can of beer, a pizza, and a TV set. But big Joe (260 pounds) was superintendent of an old, walk-up apartment building in a lower-middle-class section of New York City, so what he got was tenants banging on the pipes, tenants complaining about him and about each other, a family that wouldn't leave him alone, and a city that wanted to condemn his building. Richard Castellano starred with his real-life daughter Margaret in this ethnic comedy (among the tenants were Italians, Irish, Poles, Jews, blacks, Puerto Ricans, homosexuals, social workers, cops, and revolutionaries). Francesca was his wife, Joanne and Anthony his disrespectful kids, and Frankie his big-shot lawyer brother.

SUPER GHOST

Quiz/Audience Participation

FIRST TELECAST: *July 27, 1952*

LAST TELECAST: *September 6, 1953*

BROADCAST HISTORY:

Jul 1952–Sep 1952, NBC Sun 7:00–7:30
Jul 1953–Sep 1953, NBC Sun 7:30–8:00

EMCEE:

Bergen Evans

PANELISTS:

Shirley Stern
Robert Pollack

Super Ghost was a live game show from Chicago, based on the old word game "ghost." Each of the contestants stood before a blackboard and was given three letters of the word being used. They would add letters, one at a time, the object of the game being to avoid completing the designated word. Each time they completed a word they would become one-third a ghost and when they had completed three words they became full ghosts and "disappeared" from the game. Home viewers submitted words for the show and won money if the panel members ended up completing their word. The only two panelists who were regulars throughout the two-summer run of *Super Ghost* were a local Chicago housewife, Shirley Stern, and former drama critic Robert Pollack. A variety of guests filled the other two seats on the panel.

SURE AS FATE

Dramatic Anthology

FIRST TELECAST: *July 4, 1950*

LAST TELECAST: *April 3, 1951*

BROADCAST HISTORY:

Jul 1950, CBS Tue 8:00–9:00

Sep 1950–Apr 1951, CBS Tue 8:00–9:00

The themes that predominated in this live anthology series were of a melodramatic nature—stories of people confronted with situations not of their own making. *Sure as Fate* was tried for two weeks in July, received encouraging responses from the critics, and returned in September as a regular series. After a month as a weekly program it was cut back to alternate-week status with *Prudential Family Playhouse.* Among the performers featured were Rod Steiger, Leslie Nielsen, John Carradine, Kim Stanley, and Marsha Hunt.

SURFSIDE SIX

Detective

FIRST TELECAST: *October 3, 1960*

LAST TELECAST: *September 24, 1962*

BROADCAST HISTORY:

Oct 1960–Sep 1961, ABC Mon 8:30–9:30

Oct 1961–Sep 1962, ABC Mon 9:00–10:00

CAST:

Ken Madison .... Van Williams
Dave Thorne .... Lee Patterson
Sandy Winfield .... Troy Donahue
Daphne Dutton .... Diane McBain
Cha Cha O'Brien .... Margarita Sierra
Lt. Gene Plehn .... Richard Crane

The success of *77 Sunset Strip* had prompted both its producers, Warner Brothers, and its network, ABC, to try a series of cookie-cutter copies. *Surfside Six* fit the pattern. Just as in *Sunset Strip,* a trio of sexy, young private detectives (Ken, Dave, and Sandy) lived in an exciting city (Miami) and spent much time with beautiful women (Daphne and Cha Cha). All that was missing was a jive-talking parking-lot attendant. Surfside Six was the Miami telephone exchange that included the number of the houseboat that served as both home and office to the detectives. Anchored next to it was the yacht of kooky socialite Daphne Dutton, and across from it was the fabulous Fountainebleau Hotel, where Cha Cha worked as an entertainer in the Boom Boom Room.

Ken Madison was the only survivor of the New Orleans–based team of detectives that had been seen in the same time slot during the previous season—in *Bourbon Street Beat,* another cookie from the cutter.

SURVIVAL—ANGLIA, LTD. SERIES

Wildlife/Nature

FIRST TELECAST: *June 24, 1976*

LAST TELECAST: *September 16, 1976*

BROADCAST HISTORY:

Jun 1976–Sep 1976, NBC Thu 8:00–9:00

This summer series was composed of a collection of documentaries on various animals. Some of them were originals and others were repeats of specials that had already aired on network television. Included were "Gorilla," narrated by David Niven, "Magnificent Monsters of the Deep," narrated by Orson Welles, and "Come into My Parlor" (about spiders), narrated by Peter Ustinov.

SURVIVORS, THE

Drama

FIRST TELECAST: *September 29, 1969*

LAST TELECAST: *September 17, 1970*

BROADCAST HISTORY:

Sep 1969–Jan 1970, ABC Mon 9:00–10:00

Jun 1970–Sep 1970, ABC Thu 10:00–11:00

CAST:

Tracy Carlyle Hastings .... Lana Turner
Philip Hastings .... Kevin McCarthy
Jeffrey Hastings .... Jan Michael Vincent
Baylor Carlyle .... Ralph Bellamy
Duncan Carlyle .... George Hamilton
Belle .... Diana Muldaur

Jonathan	Louis Hayward
Jean Vale	Louise Sorel
Antaeus Riakos	Rossano Brazzi
Miguel Santerra	Robert Viharo
Marguerita	Donna Baccala
Shelia	Kathy Cannon
Tom	Robert Lipton
Sen. Mark Jennings	Clu Gulager
Eleanor Carlyle	Natalie Schaefer

Movie queen Lana Turner made her TV series debut—and swan song—in this adaptation of Harold Robbins' novel of love and lust among the jet set. Lana, as Tracy Hastings, was the center of the action as she struggled to protect her teenage son Jeffrey from (as the press release put it) "the forces that could destroy him." Among the other major protagonists were Tracy's philandering husband, Philip; her father, banking czar Baylor; and her playboy half-brother, Duncan. Continuing story lines unfolded in a new "chapter" each week, and involved the Carlyles' entanglement with South American revolutionary Miguel Santerra, Tracy's old flame Riakos (eventually revealed to be Jeffrey's real father), Baylor's lingering death, and everybody's attempts to get their hands on his millions. Pure soap opera.

The Survivors was a big-name bust, lasting only three and a half months. ABC recouped some of its cost by running repeats during the summer of 1970.

The official title of the series was *Harold Robbins' "The Survivors."*

SUSAN RAYE

Music

FIRST TELECAST: *October 2, 1950*

LAST TELECAST: *November 20, 1950*

BROADCAST HISTORY:

Oct 1950, DUM Mon/Fri 7:45–8:00

Oct 1950–Nov 1950, DUM Mon 7:30–7:45

HOSTESS:

Susan Raye

Musical interlude featuring the singing and piano stylings of Miss Raye.

SUSIE

syndicated title for *Private Secretary*

SUSPENSE

Dramatic Anthology

FIRST TELECAST: *March 1, 1949*

LAST TELECAST: *September 9, 1964*

BROADCAST HISTORY:

Mar 1949–Jun 1950, CBS Tue 9:30–10:00 (OS)

Aug 1950–Aug 1954, CBS Tue 9:30–10:00

Mar 1964–Sep 1964, CBS Wed 8:30–9:00

HOST:

Sebastian Cabot (1964)

Suspense had been a fixture on the CBS Radio Network since 1942 (where it remained for 20 years). The radio version had won a Peabody Award and a special citation from the Mystery Writers of America. In the spring of 1949 it came to television. The television plays were broadcast live from New York and featured many well-known Hollywood and Broadway actors. All of the stories dealt with people in dangerous and threatening situations of one kind or another. Some were adaptations of classic horror tales like *Dr. Jekyll and Mr. Hyde,* done in 1950 with Ralph Bell in the lead role and again a year later with Basil Rathbone. A version of *Suspicion* starred Ernest Truex and his wife Sylvia Field, William Prince had the lead in "The Waxworks," John Forsythe in Robert Louis Stevenson's "The Beach of Falsea," and Peter Lorre in "The Tortured Hand." Frequent performers during the live run of the series were Nina Foch, Mildred Natwick, Tom Drake, Barry Sullivan, and horror veterans Boris Karloff, John Carradine, and Henry Hull.

Not all of the stories were of the horror genre. Though the works of Poe and Lovecraft were adapted frequently, there were straight mysteries by Charlotte Armstrong and Quentin Reynolds, among others. Rudyard Kipling's "The Man Who Would be King" and numerous stories by Charles Dickens were also presented. On the more contemporary side, Grace Kelly starred in "50 Beautiful Girls," Arlene Francis and Lloyd Bridges in "Her Last Adventure," and Eva Gabor and Sidney Blackmer in a two-parter titled "This Is Your Confession." Jackie Cooper starred on occasion, and Cloris Leachman, Jacqueline Susann, and Mike Wallace showed up on *Suspense* as well.

In the spring of 1964, almost a full decade after the live version of *Suspense* left the air, a new series of filmed *Suspense* dramas arrived on CBS with Sebastian Cabot as host (there had never been a regular host for the live show). Some of the stars of these new stories—E. G. Marshall, James

Daly, Basil Rathbone, and Skip Homeier —were returning home, as they had also starred in episodes of the live series in the 1950s. By the end of June, however, there were no new episodes being produced. Although it was still called *Suspense*, and Sebastian Cabot remained on as host, all of the telecasts aired from July to September were actually reruns from *Schlitz Playhouse of Stars*.

SUSPENSE PLAYHOUSE

Dramatic Anthology

FIRST TELECAST: *May 24, 1971*

LAST TELECAST: *July 31, 1972*

BROADCAST HISTORY:

May 1971–Jul 1971, CBS Mon 10:00–11:00
Jul 1972, CBS Mon 10:00–11:00

The filmed plays presented in this summer anthology series were all reruns of episodes originally telecast on *Premiere* during the summer of 1968. They were all unsold pilots for proposed regular series. The three episodes that aired in the summer of 1972 had also been seen with8n the 1971 run.

SUSPICION

Suspense Anthology

FIRST TELECAST: *September 30, 1957*

LAST TELECAST: *September 6, 1959*

BROADCAST HISTORY:

Sep 1957–Sep 1958, NBC Mon 10:00–11:00
Jun 1959–Sep 1959, NBC Sun 7:30–8:30

HOST:

Dennis O'Keefe (1957)
Walter Abel (1959)

Suspicion was comprised of 20 filmed dramas and 10 live dramas that aired on NBC during the 1957–1958 season. The stories were meant to fascinate, mystify, and confound the audience, and generally dealt with people's fears and suspicions, often concerning murder. Alfred Hitchcock, who had his own series on CBS at this time, produced half of the filmed episodes. When it premiered, Dennis O'Keefe was to be the permanent host of the show. After two weeks, however, he left the series and was not replaced. In the summer of 1959 a number of the original episodes were rerun, with Walter Abel hosting them.

SWIFT SHOW, THE

Musical Variety

FIRST TELECAST: *April 1, 1948*

LAST TELECAST: *August 4, 1949*

BROADCAST HISTORY:

Apr 1948–Aug 1949, NBC Thu 8:30–9:00

EMCEE:

Lanny Ross

REGULARS:

Martha Logan
Sandra Gable (1948)
Eileen Barton (1948)
Susan Shaw (1948)
Martha Wright (1949)
Dulcy Jordan (1949)
Max Showalter (1949)
Ricki Hamilton (1949)
Frank Fontane (1949)
Harry Simeone Orchestra & Chorus

Swift and Company, which had pioneered daytime commercial network television with the *Swift Home Service Club* in 1947, moved to prime time in early 1948 with a Thursday night half-hour starring crooner Lanny Ross. Although music and light comedy remained the central theme of the show throughout its run, the specific format changed several times during the next year.

At first the program was a combination of music and a quiz segment called the "Eye-Cue Game," which had been brought over from the *Swift Home Service Club*. Contestants were asked to identify various names, places, or events from a series of visual clues. By September the quiz segment had been dropped and the setting became Lanny's elegant penthouse apartment, with regular friends and special guests dropping by to entertain. Eileen Barton played the small-town girl friend with a crush on Lanny. Soon Lanny began to get out of his apartment, in fanciful dreams set to music, and on dates with various girl friends.

In March 1949 the penthouse and the dating story lines were dropped and the program became a straight musical revue, with Lanny singing songs and entertaining guests.

Two carryovers from the *Swift Home Service Club* were Martha Logan, who gave demonstrations and commercials in the Swift Kitchen (during the "apartment" phase she was the girl upstairs), and Sandra Gable, who modeled fashions and gave home-decorating ideas.

SWIFT SHOW WAGON, THE

Variety

FIRST TELECAST: *January 8, 1955*
LAST TELECAST: *October 1, 1955*
BROADCAST HISTORY:
Jan 1955–Oct 1955, NBC Sat 7:30–8:00
HOST:
Horace Heidt

Each week this talent and variety show starring veteran bandleader Horace Heidt orginated from a different state. It highlighted performers from that state, included interviews with local civic leaders, and presented one or two native sons who had gone on to become nationally known celebrities. Each show also included a salute to the "personality of the week," someone in the state who had performed a heroic deed. The show's title derived from the fact that it moved, not unlike a wagon, from place to place across the country. The full title was *The Swift Show Wagon with Horace Heidt and the American Way.*

SWISS FAMILY ROBINSON

Adventure

FIRST TELECAST: *September 14, 1975*
LAST TELECAST: *April 11, 1976*
BROADCAST HISTORY:
Sep 1975–Apr 1976, ABC Sun 7:00–8:00
CAST:
Karl Robinson .... Martin Milner
Lotte Robinson .... Pat Delany
Fred Robinson .... Willie Aames
Ernie Robinson .... Eric Olson
Jeremiah Worth .... Cameron Mitchell
Helga Wagner .... Helen Hunt
PRODUCER:
Irwin Allen

Johann Wyss' classic children's story of a family shipwrecked in the early 1800s was brought to TV in this 1975 series. It didn't look much like the book, however. The TV *Swiss Family Robinson* was produced by Irwin Allen, famed for his "disaster" movies. Although he claimed that this was not going to be a "disaster of the week" series, there did seem to be a tidal wave, typhoon, earthquake, volcanic eruption, wild animal or other natural calamity besetting the poor Robinsons in every episode—usually staged in a rather tacky fashion (you just don't have those movie budgets in TV). In their remarkably well-equipped tree house, Karl and Lotte Robinson were stoic through it all, while their children Fred and Ernie hung on for dear life in the teeth of every gale. Jeremiah was a rascally old sailor who had previously been marooned on the island, and Helga was the only other survivor of the Robinsons' shipwreck (she was the daughter of the captain).

Quite a few visitors passed through the Robinsons' "lost" island, including pirate Jean Lafitte, who stopped off to pick up some buried treasure on his way to help General Andrew Jackson at the Battle of New Orleans.

SWITCH

Detective

FIRST TELECAST: *September 9, 1975*
LAST TELECAST: *September 3, 1978*
BROADCAST HISTORY:
Sep 1975–Nov 1975, CBS Tue 9:00–10:00
Dec 1975–Jan 1977, CBS Tue 10:00–11:00
Jan 1977–Sep 1977, CBS Sun 9:00–10:00
Sep 1977, CBS Fri 10:00–11:00
Dec 1977–Jan 1978, CBS Mon 10:00–11:00
Jun 1978–Sep 1978, CBS Sun 10:00–11:00
CAST:
Pete Ryan .... Robert Wagner
Frank McBride .... Eddie Albert
Malcolm Argos .... Charlie Callas
Maggie .... Sharon Gless
Revel .... Mindi Miller
Lt. Griffin (1975–1976) ...... Ken Swofford
Lt. Modeer (1976–1977)
.... Richard X. Slattery
Wang (1977–1978) .... James Hong

It was an unusual partnership. Pete was a former con man and Frank was a retired bunco cop. Together they had formed a private detective agency that specialized in pulling "switches" on the other con men still operating on the wrong side of the law. They would concoct elaborate schemes that would, hopefully, result in the swindlers swindling themselves. Based in Los Angeles, the two of them traveled far and wide on assorted cases. Malcolm, a small-time thief and con man who had gone straight and opened a restaurant was recruited by Pete and Frank to help them on cases, and Maggie was the firm's combination secretary-receptionist and all-around girl Friday.

By the middle of its second season, *Switch* had become a somewhat more traditional detective series, with less of the elaborate con games, and in the fall of 1977 Pete moved into a new apartment above Malcolm's bouzouki bar, where Revel was the hostess and Wang the new cook.

SWORD OF JUSTICE

Adventure

FIRST TELECAST: *September 10, 1978*

LAST TELECAST:

BROADCAST HISTORY:

Sep 1978, NBC Sun 8:00–10:00

Oct 1978– , NBC Sat 10:00–11:00

CAST:

Jack Cole .... Dack Rambo
Hector Ramirez .... Bert Rosario
Arthur Woods .... Alex Courtney

This series was billed as *Zorro* in contemporary garb. Jack Cole was not masked, but he certainly was an avenger, out to fight crime in high places, both public and private. Cole's motivation for this noble crusade was clear enough. A Park Avenue playboy, and heir to a great industrial fortune, he had suddenly been thrust from his pampered, jet-set existence into prison on a trumped up charge of embezzlement after his father's death. While behind bars he learned the skills of the criminal's trade, lock picking, telephone bugging, and all the rest, and when he emerged he was determined to use these skills against the kind of white collar criminals who had framed him. He resumed his playboy image, but only as a front for his (mostly) nocturnal crime-busting. His sign: a playing card. Helping was Hector, Jack's wisecracking Puerto Rican ex-cellmate, and always one step behind was Arthur Woods, formerly the Cole family attorney and now part of a government task force fighting high level crime.

SYMPHONY, THE

see *Chicago Symphony Chamber Orchestra*

SZYSZNYK

Situation Comedy

FIRST TELECAST: *August 1, 1977*

LAST TELECAST: *January 25, 1978*

BROADCAST HISTORY:

Aug 1977, CBS Mon 8:30–9:00

Dec 1977–Jan 1978, CBS Wed 8:30–9:00

CAST:

Nick Szysznyk .... Ned Beatty
Ms. Harrison .... Olivia Cole
Sandi Chandler (1977) .... Susan Lanier
Leonard Kriegler .... Leonard Barr
Ralph .... Jarrod Johnson
Fortwengler .... Barry Miller
Tony La Placa .... Scott Colomby
Ray Gun .... Thomas Carter

Nick Szysznyk was a retired Marine, used to the discipline and order of military life, who had taken on a new job as playground supervisor at the Northeast Community Center in a poor neighborhood in Washington, D.C. Coping with the bureaucracy in the city government that funded the center, his co-workers, and the street kids who used the center, all proved challenging to him—and to them as well. Highly successful in its initial run against repeat programming during the summer, *Szysznyk* returned in December 1977 against stronger competition and lasted only two months.

T.H.E. CAT

Adventure

FIRST TELECAST: *September 16, 1966*

LAST TELECAST: *September 1, 1967*

BROADCAST HISTORY:

Sep 1966–Sep 1967, NBC Fri 9:30–10:00

CAST:

Thomas Hewitt Edward Cat
.... Robert Loggia
Capt. MacAllister .... R. G. Armstrong
Pepi .... Robert Carricart

T.H.E. Cat was a former circus aerialist and ex-cat burglar whose name fit him very well. His current profession was that of professional bodyguard. He fought crime by guarding those clients who had been marked for death. Only T.H.E. Cat stood between them and their would-be assassins. Declining to use weapons himself, Cat relied on his quickness and agility to protect his clients and himself. Living in San Francisco, he maintained an "office" at the Casa del Gato, a nightclub owned by his friend Pepi. Pepi was a Spanish gypsy whose life had once been saved by T.H.E. Cat, and he would remain loyal to Cat until the day he died. Capt. MacAllister was the police officer with whom Cat worked most closely.

TV READER'S DIGEST

Dramatic Anthology

FIRST TELECAST: *January 17, 1955*

LAST TELECAST: *July 9, 1956*
BROADCAST HISTORY:
Jan 1955–Jul 1956, ABC Mon 8:00–8:30
HOST:
Hugh Reilly (1955)
Gene Raymond (1956)

Wholesome, frequently patriotic true stories from the pages of the *Reader's Digest* were dramatized in this filmed series. As in the *Digest,* little incidents from history and cameos from contemporary life were favorite subjects, and almost everything had a moral. Included were dramatizations of Stephen Foster's last days, the life of Pocahontas, the Scopes "Monkey" Trial of the 1920s, brainwashing attempts by the Communists in Korea, the story of a retired old-time six-gun sheriff who was recalled by his town to stop a crime wave, etc. Performers were generally lesser known, but included some future stars such as Peter Graves, Chuck Connors, and Lee Marvin.

TV RECITAL HALL

Music
FIRST TELECAST: *July 1, 1951*
LAST TELECAST: *September 6, 1954*
BROADCAST HISTORY:
Jul 1951–Aug 1951, NBC Sun 8:30–9:00
Aug 1954–Sep 1954, NBC Mon 9:00–9:30

Live performances of classical music, featuring performers in a recital-hall-type setting, were presented on a weekly basis. They originated from New York with a live audience and the selections and performers were introduced by an offstage announcer. Between August 1951 and August 1954 this show was seen on an intermittent basis, occasionally for periods on Sunday afternoons and sometimes as a one-time-only special. It returned in August 1954 with the title shortened to *Recital Hall.*

TV'S TOP TUNES

Music
FIRST TELECAST: *July 2, 1951*
LAST TELECAST: *September 3, 1955*
BROADCAST HISTORY:
Jul 1951–Aug 1951, CBS Mon/Wed/Fri 7:45–8:00
Jun 1953–Aug 1953, CBS Mon/Wed/Fri 7:45–8:00
Jun 1954–Aug 1954, CBS Mon/Wed/Fri 7:45–8:00
Jul 1955–Sep 1955, CBS Sat 10:00–10:30
REGULARS:
Peggy Lee (1951)
Mel Torme (1951)
The Fontane Sisters (1951)
Mitchell Ayres Orchestra (1951, 1955)
The Skyliners (1954)
The Anthony Choir (1954)
Helen O'Connell (1953)
Bob Eberly (1953)
Ray Anthony & His Orchestra (1953, 1954)
Tommy Mercer (1954)
Marcie Mills (1954)
Julius La Rosa (1955)

In 1951, 1953, and 1954 various artists filled in for the vacationing Perry Como on *TV's Top Tunes,* a live thrice-weekly music show that filled the remainder of the half-hour in which CBS aired its network news program. During the summer of 1955, when this series was expanded to a full half-hour on Saturday nights, its star, Julius La Rosa, had another series, *The Julius La Rosa Show,* airing three times a week in the time period that *TV's Top Tunes* had occupied during previous summers.

TAB HUNTER SHOW, THE

Situation Comedy
FIRST TELECAST: *September 18, 1960*
LAST TELECAST: *September 10, 1961*
BROADCAST HISTORY:
Sep 1960–Sep 1961, NBC Sun 8:30–9:00
CAST:
Paul Morgan .... Tab Hunter
Peter Fairfield III .... Richard Erdman
John Larsen .... Jerome Cowan
Thelma .... Reta Shaw

Paul Morgan was a swinging young bachelor who had made a living out of his lifestyle. As a cartoonist for Comics, Inc., he was the creator of the strip "Bachelor-at-Large," which detailed the adventures of an amorous young man living the good life in Southern California. The strip read almost like a diary, which it was, of the romantic exploits of its author. Paul's boss, John Larsen, never ceased to be amazed by the situations into which his prize cartoonist got himself. Paul's best friend was the wealthy, eligible, and stingy Peter Fairfield III, a fashion plate and car enthusiast who was regularly mixed up in Paul's romantic adventures. Keeping Paul's Malibu Beach apartment in order was his housekeeper, Thelma, who did not approve of his never-ending stream of beautiful women.

TABITHA

Situation Comedy

FIRST TELECAST: *November 12, 1977*

LAST TELECAST: *August 25, 1978*

BROADCAST HISTORY:

Nov 1977–Jan 1978, ABC Sat 8:00–8:30

Jun 1978–Aug 1978, ABC Fri 8:00–8:30

CAST:

Tabitha Stephens ....Lisa Hartman
Paul Thurston ....Robert Urich
Marvin Decker ....Mel Stewart
Adam Stephens ....David Ankrum
Aunt Minerva ....Karen Morrow

This briefly seen comedy was a spin off from ABC's long running hit *Bewitched.* Tabitha was the daughter of Samantha, the leading character on *Bewitched.* She was seen as a baby on that series, but by the time this one began she had grown into a bright young woman, just beginning her career as a television production assistant at station KLXA, in California. Tabitha worked for producer Marvin Decker, and her chief assignment was *The Paul Thurston Show.* Thurston was the station's handsome, but not-too-bright, star newscaster. Adam was Tabitha's brother and a fellow employee at KLXA, and Minerva was her meddlesome aunt.

Despite the similarity to *The Mary Tyler Moore Show,* Tabitha had something extra: as a witch, she could perform feats of magic, and get her own way, with a twitch of the nose. It didn't help. The series soon disappeared in a puff of Nielsen ratings.

TAKE A CHANCE

Quiz/Audience Participation

FIRST TELECAST: *October 1, 1950*

LAST TELECAST: *December 24, 1950*

BROADCAST HISTORY:

Oct 1950–Dec 1950, NBC Sun 10:30–11:00

EMCEE:

Don Ameche

Each contestant on this live quiz program was drawn from the studio audience and given an initial $5. He was then asked a series of four questions. A correct answer to the first one enabled the contestant to keep the $5 and receive a small prize. Answers to the subsequent questions were worth unspecified other winnings, some big and some small. The contestant could quit whenever he or she no longer wanted to "take a chance," but there was an incentive to go on. Correctly answering all four questions gave the contestant a shot at the jackpot question—worth $1,000 in cash and 1,000 cakes of Sweetheart soap. If a question was not answered correctly, however, the contestant had to forfeit his last prize.

TAKE A GOOD LOOK

Quiz/Panel

FIRST TELECAST: *October 22, 1959*

LAST TELECAST: *March 16, 1961*

BROADCAST HISTORY:

Oct 1959–Mar 1961, ABC Thu 10:30–11:00

HOST:

Ernie Kovacs

PANELISTS:

Hans Conried
Cesar Romero
Edie Adams (1960–1961)
Ben Alexander (1960)
Carl Reiner (1960–1961)

ACTORS:

Peggy Connelly
Bobby Lauher
Jolene Brand

Panelists were advised to "take a good look" at the contestants on this quiz show. Although they were relatively unknown, each of the contestants had once been a central figure in a headline-making news event, and the panel had to guess just who they were. To help, clues such as film clips or recordings were played, or Ernie Kovacs and a team of regulars acted out the clues. In addition to the regular panelists guest celebrities frequently appeared.

TAKE A GUESS

Quiz/Audience Participation

FIRST TELECAST: *June 11, 1953*

LAST TELECAST: *September 10, 1953*

BROADCAST HISTORY:

Jun 1953–Sep 1953, CBS Thu 8:00–8:30

MODERATOR:

John K. M. McCaffery

PANELISTS:

Margaret Lindsay
Ernie Kovacs

Dorothy Hart
John Crawford
Robin Chandler
Hans Conried

Contestants on this summer quiz show were aided by members of a celebrity panel in trying to identify something that was known only to the moderator and the audience. Each contestant started with $150. As he looked on, the panel asked questions of the moderator to determine the identity of the mystery object. However, $5 was deducted from the $150 each time one of their questions received a "yes" answer, so the contestant had an incentive to guess as quickly as possible (he could make a maximum of four guesses). The contestant won whatever was left of the original $150 after the money for the "yes" answers was subtracted. If the entire $150 was used up (due to 30 "yes" answers), or the contestant had made four incorrect answers, there were no winnings at all.

TAKE IT FROM ME

Situation Comedy

FIRST TELECAST: *November 4, 1953*
LAST TELECAST: *January 20, 1954*
BROADCAST HISTORY:
Nov 1953–Jan 1954, ABC Wed 9:00–9:30
CAST:
Jean Carroll
Alan Carney
Lynn Loring

Stand-up comedienne Jean Carroll starred as an "average" New York City housewife, complete with bumbling husband and moppet daughter, in this comedy. She opened each show with a monologue, then spiced the night's sketch with comic asides to the audience. Many of the stories involved her sly schemes to trick husband Herbie into doing whatever she wanted. The action took place in the couple's apartment and the surrounding neighborhood, which, though never identified, was presumably in Brooklyn or the Bronx. This New York orientation may have limited the show's appeal west of the Hudson River, and it lasted less than three months.

Also known as *The Jean Carroll Show*.

TALENT JACKPOT

Talent

FIRST TELECAST: *July 19, 1949*
LAST TELECAST: *August 23, 1949*
BROADCAST HISTORY:
Jul 1949–Aug 1949, DUM Tue 9:00–9:30
EMCEE:
Vinton Freedley
ASSISTANT:
Bud Collyer

Summer talent show for aspiring professionals, emceed by Broadway producer Vinton Freedley and offering a maximum prize of $250 for each of the night's five acts. The amount each act won depended on the level reached by an audience applause meter. The top winner of the night got his own winnings as well as whatever was left over from the other act's $250 maximums.

TALENT PATROL

Talent/Variety

FIRST TELECAST: *January 19, 1953*
LAST TELECAST: *September 8, 1955*
BROADCAST HISTORY:
Jan 1953–Jul 1953, ABC Mon 9:30–10:00
Jul 1953–Aug 1953, ABC Mon 8:00–8:30
Sep 1953–Oct 1953, ABC Wed 8:00–8:30
Oct 1953–Jan 1954, ABC Sat 8:00–8:30
Jan 1954–Mar 1954, ABC Thu 9:00–9:30
Apr 1954–Jul 1954, ABC Thu 8:00–8:30
Jul 1954–Oct 1954, ABC Wed 7:30–8:00
Oct 1954–Nov 1954, ABC Sun 9:30–10:00
Dec 1954–Jan 1955, ABC Mon 8:00–8:30
Jan 1955–Jun 1955, ABC Thu 8:00–8:30
Jun 1955–Sep 1955, ABC Thu 8:00–9:00
EMCEE:
Steve Allen (1953)
Bud Collyer (1953)
Arlene Francis (1953–1955)
Richard Hayes (1955)

Talent Patrol began as a military talent show, sponsored by the Army over the 88 stations of the ABC network as an aid to recruiting. All the contestants were GI's, performing a wide variety of non-military skills—impersonations, folk singing, playing musical instruments, trampoline acts, and even hula dancing! Winners got a night on the town with a pretty actress. Even the runners-up came out ahead, however, with national TV exposure, not to mention a five-day pass to go to New York and rehearse for the show. Army bands provided the musical accompaniment.

In mid-1954 the program became more of a straight variety show, featuring Army professional talent as well as celebrity guests, and the title was changed to *Soldier Parade.*

Steve Allen was the original host of the series, replaced "temporarily" by Bud Collyer after only three months and permanently by Arlene Francis in June 1953. When the program expanded to a full hour in June 1955 singer Richard Hayes, in the Army himself at the time, joined Miss Francis in the capacity of co-host.

TALENT SCOUTS

Talent/Variety

FIRST TELECAST: *July 3, 1962*

LAST TELECAST: *September 17, 1963*

BROADCAST HISTORY:

Jul 1962–Sep 1962, CBS Tue 10:00–11:00

Jul 1963–Sep 1963, CBS Tue 8:30–9:30

HOST:

Jim Backus (1962)

Merv Griffin (1963)

Each week a number of guest celebrities appeared on this show to introduce young professional performers who were being given their first network exposure on the series. In 1962 this was the summer replacement for *The Garry Moore Show* and in 1963 for *The Red Skelton Hour.* The most immediate success story from this series was impressionist Vaughn Meader. He did his imitation of President Kennedy on the first telecast of the 1962 series and had a subsequent smash recording—*The First Family.* Among the other young performers who appeared as newcomers were George Carlin, Charles Nelson Reilly, Louise Lasser, and Vic Dana.

This summer series was a revival of *Arthur Godfrey's Talent Scouts,* which had had a ten-year run on CBS ending in 1958.

TALENT VARIETIES

Variety

FIRST TELECAST: *June 28, 1955*

LAST TELECAST: *November 1, 1955*

BROADCAST HISTORY:

Jun 1955–Sep 1955, ABC Tue 7:30–8:30

Sep 1955–Nov 1955, ABC Tue 10:00–10:30

REGULARS:

Slim Wilson

The Tall Timber Trio

Originating from Springfield, Missouri, this variety show had a Country and Western flavor. Each week emcee and singer Slim Wilson introduced assorted amateur talent and occasionally performed himself.

TALES OF E.S.P.

see *E.S.P.*

TALES OF THE CITY

see *Willys Theater Presenting Ben Hecht's Tales of the City*

TALES OF THE RED CABOOSE

Adventure

FIRST TELECAST: *October 29, 1948*

LAST TELECAST: *January 14, 1949*

BROADCAST HISTORY:

Oct 1948–Jan 1949, ABC Fri 7:30–7:45

Early TV advertisers did not know what kind of use could be made of the new medium, and so can be forgiven shows like this one. *Tales of the Red Caboose* was sponsored by Lionel Trains, and consisted simply of model trains racing around on their tracks. Various races and miniaturized "adventures" were depicted, and a narrator, "Don Magee," spun yarns based on the lore of railroads.

For a similar program sponsored by rival A.C. Gilbert Co. (American Flyer) see *Roar of the Rails.*

TALES OF THE 77TH BENGAL LANCERS

Adventure

FIRST TELECAST: *October 21, 1956*

LAST TELECAST: *June 2, 1957*

BROADCAST HISTORY:

Oct 1956–Jun 1957, NBC Sun 7:00–7:30

CAST:

Lt. Michael Rhodes ....Phil Carey

Lt. William Storm ....Warren Stevens

Col. Standish ....Patrick Whyte

Set in India in the late 19th century, the stories of this fictional outfit were based on the exploits of the real Bengal Lancers, the famed British Cavalry unit. Col. Standish was the commander of the "77th" and working under him were two lieutenants who were also close friends, Michael Rhodes and William Storm. Rhodes was portrayed as a Canadian because New Jersey–born Phil Carey had trouble mastering an English accent.

TALES OF THE TEXAS RANGERS

Western

FIRST TELECAST: *December 22, 1958*

LAST TELECAST: *May 25, 1959*
BROADCAST HISTORY:
Dec 1958–May 1959, ABC Mon 7:30–8:00
CAST:
Ranger Jace Pearson ....Willard Parker
Ranger Clay Morgan ....Harry Lauter

As the title suggests, these were straightforward adventure stories concerning the exploits of one of America's most famous law-enforcement agencies. Although Rangers Pearson and Morgan were regulars, they appeared in a different setting each week, ranging from the Old West of the 1830s to modern-day Texas, using crime-detection methods appropriate to each era. The program was, in effect, a survey of the Rangers' activities over its 120-year history.

Tales of the Texas Rangers was seen on CBS as an afternoon show in 1955–1958, then moved to ABC (Thursday 5:00–5:30 P.M.) beginning in October 1958. It was on the nighttime schedule for a short run later in the 1958–1959 season. *Tales of the Texas Rangers* was also heard as a radio series in the early 1950s, with Joel McCrea in the lead role of Ranger Pearson.

TALES OF THE UNEXPECTED

Suspense Anthology
FIRST TELECAST: *February 2, 1977*
LAST TELECAST: *August 24, 1977*
BROADCAST HISTORY:
Feb 1977–Mar 1977, NBC Wed 10:00–11:00
Mar 1977, NBC Sun 9:00–11:00
Aug 1977, NBC Wed 10:00–11:00
NARRATOR:
William Conrad
EXECUTIVE PRODUCER:
Quinn Martin

This anthology show dealt in both psychological and occult suspense stories, all of which had unusual O. Henry–like twists to prolong the suspense until the very end of the episode. After five weeks on Wednesdays, the final two-hour episode of this series aired on a Sunday. Five months later, *Tales of the Unexpected* returned to its original time slot for two weeks with new episodes.

TALES OF THE UNKNOWN

see *Journey to the Unknown*

TALES OF TOMORROW

Science Fiction Anthology
FIRST TELECAST: *August 3, 1951*
LAST TELECAST: *June 12, 1953*
BROADCAST HISTORY:
Aug 1951–Jun 1953, ABC Fri 9:30–10:00

Tales of Tomorrow was one of TV's earliest adult science-fiction series, using both classic and modern stories of strange and supernatural happenings. Among the stories were "The Monsters" (from Mars), "The Dark Angel" (about a woman who never aged), H. G. Wells' "The Crystal Egg," "The Flying Saucer," "Frankenstein," and a two-part version of Jules Verne's *20,000 Leagues Under the Sea*. The program was produced by George F. Foley, Jr., and used such talent as Franchot Tone, Lon Chaney, Jr., Veronica Lake, Boris Karloff, Eva Gabor, Leslie Nielsen, and Lee J. Cobb.

During 1951 and 1953 it alternated with other series. For a time during early 1953 the program was also heard on radio.

TALES OF WELLS FARGO

Western
FIRST TELECAST: *March 18, 1957*
LAST TELECAST: *September 8, 1962*
BROADCAST HISTORY:
Mar 1957–Jul 1957, NBC Mon 8:30–9:00
Sep 1957–Sep 1961, NBC Mon 8:30–9:00
Sep 1961–Sep 1962, NBC Sat 7:30–8:30
CAST:
Jim Hardie ....Dale Robertson
Beau McCloud (1961–1962) ......Jack Ging
Jeb Gaine (1961–1962) ...William Demarest
Ovie (1961–1962) ....Virginia Christine
Mary Gee (1961–1962)
...................Mary Jane Saunders
Tina (1961–1962) ....Lory Patrick

During the five seasons in which *Tales of Wells Fargo* ran on Monday nights it had a single regular cast member, Wells Fargo agent Jim Hardie. Jim was a troubleshooter for the company, whose assignments ranged from helping employees out of personal jams to functioning as an unofficial lawman by fighting criminals who preyed on Wells Fargo shipments and passengers.

In the fall of 1961, *Tales of Wells Fargo* moved to Saturday nights and was expanded to a full hour. Also expanded was the regular cast. Although still a Wells Fargo agent, Jim Hardie was now also the owner of a ranch just outside of San Francisco. He had acquired a young assistant in Beau McCloud and a ranch foreman named Jeb Gaine. The ranch next door to his was owned by Widow Ovie, who lived with her two attractive daughters, Mary Gee and Tina. Ovie had her eye on Jeb as a possible second husband, despite his lack of interest. Most of the shows during this last season took place on the Hardie ranch and in San Francisco, although Jim still went on an occasional assignment in other parts of the West.

TALL MAN, THE

Western

FIRST TELECAST: *September 10, 1960*
LAST TELECAST: *September 1, 1962*
BROADCAST HISTORY:

Sep 1960–Sep 1962, NBC Sat 8:30–9:00

CAST:

Billy the Kid .... Clu Gulager
Dep. Sheriff Pat Garrett ..... Barry Sullivan

Set in New Mexico during the 1870s, *The Tall Man* told fictionalized stories of the adventures of two real-life characters, Sheriff Pat Garrett and William H. Bonney. The latter was more popularly known as Billy the Kid, a youthful gunfighter with a penchant for getting himself into trouble. Billy and Pat, whose honesty and forthrightness had earned him the nickname "The Tall Man," were close friends despite the fact that they were often on opposite sides of the law. Pat looked upon Billy as a younger brother or son, but knew in the back of his mind that they would eventually be forced into a showdown. Although he too was pretty handy with a gun, Pat regarded it as a tool only to be used in an emergency where there was no alternative. Billy, on the other hand, looked at his gun as the great equalizer, compensating for his inferiority in size, strength, or intelligence. His criminal activities kept bringing him and Pat closer to the day of reckoning which, although never shown on the series, culminated in Pat's killing Billy.

TAMMY

Situation Comedy

FIRST TELECAST: *September 17, 1965*
LAST TELECAST: *July 15, 1966*
BROADCAST HISTORY:

Sep 1965–Jul 1966, ABC Fri 8:00–8:30

CAST:

Tammy Tarleton .... Debbie Watson
Grandpa Tarleton .... Denver Pyle
Uncle Lucius .... Frank McGrath
John Brent .... Donald Woods
Steven Brent .... Jay Sheffield
Lavinia Tate .... Dorothy Green
Gloria Tate .... Linda Marshall
Peter Tate .... David Macklin
Dwayne Whitt .... George Furth
Cousin Cletus Tarleton .. Dennis Robertson

Tammy was the story of a winsome 18-year-old backwoods girl who moved back and forth between two worlds. One was the bayou houseboat where she and her kin lived. The other was "The Bowers," the plantation owned by wealthy John Brent, where she worked as Brent's secretary. Tammy's wistful, beguiling ways endeared her to almost everyone—except Lavinia Tate, the blue-blooded neighbor of the Brents who was always scheming to snatch some juicy plum away from Tammy for her own daughter, Gloria. Steven was John Brent's son, and Peter was Lavinia's son. Tammy's own kin included old codger Grandpa and scalawag Uncle Lucius, who had raised her after the death of her parents.

Based on the 1957 movie *Tammy and the Bachelor,* which starred Debbie Reynolds, and the movie sequels starring Sandra Dee. In 1967 there was a feature-length theatrical motion picture called, *Tammy and the Millionaire,* in which Miss Watson and most of the principals from the series appeared in their TV roles.

TAMMY GRIMES SHOW, THE

Situation Comedy

FIRST TELECAST: *September 8, 1966*
LAST TELECAST: *September 29, 1966*
BROADCAST HISTORY:

Sep 1966, ABC Thu 8:30–9:00

CAST:

Tammy Ward .... Tammy Grimes
Uncle Simon .... Hiram Sherman
Terrence Ward .... Dick Sargent
Mrs. Ratchett .... Maudie Prickett

Tammy Ward was what the ABC press releases referred to as "a madcap heiress." Given her own way, she would have spent oodles of money on just anything that hit her fancy, regardless of how useful it might be. Trying to keep the purse strings from being opened too far was her banker, Uncle Simon, a much more pecunious soul than Tammy. In addition to not being able to get her hands on her money, she had to cope with an incredibly square twin brother named Terrence and a nosy housekeeper named Mrs. Ratchett. Both Tammy and Terrence worked for Uncle Simon at the Perpetual Bank of America. This series lasted just four weeks.

TARGET: THE CORRUPTORS

Newspaper Drama

FIRST TELECAST: *September 29, 1961*

LAST TELECAST: *September 21, 1962*

BROADCAST HISTORY:

Sep 1961–Sep 1962, ABC Fri 10:00–11:00

CAST:

Paul Marino ....Stephen McNally
Jack Flood ....Robert Harland

Paul Marino was an investigative rackets reporter and Jack Flood was his undercover agent, sent to infiltrate suspected criminal-controlled or threatened businesses to provide Marino with material for his newspaper exposes and for the police. A different form of underworld corruption was detailed each week in this dramatic series—everything from bookmaking and prostitution to phony charities and protection rackets.

TARZAN

Adventure

FIRST TELECAST: *September 8, 1966*

LAST TELECAST: *September 10, 1969*

BROADCAST HISTORY:

Sep 1966, NBC Thu 7:30–8:30
Sep 1966–Sep 1968, NBC Fri 7:30–8:30
Jun 1969–Sep 1969, CBS Wed 7:30–8:30

CAST:

Tarzan ....Ron Ely
Jai ....Manuel Padilla, Jr.

Edgar Rice Burroughs' famous "Tarzan" character came to television in the person of Ron Ely, the 14th actor to play the role since *Tarzan of the Apes* had been first made as a silent movie almost half a century before. In the TV series Tarzan, who was actually the Earl of Greystroke, returned to his native jungle forest after years of formal schooling. Living among the wild creatures, with whom he could communicate, and possessed of incredibly acute senses, Tarzan waged war on renegades, poachers, and other interlopers in the jungle. Familiar with the civilized world, Tarzan preferred the honesty and openness of life in the jungle. His closest friend was the chimp Cheetah, but he was fond of all the creatures of the wilds. He was also very close to a small orphan boy named Jai. Ron Ely did many of his own stunts for this series. The famous Tarzan yell was actually a recording by another Tarzan, Johnny Weissmuller. CBS aired reruns of the NBC series during the summer of 1969, and some episodes were strung together and actually shown in theaters as feature-length films.

The character of Jane and the crude English Tarzan had used in the movie versions ("Me Tarzan—you Jane") were dropped for the purposes of this TV series.

TATE

Western

FIRST TELECAST: *June 8, 1960*

LAST TELECAST: *September 28, 1960*

BROADCAST HISTORY:

Jun 1960–Sep 1960, NBC Wed 9:30–10:00

CAST:

Tate ....David McLean

Tate was the 1960 summer replacement for the second half-hour of *The Perry Como Show*, the first half-hour being occupied by a situation comedy called *Happy*. Tate was a casualty of the Civil War. His left arm had been blasted into uselessness by an explosion during his wartime service. With only one good arm, he had found it almost impossible to get a job after the war ended. With little choice, he had become a wandering gunfighter, traveling from town to town looking for work as a fast gun. He was an imposing figure, with his shattered left arm wrapped in a rawhide-stitched black leather casing that ran from his fingertips to above the elbow.

TAXI

Situation Comedy

FIRST TELECAST: *September 12, 1978*

LAST TELECAST:

BROADCAST HISTORY:

Sept 1978– , ABC Tue 9:30–10:00

CAST:

Alex Rieger ....Judd Hirsch
Bobby Wheeler ....Jeff Conaway
Louie De Palma ....Danny DeVito
Elaine Nardo ....Marilu Henner

Tony Banta	Tony Danza
John Burns	Randall Carver
Latka Graves	Andy Kaufman

The happy cabbies of New York's Sunshine Cab Company were the focal point of this comedy. Cab driving may be fun, but it was just a job for this crew, most of whom were working part-time as they tried to make it in other fields. Alex, the most experienced and most conservative of the group, was the only full-time driver. Bobby was a frustrated actor, waiting for his big break; Elaine was an art gallery receptionist, trying to pick up a few extra bucks; Tony, the boxer who never won a fight; and John, the student and all-around lost soul. Latka was the company's mechanic, of indeterminate nationality and fractured English, and Louie was the dispatcher, a petty tyrant who ran things from a wire cage in the center of the garage.

TED KNIGHT SHOW, THE

Situation Comedy

FIRST TELECAST: *April 8, 1978*

LAST TELECAST: *May 13, 1978*

BROADCAST HISTORY:

Apr 1978–May 1978, CBS Sat 8:30–9:00

CAST:

Roger Dennis	Ted Knight
Burt Dennis	Normann Burton
Winston Dennis	Thomas Leopold
Dottie	Iris Adrian
Graziella	Cissy Colpitts
Honey	Fawne Harriman
Irma	Ellen Regan
Philadelphia	Tanya Boyd
Cheryl	Janice Kent
Joy	Deborah Harmon
Hobart Nalven	Claude Stroud

Ted Knight, the handsome, empty-headed newscaster on *The Mary Tyler Moore Show*, landed his own series with this frothy comedy about an escort service in New York City. Dennis Escorts was a strictly high-class outfit, located in a posh Manhattan apartment building, staffed by some lovely young ladies, and headed by the suave, middle-aged Roger Dennis, who clucked over his brood like a mother hen. Complicating matters was Roger's no nonsense businessman/brother, Burt, who had financed the enterprise and had incidentally saddled it with his wisecracking sister-in-law Dottie (who served as receptionist). Other cast members were Roger's college-age son Winston, who was trying to break into the business and make time with the girls, and the mailman, Hobart, who had his eyes on Dottie.

TED MACK FAMILY HOUR, THE

Musical Variety

FIRST TELECAST: *January 7, 1951*

LAST TELECAST: *November 25, 1951*

BROADCAST HISTORY:

Jan 1951–Nov 1951, ABC Sun 6:00–7:00

EMCEE:

Ted Mack

REGULARS:

The Mack Triplets
Jean Steel
Dick Byrd
Andy Roberts

Ted Mack, who was most famous for his *Original Amateur Hour*, also hosted this live Sunday night variety show during 1951. The emphasis was on family entertainment, and guest stars were generally cabaret and stage talent such as pianist Vincent Lopez, songstress Betty Ann Grove, and actor Bert Lytell. An occasional *Amateur Hour* champion also made his professional debut here.

TED STEELE SHOW, THE

Music

FIRST TELECAST: *September 29, 1948*

LAST TELECAST: *August 3, 1949*

BROADCAST HISTORY:

Sep 1948–Oct 1948, NBC Wed/Fri various 15 minute
Feb 1949–Apr 1949, DUM Sun 6:30–7:00
Apr 1949–Jul 1949, DUM Tue 9:00–9:30
Jul 1949–Aug 1949, CBS Tue/Wed/Thu 7:15–7:30

HOST:

Ted Steele

REGULARS

Mardi Bryant
Helen Wood
Michael Rich

Ted Steele was a versatile young (31) musician who had a blossoming career on radio in the 1940s. He was orchestra leader for several years on Perry Como's *Chesterfield Supper Club*, was a composer of some note ("Smoke Rings"), and also a singer, pianist, organist, and novachordist. His first break on TV came with a series of musical interludes on NBC, which originated in the WPTZ studios in Philadelphia. Ted later switched to DuMont, then to CBS, then became a local personality in New York.

TEEN TIME TUNES

Music

FIRST TELECAST: *March 14, 1949*
LAST TELECAST: *July 15, 1949*
BROADCAST HISTORY:
Mar 1949–Jul 1949, DUM Mon–Fri 6:30–6:45
REGULAR:
The Logan Trio

Dinnertime musical interlude.

TEENAGE BOOK CLUB

Discussion

FIRST TELECAST: *August 27, 1948*
LAST TELECAST: *October 29, 1948*
BROADCAST HISTORY:
Aug 1948–Oct 1948, ABC Fri 7:30–8:00
Oct 1948, ABC Fri 8:00–8:30

One of ABC's earlier series was this discussion program on books of interest to teenagers. Among the titles considered were Betty Betz's *Your Manners Are Showing,* Harry Haenigsen's comic strips, and a few classics such as *David Copperfield* and *Hamlet.*

TELEPHONE TIME

Dramatic Anthology

FIRST TELECAST: *April 8, 1956*
LAST TELECAST: *April 1, 1958*
BROADCAST HISTORY:
Apr 1956–Mar 1957, CBS Sun 6:00–6:30
Apr 1957–Jun 1957, ABC Thu 10:00–10:30
Jun 1957–Apr 1958, ABC Tue 9:30–10:00
HOST:
John Nesbitt (1956–1957)
Dr. Frank Baxter (1957–1958)

The plays presented in this film series had all been adapted from short stories by author John Nesbitt, who also served as the host of the show, introducing each episode. The subject matter ranged from contemporary to historical, with emphasis on the varied natures and qualities of people, both good and bad. He remained as the host of the series when it moved from CBS to ABC in the spring of 1957, although by this time the works of other authors had been included among the presentations. He was replaced as host in September 1957 by Dr. Frank Baxter. There were occasional appearances by such name talents as Judith Anderson, Thomas Mitchell, and Claudette Colbert, but most of the players in this series were not, at the time, major stars. A number of them—including Cloris Leachman, Michael Landon, Martin Milner, and Robert Vaughn—did become stars of their own television series in the 1960s and 1970s. On an unusual note, famed clown Emmet Kelly made his dramatic debut here in a story titled "Captain from Kopenick."

TELE-VARIETIES

see *Bristol-Myers Tele-Varieties*

TELEVISION PLAYHOUSE

see *Philco TV Playhouse*

TELEVISION PLAYHOUSE

Dramatic Anthology

FIRST TELECAST: *December 4, 1947*
LAST TELECAST: *April 11, 1948*
BROADCAST HISTORY:
Dec 1947–Apr 1948, NBC Sun 8:40–9:10

This was an early series of live television dramas presented by NBC in cooperation with the American National Theater and Academy (ANTA), a federally sponsored theater group. Both light and serious fare were presented, many by famous authors but few starring actors of any note (they would not go near television in 1947). The first presentation was "The Last of My Solid Gold Watches" by Tennessee Williams. *Television Playhouse* was a semiregular program, generally appearing every third Sunday night during the period indicated.

TELEVISION SCREEN MAGAZINE

Various

FIRST TELECAST: *November 17, 1946*
LAST TELECAST: *July 23, 1949*
BROADCAST HISTORY:
Nov 1946–Dec 1946, NBC Sun 8:00–8:30
Dec 1947–Mar 1948, NBC Thu various 30 minute
Mar 1948–Sep 1948, NBC Tue various 30 minute
Oct 1948–Jul 1949, NBC Sat various 30 minute
EMCEE/"EDITOR":
George Putnam (1948)

Alan Scott (1948, 1949)
John K. McCaffery (1948)
Millicent Fenwick (1948)
Bob Stanton (1948)
Ray Forrest (1948–1949)

REGULAR:

Bill Berns

This grab bag of features, presented magazine-style once a week, was one of NBC's earliest network series and was seen initially in three cities (New York, Philadelphia, Schenectady). At first the format was highly informal and the guests were often ordinary people—seemingly anyone who could be lured into the studio. NBC employee Walter Law and his stamp collection was an early favorite, and the very first telecast (November 17, 1946) featured the Police Athletic League Chorus. Later the program became more tightly structured, with a regular host or "editor," occasional film features, and regular segments such as Bill Berns' "While Berns Roams."

The magazine format was emphasized by a shot of pages being flipped before each feature, and regular departments such as the fashion page, personality interviews, etc.

TELL IT TO GROUCHO

Comedy Interview

FIRST TELECAST: *January 11, 1962*
LAST TELECAST: *May 31, 1962*
BROADCAST HISTORY:

Jan 1962–May 1962, CBS Thu 9:00–9:30

REGULARS:

Groucho Marx
Jack Wheeler
Patty Harmon

This filmed series was the short-lived successor to Groucho's long-running *You Bet Your Life*. It was a vehicle designed to let Groucho demonstrate his wit by zinging the guests who appeared on the show to "tell it to Groucho." Guests were interviewed by Groucho about their hobbies, problems, and/or jobs. Assisting Groucho, and participating in the discussions with the guests, were two teenagers who had been "discovered" by Groucho when they had appeared as contestants on *You Bet Your Life*.

TELL IT TO THE CAMERA

Interview

FIRST TELECAST: *December 25, 1963*
LAST TELECAST: *March 18, 1964*
BROADCAST HISTORY:

Dec 1963–Mar 1964, CBS Wed 8:30–9:00

HOST:

Red Rowe

Tell It to the Camera enabled everyday people from around the country to voice their opinions on network television. The filmed series sent a mobile unit to random locations at plants, shopping centers, schools, etc., and invited passersby to let their opinions be known, register complaints about almost anything that was bothering them, or tell what they felt were amusing or interesting stories. There was more than a coincidental resemblance between *Tell It to the Camera* and another series on the CBS schedule, *Candid Camera*. They were both produced by Allen Funt, whose entire career was wrapped up in showing normal people reacting to normal and abnormal situations.

TELLER OF TALES

see *Somerset Maugham TV Theater*

TELLTALE CLUE, THE

Police

FIRST TELECAST: *July 8, 1954*
LAST TELECAST: *September 23, 1954*
BROADCAST HISTORY:

Jul 1954–Sep 1954, CBS Thu 10:00–10:30

CAST:

Det. Lt. Richard Hale ....Anthony Ross

Detective Lieutenant Richard Hale was the head of the criminology department of the police department of a large, unnamed city. He used all of the scientific equipment and analytical skills at his disposal to find the flaws in what would have otherwise been "perfect" crimes. The step-by-step process by which he isolated the evidence that eventually led to an arrest enabled the home viewers to become familiar with modern police technology and, in certain respects, made this series a variation on the Ellery Queen–style whodunit.

TEMPERATURES RISING

Situation Comedy

FIRST TELECAST: *September 12, 1972*
LAST TELECAST: *August 29, 1974*

BROADCAST HISTORY:

Sep 1972–Jan 1974, ABC Tue 8:00–8:30
Jul 1974–Aug 1974, ABC Thu 8:00–8:30

CAST (1972–1973):

Dr. Vincent Campanelli ...James Whitmore
Dr. Jerry Noland ....Cleavon Little
Nurse Annie Carlisle ....Joan Van Ark
Nurse Mildred MacInerny ....Reva Rose
Student Nurse Ellen Turner ....Nancy Fox
Dr. David Amherst ....David Bailey

CAST (1973–1974):

Dr. Paul Mercy ....Paul Lynde
Dr. Jerry Noland ....Cleavon Little
Martha Mercy ....Sudie Bond
Miss Tillis ....Barbara Cason
Nurse "Windy" Winchester ....Jennifer Darling
Dr. Lloyd Axton ....Jeff Morrow
Dr. Charles Cleveland Claver ..John Dehner

CAST (Summer 1974):

Dr. Paul Mercy ....Paul Lynde
Dr. Jerry Noland ....Cleavon Little
Edwina Moffitt ....Alice Ghostley
Nurse Ellen Turner ....Nancy Fox
Nurse Amanda Kelly ......Barbara Rucker

ABC evidently had a good deal of faith in this medical comedy, trying three different casts and formats in two years before finally giving up. For the first season the show was set at Capital General Hospital in Washington, D.C., presided over by no-nonsense Chief of Surgery Dr. Vincent Campanelli and his all-nonsense staff. The latter consisted of prankster Jerry Noland, a free-swinging product of the ghetto and the hospital's chief bookie; sexy young nurse Annie Carlisle; her mischievous companion Mildred MacInerny; and Dr. David Amherst, the handsome love interest of practically every female in the place. There were also the patients: the old codger who liked to drag-race in his wheelchair, the paranoid young man who wanted his medication pretasted and then slipped under the door, etc.

The program returned for its second season retitled *The New Temperatures Rising Show*, with new producers, and almost completely recast. Capital General was now a private hospital, run by penny-pinching Dr. Paul Mercy (played by Paul Lynde) and owned by his meddlesome mother, Martha, who was permanently in residence and who kept calling her son via a beeper on his belt. Miss Tillis was the efficient accountant, "Windy" Winchester the romantically inclined nurse, and Dr. Axton the cheerfully fraudulent surgeon who had recently published two books, *Profit in Healing* and *Malpractice and Its Defense*. Only intern Jerry Noland remained from the first season.

The second version of *Temperatures Rising* was no more successful than the first, however, and lasted only through mid-season. Apparently viewers do not appreciate seeing doctors as the butt of comedy. The show did come back for another short run in the summer of 1974, with more new episodes, and still more changes in cast and plot. This time the meddling mother was gone, and Dr. Mercy ran the place with the help of his sister Edwina. Intern Jerry Noland was back, along with a couple of nurses.

TEMPLE HOUSTON

Western

FIRST TELECAST: *September 19, 1963*
LAST TELECAST: *September 10, 1964*
BROADCAST HISTORY:

Sep 1963–Sep 1964, NBC Thu 7:30–8:30

CAST:

Temple Houston ....Jeffrey Hunter
George Taggart ....Jack Elam

Traveling the circuit courts in the Southwest during the 1880s was Temple Houston, the handsome attorney son of Texas immortal Sam Houston. Temple found his clients, both civil and criminal, wherever the circuit court happened to be in session. In spite of his vocation as a lawyer, Temple was also quite adept as a fast-shooting gunman. His appearance was one of elegance and his oratorical skills were renowned throughout the Southwest. Also traveling with the circuit court was George Taggart, an itinerant U.S. Marshal and over-the-hill gunfighter. Taggart hired himself to the local towns and was either friend or foe of Houston, depending on the interests of Temple's clients. The real-life Temple Houston was a contemporary of both Bat Masterson and Billy the Kid, and was known to have engaged in shooting matches with them.

TENAFLY

Detective

FIRST TELECAST: *October 10, 1973*
LAST TELECAST: *August 6, 1974*

BROADCAST HISTORY:

Oct 1973–Jan 1974, NBC Wed 8:30–10:00

Apr 1974–Aug 1974, NBC Tue 8:30–10:00

CAST:

Harry Tenafly ....James McEachin

Ruth Tenafly ....Lillian Lehman

Herb Tenafly ....Paul Jackson

Lorrie ....Rosanna Huffman

Lt. Sam Church ....David Huddleston

Harry Tenafly was a rarity among television's private detectives: he was a dedicated and happy family man. He lived in Los Angeles with his wife Ruth and their son Herb. The action in the series was divided between his home life and his office life. His friend and confidant at the police department was Lt. Sam Church, who often got Harry out of jams. Unlike most other private detectives, Harry was neither chasing nor being chased by beautiful women. He was happy with his family and saw his job as only a job. *Tenafly* was one of the four rotating elements in the 1973–1974 edition of *NBC Wednesday/Tuesday Mystery Movie.*

TENNESSEE ERNIE FORD SHOW, THE

see *Ford Show Starring Tennessee Ernie Ford, The*

TEX AND JINX

Talk

FIRST TELECAST: *April 20, 1947*

LAST TELECAST: *September 5, 1949*

BROADCAST HISTORY:

Apr 1947–Jun 1947, NBC Sun 8:00–8:15

Jun 1947–Aug 1947, NBC Sun 8:00–8:30

Mar 1949–Jul 1949, CBS Mon 8:00–8:30

Jul 1949–Sep 1949, CBS Mon 9:00–9:30

REGULARS:

Tex McCrary

Jinx Falkenburg

Newspaper columnist Tex McCrary and his actress-wife Jinx Falkenburg were frequently seen during the early days of television, both in guest appearances and as hosts of their own celebrity-interview series. First seen on NBC, they later moved to CBS where their program was billed as *Preview*, "the living television magazine." In addition to these prime-time appearances they hosted *The Swift Home Service Club* (1947–1948), which NBC says was the first sponsored network daytime program, an NBC radio series and various local programs in New York. Later, in the 1950s, they returned to daytime television.

Their prime time programs were variously known as *At Home with Tex and Jinx, The Tex and Jinx Film*, and *Preview with Tex and Jinx* in addition to *Tex and Jinx.*

TEXACO STAR THEATER

see *Milton Berle Show, The*

TEXACO STAR THEATER STARRING DONALD O'CONNOR, THE

see *Donald O'Connor Texaco Show, The*

TEXACO STAR THEATER STARRING JIMMY DURANTE, THE

see *Jimmy Durante Show, The*

TEXAN, THE

Western

FIRST TELECAST: *September 29, 1958*

LAST TELECAST: *September 12, 1960*

BROADCAST HISTORY:

Sep 1958–Sep 1960, CBS Mon 8:00–8:30

CAST:

Bill Longley ....Rory Calhoun

He was not a law officer, but Big Bill Longley was often confronted with situations in which he might as well have been. In the years following the Civil War he made a name for himself throughout the state of Texas. He was a fast gun, a loyal and devoted friend, and a mortal enemy to those who broke the law or harassed those people whom he felt close to. As he traveled from town to town he helped those in need and found adventure, danger, and even an occasional romance.

TEXAS RODEO

Sports Event

FIRST TELECAST: *April 30, 1959*

LAST TELECAST: *July 2, 1959*

BROADCAST HISTORY:

Apr 1959–Jul 1959, NBC Thu 7:30–8:00

COMMENTATOR:

Paul Crutchfield

All of the standard rodeo events were shown in this weekly series filmed on location before arena audiences at rodeos in Texas and elsewhere in the Southwest. Calf roping, bronc riding, bull riding, and steer wrestling were all standard features. Such special events as wild-cow milking and barrel racing were also included in some telecasts. Veteran rodeo announcer Paul Crutchfield did the commentary for this series.

TEXAS WHEELERS, THE

Situation Comedy

FIRST TELECAST: *September 13, 1974*

LAST TELECAST: *July 24, 1975*

BROADCAST HISTORY:

Sep 1974–Oct 1974, ABC Fri 9:30–10:00
Jun 1975–Jul 1975, ABC Thu 8:30–9:00

CAST:

Zack Wheeler .... Jack Elam
Truckie Wheeler .... Gary Busey
Doobie Wheeler .... Mark Hamill
Boo Wheeler .... Karen Oberdiear
T. J. Wheeler .... Tony Becker
Sally .... Lisa Eilbacher

THEME:

"The Texas Wheelers," composed and sung by John Prine

Earthy comedy about the four motherless Wheeler children and their no-account, cantankerous, "but lovable" father Zack. With Zack spending most of his time thinking of ways to avoid work, eldest son Truckie, 24, led the clan, which consisted of Doobie (16), Boo (12), and T. J. (10). Their adventures living in rural Texas, without much money but with a lot of spirit, provided the stories for this short-lived series.

THAT GIRL

Situation Comedy

FIRST TELECAST: *September 8, 1966*

LAST TELECAST: *September 10, 1971*

BROADCAST HISTORY:

Sep 1966–Apr 1967, ABC Thu 9:30–10:00
Apr 1967–Jan 1969, ABC Thu 9:00–9:30
Feb 1969–Sep 1970, ABC Thu 8:00–8:30
Sep 1970–Sep 1971, ABC Fri 9:00–9:30

CAST:

Ann Marie .... Marlo Thomas
Don Hollinger .... Ted Bessell
Lou Marie .... Lew Parker
Helen Marie (1966–1970)
.... Rosemary DeCamp
Judy Bessemer (1966–1967) ... Bonnie Scott
Dr. Leon Bessemer (1966–1967)
.... Dabney Coleman
Jerry Bauman .... Bernie Kopell
Ruth Bauman (1967–1969)
.... Carolyn Daniels
Ruth Bauman (1969–1971) ... Alice Borden
Harvey Peck (1966–1967) ... Ronnie Schell
George Lester (1966–1967) ... George Carlin
Seymour Schwimmer (1967–1968)
.... Don Penny
Margie "Pete" Peterson (1967–1968)
.... Ruth Buzzi

Danny Thomas' daughter Marlo started a trend in TV comedies with this hit series. *That Girl* was the prototype for a wave of "independent woman" series, including *The Doris Day Show, Mary Tyler Moore,* and *Rhoda.* Marlo played Ann Marie, a high-spirited young actress who had left the comfort of her parents' home in rural Brewster, New York, to build a career in the big city. Her "big breaks" usually consisted of roles in TV commercials and bit parts in plays, so she supported herself with odd jobs in offices and department stores. New York City did bring one big break for Ann, however, as on the first telecast she met Don Hollinger, a junior executive for *Newsview* magazine, who became her first romance. They finally became engaged on a September 1970 telecast, but Don never did get to marry "that girl"—although he got as far as a stag party before the 1970–1971 season ended.

Others in Ann's world at various times were her parents, Lou (a restaurant owner) and Helen; her neighbors, the Bessemers; her friends, the Baumans, and her agents Harvey and George. Marcy (played by Reva Rose) was seen briefly as Ann Marie's married friend, during the 1970–1971 season. Danny Thomas made a few cameo appearances in the series in various roles.

THAT REMINDS ME

Stories

FIRST TELECAST: *August 13, 1948*

LAST TELECAST: *October 1, 1948*

BROADCAST HISTORY:

Aug 1948–Oct 1948, ABC Fri 8:30–9:00

EMCEE:

Walter Kiernan

REGULARS:

Governor Harold Hoffman
"Uncle Jim" Harkins

This was simply a storytelling session with newsman Walter Kiernan joined by ex-New Jersey Governor Harold Hoffman and "Uncle Jim" Harkins. The stories were generally about humorous incidents in the lives of famous people, and members of the celebrity's family were often on hand to embellish the tales. It seemed like a good idea for TV in 1948.

THAT WAS THE WEEK THAT WAS

News Satire

FIRST TELECAST: *January 10, 1964*

LAST TELECAST: *May 4, 1965*

BROADCAST HISTORY:

Jan 1964–Jul 1964, NBC Fri 9:30–10:00
Sep 1964–May 1965, NBC Tue 9:30–10:00

REGULARS:

Elliot Reid (1964)
Nancy Ames
David Frost
Henry Morgan (1964)
Phyllis Newman
Pat Englund
Buck Henry
Bob Dishy

The news of the previous week was satirized in revue style on *That Was the Week That Was,* affectionately known as "TW 3." Singer Nancy Ames was the "TW 3" girl and sang the opening and closing numbers in addition to participating in the body of the show. The emphasis of the show was on poking fun at people in high places. Included in the format were comedy sketches, blackouts, musical production numbers, and news reports. Elliot Reid was the host during its first season, to be replaced by David Frost in the fall of 1964. Britisher Frost had been host of the English version of this series, on which the American edition was based. He had been a contributor to the American version during its first season.

The satire could be very brutal. In one scene two good friends, a Catholic and a Jew, were discussing the fact that the Vatican had just exonerated the Jews from responsibility for Jesus' death. Well, they were off the hook for that one, after 2,000 years, but no, the Jew still couldn't join the Catholic's country club—that one hadn't been worked out yet. Then there was the news report from Jackson, Mississippi, where UN paratroopers had just been dropped by Guatamalan Air Force planes, to rescue Negro ministers, missionaries, and civil rights workers. The musical numbers were no less offensive. One telecast had "The Dance of the Liberal Republicans," and others such songs by writer-composer Tom Lehrer (who later recorded them on an album) as "National Brotherhood Week," "The Folk Song Army," "Smut," "Pollution," "Whatever Became of Hubert?" (Vice President Humphrey), and "The Vatican Rag."

THAT WONDERFUL GUY

Situation Comedy

FIRST TELECAST: *December 28, 1949*

LAST TELECAST: *April 28, 1950*

BROADCAST HISTORY:

Dec 1949–Mar 1950, ABC Wed 9:00–9:30
Mar 1950–Apr 1950, ABC Fri 8:30–9:00

CAST:

Harold ....Jack Lemmon
Franklin Westbrook ....Neil Hamilton

A young Jack Lemmon starred in this early situation comedy about a pompous theatrical critic and his eager but bumbling valet. Lemmon, as the valet, was a lad fresh out of a Midwestern dramatic school and fresh into New York, looking for a chance to break into the Broadway big time as an actor. While waiting for opportunity to knock, he worked for suave, cynical drama critic Franklin Westbrook. Despite slick production and smooth performances by newcomer Lemmon and old pro Neil Hamilton, this series did not attract a sponsor and lasted only four months.

Lemmon himself did somewhat better than the valet he played here. After several more television roles (see Index) he landed a part in a Broadway play in 1953, then went to Hollywood in 1954 to begin a stellar motion-picture career.

THAT'S LIFE

Music/Comedy

FIRST TELECAST: *September 24, 1968*

LAST TELECAST: *May 20, 1969*

BROADCAST HISTORY:

Sep 1968–May 1969, ABC Tue 10:00–11:00

CAST:

Robert Dickson ....Robert Morse
Gloria Quigley (Dickson) ....E. J. Peaker

MUSICAL DIRECTOR:

Elliot Lawrence

CHOREOGRAPHER:

Tony Mordante

This unusual comedy followed the romance and married life of a young couple through sketches, monologues, music and dance. Though set in the mythical town of Ridgeville, it was otherwise relatively unstructured—in a sense, a predecessor of

Love, American Style, which premiered the following fall. Both shows made heavy use of guest celebrities in cameo roles. For example, the first episode of *That's Life* opened with a monologue by George Burns, punctuated by short songs, dances, and skits. There followed a dream sequence in which Gloria imagined herself married to Rodney Wonderful (Tony Randall). Later, back in reality, Rodney arranged a blind date for Gloria and she met Bobby at a discotheque, where the music was provided by the rock group the Turtles. Their romance began, and was followed through subsequent shows as they married, set up housekeeping, had their first child, etc.

Other stars making appearances on *That's Life* included Sid Caesar, Paul Lynde, Ethel Merman, Alan King, Mahalia Jackson, Robert Goulet, Phil Silvers, the Muppets, Flip Wilson, Goldie Hawn, Louis Armstrong, Wally Cox, and many others. Creator and executive producer of the show was Marvin Marx, who was for many years Jackie Gleason's head writer.

THAT'S MY BOY

Situation Comedy

FIRST TELECAST: *April 10, 1954*

LAST TELECAST: *September 13, 1959*

BROADCAST HISTORY:

Apr 1954–Jan 1955, CBS Sat 10:00–10:30

Jun 1959–Sep 1959, CBS Sun 7:30–8:00

CAST:

"Jarring" Jack Jackson .....Eddie Mayehoff
Alice Jackson ....Rochelle Hudson
Junior Jackson ....Gil Stratton, Jr.
Henrietta Patterson ....Mabel Albertson
Bill Baker ....John Smith

"Jarring" Jack Jackson was a junior partner in the firm of Patterson and Jackson, made a comfortable living, and had a pleasant home in the suburbs. An ex-football star, and married to a former tennis star, Jack had delusions of grandeur about the future potential of his son, Junior, as an athlete. Unfortunately, Junior had neither the interest nor the ability to excel at sports. A quiet, intellectual sort, he was constantly hounded and prodded by his father into doing things he was not capable of succeeding at. Jack not only made life miserable for his son, but treating the world and everyone in it as though he was still calling signals in a football game, he also managed to make himself pretty hard for everyone else to take. During the summer of 1959 reruns of the original series were aired on Sunday evenings.

Based on the 1951 movie of the same name, which also starred Mayehoff (with Jerry Lewis as his son).

THAT'S MY MAMA

Situation Comedy

FIRST TELECAST: *September 4, 1974*

LAST TELECAST: *December 24, 1975*

BROADCAST HISTORY:

Sep 1974–Sep 1975, ABC Wed 8:00–8:30

Sep 1975–Dec 1975, ABC Wed 8:30–9:00

CAST:

Clifton Curtis ....Clifton Davis
"Mama" Eloise Curtis .....Theresa Merritt
Earl ....Theodore Wilson
Tracy (1974–1975) ....Lynne Moody
Tracy (1975) ....Joan Pringle
Leonard ....Lisle Wilson
Wildcat ....Jester Hairston
Josh ....DeForest Covan
Junior ....Ted Lange

This ethnic comedy centered on the world of Clifton Curtis, a young, hip barber in a black middle-class neighborhood of Washington, D.C. Clifton had inherited the family barbership, "Oscar's," after the death of his father. He liked his trade and his life as a bachelor, but Mama had different ideas for him, wanting him to find a nice, conservative mate, as his sister Tracy had done. Tracy's husband Leonard was successful, all right (he was an engineer), but far too square for Clifton. Others around the shop were Clifton's buddy Earl, the postman; old-timers Wildcat and Josh, who stopped in for jokes, checkers, and faulty advice; and Junior, the irrepressible street philosopher.

There were several cast changes in the fall of 1975, and Earl, the big talker with unworkable schemes, became Clifton's partner in the barbershop. (Note: Ed Bernard played Earl in the first two telecasts in 1974, while Theodore Wilson had another role in those episodes only.)

THEATER OF THE MIND

Discussion

FIRST TELECAST: *July 14, 1949*

LAST TELECAST: *September 15, 1949*

BROADCAST HISTORY:

Jul 1949–Aug 1949, NBC Thu 9:30–10:00
Aug 1949–Sep 1949, NBC Thu 9:00–9:30

MODERATOR:

Dr. Houston Peterson

An early attempt to use television to help viewers meet emotional problems of home life. The first half of each telecast consisted of a playlet revolving around a problem such as a child's adjustment to a new baby in the home, inferiority complexes, domineering parents, old age, alcoholism, etc. After the dramatization a panel of psychiatrists and other experts discussed how the problem could be faced.

THEATER TIME

Dramatic Anthology

FIRST TELECAST: *July 25, 1957*
LAST TELECAST: *September 26, 1957*
BROADCAST HISTORY:

Jul 1957–Sep 1957, ABC Thu 9:00–9:30

HOSTESS:

Anita Louise

The plays shown in this filmed series were all reruns of episodes originally aired as part of other anthology programs.

THEN CAME BRONSON

Adventure

FIRST TELECAST: *September 17, 1969*
LAST TELECAST: *September 9, 1970*
BROADCAST HISTORY:

Sep 1969–Sep 1970, NBC Wed 10:00–11:00

CAST:

Jim Bronson .... Michael Parks

Following the suicide of his best friend, big-city reporter Jim Bronson pondered the meaning of his life and wondered about the satisfaction he was getting out of it. The conclusion he reached was that he really yearned to be free of the traditional commitments of urban living. So, he gave up his job, divested himself of most of his material possessions, and left town on his deceased friend's motorcycle in search of a more meaningful existence. The places he traveled to, the people he met, and the odd jobs he took to support himself in his wanderings across the country, provided the stories in this adventure series.

THEY STAND ACCUSED

Courtroom Drama

FIRST TELECAST: *January 18, 1949*
LAST TELECAST: *December 30, 1954*
BROADCAST HISTORY:

Jan 1949–May 1949, CBS Tue 8:00–9:00
Sep 1949–Mar 1950, DUM Sun 9:00–10:00
Jun 1950–Oct 1950, DUM Sun 9:00–10:00
Oct 1950–Apr 1951, DUM Sun 10:00–11:00
Apr 1951–May 1951, DUM Sat 9:00–10:00
May 1951–Sep 1951, DUM Tue 10:00–11:00
Sep 1951–Oct 1952, DUM Sun 10:00–11:00
Sep 1954–Dec 1954, DUM Thu 8:00–9:00

They Stand Accused was one of the earliest and more popular network series to originate from Chicago. It was an unscripted, spontaneous courtroom trial with real lawyers and judges, and actors playing the parts of defendants and witnesses. Everyone ad-libbed his lines as he went along, according to the developing action. The studio audience served as the "jury," and determined the outcome of each case. Even the cases, though fictitious, had a ring of authenticity. They were plotted out by William Wines, Assistant Attorney General of the State of Illinois, who briefed the participants before each show as if they were principals in a real case about to go to trial, and then let the trial run its course.

Wines' cases sometimes involved murder, but just as often were property claims, divorces, or other civil matters. One week the jury might be deciding custody of a child, on another, whether a wealthy eccentric was capable of managing his own affairs. When it was murder there never was a question of who did it, but rather if self-defense, accident, or temporary insanity was a valid defense. So realistic was the presentation that many viewers were convinced that they were watching a real trial in progress.

They Stand Accused was first seen locally over WGN-TV in Chicago, in April 1948. One week after Chicago and New York were linked by coaxial cable in January 1949 the program was fed out to the CBS network, under the title *Cross Question*. It later moved to DuMont and changed its name to *They Stand Accused* in January 1950.

THEY'RE OFF

Quiz

FIRST TELECAST: *June 30, 1949*
LAST TELECAST: *August 18, 1949*

BROADCAST HISTORY:

Jun 1949–Aug 1949, DUM Thu 8:30–9:00

Nothing at all is known about this 1949 summer quiz show.

THICKER THAN WATER

Situation Comedy

FIRST TELECAST: *June 13, 1973*

LAST TELECAST: *August 8, 1973*

BROADCAST HISTORY:

Jun 1973–Aug 1973, ABC Wed 8:00–8:30

CAST:

Nellie Paine ....Julie Harris
Ernie Paine ....Richard Long
Jonas Paine ....Malcolm Atterbury
Lily ....Jessica Myerson
Walter ....Lou Fant

This family comedy pitted a swinging brother (Ernie) and a staid, spinster sister (Nellie) in a battle of wits. The two were brought together by their ailing, octogenarian father, Jonas, who promised them each a $75,000 inheritance if they could both live at his home and together run the family pickle factory ("Paine's Pure Pickles") for five years. As it turned out, old Jonas not only hung on to watch them bicker, but was probably going to outlive them both.

Lily was a cousin and Walter her husband. Based on the English TV series *Nearest and Dearest.*

THIN MAN, THE

Detective/Comedy

FIRST TELECAST: *September 20, 1957*

LAST TELECAST: *June 26, 1959*

BROADCAST HISTORY:

Sep 1957–Jun 1959, NBC Fri 9:30–10:00

CAST:

Nick Charles ....Peter Lawford
Nora Charles ....Phyllis Kirk

Nick and Nora Charles were wealthy New York socialites living with their wire-haired fox terrier, Asta, in a luxurious Park Avenue apartment. When he married Nora, Nick retired from his occupation as a private detective, but his underworld friends were still around to haunt him. Out of her love for Nick, Nora tried to be hospitable to his friends from the seamier side of life. Asta, with the mistaken notion that he was a bloodhound, spent much of his time sniffing out clues and suspects. The three of them were a team of super-sleuths, solving crimes together for the pure enjoyment of it.

Based on the characters created by novelist Dashiell Hammett, and portrayed in films for many years by William Powell and Myrna Loy. The name "thin man" did not refer to Nick Charles, incidentally, but to another character in the first (1934) *Thin Man* movie.

THINK FAST

Quiz/Panel

FIRST TELECAST: *March 26, 1949*

LAST TELECAST: *October 8, 1950*

BROADCAST HISTORY:

Mar 1949–Apr 1949, ABC Sat 8:30–9:00
May 1949–Sep 1949, ABC Fri 8:00–8:30
Sep 1949–Jul 1950, ABC Sun 8:00–8:30
Jul 1950–Oct 1950, ABC Sun 7:00–7:30

MODERATOR:

Dr. Mason Gross (1949–1950)
Gypsy Rose Lee (1950)

PANELISTS:

Leon Janney
David Broekman
Eloise McElhone

The five panelists (three regulars and two guests) on this wordy quiz circled a large table, each getting a chance at the "King's" throne by outtalking the others on subjects thrown out by the host.

THIS COULD BE YOU

see *Bill Gwinn Show, The*

THIS IS BROADWAY

see *This Is Show Business*

THIS IS GALEN DRAKE

see *Galen Drake Show, The*

THIS IS MUSIC

Music

FIRST TELECAST: *November 29, 1951*

LAST TELECAST: *October 9, 1952*

BROADCAST HISTORY:

Nov 1951–Jun 1952, DUM Thu 8:00–8:30
Jun 1952–Oct 1952, DUM Thu 10:00–10:30

HOST:

Alexander Gray

REGULARS:

Nancy Carr
Bruce Foote
Lucille Reed
Jackie Van (1952)
Jacqueline James (1952)

Bill Snary
Robert Trendler Orchestra

DuMont favored pleasant, unassuming musical programs such as this one because they cost very little to telecast and could be relied upon to attract a respectable, if not really large, audience. The format consisted primarily of popular songs sung by a young cast of regulars.

THIS IS MUSIC

Music

FIRST TELECAST: *June 13, 1958*
LAST TELECAST: *May 21, 1959*
BROADCAST HISTORY:
Jun 1958–Sep 1958, ABC Fri 8:30–9:00
Sep 1958, ABC Mon 7:30–8:00
Oct 1958, ABC Mon 10:00–10:30
Nov 1958–Feb 1959, ABC Thu 10:00–10:30
Mar 1959, ABC Mon 9:30–10:00
Apr 1959–May 1959, ABC Thu 10:00–10:30
EMCEE:
Colin Male
REGULARS:
Ramona Burnett
Lee Fogel
Paula Jane
Wanda Lewis
The O'Neill Dancers
Bud Chase
Bob Smith
Gail Johnson
Bob Shreeve

When the original artists mouthed the words to their hit records, as they did on *American Bandstand,* to make sure that it sounded right, it was called lip-syncing. On this live series, which originated from Cincinnati, Ohio, a group of regular performers did the same thing, but to records made famous by other artists. They mouthed the words while the records were played. *This Is Music* hopped all over the ABC schedule during the 1958–1959 season, filling otherwise empty time slots. Many of the larger stations, which scheduled syndicated programs to fill time slots that the network did not program on a regular basis, did not air this series.

THIS IS MY SONG

see *Bill Gwinn Show, The*

THIS IS NBC NEWS

News

FIRST TELECAST: *June 3, 1962*
LAST TELECAST: *September 16, 1962*
BROADCAST HISTORY:
Jun 1962–Sep 1962, NBC Sun 6:30–7:00
HOST:
Ray Scherer

Anchorman Ray Scherer opened each edition of the 1962 summer season of *This Is NBC News* with a five-minute wrap-up of the day's news. The body of the show was then devoted to a series of reports by various NBC News correspondents, on tape or filmed, covering offbeat or entertaining news events from all over the world. At the end of each show, a short summary of the major news events that had occurred during the previous week was given by Mr. Scherer. A slightly different version of this show had aired earlier on Sunday evenings during the previous summer and this version continued on Sunday afternoons until March 24, 1963.

THIS IS SHOW BUSINESS

Variety

FIRST TELECAST: *July 15, 1949*
LAST TELECAST: *September 11, 1956*
BROADCAST HISTORY:
Jul 1949–Sep 1949, CBS Fri 9:00–10:00
Oct 1949–Jan 1953, CBS Sun 7:30–8:00 (OS)
Jan 1953–Jun 1953, CBS Sat 9:00–9:30
Sep 1953–Mar 1954, CBS Tue 9:00–9:30
Jun 1956–Sep 1956, NBC Tue 9:30–10:00
EMCEE:
Clifton Fadiman
PANELISTS:
George S. Kaufman
Abe Burrows (1949–1951, 1956)
Sam Levenson (1951–1954)
Walter Slezak (1956)

The various entertainers who performed on this series were introduced by host/emcee Clifton Fadiman who chatted with them briefly before they did their acts. Following each act—there were usually three on each show—the entertainers received the opportunity to ask the panel, composed of three show-business veterans, a few questions about the contestants' own acts or on general subjects related to the entertainment world. The title of this series was *This Is Broadway* during its Friday night run in the summer of 1949. When it moved to Sunday evenings that October the title was changed to *This Is Show Business.*

During the period in which it was called *This Is Broadway*, the show was simulcast on radio and television. The NBC revival, for the summer of 1956, aired on alternate Tuesdays with *The Chevy Show*.

Probably the most famous moment in the entire run of the series came on the 1952 Christmas show, when acerbic author and panelist George S. Kaufman remarked on the commercialization of Christmas and then said, "Let's make this one program on which no one sings 'Silent Night.' " CBS received several hundred letters expressing viewer outrage at the comment, and Kaufman was briefly dropped from the show amid considerable publicity. Cooler heads prevailed, however, and he was soon reinstated.

THIS IS THE LIFE

Religious Drama

FIRST TELECAST: *September 9, 1952*

LAST TELECAST: *October 26, 1953*

BROADCAST HISTORY:

Sep 1952–Oct 1952, DUM Fri 8:00–8:30
Oct 1952–Sep 1953, ABC Sun 9:30–10:00
Apr 1953–Aug 1953, DUM Mon 8:30–9:00
Sep 1953–Oct 1953, ABC Mon 10:00–10:30

CAST:

Mr. Fisher .... Onslow Stevens
Mrs. Fisher .... Nan Boardman
Their daughter (Emily) .... Randy Stuart
Their Son .... Michael Hall
Their Son .... David Kasday
Grandpa Fisher .... Forrest Taylor
Pastor Martin .... Nelson Leigh

This religious series was produced by the Lutheran Church's Missouri Synod and depicted a Christian family's attempts to deal with the moral problems of everyday life. The "typical family" was the Fishers, who lived in the town of Middleburg, somewhere in the Midwest. Into their lives came a basketball player who had betrayed the trust of his team, a person victimized by rumors, a couple contemplating divorce, and others. The problem was unfolded in a dramatic presentation, then one member of the family, usually Grandpa or eldest child Emily, would deliver the "pitch"—the Christian solution.

The shows were provided free to any station that would air them, and were seen locally in many cities as well as in the ABC and DuMont runs indicated above. The series was described by *TV Guide* in 1954 as "the most widely circulated TV show in the world."

THIS IS TOM JONES

Musical Variety

FIRST TELECAST: *February 7, 1969*

LAST TELECAST: *January 15, 1971*

BROADCAST HISTORY:

Feb 1969–May 1969, ABC Fri 7:30–8:30
May 1969–Sep 1970, ABC Thu 9:00–10:00
Sep 1970–Jan 1971, ABC Fri 10:00–11:00

HOST:

Tom Jones

REGULARS:

The Ace Trucking Company (1970–1971)

Pop singer Tom Jones, he of the booming baritone, raw, driving energy, and ability to turn grown women into putty (read "sex appeal"), starred in his own musical variety series from 1969–1971. Jones is a Welshman and the first few telecasts originated in London and featured many English stars. Later the origination alternated between London and Hollywood, and top American stars, especially popular musicians, appeared as well. The show had a very contemporary quality, especially during the second season when the Ace Trucking Company, an improvisational comedy troupe consisting of four boys and one girl, joined as regulars.

After the last big, brassy musical number, dynamic Tom would wish his viewers goodnight in traditional Welsh, saying "Gwyn eich byd a dymunaf i chwi lawenydd bob amser." Although there was some speculation about what he was really saying (how many Americans understand Welsh?), it meant, simply, "May you always be well and be happy."

THIS IS YOUR LIFE

Testimonial

FIRST TELECAST: *October 1, 1952*

LAST TELECAST: *September 3, 1961*

BROADCAST HISTORY:

Oct 1952–Jun 1953, NBC Wed 10:00–10:30
Jun 1953–Aug 1953, NBC Tue 9:30–10:00
Jul 1953–Jun 1958, NBC Wed 9:30–10:00
Sep 1958–Sep 1960, NBC Wed 10:00–10:30
Sep 1960–Sep 1961, NBC Sun 10:30–11:00

HOST:

Ralph Edwards

ANNOUNCER:

Bob Warren

This Is Your Life was created by Ralph Edwards in the late 1940s and aired for one year each on NBC and CBS radio. It came to television in 1952 and remained on the air for nine seasons. Ralph Edwards was the host throughout the long network run and returned almost a decade later with a syndicated version.

The format of *This Is Your Life* was quite simple. Each show opened with Edwards surprising an unsuspecting individual, either in the studio or at some location not too far from it, and informing him or her that "this is your life." The guest of honor was then transported to the program's studio where his life story was presented. Edwards would read from the honored guest's *This Is Your Life* book, chronologically covering the high points in his life, and would pause periodically in the narrative for the voice of an offstage guest. The guest of honor would try to guess whose voice it was—a relative, friend, teacher, minister, business associate, etc.—and then the offstage guest would come out to reminisce about their shared experiences. This would go on until the entire life story was unfolded.

At the end of the show, Ralph Edwards gathered all the guests together on the stage and personally presented the guest of honor with momentoes—a film of the show, a camera and projector to show it on, a charm bracelet with each charm depicting a significant event in the guest of honor's life, and various other prizes. After the show, the friends and family were taken to a party at the hotel where all out-of-town guests had been staying prior to the telecast. The subjects varied from ordinary people, to show-business celebrities, to well-known businessmen. *This Is Your Life* was presented live until the start of the 1959–1960 season, at which point many of the episodes were prerecorded.

Edwards' narration of the biographies of the subjects on *This Is Your Life* tended to wring the maximum amount of emotion from both subject and audience and there was plenty of nostalgic crying done by subjects and guests. To most of the guests of honor, the confrontation with Edwards came as a complete surprise, but there were a few exceptions. Eddie Cantor was told in advance because he had a heart condition and Edwards did not want to shock him into an attack. The most celebrated subject in the long history of *This Is Your Life*, singer Lillian Roth, was also told ahead of time, but for a very different reason. She had waged a long, successful battle with alcoholism and her story was just too personal to spring on her as a surprise. That telecast was extremely inspirational, had the full sanction of Alcoholics Anonymous, and was the only episode to be aired three times, twice on kinescopes after its original live presentation in 1953.

There was always a backup kinescope ready to roll in case something went wrong when Edwards sprang his little surprise on an unsuspecting guest, but it was never needed. There were occasions, though, when the plans had to be scrapped because the subject found out in advance what was being planned. According to the *This Is Your Life* staff, Joe Louis and Ann Sheridan were two whose biographies were canceled for this reason. There was one person who was definitely off limits—Ralph Edwards himself. He had told his staff, and he meant it, that he would fire every one of them if they ever tried to pull the switch and surprise him with his "life."

THIS WEEK IN SPORTS

Sports/News

FIRST TELECAST: *September 20, 1949*

LAST TELECAST: *December 13, 1949*

BROADCAST HISTORY:

Sep 1949–Dec 1949, CBS Tue 10:00–10:15

Newsreel highlights of the week's activities in the world of sports were telecast in this series. Included were highlights from various events, films of outstanding individual plays, and short profiles of well-known sports personalities.

THIS WORLD—1954

Documentary

FIRST TELECAST: *August 4, 1954*

LAST TELECAST: *September 22, 1954*

BROADCAST HISTORY:

Aug 1954–Sep 1954, ABC Wed 9:00–9:30

Documentary films produced by the federal government on such subjects as Communism, good government, democracy, etc.

THOSE ENDEARING YOUNG CHARMS

Situation Comedy

FIRST TELECAST: *March 30, 1952*

LAST TELECAST: *June 17, 1952*
BROADCAST HISTORY:
Mar 1952–Apr 1952, NBC Sun 6:30–7:00
May 1952–Jun 1952, NBC Tue/Thu 7:15–7:30
CAST:
Ralph Charm ....Maurice Copeland
Abbe Charm ....Fern Persons
Connie Charm ....Charon Follett
Clem Charm ....Gerald Garvey
Uncle Duff ....Clarence Hartzell

This live series, originating from Chicago, told of the adventures of the Charm family, who ran a mail-order business catering to collectors of household gadgets. The family business was run by Ralph Charm and his wife Abbe, but all of the members of the household participated in it, including daughter Connie and son Clem. The strangest member of the household was Uncle Duff, whose hobby was memorizing mail-order catalogues. *Those Endearing Young Charms* had premiered on Sunday afternoons at the end of December 1951. It spent only two weeks in the 6:30–7:00 P.M. Sunday time slot and then returned early in May.

THOSE TWO
Situation Comedy
FIRST TELECAST: *November 26, 1951*
LAST TELECAST: *April 24, 1953*
BROADCAST HISTORY:
Nov 1951–Apr 1953, NBC Mon/Wed/Fri 7:30–7:45
REGULARS:
Pinky Lee
Vivian Blaine (1951–1952)
Martha Stewart (1952–1953)

This live, loosely structured musical situation-comedy series was used to fill the remainder of the half-hour in which NBC aired its network news program. Vivian was a nightclub singer whose accompanist, Pinky, was madly in love with her. Unfortunately for Pinky, she was in love with another man. The vestigial plot was primarily a backdrop allowing the stars to sing solos and duets. Miss Blaine left the series in May 1952 and was replaced by Martha Stewart.

THOSE WHITING GIRLS
Situation Comedy
FIRST TELECAST: *July 4, 1955*
LAST TELECAST: *September 30, 1957*
BROADCAST HISTORY:
Jul 1955–Sep 1955, CBS Mon 9:00–9:30
Jul 1957–Sep 1957, CBS Mon 9:00–9:30
CAST:
Margaret Whiting ....Herself
Barbara Whiting ....Herself
Mrs. Whiting ....Mabel Albertson
Artie (1957) ....Jerry Paris

There were many similarities between the real lives of the Whiting sisters, Margaret and Barbara, and the roles they portrayed in this summer replacement for *I Love Lucy*. Margaret was, and played, a popular singer and Barbara was, and played, her younger sister. They lived in Los Angeles with their mother and Barbara was a coed at UCLA. The adventures of the two girls and their relationship with their "mother" formed the bases for the stories told in the series. When it returned in 1957, Margaret had acquired an accompanist named Artie who was the one new regular in the cast.

THREE ABOUT TOWN
Music
FIRST TELECAST: *August 11, 1948*
LAST TELECAST: *October 27, 1948*
BROADCAST HISTORY:
Aug 1948–Sep 1948, ABC Wed 7:15–7:30
Sep 1948–Oct 1948, ABC Wed 8:45–9:00
HOSTESS:
Betsi Allison

Musical interlude featuring vocalist Betsi Allison and twin pianos, with songs and chatter about the theatrical world. Also seen as a local program in New York at various times during 1948.

THREE FLAMES SHOW, THE
Music
FIRST TELECAST: *June 13, 1949*
LAST TELECAST: *August 20, 1949*
BROADCAST HISTORY:
Jun 1949, NBC Mon 10:00–10:30
Jul 1949–Aug 1949, NBC Mon 9:45–10:00
Jul 1949–Aug 1949, NBC Sat 10:00–10:30
REGULARS:
The Three Flames (Tiger Haynes, guitar; Roy Testamark, piano; Bill Pollard, bass)

Live program of music and patter by the Three Flames, a popular black vocal and instrumental trio whose biggest hit was the 1947 novelty "Open the Door, Richard." They performed, appropriately enough, before a backdrop of flames. Many, though not all, of their guests were black, including trumpet players Hot Lips Page and Dizzy Gillespie, singer Dinah Washington and pianist Errol Garner.

The Three Flames were previously seen locally in New York as well as in a daytime program. They were among the first, if not *the* first, black performers to have a regular network series.

THREE FOR THE ROAD

Adventure

FIRST TELECAST: *September 14, 1975*
LAST TELECAST: *November 30, 1975*
BROADCAST HISTORY:

Sep 1975–Nov 1975, CBS Sun 7:00–8:00

CAST:

Pete Karras .... Alex Rocco
John Karras .... Vincent Van Patten
Endy Karras .... Leif Garrett

Freelance photographer Pete Karras, a widower with two teenage sons, traveled around the country on various assignments. His mode of travel, and the means by which he kept his family together, was a mobile home. The nature of Pete's job and the people that he and his sons encountered in their travels provided the material for the stories in this series, which often tended to the moralistic (after beating a bad guy to a pulp, Pete told the boys that violence is not the answer, etc.) The series had a short run.

3 GIRLS 3

Variety

FIRST TELECAST: *March 30, 1977*
LAST TELECAST: *June 29, 1977*
BROADCAST HISTORY:

Mar 1977, NBC Wed 9:00–10:00
Jun 1977, NBC Wed 9:00–10:00

REGULARS:

Debbie Allen
Ellen Foley
Mimi Kennedy

A novel programming idea, *3 Girls 3* was part musical variety show and part situation comedy. The three young stars, none of whom had any previous television experience, played three unknowns who auditioned for, and won, the starring roles in a network variety series. Part of each telecast consisted of their "show," where they were seen singing, dancing, and doing comedy sketches, and part depicted scenes at rehearsals and in their personal lives. Originally scheduled as a four-week miniseries in the spring of 1977, only the first telecast aired, with the three remaining episodes shown in June. A critical success, praised as a programming innovation, *3 Girls 3* never found much of an audience against *Baretta* and CBS movies.

THREE'S COMPANY

Music

FIRST TELECAST: *May 18, 1950*
LAST TELECAST: *September 29, 1950*
BROADCAST HISTORY:

May 1950–Jun 1950, CBS Thu 7:45–8:00
Jun 1950, CBS Wed/Thu 7:45–8:00
Jul 1950–Sep 1950, CBS Tue/Thu 7:45–8:00
Sep 1950, CBS Mon/Wed/Fri 7:45–8:00
Sep 1950, CBS Sun 9:15–9:30

REGULARS:

Martha Wright
Cy Walter
Stan Freeman
Judy Lynn

This live fifteen minute music show, which filled the remainder of the half hour in which CBS aired its network news program during the summer of 1950, featured pianists Cy Walter and Stan Freeman and the vocals of Martha Wright. When Miss Wright left the show she was replaced, effective June 28, by Judy Lynn.

THREE'S COMPANY

Situation Comedy

FIRST TELECAST: *March 15, 1977*
LAST TELECAST:
BROADCAST HISTORY:

Mar 1977–Apr 1977, ABC Thu 9:30–10:00
Aug 1977–Sep 1977, ABC Thu 9:30–10:00
Sep 1977– , ABC Tue 9:00–9:30

CAST:

Jack Tripper .... John Ritter
Janet Wood .... Joyce DeWitt
Chrissy Snow .... Suzanne Somers
Helen Roper .... Audra Lindley
Stanley Roper .... Norman Fell
Larry (1978–) .... Richard Kline

In this comedy, two contemporary young single girls found themselves in need of a roommate for their Santa Monica apartment so they decided to settle for the man they found sleeping in their bathtub—after a going-away party for their last roommate.

Jack was harmless enough, but the problem was in convincing everyone else of that.

Parents objected and humorous misunderstandings abounded, but Jack stayed. In addition to his other virtues, he was the only one of the three roommates who could cook. His favorite ploy was to intimate that he was a homosexual, and therefore uninterested in the two sexy girls (in fact, nothing did go on between them). The landlady, Mrs. Roper, who lived downstairs, worried less about what was going on upstairs than about the fact that nothing was going on in *her* love life with her husband Stanley. Away from their confused home life, Janet, the brunette, worked in a florist shop and Chrissy, the frivolous blonde, was a typist.

After a short run in the spring of 1977 *Three's Company* was picked up as a regular series on ABC's fall 1977 schedule. The comedy was based almost entirely on sexual double-entendres, and religious leaders and critics found the program almost as objectionable as *Soap,* which followed it on the Tuesday night schedule. Nevertheless viewers made it one of the major hits of the 1977–1978 season, especially after it was featured on the cover of *Newsweek* magazine in February 1978. The cover photo was a staged shot of Chrissy with her negligé seemingly falling off, and Jack leering over her shoulder—something that never happened on the show.

Based on the British series *Man about the House.*

THRILLER

Suspense Anthology

FIRST TELECAST: *September 13, 1960*

LAST TELECAST: *July 9, 1962*

BROADCAST HISTORY:

Sep 1960–Sep 1961, NBC Tue 9:00–10:00

Sep 1961–Jul 1962, NBC Mon 10:00–11:00

HOST:

Boris Karloff

Stories of normal, everyday people caught in unexpected, often terrifying, situations were broadcast weekly on *Thriller.* Famous horror-movie star Boris Karloff was the host of the series, introducing all of the stories and occasionally starring in them. Generally lesser-known actors and actresses appeared in most of the productions, which bore such evocative titles as "Parasite Mansion," "The Terror in Teakwood," "Pigeons from Hell," and "The Premature Burial."

THROUGH THE CRYSTAL BALL

Dance

FIRST TELECAST: *April 18, 1949*

LAST TELECAST: *July 4, 1949*

BROADCAST HISTORY:

Apr 1949–Jul 1949, CBS Mon 9:00–9:30

REGULAR:

Jimmy Savo

Dramatizations in dance form of popular fables were presented live on *Through the Crystal Ball.* Pantomimist Jimmy Savo was the original star, host, and narrator of the series. After he left in May there were no regular cast members. Various choreographers worked on the dance interpretation of such fables as *Alice in Wonderland,* "Cinderella," "Ali Baba," and "Casey at the Bat."

THROUGH THE CURTAIN

Discussion

FIRST TELECAST: *October 21, 1953*

LAST TELECAST: *February 24, 1954*

BROADCAST HISTORY:

Oct 1953–Feb 1954, ABC Wed 8:15–8:30

HOST:

George Hamilton Combs

REGULAR:

Leo Gruliow

The curtain referred to here was the Iron Curtain. The program's object was to bring to the American viewer a concise summary of what the Soviet citizen got in his newspapers and magazines each week, with an analysis of what these publications revealed about Soviet society. Gruliow was editor of the *Current Digest of the Soviet Press.*

THROUGH WENDY'S WINDOW

see *Wendy Barrie Show, The*

TIC TAC DOUGH

Quiz/Audience Participation

FIRST TELECAST: *September 12, 1957*

LAST TELECAST: *December 29, 1958*

BROADCAST HISTORY:

Sep 1957–Oct 1958, NBC Thu 7:30–800

Oct 1958–Dec 1958, NBC Mon 7:30–8:00

EMCEE:

Jay Jackson (1957)

Win Elliot

The format of this nighttime quiz show was essentially the same as that of its daytime counterpart which premiered in the summer of 1956 and ran until the fall of 1959. Jack Barry was the host of the daytime version and Jay Jackson hosted the nighttime show, but only for its premiere episode. He was replaced the following week by Win Elliot, who remained with it until it was canceled. The game itself was a variation of tic-tac-toe in which each contestant put his X or O in a given box by answering a question in the category covering that box. After each round (one question for each contestant) the categories were rotated to different boxes. The value of the outside-box questions was $300 and the tougher center-box question was worth $500. The winner kept the cash value of the correct questions he had answered. In a tie game, the winnings were added to the value of the next game.

TIGHTROPE

Police

FIRST TELECAST: *September 8, 1959*
LAST TELECAST: *September 13, 1960*
BROADCAST HISTORY:
Sep 1959–Sep 1960, CBS Tue 9:00–9:30
CAST:
Undercover Agent .... Mike Connors

The task of infiltrating organized crime to expose its leaders and prevent the spread of corruption was the job of the unnamed police undercover agent who was the focus of this series. The "tightrope" he walked was treacherous, for many of the police he aided had no idea who he was and would have shot him in various situations without realizing he was working on their side.

The name used by the agent was part of his cover, and changed with each episode. Originally he was supposed to be named Nick Stone, but this idea was dropped before the first telecast and thereafter only occasionally was his real name mentioned—as "Nick."

TIM CONWAY COMEDY HOUR, THE

Comedy Variety

FIRST TELECAST: *September 20, 1970*
LAST TELECAST: *December 13, 1970*
BROADCAST HISTORY:
Sep 1970–Dec 1970, CBS Sun 10:00–11:00
REGULARS:
Tim Conway
McLean Stevenson
Art Metrano
The Tom Hansen Dancers
Sally Struthers
Bonnie Boland
Belland and Somerville

Comedian Tim Conway was the host and star of this variety show which stressed sketch comedy.

TIM CONWAY SHOW, THE

Situation Comedy

FIRST TELECAST: *January 30, 1970*
LAST TELECAST: *June 19, 1970*
BROADCAST HISTORY:
Jan 1970–Jun 1970, CBS Fri 8:00–8:30
CAST:
Spud Barrett .... Tim Conway
Herbert T. Kenworth .... Joe Flynn
Mrs. K. J. Crawford .... Anne Seymour
Ronnie Crawford .... Johnnie Collins III
Becky Parks .... Emily Banks
Harry Wetzel .... Fabian Dean
Sherman Bell .... Dennis Robertson

Spud Barrett was the clumsy, oafish, but well-meaning chief pilot for Triple-A, that is, Anywhere, Anytime Airline. He was the chief pilot primarily because he was also the only pilot. Owner of the airline, and Spud's boss, was cranky Herb Kenworth who, despite being in the air-charter business, was terrified of flying. The airport out of which they flew was owned by Mrs. Crawford, who also ran her own more prosperous charter service.

TIME FOR REFLECTION

Poetry

FIRST TELECAST: *May 7, 1950*
LAST TELECAST: *October 22, 1950*
BROADCAST HISTORY:
May 1950–Oct 1950, DUM Sun 6:45–7:00
HOST:
David Ross

Poetry readings by David Ross.

TIME TO SMILE

see *Alan Young Show, The* and *Ken Murray Show, The*

TIME TUNNEL, THE

Science Fiction

FIRST TELECAST: *September 9, 1966*
LAST TELECAST: *September 1, 1967*

BROADCAST HISTORY:

Sep 1966–Jul 1967, ABC Fri 8:00–9:00
Jul 1967–Sep 1967, ABC Fri 7:30–8:30

CAST:

Dr. Tony Newman ....James Darren
Dr. Doug Phillips ....Robert Colbert
Dr. Ann MacGregor ....Lee Meriwether
Gen. Heywood Kirk ....Whit Bissel
Dr. Raymond Swain ....John Zaremba

CREATOR/PRODUCER:

Irwin Allen

Tony Newman and Doug Phillips were two young scientists working on a top-secret government project, deep below the Arizona desert. Their goal: to build a laser-actuated "time tunnel," leading to ages past and future. Unfortunately they were forced to plunge into the tunnel before it was fully tested, and found themselves lost in history, able to move from one point in time to another, but unable to get back to their starting point, 1966.

While their associates, Drs. MacGregor and Swain, worked feverishly to free them from their bondage, Tony and Doug found themselves plunged into one famous historical event after another, always knowing the outcome in advance, but unable to change it. First they were deposited on the deck of the *Titanic,* just before you-know-what. Then it was in and out of the shadows of great events from the siege of Troy (500 B.C.) to a futuristic space flight to Mars. They tried to save Marie Antoniette and President Lincoln, opposed Cortez, and watched the Battle of Jericho as the walls came a-tumbling down. They chased one villain clear from one million B.C. to one million A.D. Who wanted to go back to Arizona?

TIME WILL TELL

Quiz/Audience Participation

FIRST TELECAST: *September 3, 1954*

LAST TELECAST: *October 15, 1954*

BROADCAST HISTORY:

Sep 1954–Oct 1954, DUM Fri 10:30–11:00

EMCEE:

Ernie Kovacs

ANNOUNCER:

Bob Russell

This short-lived quiz show was intended to give comic Ernie Kovacs a chance to clown around with the contestants. And, indeed, Kovacs' interviews and asides were the principal attraction. The quiz portion consited simply of a series of questions, most requiring one-word answers, delivered rapid-fire to a panel of three contestants for 90 seconds. The contestant with the most correct answers won.

TIMMY AND LASSIE

syndicated title for *Lassie*

TIN PAN ALLEY TV

Musical Variety

FIRST TELECAST: *April 28, 1950*

LAST TELECAST: *September 29, 1950*

BROADCAST HISTORY:

Apr 1950–Sep 1950, ABC Fri 9:30–10:00

REGULARS:

Johnny Desmond
Gloria Van
Chet Roble, piano
Rex Maupin's Orchestra

This live musical program from Chicago showcased the songs of a different composer or lyricist each week. The one so honored was usually on hand; for example, lyricist Mitchell Parish watched the cast perform his "Deep Purple," "Star Dust," "Organ Grinder's Swing," and other standards on the premiere telecast. By early TV standards the production was quite elaborate, which at first gave the inexperienced studio crew some problems. *Variety* reported that on the premiere the singers were continually interrupted by loud thuds and clunks from offstage, that a dance team performing behind a vocalist worked nicely "when the camera could find them," and that a group of kids dancing around the man playing the organ grinder in "Organ Grinder's Swing" kept dancing right off the screen. Such were the problems of live TV in 1950. Presumably the problems were overcome as the series continued through the summer.

TO ROME WITH LOVE

Situation Comedy

FIRST TELECAST: *September 28, 1969*

LAST TELECAST: *September 21, 1971*

BROADCAST HISTORY:

Sep 1969–Sep 1970, CBS Sun 7:30–8:00
Sep 1970–Jan 1971, CBS Tue 9:30–10:00
Jan 1971–Sep 1971, CBS Wed 8:30–9:00

CAST:

Michael Endicott ....John Forsythe

Aunt Harriet Endicott (1969–1970)
.... Kay Medford
Alison Endicott ....Joyce Menges
Penny Endicott ....Susan Neher
Mary Jane (Pokey) Endicott
.... Melanie Fullerton
Grandpa Andy Pruitt (1970–1971)
.... Walter Brennan

Following the death of his wife, college professor Michael Endicott decided to leave his native Iowa to accept a teaching position at the American Overseas School in Rome. The adjustments made by Michael and his three daughters to a wholly alien but fascinating environment provided much of the gentle humor of this series. Michael's sister Harriet, who tried constantly to get the family to return to Iowa, was living with them in their Rome apartment through the first half of the 1969–1970 season but gave up and returned home alone. At the start of the second season Andy Pruitt, the father of Michael's late wife, joined the cast. A crotchety Iowa farmer who had sold his farm in anticipation of moving to a retirement community, he arrived for a visit in Rome and somehow never left.

TO TELL THE TRUTH

Quiz/Audience Participation

FIRST TELECAST: *December 18, 1956*
LAST TELECAST: *May 22, 1967*
BROADCAST HISTORY:

Dec 1956–Sep 1958, CBS Tue 9:00–9:30
Sep 1958–Sep 1959, CBS Tue 8:30–9:00
Oct 1959–Jun 1960, CBS Thu 7:30–8:00
Jul 1960–Sep 1960, CBS Thu 10:30–11:00
Sep 1960–Sep 1966, CBS Mon 7:30–8:00
Dec 1966–May 1967, CBS Mon 10:00–10:30

EMCEE:

Bud Collyer

PANELISTS:

Polly Bergen (1956–1961)
Hy Gardner (1956–1959)
Hildy Parks (1956–1957)
Kitty Carlisle
Ralph Bellamy (1957–1959)
Tom Poston (1958–1967)
Orson Bean (1964–1967)
Peggy Cass (1964–1967)

PRODUCERS:

Mark Goodson and Bill Todman

Contestants on *To Tell the Truth* were introduced in threes. All of them purported to be the same individual. Following the introduction, emcee Bud Collyer would read an affidavit describing the life, activities, and/or unique experiences of the person whom all the contestants claimed to be. The panel then spent an amount of time asking questions of the three contestants trying to determine which one was telling the truth and which two were lying. Following the question session, each panelist had to vote for whom he thought was really the person described in the affidavit. Wrong guesses were worth money to all three contestants, who split the winnings equally. The original title, which lasted only one episode, was *Nothing but the Truth.* The person whose description was read in the affidavit had to tell the truth, but the impostors, who had been given a briefing by the person they were pretending to be, could say anything. The famous closing line for each round: "Will the real ——— please stand up!"

TO THE QUEEN'S TASTE

Cooking

FIRST TELECAST: *May 3, 1948*
LAST TELECAST: *December 29, 1949*
BROADCAST HISTORY:

May 1948–Aug 1948, CBS Mon 8:05–8:30
Aug 1948–Apr 1949, CBS Thu 8:00–8:30
May 1949–Jul 1949, CBS Thu 9:30–10:00
Jul 1949–Sep 1949, CBS Mon 8:00–8:30
Oct 1949–Dec 1949, CBS Thu 7:00–7:30

CHEF:

Dione Lucas

This early cooking show began as a local program in New York on October 9, 1947, originating from the Cordon Bleu (a Manhattan restaurant owned by Dione Lucas). Seven months later the show became a CBS network series. Cooking expert Lucas, the Julia Child of her day, showed viewers how to prepare exotic and tasty culinary treats from varied cuisines. This series was also known as *The Dione Lucas Show,* a title that was used for later local versions after it left the CBS network.

TOAST OF THE TOWN, THE

see *Ed Sullivan Show, The*

TOM CORBETT, SPACE CADET

Children's

FIRST TELECAST: *October 2, 1950*
LAST TELECAST: *September 26, 1952*

BROADCAST HISTORY:

Oct 1950–Dec 1950, CBS Mon/Wed/Fri 6:45–7:00

Jan 1951–Sep 1952, ABC Mon/Wed/Fri 6:30–6:45

Jul 1951–Sep 1951, NBC Sat 7:00–7:30

CAST:

Tom Corbett .... Frankie Thomas
Capt. Strong (1950) .... Michael Harvey
Capt. Strong (1951–1952) .... Edward Bryce
Astro the Venusian .... Al Markim
Roger Manning .... Jan Merlin
Dr. Joan Dale .... Margaret Garland

TECHNICAL ADVISOR:

Willie Ley

WRITERS:

Frankie Thomas, Stu Brynes, Ray Morse

Tom Corbett was conceived by CBS in late 1950 to cash in on the enormous popularity of DuMont's *Captain Video*. The two programs were not directly competitive—in fact *Tom Corbett* (6:45–7:00 P.M.) led into *Captain Video* (7:00–7:30 P.M.) three nights a week—and they differed in substantial ways. *Tom Corbett* had a much larger budget and thus more realistic special effects, such as blastoffs, weightlessness, etc., all done live through various techniques of video hocus-pocus. And the emphasis was less on futuristic hardware (though there was plenty) and more on the adventures of the young cast.

Tom Corbett, curly-headed teenage cadet at the Space Academy, four centuries hence, was a figure with whom youngsters could identify. With him in training to become Solar Guards were wisecracking Cadet Roger Manning ("So what happens now, space heroes?," "Aw, go blow your jets!") and the quieter Astro, a Venusian (planetary boundaries were rather less important in the 24th century). Every week they blasted off in the spaceship *Polaris* to new adventures somewhere in space, usually against natural forces rather than the space villains who populated *Captain Video*. Their exploits were instructive as well as exciting. Program advisor Willie Ley, a noted scientist and author, worked in legitimate concepts such as variable gravity forces, asteroid belts, and anti-matter.

After three months on CBS *Tom Corbett* moved to ABC for a run of nearly two years. In addition kinescopes of the weekday serial were run on Saturdays on NBC during the summer of 1951—as summer replacement for Victor Borge! The series was also heard on ABC radio during 1952, with the same cast as the TV version. The *Tom Corbett* cast also made personal appearances to promote merchandise connected with the show (wonder if they offered the most popular of the Cadets' 24th-century aids—the Study Machine?). Late in 1952 the series moved to Saturday daytime, where it continued, off and on, until the summer of 1955.

Based on the novel *Space Cadet*, by Robert A. Heinlein.

TOM, DICK AND MARY

Situation Comedy

FIRST TELECAST: *October 5, 1964*

LAST TELECAST: *January 4, 1965*

BROADCAST HISTORY:

Oct 1964–Jan 1965, NBC Mon 8:30–9:00

CAST:

Dr. Tom Gentry .... Don Galloway
Mary Gentry .... Joyce Bulifant
Dr. Dick Moran .... Steve Franken

There is one thing you can always say for group living: it helps spread the costs of housing. It was for that reason that young Dr. Tom Gentry and his recent bride, Mary, were sharing an apartment with Tom's best friend, Dick. With Tom working as an intern and Mary as a medical secretary, the family income did not quite stretch far enough to afford their apartment at 90 Bristol Court. Dick was also an intern who had moved in with the Gentrys to share the costs of the apartment. The newlyweds were not thrilled having an extra person around, except when the rent was due. *Tom, Dick and Mary* was one of the three situation comedies that collectively made up the series *90 Bristol Court*. The other two were *Karen* and *Harris Against the World*.

TOM EWELL SHOW, THE

Situation Comedy

FIRST TELECAST: *September 27, 1960*

LAST TELECAST: *July 18, 1961*

BROADCAST HISTORY:

Sep 1960–Jul 1961, CBS Tue 9:00–9:30

CAST:

Tom Potter .... Tom Ewell
Fran Potter .... Marilyn Erskine
Irene Brady .... Mabel Albertson
Carol Potter .... Cindy Robbins

Debbie Potter ....Sherry Alberoni
Sissie Potter ....Eileen Chesis

Tom Potter was a real estate agent whose entire life, away from the office, was dominated by women. His household resembled a multi-generational girl's dormitory. In addition to his wife Fran, and his three daughters (Carol, 15; Debbie, 11; and Sissie, 7), he had to cope with a live-in mother-in-law, Grandma Brady. The problems he had living in a woman's world provided the focus of this series.

TOMA

Police

FIRST TELECAST: *October 4, 1973*
LAST TELECAST: *September 6, 1974*
BROADCAST HISTORY:
Oct 1973–Jan 1974, ABC Thu 8:00–9:00
Jan 1974–Sep 1974, ABC Fri 10:00–11:00
CAST:
Det. David Toma ....Tony Musante
Inspector Spooner ....Simon Oakland
Patty Toma ....Susan Strasberg

Like *Serpico* a few years later, *Toma* was based on the exploits of a real-life big-city cop, Det. David Toma of the Newark, New Jersey, police department. Toma was a loner, continually bucking the system, and in many ways a headache to his boss, Inspector Spooner. But he was also a master of disguise, and his quick wittedness and unorthodox methods won him national fame as a highly effective undercover agent. His targets were usually crime syndicates, racketeers, and the like. Patty Toma was his worried wife.

The real-life Dave Toma played bit parts in this series.

In a rather unusual move, actor Tony Musante left the program after only one season because he just didn't like the weekly grind of production. ABC was not unhappy with the show's performance and planned to bring *Toma* back with a new actor in the lead role. It was originally to be called *Toma Starring Robert Blake*, but despite the strong similarities in the lead role, a number of minor changes in the format resulted in a new series titled *Baretta*.

TOMBSTONE TERRITORY

Western

FIRST TELECAST: *October 16, 1957*
LAST TELECAST: *October 9, 1959*
BROADCAST HISTORY:
Oct 1957–Sep 1958, ABC Wed 8:30–9:00
Mar 1959–Oct 1959, ABC Fri 9:00–9:30
CAST:
Sheriff Clay Hollister ....Pat Conway
Harris Claibourne ....Richard Eastham
Deputy Riggs (1957) ....Gil Rankin

Western adventure set in Tombstone, Arizona, "the town too tough to die." Sheriff Hollister was the strong arm of the law, and Harris Claibourne, editor of *The Epitaph*, was the voice of the press. In addition to playing Claibourne, Eastham was also host/narrator of the series.

TOMORROW SHOW, THE

Talk

FIRST TELECAST: *October 15, 1973*
LAST TELECAST:
BROADCAST HISTORY:
Oct 1973–   , NBC Mon–Thu 1:00–2:00 A.M.
HOST:
Tom Snyder

For those insomniacs who were still looking for something to watch, other than old movies, in the wee small hours of the morning, NBC offered *The Tomorrow Show* four nights each week. Hosted by brash newsman Tom Snyder, the topics covered ranged from nudism (including a remote pickup at a California nudist colony), to discussions with draft dodgers living in Canada, to all aspects of changing American life-styles with a panel of psychologists. Sometimes light, but more often controversial, Tom Snyder's choreography often seemed to borrow a little from Edward R. Murrow's incisiveness and vintage Alan Burke guest-baiting. Tom could be sweet and ingenuous at one moment, and relentlessly probing in the next.

Tomorrow was originally produced in Los Angeles, where host Snyder worked as an anchorman on the local KNBC-TV news. When it first went on the air there was no studio audience present at the taping, a situation that changed within less than four months. After an audience had been added, Snyder would often invite its members to ask questions of his guests. When his news anchor duties shifted to New York, in December of 1974, *The Tomorrow Show* went with him. For the next two and one-half years, while working at WNBC-

TV, Snyder originated *Tomorrow* from New York City. In June 1977, however, Snyder and the show returned to California.

To those skeptical of the practicality of televising anything this late at night, *Tomorrow's* success was surprising. During its first two seasons it attracted an average of approximately three million viewers per night.

TOMORROW'S BOXING CHAMPIONS

see *Boxing*

TOMORROW'S CAREERS

Informational

FIRST TELECAST: *March 26, 1955*
LAST TELECAST: *May 29, 1956*
BROADCAST HISTORY:
Mar 1955–Jun 1955, ABC Sat 7:00–7:30
Sep 1955–Jan 1956, ABC Sat 10:00–10:30
Jan 1956–May 1956, ABC Tue 10:00–10:30
HOST:
Lynn Poole

Each week Mr. Poole discussed opportunities in a particular career area with experts in that field. One week, it might be jobs in the antique field; another week, jobs with airlines; a third week, opportunities in movie direction. Emphasis was placed on openings for students graduating from school and for those in their middle years seeking to change career paths. During its March through June 1955 run, the title of this program was simply *Tomorrow.*

TONI TWIN TIME

Variety

FIRST TELECAST: *April 5, 1950*
LAST TELECAST: *September 20, 1950*
BROADCAST HISTORY:
Apr 1950–Sep 1950, CBS Wed 9:00–9:30
HOST:
Jack Lemmon
Arlene Terry
Ardelle Terry
Ray Bloch Orchestra

This live variety show, hosted by young actor Jack Lemmon, alternated with *What's My Line* on Wednesday evenings during the summer of 1950. It was designed as a showcase for young talent, with Mr. Lemmon providing continuity and introductions. The "Toni Twins," Arlene and Ardelle Terry, acted as hostesses and did the commercials for the sponsor whose slogan "Which Twin Has the Toni?" made home-permanent history in the late 1940s.

TONIGHT ON BROADWAY

Interview/Play Excerpts

FIRST TELECAST: *April 20, 1948*
LAST TELECAST: *December 25, 1949*
BROADCAST HISTORY:
Apr 1948–May 1948, CBS Tue 7:00–7:30
Oct 1949–Dec 1949, CBS Sun 7:00–7:30
HOST:
John Mason Brown

Excerpts from current Broadway shows and interviews with the stars of those shows, broadcast directly from the stages of the theaters where the shows were being performed, were presented weekly on this series. It had originally begun as an experimental concept which premiered locally in New York on April 6, 1948, from the theater where *Mr. Roberts* was playing, moved to the CBS network two weeks later with *High Button Shoes,* and returned in the fall of 1949 for a three-month run. John Mason Brown, the host/interviewer/commentator of the series, was the president of the New York Drama Critics Circle.

TONIGHT SHOW, THE

Talk/Variety

FIRST TELECAST: *September 27, 1954*
LAST TELECAST:
BROADCAST HISTORY:
Sep 1954–Oct 1956, NBC Mon–Fri 11:30–1:00
Oct 1956–Jan 1957, NBC Mon–Fri 11:30–12:30
Jan 1957–Dec 1966, NBC Mon–Fri 11:15–1:00
Jan 1967– , NBC Mon–Fri 11:30–1:00

Because of the unusual nature of *The Tonight Show*—the several complete overhauls of its cast and format—each of the individual versions is treated separately below:

TONIGHT

(September 27, 1954–January 25, 1957)

HOST:
Steve Allen
Ernie Kovacs (1956–1957)
REGULARS:
Gene Rayburn
Steve Lawrence
Eydie Gorme
Andy Williams

Pat Marshall (1954–1955)
Pat Kirby (1955–1957)
Hy Averback (1955)
Skitch Henderson and His Orchestra
Peter Hanley (1956–1957)
Maureen Arthur (1956–1957)
Bill Wendell (1956–1957)
Barbara Loden (1956–1957)
LeRoy Holmes & Orchestra (1956–1957)

Tonight began in June 1953 as a local show on WNBT-TV, the NBC flagship station in New York. Steve Allen was the original host, and he remained with the show when it moved to the network fifteen months later. Under Allen, *Tonight* was very informal. He would open each evening seated at the piano, chatting and playing some of his own compositions (his most famous song, "This Could Be the Start of Something," was often heard). He then went to his desk, where he talked about anything that seemed to interest him. There were guest stars, in addition to his semi-regulars—only announcer Gene Rayburn and orchestra leader Skitch Henderson were on every night—but the emphasis was on Steve and his comedic ad-libbing. He would go into the audience, work up improptu sketches with other members of the cast, and do remotes outside the studio. Many of the remotes were comic man-in-the-street routines, but perhaps the most famous incident occurred when *Tonight* was doing some telecasts from Miami. Allen somehow talked the U.S. Marines into staging a nighttime landing on Miami Beach, for the benefit of his cameras—panicking tourists in nearby hotels, who thought an invasion was underway. In addition to the special features, there was a regular news summary given at about 12:30 A.M. by Gene Rayburn. The entire show was done live.

When Allen's prime time series premiered in the summer of 1956, he cut back his *Tonight* appearances to Wednesday through Friday. A series of guest hosts filled in on Mondays and Tuesdays until October 1st, when Ernie Kovacs took over as permanent Monday–Tuesday host. Kovacs had his own complete cast: Bill Wendell as announcer, and Peter Hanley, Maureen Arthur and Barbara Loden as regulars. Ernie's format was very similar to that of his various prime time shows, with most of the same characters, as well as blackouts, satires, and slapstick humor.

TONIGHT! AMERICA AFTER DARK

(January 28, 1957–July 26, 1957)

HOST:

Jack Lescoulie (Jan–Jun)
Al "Jazzbo" Collins (Jun–Jul)

REGULARS:

Judy Johnson (Mar–Jul)
Lou Stein Trio (Jan–Mar)
Mort Lindsay Quartet (Mar–Jun)
Johnny Guarnieri Quartet (Jun–Jul)
Hy Gardner
Bob Considine
Earl Wilson (Jan–Jun)
Irv Kupcinet
Vernon Scott (Jan–Feb)
Paul Coates
Lee Giroux (Mar–Jun)

When Steve Allen left in January 1957, *Tonight* was replaced by a totally different type of program. It became much more like the early-morning *Today Show*, with an emphasis on news items. Its original host was *Today* veteran Jack Lescoulie. There were reports by contributing columnists in New York, Chicago and Los Angeles, with live coverage from all three cities and elsewhere via remotes. Interviews with personalities in the news, in politics, or in show business were interspersed with live visits to night clubs, Broadway openings, or such places as research hospitals and planetariums. Regular features were Bob Considine's summary of the news of the day, "The World Tonight;" a Hy Gardner interview segment, "Face to Face;" news of the entertainment world on "Hy Gardner Time;" and news commentary, human interest stories, and interviews on "Considine's Corner."

JACK PAAR SHOW, THE

(July 29, 1957–March 30, 1962)

HOST:

Jack Paar

REGULARS:

Hugh Downs
Jose Melis & Orchestra
Tedi Thurman (1957)
Dodi Goodman (1957–1958)

SEMI-REGULARS:

Elsa Maxwell (1957–1958)
Bil Baird Puppets (1957–1958)
Betty Johnson (1957–1958)

Genevieve (1958–1962)
Cliff Arquette as
Charley Weaver (1958–1962)
Pat Harrington, Jr. as
Guido Panzini (1959–1962)
Hans Conried (1959–1962)
Peggy Cass (1958–1962)
Alexander King (1958–1962)
Joey Bishop (1958–1962)
Hermione Gingold (1958–1962)
Florence Henderson (1958–1962)
Buddy Hackett (1958–1962)
Renee Taylor (1959–1962)
Betty White (1959–1962)

Tonight! America after Dark was not successful with viewers or critics, so it was decided to return to a format closer to the original. The new host, a young comic named Jack Paar, was raided from CBS, where he had hosted several game and talk shows. Paar took over *The Tonight Show* six months after Steve Allen had left. Whereas Allen had depended on a frenetic pace and sketch comedy, Paar was at his best interviewing. He was incisive, witty and highly emotional. He could easily get emotionally involved with his guests and their stories, and was not above crying on the air when he was moved. There were still sketches, and Paar would sometimes go into the audience for interviews. "It's All Relative" was a periodic spot in which a relative of a famous person would appear and the other guests would try to figure out who he was related to; "What Is It?" was a feature in which Paar would produce some strange looking object and then explain what it was used for; there was a routine where baby pictures were shown to the audience and Paar would come up with funny captions for them; and Jose Melis had a "telephone game" in which he improvised melodies based on the last four digits of an audience member's telephone number.

Besides the fun and games, the show had a serious side. At one point Paar went on an extended crusade against the Batista dictatorship in Cuba, lauding Castro's revolution; later he tried to arrange a swap of tractors for prisoners from the Bay of Pigs invasion; several telecasts originated from the Berlin Wall; and presidential candidates Kennedy and Nixon were both guests, on separate occasions.

Paar's emotional outbursts were a major attraction of the show, and the cause of many of the controversies surrounding him. When he had first taken over as host, *The Tonight Show* was still being done live. Not too long after, it began taping early in the evening that it would be aired. It was NBC's ability to edit the tapes before air time that precipitated Paar's famous tearful walkout on the February 11, 1960, program. A "water closet" joke he had told the night before was considered in bad taste by the NBC censors and had been removed. Paar didn't think the joke was offensive and he left the show for a month. He later had a feud with Ed Sullivan over the fees paid guest stars—Paar's $320 versus Sullivan's several thousand—and eventually feuded with several newspaper columnists, notably Dorothy Kilgallen. Video tape did have its advantages, however, as it enabled Paar to cut down to a four day week. Starting July 10, 1959, the Friday show was retitled *The Best of Paar* and was composed of excerpts from previous shows.

TONIGHT SHOW, THE

(April 2, 1962–September 28, 1962)

ANNOUNCERS:

Hugh Downs
Jack Haskell
Ed Herlihy

ORCHESTRA:

Skitch Henderson

After Jack Paar's departure from the series in March 1962, *The Tonight Show* aired with a succession of substitute hosts, while awaiting the arrival of Johnny Carson (who had to wait out an ABC contract). Hosts during this period were Art Linkletter, Joey Bishop, Bob Cummings, Merv Griffin, Jack Carter, Jan Murray, Peter Lind Hayes and Mary Healy, Soupy Sales, Mort Sahl, Steve Lawrence, Jerry Lewis, Jimmy Dean, Arlene Francis, Jack E. Leonard, Hugh Downs, Groucho Marx, Hal March, and Donald O'Connor. The format was unchanged.

TONIGHT SHOW STARRING JOHNNY CARSON, THE

(October 2, 1962–

HOST:

Johnny Carson

REGULARS:

Ed McMahon

Skitch Henderson (1962–1966)
Milton Delugg (1966–1967)
Doc Severinson (1967–)
Tommy Newsom (1968–)

THEME:

"Johnny's Theme," by Paul Anka and Johnny Carson

The contrast between Jack Paar and Johnny Carson was marked. As emotional and likely to blow up as Paar was, that is how calm and unflappable Carson was. Like Paar, Carson had been spirited away from another network, in fact he had previously had shows on both CBS and ABC. His biggest asset, other than his durability, was probably his knack for salvaging disasters with a perfect reaction take (a comic expression of resignation whenever something would not work). Carson opened each show with a monologue and then spent most of the remainder of the evening chatting with guests. Unlike Paar, Carson tended to avoid anything controversial and was usually content to keep his audience amused. Features that were used on his show with varying frequency included "Stump the Band," in which members of the studio audience would ask the band to try to play obscure songs by giving them only the titles; the "Art Fern Tea Time Movie" routine with Carol Wayne as the "Matinee Lady;" sketches with the "Mighty Carson Art Players" spoofing movies, TV shows or events in the news; "Carnac the Magnificent," with Carson as an inept magician; "Carswell" with Carson as a psychic predicting the future; and the one holdover from Paar, periodic displays of strange looking contraptions with even stranger functions.

Perhaps the most celebrated telecast, and certainly the one with the most enormous audience, was that of December 17, 1969, on which Tiny Tim married Miss Vicki. Other highlights were seen on annual anniversary shows, in which Carson reprised often embarrassing moments from past years.

When Carson started, the show was originating from New York and was taped on the same evening that it aired. Johnny was on all five nights and began his monologue when the show began, at 11:15 P.M. In February 1965 he refused to do the 11:15–11:30 P.M. segment any longer, leaving that to Ed McMahon and Skitch Henderson. Many local stations carried local news until 11:30 P.M., preempting the first fifteen minutes of *The Tonight Show*, and Carson wanted to save his monologue until the full network was in place. Two years later, on January 2, 1967, this first fifteen minutes was dropped altogether. A few months later, in March 1967, Carson fought another skirmish with NBC, this time over money. This led to his walkout, which lasted for several weeks until he was finally lured back with a contract reported to provide more than $1 million per year.

In May 1972 *The Tonight Show* moved permanently from New York to Burbank (previously periodic telecasts were done from the West Coast), and for a time after that taping was done a day before the show aired. Because so much immediacy was lost, *Tonight* returned to same-night taping in May 1974. Carson also started cutting back on his appearances at about this time. After July 1971 he was no longer seen on Mondays. Then in March 1978 he obtained a highly publicized new $3 million per year contract which required him to work only three nights per week—the same as Steve Allen had in 1956 (although Allen also had a prime time show). Carson's irregular appearances opened the way for a large number of substitute hosts, some of whom have become almost as familiar to viewers as Johnny himself. Seen most often over the last 16 years has been Joey Bishop (177 appearances as guest host), followed by Bob Newhart (78), John Davidson (74), McLean Stevenson (58), Jerry Lewis (52), Joan Rivers (41), David Brenner (39), and Don Rickles (38).

For more than a decade, from January 1965 until September 1975, taped repeats of *The Tonight Show* were offered to NBC stations for airing after the 11:00 P.M. news on Saturday or Sunday.

TONY BENNETT SHOW, THE

Musical Variety

FIRST TELECAST: *August 11, 1956*

LAST TELECAST: *September 8, 1956*

BROADCAST HISTORY:

Aug 1956–Sep 1956, NBC Sat 8:00–9:00

REGULARS:

Tony Bennett
The Frank Lewis Dancers
The Spellbinders
The Carl Hoff Orchestra

The Tony Bennett Show was one of three musical variety shows that served as 1956 summer replacement for *The Perry Como Show*. All three of them featured the Frank Lewis Dancers and the singing of the Spellbinders. The only difference between them was their star and host. Patti Page starred for the first month of the summer, and was followed by Julius La Rosa, who in turn was followed by Tony Bennett.

TONY MARTIN SHOW, THE

Music

FIRST TELECAST: *April 26, 1954*
LAST TELECAST: *February 27, 1956*
BROADCAST HISTORY:

Apr 1954–Jun 1955, NBC Mon 7:30–7:45
Sep 1955–Feb 1956, NBC Mon 7:30–7:45

REGULARS:

Tony Martin
The Interludes

Singer Tony Martin starred in this live music series that filled the remainder of the half-hour in which NBC aired its network news program. Backing up Mr. Martin was a mixed vocal group, the Interludes. The show originated from Hollywood and Mr. Martin had occasional guest stars who either performed or chatted with him or both.

TONY ORLANDO AND DAWN

Musical Variety

FIRST TELECAST: *July 3, 1974*
LAST TELECAST: *December 28, 1976*
BROADCAST HISTORY:

Jul 1974, CBS Wed 8:00–9:00
Dec 1974–Jun 1976, CBS Wed 8:00–9:00
Sep 1976–Dec 1976, CBS Tue 8:00–9:00

REGULARS:

Tony Orlando
Telma Hopkins
Joyce Vincent Wilson
George Carlin (1976)
Nancy Steen (1976)
Bob Holt (1976)
Susan Lanier (1976)
Jimmy Martinez (1976)
Edie McClurg (1976)

After a number of hit records, most notably "Tie a Yellow Ribbon 'Round the Old Oak Tree," the singing group Tony Orlando and Dawn (Telma Hopkins and Joyce Vincent Wilson) was given a summer variety hour on CBS in the time slot that had been vacated by Sonny and Cher. The emphasis was on music, with guest stars joining the trio in song and comedy skits. A summer hit, it returned in December and had a very successful first year, but started to slip in the second. When it moved to Tuesday nights in the fall of 1976, there were a number of changes, including the title, which became *The Tony Orlando and Dawn Rainbow Hour*. Comedian George Carlin was added as a regular with a weekly comedy monologue, and a group of comics was also added to participate in sketches. Emphasis was shifted from music to comedy, but the series failed to last past the end of the year.

TONY RANDALL SHOW, THE

Situation Comedy

FIRST TELECAST: *September 23, 1976*
LAST TELECAST: *March 25, 1978*
BROADCAST HISTORY:

Sep 1976–Dec 1976, ABC Thu 9:00–9:30
Dec 1976–Mar 1977, ABC Thu 9:30–10:00
Sep 1977–Jan 1978, CBS Sat 9:30–10:00
Jan 1978–Mar 1978, CBS Sat 8:30–9:00

CAST:

Judge Walter Franklin .... Tony Randall
Jack Terwilliger .... Barney Martin
Miss Reubner .... Allyn Ann McLerie
Roberta "Bobby" Franklin (1976–1977) .... Devon Scott
Roberta "Bobby" Franklin (1977–1978) .... Penny Peyser
Oliver Wendell Franklin ...... Brad Savage
Mrs. Bonnie McClellan .... Rachael Roberts
Mario Lanzo .... Zane Lasky
Judge Eleanor Hooper ...... Diana Muldaur
Wyatt Franklin (1977–1978) .... Hans Conried

This comedy concerned the courtroom and home life of a middle-aged Philadelphia judge. Court of Common Pleas Judge Walter Franklin was serious about his work, sometimes a bit stuffy, but kind at heart and always had a twinkle in his eye. After two years as a widower Walter was ready for a little romance, and his attempts to both keep his dignity and charm his dates provided much of the humor. Walter played the field, although Judge Eleanor Hooper was a recurring love interest.

Jack Terwilliger was Walter's longtime, ultra-accurate court reporter, Miss Reubner the sharp-tongued, motherly secretary, Mario Lanzo the obnoxiously ingratiating assistant to the assistant District Attorney, and Mrs. McClellan the nutty housekeeper. Walter's family consisted of 18-year-old daughter Bobby, who was very much involved with current issues, and precocious 11-year-old son Oliver. Wyatt Franklin was Walter's liberal-minded father, who considered his son something of a stuffed shirt.

TOO YOUNG TO GO STEADY

Situation Comedy

FIRST TELECAST: *May 14, 1959*

LAST TELECAST: *June 25, 1959*

BROADCAST HISTORY:

May 1959–Jun 1959, NBC Thu 8:30–9:00

CAST:

Mary Blake .... Joan Bennett
Tom Blake .... Donald Cook
Pam Blake .... Brigid Bazlen
Johnny Blake .... Martin Huston
Timmy .... Lorna Gillam

The problems of teenagers Pam and Johnny Blake were the focal points of this live series that aired in the spring of 1959. Pam was a 14-year-old trying to make the transition from tomboy to young lady. Her older brother Johnny got into almost as much trouble trying to help her as he did with his own life. Pam and her girl friend Timmy were at that stage when love—or was it infatuation?—was the most important thing in their lives. Pam and Johnny's father, attorney Tom Blake, and their mother, Mary, kept a watchful eye on the activities of the kids and were generally understanding and interested in their happiness.

TOP CAT

Cartoon

FIRST TELECAST: *September 27, 1961*

LAST TELECAST: *September 26, 1962*

BROADCAST HISTORY:

Sep 1961–Sep 1962, ABC Wed 8:30–9:00

VOICES:

Top Cat .... Arnold Stang
Benny the Ball .... Maurice Gosfield
Choo Choo .... Marvin Kaplan
Spook/The Brain .... Leo DeLyon
Fancy-Fancy .... John Stephenson
Officer Dibble .... Allen Jenkins

Top Cat was the sophisticated, opportunistic leader of a pack of Broadway alley cats. Their homes were well-equipped ash cans, they made all their phone calls from the police phone on a nearby pole, got their milk and newspapers from nearby doorsteps, and ate scraps from the neighborhood delicatessen. Their only problem was Officer Dibble, the cop on the local beat. He did his best to control them but seldom succeeded.

TOP DOLLAR

Quiz/Audience Participation

FIRST TELECAST: *March 29, 1958*

LAST TELECAST: *August 30, 1958*

BROADCAST HISTORY:

Mar 1958–Aug 1958, CBS Sat 8:30–9:00

EMCEE:

Toby Reed

WORD AUTHORITY:

Dr. Bergen Evans

Three contestants participated in each round of this word-spelling game that was a variation on the old party game "ghost." The object of the game was to keep adding letters to a potential word without completing it. Each letter, after the first three, was worth $100 to the winner, and after the first person was eliminated by making a word the two remaining contestants competed to determine the winner. As long as a contestant remained undefeated, he could continue to play. Dr. Bergen Evans was the final authority on whether or not a word had been made. An added attraction for home viewers was the announcement at the end of each telecast of the serial number of a dollar bill that, if presented to the show's producers, was worth $5,000 to the bearer. The serial number was determined by the regular game. The first eight letters of the "top dollar" word of the night (the longest one created by the contestants on the show) were matched to a telephone dial and converted to the digits of the jackpot serial number for the week.

TOP PLAYS OF 1954

Dramatic Anthology

FIRST TELECAST: *June 1, 1954*

LAST TELECAST: *August 24, 1954*

BROADCAST HISTORY:

Jun 1954–Aug 1954, NBC Tue 9:30–10:00

This filmed anthology series was the 1954 summer replacement for *Armstrong Circle Theatre*. The plays which aired under this title were all reruns of episodes of *Ford*

Theatre that had been telecast during the first half of 1954.

TOP PRO GOLF

Sports

FIRST TELECAST: *April 6, 1959*

LAST TELECAST: *September 28, 1959*

BROADCAST HISTORY:

Apr 1959–Sep 1959, ABC Mon 9:30–10:30

COMMENTATOR:

Dick Danehe

Each week two professional golfers competed in an 18-hole match. The winner won $1,500 and the right to return the following week to defend his championship, while the loser took home $500. Filmed on location at various golf courses in Florida and Georgia, *Top Pro Golf* showed only the highlights of the round, avoiding coverage of holes that did not bear significantly on the outcome of the match. The big winner on this series was veteran Sam Snead. He had appeared early in the show's run and lost, but when he got another shot early in August he really took advantage of it. He won the last eight matches on this series.

TOP TEN LUCY SHOWS, THE

see *I Love Lucy*

TOPPER

Situation Comedy

FIRST TELECAST: *October 9, 1953*

LAST TELECAST: *October 14, 1956*

BROADCAST HISTORY:

Oct 1953–Sep 1955, CBS Fri 8:30–9:00
Oct 1955–Mar 1956, ABC Mon 7:30–8:00
Jun 1956–Oct 1956, NBC Sun 7:00–7:30

CAST:

Marion Kerby .... Anne Jeffreys
George Kerby .... Robert Sterling
Cosmo Topper .... Leo G. Carroll
Henrietta Topper .... Lee Patrick
Katie, the maid (1953–1954)
.... Kathleen Freeman
Mr. Schuyler .... Thurston Hall
Maggie, the cook (1954–1955)
.... Edna Skinner

On a skiing vacation in Europe, George and Marion Kerby were trapped in an avalanche along with their would-be rescuer, a St. Bernard named Neil. All three of them died—only to return to the United States to haunt their former home, now occupied by banker Cosmo Topper. George and Marion developed quite an affection for the very proper Mr. Topper, but felt that he needed to be a little less stuffy. They did everything in their powers, and those powers were considerable, to help Cosmo loosen up. Between their antics and the wanderings of the ghostly Neil, who had a penchant for oversized, brim-full brandy snifters, life in the Topper household was kept very chaotic.

After two seasons on CBS, this series was canceled, only to show up in reruns for a full season on ABC and a summer on NBC. *Topper* was based on characters created by novelist Thorne Smith. These characters were also seen later in a series of movies.

TOUCH OF GRACE, A

Situation Comedy

FIRST TELECAST: *January 20, 1973*

LAST TELECAST: *June 16, 1973*

BROADCAST HISTORY:

Jan 1973–Jun 1973, ABC Sat 8:30–9:00

CAST:

Grace Simpson .... Shirley Booth
Herbert Morrison .... J. Patrick O'Malley
Walter Bradley .... Warren Berlinger
Myra Bradley .... Marian Mercer

Oscar, Emmy, and Tony winner Shirley Booth starred in this comedy as a recently widowed, 60-ish woman who moved in with her daughter and son-in-law. There the battle of the generations began—between Grace, a perky youngster at heart, and the young couple, a pair of conservative "squares," older than their years. Grace did a lot of dating, but her steady boy friend was Herbert, a gravedigger. In the final telecast, he proposed and Grace accepted.

Based on the British TV series *For the Love of Ada.*

TRACKDOWN

Western

FIRST TELECAST: *October 4, 1957*

LAST TELECAST: *September 23, 1959*

BROADCAST HISTORY:

Oct 1957–Jan 1959, CBS Fri 8:00–8:30
Feb 1959–Sep 1959, CBS Wed 8:30–9:00

CAST:

Hoby Gilman .... Robert Culp

Set in the Southwest during the 1870s, *Trackdown* detailed the adventures of a mythical Texas Ranger, Hoby Gilman. Many of the stories told in the series were adapted from cases in the files of the Texas Rangers and it was for that reason that the show had the official approval of the State of Texas and the Rangers. That was a distinction that could be claimed by no other Western on the air.

TRAFFIC COURT

Courtroom Drama

FIRST TELECAST: *June 18, 1958*

LAST TELECAST: *March 30, 1959*

BROADCAST HISTORY:

Jun 1958–Jul 1958, ABC Wed 9:30–10:00
Jul 1958–Oct 1958, ABC Sun 9:00–9:30
Oct 1958–Nov 1958, ABC Thu 10:00–10:30
Nov 1958, ABC Mon 10:00–10:30
Mar 1959, ABC Mon 10:00–10:30

REGULAR:

Edgar Allan Jones, Jr.

This filmed series had a regular run during the summer of 1958, and was then used to fill numerous holes in the ABC schedule during the 1958–1959 season. It presented reenactments of actual traffic-court trials and arraignments. The judge was Edgar Allan Jones, Jr., who in real life was Assistant Dean of the U.C.L.A. Law School.

TRAP, THE

Dramatic Anthology

FIRST TELECAST: *April 29, 1950*

LAST TELECAST: *June 24, 1950*

BROADCAST HISTORY:

Apr 1950–Jun 1950, CBS Sat 9:00–10:00

NARRATOR:

Joseph DeSantis

The melodramas that were presented in this live anthology series were all concerned with people who had gotten themselves into situations over which they no longer had control. Fate would be the determinant of their future, of whether or not they survived the perilous predicament into which they had gotten themselves "trapped."

TRASH OR TREASURE

see *What's It Worth?*

TRAVEL CORNER

Documentary

FIRST TELECAST: *December 28, 1953*

LAST TELECAST: *September 4, 1954*

BROADCAST HISTORY:

Dec 1953–May 1954, ABC Mon 9:30–10:00
Jun 1954–Sep 1954, ABC Sat 10:00–10:30

Travel films.

TRAVELS OF JAIMIE McPHEETERS, THE

Western

FIRST TELECAST: *September 15, 1963*

LAST TELECAST: *March 15, 1964*

BROADCAST HISTORY:

Sep 1963–Mar 1964, ABC Sun 7:30–8:30

CAST:

"Doc" Sardius McPheeters .... Dan O'Herlihy
Jaimie McPheeters .... Kurt Russell
John Murrel .... James Westerfield
Shep Baggott .... Sandy Kenyon
Jenny .... Donna Anderson
Matt Kissel .... Mark Allen
Mrs. Kissel .... Meg Wyllie
Kissel Brothers .... Osmond Brothers
Henry T. Coe .... Hedley Mattingly
Othello .... Vernett Allen III
Buck Coulter (1963) .... Michael Witney
Linc Murdock .... Charles Bronson

This adventure series followed a young boy on a westward-bound wagon train in 1849. Twelve-year-old Jaimie was surrounded by a colorful cast of characters, not the least of whom was his stovepipe-hatted father, an irresponsible scalawag M.D. (they had sneaked out of Paducah, Kentucky, just ahead of their creditors to join the wagon train). Traveling with the McPheeterses in the train was 17-year-old Jenny, a rather sexy orphan, the God-fearin' Kissel family (whose children, Micah, Leviticus, Deuteronomy, and Lamentations, were portrayed by the Osmond Brothers), and blue-blooded Henry T. Coe and his valet, Othello. Continual danger was posed by the Bible-quoting but cunning thief Murrel, and his shady partner, Baggott.

Adventure followed as the wagons made their way north to St. Louis, west across the North Platte River to Ft. Bridger, down to Salt Lake City, across the Humboldt Sink and the Sierra Nevada to the Feather River and finally the gold fields of California! Wagonmaster Buck Coulter lasted only a few weeks, until he was trampled to death in the process of saving Jaimie's life. Linc Murdock, a powerful but troubled man, then became the wagonmaster for the remainder of the show's single-season journey.

Based on Robert Lewis Taylor's 1958 Pulitzer Prize–winning novel of the same name.

TREASURE HUNT

see *What's It Worth?*

TREASURE HUNT

Quiz/Audience Participation

FIRST TELECAST: *September 7, 1956*

LAST TELECAST: *June 17, 1958*

BROADCAST HISTORY:

Sep 1956–May 1957, ABC Fri 9:00–9:30

Dec 1957–Jun 1958, NBC Tue 7:30–8:00

EMCEE:

Jan Murray

ASSISTANT:

Marian Stafford (1956–1957, 1958)

Greta Thyssen (1957–1958)

Contestants on *Treasure Hunt*, usually one man and one woman, were asked a series of questions on a designated topic and got $50 for each correct answer. When one of the contestants had defeated the other in the quiz portion of the program, he won the opportunity to go on a "treasure hunt." There were a number of treasure chests on the stage and the winning contestant got to pick one. Whatever was in the chest went to the contestant. The prizes in the chests were not all winners. Everything from a head of cabbage to a check for a large sum of money was contained in various chests. The jackpot check in the ABC version was a flat $25,000. When NBC picked up *Treasure Hunt* for a nighttime version (NBC had begun airing it as a daytime show in August 1957) the jackpot check was a basic $10,000 plus $1,000 for each week that it was not discovered.

Jan Murray's sexy assistant, clad in a scanty pirate costume, was referred to on the show as the Pirate Girl. Marian Stafford was the Pirate Girl when the series was on ABC. Greta Thyssen was the first NBC nighttime pirate girl. When she left the show in January 1958, Marian, who had replaced Pat White in the daytime version in December, returned to the nighttime version as well.

TREASURE QUEST

Quiz/Audience Participation

FIRST TELECAST: *April 24, 1949*

LAST TELECAST: *September 2, 1949*

BROADCAST HISTORY:

Apr 1949–Jun 1949, ABC Sun 9:30–10:00

Jun 1949–Sep 1949, ABC Fri 8:30–9:00

HOST:

John Weigel

Quiz show in which contestants were required to identify various locations, from visual and verbal clues, with an expense-paid trip as prize. From Chicago.

Known during its first two weeks as *Bon Voyage*.

TREASURY MEN IN ACTION

Crime Drama

FIRST TELECAST: *September 11, 1950*

LAST TELECAST: *September 30, 1955*

BROADCAST HISTORY:

Sep 1950–Dec 1950, ABC Mon 8:00–8:30

Apr 1951–Apr 1954, NBC Thu 8:30–9:00 (OS)

Oct 1954–Jun 1955, ABC Thu 8:30–9:00

Jun 1955–Sep 1955, ABC Fri 8:30–9:00

CAST:

The Chief .... Walter Greaza

Action dramas based on actual cases from the files of the U.S. Treasury Department and telecast live. Walter Greaza portrayed the chief of whatever division was involved in each week's case, running to earth such assorted scoundrels as smugglers, counterfeiters, gunrunners, tax evaders (a favorite!), and moonshiners. The program invariably ended with the moral that the government always wins, and thereby received several awards and commendations from official agencies for its public service. Actual government officials sometimes appeared on the show.

The supporting cast varied from week to week, but over the years included such names as Lee Marvin, Grace Kelly, Jason Robards, Jr., James Dean, Cliff Robertson, Jack Klugman, and Charles Bronson.

TRIALS OF O'BRIEN, THE

Lawyer

FIRST TELECAST: *September 18, 1965*

LAST TELECAST: *May 6, 1966*

BROADCAST HISTORY:

Sep 1965–Nov 1965, CBS Sat 8:30–9:30

Dec 1965–May 1966, CBS Fri 10:00–11:00

CAST:

Daniel J. O'Brien .... Peter Falk

Katie .... Joanna Barnes

The Great McGonigle .... David Burns

Miss G. .... Elaine Stritch
Margaret .... Ilka Chase

The Trials of O'Brien were not confined to those that took place in the court of law. Daniel J. O'Brien was a very talented—and expensive—New York attorney whose personal life was almost more trying than his professional life. He was behind in the rent on his luxurious penthouse apartment, behind in alimony payments to his beautiful ex-wife Katie, and was one of the most unsuccessful gamblers in the city. Somehow, no matter how fast the money came in, it went out just a little bit faster. His secretary, Miss G., tried to help him maintain a better financial equilibrium, but it never quite worked out. The cases in this series were treated seriously, but O'Brien's personal problems were not. In certain ways, Peter Falk's characterization of O'Brien had parallels with his much more successful portrayal of Columbo in the 1970s. Both were extremely good at their jobs but rather sloppy and disorganized when it came to their personal lives.

TROUBLE WITH FATHER

syndicated title for *Stu Erwin Show, The*

TROUBLESHOOTERS

Adventure

FIRST TELECAST: *September 11, 1959*
LAST TELECAST: *June 17, 1960*
BROADCAST HISTORY:
Sep 1959–Jun 1960, NBC Fri 8:00–8:30
CAST:
Kodiak .... Keenan Wynn
Frank Dugan .... Bob Mathias

The number one troubleshooter of the Stenrud Corporation, a large heavy construction firm specializing in both domestic and foreign building projects, was a grizzled old veteran named Kodiak. He had held that post for five years, during which time he had coped with the problems involved in building highways, dams, airfields, skyscrapers, and atomic installations all over the world. The pace had started to become too much for him to take, and he was in the slow process of training his assistant, Frank Dugan, to take over. Frank was all the things that Kodiak was not—well educated, socially polished, soft-spoken, and innocent of the evil ways of the world. As the two of them traveled from assignment to assignment they learned from each other and acquired qualities that would stand them in good stead in the future. Kodiak became somewhat less gruff and uncivilized and Frank became stronger and more assertive.

TRUE

syndicated title for *General Electric True Theater*

TRUTH OR CONSEQUENCES

Quiz/Audience Participation

FIRST TELECAST: *September 7, 1950*
LAST TELECAST: *June 6, 1958*
BROADCAST HISTORY:
Sep 1950–May 1951, CBS Thu 10:00–10:30
May 1954–Sep 1955, NBC Tue 10:00–10:30
Sep 1955–Sep 1956, NBC Fri 8:00–8:30
Dec 1957–Jun 1958, NBC Fri 7:30–8:00
EMCEE:
Ralph Edwards (1950–1951)
Jack Bailey (1954–1956)
Steve Dunne (1957–1958)

Truth or Consequences had originally aired in 1940 as an NBC radio program with its creator, Ralph Edwards, as the emcee. A decade later it moved to television, on CBS, with its format and emcee unchanged. Contestants on the show were asked silly trick questions which they almost invariably failed to answer correctly. If they answered incorrectly, or failed to come up with any answer in a short time, Beulah the Buzzer went off. The emcee then told them that since they had failed to tell the truth, they would have to pay the consequences. Consequences consisted of elaborate stunts, some done in the studio and others done outside, some completed on that week's episode and others taking a week or more and requiring the contestant to return when the stunt was completed. Some of the stunts were funny, but more often they were also embarrassing, and occasionally they were sentimental (as when long-separated relatives were reunited within the context of the stunt).

The original TV version of this series, with Edwards as host, lasted only a single season. When it returned three years later on NBC, Jack Bailey was the emcee, later replaced by Steve Dunne. NBC aired a daytime version of the show from 1956 until 1965, and a syndicated version has been available since then.

TRY AND DO IT

Variety/Audience Participation

FIRST TELECAST: *July 4, 1948*

LAST TELECAST: *September 5, 1948*

BROADCAST HISTORY:

Jul 1948–Sep 1948, NBC Sun 8:30–9:00

HOST:

Jack Bright

REGULAR:

Thomas Leander Jones' Brass Band

Audience-participation show in which people from the studio audience performed various stunts—whistling through a mouthful of crackers, lacing up a right shoe on the left foot, etc. The program was set in a picnic ground, with Thomas Leander Jones' band providing schmaltzy music from an old-fashioned bandstand.

TURN OF FATE, A

see *Alcoa Theatre* and *Goodyear TV Playhouse*

TURNING POINT

Dramatic Anthology

FIRST TELECAST: *April 12, 1958*

LAST TELECAST: *October 4, 1958*

BROADCAST HISTORY:

Apr 1958–Oct 1958, NBC Sat 9:30–10:00

This was a collection of filmed reruns from other anthology series, with the addition of two unsold pilots for projected (but never scheduled) dramatic series.

TURNING POINT, THE

see *ABC Dramatic Shorts—1952–1953*

TURN-ON

Comedy Variety

FIRST TELECAST: *February 5, 1969*

LAST TELECAST: *February 5, 1969*

BROADCAST HISTORY:

Feb 1969, ABC Wed 8:30–9:00

REPERTORY COMPANY:

Bonnie Boland
Teresa Graves
Maura McGiveney
Cecile Ozorio
Mel Stuart
Alma Murphy
Hamilton Camp
Maxine Greene
Carlos Manteca
Chuck McCann
Bob Staats
Ken Greenwald

Turn-On is remembered as one of the most famous one-telecast fiascos in the history of television. It was publicized as the second coming of *Laugh-In*, and even had the same executive producer, George Schlatter. According to the producer, Digby Wolfe, it was to be "a visual, comedic, sensory assault involving . . . animation, videotape, stop-action film, electronic distortion, computer graphics—even people." The "star" of the show was a mock-up computer. Despite the ballyhoo, what it turned out to be was an exercise in extremely bad taste. When the show's rampant sexual double-entendres and complete depersonalization led many ABC affiliates to refuse to carry it after the first telecast, and Bristol-Myers dropped sponsorship, it was canceled.

Guest star on the first, and only, telecast was Tim Conway.

TWELVE O'CLOCK HIGH

War Drama

FIRST TELECAST: *September 18, 1964*

LAST TELECAST: *January 13, 1967*

BROADCAST HISTORY:

Sep 1964–Jan 1965, ABC Fri 9:30–10:30
Jan 1965–Sep 1965, ABC Fri 10:00–11:00
Sep 1965–Sep 1966, ABC Mon 7:30–8:30
Sep 1966–Jan 1967, ABC Fri 10:00–11:00

CAST:

Brigadier General Frank Savage (1964–1965) .... Robert Lansing
Major General Wiley Crowe (1964–1965) .... John Larkin
Major Harvey Stovall ....Frank Overton
Major Joe Cobb (1964–1965) .....Lew Gallo
Major ("Doc") Kaiser ...... Barney Phillips
Captain/Major/Colonel Joe Gallagher .... Paul Burke
Tech. Sgt. Sandy Komansky (1965–1967) .... Chris Robertson
Brigadier General Ed Britt (1965–1967) .... Andrew Duggan

EXECUTIVE PRODUCER:

Quinn Martin

This was one wartime action-adventure series in which the top brass did not stay behind the lines. It was the story of the 918th Bombardment Group of the U.S. Eighth Air Force, stationed near London during World War II. During the first season the stories centered on Brigadier General Frank Savage, as he personally led his pilots through bombing raids and narrow escapes over enemy territory. Major General Crowe was his boss, and Major Harvey Stovall his adjutant on the ground.

The action was hot and heavy, and at the start of the second season it got a little too hot for General Savage, who was killed during a mission. Colonel Joe Gallagher then assumed command, and the lead in the series for the rest of its run. (Gallagher zoomed in rank from captain to colonel during the series' run, despite getting off to a bad start in the premiere telecast. He guest-starred then as a brash young man who felt that he deserved special treatment from Savage because his father was a three-star general.) Brigadier General Britt became the new superior officer in the second season, while Tech. Sgt. Komansky was Gallagher's gunner and flight engineer.

Based on the novel by Beirne Lay, Jr., and Sy Bartlett, which was also made into a movie starring Gregory Peck (1949).

20TH CENTURY, THE

Documentary

FIRST TELECAST: *October 20, 1957*
LAST TELECAST: *January 4, 1970*
BROADCAST HISTORY:

Oct 1957–May 1958, CBS Sun 6:30–7:00
Sep 1958–Aug 1961, CBS Sun 6:30–7:00
Sep 1961–Aug 1966, CBS Sun 6:00–6:30
Jan 1967–Oct 1967, CBS Sun 6:00–6:30
Jan 1968–Oct 1968, CBS Sun 6:00–6:30
Jan 1969–Sep 1969, CBS Sun 6:00–6:30
Jan 1970, CBS Sun 6:00–6:30

NARRATOR:

Walter Cronkite

CBS News correspondent Walter Cronkite was the narrator and host of this series throughout its run. The objective of *The 20th Century* was to present filmed reports of the major events, movements, and personalities that had shaped modern world history. The subject matter ranged from politics and war to medicine and the arts. When the series returned to the air to start its tenth season in January 1967, the title and format were altered. Under the new title, *The 21st Century*, the subjects covered looked to the future, rather than the past. Advances that were taking place or were anticipated in medicine, transportation, space exploration, communications, the arts, and living conditions in general were all explored in depth.

20TH CENTURY FOX HOUR, THE

Dramatic Anthology

FIRST TELECAST: *October 5, 1955*
LAST TELECAST: *September 18, 1957*
BROADCAST HISTORY:

Oct 1955–Sep 1957, CBS Wed 10:00–11:00

HOST:

Joseph Cotten (1955–1956)
Robert Sterling (1956–1957)

The filmed dramas that were presented in this series were produced by 20th Century Fox in Hollywood. Many of them were short adaptations of films that had been released by Fox over its long history, but generally featured newer, lesser-known actors and actresses (few big-name movie stars appeared in this series). Among the adaptations presented were "The Ox-Bow Incident," "Junior Miss," "The Late George Apley," and "Miracle on 34th Street." *The 20th Century Fox Hour* aired on alternate weeks with *The U.S. Steel Hour*.

TWENTIETH CENTURY TALES

see *ABC Dramatic Shorts—1952–1953*

21ST CENTURY, THE

see *20th Century, The*

TWENTY-ONE

Quiz/Audience Participation

FIRST TELECAST: *September 12, 1956*
LAST TELECAST: *October 16, 1958*
BROADCAST HISTORY:

Sep 1956–Jan 1957, NBC Wed 10:30–11:00
Jan 1957–Sep 1958, NBC Mon 9:00–9:30
Sep 1958–Oct 1958, NBC Thu 8:30–9:00

EMCEE:

Jack Barry

Fifteen months after the premiere of *The $64,000 Question*, which was the first and most popular of the big-money quiz shows, *Twenty-One* made its debut. The format was loosely based on the card game of the same name, also known as blackjack. Two contestants competed with each other to reach a point total of 21 and win the game. They were asked the questions while in individual isolation booths. At the start of each round they were informed of the category from which the questions would come and could choose to attempt a question worth from one to eleven points, with the difficulty increasing with rising point value. The value of each point was $500, with the winner progressing to face a new opponent. In case of a tie, a new game was started with the value of each point raised by $500, a process which would continue through succeeding ties until there was a winner. The only threat to a champion was that if he lost a future game, the amount of his opponent's winnings would be deducted from his final total.

When the quiz-show scandals surfaced in 1958, initiated by a former contestant on the game show *Dotto*, *Twenty-One* was one of the biggest losers. Its producers admitted that the game had been rigged; that contestants were often given answers in advance if the producers felt that they were desirable as winners in the sense that they were people the public could identify with; and that a fraud had indeed been perpetrated on the trusting American public. Herb Stempel, a former winner on *Twenty-One*, told the detailed story of how the game had been rigged. The most popular *Twenty-One* winner, college professor Charles Van Doren, who had acquired a regular position on NBC's *Today Show* after being dethroned with winnings of $129,000, was also forced eventually to admit that he had participated in the rigging. He lost his job on *Today*, was relieved of his teaching post, and suffered inestimable embarrassment. When the dust cleared the game shows were gone, but their records of generosity to contestants remained. The biggest winner on *Twenty-One* was Elfrida Von Nardroff, who apparently had not been a participant in the fixing of the show. She came away with a final total of $220,500. In the annals of the big-money quiz shows this total was only exceeded by the $224,000 won by 11-year-old genius Robert Strom and the $252,000 won by Teddy Nadler, both on CBS game shows, *The $64,000 Question* and *The $64,000 Challenge* respectively.

21 BEACON STREET

Detective

FIRST TELECAST: *July 2, 1959*

LAST TELECAST: *March 20, 1960*

BROADCAST HISTORY:

Jul 1959–Sep 1959, NBC Thu 9:30–10:00
Dec 1959–Mar 1960, ABC Sun 10:30–11:00

CAST:

Dennis Chase .... Dennis Morgan
Lola .... Joanna Barnes
Brian .... Brian Kelly
Jim .... James Maloney

Private investigator Dennis Chase operated out of an office at 21 Beacon Street, where he and his staff worked out methods of trapping criminals. The locale was not specified; it could have been any large American metropolis. Chase's staff consisted of sexy Lola, whose beauty could be used to charm information out of people, young law school graduate Brian, and Jim, a handyman with a knack for dialects. Unlike most private-detective shows, *21 Beacon Street* developed its crime situation before the hero entered the story, and then never had him take part in the actual apprehension. Chase preferred to send the police on that errand, after determining who the culprit was. *21 Beacon Street* was the 1959 summer replacement for *The Ford Show*, and was rerun on ABC in the middle of the 1959–1960 season.

TWENTY QUESTIONS

Quiz/Panel

FIRST TELECAST: *November 26, 1949*

LAST TELECAST: *May 3, 1955*

BROADCAST HISTORY:

Nov 1949–Dec 1949, NBC Sat 8:00–8:30
Mar 1950–Jun 1951, ABC Fri 8:00–8:30 (OS)
Jul 1951–Jun 1952, DUM Fri 8:00–8:30
Jul 1952–Sep 1952, DUM Fri 8:30–9:00
Oct 1952–Sep 1953, DUM Fri 10:00–10:30
Sep 1953–Apr 1954, DUM Mon 8:00–8:30
Apr 1954–May 1954, DUM Sun 10:00–10:30
Jul 1954–May 1955, ABC Tue 8:30–9:00

HOST:

Bill Slater (1949–1952)
Jay Jackson (1953–1955)

PANELISTS:

Fred Van De Venter
Florence Rinard
Herb Polesie
Johnnie McPhee (1949–1953)
Dickie Harrison (1953–1954)
Bobby McGuire (1954–1955)

This popular quiz show was something of a family affair, having been created by the Van De Venters on radio in 1946 and featuring father (Fred), mother (Florence Rinard) and son (Bobby McGuire) together on the panel at various times. The format was based on the old parlor game of "animal, vegetable or mineral." The panel, which consisted of four regulars and one celebrity guest, could ask up to 20 questions to identify the subject at hand. Each question would be answered only by a "yes" or "no." Questions were sent in by viewers, who won a prize if they stumped the panel.

Twenty Questions originated on the Mutual Radio Network in 1946 and when first seen on TV in 1949 was simulcast on radio. There was little turnover among regular panelists during its run, except in the "teenage" chair, where Johnny McPhee was replaced by Dickie Harrison who in turn gave way to the Van De Venters' own son Bobby McGuire, who had been with the show on radio during the 1940s.

20/20

Newsmagazine

FIRST TELECAST: *June 6, 1978*

LAST TELECAST: *September 10, 1978*

BROADCAST HISTORY:

Jun 1978–Aug 1978, ABC Tue 10:00–11:00
Sep 1978, ABC Sun 7:00–8:00

HOST:

Harold Hayes and Robert Hughes (first telecast only)
Hugh Downs

CORRESPONDENTS:

Dave Marash
Sylvia Chase
Dr. Carl Sagan
Thomas Hoving
Geraldo Rivera

This ABC newsmagazine set out to emulate the success of CBS' *60 Minutes*, but got off to a disasterous start. The elements were similar to those in *60 Minutes*—personality profiles, mini-documentaries, hard-hitting investigative reports—but the coverage was so shallow, and the production so full of gimmicks, that the premiere telecast received devastating reviews. *Variety* likened it to *The National Enquirer*. In one of the fastest cast changes in history, producer Bob Shanks fired his two co-hosts—former magazine editor Harold Hayes and Australian art critic Robert Hughes—after just one telecast, brought in old pro Hugh Downs, and began tinkering with the contents. Subsequent shows were better received, though *20/20* never rivalled *60 Minutes* as an audience attraction. Correspondents included Dr. Carl Sagan on science, Geraldo Rivera with investigative reports, and Thomas Hoving on art and culture.

TWILIGHT THEATER

Dramatic Anthology

FIRST TELECAST: *April 2, 1956*

LAST TELECAST: *July 15, 1959*

BROADCAST HISTORY:

Apr 1956–Jul 1956, ABC Mon 7:30–8:00
Jul 1958–Jul 1959, CBS Wed 7:30–8:00

The title *Twilight Theater* has been used several times for filmed prime time anthology series. In 1953 it was one of the titles under which ABC aired its inventory of miscellaneous dramatic films (see *ABC Dramatic Shorts—1952–1953* for details). ABC revived the name in 1956 for a summer series consisting of 30-minute dramas and comedies featuring such Hollywood standbys as Ethel Waters, Vera Miles, Hans Conried, Charles Coburn, and Hugh O'Brien. From 1958–1959 CBS used the title *Twilight Theater* for a series of reruns of films previously seen on *Schlitz Playhouse of Stars*.

TWILIGHT ZONE, THE

Science Fiction Anthology

FIRST TELECAST: *October 2, 1959*

LAST TELECAST: *September 5, 1965*

BROADCAST HISTORY:

Oct 1959–Sep 1962, CBS Fri 10:00–10:30
Jan 1963–Sep 1963, CBS Thu 9:00–10:00
Sep 1963–Sep 1964, CBS Fri 9:30–10:00
May 1965–Sep 1965, CBS Sun 9:00–10:00

HOST:

Rod Serling

Playwright Rod Serling, who in the mid-1950s had been a prolific contributor of fine dramas for almost all of the prestigious live anthology series (his most famous being "Requiem for a Heavyweight" for *Playhouse 90*), turned to the world of science fiction with this series. In addition to serving as series host, he wrote many of the teleplays that were presented on *The Twilight Zone*. The stories were unusual and offbeat, often with ironic twists. For example, there was "Escape Clause," starring David Wayne as a hypochondriac who, in an effort to escape his dependence on pills and fear of his environment, made a pact with the Devil. In exchange for his soul he won immortality. Filled with self-assurance, he killed a man (expecting to be sentenced to die and knowing that was now impossible). Instead of the death penalty he got life imprisonment—an awfully long time for someone who was immortal. Another episode, "Time Enough at Last," starred Burgess Meredith as a bank teller who could never find enough time to read. One day at lunchtime, while he was squirreled away in the bank's vault reading a good book, there was a nuclear attack that killed everybody outside. Now he had all the time in the world to read. A happy ending—until he tripped and broke his glasses! In "The Eye of the Beholder," a young woman who had been born with a horrible facial deformity had just undergone the last possible operation to try and make her less hideous. Her head was swathed in bandages, and all the doctors and nurses were dimly seen standing in the shadows around her bed. Then the bandages were finally removed and there she was, beautiful—at least to us. Only then were the faces of the doctors and nurses revealed to be those of reptiles, for she lived in a world where our "beauty" was considered a horrible deformity. At the end of the telecast she was led away to her society's equivalent of a leper colony.

Some well-known actors appeared on *Twilight Zone,* but it was the stories rather than the performers that made the show work. Serling's original opening and closing narration to the show set the scene appropriately. The opening: "There is a fifth dimension beyond that which is known to man. It is a dimension as vast as space and as timeless as infinity. It is the middle ground between light and shadow, between science and superstition, and it lies between the pit of man's fears and the summit of his knowledge. This is the dimension of imagination. It is an area we call *The Twilight Zone.*" And at the close: ". . . and you, have you ever been there?"

After three successful seasons in a half-hour format, *The Twilight Zone* expanded to a full hour in January 1963. The longer format was abandoned the following fall, but some of the longer episodes were rerun during the summer of 1965.

TWO FOR THE MONEY

Quiz/Audience Participation

FIRST TELECAST: *September 30, 1952*

LAST TELECAST: *September 7, 1957*

BROADCAST HISTORY:

Sep 1952–Aug 1953, NBC Tue 10:00–10:30
Aug 1953–Sep 1956, CBS Sat 9:00–9:30
Mar 1957–Jun 1957, CBS Sat 10:30–11:00
Jun 1957–Sep 1957, CBS Sat 8:30–9:00

EMCEE:

Herb Shriner (1952–1956)
Walter O'Keefe (1954)
Sam Levenson (1955, 1956, 1957)

QUIZ MODERATOR:

Dr. Milton Gross

Much in the manner of *You Bet Your Life,* this quiz show was designed more as a vehicle for the comic talents of its emcee than as a straight contest. Herb Shriner, with his country humor and tales of life in Indiana, was the original emcee and remained with the show until the spring of 1956. He was spelled during the summers by Walter O'Keefe in 1954 and Sam Levenson in 1955 and 1956. Levenson returned as the full-time emcee when the show returned in the spring of 1957. Three pairs of contestants vied for cash prizes during the actual quiz portion of the show and Dr. Milton Gross, Provost and Professor of Philosophy at Rutgers University, was the authority on correctness of answers.

TWO IN LOVE

Quiz/Audience Participation

FIRST TELECAST: *June 19, 1954*

LAST TELECAST: *September 11, 1954*

BROADCAST HISTORY:

Jun 1954–Sep 1954, CBS Sat 10:30–11:00

EMCEE:

Bert Parks

Each week a couple—engaged, newly married, or celebrating a wedding anniversary—were the guests of emcee Bert Parks. Many of their relatives and friends were also invited to be on the show. The relatives and friends participated in an on-the-air discussion of the couple's romance and were asked other questions which, if answered correctly, added to the "nest egg" of cash that would be presented to the couple at the end of the show. After the first couple of weeks it was decided by the producers to have only engaged couples as guests.

TYCOON, THE

Situation Comedy

FIRST TELECAST: *September 15, 1964*

LAST TELECAST: *September 7, 1965*

BROADCAST HISTORY:

Sep 1964–Sep 1965, ABC Tue 9:00–9:30

CAST:

Walter Andrews ....Walter Brennan
Pat Burns ....Van Williams
Herbert Wilson ....Jerome Cowan
Betty Franklin ....Janet Lake
Martha Keane ....Pat McNulty
Una Fields ....Monty Margetts

The chairman of the board of the giant Thunder Corporation was Walter Andrews, a cantankerous and eccentric millionaire. Walter did things his way, and despite the complaints and misgivings of his co-workers and business associates, his approach to problems usually worked. Not one to let protocol affect his operation, Walter was a constant problem for everyone from his young assistant and private pilot Pat Burns, to company president Herbert Wilson. Walter made his home with his cute little granddaughter Martha and housekeeper Una Fields.

U.N.C.L.E.

syndicated title for *Man from U.N.C.L.E., The* and *Girl from U.N.C.L.E., The*

U.N. CASEBOOK

Documentary

FIRST TELECAST: *September 26, 1948*

LAST TELECAST: *March 6, 1949*

BROADCAST HISTORY:

Sep 1948–Oct 1948, CBS Sun 6:45–7:15
Oct 1948–Mar 1949, CBS Sun 6:30–7:00

MODERATOR:

Dr. Lyman Bryson

The many and varied functions of the United Nations were looked at individually in this documentary series. Dr. Lyman Bryson, CBS Counsellor on Public Affairs, interviewed international political and intellectual figures about the roles that the U.N. played and should play in its multiple areas of activity.

U.S. HIGHWAY 1954

Travelogue

FIRST TELECAST: *August 2, 1954*

LAST TELECAST: *September 27, 1954*

BROADCAST HISTORY:

Aug 1954–Sep 1954, ABC Mon 7:30–8:00

Travel films on American vacation spots and scenic areas such as the Grand Canon, Yosemite National Park, Cape Cod, etc.

U.S. MARINE BAND

Music

FIRST TELECAST: *July 9, 1949*

LAST TELECAST: *August 20, 1949*

BROADCAST HISTORY:

Jul 1949–Aug 1949, NBC Sat 8:00–8:30

A series of summer concerts originating in Washington, D.C., and featuring the 70-piece Marine Band, under the direction of Major William Santelmann.

U.S. MARSHAL

syndicated title for *Sheriff of Cochise, The*

U.S. ROYAL SHOWCASE, THE

Comedy Variety

FIRST TELECAST: *January 13, 1952*

LAST TELECAST: *June 29, 1952*

BROADCAST HISTORY:

Jan 1952–Jun 1952, NBC Sun 7:00–7:30

HOST:

George Abbott
Jack Carson

This live comedy variety series originated from New York City. Each show was composed of three separate acts: a performance by a well-known star comedian, a singing interlude by a popular recording artist, and a performance by a promising young comedian. Broadway producer George Abbott directed the show and acted as the host, introducing the evening's performers, but he relinquished the on-camera hosting chores to comedian Jack Carson on April 13. The new-talent segment had been dropped from the show by the time Carson had taken over as host.

U.S. STEEL HOUR, THE

Dramatic Anthology

FIRST TELECAST: *October 27, 1953*

LAST TELECAST: *June 12, 1963*

BROADCAST HISTORY:

Oct 1953–Jun 1955, ABC Tue 9:30–10:30
Jul 1955–Jun 1963, CBS Wed 10:00–11:00

United States Steel's initial venture into broadcast drama had been on ABC radio in 1945. Under the title *The Theatre Guild on the Air*, it was a showcase for authors and directors as well as performers, and presented plays from New York with distinguished casts. In 1953 The Theatre Guild moved the series to television, in effect bringing the Broadway stage to the nation's television viewers. Throughout its 10-year run as a live show originating from New York, *The U.S. Steel Hour* aired on alternate weeks with other dramatic anthologies. Ironically, *Armstrong Circle Theater*, the show with which it shared the Wednesday time slot during its eight years on CBS, had been its competition during part of the time it was on ABC.

The two years on ABC produced primarily dramatic presentations. The premiere telecast, "P.O.W." starring Gary Merrill, Richard Kiley, and Sally Forrest set the tone. Rex Harrison and his then wife Lilli Palmer were featured in "The Man in Possession," Tallulah Bankhead in an adaptation of Ibsen's *Hedda Gabler*, Thomas Mitchell and Dorothy Gish in a version of *The Rise and Fall of Silas Lapham*, and Wendell Corey and Keenan Wynn in "The Rack," by frequent contributor Rod Serling. Not all was serious, however, as Andy Griffith starred in "No Time for Sergeants" in 1955, before recreating the role on both Broadway and film.

With the move to CBS, there was more diversity in the subject matter. To be sure, there were still moving dramas—Paul Newman, Albert Salmi, and George Peppard in "Bang the Drum Slowly" in 1956, almost 20 years before the movie of the same title; Teresa Wright, Dick Van Dyke, and George C. Scott in "Trap for a Stranger"; and Mona Freeman and Cliff Robertson in "The Two Worlds of Charlie Gordon" (which became the 1968 movie *Charly* for which Mr. Robertson received a Best Actor Academy Award for his portrayal of the title role)—but there was much more. Dorothy Collins and Edward Mulhare starred in an adaptation of Oscar Wilde's *The Importance of Being Earnest*, and Jack Carson, Basil Rathbone, Jimmy Boyd, and Florence Henderson were featured in a musical titled "Huck Finn," based on the Mark Twain novel. There was even a musical revue, with Fred MacMurray, Wally Cox, Edie Adams, Carol Burnett, and Hans Conried in a bit of fluff titled "The American Cowboy." Johnny Carson, not known primarily as an actor, appeared twice in light dramas in 1960, the first time with Anne Francis in "Queen of the Orange Bowl."

In ten years on the air, *The U.S. Steel Hour* presented more than 200 live plays, and the list of noted personalities who appeared in them is substantial. Numerous people made multiple appearances and, though some of them have already been mentioned, the names that follow were featured in at least four shows: Eddie Albert, Edward Andrews, Marty Astor, Ed Begley, Ralph Bellamy, Larry Blyden, Geraldine Brooks, Jack Carson, Hans Conried, James Daly, Jeff Donnell, Patty Duke, Faye Emerson, Nina Foch, Mona Freeman, Farley Granger, Arthur Hill, Richard Kiley, June Lockhart, Diana Lynn, Biff McGuire, Barry Morse, Meg Mundy, Betsy Palmer, Gene Raymond, Cliff Robertson, Franchot Tone, and Teresa Wright.

UGLIEST GIRL IN TOWN, THE

Situation Comedy

FIRST TELECAST: *September 26, 1968*
LAST TELECAST: *January 30, 1969*
BROADCAST HISTORY:

Sep 1968–Jan 1969, ABC Thu 7:30–8:00

CAST:

Timothy Blair (Timmie) .....Peter Kastner
Julie Renfield ....Patricia Brake
Gene Blair ....Gary Marshall
Sondra Wolston ....Jenny Till

This frothy bit of comedy had a male star dressed in women's clothes as its running gag. The situation was all very logical, though somewhat farfetched. It seemed that young Hollywood talent agent Timothy Blair had fallen madly in love with an English starlet named Julie, while Julie was in town making a film. Then she flew back to London, and Timothy did not have the money to follow. Enter Timothy's brother Gene, a professional photographer assigned to shoot pictures of San Francisco hippies for a London magazine. At the last moment Gene's pictures were accidentally destroyed, and in desperation he dressed Timothy in a wig and hippie outfit and took pictures of *him* to send to London. London liked the pictures so much that they wanted that "girl"—for a major "Twiggy"-style modeling assignment.

Timothy (now dubbed "Timmie") went along with the ruse because it meant free airplane fare to England and his Julie, but once there he was faced with the necessity of maintaining the put-on in all sorts of awkward situations. What to do in a nude scene?

In almost less time than it took to explain all this, *The Ugliest Girl in Town* was on and off the ABC schedule.

UNCOVERED

syndicated title for *Vise, The*

UNDERCURRENT

Dramatic Anthology

FIRST TELECAST: *July 1, 1955*

LAST TELECAST: *September 19, 1958*

BROADCAST HISTORY:

Jul 1955–Sep 1955, CBS Fri 10:00–10:30
Jun 1956–Sep 1956, CBS Fri 10:00–10:30
Jul 1957–Sep 1957, CBS Fri 10:00–10:30
Jun 1958–Sep 1958, CBS Fri 10:00–10:30

For four summers *Undercurrent* was the replacement for *The Lineup*. During the first two years, the plays presented were all new to television. Starring in these dramas, which tended to be on the heavy side, were many future stars of television series. Among them were Brian Keith, Craig Stevens, Lloyd Bridges, Dale Robertson, Raymond Burr, and Vince Edwards. None of them, however, were major stars when these films aired. In 1957 and 1958 *Undercurrent* telecast reruns of episodes originally aired on other anthology series, the 1958 edition coming from NBC's *The Web*, which had aired the previous summer.

UNDERSEA WORLD OF JACQUES COUSTEAU, THE

Documentary

FIRST TELECAST: *May 23, 1976*

LAST TELECAST: *June 13, 1976*

BROADCAST HISTORY:

May 1976–Jun 1976, ABC Sun 7:00–8:00

PRODUCER:

Capt. Jacques-Yves Cousteau

NARRATOR:

Joseph Campanella

French scientist and explorer Capt. Jacques Cousteau has been producing TV documentaries longer than most people realize. His first network telecast was a feature on undersea archeology, presented on *Omnibus* on January 17, 1954. Widespread fame came in the late 1960s, however, when he began a long series of prime time specials for ABC depicting outdoor nature adventures from Pole to Pole. It was ABC's answer to the *National Geographic Specials*.

At first the program dealt with sea life, as seen from Cousteau's exploration ship *The Calypso* (the first special, on January 8, 1968, was "Sharks"). Later, as he began to run out of sea-born subjects, programs were done on land life as well. Rod Serling was the narrator until 1974, when he was replaced by Joseph Campanella.

The dates shown above reflect the single instance in which Cousteau specials ran consecutively for four weeks in the same time slot, qualifying as a "series" for the purposes of this book.

UNITED OR NOT

Interview

FIRST TELECAST: *July 2, 1951*

LAST TELECAST: *October 27, 1952*

BROADCAST HISTORY:

Jul 1951–Sep 1951, ABC Mon 9:00–9:30
Oct 1951–Jun 1952, ABC Tue 9:00–9:30
Jun 1952–Aug 1952, ABC Tue 8:30–9:00
Sep 1952–Oct 1952, ABC Mon 8:30–9:00

MODERATOR:

John MacVane

Interviews and discussions with guests from the United Nations, including ambassadors, specialists from various technical branches, foreign government officials, and the Secretary General, Trygve Lee.

UNIVERSAL STAR TIME

syndicated title for *Bob Hope Presents The Chrysler Theatre*

UNTOUCHABLES, THE

Police

FIRST TELECAST: *October 15, 1959*

LAST TELECAST: *September 10, 1963*

BROADCAST HISTORY:

Oct 1959–Oct 1961, ABC Thu 9:30–10:30
Oct 1961–Sep 1962, ABC Thu 10:00–11:00
Sep 1962–Sep 1963, ABC Tue 9:30–10:30

CAST:

Eliot Ness ....Robert Stack
Agent Martin Flaherty (1959–1960) .... Jerry Paris
Agent William Youngfellow .... Abel Fernandez
Agent Enrico Rossi ....Nick Georgiade
Agent Cam Allison (1960) .... Anthony George
Agent Lee Hobson (1960–1963) .... Paul Picerni
Agent Rossman (1960–1963) .... Steve London
Frank Nitti ....Bruce Gordon

NARRATOR:

Walter Winchell

PRODUCER:

Quinn Martin

With the chatter of machine-gun fire and the squeal of tires on Chicago streets, *The Untouchables* brought furious controversy—and big ratings—to ABC in the early 1960s. It was perhaps the most mindlessly violent program ever seen on TV up to that time. Critics railed and public officials were incensed, but apparently many viewers enjoyed the weekly bloodbath, which sometimes included two or three violent shootouts per episode. As *TV Guide* observed, the show was highly consistent. "In practically every episode a gang leader winds up stitched to a brick wall and full of bullets, or face down in a parking lot (and full of bullets), or face up in a gutter (and still full of bullets), or hung up in an ice box, or run down in the street by a mug at the wheel of a big black Hudson touring car."

How did they get away with it? The first defense was that the program was historically accurate, being based on the life of a real Treasury Department gangbuster in the bullet-riddled Prohibition days of the early 1930s. The agent was Eliot Ness, and he had in fact played an important role in breaking the power of the notorious Al Capone in Chicago in 1931. Ness later wrote an autobiography, which served as the basis for a two-part semi-documentary dramatization of the Capone affair, presented on *Desilu Playhouse* in April 1959.

The special was an enormous hit, and led immediately to an ABC series the next fall. It followed Ness and his small band of incorruptible agents (dubbed by a Chicago newspaper "the Untouchables") as they battled one major crime lord after another. Capone had been packed off to prison at the conclusion of the April special, so the series began with the battle between his two top lieutenants, Jake "Greasy Thumb" Guzik and Frank "The Enforcer" Nitti, for control of his empire. As the series continued, and writers were pressed to find criminals famous enough for Ness to tackle, stories wandered farther and farther from the historical record. (Ness had in real life disbanded his Untouchables after cracking the Capone case, and had nothing to do with most of the cases dramatized on TV.) *The Untouchables* went after Bugs Moran (in whose garage the St. Valentine's Day Massacre took place), Ma Barker, and such East Coast hoods as Mad Dog Coll, Dutch Schultz and Philadelphia crime boss Walter Legenza. There was even a two-part dramatization of the events leading up to the attempted assassination of President-elect Franklin D. Roosevelt at Miami Beach in 1933.

Some of this dramatic license caused problems, as when the FBI protested the depiction of Ness cornering Ma Barker (it was actually FBI agents). The estate of Al Capone sued the show for $1 million—not for inacccuracy, but for using Capone's name and likeness for profit. Italian-American groups protested the fact that so many of the hoods were given Italian names. Prison officials protested an episode which seemed to show Capone getting soft treatment in the Atlanta Penitentiary. Eventually the producers appended a disclaimer to the end of each episode stating that certain portions of *The Untouchables* had been "fictionalized."

Historical accuracy (or inaccuracy) aside, *The Untouchables* had another kind of appeal—and an excuse for violence. It was almost a fantasy, played by such colorful characters (the hoods), in such a one-dimensional style, and with such period trappings, that even the killings did not seem to be real. Eliot Ness was the upright, virtuous, and humorless enforcer of the law, and his opponents were greedy, sniveling animals. Robert Stack frankly admitted that he didn't really act in his role as Ness, but simply "re-acted" to the overplayed villains around him, and the contrast made the show work. Many fine character actors guest-starred as the thugs, such as Bruce Gordon (seen numerous times as Frank Nitti), Neville Brand (a look-alike for Capone), Nehemiah Persoff (Guzik), William Bendix (Legenza), Lloyd Nolan (Bugs Moran), Clu Gulager (baby-faced Mad Dog Coll), and Peter Falk (Nate Selko).

The Untouchables' success was spectacular but relatively short-lived. The program zoomed from the number 43 program on TV during its first season to number 8 in its second, but then, faced with the decidedly less violent competition of *Sing Along with Mitch* from 1961–1962, dropped back to number 41. There was frantic tinkering with the format during the final season—Ness became "more human," and the killings "more motivated." Investigators from other government bureaus began to appear, such as Barbara Stanwyck as a lieutenant from the Bureau of Missing Persons, and Dane Clark as an official of the U.S. Public Health Service. But *The Untouchables* was gone by 1963.

The Untouchables' original Desilu pilot and the initial episodes of the series were supervised by a young staff producer named Quinn Martin, starting a long string of TV crime-show hits for that gentleman.

UP TO PAAR

Quiz/Audience Participation

FIRST TELECAST: *July 28, 1952*

LAST TELECAST: *September 26, 1952*

BROADCAST HISTORY:

Jul 1952–Sep 1952, NBC Mon/Wed/Fri 7:00–7:30

EMCEE:

Jack Paar

Contestants on this live quiz show were drawn from the studio audience. They were interviewed by Mr. Paar and then asked a series of five questions based on current news stories. The value of each question increased, from $5 to $50. Winnings were given in the form of silver dollars and the money for each wrong answer went into the jackpot. At the end of the show all the contestants were asked the same jackpot question taken from that day's newspaper. They wrote their answers on a ballot and if anyone had the correct answer, he won $100 plus all the money lost by all the contestants on that night's show. This was Jack Paar's first network television series.

UPBEAT

Music

FIRST TELECAST: *July 5, 1955*

LAST TELECAST: *September 22, 1955*

BROADCAST HISTORY:

Jul 1955–Sep 1955, CBS Tue/Thu 7:45–8:00

REGULARS:

The Honeydreamers
Russ Case Orchestra

This twice-weekly summer series, which originated live from New York, filled the remainder of the half-hour in which CBS aired its network news program. Each week there was a different popular singer as host, performing songs he or she had made popular. Among the singers who hosted the show were Tony Bennett, Teresa Brewer, Georgia Gibbs, Polly Bergen, and the Four Lads.

VACATION PLAYHOUSE

Anthology

FIRST TELECAST: *July 22, 1963*

LAST TELECAST: *August 28, 1967*

BROADCAST HISTORY:

Jul 1963–Sep 1963, CBS Mon 8:30–9:00
Jun 1964–Sep 1964, CBS Mon 8:30–9:00
Jun 1965–Sep 1965, CBS Fri 9:30–10:00
Jul 1966–Sep 1966, CBS Mon 8:30–9:00
Jul 1967–Aug 1967, CBS Mon 8:30–9:00

Vacation Playhouse collected pilots for proposed series that had not been sold and aired them as a summer replacement series. In the four years that this show ran on Monday nights it was the replacement for *The Lucy Show* and all of the episodes were situation comedies. In 1965, when it aired as the replacement for *Gomer Pyle U.S.M.C.* on Friday nights, the episodes were adventure and mystery pilots.

VAL DOONICAN SHOW, THE

Musical Variety

FIRST TELECAST: *June 5, 1971*

LAST TELECAST: *August 14, 1971*

BROADCAST HISTORY:

Jun 1971–Aug 1971, ABC Sat 8:30–9:30

REGULARS:

Val Doonican
Bernard Cribbins
Bob Todd
The Norman Maen Dancers
The Mike Sammes Singers
Kenny Woodman's Orchestra

THEME:

"I Believe My Love Loves Me," by Tom Paxton

Irish singer Val Doonican was the star and host of this summer variety series that was taped in England. Comedians Bernard Cribbins and Bob Todd were featured regulars on the series, which also showcased both American and British guest stars.

VALENTINE'S DAY

Situation Comedy

FIRST TELECAST: *September 18, 1964*

LAST TELECAST: *September 10, 1965*

BROADCAST HISTORY:

Sep 1964–Sep 1965, ABC Fri 9:00–9:30

CAST:

Valentine Farrow .... Tony Franciosa
Rockwell "Rocky" Sin .... Jack Soo
Libby Freeman .... Janet Waldo
Molly .... Mimi Dillard
O. D. Dunstall .... Jerry Hausner
Grover Cleveland Fipple .... Eddie Quillan

The life of Valentine Farrow, a debonair young New York publishing executive, was depicted in this comedy. Valentine was continually being chased by beautiful girls, both in and out of his Park Avenue office at the publishing firm of Brackett and Dunstall, where he was senior nonfiction editor. Libby was his pretty secretary, Molly his receptionist, and O. D. Dunstall his nervous boss. At home, Valentine was no hero to his valet, the scrounging, poker-playing, con man "Rocky" Sin. Rocky had been Valentine's buddy in the Army, and had saved his neck. Now he was his chief confidant and bottle-washer. Living in the basement of Valentine's elegant East Side townhouse was Mr. Fipple, the handyman.

After a series of amorous adventures Valentine finally fell in love in the last episode, with a pretty research assistant at Brackett and Dunstall. The series didn't return for a second season, however, so it never got any further than that.

Seen in a guest role was opera singer Helen Traubel as Valentine's mother, Muriel Farrow.

VALENTINO

Romantic Monologue

FIRST TELECAST: *December 18, 1952*

LAST TELECAST: *March 5, 1953*

BROADCAST HISTORY:

Dec 1952–Mar 1953, ABC Thu 9:30–10:00

HOST:

Barry Valentino

Poetry readings, songs, and romantic monologues by Barry Valentino, who even looked a bit like his namesake, Rudolph Valentino. An obvious copy of CBS's soft-lights-and-sweet-music show, *The Continental.*

Also seen for a time as a local program in New York.

VALIANT YEARS, THE

see *Winston Churchill—The Valiant Years*

VAN CAMP'S LITTLE SHOW

Music

FIRST TELECAST: *June 27, 1950*

LAST TELECAST: *November 22, 1951*

BROADCAST HISTORY:

Jun 1950–Nov 1951, NBC Tue/Thu 7:30–7:45

HOST:

John Conte

REGULARS:

Jesse Bradley Trio

Intimate musical variety program featuring musical-comedy star Conte with a different female vocalist, and sometimes with other guests, on each show. Also known as *John Conte's Little Show* and *The Little Show.*

VAN DYKE AND COMPANY

Comedy Variety

FIRST TELECAST: *September 20, 1976*

LAST TELECAST: *December 30, 1976*

BROADCAST HISTORY:

Sep 1976, NBC Mon 10:00–11:00
Oct 1976, NBC Thu 10:00–11:00
Nov 1976–Dec 1976, NBC Thu 8:00–9:00

HOST:

Dick Van Dyke

REGULARS:

The L.A. Mime Company
Andy Kaufman

This short-lived series starred comedian Dick Van Dyke, whose previous success had been in situation comedies rather than variety programs. A true devotee of the art of pantomime, and renowned for his impression of Stan Laurel, Van Dyke made nonverbal comedy a prime ingredient in this show. In addition to the mime segments, and the recurring "bright family" sketch about the dumbest family in the world, there were appearances by guest stars from the music and comedy worlds.

VARIETY

Various

FIRST TELECAST: *April 11, 1948*

LAST TELECAST: *September 26, 1948*

BROADCAST HISTORY:

Apr 1948–Jun 1948, NBC Sun 8:30–9:00
Jul 1948–Sep 1948, NBC Sun 9:00–9:30

NBC presented what amounted to a series of specials under this umbrella title in 1948. The shows ranged from music and comedy acts to full-scale plays. Some plays were light entertainment, such as Gilbert & Sullivan, others were serious dramas. There was no host or continuing cast.

Variety was also known at times as *NBC Playhouse* or *The Players*.

VAUDEO VARIETIES

Variety

FIRST TELECAST: *January 14, 1949*

LAST TELECAST: *April 15, 1949*

BROADCAST HISTORY:

Jan 1949–Apr 1949, ABC Fri 8:00–9:00

EMCEE:

Eddie Hubbard

Hour-long variety show from Chicago, featuring emcee Eddie Hubbard and five different acts each week.

VAUDEVILLE SHOW

Musical Variety

FIRST TELECAST: *December 9, 1953*

LAST TELECAST: *December 30, 1953*

BROADCAST HISTORY:

Dec 1953, ABC Wed 9:30–10:00

ORCHESTRA:

Glenn Osser

A four-week series of re-creations of an old-time vaudeville show. Each telecast had five acts, including singers, dancers, tumblers, magicians, etc.

VAUGHN MONROE SHOW, THE

Musical Variety

FIRST TELECAST: *October 10, 1950*

LAST TELECAST: *September 8, 1955*

BROADCAST HISTORY:

Oct 1950–Jul 1951, CBS Tue 9:00–9:30
Aug 1954–Sep 1954, NBC Tue/Thu 7:30–7:45
Jul 1955–Sep 1955, NBC Tue/Thu 7:30–7:45

HOST:

Vaughn Monroe

REGULARS:

Shaye Cogan (1950–1951)
Ziggy Talent (1950–1951)
Olga Suarez (1950–1951)
Kenny Davis (1950–1951)
The Satisfiers (1954)
The Richard Hayman Orchestra (1954)
The Richard Maltby Orchestra (1955)

THEME:

"Racing with the Moon," by Vaughn Monroe, Johnny Watson, and Pauline Pope

Singer and orchestra leader Vaughn Monroe was one of the leading musical stars on radio during the late 1940s and early 1950s with his *Camel Caravan*, a Saturday night CBS variety show which ran from 1946 to 1954. He took his first plunge into the new medium of television on CBS in 1950, with a half-hour series that featured singer Shaye Cogan and comedian Ziggy Talent, plus guest stars. Most of the crooning was done by Vaughn himself, however, with his deep baritone voice and raft of melodious hits ("Racing with the Moon," "There I've Said It Again," "Ghost Riders in the Sky," etc.). After a single season as a TV series star, he returned to radio and occasional TV guest shots, but in 1954 and 1955 was back with an NBC program that served as summer replacement for *The Dinah Shore Show*. Like the CBS series it was telecast live, but the 15-minute length allowed time for little more than a few songs. By 1955 Vaughn's kind of music was becoming more nostalgic than contemporary, and thereafter he was seen with decreasing frequency in guest appearances on other shows. Perhaps his best-remembered role in TV was as commercial spokesman for RCA products. He died in 1973.

VEGA$

Detective

FIRST TELECAST: *September 20, 1978*

LAST TELECAST:

BROADCAST HISTORY:

Sep 1978– , ABC Wed 10:00–11:00

CAST:

Dan Tanna .... Robert Urich
Bernie Roth .... Tony Curtis
Beatrice .... Phyllis Davis
Angie .... Judy Landers

Binzer ....Bart Braverman
Sgt. Bella Archer ....Naomi Stevens

TV audiences never seem to tire of handsome, wisecracking private eyes, and Dan Tanna was the very latest 1978 model. Casual blue jeans, a sports car (a vintage Thunderbird), sexy assistants, glamorous Las Vegas settings, and a new homicide every Wednesday night helped make this one of the hits of the 1978–1979 season. Dan was on retainer to Bernie Roth, the fast-talking, millionaire owner of one of Vegas' bigger casinos. Binzer, a reformed hood, was Dan's legman; Angie his sexy secretary; and Beatrice his equally sexy helper (Dan used showgirls for assistants). Even Dan's police contact was female, in the person of Sgt. Bella Archer.

VERDICT IS YOURS, THE

Courtroom Drama

FIRST TELECAST: *July 3, 1958*
LAST TELECAST: *September 25, 1958*
BROADCAST HISTORY:
Jul 1958–Sep 1958, CBS Thu 8:30–9:30
COURT REPORTER:
Jim McKay

Re-enactments of actual trials were presented on this nighttime version of *The Verdict Is Yours*. Real lawyers tried the cases and real judges were on the bench. The jury was made up of members of the studio audience. Jim McKay, in the role of court reporter, established the background for each case and filled in missing details during the "trial." He also performed the same task on the daytime version which had premiered in 1957 and ran until 1962.

VERSATILE VARIETIES

Variety/Children's

FIRST TELECAST: *August 26, 1949*
LAST TELECAST: *December 14, 1951*
BROADCAST HISTORY:
Aug 1949–Jan 1951, NBC Fri 9:00–9:30 (OS)
Sep 1951–Dec 1951, ABC Fri 9:30–10:00
EMCEE:
George Givot (1949)
Harold Barry (1949–1950)
Bob Russell (1950–1951)
Lady Iris Mountbatten (1951)
"BONNY MAID":
Anne Francis (1949–1950)
ORCHESTRA:
Jerry Jerome (1949–1950)
Bernie Sands (1950–1951)

This began as a live variety show set in a nightclub, with guest singers, comedians, performing dogs, etc. Nonperforming guest celebrities were sometimes seen seated at ringside tables. George Givot, "the Greek Ambassador of Good Will," was the original host, succeeded after two months by comedian Harold Barry. Singer Bob Russell took over in the fall of 1950, as the program tended more to a presentation of new talent. Anne Francis appeared in the commercials (for floor covering) as "Bonny Maid," assisted by two other Bonny Maids and the team of "Wear and Tear."

Versatile Varieties returned in the fall of 1951 with a somewhat different format, featuring Lady Iris Mountbatten and a cast of kids who presented various children's stories and skits.

During its NBC run the program was also known as *Bonny Maid Versatile Varieties*.

VIC DAMONE SHOW, THE

see *Dean Martin Presents Vic Damone* and *Dean Martin Summer Show, The*

VIC DAMONE SHOW, THE

Musical Variety

FIRST TELECAST: *July 2, 1956*
LAST TELECAST: *September 11, 1957*
BROADCAST HISTORY:
Jul 1956–Sep 1956, CBS Mon 9:30–10:00
Jul 1957–Sep 1957, CBS Wed 8:00–9:00
REGULARS:
Vic Damone
The Spellbinders (1957)

Singer Vic Damone spent the summer of 1956 filling in for *December Bride* with a musical variety show. In addition to songs by himself and his guests, it featured aspects of Vic's personal life and interaction with the guests, many of whom were offscreen friends. The following summer Vic returned on a different night with an expanded, full-hour, variety show. The format of the 1957 series was more traditional than his first one had been, with musical and comedy numbers filling the entire hour and no side trips into Vic's personal life. A singing group, the Spellbinders, was featured regularly on the 1957 show.

VICEROY STAR THEATRE

Dramatic Anthology

FIRST TELECAST: *July 2, 1954*

LAST TELECAST: *September 24, 1954*

BROADCAST HISTORY:

Jul 1954–Sep 1954, CBS Fri 10:00–10:30

The plays presented in this filmed summer anthology series were all on the melodramatic and suspenseful side and starred personalities from the motion-picture world. Appearing were Zachary Scott, Katy Jurado, Lynn Bari, and Dennis Morgan, among others.

VICTOR BORGE SHOW, THE

Comedy Variety

FIRST TELECAST: *February 3, 1951*

LAST TELECAST: *June 30, 1951*

BROADCAST HISTORY:

Feb 1951–Jun 1951, NBC Sat 7:00–7:30

REGULARS:

Victor Borge

Internationally known pianist and comic interpreter of music Victor Borge starred in this live variety series. His satirical interpretations of classical music were only one part of the show, however, and he did play at least one piece in a straight concert rendition each week. Perhaps his most famous routine, and one that he featured periodically, was "Phonetic Punctuation," in which each punctuation mark was represented by a different noise—"Ffftt!," "Sscht!," etc. When he read quickly through an entire paragraph, substituting "Ffftt's" and "Sscht's" for every dash, comma, and period, the effect could be hilarious.

Guest stars were also a regular feature of the show, and would chat with Borge in addition to performing.

VIDEO VILLAGE

Quiz/Audience Participation

FIRST TELECAST: *July 1, 1960*

LAST TELECAST: *September 16, 1960*

BROADCAST HISTORY:

Jul 1960–Sep 1960, CBS Fri 9:00–9:30

EMCEE:

Jack Narz

ASSISTANT:

Joanne Copeland

ANNOUNCER:

Ken Williams

In a novel approach to television game shows, *Video Village* was a living board game. The contestants were the pieces, moving from square to square as determined by the roll of a giant die in a chuck-a-luck cage. The roll was accomplished with the aid of a friend or relative of the contestant. Various cash and merchandise prizes were awarded for landing on specified squares, while landing on others might cause loss of a turn, having to answer questions, or moving to another part of the board. The first person to reach the end of the board was the winner and started over again with a new contestant. Emcee Jack Narz was the mayor, assistant Joanne Copeland the assistant mayor, and announcer Ken Williams the town crier. The daytime version of this series started one week after the nighttime version and remained on the air through June 1962.

VILLAGE BARN

Musical Variety

FIRST TELECAST: *May 17, 1948*

LAST TELECAST: *May 29, 1950*

BROADCAST HISTORY:

May 1948–Oct 1948, NBC Mon 9:10–10:00
Oct 1948–Jan 1949, NBC Wed 10:10–11:00
Jan 1949–May 1949, NBC Wed 8:30–9:00
May 1949–Jul 1949, NBC Mon 10:00–10:30
Jul 1949–Sep 1949, NBC Thu 10:00–10:30
Jan 1950–May 1950, NBC Mon 9:30–10:00

EMCEE:

Zebe Carver (1948)
Dick Thomas & Dick Dudley (1948–1949)
Dick Dudley (1949)
Bob Stanton (1949)
Ray Forrest (1949)

REGULARS:

Romolo De Spirito (as *The Road Agent*, also known as *The Masked Singer*) *(1949)*
Piute Pete (1948–1949)

ORCHESTRA:

Pappy Howard and His Tumbleweed Gang
Bill Long and His Ranch Girls

Country music and down-home humor originating from New York's Village Barn, a popular night spot located at 52 West 8th Street. This was perhaps the first regular series to originate live from an actual nightclub. In addition to the music of such groups as Pappy Howard and His Tumbleweed Gang, Harry Ranch and His Kernels of Korn, and Bill Long's Ranch Girls, there was square dancing (with calls by Piute Pete), audience participation in potato sack, hobby horse, and kiddie-car races, and other unsophisticated entertainment.

VINCENT LOPEZ

Musical Variety

FIRST TELECAST: *March 7, 1949*

LAST TELECAST: *July 22, 1950*

BROADCAST HISTORY:

Mar 1949–May 1949, DUM Mon/Wed/Fri 6:45–7:00

May 1949–Jul 1949, DUM Mon–Fri 6:45–7:00

Jul 1949–Jun 1950, DUM Mon–Fri 7:30–7:45

Jan 1950–Jul 1950, DUM Sat 8:00–8:30

EMCEE:

Vincent Lopez

REGULARS:

Ann Warren

Lee Russell

Veteran bandleader and pianist Vincent Lopez ("Lopez speaking!") was seen on two different programs on the DuMont network from 1949–1950. The first was an early-evening musical interlude, running three to five nights a week. The other, seen during 1950, was a full-fledged Saturday night variety show called *Dinner Date with Vincent Lopez* and originating live from the Grill Room of the Hotel Taft in New York, where Lopez had been holding forth for many years. Featured was his full orchestra, guest performers such as Cab Calloway, Arthur Tracy, and Woody Herman, and his own regular vocalists, Ann Warren and Lee Russell. In addition to serving as emcee, Lopez did numerous interviews.

VIRGINIAN, THE

Western

FIRST TELECAST: *September 19, 1962*

LAST TELECAST: *September 8, 1971*

BROADCAST HISTORY:

Sep 1962–Sep 1971, NBC Wed 7:30–9:00

CAST:

Judge Henry Garth (1962–1966) .... Lee J. Cobb

The Virginian .... James Drury

Trampas .... Doug McClure

Steve (1962–1964) .... Gary Clarke

Molly Wood (1962–1963) ...... Pippa Scott

Betsy (1962–1965) .... Roberta Shore

Randy (1963–1966) .... Randy Boone

Emmett Ryker (1964–1966, 1967–1968) .... Clu Gulager

Jennifer (1965–1966) .... Diane Roter

John Grainger (1966–1967) .... Charles Bickford

Stacy Grainger (1966–1968) .... Don Quine

Elizabeth Grainger (1966–1967) .... Sara Lane

Clay Grainger (1967–1968) .... John McIntire

Holly Grainger (1967–1968) .... Jeanette Nolan

David Sutton (1968–1969) .... David Hartman

Jim Horn (1969–1970) ...... Tim Matheson

Col. Alan MacKenzie (1970–1971) .... Stewart Granger

Roy Tate (1970–1971) .... Lee Majors

Parker (1970–1971) .... John McLiam

This long-running drama was the first 90-minute Western series. It starred James Drury as the laconic, mysterious "Virginian," who never revealed his real name and who "forced his idea of law and order on a Wyoming Territory community in the 1890s;" and Doug McClure as the wild young cowhand Trampas. Setting for the saga was the Shiloh Ranch, owned successively by Judge Garth, the two Grainger brothers (John and Clay), and finally Col. Alan MacKenzie. Col. MacKenzie took over during the last season, at which time the program was retitled *The Men from Shiloh* and the historical period was moved up a few years.

The Virginian was one of the leading "adult Westerns," relying on strong characterizations by both regular cast and guest stars rather than on gimmicks. In many respects it resembled a weekly movie feature. Many actors and actresses appeared in regular supporting roles for varying lengths of time, among them David Hartman in 1968 and Lee Majors in 1970.

The Virginian was based on the classic 1902 novel of the same name by Owen Wister, which had been produced three times as a motion picture (the most famous being the 1929 version starring Gary Cooper and Walter Huston).

An interesting sidelight was that the original pilot for this series, produced in the late 1950s, cast Drury as a Western dandy replete with shiny hunting boots, skintight pants, lace cuffs, and a tiny pistol. It didn't sell, and so was remade several years later without the foppish accoutrements—to become one of TV's biggest hits.

VISE, THE

Suspense Anthology

FIRST TELECAST: *October 1, 1954*

LAST TELECAST: *December 16, 1955*

BROADCAST HISTORY:

Oct 1954–Dec 1955, ABC Fri 9:30–10:00

HOST:

Ron Randell

Filmed drama series produced in London, depicting people caught in "the vise" of fate due to their own misdeeds. Schemers, blackmailers, and other unseemly types always got their due in this program, and viewers invariably got a look at some very pretty girls, who always seemed to play roles in each of these internationally flavored stories. The actors were generally lesser-known British performers, but some talented newcomers who would later become internationally famous were seen here, including Honor Blackman, Patrick McGoohan, and Petula Clark. Australian actor Ron Randell was the host.

The series ended in December 1955, after which the time slot and the title *The Vise* were taken over by a new series of *Mark Saber* episodes.

VISIT WITH THE ARMED FORCES

Documentary

FIRST TELECAST: *July 3, 1950*

LAST TELECAST: *January 1, 1951*

BROADCAST HISTORY:

Jul 1950–Jan 1951, DUM Mon 8:00–8:30

Documentary films about the armed forces.

VISITOR, THE

syndicated title for *Doctor, The*

VIVA VALDEZ

Situation Comedy

FIRST TELECAST: *May 31, 1976*

LAST TELECAST: *September 6, 1976*

BROADCAST HISTORY:

May 1976–Sep 1976, ABC Mon 8:00–8:30

CAST:

Luis Valdez .... Rodolfo Hoyos
Sophia Valdez .... Carmen Zapata
Victor Valdez .... James Victor
Ernesto Valdez .... Nelson D. Cuevas
Connie Valdez .... Lisa Mordente
Pepe Valdez .... Claudio Martinez
Jerry Ramirez .... Jorge Cervera, Jr.

Noisy "gang" comedy about a close-knit Mexican-American family living in East Los Angeles. Luis ran a plumbing business with his eldest son, Victor. Sophia was the mama, Ernesto an artistic lad in training with the telephone company, Connie the irrepressible teenager, and Pepe the 12-year-old baseball fanatic. Jerry was a cousin newly arrived from Mexico.

VIVIEN KELLEMS

see *Power of Women, The*

VOICE OF FIRESTONE, THE

Music

FIRST TELECAST: *September 5, 1949*

LAST TELECAST: *June 16, 1963*

BROADCAST HISTORY:

Sep 1949–Jun 1954, NBC Mon 8:30–9:00
Jun 1954–Jun 1957, ABC Mon 8:30–9:00
Sep 1957–Jun 1959, ABC Mon 9:00–9:30 (OS)
Sep 1962–Jun 1963, ABC Sun 10:00–10:30

NARRATOR:

John Daly (1958–1959)

REGULAR:

Howard Barlow conducting the Firestone Concert Orchestra

THEME MUSIC:

"If I Could Tell You" and "In My Garden," both composed by Mrs. Harvey Firestone

Radio's venerable Monday night program of classical and semi-classical music, which had been on the air since 1928, became a TV series in 1949, when regular simulcasts began with the radio program. It survived on TV for a total of eleven seasons, but not without sparking a bitter controversy over the role that ratings and mass-audience appeal should play in TV programming. It was canceled three times, eventually leaving the air permanently in 1963, a victim of the basic rule that on American television "best" is not enough—only "biggest" counts.

The format of *Voice* changed little over the years. Stars of grand opera were the usual guests, although occasionally more "popular" talent would also appear singing Broadway show tunes and pop standards. The 25th anniversary telecast, in 1953, was an especially gala affair, with speeches and performances by many of the great stars who had appeared on *Voice* over the years, including Eleanor Steber, Rise Stevens, Thomas L. Thomas, Brian Sullivan, Robert Rounseville, and Jerome Hines.

Worthy causes were frequently promoted on the show, such as highway safety, 4-H and the UN, and in 1954 there was an essay contest on the theme "I Speak for Democracy." The winner, a 16-year-old Akron, Ohio, schoolgirl, appeared on the program to read her essay.

Though the program was certainly prestigious, to be truthful it was a bit stiff—pleasing to hear, but sometimes boring to watch. Tuxedos and starched shirts were the order of the evening, with staging to match. There were few concessions to popular taste. During the early 1950s only occasional popular talent appeared (notably Jane Froman), but from 1958–1959 a new format was announced which struck a much more equal balance between the classics and the "better" pops on each show. Jo Stafford, Fred Waring, Xavier Cugat, and Gordon MacRae were among those who appeared, along with Carlos Montoya, the Philadelphia Symphony, the Ballet Russe of Monte Carlo, and the Vienna Boys' Choir from the "serious" side. John Daly, urbane and witty as always, was added as narrator.

A further change took place from 1962–1963 when Howard Barlow was phased out as permanent conductor (he still appeared occasionally) and a rotating roster of maestros was introduced. Most frequently seen were Arthur Fiedler, Wilfred Pelletier, and Harry John Brown. James McCracken made his network TV debut during this season, and Rudolf Nureyev also appeared.

Although the audience for *Voice* was relatively small by TV standards (about two to three million viewers per week), the appreciation of those who did watch, and the considerable prestige, made Firestone quite content to continue funding the show. But in 1954, after carrying *Voice* on Monday nights at 8:30 P.M. for 26 years (first on radio and then TV), NBC insisted that a change had to be made. The program's low ratings were affecting the entire Monday night NBC lineup, and the network was finding it impossible to sell the succeeding half-hour. Firestone refused to budge, arguing that many of the program's faithful viewers would not be able to watch in a less desirable time period. So the show, both radio and TV versions, moved to ABC the following fall. ABC was at the time happy to have the business, but by 1959 that network too was beginning to taste big ratings in other parts of its schedule. A new, sales-oriented ABC management determined that *Voice* must move to 10:00 P.M. so as not to hurt the shows that followed it. Again, Firestone objected, and this time the show went off the air.

Though the audiences had been small the hue and cry when *Voice* was dropped was deafening. Sen. Mike Monroney bitterly attacked ABC for following in the footsteps of NBC in dropping the "best" of TV. There were threats of action through the FCC, and critics were unrelenting. ABC tried to appease them by putting on a similar program called *Music for a Summer Night* using the same producers, but with a smaller budget. It was not the same. All three networks offered various fringe time slots to *Voice*, which Firestone rejected. For an investment of more than $1 million per year, Firestone felt that it deserved the best. Finally in 1962, after a change of management, ABC took it back, this time at 10:00 P.M. Commendations were immediately forthcoming (Sen. Thomas E. Dodd: "You're bringing back *Voice of Firestone*, and I find that commendable"). But again "only" two and a half million viewers chose to watch, and by mid-1963 *Voice* was once again gone—this time for good.

VOICE OF FIRESTONE TELEVUES

Documentary

FIRST TELECAST: *November 4, 1946*

LAST TELECAST: *January 20, 1947*

BROADCAST HISTORY:

Nov 1946–Jan 1947, NBC Mon various 10–15 minute

The Firestone Tire and Rubber Co. was one of television's earliest advertisers, beginning this Monday night series of "Televues" on NBC's New York station on November 29, 1943, and sponsoring it continuously for more than three years. The presentations were a varied selection of short documentary films on different subjects, such as dairy farming, football, vocational guidance, etc. There was a live opening and closing for each show.

The series was fed to a two-station network during its final months.

VOLUME ONE

Dramatic Anthology

FIRST TELECAST: *June 16, 1949*

LAST TELECAST: *July 21, 1949*

BROADCAST HISTORY:

Jun 1949–Jul 1949, ABC Thu 9:30–10:00

PRODUCER/DIRECTOR/NARRATOR:

Wyllis Cooper

Famed radio writer Wyllis Cooper tried his hand at television in this six-telecast series of original dramas. Cooper was the Rod Serling of radio, producing eerie, surrealistic stories of horror and suspense, often based more on psychological terror than on actual violence. He had created, among other shows, *Lights Out* and *Quiet, Please*. His first telecast starred Jack Lescoulie, Nancy Sheridan, and Frank Thomas, Jr., in an intelligent psychological thriller which drew rave reviews. Nevertheless the series lasted for only the scheduled six weeks.

Each telecast was numbered: "Volume One, Number One," "Volume One, Number Two," etc. The radio title *Quiet, Please* was originally to be used for the series, but had to be dropped at the last minute.

VOYAGE TO THE BOTTOM OF THE SEA

Science Fiction

FIRST TELECAST: *September 14, 1964*

LAST TELECAST: *September 15, 1968*

BROADCAST HISTORY:

Sep 1964–Sep 1965, ABC Mon 7:30–8:30
Sep 1965–Sep 1968, ABC Sun 7:00–8:00

CAST:

Adm. Harriman Nelson . . Richard Basehart
Cdr./Capt. Lee Crane . . . . David Hedison
Lt. Cdr. Chip Morton . . . . . . Robert Dowdell
Chief Petty Officer Curley Jones (1964–1965) . . . . Henry Kulky
Chief Sharkey (1965–1968) . . . Terry Becker
Stu Riley (1965–1967) . . . . Allan Hunt
Kowalsky (1965–1968) . . . . Del Monroe
Patterson . . . . Paul Trinka
Doctor . . . . Richard Bull

CREATOR/PRODUCER:

Irwin Allen

One of TV's all-time favorite science-fiction adventure series, this followed the exploits of the officers and men of the *Seaview*, a glass-nosed atomic submarine that roamed the seven seas fighting villains both human and alien. The *Seaview* was the brainchild of retired Adm. Harriman Nelson, director of the super-secret Nelson Institute of Marine Research at Santa Barbara, California. The time was ten years into the future. Originally there were two subs, but the *Seaview*'s sister ship, the *Polidor*, was sunk in the third episode. Nelson's chief assistant and the commander of the *Seaview* then became Cdr. Lee Crane (he was promoted to captain in the second season). Their opponents included such dastardly villains as Dr. Gamma (Theodore Marcuse) and the sneaky Prof. Multiple (Vincent Price)—he came aboard under the pretext of presenting a puppet show, only to have the puppets come to life and run amok—plus assorted unreconstructed Nazis, lost worlds, giant orchids quivering with alien energy, globular masses of "pure intelligence" that threatened to devour the entire sub, and other fantastic creatures (remarkable, what's down there!). Some episodes were less obvious. On one, the *Seaview* picked up Old John (Carroll O'Connor), an enigmatic stranger found floating placidly in a rowboat in the middle of the Pacific.

During the second season the emphasis on gadgetry was increased, with the *Seaview* gaining the *Sea Crab*, a self-propelled two-man explorer, and the *Flying Fish*, a mini-sub which could fly through the air at fantastic speeds. Some cast changes were made, including the addition of fast-talking, handsome young surfer Stu Riley, as a kind of on-shore ally.

W.E.B.

General Drama

FIRST TELECAST: *September 13, 1978*

LAST TELECAST: *October 5, 1978*

BROADCAST HISTORY:

Sep 1978, NBC Wed 10:00–11:00
Sep 1978–Oct 1978, NBC Thu 10:00–11:00

CAST:

Ellen Cunningham . . . . Pamela Bellwood
Jack Kiley . . . . Alex Cord
Gus Dunlap . . . . Richard Basehart
Dan Costello . . . . Andrew Prine
Walter Matthews . . . . Howard Witt
Harvey Pearlstein . . . . Lee Wilcof
Christine . . . . Tisch Raye
Kevin . . . . Peter Coffield

Television showed the ability to caricature even itself, in this prime time soap opera set behind the scenes at a "major television network"—Trans Atlantic Broadcasting. Ellen Cunningham, an ambitious, talented female executive who had clawed her way up in a man's world, was head of Special Events Programming. Surrounding her was an executive suite full of unsavory characters: Jack Kiley, the ruthless head of programming; Gus Dunlap, news chief and a drunken has-been; Dan Costello, fast-talking, inebriated sales chief; Walter Matthews, hard driving head of operations; and Harvey Pearlstein, the research head obsessed with ratings. There was plenty of backbiting, maneuvering and high level treachery behind the smiling screen at T.A.B. This series was no doubt inspired by the movie *Network*, and was produced by Lin Bolen, who in real life had been one of the industry's first female programming chiefs (at NBC).

WKRP IN CINCINNATI

Situation Comedy

FIRST TELECAST: *September 18, 1978*

LAST TELECAST:

BROADCAST HISTORY:

Sep 1978– , CBS Mon 8:00–8:30

CAST:

Andy Travis .... Gary Sandy
Arthur Carlson .... Gordon Jump
Jennifer Marlowe .... Loni Anderson
Les Nessman .... Richard Sanders
Venus Flytrap .... Tim Reid
Herb Tarlek .... Frank Bonner
Bailey Quarters .... Jan Smithers
Dr. Johnny Fever .... Howard Hesseman

The arrival of a new program director, Andy Travis, brought sudden and dramatic changes to WKRP, a Cincinnati radio station that had been losing money by playing sedate music. Andy's decision to turn WKRP into a "top 40" rock 'n' roll station alienated its elderly audience, and also its few sponsors, such as the Shady Hill Rest Home and Barry's Fashions for the Short and Portly. It also created a trying time for Arthur Carlson, the inept general manager who held his job only because his mother owned the station. But mother, who had dollar signs in her eyes, decided to give Andy's plan a try. Les Nessman was the naive and gullible news director; Jennifer Marlowe, the sexy but inefficient receptionist; Herb Tarlek, the high-pressure salesman who, though married, was constantly trying to make time with Jennifer; and Bailey Quarters, Andy's enthusiastic young assistant. Jive talking Venus Flytrap and Dr. Johnny Fever were two of WKRP's more colorful disc jockeys.

WACKIEST SHIP IN THE ARMY, THE

War Adventure

FIRST TELECAST: *September 19, 1965*

LAST TELECAST: *September 4, 1966*

BROADCAST HISTORY:

Sep 1965–Sep 1966, NBC Sun 10:00–11:00

CAST:

Major Simon Butcher .... Jack Warden
Lt. (j.g.) Richard "Rip" Riddle
.... Gary Collins
Chief Petty Officer Willie Miller
.... Mike Kellin
Gunner's Mate Sherman Nagurski
.... Rudy Solari
Ship's Cook Charles Tyler ...... Don Penny
Radioman Patrick Hollis .... Mark Slade
Machinist's Mate Seymour Trivers
.... Fred Smoot
Gen. Cross .... William Zuckert
Admiral Vincent Beckett .... Charles Irving

In the spring of 1942, only months after the Japanese bombing of Pearl Harbor, the government of New Zealand presented to the United States the *Kiwi*, a 70-year-old twin-masted schooner. Obsolete and badly in need of repairs, the ship was staffed with a token crew while the U.S. Navy tried to figure out what to do with it. The Navy soon discovered that it possessed certain unique qualities that made it a useful espionage weapon. Its wooden hull did not show up on radar, its sailing power did not register on sonar, and its shallow draft allowed it to travel in waters not deep enough for larger ships. And so the *Kiwi* went to war. It was commanded by young Lt. Rip Riddle when at sea and by Maj. Simon Butcher of the Army when in port, a situation which caused numerous problems because Rip and Simon had very different views on war strategy, women, protocol, and their respective roles on the ship. Complicating things even more was the fact that Maj. Butcher, although higher in rank than Lt. Riddle, had to report to the younger man whenever the *Kiwi* was at sea, while their roles were reversed whenever it made port. The adventures of the crew in the South Pacific during the early days of the war constituted the stories, which were based on the real-life exploits of *The Echo*, a leaky two-masted schooner which New Zealand's government gave to the U.S. in 1942. The story of *The Echo* had been made into a comedy-adventure movie in 1960.

WAGON TRAIN

Western

FIRST TELECAST: *September 18, 1957*

LAST TELECAST: *September 5, 1965*

BROADCAST HISTORY:

Sep 1957–Sep 1962, NBC Wed 7:30–8:30
Sep 1962–Sep 1963, ABC Wed 7:30–8:30
Sep 1963–Sep 1964, ABC Mon 8:30–11:00
Sep 1964–Sep 1965, ABC Sun 7:30–8:30

CAST:

Major Seth Adams (1957–1961) .... Ward Bond
Flint McCullough (1957–1962) .... Robert Horton
Bill Hawks .... Terry Wilson
Charlie Wooster .... Frank McGrath
Duke Shannon (1961–1964) ... Scott Miller
Christopher Hale (1961–1965) .... John McIntire
Barnaby West (1963–1965) .... Michael Burns
Cooper Smith (1963–1965) ... Robert Fuller

Wagon Train was one of the most popular "big" Western series during the heyday of TV Westerns, in the late 1950s and early 1960s. It was big in scope (the whole American West, it seemed), big in cast (many top-name guests), and big in format (60 minutes most seasons, 90 minutes in one). The setting was a California-bound wagon train in the post–Civil War days, starting out each season from "St. Joe" (St. Joseph, Missouri) and making its way west until reaching California in the spring. In between there were endless adventures on the vast, Indian-controlled Great Plains, the endless deserts, and the towering passes of the Rocky Mountains. But what made *Wagon Train* work were the characters who passed in and out of its episodes. The program was actually a series of character studies, each week revolving around a different member of the party or a different person encountered by the train along the way. Some were God-fearin' settlers, others young adventurers, others scoundrels. The regulars in the cast, who composed the "staff" of the wagon train, were seen in co-starring or sometimes even secondary roles.

Wagon Train had only two wagonmasters in its eight years of crisscrossing the country. The first was fatherly Major Adams, replaced upon the death of actor Ward Bond in 1961 by Chris Hale (John McIntire). Flint McCullough was the original frontier scout who rode out ahead to clear the way and make peace, if possible, with often unfriendly Indians. When Robert Horton left the series (supposedly he was "fed up" with Westerns), McCullough was replaced by Duke Shannon and young Cooper Smith. Bill Hawks went all the way as the assistant wagonmaster and lead wagon driver, as did grizzled old Charlie Wooster as the cook. Barnaby West joined the regular cast during the last couple of seasons as a 13-year-old orphan boy found trudging along the trail heading west on his own.

Those were the continuing cast members, but the regular infusion of guest stars and the focus on different personalities in each episode made *Wagon Train* seem more like a new Western film every week than an ordinary TV series. The series took a season to catch on, but in its second year it was in the top ten. After three years of placing a close second to *Gunsmoke,* it became the number one program on television in the 1961–1962 season.

WAITING FOR THE BREAK

Variety

FIRST TELECAST: *March 18, 1950*

LAST TELECAST: *April 8, 1950*

BROADCAST HISTORY:

Mar 1950–Apr 1950, NBC Sat 7:30–8:00

HOST:

Hank Ladd

Four-week variety series featuring the understudies and chorus people from current Broadway hits, performing scenes and songs from their shows.

WALT DISNEY

Anthology

FIRST TELECAST: *October 27, 1954*

LAST TELECAST:

BROADCAST HISTORY:

Oct 1954–Sep 1958, ABC Wed 7:30–8:30
Sep 1958–Sep 1959, ABC Fri 8:00–9:00
Sep 1959–Sep 1960, ABC Fri 7:30–8:30
Sep 1960–Sep 1961, ABC Sun 6:30–7:30
Sep 1961–Aug 1975, NBC Sun 7:30–8:30
Sep 1975– , NBC Sun 7:00–8:00

EXECUTIVE PRODUCER/HOST:

Walt Disney (1954–1966)

As of this writing, *Walt Disney* is the longest-running prime time series in network history. It is also historic for another reason. When it premiered in 1954 it marked the first big plunge by a major Hollywood movie studio into television production. Disney changed the face of television in many ways. Previously the big studios, afraid of competition from the new medium, were television's sworn enemies, not only refusing to produce programming but denying TV the use of any of the latest or best theatrical films. Until Disney led the way, the lavish movie-style series so familiar today were an impossibility.

Luring Disney into television was a major coup for struggling ABC. Both CBS and NBC had negotiated with the moviemaker, but neither could agree to his seemingly exorbitant terms. Among other things, Mr. Disney wanted the network to help finance his proposed amusement park in Anaheim, California. Only ABC was willing to take a chance, paying a then-fabulous $500,000 plus $50,000 per program. ABC won big. Both the TV series and the park, Disneyland, were fabulous successes. The program *Disneyland* was, in fact, ABC's first major hit series.

Disneyland consisted of a mixture of cartoons, live-action adventures, documentaries, and nature stories, some made especially for TV and some former theatrical releases. A liberal number of repeat telecasts was included with each season's originals. At first *Disneyland* was divided into four rotating segments, listed at the beginning of each week's show by the cartoon character Tinkerbell (from *Peter Pan*). They were Frontierland, Fantasyland, Tomorrowland, and True Life Adventureland. The first telecast was a variety show, but what really got *Disneyland* off the ground was a three-part series of Frontierland adventures which began less than two months later—*Davy Crockett*. The exploits of the famed real-life frontiersman of the early 1800s took America by storm. The title role was played by Fess Parker (whom Disney had seen playing a bit part in the horror movie *Them*). Buddy Ebsen played his sidekick, George Russel. *Davy Crockett* lifted Fess Parker from obscurity to stardom overnight. Davy's trademark coonskin cap and other Crockett merchandise sold like wildfire to the nation's youth, and a recording of the theme song, "The Ballad of Davy Crockett," was one of the biggest hits of the mid-1950s. (Fess Parker recorded the song, but ironically a minor-league singer named Bill Hayes beat him to it and had the big hit recording. Yes, the *same* Bill Hayes who today is a romantic soap-opera idol on *Days of Our Lives!*)

The three original Crockett episodes were "Davy Crockett, Indian Fighter" (first aired December 15, 1954), "Davy Crockett Goes to Congress" (January 26, 1955), and "Davy Crockett at the Alamo" (February 23, 1955). Crockett was killed in the last episode, which created an embarrassing situation when the public began clamoring for more. Eventually a few more episodes were made, depicting incidents earlier in his life, but Crockett, for some reason, never did become a series in its own right.

Flushed with the spectacular success of Davy Crockett, Disney tried several more times to base multi-part stories on actual Western heroes. In 1958 there was "The Saga of Andy Burnett" (Jerome Courtland as the young frontiersman), followed by "The Nine Lives of Elfego Baca" (starring Robert Loggia as a peace-loving but determined lawman in Tombstone, Arizona), "Texas John Slaughter" (Tom Tryon in the lead role), and "Swamp Fox" (Leslie Nielsen as Francis Marion, the Revolutionary War hero). Even Fess Parker got another shot at superstardom playing John Grayson in the film *Westward Ho! The Wagons*, which later turned up on the TV series. That time Parker made sure he got his recording of the theme song out before Bill Hayes did, but it didn't matter because neither the show nor the song was a hit.

There were many other presentations on *Disneyland* beyond the boundaries of Frontierland. Some were adaptations of classics such as *Alice in Wonderland, The Legend of Sleepy Hollow* (narrated by Bing Crosby), *Robin Hood, Treasure Island,* and *Babes in Toyland* (with Annette Funicello, Tommy Sands, and Ray Bolger). The animated shows tended to feature well-known Disney characters such as Mickey Mouse (voice provided by Walt himself), Donald Duck, Pluto, and Goofy, sometimes in full-length stories, sometimes "narrating" documentaries on various subjects. When the series moved to NBC in 1961 a new character was added, Professor Ludwig Von Drake (voice by Paul Frees), who was supposed to be Donald's eccentric uncle and who co-hosted many of the shows, with Walt.

Documentaries within the series covered subjects ranging from space travel to how cartoons are made, and were always entertainingly presented. And of course there were plenty of plugs for the Disneyland park and its Florida counterpart, Disney World, including reports on construction in progress, big opening galas, and, later, on-location variety shows. One of the latter, "Disneyland After Dark" in April 1962, marked the network TV debut of the Osmond Brothers, who were then performing at the park.

Every season of *Disney* has brought all types of presentations, but the mix has changed with the times. In the late 1950s and early 1960s there were many Westerns and other early-American adventures. Now the emphasis has shifted more to nature stories, often about animals and their young human companions. *Disney*, in fact, has produced quite a menagerie of nonhuman "stars," to wit: "Sammy, the Way Out Seal," "Greta, the Misfit Greyhound," "Ida, the Offbeat Eagle," "Joker, the Amiable Ocelot," "Boomerang, Dog of Many Talents," "Inky the Crow," "The Horse in the Grey Flannel Suit," "Salty, the Hijacked Harbor Seal," "Ringo the Refugee Raccoon," "Stub, Best Cow Dog in the West," "Deacon, the High Noon Dog," "Twister, Bull from the Sky," and "Lefty, the Ding-a-Ling Linx." Not to mention "The Horse with the Flying Tale" and "The Hound That Thought He Was a Raccoon."

For many years Walt Disney himself introduced the telecasts, and it was through television that the master showman became a national celebrity. He was such an institution that it was a distinct shock when Walt Disney passed away suddenly on December 15, 1966. On the next Sunday's telecast the prefilmed introductions by Disney were deleted, and tributes by Chet Huntley and Dick Van Dyke were substituted. But the program itself went on as planned—appropriately, it was a tour led by Walt himself through his pride and joy, Disneyland.

In subsequent seasons there was no opening and closing host, simply voice-over narration by announcer Dick Wesson.

In recent years *Disney* has suffered the same fate as many long-running series, gradually declining in audience apparently because viewers take it for granted, or consider it "old hat." The fact that such programs may continue to provide first-rate entertainment takes second place to the quest for "novelty." Each year its renewal is more in doubt, and one day, before we realize it, it will be gone. Television will be infinitely poorer when that day comes.

The Disney series was originally titled *Disneyland*, changed to *Walt Disney Presents* in 1958, to *Walt Disney's Wonderful World of Color* in 1961 (whereupon many of the films previously seen in black-and-white on ABC were repeated in color on NBC), and *The Wonderful World of Disney* in 1969.

WALTER WINCHELL FILE, THE

Crime Anthology

FIRST TELECAST: *October 2, 1957*
LAST TELECAST: *March 28, 1958*
BROADCAST HISTORY:
Oct 1957–Dec 1957, ABC Wed 9:30–10:00
Jan 1958–Mar 1958, ABC Fri 10:00–10:30
HOST/NARRATOR:
Walter Winchell

The crime dramas presented in this anthology were adapted from stories that Walter Winchell had uncovered while working the police beat in New York City. In addition to hosting the show, he functioned as the narrator, tying together the various elements that led to the drama that was actually shown on the air.

WALTER WINCHELL SHOW, THE

News/Commentary

FIRST TELECAST: *October 5, 1952*
LAST TELECAST: *November 6, 1960*
BROADCAST HISTORY:
Oct 1952–Apr 1953, ABC Sun 6:45–7:00
Apr 1953–Jul 1953, ABC Sun 6:30–6:45
Sep 1953–Jan 1954, ABC Mon 7:00–7:15
Sep 1953–Jun 1955, ABC Sun 9:00–9:15
Oct 1960–Nov 1960, ABC Sun 10:30–11:00
REPORTER:
Walter Winchell

Syndicated newspaper columnist Walter Winchell had a highly successful radio series in the 1930s and 1940s which gave him the opportunity to report the headlines he deemed important in his uniquely fast-paced and highly opinionated style. His crusades and grudges were legendary, but everything was delivered with a theatricality (Winchell had once been in vaudeville) that kept listeners entranced. After the war he went on an extended crusade against Communism, and eventually became a staunch supporter of Senator Joseph McCarthy.

In the fall of 1952 Winchell began simulcasting his famous Sunday night news show. The sight of the grizzled reporter was a surprise to many viewers. He always wore his hat while on the air, he was noticeably older (in his 50s) than many had imagined, and he personally ran the telegraph key that was used to punctuate the news and gossip of the world that he related (though the "code" he punched out was actually meaningless garble). Even his opening line, "Good evening, Mr. and Mrs. North and South America and all the ships at sea . . . let's go to press," seemed somewhat dated on TV. The television version of his news show, although not the success that his radio program had been, remained on the air until Winchell resigned in a huff in 1955 after a disagreement with ABC executives. Five years later, it was brought back in a longer version. The revival was an immediate failure and lasted for only six weeks.

Winchell died in 1972.

WALTER WINCHELL SHOW, THE

Variety

FIRST TELECAST: *October 5, 1956*
LAST TELECAST: *December 28, 1956*
BROADCAST HISTORY:
Oct 1956–Dec 1956, NBC Fri 8:30–9:00
HOST:
Walter Winchell

In the fall of 1956, NBC gave Walter Winchell the opportunity to show that he could be as successful as his fellow columnist Ed Sullivan as the host of a weekly live variety show. The program originated from New York for its first nine weeks and then moved to Hollywood. Despite the ability of Winchell to attract as guests show-business celebrities who owed him favors, and a reasonably well-paced production, the series never caught on and was canceled after 13 weeks.

WALTONS, THE

General Drama

FIRST TELECAST: *September 14, 1972*
LAST TELECAST:
BROADCAST HISTORY:
Sep 1972– , CBS Thu 8:00–9:00
CAST:
John Walton ....Ralph Waite
Olivia Walton ....Michael Learned
Zeb (Grandpa) Walton (1972–1978) ....Will Geer
Esther (Grandma) Walton .....Ellen Corby
John Boy Walton (1972–1977) ....Richard Thomas
Mary Ellen Walton Willard ....Judy Norton-Taylor
Jim-Bob Walton ....David W. Harper
Elizabeth Walton ....Kami Cotler
Jason Walton ....Jon Walmsley
Erin Walton ...Mary Elizabeth McDonough
Ben Walton ....Eric Scott
Ike Godsey ....Joe Conley
Corabeth Godsey (1974–) ....Ronnie Claire Edwards
Sheriff Ep Bridges ....John Crawford
Mamie Baldwin ....Helen Kleeb
Emily Baldwin ....Mary Jackson
Rev. Matthew Fordwick (1972–1977) ....John Ritter
Rosemary Hunter Fordwick (1973–1977) ....Mariclare Costello
Yancy (1974–) ....Robert Donner
Flossie Brimmer (1975–) ....Nora Marlowe
Maude Gormsley (1973–) ....Merie Earle
Dr. Curtis Willard (1976–) ....Tom Bower
Rev. Hank Buchanan (1977–) ....Peter Fox
NARRATOR:
Earl Hamner, Jr.

Life in the South during the Depression was the subject of *The Waltons.* John and Olivia Walton and their seven children all lived together in rural Jefferson County, Virginia. Walton's Mountain, their property and ancestral home, was located in the Blue Ridge Mountains. The family's modest income came from the lumber mill run by John and Grandpa Zeb. It was a close-knit family, with everyone helping out most of the time, and moralistic homilies abounded. There was no sex, no violence, and very little that could be classified as action or adventure. It was just a warm family drama. Everything was seen through the eyes of John Boy, the oldest son. He had wanted to be a novelist for as long as he could remember and had written throughout high school and during his years as an English major at the local college. At the start of the 1976–1977 season he began publishing his own local paper, *The Blue Ridge Chronicle,* and by the end of the season, when his novel had been accepted by a publisher, he had decided to move to New York. That season had been full of changes, including the marriage of Mary Ellen, who was in nursing school, to young Dr. Curtis Willard in November, and her announcement that she was going to have a baby late that spring.

At the start of the 1977–1978 season *The Waltons* moved out of the Depression and into World War II. Young Rev. Fordwick enlisted in the army (John Ritter, who played the role, had a starring role in ABC's *Three's Company* that season) and was replaced by young Rev. Buchanan. Grandma Walton was ill in the hospital (actress Ellen Corby had suffered a stroke) and was not seen until the last episode of the season, when she finally came home to Walton's Mountain, even though she was still partially incapacitated. The reunion was tearful, but brief. In April 1978, shortly after the close of the regular season, actor Will Geer, who played Grandpa Walton, died at the age of 76.

Author Earl Hamner, Jr., was the creator and narrator of *The Waltons,* which was based on reminiscences of his own childhood. It was the most wholesome of TV programs and, surprisingly, did extremely well in the ratings. When it premiered in 1972 its competition was *The Flip Wilson Show* on NBC, then one of the most popular shows on television. To the surprise of both critics and TV executives *The Waltons* not only survived, but it forced Flip Wilson off the air and itself became one of the most viewed programs on TV. It was never a big hit in large cities, but it struck a chord in middle and rural America that guaranteed it a long and prosperous run.

WANTED

Documentary

FIRST TELECAST: *October 20, 1955*

LAST TELECAST: *January 5, 1956*

BROADCAST HISTORY:

Oct 1955–Jan 1956, CBS Thu 10:30–11:00

NARRATOR:

Walter McGraw

There were no actors in *Wanted.* All of the participants played themselves, be they policemen, informers, or witnesses, as this filmed documentary series reenacted the process by which wanted criminals were pursued by law-enforcement officers. Each week an actual case was followed from the criminal act and then through the process of detection. All of the cases, which were drawn from FBI files, were still active, and the criminals whose stories were shown were asked over the air to give themselves up. There were interviews with victims and members of the wanted party's family as well as the crime-and-detection aspects of the show. The narrator, Walter McGraw, also produced *Wanted.*

WANTED: DEAD OR ALIVE

Western

FIRST TELECAST: *September 6, 1958*

LAST TELECAST: *March 29, 1961*

BROADCAST HISTORY:

Sep 1958–Sep 1960, CBS Sat 8:30–9:00

Sep 1960–Mar 1961, CBS Wed 8:30–9:00

CAST:

Josh Randall .... Steve McQueen

Bounty hunters were very common in the Old West during the last half of the 19th century. They made a living from the rewards offered for capturing wanted criminals. Since it didn't matter whether or not the criminals were brought back alive, bounty hunters were not bound by the constraints that hampered lawmen, and did pretty much as they pleased. Such a man was Josh Randall. He felt little apparent emotion and was a man of few words. He was also adept at using his gun, not a normal pistol but an unusual cross between a hand gun and a rifle. His "Mare's Leg" was a 30–40 sawed-off carbine that could be handled almost like a pistol but had much more explosive impact when its cartridges hit a target.

WARNER BROTHERS PRESENTS

Various

FIRST TELECAST: *September 13, 1955*

LAST TELECAST: *September 11, 1956*

BROADCAST HISTORY:

Sep 1955–Sep 1956, ABC Tue 7:30–8:30

HOST/NARRATOR:

Gig Young

When ABC first approached the giant Warner Brothers film company it was for the purpose of obtaining the rights to theatrical films for telecasting on the network. But Warners was interested in getting into TV production, and the result was *Warner Brothers Presents,* an umbrella title for three rotating series, each based on a successful movie: *Kings Row, Cheyenne,* and *Casablanca.* From this start Warner Brothers went on to produce dozens of hit programs, and it is today an important producer of TV series.

Warners' first effort was a mixed success, however. Viewers and critics alike objected to the 10–15 minute segment at the end of each week's presentation devoted to plugging current Warner Brothers movies, and this was eventually dropped. (Gig Young was host of this segment, as well as narrator for the entire series.) *Kings Row* proved unsuccessful and was canceled at mid-season, followed soon after by *Casablanca.* Only *Cheyenne* caught on, lasting for a total of eight years on the ABC schedule. The *Warner Brothers Presents* title was discontinued after the 1955–1956 season.

See separate element titles for details.

WARREN HULL SHOW, THE

see *Ben Grauer Show, The*

WASHDAY THEATRE

see *Movies—Prior to 1961*

WASHINGTON EXCLUSIVE

Discussion

FIRST TELECAST: *June 21, 1953*

LAST TELECAST: *November 1, 1953*

BROADCAST HISTORY:

Jun 1953–Nov 1953, DUM Sun 7:30–8:00

MODERATOR:

Frank McNaughton

Public-affairs discussion program in which six former senators discussed the civil and military affairs of the nation. Produced by Martha Rountree and Lawrence Spivak.

WASHINGTON REPORT

Discussion

FIRST TELECAST: *May 22, 1951*

LAST TELECAST: *August 31, 1951*

BROADCAST HISTORY:

May 1951–Aug 1951, DUM Tue/Fri 7:45–8:00

MODERATOR:

Tris Coffin

Newsman Tris Coffin and distinguished guests from government, business, and labor discussed current events in this series originating from Washington, D.C.

WATCH MR. WIZARD

Educational

FIRST TELECAST: *May 26, 1951*

LAST TELECAST: *February 19, 1955*

BROADCAST HISTORY:

May 1951–Feb 1952, NBC Sat 6:30–7:00

Mar 1952–Feb 1955, NBC Sat 7:00–7:30

CAST:

Mr. Wizard ....Don Herbert

Watch Mr. Wizard was one of the longest-running educational children's program in the history of television. It originated from Chicago from its inception on March 3, 1951 (late on Saturday afternoons), through the conclusion of the 1954–1955 season. When it moved to New York at the start of the 1955–1956 season, it was part of the NBC Saturday morning program lineup. It remained as part of that lineup until June 27, 1965, and was revived for another season from 1971–1972.

Don Herbert was the star of the show for its entire run. As Mr. Wizard, he would show his young helper how to do interesting scientific experiments with simple things found around the house. In addition to the demonstrations, Mr. Wizard would explain the principles behind them. The original helper was Mr. Wizard's 11-year-old neighbor, a boy named Willy. By the start of the 1953–1954 season, a boy and a girl alternated as Mr. Wizard's assistant. There was considerable turnover in the children who acted as his assistants, but they were all ready with an excited "Gee, Mr. Wizard!" whenever he popped one of his scientific tricks.

WATCH THE WORLD

Documentary

FIRST TELECAST: *July 2, 1950*

LAST TELECAST: *August 20, 1950*

BROADCAST HISTORY:

Jul 1950–Aug 1950, NBC Sun 7:30–8:00

COMMENTATOR:

Don Goddard

Current events and features especially designed for youngsters, produced by NBC News in cooperation with the National Education Association. *Watch the World* was seen on Sunday afternoons during most of its 14-month run (April 1950–June 1951), with John Cameron Swayze and his family hosting. During the program's summer prime-time run, newscaster Don Goddard took over, with the vacationing Swayzes (John, his wife, son and daughter) continuing to appear in periodic filmed reports.

WAVERLY WONDERS, THE

Situation Comedy

FIRST TELECAST: *September 22, 1978*

LAST TELECAST: *October 6, 1978*

BROADCAST HISTORY:

Sep 1978–Oct 1978, NBC Fri 8:00–8:30

CAST:

Joe Casey .... Joe Namath
John Tate .... Charles Bloom
Tony Faguzzi .... Joshua Grenrock
Connie Rafkin .... Kim Lankford
Hasty Parks .... Tierre Turner
Linda Harris .... Gwynne Gilford
George Benton .... Ben Piazza

Former pro football quarterback Joe Namath took a flyer in TV comedy in this 1978 series. He starred as Joe Casey, a washed up pro basketball player turned history teacher and coach at Waverly High, in Eastfield, Wisconsin. It was questionable who was more inept, Joe in the classroom (he knew nothing about history) or his team, the Waverly Wonders, on the court (they hadn't won a game in three years). Nice kids, though: Tate, so shy he wouldn't take a shot; Faguzzi, the fumbling "Italian Stallion"; Parks, the fast-talking con artist; and Connie, the cute tomboy who was the best player of the lot. Linda Harris was the attractive principal and George Benton the stodgy former coach, known affectionately as "old prune face."

WAY OUT

Dramatic Anthology

FIRST TELECAST: *March 31, 1961*

LAST TELECAST: *July 14, 1961*

BROADCAST HISTORY:

Mar 1961–Jul 1961, CBS Fri 9:30–10:00

HOST:

Roald Dahl

The host for this dramatic anthology was well chosen. Roald Dahl was a writer of short macabre stories about people in strange and unsettling situations. The dramas in this series all fell into that category. In many respects it was like another CBS anthology series that was being aired in the following half-hour, *The Twilight Zone*. *Way Out* was noticeably less successful, however, and lasted for only three and a half months.

WAYNE AND SHUSTER TAKE AN AFFECTIONATE LOOK AT . . .

Documentary

FIRST TELECAST: *June 17, 1966*

LAST TELECAST: *July 29, 1966*

BROADCAST HISTORY:

Jun 1966–Jul 1966, CBS Fri 10:00–11:00

HOSTS:

Johnny Wayne
Frank Shuster

Each week Canadian comedians Wayne and Shuster hosted a documentary that profiled top comedians of the 20th century. Film clips were used to provide background and examples of the work of the comedians being profiled, with Wayne and Shuster providing running commentary. The people whose careers were chronicled were Bob Hope and Bing Crosby, Jack Benny, W. C. Fields, the Marx Brothers, and George Burns. In addition to the profiles of comedians, one episode presented an affectionate look at one movie form native to America, the Western.

WAYNE KING

Music

FIRST TELECAST: *September 29, 1949*

LAST TELECAST: *June 26, 1952*

BROADCAST HISTORY:

Sep 1949–Jun 1952, NBC Thu 10:30–11:00 (OS)

EMCEE:

Wayne King

REGULARS:

Nancy Evans (1949–1951)
Harry Hall
Gloria Van (1951–1952)
Barbara Becker (1951–1952)
Bob Morton (1951–1952)
The Don Large Chorus

Live program from Chicago featuring the smooth, somewhat sedate music of Wayne

King and His Orchestra. Typical, and best known, of his numbers was "The Waltz You Saved for Me." Seen only on NBC's Midwest network.

WE TAKE YOUR WORD

Quiz/Audience Participation

FIRST TELECAST: *April 1, 1950*
LAST TELECAST: *June 1, 1951*
BROADCAST HISTORY:

Apr 1950, CBS Sat 9:00–9:30
Jun 1950–Jul 1950, CBS Fri 8:00–8:30
Aug 1950, CBS Sun 9:30–10:00
Aug 1950–Sep 1950, CBS Mon 9:30–10:00
Oct 1950–Jan 1951, CBS Tue 10:30–11:00
Mar 1951–Jun 1951, CBS Fri 10:30–11:00

WORDMASTER:

John K. M. McCaffery
John Daly

PANELISTS:

Abe Burrows
Lyman Bryson (1950)

The panelists on *We Take Your Word* sought to provide the definitions, derivations, and histories of words that were sent in by viewers. Any word used on the program won for its submitter a book prize and, if the panel bungled their attempt to define it, $50. The series began on radio in January 1950 and was tried on television that April. John K. M. McCaffery was the wordmaster (moderator) of the radio version and also of the experimental TV version in April. He was replaced by John Daly when the show returned to television in June. John Daly stayed with the show through January 1951, to be replaced by its original host for its last three months. Initially there were two regular panelists and one guest. When Lyman Bryson left the show at the end of August 1950, Abe Burrows became the sole regular, with two guest panelists each week.

WE, THE PEOPLE

Interview

FIRST TELECAST: *June 1, 1948*
LAST TELECAST: *September 26, 1952*
BROADCAST HISTORY:

Jun 1948–Oct 1949, CBS Tue 9:00–9:30
Nov 1949–Jun 1951, NBC Fri 8:30–9:00
Sep 1951–Sep 1952, NBC Fri 8:30–9:00

HOST:

Dwight Weist (1948–1950)
Dan Seymour (1950–1952)

We, the People had been a feature on radio for 12 years when it moved to television in the summer of 1948. It was the first regularly scheduled series to be simulcast on both network radio and network television. Host Dwight Weist (replaced by Dan Seymour in April 1950) interviewed various guests about important events in their lives. Entertainers, politicians, and ordinary Americans appeared on the series to chat informally, often about experiences of deep personal suffering or triumph over adversary. Members of public-service organizations and individuals who had done some form of humanitarian work appeared frequently. The guests were introduced with the line, "We, the people . . . speak." The radio-TV simulcasts continued until July 1950, after which date the radio and television versions were aired at different times.

WEB, THE

Dramatic Anthology

FIRST TELECAST: *July 11, 1950*
LAST TELECAST: *October 6, 1957*
BROADCAST HISTORY:

Jul 1950–Aug 1950, CBS Tue 9:30–10:00
Aug 1950–Jul 1952, CBS Wed 9:30–10:00
Sep 1952–Sep 1954, CBS Sun 10:00–10:30
Jul 1957–Oct 1957, NBC Sun 10:00–10:30

HOST/NARRATOR:

Jonathan Blake (1950–1954)

PRODUCERS:

Mark Goodson and Bill Todman (1950–1954)

Normal, everyday people who found themselves in situations beyond their control populated the dramas telecast in this live CBS anthology series. Its producers, ironically, were Mark Goodson and Bill Todman of game-show fame.

All of the plays were adaptations of stories written by members of the Mystery Writers of America. Walter C. Brown and Hugh Pentecost were frequent contributors and even an occasional Charlotte Armstrong story, like "All the Way Home," turned up on *The Web*. Most of the actors and actresses appearing on the show were performers based in New York, where the show was produced. Included were Richard Kiley, James Daly, Eli Wallach, James Gregory, Patricia Wheel, Mary Sinclair, John Newland, and Phyllis Kirk.

Some future stars who were seen on *The Web* early in their careers were Grace Kelly in "Mirror of Delusion" in 1950, Jack Palance and Eva Marie Saint in "Last Chance" in 1953, and Paul Newman twice that summer, the second time in "One for the Road" on September 20, at the same time he was appearing on Broadway in the play *Picnic*. Newman's future wife Joanne Woodward (they would marry in 1958) starred in "Welcome Home," the final telecast of CBS' version of *The Web*, on September 26, 1954.

Hollywood veterans taking lead roles in episodes of *The Web* on CBS included John Carradine, Mildred Dunnock, Sidney Blackmer, Mildred Natwick, Henry Hull, and Chester Morris. On occasions the leads went to performers not noted for their dramatic acting ability, such as singer Jane Morgan in "Rehearsal for Death" and musical-comedy star John Raitt in "The Dark Shore." The real stars on *The Web* were the stories, however, not the performers. The overall quality of the productions was attested to when *The Web* became the first television series to win the Edgar Allan Poe Award for excellence in the presentation of suspense stories during the 1951–1952 season.

In the summer of 1957, NBC revived the title *The Web* for a series of filmed dramas with essentially the same format as the live CBS series of the early 1950s. Again, the emphasis was on story rather than star, with Alexander Scourby, Beverly Garland, James Darren, and Rex Reason the most familiar performers appearing. The NBC edition was the summer replacement for *The Loretta Young Show*.

WEDNESDAY NIGHT FIGHTS, THE

see *Boxing*

WEEK IN RELIGION, THE

Religious

FIRST TELECAST: *March 16, 1952*

LAST TELECAST: *October 18, 1954*

BROADCAST HISTORY:

Mar 1952–Sep 1952, DUM Sun 6:00–7:00
Jul 1953–Sep 1953, DUM Sun 6:00–7:00
Sep 1953–Oct 1954, DUM Sun 6:00–6:30

This ecumenical religious program was originally one-hour long and divided into three 20-minute segments: 20 minutes for the Protestants, 20 minutes for the Catholics, and 20 minutes for the Jews. A representative of each faith reported on the latest news and happenings in his denomination. There is no record of who, if anyone, got cut when the program was reduced to a half-hour.

WELCOME ABOARD

Musical Variety

FIRST TELECAST: *October 3, 1948*

LAST TELECAST: *February 20, 1949*

BROADCAST HISTORY:

Oct 1948–Feb 1949, NBC Sun 7:30–8:00

REGULARS:

Russ Morgan and His Orchestra (Oct–Nov 1948)
Vincent Lopez and His Orchestra (Nov 1948–Feb 1949)

THEME:

"Sailor's Hornpipe"

Live musical variety program with a nautical theme, including the members of the orchestra dressed in sailor suits. Top-name singers and comedians appeared as guests, with Phil Silvers and Martin and Lewis featured on the first telecast. Toward the end of the run one of the guests would serve as the emcee, with bandleader Lopez assuming a background role. The series was originally known as *Admiral Presents the Five Star Revue—Welcome Aboard*, but became *Welcome Aboard* when Admiral dropped sponsorship in December.

WELCOME BACK, KOTTER

Situation Comedy

FIRST TELECAST: *September 9, 1975*

LAST TELECAST:

BROADCAST HISTORY:

Sep 1975–Jan 1976, ABC Tue 8:30–9:00
Jan 1976–Aug 1978, ABC Thu 8:00–8:30
Sep 1978–Oct 1978, ABC Mon 8:00–8:30
Oct 1978– , ABC Sat 8:00–8:30

CAST:

Gabe Kotter .... Gabriel Kaplan
Julie Kotter .... Marcia Strassman
Vinnie Barbarino .... John Travolta
Juan Luis Pedro Phillipo de Heuvos Epstein .... Robert Hegyes
Freddie "Boom Boom" Washington .... Lawrence-Hilton Jacobs
Arnold Horshack .... Ron Palillo
Mr. Michael Woodman .... John Sylvester White
Rosalie Totzie (1975–1976) .... Debralee Scott
Verna Jean (1975–1977) .... Vernee Watson

Judy Borden (1975–1977) .... Helaine Lembeck
Todd Ludlow (1975–1977) .... Dennis Bowen
Maria (1975–1976) ....Catarina Cellino
Angie (1978) ....Melonie Haller
Beau De Labarre, (1978–) .... Stephen Shortridge
Carvelli (1978–) .....Charles Fleischer

CREATED BY:

Gabriel Kaplan and Alan Sacks

THEME:

"Welcome Back," composed and performed by John Sebastian

Welcome Back, Kotter was one of the more realistic comedies of the 1970s. Gabriel Kaplan portrayed Kotter, a Brooklyn-born teacher who returned to the inner-city high school from which he had graduated 10 years earlier to teach the toughest cases—a remedial academics group. Gabe's "sweathogs" were the outcasts of the academic system, streetwise but unable or unwilling to make it in normal classes. They were the toughest, and also the funniest, kids in school. Gabe was just as hip as they were, and with fine disregard for rules and a sense of humor he set out to help them pick up a little bit of practical, if not academic, knowledge, during their years at James Buchanan High. The four original "sweathogs" were Epstein, the Jewish Puerto Rican; "Boom Boom," the hip black; Horshack, the class yo-yo; and Barbarino, the cool, tough leader. John Travolta, playing Barbarino, became a major star through this series. He branched into popular music where he had several record hits beginning in the summer of 1976 (although the big song hit to come out of this show was the theme, as recorded by its composer John Sebastian). Travolta also began a successful movie career, with such films as *Carrie* and *Saturday Night Fever,* while he was still starring on *Kotter*. By 1978 he was seen only occasionally on the series.

Dozens of other students passed through the series, most seen only briefly. Those with the most appearances are listed above. Other regulars were Gabe's wife Julie, and Mr. Woodman, the assistant principal. Julie became pregnant at the end of the 1976–1977 season, and gave birth to twins Rachel and Robin in the fall of 1977, adding to the confusion and crowding in the Kotter's small apartment, and putting new strains on Gabe's limited income. In other developments, Angie turned up in early 1978 with the announcement that she was becoming the first female "sweathog" (she didn't last long), and a slick southerner, Beau De Labarre, joined the class the following fall. Also in the fall of 1978 Kotter was promoted to vice principal and Mr. Woodman to principal.

Welcome Back, Kotter was based on a real high school and the real experiences of Gabriel Kaplan. Kaplan had once attended the equivalent of James Buchanan High School, in Bensonhurst, Brooklyn, New York, and had been a student in a remedial class there. He credits a Miss Shepard as the teacher who inspired him, and who led, indirectly, to *Welcome Back, Kotter.* Like Kotter, she cared about her "unteachable" students.

WELCOME MAT

see *Starlit Time*

WE'LL GET BY

Situation Comedy

FIRST TELECAST: *March 14, 1975*

LAST TELECAST: *May 30, 1975*

BROADCAST HISTORY:

Mar 1975–May 1975, CBS Fri 8:30–9:00

CAST:

George Platt ....Paul Sorvino
Liz Platt ....Mitzi Hoag
Muff Platt ....Jerry Houser
Kenny Platt ....Willie Aames
Andrea Platt ....Devon Scott

The Platt family was a normal middle-class group living in a modest home in the New Jersey suburbs just outside of New York City, where George Platt worked as a lawyer. He and his wife Liz had three teenage children. Life in the Platt household, with all its conflicts, was one of love and understanding. The program was created by Alan Alda.

WELLS FARGO

see *Tales of Wells Fargo*

WENDY AND ME

Situation Comedy

FIRST TELECAST: *September 14, 1964*

LAST TELECAST: *September 6, 1965*

BROADCAST HISTORY:

Sep 1964–Sep 1965, ABC Mon 9:00–9:30

CAST:

George Burns ....Himself
Wendy Conway ....Connie Stevens
Jeff Conway ....Ron Harper
Danny Adams ....James Callahan
Mr. Bundy ....J. Pat O'Malley

This comedy was roughly patterned after the old *Burns and Allen Show* of the 1950s, and was another attempt to find a suitable format for George Burns after the retirement of his wife Gracie Allen. The setting was an apartment house in Southern California whose principal tenants were Wendy Conway, a slightly daft young bride, and her airline-pilot husband Jeff. Jeff's co-pilot and best friend was Danny, a girl-chasing bachelor who was inordinately proud of his "little black book" and "little red book." Mr. Bundy was the building superintendent.

Into the picture came George Burns, as himself. He had bought the building so he would have a place to practice his vaudeville routine—just in case anyone should ask him to perform it again. George's singing was not exactly widely admired, so he had written into every lease a provision that no tenant could evict the landlord. George, with his familiar cigar in hand, spent most of his time serving as onscreen narrator of the series. He followed Wendy through her day, commenting on the action in asides to the audience. Then he would step into the action himself.

WENDY BARRIE SHOW, THE

Interview

FIRST TELECAST: *March 14, 1949*
LAST TELECAST: *September 27, 1950*
BROADCAST HISTORY:

Mar 1949–Jun 1949, DUM Mon/Wed/Fri 7:00–7:30
Jun 1949–Jul 1949, DUM Wed 7:00–7:30
Sep 1949–Oct 1949, ABC Mon 8:30–9:00
Nov 1949–Dec 1949, ABC Wed 8:00–8:30
Dec 1949–Feb 1950, ABC Thu 9:00–9:30
Feb 1950–Jun 1950, NBC Tue/Thu 7:30–7:45
Jul 1950–Aug 1950, NBC Mon/Wed/Fri 7:30–7:45
Aug 1950–Sep 1950, NBC Wed 8:15–8:30

HOSTESS:

Wendy Barrie

Celebrity-interview and gossip show, hosted by one-time Hollywood starlet and early TV personality Wendy Barrie. Wendy's movie heyday was past by the time she went into the infant medium of television, but her vivacious charm was quite intact. Each night she welcomed viewers into a plush setting that was supposed to be her own Manhattan apartment, with outstretched arms, and such endearments as "sweet bunny," "sweetie," and "dearie" (her sign-off was always "be a good bunny"). All sorts of celebrities dropped in to chat with Wendy, and sometimes to perform, and there was show-business gossip as well as banter (Wendy had a marvelous sense of humor, even about herself). There was a definite air of glamour about it all.

Her first nighttime network series was produced in cooperation with *Photoplay* magazine and was called *Inside Photoplay,* then *Photoplay Time* (September 1949). Later it became *The Wendy Barrie Show* (December 1949) and finally *Through Wendy's Window* (August 1950). Miss Barrie was later seen on afternoon shows and on local television in New York.

WESLEY

Situation Comedy

FIRST TELECAST: *May 8, 1949*
LAST TELECAST: *August 30, 1949*
BROADCAST HISTORY:

May 1949–Jul 1949, CBS Sun 7:30–8:00
Jul 1949–Aug 1949, CBS Tue 9:30–10:00
Aug 1949, CBS Tue 8:00–8:30

CAST:

Wesley Eggleston (May–Jul) ....Donald Devlin
Wesley Eggleston (Jul–Aug) ....Johnny Stewart
Mr. Eggleston ....Frank Thomas
Mrs. Eggleston ....Mona Thomas
Grandpa ....Joe Sweeney
Elizabeth Eggleston ....Joy Reese
Alvin ....Billie Nevard

Wesley was a 12-year-old boy who was making, but ever so slowly, the transition from childhood to adulthood. He liked to play with his good buddy Alvin, with whom he had an almost brotherly relationship, fight with his teenage sister Elizabeth, and find ways of getting around his parents. This live situation comedy told of his adventures in a small rural community. The relationship between Wesley and his parents was, despite the problems inherent in all parent-child relationships, a warm and loving one. Donald Devlin, the young actor who originated the lead role in this series, left in July and was replaced by Johnny Stewart.

WEST POINT STORY, THE

General Drama

FIRST TELECAST: *October 5, 1956*

LAST TELECAST: *July 1, 1958*

BROADCAST HISTORY:

Oct 1956–Sep 1957, CBS Fri 8:00–8:30

Oct 1957–Jul 1958, ABC Tue 10:00–10:30

HOST:

Donald May (as *Cadet Charles C. Thompson*) (1956)

Produced with the cooperation of the Department of Defense, the Department of the Army, and the United States Military Academy, this series dramatized actual events and persons from the files of West Point. The names and dates of the people and situations involved were changed, but the events were real. The dramas showed cadets as real people, with the problems, joys, and tragedies that are part of every person's life. Not all of the episodes were based on contemporary life at the military academy, some looked at the academy at different periods in its history and the men who were a part of that history. Donald May was the host, in character, when *The West Point Story* premiered, but was phased out before the end of 1956.

WESTERN HOUR, THE

syndicated title for *Rifleman, The* and *Dick Powell's Zane Grey Theater* packaged as an hour show

WESTERNER, THE

Western

FIRST TELECAST: *September 30, 1960*

LAST TELECAST: *December 30, 1960*

BROADCAST HISTORY:

Sep 1960–Dec 1960, NBC Fri 8:30–9:00

CAST:

Dave Blassingame ....Brian Keith

Dave Blassingame was one of many adventurers wandering the TV version of the Old West. He was accompanied by a large mongrel named Brown (played by the same dog that had been featured in the Walt Disney movie *Old Yeller*). Though not a particularly friendly or outgoing type, Dave found settlers to defend, villains to fight, and causes to champion throughout the portion of the Southwest along the Mexican border. His avowed aim was to settle down on a ranch of his own and breed quarter horses, but his concern for the exploited pioneers he met constantly kept him postponing that move.

WESTERNERS, THE

syndicated title for *Black Saddle, Johnny Ringo, Law of the Plainsman, The,* and Westerner, The, packaged as a single series.

WESTINGHOUSE DESILU PLAYHOUSE

Dramatic Anthology

FIRST TELECAST: *October 13, 1958*

LAST TELECAST: *June 10, 1960*

BROADCAST HISTORY:

Oct 1958–Sep 1959, CBS Mon 10:00–11:00

Oct 1959–Jun 1960, CBS Fri 9:00–10:00

HOST:

Desi Arnaz

COMMERCIAL SPOKESPERSON:

Betty Furness

When *Studio One*'s live weekly anthology series went off the air after almost a full decade, sponsor Westinghouse Electric kept the time period with this series of filmed dramas. Betty Furness, who had been the spokesperson for *Studio One,* continued to show off refrigerators and ranges throughout the two years that *Desilu Playhouse* was on. The premiere telecast featured young Pier Angeli in "Bernadette," but the material ranged from light to serious. During the first season, host Desi Arnaz, whose production company was making the series, made no appearances as a performer, but two of his *I Love Lucy* gang did. Lucille Ball starred with William Lundigan and Aldo Ray in "K.O. Kitty," and William Frawley worked with Dan Duryea in "Comeback." William Bendix and Martin Balsam were featured in "The Time Element," a science-fiction story written by Rod Serling (and possibly the genesis of his later series *The Twilight Zone*). The most memorable program was a two-part story aired on April 20 and 27, 1959. Walter Winchell was the narrator, Robert Stack the star, and Keenan Wynn, Neville Brand, and Barbara Nichols featured players in "The Untouchables," which was destined to become a very successful and highly controversial series on ABC that fall.

Desi himself starred in two plays aired

during the second season, "So Tender So Profane" and "Thunder in the Night," and another "Untouchables"-type story, "Meeting at Apalachian" starring Luther Adler, Cameron Mitchell, and Jack Warden and narrated by Bob Considine was tried. Airing roughly once every five weeks within the series were a number of *Westinghouse Lucille Ball–Desi Arnaz Shows* in which the two stars recreated their roles from *I Love Lucy* along with Vivian Vance, William Frawley, and Richard Keith.

WESTINGHOUSE PLAYHOUSE

Situation Comedy

FIRST TELECAST: *January 6, 1961*

LAST TELECAST: *July 7, 1961*

BROADCAST HISTORY:

Jan 1961–Apr 1961, NBC Fri 8:30–9:00

May 1961–Jul 1961, NBC Fri 10:00–10:30

CAST:

Nan McGovern ....Nanette Fabray

Dan McGovern ....Wendell Corey

Buddy ....Bobby Diamond

Nancy ....Jacklyn O'Donnell

Mrs. Harper ....Doris Kemper

The full title of this comedy was *Westinghouse Playhouse Starring Nanette Fabray and Wendell Corey.* It was created by Miss Fabray's husband, writer-director Ranald MacDougall, and was based somewhat on her own life. Nan McGovern was a successful Broadway star who fell madly in love with Dan McGovern (whose wife had died six years previously) and married him after a very short courtship. On their way back to his home town of Hollywood, Dan admitted to Nan that he had not told his children about her. When they arrived at his home in Beverly Hills Nan found herself confronted with two rude and indifferent step-children and a less-than-enthusiastic housekeeper. Her efforts to cope with the situation and become close to her new family provided the material for the episodes in this series.

WESTINGHOUSE PREVIEW THEATRE

Comedy Anthology

FIRST TELECAST: *July 14, 1961*

LAST TELECAST: *September 22, 1961*

BROADCAST HISTORY:

Jul 1961–Sep 1961, NBC Fri 10:00–10:30

This summer series consisted of ten unsold pilots for potential situation comedy series, starring assorted TV and film personalities, and one musical program, "The Benny Goodman Show," which aired on September 15.

WESTINGHOUSE SUMMER THEATRE

see *Studio One*

WESTSIDE MEDICAL

Medical Drama

FIRST TELECAST: *March 15, 1977*

LAST TELECAST: *August 25, 1977*

BROADCAST HISTORY:

Mar 1977–Apr 1977, ABC Thu 10:00–11:00

Jun 1977–Aug 1977, ABC Thu 10:00–11:00

CAST:

Dr. Sam Lanagan ....James Sloyan

Dr. Janet Cottrell ....Linda Carlson

Dr. Philip Parker ....Ernest Thompson

Carrie ....Alice Nunn

TECHNICAL CONSULTANT:

Walter D. Dishell, M.D.

Set in Southern California, this short-lived medical drama centered around three dedicated young doctors who opened their own clinic to provide total, personalized care to their patients. Carrie was the receptionist. *Westside Medical* returned at the end of June to run for another two months with both original and repeat episodes.

WE'VE GOT EACH OTHER

Situation Comedy

FIRST TELECAST: *October 1, 1977*

LAST TELECAST: *January 14, 1978*

BROADCAST HISTORY:

Oct 1977–Jan 1978, CBS Sat 8:30–9:00

CAST:

Stuart Hibbard ....Oliver Clark

Judy Hibbard ....Beverly Archer

Damon Jerome ....Tom Poston

Dee Dee Baldwin ....Joan Van Ark

Donna ....Ren Woods

Ken Redford ....Martin Kove

The trials of a married couple whose marital roles were somewhat reversed formed the crux of this comedy. Stuart worked at home, as a copywriter for the "Herman Gutman Mail Order Catalogue" (full of improbable and useless gadgets), and did most of the cleaning and cooking. Judy commuted every day to downtown Los Angeles, where she was the assistant to professional photographer Damon Jerome, a hypertensive, absentminded man who was great with a camera but terrible at the practical aspects of his business. Both Stuart and Judy had primary sources of aggravation, his being next-door neighbor Ken Redford and hers being model Dee Dee Baldwin, who was sarcastic, demanding, and incredibly self-centered. Donna, the office secretary, tried to maintain an uneasy truce between Judy and Dee Dee, but it was almost impossible.

WHAT DO YOU HAVE IN COMMON

Quiz/Audience Participation

FIRST TELECAST: *July 1, 1954*

LAST TELECAST: *September 23, 1954*

BROADCAST HISTORY:

Jul 1954–Sep 1954, CBS Thu 9:00–9:30

EMCEE:

Ralph Story

Contestants on *What Do You Have in Common?* were brought to the stage in groups of three and informed by emcee Ralph Story that they had something in common that they must try to figure out by cross-examining each other. The first to figure out their common bond (which had been flashed on the TV screen to the viewers at home) won $500. Three groups of three participated on each show and the group that had taken the least time to figure out what they had in common won the opportunity to try for an extra $1,000 by guessing the similarity in the lives of three pictured celebrities.

WHAT DO YOU THINK?

Discussion

FIRST TELECAST: *January 17, 1949*

LAST TELECAST: *February 14, 1949*

BROADCAST HISTORY:

Jan 1949–Feb 1949, ABC Mon 8:30–9:00

Book-discussion program produced by the Great Books Foundation Forum. From Chicago.

WHAT IN THE WORLD

Quiz

FIRST TELECAST: *February 7, 1953*

LAST TELECAST: *September 5, 1953*

BROADCAST HISTORY:

Feb 1953–Sep 1953, CBS Sat 6:30–7:00

MODERATOR:

Dr. Froelich Rainey

PANELISTS:

Dr. Carleton Coon
Dr. Schuyler Cammann

The moderator of this live museum quiz was Dr. Froelich Rainey, director of the University of Pennsylvania Museum. Each week the two regular panelists, both professors in the Anthropology Department of the University of Pennsylvania, along with a third, guest panelist were shown works of art from the museum and asked to identify them. The identifications included background on the origins and original uses of the pieces, as well as possible explanations of the circumstances surrounding their discovery. This Peabody Award—winning series, broadcast live from Philadelphia, had actually premiered in April 1951 and continued until March 1955. For most of its run, however, it aired as a Saturday or Sunday afternoon program.

WHAT REALLY HAPPENED TO THE CLASS OF '65?

Dramatic Anthology

FIRST TELECAST: *December 8, 1977*

LAST TELECAST: *July 27, 1978*

BROADCAST HISTORY:

Dec 1977–Mar 1978, NBC Thu 10:00–11:00
May 1978–Jul 1978, NBC Thu 10:00–11:00

CAST:

Sam Ashley ....Tony Bill

A different graduate of Bret Harte High School, class of '65, was the subject of this dramatic anthology each week. Their post-high school stories were told from the perspective of a decade later: the class hustler, who had become a Vietnam War amputee; the class dreamers, who had become involved in a get rich quick scheme; "everybody's girl," who could never escape from her reputation for promiscuity.

A different cast appeared each week, with the only continuing role being that of Sam Ashley, who was a graduate of the class himself and who had returned to teach at the school. He served solely as narrator. Others appearing in individual telecasts included Leslie Nielsen, Jane Curtin, Larry Hagman, Linda Purl, and Meredith Baxter-Birney.

The series was based on the book of the same name.

WHAT'S GOING ON?

Quiz/Panel

FIRST TELECAST: *November 28, 1954*

LAST TELECAST: *December 26, 1954*

BROADCAST HISTORY:

Nov 1954–Dec 1954, ABC Sun 9:30–10:00

MODERATOR:

Lee Bowman

PANELISTS:

Kitty Carlisle
Hy Gardner
Audrey Meadows
Cliff Norton
Gene Raymond
Susan Oakland

This show featured a panel of six celebrities, divided into two groups, the "ins" and the "outs." The "ins" remained inside the studio and had to guess what the "outs," gathered outside at some remote location, were doing. The program lasted exactly five weeks.

WHAT'S HAPPENING

Situation Comedy

FIRST TELECAST: *August 5, 1976*

LAST TELECAST:

BROADCAST HISTORY:

Aug 1976, ABC Thu 8:30–9:00
Nov 1976–Dec 1976, ABC Sat 8:30–9:00
Dec 1976–Jan 1978, ABC Thu 8:30–9:00
Jan 1978–Apr 1978, ABC Sat 8:00–8:30
Apr 1978– , ABC Thu 8:30–9:00

CAST:

Roger Thomas ("Raj") ...... Ernest Thomas
Rerun .... Fred Berry
Dwayne .... Haywood Nelson
Mrs. Thomas (Mama) .... Mabel King
Dee Thomas .... Danielle Spencer
Shirley .... Shirley Hemphill
Bill Thomas (1976–1977) .... Thalmus Rasulala
Marvin (1976–1977) .... Bryan O'Dell

MUSIC:

Henry Mancini

Urban comedy about three spirited black kids in a large American city. Raj was the studious dreamer, who wanted to be a writer; Rerun the jolly, overweight clown who often wound up with his foot in his mouth; and Dwayne the shy tag-along, always striving to be "cool." When not involved in some sort of scrape, the three could be found hanging out at a soda shop near the school, where Shirley was the waitress. Family problems arose when Raj clashed with his no-nonsense Mother, who worked as a maid, and with his pesky little sister, Dee. Mama's no-good ex-husband Bill, the kids' father was seen in occasional episodes, as was Marvin, the gossipy reporter for the high school newspaper.

First seen as a summer replacement show, *What's Happening* was given a spot on the regular ABC schedule in the fall of 1976. The program was loosely based on the movie *Cooley High*.

WHAT'S HAPPENING TO AMERICA

Discussion

FIRST TELECAST: *July 12, 1968*

LAST TELECAST: *August 16, 1968*

BROADCAST HISTORY:

Jul 1968–Aug 1968, NBC Fri 10:00–11:00

HOST:

Edwin Newman

NBC News correspondent Edwin Newman was the host and moderator of this series of four discussions with prominent figures about the contradictions in American life: the gap between the rich and the poverty-stricken, the disparity between the good times experienced by some and the bad times by others, and the recently apparent tension and violence on the political scene. This series did not air on either August 2 or August 9.

WHAT'S IN A WORD

Quiz/Audience Participation

FIRST TELECAST: *July 22, 1954*

LAST TELECAST: *September 9, 1954*

BROADCAST HISTORY:

Jul 1954–Sep 1954, CBS Thu 8:00–8:30

MODERATOR:

Clifton Fadiman

PANELISTS:

Faye Emerson
Audrey Meadows
Jim Moran
Mike Wallace

Contestants on this word-association panel show made up simple two-word rhymes, like Fickle Pickle or Nice Rice, and won money depending on how successful the panel was at guessing what the rhyme was. The moderator provided clues to the noun portion of the rhyme and, to narrow down the possibilities, the panelists tried to make an association that was correct. The contestant won $5 for each clue used before the panel narrowed down and correctly identified the noun. At that point the moderator would give a definition of the adjective. The contestant then won an additional $5 for each wrong guess until the panel identified the adjective to complete the rhyme.

WHAT'S IT ALL ABOUT, WORLD?

Comedy Variety

FIRST TELECAST: *February 6, 1969*
LAST TELECAST: *May 1, 1969*
BROADCAST HISTORY:
Feb 1969–May 1969, ABC Thu 9:00–10:00
HOST:
Dean Jones
REGULARS:
Dick Clair
Jenna McMahon
Gerri Granger
Alex Dreier
Dennis Allen
Scoey Mitchlll
Ron Prince
Maureen Arthur
Bayn Johnson
Kevin Carlisle Dancers
Denny Vaughan Orchestra

Not exactly a *Laugh-In*, not as bitingly satirical as *That Was the Week That Was*, not as controversial as *The Smothers Brothers Show*, *What's It All About, World?* nevertheless had some elements of each of those programs. It was a satirical revue that made fun of contemporary mores and hallowed institutions in a light, relatively inoffensive way. Comedy routines, fake documentaries, and musical production numbers were included, such as "The Rumor Factory" and "Hollywood behind the Nixons." Among the regulars were the comedy team of Clair and McMahon, singer Gerri Granger, commentator Alex Dreier, and nine-year-old Bayn Johnson.

The show was produced by Saul Ilson and Ernest Chambers, who were also responsible for *The Smothers Brothers Show* (the Smothers Brothers made a guest appearance here).

WHAT'S IT FOR

Quiz/Audience Participation

FIRST TELECAST: *October 12, 1957*
LAST TELECAST: *January 4, 1958*
BROADCAST HISTORY:
Oct 1957–Jan 1958, NBC Sat 10:00–10:30
EMCEE:
Hal March
REGULARS:
Betsy Palmer
Hans Conried
Abe Burrows
Toni Gilman (1957)
Lisa Ferraday

Strange inventions with presumably practical uses (an automatic hammock swinger, an umbrella skirt, etc.) were demonstrated each week for the panelists and audience of this program. After the demonstration an offstage announcer would inform the audience what the purpose of the invention was. The panel then had four minutes, one for each panel member, to guess the use of the invention by asking questions of the inventor or the inventor's representative, who had performed the demonstration. If the panel was stumped the inventor received $100, and if they guessed the function of the invention he received $50. The three original regular panel members were Betsy Palmer, Hans Conried, and Abe Burrows, with a rotating fourth member. Toni Gilman became a fourth regular member in November and Lisa Ferraday replaced Miss Gilman in December.

WHAT'S IT WORTH

Art Appraisal

FIRST TELECAST: *May 21, 1948*
LAST TELECAST: *October 11, 1953*
BROADCAST HISTORY:
May 1948–Jun 1948, CBS Fri 9:00–9:30
Jul 1948–Dec 1948, CBS Fri 8:00–8:30
Dec 1948–Jan 1949, CBS Fri 8:30–9:00
Jan 1949–Mar 1949, CBS Tue 9:30–10:00
Oct 1952, DUM Wed 8:30–9:00
Nov 1952–Sep 1953, DUM Thu 9:00–9:30
Sep 1953–Oct 1953, DUM Sun 6:00–6:30
APPRAISER:
Sigmund Rothschild
EMCEE:
Nelson Case (1952–1953)
Bill Wendell (1953)

As the resident authority on *What's It Worth?*, art restorer and copyist Sigmund Rothschild invited viewers to submit objects for appraisal. The objects could be family heirlooms, things discovered buried in attics, pets, or anything else of questionable value. Aided by visiting appraisers, Mr. Rothschild would establish the value of the object and discuss its discovery or history with its owners. The series left network TV in March 1949 but remained on as a local program in New York for another three months.

A little over a year later, on November 9, 1950, Mr. Rothschild made his first appearance as an occasional visitor to the late afternoon weekday daytime series, *The Kate Smith Hour.* He did essentially the same thing he had done on CBS—pointing out the distinguishing characteristics that made objects either valuable or worthless. He left Miss Smith in January 1952 but turned up that fall on DuMont with his own show, *Trash or Treasure,* the same title his feature had used within *The Kate Smith Hour.* The DuMont show utilized an emcee, Nelson Case, until March 1953 and Bill Wendell thereafter. The title was changed to *Treasure Hunt* (not to be confused with the later quiz show of that name) in April 1953.

WHAT'S MY LINE

Quiz/Audience Participation

FIRST TELECAST: *February 16, 1950*
LAST TELECAST: *September 3, 1967*
BROADCAST HISTORY:

Feb 1950–Mar 1950, CBS Thu 8:00–8:30
Apr 1950–Sep 1950, CBS Wed 9:00–9:30
Oct 1950–Sep 1967, CBS Sun 10:30–11:00

MODERATOR:

John Daly

PANELISTS:

Arlene Francis
Dorothy Kilgallen (1950–1965)
Louis Untermeyer (1950–1951)
Hal Block (1950–1953)
Bennett Cerf (1951–1967)
Steve Allen (1953–1954)
Fred Allen (1954–1956)

PRODUCERS:

Mark Goodson and Bill Todman

What's My Line was the longest-running game show in the history of nighttime network television. For 18 seasons it ran, on alternate weeks from its premiere in February 1950 until the following September, and then in the 10:30 P.M. time period on Sundays for the next 17 years. The format was exceedingly simple. Contestants were quizzed by the panel members who tried to determine what they did for a living. Each time the contestant could answer no to a question it was worth $5 and a total of ten no's ended the game. The panel was forced to don blindfolds for the "mystery guest," a celebrity who tried to avoid identification by disguising his voice.

The panel on the initial telecast consisted of Dr. Richard Hoffman, Lewis Untermeyer, former New Jersey Governor Harold Hoffman, and Dorothy Kilgallen. Arlene Francis joined the panel on the second telecast and Bennett Cerf in March 1951. Kilgallen, Cerf, and Francis were continuing regulars for 15 years. Miss Kilgallen died of an overdose of medication following her appearance on November 7, 1965. After her death, there were only two regulars and two weekly guest panelists, rather than the three regulars and one guest panelist that had been the format previously. *What's My Line* has remained a success in syndication since its network cancellation.

WHAT'S MY NAME

see *Paul Winchell–Jerry Mahoney Show, The*

WHAT'S NEW

see *Gulf Road Show Starring Bob Smith, The*

WHAT'S ON YOUR MIND

see *How Did They Get That Way*

WHAT'S THE STORY?

Quiz/Panel

FIRST TELECAST: *July 25, 1951*
LAST TELECAST: *September 23, 1955*
BROADCAST HISTORY:

Jul 1951–Oct 1951, DUM Wed 9:00–9:30
Oct 1951–Feb 1952, DUM Tue 8:00–8:30
Feb 1952–May 1952, DUM Tue 10:30–11:00
Jun 1952–May 1953, DUM Thu 9:30–10:00
May 1953–Jun 1953, DUM Wed 7:30–8:00
Jun 1953–Sep 1953, DUM Sun 10:00–10:30
Sep 1953–Apr 1954, DUM Thu 9:00–9:30
Apr 1954–Sep 1954, DUM Thu 8:00–8:30
Sep 1954–Feb 1955, DUM Thu 9:00–9:30
Mar 1955–Jun 1955, DUM Wed 8:00–8:30
Jul 1955–Sep 1955, DUM Fri 7:30–8:00

MODERATOR:

Walt Raney (1951)
Walter Kiernan (1951–1953)
Al Capp (1953)
John K. M. McCaffery (1953–1955)

PANELISTS:
Harriet Van Horne (1952–1955)
Robert Sullivan (1952–1953)
Jimmy Cannon (1952–1955)

To this innocuous panel show belongs the unique distinction of being the last surviving entertainment show on the dying DuMont TV network—only a few scattered sports events were continued into 1956. After *What's the Story?* left the air in September 1955, and the remaining boxing matches petered out in 1956, the DuMont network was but a memory.

For four years, however, *What's the Story?* had a reasonably successful career. It consisted of a celebrity panel which attempted to identify important news events from clues provided by the moderator and his helpers. Panelists were generally well-known newspaper columnists, with Harriet Van Horne of the *New York World Telegram*, Robert Sullivan of the New York *Daily News* and Jimmy Cannon of the *Post* the longest-running regulars. Bosley Crowther of the *New York Times* made frequent guest appearances, and John McCaffery's English bulldog, Porthos, was the show's mascot for a time.

WHAT'S YOUR BID

Auction

FIRST TELECAST: *February 14, 1953*
LAST TELECAST: *July 5, 1953*
BROADCAST HISTORY:
Feb 1953–Apr 1953, ABC Sat 7:30–8:00
May 1953–Jul 1953, DUM Sun 10:00–10:30
HOST:
Leonard Rosen (ABC)
Robert Alda (DUM)
ANNOUNCER:
John Reed King (ABC)
Dick Shepard (DUM)

What's Your Bid was a switch on the usual TV giveaway in that the studio audience was supposed to bring its own money to the show—and use it to bid on merchandise such as radios, cars, mink coats, home freezers, etc. Bidders at least got their money's worth (if they bid more than an item was worth, something extra was thrown in) and the proceeds all went to charity. A feature of each show was the auctioning of an item brought in by a famous celebrity, and having some special connection with that celebrity. Some straight giveaway segments were also worked in, but this early form of "pay TV" did not catch on and was soon canceled. Leonard Rosen, the first host and auctioneer, was known on the show as "Liberal Bill."

WHEEL OF FORTUNE

Quiz/Audience Participation

FIRST TELECAST: *July 7, 1953*
LAST TELECAST: *September 15, 1953*
BROADCAST HISTORY:
Jul 1953–Sep 1953, CBS Tue 8:30–9:00
HOST:
Todd Russell

All of the contestants on *Wheel of Fortune* were people who had distinguished themselves as good samaritans or heroes. They were brought on the show and received rewards for their good deeds. After host Todd Russell related their individual stories for the audience, a giant carnival-type wheel was spun to determine the nature of the "reward" that they would receive. A special "lucky" section on the wheel could bring the contestant a $1,000 bonus if he could answer a special jackpot question correctly. This summer series was identical to the daytime version which had premiered the previous October.

WHEN THINGS WERE ROTTEN

Situation Comedy

FIRST TELECAST: *September 10, 1975*
LAST TELECAST: *December 24, 1975*
BROADCAST HISTORY:
Sep 1975–Dec 1975, ABC Wed 8:00–8:30
CAST:
Robin Hood .... Dick Gautier
Friar Tuck .... Dick Van Patten
Alan-a-Dale .... Bernie Kopell
Bertram/Renaldo .... Richard Dimitri
The Sheriff of Nottingham ... Henry Polic II
Maid Marian .... Misty Rowe
Little John .... David Sabin
Prince John .... Ron Rifkin
Princess Isabelle .... Jane A. Johnston
CREATOR/PRODUCER:
Mel Brooks

Mel Brooks created this wild satire on Robin Hood and His Merry Men of Sherwood Forest, in 12th-century England. Instead of the boldly heroic Robin of legend, he was portrayed as a complete nitwit, and his men a band of incompetents who only succeeded because of the even greater incompetence of the evil Prince John and his henchman, the Sheriff of Nottingham. Much of the humor in this fast-paced, movie-style comedy was based on nonsequiturs and historical anachronisms, such as the episode in which Prince John hired the four fastest woodcutters in the kingdom to chop down the entire Sherwood Forest—to make way for a new housing development for wealthy burghers. In the premiere telecast, the Prince lured Robin into a trap by staging an archery contest to determine who was the greatest bowman in the land. Robin, vain as ever, came in disguise to win the title but was seized and thrown into the dungeon. Whereupon his men disguised themselves as a traveling conga band and bongoed their way into the castle to rescue him.

Maid Marian was Robin's sexy, but empty-headed love interest.

Critics applauded this series as one of the most inventive of the season, but viewers paid no attention to it and it was soon canceled.

WHERE WAS I?

Quiz/Panel

FIRST TELECAST: *September 2, 1952*

LAST TELECAST: *October 6, 1953*

BROADCAST HISTORY:

Sep 1952–May 1953, DUM Tue 9:00–9:30
May 1953–Jun 1953, DUM Tue 10:00–10:30
Jul 1953–Oct 1953, DUM Tue 9:30–10:00

EMCEE:

Dan Seymour (1952)
Ken Roberts (1952)
John Reed King (1952–1953)

PANELISTS:

Nancy Guild
Peter Donald
Samuel Grafton (1953)
Virginia Graham (1952)
Bill Cullen (1953)
Barbara Barondess MacLean (1953)
Skitch Henderson (1953)
Mort Green (1953)

In this picture quiz the panel had to identify a given location from a set of photographs, and some verbal clues. The original host, Dan Seymour, lasted less than a month, followed by Ken Roberts for about two months and then John Reed King for the remainder of the run of the show. There was quite a bit of turnover in panelists as well.

WHERE'S HUDDLES

Cartoon

FIRST TELECAST: *July 1, 1970*

LAST TELECAST: *September 9, 1970*

BROADCAST HISTORY:

Jul 1970–Sep 1970, CBS Wed 7:30–8:00

VOICES:

Bubba McCoy .... Mel Blanc
Sports announcer .... Dick Enberg
Freight Train .... Herb Jeffries
Claude Pertwee .... Paul Lynde
Fumbles .... Don Messick
Ed Huddles .... Cliff Norton
Mad Dog Maloney .... Alan Reed
Marge Huddles .... Jean Vanderpyl
Penny McCoy .... Marie Wilson

This animated summer series was the story of two professional football players for the Rhinos, quarterback Ed Huddles and center Bubba McCoy. They were next-door neighbors and best friends, as well as teammates, and their adventures on and off the field were the subjects of the episodes of the show.

WHERE'S RAYMOND?

see *Ray Bolger Show, The*

WHISPERING SMITH

Western/Detective

FIRST TELECAST: *May 15, 1961*

LAST TELECAST: *September 18, 1961*

BROADCAST HISTORY:

May 1961–Sep 1961, NBC Mon 9:00–9:30

CAST:

Det. Tom "Whispering" Smith
.... Audie Murphy
Det. George Romack .... Guy Mitchell
Chief John Richards .... Sam Buffington

Set in Denver, Colorado, in the 1870s, *Whispering Smith* was based on the adventures of the first police detective to bring modern methods of analysis, tracing technique, and apprehension to the practice of law enforcement in the West. Denver police detective Tom Smith, better known by his nickname "Whispering," was this pioneer Western criminologist. His partner and sidekick George Romack was played by singer-turned-actor Guy Mitchell. Sam Buffington, who played the chief of the Denver Police Department, died during the filming of the series and was seen in only a portion of the episodes. Actual cases from the file of the Denver Police Department provided the cases depicted in *Whispering Smith.*

This series was originally scheduled for the 1959–1960 fall season but, after co-star Guy Mitchell suffered a broken shoulder with only seven episodes completed, it was temporarily postponed.

WHITE CAMELLIA, THE

see *ABC Dramatic Shorts—1952–1953*

WHO IN THE WORLD

Interview

FIRST TELECAST: *June 24, 1962*

LAST TELECAST: *September 16, 1962*

BROADCAST HISTORY:

Jun 1962–Sep 1962, CBS Sun 9:30–10:00

HOST:

Warren Hull

Each week host Warren Hull interviewed three to five people who had made headlines in the nation's newspapers during the previous seven days. At least that was the original idea behind the show. A shortage of available headline-makers forced the area from which guests were drawn to be broadened to include people who had human-interest stories to tell. The program's producer found the world's first airline stewardess and the 1,000th member of the Peace Corps, among others, for Warren Hull to chat with.

WHO PAYS

Quiz/Audience Participation

FIRST TELECAST: *July 2, 1959*

LAST TELECAST: *September 24, 1959*

BROADCAST HISTORY:

Jul 1959–Sep 1959, NBC Thu 8:00–8:30

EMCEE:

Mike Wallace

REGULARS:

Gene Klavan
Cedric Hardwicke
Celeste Holm

The object of *Who Pays* was for the three regular panelists to determine which celebrity or public figure was the employer of each pair of contestants. The employees were questioned by the panelists in two rounds. The first round gave each panelist one minute to ask specific questions of the two employees (who were chauffeurs, doctors, gardeners, hair stylists, etc.). At the end of the round the panelists pooled their information and decided whether or not to guess the identity of the employer. If they guessed correctly, the employees split $100 and if they guessed incorrectly the employees split $200. If the panelists felt they had too little information to hazard a guess, a second round was played with the dollar value to the employees doubling.

WHO SAID THAT?

Quiz/Panel

FIRST TELECAST: *December 9, 1948*

LAST TELECAST: *July 26, 1955*

BROADCAST HISTORY:

Dec 1948–Jan 1949, NBC Mon 10:00–10:30
Jan 1949–Mar 1949, NBC Sun 10:30–11:00
Apr 1949–Dec 1949, NBC Sat 9:00–9:30
Jan 1950–Jul 1954, NBC Mon 10:30–11:00
Feb 1955–Apr 1955, ABC Wed 9:00–9:30
May 1955–Jul 1955, ABC Tue 8:30–9:00

EMCEE:

Robert Trout (1948–1951)
Walter Kiernan (1951–1954)
John Daly (1955)

PANELISTS:

John Cameron Swayze (1948–1951)
Bill Henry (1952–1953)
June Lockhart (1952–1955)
Morey Amsterdam (1954)
H. V. Kaltenborn (1954)
Bob Considine (1955)
John Mason Brown (1955)

Live quiz show based on quotations from the news. A panel of newsmen and celebrities was read a quotation from the current headlines, and then asked to identify "who said that," and something about the circumstances. Failure to come up with the correct answer resulted in forfeiture of cash to the prize jackpot, which at one time was represented by a goldfish bowl into which panel members stuffed bills. The jackpot was awarded to a home viewer if the quote had been sent in by one, or to a charity. Variations such as a famous guest who, seen only in silhouette, personally delivered his own quote, famous quotes from the past, and partial quotes which had to be completed were also introduced from time to time. During most of the show's run there was only a single permanent panelist (or "anchorman"), plus guests, but toward the end several permanent panelists were used. Among the panelists appearing irregularly, but frequently, were Frank Coniff, Earl Wilson, Al Capp, Quentin Reynolds, Bennett Cerf, Oscar Levant, and Kitty Carlisle.

The program was originally edited by Fred Friendly, and was also heard on radio for a time.

WHO'S THE BOSS?

Quiz/Panel

FIRST TELECAST: *February 19, 1954*

LAST TELECAST: *August 20, 1954*

BROADCAST HISTORY:

Feb 1954–Jun 1954, ABC Fri 9:30–10:00

Jul 1954–Aug 1954, ABC Fri 8:30–9:00

EMCEE:

Walter Kiernan (Feb–Jul)

Mike Wallace (Jul–Aug)

PANEL:

Peggy McKay

Dick Kollmar

Sylvia Lyons

Horace Sutton

Secretaries to famous personalities from the worlds of show business, politics, and sports were the guests on this show. The panel attempted to identify the names of their bosses through indirect questioning, with prizes being awarded after each round that the secretary continued to stump the panel.

WHO'S THERE

Quiz/Audience Participation

FIRST TELECAST: *July 14, 1952*

LAST TELECAST: *September 15, 1952*

BROADCAST HISTORY:

Jul 1952–Sep 1952, CBS Mon 9:30–10:00

EMCEE:

Arlene Francis

PANELISTS:

Bill Cullen

Robert Coote

Roger Price

The panelists on *Who's There* tried to identify famous celebrities from various articles of clothing or props that had been characteristic of, or identified with, the celebrities. There were two regular panelists —originally Bill Cullen and Robert Coote—and one guest panelist. Cullen was replaced in midsummer by Roger Price.

WHO'S WATCHING THE KIDS

Situation Comedy

FIRST TELECAST: *September 22, 1978*

LAST TELECAST:

BROADCAST HISTORY:

Sep 1978– , NBC Fri 8:30–9:00

CAST:

Stacy Turner ....Caren Kaye

Angie Vitola ....Lynda Goodfriend

Frankie "the Fox" Vitola ......Scott Baio

Melissa Turner ....Tammy Lauren

Mitzi Logan ....Marcia Lewis

Christopher Day ....Larry Breeding

Memphis O'Hara ....Lorrie Mahaffey

Bert Gunkel ....Jim Belushi

The kids in this comedy were 15-year-old Frankie and 9-year-old Melissa, two hyperactive and worldly-wise youngsters who lived with their showgirl older sisters in a Las Vegas apartment. Angie and Stacy spent much of their time performing at a third-rate local nightspot, the Club Sand Pile, so help was enlisted from neighbor Christopher Day to "watch the kids." Macho, streetwise Frankie and bookish, know-it-all Melissa were more than a match for all three adults. Christopher was a reporter whose ambition was to become a hard hitting, investigative journalist, but so far he had made it only to reading the weather and garden news on a local TV station. Mitzi was the rotund emcee at the Club Sand Pile, and also the girls' landlady; Memphis was a singer at the club.

The pilot for this comedy, which had a slightly different storyline, aired on May 19, 1978 under the title *Legs*.

WHO'S WHO

New Magazine

FIRST TELECAST: *January 4, 1977*

LAST TELECAST: *June 26, 1977*

BROADCAST HISTORY:

Jan 1977–May 1977, CBS Tue 8:00–9:00

Jun 1977, CBS Sun 10:00–11:00

REPORTERS:

Dan Rather

Barbara Howar

Charles Kuralt

If *60 Minutes* was the television equivalent of *Time* magazine, this series, produced by the same team, was patterned after *People* magazine. Although *60 Minutes* often did profiles on individuals, it also included in-depth studies of broader issues. *Who's*

Who concentrated only on people. Dan Rather and Barbara Howar did pieces on the famous—Richard Burton, Leopold Stokowsky, Lily Tomlin, Jodie Foster, Jack Nicklaus, UN Ambassador Andrew Young, and First Lady Rosalynn Carter. Charles Kuralt focused on more obscure subjects. His "On the Road" segment included chats with an 89-year-old kite flyer in Farmland, Indiana; a champion boomerang thrower living on an island in the Gulf of Mexico; a nightclub owner in Vicksburg, Mississippi, who had booked top black jazz performers into his place in the 1930s and 1940s; and the inventor of the supermarket shopping cart, in Oklahoma City.

WHO'S WHOSE

Quiz/Audience Participation

FIRST TELECAST: *June 25, 1951*
LAST TELECAST: *June 25, 1951*
BROADCAST HISTORY:
Jun 1951, CBS Mon 9:30–10:00
EMCEE:
Phil Baker
PANELISTS:
Robin Chandler
Art Ford
Basil Davenport
Emily Kimbrough

The object of this summer show was for the celebrity panel (three regulars and one guest) to guess which of three people was the spouse of a fourth contestant. The panelists had an opportunity to question all four people, three of one sex and the fourth of the other, in the attempt to determine who was whose. Since the show only lasted one week, it obviously did not work too well.

WHY?

Quiz/Panel

FIRST TELECAST: *January 12, 1953*
LAST TELECAST: *April 20, 1953*
BROADCAST HISTORY:
Jan 1953–Apr 1953, ABC Mon 10:00–10:30
EMCEE:
John Reed King
ASSISTANT:
Bill Cullen

In this quiz show based on the old "five W's," Bill Cullen read the panel the who, what, where, and when of a situation. The panel then had to guess the "why?" The three members of each night's panel were drawn from all walks of life.

WICHITA TOWN

Western

FIRST TELECAST: *September 30, 1959*
LAST TELECAST: *September 23, 1960*
BROADCAST HISTORY:
Sep 1959–Apr 1960, NBC Wed 10:30–11:00
Jun 1960–Sep 1960, NBC Fri 8:30–9:00
CAST:
Marshal Mike Dunbar ....Joel McCrea
Ben Matheson ....Jody McCrea
Rico Rodriguez ....Carlos Romero
Dr. Nat Wyndham ....George Neise
Aeneas MacLinahan ....Bob Anderson
Joe Kingston ....Robert Foulk

In the decade following the Civil War the town of Wichita, on the fringes of the lawless Western frontier in the Kansas Territory, was a young city trying to grow and prosper. The town's leading citizen was Mike Dunbar, a man who had led a cattle drive to Wichita and decided to stay on as marshal to help establish law and order in the community. Dunbar was aided by his two deputies, Ben Matheson and Rico Rodriguez, the former a foreman at the nearby Circle J Ranch, and the latter a reformed Mexican gunfighter. Also seen regularly in the series were Dr. Nat Wyndham, Wichita's first doctor, Aeneas MacLinahan, the town blacksmith, and Joe Kingston, the bartender in the local saloon.

Joel and Jody McCrea, who played marshal and deputy in this Western, were in real life father and son.

WIDE COUNTRY, THE

Western

FIRST TELECAST: *September 20, 1962*
LAST TELECAST: *September 12, 1963*
BROADCAST HISTORY:
Sep 1962–Sep 1963, NBC Thu 7:30–8:30
CAST:
Mitch Guthrie ....Earl Holliman
Andy Guthrie ....Andrew Prine

Western drama revolving around champion bronco rider Mitch Guthrie, as he encountered the adventures of contemporary rodeo life, while trying to persuade his kid brother Andy not to become a "rodeo bum" like himself.

WIFE SAVER, THE

Household Hints

FIRST TELECAST: *May 22, 1947*

LAST TELECAST: *June 26, 1947*

BROADCAST HISTORY:

May 1947–Jun 1947, NBC Thu 8:30–9:00

HOST:

Allen Prescott

Longtime radio favorite Allen Prescott tried his popular *Wife Saver* routine (first heard in 1932) on television in 1947. The format consisted of Prescott in the kitchen demonstrating household gadgets and explaining ways of solving problems around the house, such as keeping twine unraveled or bureau drawers unstuck, all interspersed with a steady patter of gags. The humor plus the useful hints should have made this a popular show, but it lasted only six weeks.

WILD KINGDOM

Wildlife/Nature

FIRST TELECAST: *January 7, 1968*

LAST TELECAST: *April 11, 1971*

BROADCAST HISTORY:

Jan 1968–Jun 1968, NBC Sun 7:00–7:30
Jan 1969–Jun 1969, NBC Sun 7:00–7:30
Sep 1969–Jun 1970, NBC Sun 7:00–7:30
Sep 1970–Apr 1971, NBC Sun 7:00–7:30

REGULARS:

Marlin Perkins
Jim Fowler
Stan Brock

The full title of this long-running nature series was *Mutual of Omaha's Wild Kingdom*. It starred famed naturalist and zoo director Marlin Perkins, with the aid of fellow naturalist Jim Fowler and, later, Stan Brock. The series covered such diverse topics as animal survival in the wilds, treatment of animals in captivity, the environments of primitive peoples, and the interrelationships between both primitive peoples and their animal neighbors and different species of animals with each other. An outgrowth of an earlier NBC series, *Zoo Parade*, which had originated almost exclusively from Chicago's Lincoln Park Zoo and which also starred Mr. Perkins, *Wild Kingdom* spent much more time away from the zoo setting. When it premiered on January 6, 1963, *Wild Kingdom* was telecast on Sunday afternoons, as its predecessor had been. It moved into the evening hours in January 1968. Following its cancellation by NBC at the end of the 1970–1971 season, *Wild Kingdom* went into syndication. It is currently still in production and carried in most of the U.S. by local stations.

WILD WILD WEST, THE

Western

FIRST TELECAST: *September 17, 1965*

LAST TELECAST: *September 7, 1970*

BROADCAST HISTORY:

Sep 1965–Sep 1969, CBS Fri 7:30–8:30
Jul 1970–Sep 1970, CBS Mon 10:00–11:00

CAST:

James T. West .... Robert Conrad
Artemus Gordon .... Ross Martin

James T. West was the James Bond of Westerns. West was an undercover agent for President Grant whose assignments usually involved exposing or undermining the attempts of various radical, revolutionary, or criminal groups to take over all or part of the U.S. Helping him was his friend and assistant, Artemus Gordon, a master of disguises and dialects. The two of them traveled in a special railroad car that supplied them with the materials to concoct all sorts of bizarre weapons and devices to foil their adversaries. Beautiful women, contrived situations, and fantastic devices populated this series throughout its four-year run. CBS aired reruns during the summer of 1970.

WILLY

Lawyer

FIRST TELECAST: *September 18, 1954*

LAST TELECAST: *July 7, 1955*

BROADCAST HISTORY:

Sep 1954–Mar 1955, CBS Sat 10:30–11:00
Apr 1955–Jul 1955, CBS Thu 10:30–11:00

CAST:

Willa Dodger .... June Havoc
Franklin Dodger .... Denny Richards, Jr.
Emily Dodger .... Mary Treen
Papa Dodger .... Lloyd Corrigan
Charlie Bush .... Whitfield Connor
Perry Bannister (1955) .... Hal Peary

Following her graduation from law school, Willa Dodger opened a legal practice in her home town of Renfrew, New Hampshire. There were not many exciting cases in that little hamlet so, in mid-season, Willy got an offer to work as legal counsel to a vaudeville organization run by Perry Bannister. She left her family and her boy friend, Charlie Bush, and relocated to the big city. Her adventures, whether in rural New England or cosmopolitan New York, were on the lighter side and rarely involved her in serious legal cases.

WILLYS THEATRE PRESENTING BEN HECHT'S TALES OF THE CITY

Dramatic Anthology

FIRST TELECAST: *June 25, 1953*

LAST TELECAST: *September 17, 1953*

BROADCAST HISTORY:

Jun 1953–Sep 1953, CBS Thu 8:30–9:00

NARRATOR:

Ben Hecht

Author Ben Hecht, whose most famous and award-winning work was the play *The Front Page,* was the narrator of this anthology series composed of adaptations of his stories. He was never seen onscreen, only heard with his introductions and closing remarks. The live dramas aired on alternate weeks with *Four Star Playhouse.*

WIN WITH A WINNER

Quiz/Audience Participation

FIRST TELECAST: *June 24, 1958*

LAST TELECAST: *September 9, 1958*

BROADCAST HISTORY:

Jun 1958–Sep 1958, NBC Tue 7:30–8:00

EMCEE:

Sandy Becker
Win Elliott

POSTCARD GIRL:

Marilyn Toomey
Rita Hayes

This rather complicated summer quiz show encouraged home viewers to root for their favorite contestant and possibly share in the prizes. At the end of each show the next week's contestants were introduced, and viewers were invited to write in with their prediction of who would be the top money winner, as well as (during the first month at least) the order of finish. Those with the right choice were candidates for cash prizes, and anyone predicting the entire order of finish got a bonus prize.

The game itself generally resembled a horserace. The five (later four) contestants were each given the same question. A correct answer added the value of that question, usually $100 or $200, to their total, while a wrong answer subtracted the same amount from their previous winnings. In addition one contestant in each round had the opportunity to double his winnings—or losses. A running tally was kept of each contestant's total in the race, but only the top winner got to keep his money. The others got consolation prizes.

A "postcard girl" picked home-viewer predictions out of a large drum during the course of the show, and all those predicting the top contestant would "win with the winner," splitting the same amount of money that he had won.

Sandy Becker and Marilyn Toomey, the original host and postcard girl, were replaced by Win Elliot and Rita Hayes on July 22.

WINDOW ON MAIN STREET

Situation Comedy

FIRST TELECAST: *October 2, 1961*

LAST TELECAST: *September 12, 1962*

BROADCAST HISTORY:

Oct 1961–Feb 1962, CBS Mon 8:30–9:00
Feb 1962–Sep 1962, CBS Wed 8:00–8:30

CAST:

Cameron Garrett Brooks .....Robert Young
Chris Logan ....Constance Moore
Lloyd Ramsey ....Ford Rainey
Arny Logan ....Brad Berwick
Wally Evans ....James Davidson
Peggy Evans ....Carol Byron
Miss Wycliffe ....Coleen Gray

Writer Cameron Brooks returned to his home town of Millsburg in search of materials for stories. He moved into the Majestic Hotel and resumed an old friendship with Lloyd Ramsey, editor of the local newspaper. The people he knew, as well as those he met at the hotel, served as subjects for his stories. In the spring, when the Majestic was temporarily closed for renovations, Cameron took a room in the home of Wally and Peggy Evans.

Robert Young, the star of this series, had just completed a six-year run in the highly popular *Father Knows Best* (reruns of which were still being telecast in prime time). He was looking for a different type of series to display his talents, but *Window on Main Street* was not successful and so Young subsequently went into retirement—until 1969, when *Marcus Welby* came along.

WINDOW ON THE WORLD

Variety

FIRST TELECAST: *January 27, 1949*

LAST TELECAST: *April 14, 1949*

BROADCAST HISTORY:

Jan 1949–Apr 1949, DUM Thu 9:00–9:30

Hollywood comedian Gil Lamb, actress-singer Irene Manning, and others were seen on this short-lived show.

WINDOWS

Dramatic Anthology

FIRST TELECAST: *July 8, 1955*

LAST TELECAST: *August 26, 1955*

BROADCAST HISTORY:

Jul 1955–Aug 1955, CBS Fri 10:30–11:00

This live dramatic series, originating from New York, was the 1955 summer replacement for *Person to Person.* Each episode of the series opened on an ordinary window through which the camera moved to begin the unfolding of the story. All of the stories were designed to show real people confronting real problems, such as a woman alcoholic and her effect on her family, a boy's adulation for an ex-circus clown, and an illiterate woman's determined struggle to learn how to read.

WINDY CITY JAMBOREE

Country Music

FIRST TELECAST: *March 19, 1950*

LAST TELECAST: *June 18, 1950*

BROADCAST HISTORY:

Mar 1950–Jun 1950, DUM Sun 9:00–10:00

REGULARS:

Danny O'Neil
Gloria Van

Barn dance with variety acts, originating from Chicago.

WINGO

Quiz/Audience Participation

FIRST TELECAST: *April 1, 1958*

LAST TELECAST: *May 6, 1958*

BROADCAST HISTORY:

Apr 1958–May 1958, CBS Tue 8:30–9:00

EMCEE:

Bob Kennedy

This short-lived entry in the big-money quiz-show sweepstakes pitted two contestants against each other in answering questions of general and varied knowledge. The winner of each round won $1,000, the opportunity to continue against a new challenger, and a shot at the "Wingo" portion of the show. This part of the game, which depended on pure luck, offered the ultimate jackpot of $250,000 to any contestant who succeeded in matching the letters spelling the show's title in an elaborate word game. Contestants who continued to compete risked a part of their winnings in the event that they were defeated by a subsequent challenger.

WINNER TAKE ALL

Quiz/Audience Participation

FIRST TELECAST: *July 8, 1948*

LAST TELECAST: *October 3, 1950*

BROADCAST HISTORY:

Jul 1948–Aug 1948, CBS Thu 9:30–10:00
Aug 1948–Jan 1949, CBS Wed 8:30–9:00
Apr 1950–Jul 1950, CBS Thu 9:45–10:30
Jul 1950–Oct 1950, CBS Tue 9:00–9:30

EMCEE:

Bud Collyer

The format of *Winner Take All* was very simple. Two contestants competed with each other answering questions given them by the emcee. One of them had a bell and the other had a buzzer. The first one to announce his/her readiness to answer (by ringing or buzzing) was given an opportunity to answer the question. Each correct answer was worth a point and three points won the game. The winner won merchandise prizes and the right to meet new challengers until defeated. *Winner Take All* had been on CBS radio since the mid–1940s and the radio version, with a different emcee, was still being aired when the show moved to television in 1948. During the 15 months that it was not on the network, from January 1949 to April 1950, it continued as a local program in New York, returning to the network for its final six months as a nighttime series. It then became a daytime show, with a new emcee, lasting until the following April. The daytime version, hosted by radio personality Barry Gray, was much different from the evening *Winner Take All.* Regular members of the daytime cast performed sketches to challenge contestants' knowledge, and did song and dance numbers as well.

WINSTON CHURCHILL—THE VALIANT YEARS

Documentary

FIRST TELECAST: *November 27, 1960*

LAST TELECAST: *April 5, 1963*

BROADCAST HISTORY:

Nov 1960–Jun 1961, ABC Sun 10:30–11:00
Sep 1962–Dec 1962, ABC Sun 6:30–7:00
Dec 1962–Apr 1963, ABC Fri 7:30–8:00

NARRATORS:

Gary Merrill
Richard Burton

Churchill's role in the years leading into and during World War II was chronicled in this award-winning documentary series. The basis for each episode was memoirs that Churchill the historian had kept to describe the activities of Churchill the statesman. Old film clips, letters, and contemporary backgrounds were woven together to paint a picture of Churchill's role at that critical period of world history. Gary Merrill was the formal narrator with Richard Burton doing selected dramatic readings. The series was rerun in its entirety during the 1962–1963 season.

WIRE SERVICE

Newspaper

FIRST TELECAST: *October 4, 1956*

LAST TELECAST: *September 13, 1959*

BROADCAST HISTORY:

Oct 1956–Feb 1957, ABC Thu 9:00–10:00
Feb 1957–Sep 1957, ABC Mon 7:30–8:30
Feb 1959–Sep 1959, ABC Sun 9:30–10:30

CAST:

Dan Miller .... Dane Clark
Dean Evans .... George Brent
Katherine Wells ... Mercedes McCambridge

The three stars of this series each played a roving reporter for the Trans-Globe wire service. Each of them traveled all over the country and the world, tracking down stories involving crime and high adventure. The three reporters worked independently and appeared in separate stories, on a rotating basis.

In 1959 the *Wire Service* episodes starring Dane Clark were rerun under the title *Deadline for Action.*

WISDOM OF THE AGES

Discussion

FIRST TELECAST: *December 16, 1952*

LAST TELECAST: *June 30, 1953*

BROADCAST HISTORY:

Dec 1952–Jun 1953, DUM Tue 9:30–10:00

MODERATOR:

Jack Barry

PANELISTS:

Ronnie Mulluzzo (Age 8)
Marcia Van Dyke (28)
Leo Cherne (40)
Mrs. H. V. Kaltenborn (64)
Thomas Clark (82)

Quizmaster Jack Barry had been highly successful with a panel show featuring youngsters *(Juvenile Jury)* and another with oldsters *(Life Begins at Eighty),* so it was natural to try a show that spanned all age groups. As on the prototype programs, the format was simply for the panel to discuss, from the perspective of their various generations, the often humorous problems and questions submitted by viewers. The panel consisted of one member under 20, one 20–40, one 40–60, one 60–80, and one over 80. The panelists most frequently seen during the show's six-month run are listed above. Interestingly enough, though each age group had its own unique point of view, it was the two extremes—the eight- and the 82-year-old—who were most often in agreement.

WITNESS, THE

Courtroom Anthology

FIRST TELECAST: *September 29, 1960*

LAST TELECAST: *January 26, 1961*

BROADCAST HISTORY:

Sep 1960–Dec 1960, CBS Thu 7:30–8:30
Dec 1960–Jan 1961, CBS Thu 9:00–10:00

CAST:

Court Reporter .... Verne Collett
Court Clerk .... William Griffis

COMMITTEE MEMBERS:

Charles Haydon
Paul McGrath
William Smithers
Frank Milan

In a format that was similar to a Congressional investigation, this series attempted to dramatize the exploits and life-styles of gangsters and rogues from the past and present. Detailed research was done on all of the "witnesses" who were brought before the committee to explain and/or defend their activities. The first of these hearings starred Telly Savalas as Charles "Lucky" Luciano. Among the other figures whose lives were exposed on this show were Bugsy Siegel, Dutch Schultz, Al Capone, John Dillinger, James Walker (former New York City mayor), and Ma Barker. The committee members asking the questions were all real attorneys and members of the New York Bar Association.

WOMAN TO REMEMBER, A

Romantic Drama

FIRST TELECAST: *May 2, 1949*

LAST TELECAST: *July 15, 1949*

BROADCAST HISTORY:

May 1949–Jul 1949, DUM Mon–Fri 7:30–7:45

CAST:

Christine Baker ....Patricia Wheel
Steve Hammond ....John Raby
Charley Anderson ....Frankie Thomas
Bessie Thatcher ....Ruth McDevitt

A Woman to Remember was an early attempt to bring soap opera—radio soap opera, at that—to early-evening television. The leading character, Christine Baker, was even depicted as a radio soap-opera queen, engaged to handsome Steve Hammond, but beset by scheming rivals, notably shrewish Carol Winstead. Charley Anderson, the young sound man on Christine's show, and Bessie, another actress, were allies.

A Woman to Remember was first seen as a daytime serial, beginning February 21, 1949.

WONDER WOMAN

Adventure

FIRST TELECAST: *December 18, 1976*

LAST TELECAST:

BROADCAST HISTORY:

Dec 1976–Jan 1977, ABC Sat 8:00–9:00
May 1977–Jul 1977, ABC Sat 8:00–9:00
Sep 1977– , CBS Fri 8:00–9:00

CAST:

Yeoman Diana Prince/"Wonder Woman" .... Lynda Carter
Maj. Steve Trevor/Steve Trevor, Jr. .... Lyle Waggoner
Gen. Blankenship (1976–1977) .... Richard Eastham
Corp. Etta Candy (1976–1977) .... Beatrice Colen
Joe Atkinson (1977) ......Normann Burton

Wonder Woman, based on Charles Moulton's comic-book superheroine of the 1940s, developed gradually into a regular TV series. It was first seen as a TV movie in March 1974 (with Cathy Lee Crosby in the title role), then in another try in November 1975 (with Lynda Carter), then in a series of specials called *The New Original Wonder Woman* beginning in March 1976. After popping up in various spots all over the ABC schedule, it had a short consecutive-weeks run in December 1976–January 1977. Finally, in the fall of 1977, it moved to CBS and became a regular weekly series.

The show was comic strip, pure and simple, set in the 1940s. Wonder Woman came from a "lost" island where a band of Amazon women had fled *ca.* 200 B.C. to escape male domination by the ancient Greeks and Romans. On Paradise Island they found the magic substance Feminum, which when molded into a golden belt gave them superhuman strength and in golden bracelets could deflect bullets. It didn't help their love life much, though, so when Major Steve Trevor of the U.S. Army crash-landed on the island during World War II, Wonder Woman fell in love and returned with him to the U.S. in the guise of his secretary. Major Trevor did not know of her powers, but when trouble threatened, Yeoman Prince could disappear for awhile, and whirl herself into Wonder Woman! She then reappeared, clad in sexy tights and draped in a cape that looked something like the American flag.

Her opponents were mostly Nazi agents, plus a few aliens from outer space, all of whom were dispatched in slam-bang-biff-pow style. Once the Nazis even found and occupied Paradise Island in their quest for Feminum, and they had their own Wonder Woman in Fausta. Seen occasionally on Diana's side was her younger sister Drusilla, the "Wonder Girl" (played by Debra Winger).

When the series moved to CBS in the fall 1977 there were a number of changes made. The title was now *The New Adventures of Wonder Woman* and the period was contemporary, rather than World War II. The heroine returned to America to fight terrorists and subversive elements for the Inter-Agency Defense Command (IADC), where her boss was Joe Atkinson. Working closely with her was Steve Trevor, Jr., the son of the Major Trevor with whom she had been associated during World War II. Since she had not aged at all—residents of Paradise Island had life spans measured in centuries, not decades—and Steve, Jr. was a dead ringer for his father, the couple seemed virtually unchanged. By the end of 1977 Mr. Atkinson had been phased out of the show and Steve had been promoted to Diana Prince's boss, leaving her to go alone on missions. A primary source of information for all IADC agents was the Internal Retrieval Associative Computer. This wonderful device, called IRA by the staff, could actually communicate by voice with the agents. Despite the fact that Diana was no longer wearing glasses to conceal her real identity, as she had done in the ABC version of *Wonder Woman*, only IRA knew who she really was.

Lynda Carter, who portrayed Wonder Woman, did fit the part. A former "Miss World—U.S.A.," she was a very athletic, tall (5′10″, not 6′ as some publicity releases claimed), and extremely well-endowed.

WONDERFUL JOHN ACTON, THE

General Drama

FIRST TELECAST: *July 5, 1953*

LAST TELECAST: *September 22, 1953*

BROADCAST HISTORY:

July 1953–Aug 1953, NBC Sun 10:00–10:30

Sep 1953, NBC Tue 8:30–9:00

CAST:

John Acton ....Harry Holcombe

Uncle Terrence ....Ian Martin

Julia Acton ....Virginia Dwyer

Kevin Acton ....Ronnie Walken

Aunt Bessie ....Jane Rose

Peter Bodkin, Sr. ....Pat Harrington

Birdie Bodkin ....Mary Michael

Narrator ....Luis Van Roten

Set in the Ohio River Valley town of Ludlow, Kentucky, *The Wonderful John Acton* was the story of an Irish family in 1919, John Acton was the county clerk and owned a combination candy and notions store, with his living quarters in the back. The stories were narrated by John's grandson, Kevin Acton, who reminisced about his childhood growing up in small-town America. Kevin revered his grandfather and had always considered him someone "wonderful." As narrator, the adult Kevin was never seen in this live dramatic series.

WONDERFUL WORLD OF DISNEY, THE

see *Walt Disney*

WORD OF LIFE SONGTIME, THE

see *Songtime*

WORDS AND MUSIC

Music

FIRST TELECAST: *August 2, 1949*

LAST TELECAST: *September 8, 1949*

BROADCAST HISTORY:

Aug 1949–Sep 1949, NBC Tue/Thu 7:30–7:45

REGULARS:

Barbara Marshall

Jerry Jerome Trio

Live musical interlude featuring singer-pianist Barbara Marshall.

WORLD IN YOUR HOME, THE

Documentary

FIRST TELECAST: *December 22, 1944*

LAST TELECAST: *January 9, 1948*

BROADCAST HISTORY:

Dec 1944–Jan 1948, NBC Fri 8:45–9:00 (approx.)

One of the very earliest regular network features on TV seems to have been this weekly educational film sponsored by RCA Victor. It ran for more than three years in the same time slot, from 1944 to 1948. Network records are sketchy that far back and it is not known exactly when *The World in Your Home* became a network show (it originated from New York), but New York, Philadelphia, and Schenectady were linked by NBC-TV in 1944 and it is quite possible that it was fed to all three stations from the beginning.

WORLD OF MR. SWEENEY, THE

Situation Comedy

FIRST TELECAST: *June 30, 1954*

LAST TELECAST: *August 20, 1954*

BROADCAST HISTORY:

Jun 1954–Aug 1954, NBC Tue/Wed/Fri 7:30–7:45

CAST:

Cicero P. Sweeney ....Charlie Ruggles

Kippy Franklin ....Glen Walken

Marge Franklin ....Helen Wagner

Following a season as one of the segments of *The Kate Smith Evening Hour*, *The World of Mr. Sweeney* struck out on its own during the summer of 1954. Cicero P. Sweeney was the owner of a small-town general store who, in addition to providing groceries to the townspeople, was a sounding board for their problems and provider of good advice. Each episode revolved around different members of the local community and Sweeney's solutions to their problems. The only regulars other than Sweeney himself were his grandson Kippy and Kippy's mother Marge. *The World of Mr. Sweeney* was produced live from New York throughout its nighttime run. In October 1954 it moved to the NBC Monday–Friday daytime lineup where it stayed until December 1955.

Despite its relatively short run, *The World of Mr. Sweeney* was recently cited as holding the all-time record for the largest number of episodes of a comedy series ever presented on the NBC network—mostly because of its 14 months in daytime, where it ran five times a week. In all, 345 installments were presented.

WORLD OF TALENT

see *Dick Clark's World of Talent*

WORLD WAR I

Documentary

FIRST TELECAST: *September 22, 1964*

LAST TELECAST: *September 5, 1965*

BROADCAST HISTORY:

Sep 1964–Dec 1964, CBS Tue 8:00–8:30
Dec 1964–Sep 1965, CBS Sun 6:30–7:00

NARRATOR:

Robert Ryan

This was a documentary series recalling the background causes, conduct, and aftermath of World War I. The emotional reactions of the leaders and peoples most directly involved, as well as the social, political and economic fabric of the times, were analyzed in depth.

WORLD WIDE '60

Documentary

FIRST TELECAST: *January 23, 1960*

LAST TELECAST: *August 27, 1960*

BROADCAST HISTORY:

Jan 1960–Aug 1960, NBC Sat 9:30–10:30

HOST:

Frank McGee

NBC News correspondent Frank McGee served as host and narrator of this series of public-affairs documentaries. The subject matter ranged from alcoholism, to old age, to architecture, to missiles, to jazz, to the problems of refugees. The premiere telecast of this series covered the first year of Fidel Castro's regime in Cuba.

WRANGLER

Western

FIRST TELECAST: *August 4, 1960*

LAST TELECAST: *September 15, 1960*

BROADCAST HISTORY:

Aug 1960–Sep 1960, NBC Thu 9:30–10:00

CAST:

Pitcairn, the Wrangler ....Jason Evers

Wrangler was the 1960 summer replacement for *The Ford Show Starring Tennessee Ernie Ford*. Pitcairn, the Wrangler, was an adventurer who traveled about the Old West working sometimes as a ranch hand, sometimes as a gunfighter, and sometimes as a good samaritan. This short-lived summer series was filled with rustlers, horse thieves, hostile Indians, and all the other low-brow characters so prevalent in superficial Western shoot-em-ups.

WREN'S NEST

Situation Comedy

FIRST TELECAST: *January 13, 1949*

LAST TELECAST: *April 30, 1949*

BROADCAST HISTORY:

Jan 1949–Apr 1949, ABC Thu/Fri/Sat 7:15–7:30

CAST:

Sam Wren
Virginia Sale

One of the many "Mr. and Mrs." comedies of early television was this thrice-weekly series about the home life of a suburban New York couple and their 12-year-old twins. The Wrens were also married in real life, and both had appeared in numerous Hollywood films. (Virginia's screen career lasted from the 1920s to the 1960s, and recently, at the age of 80, she completed a one-woman national tour doing her comedy-drama act in theaters, schools, and clubs.)

WRESTLING

Sports

FIRST TELECAST: *July 30, 1948*

LAST TELECAST: *March 5, 1955*

BROADCAST HISTORY:

Monday—
Sep 1949–Jan 1950, DUM 9:30–11:00
Jan 1950–Feb 1952, DUM 9:00–11:00
Feb 1952–Mar 1952, DUM 9:30–11:00

Tuesday—
Oct 1948–Jul 1949, NBC
10:00–Conclusion
Jan 1950–Aug 1950, CBS
10:00–Conclusion
Wednesday—
Aug 1948–Sep 1950, ABC
9:30–Conclusion
Sep 1950–Apr 1951, ABC
10:00–Conclusion
Apr 1951–Sep 1951, ABC 9:30–11:00
Jun 1952–Sep 1952, ABC 10:00–11:15
Sep 1952–Oct 1953, ABC 9:30–11:15
Oct 1953–Sep 1954, ABC
10:00–Midnight
Thursday—
Oct 1948–Jan 1949, DUM
9:00–Conclusion
Friday—
Jul 1948–Dec 1948, DUM
9:00–Conclusion
Saturday—
Sep 1949–May 1951, DUM
10:00–Conclusion
May 1951–Mar 1955, DUM
9:30–Conclusion

Professional wrestling, the world of the "grunt and groaners," was a regular and popular form of entertainment on early, live network television, particularly on ABC and DuMont. Names like Gorgeous George, Antonino "Argentina" Rocca, and The Mighty Atlas were household words among the owners of TV sets in the late 1940s and early 1950s, as well as among those who watched the matches at their local bars. The two longest-running wrestling shows originated from Chicago—Jack Brickhouse doing the play-by-play from Marigold Garden every Saturday night on DuMont for almost six years and Wayne Griffin announcing from Rainbo Arena for ABC for roughly the same length of time. DuMont's other long-running wrestling show originated from various arenas around the New York City area (Jerome Arena, Jamaica Arena, Sunnyside Gardens, and Columbia Park Arena) with Dennis James at the mike. Bill Johnston, Jr., did commentary for CBS's New York–based show (from the Bronx Winter Garden Arena and St. Nicholas Arena), and NBC's show was covered by Bob Stanton (from St. Nicholas Arena).

The most famous of these early wrestling announcers was probably DuMont's Dennis James, whose simplified explanations and infectious enthusiasm made the sport palatable even to little old ladies. His oft-repeated phrase "Okay, Mother" became so identified with him that it was later used for the title of one of his numerous daytime game shows. That a game show emcee like James could become wrestling's most famous commentator was perhaps symbolic of the fact that on TV wrestling was more show business than sport.

WYATT EARP

see *Life and Legend of Wyatt Earp, The*

XAVIER CUGAT SHOW, THE

Music

FIRST TELECAST: *February 27, 1957*
LAST TELECAST: *May 24, 1957*
BROADCAST HISTORY:
Feb 1957–May 1957, NBC Wed/Fri
7:30–7:45
REGULARS:
Xavier Cugat
Abbe Lane

Latin bandleader Xavier Cugat and his then wife Abbe Lane starred in this live 15-minute musical variety show that filled the remainder of the half-hour in which NBC aired its nightly network news program. Cugie led the band and played his violin, Abbe sang Latin numbers and danced, and occasional guest stars joined them for variety.

YANCY DERRINGER

Action/Adventure

FIRST TELECAST: *October 2, 1958*
LAST TELECAST: *September 24, 1959*
BROADCAST HISTORY:
Oct 1958–Sep 1959, CBS Thu 8:30–9:00
CAST:
Yancy Derringer ....Jock Mahoney
Pahoo-Ka-Ta-Wah ....X. Brands
John Colton ....Kevin Hagen
Amanda Eaton ....Julie Adams

Set in New Orleans in the years after the Civil War, *Yancy Derringer* followed the exploits of an ex-Confederate soldier turned cardsharp and adventurer in a wide-open city. Yancy did have a steady occupation, that of special agent working for John Colton, Civil Administrator of the City of New Orleans. His job was to prevent crimes when possible, and to capture the criminals when it was not. Yancy was a smooth operator, dapper and suave with the ladies, and he carried a tiny pistol in his fancy hat. His constant companion and aide was an Indian named Pahoo. Together they formed a team that was not police, not detective, and not secret agent, but a little bit of all three.

YEAR AT THE TOP, A

Situation Comedy

FIRST TELECAST: *August 5, 1977*
LAST TELECAST: *September 4, 1977*
BROADCAST HISTORY:
Aug 1977, CBS Fri 8:00–8:30
Aug 1977–Sep 1977, CBS Sun 8:30–9:00
CAST:
Greg .... Greg Evigan
Paul .... Paul Shaffer
Frederick J. Hanover .... Gabriel Dell
Miss Worley .... Priscilla Morrill
Grandma Belle Durbin .... Nedra Volz
EXECUTIVE PRODUCER:
Norman Lear
MUSIC SUPERVISOR:
Don Kirshner

This summer series, long delayed in getting on the air because of production and conceptual problems (it was originally supposed to premiere in January, with a completely different cast), was about two young rock musicians in search of fame and fortune. Greg and Paul moved to Hollywood from their home in Boise, Idaho, and were looking for an agent to help them get their big break. The promoter they found was Frederick J. Hanover, renowned for discovering and creating pop music stars. He offered them the chance at stardom, but there was one little catch. Hanover was the son of the Devil and, in exchange for their year as pop music superstars, Greg and Paul would have to sign away their souls. Hanover gave them tastes of what their "year at the top" could be like, and tried various ways of tempting them to sign the contract, but circumstances and misgivings on Greg and Paul's part prevented it from happening, at least in the five weeks that *A Year at the Top* ran.

YES YES NANETTE

syndicated title for *Westinghouse Playhouse*

YOU ARE AN ARTIST

see *Ben Grauer Show, The*

YOU ARE AN ARTIST

Art Instruction

FIRST TELECAST: *November 1, 1946*
LAST TELECAST: *January 17, 1950*
BROADCAST HISTORY:
Nov 1946–Dec 1946, NBC Fri 8:15–8:30
Dec 1946–Aug 1948, NBC Thu 9:00–9:15
Sep 1948–Oct 1948, NBC Wed 7:30–7:50
Nov 1948–Mar 1949, NBC Tue 7:30–7:45
Mar 1949–Apr 1949, NBC Thu 7:30–7:45
Jul 1949–Sep 1949, NBC Sat 7:30–7:45
Jan 1950, NBC Tue 11:00–11:15
HOST:
Jon Gnagy

Jon Gnagy might seem an unlikely choice to be one of the very first personalities to have his own network television series. An obscure but articulate young artist, he first appeared on NBC's *Radio City Matinee*, a grab bag of features telecast locally over WNBT, New York, in the early and mid-1940s. In November 1946, he was given a 15-minute time slot of his own and his program, *You Are an Artist*, was fed to a small network of stations on the East Coast. A month later the Gulf Oil Company was persuaded to assume sponsorship of the show, thus insuring its survival (and making Gulf one of the first sponsors of a network series).

Sporting a goatee, a plaid shirt, and sometimes a beret, Gnagy would execute drawings before the camera while describing his technique in simple, understandable terms as he went along. Later he added a segment in which he analyzed a famous painting lent by the Museum of Modern Art (and brought into the studio by two armed guards). He varied little from this simple format from 1946 to 1949, but around him the medium of television changed dramatically. In 1949 the program, by then a gentle reminder of an earlier day (only 3 years back!), quietly moved into daytime, then became a local New York show. It had a final three-week run on the network in January 1950.

Though soon forgotten amid the rush of superproductions and big names flooding into the new medium, Jon Gnagy and *You Are an Artist* were true video pioneers. Where is he today?

YOU ARE THERE

Documentary Drama

FIRST TELECAST: *February 1, 1953*

LAST TELECAST: *October 13, 1957*

BROADCAST HISTORY:

Feb 1953–Jun 1953, CBS Sun 6:00–6:30
Sep 1953–Oct 1957, CBS Sun 6:30–7:00 (OS)

REPORTER:

Walter Cronkite

Reenactments of major events in the history of the world, with the emphasis on those of the last century, were presented on this weekly series. CBS News correspondent Walter Cronkite served as the anchorman as the events "occurred" and reports and interviews came in from various reporters. The initial telecast was "The Landing of the Hindenburg" and the last one was "The Scuttling of the Graf Spee." In between there were programs on "The Salem Witchcraft Trials," "The Gettysburg Address," and "The Fall of Troy."

Perhaps best remembered are the program's closing lines: "What sort of a day was it? A day like all days, filled with those events that alter and illuminate our times . . . and you were there."

You Are There was first heard as a CBS radio show in 1947, with John Daly as host.

YOU ASKED FOR IT

Audience Participation

FIRST TELECAST: *December 29, 1950*

LAST TELECAST: *September 27, 1959*

BROADCAST HISTORY:

Dec 1950–Dec 1951, DUM Fri 8:30–9:00
Dec 1951–Mar 1952, ABC Mon 9:00–9:30
Apr 1952–Jan 1958, ABC Sun 7:00–7:30
Jan 1958–Apr 1958, ABC Sun 9:30–10:00
Apr 1958–Sep 1959, ABC Sun 7:00–7:30

HOST:

Art Baker (1950–1958)
Jack Smith (1958–1959)

When this series premiered on the DuMont television network in December 1950, it was named *The Art Baker Show*, after its creator and host. That title was changed on April 13, 1951, to the more descriptive *You Asked for It*.

The format of the show was very simple. Viewers were asked to send in a postcard describing something they wanted to see and the program's staff made every attempt to provide it. For almost a decade *You Asked for It* thrived, taking viewers into the vault at Fort Knox, bringing to them strange people with unusual talents, showing them $1,000,000 in one-dollar bills, and almost anything else that the viewers wanted to see. Jack Smith replaced Art Baker as host when the program moved to 9:30 P.M. Sunday night on January 26, 1958.

Although *You Asked for It* is most associated with this particular format, it was actually anticipated by a nearly identical program on NBC from 1948–1949 called *I'd Like to See*.

YOU BET YOUR LIFE

Quiz/Audience Participation

FIRST TELECAST: *October 5, 1950*

LAST TELECAST: *September 21, 1961*

BROADCAST HISTORY:

Oct 1950–Jun 1951, NBC Thu 8:00–8:30
Oct 1951–Sep 1958, NBC Thu 8:00–8:30
Sep 1958–Sep 1961, NBC Thu 10:00–10:30

EMCEE:

Groucho Marx

ANNOUNCER:

George Fenneman

THEME:

"Hooray for Captain Spaulding," by Bert Kalmar and Harry Ruby

Comedian Groucho Marx, of the rapier-like wit and sarcastic asides, was the emcee and star of this filmed quiz show, which had begun on radio in 1947. Although it was ostensibly a quiz, the series' most important asset was the humor injected by Groucho into the interviews he did with contestants before they had a chance to play the game. Contestants were picked primarily on the potential they had to be foils for Groucho's barbs, which they seemed to love.

At the start of each show the audience was informed of the night's secret word—"It's a common word, something you see every day." If any of the contestants happened to say it while they were on the air, they won an extra $100. When they said the word a dilapidated stuffed duck would drop from the ceiling with the $100 attached (sometimes it would be brought out by a sexy "Secret Word Girl"). The quiz consisted of question-and-answer rounds in which contestants bet all or part of an initial purse on their ability to answer the questions in a chosen category. The questions were not really difficult, and the two members of a team could collaborate ("Remember, only one answer between you"), but sometimes they lost the whole thing. Then there was always the consolation prize, which could be won by answering a nonsense question like "Who is buried in Grant's Tomb?" As Groucho liked to say, "Nobody leaves here broke."

During the period in which *You Bet Your Life* was aired on both TV and radio, an hour-long session was filmed and then edited down to provide both 30-minute versions of the show—as well as to edit out any risqué remarks by Groucho. The same contestants appeared on both radio and TV versions, though the two were not exactly alike. The reruns that aired on TV during the summer were titled *The Best of Groucho* and the entire program was retitled *The Groucho Show* during its last season.

YOU DON'T SAY

Quiz/Audience Participation

FIRST TELECAST: *January 7, 1964*
LAST TELECAST: *May 5, 1964*
BROADCAST HISTORY:
Jan 1964–May 1964, NBC Tue 8:30–9:00
EMCEE:
Tom Kennedy

You Don't Say was a game in which two teams of two members each (one member being the contestant and the other member a celebrity) competed in trying to guess the name of a famous person. One member of each team would be told the identity of the person and would then give clues to his partner in the form of incomplete sentences, with the missing word at the end of the sentence being the clue. The winner of each game got $100 and the chance to go to the bonus board to win more money. The board contained word clues to a different famous person's name. The clues were revealed, one at a time, and the members of the winning team tried to guess who the famous person was. Correct identification after one clue was worth $300, after two clues worth $200, and after all three clues worth $100. The daytime version of *You Don't Say*, on which the nighttime version was based, ran from April 1963 to September 1969 and was revived for a six-month period in 1975.

YOU'LL NEVER GET RICH

see *Phil Silvers Show, The*

YOUNG AND GAY

see *Girls, The*

YOUNG BROADWAY

Music

FIRST TELECAST: *December 22, 1948*
LAST TELECAST: *June 23, 1949*
BROADCAST HISTORY:
Dec 1948–Mar 1949, NBC Wed 7:30–7:50
Apr 1949–Jun 1949, NBC Thu 10:00–10:30

Live musical program featuring young performers who were just getting their start in show business. For a time each program was built around a current Broadway play, but with the understudies rather than the stars performing the lead roles. Performers as varied as Roberta Quinlan and Marguerite Piazza appeared on the program.

YOUNG DAN'L BOONE

Adventure

FIRST TELECAST: *September 12, 1977*
LAST TELECAST: *October 4, 1977*
BROADCAST HISTORY:
Sep 1977, CBS Mon 8:00–9:00
Oct 1977, CBS Tue 8:00–9:00
CAST:
Daniel Boone ....Rick Moses
Rebecca Ryan ....Devon Ericson
Hawk ....Ji-Tu Cumbuka
Peter Dawes ....John Joseph Thomas
Tsiskwa ....Eloy Phil Casados

Fess Parker had spent six successful seasons in the latter half of the 1960s playing an older version of the legendary Daniel Boone and CBS brought a younger version of the Kentucky woodsman to television in the fall of 1977. In his mid-20s, and not yet married, Daniel did his exploring with Peter Dawes, a 12-year-old English boy; Hawk, a runaway slave; and a Cherokee Indian friend named Tsiskwa. Waiting for him to settle down was his sweetheart, Rebecca. One of the failures of the 1977–1978 season, *Young Dan'l Boone* lasted only four weeks, three in its original Monday time slot and a fourth on Tuesday, October 4.

YOUNG LAWYERS, THE

General Drama

FIRST TELECAST: *September 21, 1970*

LAST TELECAST: *May 5, 1971*
BROADCAST HISTORY:
Sep 1970–Jan 1971, ABC Mon 7:30–8:30
Jan 1971–May 1971, ABC Wed 10:00–11:00
CAST:
Attorney David Barrett ....Lee J. Cobb
Aaron Silverman ....Zalman King
Pat Walters ....Judy Pace
Chris Blake (1971) ....Philip Clark

Drama about law students operating a Boston "Neighborhood Law Office" that provided free legal assistance to indigent clients. Slumlords, drug busts, police brutality, and rip-offs of the poor constituted most of their cases. In TV fashion the crew was suitably mixed: Aaron was the scrappy, tousle-haired young idealist, Pat was the well-educated but street-wise black chick, and Chris the earnest young middle-class WASP who was added to the cast in January, for contrast. Their experienced supervisor was David Barrett.

YOUNG MR. BOBBIN

Situation Comedy
FIRST TELECAST: *August 26, 1951*
LAST TELECAST: *May 18, 1952*
BROADCAST HISTORY:
Aug 1951–May 1952, NBC Sun 7:30–8:00
CAST:
Alexander Hawthorne Bobbin
.... Jackie Kelk
Aunt Clara ....Jane Seymour
Aunt Bertha ....Nydia Westman
Nancy ....Pat Hosley
Susie ....Laura Weber
Mr. Deacon ....Cameron Prud'homme
Mr. Willis ....Cort Benson

At age 18, Alexander Bobbin had just graduated from high school and begun seeking his fortune. At his age, however, his aspirations tended to exceed his abilities. This live situation comedy focused on the struggles of the young man to establish himself and attain maturity. Alexander lived in an old house with the two maiden aunts who had raised him: organized, resourceful Aunt Clara, and confused, flighty Aunt Bertha. He was in love with Nancy, the girl next door, who liked him but was determined not to let him think he was the only man in her life. His strongest ally in his effort to win Nancy was Susie, her tomboy sister who tried to help him despite her apparent teasing.

YOUNG PEOPLE'S CHURCH OF THE AIR

see *Youth on the March*

YOUNG REBELS, THE

Adventure
FIRST TELECAST: *September 20, 1970*
LAST TELECAST: *January 3, 1971*
BROADCAST HISTORY:
Sep 1970–Jan 1971, ABC Sun 7:00–8:00
CAST:
Jeremy Larkin ....Rick Ely
Isak Poole ....Lou Gossett
Henry Abington ....Alex Henteloff
Elizabeth Coates ....Hilarie Thompson
General the Marquis de Lafayette
.... Philippe Forquet

This series was supposed to allow the youthful social rebels of the late 1960s and early 1970s (or those who fantasized along with them) to relate to the American Revolution. The four young leads were members of the fictional Yankee Doodle Society, based in Chester, Pennsylvania, in the year 1777. Their goal was to harass the British behind their lines and to serve as spies for the American forces. Everyone was under 30, and British rule was the "system" they sought to overturn. Jeremy, the son of the town's mayor, was the long-haired leader; Elizabeth, his teenage girl friend and helper; Isak, an ex-slave; and Henry, the brains of the outfit. Henry greatly admired Benjamin Franklin, and even looked a lot like him, with a calm, intellectual detachment and tiny spectacles on his nose. General Lafayette, the 20-year-old French nobleman who had come to aid the rebels, was a frequent ally, and various other youthful patriots also passed through the stories (including that eternal teenager Brandon De Wilde as young Nathan Hale).

YOUR BIG MOMENT

see *Blind Date*

YOUR CHEVROLET SHOWROOM

Variety
FIRST TELECAST: *November 20, 1953*
LAST TELECAST: *February 12, 1954*
BROADCAST HISTORY:
Nov 1953–Feb 1954, ABC Fri 10:00–11:00
EMCEE:
Cesar Romero

This hour of music and comedy premiered locally in New York on October 25, 1953, and went on the full ABC network a month later. Unfortunately the biggest name guests appeared on the first few telecasts, which were seen only in New York, and by the time network telecasting had begun Cesar Romero found himself playing host to good but non-superstar acts such as Earl Wrightson, Connee Boswell, and the Russ Morgan Orchestra, plus legions of unknown singers, dancers, and comedians. The program was known for its first few weeks simply as *Chevrolet Showroom*.

YOUR ESSO REPORTER

News

FIRST TELECAST: *July 12, 1951*

LAST TELECAST: *September 13, 1951*

BROADCAST HISTORY:

Jul 1951–Sep 1951, CBS Thu 9:00–9:30

Your Esso Reporter had been a regular feature of CBS radio since the late 1930s, and the company had also sponsored one of the very earliest regular network TV newscasts, which began almost as soon as NBC was able to organize its first three-station East Coast network in 1946. During the summer of 1951 Esso sponsored this weekly roundup of the major news events from around the world, with the CBS News correspondents based in various world capitals all participating. In a rather unusual situation, the 1951 series was seen only in the East and the Far West, where Esso was marketed. The Midwest portion of the CBS-TV network got *Meet Corliss Archer* instead.

YOUR FUNNY, FUNNY FILMS

Comedy

FIRST TELECAST: *July 8, 1963*

LAST TELECAST: *September 9, 1963*

BROADCAST HISTORY:

Jul 1963–Sep 1963, ABC Mon 8:30–9:00

HOST:

George Fenneman

Home movies taken by amateurs, with the emphasis on intentionally (and sometimes unintentionally) humorous sequences. A few celebrities also appeared with their home movies. The first telecast consisted of (1) a five-year-old's birthday party, as he demolished a cake, then learned to ride a bicycle and roller skate; (2) a World War II "epic" made by a 12-year-old and his friends; (3) some amateur films made in the 1920s. The "Short Shorts" feature consisted of a string of brief clips, such as a youngster experimenting with shoe polish, a woman ostensibly climbing a mountain, a little girl dancing, a wood-chopping scene, and a tiny Romeo trying to steal a kiss from his little girl friend. A lot of kids were seen in this series, which in some ways resembled *Candid Camera*.

YOUR HIT PARADE

Music

FIRST TELECAST: *July 10, 1950*

LAST TELECAST: *August 30, 1974*

BROADCAST HISTORY:

Jul 1950–Aug 1950, NBC Mon 9:00–9:30
Oct 1950–Jun 1958, NBC Sat 10:30–11:00 (OS)
Oct 1958–Apr 1959, CBS Fri 7:30–8:00
Aug 1974, CBS Fri 8:00–8:30

VOCALISTS:

Eileen Wilson (1950–1952)
Snooky Lanson (1950–1957)
Dorothy Collins (1950–1957, 1958–1959)
Sue Bennett (1951–1952)
June Valli (1952–1953)
Russell Arms (1952–1957)
Gisele MacKenzie (1953–1957)
Tommy Leonetti (1957–1958)
Jill Corey (1957–1958)
Alan Copeland (1957–1958)
Virginia Gibson (1957–1958)
Johnny Desmond (1958–1959)
Kelly Garrett (1974)
Chuck Woolery (1974)
Sheralee (1974)

DANCERS:

The Hit Paraders (chorus & dancers) (1950–1958)
Peter Gennaro Dancers (1958–1959)
Tom Hansen Dancers (1974)

ANNOUNCERS:

Andre Baruch (1950–1957)
Del Sharbutt (1957–1958)

ORCHESTRA:

Raymond Scott (1950–1957)
Harry Sosnick (1958–1959)
Milton Delugg (1974)

THEME:

"Lucky Day"; "So Long for Awhile" (closing)

The legendary *Lucky Strike Hit Parade*, which had been a radio standby since 1935, was first seen on television during the summer of 1950, as a four-time-only replacement for *Robert Montgomery Pre-*

sents. It became a regular series the following October, simulcast with the radio version.

The format was essentially unchanged from radio, presenting the seven most popular songs in America as performed by a regular cast of singers and the Hit Parade Orchestra. Songs were not necessarily presented in rank order, although the rank of each was prominently featured and number one was always presented last, with great fanfare. Two or three "extras"—usually standards—were also included. Elaborate production numbers marked *Your Hit Parade*, and since many songs stayed on the charts for months, considerable ingenuity was required to vary the treatment of a song from week to week. Among the songs that remained in the number one spot for long periods in the early 1950s were "Too Young" (12 weeks), "Because of You" (11 weeks), and "Hey There" (10 weeks).

The survey strove to sound official. Each week listeners were told that "*Your Hit Parade* survey checks the best sellers on sheet music and phonograph records, the songs most heard on the air and most played on the automatic coin machines . . . an accurate, authentic tabulation of America's taste in popular music." No explanation of exactly how the surveying was done was ever revealed, however, and the actual compiling took place in great secrecy at Batten, Barton, Durstine & Osborne, which was sponsor American Tobacco Company's advertising agency.

The ballads of the early 1950s were fine for TV presentation by a regular cast of singers, but trouble began to brew for *Your Hit Parade* in 1955 when a new kind of music invaded the charts—rock 'n' roll. Not only were the Hit Parade regulars ill-suited to perform this new, raucous music, but the youngsters who bought the records wanted to see only the original performers. There was something ludicrous about Snooky Lanson attempting "Hound Dog" in a different setting each week (usually as a childish novelty).

Although most of the Hit Parade singers were recording artists in their own right, only one of them ever had a hit big enough to appear on the program's top seven while a regular on the show. That was Gisele MacKenzie's "Hard to Get," which made the list briefly in 1955. Ironically, one-time Hit Parade regular June Valli had the biggest hit of her career, "Crying in the Chapel," only two months after leaving the show in June 1953.

In September 1957 the entire cast was replaced by a younger, more "contemporary" crew, none of whom were popular rock artists, however. The age-old format itself was extensively revamped the following February, with the hit parade reduced to five songs, plus five more melodious "extras" and a big $200,000 "Mystery Tune" contest. None of this tinkering solved the problems created by drastically changing musical styles, and after a final season on CBS (during which the top-tunes list was drawn from *Billboard* magazine) the program expired on April 24, 1959. An abortive attempt was made at reviving the show in the summer of 1974, with the emphasis on *Your Hit Parade* songs from selected broadcasts of specific weeks in the 1940s and 1950s, mixed with currently popular hits performed by the original artists.

YOUR KAISER DEALER PRESENTS KAISER-FRAZER "ADVENTURES IN MYSTERY" STARRING BETTY FURNESS IN "BYLINE"

see *Byline*

YOUR LUCKY CLUE

Quiz/Audience Participation

FIRST TELECAST: *July 13, 1952*

LAST TELECAST: *August 31, 1952*

BROADCAST HISTORY:

Jul 1952–Aug 1952, CBS Sun 7:30–8:00

EMCEE:

Basil Rathbone

Each week two teams competed with each other to solve dramatized mysteries. One team was composed of two professional detectives and the other of two amateur criminologists. The audience was made aware of where the clues were in each dramatization, but the contestants were not. Each team tried to solve the case before the other team did, and before the emcee disclosed the solution. Basil Rathbone, long known as the Sherlock Holmes of motion pictures (he played the role in most of the adaptations of A. Conan Doyle's stories), was a logical choice as emcee.

YOUR LUCKY STRIKE HIT PARADE

see *Your Hit Parade*

YOUR NEIGHBOR THE WORLD

Documentary

FIRST TELECAST: *April 6, 1958*

LAST TELECAST: *October 8, 1959*

BROADCAST HISTORY:

Apr 1958–Jan 1959, ABC Sun various 30 minute

May 1959–Oct 1959, ABC Thu 10:00–10:30

Documentary films about different peoples and cultures around the world, from high fashion in Paris to natives in the Belgian Congo.

YOUR PLAY TIME

Dramatic Anthology

FIRST TELECAST: *June 14, 1953*

LAST TELECAST: *September 3, 1955*

BROADCAST HISTORY:

Jun 1953–Sep 1953, CBS Sun 7:30–8:00

Jun 1954–Sep 1954, CBS Sun 7:30–8:00

Jun 1955–Sep 1955, NBC Sat 10:30–11:00

For three consecutive summers series bearing the title *Your Play Time* aired as replacements for other shows. In 1953 and 1954, on CBS, the show was the summer replacement for two alternating CBS programs, *The Jack Benny Show* and *Private Secretary*. In 1953 some of the plays were done live and others on film. They tended to be on the melodramatic side with settings in foreign locales. 1954's offerings, both comedy and drama, were entirely on film and generally took place in domestic settings. Featured were such lesser-known stars as George Nader, Hillary Brooke, Jack Haley, Peter Graves, Ruth Warrick, and Tommy Rettig.

The *Your Play Time* that was telecast by NBC in the summer of 1955 was made up of reruns from other anthology series, primarily *Pepsi-Cola* and *Studio 57*. It was the summer replacement for *Your Hit Parade*.

YOUR PRIZE STORY

Dramatic Anthology

FIRST TELECAST: *April 2, 1952*

LAST TELECAST: *May 28, 1952*

BROADCAST HISTORY:

Apr 1952–May 1952, NBC Wed 10:00–10:30

This live weekly dramatic show was unique in that its sponsor, Hazel Bishop, requested viewers to submit story ideas. The person sending in a story that was accepted and adapted for television received a cash prize of $1,000. It had to be a true story and literary skill was not required. The viewer was to tell it in his own words and let the program's staff rewrite it for airing. The presentations were done with very little in the way of scenery or props, much in the manner of little-theater performances.

Evidently the public was not bubbling over with good ideas for TV shows, as the series lasted less than two months.

YOUR SHOW OF SHOWS

Comedy Variety

FIRST TELECAST: *February 25, 1950*

LAST TELECAST: *June 5, 1954*

BROADCAST HISTORY:

Feb 1950–Jun 1954, NBC Sat 9:00–10:30

REGULARS:

Sid Caesar
Imogene Coca
Carl Reiner
Howard Morris (1951–1954)
Robert Merrill (1950–1951)
Marguerite Piazza (1950–1953)
Bill Hayes (1950–1953)
Jerry Ross & Nellie Fisher (1950–1952)
Mata & Hari (1950–1953)
Tom Avera (1950)
Hamilton Dancers
Jack Russell
Billy Williams Quartet
Judy Johnson (1950–1953)
Earl Redding (1950–1951)
Aariana Knowles (1951–1952)
Dick DeFreitas (1950–1953)
Bambi Linn & Rod Alexander (1952–1954)
James Starbuck
Show of Shows Ballet Company
Charles Sanford Orchestra

PRODUCER:

Max Liebman

WRITERS:

Mel Brooks, Neil Simon, Woody Allen, Lucille Kallen, Larry Gelbart, Mel Tolkin, others

One of the classics of television's "Golden Age," *Your Show of Shows* was the successor to Caesar and Coca's 1949 *Admiral Broadway Revue*. At the outset, *Your Show of Shows* was actually half of a larger show, being the New York element of NBC's *Saturday Night Revue*. The other portion, from Chicago, was *The Jack Carter Show*, on between 8:00 and 9:00 P.M. At the end of the 1950–1951 season Carter and the *Saturday Night Revue* umbrella title were dropped.

Your Show of Shows was surely one of the most ambitious undertakings on television, *ever*. It was 90 minutes of live, original comedy, every week. And it was good. In addition to Caesar and Coca's sketches there was a large corps of regular singers and dancers, plus top-name guest stars. As a matter of fact, the nominal host of each program was a different big-name guest star (Burgess Meredith hosted the first two shows). Ballet sequences and scenes from grand opera were also featured, to give the show an undeniably "classy" air.

But it was the comic genius of Caesar and Coca for which the program is remembered. They appeared in such regular routines as "History As She Ain't," Caesar's roving reporter, monologues and mime, as well as in large-scale satires on current films and other hit TV shows. Caesar and his writers were movie buffs, and many of Hollywood's most pretentious epics got the full treatment, ranging from antique silent films (the drunken father) to contemporary hits such as *Shane* (in which Caesar played the unbelievably fearless gunfighter Strange) and *From Here to Eternity* ("From Here to Obscurity").

Carl Reiner and Howard Morris, who joined the supporting cast in 1950 and 1951 respectively, were gradually given more prominent roles and by the final season Caesar, Coca, Reiner, and Morris constituted a four-person repertory group employed in many of the skits. Caesar could take on many roles. He was the double-talking foreigner (he was a master of dialects), the henpecked husband, or the greasy-haired cad. Coca was nearly as versatile, while Reiner would most often be the slick, presumptuous salesman type, and Howard Morris the little guy determined to prove that he was as good as *anybody*—even if he wasn't. Among the notable routines developed during the show's long run were Caesar and Coca's husband-and-wife skit, "The Hickenloopers"; the fable of the great clock in the little town of Baverhoff, Bavaria, whose mechanical figures always seemed to go haywire when the hour struck; Coca as the happy-go-lucky tramp; Caesar as an Italian opera star babbling gibberish in *Galapacci*, or as the supercool jazz musician Progress Hornsby, or as the visiting authority on almost anything, usually being interviewed at the airport, with such dialogue as this:

ARCHEOLOGIST: "After many years, I haff found ze secret of Titten-Totten's Tomb!"

INTERVIEWER (excitedly): "What is it, Professor?"

ARCHEOLOGIST: "I should tell *you?*"

Your Show of Shows finally left the air in June 1954, as Caesar and Coca parted to pursue separate careers. Most series end their runs forgotten or in reruns, but in what must have been one of the more unusual farewells in TV history, the last telecast of *Your Show of Shows* was a big, tearful, nostalgic recap of the best sketches of the past years, ending with the by-then famous finale number "Stars over Broadway." Even the president of NBC, Pat Weaver, showed up to thank everyone for four excellent years and to wish them well in their future separate series.

Caesar and Coca never again quite captured the magic of those four years, either separately or together. The combination of fresh talent, excellent supporting cast, gifted writers (including such future stars as Mel Brooks, Neil Simon, and a young Woody Allen), and perhaps the times themselves had been "right"—but only once. In recent years excerpts from the shows have been packaged by producer Max Liebman and shown in theaters under the title *Ten from Your Show of Shows*.

YOUR SHOW TIME

Dramatic Anthology

FIRST TELECAST: *January 21, 1949*

LAST TELECAST: *July 15, 1949*

BROADCAST HISTORY:

Jan 1949–Jul 1949, NBC Fri 9:30–10:00

HOST:

Arthur Shields

Filmed dramatizations of classic short stories by many of the world's most famous authors, including Guy de Maupassant, Robert Louis Stevenson, Henry James, and Sir Arthur Conan Doyle. Each telecast opened in an old bookshop where host Arthur Shields was seen seated behind an old-fashioned desk, from which he introduced "tonight's story."

This program was notable as the recipient of the very first "Emmy" award presented to a network show. The award was for the premiere telecast, "The Necklace," starring John Beal.

YOUR SPORTS SPECIAL

Sports News

FIRST TELECAST: *October 8, 1948*

LAST TELECAST: *November 4, 1949*

BROADCAST HISTORY:

Oct 1948–Jan 1949, CBS Fri 7:00–7:15
Jan 1949–Nov 1949, CBS Various 7:00–7:15

REPORTERS:

Carswell Adams
Dolly Stark

Sports reporter Carswell Adams and former major-league umpire Dolly Stark were the hosts of this sports news and interview show. Originally seen on Friday nights, it expanded in January 1949 to an irregular schedule that varied from two to five times per week for the next ten months.

YOUR STORY THEATRE

Dramatic Anthology

FIRST TELECAST: *December 1, 1950*

LAST TELECAST: *February 2, 1951*

BROADCAST HISTORY:

Dec 1950–Feb 1951, DUM Fri 8:00–8:30

Series of half-hour filmed dramas, starring such Hollywood standbys as Robert Alda, Hurd Hatfield, Marjorie Lord, William Frawley, Sterling Holloway, etc. Stories included both original scripts and adaptations from Henry James, Robert Louis Stevenson, Frank R. Stockton ("The Lady or the Tiger"), and other noted authors.

YOUR —— TV THEATER

syndicated title for *Fireside Theater*

YOUR WITNESS

Courtroom

FIRST TELECAST: *September 19, 1949*

LAST TELECAST: *September 26, 1950*

BROADCAST HISTORY:

Sep 1949–Oct 1949, ABC Mon 8:00–8:30
Dec 1949–May 1950, ABC Sun 9:00–9:30
Aug 1950–Sep 1950, ABC Wed 9:00–9:30

WITH:

Edmund Lowe

Wednesday was courtroom night in 1950, with *Your Witness* following *On Trial* on the ABC schedule, and running opposite *Famous Jury Trials* on DuMont. This was a low-budget courtroom drama/mystery, and originated from Chicago.

YOU'RE IN THE PICTURE

Quiz/Audience Participation

FIRST TELECAST: *January 20, 1961*

LAST TELECAST: *January 20, 1961*

BROADCAST HISTORY:

Jan 1961, CBS Fri 9:30–10:00

HOST:

Jackie Gleason

PANELISTS:

Keenan Wynn
Pat Carroll
Jan Sterling
Arthur Treacher

This was one of those rare series that was so bad it was canceled after exactly one telecast. It was certainly one of the major fiascos in Jackie Gleason's career. The four celebrity panelists on the show were seen situated behind an oversized comic cutout of the kind found in amusement-park photography booths. They had no idea what the picture through which they had stuck their heads, and sometimes their hands, represented. The object was for the panel to guess what the picture was, by asking questions of host/emcee Gleason. When they had successfully identified the picture, a new one would be substituted and they would start over. Jackie's wit was supposed to add to the humor of the show, which was played primarily for laughs.

The first telecast was so bad, however, that the program never aired again. On the following Friday night Jackie spent the entire half-hour apologizing for the disastrous first episode. For the remainder of the season he filled the time slot with an interview show, hosting different celebrities each week, under the title *The Jackie Gleason Show* (not to be confused with his comedy variety series of the same name). *You're in the Picture* was never heard of again.

YOU'RE INVITED

Comedy Variety

FIRST TELECAST: *July 1, 1948*

LAST TELECAST: *September 20, 1948*

BROADCAST HISTORY:

Jul 1948–Aug 1948, ABC Wed 8:00–8:30
Aug 1948–Sep 1948, ABC Mon 9:00–9:30

EMCEE:
Romo Vincent

Jovial, rotund comic Romo Vincent hosted this early variety show, which took place in a house-party setting. At the start of each show he greeted his audience at the front door and invited them in to see the singers, dancers, and ventriloquists who were that week's guests. There was also an audience-participation segment.

YOU'RE ON YOUR OWN

Quiz/Audience Participation

FIRST TELECAST: *December 22, 1956*
LAST TELECAST: *March 16, 1957*
BROADCAST HISTORY:
Dec 1956–Mar 1957, CBS Sat 10:30–11:00
EMCEE:
Steve Dunne

Contestants on *You're on Your Own* had free access to anything on the stage that would help them find the answers to the questions posed by emcee Steve Dunne. They need not know everything, only be able to use the correct source; directories, record albums, telephone books, etc. The faster they were at ferreting out the correct answers, the more money they could win—as much as $25,000 on a single night.

YOURS FOR A SONG

Quiz/Audience Participation

FIRST TELECAST: *November 14, 1961*
LAST TELECAST: *September 18, 1962*
BROADCAST HISTORY:
Nov 1961–Sep 1962, ABC Tue 9:30–10:00
EMCEE:
Bert Parks

Contestants on this live half-hour game show won money by filling in the missing words to song lyrics that were flashed on a screen. Whenever a contestant won a round, in addition to the prize money he won the right to face a new challenger. In addition to serving as quizmaster, Bert Parks got a chance to sing in this one.

YOUTH ON THE MARCH

Religious

FIRST TELECAST: *October 9, 1949*
LAST TELECAST: *June 7, 1953*
BROADCAST HISTORY:
Oct 1949–May 1952, ABC Sun 10:30–11:00 (OS)
Oct 1952–Jun 1953, DUM Sun 10:30–11:00
HOST:
Rev. Percy Crawford

This program of inspirational songs, hymns, and sermons was a fixture on Sunday nights for nearly four years, first on ABC and then on DuMont. It was presented by the Young People's Church of the Air and presided over by Rev. Percy Crawford, with mixed choir and men's glee club.

YOUTH TAKES A STAND

Discussion

FIRST TELECAST: *August 18, 1953*
LAST TELECAST: *September 15, 1953*
BROADCAST HISTORY:
Aug 1953–Sep 1953, CBS Tue 10:30–11:00
MODERATOR:
Marc Cramer
Alan Jackson

In an effort to get intelligent audience feedback to its television news effort, CBS invited four young scholars from high schools and junior colleges to participate in a discussion of current events and world affairs with a different CBS-TV reporter each week. The first moderator for the sessions during the show's prime time run was the series' co-producer, Marc Cramer. A different panel of students, selected by CBS stations around the country in cooperation with various public, parochial, and private school organizations, appeared on each telecast to chat with such reporters as Charles Collingwood and Douglas Edwards. Mr. Cramer was replaced by CBS News reporter Alan Jackson before the series moved into a late-afternoon time slot on Sundays. It remained on the air until March 1955 with Jim McKay replacing Jackson as moderator in March 1954.

YOUTH WANTS TO KNOW

Forum

FIRST TELECAST: *September 8, 1951*
LAST TELECAST: *August 24, 1954*
BROADCAST HISTORY:
Sep 1951–Oct 1951, NBC Sat 7:00–7:30
Jun 1952–Sep 1952, NBC Wed 8:30–9:00
Jul 1954–Aug 1954, NBC Sat 7:30–8:00
MODERATOR:
Theodore Granik

This series gave high school and college students the opportunity to ask questions of major figures in the world of politics, business, and international affairs. The subjects covered were generally related to major issues that affected large parts of the world and large numbers of its people. *Youth Wants to Know* originated live from Washington, D.C., and students from the Washington area participated. Mr. Granik and the guest were seated on a platform in front of the students and the entire operation was run like a press conference, with Mr. Granik picking the questioners. The students prepared their own questions. When this series premiered in 1951, its title was *The American Youth Forum*. It was changed to *Youth Wants to Know* in January 1952. At times, though not always, it was simulcast on radio, and it continued to run irregularly on Sunday afternoons until October 1958.

ZANE GREY THEATER

see *Dick Powell's Zane Grey Theater*

ZORRO

Western

FIRST TELECAST: *October 10, 1957*

LAST TELECAST: *September 24, 1959*

BROADCAST HISTORY:

Oct 1957–Sep 1959, ABC Thu 8:00–8:30

CAST:

Don Diego de la Vega ("Zorro") .... Guy Williams
Don Alejandro ....George J. Lewis
Bernardo ....Gene Sheldon
Capt. Monastario ....Britt Lomond
Sgt. Garcia ....Henry Calvin
Nacho Torres ....Jan Arvan
Elena Torres ....Eugenia Paul
Magistrate Galindo ......Vinton Hayworth
Anna Maria Verdugo (1958–1959) .... Jolene Brand
Señor Gregorio Verdugo (1958–1959) .... Eduard Franz
Cpl. Reyes (1958–1959) ......Don Diamond

PRODUCER:

Walt Disney

THEME:

"Theme from Zorro," by Norman Foster and George Burns

Guy Williams starred as a swashbuckling masked hero in Spanish California in this popular series. The year was 1820, and young Don Diego, the only son of wealthy Don Alejandro, was returning home from Spain in response to his father's appeals. Monastario, a ruthless army officer, had become commandant of the Fortress de los Angeles, and was tyrannizing the local dons and their peons. Arriving in California, Don Diego presented himself as a lazy, foppish aristocrat, much to his father's dismay. Secretly, however, he donned mask and sword and set out to aid the oppressed and foil the schemes of the evil Monastario. His name on these forays was Zorro—for the sign of the "Z" he cut with his sword—and his loyal manservant was the deaf mute Bernardo.

The plots were pretty simple, and there was a lot of derring-do (especially in the sword fights), making *Zorro* a great favorite with children. Helping Zorro's crusade was the fact that his chief adversaries, Monastario and his henchman, the fat, dimwitted Sgt. Garcia, were both quite incompetent. Another element of interest was that the stories continued from episode to episode, in semi-serial fashion, even though they were so basic that they could be joined at any point.

Among the other regulars were Anna Maria Verdugo, Zorro's love interest (introduced in the second season); Nacho Torres, an escaped political prisoner, and his daughter Elena; and Zorro's black and white stallions, Tornado and Phantom. Many characters came and went in three- or four-installment subplots within the main series, including a young señorita named Anita Cabrillo, played by Annette Funicello, who even got a chance to sing a few songs on the show. Her role was a birthday present from series producer Walt Disney, who had originally brought Annette to stardom as a *Mickey Mouse Club* mouseketeer only a few years before.

The theme song from the show ("Zorro—the fox so cunning and free/ Zorro—make the sign of the Z!") was a hit-parade favorite in 1958. It was first recorded by Henry Calvin, of all people (fat Sgt. Garcia!), but the hit version was by a pop group, the Chordettes.

APPENDIX 1

PRIME TIME SCHEDULES: 1946–1978

On the following pages are complete prime time network schedules for each season from 1946–1947 through 1978–1979. Television programming changes constantly, and schedules such as these can only offer an approximation of what was on during any given week. However, the industry has long had a custom of introducing new series in September or October of each year, and it is these introductory "fall schedules" that are shown here.

During the 1950s and 1960s most of the series introduced in the fall of each year lasted for at least three months, and often for a full year, even when they were unsuccessful. Industry practice was to contract in advance for from 13 to 26 original episodes of a series, with repeats during the summer. In recent years, however, intense network competition has led to the dropping of unsuccessful series as soon as three or four weeks after their premieres, and occasionally a TV dud, like a Broadway flop, will even close on its opening night. The principal fall programs are shown here, no matter how short their actual runs.

Times given are those at which the programs were seen in most cities. Newscasts will be found in the main body of the book under *News*, feature film series under *Movies*, sports events under the name of the sport, etc. (Miscellaneous collections of film shorts, used to fill time, are included on the schedules but are not in the book.) A blank indicates that there was no network programming in the time slot. This does not necessarily mean there was nothing on TV—individual stations usually filled in with their own local shows—although in the earliest days there sometimes was only a test pattern to watch.

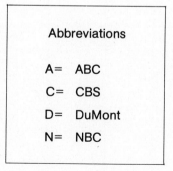

Abbreviations

A= ABC

C= CBS

D= DuMont

N= NBC

PRIME TIME SCHEDULE: 1946

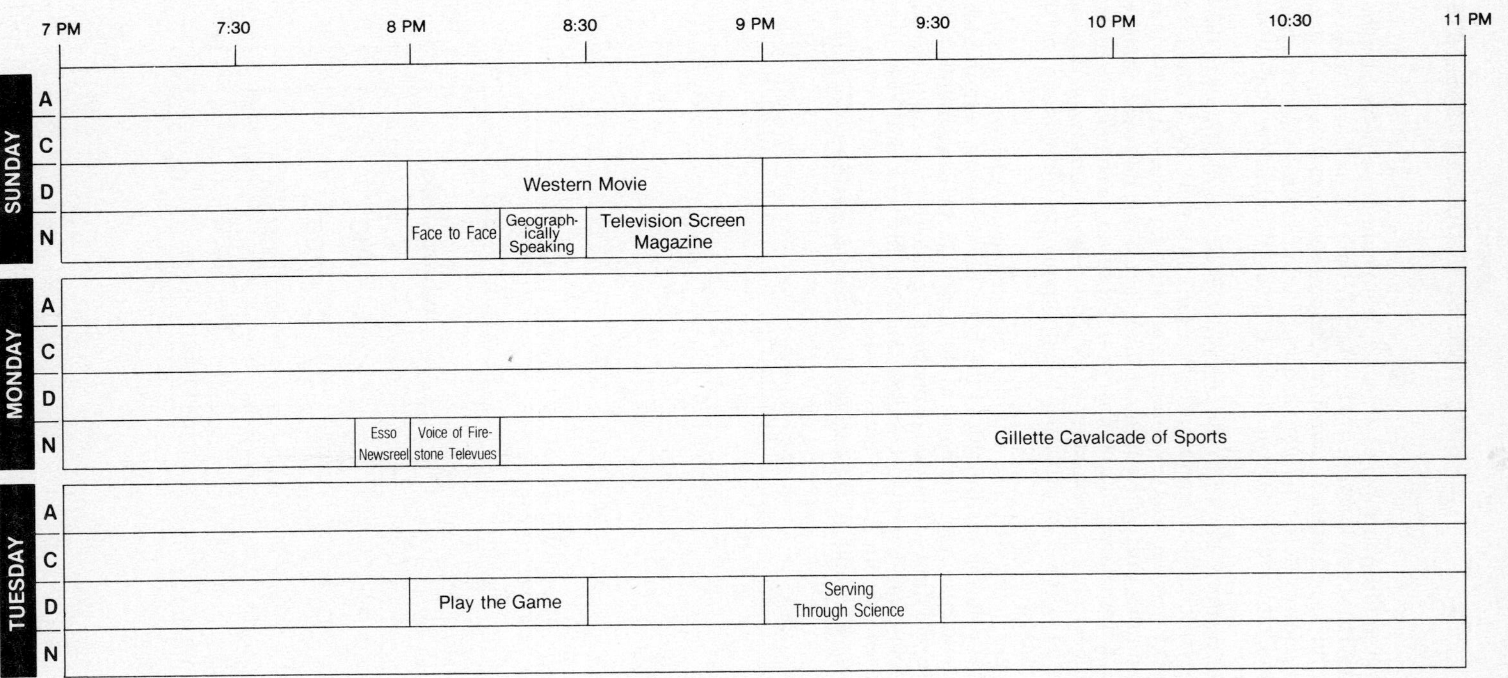

Day	Network	7 PM	7:30	8 PM	8:30	9 PM	9:30	10 PM	10:30
SUNDAY	A								
	C								
	D			Western Movie					
	N			Face to Face / Geographically Speaking	Television Screen Magazine				
MONDAY	A								
	C								
	D								
	N		Esso Newsreel	Voice of Firestone Televues		Gillette Cavalcade of Sports			
TUESDAY	A								
	C								
	D			Play the Game		Serving Through Science			
	N								

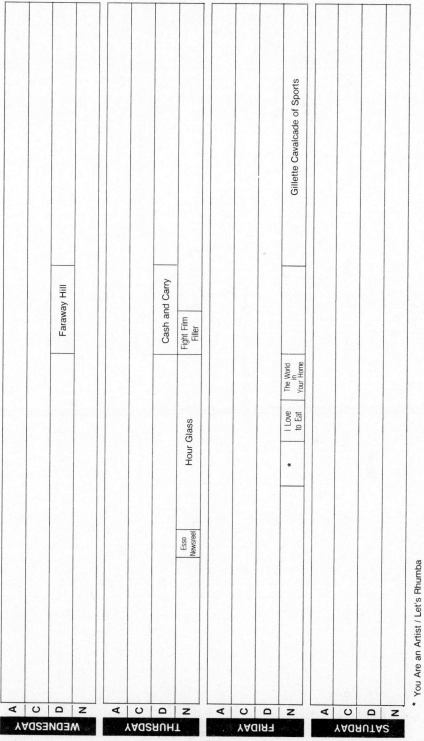

Day	Network	Programs
WEDNESDAY	A	
	C	
	D	Faraway Hill
	N	
THURSDAY	A	
	C	
	D	Cash and Carry
	N	Esso Newsreel; Hour Glass; Fight Film Filler
FRIDAY	A	
	C	
	D	
	N	*; I Love to Eat; The World in Your Home; Gillette Cavalcade of Sports
SATURDAY	A	
	C	
	D	
	N	

* You Are an Artist / Let's Rhumba

PRIME TIME SCHEDULE: 1947

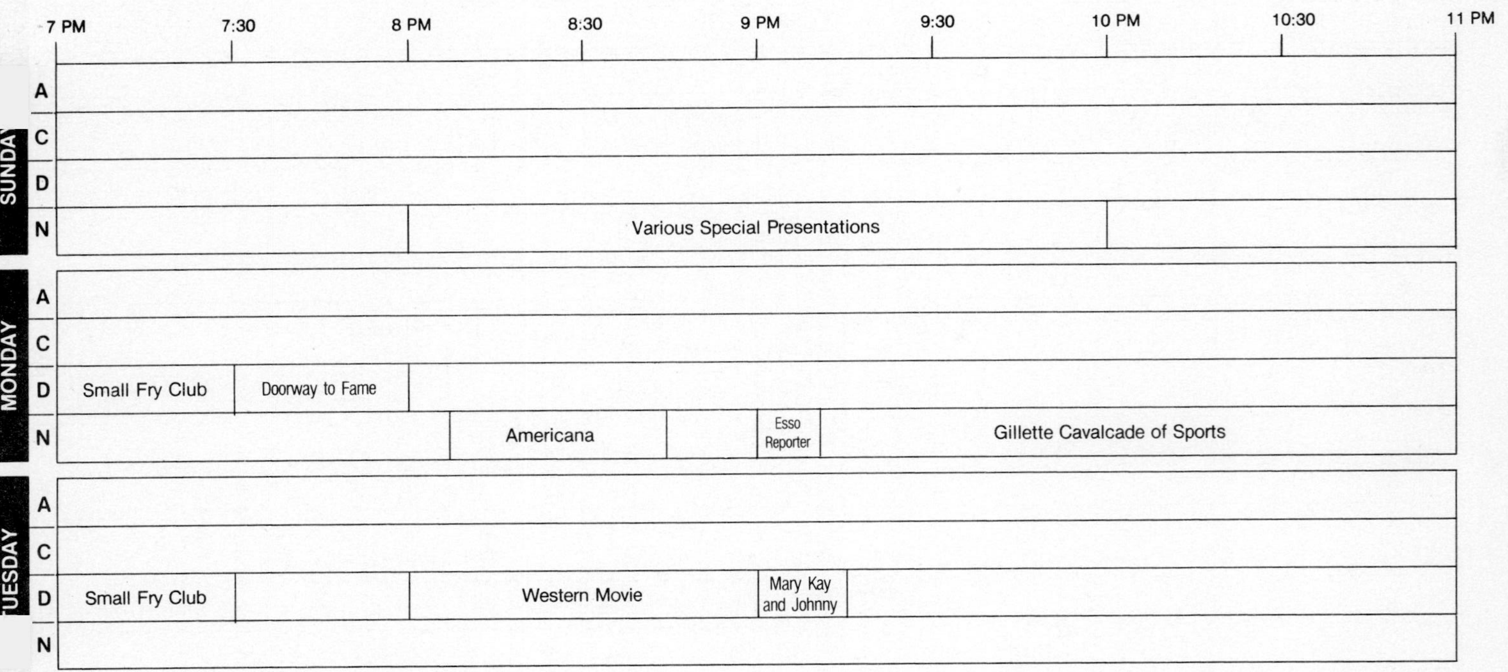

7 PM
7:30
8 PM
8:30
9 PM
9:30
10 PM
10:30
11 PM
SUNDAY
A
C
D
N
Various Special Presentations
MONDAY
A
C
D
Small Fry Club
Doorway to Fame
N
Americana
Esso Reporter
Gillette Cavalcade of Sports
TUESDAY
A
C
D
Small Fry Club
Western Movie
Mary Kay and Johnny
N

Day	Network	Programs
WEDNESDAY	A	
	C	
	D	Small Fry Club
	N	Kraft Television Theatre; *
THURSDAY	A	
	C	
	D	Small Fry CLub; Birthday Party; Charade Quiz
	N	†; Musical Merry-Go-Round; Eye Witness; You Are An Artist
FRIDAY	A	
	C	
	D	Small Fry Club
	N	Campus Hoopla; The World in Your Home; Gillette Cavalcade of Sports
SATURDAY	A	
	C	
	D	
	N	

* In the Kelvinator Kitchen

† NBC TV Newsreel

PRIME TIME SCHEDULE: 1948

Day		7 PM		7:30		8 PM		8:30		9 PM		9:30		10 PM		10:30	
SUNDAY	A	Pauline Fredericks		Southernaires Quartet		Hollywood Screen Test		Actors Studio		Movie							
SUNDAY	C	Newsweek in Review		Studio One / Various				Riddle Me This		Toast of the Town				America Speaks		News	
SUNDAY	D	Original Amateur Hour															
SUNDAY	N	Mary Kay and Johnny	News	Welcome Aboard		Author Meets the Critics		Meet the Press		Philco TV Playhouse							
MONDAY	A	News		Kiernan's Corner		Quizzing the News		Film Shorts									
MONDAY	C		Places Please	News	Face the Music			Arthur Godfrey's Talent Scouts		Basketball							
MONDAY	D	Doorway to Fame		††	Champagne and Orchids	Court of Current Issues											
MONDAY	N			America Song	News	Chevrolet Tele-Theater		Americana		Newsreel	Boxing from St. Nicholas Arena						
TUESDAY	A	News		Movieland Quiz		Film Shorts		America's Town Meeting of the Air									
TUESDAY	C	Roar of the Rails		News	Face the Music					We, the People		People's Platform					
TUESDAY	D			††	INS Telenews					Boxing							
TUESDAY	N			Musical Miniatures	News	Texaco Star Theater				Mary Margaret McBride		News / Films	Wrestling from St. Nicholas Arena				

11 PM

Day	Network										
WEDNESDAY	A	News		Critic at Large	Gay Nineties Revue	Film Shorts	Three About Town	Wrestling from Washington, D.C.			
	C		Places Please	News	Face the Music	Kobbs Korner	Winner Take All		Boxing from Westchester	News	
	D	Birthday Party	††	Film Shorts	Photographic Horizons	The Growing Paynes	Boxing from Jamaica Arena				
	N		You Are an Artist	News	Girl About Town	Picture This	Ted Steele	Story of the Week	Kraft Television Theatre	News Reel	Village Barn
THURSDAY	A	News	Film Shorts	Fashion Story	Club Seven	Movie					
	C		News	Face the Music	To the Queen's Taste	Movies / Sports					
	D	Adventures of Okey Doky	††		Film Shorts	Charade Quiz	Wrestling / Football				
	N		Paris Cavalcade of Fashion	Musical Miniatures	*	News	NBC Presents	The Nature of Things	Swift Show	Gulf Road Show with Bob Smith	Bigelow Show
FRIDAY	A	News		Tales of Red Caboose	Film Shorts	Teenage Book Club	Various	Break the Bank			
	C	Your Sports Special	Places Please	News	Face the Music	†	What's It Worth	Cap'n Billy's Mississippi Music Hall			
	D	Key to the Missing	††	Film Shorts	Fashions on Parade	Film Shorts	Wrestling from Jamaica Arena				
	N		Musical Merry-Go-Round	News	Musical Miniatures	Stop Me If You've Heard This One	I'd Like to See	News	Gillette Cavalcade of Sports		
SATURDAY	A	News	Film Shorts	Sports with Joe Hasel		Play the Game	Film Shorts	Basketball			
	C			Basketball							
	D										
	N		Television Screen Magazine	Saturday Night Jamboree	Basketball						

* Sportswoman of the Week
† Sportsman's Quiz
†† Camera Headlines (News)

PRIME TIME SCHEDULE: 1949

Day	Network	7 PM	7:30	8 PM	8:30	9 PM	9:30	10 PM	10:30
SUNDAY	A	Paul Whiteman's Goodyear Revue	ABC Penthouse Players	Think Fast	The Little Revue	Let There Be Stars		Celebrity Time	Youth on the March
	C	Tonight on Broadway	This Is Show Business	Toast of the Town		Fred Waring Show		News	
	D	Front Row Center		Chicagoland Mystery Players	Cinema Varieties	Cross Question			
	N	Leave It to the Girls	Aldrich Family	Chesterfield Supper Club	Colgate Theatre	Philco TV Playhouse		Garroway at Large	
MONDAY	A								
	C	Roar of the Rails	News / Sonny Kendis / *	Silver Theater	Arthur Godfrey's Talent Scouts	Candid Camera	The Goldbergs	Studio One	
	D	Captain Video	Manhattan Spotlight / Vincent Lopez	Newsweek Views the News	Al Morgan	And Everything Nice	Wrestling		
	N	Kukla, Fran & Ollie	Mohawk Showroom / News	Chevrolet Tele-Theater	Voice of Firestone	Lights Out	Cities Service Band of America	Quiz Kids	
TUESDAY	A							Tomorrow's Boxing Champions	
	C	Strictly for Laughs	News / Sonny Kendis / *	Movies / Specials		Actors Studio	Suspense	This Week in Sports	
	D	Captain Video	Vincent Lopez	Court of Current Issues		The O'Neills	Feature Theatre		
	N	Kukla, Fran & Ollie	Mohawk Showroom / News	Texaco Star Theater		Fireside Theatre	Life of Riley	Original Amateur Hour	

Day	Net										
WEDNESDAY	A					Photoplay Time	Look Photocrime	Author Meets the Critics	Wrestling from Chicago		
	C	Strictly for Laughs		News	At Home	Arthur Godfrey & His Friends		Bigelow Show	Boxing from St. Nicholas Arena		
	D	Captain Video		Manhattan Spotlight	Vincent Lopez	Movies		The Plainclothesman	Famous Jury Trials		
	N	Kukla, Fran & Ollie		Mohawk Showroom	News	Crisis	The Clock	Kraft Television Theatre		Break the Bank	
THURSDAY	A			Lone Ranger		Stop the Music		Crusade In Europe	Starring Boris Karloff	Roller Derby	
	C	Dione Lucas		News	Sonny Kendis *	Front Page	Inside U.S.A. / Romance	Ed Wynn Show			
	D	Captain Video		Manhattan Spotlight	Vincent Lopez	Mystery Theater		Morey Amsterdam Show	Boxing from Sunnyside Gardens		
	N	Kukla, Fran & Ollie		Mohawk Showroom	News	Hollywood Premiere	Mary Kay and Johnny	Fireball Fun-For-All		Martin Kane, Private Eye	
FRIDAY	A					Majority Rules	Blind Date	Auction-Aire	Fun for the Money	Roller Derby	
	C	Strictly for Laughs		News	Sonny Kendis *	Mama	Man Against Crime	Ford Theatre / 54th Street Revue		People's Platform	Capitol Cloakroom
	D	Captain Video		Manhattan Spotlight	Vincent Lopez	Hands of Mystery	Headline Clues	Fishing and Hunting Club	Film	Amateur Boxing from Chicago	
	N	Kukla, Fran & Ollie		Mohawk Showroom	News	One Man's Family	We, the People	Bonny Maid Versatile Varieties	Big Story/ Various	Gillette Cavalcade of Sports	
SATURDAY	A			Hollywood Screen Test		Paul Whiteman's TV Teen Club		Roller Derby			
	C			Quincy Howe-News	Blues by Bargy *			Premiere Playhouse			
	D					Spin the Picture		Cavalcade of Stars		Wrestling from Chicago	
	N			The Nature of Things	News	Twenty Questions	Sessions Stud's Place	Who Said That?	Meet the Press	Black Robe	

* Herb Shriner Show

PRIME TIME SCHEDULE: 1950

Day	Net	7 PM	7:30	7:45	8 PM	8:30	9 PM	9:30	10 PM	10:30
SUNDAY	A	Paul Whiteman's Revue	Showtime, U.S.A.		Hollywood Premiere Theatre	Sit or Miss	Soap Box Theatre	Marshall Plan in Action	Old Fashioned Meeting	Youth on the March
	C	Gene Autry Show	This is Show Business		Toast of the Town		Fred Waring Show		Celebrity Time	What's My Line
	D	Starlit Time			Rhythm Rodeo		Arthur Murray Party		They Stand Accused	
	N	Leave It to the Girls	Aldrich Family		Colgate Comedy Hour		Philco TV Playhouse		Garroway at Large	Take a Chance
MONDAY	A	Club Seven	Hollywood Screen Test		Treasury Men in Action	Dick Tracy	College Bowl	On Trial	Feature Film	
	C	Stork Club		Perry Como	Lux Video Theatre	Arthur Godfrey's Talent Scouts	Horace Heidt Show	The Goldbergs	Studio One	
	D	Captain Video	Susan Raye	Manhattan Spotlight	Visit with the Armed Forces	Al Morgan	Wrestling from Columbia Park			
	N	Kukla, Fran & Ollie	Mohawk Showroom		Speidel Show	Voice of Firestone	Lights Out	Robert Montgomery Presents Lucky Strike Time/Musical Comedy Time		Who Said That?
TUESDAY	A	Club Seven	Beulah		Game of the Week	Buck Rogers	Billy Rose Show	Can You Top This?	Life Begins at Eighty	Roller Derby
	C	Stork Club		Faye Emerson	Prudential Family Playhouse/ Sure as Fate		Vaughn Monroe Musical Variety	Suspense	Danger	We Take Your Word
	D	Captain Video		Joan Edwards	Court of Current Issues	Johns Hopkins Science Review	Cavalcade of Bands		Star Time	
	N	Kukla, Fran & Ollie	Little Show		Texaco Star Theater		Fireside Theatre	Circle Theatre	Original Amateur Hour	

WEDNESDAY	A	Club Seven	Chance of a Lifetime		First Nighter		Don McNeill TV Club		Chicago Wrestling	
	C	Stork Club		Perry Como	Arthur Godfrey and His Friends		Teller of Tales		Blue Ribbon Bouts	
	D	Captain Video	Most Important People	Manhattan Spotlight			Famous Jury Trials	The Plainclothesman	Broadway to Hollywood	
	N	Kukla, Fran & Ollie	Mohawk Showroom		Four Star Revue		Kraft Television Theatre		Break the Bank	Stars Over Hollywood
THURSDAY	A	Club Seven	Lone Ranger		Stop the Music		Holiday Hotel	Blind Date	I Cover Times Square	Roller Derby
	C	Stork Club		Faye Emerson	Show Goes On		Alan Young Show	Big Town	Truth or Consequences	Nash Airflyte Theater
	D	Captain Video	Manhattan Spotlight	Joan Edwards			Adventures of Ellery Queen	Boxing from Dexter Arena		
	N	Kukla, Fran & Ollie	Little Show		You Bet Your Life	Hawkins Falls	Kay Kyser's Kollege of Musical Knowledge		Martin Kane, Private Eye	Wayne King
FRIDAY	A	Club Seven	Life with Linkletter		Twenty Questions	Pro Football Highlights	Pulitzer Prize Playhouse		Penthouse Party	Stud's Place
	C	Stork Club		Perry Como	Mama	Man Against Crime	Ford Theatre / Magnavox Theater		Morton Downey Show	Beat the Clock
	D	Captain Video	Most Important People	Manhattan Spotlight	Film Filler	Hold That Camera	Hands of Mystery	Inside Detective	Cavalcade of Stars	
	N	Kukla, Fran & Ollie	Mohawk Showroom		Quiz Kids	We, the People	Bonny Maid Versatile Varieties	Big Story/ The Clock	Gillette Cavalcade of Sports	Greatest Fights
SATURDAY	A	Sandy Dreams	Stu Erwin Show		Paul Whiteman's Teen Club		Roller Derby			
	C	Big Top	Week in Review	Faye Emerson	Ken Murray Show		Frank Sinatra Show		Sing It Again	
	D	Captain Video			Country Style		Madison Square Garden			
	N	Hank McCune	One Man's Family		Jack Carter Show		Your Show of Shows			Your Hit Parade

PRIME TIME SCHEDULE: 1951

		7 PM	7:30		8 PM	8:30	9 PM	9:30	10 PM	10:30
SUNDAY	A	Paul Whiteman's Goodyear Revue	Music in Velvet		Admission Free		Film Filler	Marshall Plan in Action	Hour of Decision	Youth on the March
	C	Gene Autry Show	This Is Show Business		Toast of the Town		Fred Waring Show		Goodrich Celebrity Time	What's My Line
	D						Rocky King, Detective	The Plainclothesman	They Stand Accused	
	N	Chesterfield Sound Off Time	Young Mr. Bobbin		Colgate Comedy Hour		Philco TV Playhouse/ Goodyear TV Playhouse		Red Skelton Show	Leave It to the Girls
MONDAY	A		Hollywood Screen Test		Mr. District Attorney/ Amazing Mr. Malone	Life Begins at Eighty	Curtain Up		Bill Gwinn Show	Stud's Place
	C			Perry Como	Lux Video Theatre	Arthur Godfrey's Talent Scouts	I Love Lucy	It's News to Me	Studio One	
	D	Captain Video			Stage Entrance	Johns Hopkins Science Review	Wrestling from Columbia Park			
	N	Kukla, Fran & Ollie	Mohawk Showroom		Speidel Show	Voice of Firestone	Lights Out	Robert Montgomery Presents/ Somerset Maugham TV Theatre		
TUESDAY	A		Beulah		Charlie Wild, Private Detective	How Did They Get That Way	United or Not	On Trial	Film Filler	Chicago Symphony Chamber Orchestra
	C			Stork Club	Frank Sinatra Show		Crime Syndicated	Suspense	Danger	
	D	Captain Video			What's the Story?	Keep Posted	Cosmopolitan Theatre		Hands of Destiny	
	N	Kukla, Fran & Ollie	Little Show		Texaco Star Theater		Fireside Theatre	Armstrong Circle Theatre	Original Amateur Hour	

Day	Network										
WEDNESDAY	A		Chance of a Lifetime		Paul Dixon Show		Don McNeill's TV Club/ Arthur Murray Party	The Clock	Celanese Theatre/ King's Crossroads		
	C			Perry Como	Arthur Godfrey & His Friends		Strike It Rich	The Web	Pabst Blue Ribbon Bouts		Sports Spot
	D	Captain Video					Gallery of Mme. Liu-Tsong	Shadow of the Cloak			
	N	Kukla, Fran & Ollie	Mohawk Showroom		Kate Smith Evening Hour		Kraft Television Theatre		Break the Bank	Freddy Martin Show	
THURSDAY	A		Lone Ranger		Stop the Music		Herb Shriner Show	Gruen Guild Theater	Paul Dixon Show	Masland at Home Show	Carmel Myers Show
	C			Stork Club	George Burns & Gracie Allen Show/Garry Moore Show	Amos 'n' Andy	Alan Young Show	Big Town	Racket Squad	Crime Photographer	
	D	Captain Video			Georgetown University Forum	Broadway to Hollywood	Adventures of Ellery Queen		Bigelow Theatre		Football This Week
	N	Kukla, Fran & Ollie	Little Show		You Bet Your Life	Treasury Men in Action	Ford Festival		Martin Kane, Private Eye	Wayne King	
FRIDAY	A		Say It with Acting/ Life with Linkletter		Mystery Theatre	Stu Erwin Show	Crime with Father	Tales of Tomorrow/ Versatile Varieties	Dell O'Dell Show	America in View	
	C			Perry Como	Mama	Man Against Crime	Schlitz Playhouse of Stars		Live Like a Millionaire	Hollywood Opening Night	
	D	Captain Video			Twenty Questions	You Asked for It	Down You Go	Front Page Detective	Cavalcade of Stars		
	N	Kukla, Fran & Ollie	Mohawk Showroom		Quiz Kids	We, the People	Big Story	Aldrich Family	Gillette Cavalcade of Sports		Greatest Fights
SATURDAY	A	Hollywood Theatre Time	Jerry Colonna Show		Paul Whiteman's Teen Club		Lesson in Safety	America's Health			
	C	Sammy Kaye Variety Show	Beat the Clock		Ken Murray Show		Faye Emerson's Wonderful Town	Show Goes On	Songs for Sale		
	D							Pro Wrestling from Chicago			
	N	American Youth Forum	One Man's Family		All Star Revue		Your Show of Shows			Your Hit Parade	

PRIME TIME SCHEDULE: 1952

		7 PM		7:30		8 PM		8:30		9 PM		9:30		10 PM		10:30		11 PM
SUNDAY	A	You Asked for It		Hot Seat		All-Star News				Playhouse #7		This Is the Life		Hour of Decision	Film Filler	Anywhere, U.S.A.		
	C	Gene Autry Show		This Is Show Business		Toast of the Town				Fred Waring Show		Break the Bank		The Web		What's My Line		
	D	Georgetown University Forum								Rocky King, Detective		The Plainclothesman		Arthur Murray Show		Youth on the March		
	N	Red Skelton Show		Doc Corkle		Colgate Comedy Hour				Philco TV Playhouse/ Goodyear TV Playhouse				The Doctor				
MONDAY	A			Hollywood Screen Test		Inspector Mark Saber		United or Not		All-Star News								
	C				Perry Como	Lux Video Theatre		Arthur Godfrey's Talent Scouts		I Love Lucy		Life with Luigi		Studio One				
	D	Captain Video				Pentagon		Johns Hopkins Science Review		Guide Right		Football Sidelines	Famous Fights	Boxing from Eastern Parkway				
	N			Those Two		What's My Name		Voice of Firestone		Hollywood Opening Night		Robert Montgomery Presents				Who Said That?		
TUESDAY	A			Beulah														
	C				Heaven for Betsy	Leave it to Larry		Red Buttons Show		Crime Syndicated/ City Hospital		Suspense		Danger				
	D	Captain Video				Power of Women		Keep Posted		Where Was I?		Quick on the Draw						
	N		Short Short Dramas	Dinah Shore		Texaco Star Theater				Fireside Theatre		Armstrong Circle Theatre		Two for the Money		Club Embassy	On the Line with Considine	

<table>
<tr><td rowspan="4">WEDNESDAY</td><td>A</td><td colspan="2"></td><td colspan="2">Name's the Same</td><td colspan="4">All-Star News</td><td colspan="2">Adventures of Ellery Queen</td><td colspan="6">Chicago Wrestling</td></tr>
<tr><td>C</td><td colspan="2"></td><td></td><td>Perry Como</td><td colspan="4">Arthur Godfrey & His Friends</td><td colspan="2">Strike It Rich</td><td colspan="2">Man Against Crime</td><td colspan="3">Pabst Blue Ribbon Bouts</td><td>Sports Spot</td></tr>
<tr><td>D</td><td colspan="2">Captain Video</td><td colspan="2">New York Giants Quarterback Huddle</td><td colspan="2"></td><td colspan="2">Trash or Treasure</td><td colspan="4">Stage a Number</td><td colspan="4"></td></tr>
<tr><td>N</td><td colspan="2"></td><td>Those Two</td><td></td><td colspan="2">I Married Joan</td><td colspan="2">Scott Music Hall/ Cavalcade of America</td><td colspan="4">Kraft Television Theatre</td><td colspan="2">This is Your Life</td><td colspan="2"></td></tr>
<tr><td rowspan="4">THURSDAY</td><td>A</td><td colspan="2"></td><td colspan="2">Lone Ranger</td><td colspan="2">All-Star News</td><td colspan="2">Chance of a Lifetime</td><td colspan="2">Politics on Trial</td><td colspan="2">On Guard</td><td colspan="4"></td></tr>
<tr><td>C</td><td colspan="2"></td><td></td><td>Heaven for Betsy</td><td colspan="2">George Burns and Gracie Allen Show</td><td colspan="2">Amos 'n' Andy/ Four Star Playhouse</td><td colspan="2">Pick the Winner</td><td colspan="2">Big Town</td><td colspan="2">Racket Squad</td><td colspan="2">I've Got a Secret</td></tr>
<tr><td>D</td><td colspan="2">Captain Video</td><td colspan="4"></td><td colspan="2">Broadway to Hollywood</td><td colspan="2">Pick the Winner</td><td colspan="2">What's the Story?</td><td colspan="2">Author Meets the Critics</td><td colspan="2"></td></tr>
<tr><td>N</td><td></td><td>Short Short Dramas</td><td>Dinah Shore</td><td></td><td colspan="2">You Bet Your Life</td><td colspan="2">Treasury Men in Action</td><td colspan="2">Dragnet/ Gangbusters</td><td colspan="2">Ford Theatre</td><td colspan="2">Martin Kane, Private Eye</td><td colspan="2"></td></tr>
<tr><td rowspan="4">FRIDAY</td><td>A</td><td colspan="2"></td><td colspan="2">Stu Erwin Show</td><td colspan="2">Adventures of Ozzie & Harriet</td><td colspan="4">All-Star News</td><td colspan="2">Tales of Tomorrow</td><td colspan="4"></td></tr>
<tr><td>C</td><td colspan="2"></td><td></td><td>Perry Como</td><td colspan="2">Mama</td><td colspan="2">My Friend Irma</td><td colspan="2">Schlitz Playhouse of Stars</td><td colspan="2">Our Miss Brooks</td><td colspan="2">Mr. & Mrs. North</td><td colspan="2"></td></tr>
<tr><td>D</td><td colspan="2">Captain Video</td><td colspan="2"></td><td colspan="2">Steve Randall</td><td colspan="2">Dark of Night</td><td colspan="2">Life Begins at Eighty</td><td colspan="2"></td><td colspan="2">Twenty Questions</td><td colspan="2">Down You Go</td></tr>
<tr><td>N</td><td>Herman Hickman Show</td><td></td><td>Those Two</td><td></td><td colspan="2">RCA Victor Show</td><td colspan="2">Gulf Playhouse</td><td colspan="2">Big Story</td><td colspan="2">Aldrich Family</td><td colspan="3">Gillette Cavalcade of Sports</td><td>Greatest Fights</td></tr>
<tr><td rowspan="4">SATURDAY</td><td>A</td><td colspan="2">Paul Whiteman's TV Teen Club</td><td colspan="2">Live Like a Millionaire</td><td colspan="8">Feature Playhouse</td><td colspan="4"></td></tr>
<tr><td>C</td><td colspan="2">Stork Club</td><td colspan="2">Beat the Clock</td><td colspan="4">Jackie Gleason Show</td><td colspan="2">Jane Froman's U.S.A. Canteen</td><td colspan="2">Meet Millie</td><td colspan="2">Balance Your Budget/ Quiz Kids</td><td colspan="2">Battle of the Ages</td></tr>
<tr><td>D</td><td colspan="2"></td><td colspan="2">Pet Shop</td><td colspan="6"></td><td colspan="6">Pro Wrestling from Chicago</td></tr>
<tr><td>N</td><td colspan="2">Mr. Wizard</td><td colspan="2">My Little Margie</td><td colspan="4">All Star Revue</td><td colspan="6">Your Show of Shows</td><td colspan="2">Your Hit Parade</td></tr>
</table>

PRIME TIME SCHEDULE: 1953

Day	Net	7 PM	7:30	8 PM	8:30	9 PM	9:30	10 PM	10:30
SUNDAY	A	You Asked for It	Frank Leahy Show Notre Dame Football			Walter Winchell Show Orchid Award	Peter Potter Show		Hour of Decision
	C	Quiz Kids	Jack Benny Show/ Private Secretary	Toast of the Town		G.E. Theater/ Fred Waring Show	Man Behind the Badge	The Web	What's My Line
	D	Georgetown University Forum	Washington Exclusive			Rocky King, Detective	The Plainclothesman	Dollar a Second	Man Against Crime
	N	Paul Winchell Show	Mr. Peepers	Colgate Comedy Hour		Philco TV Playhouse/ Goodyear TV Playhouse		Letter to Loretta	Man Against Crime
MONDAY	A	Walter Winchell	Jamie	Sky King	Of Many Things	Junior Press Conference	Big Picture	This Is the Life	
	C		Perry Como	George Burns and Gracie Allen Show	Arthur Godfrey's Talent Scouts	I Love Lucy	Red Buttons Show	Studio One	
	D	Captain Video		Twenty Questions	Big Issue	Boxing from Eastern Parkway			
	N		Arthur Murray Party	Name That Tune	Voice of Firestone	RCA Victor Show Starring Dennis Day	Robert Montgomery Presents		Who Said That?
TUESDAY	A		Cavalcade of America			Make Room for Daddy	U.S. Steel Hour/Motorola TV Theatre		Name's the Same
	C		Jane Froman	Gene Autry Show	Red Skelton Show	This Is Show Business	Suspense	Danger	See It Now
	D	Captain Video		Life Is Worth Living	Pantomime Quiz				
	N		Dinah Shore	Buick Berle Show		Fireside Theatre	Armstrong Circle Theatre	Judge for Yourself	On the Line with Considine It Happened In Sports

<table>
<tr><td rowspan="4">WEDNESDAY</td><td>A</td><td colspan="2"></td><td colspan="2">Inspector Mark Saber</td><td>At Issue</td><td>Through the Curtain</td><td colspan="2">America in View</td><td colspan="8">Wrestling from Rainbo</td></tr>
<tr><td>C</td><td colspan="3"></td><td>Perry Como</td><td colspan="4">Arthur Godfrey & His Friends</td><td colspan="2">Strike It Rich</td><td colspan="2">I've Got a Secret</td><td colspan="3">Pabst Blue Ribbon Bouts</td><td>Sports Spot</td></tr>
<tr><td>D</td><td>Captain Video</td><td colspan="3"></td><td colspan="2">Johns Hopkins Science Review</td><td colspan="2">Joseph Schildkraut Presents</td><td colspan="2">Colonel Humphrey Flack</td><td colspan="2">On Your Way</td><td colspan="2">Stars on Parade</td><td colspan="2">Music Show</td></tr>
<tr><td>N</td><td colspan="2"></td><td>Coke Time</td><td></td><td colspan="2">I Married Joan</td><td colspan="2">My Little Margie</td><td colspan="4">Kraft Television Theatre</td><td colspan="4">This Is Your Life</td></tr>
<tr><td rowspan="4">THURSDAY</td><td>A</td><td colspan="2"></td><td colspan="2">Lone Ranger</td><td colspan="2">Quick as a Flash</td><td colspan="2">Where's Raymond</td><td colspan="2">Back That Fact</td><td colspan="4">Kraft Television Theatre</td><td colspan="2"></td></tr>
<tr><td>C</td><td colspan="3"></td><td>Jane Froman</td><td colspan="2">Meet Mr. McNutley</td><td colspan="2">Four Star Playhouse</td><td colspan="2">Lux Video Theatre</td><td colspan="2">Big Town</td><td colspan="2">Philip Morris Playhouse</td><td colspan="2">Place the Face</td></tr>
<tr><td>D</td><td>Captain Video</td><td colspan="3"></td><td colspan="2">New York Giants Quarterback Huddle</td><td colspan="2">Broadway to Hollywood</td><td colspan="2">What's the Story?</td><td colspan="6"></td></tr>
<tr><td>N</td><td colspan="2"></td><td>Dinah Shore</td><td></td><td colspan="2">You Bet Your Life</td><td colspan="2">Treasury Men in Action</td><td colspan="2">Dragnet</td><td colspan="2">Ford Theatre</td><td colspan="2">Martin Kane, Private Eye</td><td colspan="2"></td></tr>
<tr><td rowspan="4">FRIDAY</td><td>A</td><td colspan="2"></td><td colspan="2">Stu Erwin Show</td><td colspan="2">Adventures of Ozzie & Harriet</td><td colspan="2">Pepsi-Cola Playhouse</td><td colspan="2">Pride of the Family</td><td colspan="2">Comeback Story</td><td colspan="2">Showcase Theater</td><td colspan="2"></td></tr>
<tr><td>C</td><td colspan="3"></td><td>Perry Como</td><td colspan="2">Mama</td><td colspan="2">Topper</td><td colspan="2">Schlitz Playhouse of Stars</td><td colspan="2">Our Miss Brooks</td><td colspan="2">My Friend Irma</td><td colspan="2">Person to Person</td></tr>
<tr><td>D</td><td colspan="4"></td><td colspan="2">Front Page Detective</td><td colspan="2">Melody Street</td><td colspan="2">Life Begins at Eighty</td><td colspan="2">Nine Thirty Curtain</td><td colspan="2">Chance of a Lifetime</td><td colspan="2">Down You Go</td></tr>
<tr><td>N</td><td colspan="2"></td><td>Coke Time</td><td></td><td colspan="2">Dave Garroway Show</td><td colspan="2">Life of Riley</td><td colspan="2">Big Story</td><td colspan="2">Campbell Soundstage</td><td colspan="3">Gillette Cavalcade of Sports</td><td>Greatest Fights</td></tr>
<tr><td rowspan="4">SATURDAY</td><td>A</td><td colspan="2">Paul Whiteman's TV Teen Club</td><td colspan="2">Leave It to the Girls</td><td colspan="2">Talent Patrol</td><td colspan="2">Music at the Meadowbrook</td><td colspan="3">Saturday Night Fights</td><td>Fight Talk</td><td colspan="2">Madison Square Garden Highlights</td><td colspan="2"></td></tr>
<tr><td>C</td><td colspan="2">Meet Millie</td><td colspan="2">Beat the Clock</td><td colspan="4">Jackie Gleason Show</td><td colspan="2">Two for the Money</td><td colspan="2">My Favorite Husband</td><td colspan="2">Medallion Theater</td><td colspan="2">Revlon Mirror Theatre</td></tr>
<tr><td>D</td><td colspan="4"></td><td colspan="12">Pro Football</td></tr>
<tr><td>N</td><td colspan="2">Mr. Wizard</td><td colspan="2">Ethel & Albert</td><td colspan="2">Bonino</td><td colspan="2">Original Amateur Hour</td><td colspan="6">Your Show of Shows</td><td colspan="2">Your Hit Parade</td></tr>
</table>

PRIME TIME SCHEDULE: 1954

		7 PM		7:30		8 PM	8:30	9 PM		9:30	10 PM	10:30
SUNDAY	A	You Asked for It		Pepsi-Cola Playhouse		Flight #7	Big Picture	Walter Winchell Show	Martha Wright Show	Dr. I.Q.	Break the Bank	
	C	Lassie		Jack Benny Show / Private Secretary		Toast of the Town		G.E. Theater		Honestly Celeste	Father Knows Best	What's My Line
	D	Author Meets the Critic		Opera Cameos				Rocky King, Detective		Life Begins at Eighty	Music Show	
	N	People Are Funny		Mr. Peepers		Colgate Comedy Hour		Philco TV Playhouse / Goodyear TV Playhouse			Loretta Young Show	The Hunter
MONDAY	A	Kukla, Fran & Ollie		Name's the Same		Come Closer	Voice of Firestone	Junior Press Conference		Boxing from Eastern Parkway		
	C				Perry Como	George Burns and Gracie Allen Show	Arthur Godfrey's Talent Scouts	I Love Lucy		December Bride	Studio One	
	D	Captain Video				Ilona Massey Show		Boxing from St. Nicholas Arena				
	N			Tony Martin		Caesar's Hour		Medic		Robert Montgomery Presents		
TUESDAY	A	Kukla, Fran & Ollie		Cavalcade of America			Twenty Questions	Make Room for Daddy		U.S. Steel Hour/Elgin TV Hour		Stop the Music
	C				Jo Stafford	Red Skelton Show	Halls of Ivy	Meet Millie		Danger	Life with Father	See It Now
	D	Captain Video				Life Is Worth Living	Studio 57	One Minute Please				
	N			Dinah Shore		Buick Berle Show		Fireside Theatre		Armstrong Circle Theatre	Truth or Consequences	It's a Great Life

(11 PM)

WEDNESDAY	A	Kukla, Fran & Ollie		Disneyland			Stu Erwin Show	Masquerade Party	Enterprise				
	C				Perry Como	Arthur Godfrey & His Friends		Strike It Rich	I've Got a Secret		Pabst Blue Ribbon Bouts		Sports Spot
	D	Captain Video						Chicago Symphony			Down You Go		
	N			Coke Time		I Married Joan	My Little Margie	Kraft Television Theatre			This Is Your Life	Big Town	
THURSDAY	A	Kukla, Fran & Ollie		Lone Ranger		Mail Story	Treasury Men In Action	So You Want to Lead a Band	Kraft Television Theatre				
	C				Jane Froman	Ray Milland Show	Climax		Four Star Playhouse		Public Defender	Name That Tune	
	D	Captain Video				They Stand Accused		What's the Story?					
	N			Dinah Shore		You Bet Your Life	Justice	Dragnet	Ford Theatre		Lux Video Theatre		
FRIDAY	A	Kukla, Fran & Ollie		Adventures of Rin Tin Tin		Adventures of Ozzie & Harriet	Ray Bolger Show	Dollar a Second	The Vise				
	C				Perry Como	Mama	Topper	Schlitz Playhouse of Stars	Our Miss Brooks		The Lineup	Person to Person	
	D	Captain Video						The Stranger			Chance of a Lifetime	Time Will Tell	
	N			Coke Time		Red Buttons Show	Life of Riley	Big Story	Dear Phoebe		Gillette Cavalcade of Sports		Great Moments In Sports
SATURDAY	A			Compass		Dotty Mack Show		Saturday Night Fights		Fight Talk	Stork Club		
	C	Gene Autry Show		Beat the Clock		Jackie Gleason Show		Two for the Money	My Favorite Husband		That's My Boy	Willy	
	D					Pro Football							
	N	Mr. Wizard		Ethel & Albert		Mickey Rooney Show	Place the Face	Imogene Coca Show	Texaco Star Theater		George Gobel Show	Your Hit Parade	

PRIME TIME SCHEDULE: 1955

<table>
<tr><th></th><th></th><th>7 PM</th><th>7:30</th><th>8 PM</th><th>8:30</th><th>9 PM</th><th>9:30</th><th>10 PM</th><th>10:30</th></tr>
<tr><td rowspan="3">SUNDAY</td><td>A</td><td>You Asked for It</td><td colspan="3">Famous Film Festival</td><td>Chance of a Lifetime</td><td>Original Amateur Hour</td><td>Life Begins at Eighty</td><td></td></tr>
<tr><td>C</td><td>Lassie</td><td>Jack Benny Show/ Private Secretary</td><td colspan="2">Ed Sullivan Show</td><td>G.E. Theater</td><td>Alfred Hitchcock Presents</td><td>Appointment with Adventure</td><td>What's My Line</td></tr>
<tr><td>N</td><td>It's a Great Life</td><td>Frontier</td><td colspan="2">Colgate Variety Hour</td><td colspan="2">Goodyear TV Playhouse/Alcoa Hour</td><td>Loretta Young Show</td><td>Justice</td></tr>
<tr><td rowspan="3">MONDAY</td><td>A</td><td>Kukla, Fran & Ollie</td><td>Topper</td><td>TV Reader's Digest</td><td>Voice of Firestone</td><td>Dotty Mack Show</td><td>Medical Horizons</td><td>Big Picture</td><td></td></tr>
<tr><td>C</td><td></td><td>Adventures of Robin Hood</td><td>George Burns and Gracie Allen Show</td><td>Arthur Godfrey's Talent Scouts</td><td>I Love Lucy</td><td>December Bride</td><td colspan="2">Studio One</td></tr>
<tr><td>N</td><td></td><td>Tony Martin Show</td><td colspan="2">Caesar's Hour</td><td>Medic</td><td colspan="2">Robert Montgomery Presents</td><td></td></tr>
<tr><td rowspan="3">TUESDAY</td><td>A</td><td>Kukla, Fran & Ollie</td><td colspan="2">Warner Brothers Presents</td><td>Life and Legend of Wyatt Earp</td><td>Make Room for Daddy</td><td>DuPont Cavalcade Theater</td><td>Talent Varieties</td><td></td></tr>
<tr><td>C</td><td></td><td>Name That Tune</td><td>Navy Log</td><td>You'll Never Get Rich</td><td>Meet Millie</td><td>Red Skelton Show</td><td>$64,000 Question</td><td>My Favorite Husband</td></tr>
<tr><td>N</td><td></td><td>Dinah Shore Show</td><td colspan="2">Martha Raye Show/Milton Berle Show/ Chevy Show</td><td>Fireside Theatre</td><td colspan="2">Armstrong Circle Theatre/ Pontiac Presents Playwrights '56</td><td>Big Town</td></tr>
</table>

Day	Network								
WEDNESDAY	A	Kukla, Fran & Ollie	Disneyland		MGM Parade	Masquerade Party	Break the Bank	Wednesday Night Fights	
	C		Brave Eagle	Arthur Godfrey & His Friends		The Millionaire	I've Got a Secret	20th Century-Fox Hour/U.S. Steel Hour	
	N		Coke Time	Screen Director's Playhouse	Father Knows Best	Kraft Television Theatre		This Is Your Life	Midwestern Hayride
THURSDAY	A	Kukla, Fran & Ollie	Lone Ranger	Life Is Worth Living	Stop the Music	Star Tonight	Down You Go	Outside U.S.A.	
	C		Sgt. Preston of the Yukon	Bob Cummings Show	Climax		Four Star Playhouse	Johnny Carson Show	Wanted
	N		Dinah Shore Show	You Bet Your Life	People's Choice	Dragnet	Ford Theatre	Lux Video Theatre	
FRIDAY	A	Kukla, Fran & Ollie	Adventures of Rin Tin Tin	Adventures of Ozzie & Harriet	Crossroads	Dollar a Second	The Vise	Ethel & Albert	
	C		Adventures of Champion	Mama	Our Miss Brooks	The Crusader	Schlitz Playhouse of Stars	The Lineup	Person to Person
	N		Coke Time	Truth or Consequences	Life of Riley	Big Story	Star Stage	Gillette Cavalcade of Sports	Red Barber's Corner
SATURDAY	A		Ozark Jubilee			Lawrence Welk Show		Tomorrow's Careers	
	C	Gene Autry Show	Beat the Clock	Stage Show	The Honeymooners	Two for the Money	It's Always Jan	Gunsmoke	Damon Runyon Theatre
	N		Big Surprise	Perry Como Show		People Are Funny	Texaco Star Theater Starring Jimmy Durante	George Gobel Show	Your Hit Parade

PRIME TIME SCHEDULE: 1956

		7 PM	7:30	8 PM	8:30	9 PM	9:30	10 PM	10:30
SUNDAY	A	You Asked for It	Original Amateur Hour		Press Conference	Omnibus			
	C	Lassie	Jack Benny Show/ Private Secretary	Ed Sullivan Show		G.E. Theater	Alfred Hitchcock Presents	$64,000 Challenge	What's My Line
	N	Tales of the 77th Bengal Lancers	Circus Boy	Steve Allen Show		Goodyear TV Playhouse/Alcoa Hour		Loretta Young Show	National Bowling Champions
MONDAY	A	Kukla, Fran & Ollie	Bold Journey	Danny Thomas Show	Voice of Firestone	Life Is Worth Living	Lawrence Welk Talent Show		
	C		Adventures of Robin Hood	George Burns and Gracie Allen Show	Arthur Godfrey's Talent Scouts	I Love Lucy	December Bride	Studio One	
	N		Nat "King" Cole Show	Adventures of Sir Lancelot	Stanley	Medic	Robert Montgomery Presents		
TUESDAY	A	Kukla, Fran & Ollie	Conflict/Cheyenne		Life and Legend of Wyatt Earp	Broken Arrow	DuPont Theater	It's Polka Time	
	C		Name That Tune	Phil Silvers Show	The Brothers	Herb Shriner Show	Red Skelton Show	$64,000 Question	Do You Trust Your Wife?
	N		Jonathan Winters Show	Big Surprise	Noah's Ark	Jane Wyman Show	Armstrong Circle Theatre/Kaiser Aluminum Hour		Break the $250,000 Bank

WEDNESDAY	A	Kukla, Fran & Ollie	Disneyland		Navy Log	Adventures of Ozzie & Harriet	Ford Theatre	Wednesday Night Fights	
	C		Giant Step	Arthur Godfrey Show		The Millionaire	I've Got a Secret	20th Century-Fox Hour/U.S. Steel Hour	
	N		Eddie Fisher Show	Adventures of Hiram Holliday	Father Knows Best	Kraft Television Theatre		This Is Your Life	Twenty-One
THURSDAY	A	Kukla, Fran & Ollie	Lone Ranger	Circus Time		Wire Service		Ozark Jubilee	
	C		Sgt. Preston of the Yukon	Bob Cummings Show	Climax		Playhouse 90		
	N		Dinah Shore Show	You Bet Your Life	Dragnet	People's Choice	Ford Show Starring Tennessee Ernie Ford	Lux Video Theatre	
FRIDAY	A	Kukla, Fran & Ollie	Adventures of Rin Tin Tin	Adventures of Jim Bowie	Crossroads	Treasure Hunt	The Vise	Ray Anthony Show	
	C		My Friend Flicka	West Point Story	Dick Powell's Zane Grey Theater	The Crusader	Schlitz Playhouse	The Lineup	Person to Person
	N		Eddie Fisher Show	Life of Riley	Walter Winchell Show	On Trial	Big Story	Gillette Cavalcade of Sports	Red Barber's Corner
SATURDAY	A		Famous Film Festival			Lawrence Welk Show		Masquerade Party	
	C	Beat the Clock	The Buccaneers	Jackie Gleason Show		Gale Storm Show	Hey Jeannie	Gunsmoke	High Finance
	N		People Are Funny	Perry Como Show		Caesar's Hour		George Gobel Show	Your Hit Parade

PRIME TIME SCHEDULE: 1957

Day	Network	7 PM	7:30	8 PM	8:30	9 PM	9:30	10 PM	10:30
SUNDAY	A	You Asked for It	Maverick		Bowling Stars	Open Hearing	All-American Football Game of the Week		
	C	Lassie	Jack Benny Show/ Bachelor Father	Ed Sullivan Show		G.E. Theater	Alfred Hitchcock Presents	$64,000 Challenge	What's My Line
	N	Original Amateur Hour	Sally	Steve Allen Show		Dinah Shore Chevy Show		Loretta Young Show	
MONDAY	A		American Bandstand	Guy Mitchell Show	Bold Journey	Voice of Firestone	Lawrence Welk's Top Tunes and New Talent Show		
	C		Robin Hood	George Burns and Gracie Allen Show	Arthur Godfrey's Talent Scouts	Danny Thomas Show	December Bride	Studio One in Hollywood	
	N		Price Is Right	Restless Gun	Tales of Wells Fargo	Twenty-One	Turn of Fate	Suspicion	
TUESDAY	A		Cheyenne/Sugarfoot		Life and Legend of Wyatt Earp	Broken Arrow	Telephone Time	West Point Story	
	C		Name That Tune	Phil Silvers Show	Eve Arden Show	To Tell the Truth	Red Skelton Show	$64,000 Question	Assignment Foreign Legion
	N		Nat "King" Cole Show	Eddie Fisher Show/George Gobel Show		Meet McGraw	Bob Cummings Show	The Californians	

WEDNESDAY	A		Disneyland		Tombstone Territory	Adventures of Ozzie & Harriet	Walter Winchell File	Wednesday Night Fights	Famous Fights
	C		I Love Lucy	Big Record		The Millionaire	I've Got a Secret	Armstrong Circle Theatre/U.S. Steel Hour	
	N		Wagon Train		Father Knows Best	Kraft Television Theatre		This Is Your Life	
THURSDAY	A		Circus Boy	Zorro	Real McCoys	Pat Boone—Chevy Showroom	O.S.S.	Navy Log	
	C		Sgt. Preston of the Yukon	Harbourmaster	Climax		Playhouse 90		
	N		Tic Tac Dough	You Bet Your Life	Dragnet	People's Choice	Ford Show Starring Tennessee Ernie Ford	Lux Show Starring Rosemary Clooney	Jane Wyman Show
FRIDAY	A		Adventures of Rin Tin Tin	Adventures of Jim Bowie	Patrice Munsel Show	Frank Sinatra Show	Date with the Angels	Colt .45	
	C		Leave It to Beaver	Trackdown	Dick Powell's Zane Grey Theatre	Mr. Adams & Eve	Schlitz Playhouse	The Lineup	Person to Person
	N		Saber of London	Court of Last Resort	Life of Riley	M Squad	Thin Man	Gillette Cavalcade of Sports	Red Barber's Corner
SATURDAY	A		Keep It in the Family	Country Music Jubilee		Lawrence Welk's Dancing Party		Mike Wallace Interviews	
	C		Perry Mason		Dick & the Duchess	Gale Storm Show	Have Gun, Will Travel	Gunsmoke	
	N		People Are Funny	Perry Como Show		Polly Bergen Show/Club Oasis	Gisele MacKenzie Show	What's It For	Your Hit Parade

PRIME TIME SCHEDULE: 1958

Day	Network	7 PM	7:30	8 PM	8:30	9 PM	9:30	10 PM	10:30
SUNDAY	A	You Asked for It	Maverick		The Lawman	Colt .45	Encounter		
	C	Lassie	Jack Benny Show/ Bachelor Father	Ed Sullivan Show		G.E. Theater	Alfred Hitchcock Presents	$64,000 Question	What's My Line
	N	Saber of London	Northwest Passage	Steve Allen Show		Dinah Shore Chevy Show		Loretta Young Show	
MONDAY	A		Jubilee U.S.A.		Bold Journey	Voice of Firestone	Anybody Can Play	This Is Music	
	C		Name That Tune	The Texan	Father Knows Best	Danny Thomas Show	Ann Sothern Show	Desilu Playhouse	
	N		Tic Tac Dough	Restless Gun	Tales of Wells Fargo	Peter Gunn	Alcoa/Goodyear TV Playhouse	Arthur Murray Party	
TUESDAY	A		Cheyenne/Sugarfoot		Life and Legend of Wyatt Earp	The Rifleman	Naked City	Confession	
	C		Stars in Action	Keep Talking	To Tell the Truth	Arthur Godfrey Show	Red Skelton Show	Garry Moore Show	
	N		Dragnet	George Gobel Show/Eddie Fisher Show		George Burns Show	Bob Cummings Show	The Californians	

WEDNESDAY	A		Lawrence Welk's Plymouth Show		Adventures of Ozzie & Harriet	Donna Reed Show	Patti Page Olds Show	Wednesday Night Fights	
	C		Twilight Theater	Pursuit		The Millionaire	I've Got a Secret	Armstrong Circle Theatre/U.S. Steel Hour	
	N		Wagon Train		Price Is Right	Milton Berle in the Kraft Music Hall	Bat Masterson	This Is Your Life	
THURSDAY	A		Leave It to Beaver	Zorro	Real McCoys	Pat Boone — Chevy Showroom	Rough Riders	Traffic Court	
	C		I Love Lucy	December Bride	Yancy Derringer	Dick Powell's Zane Grey Theatre	Playhouse 90		
	N		Jefferson Drum	Ed Wynn Show	Twenty-One	Behind Closed Doors	Ford Show Starring Tennessee Ernie Ford	You Bet Your Life	Masquerade Party
FRIDAY	A		Adventures of Rin Tin Tin	Walt Disney Presents		Man with a Camera	77 Sunset Strip		
	C		Your Hit Parade	Trackdown	Jackie Gleason Show	Phil Silvers Show	Lux Playhouse / Schlitz Playhouse	The Lineup	Person to Person
	N		Buckskin	Adventures of Ellery Queen		M Squad	Thin Man	Gillette Cavalcade of Sports	Fight Beat
SATURDAY	A		Dick Clark Show	Jubilee U.S.A.		Lawrence Welk's Dodge Dancing Party		Sammy Kaye's Music from Manhattan	
	C		Perry Mason		Wanted: Dead or Alive	Gale Storm Show	Have Gun, Will Travel	Gunsmoke	
	N		People Are Funny	Perry Como Show		Steve Canyon	Cimarron City		Brains & Brawn

PRIME TIME SCHEDULE: 1959

Day	Network	7 PM	7:30	8 PM	8:30	9 PM	9:30	10 PM	10:30
SUNDAY	A	Colt .45	Maverick		The Lawman	The Rebel	The Alaskans		Dick Clark's World of Talent
	C	Lassie	Dennis the Menace	Ed Sullivan Show		G.E. Theater	Alfred Hitchcock Presents	Jack Benny Show/ George Gobel Show	What's My Line
	N	Riverboat		Sunday Showcase		Dinah Shore Chevy Show		Loretta Young Show	
MONDAY	A		Cheyenne		Bourbon Street Beat		Adventures in Paradise		Man with a Camera
	C		Masquerade Party	The Texan	Father Knows Best	Danny Thomas Show	Ann Sothern Show	Hennesey	DuPont Show with June Allyson
	N		Richard Diamond, Private Detective	Love & Marriage	Tales of Wells Fargo	Peter Gunn	Alcoa/Goodyear TV Playhouse	Steve Allen Plymouth Show	
TUESDAY	A		Sugarfoot/Bronco		Life and Legend of Wyatt Earp	The Rifleman	Philip Marlowe	Alcoa Presents	Keep Talking
	C			Dennis O'Keefe Show	Many Loves of Dobie Gillis	Tightrope	Red Skelton Show	Garry Moore Show	
	N		Laramie		Fibber McGee & Molly	Arthur Murray Party	Startime		

<table>
<tr><td rowspan="3">WEDNESDAY</td><td>A</td><td></td><td>Court of Last Resort</td><td>Hobby Lobby Show</td><td>Adventures of Ozzie & Harriet</td><td colspan="2">Hawaiian Eye</td><td colspan="2">Wednesday Night Fights</td></tr>
<tr><td>C</td><td></td><td colspan="2">The Lineup</td><td>Men into Space</td><td>The Millionaire</td><td>I've Got a Secret</td><td colspan="2">Armstrong Circle Theatre/U.S. Steel Hour</td></tr>
<tr><td>N</td><td></td><td colspan="2">Wagon Train</td><td>Price Is Right</td><td colspan="2">Perry Como's Kraft Music Hall</td><td>This Is Your Life</td><td>Wichita Town</td></tr>
<tr><td rowspan="3">THURSDAY</td><td>A</td><td></td><td>Gale Storm Show</td><td>Donna Reed Show</td><td>Real McCoys</td><td>Pat Boone — Chevy Showroom</td><td colspan="2">The Untouchables</td><td>Take a Good Look</td></tr>
<tr><td>C</td><td></td><td>To Tell the Truth</td><td>Betty Hutton Show</td><td>Johnny Ringo</td><td>Dick Powell's Zane Grey Theatre</td><td colspan="3">Playhouse 90/Big Party</td></tr>
<tr><td>N</td><td></td><td>Law of the Plainsman</td><td>Bat Masterson</td><td>Staccato</td><td>Bachelor Father</td><td>Ford Show Starring Tennessee Ernie Ford</td><td>You Bet Your Life</td><td>The Lawless Years</td></tr>
<tr><td rowspan="3">FRIDAY</td><td>A</td><td></td><td colspan="2">Walt Disney Presents</td><td>Man from Blackhawk</td><td colspan="2">77 Sunset Strip</td><td>Robert Taylor: The Detectives</td><td>Black Saddle</td></tr>
<tr><td>C</td><td></td><td colspan="2">Rawhide</td><td>Hotel de Paree</td><td colspan="2">Desilu Playhouse</td><td>Twilight Zone</td><td>Person to Person</td></tr>
<tr><td>N</td><td></td><td>People Are Funny</td><td>The Troubleshooters</td><td colspan="2">Bell Telephone Hour</td><td>M Squad</td><td>Gillette Cavalcade of Sports</td><td>Phillies Jackpot Bowling</td></tr>
<tr><td rowspan="3">SATURDAY</td><td>A</td><td></td><td>Dick Clark Show</td><td>High Road</td><td>Leave It to Beaver</td><td colspan="2">Lawrence Welk Show</td><td colspan="2">Jubilee U.S.A.</td></tr>
<tr><td>C</td><td></td><td colspan="2">Perry Mason</td><td>Wanted: Dead or Alive</td><td>Mr. Lucky</td><td>Have Gun, Will Travel</td><td>Gunsmoke</td><td>Markham</td></tr>
<tr><td>N</td><td></td><td colspan="2">Bonanza</td><td>Man & the Challenge</td><td>The Deputy</td><td colspan="2">Five Fingers</td><td>It Could Be You</td></tr>
</table>

PRIME TIME SCHEDULE: 1960

		7 PM	7:30	8 PM	8:30	9 PM	9:30	10 PM	10:30
SUNDAY	A	Walt Disney Presents	Maverick		The Lawman	The Rebel	The Islanders		Walter Winchell Show
	C	Lassie	Dennis the Menace	Ed Sullivan Show		G.E. Theater	Jack Benny Show	Candid Camera	What's My Line
	N	Shirley Temple's Storybook		National Velvet	Tab Hunter Show	Dinah Shore Chevy Show		Loretta Young Show	This Is Your Life
MONDAY	A		Cheyenne		Surfside Six		Adventures in Paradise		Peter Gunn
	C		To Tell the Truth	Pete & Gladys	Bringing Up Buddy	Danny Thomas Show	Andy Griffith Show	Hennesey	Presidential Countdown
	N		Riverboat		Tales of Wells Fargo	Klondike	Dante	Barbara Stanwyck Show	Jackpot Bowling
TUESDAY	A	Expedition	Bugs Bunny Show	The Rifleman	Life and Legend of Wyatt Earp	Stagecoach West		Alcoa Presents	
	C			Father Knows Best	Many Loves of Dobie Gillis	Tom Ewell Show	Red Skelton Show	Garry Moore Show	
	N		Laramie		Alfred Hitchcock Presents	Thriller			

WEDNESDAY	A		Hong Kong		Adventures of Ozzie & Harriet	Hawaiian Eye		Naked City	
	C		Aquanauts		Wanted: Dead or Alive	My Sister Eileen	I've Got a Secret	Armstrong Circle Theatre/U.S. Steel Hour	
	N		Wagon Train		Price Is Right	Perry Como's Kraft Music Hall		Peter Loves Mary	
THURSDAY	A		Guestward Ho!	Donna Reed Show	Real McCoys	My Three Sons	The Untouchables		Take a Good Look
	C		The Witness		Dick Powell's Zane Grey Theatre	Angel	Peck's Bad Girl	Person to Person	DuPont Show with June Allyson
	N		The Outlaws		Bat Masterson	Bachelor Father	Ford Show Starring Tennessee Ernie Ford	Groucho Show	
FRIDAY	A		Matty's Funday Funnies	Harrigan & Son	The Flintstones	77 Sunset Strip		Robert Taylor: The Detectives	Law & Mr. Jones
	C		Rawhide		Route 66		Mr. Garlund	Twilight Zone	Eyewitness to History
	N		Dan Raven		The Westerner	Bell Telephone Hour		Michael Shayne	
SATURDAY	A		Roaring Twenties		Leave It to Beaver	Lawrence Welk Show		Fight of the Week	Make That Spare
	C		Perry Mason		Checkmate		Have Gun, Will Travel	Gunsmoke	
	N		Bonanza		Tall Man	The Deputy	Nation's Future		

PRIME TIME SCHEDULE: 1961

Day	Network	7 PM	7:30	8 PM	8:30	9 PM	9:30	10 PM	10:30
SUNDAY	A	Maverick	Follow the Sun		The Lawman	Bus Stop		Adventures in Paradise	
	C	Lassie	Dennis the Menace	Ed Sullivan Show		G.E. Theater	Jack Benny Show	Candid Camera	What's My Line
	N	Bullwinkle Show	Walt Disney's Wonderful World of Color		Car 54, Where Are You?	Bonanza		DuPont Show of the Week	
MONDAY	A	Expedition	Cheyenne		The Rifleman	Surfside Six		Ben Casey	
	C		To Tell the Truth	Pete & Gladys	Window on Main Street	Danny Thomas Show	Andy Griffith Show	Hennesey	I've Got a Secret
	N			National Velvet	Price Is Right	87th Precinct		Thriller	
TUESDAY	A		Bugs Bunny Show	Bachelor Father	Calvin & the Colonel	New Breed		Alcoa Premiere	
	C		Marshal Dillon	Dick Van Dyke Show	Many Loves of Dobie Gillis	Red Skelton Show	Ichabod & Me	Garry Moore Show	
	N		Laramie		Alfred Hitchcock Presents	Dick Powell Show		Cain's Hundred	

Day	Network								
WEDNESDAY	A		Steve Allen Show		Top Cat	Hawaiian Eye		Naked City	
	C		Alvin Show	Father Knows Best	Checkmate		Mrs. G. Goes to College	U.S. Steel Hour/Armstrong Circle Theatre	
	N		Wagon Train		Joey Bishop Show	Perry Como's Kraft Music Hall		Bob Newhart Show	David Brinkley's Journal
THURSDAY	A		Adventures of Ozzie & Harriet	Donna Reed Show	Real McCoys	My Three Sons	Margie	The Untouchables	
	C		Frontier Circus		Bob Cummings Show	The Investigators		CBS Reports	
	N		The Outlaws		Dr. Kildare		Hazel	Sing Along with Mitch	
FRIDAY	A		Straightaway	The Hathaways	The Flintstones	77 Sunset Strip		Target: The Corruptors	
	C		Rawhide		Route 66		Father of the Bride	Twilight Zone	Eyewitness
	N		International Showtime		Robert Taylor's Detectives		Bell Telephone Hour/Dinah Shore Show		Here & Now
SATURDAY	A	Matty's Funday Funnies	Roaring Twenties		Leave It to Beaver	Lawrence Welk Show		Fight of the Week	Make That Spare
	C		Perry Mason		The Defenders		Have Gun, Will Travel	Gunsmoke	
	N		Tales of Wells Fargo		Tall Man	NBC Saturday Night Movie			

PRIME TIME SCHEDULE: 1962

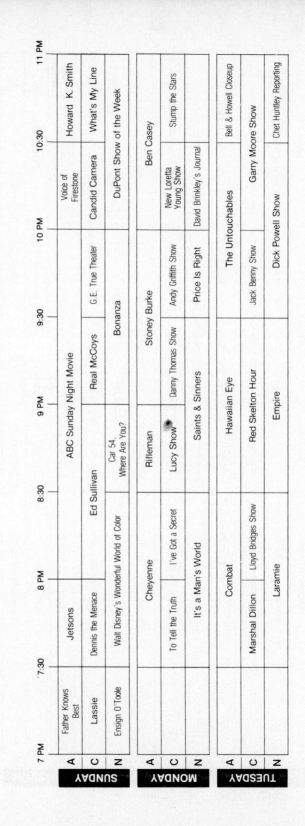

<table>
<tr><th></th><th></th><th>7 PM</th><th>7:30</th><th>8 PM</th><th>8:30</th><th>9 PM</th><th>9:30</th><th>10 PM</th><th>10:30</th><th>11 PM</th></tr>
<tr><td rowspan="3">SUNDAY</td><td>A</td><td>Father Knows Best</td><td>Jetsons</td><td colspan="4">ABC Sunday Night Movie</td><td>Voice of Firestone</td><td>Howard K. Smith</td><td></td></tr>
<tr><td>C</td><td>Lassie</td><td>Dennis the Menace</td><td colspan="2">Ed Sullivan</td><td>Real McCoys</td><td>G.E. True Theater</td><td>Candid Camera</td><td>What's My Line</td><td></td></tr>
<tr><td>N</td><td>Ensign O'Toole</td><td colspan="2">Walt Disney's Wonderful World of Color</td><td>Car 54, Where Are You?</td><td colspan="2">Bonanza</td><td colspan="2">DuPont Show of the Week</td><td></td></tr>
<tr><td rowspan="3">MONDAY</td><td>A</td><td></td><td colspan="2">Cheyenne</td><td>Rifleman</td><td colspan="2">Stoney Burke</td><td colspan="2">Ben Casey</td><td></td></tr>
<tr><td>C</td><td></td><td>To Tell the Truth</td><td>I've Got a Secret</td><td>Lucy Show</td><td>Danny Thomas Show</td><td>Andy Griffith Show</td><td>New Loretta Young Show</td><td>Stump the Stars</td><td></td></tr>
<tr><td>N</td><td></td><td colspan="2">It's a Man's World</td><td colspan="2">Saints & Sinners</td><td>Price Is Right</td><td>David Brinkley's Journal</td><td></td><td></td></tr>
<tr><td rowspan="3">TUESDAY</td><td>A</td><td></td><td colspan="2">Combat</td><td colspan="2">Hawaiian Eye</td><td colspan="2">The Untouchables</td><td>Bell & Howell Closeup</td><td></td></tr>
<tr><td>C</td><td></td><td>Marshal Dillon</td><td>Lloyd Bridges Show</td><td colspan="2">Red Skelton Hour</td><td>Jack Benny Show</td><td colspan="2">Garry Moore Show</td><td></td></tr>
<tr><td>N</td><td></td><td colspan="2">Laramie</td><td colspan="2">Empire</td><td colspan="2">Dick Powell Show</td><td>Chet Huntley Reporting</td><td></td></tr>
</table>

Day	Network								
WEDNESDAY	A		Wagon Train		Going My Way		Our Man Higgins	Naked City	
	C		CBS Reports		Many Loves of Dobie Gillis	Beverly Hillbillies	Dick Van Dyke Show	Armstrong Circle Theatre/U.S. Steel Hour	
	N		The Virginian			Perry Como's Kraft Music Hall		Eleventh Hour	
THURSDAY	A		Adventures of Ozzie & Harriet	Donna Reed Show	Leave It to Beaver	My Three Sons	McHale's Navy	Alcoa Premiere	
	C		Mr. Ed	Perry Mason		The Nurses		Alfred Hitchcock Hour	
	N		Wide Country		Dr. Kildare		Hazel	Andy Williams Show	
FRIDAY	A		Gallant Men		Flintstones	I'm Dickens — He's Fenster	77 Sunset Strip		
	C		Rawhide		Route 66		Fair Exchange		Eyewitness
	N		International Showtime		Sing Along with Mitch		Don't Call Me Charlie	Jack Paar Show	
SATURDAY	A	Beany & Cecil	Roy Rogers & Dale Evans Show		Mr. Smith Goes to Washington	Lawrence Welk Show		Fight of the Week	Make That Spare
	C		Jackie Gleason Show		Defenders		Have Gun, Will Travel	Gunsmoke	
	N		Sam Benedict		Joey Bishop Show	NBC Saturday Night Movie			

PRIME TIME SCHEDULE: 1963

Day	Net	7 PM	7:30	8 PM	8:30	9 PM	9:30	10 PM	10:30
SUNDAY	A		Travels of Jaimie McPheeters		Arrest and Trial			100 Grand	ABC News Reports
	C	Lassie	My Favorite Martian	Ed Sullivan Show		Judy Garland Show		Candid Camera	What's My Line
	N	Bill Dana Show	Walt Disney's Wonderful World of Color		Grindl	Bonanza		DuPont Show of the Week	
MONDAY	A		Outer Limits		Wagon Train			Breaking Point	
	C		To Tell the Truth	I've Got a Secret	Lucy Show	Danny Thomas Show	Andy Griffith Show	East Side / West Side	
	N		NBC Monday Night Movie				Hollywood & the Stars	Sing Along with Mitch	
TUESDAY	A		Combat		McHale's Navy	Greatest Show on Earth		The Fugitive	
	C		Marshal Dillon	Red Skelton Hour		Petticoat Junction	Jack Benny Show	Garry Moore Show	
	N		Mr. Novak		Redigo	Richard Boone Show		Bell Telephone Hour	

WEDNESDAY	A		Adventures of Ozzie & Harriet	Patty Duke Show	Price Is Right	Ben Casey		Channing	
	C		Chronicle / CBS Reports		Glynis Johns Show	Beverly Hillbillies	Dick Van Dyke Show	Danny Kaye Show	
	N		The Virginian			Espionage		Eleventh Hour	
THURSDAY	A		The Flintstones	Donna Reed Show	My Three Sons	Jimmy Dean Show		Edie Adams Show/ Sid Caesar Show	
	C		Password	Rawhide		Perry Mason		The Nurses	
	N		Temple Houston		Dr. Kildare		Hazel	Kraft Suspense Theater	
FRIDAY	A		77 Sunset Strip		Burke's Law		Farmer's Daughter	Fight of the Week	Make That Spare
	C		Great Adventure		Route 66		Twilight Zone	Alfred Hitchcock Hour	
	N		International Showtime		Bob Hope Presents the Chrysler Theatre		Harry's Girls	Jack Paar Show	
SATURDAY	A		Hootenanny		Lawrence Welk Show		Jerry Lewis Show		
	C		Jackie Gleason Show		Phil Silvers Show	The Defenders		Gunsmoke	
	N		The Lieutenant		Joey Bishop Show	NBC Saturday Night Movie			

PRIME TIME SCHEDULE: 1964

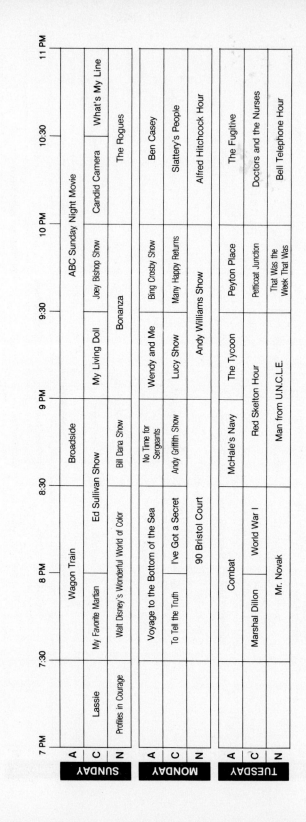

Day	Network	7 PM	7:30	8 PM	8:30	9 PM	9:30	10 PM	10:30
SUNDAY	A		Wagon Train		Broadside	ABC Sunday Night Movie			
	C	Lassie	My Favorite Martian	Ed Sullivan Show		My Living Doll	Joey Bishop Show	Candid Camera	What's My Line
	N	Profiles in Courage	Walt Disney's Wonderful World of Color		Bill Dana Show	Bonanza		The Rogues	
MONDAY	A		Voyage to the Bottom of the Sea		No Time for Sergeants	Wendy and Me	Bing Crosby Show	Ben Casey	
	C		To Tell the Truth	I've Got a Secret	Andy Griffith Show	Lucy Show	Many Happy Returns	Slattery's People	
	N		90 Bristol Court			Andy Williams Show		Alfred Hitchcock Hour	
TUESDAY	A		Combat		McHale's Navy	The Tycoon	Peyton Place	The Fugitive	
	C		Marshal Dillon	World War I	Red Skelton Hour		Petticoat Junction	Doctors and the Nurses	
	N		Mr. Novak		Man from U.N.C.L.E.		That Was the Week That Was	Bell Telephone Hour	

Day	Network								
WEDNESDAY	A		Adventures of Ozzie & Harriet	Patty Duke Show	Shindig	Mickey	Burke's Law		ABC Scope
	C		CBS Reports		Beverly Hillbillies	Dick Van Dyke Show	Cara Williams Show	Danny Kaye Show	
	N		The Virginian			NBC Wednesday Night Movie			
THURSDAY	A		The Flintstones	Donna Reed Show	My Three Sons	Bewitched	Peyton Place	Jimmy Dean Show	
	C		The Munsters	Perry Mason		Password	Baileys of Balboa	The Defenders	
	N		Daniel Boone		Dr. Kildare		Hazel	Kraft Suspense Theater	
FRIDAY	A		Jonny Quest	Farmer's Daughter	Addams Family	Valentine's Day	Twelve O'Clock High		
	C		Rawhide		The Entertainers		Gomer Pyle, U.S.M.C	The Reporter	
	N		International Showtime		Bob Hope Presents the Chrysler Theatre		Jack Benny Program	Jack Paar Show	
SATURDAY	A		Outer Limits		Lawrence Welk Show		Hollywood Palace		
	C		Jackie Gleason Show		Gilligan's Island	Mr. Broadway		Gunsmoke	
	N		Flipper	Famous Adventures of Mr. Magoo	Kentucky Jones	NBC Saturday Night Movie			

PRIME TIME SCHEDULE: 1965

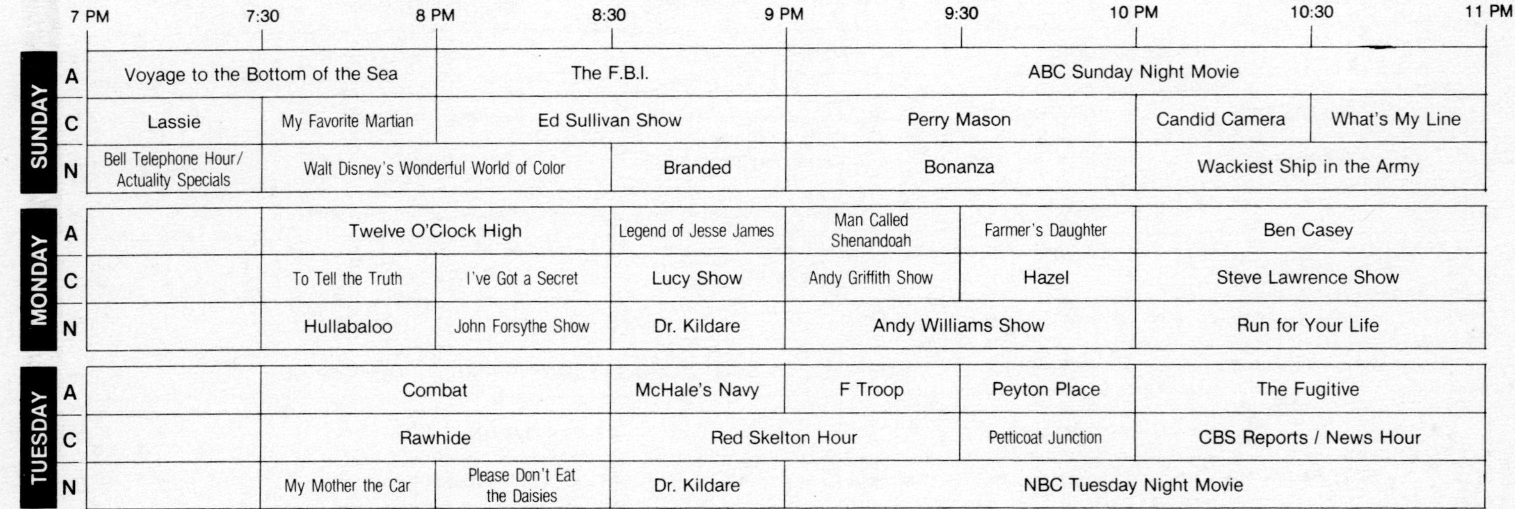

<table>
<tr><th></th><th></th><th>7 PM</th><th>7:30</th><th>8 PM</th><th>8:30</th><th>9 PM</th><th>9:30</th><th>10 PM</th><th>10:30</th></tr>
<tr><td rowspan="3">SUNDAY</td><td>A</td><td colspan="2">Voyage to the Bottom of the Sea</td><td colspan="2">The F.B.I.</td><td colspan="4">ABC Sunday Night Movie</td></tr>
<tr><td>C</td><td>Lassie</td><td>My Favorite Martian</td><td colspan="2">Ed Sullivan Show</td><td colspan="2">Perry Mason</td><td>Candid Camera</td><td>What's My Line</td></tr>
<tr><td>N</td><td>Bell Telephone Hour/ Actuality Specials</td><td colspan="2">Walt Disney's Wonderful World of Color</td><td>Branded</td><td colspan="2">Bonanza</td><td colspan="2">Wackiest Ship in the Army</td></tr>
<tr><td rowspan="3">MONDAY</td><td>A</td><td></td><td colspan="2">Twelve O'Clock High</td><td>Legend of Jesse James</td><td>Man Called Shenandoah</td><td>Farmer's Daughter</td><td colspan="2">Ben Casey</td></tr>
<tr><td>C</td><td></td><td>To Tell the Truth</td><td>I've Got a Secret</td><td>Lucy Show</td><td>Andy Griffith Show</td><td>Hazel</td><td colspan="2">Steve Lawrence Show</td></tr>
<tr><td>N</td><td></td><td>Hullabaloo</td><td>John Forsythe Show</td><td>Dr. Kildare</td><td colspan="2">Andy Williams Show</td><td colspan="2">Run for Your Life</td></tr>
<tr><td rowspan="3">TUESDAY</td><td>A</td><td></td><td colspan="2">Combat</td><td>McHale's Navy</td><td>F Troop</td><td>Peyton Place</td><td colspan="2">The Fugitive</td></tr>
<tr><td>C</td><td></td><td colspan="2">Rawhide</td><td colspan="2">Red Skelton Hour</td><td>Petticoat Junction</td><td colspan="2">CBS Reports / News Hour</td></tr>
<tr><td>N</td><td></td><td>My Mother the Car</td><td>Please Don't Eat the Daisies</td><td>Dr. Kildare</td><td colspan="4">NBC Tuesday Night Movie</td></tr>
</table>

WEDNESDAY	A		Adventures of Ozzie & Harriet	Patty Duke Show	Gidget	Big Valley		Amos Burke — Secret Agent
	C		Lost in Space		Beverly Hillbillies	Green Acres	Dick Van Dyke Show	Danny Kaye Show
	N		The Virginian			Bob Hope Presents the Chrysler Theatre		I Spy
THURSDAY	A		Shindig	Donna Reed Show	O.K. Crackerby	Bewitched	Peyton Place	Long, Hot Summer
	C		The Munsters	Gilligan's Island	My Three Sons	CBS Thursday Night Movie		
	N		Daniel Boone		Laredo		Mona McCluskey	Dean Martin Show
FRIDAY	A		The Flintstones	Tammy	Addams Family	Honey West	Peyton Place	Jimmy Dean Show
	C		Wild Wild West		Hogan's Heroes	Gomer Pyle, U.S.M.C.	Smothers Brothers Show	Slattery's People
	N		Camp Runamuck	Hank	Convoy		Mr. Roberts	Man from U.N.C.L.E.
SATURDAY	A		Shindig	King Family Show	Lawrence Welk Show		Hollywood Palace	ABC Scope
	C		Jackie Gleason Show		Trials of O'Brien		The Loner	Gunsmoke
	N		Flipper	I Dream of Jeannie	Get Smart	NBC Saturday Night Movie		

PRIME TIME SCHEDULE: 1966

Day	Network	7 PM	7:30	8 PM	8:30	9 PM	9:30	10 PM	10:30
SUNDAY	A	Voyage to the Bottom of the Sea		The F.B.I.		ABC Sunday Night Movie			
	C	Lassie	It's About Time	Ed Sullivan Show		Garry Moore Show		Candid Camera	What's My Line
	N	Actuality Specials/ Bell Telephone Hour	Walt Disney's Wonderful World of Color		Hey Landlord	Bonanza		Andy Williams Show	
MONDAY	A		Iron Horse		Rat Patrol	Felony Squad	Peyton Place	Big Valley	
	C		Gilligan's Island	Run Buddy Run	Lucy Show	Andy Griffith Show	Family Affair	Jean Arthur Show	I've Got a Secret
	N		The Monkees	I Dream of Jeannie	Roger Miller Show	Road West		Run for Your Life	
TUESDAY	A		Combat		The Rounders	Pruitts of Southampton	Love on a Rooftop	The Fugitive	
	C		Daktari		Red Skelton Hour		Petticoat Junction	CBS News Hour	
	N		Girl from U.N.C.L.E.		Occasional Wife	NBC Tuesday Night Movie			

Day	Network								
WEDNESDAY	A		Batman	The Monroes		Man Who Never Was	Peyton Place	ABC Stage '67	
	C		Lost in Space		Beverly Hillbillies	Green Acres	Gomer Pyle, U.S.M.C.	Danny Kaye Show	
	N		The Virginian			Bob Hope Presents the Chrysler Theatre		I Spy	
THURSDAY	A		Batman	F Troop	Tammy Grimes Show	Bewitched	That Girl	Hawk	
	C		Jericho		My Three Sons	CBS Thursday Night Movie			
	N		Daniel Boone		Star Trek		The Hero	Dean Martin Show	
FRIDAY	A		Green Hornet	Time Tunnel		Milton Berle Show		Twelve O'Clock High	
	C		Wild Wild West		Hogan's Heroes	CBS Friday Night Movie			
	N		Tarzan		Man from U.N.C.L.E.		T.H.E. Cat	Laredo	
SATURDAY	A		Shane		Lawrence Welk Show		Hollywood Palace		ABC Scope
	C		Jackie Gleason Show		Pistols 'n' Petticoats	Mission: Impossible		Gunsmoke	
	N		Flipper	Please Don't Eat the Daisies	Get Smart	NBC Saturday Night Movie			

PRIME TIME SCHEDULE: 1967

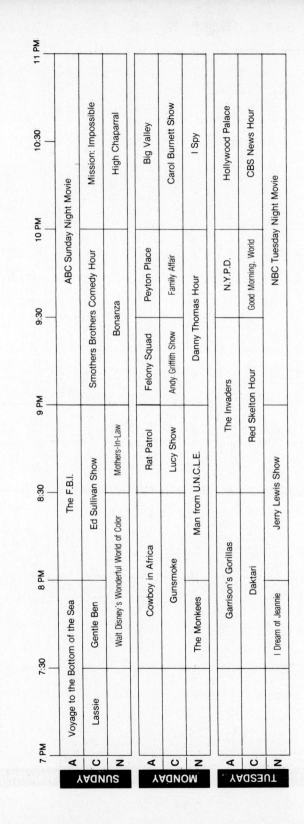

Day	Network	7 PM	7:30	8 PM	8:30	9 PM	9:30	10 PM	10:30
SUNDAY	A	Voyage to the Bottom of the Sea		The F.B.I.		ABC Sunday Night Movie			
	C	Lassie	Gentle Ben	Ed Sullivan Show		Smothers Brothers Comedy Hour		Mission: Impossible	
	N		Walt Disney's Wonderful World of Color		Mothers-In-Law	Bonanza		High Chaparral	
MONDAY	A		Cowboy in Africa		Rat Patrol	Felony Squad	Peyton Place	Big Valley	
	C		Gunsmoke		Lucy Show	Andy Griffith Show	Family Affair	Carol Burnett Show	
	N		The Monkees	Man from U.N.C.L.E.		Danny Thomas Hour		I Spy	
TUESDAY	A		Garrison's Gorillas		The Invaders		N.Y.P.D.	Hollywood Palace	
	C		Daktari		Red Skelton Hour		Good Morning, World	CBS News Hour	
	N		I Dream of Jeannie	Jerry Lewis Show		NBC Tuesday Night Movie			

WEDNESDAY	A		Legend of Custer		Second 100 Years	ABC Wednesday Night Movie			
	C		Lost in Space		Beverly Hillbillies	Green Acres	He & She	Dundee and the Culhane	
	N		The Virginian			Kraft Music Hall		Run for Your Life	
THURSDAY	A		Batman	Flying Nun	Bewitched	That Girl	Peyton Place	Good Company	
	C		Cimarron Strip			CBS Thursday Night Movie			
	N		Daniel Boone		Ironside		Dragnet	Dean Martin Show	
FRIDAY	A		Off To See the Wizard		Hondo		Guns of Will Sonnett	Judd, for the Defense	
	C		Wild Wild West		Gomer Pyle, U.S.M.C.	CBS Friday Night Movie			
	N		Tarzan		Star Trek		Accidental Family	Actuality Specials/Bell Telephone Hour	
SATURDAY	A		Dating Game	Newlywed Game	Lawrence Welk Show		Iron Horse		ABC Scope
	C		Jackie Gleason Show		My Three Sons	Hogan's Heroes	Petticoat Junction	Mannix	
	N		Maya		Get Smart	NBC Saturday Night Movie			

PRIME TIME SCHEDULE: 1968

Day	Network	7 PM	7:30	8 PM	8:30	9 PM	9:30	10 PM	10:30
SUNDAY	A	Land of the Giants		The F.B.I.		ABC Sunday Night Movie			
	C	Lassie	Gentle Ben	Ed Sullivan Show		Smothers Brothers Comedy Hour		Mission: Impossible	
	N	New Adventures of Huck Finn	Walt Disney's Wonderful World of Color		Mothers-In-Law	Bonanza		Beautiful Phyllis Diller Show	
MONDAY	A		The Avengers		Peyton Place	The Outcasts		Big Valley	
	C		Gunsmoke		Here's Lucy	Mayberry R.F.D.	Family Affair	Carol Burnett Show	
	N		I Dream of Jeannie	Rowan & Martin's Laugh-In		NBC Monday Night Movie			
TUESDAY	A		Mod Squad		It Takes a Thief		N.Y.P.D.	That's Life	
	C		Lancer		Red Skelton Hour		Doris Day Show	CBS News Hour / 60 Minutes	
	N		Jerry Lewis Show		Julia	NBC Tuesday Night Movie			

WEDNESDAY	A		Here Come the Brides		Peyton Place	ABC Wednesday Night Movie			
	C		Daktari		Good Guys	Beverly Hillbillies	Green Acres	Jonathan Winters Show	
	N		The Virginian			Kraft Music Hall		The Outsider	
THURSDAY	A		Ugliest Girl in Town	Flying Nun	Bewitched	That Girl	Journey to the Unknown		
	C		Blondie	Hawaii Five-0		CBS Thursday Night Movie			
	N		Daniel Boone		Ironside		Dragnet	Dean Martin Show	
FRIDAY	A		Operation: Entertainment		Felony Squad	Don Rickles Show	Guns of Will Sonnett	Judd, for the Defense	
	C		Wild Wild West		Gomer Pyle, U.S.M.C.	CBS Friday Night Movie			
	N		High Chaparral		Name of the Game			Star Trek	
SATURDAY	A		Dating Game	Newlywed Game	Lawrence Welk Show		Hollywood Palace		
	C		Jackie Gleason Show		My Three Sons	Hogan's Heroes	Petticoat Junction	Mannix	
	N		Adam 12	Get Smart	Ghost & Mrs. Muir	NBC Saturday Night Movie			

PRIME TIME SCHEDULE: 1969

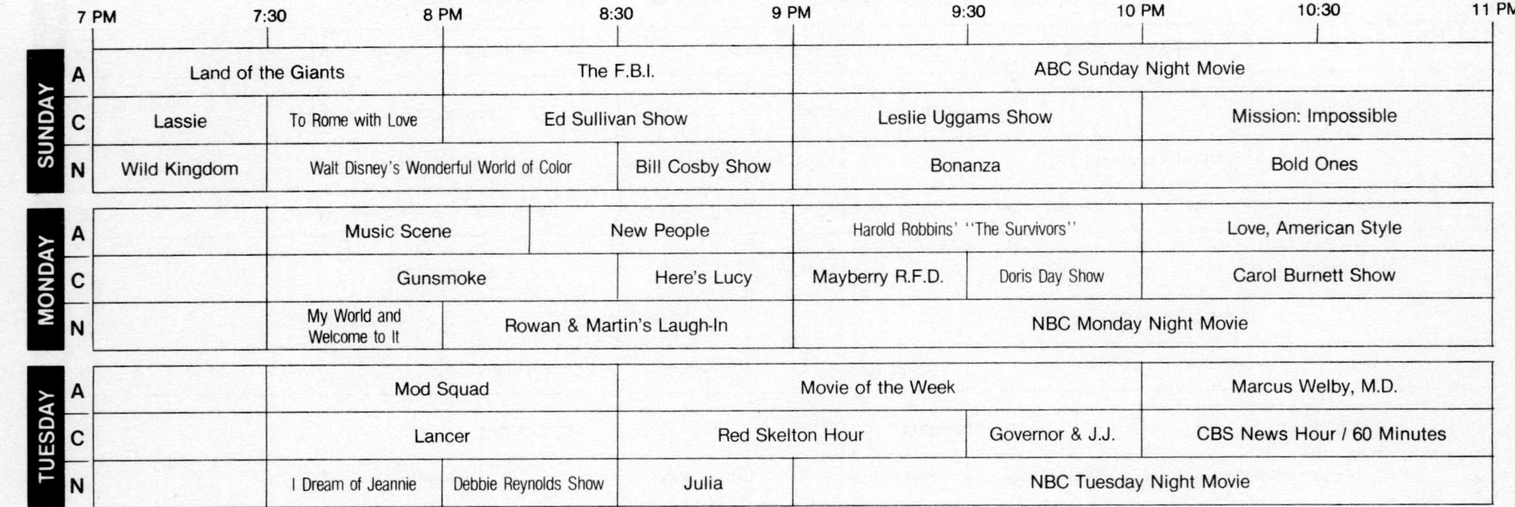

		7 PM	7:30	8 PM	8:30	9 PM	9:30	10 PM	10:30
SUNDAY	A	Land of the Giants		The F.B.I.		ABC Sunday Night Movie			
	C	Lassie	To Rome with Love	Ed Sullivan Show		Leslie Uggams Show		Mission: Impossible	
	N	Wild Kingdom	Walt Disney's Wonderful World of Color		Bill Cosby Show	Bonanza		Bold Ones	
MONDAY	A		Music Scene		New People	Harold Robbins' "The Survivors"		Love, American Style	
	C		Gunsmoke		Here's Lucy	Mayberry R.F.D.	Doris Day Show	Carol Burnett Show	
	N		My World and Welcome to It	Rowan & Martin's Laugh-In		NBC Monday Night Movie			
TUESDAY	A		Mod Squad		Movie of the Week			Marcus Welby, M.D.	
	C		Lancer		Red Skelton Hour		Governor & J.J.	CBS News Hour / 60 Minutes	
	N		I Dream of Jeannie	Debbie Reynolds Show	Julia	NBC Tuesday Night Movie			

Day	Network								
WEDNESDAY	A		Flying Nun	Courtship of Eddie's Father	Room 222	ABC Wednesday Night Movie			
	C		Glen Campbell Goodtime Hour		Beverly Hillbillies	Medical Center		Hawaii Five-0	
	N		The Virginian			Kraft Music Hall		Then Came Bronson	
THURSDAY	A		Ghost & Mrs. Muir	That Girl	Bewitched	This Is Tom Jones		It Takes a Thief	
	C		Family Affair	Jim Nabors Hour		CBS Thursday Night Movie			
	N		Daniel Boone		Ironside		Dragnet	Dean Martin Show	
FRIDAY	A		Let's Make a Deal	Brady Bunch	Mr. Deeds Goes to Town	Here Come the Brides		Jimmy Durante Presents Lennon Sisters	
	C		Get Smart	Good Guys	Hogan's Heroes	CBS Friday Night Movie			
	N		High Chaparral		Name of the Game			Bracken's World	
SATURDAY	A		Dating Game	Newlywed Game	Lawrence Welk Show		Hollywood Palace		
	C		Jackie Gleason Show		My Three Sons	Green Acres	Petticoat Junction	Mannix	
	N		Andy Williams Show		Adam 12	NBC Saturday Night Movie			

PRIME TIME SCHEDULE: 1970

<table>
<tr><th></th><th></th><th>7 PM</th><th>7:30</th><th>8 PM</th><th>8:30</th><th>9 PM</th><th>9:30</th><th>10 PM</th><th>10:30</th></tr>
<tr><td rowspan="3">SUNDAY</td><td>A</td><td colspan="2">Young Rebels</td><td colspan="2">The F.B.I.</td><td colspan="4">ABC Sunday Night Movie</td></tr>
<tr><td>C</td><td>Lassie</td><td>Hogan's Heroes</td><td colspan="2">Ed Sullivan Show</td><td colspan="2">Glen Campbell Goodtime Hour</td><td colspan="2">Tim Conway Comedy Hour</td></tr>
<tr><td>N</td><td>Wild Kingdom</td><td colspan="2">Wonderful World of Disney</td><td>Bill Cosby Show</td><td colspan="2">Bonanza</td><td colspan="2">Bold Ones</td></tr>
<tr><td rowspan="3">MONDAY</td><td>A</td><td></td><td colspan="2">Young Lawyers</td><td>Silent Force</td><td colspan="4">ABC Monday Night Football</td></tr>
<tr><td>C</td><td></td><td colspan="2">Gunsmoke</td><td>Here's Lucy</td><td>Mayberry R.F.D.</td><td>Doris Day Show</td><td colspan="2">Carol Burnett Show</td></tr>
<tr><td>N</td><td></td><td>Red Skelton Show</td><td colspan="2">Rowan & Martin's Laugh-In</td><td colspan="4">NBC Monday Night Movie</td></tr>
<tr><td rowspan="3">TUESDAY</td><td>A</td><td></td><td colspan="2">Mod Squad</td><td colspan="3">Movie of the Week</td><td colspan="2">Marcus Welby, M.D.</td></tr>
<tr><td>C</td><td></td><td>Beverly Hillbillies</td><td>Green Acres</td><td colspan="2">Hee Haw</td><td>To Rome with Love</td><td colspan="2">CBS News Hour / 60 Minutes</td></tr>
<tr><td>N</td><td></td><td colspan="2">Don Knotts Show</td><td>Julia</td><td colspan="4">NBC Tuesday Night Movie</td></tr>
</table>

Day	Network								
WEDNESDAY	A		Courtship of Eddie's Father	Make Room for Granddaddy	Room 222	Johnny Cash Show		Dan August	
	C		Storefront Lawyers		Governor & J.J.	Medical Center		Hawaii Five-0	
	N		Men from Shiloh			Kraft Music Hall		Four in One	
THURSDAY	A		Matt Lincoln		Bewitched	Barefoot in the Park	Odd Couple	The Immortal	
	C		Family Affair	Jim Nabors Hcur		CBS Thursday Night Movie			
	N		Flip Wilson Show		Ironside		Nancy	Dean Martin Show	
FRIDAY	A		Brady Bunch	Nanny and the Professor	Partridge Family	That Girl	Love, American Style	This Is Tom Jones	
	C		The Interns		The Headmaster	CBS Friday Night Movie			
	N		High Chaparral		Name of the Game			Bracken's World	
SATURDAY	A		Let's Make a Deal	Newlywed Game	Lawrence Welk Show		Most Deadly Game		
	C		Mission: Impossible		My Three Sons	Arnie	Mary Tyler Moore Show	Mannix	
	N		Andy Williams Show		Adam 12	NBC Saturday Night Movie			

PRIME TIME SCHEDULE: 1971

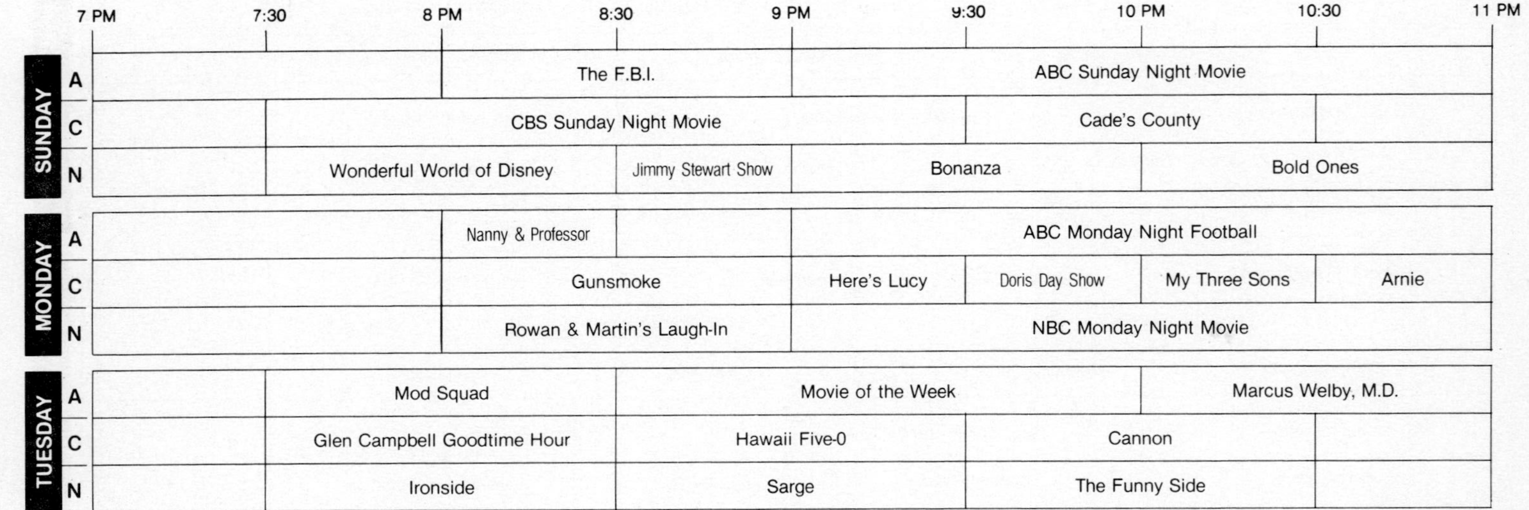

Day	Network	7 PM	7:30	8 PM	8:30	9 PM	9:30	10 PM	10:30
SUNDAY	A			The F.B.I.		ABC Sunday Night Movie			
	C		CBS Sunday Night Movie				Cade's County		
	N		Wonderful World of Disney		Jimmy Stewart Show	Bonanza		Bold Ones	
MONDAY	A			Nanny & Professor		ABC Monday Night Football			
	C			Gunsmoke		Here's Lucy	Doris Day Show	My Three Sons	Arnie
	N			Rowan & Martin's Laugh-In		NBC Monday Night Movie			
TUESDAY	A		Mod Squad		Movie of the Week			Marcus Welby, M.D.	
	C		Glen Campbell Goodtime Hour		Hawaii Five-0		Cannon		
	N		Ironside		Sarge		The Funny Side		

WEDNESDAY	A		Bewitched	Courtship of Eddie's Father	Smith Family	Shirley's World	Man and the City	
	C		Carol Burnett Show		Medical Center		Mannix	
	N		Adam 12	NBC Mystery Movie			Night Gallery	
THURSDAY	A		Alias Smith & Jones		Longstreet		Owen Marshall	
	C		Bearcats		CBS Thursday Night Movie			
	N		Flip Wilson Show		Nichols		Dean Martin Show	
FRIDAY	A		Brady Bunch	Partridge Family	Room 222	Odd Couple	Love, American Style	
	C		Chicago Teddy Bears	O'Hara, U.S. Treasury		New CBS Friday Night Movies		
	N		The D.A.	NBC World Premiere Movie				
SATURDAY	A		Getting Together	ABC Movie of the Weekend			The Persuaders	
	C		All in the Family	Funny Face	New Dick Van Dyke Show	Mary Tyler Moore Show	Mission: Impossible	
	N		The Partners	The Good Life	NBC Saturday Night Movie			

PRIME TIME SCHEDULE: 1972

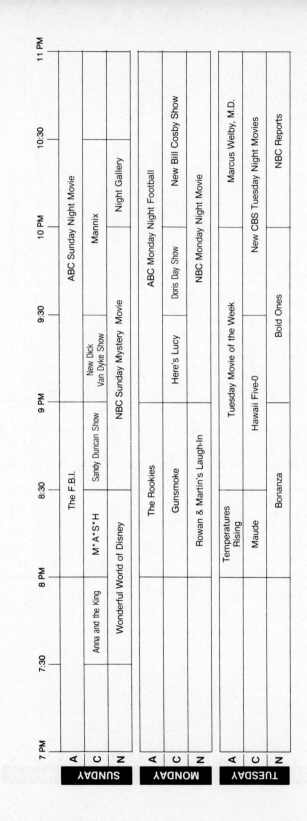

Day	Network	7 PM	7:30	8 PM	8:30	9 PM	9:30	10 PM	10:30
SUNDAY	A			The F.B.I.		ABC Sunday Night Movie			
	C		Anna and the King	M*A*S*H	Sandy Duncan Show	New Dick Van Dyke Show	Mannix		
	N		Wonderful World of Disney		NBC Sunday Mystery Movie			Night Gallery	
MONDAY	A			The Rookies		ABC Monday Night Football			
	C			Gunsmoke		Here's Lucy	Doris Day Show	New Bill Cosby Show	
	N			Rowan & Martin's Laugh-In		NBC Monday Night Movie			
TUESDAY	A			Temperatures Rising	Tuesday Movie of the Week			Marcus Welby, M.D.	
	C			Maude	Hawaii Five-0		New CBS Tuesday Night Movies		
	N			Bonanza		Bold Ones		NBC Reports	

<table>
<tr><td rowspan="3">WEDNESDAY</td><td>A</td><td></td><td>Paul Lynde Show</td><td colspan="3">Wednesday Movie of the Week</td><td>Julie Andrews Hour</td></tr>
<tr><td>C</td><td></td><td colspan="2">Carol Burnett Show</td><td colspan="2">Medical Center</td><td>Cannon</td></tr>
<tr><td>N</td><td></td><td>Adam 12</td><td colspan="3">NBC Wednesday Mystery Movie</td><td>Search</td></tr>
<tr><td rowspan="3">THURSDAY</td><td>A</td><td></td><td colspan="2">Mod Squad</td><td colspan="2">The Men</td><td>Owen Marshall</td></tr>
<tr><td>C</td><td></td><td colspan="2">The Waltons</td><td colspan="3">CBS Thursday Night Movie</td></tr>
<tr><td>N</td><td></td><td colspan="2">Flip Wilson Show</td><td colspan="2">Ironside</td><td>Dean Martin Show</td></tr>
<tr><td rowspan="3">FRIDAY</td><td>A</td><td></td><td>Brady Bunch</td><td>Partridge Family</td><td>Room 222</td><td>Odd Couple</td><td>Love, American Style</td></tr>
<tr><td>C</td><td></td><td colspan="2">Sonny & Cher Comedy Hour</td><td colspan="3">CBS Friday Night Movie</td></tr>
<tr><td>N</td><td></td><td>Sanford & Son</td><td>Little People</td><td colspan="2">Ghost Story</td><td>Banyon</td></tr>
<tr><td rowspan="3">SATURDAY</td><td>A</td><td></td><td colspan="2">Alias Smith & Jones</td><td colspan="2">Streets of San Francisco</td><td>The Sixth Sense</td></tr>
<tr><td>C</td><td></td><td>All in the Family</td><td>Bridget Loves Bernie</td><td>Mary Tyler Moore Show</td><td>Bob Newhart Show</td><td>Mission: Impossible</td></tr>
<tr><td>N</td><td></td><td colspan="2">Emergency</td><td colspan="3">NBC Saturday Night Movie</td></tr>
</table>

PRIME TIME SCHEDULE: 1973

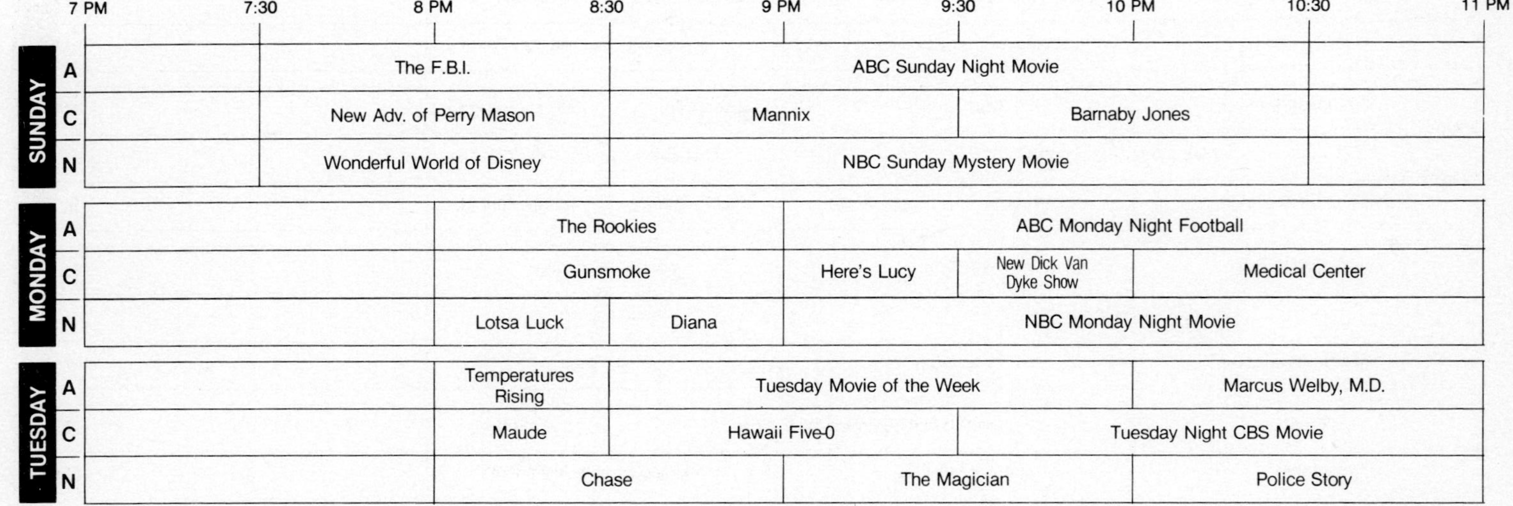

Day	Network	7 PM	7:30	8 PM	8:30	9 PM	9:30	10 PM	10:30
SUNDAY	A		The F.B.I.		ABC Sunday Night Movie				
	C		New Adv. of Perry Mason		Mannix		Barnaby Jones		
	N		Wonderful World of Disney		NBC Sunday Mystery Movie				
MONDAY	A			The Rookies		ABC Monday Night Football			
	C			Gunsmoke		Here's Lucy	New Dick Van Dyke Show	Medical Center	
	N			Lotsa Luck	Diana	NBC Monday Night Movie			
TUESDAY	A			Temperatures Rising	Tuesday Movie of the Week			Marcus Welby, M.D.	
	C			Maude	Hawaii Five-0		Tuesday Night CBS Movie		
	N			Chase		The Magician		Police Story	

Day	Network						
WEDNESDAY	A		Bob & Carol & Ted & Alice	Wednesday Movie of the Week			Owen Marshall
	C		Sonny & Cher Comedy Hour		Cannon		Kojak
	N		Adam 12	NBC Wednesday Mystery Movie			Love Story
THURSDAY	A		Toma		Kung Fu		Streets of San Francisco
	C		The Waltons		CBS Thursday Night Movie		
	N		Flip Wilson Show		Ironside		NBC Follies
FRIDAY	A		Brady Bunch	Odd Couple	Room 222	Adam's Rib	Love, American Style
	C		Calucci's Dept.	Roll Out	CBS Friday Night Movie		
	N		Sanford & Son	The Girl with Something Extra	Needles & Pins	Brian Keith Show	Dean Martin Show
SATURDAY	A		Partridge Family	ABC Suspense Movie			Griff
	C		All in the Family	M*A*S*H	Mary Tyler Moore Show	Bob Newhart Show	Carol Burnett Show
	N		Emergency		NBC Saturday Night Movie		

PRIME TIME SCHEDULE: 1974

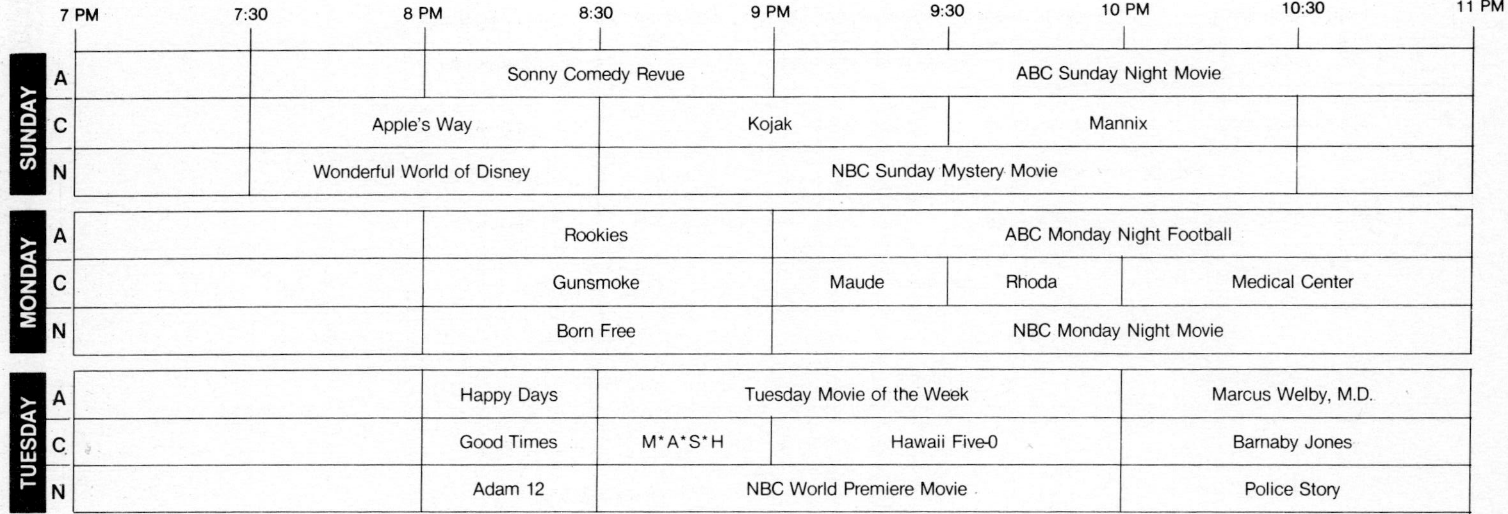

Day	Network	7 PM	7:30	8 PM	8:30	9 PM	9:30	10 PM	10:30
SUNDAY	A			Sonny Comedy Revue		ABC Sunday Night Movie			
	C		Apple's Way		Kojak		Mannix		
	N		Wonderful World of Disney		NBC Sunday Mystery Movie				
MONDAY	A			Rookies		ABC Monday Night Football			
	C			Gunsmoke		Maude	Rhoda	Medical Center	
	N			Born Free		NBC Monday Night Movie			
TUESDAY	A			Happy Days	Tuesday Movie of the Week			Marcus Welby, M.D.	
	C			Good Times	M*A*S*H	Hawaii Five-0		Barnaby Jones	
	N			Adam 12	NBC World Premiere Movie			Police Story	

11 PM

WEDNESDAY	A		That's My Mama	Wednesday Movie of the Week			Get Christie Love	
	C		Sons & Daughters		Cannon		Manhunter	
	N		Little House on the Prairie		Lucas Tanner		Petrocelli	
THURSDAY	A		Odd Couple	Paper Moon	Streets of San Francisco		Harry-O	
	C		The Waltons		CBS Thursday Night Movie			
	N		Sierra		Ironside		Movin' On	
FRIDAY	A		Kodiak	Six Million Dollar Man		Texas Wheelers	Kolchak: The Night Stalker	
	C		Planet of the Apes		CBS Friday Night Movie			
	N		Sanford & Son	Chico and the Man	Rockford Files		Police Woman	
SATURDAY	A		The New Land		Kung Fu		Nakia	
	C		All in the Family	Paul Sand in Friends and Lovers	Mary Tyler Moore Show	Bob Newhart Show	Carol Burnett Show	
	N		Emergency		NBC Saturday Night Movie			

PRIME TIME SCHEDULE: 1975

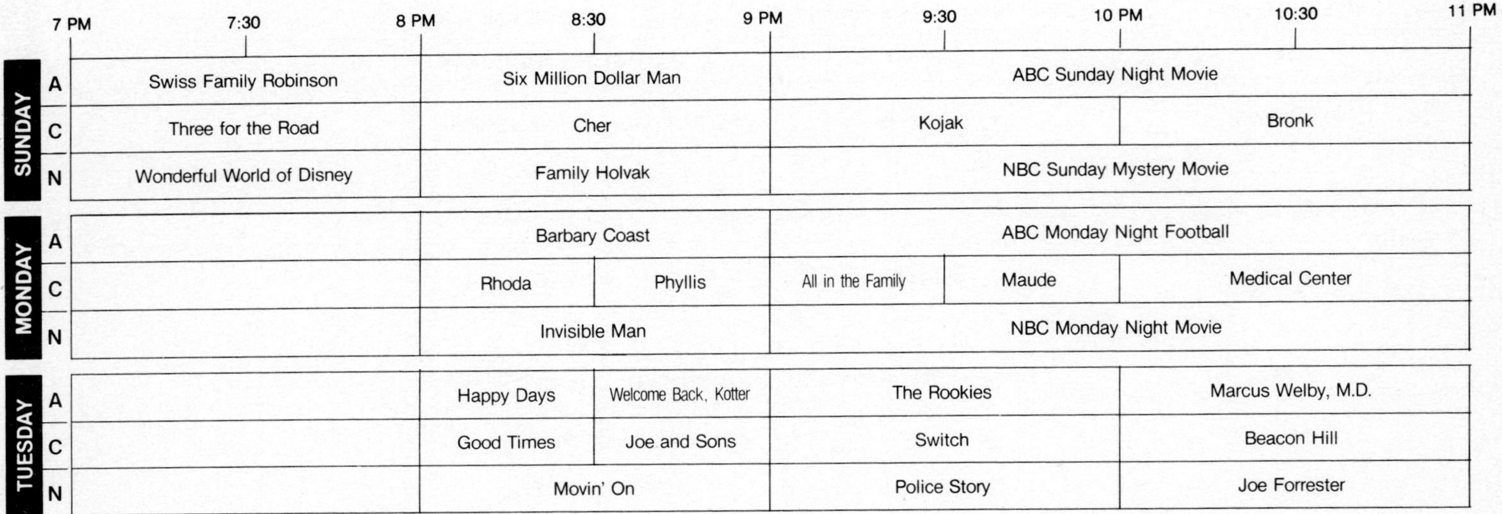

Day	Net	7 PM	7:30	8 PM	8:30	9 PM	9:30	10 PM	10:30
SUNDAY	A	Swiss Family Robinson		Six Million Dollar Man		ABC Sunday Night Movie			
	C	Three for the Road		Cher		Kojak		Bronk	
	N	Wonderful World of Disney		Family Holvak		NBC Sunday Mystery Movie			
MONDAY	A			Barbary Coast		ABC Monday Night Football			
	C			Rhoda	Phyllis	All in the Family	Maude	Medical Center	
	N			Invisible Man		NBC Monday Night Movie			
TUESDAY	A			Happy Days	Welcome Back, Kotter	The Rookies		Marcus Welby, M.D.	
	C			Good Times	Joe and Sons	Switch		Beacon Hill	
	N			Movin' On		Police Story		Joe Forrester	

WEDNESDAY	A		When Things Were Rotten	That's My Mama	Baretta		Starsky & Hutch	
	C		Tony Orlando & Dawn		Cannon		Kate McShane	
	N		Little House on the Prairie		Doctors' Hospital		Petrocelli	
THURSDAY	A		Barney Miller	On the Rocks	Streets of San Francisco		Harry-O	
	C		The Waltons		CBS Thursday Night Movie			
	N		The Montefuscos	Fay	Ellery Queen		Medical Story	
FRIDAY	A		Mobile One		ABC Friday Night Movie			
	C		Big Eddie	M*A*S*H	Hawaii Five-0		Barnaby Jones	
	N		Sanford & Son	Chico and the Man	Rockford Files		Police Woman	
SATURDAY	A		Saturday Night Live with Howard Cosell		S.W.A.T.		Matt Helm	
	C		The Jeffersons	Doc	Mary Tyler Moore Show	Bob Newhart Show	Carol Burnett Show	
	N		Emergency		NBC Saturday Night Movie			

PRIME TIME SCHEDULE: 1976

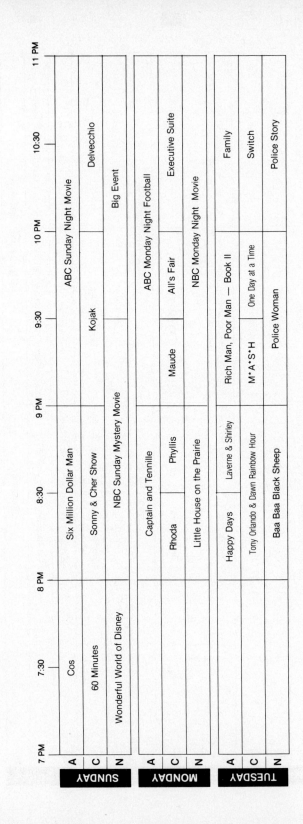

		7 PM	7:30	8 PM	8:30	9 PM	9:30	10 PM	10:30
SUNDAY	A	Cos		Six Million Dollar Man		ABC Sunday Night Movie			
	C	60 Minutes		Sonny & Cher Show		Kojak		Delvecchio	
	N	Wonderful World of Disney		NBC Sunday Mystery Movie			Big Event		
MONDAY	A			Captain and Tennille		ABC Monday Night Football			
	C			Rhoda	Phyllis	Maude	All's Fair	Executive Suite	
	N			Little House on the Prairie		NBC Monday Night Movie			
TUESDAY	A			Happy Days	Laverne & Shirley	Rich Man, Poor Man — Book II		Family	
	C			Tony Orlando & Dawn Rainbow Hour		M*A*S*H	One Day at a Time	Switch	
	N			Baa Baa Black Sheep		Police Woman		Police Story	

Day	Network								
WEDNESDAY	A			Bionic Woman		Baretta		Charlie's Angels	
	C			Good Times	Ball Four	All in the Family	Alice	Blue Knight	
	N			The Practice	NBC Movie of the Week			The Quest	
THURSDAY	A			Welcome Back, Kotter	Barney Miller	Tony Randall Show	Nancy Walker Show	Streets of San Francisco	
	C			The Waltons		Hawaii Five-0		Barnaby Jones	
	N			Gemini Man		NBC's Best Sellers		Van Dyke & Company	
FRIDAY	A			Donny & Marie		ABC Friday Night Movie			
	C		Campaign '76	Spencer's Pilots		CBS Friday Night Movie			
	N			Sanford & Son	Chico and the Man	Rockford Files		Serpico	
SATURDAY	A			Holmes & Yo-Yo	Mr. T and Tina	Starsky & Hutch		Most Wanted	
	C			The Jeffersons	Doc	Mary Tyler Moore Show	Bob Newhart Show	Carol Burnett Show	
	N			Emergency		NBC Saturday Night Movie			

PRIME TIME SCHEDULE: 1977

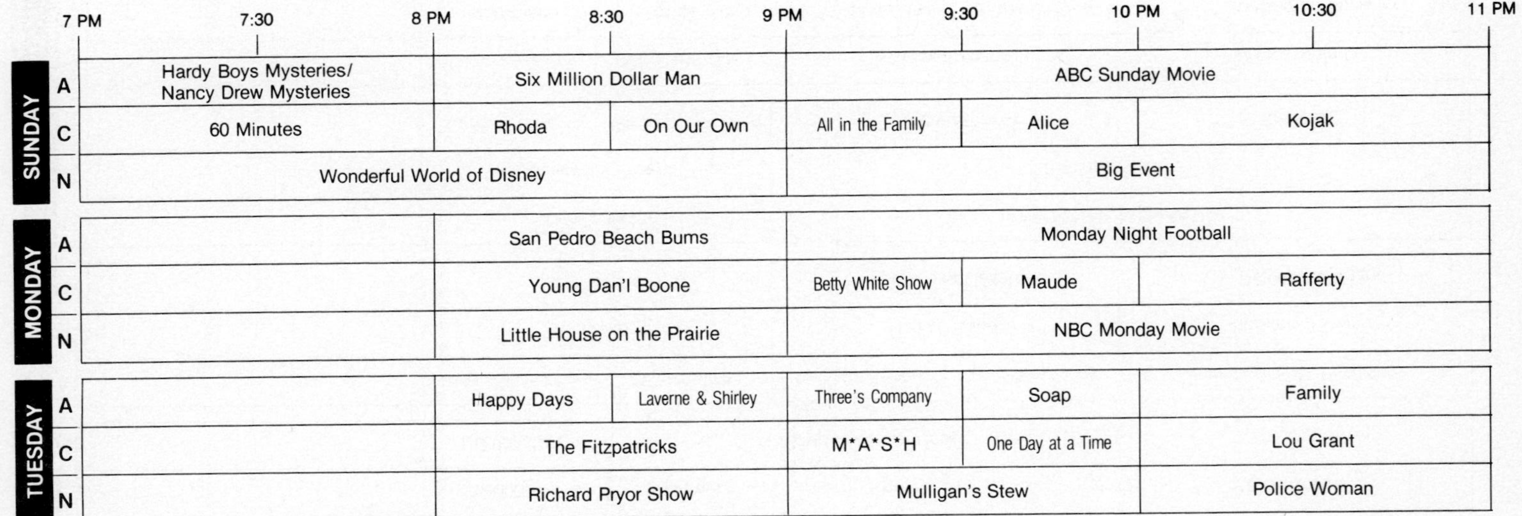

Day	Network	7 PM	7:30	8 PM	8:30	9 PM	9:30	10 PM	10:30
SUNDAY	A	Hardy Boys Mysteries/ Nancy Drew Mysteries		Six Million Dollar Man		ABC Sunday Movie			
	C	60 Minutes		Rhoda	On Our Own	All in the Family	Alice	Kojak	
	N	Wonderful World of Disney				Big Event			
MONDAY	A			San Pedro Beach Bums		Monday Night Football			
	C			Young Dan'l Boone		Betty White Show	Maude	Rafferty	
	N			Little House on the Prairie		NBC Monday Movie			
TUESDAY	A			Happy Days	Laverne & Shirley	Three's Company	Soap	Family	
	C			The Fitzpatricks		M*A*S*H	One Day at a Time	Lou Grant	
	N			Richard Pryor Show		Mulligan's Stew		Police Woman	

WEDNESDAY	A		Eight Is Enough		Charlie's Angels		Baretta
	C		Good Times	Busting Loose	CBS Wednesday Movie		
	N		Life and Times of Grizzly Adams		Oregon Trail		Big Hawaii
THURSDAY	A		Welcome Back, Kotter	What's Happening	Barney Miller	Carter Country	Redd Foxx Show
	C		The Waltons		Hawaii Five-0		Barnaby Jones
	N		Chips		Man from Atlantis		Rosetti and Ryan
FRIDAY	A		Donny and Marie		ABC Friday Movie		
	C		New Adventures of Wonder Woman		Logan's Run		Switch
	N		Sanford Arms	Chico and the Man	Rockford Files		Quincy, M.E.
SATURDAY	A		Fish	Operation Petticoat	Starsky and Hutch		Love Boat
	C		Bob Newhart Show	We've Got Each Other	The Jeffersons	Tony Randall Show	Carol Burnett Show
	N		Bionic Woman		NBC Saturday Movie		

PRIME TIME SCHEDULE: 1978

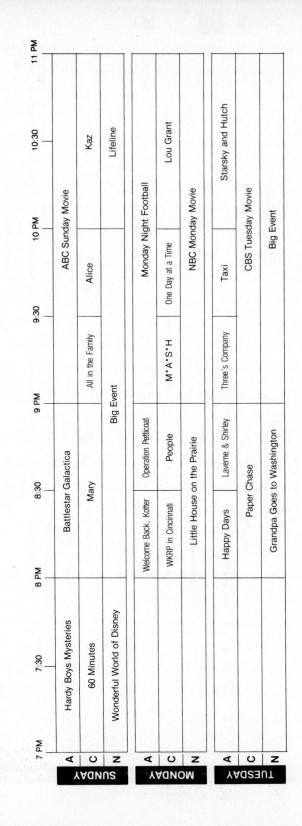

Day	Network	7 PM	7:30	8 PM	8:30	9 PM	9:30	10 PM	10:30
SUNDAY	A	Hardy Boys Mysteries		Battlestar Galactica		ABC Sunday Movie			
	C	60 Minutes		Mary		All in the Family	Alice	Kaz	
	N	Wonderful World of Disney		Big Event				Lifeline	
MONDAY	A			Welcome Back, Kotter	Operation Petticoat	Monday Night Football			
	C			WKRP in Cincinnati	People	M*A*S*H	One Day at a Time	Lou Grant	
	N			Little House on the Prairie		NBC Monday Movie			
TUESDAY	A			Happy Days	Laverne & Shirley	Three's Company	Taxi	Starsky and Hutch	
	C			Paper Chase		CBS Tuesday Movie			
	N			Grandpa Goes to Washington		Big Event			

WEDNESDAY	A		Eight Is Enough		Charlie's Angels		Vega$	
	C		The Jeffersons	In the Beginning	CBS Wednesday Movie			
	N		Dick Clark's Live Wednesday		NBC Wednesday Movie			
THURSDAY	A		Mork & Mindy	What's Happening	Barney Miller	Soap	Family	
	C		The Waltons		Hawaii Five-0		Barnaby Jones	
	N		Project U.F.O.		Quincy, M.E.		W.E.B.	
FRIDAY	A		Donny and Marie		ABC Friday Movie			
	C		New Adventures of Wonder Woman		Incredible Hulk		Flying High	
	N		Waverly Wonders	Who's Watching the Kids	Rockford Files		Eddie Capra Mysteries	
SATURDAY	A		Carter Country	Apple Pie	Love Boat		Fantasy Island	
	C		Rhoda	Good Times	American Girls		Dallas	
	N		Chips		Specials		Sword of Justice	

APPENDIX 2
EMMY AWARD WINNERS

The "Emmy" awards are given each year in recognition of excellence in television performance and production. The following are the principal awards presented over the years to nighttime network series and the people connected with them, including actors, writers, and directors. Also included, for the sake of completeness, are awards for nighttime "one-time-only" specials and Public Broadcasting Service programs, even though these are not otherwise within the scope of this book.

The National Academy of Television Arts and Sciences also presents many other "Emmy" awards not listed here, in such areas as local programming, daytime and sports programming, and in numerous technical areas such as film editing, sound mixing, and technical direction.

1948 (presented January 25, 1949)
BEST FILM MADE FOR TELEVISION: "The Necklace," *Your Show Time* (NBC)

1949 (presented January 27, 1950)
BEST LIVE SHOW: *The Ed Wynn Show* (CBS)
BEST KINESCOPE SHOW: *Texaco Star Theater* (NBC)
MOST OUTSTANDING LIVE PERSONALITY: Ed Wynn (CBS)
MOST OUTSTANDING KINESCOPE PERSONALITY: Milton Berle (NBC)
BEST FILM MADE FOR AND VIEWED ON TELEVISION: *The Life of Riley* (NBC)

1950 (presented January 23, 1951)
BEST ACTOR: Alan Young (CBS)
BEST ACTRESS: Gertrude Berg (CBS)
MOST OUTSTANDING PERSONALITY: Groucho Marx (NBC)
BEST VARIETY SHOW: *The Alan Young Show* (CBS)
BEST DRAMATIC SHOW: *Pulitzer Prize Playhouse* (ABC)
BEST GAME AND AUDIENCE PARTICIPATION SHOW: *Truth or Consequences* (CBS)

1951 (presented February 18, 1952)
BEST DRAMATIC SHOW: *Studio One* (CBS)
BEST COMEDY SHOW: *The Red Skelton Show* (CBS)
BEST VARIETY SHOW: *Your Show of Shows* (NBC)
BEST ACTOR: Sid Caesar (NBC)
BEST ACTRESS: Imogene Coca (NBC)
BEST COMEDIAN OR COMEDIENNE: Red Skelton (NBC)

1952 (presented February 5, 1953)
BEST DRAMATIC PROGRAM: *Robert Montgomery Presents* (NBC)
BEST VARIETY PROGRAM: *Your Show of Shows* (NBC)
BEST PUBLIC AFFAIRS PROGRAM: *See It Now* (CBS)
BEST MYSTERY, ACTION, OR ADVENTURE PROGRAM: *Dragnet* (NBC)
BEST SITUATION COMEDY: *I Love Lucy* (CBS)
BEST AUDIENCE PARTICIPATION, QUIZ, OR PANEL PROGRAM: *What's My Line* (CBS)
BEST ACTOR: Thomas Mitchell
BEST ACTRESS: Helen Hayes
BEST COMEDIAN: Jimmy Durante (NBC)
BEST COMEDIENNE: Lucille Ball (CBS)
MOST OUTSTANDING PERSONALITY: Bishop Fulton J. Sheen (DUM)

1953 (presented February 11, 1954)
BEST DRAMATIC PROGRAM: *The U.S. Steel Hour* (ABC)

BEST SITUATION COMEDY: *I Love Lucy* (CBS)
BEST VARIETY PROGRAM: *Omnibus* (CBS)
BEST PROGRAM OF NEWS OR SPORTS: *See It Now* (CBS)
BEST PUBLIC AFFAIRS PROGRAM: *Victory at Sea* (NBC)
BEST CHILDREN'S PROGRAM: *Kukla, Fran & Ollie* (NBC)
BEST NEW PROGRAMS: *Make Room for Daddy* (CBS) and *The U.S. Steel Hour* (ABC)
BEST MALE STAR OF REGULAR SERIES: Donald O'Connor, *Colgate Comedy Hour* (NBC)
BEST FEMALE STAR OF REGULAR SERIES: Eve Arden, *Our Miss Brooks* (CBS)
BEST SERIES SUPPORTING ACTOR: Art Carney, *The Jackie Gleason Show* (CBS)
BEST SERIES SUPPORTING ACTRESS: Vivian Vance, *I Love Lucy* (CBS)
BEST MYSTERY, ACTION, OR ADVENTURE PROGRAM: *Dragnet* (NBC)
BEST AUDIENCE PARTICIPATION, QUIZ, OR PANEL PROGRAM: *This Is Your Life* (NBC) and *What's My Line* (CBS)
MOST OUTSTANDING PERSONALITY: Edward R. Murrow (CBS)

1954 (presented March 7, 1955)
MOST OUTSTANDING NEW PERSONALITY: George Gobel (NBC)
BEST CULTURAL, RELIGIOUS, OR EDUCATIONAL PROGRAM: *Omnibus* (CBS)
BEST SPORTS PROGRAM: *The Gillette Cavalcade of Sports* (NBC)
BEST CHILDREN'S PROGRAM: *Lassie* (CBS)
BEST WESTERN OR ADVENTURE SERIES: *Stories of the Century* (syndicated)
BEST NEWS REPORTER OR COMMENTATOR: John Daly (ABC)
BEST AUDIENCE, GUEST PARTICIPATION, OR PANEL PROGRAM: *This Is Your Life* (NBC)
BEST ACTOR IN A SINGLE PERFORMANCE: Robert Cummings, "Twelve Angry Men," *Studio One* (CBS)
BEST ACTRESS IN A SINGLE PERFORMANCE: Judith Anderson, "Macbeth," *Hallmark Hall of Fame* (NBC)
BEST MALE SINGER: Perry Como (NBC)
BEST FEMALE SINGER: Dinah Shore (NBC)
BEST SUPPORTING ACTOR IN A REGULAR SERIES: Art Carney, *The Jackie Gleason Show* (CBS)
BEST SUPPORTING ACTRESS IN A REGULAR SERIES: Audrey Meadows, *The Jackie Gleason Show* (CBS)
BEST ACTOR STARRING IN A REGULAR SERIES: Danny Thomas, *Make Room for Daddy* (ABC)
BEST ACTRESS STARRING IN A REGULAR SERIES: Loretta Young, *The Loretta Young Show* (NBC)
BEST MYSTERY OR INTRIGUE SERIES: *Dragnet* (NBC)
BEST VARIETY SERIES INCLUDING MUSICAL VARIETIES: *Disneyland* (ABC)
BEST SITUATION COMEDY SERIES: *Make Room for Daddy* (ABC)
BEST DRAMATIC SERIES: *The U.S. Steel Hour* (ABC)
BEST INDIVIDUAL PROGRAM OF THE YEAR: "Operation Undersea," *Disneyland* (ABC)
BEST WRITTEN DRAMATIC MATERIAL: Reginald Rose, "Twelve Angry Men," *Studio One* (CBS)
BEST WRITTEN COMEDY MATERIAL: James Allardice, Jack Douglas, Hal Kanter, and Harry Winkler, *The George Gobel Show* (NBC)
BEST DIRECTION: Franklin Schaffner, "Twelve Angry Men," *Studio One* (CBS)

1955 (presented March 17, 1956)
BEST CHILDREN'S SERIES: *Lassie* (CBS)
BEST DOCUMENTARY PROGRAM (RELIGIOUS, INFORMATIONAL, EDUCATIONAL, OR INTERVIEW): *Omnibus* (CBS)
BEST AUDIENCE PARTICIPATION SERIES (QUIZ, PANEL, ETC.): *The $64,000 Question* (CBS)

BEST ACTION OR ADVENTURE SERIES: *Disneyland* (ABC)
BEST COMEDY SERIES: *The Phil Silvers Show* (CBS)
BEST VARIETY SERIES: *The Ed Sullivan Show* (CBS)
BEST MUSIC SERIES: *Your Hit Parade* (NBC)
BEST DRAMATIC SERIES: *Producers' Showcase* (NBC)
BEST SINGLE PROGRAM OF THE YEAR: "Peter Pan," *Producers' Showcase* (NBC)
BEST ACTOR (SINGLE PERFORMANCE): Lloyd Nolan, "The Caine Mutiny Court-Martial," *Ford Star Jubilee* (CBS)
BEST ACTRESS (SINGLE PERFORMANCE): Mary Martin, "Peter Pan," *Producers' Showcase* (NBC)
BEST ACTOR (CONTINUING PERFORMANCE): Phil Silvers, *The Phil Silvers Show* (CBS)
BEST ACTRESS (CONTINUING PERFORMANCE): Lucille Ball, *I Love Lucy* (CBS)
BEST ACTOR IN A SUPPORTING ROLE: Art Carney, *The Jackie Gleason Show* (CBS)
BEST ACTRESS IN A SUPPORTING ROLE: Nanette Fabray, *Caesar's Hour* (NBC)
BEST COMEDIAN: Phil Silvers (CBS)
BEST COMEDIENNE: Nanette Fabray (NBC)
BEST MALE SINGER: Perry Como (NBC)
BEST FEMALE SINGER: Dinah Shore (NBC)
BEST MC OR PROGRAM HOST (MALE OR FEMALE): Perry Como (NBC)
BEST NEWS COMMENTATOR OR REPORTER: Edward R. Murrow (CBS)
BEST ORIGINAL TELEPLAY WRITING: Rod Serling, "Patterns," *Kraft Television Theatre* (NBC)
BEST COMEDY WRITING: Nat Hiken, Barry Blitser, Arnold Auerbach, Harvey Orkin, Vincent Bogert, Arnold Rosen, Coleman Jacoby, Tony Webster, and Terry Ryan, *The Phil Silvers Show* (CBS)
BEST TELEVISION ADAPTATION: Paul Gregory and Franklin Schaffner, "The Caine Mutiny Court-Martial," *Ford Star Jubilee* (CBS)
BEST PRODUCER (LIVE SERIES): Fred Coe, *Producers' Showcase* (NBC)
BEST PRODUCER (FILM SERIES): Walt Disney, *Disneyland* (ABC)
BEST DIRECTOR (LIVE SERIES): Franklin Schaffner, "The Caine Mutiny Court-Martial," *Ford Star Jubilee* (CBS)
BEST DIRECTOR (FILM SERIES): Nat Hiken, *The Phil Silvers Show* (CBS)

1956 (presented March 16, 1957)
BEST SINGLE PROGRAM OF THE YEAR: "Requiem for a Heavyweight," *Playhouse 90* (CBS)
BEST NEW PROGRAM SERIES: *Playhouse 90* (CBS)
BEST SERIES (HALF HOUR OR LESS): *The Phil Silvers Show* (CBS)
BEST SERIES (ONE HOUR OR MORE): *Caesar's Hour* (NBC)
BEST PUBLIC SERVICE SERIES: *See It Now* (CBS)
BEST CONTINUING PERFORMANCE BY AN ACTOR IN A DRAMATIC SERIES: Robert Young, *Father Knows Best* (NBC)
BEST CONTINUING PERFORMANCE BY AN ACTRESS IN A DRAMATIC SERIES: Loretta Young, *The Loretta Young Show* (NBC)
BEST CONTINUING PERFORMANCE BY A COMEDIAN IN A SERIES: Sid Caesar, *Caesar's Hour* (NBC)
BEST CONTINUING PERFORMANCE BY A COMEDIENNE IN A SERIES: Nanette Fabray, *Caesar's Hour* (NBC)
BEST SINGLE PERFORMANCE BY AN ACTOR: Jack Palance, "Requiem for a Heavyweight," *Playhouse 90* (CBS)
BEST SINGLE PERFORMANCE BY AN ACTRESS: Claire Trevor, "Dodsworth," *Producers' Showcase* (NBC)
BEST SUPPORTING PERFORMANCE BY AN ACTOR: Carl Reiner, *Caesar's Hour* (NBC)
BEST SUPPORTING PERFORMANCE BY AN ACTRESS: Pat Carroll, *Caesar's Hour* (NBC)

BEST MALE PERSONALITY (CONTINUING PERFORMANCE): Perry Como (NBC)
BEST FEMALE PERSONALITY (CONTINUING PERFORMANCE): Dinah Shore (NBC)
BEST NEWS COMMENTATOR: Edward R. Murrow (CBS)
BEST TELEPLAY WRITING (HALF HOUR OR LESS): James P. Cavanagh, "Fog Closes In," *Alfred Hitchcock Presents* (CBS)
BEST TELEPLAY WRITING (ONE HOUR OR MORE): Rod Serling, "Requiem for a Heavyweight," *Playhouse 90* (CBS)
BEST COMEDY WRITING (VARIETY OR SITUATION COMEDY): Nat Hiken, Billy Friedberg, Tony Webster, Leonard Stern, Arnold Rosen, and Coleman Jacoby, *The Phil Silvers Show* (CBS)
BEST DIRECTION (HALF HOUR OR LESS): Sheldon Leonard, "Danny's Comeback," *The Danny Thomas Show* (ABC)
BEST DIRECTION (ONE HOUR OR MORE): Ralph Nelson, "Requiem for a Heavyweight," *Playhouse 90* (CBS)

1957 (presented April 15, 1958)

BEST SINGLE PROGRAM OF THE YEAR: "The Comedian," *Playhouse 90* (CBS)
BEST NEW PROGRAM SERIES OF THE YEAR: *The Seven Lively Arts* (CBS)
BEST DRAMATIC ANTHOLOGY SERIES: *Playhouse 90* (CBS)
BEST DRAMATIC SERIES WITH CONTINUING CHARACTERS: *Gunsmoke* (CBS)
BEST COMEDY SERIES: *The Phil Silvers Show* (CBS)
BEST MUSICAL, VARIETY, AUDIENCE PARTICIPATION, OR QUIZ SERIES: *The Dinah Shore Chevy Show* (NBC)
BEST PUBLIC SERVICE PROGRAM OR SERIES: *Omnibus* (ABC and NBC)
BEST CONTINUING PERFORMANCE BY AN ACTOR IN A LEADING ROLE IN A DRAMATIC OR COMEDY SERIES: Robert Young, *Father Knows Best* (NBC)
BEST CONTINUING PERFORMANCE BY AN ACTRESS IN A LEADING ROLE IN A DRAMATIC OR COMEDY SERIES: Jane Wyatt, *Father Knows Best* (NBC)
BEST CONTINUING PERFORMANCE (MALE) IN A SERIES BY A COMEDIAN, SINGER, HOST, DANCER, MC, ANNOUNCER, NARRATOR, PANELIST, OR ANY PERSON WHO ESSENTIALLY PLAYS HIMSELF: Jack Benny, *The Jack Benny Show* (CBS)
BEST CONTINUING PERFORMANCE (FEMALE) IN A SERIES BY A COMEDIENNE, SINGER, HOSTESS, DANCER, MC, ANNOUNCER, NARRATOR, PANELIST, OR ANY PERSON WHO ESSENTIALLY PLAYS HERSELF: Dinah Shore, *The Dinah Shore Chevy Show* (NBC)
ACTOR—BEST SINGLE PERFORMANCE (LEAD OR SUPPORT): Peter Ustinov, "The Life of Samuel Johnson," *Omnibus* (NBC)
ACTRESS—BEST SINGLE PERFORMANCE (LEAD OR SUPPORT): Polly Bergen, "The Helen Morgan Story," *Playhouse 90* (CBS)
BEST CONTINUING SUPPORTING PERFORMANCE BY AN ACTOR IN A DRAMATIC OR COMEDY SERIES: Carl Reiner, *Caesar's Hour* (NBC)
BEST CONTINUING SUPPORTING PERFORMANCE BY AN ACTRESS IN A DRAMATIC OR COMEDY SERIES: Ann B. Davis, *The Bob Cummings Show* (CBS and NBC)
BEST NEWS COMMENTARY: Edward R. Murrow, *See It Now* (CBS)
BEST TELEPLAY WRITING (HALF HOUR OR LESS): Paul Monash, "The Lonely Wizard," *Schlitz Playhouse of Stars* (CBS)
BEST TELEPLAY WRITING (ONE HOUR OR MORE): Rod Serling, "The Comedian," *Playhouse 90* (CBS)
BEST COMEDY WRITING: Nat Hiken, Billy Friedberg, Phil Sharp, Terry Ryan, Coleman Jacoby, Arnold Rosen, Sydney Zelinka, A. J. Russell, and Tony Webster, *The Phil Silvers Show* (CBS)
BEST DIRECTION (HALF HOUR OR LESS): Robert Stevens, "The Glass Eye," *Alfred Hitchcock Presents* (CBS)
BEST DIRECTION (ONE HOUR OR MORE): Bob Banner, *The Dinah Shore Chevy Show* (NBC)

1958–1959 (presented May 6, 1959)

MOST OUTSTANDING SINGLE PROGRAM OF THE YEAR: "An Evening with Fred Astaire" (NBC)

BEST DRAMATIC SERIES (ONE HOUR OR LONGER): *Playhouse 90* (CBS)

BEST DRAMATIC SERIES (LESS THAN ONE HOUR): *Alcoa-Goodyear Theatre* (NBC)

BEST COMEDY SERIES: *The Jack Benny Show* (CBS)

BEST MUSICAL OR VARIETY SERIES: *The Dinah Shore Chevy Show* (NBC)

BEST WESTERN SERIES: *Maverick* (ABC)

BEST PUBLIC SERVICE PROGRAM OR SERIES: *Omnibus* (NBC)

BEST NEWS REPORTING SERIES: *The Huntley-Brinkley Report* (NBC)

BEST PANEL, QUIZ, OR AUDIENCE PARTICIPATION SERIES: *What's My Line* (CBS)

BEST SPECIAL DRAMATIC PROGRAM (ONE HOUR OR LONGER): "Little Moon of Alban," *Hallmark Hall of Fame* (NBC)

BEST SPECIAL MUSICAL OR VARIETY PROGRAM (ONE HOUR OR LONGER): "An Evening with Fred Astaire" (NBC)

BEST ACTOR IN A LEADING ROLE (CONTINUING CHARACTER) IN A DRAMATIC SERIES: Raymond Burr, *Perry Mason* (CBS)

BEST ACTRESS IN A LEADING ROLE (CONTINUING CHARACTER) IN A DRAMATIC SERIES: Loretta Young, *The Loretta Young Show* (NBC)

BEST ACTOR IN A LEADING ROLE (CONTINUING CHARACTER) IN A COMEDY SERIES: Jack Benny, *The Jack Benny Show* (CBS)

BEST ACTRESS IN A LEADING ROLE (CONTINUING CHARACTER) IN A COMEDY SERIES: Jane Wyatt, *Father Knows Best* (CBS and NBC)

BEST SUPPORTING ACTOR (CONTINUING CHARACTER) IN A DRAMATIC SERIES: Dennis Weaver, *Gunsmoke* (CBS)

BEST SUPPORTING ACTRESS (CONTINUING CHARACTER) IN A DRAMATIC SERIES: Barbara Hale, *Perry Mason* (CBS)

BEST SUPPORTING ACTOR (CONTINUING CHARACTER) IN A COMEDY SERIES: Tom Poston, *The Steve Allen Show* (NBC)

BEST SUPPORTING ACTRESS (CONTINUING CHARACTER) IN A COMEDY SERIES: Ann B. Davis, *The Bob Cummings Show* (NBC)

BEST PERFORMANCE BY AN ACTOR (CONTINUING CHARACTER) IN A MUSICAL OR VARIETY SERIES: Perry Como, *The Perry Como Show* (NBC)

BEST PERFORMANCE BY AN ACTRESS (CONTINUING CHARACTER) IN A MUSICAL OR VARIETY SERIES: Dinah Shore, *The Dinah Shore Chevy Show* (NBC)

BEST SINGLE PERFORMANCE BY AN ACTOR: Fred Astaire, "An Evening with Fred Astaire" (NBC)

BEST SINGLE PERFORMANCE BY AN ACTRESS: Julie Harris, "Little Moon of Alban," *Hallmark Hall of Fame* (NBC)

BEST NEWS COMMENTATOR OR ANALYST: Edward R. Murrow (CBS)

BEST DIRECTION OF A SINGLE PROGRAM OF A DRAMATIC SERIES (LESS THAN ONE HOUR): Jack Smight, "Eddie," *Alcoa-Goodyear Theatre* (NBC)

BEST DIRECTION OF A SINGLE DRAMATIC PROGRAM (ONE HOUR OR LONGER): George Schaefer, "Little Moon of Alban," *Hallmark Hall of Fame* (NBC)

BEST DIRECTION OF A SINGLE PROGRAM OF A COMEDY SERIES: Peter Tewksbury, "Medal for Margaret," *Father Knows Best* (CBS)

BEST DIRECTION OF A SINGLE MUSICAL OR VARIETY PROGRAM: Bud Yorkin, "An Evening with Fred Astaire" (NBC)

BEST WRITING OF A SINGLE PROGRAM OF A DRAMATIC SERIES (LESS THAN ONE HOUR): Alfred Brenner and Ken Hughes, "Eddie," *Alcoa-Goodyear Theatre* (NBC)

BEST WRITING OF A SINGLE DRAMATIC PROGRAM (ONE HOUR OR LONGER): James Costigan, "Little Moon of Alban," *Hallmark Hall of Fame* (NBC)

BEST WRITING OF A SINGLE PROGRAM OF A COMEDY SERIES: Sam Perrin, George Baker, Hal Goldman, and Al Gordon, "Jack Benny Show with Ernie Kovacs," *The Jack Benny Show* (CBS)

BEST WRITING OF A SINGLE MUSICAL OR VARIETY PROGRAM: Bud Yorkin and Herbert Baker, "An Evening with Fred Astaire" (NBC)

1959–1960 (presented June 20, 1960)

OUTSTANDING PROGRAM ACHIEVEMENT IN THE FIELD OF HUMOR: "The Art Carney Special" (NBC)

OUTSTANDING PROGRAM ACHIEVEMENT IN THE FIELD OF DRAMA: *Playhouse 90* (CBS)

OUTSTANDING PROGRAM ACHIEVEMENT IN THE FIELD OF VARIETY: "The Fabulous Fifties" (CBS)

OUTSTANDING PROGRAM ACHIEVEMENT IN THE FIELD OF NEWS: *The Huntley-Brinkley Report* (NBC)

OUTSTANDING PROGRAM ACHIEVEMENT IN THE FIELD OF PUBLIC AFFAIRS AND EDUCATION: *The Twentieth Century* (CBS)

OUTSTANDING SINGLE PERFORMANCE BY AN ACTOR (LEAD OR SUPPORT): Laurence Olivier, "The Moon and Sixpence" (NBC)

OUTSTANDING SINGLE PERFORMANCE BY AN ACTRESS (LEAD OR SUPPORT): Ingrid Bergman, "The Turn of the Screw," *Ford Startime* (NBC)

OUTSTANDING PERFORMANCE BY AN ACTOR IN A SERIES (LEAD OR SUPPORT): Robert Stack, *The Untouchables* (ABC)

OUTSTANDING PERFORMANCE BY AN ACTRESS IN A SERIES (LEAD OR SUPPORT): Jane Wyatt, *Father Knows Best* (CBS)

OUTSTANDING PERFORMANCE IN A VARIETY OR MUSICAL PROGRAM OR SERIES: Harry Belafonte, "Tonight with Belafonte," *The Revlon Revue* (CBS)

OUTSTANDING WRITING ACHIEVEMENT IN DRAMA: Rod Serling, *The Twilight Zone* (CBS)

OUTSTANDING WRITING ACHIEVEMENT IN COMEDY: Sam Perrin, George Balzer, Al Gordon, and Hal Goldman, *The Jack Benny Show* (CBS)

OUTSTANDING WRITING ACHIEVEMENT IN THE DOCUMENTARY FIELD: Howard K. Smith and Av Westin, "The Population Explosion" (CBS)

OUTSTANDING DIRECTORIAL ACHIEVEMENT IN DRAMA: Robert Mulligan, "The Moon and Sixpence" (NBC)

OUTSTANDING DIRECTORIAL ACHIEVEMENT IN COMEDY: Ralph Levy and Bud Yorkin, *The Jack Benny Hour Specials* (CBS)

1960–1961 (presented May 16, 1961)

THE PROGRAM OF THE YEAR: "Macbeth," *Hallmark Hall of Fame* (NBC)

OUTSTANDING PROGRAM ACHIEVEMENT IN THE FIELD OF HUMOR: *The Jack Benny Show* (CBS)

OUTSTANDING PROGRAM ACHIEVEMENT IN THE FIELD OF DRAMA: "Macbeth," *Hallmark Hall of Fame* (NBC)

OUTSTANDING PROGRAM ACHIEVEMENT IN THE FIELD OF VARIETY: "Astaire Time" (NBC)

OUTSTANDING PROGRAM ACHIEVEMENT IN THE FIELD OF NEWS: *The Huntley-Brinkley Report* (NBC)

OUTSTANDING PROGRAM ACHIEVEMENT IN THE FIELD OF PUBLIC AFFAIRS AND EDUCATION: *The Twentieth Century* (CBS)

OUTSTANDING SINGLE PERFORMANCE BY AN ACTOR IN A LEADING ROLE: Maurice Evans, "Macbeth," *Hallmark Hall of Fame* (NBC)

OUTSTANDING SINGLE PERFORMANCE BY AN ACTRESS IN A LEADING ROLE: Judith Anderson, "Macbeth," *Hallmark Hall of Fame* (NBC)

OUTSTANDING PERFORMANCE BY AN ACTOR IN A SERIES (LEAD): Raymond Burr, *Perry Mason* (CBS)

OUTSTANDING PERFORMANCE BY AN ACTRESS IN A SERIES (LEAD): Barbara Stanwyck, *The Barbara Stanwyck Show* (NBC)

OUTSTANDING PERFORMANCE IN A SUPPORTING ROLE BY AN ACTOR OR ACTRESS IN A SINGLE PROGRAM: Roddy McDowall, "Not without Honor," *Equitable's American Heritage* (NBC)

OUTSTANDING PERFORMANCE IN A SUPPORTING ROLE BY AN ACTOR OR ACTRESS IN A SERIES: Don Knotts, *The Andy Griffith Show* (CBS)

OUTSTANDING PERFORMANCE IN A VARIETY OR MUSICAL PROGRAM OR SERIES: Fred Astaire, "Astaire Time" (NBC)
OUTSTANDING WRITING ACHIEVEMENT IN DRAMA: Rod Serling, *The Twilight Zone* (CBS)
OUTSTANDING WRITING ACHIEVEMENT IN COMEDY: Sherwood Schwartz, Dave O'Brien, Al Schwartz, Martin Ragaway, and Red Skelton, *The Red Skelton Show* (CBS)
OUTSTANDING WRITING ACHIEVEMENT IN THE DOCUMENTARY FIELD: Victor Wolfson, *Winston Churchill—The Valiant Years* (ABC)
OUTSTANDING DIRECTORIAL ACHIEVEMENT IN DRAMA: George Schaefer, "Macbeth," *Hallmark Hall of Fame* (NBC)
OUTSTANDING DIRECTORIAL ACHIEVEMENT IN COMEDY: Sheldon Leonard, *The Danny Thomas Show* (CBS)

1961–1962 (presented May 22, 1962)
THE PROGRAM OF THE YEAR: "Victoria Regina," *Hallmark Hall of Fame* (NBC)
OUTSTANDING PROGRAM ACHIEVEMENT IN THE FIELD OF HUMOR: *The Bob Newhart Show* (NBC)
OUTSTANDING PROGRAM ACHIEVEMENT IN THE FIELD OF DRAMA: *The Defenders* (CBS)
OUTSTANDING PROGRAM ACHIEVEMENT IN THE FIELD OF VARIETY: *The Garry Moore Show* (CBS)
OUTSTANDING PROGRAM ACHIEVEMENT IN THE FIELD OF NEWS: *The Huntley-Brinkley Report* (NBC)
OUTSTANDING PROGRAM ACHIEVEMENT IN THE FIELD OF EDUCATIONAL AND PUBLIC AFFAIRS PROGRAMMING: *David Brinkley's Journal* (NBC)
OUTSTANDING SINGLE PERFORMANCE BY AN ACTOR IN A LEADING ROLE: Peter Falk, "The Price of Tomatoes," *The Dick Powell Show* (NBC)
OUTSTANDING SINGLE PERFORMANCE BY AN ACTRESS IN A LEADING ROLE: Julie Harris, "Victoria Regina," *Hallmark Hall of Fame* (NBC)
OUTSTANDING CONTINUED PERFORMANCE BY AN ACTOR IN A SERIES (LEAD): E. G. Marshall, *The Defenders* (CBS)
OUTSTANDING CONTINUED PERFORMANCE BY AN ACTRESS IN A SERIES (LEAD): Shirley Booth, *Hazel* (NBC)
OUTSTANDING PERFORMANCE IN A SUPPORTING ROLE BY AN ACTOR: Don Knotts, *The Andy Griffith Show* (CBS)
OUTSTANDING PERFORMANCE IN A SUPPORTING ROLE BY AN ACTRESS: Pamela Brown, "Victoria Regina," *Hallmark Hall of Fame* (NBC)
OUTSTANDING PERFORMANCE IN A VARIETY OR MUSICAL PROGRAM OR SERIES: Carol Burnett, *The Garry Moore Show* (CBS)
OUTSTANDING WRITING ACHIEVEMENT IN DRAMA: Reginald Rose, *The Defenders* (CBS)
OUTSTANDING WRITING ACHIEVEMENT IN COMEDY: Carl Reiner, *The Dick Van Dyke Show* (CBS)
OUTSTANDING WRITING ACHIEVEMENT IN THE DOCUMENTARY FIELD: Lou Hazam, "Vincent Van Gogh: A Self-Portrait" (NBC)
OUTSTANDING DIRECTORIAL ACHIEVEMENT IN DRAMA: Franklin Schaffner, *The Defenders* (CBS)
OUTSTANDING DIRECTORIAL ACHIEVEMENT IN COMEDY: Nat Hiken, *Car 54, Where Are You?* (NBC)

1962–1963 (presented May 26, 1963)
THE PROGRAM OF THE YEAR: "The Tunnel" (NBC)
OUTSTANDING PROGRAM ACHIEVEMENT IN THE FIELD OF HUMOR: *The Dick Van Dyke Show* (CBS)
OUTSTANDING PROGRAM ACHIEVEMENT IN THE FIELD OF DRAMA: *The Defenders* (CBS)

OUTSTANDING PROGRAM ACHIEVEMENT IN THE FIELD OF MUSIC: "Julie and Carol at Carnegie Hall" (CBS)

OUTSTANDING ACHIEVEMENT IN THE FIELD OF VARIETY: *The Andy Williams Show* (NBC)

OUTSTANDING PROGRAM ACHIEVEMENT IN THE FIELD OF PANEL, QUIZ, OR AUDIENCE PARTICIPATION: *The G. E. College Bowl* (CBS)

OUTSTANDING PROGRAM ACHIEVEMENT IN THE FIELD OF CHILDREN'S PROGRAMMING: *Walt Disney's Wonderful World of Color* (NBC)

OUTSTANDING ACHIEVEMENT IN THE FIELD OF DOCUMENTARY PROGRAMS: "The Tunnel," Reuven Frank (NBC)

OUTSTANDING ACHIEVEMENT IN THE FIELD OF NEWS: *The Huntley-Brinkley Report* (NBC)

OUTSTANDING PROGRAM ACHIEVEMENT IN THE FIELD OF NEWS COMMENTARY OR PUBLIC AFFAIRS: *David Brinkley's Journal* (NBC)

OUTSTANDING ACHIEVEMENT IN INTERNATIONAL REPORTING OR COMMENTARY: Piers Anderson, Berlin correspondent, "The Tunnel" (NBC)

OUTSTANDING SINGLE PERFORMANCE BY AN ACTOR IN A LEADING ROLE: Trevor Howard, "The Invincible Mr. Disraeli," *Hallmark Hall of Fame* (NBC)

OUTSTANDING SINGLE PERFORMANCE BY AN ACTRESS IN A LEADING ROLE: Kim Stanley, "A Cardinal Act of Mercy," *Ben Casey* (ABC)

OUTSTANDING CONTINUED PERFORMANCE BY AN ACTOR IN A SERIES (LEAD): E. G. Marshall, *The Defenders* (CBS)

OUTSTANDING CONTINUED PERFORMANCE BY AN ACTRESS IN A SERIES (LEAD): Shirley Booth, *Hazel* (NBC)

OUTSTANDING PERFORMANCE IN A SUPPORTING ROLE BY AN ACTOR: Don Knotts, *The Andy Griffith Show* (CBS)

OUTSTANDING PERFORMANCE IN A SUPPORTING ROLE BY AN ACTRESS: Glenda Farrell, "A Cardinal Act of Mercy," *Ben Casey* (ABC)

OUTSTANDING PERFORMANCE IN A VARIETY OR MUSICAL PROGRAM OR SERIES: Carol Burnett, "Julie and Carol at Carnegie Hall" (CBS) and "Carol and Company" (CBS)

OUTSTANDING WRITING ACHIEVEMENT IN DRAMA: Robert Thom and Reginald Rose, "The Madman," *The Defenders* (CBS)

OUTSTANDING WRITING ACHIEVEMENT IN COMEDY: Carl Reiner, *The Dick Van Dyke Show* (CBS)

OUTSTANDING DIRECTORIAL ACHIEVEMENT IN DRAMA: Stuart Rosenberg, "The Madman," *The Defenders* (CBS)

OUTSTANDING DIRECTORIAL ACHIEVEMENT IN COMEDY: John Rich, *The Dick Van Dyke Show* (CBS)

1963–1964 (presented May 25, 1964)

THE PROGRAM OF THE YEAR: "The Making of the President 1960" (ABC)

OUTSTANDING PROGRAM ACHIEVEMENT IN THE FIELD OF COMEDY: *The Dick Van Dyke Show* (CBS)

OUTSTANDING PROGRAM ACHIEVEMENT IN THE FIELD OF DRAMA: *The Defenders* (CBS)

OUTSTANDING PROGRAM ACHIEVEMENT IN THE FIELD OF MUSIC: *The Bell Telephone Hour* (NBC)

OUTSTANDING PROGRAM ACHIEVEMENT IN THE FIELD OF VARIETY: *The Danny Kaye Show* (CBS)

OUTSTANDING ACHIEVEMENT IN THE FIELD OF DOCUMENTARY PROGRAMS: "The Making of the President 1960" (ABC)

OUTSTANDING PROGRAM ACHIEVEMENT IN THE FIELD OF NEWS REPORTS: *The Huntley-Brinkley Report* (NBC)

OUTSTANDING PROGRAM ACHIEVEMENT IN THE FIELD OF NEWS COMMENTARY OR PUBLIC AFFAIRS: "Cuba: Parts I and II—The Bay of Pigs and the Missile Crisis," *NBC White Paper* (NBC)

OUTSTANDING SINGLE PERFORMANCE BY AN ACTOR IN A LEADING ROLE: Jack Klugman, "Blacklist," *The Defenders* (CBS)

OUTSTANDING SINGLE PERFORMANCE BY AN ACTRESS IN A LEADING ROLE: Shelley Winters, "Two Is the Number," *Bob Hope Presents the Chrysler Theatre* (NBC)

OUTSTANDING CONTINUED PERFORMANCE BY AN ACTOR IN A SERIES (LEAD): Dick Van Dyke, *The Dick Van Dyke Show* (CBS)

OUTSTANDING CONTINUED PERFORMANCE BY AN ACTRESS IN A SERIES (LEAD): Mary Tyler Moore, *The Dick Van Dyke Show* (CBS)

OUTSTANDING PERFORMANCE IN A SUPPORTING ROLE BY AN ACTOR: Albert Paulsen, "One Day in the Life of Ivan Denisovich," *Bob Hope Presents the Chrysler Theatre* (NBC)

OUTSTANDING PERFORMANCE IN A SUPPORTING ROLE BY AN ACTRESS: Ruth White, "Little Moon of Alban," *Hallmark Hall of Fame* (NBC)

OUTSTANDING PERFORMANCE IN A VARIETY OR MUSICAL PROGRAM OR SERIES: Danny Kaye, *The Danny Kaye Show* (CBS)

OUTSTANDING WRITING ACHIEVEMENT IN DRAMA (ORIGINAL): Ernest Kinoy, "Blacklist," *The Defenders* (CBS)

OUTSTANDING WRITING ACHIEVEMENT IN DRAMA (ADAPTATION): Rod Serling, "It's Mental Work" (from the story by John O'Hara), *Bob Hope Presents the Chrysler Theatre* (NBC)

OUTSTANDING WRITING ACHIEVEMENT IN COMEDY OR VARIETY: Carl Reiner, Sam Denoff, and Bill Persky, *The Dick Van Dyke Show* (CBS)

OUTSTANDING DIRECTORIAL ACHIEVEMENT IN DRAMA: Tom Gries, "Who Do You Kill," *East Side/West Side* (CBS)

OUTSTANDING DIRECTORIAL ACHIEVEMENT IN COMEDY: Jerry Paris, *The Dick Van Dyke Show* (CBS)

OUTSTANDING DIRECTORIAL ACHIEVEMENT IN VARIETY OR MUSIC: Robert Scheerer, *The Danny Kaye Show* (CBS)

1964–1965 (presented September 12, 1965)

OUTSTANDING PROGRAM ACHIEVEMENTS IN ENTERTAINMENT: *The Dick Van Dyke Show*, Carl Reiner, producer (CBS); "The Magnificent Yankee," *Hallmark Hall of Fame*, George Schaefer, producer (NBC); "My Name Is Barbra," Richard Lewine, producer (CBS)

OUTSTANDING INDIVIDUAL ACHIEVEMENTS IN ENTERTAINMENT (ACTORS AND PERFORMERS): Lynn Fontanne, "The Magnificent Yankee," *Hallmark Hall of Fame* (NBC); Alfred Lunt, "The Magnificent Yankee," *Hallmark Hall of Fame* (NBC); Barbra Streisand, "My Name Is Barbra" (CBS); Dick Van Dyke, *The Dick Van Dyke Show* (CBS)

OUTSTANDING INDIVIDUAL ACHIEVEMENT IN ENTERTAINMENT (WRITER): David Karp, "The 700-Year-Old Gang," *The Defenders* (CBS)

OUTSTANDING INDIVIDUAL ACHIEVEMENT IN ENTERTAINMENT (DIRECTOR): Paul Bogart, "The 700-Year-Old Gang," *The Defenders* (CBS)

OUTSTANDING PROGRAM ACHIEVEMENTS IN NEWS, DOCUMENTARIES, INFORMATION, AND SPORTS: "I, Leonardo da Vinci," *The Saga of Western Man*, John H. Secondari and Helen Jean Rogers, producers (ABC); "The Louvre," Lucy Jarvis, producer, and John J. Sughrue, co-producer (NBC)

OUTSTANDING INDIVIDUAL ACHIEVEMENT IN NEWS, DOCUMENTARIES, INFORMATION, AND SPORTS (DIRECTOR): John J. Sughrue, "The Louvre" (NBC)

OUTSTANDING INDIVIDUAL ACHIEVEMENT IN NEWS, DOCUMENTARIES, INFORMATION, AND SPORTS (WRITER): Sidney Carroll, "The Louvre" (NBC)

1965–1966 (presented May 22, 1966)

OUTSTANDING COMEDY SERIES: *The Dick Van Dyke Show*, Carl Reiner, producer (CBS)

OUTSTANDING VARIETY SERIES: *The Andy Williams Show*, Bob Finkel, producer (NBC)

OUTSTANDING VARIETY SPECIAL: "Chrysler Presents the Bob Hope Christmas Special," Bob Hope, executive producer (NBC)

OUTSTANDING DRAMATIC SERIES: *The Fugitive,* Alan Armer, producer (ABC)

OUTSTANDING DRAMATIC PROGRAM: "The Ages of Man," David Susskind and Daniel Melnick, producers (CBS)

OUTSTANDING MUSICAL PROGRAM: "Frank Sinatra: A Man and His Music," Dwight Hemion, producer (NBC)

OUTSTANDING CHILDREN'S PROGRAM: "A Charlie Brown Christmas," Lee Mendelson and Bill Melendez, producers (CBS)

OUTSTANDING PERFORMANCE BY AN ACTOR IN A LEADING ROLE IN A DRAMA: Cliff Robertson, "The Game," *Bob Hope Presents the Chrysler Theatre* (NBC)

OUTSTANDING PERFORMANCE BY AN ACTRESS IN A LEADING ROLE IN A DRAMA: Simone Signoret, "A Small Rebellion," *Bob Hope Presents the Chrysler Theatre* (NBC)

OUTSTANDING CONTINUED PERFORMANCE BY AN ACTOR IN A LEADING ROLE IN A DRAMATIC SERIES: Bill Cosby, *I Spy* (NBC)

OUTSTANDING CONTINUED PERFORMANCE BY AN ACTRESS IN A LEADING ROLE IN A DRAMATIC SERIES: Barbara Stanwyck, *The Big Valley* (ABC)

OUTSTANDING CONTINUED PERFORMANCE BY AN ACTOR IN A LEADING ROLE IN A COMEDY SERIES: Dick Van Dyke, *The Dick Van Dyke Show* (CBS)

OUTSTANDING CONTINUED PERFORMANCE BY AN ACTRESS IN A LEADING ROLE IN A COMEDY SERIES: Mary Tyler Moore, *The Dick Van Dyke Show* (CBS)

OUTSTANDING PERFORMANCE BY AN ACTOR IN A SUPPORTING ROLE IN A DRAMA: James Daly, "Eagle in a Cage," *Hallmark Hall of Fame* (NBC)

OUTSTANDING PERFORMANCE BY AN ACTRESS IN A SUPPORTING ROLE IN A DRAMA: Lee Grant, *Peyton Place* (ABC)

OUTSTANDING PERFORMANCE BY AN ACTOR IN A SUPPORTING ROLE IN A COMEDY: Don Knotts, "The Return of Barney Fife," *The Andy Griffith Show* (CBS)

OUTSTANDING PERFORMANCE BY AN ACTRESS IN A SUPPORTING ROLE IN A COMEDY: Alice Pearce, *Bewitched* (ABC)

OUTSTANDING WRITING ACHIEVEMENT IN DRAMA: Millard Lampell, "Eagle in a Cage," *Hallmark Hall of Fame* (NBC)

OUTSTANDING WRITING ACHIEVEMENT IN COMEDY: Bill Persky and Sam Denoff, "Coast to Coast Big Mouth," *The Dick Van Dyke Show* (CBS)

OUTSTANDING WRITING ACHIEVEMENT IN VARIETY: Al Gordon, Hal Goldman, and Sheldon Keller, "An Evening with Carol Channing" (CBS)

OUTSTANDING DIRECTORIAL ACHIEVEMENT IN DRAMA: Sidney Pollack, "The Game," *Bob Hope Presents the Chrysler Theatre* (NBC)

OUTSTANDING DIRECTORIAL ACHIEVEMENT IN COMEDY: William Asher, *Bewitched* (ABC)

OUTSTANDING DIRECTORIAL ACHIEVEMENT IN VARIETY OR MUSIC: Alan Handley, "The Julie Andrews Show" (NBC)

ACHIEVEMENTS IN NEWS AND DOCUMENTARIES (PROGRAMS): "American White Paper: United States Foreign Policy," Fred Freed, producer (NBC); "KKK—The Invisible Empire," *CBS Reports,* David Lowe, producer (CBS); "Senate Hearings on Vietnam," Chet Hagen, producer (NBC)

SPECIAL CLASSIFICATIONS OF INDIVIDUAL ACHIEVEMENTS: Burr Tillstrom, "Berlin Wall" hand ballet, *That Was the Week That Was* (NBC)

1966–1967 (presented June 4, 1967)

OUTSTANDING COMEDY SERIES: *The Monkees,* Bert Schneider and Bob Rafelson, producers (NBC)

OUTSTANDING VARIETY SERIES: *The Andy Williams Show,* Edward Stephenson and Bob Finkel, producers (NBC)

OUTSTANDING VARIETY SPECIAL: "The Sid Caesar, Imogene Coca, Carl Reiner, Howard Morris Special," Jack Arnold, producer (CBS)

OUTSTANDING DRAMATIC SERIES: *Mission: Impossible,* Joseph Gantman and Bruce Geller, producers (CBS)

OUTSTANDING DRAMATIC PROGRAM: "Death of a Salesman," David Susskind and Daniel Melnick, producers (CBS)
OUTSTANDING MUSICAL PROGRAM: "Brigadoon," Fielder Cook, producer (ABC)
OUTSTANDING CHILDREN'S PROGRAM: "Jack and the Beanstalk," Gene Kelly, producer (NBC)
OUTSTANDING SINGLE PERFORMANCE BY AN ACTOR IN A LEADING ROLE IN A DRAMA: Peter Ustinov, "Barefoot in Athens," *Hallmark Hall of Fame* (NBC)
OUTSTANDING SINGLE PERFORMANCE BY AN ACTRESS IN A LEADING ROLE IN A DRAMA: Geraldine Page, "A Christmas Memory," *ABC Stage 67* (ABC)
OUTSTANDING CONTINUED PERFORMANCE BY AN ACTOR IN A LEADING ROLE IN A DRAMATIC SERIES: Bill Cosby, *I Spy* (NBC)
OUTSTANDING CONTINUED PERFORMANCE BY AN ACTRESS IN A LEADING ROLE IN A DRAMATIC SERIES: Barbara Bain, *Mission: Impossible* (CBS)
OUTSTANDING CONTINUED PERFORMANCE BY AN ACTOR IN A LEADING ROLE IN A COMEDY SERIES: Don Adams, *Get Smart* (NBC)
OUTSTANDING CONTINUED PERFORMANCE BY AN ACTRESS IN A LEADING ROLE IN A COMEDY SERIES: Lucille Ball, *The Lucy Show* (CBS)
OUTSTANDING PERFORMANCE BY AN ACTOR IN A SUPPORTING ROLE IN A DRAMA: Eli Wallach, "The Poppy Is Also a Flower," *Xerox Special* (ABC)
OUTSTANDING PERFORMANCE BY AN ACTRESS IN A SUPPORTING ROLE IN A DRAMA: Agnes Moorehead, "Night of the Vicious Valentine," *The Wild Wild West* (CBS)
OUTSTANDING PERFORMANCE BY AN ACTOR IN A SUPPORTING ROLE IN A COMEDY: Don Knotts, "Barney Comes to Mayberry," *The Andy Griffith Show* (CBS)
OUTSTANDING PERFORMANCE BY AN ACTRESS IN A SUPPORTING ROLE IN A COMEDY: Frances Bavier, *The Andy Griffith Show* (CBS)
OUTSTANDING WRITING ACHIEVEMENT IN DRAMA: Bruce Geller, *Mission: Impossible* (CBS)
OUTSTANDING WRITING ACHIEVEMENT IN COMEDY: Buck Henry and Leonard Stern, "Ship of Spies," *Get Smart* (NBC)
OUTSTANDING WRITING ACHIEVEMENT IN VARIETY: Mel Brooks, Sam Denoff, Bill Persky, Carl Reiner, and Mel Tolkin, "The Sid Caesar, Imogene Coca, Carl Reiner, Howard Morris Special" (CBS)
OUTSTANDING DIRECTORIAL ACHIEVEMENT IN DRAMA: Alex Segal, "Death of a Salesman" (CBS)
OUTSTANDING DIRECTORIAL ACHIEVEMENT IN COMEDY: James Frawley, "Royal Flush," *The Monkees* (NBC)
OUTSTANDING DIRECTORIAL ACHIEVEMENT IN VARIETY OR MUSIC: Fielder Cook, "Brigadoon" (ABC)
ACHIEVEMENTS IN NEWS AND DOCUMENTARIES (PROGRAMS): "China: The Roots of Madness," Mel Stuart, producer (syndicated); "Hall of Kings," Harry Rasky, producer (ABC); "The Italians," Bernard Birnbaum, producer (CBS)
ACHIEVEMENTS IN NEWS AND DOCUMENTARIES (INDIVIDUAL): Theodore H. White, writer, "China: The Roots of Madness" (syndicated)
SPECIAL CLASSIFICATIONS OF INDIVIDUAL ACHIEVEMENTS: Art Carney, *The Jackie Gleason Show* (CBS); Truman Capote and Eleanor Perry, adaptation of "A Christmas Memory," *ABC Stage 67* (ABC); Arthur Miller, adaptation of "Death of a Salesman" (CBS)

1967–1968 (presented May 19, 1968)

OUTSTANDING ACHIEVEMENT WITHIN REGULARLY SCHEDULED NEWS PROGRAMS: "1st Cavalry, Con Thien," and other segments, *The CBS Evening News with Walter Cronkite*, CBS news correspondent John Laurence and CBS news cameraman Keith Kay (CBS); "Crisis in the Cities," *Public Broadcast Laboratory*, Av Westin, executive producer (NET)
OUTSTANDING ACHIEVEMENT IN NEWS DOCUMENTARIES: "Africa," James Fleming, executive producer (ABC); "Summer '67: What We Learned," Fred Freed, producer

(NBC); "CBS Reports: What about Ronald Reagan?" *CBS News Hour*, Harry Reasoner, writer (CBS); "Same Mud, Same Blood," Vo Huynh, cameraman (NBC)

OUTSTANDING ACHIEVEMENT IN CULTURAL DOCUMENTARIES: "Eric Hoffer, the Passionate State of Mind," *CBS News Hour*, Jack Beck, producer (CBS); "Gauguin in Tahiti: The Search for Paradise," *CBS News Hour*, Martin Carr, producer (CBS); "John Steinbeck's America and the Americans," Lee Mendelson, producer (NBC); "Dylan Thomas: The World I Breathe," *NET Festival*, Perry Miller Adato, producer (NET); Nathaniel Dorsky, art photographer, "Gauguin in Tahiti: The Search for Paradise," *CBS News Hour* (CBS); Harry Morgan, writer, "The Wyeth Phenomenon," *Who, What, When, Where, Why* (CBS); Thomas A. Priestley, director of photography, and Robert Loweree, film editor, "John Steinbeck's America and Americans" (NBC)

OTHER OUTSTANDING NEWS AND DOCUMENTARY ACHIEVEMENTS: *The Twenty-first Century*, Isaac Kleinerman, producer (CBS); "Science and Religion: Who Will Play God?" *CBS News Special*, Ben Flynn, producer (CBS); *Our World*, George Delerue, composer (NET)

OUTSTANDING COMEDY SERIES: *Get Smart*, Burt Nodella, producer (NBC)

OUTSTANDING DRAMATIC SERIES: *Mission: Impossible*, Joseph E. Gantman, producer (CBS)

OUTSTANDING DRAMATIC PROGRAM: "Elizabeth the Queen," *Hallmark Hall of Fame*, George Schaefer, producer (NBC)

OUTSTANDING MUSICAL OR VARIETY SERIES: *Rowan and Martin's Laugh-In*, George Schlatter, producer (NBC)

OUTSTANDING MUSICAL OR VARIETY PROGRAM: "Rowan and Martin's Laugh-In Special," George Schlatter, producer (NBC)

OUTSTANDING SINGLE PERFORMANCE BY AN ACTOR IN A LEADING ROLE IN A DRAMA: Melvin Douglas, "Do Not Go Gentle into That Good Night," *CBS Playhouse* (CBS)

OUTSTANDING SINGLE PERFORMANCE BY AN ACTRESS IN A LEADING ROLE IN A DRAMA: Maureen Stapleton, "Among the Paths to Eden," *Xerox Special Event* (ABC)

OUTSTANDING CONTINUED PERFORMANCE BY AN ACTOR IN A LEADING ROLE IN A DRAMATIC SERIES: Bill Cosby, *I Spy* (NBC)

OUTSTANDING CONTINUED PERFORMANCE BY AN ACTRESS IN A LEADING ROLE IN A DRAMATIC SERIES: Barbara Bain, *Mission: Impossible* (CBS)

OUTSTANDING CONTINUED PERFORMANCE BY AN ACTOR IN A LEADING ROLE IN A COMEDY SERIES: Don Adams, *Get Smart* (NBC)

OUTSTANDING CONTINUED PERFORMANCE BY AN ACTRESS IN A LEADING ROLE IN A COMEDY SERIES: Lucille Ball, *The Lucy Show* (CBS)

OUTSTANDING PERFORMANCE BY AN ACTOR IN A SUPPORTING ROLE IN A DRAMA: Milburn Stone, *Gunsmoke* (CBS)

OUTSTANDING PERFORMANCE BY AN ACTRESS IN A SUPPORTING ROLE IN A DRAMA: Barbara Anderson, *Ironside* (NBC)

OUTSTANDING PERFORMANCE BY AN ACTOR IN A SUPPORTING ROLE IN A COMEDY: Werner Klemperer, *Hogan's Heroes* (CBS)

OUTSTANDING PERFORMANCE BY AN ACTRESS IN A SUPPORTING ROLE IN A COMEDY: Marion Lorne, *Bewitched* (ABC)

OUTSTANDING WRITING ACHIEVEMENT IN DRAMA: Loring Mandel, "Do Not Go Gentle into That Good Night," *CBS Playhouse* (CBS)

OUTSTANDING WRITING ACHIEVEMENT IN COMEDY: Alan Burns and Chris Hayward, "The Coming-Out Party," *He & She* (CBS)

OUTSTANDING WRITING ACHIEVEMENT IN MUSIC OR VARIETY: Paul Keyes, Hugh Wedlock, Allan Manings, Chris Beard, David Panich, Phil Hahn, Jack Hanrahan, Coslough Johnson, Marc London, and Digby Wolfe, *Rowan and Martin's Laugh-In* (NBC)

OUTSTANDING DIRECTORIAL ACHIEVEMENT IN DRAMA: Paul Bogart, "Dear Friends," *CBS Playhouse* (CBS)

OUTSTANDING DIRECTORIAL ACHIEVEMENT IN COMEDY: Bruce Bilson, "Maxwell Smart, Private Eye," *Get Smart* (NBC)

OUTSTANDING DIRECTORIAL ACHIEVEMENT IN MUSIC OR VARIETY: Jack Haley, Jr, "Movin' with Nancy" (NBC)

SPECIAL CLASSIFICATION OF OUTSTANDING INDIVIDUAL ACHIEVEMENT: Art Carney, *The Jackie Gleason Show* (CBS); Pat Paulsen, *The Smothers Brothers Comedy Hour* (CBS)

1968–1969 (presented June 8, 1969)

OUTSTANDING COMEDY SERIES: *Get Smart*, Arne Sultan, executive producer; Burt Nodella, producer (NBC)

OUTSTANDING DRAMATIC SERIES: *NET Playhouse*, Curtis Davis, executive producer (NET)

OUTSTANDING DRAMATIC PROGRAM: "Teacher, Teacher," Henry Jaffe, executive producer; George Lefferts, producer, *Hallmark Hall of Fame* (NBC)

OUTSTANDING MUSICAL OR VARIETY SERIES: *Rowan and Martin's Laugh-In*, George Schlatter, executive producer; Paul Keyes and Carolyn Raskin, producers (NBC)

OUTSTANDING VARIETY OR MUSICAL PROGRAM: "The Bill Cosby Special," Roy Silver, executive producer; Bill Hobin, Bill Persky, and Sam Denoff, producers (NBC)

OUTSTANDING SINGLE PERFORMANCE BY AN ACTOR IN A LEADING ROLE: Paul Scofield, "The Male of the Species," *Prudential's On Stage* (NBC)

OUTSTANDING SINGLE PERFORMANCE BY AN ACTRESS IN A LEADING ROLE: Geraldine Page, "The Thanksgiving Visitor" (ABC)

OUTSTANDING CONTINUED PERFORMANCE BY AN ACTOR IN A LEADING ROLE IN A DRAMATIC SERIES: Carl Betz, *Judd, for the Defense* (ABC)

OUTSTANDING CONTINUED PERFORMANCE BY AN ACTRESS IN A LEADING ROLE IN A DRAMATIC SERIES: Barbara Bain, *Mission: Impossible* (CBS)

OUTSTANDING CONTINUED PERFORMANCE BY AN ACTOR IN A LEADING ROLE IN A COMEDY SERIES: Don Adams, *Get Smart* (NBC)

OUTSTANDING CONTINUED PERFORMANCE BY AN ACTRESS IN A LEADING ROLE IN A COMEDY SERIES: Hope Lange, *The Ghost and Mrs. Muir* (NBC)

OUTSTANDING SINGLE PERFORMANCE BY AN ACTOR IN A SUPPORTING ROLE: no award given

OUTSTANDING SINGLE PERFORMANCE BY AN ACTRESS IN A SUPPORTING ROLE: Anna Calder-Marshall, "The Male of the Species," *Prudential's On Stage* (NBC)

OUTSTANDING CONTINUED PERFORMANCE BY AN ACTOR IN A SUPPORTING ROLE IN A SERIES: Werner Klemperer, *Hogan's Heroes* (CBS)

OUTSTANDING CONTINUED PERFORMANCE BY AN ACTRESS IN A SUPPORTING ROLE IN A SERIES: Susan Saint James, *The Name of the Game* (NBC)

OUTSTANDING WRITING ACHIEVEMENT IN DRAMA: J. P. Miller, "The People Next Door," *CBS Playhouse* (CBS)

OUTSTANDING WRITING ACHIEVEMENT IN COMEDY, VARIETY, OR MUSIC: Alan Blye, Bob Einstein, Murray Roman, Carl Gottlieb, Jerry Music, Steve Martin, Cecil Tuck, Paul Wayne, Cy Howard, and Mason Williams, *The Smothers Brothers Comedy Hour* (CBS)

OUTSTANDING DIRECTORIAL ACHIEVEMENT IN DRAMA: David Greene, "The People Next Door," *CBS Playhouse* (CBS)

OUTSTANDING PROGRAM ACHIEVEMENT (SPECIAL CLASSIFICATION): *Firing Line with William F. Buckley, Jr.*, Warren Steibel, producer (syndicated); *Wild Kingdom*, Don Meier, producer (NBC)

OUTSTANDING INDIVIDUAL ACHIEVEMENT (SPECIAL CLASSIFICATION): Arte Johnson, *Rowan and Martin's Laugh-In* (NBC); Harvey Korman, *The Carol Burnett Show* (CBS)

OUTSTANDING ACHIEVEMENT WITHIN REGULARLY SCHEDULED NEWS PROGRAMS: "Coverage of Hunger in the United States," *The Huntley-Brinkley Report*, Wallace Westfeldt, executive producer (NBC). "On the Road," *The CBS Evening News with Walter Cronkite*, Charles Kuralt, correspondent; James Wilson, cameraman; Robert Funk, soundman (CBS). "Police After Chicago," *The CBS Evening News with Walter Cronkite*, John Laurence, correspondent (CBS)

OUTSTANDING ACHIEVEMENT IN COVERAGE OF SPECIAL EVENTS: "Coverage of Martin Luther King Assassination and Aftermath," *CBS News Special Reports* and Broadcasts, Robert Wussler, Ernest Leiser, Don Hewitt, and Burton Benjamin, executive producers (CBS)

OUTSTANDING NEWS DOCUMENTARY PROGRAM ACHIEVEMENTS: "CBS Reports: Hunger in America," *CBS News Hour*, Martin Carr, producer (CBS); "Law and Order," *Public Broadcast Laboratory*, Frederick Wiseman, producer (NET)

OUTSTANDING NEWS DOCUMENTARY INDIVIDUAL ACHIEVEMENT: Perry Wolff and Andrew A. Rooney, writers, "Black History: Lost, Stolen or Strayed" [*Of Black America series*], *CBS News Hour* (CBS)

OUTSTANDING CULTURAL DOCUMENTARY AND "MAGAZINE TYPE" PROGRAM OR SERIES ACHIEVEMENT (PROGRAMS): "Don't Count the Candles," *CBS News Hour*, William K. McClure, producer (CBS); "Justice Black and the Bill of Rights," *CBS News Special*, Burton Benjamin, producer (CBS); "Man Who Dances: Edward Villela," *The Bell Telephone Hour*, Robert Drew and Mike Jackson, producers (NBC); "The Great American Novel," *CBS News Hour*, Arthur Barron, producer (CBS)

OUTSTANDING CULTURAL DOCUMENTARY AND "MAGAZINE TYPE" PROGRAM OR SERIES ACHIEVEMENT: (INDIVIDUAL): Walter Dombrow and Jerry Sims, cinematographers, "The Great American Novel," *CBS News Hour* (CBS); Tom Pettit, producer, "CBW: The Secrets of Secrecy," *First Tuesday* (NBC); Lord Snowden, cinematographer, "Don't Count the Candles," *CBS News Hour* (CBS)

1969–1970 (presented June 7, 1970)

OUTSTANDING COMEDY SERIES: *My World and Welcome to It*, Sheldon Leonard, executive producer; Danny Arnold, producer (NBC)

OUTSTANDING DRAMATIC SERIES: *Marcus Welby, M.D.*, David Victor, executive producer; David J. O'Connell, producer (ABC)

OUTSTANDING DRAMATIC PROGRAM: "A Storm in Summer," *Hallmark Hall of Fame*, M. J. Rifkin, executive producer; Alan Landsburg, producer (NBC)

OUTSTANDING VARIETY OR MUSICAL SERIES: *The David Frost Show*, Peter Baker, producer (syndicated)

OUTSTANDING VARIETY OR MUSICAL PROGRAM (VARIETY AND POPULAR MUSIC): "Annie, the Women in the Life of a Man," Joseph Cates, executive producer; Martin Charnin, producer (CBS)

OUTSTANDING VARIETY OR MUSICAL PROGRAM (CLASSICAL MUSIC): "Cinderella," John Barnes and Curtis Davis, executive producers; Norman Campbell, producer (NET)

OUTSTANDING NEW SERIES: *Room 222*, Gene Reynolds, producer (ABC)

OUTSTANDING SINGLE PERFORMANCE BY AN ACTOR IN A LEADING ROLE: Peter Ustinov, "A Storm in Summer," *Hallmark Hall of Fame* (NBC)

OUTSTANDING SINGLE PERFORMANCE BY AN ACTRESS IN A LEADING ROLE: Patty Duke, "My Sweet Charlie," *NBC World Premiere Movie* (NBC)

OUTSTANDING CONTINUED PERFORMANCE BY AN ACTOR IN A LEADING ROLE IN A DRAMATIC SERIES: Robert Young, *Marcus Welby, M.D.* (ABC)

OUTSTANDING CONTINUED PERFORMANCE BY AN ACTRESS IN A LEADING ROLE IN A DRAMATIC SERIES: Susan Hampshire, *The Forsythe Saga* (NET)

OUTSTANDING CONTINUED PERFORMANCE BY AN ACTOR IN A LEADING ROLE IN A COMEDY SERIES: William Windom, *My World and Welcome to It* (NBC)

OUTSTANDING CONTINUED PERFORMANCE BY AN ACTRESS IN A LEADING ROLE IN A COMEDY SERIES: Hope Lange, *The Ghost and Mrs. Muir* (ABC)

OUTSTANDING PERFORMANCE BY AN ACTOR IN A SUPPORTING ROLE IN DRAMA: James Brolin, *Marcus Welby, M.D.* (ABC)

OUTSTANDING PERFORMANCE BY AN ACTRESS IN A SUPPORTING ROLE IN DRAMA: Gail Fisher, *Mannix* (CBS)

OUTSTANDING PERFORMANCE BY AN ACTOR IN A SUPPORTING ROLE IN COMEDY: Michael Constantine, *Room 222* (ABC)

OUTSTANDING PERFORMANCE BY AN ACTRESS IN A SUPPORTING ROLE IN COMEDY: Karen Valentine, *Room 222* (ABC)

OUTSTANDING WRITING ACHIEVEMENT IN DRAMA: Richard Levinson and William Link, "My Sweet Charlie," *NBC World Premiere Movie* (NBC)

OUTSTANDING WRITING ACHIEVEMENT IN COMEDY, VARIETY, OR MUSIC: Gary Belkin, Peter Bellwood, Herb Sargent, Thomas Meehan, and Judith Viorst, "Annie, the Women in the Life of a Man" (CBS)

OUTSTANDING DIRECTORIAL ACHIEVEMENT IN DRAMA: Paul Bogart, "Shadow Game," *CBS Playhouse* (CBS)

OUTSTANDING DIRECTORIAL ACHIEVEMENT IN COMEDY, VARIETY, OR MUSIC: Dwight Hemion, "The Sound of Burt Bacharach," *Kraft Music Hall* (NBC)

SPECIAL CLASSIFICATION OF OUTSTANDING PROGRAM AND INDIVIDUAL ACHIEVEMENT: *Wild Kingdom*, Don Meier, producer (NBC)

OUTSTANDING ACHIEVEMENT WITHIN REGULARLY SCHEDULED NEWS PROGRAMS: "An Investigation of Teenage Drug Addiction—Odyssey House," *The Huntley-Brinkley Report*, Wallace Westfeldt, executive producer; Les Crystal, producer (NBC). "Can the World Be Saved?" *The CBS Evening News with Walter Cronkite*, Ronald Bonn, producer (CBS)

OUTSTANDING ACHIEVEMENT IN MAGAZINE-TYPE PROGRAMMING: *Black Journal*, William Greaves, executive producer (NET); Tom Pettit, reporter-writer, "Some Footnotes to 25 Nuclear Years," *First Tuesday* (NBC)

OUTSTANDING ACHIEVEMENT IN NEWS DOCUMENTARY PROGRAMMING: "Hospital," *NET Journal*, Frederick Wiseman, producer (NET). "The Making of the President 1968," M. J. Rifkin, executive producer; Mel Stuart, producer (CBS)

OUTSTANDING ACHIEVEMENT IN CULTURAL DOCUMENTARY PROGRAMMING: "Artur Rubinstein," George A. Vicas, producer (NBC). Artur Rubinstein, commentator, "Artur Rubinstein" (NBC). "Fathers and Sons," *CBS News Hour*, Ernest Leiser, executive producer; Harry Morgan, producer (CBS). "The Japanese," *CBS News Hour*, Perry Wolff, executive producer; Igor Oganesoff, producer (CBS). Edwin O. Reischauer, commentator, "The Japanese," *CBS News Hour* (CBS)

1970–1971 (presented May 9, 1971)

OUTSTANDING SERIES—COMEDY: *All in the Family*, Norman Lear, producer (CBS)

OUTSTANDING SERIES—DRAMA: *The Senator* [*The Bold Ones*], David Levinson, producer (NBC)

OUTSTANDING SINGLE PROGRAM—DRAMA OR COMEDY: "The Andersonville Trial," *Hollywood Television Theatre*, Lewis Freedman, producer (PBS)

OUTSTANDING VARIETY SERIES—MUSICAL: *The Flip Wilson Show*, Monte Kay, executive producer; Bob Henry, producer (NBC)

OUTSTANDING VARIETY SERIES—TALK: *The David Frost Show*, Peter Baker, producer (syndicated)

OUTSTANDING SINGLE PROGRAM—VARIETY OR MUSICAL (VARIETY AND POPULAR MUSIC): "Singer Presents Burt Bacharach," Gary Smith and Dwight Hemion, producers (CBS)

OUTSTANDING SINGLE PROGRAM—VARIETY OR MUSICAL (CLASSICAL MUSIC): "Leopold Stokowski," *NET Festival*, Curtis W. Davis, executive producer; Thomas Stevin, producer (PBS)

OUTSTANDING NEW SERIES: *All in the Family*, Norman Lear, producer (CBS)

OUTSTANDING SINGLE PERFORMANCE BY AN ACTOR IN A LEADING ROLE: George C. Scott, "The Price," *Hallmark Hall of Fame* (NBC)

OUTSTANDING SINGLE PERFORMANCE BY AN ACTRESS IN A LEADING ROLE: Lee Grant, "The Neon Ceiling," *World Premiere NBC Monday Night at the Movies* (NBC)

OUTSTANDING CONTINUED PERFORMANCE BY AN ACTOR IN A LEADING ROLE IN A DRAMATIC SERIES: Hal Holbrook, *The Senator* [*The Bold Ones*] (NBC)

OUTSTANDING CONTINUED PERFORMANCE BY AN ACTRESS IN A LEADING ROLE

IN A DRAMATIC SERIES: Susan Hampshire, *The First Churchills* [*Masterpiece Theatre*] (PBS)

OUTSTANDING CONTINUED PERFORMANCE BY AN ACTOR IN A LEADING ROLE IN A COMEDY SERIES: Jack Klugman, *The Odd Couple* (ABC)

OUTSTANDING CONTINUED PERFORMANCE BY AN ACTRESS IN A LEADING ROLE IN A COMEDY SERIES: Jean Stapleton, *All in the Family* (CBS)

OUTSTANDING PERFORMANCE BY AN ACTOR IN A SUPPORTING ROLE IN DRAMA: David Burns, "The Price," *Hallmark Hall of Fame* (NBC)

OUTSTANDING PERFORMANCE BY AN ACTRESS IN A SUPPORTING ROLE IN DRAMA: Margaret Leighton, "Hamlet," *Hallmark Hall of Fame* (NBC)

OUTSTANDING PERFORMANCE BY AN ACTOR IN A SUPPORTING ROLE IN COMEDY: Edward Asner, *The Mary Tyler Moore Show* (CBS)

OUTSTANDING PERFORMANCE BY AN ACTRESS IN A SUPPORTING ROLE IN COMEDY: Valerie Harper, *The Mary Tyler Moore Show* (CBS)

OUTSTANDING DIRECTORIAL ACHIEVEMENT IN DRAMA (SERIES): Daryl Duke, "The Day the Lion Died," *The Senator* [*The Bold Ones*] (NBC)

OUTSTANDING DIRECTORIAL ACHIEVEMENT IN DRAMA (SINGLE PROGRAM): Fielder Cook, "The Price," *Hallmark Hall of Fame* (NBC)

OUTSTANDING DIRECTORIAL ACHIEVEMENT IN COMEDY (SERIES): Jay Sandrich, "Toulouse-Lautrec Is One of My Favorite Artists," *The Mary Tyler Moore Show* (CBS)

OUTSTANDING DIRECTORIAL ACHIEVEMENT IN VARIETY OR MUSIC (SERIES): Mark Warren, *Rowan and Martin's Laugh-In*, 10/26/70 (NBC)

OUTSTANDING DIRECTORIAL ACHIEVEMENT IN VARIETY OR MUSIC (SPECIAL): Sterling Johnson, "Timex Presents Peggy Fleming at Sun Valley" (NBC)

OUTSTANDING WRITING ACHIEVEMENT IN DRAMA (SERIES): Joel Oliansky, "To Taste of Death But Once," *The Senator* [*The Bold Ones*] (NBC)

OUTSTANDING WRITING ACHIEVEMENT IN DRAMA, ORIGINAL TELEPLAY (SPECIAL): Tracy Keenan Wynn and Marvin Schwartz, "Tribes," *Movie of the Week* (ABC)

OUTSTANDING WRITING ACHIEVEMENT IN DRAMA, ADAPTATION (SPECIAL): Saul Levitt, "The Andersonville Trial" (PBS)

OUTSTANDING WRITING ACHIEVEMENT IN COMEDY (SERIES): James L. Brooks and Allan Burns, "Support Your Local Mother," *The Mary Tyler Moore Show* (CBS)

OUTSTANDING WRITING ACHIEVEMENT IN VARIETY OR MUSIC (SERIES): Herbert Baker, Hal Goodman, Larry Klein, Bob Weiskopf, Bob Schiller, Norman Steinberg, and Flip Wilson, *The Flip Wilson Show*, with Lena Horne and Tony Randall, 12/10/70 (NBC)

OUTSTANDING WRITING ACHIEVEMENT IN COMEDY, VARIETY, OR MUSIC (SPECIAL): Bob Ellison and Marty Farrell, "Singer Presents Burt Bacharach" (CBS)

OUTSTANDING ACHIEVEMENT WITHIN REGULARLY SCHEDULED NEWS PROGRAMS (PROGRAMS): "Five Part Investigation of Welfare," *The NBC Nightly News*, Wallace Westfeldt, executive producer; David Teitelbaum, producer (NBC)

OUTSTANDING ACHIEVEMENT WITHIN REGULARLY SCHEDULED NEWS PROGRAMS (INDIVIDUALS): Bruce Morton, correspondent, "Reports from the Lt. Calley Trial," *The CBS Evening News with Walter Cronkite* (CBS)

OUTSTANDING ACHIEVEMENT IN NEWS DOCUMENTARY PROGRAMMING (PROGRAMS): "The Selling of the Pentagon," Perry Wolff, executive producer; Peter Davis, producer (CBS). "The World of Charlie Company," Ernest Leiser, executive producer; Russ Bensley, producer (CBS). "NBC White Paper: Pollution Is a Matter of Choice," Fred Freed, producer (NBC)

OUTSTANDING ACHIEVEMENT IN NEWS DOCUMENTARY PROGRAMMING (INDIVIDUALS): John Laurence, correspondent, "The World of Charlie Company" (CBS); Fred Freed, writer, "NBC News White Paper: Pollution Is a Matter of Choice" (NBC)

OUTSTANDING ACHIEVEMENT IN MAGAZINE-TYPE PROGRAMMING (PROGRAMS): "Gulf of Tonkin Segment," *60 Minutes*, Joseph Wershba, producer; *The Great American Dream Machine*, A. H. Perlmutter and Jack Willis, executive producers (PBS)

OUTSTANDING ACHIEVEMENT IN MAGAZINE-TYPE PROGRAMMING (INDIVIDUALS): Mike Wallace, correspondent, *60 Minutes* (CBS)

OUTSTANDING ACHIEVEMENT IN CULTURAL DOCUMENTARY PROGRAMMING (PROGRAMS): "The Everglades," Craig Fisher, producer (NBC); "The Making of Butch Cassidy & the Sundance Kid," Ronald Preissman, producer (NBC); "Arthur Penn, 1922–: Themes and Variants," Robert Hughes, producer (PBS)

OUTSTANDING ACHIEVEMENT IN CULTURAL DOCUMENTARY PROGRAMMING (INDIVIDUALS): Nana Mahomo, narrator, "A Black View of South Africa" (CBS); Robert Guenette and Theodore H. Strauss, writers, "They've Killed President Lincoln" (NBC); Robert Young, director, "The Eskimo: Fight for Life" (CBS)

SPECIAL CLASSIFICATION OF OUTSTANDING INDIVIDUAL ACHIEVEMENT: Harvey Korman, *The Carol Burnett Show* (CBS)

1971–1972 (presented May 6, 1972)

OUTSTANDING SERIES—COMEDY: *All in the Family*, Norman Lear, producer (CBS)

OUTSTANDING SERIES—DRAMA: *Elizabeth R* [*Masterpiece Theatre*], Christopher Sarson, executive producer; Roderick Graham, producer (PBS)

OUTSTANDING SINGLE PROGRAM—DRAMA OR COMEDY: "Brian's Song," *Movie of the Week*, Paul Junger Witt, producer (ABC)

OUTSTANDING VARIETY SERIES—MUSICAL: *The Carol Burnett Show*, Joe Hamilton, executive producer; Arnie Rosen, producer (CBS)

OUTSTANDING VARIETY SERIES—TALK: *The Dick Cavett Show*, John Gilroy, producer (ABC)

OUTSTANDING SINGLE PROGRAM (VARIETY AND POPULAR MUSIC): "Jack Lemmon in 'S Wonderful, 'S Marvelous, 'S Gershwin," *Bell System Family Theatre*, Joseph Cates, executive producer; Martin Charnin, producer (NBC)

OUTSTANDING SINGLE PROGRAM (CLASSICAL MUSIC): "Beethoven's Birthday: A Celebration in Vienna with Leonard Bernstein," James Krayer, executive producer; Humphrey Burton, producer (CBS)

OUTSTANDING NEW SERIES: *Elizabeth R* [*Masterpiece Theatre*], Christopher Sarson, executive producer; Roderick Graham, producer (PBS)

OUTSTANDING SINGLE PERFORMANCE BY AN ACTOR IN A LEADING ROLE: Keith Mitchell, "Catherine Howard," *The Six Wives of Henry VIII* (CBS)

OUTSTANDING SINGLE PERFORMANCE BY AN ACTRESS IN A LEADING ROLE: Glenda Jackson, "Shadow in the Sun," *Elizabeth R* [*Masterpiece Theatre*] (PBS)

OUTSTANDING CONTINUED PERFORMANCE BY AN ACTOR IN A LEADING ROLE IN A DRAMATIC SERIES: Peter Falk, *Columbo* [*NBC Mystery Movie*] (NBC)

OUTSTANDING CONTINUED PERFORMANCE BY AN ACTRESS IN A LEADING ROLE IN A DRAMATIC SERIES: Glenda Jackson, *Elizabeth R* [*Masterpiece Theatre*] (PBS)

OUTSTANDING CONTINUED PERFORMANCE BY AN ACTOR IN A LEADING ROLE IN A COMEDY SERIES: Carroll O'Connor, *All in the Family* (CBS)

OUTSTANDING CONTINUED PERFORMANCE BY AN ACTRESS IN A LEADING ROLE IN A COMEDY SERIES: Jean Stapleton, *All in the Family* (CBS)

OUTSTANDING PERFORMANCE BY AN ACTOR IN A SUPPORTING ROLE IN DRAMA: Jack Warden, "Brian's Song," *Movie of the Week* (ABC)

OUTSTANDING PERFORMANCE BY AN ACTRESS IN A SUPPORTING ROLE IN DRAMA: Jenny Agutter, "The Snow Goose," *Hallmark Hall of Fame* (NBC)

OUTSTANDING PERFORMANCE BY AN ACTOR IN A SUPPORTING ROLE IN COMEDY: Edward Asner, *The Mary Tyler Moore Show* (CBS)

OUTSTANDING PERFORMANCE BY AN ACTRESS IN A SUPPORTING ROLE IN COMEDY: (TIE) Valerie Harper, *The Mary Tyler Moore Show* (CBS); Sally Struthers, *All in the Family* (CBS)

OUTSTANDING ACHIEVEMENT BY A PERFORMER IN MUSIC OR VARIETY: Harvey Korman, *The Carol Burnett Show* (CBS)

OUTSTANDING ACHIEVEMENT WITHIN REGULARLY SCHEDULED NEWS PROGRAMS (PROGRAMS): "Defeat of Dacca," *The NBC Nightly News*, Wallace Westfeldt, executive producer; Robert Mulholland and David Teitelbaum, producers (NBC)

OUTSTANDING ACHIEVEMENT WITHIN REGULARLY SCHEDULED NEWS PRO-

GRAMS (INDIVIDUALS): Phil Brady, reporter, "Defeat of Dacca," *The NBC Nightly News* (NBC); Bob Schieffer, Phil Jones, Don Webster, and Bill Plante, correspondents, "The Air War," *The CBS Evening News with Walter Cronkite* (CBS)

OUTSTANDING ACHIEVEMENT FOR REGULARLY SCHEDULED MAGAZINE-TYPE PROGRAMS (PROGRAMS): *The Great American Dream Machine,* A. H. Perlmutter, executive producer (PBS); *Chronolog,* Eliot Frankel, executive producer (NBC)

OUTSTANDING ACHIEVEMENT FOR REGULARLY SCHEDULED MAGAZINE-TYPE PROGRAMS (INDIVIDUALS): Mike Wallace, correspondent, *60 Minutes* (CBS)

OUTSTANDING DOCUMENTARY PROGRAM ACHIEVEMENT (PROGRAMS OF CURRENT SIGNIFICANCE): "A Night in Jail, A Night in Court," *CBS Reports,* Burton Benjamin, executive producer; John Sharnik, producer (CBS). "This Child Is Rated X: An NBC News White Paper on Juvenile Justice," Martin Carr, producer (NBC)

OUTSTANDING DOCUMENTARY PROGRAM ACHIEVEMENT (CULTURAL PROGRAMS): "Hollywood: The Dream Factory," *The Monday Night Special,* Nicolas Noxon, executive producer; Irwin Rosten and Bud Friedman, producers (ABC). "A Sound of Dolphins," *The Undersea World of Jacques Cousteau,* Jacques Cousteau and Marshall Flaum, executive producers; Andy White, producer (ABC). "The Unsinkable Sea Otter," *The Undersea World of Jacques Cousteau,* Jacques Cousteau and Marshall Flaum, executive producers; Andy White, producer (ABC)

OUTSTANDING DOCUMENTARY PROGRAM ACHIEVEMENT (INDIVIDUALS): Louis J. Hazam, writer, "Venice Be Damned" (NBC); Robert Northshield, writer, "Suffer the Little Children—An ABC News White Paper on Northern Ireland" (NBC)

OUTSTANDING DIRECTORIAL ACHIEVEMENT IN DRAMA (SERIES): Alexander Singer, "The Invasion of Kevin Ireland," *The Lawyers* [*The Bold Ones*] (NBC)

OUTSTANDING DIRECTORIAL ACHIEVEMENT IN DRAMA (SINGLE PROGRAM): Tom Gries, "The Glass House," *The New CBS Friday Night Movies* (CBS)

OUTSTANDING DIRECTORIAL ACHIEVEMENT IN COMEDY (SERIES): John Rich, "Sammy's Visit," *All in the Family* (CBS)

OUTSTANDING DIRECTORIAL ACHIEVEMENT IN VARIETY OR MUSIC (SERIES): Art Fisher, *The Sonny and Cher Comedy Hour,* with Tony Randall, 1/31/72 (CBS)

OUTSTANDING DIRECTORIAL ACHIEVEMENT IN COMEDY, VARIETY, OR MUSIC (SPECIAL): Walter C. Miller and Martin Charnin, "Jack Lemmon in 'S Wonderful, 'S Marvelous, 'S Gershwin," *Bell System Family Theatre* (NBC)

OUTSTANDING WRITING ACHIEVEMENT IN DRAMA (SERIES): Richard L. Levinson and William Link, "Death Lends a Hand," *Columbo* [*NBC Mystery Movie*] (NBC)

OUTSTANDING WRITING ACHIEVEMENT IN DRAMA, ORIGINAL TELEPLAY: Allan Sloane "To All My Friends on Shore" (CBS)

OUTSTANDING WRITING ACHIEVEMENT IN DRAMA, ADAPTATION: William Blinn, "Brian's Song," *Movie of the Week* (ABC)

OUTSTANDING WRITING ACHIEVEMENT IN COMEDY (SERIES): Burt Styler, "Edith's Problem," *All in the Family* (CBS)

OUTSTANDING WRITING ACHIEVEMENT IN VARIETY OR MUSIC (SERIES): Don Hinkley; Stan Hart, Larry Siegel, Woody Kling, Roger Beatty, Art Baer, Ben Joelson, Stan Burns, Mike Marmer, and Arnie Rosen, *The Carol Burnett Show,* with Tim Conway and Ray Charles, 1/26/72 (CBS)

OUTSTANDING WRITING ACHIEVEMENT IN COMEDY, VARIETY, OR MUSIC (SPECIAL): Anne Howard Bailey, "The Trial of Mary Lincoln," *NET Opera Theatre* (PBS)

SPECIAL CLASSIFICATION OF OUTSTANDING PROGRAM AND INDIVIDUAL ACHIEVEMENT (GENERAL PROGRAMMING): "The Pentagon Papers," *PBS Special,* David Prowitt, executive producer; Martin Clancy, producer (PBS)

SPECIAL CLASSIFICATION OF OUTSTANDING PROGRAM AND INDIVIDUAL ACHIEVEMENT (DOCU-DRAMA): "The Search for the Nile—Parts I–VI," Christopher Railing, producer (NBC)

SPECIAL CLASSIFICATION OF OUTSTANDING PROGRAM AND INDIVIDUAL ACHIEVEMENT (INDIVIDUALS): Michael Hastings and Derek Marlowe, writers, "The Search for the Nile—Parts I–VI" (NBC)

1972–1973 (presented May 22, 1973)

OUTSTANDING COMEDY SERIES: *All in the Family*, Norman Lear, executive producer; John Rich, producer (CBS)

OUTSTANDING DRAMA SERIES—CONTINUING: *The Waltons*, Lee Rich, executive producer; Robert L. Jacks, producer (CBS)

OUTSTANDING DRAMA/COMEDY—LIMITED EPISODES: *Tom Brown's Schooldays* [*Masterpiece Theatre*], John D. McRae, producer (PBS)

OUTSTANDING VARIETY MUSICAL SERIES: *The Julie Andrews Hour*, Nick Vanoff and William O. Harbach, producers (ABC)

OUTSTANDING SINGLE PROGRAM—DRAMA OR COMEDY: "A War of Children," *The New CBS Tuesday Night Movies*, Roger Gimbel, executive producer; George Schaefer, producer (CBS)

OUTSTANDING SINGLE PROGRAM—VARIETY AND POPULAR MUSIC: "Singer Presents Liza with a 'Z'," Bob Fosse and Fred Ebb, producers (NBC)

OUTSTANDING SINGLE PROGRAM—CLASSICAL MUSIC: "The Sleeping Beauty," J. W. Barnes and Robert Kotlowitz, executive producers; Norman Campbell, producer (PBS)

OUTSTANDING NEW SERIES: *America*, Michael Gill, producer (NBC)

OUTSTANDING SINGLE PERFORMANCE BY AN ACTOR IN A LEADING ROLE: Laurence Olivier, "A Long Day's Journey into Night" (ABC)

OUTSTANDING SINGLE PERFORMANCE BY AN ACTRESS IN A LEADING ROLE: Cloris Leachman, "A Brand New Life," *Tuesday Movie of the Week* (ABC)

OUTSTANDING CONTINUED PERFORMANCE BY AN ACTOR IN A LEADING ROLE (DRAMA SERIES—CONTINUING): Richard Thomas, *The Waltons* (CBS)

OUTSTANDING CONTINUED PERFORMANCE BY AN ACTOR IN A LEADING ROLE (DRAMA/COMEDY—LIMITED EPISODES): Anthony Murphy, *Tom Brown's Schooldays* [*Masterpiece Theatre*] (PBS)

OUTSTANDING CONTINUED PERFORMANCE BY AN ACTRESS IN A LEADING ROLE (DRAMA SERIES—CONTINUING): Michael Learned, *The Waltons* (CBS)

OUTSTANDING CONTINUED PERFORMANCE BY AN ACTRESS IN A LEADING ROLE (DRAMA/COMEDY—LIMITED EPISODES): Susan Hampshire, *Vanity Fair* [*Masterpiece Theatre*] (PBS)

OUTSTANDING CONTINUED PERFORMANCE BY AN ACTOR IN A LEADING ROLE IN A COMEDY SERIES: Jack Klugman, *The Odd Couple* (ABC)

OUTSTANDING CONTINUED PERFORMANCE BY AN ACTRESS IN A LEADING ROLE IN A COMEDY SERIES: Mary Tyler Moore, *The Mary Tyler Moore Show* (CBS)

OUTSTANDING PERFORMANCE BY AN ACTOR IN A SUPPORTING ROLE IN DRAMA: Scott Jacoby, "That Certain Summer," *Wednesday Movie of the Week* (ABC)

OUTSTANDING PERFORMANCE BY AN ACTRESS IN A SUPPORTING ROLE IN DRAMA: Ellen Corby, *The Waltons* (CBS)

OUTSTANDING PERFORMANCE BY AN ACTOR IN A SUPPORTING ROLE IN COMEDY: Ted Knight, *The Mary Tyler Moore Show* (CBS)

OUTSTANDING PERFORMANCE BY AN ACTRESS IN A SUPPORTING ROLE IN COMEDY: Valerie Harper, *The Mary Tyler Moore Show* (CBS)

OUTSTANDING ACHIEVEMENT BY A SUPPORTING PERFORMER IN MUSIC OR VARIETY: Tim Conway, *The Carol Burnett Show*, 2/17/73 (CBS)

OUTSTANDING DIRECTORIAL ACHIEVEMENT IN DRAMA (SERIES): Jerry Thorpe, "An Eye for an Eye," *Kung Fu* (ABC)

OUTSTANDING DIRECTORIAL ACHIEVEMENT IN DRAMA (SINGLE PROGRAM): Joseph Sargent, "The Marcus-Nelson Murders," *The CBS Thursday Night Movies* (CBS)

OUTSTANDING DIRECTORIAL ACHIEVEMENT IN COMEDY (SERIES): Jay Sandrich, "It's Whether You Win or Lose," *The Mary Tyler Moore Show* (CBS)

OUTSTANDING DIRECTORIAL ACHIEVEMENT IN VARIETY OR MUSIC (SERIES): Bill Davis, *The Julie Andrews Hour*, with "Liza Doolittle" and "Mary Poppins," 9/13/72 (ABC)

OUTSTANDING DIRECTORIAL ACHIEVEMENT IN VARIETY OR MUSIC (SPECIAL): Bob Fosse, "Singer Presents Liza with a 'Z' " (NBC)

OUTSTANDING WRITING ACHIEVEMENT IN DRAMA (SERIES): John McGreevey, "The Scholar," *The Waltons* (CBS)

OUTSTANDING WRITING ACHIEVEMENT IN DRAMA, ORIGINAL TELEPLAY (SINGLE PROGRAM): Abby Mann, "The Marcus-Nelson Murders," *The CBS Thursday Night Movies* (CBS)

OUTSTANDING WRITING ACHIEVEMENT IN DRAMA, ADAPTATION (SINGLE PROGRAM): Eleanor Perry, "The House without a Christmas Tree" (CBS)

OUTSTANDING WRITING ACHIEVEMENT IN COMEDY (SERIES): Michael Ross, Bernie West, and Lee Kalcheim, "The Bunkers and the Swingers," *All in the Family* (CBS)

OUTSTANDING WRITING ACHIEVEMENT IN VARIETY OR MUSIC (SERIES): Stan Hart, Larry Siegel, Gail Parent, Woody Kling, Roger Beatty, Tom Patchett, Jay Tarses, Robert Hilliard, Arnie Kogen, Bill Angelos, and Buz Kohan, *The Carol Burnett Show*, with Steve Lawrence and Lily Tomlin, 11/8/72 (CBS)

OUTSTANDING WRITING ACHIEVEMENT IN COMEDY, VARIETY, OR MUSIC (SPECIAL): Renee Taylor and Joseph Bologna, "Acts of Love—And Other Comedies" (ABC)

OUTSTANDING ACHIEVEMENT WITHIN REGULARLY SCHEDULED NEWS PROGRAMS (PROGRAM SEGMENTS): "The U.S./Soviet Wheat Deal: Is There a Scandal?" *The CBS Evening News with Walter Cronkite*, Paul Greenberg and Russ Bensley, executive producers; Stanhope Gould and Linda Mason, producers (CBS)

OUTSTANDING ACHIEVEMENT WITHIN REGULARLY SCHEDULED NEWS PROGRAMS (INDIVIDUALS): Walter Cronkite, Dan Rather, Daniel Schorr, and Joel Blocker, correspondents, "The Watergate Affair," *CBS Evening News with Walter Cronkite* (CBS); David Dick, Dan Rather, Roger Mudd, and Walter Cronkite, correspondents, "Coverage of the Shooting of Governor Wallace," *CBS Evening News with Walter Cronkite* (CBS); Eric Sevareid, correspondent, "LBJ—The Man and the President," *CBS Evening News with Walter Cronkite* (CBS)

OUTSTANDING ACHIEVEMENT FOR REGULARLY SCHEDULED MAGAZINE-TYPE PROGRAMS (PROGRAMS): "Poppy Fields of Turkey—The Heroin Labs of Marseilles—The New York Connection," *60 Minutes*, Don Hewitt, executive producer; William McClure, John Tiffin, and Philip Scheffler, producers (CBS). "The Selling of Colonel Herbert," *60 Minutes*, Don Hewitt, executive producer; Barry Lando, producer (CBS). *60 Minutes*, Don Hewitt, executive producer (CBS)

OUTSTANDING ACHIEVEMENT FOR REGULARLY SCHEDULED MAGAZINE-TYPE PROGRAMS (INDIVIDUALS): Mike Wallace, correspondent, "The Selling of Colonel Herbert," *60 Minutes* (CBS); Mike Wallace, correspondent, *60 Minutes* (CBS)

OUTSTANDING ACHIEVEMENT IN COVERAGE OF SPECIAL EVENTS (INDIVIDUALS): Jim McKay, commentator, "Coverage of the Munich Olympic Tragedy," *ABC Special* (ABC)

OUTSTANDING DOCUMENTARY PROGRAM ACHIEVEMENT (CURRENT EVENTS): "The Blue Collar Trap," *NBC News White Paper*, Fred Freed, producer (NBC). "The Mexican Connection," *CBS Reports*, Burton Benjamin, executive producer; Jay McMullen, producer (CBS). "One Billion Dollar Weapon and Now the War Is Over—The American Military in the 1970's," *NBC Reports*, Fred Freed, executive producer; Al Davis, producer (NBC)

OUTSTANDING DOCUMENTARY PROGRAM ACHIEVEMENT (CULTURAL): *America*, Michael Gill, executive producer (NBC). "Jane Goodall and the World of Animal Behavior—The Wild Dogs of Africa," Marshall Flaum, executive producer; Hugo Van Lawick, Bill Travers, and James Hill, producers (ABC)

OUTSTANDING DOCUMENTARY PROGRAM ACHIEVEMENT (INDIVIDUALS): Alistair Cooke, narrator, *America* (NBC); Alistair Cooke, writer, "A Fireball in the Night," *America* (NBC); Hugo Van Lawick, director, "Jane Goodall and the World of Animal Behavior—The Wild Dogs of Africa" (ABC)

SPECIAL CLASSIFICATION OF OUTSTANDING PROGRAM AND INDIVIDUAL ACHIEVEMENT: *The Advocates*, Greg Harney, executive producer; Tom Burrows,

Russ Morash, and Peter McGhee, producers (PBS). "VD Blues," *The Special of the Week*, Don Fouser, producer (PBS)

1973–1974 (presented May 28, 1974)

OUTSTANDING COMEDY SERIES: *M*A*S*H*, Gene Reynolds and Larry Gelbart, producers (CBS)

OUTSTANDING DRAMA SERIES: *Upstairs, Downstairs* [*Masterpiece Theatre*], Rex Firkin, executive producer; John Hawkesworth, producer (PBS)

OUTSTANDING MUSIC-VARIETY SERIES: *The Carol Burnett Show*, Joe Hamilton, executive producer; Ed Simmons, producer (CBS)

OUTSTANDING LIMITED SERIES: *Columbo* [*NBC Sunday Mystery Movie*], Dean Hargrove and Roland Kibbee, executive producers; Douglas Benton, Robert F. O'Neill, and Edward K. Dodds, producers (NBC)

OUTSTANDING SPECIAL—COMEDY OR DRAMA (SINGLE SPECIAL PROGRAM): "The Autobiography of Miss Jane Pittman," Robert Christiansen and Rick Rosenberg, producers (CBS)

OUTSTANDING COMEDY-VARIETY, VARIETY, OR MUSIC SPECIAL (SINGLE SPECIAL PROGRAM): "Lily," Irene Pinn, executive producer; Herb Sargent and Jerry McPhie, producers (CBS)

OUTSTANDING CHILDREN'S SPECIAL (EVENING): "Marlo Thomas and Friends in Free to Be . . . You and Me," Marlo Thomas and Carole Hart, producers (ABC)

BEST LEAD ACTOR IN A COMEDY SERIES: Alan Alda, *M*A*S*H* (CBS)

BEST LEAD ACTOR IN A DRAMA SERIES: Telly Savalas, *Kojak* (CBS)

BEST LEAD ACTOR IN A LIMITED SERIES: William Holden, *The Blue Knight* (NBC)

BEST LEAD ACTOR IN A DRAMA (FOR A SPECIAL PROGRAM—COMEDY OR DRAMA; OR A SINGLE APPEARANCE IN A COMEDY OR DRAMA SERIES): Hal Holbrook, "Pueblo," *ABC Theatre* (ABC)

ACTOR OF THE YEAR—SERIES: Alan Alda, *M*A*S*H* (CBS)

ACTOR OF THE YEAR—SPECIAL: Hal Holbrook, "Pueblo," *ABC Theatre* (ABC)

BEST LEAD ACTRESS IN A COMEDY SERIES: Mary Tyler Moore, *The Mary Tyler Moore Show* (CBS)

BEST LEAD ACTRESS IN A DRAMA SERIES: Michael Learned, *The Waltons* (CBS)

BEST LEAD ACTRESS IN A LIMITED SERIES: Mildred Natwick, *The Snoop Sisters* [*NBC Tuesday Mystery Movie*] (NBC)

BEST LEAD ACTRESS IN A DRAMA (FOR A SPECIAL PROGRAM—COMEDY OR DRAMA; OR A SINGLE APPEARANCE IN A COMEDY OR DRAMA SERIES): Cicely Tyson, "The Autobiography of Miss Jane Pittman" (CBS)

ACTRESS OF THE YEAR—SERIES: Mary Tyler Moore, *The Mary Tyler Moore Show* (CBS)

ACTRESS OF THE YEAR—SPECIAL: Cicely Tyson, "The Autobiography of Miss Jane Pittman" (CBS)

BEST SUPPORTING ACTOR IN COMEDY (FOR A SPECIAL PROGRAM; A ONE-TIME APPEARANCE IN A SERIES; OR A CONTINUING ROLE): Rob Reiner, *All in the Family* (CBS)

BEST SUPPORTING ACTOR IN DRAMA (FOR A SPECIAL PROGRAM; A ONE-TIME APPEARANCE IN A SERIES; OR A CONTINUING ROLE): Michael Moriarty, "The Glass Menagerie" (ABC)

BEST SUPPORTING ACTOR IN COMEDY-VARIETY, VARIETY, OR MUSIC (FOR A SPECIAL PROGRAM; A ONE-TIME APPEARANCE IN A SERIES; OR A CONTINUING ROLE): Harvey Korman, *The Carol Burnett Show* (CBS)

SUPPORTING ACTOR OF THE YEAR: Michael Moriarty, "The Glass Menagerie" (ABC)

BEST SUPPORTING ACTRESS IN COMEDY (FOR A SPECIAL PROGRAM; A ONE-TIME APPEARANCE IN A SERIES; OR A CONTINUING ROLE): Cloris Leachman, "The Lars Affair," *The Mary Tyler Moore Show*, 9/15/73 (CBS)

BEST SUPPORTING ACTRESS IN DRAMA (FOR A SPECIAL PROGRAM; A ONE-TIME APPEARANCE IN A SERIES; OR A CONTINUING ROLE): Joanna Miles, "The Glass Menagerie" (ABC)

BEST SUPPORTING ACTRESS IN COMEDY-VARIETY, VARIETY, OR MUSIC (FOR A SPECIAL PROGRAM; A ONE-TIME APPEARANCE IN A SERIES; OR A CONTINUING ROLE): Brenda Vaccaro, "The Shape of Things" (CBS)

SUPPORTING ACTRESS OF THE YEAR: Joanna Miles, "The Glass Menagerie" (ABC)

BEST DIRECTING IN DRAMA (A SINGLE PROGRAM OF A SERIES WITH CONTINUING CHARACTERS AND/OR THEME): Robert Butler, *The Blue Knight*, Part III, 11/15/73 (NBC)

BEST DIRECTING IN DRAMA (A SINGLE PROGRAM—COMEDY OR DRAMA): John Korty, "The Autobiography of Miss Jane Pittman" (CBS)

BEST DIRECTING IN COMEDY (A SINGLE PROGRAM OF A SERIES WITH CONTINUING CHARACTERS AND/OR THEME): Jackie Cooper, "Carry On Hawkeye," *M*A*S*H*, 11/24/73 (CBS)

BEST DIRECTING IN VARIETY OR MUSIC (A SINGLE PROGRAM OF A SERIES): Dave Powers, "The Australia Show," *The Carol Burnett Show*, 12/8/73 (CBS)

BEST DIRECTING IN COMEDY-VARIETY, VARIETY, OR MUSIC (A SPECIAL PROGRAM): Dwight Hemion, "Barbra Streisand . . . And Other Musical Instruments" (CBS)

DIRECTOR OF THE YEAR—SERIES: Robert Butler, *The Blue Knight*, Part III, 11/15/73 (NBC)

DIRECTOR OF THE YEAR—SPECIAL: Dwight Hemion, "Barbra Streisand . . . And Other Musical Instruments" (CBS)

BEST WRITING IN DRAMA (A SINGLE PROGRAM OF A SERIES WITH CONTINUING CHARACTERS AND/OR THEME): Joanna Lee, "The Thanksgiving Story," *The Waltons*, 11/15/73 (CBS)

BEST WRITING IN DRAMA, ORIGINAL TELEPLAY (A SINGLE PROGRAM—COMEDY OR DRAMA): Fay Kanin, "Tell Me Where It Hurts," *G.E. Theater* (CBS)

BEST WRITING IN DRAMA, ADAPTATION (A SINGLE PROGRAM—COMEDY OR DRAMA): Tracy Keenan Wynn, "The Autobiography of Miss Jane Pittman" (CBS)

BEST WRITING IN COMEDY (A SINGLE PROGRAM OF A SERIES WITH CONTINUING CHARACTERS AND/OR THEME): Treva Silverman, "The Lou and Edie Story," *The Mary Tyler Moore Show*, 10/6/73 (CBS)

BEST WRITING IN VARIETY OR MUSIC (A SINGLE PROGRAM OF A SERIES): Ed Simmons, Gary Belkin, Roger Beatty, Arnie Kogen, Bill Richmond, Gene Perret, Rudy De Luca, Barry Levinson, Dick Clair, Jenna McMahon, and Barry Harman, *The Carol Burnett Show*, with Tim Conway and Bernadette Peters, 2/16/74 (CBS)

BEST WRITING IN COMEDY-VARIETY, VARIETY, OR MUSIC (A SPECIAL PROGRAM): Herb Sargent, Rosalyn Drexler, Lorne Michaels, Richard Pryor, Jim Rusk, James R. Stein, Robert Illes, Lily Tomlin, George Yanok, Jane Wagner, Rod Warren, Ann Elder, and Karyl Geld, "Lily" (CBS)

WRITER OF THE YEAR—SERIES: Treva Silverman, "The Lou and Edie Story," *The Mary Tyler Moore Show*, 10/6/73 (CBS)

WRITER OF THE YEAR—SPECIAL: Fay Kanin, "Tell Me Where It Hurts," *G.E. Theater* (CBS)

SPECIAL CLASSIFICATION OF OUTSTANDING PROGRAM AND INDIVIDUAL ACHIEVEMENT: *The Dick Cavett Show*, John Gilroy, producer (ABC); Tom Snyder, host, *Tomorrow* (NBC)

OUTSTANDING INDIVIDUAL ACHIEVEMENT IN CHILDREN'S PROGRAMMING: Charles M. Schultz, writer, "A Charlie Brown Thanksgiving" (CBS)

OUTSTANDING ACHIEVEMENT WITHIN REGULARLY SCHEDULED NEWS PROGRAMS: "Coverage of the October War from Israel's Northern Front," *CBS Evening News with Walter Cronkite*, John Laurence, correspondent, October 1973 (CBS). "The Agnew Resignation," *CBS Evening News with Walter Cronkite*, Paul Greenberg, executive producer; Ron Bonn, Ed Fouhy, John Lane, Don Bowers, John Armstrong, and Robert Mean, producers; Walter Cronkite, Robert Schakne, Fred Graham, Robert Pierpoint, Roger Mudd, Dan Rather, John Hart, and Eric Sevareid, correspondents, 10/10/73 (CBS). "The Key Biscayne Bank Charter Struggle," *CBS Evening News with Walter Cronkite*, Ed Fouhy, producer; Robert Pierpoint, correspondent, 10/15–10/17/73 (CBS). "Reports on World Hunger," *NBC Nightly News*, Lester M. Crystal, executive producer;

Richard Fischer and Joseph Angotti, producers; Tom Streithorst, Phil Brady, John Palmer, and Liz Trotta, correspondents, March–June 1974 (NBC)

OUTSTANDING ACHIEVEMENT FOR REGULARLY SCHEDULED MAGAZINE-TYPE PROGRAMS: "America's Nerve Gas Arsenal," *First Tuesday*, Eliot Frankel, executive producer; William B. Hill and Anthony Potter, producers; Tom Pettit, correspondent, 6/5/73 (NBC). "The Adversaries," *Behind the Lines*, Carey Winfrey, executive producer; Peter Forbath, producer/reporter; Brendan Gill, host/moderator, 3/28/74 (PBS); "A Question of Impeachment," *Bill Moyers' Journal*, Jerome Toobin, executive producer; Martin Clancy, producer; Bill Moyers, broadcaster, 1/22/74 (PBS)

OUTSTANDING DOCUMENTARY PROGRAM ACHIEVEMENTS (CURRENT EVENTS): "Fire!", *ABC News Close Up*, Pamela Hill, producer; Jules Bergman, correspondent/narrator (ABC). "CBS News Special Report: The Senate and the Watergate Affair," Lesley Midgley, executive producer; Hal Haley, Bernard Birnbaum, and David Browning, producers; Dan Rather, Roger Mudd, Daniel Schorr, and Fred Graham, correspondents (CBS)

OUTSTANDING DOCUMENTARY PROGRAM ACHIEVEMENTS (CULTURAL): "Journey to the Outer Limits," *National Geographic Specials*, Nicholas Clapp and Dennis Kane, executive producers; Alex Grasshoff, producer (ABC). *The World at War*, Jeremy Isaacs, producer (syndicated). "CBS Reports: The Rockefellers," Burton Benjamin, executive producer; Howard Stringer, producer; Walter Cronkite, correspondent (CBS)

OUTSTANDING INTERVIEW PROGRAM (FOR A SINGLE PROGRAM OF A SERIES): "Solzhenitsyn," *CBS News Special*, Burton Benjamin, producer; Walter Cronkite, correspondent, 6/24/74 (CBS). "Henry Steele Commager," *Bill Moyers' Journal*, Jerome Toobin, executive producer; Martin Clancy, producer; Bill Moyers, broadcaster, 3/26/74 (PBS)

OUTSTANDING TELEVISION NEWS BROADCASTER: Harry Reasoner, *ABC News* (ABC); Bill Moyers, "Essay on Watergate," *Bill Moyers' Journal*, 10/31/73 (PBS)

1974–1975 (presented May 19, 1975)

OUTSTANDING COMEDY SERIES: *The Mary Tyler Moore Show*, James L. Brooks and Allan Burns, executive producers; Ed Weinburger and Stan Daniels, producers (CBS)

OUTSTANDING DRAMA SERIES: *Upstairs, Downstairs* [*Masterpiece Theatre*], Rex Firkin, executive producer; John Hawkesworth, producer (PBS)

OUTSTANDING COMEDY-VARIETY OR MUSIC SERIES: *The Carol Burnett Show*, Joe Hamilton, executive producer; Ed Simmons, producer (CBS)

OUTSTANDING LIMITED SERIES: *Benjamin Franklin*, Lewis Freedman, executive producer; George Lefferts and Glenn Jordan, producers (CBS)

OUTSTANDING SPECIAL—DRAMA OR COMEDY: "The Law," *NBC World Premiere Movie*, William Sackheim, producer, 10/22/74 (NBC)

OUTSTANDING SPECIAL—COMEDY-VARIETY OR MUSIC: "An Evening with John Denver," Jerry Weintraub, executive producer; Al Rogers and Rich Eustis, producers (ABC)

OUTSTANDING CLASSICAL MUSIC PROGRAM (FOR A SPECIAL PROGRAM OR FOR A SERIES): "Profile in Music: Beverly Sills," *Festival '75*, Patricia Foy, producer, 3/10/75 (PBS)

OUTSTANDING LEAD ACTOR IN A COMEDY SERIES: Tony Randall, *The Odd Couple* (ABC)

OUTSTANDING LEAD ACTOR IN A DRAMA SERIES: Robert Blake, *Baretta* (ABC)

OUTSTANDING LEAD ACTOR IN A LIMITED SERIES: Peter Falk, *Columbo* [*NBC Sunday Mystery Movie*] (NBC)

OUTSTANDING LEAD ACTOR IN A SPECIAL PROGRAM—DRAMA OR COMEDY (FOR A SPECIAL PROGRAM; OR A SINGLE APPEARANCE IN A DRAMA OR COMEDY SERIES): Laurence Olivier, "Love Among the Ruins," *ABC Theatre* (ABC)

OUTSTANDING LEAD ACTRESS IN A COMEDY SERIES: Valerie Harper, *Rhoda* (CBS)

OUTSTANDING LEAD ACTRESS IN A DRAMA SERIES: Jean Marsh, *Upstairs, Downstairs* [*Masterpiece Theatre*] (PBS)

OUTSTANDING LEAD ACTRESS IN A LIMITED SERIES: Jessica Walter, *Amy Prentiss* [*NBC Sunday Mystery Movie*] (NBC)

OUTSTANDING LEAD ACTRESS IN A SPECIAL PROGRAM—DRAMA OR COMEDY (FOR A SPECIAL PROGRAM; OR A SINGLE APPEARANCE IN A DRAMA OR COMEDY SERIES): Katharine Hepburn, "Love Among the Ruins," *ABC Theatre* (ABC)

OUTSTANDING CONTINUING PERFORMANCE BY A SUPPORTING ACTOR IN A COMEDY SERIES: Ed Asner, *The Mary Tyler Moore Show* (CBS)

OUTSTANDING CONTINUING PERFORMANCE BY A SUPPORTING ACTOR IN A DRAMA SERIES: Will Geer, *The Waltons* (CBS)

OUTSTANDING CONTINUING OR SINGLE PERFORMANCE BY A SUPPORTING ACTOR IN VARIETY OR MUSIC (FOR A CONTINUING ROLE IN A REGULAR OR LIMITED SERIES; OR A ONE-TIME APPEARANCE IN A SERIES; OR A SPECIAL): Jack Albertson, *Cher*, 3/2/75 (CBS)

OUTSTANDING SINGLE PERFORMANCE BY A SUPPORTING ACTOR IN A COMEDY OR DRAMA SPECIAL: Anthony Quayle, "QB VII," Parts 1 & 2, *ABC Movie Special* (ABC)

OUTSTANDING SINGLE PERFORMANCE BY A SUPPORTING ACTOR IN A COMEDY OR DRAMA SERIES (FOR A ONE-TIME APPEARANCE IN A REGULAR OR LIMITED SERIES): Patrick McGoohan, "By Dawn's Early Light," *Columbo* [*NBC Sunday Mystery Movie*], 10/27/74 (NBC)

OUTSTANDING CONTINUING PERFORMANCE BY A SUPPORTING ACTRESS IN A COMEDY SERIES: Betty White, *The Mary Tyler Moore Show* (CBS)

OUTSTANDING CONTINUING PERFORMANCE BY A SUPPORTING ACTRESS IN A DRAMA SERIES: Ellen Corby, *The Waltons* (CBS)

OUTSTANDING CONTINUING OR SINGLE PERFORMANCE BY A SUPPORTING ACTRESS IN VARIETY OR MUSIC (FOR A CONTINUING ROLE IN A REGULAR OR LIMITED SERIES; OR A ONE-TIME APPEARANCE IN A SERIES: OR A SPECIAL): Cloris Leachman, *Cher*, 3/2/75 (CBS)

OUTSTANDING SINGLE PERFORMANCE BY A SUPPORTING ACTRESS IN A COMEDY OR DRAMA SPECIAL: Juliet Mills, "QB VII," Parts 1 & 2, *ABC Movie Special* (ABC)

OUTSTANDING SINGLE PERFORMANCE BY A SUPPORTING ACTRESS IN A COMEDY OR DRAMA SERIES (FOR A ONE-TIME APPEARANCE IN A REGULAR OR LIMITED SERIES): (TIE) Cloris Leachman, "Phyllis Whips Inflation," *The Mary Tyler Moore Show*, 1/18/75 (CBS); Zohra Lampert, "Queen of the Gypsies," *Kojak*, 1/19/75 (CBS)

OUTSTANDING DIRECTING IN A DRAMA SERIES (A SINGLE EPISODE OF A REGULAR OR LIMITED SERIES WITH CONTINUING CHARACTERS AND/OR THEME): Bill Bain, "A Sudden Storm," *Upstairs, Downstairs* [*Masterpiece Theatre*], 12/22/74 (PBS)

OUTSTANDING DIRECTING IN A COMEDY SERIES (A SINGLE EPISODE OF A REGULAR OR LIMITED SERIES WITH CONTINUING CHARACTERS AND/OR THEME): Gene Reynolds, "O.R." *M*A*S*H*, 10/8/74 (CBS)

OUTSTANDING DIRECTING IN A COMEDY-VARIETY OR MUSIC SERIES (A SINGLE EPISODE OF A REGULAR OR LIMITED SERIES): Dave Powers, *The Carol Burnett Show*, with Alan Alda, 12/21/74 (CBS)

OUTSTANDING DIRECTING IN A COMEDY-VARIETY OR MUSIC SPECIAL: Bill Davis, "An Evening with John Denver" (ABC)

OUTSTANDING DIRECTING IN A SPECIAL PROGRAM—DRAMA OR COMEDY: George Cukor, "Love Among the Ruins," *ABC Theatre* (ABC)

OUTSTANDING WRITING IN A DRAMA SERIES (A SINGLE EPISODE OF A REGULAR OR LIMITED SERIES WITH CONTINUING CHARACTERS AND/OR THEME): Howard Fast, "The Ambassador," *Benjamin Franklin*, 11/21/74 (CBS)

OUTSTANDING WRITING IN A COMEDY SERIES (A SINGLE EPISODE OF A REGULAR OR LIMITED SERIES WITH CONTINUING CHARACTERS AND/OR THEME): Ed Weinberger and Stan Daniels, "Mary Richards Goes to Jail," *The Mary Tyler Moore Show*, 9/14/74 (CBS)

OUTSTANDING WRITING IN A COMEDY-VARIETY OR MUSIC SERIES (A SINGLE EPISODE OF A REGULAR OR LIMITED SERIES): Ed Simmons, Gary Belkin, Roger Beatty, Arnie Kogen, Bill Richmond, Gene Perret, Rudy DeLuca, Barry Levinson, Dick Clair, and Jenna McMahon *The Carol Burnett Show*, with Alan Alda, 12/21/74 (CBS)

OUTSTANDING WRITING IN A COMEDY-VARIETY OR MUSIC SPECIAL: Bob Wells, John Bradford, and Cy Coleman, "Shirley MacLaine: If They Could See Me Now" (CBS)

OUTSTANDING WRITING IN A SPECIAL PROGRAM—DRAMA OR COMEDY—ORIGINAL TELEPLAY: James Costigan, "Love Among the Ruins," *ABC Theatre* (ABC)

OUTSTANDING WRITING IN A SPECIAL PROGRAM—DRAMA OR COMEDY—ADAPTATION: David W. Rintels, "IBM Presents Clarence Darrow" (NBC)

OUTSTANDING CHILDREN'S SPECIAL (EVENING): "Yes Virginia, There Is a Santa Claus," Burt Rosen, executive producer; Bill Melendez and Mort Green, producers (ABC)

SPECIAL CLASSIFICATION OF OUTSTANDING PROGRAM ACHIEVEMENT: "The American Film Institute Salute to James Cagney," George Stevens, Jr., executive producer; Paul W. Keyes, producer (CBS)

SPECIAL CLASSIFICATION OF OUTSTANDING INDIVIDUAL ACHIEVEMENT: Alistair Cooke, host, *Masterpiece Theatre* (PBS)

1975–1976 (presented May 17, 1976)

OUTSTANDING COMEDY SERIES: *The Mary Tyler Moore Show*, James L. Brooks and Allan Burns, executive producers; Ed Weinberger and Stan Daniels, producers (CBS)

OUTSTANDING DRAMA SERIES: *Police Story*, David Gerber and Stanley Kallis, executive producers; Liam O'Brien and Carl Pingitore, producers (NBC)

OUTSTANDING COMEDY-VARIETY OR MUSIC SERIES: *NBC's Saturday Night Live*, Lorne Michaels, producer (NBC)

OUTSTANDING LIMITED SERIES: *Upstairs, Downstairs* [*Masterpiece Theatre*], Rex Firkin, executive producer; John Hawkesworth, producer (PBS)

OUTSTANDING SPECIAL—DRAMA OR COMEDY: "Eleanor and Franklin," *ABC Theatre*, David Susskind, executive producer; Harry Sherman and Audrey Mass, producers (ABC)

OUTSTANDING SPECIAL—COMEDY-VARIETY OR MUSIC: "Gypsy in My Soul," William O. Harbach, executive producer; Cy Coleman and Fred Ebb, producers (CBS)

OUTSTANDING CLASSICAL MUSIC PROGRAM: "Bernstein and the New York Philharmonic," *Great Performances*, Klaus Hallig and Harry Kraut, executive producers; David Griffiths, producer, 11/26/75 (PBS)

OUTSTANDING LEAD ACTOR IN A COMEDY SERIES: Jack Albertson, *Chico and the Man* (NBC)

OUTSTANDING LEAD ACTOR IN A DRAMA SERIES: Peter Falk, *Columbo* [*NBC Sunday Mystery Movie*] (NBC)

OUTSTANDING LEAD ACTOR IN A LIMITED SERIES: Hal Holbrook, "Sandburg's Lincoln" (NBC)

OUTSTANDING LEAD ACTOR IN A DRAMA OR COMEDY SPECIAL: Anthony Hopkins, "The Lindbergh Kidnapping Case," *NBC World Premiere Movie* (NBC)

OUTSTANDING LEAD ACTOR FOR A SINGLE APPEARANCE IN A DRAMA OR COMEDY SERIES: Edward Asner, *Rich Man, Poor Man*, 2/1/76 (ABC)

OUTSTANDING LEAD ACTRESS IN A COMEDY SERIES: Mary Tyler Moore, *The Mary Tyler Moore Show* (CBS)

OUTSTANDING LEAD ACTRESS IN A DRAMA SERIES: Michael Learned, *The Waltons* (CBS)

OUTSTANDING LEAD ACTRESS IN A LIMITED SERIES: Rosemary Harris, *Notorious Woman* [*Masterpiece Theatre*] (PBS)

OUTSTANDING LEAD ACTRESS IN A DRAMA OR COMEDY SPECIAL: Susan Clark, "Babe" (CBS)

OUTSTANDING LEAD ACTRESS FOR A SINGLE APPEARANCE IN A DRAMA OR COMEDY SERIES: Kathryn Walker, "John Adams, Lawyer," *The Adams Chronicles*, 1/20/76 (PBS)

OUTSTANDING CONTINUING PERFORMANCE BY A SUPPORTING ACTOR IN A COMEDY SERIES: Ted Knight, *The Mary Tyler Moore Show* (CBS)

OUTSTANDING CONTINUING PERFORMANCE BY A SUPPORTING ACTOR IN A DRAMA SERIES: Anthony Zerbe, *Harry-O* (ABC)

OUTSTANDING CONTINUING OR SINGLE PERFORMANCE BY A SUPPORTING ACTOR IN VARIETY OR MUSIC: Chevy Chase, *NBC's Saturday Night Live*, 1/17/76 (NBC)

OUTSTANDING SINGLE PERFORMANCE BY A SUPPORTING ACTOR IN A COMEDY OR DRAMA SPECIAL: Ed Flanders, "A Moon for the Misbegotten," *ABC Theatre* (ABC)

OUTSTANDING SINGLE PERFORMANCE BY A SUPPORTING ACTOR IN A COMEDY OR DRAMA SERIES: Gordon Jackson, "The Beastly Hun," *Upstairs, Downstairs* [*Masterpiece Theatre*], 1/18/76 (PBS)

OUTSTANDING CONTINUING PERFORMANCE BY A SUPPORTING ACTRESS IN A COMEDY SERIES: Betty White, *The Mary Tyler Moore Show* (CBS)

OUTSTANDING CONTINUING PERFORMANCE BY A SUPPORTING ACTRESS IN A DRAMA SERIES: Ellen Corby, *The Waltons* (CBS)

OUTSTANDING CONTINUING OR SINGLE PERFORMANCE BY A SUPPORTING ACTRESS IN VARIETY OR MUSIC: Vicki Lawrence, *The Carol Burnett Show*, 2/7/76 (CBS)

OUTSTANDING SINGLE PERFORMANCE BY A SUPPORTING ACTRESS IN A COMEDY OR DRAMA SPECIAL: Rosemary Murphy, "Eleanor and Franklin," *ABC Theatre* (ABC)

OUTSTANDING SINGLE PERFORMANCE BY A SUPPORTING ACTRESS IN A COMEDY OR DRAMA SERIES: Fionnuala Flanagan, *Rich Man, Poor Man*, 2/2/76 (ABC)

OUTSTANDING DIRECTING IN A DRAMA SERIES (A SINGLE EPISODE OF A REGULAR OR LIMITED SERIES WITH CONTINUING CHARACTERS AND/OR THEME): David Greene, "Episode 8," *Rich Man, Poor Man*, 3/15/76 (ABC)

OUTSTANDING DIRECTING IN A COMEDY SERIES (A SINGLE EPISODE OF A REGULAR OR LIMITED SERIES WITH CONTINUING CHARACTERS AND/OR THEME): Gene Reynolds, "Welcome to Korea," *M*A*S*H*, 9/12/75 (CBS)

OUTSTANDING DIRECTING IN A COMEDY-VARIETY OR MUSIC SERIES (A SINGLE EPISODE OF A REGULAR OR LIMITED SERIES): Dave Wilson, *NBC's Saturday Night Live*, with host Paul Simon, 10/18/75 (NBC)

OUTSTANDING DIRECTING IN A COMEDY-VARIETY OR MUSIC SPECIAL: Dwight Hemion, "Steve and Eydie: 'Our Love Is Here to Stay' " (CBS)

OUTSTANDING DIRECTING IN A SPECIAL PROGRAM—DRAMA OR COMEDY: Daniel Petrie, "Eleanor and Franklin," *ABC Theatre* (ABC)

OUTSTANDING WRITING IN A DRAMA SERIES (A SINGLE EPISODE OF A REGULAR OR LIMITED SERIES WITH CONTINUING CHARACTERS AND/OR THEME): Sherman Yellen, "John Adams, Laywer," *The Adams Chronicles*, 1/20/76 (PBS)

OUTSTANDING WRITING IN A COMEDY SERIES (A SINGLE EPISODE OF A REGULAR OR LIMITED SERIES WITH CONTINUING CHARACTERS AND/OR THEME): David Lloyd, "Chuckles Bites the Dust," *The Mary Tyler Moore Show*, 10/25/75 (CBS)

OUTSTANDING WRITING IN A COMEDY-VARIETY OR MUSIC SERIES (A SINGLE EPISODE OF A REGULAR OR LIMITED SERIES): Anne Beatts, Chevy Chase, Al Franken, Tom Davis, Lorne Michaels, Marilyn Suzanne Miller, Michael O'Donoghue, Herb Sargent, Tom Schiller, Rosie Schuster, and Alan Zweibel, *NBC's Saturday Night Live*, with host Elliott Gould, 1/10/76 (NBC)

OUTSTANDING WRITING IN A COMEDY-VARIETY OR MUSIC SPECIAL: Jane Wagner, Lorne Michaels, Ann Elder, Christopher Guest, Earl Pomerantz, Jim Rusk, Lily Tomlin, Rod Warren, and George Yanok, "Lily Tomlin" (ABC)

OUTSTANDING WRITING IN A SPECIAL PROGRAM—DRAMA OR COMEDY—ORIGINAL TELEPLAY: James Costigan, "Eleanor and Franklin," *ABC Theatre* (ABC)

OUTSTANDING WRITING IN A SPECIAL PROGRAM—DRAMA OR COMEDY—ADAPTATION: David W. Rintels, "Fear on Trial" (CBS)

OUTSTANDING EVENING CHILDREN'S SPECIAL: (TIE) "You're a Good Sport, Charlie Brown," Lee Mendelson, executive producer; Bill Melendez, producer (CBS). "Huckleberry Finn," Steven North, producer (ABC)

SPECIAL CLASSIFICATION OF OUTSTANDING PROGRAM AND INDIVIDUAL ACHIEVEMENT: *Bicentennial Minutes*, Bob Markell, executive producer; Gareth Davies and Paul Walgner, producers (CBS). *The Tonight Show Starring Johnny Carson*, Fred De Cordova, producer (NBC). Ann Marcus, Jerry Adelman, and Daniel Gregory Browne, writers, *Mary Hartman, Mary Hartman* (syndicated)

1976–1977 (presented September 12, 1977)

OUTSTANDING COMEDY SERIES: *The Mary Tyler Moore Show*, Allan Burns and James L. Brooks, executive producers; Ed Weinberger and Stan Daniels, producers (CBS)

OUTSTANDING DRAMA SERIES: *Upstairs, Downstairs* [*Masterpiece Theatre*], John Hawkesworth and Joan Sullivan, producers (PBS)

OUTSTANDING COMEDY-VARIETY OR MUSIC SERIES: *Van Dyke and Company*, Byron Paul, executive producer; Allan Blye and Bob Einstein, producers (NBC)

OUTSTANDING LIMITED SERIES: *Roots* [*ABC Novel for Television*], David L. Wolper, executive producer; Stan Margulies, producer (ABC)

OUTSTANDING SPECIAL—DRAMA OR COMEDY: (TIE) "Eleanor and Franklin: The White House Years," *ABC Theatre*, David Susskind, executive producer; Harry R. Sherman, producer (ABC). "Sybil," *The Big Event/NBC World Premiere Movie*, Peter Dunne and Philip Capice, executive producers; Jacqueline Babbin, producer (NBC)

OUTSTANDING SPECIAL—COMEDY-VARIETY OR MUSIC: "The Barry Manilow Special," Miles Lourie, executive producer; Steve Binder, producer (ABC)

OUTSTANDING CLASSICAL PROGRAM IN THE PERFORMING ARTS: "American Ballet Theatre: Swan Lake Live from Lincoln Center," *Great Performances*, John Goberman, producer, 6/30/76 (PBS)

OUTSTANDING LEAD ACTOR IN A COMEDY SERIES: Carroll O'Connor, *All in the Family* (CBS)

OUTSTANDING LEAD ACTOR IN A DRAMA SERIES: James Garner, *The Rockford Files* (NBC)

OUTSTANDING LEAD ACTOR IN A LIMITED SERIES: Christopher Plummer, "The Moneychangers," *The Big Event/NBC World Premiere Movie* (NBC)

OUTSTANDING LEAD ACTOR IN A DRAMA OR COMEDY SPECIAL: Ed Flanders, "Harry S Truman: Plain Speaking" (PBS)

OUTSTANDING LEAD ACTOR FOR A SINGLE APPEARANCE IN A DRAMA OR COMEDY SERIES: Louis Gossett, Jr., *Roots*—Part Two, 1/24/77 (ABC)

OUTSTANDING LEAD ACTRESS IN A COMEDY SERIES: Beatrice Arthur, *Maude* (CBS)

OUTSTANDING LEAD ACTRESS IN A DRAMA SERIES: Lindsay Wagner, *The Bionic Woman* (ABC)

OUTSTANDING LEAD ACTRESS IN A LIMITED SERIES: Patty Duke Astin, *Captains and the Kings, NBC's Best Sellers* (NBC)

OUTSTANDING LEAD ACTRESS IN A DRAMA OR COMEDY SPECIAL: Sally Field, "Sybil," *The Big Event/NBC World Premiere Movie* (NBC)

OUTSTANDING LEAD ACTRESS FOR A SINGLE APPEARANCE IN A DRAMA OR COMEDY SERIES: Beulah Bondi, "The Pony Cart," *The Waltons*, 12/2/76 (CBS)

OUTSTANDING CONTINUING PERFORMANCE BY A SUPPORTING ACTOR IN A COMEDY SERIES: Gary Burghoff, *M*A*S*H* (CBS)

OUTSTANDING CONTINUING PERFORMANCE BY A SUPPORTING ACTOR IN A DRAMA SERIES: Gary Frank, *Family* (ABC)

OUTSTANDING CONTINUING OR SINGLE PERFORMANCE BY A SUPPORTING ACTOR IN VARIETY OR MUSIC: Tim Conway, *The Carol Burnett Show* (CBS)

OUTSTANDING PERFORMANCE BY A SUPPORTING ACTOR IN A COMEDY OR DRAMA SPECIAL: Burgess Meredith, "Tailgunner Joe," *The Big Event*, 2/6/77 (NBC)

OUTSTANDING SINGLE PERFORMANCE BY A SUPPORTING ACTOR IN A COMEDY OR DRAMA SERIES: Edward Asner, *Roots*—Part One, 1/23/77 (ABC)

OUTSTANDING CONTINUING PERFORMANCE BY A SUPPORTING ACTRESS IN A COMEDY SERIES: Mary Kay Place, *Mary Hartman, Mary Hartman* (syndicated)

OUTSTANDING CONTINUING PERFORMANCE BY A SUPPORTING ACTRESS IN A DRAMA SERIES: Kristy McNichol, *Family* (ABC)

OUTSTANDING CONTINUING OR SINGLE PERFORMANCE BY A SUPPORTING ACTRESS IN VARIETY OR MUSIC: Rita Moreno, *The Muppet Show* (syndicated)

OUTSTANDING PERFORMANCE BY A SUPPORTING ACTRESS IN A COMEDY OR DRAMA SPECIAL: Diana Hyland, "The Boy in the Plastic Bubble," *The ABC Friday Night Movie*, 11/12/76 (ABC)

OUTSTANDING SINGLE PERFORMANCE BY A SUPPORTING ACTRESS IN A COMEDY OR DRAMA SERIES: Olivia Cole, *Roots*—Part Eight, 1/30/77 (ABC)

OUTSTANDING DIRECTING IN A DRAMA SERIES (A SINGLE EPISODE OF A REGULAR OR LIMITED SERIES WITH CONTINUING CHARACTERS AND/OR THEME): David Greene, *Roots*—Part One, 1/23/77 (ABC)

OUTSTANDING DIRECTING IN A COMEDY SERIES (A SINGLE EPISODE OF A REGULAR OR LIMITED SERIES WITH CONTINUING CHARACTERS AND/OR THEME): Alan Alda, "Dear Sigmund," *M*A*S*H*, 11/9/76 (CBS)

OUTSTANDING DIRECTING IN A COMEDY-VARIETY OR MUSIC SERIES (A SINGLE EPISODE OF A REGULAR OR LIMITED SERIES): Dave Powers, *The Carol Burnett Show*, with Eydie Gorme, 2/12/77 (CBS)

OUTSTANDING DIRECTING IN A COMEDY-VARIETY OR MUSIC SPECIAL: Dwight Hemion, "America Salutes Richard Rodgers: The Sound of His Music" (CBS)

OUTSTANDING DIRECTING IN A SPECIAL PROGRAM—DRAMA OR COMEDY: Daniel Petrie, "Eleanor and Franklin: The White House Years," *ABC Theatre* (ABC)

OUTSTANDING WRITING IN A DRAMA SERIES (A SINGLE EPISODE OF A REGULAR OR LIMITED SERIES WITH CONTINUING CHARACTERS AND/OR THEME): William Blinn, *Roots*—Part Two, 1/24/77 (ABC)

OUTSTANDING WRITING IN A COMEDY SERIES (A SINGLE EPISODE OF A REGULAR OR LIMITED SERIES WITH CONTINUING CHARACTERS AND/OR THEME): Allan Burns, James L. Brooks, Ed Weinberger, Stan Daniels, David Lloyd, and Bob Ellison, "The Final Show," *The Mary Tyler Moore Show*, 3/19/77 (CBS)

OUTSTANDING WRITING IN A COMEDY-VARIETY OR MUSIC SERIES (A SINGLE EPISODE OF A REGULAR OR LIMITED SERIES): Anne Beatts, Dan Aykroyd, Al Franken, Tom Davis, James Downey, Lorne Michaels, Marilyn Suzanne Miller, Michael O'Donoghue, Herb Sargent, Tom Schiller, Rosie Schuster, Alan Zweibel, John Belushi, and Bill Murray, *NBC's Saturday Night Live*, with host Sissy Spacek, 3/12/77 (NBC)

OUTSTANDING WRITING IN A COMEDY-VARIETY OR MUSIC SPECIAL: Alan Buz Kohan and Ted Strauss, "America Salutes Richard Rodgers: The Sound of His Music" (CBS)

OUTSTANDING WRITING IN A SPECIAL PROGRAM—DRAMA OR COMEDY—ORIGINAL TELEPLAY: Lane Slate, "Tailgunner Joe," *The Big Event*, 2/6/77 (NBC)

OUTSTANDING WRITING IN A SPECIAL PROGRAM—DRAMA OR COMEDY—ADAPTATION: Stewart Stern, "Sybil," *The Big Event/NBC World Premiere Movie* (NBC)

OUTSTANDING EVENING CHILDREN'S SPECIAL: "Ballet Shoes, Parts 1 & 2," *Piccadilly Circus*, 12/27 & 12/28/76 (PBS)

SPECIAL CLASSIFICATION OF OUTSTANDING PROGRAM ACHIEVEMENT: *The Tonight Show Starring Johnny Carson*, Fred De Cordova, producer (NBC)

1977–1978 (presented September 17, 1978)

OUTSTANDING COMEDY SERIES: *All in the Family* (CBS)

OUTSTANDING DRAMA SERIES: *The Rockford Files* (NBC)

OUTSTANDING COMEDY-VARIETY OR MUSIC SERIES: *The Muppet Show* (syndicated)

OUTSTANDING LIMITED SERIES: *Holocaust* (NBC)

OUTSTANDING INFORMATION SERIES: *The Body Human* (CBS)

OUTSTANDING SPECIAL—DRAMA OR COMEDY: "The Gathering" (ABC)

OUTSTANDING SPECIAL—COMEDY-VARIETY OR MUSIC: "Bette Midler—Ole Red Hair Is Back" (NBC)

OUTSTANDING INFORMATION SPECIAL: "The Great Whales: National Geographic" (PBS)

OUTSTANDING CLASSICAL PROGRAM IN THE PERFORMING ARTS: "American Ballet Theatre: 'Giselle' Live from Lincoln Center" (PBS)

OUTSTANDING LEAD ACTOR IN A COMEDY SERIES: Carroll O'Connor, *All in the Family* (CBS)

OUTSTANDING LEAD ACTOR IN A DRAMA SERIES: Edward Asner, *Lou Grant* (CBS)

OUTSTANDING LEAD ACTOR IN A LIMITED SERIES: Michael Moriarty, *Holocaust* (NBC)

OUTSTANDING LEAD ACTOR IN A DRAMA OR COMEDY SPECIAL: Fred Astaire, "A Family Upside Down" (NBC)

OUTSTANDING LEAD ACTOR FOR A SINGLE APPEARANCE IN A DRAMA OR COMEDY SERIES: Barnard Hughes, "Judge," *Lou Grant* (CBS)

OUTSTANDING LEAD ACTRESS IN A COMEDY SERIES: Jean Stapleton, *All in the Family* (CBS)

OUTSTANDING LEAD ACTRESS IN A DRAMA SERIES: Sada Thompson, *Family* (ABC)

OUTSTANDING LEAD ACTRESS IN A LIMITED SERIES: Meryl Streep, *Holocaust* (NBC)

OUTSTANDING LEAD ACTRESS IN A DRAMA OR COMEDY SPECIAL: Joanne Woodward, "See How She Runs," *General Electric Theater* (CBS)

OUTSTANDING LEAD ACTRESS FOR A SINGLE APPEARANCE IN A DRAMA OR COMEDY SERIES: Rita Moreno, "The Paper Palace," *The Rockford Files* (NBC)

OUTSTANDING CONTINUING PERFORMANCE BY A SUPPORTING ACTOR IN A COMEDY SERIES: Rob Reiner, *All in the Family* (CBS)

OUTSTANDING CONTINUING PERFORMANCE BY A SUPPORTING ACTOR IN A DRAMA SERIES: Robert Vaughn, *Washington: Behind Closed Doors* (ABC)

OUTSTANDING CONTINUING OR SINGLE PERFORMANCE BY A SUPPORTING ACTOR IN VARIETY OR MUSIC: Tim Conway, *The Carol Burnett Show* (CBS)

OUTSTANDING PERFORMANCE BY A SUPPORTING ACTOR IN A COMEDY OR DRAMA SPECIAL: Howard Da Silva, "Verna: USO Girl," *Great Performances* (PBS)

OUTSTANDING SINGLE PERFORMANCE BY A SUPPORTING ACTOR IN A COMEDY OR DRAMA SERIES: Ricardo Montalban, *How the West Was Won*—Part Two (ABC)

OUTSTANDING CONTINUING PERFORMANCE BY A SUPPORTING ACTRESS IN A COMEDY SERIES: Julie Kavner, *Rhoda* (CBS)

OUTSTANDING CONTINUING PERFORMANCE BY A SUPPORTING ACTRESS IN A DRAMA SERIES: Nancy Marchand, *Lou Grant* (CBS)

OUTSTANDING CONTINUING OR SINGLE PERFORMANCE BY A SUPPORTING ACTRESS IN VARIETY OR MUSIC: Gilda Radner, *NBC's Saturday Night Live* (NBC)

OUTSTANDING PERFORMANCE BY A SUPPORTING ACTRESS IN A COMEDY OR DRAMA SPECIAL: Eva La Gallienne, "The Royal Family" (PBS)

OUTSTANDING SINGLE PERFORMANCE BY A SUPPORTING ACTRESS IN A COMEDY OR DRAMA SERIES: Blanche Baker, *Holocaust*—Part One (NBC)

OUTSTANDING DIRECTING IN A DRAMA SERIES (A SINGLE EPISODE OF A REGULAR OR LIMITED SERIES WITH CONTINUING CHARACTERS AND/OR THEME): Marvin J. Chomsky, *Holocaust*, entire series (NBC)

OUTSTANDING DIRECTING IN A COMEDY SERIES (A SINGLE EPISODE OF A REGULAR OR LIMITED SERIES WITH CONTINUING CHARACTERS AND/OR THEME): Paul Bogart, "Edith's 50th Birthday," *All in the Family* (CBS)

OUTSTANDING DIRECTING IN A COMEDY-VARIETY OR MUSIC SERIES (A SINGLE EPISODE OF A REGULAR OR LIMITED SERIES): Dave Powers, *The Carol Burnett Show*, with Steve Martin and Betty White (CBS)

OUTSTANDING DIRECTING IN A COMEDY-VARIETY OR MUSIC SPECIAL: Dwight Hemion, "The Sentry Collection Presents Ben Vereen—His Roots" (ABC)

OUTSTANDING DIRECTING IN A SPECIAL PROGRAM—DRAMA OR COMEDY: David Lowell Rich, "The Defection of Simas Kudirka" (CBS)

OUTSTANDING WRITING IN A DRAMA SERIES: Gerald Green, *Holocaust* (NBC)

OUTSTANDING WRITING IN A COMEDY SERIES: Harve Broston, Barry Harman, Bob Schiller, and Bob Weiskopf, *All in the Family* (CBS)

OUTSTANDING WRITING IN A COMEDY-VARIETY OR MUSIC SERIES: Roger Beatty, Dick Clair, Tim Conway, Rick Hawkins, Robert Illes, Jenna McMahon, Gene Perret, Bill

Richmond, Liz Sage, Larry Siegel, Franelle Silver, Ed Simmons, and James Stein, *The Carol Burnett Show* (CBS)

OUTSTANDING WRITING IN A COMEDY-VARIETY OR MUSIC SPECIAL: Chevy Chase, Tom Davis, Al Franken, Charles Grodin, Lorne Michaels, Paul Simon, Lily Tomlin, and Alan Zweibel, "The Paul Simon Special" (NBC)

OUTSTANDING WRITING IN A SPECIAL PROGRAM—DRAMA OR COMEDY—ORIGINAL TELEPLAY: George Rubino, "The Last Tenant" (ABC)

OUTSTANDING WRITING IN A SPECIAL PROGRAM—DRAMA OR COMEDY—ADAPTATION: Caryl Ledner, "Mary White" (ABC)

OUTSTANDING EVENING CHILDREN'S SPECIAL: "Halloween Is Grinch Night" (ABC)

SPECIAL CLASSIFICATION OF OUTSTANDING PROGRAM ACHIEVEMENT: *The Tonight Show Starring Johnny Carson* (NBC)

APPENDIX 3
TOP-RATED PROGRAMS BY SEASON

The following are listings of the top-rated evening series during each season, ranked by audience size. The Nielsen rating is the percent of all TV-equipped homes tuned to the program on an average night, as measured by the A.C. Nielsen Company. Thus a rating of 61.6 for the *Texaco Star Theater* from 1950–1951 means that on the average, 61.6 percent of all homes that had a TV were tuned to this show.

A.C. Nielsen changed its system of computing ratings in 1960, so ratings prior to and after that date are not precisely comparable. It should also be noted that since the Nielsen system is basically a service for advertisers, only sponsored programs are measured. However, it is unlikely that any unsponsored series (usually public affairs or news) has ever regularly achieved audience levels comparable to those of the commercial programs shown here.

October 1950–April 1951

	Program	Network	Rating
1.	Texaco Star Theater	NBC	61.6
2.	Fireside Theatre	NBC	52.6
3.	Philco TV Playhouse	NBC	45.3
4.	Your Show of Shows	NBC	42.6
5.	The Colgate Comedy Hour	NBC	42.0
6.	Gillette Cavalcade of Sports	NBC	41.3
7.	The Lone Ranger	ABC	41.2
8.	Arthur Godfrey's Talent Scouts	CBS	40.6
9.	Hopalong Cassidy	NBC	39.9
10.	Mama	CBS	39.7
11.	Robert Montgomery Presents	NBC	38.8
12.	Martin Kane, Private Eye	NBC	37.8
13.	Man Against Crime	CBS	37.4
14.	Kraft Television Theatre	NBC	37.0
15.	The Toast of the Town	CBS	36.5

October 1951–April 1952

	Program	Network	Rating
1.	Arthur Godfrey's Talent Scouts	CBS	53.8
2.	Texaco Star Theater	NBC	52.0
3.	I Love Lucy	CBS	50.9
4.	The Red Skelton Show	NBC	50.2
5.	The Colgate Comedy Hour	NBC	45.3
6.	Arthur Godfrey and His Friends	CBS	43.3
7.	Fireside Theatre	NBC	43.1
8.	Your Show of Shows	NBC	43.0
9.	The Jack Benny Show	CBS	42.8
10.	You Bet Your Life	NBC	42.1
11.	Mama	CBS	41.3
12.	Philco TV Playhouse	NBC	40.4
13.	Amos 'n' Andy	CBS	38.9
14.	Gangbusters	NBC	38.7
15.	Big Town	CBS	38.5

October 1952–April 1953

	Program	Network	Rating
1.	I Love Lucy	CBS	67.3
2.	Arthur Godfrey's Talent Scouts	CBS	54.7
3.	Arthur Godfrey and His Friends	CBS	47.1
4.	Dragnet	NBC	46.8
5.	Texaco Star Theater	NBC	46.7
6.	The Buick Circus Hour	NBC	46.0
7.	The Colgate Comedy Hour	NBC	44.3
8.	Gangbusters	NBC	42.4
9.	You Bet Your Life	NBC	41.6
10.	Fireside Theatre	NBC	40.6
11.	The Red Buttons Show	CBS	40.2
12.	The Jack Benny Show	CBS	39.0
13.	Life with Luigi	CBS	38.5
14.	Pabst Blue Ribbon Bouts	CBS	37.9
15.	Goodyear TV Playhouse	NBC	37.8

October 1953–April 1954

	Program	Network	Rating
1.	I Love Lucy	CBS	58.8
2.	Dragnet	NBC	53.2
3.	Arthur Godfrey's Talent Scouts	CBS	43.6
4.	You Bet Your Life	NBC	43.6
5.	The Chevy Show (Bob Hope)	NBC	41.4
6.	The Milton Berle Show	NBC	40.2
7.	Arthur Godfrey and His Friends	CBS	38.9
8.	The Ford Show	NBC	38.8
9.	The Jackie Gleason Show	CBS	38.1
10.	Fireside Theatre	NBC	36.4
11.	The Colgate Comedy Hour	NBC	36.2
12.	This Is Your Life	NBC	36.2
13.	The Red Buttons Show	CBS	35.3
14.	The Life of Riley	NBC	35.0
15.	Our Miss Brooks	CBS	34.2

October 1954–April 1955

	Program	Network	Rating
1.	I Love Lucy	CBS	49.3
2.	The Jackie Gleason Show	CBS	42.4
3.	Dragnet	NBC	42.1
4.	You Bet Your Life	NBC	41.0
5.	The Toast of the Town	CBS	39.6
6.	Disneyland	ABC	39.1
7.	The Chevy Show (Bob Hope)	NBC	38.5
8.	The Jack Benny Show	CBS	38.3
9.	The Martha Raye Show	NBC	35.6
10.	The George Gobel Show	NBC	35.2
11.	Ford Theater	NBC	34.9
12.	December Bride	CBS	34.7
13.	Buick-Berle Show	NBC	34.6
14.	This Is Your Life	NBC	34.5
15.	I've Got a Secret	CBS	34.0

October 1955–April 1956

	Program	Network	Rating
1.	The $64,000 Question	CBS	47.5
2.	I Love Lucy	CBS	46.1
3.	The Ed Sullivan Show	CBS	39.5
4.	Disneyland	ABC	37.4
5.	The Jack Benny Show	CBS	37.2
6.	December Bride	CBS	37.0
7.	You Bet Your Life	NBC	35.4
8.	Dragnet	NBC	35.0
9.	The Millionaire	CBS	33.8
10.	I've Got a Secret	CBS	33.5
11.	General Electric Theater	CBS	32.9
12.	Private Secretary	CBS	32.4
13.	Ford Theater	NBC	32.4
14.	The Red Skelton Show	CBS	32.3
15.	The George Gobel Show	NBC	31.9

October 1956–April 1957

	Program	Network	Rating
1.	I Love Lucy	CBS	43.7
2.	The Ed Sullivan Show	CBS	38.4
3.	General Electric Theater	CBS	36.9
4.	The $64,000 Question	CBS	36.4
5.	December Bride	CBS	35.2
6.	Alfred Hitchcock Presents	CBS	33.9
7.	I've Got a Secret	CBS	32.7
8.	Gunsmoke	CBS	32.7
9.	The Perry Como Show	NBC	32.6
10.	The Jack Benny Show	CBS	32.3
11.	Dragnet	NBC	32.1
12.	Arthur Godfrey's Talent Scouts	CBS	31.9
13.	The Millionaire	CBS	31.8
14.	Disneyland	ABC	31.8
15.	The Red Skelton Show	CBS	31.4

October 1957–April 1958

	Program	Network	Rating
1.	Gunsmoke	CBS	43.1
2.	The Danny Thomas Show	CBS	35.3
3.	Tales of Wells Fargo	NBC	35.2
4.	Have Gun Will Travel	CBS	33.7
5.	I've Got a Secret	CBS	33.4
6.	The Life and Legend of Wyatt Earp	ABC	32.6
7.	General Electric Theater	CBS	31.5
8.	The Restless Gun	NBC	31.4
9.	December Bride	CBS	30.7
10.	You Bet Your Life	NBC	30.6
11.	The Perry Como Show	NBC	30.5
12.	Alfred Hitchcock Presents	CBS	30.3
13.	Cheyenne	ABC	30.3
14.	The Ford Show	NBC	29.7
15.	The Red Skelton Show	CBS	28.9
16.	The Gale Storm Show	CBS	28.8
17.	The Millionaire	CBS	28.5
18.	The Lineup	CBS	28.4
19.	This Is Your Life	NBC	28.1
20.	The $64,000 Question	CBS	28.1
21.	Zane Grey Theater	CBS	27.9
22.	Lassie	CBS	27.8
23.	Wagon Train	NBC	27.7
24.	Sugarfoot	ABC	27.7
25.	Father Knows Best	NBC	27.7

October 1958–April 1959

	Program	Network	Rating
1.	Gunsmoke	CBS	39.6
2.	Wagon Train	NBC	36.1
3.	Have Gun Will Travel	CBS	34.3
4.	The Rifleman	ABC	33.1
5.	The Danny Thomas Show	CBS	32.8
6.	Maverick	ABC	30.4
7.	Tales of Wells Fargo	NBC	30.2
8.	The Real McCoys	ABC	30.1
9.	I've Got a Secret	CBS	29.8
10.	The Life and Legend of Wyatt Earp	ABC	29.1
11.	The Price Is Right	NBC	28.6
12.	The Red Skelton Show	CBS	28.5
13.	Zane Grey Theater	CBS	28.3
14.	Father Knows Best	CBS	28.3
15.	The Texan	CBS	28.2
16.	Wanted: Dead or Alive	CBS	28.0
17.	Peter Gunn	NBC	28.0
18.	Cheyenne	ABC	27.9
19.	Perry Mason	CBS	27.5
20.	The Ford Show	NBC	27.2
21.	Sugarfoot	ABC	27.0
22.	The Ann Sothern Show	CBS	27.0
23.	The Perry Como Show	NBC	27.0
24.	Alfred Hitchcock Presents	CBS	26.8
25.	Name That Tune	CBS	26.7

October 1959–April 1960

	Program	Network	Rating
1.	Gunsmoke	CBS	40.3
2.	Wagon Train	NBC	38.4
3.	Have Gun Will Travel	CBS	34.7
4.	The Danny Thomas Show	CBS	31.1
5.	The Red Skelton Show	CBS	30.8
6.	Father Knows Best	CBS	29.7
7.	77 Sunset Strip	ABC	29.7
8.	The Price Is Right	NBC	29.2
9.	Wanted: Dead or Alive	CBS	28.7
10.	Perry Mason	CBS	28.3
11.	The Real McCoys	ABC	28.2
12.	The Ed Sullivan Show	CBS	28.0
13.	The Bing Crosby Show	ABC	27.7
14.	The Rifleman	ABC	27.5
15.	The Ford Show	NBC	27.4
16.	The Lawman	ABC	26.2
17.	Dennis the Menace	CBS	26.0
18.	Cheyenne	ABC	25.9
19.	Rawhide	CBS	25.8
20.	Maverick	ABC	25.2
21.	The Life and Legend of Wyatt Earp	ABC	25.0
22.	Mr. Lucky	CBS	24.4
23.	Zane Grey Theater	CBS	24.4
24.	General Electric Theater	CBS	24.4
25.	The Ann Sothern Show	CBS	24.2

October 1960–April 1961

	Program	Network	Rating
1.	Gunsmoke	CBS	37.3
2.	Wagon Train	NBC	34.2
3.	Have Gun Will Travel	CBS	30.9
4.	The Andy Griffith Show	CBS	27.8
5.	The Real McCoys	ABC	27.7
6.	Rawhide	CBS	27.5
7.	Candid Camera	CBS	27.3
8.	The Untouchables	ABC	27.0
9.	The Price Is Right	NBC	27.0
10.	The Jack Benny Show	CBS	26.2
11.	Dennis the Menace	CBS	26.1
12.	The Danny Thomas Show	CBS	25.9
13.	My Three Sons	ABC	25.8
14.	77 Sunset Strip	ABC	25.8
15.	The Ed Sullivan Show	CBS	25.0
16.	Perry Mason	CBS	24.9
17.	Bonanza	NBC	24.8
18.	The Flintstones	ABC	24.3
19.	The Red Skelton Show	CBS	24.0
20.	Alfred Hitchcock Presents	CBS	23.8
21.	Celebrity Talent Scouts	CBS	23.7
22.	General Electric Theater	CBS	23.4
23.	Checkmate	CBS	23.2
24.	What's My Line	CBS	23.1
25.	The Many Loves of Dobie Gillis	CBS	23.0

October 1961–April 1962

	Program	Network	Rating
1.	Wagon Train	NBC	32.1
2.	Bonanza	NBC	30.0
3.	Gunsmoke	CBS	28.3
4.	Hazel	NBC	27.7
5.	Perry Mason	CBS	27.3
6.	The Red Skelton Show	CBS	27.1
7.	The Andy Griffith Show	CBS	27.0
8.	The Danny Thomas Show	CBS	26.1
9.	Dr. Kildare	NBC	25.6
10.	Candid Camera	CBS	25.5
11.	My Three Sons	ABC	24.7
12.	The Garry Moore Show	CBS	24.6
13.	Rawhide	CBS	24.5
14.	The Real McCoys	ABC	24.2
15.	Lassie	CBS	24.0
16.	Sing Along with Mitch	NBC	24.0
17.	Dennis the Menace	CBS	23.8
18.	Ben Casey	ABC	23.7
19.	The Ed Sullivan Show	CBS	23.5
20.	Car 54, Where Are You?	NBC	23.2
21.	The Flintstones	ABC	22.9
22.	The Many Loves of Dobie Gillis	CBS	22.9
23.	Walt Disney's Wonderful World of Color	NBC	22.7
24.	The Joey Bishop Show	NBC	22.6
25.	The Perry Como Show	NBC	22.5

October 1962–April 1963

	Program	Network	Rating
1.	The Beverly Hillbillies	CBS	36.0
2.	Candid Camera	CBS	31.1
3.	The Red Skelton Show	CBS	31.1
4.	Bonanza	NBC	29.8
5.	The Lucy Show	CBS	29.8
6.	The Andy Griffith Show	CBS	29.7
7.	Ben Casey	ABC	28.7
8.	The Danny Thomas Show	CBS	28.7
9.	The Dick Van Dyke Show	CBS	27.1
10.	Gunsmoke	CBS	27.0
11.	Dr. Kildare	NBC	26.2
12.	The Jack Benny Show	CBS	26.2
13.	What's My Line	CBS	25.5
14.	The Ed Sullivan Show	CBS	25.3
15.	Hazel	NBC	25.1
16.	I've Got a Secret	CBS	24.9
17.	The Jackie Gleason Show	CBS	24.1
18.	The Defenders	CBS	23.9
19.	The Garry Moore Show	CBS	23.3
20.	To Tell the Truth	CBS	23.3
21.	Lassie	CBS	23.3
22.	Rawhide	CBS	22.8
23.	Perry Mason	CBS	22.4
24.	Walt Disney's Wonderful World of Color	NBC	22.3
25.	Wagon Train	ABC	22.0

October 1963–April 1964

	Program	Network	Rating
1.	The Beverly Hillbillies	CBS	39.1
2.	Bonanza	NBC	36.9
3.	The Dick Van Dyke Show	CBS	33.3
4.	Petticoat Junction	CBS	30.3
5.	The Andy Griffith Show	CBS	29.4
6.	The Lucy Show	CBS	28.1
7.	Candid Camera	CBS	27.7
8.	The Ed Sullivan Show	CBS	27.5
9.	The Danny Thomas Show	CBS	26.7
10.	My Favorite Martian	CBS	26.3
11.	The Red Skelton Show	CBS	25.7
12.	I've Got a Secret	CBS	25.0
13.	Lassie	CBS	25.0
14.	The Jack Benny Show	CBS	25.0
15.	The Jackie Gleason Show	CBS	24.6
16.	The Donna Reed Show	ABC	24.5
17.	The Virginian	NBC	24.0
18.	The Patty Duke Show	ABC	23.9
19.	Dr. Kildare	NBC	23.6
20.	Gunsmoke	CBS	23.5
21.	Walt Disney's Wonderful World of Color	NBC	23.0
22.	Hazel	NBC	22.8
23.	McHale's Navy	ABC	22.8
24.	To Tell the Truth	CBS	22.6
25.	What's My Line	CBS	22.6

October 1964–April 1965

	Program	Network	Rating
1.	Bonanza	NBC	36.3
2.	Bewitched	ABC	31.0
3.	Gomer Pyle, U.S.M.C.	CBS	30.7
4.	The Andy Griffith Show	CBS	28.3
5.	The Fugitive	ABC	27.9
6.	The Red Skelton Hour	CBS	27.4
7.	The Dick Van Dyke Show	CBS	27.1
8.	The Lucy Show	CBS	26.6
9.	Peyton Place II	ABC	26.4
10.	Combat	ABC	26.1
11.	Walt Disney's Wonderful World of Color	NBC	25.7
12.	The Beverly Hillbillies	CBS	25.6
13.	My Three Sons	ABC	25.5
14.	Branded	NBC	25.3
15.	Petticoat Junction	CBS	25.2
16.	The Ed Sullivan Show	CBS	25.2
17.	Lassie	CBS	25.1
18.	The Munsters	CBS	24.7
19.	Gilligan's Island	CBS	24.7
20.	Peyton Place I	ABC	24.6
21.	The Jackie Gleason Show	CBS	24.4
22.	The Virginian	NBC	24.0
23.	The Addams Family	ABC	23.9
24.	My Favorite Martian	CBS	23.7
25.	Flipper	NBC	23.4

October 1965–April 1966

	Program	Network	Rating
1.	Bonanza	NBC	31.8
2.	Gomer Pyle, U.S.M.C.	CBS	27.8
3.	The Lucy Show	CBS	27.7
4.	The Red Skelton Hour	CBS	27.6
5.	Batman (Thurs.)	ABC	27.0
6.	The Andy Griffith Show	CBS	26.9
7.	Bewitched	ABC	25.9
8.	The Beverly Hillbillies	CBS	25.9
9.	Hogan's Heroes	CBS	24.9
10.	Batman (Wed.)	ABC	24.7
11.	Green Acres	CBS	24.6
12.	Get Smart	NBC	24.5
13.	The Man from U.N.C.L.E.	NBC	24.0
14.	Daktari	CBS	23.9
15.	My Three Sons	CBS	23.8
16.	The Dick Van Dyke Show	CBS	23.6
17.	Walt Disney's Wonderful World of Color	NBC	23.2
18.	The Ed Sullivan Show	CBS	23.2
19.	The Lawrence Welk Show	ABC	22.4
20.	I've Got a Secret	CBS	22.4
21.	Petticoat Junction	CBS	22.3
22.	Gilligan's Island	CBS	22.1
23.	Wild, Wild West	CBS	22.0
24.	The Jackie Gleason Show	CBS	22.0
25.	The Virginian	NBC	22.0

October 1966–April 1967

	Program	Network	Rating
1.	Bonanza	NBC	29.1
2.	The Red Skelton Hour	CBS	28.2
3.	The Andy Griffith Show	CBS	27.4
4.	The Lucy Show	CBS	26.2
5.	The Jackie Gleason Show	CBS	25.3
6.	Green Acres	CBS	24.6
7.	Daktari	CBS	23.4
8.	Bewitched	ABC	23.4
9.	The Beverly Hillbillies	CBS	23.4
10.	Gomer Pyle, U.S.M.C.	CBS	22.8
11.	The Virginian	NBC	22.8
12.	The Lawrence Welk Show	ABC	22.8
13.	The Ed Sullivan Show	CBS	22.8
14.	The Dean Martin Show	NBC	22.6
15.	Family Affair	CBS	22.6
16.	The Smothers Brothers Comedy Hour	CBS	22.2
17.	Friday Night Movies	CBS	21.8
18.	Hogan's Heroes	CBS	21.8
19.	Walt Disney's Wonderful World of Color	NBC	21.5
20.	Saturday Night at the Movies	NBC	21.4
21.	Dragnet	NBC	21.2
22.	Get Smart	NBC	21.0
23.	Petticoat Junction	CBS	20.9
24.	Rat Patrol	ABC	20.9
25.	Daniel Boone	NBC	20.8

October 1967–April 1968

	Program	Network	Rating
1.	The Andy Griffith Show	CBS	27.6
2.	The Lucy Show	CBS	27.0
3.	Gomer Pyle, U.S.M.C.	CBS	25.6
4.	Gunsmoke	CBS	25.5
5.	Family Affair	CBS	25.5
6.	Bonanza	NBC	25.5
7.	The Red Skelton Show	CBS	25.3
8.	The Dean Martin Show	NBC	24.8
9.	The Jackie Gleason Show	CBS	23.9
10.	Saturday Night at the Movies	NBC	23.6
11.	Bewitched	ABC	23.5
12.	The Beverly Hillbillies	CBS	23.3
13.	The Ed Sullivan Show	CBS	23.2
14.	The Virginian	NBC	22.9
15.	Friday Night Movie	CBS	22.8
16.	Green Acres	CBS	22.8
17.	The Lawrence Welk Show	ABC	21.9
18.	The Smothers Brothers Comedy Hour	CBS	21.7
19.	Gentle Ben	CBS	21.5
20.	Tuesday Night at the Movies	NBC	21.4
21.	Rowan & Martin's Laugh-In	NBC	21.3
22.	The F.B.I.	ABC	21.2
23.	Thursday Night Movie	CBS	21.1
24.	My Three Sons	CBS	20.8
25.	Walt Disney's Wonderful World of Color	NBC	20.7

October 1968–April 1969

	Program	Network	Rating
1.	Rowan & Martin's Laugh-In	NBC	31.8
2.	Gomer Pyle, U.S.M.C.	CBS	27.2
3.	Bonanza	NBC	26.6
4.	Mayberry R.F.D.	CBS	25.4
5.	Family Affair	CBS	25.2
6.	Gunsmoke	CBS	24.9
7.	Julia	NBC	24.6
8.	The Dean Martin Show	NBC	24.1
9.	Here's Lucy	CBS	23.8
10.	The Beverly Hillbillies	CBS	23.5
11.	Mission: Impossible	CBS	23.3
12.	Bewitched	ABC	23.3
13.	The Red Skelton Hour	CBS	23.3
14.	My Three Sons	CBS	22.8
15.	The Glen Campbell Goodtime Hour	CBS	22.5
16.	Ironside	NBC	22.3
17.	The Virginian	NBC	21.8
18.	The F.B.I.	ABC	21.7
19.	Green Acres	CBS	21.6
20.	Dragnet	NBC	21.4
21.	Daniel Boone	NBC	21.3
22.	Walt Disney's Wonderful World of Color	NBC	21.3
23.	The Ed Sullivan Show	CBS	21.2
24.	The Carol Burnett Show	CBS	20.8
25.	The Jackie Gleason Show	CBS	20.8

October 1969–April 1970

	Program	Network	Rating
1.	Rowan & Martin's Laugh-In	NBC	26.3
2.	Gunsmoke	CBS	25.9
3.	Bonanza	NBC	24.8
4.	Mayberry R.F.D.	CBS	24.4
5.	Family Affair	CBS	24.2
6.	Here's Lucy	CBS	23.9
7.	The Red Skelton Hour	CBS	23.8
8.	Marcus Welby, M.D.	ABC	23.7
9.	Walt Disney's Wonderful World of Color	NBC	23.6
10.	The Doris Day Show	CBS	22.8
11.	The Bill Cosby Show	NBC	22.7
12.	The Jim Nabors Hour	CBS	22.4
13.	The Carol Burnett Show	CBS	22.1
14.	The Dean Martin Show	NBC	21.9
15.	My Three Sons	CBS	21.8
16.	Ironside	NBC	21.8
17.	The Johnny Cash Show	ABC	21.8
18.	The Beverly Hillbillies	CBS	21.7
19.	Hawaii Five-O	CBS	21.1
20.	The Glen Campbell Goodtime Hour	CBS	21.0
21.	Hee Haw	CBS	21.0
22.	Movie of the Week	ABC	20.9
23.	Mod Squad	ABC	20.8
24.	Saturday Night Movie	NBC	20.6
25.	Bewitched	ABC	20.6

October 1970–April 1971

	Program	Network	Rating
1.	Marcus Welby, M.D.	ABC	29.6
2.	The Flip Wilson Show	NBC	27.9
3.	Here's Lucy	CBS	26.1
4.	Ironside	NBC	25.7
5.	Gunsmoke	CBS	25.5
6.	ABC Movie of the Week	ABC	25.1
7.	Hawaii Five-O	CBS	25.0
8.	Medical Center	CBS	24.5
9.	Bonanza	NBC	23.9
10.	The F.B.I.	ABC	23.0
11.	Mod Squad	ABC	22.7
12.	Adam-12	NBC	22.6
13.	Rowan & Martin's Laugh-In	NBC	22.4
14.	The Wonderful World of Disney	NBC	22.4
15.	Mayberry R.F.D.	CBS	22.3
16.	Hee Haw	CBS	21.4
17.	Mannix	CBS	21.3
18.	The Men from Shiloh	NBC	21.2
19.	My Three Sons	CBS	20.8
20.	The Doris Day Show	CBS	20.7
21.	The Smith Family	ABC	20.6
22.	The Mary Tyler Moore Show	CBS	20.3
23.	NBC Saturday Movie	NBC	20.1
24.	The Dean Martin Show	NBC	20.0
25.	The Carol Burnett Show	CBS	19.8

October 1971–April 1972

	Program	Network	Rating
1.	All in the Family	CBS	34.0
2.	The Flip Wilson Show	NBC	28.2
3.	Marcus Welby, M.D.	ABC	27.8
4.	Gunsmoke	CBS	26.0
5.	ABC Movie of the Week	ABC	25.6
6.	Sanford and Son	NBC	25.2
7.	Mannix	CBS	24.8
8.	Funny Face	CBS	23.9
9.	Adam 12	NBC	23.9
10.	The Mary Tyler Moore Show	CBS	23.7
11.	Here's Lucy	CBS	23.7
12.	Hawaii Five-O	CBS	23.6
13.	Medical Center	CBS	23.5
14.	The NBC Mystery Movie	NBC	23.2
15.	Ironside	NBC	23.0
16.	The Partridge Family	ABC	22.6
17.	The F.B.I.	ABC	22.4
18.	The New Dick Van Dyke Show	CBS	22.2
19.	The Wonderful World of Disney	NBC	22.0
20.	Bonanza	NBC	21.9
21.	Mod Squad	ABC	21.5
22.	Rowan & Martin's Laugh-In	NBC	21.4
23.	The Carol Burnett Show	CBS	21.2
24.	The Doris Day Show	CBS	21.2
25.	ABC NFL Football	ABC	20.9

October 1972–April 1973

	Program	Network	Rating
1.	All in the Family	CBS	33.3
2.	Sanford and Son	NBC	27.6
3.	Hawaii Five-O	CBS	25.2
4.	Maude	CBS	24.7
5.	Bridget Loves Bernie	CBS	24.2
6.	Sunday Mystery Movie	NBC	24.2
7.	The Mary Tyler Moore Show	CBS	23.6
8.	Gunsmoke	CBS	23.6
9.	The Wonderful World of Disney	NBC	23.5
10.	Ironside	NBC	23.4
11.	Adam 12	NBC	23.3
12.	The Flip Wilson Show	NBC	23.1
13.	Marcus Welby, M.D.	ABC	22.9
14.	Cannon	CBS	22.4
15.	Here's Lucy	CBS	21.9
16.	The Bob Newhart Show	CBS	21.8
17.	Tuesday Movie of the Week	ABC	21.5
18.	ABC NFL Football	ABC	21.0
19.	The Partridge Family	ABC	20.6
20.	The Waltons	CBS	20.6
21.	Medical Center	CBS	20.4
22.	The Carol Burnett Show	CBS	20.3
23.	ABC Sunday Movie	ABC	20.0
24.	The Rookies	ABC	20.0
25.	Escape	NBC	19.9

September 1973–April 1974

	Program	Network	Rating
1.	All in the Family	CBS	31.2
2.	The Waltons	CBS	28.1
3.	Sanford and Son	NBC	27.5
4.	M*A*S*H	CBS	25.7
5.	Hawaii Five-O	CBS	24.0
6.	Maude	CBS	23.5
7.	Kojak	CBS	23.3
8.	The Sonny and Cher Comedy Hour	CBS	23.3
9.	The Mary Tyler Moore Show	CBS	23.1
10.	Cannon	CBS	23.1
11.	The Six Million Dollar Man	ABC	22.7
12.	The Bob Newhart Show	CBS	22.3
13.	The Wonderful World of Disney	NBC	22.3
14.	The NBC Sunday Mystery Movie	NBC	22.2
15.	Gunsmoke	CBS	22.1
16.	Happy Days	ABC	21.5
17.	Good Times	CBS	21.4
18.	Barnaby Jones	CBS	21.4
19.	ABC Monday Night Football	ABC	21.2
20.	CBS Friday Night Movie	CBS	21.2
21.	Tuesday Movie of the Week	ABC	21.0
22.	The Streets of San Francisco	ABC	20.8
23.	Adam 12	NBC	20.7
24.	ABC Sunday Night Movie	ABC	20.7
25.	The Rookies	ABC	20.3

September 1974–April 1975

	Program	Network	Rating
1.	All in the Family	CBS	30.2
2.	Sanford and Son	NBC	29.6
3.	Chico and The Man	NBC	28.5
4.	The Jeffersons	CBS	27.6
5.	M*A*S*H	CBS	27.4
6.	Rhoda	CBS	26.3
7.	Good Times	CBS	25.8
8.	The Waltons	CBS	25.5
9.	Maude	CBS	24.9
10.	Hawaii Five-O	CBS	24.8
11.	The Mary Tyler Moore Show	CBS	24.0
12.	The Rockford Files	NBC	23.7
13.	Little House on the Prairie	NBC	23.5
14.	Kojak	CBS	23.3
15.	Police Woman	NBC	22.8
16.	S.W.A.T.	ABC	22.6
17.	The Bob Newhart Show	CBS	22.4
18.	The Wonderful World of Disney	NBC	22.0
19.	The Rookies	ABC	22.0
20.	Mannix	CBS	21.6
21.	Cannon	CBS	21.6
22.	Cher	CBS	21.3
23.	The Streets of San Francisco	ABC	21.3
24.	The NBC Sunday Mystery Movie	NBC	21.3
25.	Paul Sand in Friends and Lovers	CBS	20.7

September 1975–April 1976

	Program	Network	Rating
1.	All in the Family	CBS	30.1
2.	Rich Man, Poor Man	ABC	28.0
3.	Laverne & Shirley	ABC	27.5
4.	Maude	CBS	25.0
5.	The Bionic Woman	ABC	24.9
6.	Phyllis	CBS	24.5
7.	Sanford and Son	NBC	24.4
8.	Rhoda	CBS	24.4
9.	The Six Million Dollar Man	ABC	24.3
10.	ABC Monday Night Movie	ABC	24.2
11.	Happy Days	ABC	23.9
12.	One Day at a Time	CBS	23.1
13.	ABC Sunday Night Movie	ABC	23.0
14.	The Waltons	CBS	22.9
15.	M*A*S*H	CBS	22.9
16.	Starsky and Hutch	ABC	22.5
17.	Good Heavens	ABC	22.5
18.	Welcome Back, Kotter	ABC	22.1
19.	The Mary Tyler Moore Show	CBS	21.9
20.	Kojak	CBS	21.8
21.	The Jeffersons	CBS	21.5
22.	Baretta	ABC	21.3
23.	The Sonny & Cher Show	CBS	21.2
24.	Good Times	CBS	21.0
25.	Chico and the Man	NBC	20.8

September 1976–April 1977

	Program	Network	Rating
1.	Happy Days	ABC	31.5
2.	Laverne & Shirley	ABC	30.9
3.	ABC Monday Night Movie	ABC	26.0
4.	M*A*S*H	CBS	25.9
5.	Charlie's Angels	ABC	25.8
6.	The Big Event	NBC	24.4
7.	The Six Million Dollar Man	ABC	24.2
8.	ABC Sunday Night Movie	ABC	23.4
9.	Baretta	ABC	23.4
10.	One Day at a Time	CBS	23.4
11.	Three's Company	ABC	23.1
12.	All in the Family	CBS	22.9
13.	Welcome Back, Kotter	ABC	22.7
14.	The Bionic Woman	ABC	22.4
15.	The Waltons	CBS	22.3
16.	Little House on the Prairie	NBC	22.3
17.	Barney Miller	ABC	22.2
18.	60 Minutes	CBS	21.9
19.	Hawaii Five-O	CBS	21.9
20.	NBC Monday Night Movie	NBC	21.8
21.	Rich Man, Poor Man, Book II	ABC	21.6
22.	ABC NFL Football	ABC	21.2
23.	Eight Is Enough	ABC	21.1
24.	The Jeffersons	CBS	21.0
25.	What's Happening	ABC	20.9

September 1977–April 1978

	Program	Network	Rating
1.	Laverne & Shirley	ABC	31.6
2.	Happy Days	ABC	31.4
3.	Three's Company	ABC	28.3
4.	60 Minutes	CBS	24.4
5.	Charlie's Angels	ABC	24.4
6.	All in the Family	CBS	24.4
7.	Little House on the Prairie	NBC	24.1
8.	Alice	CBS	23.2
9.	M*A*S*H	CBS	23.2
10.	One Day at a Time	CBS	23.0
11.	How the West Was Won	ABC	22.5
12.	Eight Is Enough	ABC	22.2
13.	Soap	ABC	22.0
14.	The Love Boat	ABC	21.9
15.	NBC Monday Night Movie	NBC	21.7
16.	Monday Night Football	ABC	21.5
17.	Fantasy Island	ABC	21.4
18.	Barney Miller	ABC	21.4
19.	The Amazing Spider-Man	CBS	21.2
20.	Project U.F.O.	NBC	21.2
21.	ABC Sunday Night Movie	ABC	20.8
22.	The Waltons	CBS	20.8
23.	Barnaby Jones	CBS	20.6
24.	Hawaii Five-O	CBS	20.4
25.	ABC Monday Night Movie	ABC	20.3

APPENDIX 4

LONGEST RUNNING SERIES

The following is a listing of the longest running series on nighttime network television, excluding movies and newscasts. A series is counted as having aired in a season if it was on for at least two months during that season. Seasons in which a series aired at other times of the day (for example, in the daytime), or on local stations, are not counted.

Meet the Press is the longest running series in all of television, having been on the air continuously since 1947. Only the eighteen seasons which it spent on the nighttime schedule (post 6:00 P.M.) are shown here, however.

Alternate titles are given in parentheses. The 1978–1979 season has been counted for all series running as of September 30, 1978.

25 Seasons

The Tonight Show (The Jack Paar Show, Tonight! America After Dark, The Tonight Show Starring Johnny Carson)
Walt Disney (Disneyland, Walt Disney Presents, Walt Disney's Wonderful World of Color, The Wonderful World of Disney)

24 Seasons

The Ed Sullivan Show (The Toast of the Town)

20 Seasons

Gunsmoke
The Red Skelton Show (The Red Skelton Hour)

18 Seasons

Meet the Press
What's My Line

17 Seasons

Lassie
The Lawrence Welk Show (Lawrence Welk's Dodge Dancing Party)

16 Seasons

Kraft Television Theatre (Kraft Suspense Theater, Kraft Mystery Theater)

15 Seasons

I've Got a Secret
The Jack Benny Show
The Jackie Gleason Show (The Honeymooners)
The Perry Como Show (Chesterfield Supper Club)

14 Seasons

The Adventures of Ozzie & Harriet
Armstrong Circle Theatre (Circle Theatre)
Bonanza
The Gillette Cavalcade of Sports (The Cavalcade of Sports)

13 Seasons

The Danny Thomas Show (Make Room for Daddy, Make Room for Granddaddy)
The Dinah Shore Show (The Dinah Shore Chevy Show)

12 Seasons

Dragnet
The Lucy Show (Here's Lucy)
My Three Sons
The Original Amateur Hour
Pabst Blue Ribbon Bouts (International Boxing Club Bouts, The Wednesday Night Fights)
The 20th Century (The 21st Century)

11 Seasons

Arthur Godfrey's Talent Scouts
The Arthur Murray Party
CBS Reports/News Hour/News Special
Candid Camera (Candid Microphone)
The Carol Burnett Show
Fireside Theatre (Jane Wyman's Fireside Theater, The Jane Wyman Show)
General Electric Theater (General Electric True)

Hawaii Five-O
The Milton Berle Show (The Texaco Star Theater, The Buick-Berle Show, Milton Berle Starring in the Kraft Music Hall)
Pantomime Quiz (Stump the Stars)
60 Minutes
To Tell the Truth
The Voice of Firestone
You Bet Your Life (The Groucho Show)

10 Seasons

Alfred Hitchcock Presents (The Alfred Hitchcock Hour)
Arthur Godfrey and His Friends (The Arthur Godfrey Show)
Perry Mason (The New Adventures of Perry Mason)
Studio One
The U.S. Steel Hour
Your Hit Parade

9 Seasons

All in the Family
The Andy Williams Show
Beat the Clock
The Beverly Hillbillies
Break the Bank
The Dean Martin Show
The F.B.I.
Father Knows Best
Goodyear TV Playhouse (Goodyear Theater)
Masquerade Party
Monday Night Football
This Is Your Life
The Virginian (The Men from Shiloh)
You Asked for It (The Art Baker Show)

8 Seasons

The Alcoa Hour (Alcoa Theatre, Alcoa Presents, Alcoa Premiere)
The Andy Griffith Show
The Bell Telephone Hour
Bewitched
Cheyenne
The Donna Reed Show
The George Burns and Gracie Allen Show
The Garry Moore Show
I Love Lucy (The Sunday Lucy Show, The Lucy Show, The Top 10 Lucy Shows)
Ironside
The Lone Ranger
The Loretta Young Show (A Letter to Loretta)
Lux Video Theatre (Lux Playhouse)
Mama
Mannix
Mark Saber (Mystery Theater, Inspector Mark Saber—Homicide Squad, The Vise, Saber of London)
Midwestern Hayride
Person to Person
Rawhide
Robert Montgomery Presents
Schlitz Playhouse of Stars (Schlitz Playhouse)
The Steve Allen Show
Wagon Train

7 Seasons

Adam 12
Barnaby Jones
The Big Story
Captain Video and His Video Rangers
The Eddie Fisher Show (Coke Time with Eddie Fisher)
The Gene Autry Show
The Hollywood Palace
Kukla, Fran & Ollie
Life Begins at Eighty
The Life of Riley
M*A*S*H
Marcus Welby, M.D.
The Mary Tyler Moore Show
McCloud
Medical Center
Mission: Impossible
Monday Night Baseball
Name That Tune
People Are Funny
Petticoat Junction
Philco TV Playhouse
The Price Is Right
The Quiz Kids
Red Barber's Corner (Red Barber's Clubhouse, The Peak of the Sports News)
Suspense
This Is Show Business
The Waltons
Who Said That?

6 Seasons

The Author Meets the Critics
Big Town
The Bob Newhart Show
Broadway to Hollywood—Headline Clues
The Colgate Comedy Hour
Columbo
Daniel Boone

December Bride
Dick Powell's Zane Grey Theater
Down You Go
Emergency
The Flintstones
Focus
The Fred Waring Show
The George Gobel Show
The Gillette Summer Sports Reel
The Goldbergs
Gomer Pyle, U.S.M.C.
Good Times
Green Acres
Happy Days
Have Gun Will Travel
Hogan's Heroes
Hollywood Screen Test
Leave It to Beaver
The Life and Legend of Wyatt Earp
Life Is Worth Living
The Lineup
Man Against Crime
Maude
McMillan and Wife (McMillan)
The Millionaire
NBC Mystery Movie (NBC Sunday/Tuesday/Wednesday Mystery Movie)
Ozark Jubilee (Country Music Jubilee, Jubilee U.S.A.)
Paul Whiteman's TV Teen Club
The Real McCoys
Rocky King, Inside Detective (Inside Detective)
Rowan & Martin's Laugh-In
The Sammy Kaye Show (So You Want to Lead a Band, Music from Manhattan)
Sanford and Son
77 Sunset Strip
The Sonny and Cher Comedy Hour (The Sonny and Cher Show)
Stop the Music
Twenty Questions
The Twilight Zone
The Web

APPENDIX 5
SERIES AIRING IN PRIME TIME ON MORE THAN ONE NETWORK

On All 4 Networks

The Arthur Murray Party
Down You Go
The Original Amateur Hour
Pantomime Quiz

On 3 Networks

The Adventures of Ellery Queen (The Further Adventures of Ellery Queen, Ellery Queen) (DUM, ABC, NBC)
The Andy Williams Show (ABC, CBS, NBC)
Animal World (NBC, CBS, ABC)
The Author Meets the Critics (NBC, ABC, DUM)
Bachelor Father (CBS, NBC, ABC)
Big Town (CBS, DUM, NBC)
Blind Date (Your Big Moment) (ABC, NBC, DUM)
Break the Bank (ABC, NBC, CBS)
Candid Camera (Candid Microphone) (ABC, NBC, CBS)
Charlie Wild, Private Detective (CBS, ABC, DUM)
Dollar a Second (DUM, NBC, ABC)
The Eddy Arnold Show (CBS, NBC, ABC)
Ethel and Albert (NBC, CBS, ABC)
Father Knows Best (CBS, NBC, ABC)
Ford Theatre (CBS, NBC, ABC)
The Goldbergs (CBS, NBC, DUM)
Life Begins at Eighty (NBC, ABC, DUM)
Man Against Crime (CBS, DUM, NBC)
Mary Kay and Johnny (DUM, NBC, CBS)
Masquerade Party (NBC, CBS, ABC)
The Sammy Kaye Show (So You Want to Lead a Band, Music from Manhattan) (NBC, CBS, ABC)
The Smothers Brothers Comedy Hour (The Smothers Brothers Summer Show, The Smothers Brothers Show) (CBS, ABC, NBC)
The Steve Allen Show (CBS, NBC, ABC)
The Ted Steele Show (NBC, DUM, CBS)
Tom Corbett: Space Cadet (CBS, ABC, NBC)
Topper (CBS, ABC, NBC)
Twenty Questions (NBC, ABC, DUM)
The Wendy Barrie Show (Inside Photoplay, Photoplay Time, Through Wendy's Window) (DUM, ABC, NBC)

On 2 Networks

Actor's Studio (The Play's the Thing) (ABC, CBS)
Adventure Theater (NBC, CBS)
The Alan Dale Show (DUM, CBS)
Alfred Hitchcock Presents (The Alfred Hitchcock Hour) (CBS, NBC)
The Amazing Dunninger (The Dunninger Show) (ABC, NBC)
Armstrong Circle Theatre (NBC, CBS)
Bank on the Stars (CBS, NBC)
The Battle of the Ages (DUM, CBS)
The Bigelow Show (NBC, CBS)
Bigelow Theatre (CBS, DUM)
The Bionic Woman (ABC, NBC)
The Black Saddle (NBC, ABC)
Blondie (CBS, NBC)
The Bob Cummings Show (NBC, CBS)
Cavalcade of America (DuPont Cavalcade Theater, DuPont Theater) (NBC, ABC)
Celebrity Time (Goodrich Celebrity Time) (CBS, ABC)
Chance of a Lifetime (ABC, DUM)
The Charlie Farrell Show (CBS, NBC)
Circus Boy (NBC, ABC)
Claudia, The Story of a Marriage (NBC, CBS)
The Clock (NBC, ABC)
The Continental (CBS, ABC)
The Court of Last Resort (NBC, ABC)
Dan August (ABC, CBS)
The Danny Thomas Show (Make Room for Daddy) (ABC, CBS)
The Detectives Starring Robert Taylor (Robert Taylor's Detectives) (ABC, NBC)
Doorway to Danger (NBC, ABC)
The Dotty Mack Show (Girl Alone) (DUM, ABC)
Drew Pearson (ABC, DUM)
The Earl Wrightson Show (Earl Wrightson at Home, The at Home Show, The Masland at Home Party) (ABC, CBS)
Eddie Condon's Floor Show (NBC, CBS)
Empire (NBC, ABC)
Ensign O'Toole (NBC, ABC)
The Ernie Kovacs Show (CBS, NBC)
The Family Holvak (NBC, CBS)
Famous Fights (DUM, ABC)
The Faye Emerson Show (Fifteen with Faye) (CBS, NBC)
Fireside Theatre (Jane Wyman's Fireside Theater, The Jane Wyman Show) (NBC, ABC)

The Gale Storm Show (CBS, ABC)
The George Gobel Show (NBC, CBS)
Get Smart (NBC, CBS)
The Ghost and Mrs. Muir (NBC, ABC)
Harbourmaster (Adventures at Scott Island) (CBS, ABC)
Hawk (ABC, NBC)
Hazel (NBC, CBS)
The Herb Shriner Show (Herb Shriner Time) (CBS, ABC)
Hey Jeannie (The Jeannie Carson Show) (CBS, ABC)
Hollywood Opening Night (CBS, NBC)
The Hunter (CBS, NBC)
It Pays to Be Ignorant (CBS, NBC)
The Jack Benny Show (CBS, NBC)
The Jimmy Dean Show (CBS, ABC)
The Jimmy Durante Show (NBC, CBS)
The Joey Bishop Show (NBC, CBS)
The John Davidson Show (ABC, NBC)
The Johnny Cash Show (ABC, CBS)
Johnny Staccato (NBC, ABC)
The Johns Hopkins Science Review (CBS, DUM)
The Joseph Cotten Show (On Trial) (NBC, CBS)
Juvenile Jury (NBC, CBS)
Keep Talking (CBS, ABC)
Kraft Television Theatre (NBC, ABC)
Kukla, Fran & Ollie (NBC, ABC)
Law of the Plainsman (NBC, ABC)
Leave It to Beaver (CBS, ABC)
Leave It to the Girls (NBC, ABC)
Let's Make a Deal (NBC, ABC)
The Liberace Show (NBC, CBS)
Life Is Worth Living (DUM, ABC)
Live Like a Millionaire (CBS, ABC)
Lux Video Theatre (Lux Playhouse) (CBS, NBC)
Madison Square Garden Highlights (ABC, DUM)
Mark Saber (Mystery Theater, Inspector Mark Saber—Homicide Squad, The Vise, Saber of London) (ABC, NBC)
Meet McGraw (NBC, ABC)
Meet Your Congress (NBC, DUM)
Midwestern Hayride (NBC, ABC)
The Milton Berle Show (NBC, ABC)
Mr. & Mrs. North (CBS, NBC)
The Morey Amsterdam Show (CBS, DUM)
My Friend Flicka (CBS, NBC)
My Little Margie (CBS, NBC)
My Three Sons (ABC, CBS)
My World and Welcome to It (NBC, CBS)
Name That Tune (NBC, CBS)
Navy Log (CBS, ABC)
Omnibus (CBS, ABC)
On the Line with Considine (NBC, ABC)
On Your Way (DUM, ABC)
The Perry Como Show (The Chesterfield Supper Club) (NBC, CBS)
Peter Gunn (NBC, ABC)
Pick the Winner (CBS, DUM)
Place the Face (NBC, CBS)
Press Conference (Martha Rountree's Press Conference) (NBC, ABC)
The Price Is Right (NBC, ABC)
The Pride of the Family (ABC, CBS)
Private Secretary (CBS, NBC)
Quiz Kids (NBC, CBS)
The Real McCoys (ABC, CBS)
The Rebel (ABC, NBC)
Rebound (ABC, DUM)
Red Barber's Corner (Red Barber's Clubhouse, The Peak of the Sports News) (CBS, NBC)
The Red Buttons Show (CBS, NBC)
The Red Skelton Show (NBC, CBS)
Revlon Mirror Theatre (NBC, CBS)
Richard Diamond, Private Detective (CBS, NBC)
Say It with Acting (NBC, ABC)
Screen Director's Playhouse (NBC, ABC)
Shirley Temple's Storybook (ABC, NBC)
Somerset Maugham TV Theatre (Teller of Tales) (CBS, NBC)
The Spike Jones Show (NBC, CBS)
Steve Canyon (NBC, ABC)
The Stork Club (CBS, ABC)
Stud's Place (NBC, ABC)
Tarzan (NBC, CBS)
Telephone Time (CBS, ABC)
Tex and Jinx (NBC, CBS)
They Stand Accused (CBS, DUM)
This Is Show Business (CBS, NBC)
This Is the Life (DUM, ABC)
The Tony Randall Show (ABC, CBS)
Treasure Hunt (ABC, NBC)
Treasury Men in Action (ABC, NBC)
Truth or Consequences (CBS, NBC)
21 Beacon Street (NBC, ABC)
Two for the Money (NBC, CBS)
The U.S. Steel Hour (ABC, CBS)
The Vaughn Monroe Show (CBS, NBC)
Versatile Varieties (NBC, ABC)
The Voice of Firestone (NBC, ABC)
Wagon Train (NBC, ABC)
Walt Disney (Disneyland, Walt Disney Presents, Walt Disney's Wonderful World of Color, The Wonderful World of Disney) (ABC, NBC)
We, the People (CBS, NBC)
The Web (CBS, NBC)
The West Point Story (CBS, ABC)

What's It Worth (Trash or Treasure, Treasure Hunt) (CBS, DUM)
What's Your Bid (ABC, DUM)
Who Said That? (NBC, ABC)
Wonder Woman (The New Adventures of Wonder Woman) (ABC, CBS)
You Asked for It (DUM, ABC)
Your Hit Parade (NBC, CBS)
Your Play Time (CBS, NBC)
Youth on the March (ABC, DUM)

APPENDIX 6
SONG HITS FROM TELEVISION

Radio has been more closely associated with the popular record field than has television, but there have been a number of instances of major song hits created by TV—sometimes by a single telecast. The audiences to television shows are enormous, and represent an excellent opportunity to expose new songs. Listed below are some notable song hits resulting directly from TV broadcasts. Not included are routine performances on variety or music shows, or extraneous "plugs" by television stars of their latest records (as on *The Partridge Family, The Monkees,* etc.). The artist who had the hit version is listed, along with the year and the highest position reached on the national hit parade, as compiled by *Billboard* magazine. An asterisk (*) indicates a million seller. See under individual program titles for more information.

Hit Songs from Individual Telecasts

(Chronological order)

"I Believe" sung by Jane Froman on *Jane Froman's U.S.A. Canteen;* Frankie Laine* (1953, #2); Jane Froman (1953, #11)

"No Other Love," based on a main theme from *Victory at Sea* (series of specials; 1952–1953); Perry Como (1953, #2)

"Let Me Go Lover" sung by Joan Weber on *Studio One* (November 15, 1954); Joan Weber* (1954, #1)

"The Ballad of Davy Crockett" sung by Fess Parker on *Disneyland* (December 15, 1954); Bill Hayes* (1955, #1); Fess Parker (1955, #5); Tennessee Ernie Ford (1955, #6); Walter Schumann (1955, #29)

"Play Me Hearts and Flowers" sung by Johnny Desmond on *Philco Playhouse* (March 6, 1955); Johnny Desmond (1955, #16)

"Hard to Get" sung by Gisele MacKenzie on *Justice* (May 12, 1955); Gisele MacKenzie (1955, #5)

"Love and Marriage" sung by Frank Sinatra on *Producer's Showcase* production of "Our Town" (September 19, 1955); Frank Sinatra* (1955, #5)

"Theme Song from 'Song for a Summer Night' " introduced by Mitch Miller and His Orchestra in the *Studio One* production, "Song for a Summer Night" (July 9, 1956); Mitch Miller and His Orchestra (1956, #10)

"Teenage Crush" sung by Tommy Sands on *Kraft Television Theatre* production of "The Singing Idol" (January 30, 1957); Tommy Sands* (1957, #3)

"Start Movin' " sung by Sal Mineo on *Kraft Television Theatre* production of "Drummer Man" (May 1, 1957); Sal Mineo* (1957, #10)

"Love Me to Pieces" sung by Jill Corey on *Studio One Summer Theatre* production of "Love Me to Pieces" (July 15, 1957); Jill Corey (1957, #18)

"Come to Me" sung by Julie Wilson on *Kraft Television Theatre* production of "Come to Me" (December 4, 1957); Johnny Mathis (1958, #43)

"Kookie, Kookie, Lend Me Your Comb" sung by Edd Byrnes on *77 Sunset Strip* (October 16, 1959); Edd Byrnes and Connie Stevens* (1959, #4)

"Tracy's Theme" introduced on the dramatic special "Philadelphia Story" (December 7, 1959); Spencer Ross Orchestra (1960, #13)

Hit Theme Songs from Series

All in the Family
("Those Were the Days"), Carroll O'Connor & Jean Stapleton (1971, #43)

Baretta
("Keep Your Eye on the Sparrow"), Rhythm Heritage (1976, #20)

Batman, The Marketts (1966, #17), Neal Hefti & Orchestra (1966, #35)

Ben Casey, Valjean (1962, #28)

Beverly Hillbillies
("The Ballad of Jed Clampett"), Lester Flatt & Earl Scruggs (1962, #44)

Bonanza, Al Caiola (1961, #19)

Charlie's Angels, Henry Mancini (1977, #45)

Dr. Kildare, Richard Chamberlain (1962, #10)

Dragnet, Ray Anthony Orchestra (1953, #3)

Happy Days, Pratt & McClain (1976, #5)

Have Gun Will Travel
("Ballad of Paladin"), Duane Eddy (1962, #33)

Hawaii Five-O, The Ventures (1969, #4)

Here Come the Brides
("Seattle"), Perry Como (1969, #38)

I Love Lucy
("Disco Lucy"), Wilton Place Street Band (1977, #24)

Laverne and Shirley
("Making Our Dreams Come True"), Cyndi Grecco (1976, #25)

Medic
("Blue Star"), Felicia Sanders (1955, #29)

The Men, Isaac Hayes (1972, #38)

Mission: Impossible, Lalo Schifrin (1968, #41)

Mr. Lucky, Henry Mancini Orchestra (1960, #21)

My Three Sons, Lawrence Welk Orchestra (1961, #55)

Peter Gunn, Ray Anthony Orchestra (1959, #8), Duane Eddy (1960, #27)

The Rockford Files, Mike Post (1975, #10)

Route 66, Nelson Riddle Orchestra (1962, #30)

S.W.A.T., Rhythm Heritage* (1975, #1)

Secret Agent
("Secret Agent Man"), Johnny Rivers* (1966, #3), The Ventures (1966, #54)

Welcome Back, Kotter
("Welcome Back"), John Sebastian* (1976, #1)

Zorro, The Chordettes (1958, #17)

INDEX

A

B

E

G

H

I

J

K

L

N

O

P

S

T

U

V

W

Y

Z

ABOUT THE AUTHORS

Tim Brooks is Director of Television Network Research for NBC. He holds degrees from Dartmouth College and Syracuse University, and has worked for Westinghouse Broadcasting Corp., Capital Cities Broadcasting Corp., and CBS in research and promotion capacities. He has also written numerous articles on the history of the record industry, and is currently working on a book about early recordings. A native of New Hampshire, Mr. Brooks now lives in Jackson Heights, New York.

Earle Marsh is Manager of Special Projects for the CBS national television research department. A graduate of Northwestern University, he has previously held positions with the A. C. Nielsen Company and NBC, as well as CBS. In addition to working in network television research, he has done research for local television stations and network radio. A native of Cleveland, Ohio, Mr. Marsh currently resides in Yonkers, New York.